DATE			

Handbook of
Cross-Cultural
Human
Development

The Garland Anthropology
and Human Development Series

General Editor
Richard A. Shweder
The University of Chicago

The aim of this series is to promote scholarship and
research in the human sciences, with special reference to
cross-cultural and developmental enquiry.

Handbook of Cross-Cultural Human Development

EDITED BY

Ruth H. Munroe
Pitzer College
Claremont, California

Robert L. Munroe
Pitzer College
Claremont, California

Beatrice B. Whiting
Harvard University
Cambridge, Massachusetts

Garland STPM Press
New York & London

Copyright © 1981 by Garland Publishing, Inc.

All rights reserved. No part of this work covered by the copyright hereon may be reproduced or used in any form or by any means—graphic, electronic, or mechanical, including photocopying, recording, taping, or information storage and retrieval systems—without permission of the publisher.

15 14 13 12 11 10 9 8 7 6 5 4 3 2 1

Library of Congress Cataloging in Publication Date
Main entry under title:

Handbook of cross-cultural human development.

Bibliography: p.
Includes index.
1. Child psychology.   2. Cross-cultural studies.
I. Munroe, Robert L.   II. Munroe, Ruth H.   III. Whiting, Beatrice Blyth.
BF721.H243   155.8   79-12028
ISBN 0-8240-7045-3

Published by Garland STPM Press
136 Madison Avenue, New York, New York 10016

Printed in the United States of America

Contents

List of Contributors

Margaret K. Bacon, Department of Anthropology, Livingston College, Rutgers University.

Herbert Barry, III, School of Pharmacy, and Department of Anthropology, University of Pittsburgh.

John W. Berry, Department of Psychology, Queen's University at Kingston, Ontario, Canada.

Ben G. Blount, Department of Anthropology, University of Georgia.

Gwen J. Broude, Department of Psychology, Vassar College.

Judith K. Brown, Department of Sociology and Anthropology, Oakland University.

Roger V. Burton, Department of Psychology, State University of New York, Buffalo.

Carolyn Pope Edwards, School of Education, University of Massachusetts, Amherst.

Carol R. Ember, Department of Anthropology, Hunter College and the Graduate School of the City University of New York.

John L. Fischer, Department of Anthropology, Tulane University.

Ronald Gallimore, Department of Psychiatry and Biobehavioral Science, School of Medicine, University of California, Los Angeles.

Alan Howard, Department of Anthropology, University of Hawaii.

Jerome Kagan, Department of Psychology and Social Relations, Harvard University.

Melvin J. Konner, Department of Anthropology, Harvard University.

Thomas K. Landauer, Laboratory of Acoustical and Behavioral Research, Bell Laboratories, Murray Hill, New Jersey.

Robert A. LeVine, Laboratory of Human Development, Graduate School of Education, Harvard University.

David C. McClelland, Department of Psychology and Social Relations, Harvard University.

Howard V. Meredith, College of Health and Physical Education, University of South Carolina.

Robert L. Munroe, Department of Anthropology, Pitzer College (Claremont Colleges).

Ruth H. Munroe, Department of Psychology, Pitzer College (Claremont Colleges).

Jane M. Murphy, Department of Psychiatry, Harvard Medical School.

Sara Beth Nerlove, Health and Population Study Center, Human Affairs Research Centers, Battelle Memorial Institute, Washington, D. C.

Douglass Price-Williams, Departments of Psychiatry and Anthropology, University of California, Los Angeles.

Janet Reis, Department of Psychology, Northwestern University.

Robert A. Scott, Department of Sociology, Princeton University.

Susan Seymour, Department of Anthropology, Pitzer College (Claremont Colleges).

Ann Stanton Snipper, Department of Human Services Studies, Cornell University.

Charles M. Super, Graduate School of Education, School of Public Health, and School of Medicine, Harvard University.

Thomas S. Weisner, Departments of Psychiatry and Anthropology, University of California, Los Angeles.

Beatrice B. Whiting, Graduate School of Education, Harvard University.

John W. M. Whiting, Department of Anthropology and Social Relations, Harvard University.

Preface

Although individuals have been involved in cross-cultural research on psychological processes since the turn of the century—the Torres Strait expedition being one of the first research projects dedicated to exploring differences in sample populations —there was little interest in systematic cross-cultural studies of human development until the late twenties and early thirties. In the 1930s, a group of scholars under the guidance of George Peter Murdock began to carry out cross-cultural studies based on published ethnographic data, and some of these investigations were developmentally oriented. But until the last decade or so, with infrequent exceptions (most notably the research of Margaret Mead and her students, the Kluckhohn values project, and the collaborative research organized by John Whiting, Irvin Child, and William Lambert), few had attempted to gather comparable data in a sample of different cultures. More recently there have been a series of studies conducted in various parts of the world using comparable instruments. The field of cross-cultural human development is thus relatively new, and the papers that make up this *Handbook* reflect the fact that not all topics have reached a level of maturity sufficient to allow a "state-of-the-art" review.

The recent emergence of the discipline prompted us to ask authors to write articles with a prospective orientation. We asked that they review primarily those studies that they considered important and indicative of areas where, based on existing cross-cultural work, future research looked promising. We requested that they emphasize these areas and the hypotheses that appeared to be most worth testing. The volume is therefore a prospectus as much as a review of the field.

We also decided to limit the coverage of comparative cognitive development since it has been and is being reviewed in a number of volumes (cf. Berry, 1976; Berry & Dasen, 1974; Cole & Scribner, 1974; Dasen, 1977; Glick, 1975; Lloyd, 1972; Triandis, 1979). There are two chapters in this book which deal exclusively with cognitive development as investigated with instruments developed and standardized in the United States and Europe (cf. chapters by Berry and Price-Williams). The chapter by Nerlove and Snipper reviews studies using natural indicators as well as the standard tests.

Most of the research on human development has been undertaken by European and American psychologists. The subjects of their research have been predominantly parents and children native to the United States and the Continent. The findings, however, are presented as relevant to the human race. When challenged, all are quick to add the phrase "in our culture." Until recently, however, few have had the motivation or the opportunity to consider the implications of this phrase. What influences can *culture* have on human development? What are the components of this concept which are of particular relevance to the principles of development derived from psychological research?

For example, age, sex, and social class are the three variables that have been used most frequently in child development research. Each of these, however, is a "packaged variable." The experiences of an infant and 2-year-old in our society are strikingly different from the experience of children brought up in nonindustrial societies and warm climates (cf. chapters by Super and by Whiting). When we trace the normal development of infants in our society, are we aware of the effect of the early separation of the infant from body contact and other differences in its environment and experiences? Have we considered the effect of sleeping in a single bed in a room of one's own? Can we discriminate what is universally true of development from that which is the product of these environmental influences?

Similarly, in attempting to isolate biological determinants of sex differences, we need to be sure that we have controlled for the various environmental and cultural influences (cf. chapter by Ember). How many of the sex differences reported in the literature are the direct result of the isolation of young mothers who are not in the work force from other adults, or of the number of years spent by the mother and children in coeducational age-graded schools? When we compare child development and parental practices in social classes and ethnic subgroups within the United States, are we able to isolate the factors that bear on school achievement? Can we separate sociocultural constraints from such influences as hunger, anxiety about money, or membership in a minority group (cf. chapter by Howard and Scott)?

As students of human development, we neglect many of the effects of environmental, economic, social structural and ideational variables because of cultural blindness —a blindness resulting from lack of knowledge of the possible variations of experience. Knowledge of the daily life of adults and children in other parts of the world and a study of the cultures of a worldwide sample of societies facilitate the identification of environmental constraints and their cultural consequences, factors we have previously failed to see.

The variables we do not see or identify in our research are often normative and universal in our culture so that we fail to realize their influence. It is difficult for us, for example, to study the effects of age grading on our children, as we have no control groups of normals who do not spend at least six hours a day in school in age-graded peer groups. In fact it is becoming difficult to find any culture that is not now providing age-graded school for all children.

There are two strategies students of human development can use to help them identify hidden variables. One is the cross-cultural study of human development as described in ethnographic literature; the other, the field study of socialization and the developmental process. From the late nineteenth century to the present, anthropologists and other social scientists have been collecting and publishing detailed monographs on the culture and daily life events in a worldwide sample of societies. Familiarity with this literature alerts researchers to the new variables. For example, detailed comparison of child training practices and environmental constraints lead to modification and revision of developmental hypotheses. John Whiting's (1968) cross-cultural analysis of the relation of age to emotional disturbance at weaning is an example of such a study. Researchers in the United States had concluded that emotional disturbance at weaning was a function of age such that a child of 8 months cried more and showed other symptoms of distress significantly more than an infant of 3 or 4 months. Whiting, drawing information on weaning practices and the reported responses to weaning from ethnographic sources, demonstrated that the relation was curvilinear rather than linear. The ethnographic literature suggested that disturbance increased to a maximum at around 18 months to 2 years of age but decreased thereafter. It is interesting to note the similarity between this finding and recent research on fear of strangers and separation anxiety (cf. chapters by Kagan and Super).

Ideally, once a new variable is identified by a cross-cultural study based on a search of the literature, research should be designed to test relevant hypotheses in a sample where there is culturally acceptable variation. It is possible to stratify samples both across cultures and within discrete cultures on dimensions of social structure and economic features. This strategy, however, requires special field research to test the hypotheses in appropriate sites. Examples of such research are cited in Ember's discussion of sex differences and Landauer and Whiting's chapter on stress and physical growth. In these papers the research is both across cultures based on the ethnographic literature and within a culture where relevant variables are distributed in such a way as to make possible comparison between sub-samples.

Only one of the chapters deals specifically with the myriad of methodological problems that face cross-culturalists (cf. Barry's discussion of the use of ethnographic descriptions). However, in evaluating research, many authors assessed the adequacy of sampling, the face validity of the scales, and the adequacy of the statistical procedures. In studies based on the literature there is the nagging problem of the independence of cases. Numerous strategies for solving "Galton's problem" have been advanced. These are represented in the chapters that follow. The solutions all have advantages and disadvantages. The Standard Cross-Cultural Sample developed by Murdock and White (1969) and published in *Ethnology* has worldwide coverage and allows examination of many cultures that are no longer viable. This sample was drawn with the intention of obtaining descriptions of societies in the period before they had changed as a result of contact with the emerging modern world. However, such descriptions are often based on cultural reconstructions developed from recollections of informants. These accounts are adequate for highly salient features of the culture, but they frequently include highly inferential statements, and they typically underdescribe less salient practices, including socialization and developmental material. The blue ribbon sample of societies selected by the Human Relations Area Files (Lagacé, 1976) to improve coverage for future research and for indexing purposes is also a valuable resource, but like the Standard Cross-Cultural Sample, it is highly biased toward nonindustrial cases. Although these predrawn samples are very useful for exploratory work, serious study should pay attention to the question of representation of the industrial era and to the need for solid coverage of the variables of interest. Attention also should be given to operational definitions of ratings and scales published in the *Ethnographic Atlas* (Murdock, 1967) and various studies based on the Standard Cross-Cultural Sample, as the simple labels for scales are often misleading.

Another nagging problem is the level of inference required in rating societies on relevant scales. Some studies lean heavily on high inference variables such as level of anxiety; others seek to find low inference variables and use them as indices of more complex phenomena (see infant-carrying devices as a measure of mother-infant proximity in the chapter by Whiting). The social structure variables are often complex constructs as Bacon points out in her summary of the research on the use of alcohol.

No attempt is made in the volume to discuss the problem of sampling in field studies where the lack of census material, detailed survey data, and published monographs make it necessary for the researcher to collect a massive amount of data on his sample population. As a result, limited by both time and the size of many target communities, the study samples are small. The solution to the problems is probably a combination of intensive and extensive research, the latter using instruments that are derived from the detailed knowledge of a few families and pretested for validity.

The work of cross-culturalists is beset with the problem of validity. It is, for example, a central concern in Edwards' review of the cross-cultural research on moral reasoning. To establish validity, however, requires spending time in the field, especially if one's research variables are not easily observed. The day has passed when a researcher can translate an interview or test procedure developed in the States and feel confident that he is measuring comparable phenomena in different cultures. Even the most avid jet set cross-culturalists are addressing the problem of the validity of their instruments. (Cf. Cole and Scribner, 1974, and Harkness and Super, 1977, for discussions of the problems of testing cross-culturally.) Important aid has come from the ethnoscientists who have devised techniques for exploring the meaning of linguistic concepts. In many societies a strict experimental or formal testing situation would be culturally inappropriate. Promising alternatives to the laboratory are field experiments in naturally occurring settings and standardized behavior observations, which have evolved from the stock-in-trade of the anthropological method, the technique of participant observation. Important innovative work is represented by the research of Gallimore, Howard and Nerlove, all of whom have devised experiments in the field to test hypotheses about the interpretation of behavior in naturally occurring settings (cf. Chapters 6; 13; and 21 in this volume) (Gallimore, Boggs, & Jordan, 1974; Howard, 1974; Nerlove, Roberts, Klein, Yarbrough, & Habicht, 1974).

Most of the chapters are reviews of studies concerning the genesis of adult behavior and its function in the life cycle. The studies attempt to isolate both psychological and sociocultural processes associated with such diverse cultural forms as themes in folktales, drinking behavior, ritual behavior, deviance, sexual behavior and moral reasoning. The authors have chosen to review those topics on which they have done cross-cultural work.

Several themes in the volume are pervasive in the literature on cross-cultural human development. The pioneering works of Margaret Mead and Ruth Benedict, which marked the first major attempts to place the individual in a sociocultural nexus, tended to conceptualize both culture and personality as monolithic entities. Culture, conceived as the heritage of learned symbolic behavior characteristic of a people, still persisted as an explanatory construct in anthropology after World War II. In recent years the summary nature of this concept, together with a growing recognition of intracultural diversity, has led to increasing dissatisfaction with its use in this broad form and to its reconceptualization in more narrow, specialized senses. Correspondingly, in psychology the concept of personality was defined in terms of stable response tendencies or traits. But what has been learned through a great mass of empirical findings is the failure of trait theory to yield accurate predictions of social behavior across varying situations. Thus both fields have moved toward a greater specificity, and in cross-cultural research this shift has been reflected in the decline of interest in the effects of culture on personality and the rise of interest in the effects of particular cultural practices on both developmental processes and particular aspects of personality. The situational or contextual effects on social behavior have been examined more fully.

A second theme is the assignment of a special place to early experience. Not all the chapters assume that infant experience is of primary importance—indeed, one author argues that his previously positive attitude about this question has been entirely wrong—but a large proportion of the authors find the assumption congenial. For example, prolonged body contact between infant and mother and the nature of early attachment and object relations are preverbal experiences that may have lasting effects (cf. chapters by Broude, Brown, LeVine, Super, and Whiting). Following infancy, role assignments and other learning experiences of childhood appear to entail a narrowing of developmental options (cf. chapters by Ember, Gallimore, and Nerlove and Snipper). Furthermore, consistent experiences throughout early life may have a cumulative effect (cf. chapter by Burton and Reis). The existence of cut-off ages, or perhaps even critical periods, needs to be explored.

A third theme has to do with universals. One issue often discussed in connection with universals is better viewed as the question of the generalizability of findings: Given a relationship discovered in one society, does it hold up in all societies? Throughout the first half of this century, anthropology as a whole adopted a position of extreme cultural relativism that emphasized the uniqueness and the value of every sociocultural system. The discipline therefore took a skeptical stance on the problem of generalizability. Psychologists, on the contrary, have usually assumed that a relationship was general unless shown otherwise, a tendency that can be seen in positions as diverse as those of Freud, Piaget, and Skinner. In recent years, as many anthropologists have begun pursuing developmental questions and increasing numbers of developmental psychologists have moved toward cross-cultural research, the positions have come closer together, and it is probably fair to say that a modulated nomothetic viewpoint is typical of the field today. Certainly most of the chapters in this volume demonstrate that the discovery of general relationships stands as an important goal in cross-cultural developmental study.

Another aspect of the theme on universals concerns the identity and the sources of invariant aspects of development. The contribution of biological, social, cultural, and environmental variables to the emergence of these developmental nodes, and to the timing and order of their appearance, can be investigated through cross-cultural data. Further, even for universals, their degree of elaboration and level of complexity is not necessarily identical everywhere; and again the impact of all these types of variables can be assessed by means of cross-cultural work, as various chapters indicate.

There are many who worry about the violation of data that results from abstracting it from its cultural context. There is no doubt that many nuances of meaning and subtle differences are of necessity overlooked in making comparisons. The beauty of a cultural phenomenon may be destroyed in the process of abstraction. (Snowflakes have an individual configuration, each lovelier than the last; but they share many characteristics.) Temporarily the cross-culturalist is concerned primarily with those qualities shared by all.

We do not pretend to have reviewed all cross-cultural studies but instead offer a large sample of the types of studies that are being conducted, many by members of the editors' lineage founded by George Peter Murdock, a student of Sumner and Keller. Our aim is to encourage cross-cultural research and in particular to encourage anthropologists, sociologists, and psychologists to collect comparable data. We believe that there are laws that govern human development and that they can only be discovered by the systematic testing of hypotheses within and across cultures.

RUTH H. MUNROE
ROBERT L. MUNROE
BEATRICE B. WHITING

ACKNOWLEDGMENTS

The editors are greatly indebted to Richard Shweder, Editor of Garland's series on Anthropology and Human Development, for his aid in the planning of this volume, to Stuart Anderson for his diligent and painstaking editorial assistance, and to Beverly Scales and Stella Vlastos for their long-term help with typing of manuscripts and correspondence concerning the *Handbook*. The Research and Development Committee of Pitzer College gave several substantial grants-in-aid which assisted materially in the preparation of the volume.

NOTE

The terms "biological" and "biologic" are used interchangeably throughout the volume, as are several other sets of variants, e.g., "methodological" and "methodologic," "egological" and "ecologic."

REFERENCES

Berry, J. W. *Human ecology and cognitive style.* New York: Wiley, 1976.

Berry, J. W., & Dasen, P. R. (Eds.). *Culture and cognition: Readings in cross-cultural psychology.* London: Methuen, 1974.

Cole, M., & Scribner, S. *Culture and thought: A psychological introduction.* New York: Wiley, 1974.

Dasen, P. R. (Ed). *Piagetian psychology: Cross-cultural contributions.* New York: Gardner, 1977.

Gallimore, R., Boggs, J. W., & Jordan, C. *Culture, behavior and education.* Beverly Hills, Ca.: Sage, 1974.

Glick, J. Cognitive development in cross-cultural perspective. In F. D. Horowitz (Ed.), *Review of child development research,* (Vol. 4). Chicago: University of Chicago Press, 1975.

Harkness, S., & Super, C. M. Why African children are so hard to test. *Annals of the New York Academy of Sciences,* 1977, *285,* 326–331.

Howard, A. *Ain't no big thing.* Honolulu: University of Hawaii Press, 1974.

Lagacé, R. O. *Sixty cultures: A guide to the HRAF probability sample files.* New Haven: HRAF Press, 1976.

Lloyd, B. B. *Perception and cognition: A cross-cultural perspective.* Harmondsworth, England: Penguin, 1972.

Murdock, G. P. Ethnographic atlas. *Ethnology,* 1967, *6,* 109–236.

Murdock, G. P., & White, D. R. Standard cross-cultural sample. *Ethnology,* 1969, *8,* 329–369.

Nerlove, S. B., Roberts, J. M., Klein, R. E., Yarbrough, C., & Habicht, J. *Natural indicators of cognitive development: An observational study of rural Guatemalan children. Ethos,* 1974, *2,* 265–295.

Triandis, H. C. (Ed.). *Handbook of cross-cultural psychology.* Boston: Allyn and Bacon, 1979.

Whiting, J. W. M. Methods and problems in cross-cultural research. In G. Lindzey & E. Aronson (Eds.), *The handbook of social psychology.* (Vol. 2). Reading, Ma: Addison-Wesley, 1968.

Part I

Perspectives

1

Evolution of Human Behavior Development

Melvin J. Konner

It should, by now, be . . . obvious that there is, indeed, a general theory of behavior and that that theory is . . . evolution, to just the same extent and in almost exactly the same ways in which evolution is the general theory of morphology.
(Roe & Simpson, 1958, p.2)

This chapter considers theoretically what developmentalists may stand to gain by giving attention—that elusive and precious commodity—to the science of evolution; that is to say, substantial attention, something beyond the lip service offered casually in the first few pages of the textbooks. Owing to various excesses of biological determinism, developmentalists—who historically have concerned themselves with the making of policy to maximize human potential—have more or less sworn off biology. To put it more exactly, they have, in general, signified their intention to operate with the variance remaining within the limits provided by biology.

Thus many developmentalists find motor development boring, except insofar as it is deemed responsive to experience. The question of population differences in behavior is so deeply politicized that one can scarcely approach it without some armor of ideology, and the question of sex differences is gaining the same distinction. As for comparative developmental research—well, a child is neither rat, nor dog, nor duckling, nor monkey. So goes the objection we hear quite regularly.

Having some familiarity with all five of those sorts of animals, one can scarcely dissent from this opinion. A child is indeed none of those things, nor, for that matter, is a duckling a dog (or a rat a monkey). Yet, one insists, there is much knowledge to be gained about each of those creatures by looking at all of them.

Backing away from biology was a wise step when it happened. In the early part of this century Haeckel's "biogenetic law"—to the effect that the course of development recapitulates the phyletic history of the organism—was overapplied so literally and indiscriminately that it rapidly outlived its usefulness (which was, incidentally, as a pillar of the edifice of evidence for evolution, rather than as a theory of development). At length it resulted in one of the most famous pieces of silliness in the history of psychology, its sad monument in a field which had grown away from it (Freud, 1938).

At the same time the excesses of "social Darwinism"—which, as we now understand, was not Darwinian—caused evolution to become identified with political and social reaction. In the United States, Yerkes, Terman, and other psychometricians, allied with eugenicists in biology and racists in politics, succeeded in turning down to a trickle, by the early 1930s, a current of immigration which could have saved the Jews of Europe (Kamin, 1974). On the other side of the ocean Lorenz and other continental ethologists, to their everlasting detriment and shame, allied themselves in the name of biology with the most pernicious ideology in human history (Eisenberg, 1972).

Thus decent people entering anthropology or psychology to consider various issues in human behavior development were understandably chary of evolution. The work of Gesell and Amatruda (1965) and McGraw (1963) on motor development came ultimately to be largely ignored, sex differences came to be explained by sex role learning (Kagan, 1964), and the laws of operant conditioning were stretched in attempts to account for such phenomena as language acquisition (Skinner, 1957) and the infant's tie to its caretaker (Gewirtz, 1972).

But with the front door firmly barred, biology was again found in the house, not only having sneaked in through the basement and seeped in around the windows, but also having walked calmly in through various other unlocked doors. Piaget's biologizing slipped by, perhaps because he slyly refused to take a stand on the nature-nurture controversy. Still, it became apparent that he was dealing with phenomena whose variance mostly was accounted for by maturation (Flavell, 1963), a fact not surprising when it is considered that he began life as a zoologist. The quantum advance of the 1960s in developmental psycholinguistics laid permanently to rest the notion that first language acquisition could ever be accounted for by conventional learning theory (Lenneberg, 1964; R. Brown, 1973). Perceptual and cognitive development in infancy (Bower, 1974; Kagan, 1970) acquired an increasingly maturational cast. Finally, work on the development of fear (Hebb, 1946; Bronson, 1972) and of primary attachment (Bowlby, 1969; 1973; Ainsworth, 1967) became "biologized" and set in the context of evolution.

Also, there were some unwanted presences. Scientists and nonscientists alike were addressing the public with poorly formulated notions about the biological basis of aggressiveness (Morris, 1968), territoriality (Ardrey, 1966), and intelligence (Herrnstein, 1973) before those notions were subject to adequate scientific scrutiny. None of them has survived even a few years of such scrutiny, but their hold on the public, of course, outlives their real credibility, and that hold itself is a subject worthy of study.

More recently, somewhat more serious efforts have been made to bring to the attention of scientists (Wilson, 1975) and the public (Wilson, 1978) the findings and implications of a newly named subfield of zoology, sociobiology. This subfield attempts to integrate theory and data in population genetics, ecology, evolution, and animal behavior to produce a comprehensive conception of the adaptive basis of behavior. Although intrinsically more valuable than the earlier, popular formulations, this viewpoint has lent itself rather easily to serious misinterpretation by making a premature bid for public acclaim through unwarranted generalizations about human behavior, together with explicit predictions that sociobiology would soon replace or "cannibalize" all the other major fields of behavioral science and even some fields of the humanities (Wilson, 1975). It thus expectably provoked much criticism from psychologists, anthropologists, and other behavioral scientists, ranging from the informed and constructive (Campbell, 1975) to the confused and useless (Sahlins, 1976). Although the latest presentation of the viewpoint (Wilson, 1978) is much more restrained in its claims and quite well informed about human behavioral biology, the damage, in terms of scientific communication, may have already been done; behavioral and social scientists may be sufficiently alienated from the viewpoint so as to be unwilling to read the more mature formulation.

The resistance found among behavioral scientists to behavioral biology is thus understandable and, in certain respects, valuable. However, at last it is unwise, since if responsible scientists fail to consider the biology of behavior, irresponsible ones will do so, and we will all spend a great deal of time explaining what is wrong with their notions. The study of behavior, which is a feature of living organisms, is simply a branch of biology, and behavior development research above all should be cognizant of this; with the exception of behaviorism and associationism in perception, every major advance in behavior development research has been biological (Freud, 1920; Piaget, 1971; Gesell & Amatruda, 1965; Carmichael, 1970; Bower, 1974; Bowlby, 1969; R. Brown, 1973). Thus in fields as widely disparate as affect and psychopathology, cognition, motor systems, parental behavior, infant perception, attachment, and language, developmental process is viewed as largely maturational. This view always contains a genetic and evolutionary stance, even where such a stance is not explicit.

In the last few years biological and, more specifically, evolutionary perspectives have if anything increased their influence in the field of behavior development. Some examples follow:

1. Following a suggestion made by Bell (1968), a number of investigators of parent–infant interaction have begun to reinterpret the direction of effect in correlations between infant and caretaker behavior, focusing attention on the effects of the infant on the caretaker (Lewis & Rosenblum, 1973). This outlook recognizes that infants are highly individual at birth, largely for genetic reasons, and that caretakers inevitably respond to this individuality, being shaped by the infant almost as much as they shape it. An instrument for subtle assessment of individuality in neonatal behavior and responsiveness has come into widespread use (Brazelton, 1973), but its predictive validity, if any, is unknown.

2. Notwithstanding the extremes of controversy that arose over race differences in intelligence (Herrnstein, 1973; Kamin, 1974; for a less ideologized view of the problem, see Loehlin, Lindzey, & Spuhler, 1975), several respected investigators of infant behavior and capacity have begun or continued to focus on the question of population differences in infant measures (although not on "intelligence") and have given serious consideration to the hypothesis that these differences are due to genetic rather than cultural causes. Freedman (1974) has used the Brazelton Neonatal Assessment Scale to search for differences in human behavior at birth and found that neonates who are descendants of East Asians differ from those of European descent in that the former are less irritable, habituate more rapidly, and are more easily consolable. Such differences have been found, at least in part, by other investigators, although intrauterine as well as genetic causes may be implicated (Chisholm, 1978). Wolff (1972; 1973; 1977) has observed that infants of East Asian and European descent differ in their sensitivity to alcohol, the former showing a greater facial flushing response (measured at the earlobe with a transillumination densitometer) in infancy as in adulthood. He believes this difference

to be genetic, speculates on possible enzyme differences, and suggests that the differences may be tied to emotion-related facial flushing (blushing), also more frequent in individuals of East Asian descent, at least in adulthood. Kagan, Kearsley, and Zelazo (1978) have compared infants of East Asian and European descent in situations likely to evoke timidity. They find within and between group differences in this measure, together with associated differences in heart rate stability, that are consistent with temperamental differences stable across age. They do not conclude that such differences are genetic, but they consider this hypothesis a viable one. Wolff (1977) notes in passing that the complete denial of such genetically based temperamental differences between people constitutes a kind of denial of individuality.

3. Several new lines of research have indicated the increasing emphasis placed by developmental scientists on maturation rather than learning in the explanation of behavior development. At least one attempt has been made (Lecours, 1975) to give neuroanatomic substance to the proposed Language Acquisition Device (LAD) of the developmental psycholinguists. They hypothesized (e.g., Lenneberg, 1964) the existence of universal specific brain growth patterns that would account for the great strides in language competence taken between ages 1 and 5 years, irrespective of wide variation in the language environment. Lecours shows very plausible links between the pattern of myelination of relevant brain systems and proposed universals of language development. A similar attempt has been made to relate proposed universals of social development in the first year (specifically, the development of smiling in the first few months and the development of fear of strangers in the second half-year) to myelination in specific brain systems (Konner, 1979). Explorations of the cognitive abilities of adolescents have resulted in the hypothesis that verbal and spatial abilities are influenced by the timing of puberty, owing to the presumed effect of this timing on the degree of lateralization of the cerebral hemispheres (Waber, 1976; Petersen, 1976). (These brain–behavior relationships are all still hypothetical, but they serve to illustrate several new directions of investigation.)

4. Maturation has also been reemphasized by investigators of the question of continuity in behavior development and of the importance of early experience. Kagan in particular (Kagan & Klein, 1973; Kagan et al., 1978) has reversed his earlier belief in the importance of early experience and the prominence of continuity. He argues that new evidence on recovery from early damage and deprivation (e.g., Suomi & Harlow, 1972), on the absence of long-term stability in early group differences (Caldwell, 1964), and on the small amount of variance (usual maximum, 10 percent) explained by early (before age 5) predictors of later measures, especially measures of intelligence (McCall, 1978; Lewis & McGurk, 1972), all point to the importance of developmental processes that subvert continuity, processes that would have to be maturational. Kagan hypothesizes that certain features of human behavior and ability are such fundamental features of nervous system function that they will unfold in almost any environment (cf. the canalization concept in genetics—Waddington, 1942) in a fashion highly resilient with respect to deviation. He notes that one would expect natural selection to have favored such resilience, cushioning crucial abilities against environmental insult. He uses the biological metaphor of metamorphosis, as in the transformation of caterpillars into butterflies, to emphasize the maturational nature of the emergence of such abilities. This view has been shared by other major theorists (e.g.

McCall, 1978, with respect to the growth of intelligence). While it is premature to accept the view that continuity is nonexistent and early experience unimportant, it can now be said that developmental psychology has failed to convincingly demonstrate their importance, at least within the normal range of variation. (Although usually applied to species-wide universals, the concept of canalization was recently applied to individual differences. In a study of the growth of mental abilities of identical and nonidentical twins, the identical twins increased in concordance from 3 months to 6 years of age, while the nonidentical twins decreased in concordance to the point of their concordance level with nontwin siblings, suggesting the existence of a goal-corrected or "canalizing" genetic plan more apparent later than earlier [R. Wilson, 1978].)

5. The process of differentiation of behavior by sex or gender has received very intensive study during the last few years. The extent to which conditioning, imitation, culture, and sexist ideology figure in this process is well documented. Nevertheless, as conceded in the most widely read and accepted recent major review of the literature (Maccoby & Jacklin, 1974), if all major external differentiating factors were removed there would probably remain a residue of difference (beyond the most obvious differences in reproductive behavior) explainable only by reference to biological factors. One such factor, derived mainly from animal experiments (e.g., Raisman & Field, 1971) but supported by some human clinical evidence as well (Ehrhardt, 1978), is pre- or perinatal sex differentiation of the hypothalamus. Certainly in several mammal species, and probably in humans, androgens circulating very early in life exert a formative influence on neural connectivity in this brain area, as well as on later reproductive and aggressive behavior, both pre- and postpubertally. This is consistent with much evidence from evolutionary biology suggesting that natural selection has prepared males and females for adaptive purposes that are not completely overlapping (e.g. Trivers, 1972). Cross-cultural research using modern, well-validated techniques for the observational measurement and analysis of children's social behavior under natural conditions (B. Whiting & J. Whiting, 1975; Edwards & Whiting, 1973; Blurton Jones & Konner, 1973) has suggested that the sex or gender differences in aggressive and nurturant behavior we observe in American and English children are not limited to Anglo-Saxon cultures and may indeed be cross-cultural universals. If so, such differences are consistent with the notion that normally circulating androgens influence the development of behaviorally significant portions of the human brain. Whether or not this notion is true, it is highly likely that the marked hormonal and maturational differences between males and females during adolescence influence sex and gender differences in behavioral dispositions both during adolescence and subsequently.

6. At least four investigators of human development have incorporated the evolutionary perspective in a fundamental, organizing fashion into their research. Bowlby (1969; 1973) has continued his three-volume work on attachment, separation, and loss, an attempt to bring the psychoanalytic theory of object relations into line with evolutionary theory (stressing the adaptive significance of the attachment bond) as well as with modern research in developmental ethology and developmental psychology. His remarkable synthesis is a major contribution that has influenced many other investigators. In terms of evolutionary theory, it is marred only by its failure to take note of the evolutionary sources of parent-offspring conflict (Trivers 1974), as powerful and natural a force as parent-offspring

bonding. Freedman (1974) has summarized 17 years of work on various aspects of the genetic basis of behavior, mainly in human infants, viewed in an evolutionary perspective. Much of this work can be criticized methodologically, but is solid enough to have to be dealt with in some way, if only by replication. His evolutionary thinking is up to date and useful in some areas (e.g., universals of human infant behavior; evolution of sex differences) but very weak in others, especially the phylogeny of human population differences. His explanation of the adaptive significance of population differences in newborn behavior is incomplete and unconvincing at best and should probably await full confirmation of the existence and character of the differences. Nevertheless, he is to be commended for attempting to deal with a difficult and important set of problems in an integrative way. Fishbein (1976) has provided an admirable integrative synthesis of current knowledge of cognitive development with several aspects of evolutionary and embryologic thinking. Relying heavily on Waddington's (1942) concept of canalization, he argues that a wide variety of children's competences, including motor, cognitive, social, and moral competences, are more highly canalized than previously recognized; because of their great adaptive significance during the course of human evolution, the genes guide children's development through and toward these competences in a fairly fixed manner. Although the general points about the adaptive significance of developing behavior and the embryologic nature of some aspects of postnatal behavior development are well supported and convincing, evolutionary theory does not appear to make a tight fit with many specific aspects of children's competence discussed. This fit will presumably be improved in the future. Fishbein's treatment will have to be improved especially in the areas of social and moral competence, where several new contributions in evolutionary theory (see below) will have to be taken into account. Finally, Konner (1972; 1975; 1977; 1978; 1979; Blurton Jones & Konner, 1973; West & Konner, 1976) has presented data on development in infancy and early childhood in a population representative of the basic human sociocultural adaptation, the !Kung San. For a variety of reasons, great caution should be exercised in attempting to generalize from these data to hunting–gathering societies in general and, even more so, to societies of the distant past. Nevertheless, these findings provide one of the few real routes away from speculation in the area of human behavior development in evolutionary perspective and are an obvious natural testing ground for the theories of Bowlby, Trivers, Freedman, Fishbein, and others as to the adaptive significance of developing behavior. These findings, with related speculations, will be treated extensively in the last section of this chapter. The intervening two sections deal with *natural selection theory* as applied to behavior development and parental behavior and with the *phylogeny* of behavior development and parental behavior, respectively. These two distinct currents in the theory of evolution have flourished robustly and grown beyond recognition since half a century ago, when the "modern synthesis," which forms the basis of most people's education in this area, was taking shape.

NATURAL SELECTION THEORY, BEHAVIOR DEVELOPMENT, AND PARENTAL BEHAVIOR

Natural selection has two components which, for purposes of analysis, are usefully separated. The one which comes most quickly to mind is differential viability. Some individuals are more likely than others to die and are said to be less well adapted.

It should be noted, as it often is not, that selection through differential viability operates at each stage of the life cycle from before conception to the end of the breeding period, and not just at maturity. Consequently, an immature individual is constantly balancing two forms of viability—the necessity to survive currently and the necessity to develop toward viability at maturity. There may be tension between these forms of viability, as in the obvious case in which becoming "tied to a parent's apron-strings" may improve current, but reduce ultimate, viability. Much more subtle interactions are possible; since it is considered that each life cycle stage may affect all subsequent ones, the balance of selective effects may be very complex.

It will be useful also to introduce the concept of a *selection funnel.* This will be taken to mean a stage of the life cycle in which mortality is very high and in which selection consequently may operate more intensively. A sufficiently intense selection will produce optimal viability at this stage, even though the adaptation necessary may, in the life of the individual, result in suboptimal viability at later stages. Selection funnels may be as common as the reverse case, in which an adaptively neutral feature of the juvenile, such as, perhaps, play behavior, results in improved viability in the adult.

However, differential viability, in spite of its complexity, is only half the picture of natural selection. In fact, if a population were to have strictly uniform viability— if all the individuals died at the same age—evolution would still proceed apace, by means of sexual selection. Though viability were uniform, reproductive success—the number of offspring left to the subsequent generation—would vary because sexual attractiveness and sexual effectiveness would vary. If we add to our model population the possibility of death during infancy, we have another source of variability— differential caretaking effectiveness. Thus in addition to balancing current against future viability the immature individual must balance both against future sexual attractiveness, sexual effectiveness, caretaking effectivness, and other influences on reproductive process. Again, these effects may sometimes oppose each other. An individual may die young but have left so many offspring that selection favors his or her genotype in spite of an early death. To win at selection roulette means only to maximize surviving offspring, a complex sum of all these selective effects.

Some aspects of natural selection theory which have specific implications for infant and parent behavior are now considered along with past applications of the specific concept, difficulties with it, and testable predictions arising from it. It is hoped in this way to make the heuristic and explanatory value of these concepts apparent.

Selection Funnels

At some stages of the life cycle mortality is exceptionally high or arises from causes later to disappear or diminish in importance, and selection acting at this stage thus affects all subsequent phases of the organism. In this way the ABO and Rh blood-type distributions of the adult population are determined not primarily by the (very slight) selection pressures operating on them in adulthood but by maternal–fetal incompatability during fetal life.

Bowlby's (1969) view of attachment rests, in effect, on this concept. Heightened effects of selection by predation at the time of infancy, he argues, have produced in many infant birds and mammals a set of innate proximity-maintaining mechanisms which, by reducing the distance between infant and parent, reduce the rate of predation. Several problems arise.

1. Bowlby assumes that because this pattern has been selected for in infancy, interference with it will have deleterious consequences for current or later (adult) phases of the organism. In fact, if a selection funnel is narrow enough, it may produce adaptations in the early phase which result ontogenetically in later-phase adaptations which are selectively neutral or even deleterious. In other words, it is possible that early attachment to a mother or single permanent mother-substitute, so crucial for reduction of the predation rate in infancy, has deleterious consequences for the mental health of the adult and that the appropriate response to the present reduced predation rate is to *reduce* the strength or exclusiveness of that attachment. It is also possible that, as Bowlby argues, eons of selection have produced later-phase adaptations which result from strong infant attachment but which are advantageous for the organism, or that, as Kagan would argue, early attachment patterns have few or no later-phase consequences. The respective validity of these competing hypotheses can be assessed only by means of longitudinal intervention studies and not by evolutionary analysis. However, the latter theory points to the problems of importance.
2. Bowlby's stress on the infant's current survival also leads to neglect of possible adaptive *advantages* for later phases of the organism. Observations of infants in the human environment of evolutionary adaptedness (Konner, 1972; 1977) reveal that no infant deaths occur through loss or predation and that the 20 percent mortality in the first year (Howell, 1976) results from infectious disease. This may occur, of course, because the adaptation provided by attachment is essentially perfect. However, observation suggests that proximity to caretakers results in transmission of behaviors essential for subsistence activity and for social and sexual activity. Experiments on rhesus monkeys have shown that interference with the earliest attachments can place the individual at a severe reproductive disadvantage by impairing later sexual and parental behavior (Harlow, 1963). This would constitute as strong a selection force favoring attachment as any pressure arising from current viability. An elaboration of this concept follows.

Teleological Selection

Teleological selection will be taken to refer to early-phase characteristics of the organism which although selectively neutral or deleterious for that phase, are favored for overwhelming later-phase advantages. The evolution of altriciality, or prolonged immaturity, is usually accounted for by some variant of this process. Increasing altriciality, so the argument goes, in the evolution of man, with its attendant disadvantages—greater early mortality, greater cost to the parent, slower reproductive rate due to longer generations and reduced litter size—is nevertheless favored because of overwhelming advantages accruing to the adult, including larger body and brain size and a larger set of acquired associations and responses.[1]

Beyond this cliché, which will receive critical scrutiny below, of what use is the concept? In recent years it has been applied by investigators studying the details of the development of skill in infancy (Bruner & Bruner, 1968). Sucking patterns of the newborn, it is argued, in addition to their obvious effect on current viability, serve as the ontogenetic foundation of later-phase information processing and mother–infant interaction schemes which are uniquely human. Thus evolution, ever conservative, gives a new ontogenetic function to a phylogenetically old system. Furthermore, it is argued, the system becomes modified in ways that have nothing to do with current viability but only with effects on later-phase adaptations. Claims have been made for a uniquely human burst-pause pattern in newborn sucking, unrelated to feeding or breathing, having as its sole purpose the eliciting of the mother's attention so that a rhythmic mother–infant interaction pattern, essential for later-phase viability, will begin to form (Kaye & Brazelton, 1971).

While we can cavil at the extent to which these workers have stressed, again, the old idea of human uniqueness, and while we note that there is no evidence that sucking patterns have any influence on later information processing or mother–infant relations, still the invocation of evolutionary process is leading to experiments which might not otherwise have been made. We can hope and expect that more attention will be given to the sucking pattern in nonhuman primates and to the question of late effects of the early pattern.

Selection for Plasticity and Resilience in Development

It has been argued (Kagan, 1977) that selection can be expected to have produced a developing nervous system which will be relatively impervious to insult and whose major behavioral functions will be maintained and emerge normally in spite of wide environmental fluctuations. This corresponds to the notion of canalization in evolutionary biology and embryology (Waddington, 1942), according to which selection is held to have endowed organisms with a small number of developmental tracks, progress along which is regulated by negative feedback. Thus departures from the track (for example, effects of early insults) will be tolerated temporarily but will result in final correction, so that the end point reached by the organism will not have been altered. This means not that normal development is environment-independent but rather that so wide a range of stimuli can provoke or restore progress along developmental tracks that the normal outcome is very nearly certain. Broadly speaking, this is a sound view, but it faces three problems.

1. While this would seem to be equally true for all organisms, the fact is that organisms vary greatly in the environment-dependency of their developing nervous systems. Thus factors other than the necessity to protect vital functions must be operating.
2. It is difficult to see how natural selection would produce a nervous system with functions developing independent of features of the environment which are continuously present. With respect to such features, selection would lose its cutting edge. Thus the visual system of kittens does not develop normally without an input of patterned light (Wiesel & Hubel, 1965; Hirsch & Spinnelli, 1970). Why, one may ask, did natural selection not give them a *really* good visual system, one that would grow reliably with or without patterned light? The reason is probably that since kittens have never been called upon to grow the system in darkness there was no disadvantage for those that were unable to do so. How generally this principle may be applied remains to be seen, however.
3. The developing nervous systems of many organisms, including those with the least plastic behavioral functions, may exhibit highly specific forms of environment dependency. For example, salmon become imprinted on the odor of the stream they are raised in; this accounts for their ability to return after long migrations (Hasler, 1960; 1974). Moths will feed preferentially on the species of leaf they lived on as caterpillars (Thorpe, 1939), a simple effect surviving metamorphosis. A similar process appears to be operating to determine habitat selection in damselflies (Johnson, 1966). The infantile attachment objects of members

of many bird species will determine their sexual choice as adults (Hess, 1974). This effect is subsequently modifiable, but at greater cost, and is in any case readily reinstated.[2] Finally, learning paradigms in which rats are trained early in life and then the habits are allowed to become extinct show that later in life such habits are much more easily reengrained ("reinstatement") than established anew in controls, in spite of the fact that experimental and control animals do not differ at all in base-level responding on the task (Campbell & Jaynes, 1966). This interesting phenomenon may have wide applicability and should alert those investigators of early experience effects who study only base-level adult responding to the hazards of accepting the null hypothesis.

Even for those species whose behavioral repertoire is limited and relatively fixed (and certainly for species which do not fit this description) we must recognize the existence of *facultative* as opposed to obligatory adaptations. The former result from selection for a *series* of adaptations in an organism which inhabits several different niches. Facultative adaptations require a switching mechanism which will enable the animal to "select" (not necessarily consciously or voluntarily) among the several possibilities of the genome, and the switch must be responsive to information in the environment. Early experience may be a part of the switch in certain animals. That is, the environment may signal the developing infant nervous system that certain facultative adaptations will be required in adulthood and "tell" it to produce those rather than others. The well-known (although poorly understood) mechanism by which rats stressed in infancy become larger and less fearful as adults (e.g., Levine & Mullins, 1966; Denenberg, 1964) could conceivably have resulted from such selection. (One would have to suppose either that being smaller and more fearful is an advantage in some environments or that it is tied to some other parameter which is important. Either of these suppositions is reasonable.)

Genetic Assimilation

By this mechanism characteristics, whether morphological or behavioral, which are at first acquired during individual life history come eventually to be genetically determined (Waddington, 1953). While at first blush this seems to have a Lamarckian cast, it is really not mysterious. Members of a population who can acquire the character lead the population into niches where the character is an advantage. The same individuals are likely to be among the first who exhibit some *genetic* adaptation for the character, and these will be selected for in the ordinary way. (Of course, this must be a situation in which lability for the character is not at a premium.) A related mechanism, usually called the Baldwin effect (Mayr, 1958), specifies that the initial acquired character be behavioral but that the genetic adaptations which follow may be of a wide variety *not* limited to genetic changes underlying the behavior. For example, a bird population acquires a taste for a new berry by experiment; adaptations may follow affecting the genetic basis of beak shape, color perception, and digestive enzyme systems. When we consider that entering a new niche is typically the first step in species formation (Mayr, 1963) and that for animals, at least, a new niche is entered by means of behavior, we may conclude that something like the Baldwin effect must be very important in animal evolution. The human or protohuman invention of the infant-carrying sling may thus have paved the way for the increase in human altriciality at birth, with its many important consequences. (Some of these are considered below.) The recently demonstrated fact that chimpanzees can acquire some rudiments of language (e.g. Rumbaugh, von Glaserfeld, Warner, Pisani, & Gill, 1974) suggests that genetic assimilation may have been involved in the evolution of the human capacity for language. Finally, since juveniles are typically the most experimental members of a species, exhibiting many useless behaviors usually called play, we may expect that it is often they who take the lead into a new niche. The first step in the evolution of language may, indeed, have been taken by a population of infants and mothers babbling at each other.

Selection for Litter Size and Birth Spacing

It has been known for many years that animals exhibiting parental care cannot usually maximize their reproductive success by maximizing litter or clutch size or minimizing birth spacing (Lack, 1954) because there is a quickly reached point of diminishing returns at which investment by parents is thinned so as to jeopardize all the offspring. Optimal litter or clutch size varies with environmental quality, but in any environment there is a point at which the total number of surviving offspring will be decreased by a further increase in clutch size. This phenomenon operates in humans in relation to birth spacing as well as litter size. Before the advent of modern medicine the number of children surviving from 100 twin pairs was smaller than the number surviving from 100 singletons, giving humans an optimal litter size of 1 (Trivers, 1974). Particularly in developing countries, but also in the United States (Morley, 1973), neonatal, infant, and early childhood mortality increases with decreasing birth interval.

In human hunter–gatherers, as well as in great apes, natural birth spacing is about 4 years. Many questions may be raised regarding the implications of shorter spacing, among which are direct effects on the young child of reduced length of intensive care, variations in the intensity of sibling rivalry, and strain on the mother, with its probable attendant ill effects on the children. One wonders, also, if the strong birth order effects usually found in the study of achievement motivation are related in any way to length of birth spacing.

Inclusive Fitness Theory and Parental Investment Strategy

Important recent advances in natural selection theory have transformed our understanding of parental altruistic behavior, among other forms of social behavior, and more generally of parent–offspring relations. These advances have decisively liberated the study of social behavior from such concepts as "group selection" and "survival of the species." (Both these concepts are now widely considered untenable.) The advances are summarized as follows:[3]

Inclusive fitness. Invoked initially to explain the remarkable altruism of the social insects, this concept extends the notion of individual fitness to include the individual's blood relatives. A gene for altruism will spread through a population, in spite of the cost to the individual altruist, provided the altruist preferentially helps those most likely to share the gene. These will be the subject's relatives, and the likelihood of a shared gene (and thus of a given degree of altruism) will vary closely with the degree of relatedness (Hamilton, 1964).

Parental investment and sexual selection. In species in which one sex invests more than the other in offspring, this sex will become a limiting resource, and members of the other sex (males, in most birds and mammals) will compete among themselves for access to the first (females). The result will be greater male than female variability in reproductive success (RS; number of offspring), and a variety of special adaptations for fighting in males and nurturance in females. Female choice will be seen to guide the course of male evolution by selecting only certain males for fertilization of ova. Sexual dimorphism of varying degrees will result. Species, or populations within species, will be seen to vary systematically along certain parameters. Those high in sexual dimorphism will exhibit high male variability in RS, high promiscuity (or polygamy) in the successful males, low male parental investment, and high male–male competition. Those at the other end of the continuum will exhibit pair bonding with relatively low male promiscuity, low male variability in RS, low male–male competition, and high male parental investment (Trivers, 1972). Humans are generally considered to be near but not *at* this end of the continuum; many species of birds are more strongly pair bonded. It should be remembered that these adaptations may be facultative; that is, the same species may exhibit different reproductive strategies in different environments.

Parent–offspring conflict.   Parent and offspring may be expected to "disagree" over the degree of parental investment, since the offspring is related to itself more closely than to future siblings, whereas the parent is equally related to all of them. At a certain point in the offspring's growth, the parent will "decide" that the offspring is viable and will want to direct its energy to the production of subsequent offspring, while the offspring will be demanding more investment. At a later point, the offspring's "desire" to have siblings, which arises from the same selection pressure that makes parents want offspring, will be sufficient to overcome its own selfishness. The period intervening will be the period of weaning conflict, during which the offspring will be expected to exhibit "tantrums"—signals which deceive the parent into perceiving distress where there is no distress so as to cajole out of it more investment. Such tantrums are found in a wide variety of species (Trivers, 1974).

Sex ratio theory.   Because males are more variable than females in their reproductive success, parents in good environments will be expected to vary the sex ratio of their offspring in favor of males so as to maximize the number of offspring in the third (F_2) generation. Parents in poor environments will be expected to want more females, since inferior males are likely to leave no offspring (Fisher, 1958; Trivers & Willard, 1973).

Theory of competition.   The relevant portion of this body of theory holds that competition will be selected to be different among relatives than among nonrelatives. The closer the relationship, the less likely the competitor will be to inflict real harm and the more likely to protest strongly over a small degree of harm inflicted on himself. (In other words, the relatedness will make him or her behave like a parent in the former case and an offspring in the latter [Popp & DeVore, 1975].)

Relations among juveniles.   Except where preparation for adult competition is at a premium and where population structure makes this possible, juveniles will be expected to aggregate in mixed-age rather than same-age play groups. An individual will be at an advantage choosing an older playmate because of possible investment by that playmate, including transfer of nongenetic information, particularly if the two are related. An individual will be at an advantage choosing a younger playmate because of possible practice of parental behavior. However, where competition among adults is of very great importance, individual juveniles will be expected to try to accustom themselves to it by associating with others as nearly as possible equal in ability (Konner, 1975).

Among investigatable questions raised by this body of theory, the following may be of interest to child psychologists:

1. How do adoptive parents differ from biological parents in parental investment? What causes adoption under various circumstances?
2. What explains variation in human male parental investment?
3. At what age and in what circumstances can children be expected to desire younger siblings, if they have none?
4. Does parental differentiation in caretaking of boys and girls vary systematically with environmental quality, as sex ratio theory predicts?
5. Do identical and fraternal twin pairs differ in their competitive behavior?
6. How does varying the age discrepancy between two children affect their interaction?

Many other testable hypotheses readily come to mind. It should be noted that invoking natural selection in these instances does not rule out more conventional explanations. Natural selection is the final cause theory in biology. Its dictates must be met, but they may be met with a wide variety of proximate mechanisms, by means of a wide variety of efficient causes. Unraveling those efficient causes is the business of most of the life sciences, including behavioral science. Yet selection theory may point the way to some of the more interesting ones.

PHYLOGENY OF PARENTAL BEHAVIOR AND OF BEHAVIOR DEVELOPMENT

Apart from the question of how selection may be expected to influence various behaviors during evolution, from considerations arising from Darwinian assumptions, there is the question of what has actually happened in evolution. How are various features of behavior and development distributed taxonomically, and what can we infer from that distribution (and from the fossil evidence) about the history of those behaviors? What are the broad trends and modes of change affecting behavior and development, not at the population level, where specific selective forces are seen to be operating *currently,* but at the phyletic level, where processes requiring thousands of generations may be in evidence?

Four Misconceptions

"Ontogeny recapitulates phylogeny." Wrong; but, properly stated, there is a piece of the truth here. Evolution is opportunistic; it builds on what it has. Therefore embryologic and other developmental events are conserved, while evolution builds on later phases of the organism. In other words, ontogeny recapitulates not the adult phases of ancestral forms but, to some extent, the early ontogeny of those forms. Put yet another way, the early phases of related forms can be expected to resemble one another more than the adult phases of these forms. But we must never look, in human infancy and childhood, for characteristics resembling those of *adults* of other animals. (Carried to a bizarre extreme, this has at times resulted in the contention that mental functioning in Western children resembles that of adults of other human populations. Evidence for this contention is, to put it mildly, hard to find. In addition, it makes a travesty of everything we know about the biology and evolution of human populations.)

"The higher the animal, the slower its development, the less developed it is at birth, and the more plastic is its behavioral repertoire." No. First, there is no acceptable way of arraying animals in a hierarchy. Attempts to do this have been very heavily criticized (e.g., Lockhard, 1971). What is interesting about animals is how they differ, not how they rank. Second, plasticity is very variable even in closely related animals and is by no means always linked to slow development. Of two subspecies of deermice (*Peromyscus maniculatus*) the one that develops faster is more affected by early experience (Rosen & Hart, 1963). A review of sensory-motor development in two prosimian, one Old World monkey, and two New World monkey species (Ehrlich, 1974), reveals no trends at all in the rate of emergence of the behavior and no relation to the wide differences in learning ability among these animals in adulthood. Variation within a species in time of emergence of the behaviors proves in some instances greater than variation among widely disparate phyla.

Very broadly speaking, of course, it may be said that behavioral plasticity increases as we come closer to man (Lorenz, 1965), but more specific expectations than this one should not be held. Plasticity should not be expected to vary with rate of development, and it should be understood that plasticity may vary with stage of the life cycle in unexpected ways, related organisms being more or less plastic at earlier or later stages of their development.

Above all, no simple notions should be held about state of development at birth. This is determined not by broad phyletic trends but by necessities specific to individual species, such as the level of predation, the possibility of nest building, the time available for gestation, and the overall length of the lifespan. State of development at birth need not be correlated with overall rate of development or ultimate behavioral plasticity in any way. Finally, it should not be expected that the rate of development *or* the state of development at birth *in different behavioral and organ systems* will be intercorrelated. Newborn kangaroos and opossums, otherwise the most altricial of all mammals, have highly developed forelimbs and a poorly understood orienting system which carry them from the uterus, across a great expanse of belly, into the pouch, and to the teat, with no assistance from their mothers. Among ungulates, fairly closely related species differ in whether or not the newborn is able to follow the mother immediately; it *is* in species (such as wildebeest) which are highly migratory; in a number of others it is "cached" in a shifting hiding place, and the mother returns periodically until it is able to follow well. Here, again, the state of development at birth is determined by the specific demands of the niche and is unrelated to behavioral plasticity. Hares and rabbits, close relatives, differ as dramatically in their state of development at birth as virtually any other pair of mammals (Bourliere, 1955). Humans and other higher primates are precocial in most sensory systems and altricial in most motor systems (except for, in monkeys, clinging). (An extensive discussion of these and other aspects of altriciality and precociality is given by Ewer, 1968). Thus it seems that state of development at birth, which as we will see determines many other aspects of infant and parent behavior, is in turn the result of specific adaptation, usually at birth by means of the process we have called the "selection funnel" and follows no grand phylogenetic logic nor does it bear any relation to ultimate adult plasticity of the organism.

Here again, the misconception has been carried to bizarre extremes. African motor precocity has been viewed as consistent with an alleged African intellectual inferiority in adulthood because of some half-baked and silly notions about phylogeny. Of course, there is no good evidence for African intellectual inferiority and no evidence whatever for any correlation, positive or negative, between infant motor development and later intellectual capacity. We may point out as well that there is no basis in evolutionary theory for expecting such a relationship.

"If a behavior is phyletically widespread, it must be a 'fixed action pattern' or 'instinct' and thus genetically based; in this event there is no sense trying to change it." Each step of this syllogism is wrong.

1. Analogy is not homology. Widely disparate animals may face similar puzzles posed to them by natural selection, and their solutions may look similar, and serve similar functions, *without* having similar mechanisms. The wings of flies come from the thorax; of birds, from forelimbs; of bats, from fingers; and of man, from Eastern Airlines. Bowlby (1969) correctly points out that human infant attachment formation and precocial bird imprinting serve similar adaptive functions. But we need know scarcely more than that one is completed in several days and the other requires several months to know that their underlying mechanisms must differ in important ways. The point is that both mechanisms must be investigated separately. All the comparision can do is point to *possible* features of attachment formation in humans which have received inadequate study.[4]

2. "Fixed action patterns," the building blocks of what used to be called instincts (Lorenz, 1965), are arrived at by as wide a variety of routes as there are species to exhibit them. For us to accept that a fixed action pattern or a response to a given stimulus ("releasing mechanism") is not learned, we must have the evidence of the deprivation experiment, by means of which the relevant information or experience is withheld from the animal during its growth. In this fashion numerous features of the behavior of virtually any organism studied can be shown to be innate, or at least that, as Lorenz points out (1965, p. 27), to say that they are is "less inexact than the statement that a steam locomotive or the Eiffel Tower are built entirely of metal." In human infants, smiling, crying from discomfort, bipedal walking, and language competence are examples of behavioral or cognitive characteristics not dependent on learning for their emergence. However, and here we depart from the classical ethologists, many fixed and perfectly stereotypic action patterns and, more especially, releasing mechanisms, in a wide variety of species, may emerge by routes which depend in important ways on experience. Already mentioned among these are food choice in moths, habitat choice in damselflies, homing in salmon, sexual choice in some pair-bonding birds, and sexual performance in rhesus monkeys. The same evidently applies to mouse killing by rats (Denenberg, Pachke, & Zarrow, 1968) and maternal behavior in rhesus monkeys (Arling & Harlow, 1967). It has even been argued (Lehrmann, 1953) that the pecking behavior of chicks immediately after hatching is *acquired* during gestation through the training of head movements by the beat of the fetal heart. While this particular instance may be criticized (Lorenz, 1965), the concept is important because it makes a further distinction: behaviors (and releasers) which are *innate* need not be *genetically determined.* (Various routes to species-specific fixed action patterns are discussed by Moltz and Robbins, 1965.) Again, the specific determination of each pattern must be investigated individually.

3. A proper discussion of this point is beyond the scope of this chapter, but because the specter of biology seems to cast such a sombre shadow over the making of public policy, it must be mentioned. The belief is held by some psychologists that if a behavior, ability, or behavior disorder is genetically determined, it is a waste of time to try to change it (Jensen, 1969). Wearers of eyeglasses and takers of insulin can testify to the folly of this view. While these are palliative measures and not cures, medical institutes forge bravely ahead from day to day searching for ways of altering conditions in people who have them because of simple gene action. Behavioral scientists can do the same.

"If animals are so variable, we may as well pay attention to those most closely related to man, since this is where we will learn the most."   This view guides the funding of research on monkeys and apes and the comparative thinking of most behavioral scientists. It is not completely false, but is wrong enough to require comment. Closeness of phyletic relationship is only one of four bases for comparing two species, and it sometimes may be misleading. The other three are similarity of reproductive strategy, similarity of ecological adaptation, and similarity of major sensory processes used in communication. The chimpanzee, our closest relative and surely worthy of study, differs from humans living under natural conditions in having a much smaller territorial or home range, doing much less hunting, and exhibiting much less pair bonding (Goodall, 1965). Hunting mammals such as lions exhibit much more humanlike patterns of sharing behavior (Schaller, 1972) and teaching behavior (Schenkel, 1966) with respect to offspring than do any higher primates. Foxes, which are pair-bonding hunting mammals and thus an excellent model for certain aspects of human parent–offspring relations, have scarcely been studied at all.

Rhesus monkeys, the model on which we rely almost completely for laboratory manipulation of the growth of social relations, may not be appropriate at all. The major difficulties are that under natural conditions rhesus monkeys live in very large troops, are highly promiscuous, and are very careful to keep their infants from other individuals. These are important differences distinguishing them from human foragers. Indeed, it has been shown that in two closely related species of macaque (bonnet and pigtail) the response of infants to removal of their mothers when the pair are living in a social context derives from just such differences in the species' normal guarding of infants (Rosenblum, 1971a; 1976). The responses of the infants are diametric opposites: the bonnet infant is soon adopted by another female and is soon behaving normally; the pigtail infant enters a profound depression from which it never fully recovers. In these and other respects, the pigtail resembles the rhesus, our favorite subject for study; the bonnet, studied only in one or two laboratories, resembles humans.[5]

A final example will illustrate the principle of comparision because of similarity in the sensory processes relied on for communication. Much has been made in recent years of the fact that the redoubtable rhesus monkey relies largely on olfactory signaling for communication in courtship (Michael & Keverne, 1968). While the possibility of similar effects in humans could receive more attention than it has, it may be of greater interest to study the ring dove (Lott, Scholz, & Lehrman, 1967), which we know relies overwhelmingly (as people do) on *visual* signaling in courtship. Thus a close relative, the rhesus, with its much better sense of smell than ours, is of less value as a model than a remote relative, the ring dove, which, like humans, has a poor sense of smell and an excellent sense of vision (and, incidentally, is pair bonding, as people are). Similar considerations *may* apply regarding the development of attachment in infancy, although we must note the recent intriguing demonstration that human infants show preferential head turning toward their own mothers' breast pads, as opposed to another mother's, using olfactory discrimination, at the age of 6 days (MacFarlane, 1974).

Process in the Phylogeny of Development

This review would be incomplete without mention of some basic concepts of phylogenesis derived from comparative embryology. They provide descriptive generalizations regarding events which are known to have happened during the evolution of ontogeny in various phyla (DeBeer, 1951). These processes are of a much more inductive sort and describe much more long-term events than the processes discussed earlier in the chapter. They are descriptive summaries of the history of various organisms, rather than deductive principles of change in adaptation.

At least eight such processes have been named. The names will not be repeated here, except for the most famous of these, *neoteny,* which is usually held to have operated in human evolution. As a result of this process, the rate of general body growth becomes slowed relative to the pacing of sexual maturation in such a way as to make the adult of the descendent resemble the juvenile of the ancestor. For this reason, it is said, human adults resemble ape infants and juveniles in various physical characteristics more than we do adult apes.

Little purpose will be served by describing the rest of the terms and concepts (see DeBeer, 1951, for a review). The main point, which summarizes all of them, is this: the speed of growth in specific organ systems, the age at termination of growth in specific systems, the age at sexual maturity, the length of gestation, and the length of life *all may evolve independently of one another.* DeBeer called such processes "heterochrony." New characters may appear at one phase of development and then shift to another phase or come to occupy more than one phase. Old characteristics may disappear by means of the same processes in similar phase-specific fashion. Such events affecting ontogeny must, indeed, be among the major processes by which the form of organisms changes over the history of life.

The concept of *allometry* is usually invoked to describe the relationship between the size and weight of organ systems whose rates of growth are not related linearly. It provides descriptive equations, usually simple exponential equations of the form $y = bx^k$, where y and x are the respective organs or body parts and b and k are constants (Sinclair, 1973). These equations summarize the shape changes of organisms, whether during evolution or during individual development.

Its significance in phylogency is that we may observe major shape changes during the evolution of a body part the significance of which is attributable to other body size changes and which needs no separate adaptive explanation. In the evolution of the horse, for example, the face has lengthened as body size has increased. This is because face length is determined by area of tooth surface necesaary for chewing, which, since it depends on the amount eaten, depends on body mass. Body mass increases as the cube of body length, and tooth surface as the square of face length. Therefore face length must increase faster than (as the 3/2 power of) body length. A recent attempt has been made to apply the same kind of reasoning to the study of human brain evolution (Pilbeam & Gould, 1974).

Its significance in individual behavior development lies in the manner in which allometric shape changes affect the behavior of parents and children. It has been noted, for example, that humans, as well as all other mammals and birds, because of allometric shape changes during growth, have young with a characteristic "infant shape," including a head very large and limbs short with respect to the torso, a flat face, and eyes very large with respect to the face. These features, in addition to small size and behavioral clumsiness, are proposed as releasing mechanisms for parental behavior (Lorenz, 1965) and their universality held to explain the potential for cross-fostering of species, including human affection for young of other species. Allometric shape changes during growth remove the features and correspondingly reduce the power of the child to release parental behavior.

Among other consequences of allometric shape changes for behavior development, it may be noted that among other problems faced by children learning to walk, their centers of gravity are higher than they will be later, and, among other problems faced by adolescents learning virtually everything, they have to face the embarrassment of having feet and hands that grow faster than the rest of them.

A major new treatment of the evolution of ontogeny, which has restored the field to common-sense usefulness and scientific respectability (while stirring up a bit of interesting controversy), has been contributed by Gould (1977). His book, which covers all aspects of heterochrony and many aspects of allometry, is divided into two parts. The first, of interest mainly to historians of science, retraces the (frequently false) steps of his predecessors in the field. The second, substantive portion presents a modern synthesis of DeBeer's ideas with Gould's system for rationalizing them, tested against much modern data in ontogeny and phylogeny, especially of marine and other invertebrates. The book ends with a treatment of human evolution and a reconsideration of the Bolk fetalization thesis and the concept of human neoteny. According to this thesis the human being is, in Bolk's words, "a sexually mature fetal ape" (quoted by Gould, 1977, p . 361). This *condition,* called *pedomorphosis,* could have been attained by *neoteny*—absolute deceleration of somatic growth in relation to sexual maturation—or by its opposite—acceleration of gonadal maturity in relation to a more fixed pace of somatic growth *(progenesis).* In view of the slow absolute rate of human somatic development when compared with that of apes, neoteny seems the only choice. (Indeed—although Gould does not mention this—the facts of comparative development of humans and other higher primates (Schultz, 1963; Tanner, 1962) would seem to require an absolute slowing of gonadal maturation exceeded by a substantially *greater* absolute deceleration in somatic growth.)

Resting on and synthesizing the work of Portmann (1945), Count (1947), Holt, Chee, Mellits and Hill (1975), and others, Gould argues that the key, if not the sole, difference between humans and other higher primates is that the steep prenatal slope of log brain weight on log body weight, identical in all, continues longer in humans relative to birthweight and relative to body weight. In the other higher primates the slope drops at the time of birth; in humans it continues as steeply for almost two more years. To paraphrase Portmann, humans should be born about 21 months later than we are, in terms of brain growth rate. Such a perspective certainly lends greater credence to the notion that infant behavior development in humans has more to do with a sort of postnatal neuroembryology than with learning (Konner, 1979). It also raises serious questions about the appropriateness of all of the currently used monkey and ape models of human infant behavior and deprivation.

Gould argues that a very minor genetic change could alter this growth rate, which in turn could account for most of the morphological differences between humans and apes. He even attempts to revive the discredited notion of saltation—sudden major morphological change instead of gradualism—to account for the emergence of new species. This may be plausible with the asexually reproducing marine invertebrates Gould has done so much work on; these could presumably mutate and go about their reproductive business. For sexually reproducing vertebrates the microevolutionary scenario is as unlikely as it was at the turn of the century: how does the "hopeful monster" find a mate? However, heterochrony—and its specific hominid version, neoteny—are perfectly compatible with polygenic gradualism and will probably soon play a major role in the synthetic theory of evolution.

THE EVOLUTION OF HUMAN BEHAVIOR DEVELOPMENT

To be of real use to us, this body of theory must, of course, generate hypotheses and guide us in our choice of laboratory animal models; but it must do more. It must help us to place the human species in relation to other animals in such a way that we can reconstruct the history of the facts we are most concerned with—the facts of the behavior, and the growth, of parents and children. Only then will evolution illuminate these facts.

An extensive review of the data now available is not possible here. Even if it were, great gaps would still remain in the picture. Still we may touch upon a few areas of interest. In each case, probable events leading from our higher primate ancestors to the condition found in human hunter–gatherers, will be suggested. This will be followed by an account of the range of adaptations seen in intermediate-level societies, including traditional farming and pastoral societies, in which certain ecological possibilities and restrictions of the hunting–gathering societies do not obtain, and by a brief account of the modern industrial adaptation, particularly as seen currently in the United States and England.

Several notes of caution are required. First, the process of transformation from higher primates to human hunter–gatherers is evolutionary in the biological sense; the subsequent transitions are instances of sociohistorical change, such as may in a modern nation take place in the course of a few decades, and involving, so far as we can surmise, no genetic change whatever. Put another way, there is no important difference, biologically, between modern human hunter–gatherers and the inhabitants of modern industrial states that can help us to understand the differences in behavior development and parental behavior that distinguish these two sociocultural adaptations.

Second, the brief characterization of each adaptation, as well as that of the "intermediate-level" societies, is necessarily an oversimplification. Hunting–gathering is understood here to exclude equestrian (mounted) hunters, since our purpose is to make inferences about the circumstances obtaining during most of human evolution, whereas mounted hunting is a recent sociohistorical novelty. Of the nonmounted hunter–gatherers (sometimes called "classical" hunter–gatherers), detailed and accurate information about infancy and childhood is available only for the !Kung San (Konner, 1972; 1975; 1977; 1978; 1979; Blurton Jones & Konner, 1973; West & Konner, 1976; Gaulin & Konner, 1977), and generalizations beyond the !Kung to other hunter–gatherers must be made with caution.

Nevertheless, it is possible to examine ethnographic descriptions of other classical hunter–gatherers (e.g. Turnbull, 1965; Holmberg, 1969) and find fairly detailed accounts of infancy and childhood that accord very well with that for the !Kung, although such groups as the Ituri Pygmies and the Siriono of Bolivia can have no common historical origin with the !Kung. Of greater interest than these isolated supporting instances is cross-cultural statistical survey research on child training practices. Much of this research has been summarized by Textor (1967). Although random perusal of Textor's summary carries with it a well-known risk of unwarranted rejection of the null hypothesis (it is essentially a compendium of all significant relationships among variables derived from all past nomothetic cross-cultural survey research, with the nonsignificant relationships omitted), deliberate hypothesis testing carries much less risk. Testing the hypothesis that hunting–gathering societies would resemble the !Kung San in infant and child care practices more than would other nonindustrial societies produces evidence that hunter–gatherers are indeed distinctive and more similar to the !Kung. Unfortunately, the variables assessed in most of the older nomothetic surveys are not the ones we are most interested in, in the light of modern theory in developmental psychology. Still, the data reported by Textor indicate a consistent tendency for societies relying on food gathering to exhibit more indulgent infant and child training practices than do other nonindustrial societies. Specifically, "pain inflicted on infant" is lower ($p < 0.05$) and "overall indulgence of infant" ($p < 0.05$) and "anal satisfaction potential" ($p < 0.01$) are higher in societies subsisting primarily by food gathering ($n = 19\text{--}40$) than in those subsisting by other means ($n = 22\text{--}34$). In childhood, "anxiety over responsible behavior" ($p < 0.01$), "anxiety over obedient behavior" ($p < 0.01$), and "anxiety over self-reliant behavior" ($p < 0.05$) are lower in food gathering ($n = 30\text{--}35$) than in other societies ($n = 37\text{--}42$). Only at adolescence, when "female initiation rites ($p < 0.01$) are more severe in foraging societies $n = 38$) than in nonforaging ones ($n = 27$), is the pattern of difference in indulgence reversed. Also, adolescent peer groups are less common ($p < 0.05$) in foraging ($n = 23$) than in nonforaging societies ($n = 14$), consistent with other findings and demographic predictions indicating the unlikelihood of same-age peer groups at any time during childhood in hunting–gathering societies.[6]

Furthermore, Lozoff and Brittenham (1978) compared ten tropical hunting–gathering societies with 176 other nonindustrial societies on infant care practices rated by Barry and Paxson (1971). The ten (!Kung San, Hadza, Mbuti, Semang, Vedda, Tiwi, Siriono, Botocudo, Shavante, and Chenchu) were all those that met the criteria of living between the latitudes of 22°30' N and 22°30' S and having less than 10 percent dependence on agriculture, animal husbandry, and fishing for their subsistence, as coded by Murdock and Morrow (1970). Unfortunately, the authors do not test the differences they report for statistical significance. Nevertheless, it is clear that very close mother–infant contact, late weaning, and indulgent responsiveness to infant crying are highly characteristic of hunting–gathering societies in the tropics. Late weaning is also characteristic of other nonindustrial societies, and there too the mother is the principal caretaker in infancy, but other aspects of the mother–infant bond measured by Barry and Paxson make it seem closer and more indulgent in hunter–gatherers.

Lozoff and Brittenham also attempt a comparision of the Barry and Paxson codes for intermediate-level societies with published research and recommendations concerning the United States. Whether measured by body contact, sleeping distance, response to crying, or weaning age, mother–infant contact and maternal indulgence of infants appear to be lower in the United States than in the 176 nonindustrial non–hunter–gatherers. This finding supports that of Whiting and Child (1953), who reported that patterns of infant and child care and training in Chicago during the 1940s were substantially above the median of their ratings for the comparable customs of a large representative sample of nonindustrial societies (including hunter–gatherers), except in the area of aggressiveness training, where the Chicagoans were more indulgent. In oral socialization, anal socialization, sex and modesty training, and independence training they were considered very strict or at least more strict than average for the nonindustrial societies. This comparison was done independently of, and for different theoretical purposes than, the much later comparision made by Lozoff and Brittenham using the Barry and Paxson ratings.

It has sometimes been suggested that while "primitive" societies use more physical contact and more indulgent nursing practices in nurturing their offspring, industrial societies compensate by offering more interaction using "distal" mechanisms —eyes, ears, and voice. For example, in a comparison of mother–infant interaction in Boston with that in a rural Guatemalan village, it was found that the total number of interactions was about the same but that in Guatemala about 80 percent of the interactions were physical, whereas in Boston about 80 percent were verbal or vocal (Klein, Lasky, Yarbrough, Habicht, & Sellers, 1977; Sellers, 1973). Suspecting that this was not a generally applicable distinction between industrial and nonindustrial societies, Konner (1977) compared the Guatemalan data with data on interaction among the !Kung, collected by a very similar method. The Boston data, also using the same method of observation recording, showed that the professional-class infants had somewhat more verbal interaction than did the working-class infants (Tulkin, 1977), but the cross-cultural comparision showed that the Guatemalan infants indeed received much less verbal stimulation than did even those of the Boston working class (4 percent as opposed to 10 percent of observed 5-sec blocks contained a caretaker vocalization). !Kung observations, however, showed levels of infant vocalization, caretaker vocalization, and reciprocal vocalization equal to those of the Boston working class (Konner, 1977, p. 300). Thus "distal" and "proximal" or contact mechanisms of mother–infant interaction are not reciprocals of one another, the one inevitably declining as the other rises during the course of sociohistorical change. !Kung infants receive levels of distal stimulation comparable to those of the Boston infants while getting much higher levels of physical contact, more indulgent weaning, and a higher percentage of responsiveness to crying.

It is important to note that the range of variability in intermediate-level societies (those relying primarily on agriculture, animal husbandry, and/or fishing for subsistence) is very great—greater than that for hunting–gathering societies (even if not restricted to the tropics) and much greater than that for industrialized societies, which become more similar as they modernize—and they constitute the vast majority of the empirical base on which modern anthropology rests. The variation in their child care practices is not random with respect to their basic modes of subsistence and other aspects of their ecological situation. Some of this variation will be considered below. Here it may be noted merely that the comparison of industrial with nonindustrial societies on indulgence may also be made among nonindustrial societies, comparing those of greater with those of lesser political complexity. Textor (1967) compares on various measures of child rearing societies exhibiting the large or small state with those in which the highest level of political integration is the minimal state, autonomous community, or family. Like the earlier-mentioned comparison in Textor's summary (foraging versus nonforaging societies), this one is merely an ingenious and orderly concatenation of previously published data and contains no new coding of the ethnographic literature. The hypothesis of decreasing indulgence with increasing political complexity is confirmed on six measures of infant and child care comparable to the ones mentioned in the foraging–nonforaging comparison discussed above. (It should be noted that these various measures of infant and child care are not necessarily mutually independent.) In addition, three other variables relating to child life show significant differences in this comparison. Punishment of premarital sex is more severe in 89 more complex than in 90 less complex societies ($p < 0.001$). Exclusive mother–child households (father sleeps elsewhere, no extended family) are more likely in more complex societies ($p < 0.001$). Desire for children is higher in more complex than less complex societies.[7] Thus, paradoxically, indulgence of children is lower where expressed desire for children is higher. (Perhaps the desire is expressed primarily by men, who then turn them over to women, usually in exclusive mother–child households, for their succorance.)

What follows, then, is a series of speculations, or "just so" stories, about the evolution of human behavior development and the context in which it occurs, from the presumed protohuman higher-primate condition to the present-day industrial state, based on solid knowledge of higher primates (monkeys and apes), reasonably solid although incomplete knowledge of human hunter–gatherers of the present day, and solid knowledge of both nonindustrial and industrial nonforaging societies. The evolutionary (i.e., up to the hunting–gathering stage) and subsequent sociohistorical sequences proposed are no more than plausible hypothetical arrangements of the available knowledge, using a strategy something like that of the comparative anatomist who tries to reconstruct the evolution of soft body parts. That is, data on contemporaneous forms are made to appear sequential or at least to provide reasonable inferences about sequences. How reasonable they turn out to be will depend on the development of new knowledge about the several stages, particularly about the hunting–gathering stage, where knowledge is weakest. Hunter–gatherer studies are currently the most urgent and most neglected area of anthropology.

Carrying Methods and the Behavioral Status of Newborns

Phylogenetic Background

Higher-primate newborns are generally precocial in sensory systems and altricial in motor systems, except for clinging ability, which in most monkeys is present at birth (Ewer, 1968). Humans are more altricial motorically at birth than monkeys or apes. They develop more slowly than apes, which develop more slowly than monkeys. Monkeys have the shortest and humans the longest lifespan. Comparing humans to chimpanzees, it is not clear that there has been a *relative* slowing of development in all growth systems. It seems instead that an absolute lengthening of the lifespan can account for many of the differences in rate of development. This lengthening may account for the more altricial condition of humans at birth if we assume that gestation could not be lengthened (see note 1). Surely the human invention of the sling for carrying infants must have been an important step in making this more altricial condition possible; human neonates do not ordinarily cling and so must be carried. Also, to evolve a slower rate of development often requires reduced selection pressure against offspirng (Emlen, 1973, p. 141), which the sling would provide. This suggests that the exceptionally altricial condition of human newborns has evolved very recently, probably in the last million years. This notion is supported by the fact that the social smile, which makes human infants most attractive to mothers, does not appear until the second month, and infants are unattractive at birth, suggesting that selection has not had time to reduce the age of emergence of social smiling. (A similar argument was made by Richards [1966] for the golden hamster. In this species the length of gestation is shorter than in other rodents, and mothers are more responsive to pups at several days of age than they are at birth, suggesting that the gestation period has shortened recently and selection has not had time to make the necessary adjustments in the releasing characteristics of the pups.)

However, while birth is occurring relatively earlier in a maturational plan that has slowed overall, with little change in the proportion of specific somatic growth phases to the whole lifespan and to each other, this is not the end of the story. In addition to overall slowing, brain growth in humans has slowed relative to somatic growth. This is evident even in comparing human development to that of our nearest higher-primate relatives, the great apes (Gould, 1977; Elias, n.d.) and is a principal illustration of the operation of Gould's concept of heterochrony in phylogeny (see above, Process in the Phylogeny of Development).

The combined effect of these two processes is to produce an infant of exceptional helplessness, not only in the motoric but even in the social realm. This condition could have evolved only in coadaptation with an evolving parental care pattern of exceptional ingenuity, perhaps impossible without humanlike intelligence, one inclusive of an appropriate carrying device, which may have been one of the early tools that helped make human evolution possible. In view of the fact that half of the very high infant mortality in some hunter–gatherer societies (10–20 percent in the first year: Howell, 1976; Harpending, 1976) occurs in the first week (Howell, 1976), the opportunity for natural selection to operate during the neonatal period must have been very great throughout human evolution, although it must be noted that high mortality is not in itself evidence of the operation of natural selection, since mortality can be mostly random rather than directional with respect to characteristics of the organism (Howell, in press, 1979b).

Intermediate-Level Societies

There is now weak evidence that there are differences in the behavior and responsiveness of infants in different human populations at birth (Freedman, 1974; see the first two examples of the influence of evolutionary perspectives, in the introductory pages of this chapter). However, speculations aside, there is no evidence that such differences bear any relationship to patterns of carrying or any other patterns of care or to any aspects of the ecological situation that might lead one to view these possible population differences as adaptations.

Characteristics of the infants aside, there are extensive variations of carrying method of young infants in nonindustrial societies, and these have been closely studied by J. Whiting (1971) (see Chapter 7 in this volume). Variations include almost constant carrying in a sling at the mother's side, back, or front, with or without direct skin contact; some carrying with some time in a crib, cradle, or hammock, or on a blanket on the ground or floor; very little or no carrying, with infant tied in a cradleboard or swaddled tightly. These variations were found to be systematically related to the ecological conditions of the society into which the infant was born, with climate having the most powerful influence. In the tropics (between latitudes 20° N and 20° S) 40 of 48 societies had close and frequent physical contact, usually with carrying devices, whereas 29 of 37 societies situated outside those

latitudes used heavy swaddling or cradleboards, irrespective of the continental location of the societies. Thus Whiting questions whether hunting–gathering is a necessary or sufficient condition for close physical contact and sling carrying. However, the
two exceptions he mentions to the generalization about cold-climate societies are the
Eskimo and the Yahgan of Patagonia, both of whom have close physical contact and
both of whom are nontropical, nonmounted, "classical" hunter–gatherers. This
suggests that hunting–gathering may be a sufficient condition for close contact,
although not a necessary one. In any case, since the great majority of the events of
human evolution took place in tropical regions, the inference that early humans had
close physical contact, probably with use of a sling, is still likely to be sound. Such
carrying is also characteristic of many nonforaging nonindustrial societies in tropical
regions. Thus societies of the middle range run the gamut from close contact in a
sling to little or no contact in a tightly tied cradleboard. It is likely that the two
variables of level of subsistence organization and, perhaps more important, ambient
temperature would together explain much of the variation in carrying method. It
may be correct to say that leaving behind the hunting–gathering mode of subsistence
permitted, but did not cause, a decrease in the use of direct contact in a sling as the
principal carrying method.

Modern United States
Since the sling is not very much in use, the Western neonate experiences fewer
motor challenges, less tactile and vestibular stimulation, and less direct maternal
proximity and is kept almost exclusively horizontal in posture instead of largely
vertical, in comparison with the condition of neonates in hunter–gatherer societies
(Konner, 1977). Judging from the similarity of the hunter–gatherer neonatal condition to that of other higher primates, with respect to these variables, we may infer
that we have experienced a sudden change in a pattern which is very old, perhaps
tens of millions of years old. The consequences of the change, if any, are unclear,
but it is worthy of note that the use of infant sling is now showing a slight tendency
to reemerge in certain Western populations.

Nursing Behavior of Infants and Mothers
Age at weaning, frequency of suckling bouts, and rate of sucking within bouts have
all received substantial attention in the comparative literature. These will be considered in turn.

Age at Weaning
Phylogenetic background. Weaning is precipitated by the gestation of a subsequent offspring, and the attendant maternal rejection of the preceding offspring, in
most species. In many Old World monkeys this occurs at about 1 year of age,
although in baboons it is usually 2 years (DeVore, 1965). In chimpanzees (Goodall,
1967; Clark, 1977), and in at least some groups of human hunter–gatherers (Konner,
1972; 1977), it occurs at about 4 years. In each case the age at weaning is equivalent
to approximately one-fourth to one-third the age at sexual maturity for females
(Tanner, 1962; Schultz, 1968), so that in spite of the absolute lengthening of the
nursing period its relative length has not changed much during the course of higher-
primate evolution (until recently in human populations).

Intermediate-level societies. Age at weaning in nonforaging nonindustrial societies ranges from immediately after birth in the Marquesan Islands (Linton, 1939)

to a number of societies that wean as late as do the !Kung (4 or more years). As was the case with reduced direct-contact carrying, leaving the hunting–gathering subsistence mode behind would appear to permit rather than constrain societies to choose earlier weaning. This presumably depends in part on the availability of suitable weaning foods. (The relative acceptability of cow's milk and cereal gruels to infants suggests some obvious hypotheses about the relationship of subsistence mode to weaning age.) The decline of weaning age in the last few years among !Kung hunter–gatherers as they become more settled and cow's milk becomes more easily available to them (Konner & Worthman, n.d.) underscores the possibility of such a relationship. Nevertheless, 83 percent of 176 societies in the Barry and Paxson (1971) sample that were *not* hunter–gatherers had weaning ages of 2 years or later. Thus weaning is late in intermediate-level societies, although perhaps not as late as in hunter–gatherers. Most of the world's settled agricultural populations appear to have a birth interval, and consequently a weaning age, of 2–3 years (Morley, 1973, p. 306).

Modern United States. In 1972 about 10 percent of United States infants were breastfed at 3 months of age, and about 5 percent at 6 months (Fomon, 1974, p. 9). This contrasts with the level of 58 percent breastfed at 1 year of age during the period 1911–1916 (Fomon, 1974, p. 2). Similar declines and similarly low current levels have been observed in Great Britain, Sweden, Poland, and other modern industrial countries. This change is not due only to bottle feeding, since age at first solid food has also declined. More alarmingly from the public health standpoint, many Third World rural populations are now seeing a similar decline in breastfeeding (Fomon, 1974, pp. 1–16; Morley, 1973). The American Academy of Pediatrics (1978) now officially recommends breastfeeding, but this recommendation is unlikely to halt the worldwide trend, which is almost a hallmark of modernization. Research has failed to demonstrate significant psychological consequences of mode of infant feeding (Caldwell, 1964). However, this research, limited to within the United States, could only compare infants breastfed for a few months with infants bottle fed. This scarcely addresses the issue of possible consequences of the different treatments observed in the cross-cultural and historical material. Thus the consequences of the great drop in age at weaning, for individual development, must be considered an open question.

Frequency of Suckling Bouts
Phylogenetic background. Comparative work (Ewer, 1968; Ben Shaul, 1962; Blurton Jones, 1972b) has suggested that mammals may be usefully divided into two groups, characterized as "continual" or "spaced" feeders in early infancy. Continual feeders are those whose infants cling to them, such as most primates, bats, and marsupials, and those whose infants follow them, such as the most precocial ungulates. Spaced feeders are those which leave their infants in nests, such as tree shrews and rabbits, or in movable caches, such as eland and certain other ungulates. Milk composition (Ben Shaul, 1962) and sucking rate (Wolff, 1968, cited by Blurton Jones, 1972b) are correlated with spacing of feeds as follows: Continual feeders have more dilute milk, with lower fat and protein content, and suck slowly. Spaced feeders have more concentrated milk and suck quickly. The milk composition and sucking rates of higher primates, including people, is consistent with a classification of them as continual feeders. This is indeed the case for most monkeys (Horwich, 1974),

chimpanzees (Clark, 1977), and human hunter–gatherers (Konner, 1972; 1975; 1976; 1977; 1978; 1979;), all of which suckle several times an hour.

Intermediate-level societies. Temporal patterns of suckling bout distribution have not been closely studied in these societies, but descriptive ethnographic material is available. Here again, the range of variation is very great. While feeding frequency following the !Kung pattern evidently occurs in some cases, in others this is precluded by the organization of subsistence activities. The key variable here appears to be mother's work load (Nerlove 1974; B. Whiting, 1963; 1972; B. Whiting & J. Whiting, 1975). In many intermediate-level societies the organization of work and nurturance results in several-hour separations of mother and infant, which precludes the possibility of very frequent suckling. In the typical situation the mother might be working in the garden during part of the day, while her infant is with a young girl or young woman (often an older sibling of the infant), at a remove from the mother, in the home village compound. A quantitative analysis of this pattern of distribution of care for one society (the Kikuyu of Kenya), with some proposed developmental consequences is given by Leiderman and Leiderman (1977). Unfortunately, these authors do not present data on nursing, but after the first few months of life the infant is in the care of someone other than the mother a large majority of the time. Presumably, when the infant is with the mother highly frequent nursing would still be possible.

Modern United States. We are now spaced feeders. When this change occurred is unknown, and what its consequences may be are a matter for speculation. Studies showing no significant sequelae of the choice between "demand" and "scheduled" (every 4 hr) feeds are of slender interest in this context, since in American homes "demand" feeding seems to sort itself out to about six four-hourly feeds a day (Aldrich & Hewitt, 1947), raising questions about the definitional criteria of a "demand." Not merely the possible long-term psychological effects, for individual development, of the change from continual to spaced feeding, but also the immediate effects on such phenomena as infant feeding difficulty and "colic," infant sleep–activity cycles, infant blood glucose dynamics, maternal success in sustained milk production, maternal mood, and likelihood of conception are largely unknown. Konner and Worthman (n.d.) have found evidence for profound suppression of gonadal hormone secretion in !Kung nursing women, with the degree of suppression a function of length of interval between nursing bouts. They hypothesize the existence of a prolactin-mediated, timing-dependent suppression of gonadal function by nipple stimulation. If they are right, their hypothesis would help to account for the well-known failure of breastfeeding to prevent conception in modern populations, where spaced feeding is the rule.

Rate of Sucking within Bouts
Phylogenetic background. Much work (Bruner & Bruner, 1968; Kaye & Brazelton, 1971; J.V. Brown, 1973) has centered around the differences between human and ape newborns in their pattern of nonnutritive sucking, and improbable arguments have been mounted regarding the presumed adaptive value of the differences. The essential differences seem to be that humans exhibit a unique burst–pause pattern and are more easily distracted from sucking. Two remarks are of interest here. First, developmental studies are necessary to show that the human newborn's unique pattern is not merely a consequence of greater human altriciality at birth,

only to disappear during the ensuing weeks. Second, since neither human hunter–gatherers nor apes typically provide their infants with anything other than the breast to suck, we must wonder how a nonnutritive sucking pattern with such complex presumed adaptive consequences could have been selected for. If, as is likely, some of the extensive suckling at the breast is nonnutritive, then it should exist (and lead to adaptations) in apes as well as humans. Clearly this area of phylogenetic thinking would benefit from closer scrutiny of the natural phenomena in question.

There appears to be no evidence regarding cross-cultural, population, or historical variation in sucking rates or burst–pause patterns within suckling bouts. A demonstration of cross-cultural validity to the burst–pause pattern and to its use in mother–infant communication would lend some credence to its hypothesized adaptive functions.

Maternal and Infant Attachment

Phylogenetic background.   Evolutionary views of the infant's attachment to its primary caretaker (Bowlby, 1969; 1973; Konner, 1972; 1977; DeVore & Konner, 1974) and of the mother's attachment to the infant (Kennell, Jerauld, Wolfe, Chesler, Kreger, McAlpine, Steffa, & Klaus, 1974; Klaus & Kennell, 1976) have been presented over the past decade. Bowlby discusses many similarities in the growth of attachment in infants in various species but argues that humans have distinguished themselves by coming to rely on distal mechanisms of mother–infant communication for the formation of attachment. He cites the human newborn's poor clinging ability as evidence for an evolutionary step away from physical contact–dependent proximal mechanisms. It will be clear from the foregoing discussion and from other works (Konner, 1972; 1977) that humans, in their environment of evolutionary adaptedness, exhibit a mother–infant bond in which both continual physical contact and continual prolonged nursing figure importantly, just as they do in other higher primates. The infant sling, and not distance from the infant, is what has obviated the necessity for strong newborn clinging in humans. Indeed, the gradualness of this transition is evident when it is considered that none of the great apes is able to cling well at birth and that all are supported for a time by the cradling arm of the mother, who walks three-leggedly for the first few weeks of the infant's life (Goodall, 1967; Schaller, 1963; Rodman, 1973).[8] (See Carrying Methods and the Behavioral Status of Newborns, above, for a more extensive treatment of infant carrying methods.)

Mother–infant sleeping distance is one of the most neglected features of the caretaking environment, even though bedtime protest is among the most ubiquitous problems of infant care in the United States (Spock, 1976). In all higher primates and among !Kung hunter–gatherers mother and infant sleep in immediate proximity (if not direct physical contact) in the same bed (or nest). Almost all !Kung mothers report that their infants wake during the night to nurse, two to many times nightly, until the age of weaning. It is likely that some additional nighttime nursing bouts take place while one or both partners in the nursing relationship are in a sleeping or semiwaking state. This pattern was probably selected for early in higher-primate evolution. An infant sleeping alone, even among human hunter–gatherers, would be subject to almost certain death by predation.

In addition to these components of the bond which clearly affect both mother and infant, it has been suggested (Kennell et al., 1974; Klaus & Kennell, 1976) that events in the first days or even the first hours of life may affect the mother's subsequent attachment to the infant. It is true that in all placental mammals there is extensive mother–infant contact, including handling or licking stimulation of the infant, during the immediate postparturitional period (Ewer, 1968), and in some mammals such contact appears to be important in the development of maternal attachment (Klopfer & Klopfer, 1968). Human hunter–gatherers exhibit immediate extensive stimulation of the infant and continuous mother–infant contact during the hours and days after birth. Although it seems unlikely that events of the first few hours could be crucial, and there is evidence that effects of contact during the first few days are not lasting, the comparative evidence (Klopfer & Klopfer, 1968; Leiderman & Seashore, 1974) warrants further study of these phenomena.

Intermediate-level societies.   Some aspects of maternal and infant attachment in these societies have been discussed in the sections on carrying methods and nursing patterns, above. On the dimension of mother–infant sleeping distance, there is surprisingly little variation in the whole range of nonindustrial societies (although there is considerable variation in father–infant sleeping distance—see below). Of 90 societies in the Barry and Paxson (1971) sample for which information is available, the mother and infant sleep in the same bed in 41, in the same room with bed unspecified in 30, and in the same room in separate beds in 19. In none of the 90 cases do mother and infant sleep in separate rooms. This feature of the mother–infant bond was simply not permitted to vary very much against different ecological backgrounds until the coming of the industrial state.

There is available substantial cross-cultural information about the birth process, its context, and the immediate postpartum period. Traditional ethnographers were quite diligent in recording this set of behaviors, which they seemed to view as customs rather than as psychology. Behaviors range from preferred solitary delivery to delivery-as-community-party, and attitudes range from birth-as-pollution to birth-as-celebration. Supportive behavior toward the mother appears to be universal, and asistance in the delivery by older women, frequently nonspecialists and relatives, is the rule rather than the exception (Newton & Newton, 1972).

Modern United States.   Our dominant culture derives from that of the agricultural peoples of northern Europe for whom the use of cradles and swaddling was the rule. As compared with !Kung hunter–gatherers and with the more indulgent of the intermediate-level societies, the regulation of the amount of contact between mother and infant rests much more in the power of the mother in the United States, and infants have to adapt as best they can. This is nowhere more clear than in sleeping arrangements. Departing from the universal pattern for nonindustrial societies, we often have infants sleeping in separate rooms from their mothers (and fathers), alone or with siblings too young to nurture them. It may be that the "syndrome" of bedtime protest that afflicts so many infants and toddlers (Spock, 1976) and the "syndrome" of night waking that afflicts a third of English 1-year-olds (Bernal, 1973) are mere artifacts of our sleeping arrangements—that is, without mother–infant separation bedtime protest might not occur, and night waking might occur but not become a "problem." (Anecdotal evidence of possible new developments in sleeping arrangements is also available. A well-known pediatrician who writes a regular column for a mass circulation national women's magazine wrote a column recently explaining how to get infants to sleep in a separate room, and why this was advisable. He was deluged with letters from women who sleep with their babies—so many, in fact, that he was moved to write a second column saying that sleeping with infants was all right too [T. B. Brazelton: Personal Communication] —a picture of medical advice negotiating a sea of other cultural forces.)

In the United States, over the last 150 years the event of birth has been removed progressively farther from its social context and from the control of the laboring woman and those close to her. Midwifery has been replaced by obstetrics, the home by the hospital, "natural" childbirth by drugs and technology. The percentage of women delivering in hospitals has changed from 5 percent to 100 percent in this century (Wertz & Wertz, 1977). These changes have been associated with dramatic decreases in maternal and neonatal mortality, although the association is far from perfect, and where it is close it may not be causal. (Most mortality was due to infection and may have responded to public health measures more than to obstetric interventions.) The trends toward more intervention and more technology are continuing. However, side by side with them, there is emerging a sense among some prospective parents that birth is now safe enough for most women so that psychological, social, and spiritual factors may be responsibly taken into account. Partly because of the feminist movement of the 1970s and partly because of the influence of physicians such as Lamaze, Leboyer, Kennell, and Klaus, midwifery, prepared childbirth, home birth, and family-centered hospital birth are winning many adherents. Its occasional polemical excesses aside, this movement does seem to have the potential for restoring to childbearing women the rich social context in which children were once born. However, lest it be thought that postobstetrics "natural" childbirth is really *natural* childbirth, one must hasten to add that *natural* childbirth is—and was —a faulty process full of fear and pain that ended all too frequently in death. Nevertheless, it does seem that psychological and physical preparedness, congenial surroundings, and family support, backed up by modern public health and medical measures, may indeed restore something that has been lost, and in so doing promote mother–infant—and father–infant—attachment.

Other Early Relationships

Male Parental Investment
Patterns of male participation in the care of offspring, direct as well as indirect, in evolutionary and cross-cultural perspective have been recently extensively reviewed (West & Konner, 1976) and will be summarized here only briefly.

Phylogenetic background. Male parental investment has increased greatly during our evolution from our primate ancestors, but this has not taken the form of an increase in the amount of interaction between males and their offspring. Rather, it has taken the form of economic investment, which in nonhuman primates is nil as they do not provision offspring. Still, this does represent a greater investment by human males, as would be predicted from the fact that humans are more or less pair-bonding (see Parental Investment and Sexual Selection, above). It is worth noting, however, that males among marmosets (*Callitrichidae*), also pair-bonding primates, exhibit extensive interaction with infants, carrying them 70 percent of the time (there are usually twins) and giving them to their mothers only to nurse (Epple, 1975; Mason, 1966). Gibbons (*Hylobatidae*) are also highly pair bonding, yet do not exhibit this extremely high male parental investment; perhaps it is the birth of twins that requires such high male investment in marmosets. Either of these groups of species would be interesting models of human fathering, as would several canid species (especially the coyote, with its strong isolated pair bond [Gier, 1975]), which simulate better the less direct, or "economic," aspects of human fatherhood, and as would many of the approximately 8000 species of monogamous birds, some of which, such as the ring dove (*Streptopelia risoria;* Lehrman, 1965; Lott, Scholz, & Lehrman, 1967) have males that are fully physiologically adapted to parental care. (For good reviews of male parental behavior in primates, see Mitchell & Brandt, 1972, or Redican & Mitchell, 1973.)

Male behavior toward infants in higher primates is not always appropriately viewed as "parental." In Japanese monkeys, for example, subdominant males seem to use infants they are carrying to jockey for position among the leading males in a large hierarchical troop (Itani, 1963), a behavior known as agonistic buffering. They also seem to carry preferentially yearling females, some of whom are destined later to become objects of very different solicitations from the same males. This sort of system is carried to an extreme by hamadryas baboons (*Papio hamadryas*)—males adopt prepubescent females into their harems, carefully protecting and restricting them until they are fully mature and breeding harem members (Kummer, 1968). In Barbary apes (*Macaca sylvana*) males are unusually solicitous toward infants, a pattern that is poorly understood but that may be another form of agonistic buffering (Burton, 1972). It may also be of very recent "cultural" origin, suggesting that the pattern of male caretaking in this species is far from fixed. Finally, in some primate species (Hrdy, 1979), especially Hanuman langurs (*Presbytis entellus;* Hrdy 1977), it has been shown that males will sometimes deliberately and systematically kill infants of strange females, an event usually followed shortly thereafter by impregnation of the female by the infanticidal male. These various systems in which males benefit as much or more from their interactions with young than do the young must also be kept in mind as possible models for certain aspects of the behavior of human adult males toward human young.

As mentioned above, the principal form of male parental investment in all human societies is indirect—economic, and defensive or protective. The protective functions are common to many (perhaps all) higher primates, but the economic or food-contributing function is unique (among primates) to humans, with only trivial exceptions. It is the product of hominid evolution and is associated with the emergence of the partially carnivorous human adaptation (Washburn, 1978). !Kung hunter–gatherers are rated by Barry and Paxson (1971) as having fathers with "regular close relationships" with both infants and young children. This is the highest rating for father involvement, shared by only 4 percent of ratable societies for infancy and only 9 percent for early childhood (West & Konner, 1976). Nevertheless, it is very limited, especially when compared to the care provided by mothers. !Kung fathers account for about 10 percent of vocalizations to the infant during the first 3 months of life (Konner, 1977). For infants of both sexes over the first 2 years of life the combined incidence of father participation in an infant observation is 13.7 percent, whereas mother participation in observations in this period is universal (see West & Konner, 1976, for further quantitative details). Interestingly, the type of proximity (physical contact, face to face, within 0.6 m [2 ft], more than 0.6 m [2 ft] away) shows similar proportional distributions for father and mother despite the large difference in absolute incidence.

Lozoff and Brittenham (1978) find that their small sample of hunting–gathering societies have closer father–infant and father–child contact than the other nonindustrial societies. However, it is unlikely that absolute levels of father participation differ very much from those of the !Kung, who get the highest rating. Thus in the evolution of human hunter–gatherers from their ancestors the story is not one of greatly increased direct care but one of greatly increased indirect investment in the form of hunted meat, while preserving the usual higher-primate male's defensive–protective functions. Lancaster (1978) has suggested that the much lower mortality between weaning and reproductive maturity characteristic of human hunter–gatherers as compared with other higher primates under natural conditions stems from the fact that only humans among higher primates feed their offspring significantly during this period. This suggests that such investment, on the part of the father as well as the mother, may have been strongly selected for.

Intermediate-level societies. There is no human society in which males have primary responsibility for care of offspring or even share this responsibility equally with females (West & Konner, 1976). For all nonindustrial societies the distributions are as follows, for infancy: "no close proximity," 5 percent; rare proximity," 15 percent; "occasional proximity," 37 percent; "frequent proximity," 39 percent; and "regular close relationship," 4 percent. For early childhood, the figures are 1, 11, 19, 60, and 9 percent, respectively (Barry & Paxson, 1971; West & Konner, 1976). For older children, five intensively studied intermediate-level societies had fathers present in 3–14 percent of the observations of 3–11-year-olds of both sexes (B. Whiting & J. Whiting, 1975, p. 45; see B. Whiting, 1963, for ethnographic details). J. Whiting and B. Whiting (1975) have shown that father involvement in infant care is part of a general dimension that they call husband–wife aloofness or intimacy, and that cultures with distant fathers are those with distant husbands. These societies are unlikely to be hunter–gatherers but are likely to be those that have important material resources that need defending, drawing the father into military activity. They are also likely to be polygynous, which draws the father away for other reasons. West and Konner (1976) also find that the absence of an extended family (which when present provides nonpaternal sources of aid to the mother) and a heavy work load for the mother both predispose societies toward closer fathering.

Modern United States. The traditional role of fathers in the United States does not appear to be unusual against the background of nonindustrial societies as a whole, although fathers may be slightly more distant here than among !Kung hunter–gatherers (B. Whiting & J. Whiting, 1975; B. Whiting, 1963; West & Konner, 1976; for a summary of research on fathering in the United States, see Lamb, 1976). Efforts are being made at present in some sectors of our population to give fathers and mothers equal roles in child care, even in infancy. This intriguing experiment bears watching.

Relations among Infants and Juveniles
This problem has been extensively reviewed recently (Konner, 1975), and the results will be summarized here very briefly.

Phylogenetic background. In all higher primates, including human hunter–gatherers, the very close mother–infant bond is mitigated, for the mother, by the presence of other adults[9](Hrdy, 1974) and, for the infant, by the presence of a multiaged juvenile play group, an easy object for the infant's transition to a wider social world (Konner, 1975). Same-age peer relations are nonexistent in human hunter–gatherers and in apes because of demographic considerations but tend to be more possible in monkeys, although even here exclusively same-age peer groups are rare. Thus there appears to have been a gradual increase in the multiaged nature of the juvenile play group during the evolution of apes and humans from our monkey ancestors. This multiage child group appears to function more efficiently than a same-age peer group in assisting with infant care, integrating the infant into a larger social group, intergenerational transfer of culturally and ecologically important information, and practice of infant and child care. Such groups constitute the dominant context of child life after infancy in hunting–gathering societies.

Intermediate-level societies. As usual, the range of variation is great, but three patterns become more common. First, total nonmaternal care in early childhood increases. Second, the use of children as infant *caretakers* increases. This type of child nurse, an institution in many agricultural societies where women's work load is heavy, is quite different from the care offered infants by children in the hunter–gatherer multiage child group in that the mother is farther away and the child has more responsibility for longer stretches (see B. Whiting, 1963, for detailed ethnographic description; Leiderman & Leiderman, 1977, for a quantitative account of the institution in a Kikuyu (Kenya) village; and B. Whiting & J. Whiting, 1975, for quantitative cross-cultural data). Third, same-age peer groups become demographically possible, and adolescent peer groups actually increase in frequency (Harley, 1963). (See Konner, 1975, for more details on all these changes.)

Modern United States. Same-age peer groups are ubiquitous in our culture, both in and out of school and at all ages including infancy. The culture seems to hold the belief that it is best for children to be with other children their own age. (This belief is carried even further in some nonindustrial cultures; see M. Wilson, 1951.) It is likely that same-age peer groups promote efficiency in the learning of competition strategies, and they may even be indispensable in a society in which the quintessential social act is comparing oneself to someone else. Nevertheless, it may be useful for us to consider what this system may be costing us in terms of the special adaptive functions of multiage child groups (Konner, 1975).

Observational Learning, Teaching, and Play
In all animals some accumulation of information about the environment and some acquisition, or at least sharpening, of skills must be effected during development. Three means for achieving these purposes can be considered.

Phylogenetic Background
Observational learning. Improvement of rate of learning by observation of conspecifics has been shown for a number of mammals (e.g., Chesler, 1969). In herbivorous mammals, especially those whose infants follow them or are carried around by them, transmission of information about food sources and food extraction is effected by this means. This is clearly one of the adaptive functions served by the mother–infant bond in nonhuman higher primates and in human hunter–gatherers, in addition to the predation-reducing function. (It appears [Chesler, 1969] that the mother is a more effective object for observational learning enhancement in kittens than is a strange conspecific, as might be expected.) Even quite complex skills, such as termite fishing in chimpanzees (Goodall, 1967), can be acquired, or have their acquisition facilitated, in this manner. Infants among human hunter–gatherers acquire the rudiments of digging for roots, cracking nuts, and pounding with a mortar

and pestle by the end of the second year of life by observing their mothers engaging in these skills and imitating them (Konner, 1972).

Teaching. As distinct from observational learning, teaching requires actual efforts by adults or older juveniles to aid in the process of acquisition. Not merely being available for observation but also deliberate modeling when the action is really purposeless, active encouragement, or simplifying the task to provide graded steps are required. Such behavior is rarely observed in nonhuman primates, and efforts to stretch certain features of their parental behavior to make it seem more like teaching (e.g., Whiten, 1975) impress one more strongly with how little teaching they really do. Carnivores, on the other hand, including lions (Schenkel, 1966), tigers (Schaller, 1967), and otters (Ewer, 1968), commonly engage in substantial teaching behavior which functions to transmit hunting and prey-catching skills. Feline mothers bring back half-dead prey which their young then kill and eat, lead cubs and kittens on expeditions whose main purpose seems to be acquainting the young with stalking, and injure and lame prey on the hunt, leaving the young to finish it off and intervening when the prey shows signs of escaping. Human hunter-gatherers have available, of course, a unique means of information transfer: language. Most teaching about hunting occurs in the form of storytelling and answering questions, means unavailable to hunting cats. Thus it is not surprising that the teaching actions described above for cats occur very infrequently in human hunters and that linguistic information transfer, observational learning, and play are the main means of acquiring hunting skills. Fathers sometimes make play bow and arrow sets for their sons, but the boys often make these themselves. It must also be noted that boys learn much that will be useful in later hunting—tracks, game movements, and local landscape—while following their mothers during gathering trips. Girls acquire much of the information they need about food gathering during the same expeditions, also, with little active teaching.

Play. Much print has been expended regarding the functions of play (e.g. Lorenz, 1965; Loizos, 1966; Ewer, 1968), and the evidence suggests that it serves the functions of exercise, acquisition of information about the environment and about conspecifics, and sharpening, or, more rarely, acquisition of subsistence and social skills. In some mammals it is clear that the deprivation of opportunities for play in early life have serious deleterious consequences for social and reproductive skills.It may be noted (Ewer, 1968) that, broadly speaking, the most intelligent mammals (primates, cetacea, and carnivora) are the most playful; the two qualities probably increase synergistically. Also, if an animal is very short lived, the young do not appear to play very much, probably because there is too little time for them to gain much from playing (Ewer, 1968). Hypotheses such as this one relating play to lifespan (as well as to body size, type of selection a species has been under, and other variables) have been mathematically modeled, numerically tested, supported, and extended by Fagen (1977). His findings and predictions are (1) that play should be more likely in stable populations near the carrying capacity of their environments, (2) that there should be considerable variation among populations within species as to the scheduling of play over the life cycle, since the model predicts several different adaptive optima, (3) that younger animals should play more, although adults of some species should play, and (4) that behavior patterns should appear in play as soon as they appear in the general behavioral repertoire. Such hypotheses resulting from computer simulations require extensive empirical testing, but they do provide valuable insights into the adaptive significance of this puzzling set of behaviors.

Finally, the composition of play groups has received comparative attention (Konner, 1975), as summarized in Relations Among Infants and Juveniles. Because of the multiaged nature of hunter–gatherer and other higher-primate play groups, information acquisition and practice of skills are effected in a context in which teaching, observational learning, and play are combined and, in effect, become one process.

Intermediate-Level Societies

Observational learning and play continue to be important and pervasive, while deliberate and distinct teaching efforts continue to be relatively unimportant, either falling into the context of observational learning or confined to rare occasions such as initiation rituals. The major new development at this level of subsistence organization is task assignment. Chores are a central feature of child life (B. Whiting & J. Whiting, 1975) and are quite essential to the ongoing subsistence strategy of the whole society (B. Whiting, 1972). Task assignment, if not gender appropriate for the society, many influence other gender-related social behavior (Ember, 1973). For five nonindustrial nonforaging societies (Nyansongo, Juxtlahuaca, Taira, Tarong, Khalapur) on three continents (B. Whiting, 1963), the mean percentage of child observations that include *work* was 16.6 (range 8–41) percent, while the figures for *play* and *casual social interaction* were 44.2 (17–76) and 33.6 (11–46 percent, respectively. In "Orchard Town," a community in New England, the percentage for work, play, and casual social interaction were 2, 30, and 52 percent, respectively, the major difference being in the absence of work. However, in Orchard Town, situations involving formal *learning* occupied 16 percent of observations, while the figure for the five other societies was 5.2 (0–9) percent. Thus there is almost a reversal of the relative proportions of work and learning when the industrial and nonindustrial nonforaging societies are compared, with not much difference in the other measures. (Data are from B. Whiting & J. Whiting, 1975, p. 48.) Directly comparable measures are not available for hunting–gathering societies, but task assignment of any kind among the !Kung San in this age group (3–11 years) is nil. On a large cross-cultural sample (Barry, Bacon, and Child, 1957) showed that pressure on children for responsibility and obedience is a function of subsistence economy, and, as noted earlier, hunting–gathering societies put less of this pressure on children than do other nonindustrial societies. Presumably the key variable here is task assignment.

Modern United States

Compared with that for hunter–gatherers, the percentage of information transfer accounted for by deliberate teaching is much greater, while that accounted for by observational learning and play is proportionately less. Work, in the sense of economically meaningful chores, is practically nonexistent, but this can be seen as a return to the hunter–gatherer pattern. The context of information transfer has become overwhelming that of adult to child or adult to same-age peer group of children, rather than from older to younger child. Usually this change is attributed to the greater amount, greater complexity, and less organic nature of the information to be transferred. Undoubtedly this explanation has some merit, but it will be of interest to follow the emergent trends toward mixed-age grouping, individual pacing, and "open" (playful?) classrooms in schools and to attempt to assess the efficiency of these other very ancient means of information transfer.

Stages and Patterns of Growth

Phylogenetic background. The concept of heterochrony has its greatest applicability here, where we consider the relatively fixed aspects of pacing and pattern in human behavioral growth. Determinants of the infant's condition at birth have already been considered (see Process in the Phylogeny of Development and Carrying Methods and the Behavioral Status of Newborns, above). Two other benchmarks of human behavioral growth that have been considered in phylogenetic perspective are the "five-to-seven shift" and adolescence. The five-to-seven shift is a series of apparently maturational changes that occur approximately at ages 5–7 years, do not depend on the onset of schooling, and appear to be cross-cultural universals (White, 1974). Included are a slight physical growth spurt, or at least a cessation of the otherwise steady decline in growth velocity with age; changes in learning ability; the onset of Piaget's "concrete operations"; emotional "readiness" for schooling or other responsibilities; characteristic changes in evoked potentials over the visual cortex; and other changes. The principal authority on the five-to-seven shift (White, 1970), influenced by Gould (1977), now considers this phenomenon to be understandable in the light of the Bolk thesis of human neoteny (see Process in the Phylogeny of Development, above). White reasons that the neotenic slowing of human somatic growth entailed, among other things, postponement of the adolescent growth spurt. He suggests that the five-to-seven shift is a vestige of what was, in some ancestral apelike creature, the beginning of the adolescent growth spurt. Since there is a growth spurt in great apes (at least in chimpanzees) at puberty, and since it does begin much earlier than in humans, the theory is plausible in light of the comparative evidence (see Tanner, 1962). However, it would have to be shown first that there is no midgrowth spurt (at, say, age 3 or 4 years) in apes that would be homologous with the human five-to-seven shift; this would suggest some other phylogenetic or adaptive explanation for the midgrowth spurt.

It is of interest also to note that the five-to-seven shift begins soon after the time when, in hunting–gathering populations, a child's next sibling is born. It is tempting to speculate that selection has provided for a quantum step in the direction of physical and behavioral adulthood not long after the child's dependence on its mother has to be sharply curtailed. (This presumes, of course, that there is a five-to-seven shift in hunter–gatherers, which has not yet been shown.) The adaptive purpose of the 4-year birth spacing itself seems to have to do with the mother's work load—the bioenergetics of the amount of weight she can carry over the daily distances she has to walk in tropical temperatures; this weight includes small children. (See Blurton Jones & Sibly, 1978, for a quantitative modeling experiment on this problem as it relates to the !Kung.)

It must also be noted that puberty and adolescence themselves take place considerably later in hunting–gathering populations than among ourselves. For example, among the !Kung the mean age at first menstruation (menarche) is 16.5 years (Howell, 1976; 1979), while in Newton, Mass. in the 1970s it was 12.65 years (Zacharias, Rand & Wurtman, 1976). The onset of motherhood was thus quite late among the !Kung (mean age 19.5 years: Howell, 1976; 1979) due to the late age of reproductive maturity. Late menarche may also be followed by a period of infertile cycling, which lasts one or more years in many nonindustrial human populations, as well as in some nonhuman primates (Montagu, 1957).

For quantitative and retrospective accounts of !Kung child life from weaning to maturity, see Draper (1976) and Shostak (1976), respectively. These studies underscore the absence of responsibility in childhood and the importance of observational learning and play in the acquisition of subsistence, social, and reproductive behavior.

Intermediate-level societies. As noted above, chores are an essential part of child life in most nonindustrial nonforaging societies and are essential to family subsistence as well. In a cross-cultural study 50 nonindustrial societies were examined with respect to the ages at which task assignment was made (Rogoff, Sellers, Pirrotta, Fox, & White, 1975), as well as for other indications of the age-related expectations parents had for children. For 16 of 27 variables 5–7 years was the modal age at which an important change in child life occurred, including responsibility for care of younger children, animal tending, household chores, and gathering. Teaching, new forms of punishment for children's transgressions, and segregation of child groups by gender all tend to occur at this time as well. This suggests that cultures are responding to universal characteristics of children's mental growth at this age.

The study also noted widespread cross-cultural commonality in the occurrence of certain events at puberty, including independence from the family situation, initiation into adult status, onset of sexual attractiveness, and assumption of completely adult clothing. As for the timing of puberty, nonindustrial societies have been shown to have later puberty than industrial ones in many studies. In developing countries there is a rural–urban distinction of 1 year or more wherever adequate data are available (Eveleth & Tanner, 1976; Tanner & Eveleth, 1975). Menarche also occurred later during the European past than it does today, with major changes in the last 150 years (Tanner, 1970; Laslett, 1965; 1977; Frisch, 1978). These differences are almost certainly caused by environmental rather than genetic reasons (Tanner, 1970; Frisch, 1978; Zacharias & Wurtman, 1968). To summarize a great deal of information very briefly, it is reasonable to propose that natural selection has made the timing of puberty to an important extent a facultative adaptation—one in which the phenotype varies in predictable (and restricted) ways with environmental variation that the species may be expected to encounter. In this instance, the timing of reproductive maturation has been designed by evolution to respond to improvement in environmental quality with earlier breeding.

Modern United States. Although there are few economically relevant tasks performed by our children, they do go to school, which involves long-term economic consequences and immediate, sometimes heavy, responsibility. The onset of schooling does appear to take cognizance of the child's biological "readiness" as provided by the five-to-seven shift.

The recent changes in the timing of puberty, commonly known as secular trends, have been mentioned. It is now certain that in many of the world's populations, especially in European and American ones, there has been a dramatic increase in adult stature, decrease in the age at menarche, and decrease in the age at termination of growth in stature. The age at menarche has dropped about 4 years and the age of termination of growth more than 5 years during the last century (Tanner, 1970).[10] This is not the place to discuss the causes of these trends, but it may be noted that they constitute a biological change in the course of growth which has enormous potential ramifications. The central challenge they present to psychologists is to determine whether or not emotional and intellectual growth patterns are changing at a similar rate. If they are not, then clearly earlier onset of sexual maturity presents threats to mental health and social welfare which must be guarded against. For example, adolescent pregnancy (Konner, 1978), a serious public health problem at present in the United States, may be in part the result of a biological novelty—reproductive and hormonal maturity occurring so early that experience, mental growth, and transmission of social mores cannot catch up. Natural selection may not have been able to anticipate an environment of such consistently high quality in its design of the facultative adaptation. The result may be disruption of a delicately balanced system of reproductive maturation in a context of enriching social experience. It is conceivable that similar remarks could be made in regard to the incidence of juvenile delinquency.

On the other hand, if some intellectual and emotional growth patterns have accelerated greatly during the last 150 years, then clearly our view of adolescent rights and privileges, and our notion of what an adult is, need to be substantially revised.

SUMMARY AND CONCLUSION

Evolutionary concepts and facts relevant to the understanding of the development of behavior have been presented. First, elements of natural selection theory as it applies to parent and child behavior were outlined. Second, major misconceptions about the phylogeny of behavior and development were discussed. Third, broad processes of the phylogeny of development were mentioned. Finally, an attempt was made to array the comparative evidence in such a way as to infer the evolutionary history of some aspects of infant behavior, parent behavior, and developmental process. These histories were then set against the very recent changes in these characters, changes probably too recent for selection to have adequately responded to them.

According to the most widely accepted and heuristically useful model of human development in its social and cultural context (B. Whiting & J. Whiting, 1975, p. 1), the growth of behavior through life is determined by experience in infancy and childhood, which in turn are caused in large part by the structure of the society's socioecological or "maintenance" systems. These in turn are responses to each society's peculiar environmental and historical situation. The adult's behavioral dispositions and character, formed in the crucible of early experience, produce or at least influence "projective–expressive systems" such as art, religion, magic, and certain social problems such as crime and suicide. A modified version of this model is shown in Figure 1–1. There are two important changes suggested. The first is the introduction of an "adult's learning environment," which mediates directly between maintenance systems and the adult's behavior and character. This change reflects our current understanding that experience is influential in fundamental ways at all phases of the life cycle and not just in childhood.

The second modification is the addition of "natural selection and phylogeny" as the background, ultimate causes not of any of the boxes in the model but of all the arrows. The arrows represent, so to speak, the equations by which the social system and the individual translate environmental influences into behavioral and social phenotype. These equations are what might be called generously restrictive—they provide degrees of freedom that are substantial but specifiable and that are neither random nor infinite in number. These equations, provided by the genes as the result

FIGURE 1-1. Modified Whiting and Whiting model of the environmental determinants of behavior.

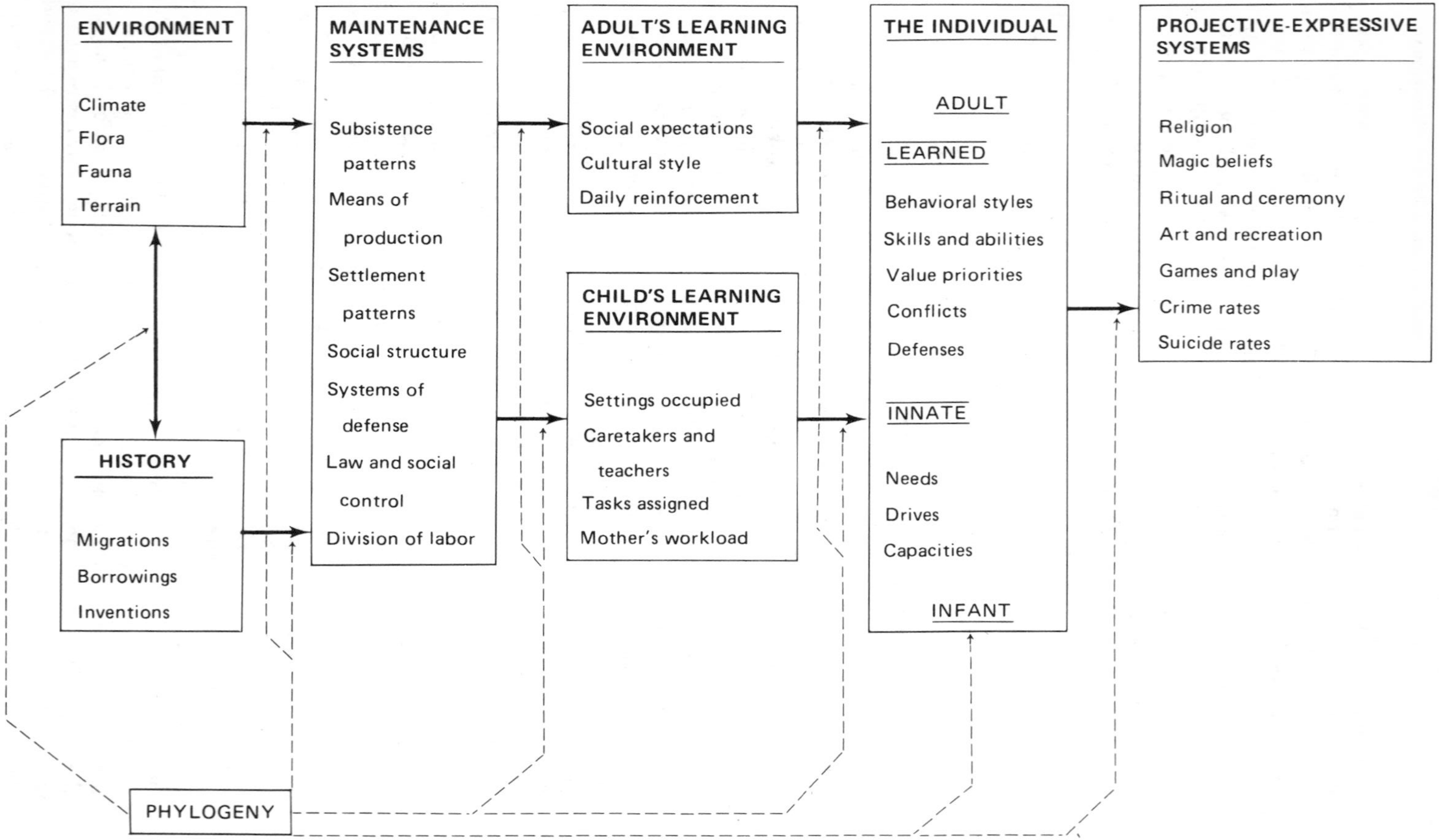

of natural selection during the long course of phylogeny, have been the main subject of this chapter.

Much nonsense has been written about the evolution of behavior and development, and glib talk has put many sensible people off it as a useful area for study. It is hoped that this review may function to tighten up some of the loose thinking and persuade some skeptics that there is indeed value in it. Not only must it guide our choice of subjects for laboratory and field comparative study, not only can it point to phenomena needing study in human children, but it may, by providing historical depth, affect our concept of our nature and so, as well, of our future.

ACKNOWLEDGMENTS

I thank I. DeVore, N. G. Blurton Jones, J. Whiting, J. Kagan, M. Elias, and M. Shostak for helpful discussions, and B. de Zalduondo for help in organizing and preparing the manuscript. Part of this work was supported by the Foundations Fund for Research in Psychiatry and by the Harry Frank Guggenheim Foundation.

NOTES

1. One aspect of this concerns the evolution of the ontogeny of the human skull. In order to pass a large brain through the narrow pelvic corridor of an erect biped, it became necessary to have disarticulated skull plates beyond the time of birth. Now, no one would suggest that to expose the infant's brain for a year or more to the jeopardy of sharp objects and poking fingers is adaptive, yet it is the inevitable consequence of an ontogenetically prior adaptation which is so strongly selected for that its advantage outweighs the later disadvantage. This instance is further complicated by the fact that the disarticulated sutures have arisen to protect the large brain which is to become a real advantage only much later in the life cycle, which, in other words, has been favored by teleological selection. Finally, the necessity for the adaptation arose in the first place because of selection for erect posture in the adult female, a process seemingly far removed from any infant adaptation. This simple case illustrates the complexities which call for caution in attempts to analyze the adaptive value of infant characters.

2. Over the years, much qualification of the original concept of imprinting has made it less mysterious than it seemed at first but has not really changed its essential outlines.

3. The interested reader is strongly urged to consult the original papers. They have begun to cause a paradigm shift in zoology and ethology and promise to have a similar impact in anthropology and psychology. It appears likely that they will be looked upon in the future as quantum advances in sciences of behavior.

4. Incidentally, the converse notion—if only humans do it, it must be learned—is also false. Smiling and language competence, both fixed action patterns and, strictly speaking, limited to humans, are clearly not learned in any usual sense of the word.

5. Higher primates differ widely from species to species, and according to no obvious pattern, in the extent to which females will permit their offspring to be handled by other animals. For a review of this interesting, if puzzling, variation, see Hrdy (1974).

6. In making these comparisions Textor relied on the following previous studies: Whiting and Child (1953) for pain, overall indulgence and anal satisfaction; Barry, Bacon, and Child (1967) for anxiety in childhood; J. Brown (1963) for initiation rites; and Harley (1963) for peer groups.

7. In addition to sources mentioned in note 6, Textor relied on Westbrook (1963) for attitudes toward premarital sex; on Whiting and D'Andrade (in Stephens, 1962, p. 245) for mother–child households; and on Ayres (1954) for desire for children.

8. Orangutans (*Pongo pygmaeus*) may be an exception to this; their clinging is exceptional, since they are the most arboreal of the great apes (see Horr, 1977).

9. Again, orangutans are exceptional. The most solitary of all higher primates, their basic social unit consists of only mother and offspring.

10. These trends seem to be ending in populations with very high socioeconomic status, where they may also have started earlier. Thus the trends are not expected to continue indefinitely.

REFERENCES

Ainsworth, M. D. S. *Infancy in Uganda: Infant care and the growth of attachment.* Baltimore: Johns Hopkins Press 1967.

Aldrich, C. A., & Hewitt, E. S. A self-regulating feeding program for infants. *Journal of the American Medical Association,* 1947, *135,* 340–342.

American Academy of Pediatrics. Breast-feeding. A commentary in celebration of the International Year of the Child, 1979, *Pediatrics,* 1978, *62,* 591–601.

Ardrey, R. *The territorial imperative.* New York: Atheneum, 1966.

Arling, G. L., & Harlow, H. F. Effects of social deprivation on maternal behavior of rhesus monkeys. *Journal of Comparative and Physiological Psychology,* 1967, *64,* 371–377.

Ayres, B. *A cross-cultural study of factors relating to pregnancy taboos.* Unpublished doctoral dissertation, Radcliffe College, 1954.

Barry, H., III, Bacon, M. K., & Child, I. L. A cross-cultural survey of some sex differences in socialization. *Journal of Abnormal and Social Psychology,* 1957, *55,* 327–332.

Barry, H., III, Bacon, M. K., & Child, I. L. Definitions, ratings and bibliographic sources for child training practices of 110 cultures. In C. S. Ford (Ed.), *Cross cultural approaches.* New Haven: HRAF Press, 1967.

Barry, H., III, & Paxson, L. Infancy and early childhood: Cross-cultural codes. 2. *Ethnology,* 1971, *10,* 466–508.

Bell, R. Q. A reinterpretation of the direction of effects in studies of socialization. *Psychological Review,* 1968, *4,* 63–72.

Ben Shaul, D. M. The composition of the milk of wild animals. *International Zoological Year Book,* 1962, *4* 333–342.

Bernal, J. Night-waking in children from birth to 14 months. *Developmental Medicine and Child Neurology, 1973, 15,* 787–801.

Blurton Jones, N. G. (Ed.). *Ethological studies of child behaviour.* Cambridge: Cambridge University Press, 1972. (a)

Blurton Jones, N. G. Comparative aspects of mother-child contact. In N. G. Blurton Jones (Ed.), *Ethological studies of child behaviour.* Cambridge: Cambridge University Press, 1972. (b)

Blurton Jones, N. G., & Konner, M. J. Sex differences in the behavior of Bushman and London two- to five-year-olds. In J. Crook & R. Michael (Eds.), *Comparative ecology and behavior of primates.* New York: Academic Press, 1973.

Blurton Jones, N. G., & Sibly, R. M. Testing adaptiveness of culturally determined behaviour: Do Bushman women maximize their reproductive success by spacing births widely and foraging seldom? In *Human behavior and adaptation* (Symposium No. 18 of the Society for the Study of Human Biology). London: Taylor & Francis, 1978.

Bourliere, F. *Natural history of mammals.* London: Harrap, 1955.

Bower, T. G. R. *Development in infancy.* San Francisco: W. H. Freeman & Co., 1974.

Bowlby, J. *Attachment and loss* (Vol. 1), *Attachment.* London: Hogarth Press and the Institute of Psycho-analysis, 1969.

Bowlby, J. *Attachment and loss* (Vol. 2), *Separation.* London: Hogarth Press 1973.

Brazelton, T. B. *Neonatal behavioral assessment scale.* Philadelphia: J. B. Lippincott Co., 1973.

Bronson, G. W. Infants' reactions to unfamiliar persons and novel objects. *Monographs of the Society for Research in Child Development,* 1972, *37* (3).

Brown, J. K. A cross-cultural study of female initiation rites. *American Anthropologist,* 1963, *65,* 837–853.

Brown, J. V. Non-nutritive sucking in great ape and human newborns: Some phylogenetic and ontogenetic characteristics. In J. F. Bosma (Ed.), *Fourth symposium on oral sensation and perception: Development in the fetus and infant.* Washington, D.C.: U.S. Government Printing Office, 1973.

Brown, R. *A first language.* Cambridge Mass.: Harvard University Press, 1973.

Bruner, J., & Bruner, B. *Process of cognitive growth: Infancy.* Worcester, Mass.: Clark University Press, 1968.

Burton, F. D. The integration of biology and behavior in the socialization of Macaca sylvana of Gibraltar. In F. E. Poirier (Ed.), *Primate socialization.* New York: Random House, 1972.

Caldwell, B. The effects of infant care. In M. L. Hoffman & L. W. Hoffman (Eds.), *Review of child development research* (Vol. 1). New YOrk: Russell Sage Foundation, 1964.

Campbell, B. A., & Jaynes, J. Reinstatement. *Psychological Review,* 1966, *73,* 487–490.

Campbell, D. T. On the conflicts between biological and social evolution and between psychology and moral tradition. *American Psychologist,* 1975, *30,* 1103–1126.

Carmichael, L. The onset and early development of behavior. In P. H. Mussen (Ed.), *Carmichael's manual of child psychology* (Vol. 1) (3rd ed.). New York: John Wiley & Sons; 1970.

Chesler, P. Maternal influence in learning by observation in kittens. *Science,* 1969, *166,* 901–903.

Chevalier-Skolnikoff, S., & Poirier, F. E. (Eds.) *Primate bio-social development: Biological, social and ecological determinants.* New York: Garland Publishing, 1977.

Chisholm, J. S. *Developmental ethology of the Navajo.* Unpublished doctoral dissertation, Rutgers University, 1978.

Clark, C. B. A preliminary report on weaning among chimpanzees of the Gombe National Park, Tanzania. In S. Chevalier-Skolnikoff & F. E. Poirier (Eds.), *Primate bio-social development: Biological, social, and ecological determinants.* New York: Garland Publishing, 1977.

Count, E. W. Brain and body weight in man: Their antecedents in growth and evolution. *Annals of the New York Academy of Science,* 1947, *46,* 993–1122.

DeBeer, G. R. *Embryos and ancestors.* Oxford: Oxford University Press, 1951.

Denenberg, V. H. Critical periods, stimulus input, and emotional reactivity: A theory of infantile stimulation. *Psychological Review,* 1964, *71,* 335–351.

Denenberg, V. H., Pachke, R., & Zarrow, M. X. Killing of mice by rats prevented by early interaction between the two species. *Psychonomic Science,* 1968, *11* (39).

DeVore, I. (Ed.). *Primate behavior.* New York: Holt, Rinehart & Winston, 1965.

DeVore, I., & Konner, M. J. Infancy in hunter-gatherer life: An ethological perspective. In N. White (Ed.), *Ethology and psychiatry.* Toronto: University of Toronto Press, 1974.

Draper, P. Social and economic constraints on child life among the !Kung. In R. B. Lee & I. DeVore (Eds.), *Kalahari hunter-gatherers.* Cambridge, Mass.: Harvard University Press, 1976.

Ehrhardt, A. A. Behavorial sequelae of prenatal hormone exposure in animals and man. In M. A. Lipton, A. D. Mascio, & K. F. Killman (Eds.), *Psychopharmacology: A generation of progress.* New York: Raven Press, 1978.

Ehrlich, A. Infant development in two prosimian species: Greater galago and slow laoris. *Developmental Pyschobiology,* 1974, *7,* 439–454.

Eisenberg, L. The human nature of human nature. *Science,* 1972, *176,* 123–128.

Elias, M. F. Relative maturity of *Cebus* and squirrel monkeys at birth and during infancy. *Developmental Psychobiology,* 1977, *10,* 519–528.

Elias, M. F. *Heterochrony in ontogeny of orang-utans and humans.* Unpublished manuscript, n.d.

Ember, C. R. Feminine task assignment and the social behavior of boys. *Ethos,* 1973, *1,* 424–439.

Emlen, J. M. *Ecology: An evolutionary approach.* Reading, Mass.: Addison-Wesley, 1973.

Epple, G. The behavior of marmoset monkeys (*Callithricidae*). In L. A. Rosenblum (Ed.), *Primate behavior: Developments in field and laboratory research* (Vol. 4). New York: Academic Press, 1975.

Eveleth, P., & Tanner, J. M. *Worldwide variation in human growth.* London: Cambridge University Press, 1976.

Ewer, R. F. *Ethology of mammals.* London: Elek, 1968.

Fagen, R. M. Selection for optimal age-dependent schedules of play behavior. *American Naturalist,* 1977, *111,* 395–414.

Fishbein, H. D. *Evolution, development, and children's learning.* Pacific Palisades, Calif.: Goodyear, 1976.

Fisher, R. A. *The genetical theory of natural selection.* New York: Dover Publishing Co., 1958.

Flavell, J. H. *The developmental psychology of Jean Piaget.* Princeton: D. Van Nostrand, 1963.

Fomon, S. J. *Infant nutrition* (2nd ed.). Philadelphia: W. B. Saunders, 1974.

Freedman, D. G. *Human infancy: An evolutionary perspective.* Hillsdale, N.J.: Lawrence Erlbaum Associates, 1974.

Frisch, R. E. Population, food intake, and fertility. *Science,* 1978, *199,* 22–30.

Freud, S. Totem and taboo. In A. A. Brill (Ed.), *The basic writings of Sigmund Freud.* New York: Random House, 1938.

Freud, S. *A general introduction to psychoanalysis.* New York: Washington Square Press, 1920.

Gardner, P. M. The Paliyans. In M. G. Bicchieri (Ed.), *Hunters and gatherers today.* New York: Holt, Rinehart & Winston, 1972.

Gaulin, S., & Konner, M. J. On the natural diet of primates, including humans. In J. Wurtman & R. J. Wurtman (Eds.), *Nutrition and the brain.* Vol. 1. New York: Raven Press, 1977.

Gesell, A., & Amatruda, C. S. *Developmental diagnosis, normal and abnormal child development.* New York: Harper & Row, 1965.

Gewirtz, J. L. (Ed.). *Attachment and dependency.* Washington, D.C.: V. H. Winston and Sons, 1972.

Gier, H. T. Ecology and social behavior of the coyote. In M. W. Fox (Ed.), *The wild canids.* New York: Van Nostrand Reingold, 1975.

Goodall, J. Chimpanzees of the Gombe Stream Reserve. In I. DeVore (Ed.), *Primate behavior: Field studies of monkeys and apes.* New York: Holt, Rinehart & Winston, 1965.

Goodall, J. Mother-offspring relationships in chimpanzees. In D. Morris (Ed.), *Primate ethology*. Chicago: Aldine Press, 1967.

Gould, S. J. *Ontogeny and phylogeny*. Cambridge, Mass.: Belknap Press, 1977.

Hamilton, W. D. The genetical evolution of social behavior, I & II. *Journal of Theoretical Biology*, 1964, *7*, 1–16 17–52.

Harley, J. K. *Adolescent youths in peer groups: A cross-cultural study*. Unpublished doctoral dissertation, Harvard University, 1963.

Harlow, H. F. The maternal affectional system. In B. M. Foss (Ed.), *Determinants of infant behavior* (Vol. 2). London: Methuen, 1963.

Harlow, H. F. Age-mate or peer affectional system. In D. Lehrman, R. Hinde, & E. Shaw (Eds.), *Advances in the study of behavior* (Vol. 2). New York: Academic Press, 1969.

Harpending, H. Regional variation in !Kung populations. In R. B. Lee & I. DeVore (Eds.), *Kalahari hunter-gatherers: Studies of the !Kung San and their neighbors*. Cambridge, Mass.: Harvard University Press, 1976.

Hasler, A. D. Guideposts of migrating fishes. *Science*, 1960, *131*, 785–792.

Hasler, A. D. *Olfactory imprinting in migrating salmon*. Paper presented at the Fourth Annual Meeting of the Society for Neuroscience, St. Louis, October 20–24, 1974.

Hebb, D. O. On the nature of fear. *Psychological Review*, 1946, *53*, 259–276.

Herrnstein, R. J. *I.Q. in the meritocracy*. Boston: Little, Brown, 1973.

Hess, E. *Imprinting*. Chicago: University of Chicago Press, 1974.

Hirsch, H., & Spinnelli, D. Visual experience modifies distribution of horizontally and vertically oriented receptive fields in cats. *Science*, 1970, *168*, 869–871.

Holmberg, A. R. *Nomads of the long bow: The Siriono of eastern Bolivia*. Garden City, N. Y.: Natural History Press, 1969.

Holt, A. B., Cheek, D. B., Mellits, E. D., & Hill, D. E. Brain size and the relation of the primate to the nonprimate. In D. B. Cheek (Ed.), *Fetal and postnatal cellular growth: Hormones and nutrition*. New York: John Wiley & Sons, 1975.

Horr, D. A. Orang-utan maturation: Growing up in a female world. In S. Chevalier-Skolnikoff & F. E. Poirier (Eds.), *Primate bio-social development: Biological, social, and ecological determinants*. New York: Garland Publishing, 1977.

Horwich, R. H. Regressive periods in primate behavioral development with reference to other mammals. *Primates*, 1974, *15*, 141–149.

Howell, N. The population of the Dobe area !Kung. In R. Lee & I. DeVore (Eds.), *Kalahari hunter-gatherers: Studies of the !Kung San and their neighbors*. Cambridge, Mass.: Harvard University Press, 1976.

Howell, N. *Demography of the Dobe area !Kung*. New York: Academic Press, 1979.(a)

Howell, N. Selection intensity of the !Kung and other hunter-gatherers. In I. DeVore (Ed.), *Sociobiology and anthropology: The implications for theory*. Chicago: Aldine, 1979.(b)

Hrdy, S. B. The care and exploitation of non-human primate infants by conspecifics other than the mother. In J. S. Rosenblatt, R. A. Hinde, & E. Shaw (Eds.), *Advances in the study of behavior* (Vol. 6). New York: Academic Press, 1974.

Hrdy, S. B. *The langurs of Abu: Female and male strategies of reproduction*. Cambridge, Mass.: Harvard University Press, 1977.

Hrdy, S. B. Infanticide among primates. In I. DeVore (Ed.), *Sociobiology and anthropology: The implications for theory*. Chicago: Aldine, 1978.

Itani, J. Paternal care in the wild Japanese monkey. In C. H. Southwick (Ed.), *Primate social behavior*. Princeton: Van Nostrand, 1963.

Jensen, A. R. How much can we boost IQ and scholastic achievement? *Harvard Educational Review*, 1969, *39*, 1–123.

Johnson, C. Environmental modification of habitat selection in adult damselflies. *Ecology*, 1966, *47*, 674–676.

Kagan, J. Acquisition and significance of sex typing and sex role identity. In M. L. Hoffman & L. W. Hoffman (Eds.), *Review of child development research* (Vol. 1). New York: Russell Sage Foundation, 1964.

Kagan, J. Attention and psychological change in the young child. *Science,* 1970, *170,* 826–832.

Kagan, J. The uses of cross-cultural research in early development. In T. H. Leiderman, S. R. Tulkin, & A. Rosenfeld (Eds.), *Culture and infancy.* New York: Academic Press, 1977.

Kagan, J., Kearsley, R. B., & Zelazo, P. R. *Infancy: Its place in human development.* Cambridge, Mass.: Harvard University Press, 1978.

Kagan, J., & Klein, R. E. Crosscultural perspectives on early development. *American Psychologist,* 1973, *28,* 947–961.

Kamin, L. J. *The science and politics of I.Q.* New York: John Wiley & Sons, 1974.

Kaye, K., & Brazelton, T. B. Mother-infant interaction in the organization of sucking. Paper presented at the Annual Meeting of the Society for Research in Child Development, Minneapolis, April 1971.

Kennell, J., Jerauld, R., Wolfe, H., Chesler, D., Kreger, N., McAlpine, W., Steffa, M., & Klaus, M. Maternal behavior one year after early and extended post partum contact. *Developmental Medicine and Child Neurology,* 1974, *16,* 172–179.

Klaus, M. H., & Kennell, J. H. *Maternal-infant bonding.* St. Louis: C. V. Mosby, 1976.

Klein, R. E., Lasky, R. E., Yarbrough, C., Habicht, J. P., & Sellers, M. J. Relationship of infant/caretaker interaction, social class, and nutritional status to developmental test performance among Guatemalan infants. In P. H. Leiderman, S. R. Tulkin, & A. Rosenfeld (Eds.), *Culture and infancy.* New York Academic Press, 1977.

Klopfer, D. H., & Klopfer, M. Maternal "imprinting" in goats: Fostering of alien young. *Zeitschrift fur Tierpsychologie,* 1968, *25,* 862–866.

Konner, M. J. Aspects of the developmental ethology of a foraging people. In N. G. Blurton Jones (Ed.), *Ethological studies of child behaviour.* Cambridge, Engl.: Cambridge University Press, 1972.

Konner, M. J. Relations among infants and juveniles in comparative perspective. In M. Lewis & L. Rosenblum (Eds.) *The origins of behavior* (Vol. 3), *Friendship and peer relations.* New York: John Wiley & Sons, 1975.

Konner, M. J. Infancy among the Kalahari Desert San. In P. H. Leiderman, S. R. Tulkin, & A. Rosenfeld (Eds.), *Culture and infancy.* New York: Academic Press, 1977.

Konner, M. J. *Adolescent pregnancy: An anthropological perspective.* Paper delivered at the March of Dimes Conference on Adolescent Pregnancy, Boston, April 1978.

Konner, M. J. Biological bases of social development. In M. Kent, J. Rolf, & B. Jaffe (Eds.), *Primary prevention of psychopathology* (Vol. 3). Hanover, N. H.: University of New England Press, 1979.

Konner, M. J., & Worthman, C. Nursing frequency, gonadal hormones, and birth spacing among !Kung hunter-gatherers. Submitted for publication, 1979.

Kummer, H. *Social organization of Hamadryas baboons.* Chicago: University of Chicago Press, 1968.

Lack, D. *The natural regulation of animal numbers.* London: Oxford University Press, 1954.

Lamb, M. E. (Ed.). *The role of the father in child development.* New York: John Wiley & Sons; 1976.

Lancaster, J. Demographic aspects of primate field studies. Presentation at the Social Science Research Council conference on Biosocial foundations of parenting and offspring development, New York, December, 1978.

Laslett, P. *The world we have lost: England before the industrial age.* New York: Scribners, 1965.

Laslett, P. *Family life and illicit love in earlier generations.* Cambridge, Engl.: Cambridge University Press, 1977.

Lecours, A. R. Myelogenetic correlates of the development of speech and language. In UNESCO, *Foundations of language development* (Vol. 1), *A multidisciplinary approach.* New York: Academic Press, 1975.

Lee, R. B. *The !Kung San: men, women and work in a foraging society.* Cambridge: Cambridge University Press, in press.

Lehrman, D. A critique of Konrad Lorenz' theory of instinctive behavior. *Quarterly Review of Biology,* 1953, *28,* 337–363.

Lehrman, D. S. Interaction between internal and external environments in the regulation of the reproductive cycle of the ring dove. In F. A. Beach (Ed.), *Sex and behavior.* New York: John Wiley & Sons, 1965.

Leiderman, P. H., & Leiderman, G. F. Economic change and infant care in an East African agricultural community. In P. H. Leiderman, S. R. Tulkin, & A. Rosenfeld (Eds.), *Culture and infancy.* New York: Academic Press, 1977.

Leiderman, H. P. & Seashore, M. J.: Mother-infant neonatal separation: Some delayed consequences. Paper presented at CIBA Foundation Conference on Parent-Infant Relationships, London, England, 1974.

Leiderman, P. H., Tulkin, S. R., & Rosenfeld, A. (Eds.). *Culture and infancy.* New York: Academic Press, 1977.

Lenneberg, E. H. A biological perspective of language. In E. H. Lenneberg (Ed.), *New directions in the study of language.* Cambridge, Mass.: MIT Press, 1964.

Lenneberg, E. H. *Biological foundations of language.* New York: John Wiley & Sons, 1967.

Levine, S., & Mullins, R. F., Jr. Hormonal influences in brain organization in infant rats. *Science,* 1966, *152,* 1585–1592.

Lewis, M., & McGurk, H. Evaluation of infant intelligence. *Science,* 1972. *178,* 1174–1177.

Lewis, M., & Rosenblum, L. *The effect of the infant on its caregiver.* New York: John Wiley & Sons, 1973.

Linton, R. Marquesan culture. In A. Kardiner (Ed.), *The individual and his society, the psychodynamics of primitive social organization.* New York; Columbia University Press, 1939.

Lockhard, R. Reflections on the fall of comparative psychology: Is there a message for us all? *American Psychologist,* 1971, *26,* 168–179.

Loehlin, J. C., Lindzey, G., & Spuhler, J. N. *Race differences in intelligence.* San Francisco: W. H. Freeman, 1975.

Loizos, C. Play in mammals. In P. Jewell & C. Loizos (Eds.), *Play, territoriality and exploration in mammals.* New York: Academic Press, 1966.

Lorenz, K. Z. *Evolution and modification of behavior.* Chicago: University of Chicago Press, 1965.

Lott, D., Scholz, D. S., & Lehrman, D. S. Exteroceptive stimulation of the reproductive system of the female ring dove (Streptopelia risoria) by the mate and the colony milieu. *Animal Behavior,* 1967, *15,* 433–437.

Lozoff, B., & Brittenham, G. *Infant care: Cache or carry.* Paper presented at the Meeting of the Society for Pediatric Research, New York, Spring 1978.

Maccoby, E. E., & Jacklin, C. N. *The psychology of sex differences.* Stanford, Calif.: Stanford University Press, 1974.

MacFarlane, A. *Olfaction in the development of social preferences in the human neonate.* Paper presented at the CIBA Foundation Symposium on the Parent–Infant Relationship, London, November 1974.

Mason, W. A. Social organization of the South American monkey, Callicebus ma-loch: A preliminary report. *Tulane Studies in Zoology,* 1966, *13,* 23–28.

Mayr, E. Behavior and systematics. In A. Roe & G. G. Simpson (Eds.), *Behavior and evolution.* New Haven: Yale University Press, 1958.

Mayr, E. *Animal species and evolution.* Cambridge, Mass.: Harvard University Press, 1963.

McCall, R. B. The development of intellectual functioning in infancy and the prediction of later I.Q. In J. D. Osofsky (Eds.), *The handbook of infant development.* New York: Wiley, 1978.

McGraw, M. *The neuromuscular maturation of the human infant.* New York: Hafner Publishing, 1963.

Michael, R. P., & Keverne, E. Pheromones in the communication of sexual status in primates. *Nature,* 1968, *218,* 746–749.

Mitchell, G., & Brandt, E. Paternal behavior in primates. In F. E. Poirier (Ed.), *Primate socialization.* New York: Random House, 1972.

Moltz, H., & Robbins, D. Maternal behavior of primiparous and multiparous rats. *Journal of Comparative Physiological Psychology,* 1965, *60,* 417–421.

Montagu, M. F. A. *The reproductive development of the female* (2nd ed.). New York: Julian Press, 1957.

Morley, D. *Pediatric priorities in the developing world.* London: Butterworths, 1973.

Morris, D. *The naked ape.* New York: McGraw-Hill, 1968.

Murdock, G. P., & Morrow, D. O. Subsistence economy and supportive practices: Cross-cultural codes. 1. *Ethnology,* 1970, *9,* 302–330.

Nerlove, S. B. Women's workload and infant feeding practices: A relationship with demographic implications. *Ethnology,* 1974, *13,* 207–214.

Newton, N., & Newton, M. Childbirth in crosscultural perspective. In J. G. Howells (Ed.), *Modern perspectives in psycho-obstetrics.* Edinburgh: Oliver and Boyd, 1972.

Nicolson, N. A. A comparison of early behavioral development in wild and captive chimpanzees. In S. Chevalier-Skolnikoff & F. E. Poirier (Eds.), *Primate bio-social development: Biological, social, and ecological determinants.* New York: Garland Publishing, 1977.

Petersen, A. C. Physical androgyny and cognitive functioning in adolescence. *Developmental Psychology,* 1976, *12,* 524–533.

Piaget, J. *Biology and knowledge.* Chicago: University of Chicago Press, 1971.

Pilbeam, K., & Gould, S. Size and scaling in human evolution. *Science,* 1974, *186,* 892–901.

Poirier, F. E. (Ed.) *Primate socialization.* New York: Random House, 1972.

Popp, J., & DeVore, I. Aggressive competition and social dominance theory. In D. Hamburg & J. Goodall (Eds.), *The behavior of the great apes.* New York: Holt, Rinehart & Winston, 1975.

Portmann, A. Die Ontogenese des Menschen als Problem der Evolutionsforschung. *Verhandlungen der Schweizerischen Naturforschenden Gesellschaft,* 1945, *125,* 44–53.

Raisman, G., & Field, P. M. Sexual dimorphism in the pre-optic area of the rat. *Science,* 1971, *173,* 731–733.

Redican, W. K., & Mitchell, G. A longitudinal study of parental behavior in adult male rhesus monkeys: 1. Observations on the first dyad. *Developmental Psychology,* 1973, *8,* 135–136.

Richards, M. P. M. Activity measured by running wheels and observation during the oestrous cycle, pregnancy and pseudopregnancy in the golden hamster. *Animal Behaviour,* 1966, *14,* 303–309.

Rodman, P. Population composition and adaptive organization among orangutans of the Kutai Reserve. In R. Michael & J. Crook (Eds.), *Comparative ecology and behavior of primates.* New York: Academic Press, 1973.

Roe, A., & Simpson, G. G. *Behavior and evolution.* New Haven: Yale University Press, 1958.

Rogoff, B., Sellers, M. J., Pirrotta, S., Fox, N., & White, S. H. Age of assignment of roles and responsibilities to children: A cross-cultural survey. *Human Development,* 1975, *18,* 353–369.

Rosen, J., & Hart, F. Effects of early social isolation upon adult timidity and dominance in *Peromyscus. Psychological Reports,* 1963, *13,* 47–50.

Rosenblum, L. A. Infant attachment in monkeys. In R. Schaffer (Ed.), *The origins of human social relations.* New York: Academic Press, 1971. (a)

Rosenblum, L. A. The ontogeny of mother-infant relations in macaques. In H. Moltz (Ed.), *Ontogeny of vertebrate behavior.* New York: Academic Press, 1971. (b)

Rumbaugh, D., von Glaserfeld, E., Warner, H., Pisani, P., & Gill, T. Lana (chimpanzee) learning language: A progress report. *Brain and Language,* 1974, *1,* 205–212.

Sahlins, M. *The use and abuse of biology.* Ann Arbor: University of Michigan Press, 1976.

Schaller, G. *The mountain gorilla: Ecology and behavior.* Chicago: University of Chicago Press, 1963.

Schaller, G. *The deer and the tiger.* Chicago: University of Chicago Press, 1967.

Schaller, G. *The Serengeti lion: A study of predator-prey relations.* Chicago: University of Chicago Press, 1972.

Schenkel, R. Play, exploration and territoriality in the wild lion. In P. Jewell & C. Loizos (Eds.), *Play, exploration and territory in mammals* (Symposium of the Zoological Society of London, No. 18). London: Zoological Society of London, 1966.

Schultz, A. H. Age changes, sex differences, and variability as factors in the classification of primates. In S. L. Washburn (Ed.), *Classification and human evolution.* Chicago: Aldine, 1963.

Schultz, A. H. The recent hominoid primates. In S. L. Washburn & P. C. Jay (Eds.), *Perspectives in human evolution.* New York: Holt, Rinehart & Winston, 1968.

Scott, J. The effects of early experience on social behavior and organization. In W. Etkin (Ed.), *Social behavior and organization among vertebrates.* Chicago: University of Chicago Press, 1964.

Sellers, M. J. Personal communication, 1973.

Shostak, M. A !Kung woman's memories of childhood. In R. B. Lee & I. DeVore (Eds.), *Kalahari hunter-gatherers: Studies of the !Kung San and their neighbors.* Cambridge, Mass.: Harvard University Press, 1976.

Sinclair, D. *Human growth after birth.* London: Oxford University Press, 1973.

Skinner, B. F. *Verbal behavior.* New York: Appleton-Century-Crofts, 1957.

Spock, B. *Baby and child care.* New York: Pocket Books, 1976.

Stephens, W. N. *The Oedipus complex.* Glencoe, Ill.: Free Press, 1962.

Suomi, S. J.; & Harlow, H. F. Social rehabilitation of isolate-reared monkeys. *Developmental Psychology,* 1972, *6,* 487–496.

Tanner, J. M. *Growth at adolescence* (2nd ed.). Philadelphia: Davis, 1962.

Tanner, J. M. Physical growth. In P. Mussen (Ed.), *Carmichael's manual of child psychology* (Vol. 1) (3rd ed.). New York: John Wiley & Sons, 1970.

Tanner, J. M., & Eveleth, P. Variability between populations in growth and development at puberty. In S. Berenberg (Ed.), *Puberty: Biologic and psycho-social components.* Leiden: Stenfert Kroese, 1975.

Textor, R. B. *A cross-cultural summary.* New Haven: HRAF Press, 1967.

Thorpe, W. H. Further studies on pre-imaginal olfactory conditioning in insects. *Proceedings of the Royal Society of London,* 1939, *127,* 424–433.

Trivers, R. L. Parental investment and sexual selection. In B. Campbell (Ed.), *Sexual selection and the descent of man, 1871–1971.* Chicago: Aldine, 1972.

Trivers, R. L. Parent-offspring conflict. *American Zoologist,* 1974, *14,* 249–264.

Trivers, R. L., & Willard, D. E. Natural selection of parental ability to vary the sex ratio of offspring. *Science,* 1973, *179,* 90–92.

Tulkin, S. R. Social class differences in maternal and infant behavior. In P. H. Leiderman, S. R. Tulkin, & A. Rosenfeld (Eds.), *Culture and infancy.* New York: Academic Press, 1977.

Tulkin, S. R., & Leiderman, P. H. Mother and infant in Japan and America: A synthesis of several recent papers of William Caudill. In *Cultural and social influences in infancy and early childhood* (Burg Wartenstein Symposium No. 57). Wenner-Gren Foundation for Anthropological Research, 1973.

Turnbull, C. M. *Wayward servants: The two worlds of the African Pygmies.* Garden City, N. Y.: Natural History Press, 1965.

Waber, D. P. Sex differences in cognition: A function of maturational rate? *Science,* 1976, *192,* 572–574.

Waddington, C. H. Canalisation of development and the inheritance of acquired characters. *Nature,* 1942, *150,* 563.

Waddington, C. H. Genetic assimilation of an acquired character. *Evolution,* 1953, *7,* 118.

Washburn, S. L. The evolution of man. *Scientific American,* 1978, *239,* 194–208.

Wertz, R. W., & Wertz, D. C. *Lying-in: A history of childbirth in America.* New York: The Free Press, 1977.

West, M. M., & Konner, M. J. The role of the father: An anthropological perspective. In M. E. Lamb (Ed.), *The role of the father in child development.* New York: John Wiley & Sons, 1976.

Westbrook, J. T. Unpublished codings. Published in modified form: Murdock, G. P. Ethnographic Atlas: A summary. *Ethnology,* 1967, *6,* 109–236.

White, S. Some general outlines of the matrix of developmental changes between five and seven years. *Bulletin of the Orton Society,* 1970, *20,* 41–57.

White, S. Review of mental health: From infancy to adolescence and social change in the mental health of children. *Contemporary Psychology,* 1974, *19,* 497–498.

White, S. Personal communication, 1978.

Whiten, A. *Observations of teaching behavior in a gorilla.* Unpublished manuscript, Department of Psychology, Oxford University, 1975.

Whiting, B. B. (Ed.). *Six cultures.* New York: John Wiley & Sons, 1963.

Whiting, B. B. Work and the family: Cross-cultural perspectives. Paper prepared for the conference on "Women: Resource for a Changing World," held at the Radcliffe Institute, Cambridge, Mass., April 1972.

Whiting, B. B., & Edwards, C. P. A cross-cultural analysis of sex differences in the behavior of children aged three through eleven. *Journal of social psychology,* 1973, *91,* 171–188.

Whiting, B. B., & Whiting, J. W. M. *Children of six cultures: A psychocultural analysis.* Cambridge Mass.: Harvard University Press, 1975.

Whiting, J. W. M. *Causes and consequences of the amount of body contact between mother and infant.* Paper delivered at the 70th Annual Meeting of the American Anthropological Association, New York, 1971.

Whiting, J. W. M., & Child, I. L. *Child training and personality: A cross-cultural study.* New Haven: Yale University Press, 1953.

Whiting, J. W. M., & Whiting, B. B. Aloofness and intimacy between husbands and wives. *Ethos,* 1975, *3,* 183–207.

Wiesel, T., & Hubel, D. Extent of recovery from the effects of visual deprivation in kittens. *Journal of Neurophysiology,* 1965, *28,* 1060–1072.

Wilson, E. O. *Sociobiology: The new synthesis.* Cambridge, Mass.: Belknap Press, 1975.

Wilson, E. O. *On human nature.* Cambridge, Mass.: Harvard University Press, 1978.

Wilson, M. *Good company: A study of Nyakyusa age-villages.* Oxford: Oxford University Press, 1951.

Wilson, R. S. Synchronies in mental development: An epigenetic perspective. *Science,* 1978, *202,* 939–948.

Wolff, P. H. Sucking patterns of infant mammals. *Brain, Behavior and Evolution,* 1968, *1,* 354–367.

Wolff, P. H. Ethnic difference in alcohol sensitivity. *Science,* 1972, *175,* 449–450.

Wolff, P. H. Vasomotor sensitivity to alcohol in diverse Mongoloid populations. *American Journal of Human Genetics,* 1973, *25,* 193–199.

Wolff, P. H. Biological variations and cultural diversity: An exploratory study. In P. H. Leiderman, S. R. Tulkin, & A. Rosenfeld (Eds.), *Culture and infancy.* New York: Academic Press, 1977.

Zacharias, L., Rand, W., & Wurtman, R. A prospective study of sexual development and growth in American girls. *Obstetrical and Gynecological Survey,* 1976, *31,* 325–337.

Zacharias, L., & Wurtman, R. Age at menarche: Genetic and environmental influences. *New England Journal of Medicine,* 1968, *280,* 868–875.

2

Universals in
Human Development

Jerome Kagan

Although a great many social scientists who are now approaching retirement were confident of the existence of universal laws governing the behavior of individuals or societies, the succeeding generation has had that faith challenged by repeated failures to replicate in one cultural setting hardy findings found in another. For example, in a recent study of recognition memory, American children were much better at detecting the addition of a new element to a photograph that had been inspected earlier than in detecting the rearrangement of the elements in the original photograph, but children of the same age living in San Pedro la Laguna in the Guatemalan highlands were equally proficient at recognizing both alterations in the original scene (Newcombe, Rogoff, & Kagan, 1977). There are two aspects of the problem of universals in psychological functioning. One concerns the generalizability of a particular functional relation; for example, is the sequence of morphemes Brown (1973) describes for English found in other languages? A second concerns the breadth of a hypothetical competence; for example, does performance on a test of recall of words reflect a general ability at recall memory or only recall memory for words (or, even more extremely, recall memory for the particular words used in the study)?

Although some functional relations involving cognitive processes have survived evaluation with diverse materials and samples, most studies imply that cognitive competences are typically specific to problem contexts and materials. Recall memory for verbal information is not always correlated with recall memory for visual scenes and is poorly correlated with recognition memory for visual scenes (Rogoff, 1977). The corpus of accumulated data suggests that we should not compose propositions that use terms like memory or perceptual ability, but rather invent constructs that specify the nature of the problem being solved. Since persons from different cultures are not likely to interpret a particular set of psychological materials in the same way, the specificity of cognitive talents has implications for universal principles of cognitive functioning.

The usual, not unreasonable, rebuttal to this pessimistic conclusion is that although performances may vary across contexts, as chemical reactions vary with acidity, pressure, and temperature, the potential for a particular performance is universal. Most psychologists hold the presupposition that there is a core set of universal competences that emerges in accord with a universal growth sequence. Let us examine that belief more closely.

Suppose biologists did not assume, as they do, a universal embryogenesis for the sea urchin. If hypothetical biologists placed each of three sea urchin eggs in three growth media differing in acidity and temperature and discovered three different courses of morphologic development, they might not conclude that there was a universal developmental course with variations depending upon local conditions. Rather, the biologists might decide that there were different ontogenies depending upon the conditions of growth. That conclusion would irritate some traditional biologists, who would reply that there is a universal sea urchin and an optimal ontogeny; namely, the potential contained in the genome. It is assumed the universal form is the one that occurs most often in nature; the others are variations on that ideal. Since each fertilized egg needs an environment in which to grow, how does one ever discover the ideal contained in the genome of the zygote? All one can ever know is what happened under the environment that existed during embryogenesis.

Typically, scientists assume that the modal form in nature is the universal rather than take the philosopher's definition of universal (as opposed to particular), which consists of the characteristics common to a variety of particulars (that is, a concept). This latter meaning of universal is not identical with the meaning implied by noting the most frequently occurring particular. Since the modal form might change if the earth's temperature changed, is it reasonable to assume that the most frequent form is nature's ideal and others merely unintended variations? Perhaps there is some merit in the position taken more recently by geneticists, namely, that the genome sets only a range of outcomes. The particular sequence actualized will depend on local conditions. Hence there is no outcome that is absolutely more universal or more fundamental than another. Biologists might contend that although there is enormous variety in possible outcomes, some are more in accord with the genome than others. They would argue that heterosexuality, for example, is more compatible with man's genome than homosexuality. That statement derives support from intuition and theoretical strength from the data and logic that relate sexuality to evolution. Hence the popular view is that there is a correlation between the genome and selected behavior outcomes across variations in environment. The task is to specify the classes of behavior that are seriously controlled by our inheritance and those that are not, since the former will define the universals in psychological growth.

Consider a candidate for a class of universals taken from early infant development. Between about 7 and 20 months of age, human infants are particularly vulnerable to inhibition and distress when faced with a discrepant event that cannot be assimilated. Examples include unfamiliar adults, children, or separation from a caretaker. The specific events that generate the mood of uncertainty and the ages at which the apprehension appears and declines will depend on local conditions. Thus the statement that stranger and separation anxiety are universals perhaps should be replaced with the following proposition: human infants between 7 and 20 months of age will show a low threshold for uncertainty to certain classes of discrepant events, but the specific event that provokes the fear will depend on local conditions of growth. A Fiji 12-month-old is likely to show extreme fear to a small doll because it is extremely discrepant from his or her experience; such a behavior is rare among American infants. If an infant is continually exposed to unfamiliar adults, admittedly an unlikely script, anxiety to a stranger is not likely to appear at 8 months of age. Thus it may be theoretically useful to replace statements about universal competences with those that specify a particular response to a specific situation.

The Bases for Limits
Since we believe it is impossible to invent any environment that will permit a 3-month-old to talk or a 6-year-old to worry about his generativity, it is generally acknowledged that the genome sets limits on behavioral outcomes. We should also note that there are novelties that seem to be primarily environmental rather than genetic in origin. The feelings of depersonalization that exist in large cities might not be understandable to hunter–gatherers or early Roman agriculturalists. The potential for depersonalization may have been present, but it was not realized. We do not know what psychological potentials exist for the human species because of serious limitations on realizable environments. Both genome and environment limit the variations that will be finally expressed. With the above as introduction, let us turn to some data that suggest a universal psychological sequence during the period of infancy.

GROWTH OF RETRIEVAL PROCESSES DURING THE LATTER HALF OF THE FIRST YEAR

A great deal of data gathered by many investigators during the last decade suggests that a set of competences is maturing during the last half of the first year. These competences seem to explain a variety of phenomena that emerge during this interval. Let us consider some of the reactions that emerge during the last 4–5 months of the first year in varied cultural settings.

After 7 or 8 months of age the human infant frequently displays greater attention to a variety of discrepant events than when at age 6 or 7 months. For example, if representations of human faces are shown to children 4–36 months, attention is prolonged at 4 months, lower at 8 months, and increases through the second and third years (Kagan, 1972). This developmental function for attention to facial masks was found not only among American infants, but also among a group of rural Mexican children (Finley, Kagan, & Layne, 1972) and Guatemalan children (Sellers, Klein, Kagan, & Minton, 1972). This U-shaped growth function also holds for attentiveness to nonvisual events as well as to human speech (Kagan, Kearsley, & Zelazo, 1978).

A group of 95 children were seen over the period 3½–29 months of age. About a third of these children were attending a daycare center 5 days a week while the remaining children were being reared totally at home. Two episodes were administered across this interval. One was a visual episode. The event consisted of a box with a rod at one end and three lightbulbs at the other. A hand came out and touched the orange rod and moved it across a traverse of 180° toward three lightbulbs which lit when the rod contacted them. The event was repeated eight or ten times, depending on the child's age, followed by five transformations in which the hand touched the rod, the rod did not move, and 3 sec later the lights went on. Following these five transformation trials there were three representations of the original standard.

In an auditory episode, the child heard a 4 sec meaningful phrase for 10 or 12 trials, followed by 5 transformation trials of either a phrase of nonsense or a change in word order, followed by 3 representations of the standard. The variable of interest was attentiveness to the stimulus, either the visual event or the auditory information. The main variable for the auditory episode was called *search*, which was defined as the maintenance of a quiet, alert posture together with saccadic movements of the eyes during the presentation of the auditory episode. There was a U-shaped function for attentiveness for all phases of the auditory episode and for the three return trials of the visual episode, with a trough in attention at 7½ months. A similar growth function emerged for a longitudinal sample of Guatemalan infants living in rural subsistence farming villages in the eastern part of the country. These infants were administered the same light episode in a manner comparable to the procedure used in the United States. These infants also displayed the U-shaped growth function with a trough at 7½ months. In addition, the auditory episode was administered to a much more isolated group of 87 Guatemalan native tribal (Mayan) children between 5 and 21 months of age living on Lake Atitlan in the northwest highlands of the country. The children heard a recording of a phrase in dialect (best translated as "Come here, I'll pick you up") for 12 repeated presentations followed by 5 transformations and then 3 representations of the original standard. The occurrence of search behavior showed a U-shaped function with a trough at 7–8 months of age. Thus both American as well as moderately isolated Guatemalan infants seem to pass through a brief stage at 7–9 months of age when attentiveness to visual and auditory events is at a nadir, after which it begins to increase.

Additionally, prior to 7–8 months the human infant typically shows little or no inhibition in reaching for a novel object that is presented after repeated presentations of a familiarized standard. By contrast, the 1-year-old shows a short but obvious delay before reaching for an unexpected toy (Parry, 1973; Schaffer, Greenwood, & Parry, 1972).

Further, the infant who has just begun to crawl does not always show avoidance of the deep side of the visual cliff until after age 7 months even though capable of perceiving the difference between the deep and shallow sides (Campos, Hiatt, Ramsay, Henderson, & Sveda, in press). Inhibition is also the dominant initial reaction of 1-year-olds when they encounter an unfamiliar child. The child usually stops playing, becomes quiet, and may even retreat to a familiar caretaker (Kagan, Kearsley, & Zelazo, 1978). These observations hold for American as well as Israeli children being raised in a kibbutz (Zaslow, 1977). What is impressive about the 1-year-old's initial reaction to an unfamiliar peer, in contrast to the behavior of two young baboons, is the muting of strong emotion in the human child. The human child rarely shows excessive fear or violent attack toward the stranger. Perhaps nature intended this buffering of emotion in order to facilitate social bonding and communication of information between members from different family groups.

Additionally, there is a dramatic increase in the likelihood of wariness, inhibition of play, and occasionally crying to those events that are discrepant transformations of earlier experience. Scarr and Salapatek (1970) exposed infants 2–23 months of age to six different discrepant or novel events—a stranger approaching the child, a visual cliff, a jack-in-the- box, a mechanical dog that moved, facial masks, and a loud noise. Infants younger than 7 months rarely showed any signs of anxiety to any of these events. Peak display of uncertainty occurred between 11 and 18 months and then declined. Infants older than 1 year also show signs of anxiety to a videotape sequence illustrating another child or a videotape recording of the subject. Ten-month-olds do not display these signs of apprehension, but smile or babble (Amsterdam & Greenberg, 1977). Many studies in different settings have shown that an unfamiliar adult elicits signs of anxiety in infants 7–12 months of age. The growth function for separation distress (that is, the tendency to cry and show inhibition of play following departure of a primary caretaker) is similar among children being raised in the United States, barrios in urban Guatemala, subsistence tribal villages in the Guatemalan highlands, Israeli kibbutzim, and !Kung San bands in Botswana

(Kagan, 1976). Even infants diagnosed as showing "failure to thrive" show inhibition of play following departure of the caretaker (Jameson & Gordon, 1977). Signs of separation distress emerge at about 8 months, rise to a peak at 13–15 months, and then begin to decline.

Children who are blind from birth show a similar developmental course for separation distress (Fraiberg, 1975). Separation protest emerges between 10 and 19 months in blind children, with a median age of 11 months.

In earlier publications we suggested that the temporal concordance of increased attentiveness, as well as inhibition, wariness, and distress to discrepancy, are due to the emergence of several related cognitive competencies which seem to occur in children in many societies. The competencies include the ability (1) to retrieve a schema related to the child's present experience, despite minimal incentive cues in the immediate field, and (2) to retain that schema in memory while the child compares the retrieved structure with the present in an attempt to resolve the discrepancy or inconsistency. The wariness is the result of the child's failure to resolve the inconsistency between discrepant event and schemata, despite an attempt to do so. Support for these hypotheses comes from two complementary studies.

In the first study a group of eight healthy, middle-class, white American children were observed monthly in home and laboratory from 6 to 13 months of age and administered a series of tests, many of which were intended to assess the growth of memorial competence. Children were administered stage IV object permanence tasks with variations, as well as the A/not B procedure, in which the child first finds a toy at location A several times, after which the toy is hidden at location B; the time interval between the hiding of the toy at location B and permitting the child to reach was varied. There was remarkable agreement among the eight children in the age at which the infants met the criterion for each of the tasks. By about 8 months, all children had passed the criterion for state IV object permanence, followed a month later by successful performance on the A/not-B problems with a three second delay. By 10 months, all had solved the A/not-B problem with a 7-sec delay. Separation distress occurred in all eight children by 10 months of age, the time when the memory ability was growing (Fox, Kagan, & Weiskopf, 1979).

A related study was conducted with native (Mayan) children growing up in one of two subsistence farming villages on Lake Atitlan in the highlands of northwest Guatemala. The sample included 87 infants, 5–21 months of age, who were tested by a local woman with the mother present. The coder was a white woman who lived in each of the villages during the course of data gathering. Some of the procedures given to these children overlapped with those given to the American sample, including object permanence and separation distress, as well as vacillation to the paired presentation of an old and an unfamiliar object. In general, children in both of the villages displayed a similar sequence of development, and it resembled the growth function for Cambridge children. Vacillation to the presentation of a new and old event was the first behavior to appear in both American and Guatemalan children, followed by the emergence of inhibition to novelty, stage IV object permanence, and separation distress. Although the Cambridge children tended to be a few months advanced over the more isolated Guatemalan infants in the emergence of object permanence and vacillation, the sequence of milestones was similar in both cultures (Kagan, Klein, Finley, Rogoff, & Nolan, 1979).

More direct support for this notion comes from the dissertation research of Leslie Brody. Brody (1977) trained 8- and 12-month-olds to touch after the "light" went off one of two stimuli (resembling faces) that had been lit. She varied the delay between the offset of the lighted facial stimulus and when she allowed the child to make the operant touching response. The delays were 0, 3, 6, or 9 sec. There was a dramatic difference between the 8- and 12-month-olds in the ability to tolerate the delays. The 12-month-olds could solve the problem at the longest delay, while none of the 8-month-olds could do so.

In a similar study with a longitudinal design, ten infants were seen monthly from 8 to 12 months of age. Infants had to retrieve toys they watched being hidden under one of two identical cloths. Delays—1, 3, or 7 sec—and interference—no screen, transparent screen, or an opaque screen—were varied, and all infants were tested under all conditions. There was a steady improvement in the performance of all children across the 4 months of study. No 8-month-old infant was able to retrieve the object at a 1-sec delay when an opaque screen was lowered during the brief interval, but four 8-month-olds solved the problem with a 7-sec delay if no screen was lowered. By 1 year, all infants could retrieve the toy when the opaque screen was lowered for 1 or 3 sec, and seven of the ten infants could solve the problem when the opaque screen was lowered for the maximum duration of 7 sec (Szpak, 1977).

The new capacity to retrieve structures for events not in the immediate field may help to explain some of the phenomena listed earlier. The reason why 9- and 10-month-old children are more attentive that 7-month-olds to a particular stimulus is that the former retrieve a representation of the repeated experience, hold it in memory, and try to relate it to the discrepant events in their perceptual field. If the events are facial masks, they retrieve the representation of regular faces and try to generate the relation between their knowledge of the normal face and the masks in front of them. As long as a trace of the past event remains articulated and the infants continue to relate it to present experience in the service of understanding, they will remain attentive. Similarly, the appearance of motor inhibition in reaching for an unexpected object implies that the child pauses while generating structures representative of the earlier event. During the period when that mental work is occurring, the child remains inhibited.

The theoretical position being developed here implies that successful retrieval of a toy in stages IV and V of the object concept sequence may be due, in large measure, to the enhanced ability to retrieve structures for past events. Although Piaget acknowledged the role of memory in the object concept, he dismissed it as a major factor because the infants seemed to be so attentive to the placement of the object. He equated attentiveness to an event in the perceptual field with the capacity to retrieve and hold the representation on the stage of memory after the event had terminated. He did not seem to appreciate that these are quite different processes, even though he acknowledged that memory might play a role.

Such then are the three possible explanations for the phenomenon: defect of memory, defect of spatial localization, or defect of objectification. But far from trying to choose among them, we should on the contrary try to show that these three explanations, seemingly different, in reality only constitute a single explanation seen from three distinct points of view. It is only if one retained one of the three explanations to the exclusion of the two others that it would be disputable. But if all three are accepted, they are complementary. (Piaget, 1954, pp. 63–64)

The emphasis on the process of memory, rather than the structure called the object concept, in interpreting the child's behavior between 8 and 12 months of age is in accord with work on cognitive development in older children. The improvement in recognition and recall memory after 6 years of age may be due to activation of processes involving organization, rehearsal, and retrieval rather than new knowledge structures. The ability to answer the class inclusion question properly may be due, in part, to the ability to hold the entire question in short-term memory and examine it mentally without the information vanishing. It may not be due necessarily to the presence of a new operation that represents the nesting of hierarchically organized classes.

We believe the growth function for separation distress, which has been replicated in several cultural settings, requires as a necessary but not sufficient condition enhanced ability to retrieve schemata for past events and to hold them on the stage of awareness for a longer period of time. After the mother departs, the 10-month-old generates from memory the schema of her former presence and holds that representation in memory while comparing it with the present. The child that cannot resolve the inconsistency becomes uncertain and may cry. That sequence is not completely adequate for several reasons. First, the 1-year-old occasionally cries as the mother walks toward the exit, before she has left the room. Second, the child will not cry in similar situations when comparison of past and present cannot resolve the discrepancy. The 1-year-old becomes puzzled but does not cry when failing to find a toy under a cover after having watched an adult place an object there several seconds earlier. Therefore we must postulate additional processes to explain the robust separation findings.

One possibility is that the enhanced ability to retrieve and to hold a representation of the past is correlated with the ability to generate anticipations of the future. We think 8- to 9-month-olds have a new capacity to attempt to predict future events and to generate responses to deal with unexpected situations. Children now begin to cope instrumentally with unfamiliar experience, aside from merely assimilating it. If they cannot generate a prediction or an instrumental behavior, they become vulnerable to distress. If they can generate either a prediction or an adequate response, they may laugh. We do not think that 8-to-12-month-olds' ability to predict leads them to anticipate pain or danger because it is hard to believe that infants all over the world, even those that are with their mothers for most of the day, suddenly expect a painful or unpleasant event to occur when they are between 8 and 12 months of age. Thus we think of the distress as independent of the frequency with which the infants have experienced past unpleasantness when their mothers were absent. Moreover, children whose mothers leave them often (for example, children in a daycare center) do not show separation distress earlier or with more intensity than those who have their mother with them continually. The importance of having an action routine to initiate in a potentially uncertain situation is seen in the child's reaction to an unfamiliar adult. If the stranger actively initiates interaction with the 1-year-old, therefore providing incentives for a counterreaction from the child, the infant is less likely to cry or stay close to the mother than if the stranger sits passively (Ross & Goldman, 1977).

One puzzle remains. The presence of either a familiar person or a familiar setting will reduce dramatically the occurrence of uncertainty and crying to maternal departure, as it does for encounters with strangers. Why does the presence of a parent reduce the likelihood of fear to a wide variety of discrepant events? One possibility is that there is a continuum of uncertainty. Within that continuum each child has a threshold level which, when crossed, leads to distress. A second possibility is that the context is an essential part of the child's conceptualization of any figural event; the infant implicitly classifies all contexts into familiar and unfamiliar ones. This is unlikely, since the child sometimes reacts with inhibition and fear to a discrepancy while sitting on the mother's lap.

A third candidate for explanation is that the presence of a familiar person provides the child with opportunities for behaviors to issue when uncertainty mounts. Recognition of the opportunity to issue a behavior mutes the uncertainty. The distress does not occur when the mother leaves the child with the father because the father's presence provides the child with a potential target for a set of behaviors. This is a profoundly cognitive interpretation, since the infant does not have to move toward the father but has to know only that he is present. The blind 1-year-old does not have to see the mother to be protected against separation distress; the child must know only that she is in the room.

In sum, the protest of separation during the latter part of the first year requires a postulation of at least four processes: (1) the ability to retrieve from memory schemata of past events with minimal incentive cues and to hold those representations in a stage of short-term memory so that comparison of past and present is possible; (2) the attempt to predict possible future events or generate instrumental reactions to deal with discrepant experience; (3) the inability to resolve the inconsistency between past and present or to predict future possibilities or to generate a coping reaction; (4) if there is no opportunity to issue a behavior to the preceding state of uncertainty the distress mounts and crying is likely to occur.

SUMMARY AND CONCLUSIONS

The data suggest that two complementary abilities emerge in most infants around the world during the last 4 months of the first year. They include the increased ability to hold past and current experiences in short-term memory and the disposition to generate cognitive structures that are attempts to relate past and present, as well as possible reactions to cope with the unexpected. The enhancement in short-term memory permits the infant more time to work at the puzzles inherent in discrepant events. The child that fails in this mission is in a state of uncertainty. We believe these universal maturational milestones are likely to be the consequence of changes in the central nervous system. It may not be a coincidence that the proportion of quiet sleep shows a major increase at 9–months of age. Moreover, the occurrence of sleep spindles in the EEG (12–14 hz and prominent in the precentral area) during stage II sleep shows a large decrease during the last half of the first year (Tanguay, Ornitz, Kaplan, & Bozzo, 1975). Since many physiologists believe that the neural control of sleep shifts from brainstem to forebrain mechanisms during the first year (McGinty, 1971), it is reasonable to suggest that the diverse behavioral changes that suddenly and rather uniformly appear toward the end of the first year are released by structural and biochemical events that are essential components of ontogenesis.

In closing, we might note that Freud was approaching a similar insight toward the end of his career. In a rarely quoted paragraph, Freud questioned the formative power he assigned earlier to variations in experience with caretakers. He implied that muturational forces would guarantee that infants would display some common developmental profile:

> The phylogenetic foundation has so much the upper hand over personal accidental experience that it makes no difference whether a child has really sucked at the

breast or has been brought up on the bottle and never enjoyed the tenderness of a mother's care. In both cases the child's development takes the same path. (Freud, 1964, p. 188)

Some Implications

If we view these data as a specific instance of a universal sequence in human development and assume it is typical of others to be discovered, we can analyze its characteristics and perhaps draw implications. First, the central psychological process that permitted the behaviors of inhibition, fear, and increased attentiveness to appear were cognitive—an increase in memorial capacity and attempts to predict the future. Second, the behavioral sequellae of that new competence were varied and phenotypically different. Finally, it is likely that the new cognitive competences could not emerge until prior biologic events tied closely to the maturation of the central nervous system had transpired. This trio of characteristics is also potentially applicable to the changes we see in adolescence. A variety of phenotypically different behaviors emerge which, if Piaget is correct, are likely to be due to emerging cognitive competences. For example, it is believed that the 12-year-old has acquired the ability to examine the logic and consistency of existing beliefs. The emergence of this ability, which may be dependent on biologic changes in the central nervous system, is catalyzed by experiences that confront the adolescent with phenomena and attitudes that are not easily interpreted with an existing ideology. These intrusions nudge the preadolescent to begin an analytic reexamination of all of his or her knowledge. The detailed example from infancy and the brief allusion to adolescence imply that we should be alert to concordant changes in behavior, cognitive functions, and biology as probable signs that some universal node is being traversed.

REFERENCES

Amsterdam, B., & Greenberg, L. M. Self-conscious behavior of infants: A videotape study. *Developmental Psychobiology,* 1977, *10,* 1–6.

Brody, L. The enhancement of recall memory in infancy. Unpublished doctoral dissertation, Harvard University, 1977.

Brown, R. W. *A first language: The early stages.* Cambridge, Mass.: Harvard University Press, 1973.

Campos, J. J., Hiatt, S., Ramsay, D., Henderson, C., & Svedja, M. The development of fear on the visual cliff. In M. Lewis & L. Rosenblum (Eds.), *Origins of affect.* New York: Plenum, in press.

Finley, G. E., Kagan, J., & Layne, O. Development of young children's attention to normal and distorted stimuli. *Developmental Psychology,* 1972, *6,* 288–292.

Fox, N., Kagan, J., & Weiskopf, S. The growth of memory during infancy. *Genetic Psychology Monographs,* 1979, *99,* 91–130.

Fraiberg, S. The development of human attachment in infants blind from birth. *Merrill-Palmer Quarterly,* 1975, *21,* 315–334.

Freud, S. *An outline of psychoanalysis.* In The standard edition of the works of Sigmund Freud (Vol. 23). London: Hogarth Press, 1964, pp. 141–208.

Jameson, J., & Gordon, A. Separation protest in children with the failure-to-thrive syndrome. Unpublished paper, 1977.

Kagan, J. Do infants think? *Scientific American,* 1972, *226,* 74–83.

Kagan, J. Emergent themes in human development. *American Scientist,* 1976, *64,* 186–196.

Kagan, J., Kearsley, R. B., & Zelazo, P. *The place of infancy in human development.* Cambridge, Mass.: Harvard University Press, 1978.

Kagan, J., Klein, R. E., Finley, G. E., Rogoff, B., & Nolan, E. A crosscultural study of cognitive development. *Monographs of the Society for Research in Child Development,* 1979, *180.*

McGinty, T. J. Encephalization and the neural control of sleep. In M. B. Sturman, D. J. McGinty, & A. Adinolfi (Eds.), *Brain development and behavior.* New York: Academic Press, 1971, pp. 335–358.

Newcombe, N., Rogoff, B., & Kagan, J. Developmental changes in recognition memory for pictures of objects and scenes. *Developmental Psychology,* 1977, *13,* 337–341.

Parry, M. H. Infant wariness and stimulus discrepancy. *Journal of Experimental Child Psychology,* 1973, *16,* 377–387.

Piaget, J. *The construction of reality in the child.* New York: Basic Books, 1954.

Rogoff, B. A portrait of memory in cultural context. Unpublished doctoral dissertation, Harvard University, 1977.

Ross, H. S., & Goldman, B. D. Infants' sociability towards strangers. *Child Development,* 1977, *48,* 638–642.

Scarr, S., & Salapatek, P. Patterns of fear development during infancy. *Merrill-Palmer Quarterly,* 1970, *16,* 53–90.

Schaffer, H. R., Greenwood, A., & Parry, M. H. The onset of wariness. *Child Development,* 1972, *43,* 165–175.

Sellers, M. J., Klein, R. E., Kagan, J., & Minton, C. Developmental determinants of attention: A crosscultural replication. *Developmental Psychology,* 1972, *6,* 185.

Szpak, M. P. A study of infant memory and play. Unpublished undergraduate honors thesis, Harvard University, 1977.

Tanguay, P. E., Ornitz, E. M., Kaplan, A., & Bozzo, E. S. Evolution of sleep spindles in childhood. *Electroencephalography and Clinical Neurophysiology,* 1975, *38,* 175–181.

Zaslow, M. A study of social behavior. Unpublished doctoral dissertation, Harvard University, 1977.

3

Psychoanalytic Theory and the Comparative Study of Human Development

Robert A. LeVine

The relationship of psychoanalysis to the academic disciplines concerned with behavioral development is paradoxical. Freud's writings are acknowledged as a major source of theoretical inspiration for research, but psychoanalysis is most frequently rejected by psychological investigators as being untestable in theory and unscientific in method. Social and biological scientists from outside academic psychology and psychiatry nevertheless continue to rediscover Freud, claiming to find in his work valuable ideas that no other psychology offers. While some contemporary scholars regard psychoanalytic theory as an archaic speculative fallacy equivalent to alchemy, others see in it the cornerstone of a more sophisticated scientific conception of psychological processes. It is not difficult to understand the case against psychoanalysis by those of an empiricist persuasion; what requires explanation is its continued appeal as a theory after decades of empirical attack.

Social and biological scientists continue to be interested in psychoanalysis because it is the only extant psychology that is concerned with the psychological organization of the individual and therefore generates the only theoretical models of personality as a system. American academic psychologists, after the decline of Hull's behavior theory (1951), relinquished the aspiration to build or defend a comprehensive view of human psychological functioning, insofar as doing so would require hypothetical constructs that could not yet be made operational. (See Koch, 1975, for an extended review of this transition.) They have adopted the position of specialized empirical investigators of response patterns within narrowly defined psychological domains, leaving broader relationships and systemic patterns to the future—or to the "undisciplined speculations" of psychoanalysis. Thus the systems-theory approach, although widely used in other biological and social sciences, has had extremely limited application in psychology, and the nonpsychologist searches in vain for a usable conception of psychological organization in the academic research literature before turning to psychoanalysis.

This situation is pertinent to the comparative study of human development not only because the growth of organization is central to what we usually mean by "development" but also because the most interesting and important psychological differences between human populations seem to reside not in the discrete functional processes of perception, memory, reasoning, emotion, and so forth but in their *organization* toward culturally distinctive goals. As empirical psychologists provide us with an increasingly detailed portrait of the universal human capacities for processing information, it becomes increasingly clear that the primary locus of cultural diversity is in the uses to which these capacities are put, their relations to cultural standards and personal intentions. To deal with these relations at the level of the individual, we need a conception of how his or her psychological processes are organized, and this leads to a consideration of psychoanalytic theory.

Psychoanalytic theory, broadly conceived, includes the following elements:

1. A conception of an individual psychological organization which integrates cognition, affect, and overt behavior in sequences of action and ideas united by meanings with which objects are repetitively endowed, functions to attain homeostatic and adaptive goals for the individual in pleasure-seeking, moralistic, and utilitarian activities, and is hierarchically ordered so that more highly developed cognitive structures supersede but do not eliminate more primitive thought processes and the memories, meanings, and goals acquired through them.
2. A functional account of the process through which the individual psychological organization preserves itself: defense mechanisms operating to conceal or distort anxiety-arousing self-perceptions.
3. An account of psychological disintegration, in which higher-order cognitive structures give way under stress and in altered states of consciousness, with the individual regressing to more primitive levels of cognition–affect organization.

In this perspective, psychoanalytic theory provides a framework for conceptualizing individual mental processes as a system of interdependent parts, hierarchically organized, with processes for maintaining a steady state, for growth and disintegration. It does not compete with the empirical psychologies of perception, cognition, memory, language, affect, and learning, with which it should be entirely consistent, but deals with a higher level they do not touch, viz., their organization in the experience and behavior of the individual. This is a level in which cultural beliefs and values are salient, providing the individual with the collective meanings, standards, and expectancies that form the context of personal experience and the reference points for evaluation of self and others. The comparative study of human development cannot do without this level of analysis, and it must bring some conceptual framework to investigation at that level; hence the relevance of psychoanalytic theory.

There are numerous contemporary versions of psychoanalytic theory, and although all contain the three elements outlined above, they vary in many other ways. This is due in part to the fact that Freud altered his theoretical views several times over a period of almost 50 years without revising earlier formulations on many important topics (Holzman, 1971). His followers were left with the task of making these revisions after his death or accepting a body of theory full of potential and actual contradictions and inconsistencies. But Freud's insistence on presenting psychoanalysis as a comprehensive theoretical system, together with the opposition of those who sought to replace it with fundamentally differing doctrines, made his followers reluctant to engage in revising his theory without abandoning it altogether. Thus Erik Erikson (1950; 1959) superimposed his psychosocial conception of development on Freud's psychosexual stages while leaving the latter largely intact. David Rapaport (1959) explicitly recognized the need for an overall theoretical reassessment and initiated it before his death in 1960, but it is only in recent years that major restatements of theory have been forthcoming, (e.g., Gedo & Goldberg, 1973; Schafer, 1976; Kohut, 1977). These efforts reflect the concerns of psychoanalysts for a theory that is faithful to the clinical evidence as they see it. They are moving away from libido economics and other reified aspects of Freudian metapsychology toward phenomenological concepts based more heavily on the contents of experience, with fewer doctrinaire assumptions about the nature of early development. The relationship of these efforts to nonclinical research, however, remains largely undeveloped.

Since contemporary psychoanalytic theorists do not speak directly to the concerns of comparative research on human development, investigators in this field must find in psychoanalysis what is most useful for their own work and make whatever revisions of Freud seem necessary from a cross-cultural viewpoint. I have elsewhere stated what I find most valuable for anthropology in psychoanalytic *method* (LeVine, 1973, pp. 185–202). In this chapter I shall present in outline some components of a psychoanalytic conceptual framework that could be used to guide cross-cultural data collection. This framework should preserve the psychoanalytic focus on intrapsychic organization and its development while making as few a priori assumptions as possible about the nature of that organization among diverse peoples. Much of the Freudian theoretical inheritance must be omitted from such a framework. I join psychoanalytic thinkers such as Schaefer (1976) in dropping libido and the metapsychological concepts of drive and energy from my working formulation. I reject also the psychosexual stages of libidinal development (oral, anal, phallic-genital) and associated concepts such as the latency period on the grounds that they are not consistent with observational evidence in our own and other cultures. In any event, these stages remain, 70 years after their formulation, based largely on reconstructive evidence from adult patients without substantial confirmation from the direct observation of children. To presume their existence is to block the unbiased observation that is so badly needed in comparative research. The Oedipus complex is somewhat different; I would join Parsons (1969) in assuming the universality of a family romance in some form, while leaving its content open to investigation in each culture. Similarly, I assume the universality of pleasure seeking, morality, and adaptation as individual functions without positing intrapsychic agencies of id, ego, and superego as pancultural. There is enough evidence that these functions are regulated at the interpersonal level in many societies to warrant keeping an open mind about whether or not they are structuralized at the intrapsychic level in any particular society. In comparative work, as in the psychoanalytic situation, the observer should permit individuals to speak for themselves, revealing their mental contents as fully and spontaneously as possible. This is a principle of psychoanalytic clinical method that is often obscured in the heavily interpretive published literature of psychoanalysis.

The student whose knowledge of psychoanalysis comes from textbooks may wonder what is left when the trichotomies of oral/anal/genital and id/ego/superego are dropped from its theoretical assumptions. The elements outlined above give some indications—a psychological organization conceived in functional and developmental terms, its defensive processes, and its adaptive and maladaptive responses to environmental pressures. Modern psychoanalytic theory also offers a conception of thought, conscious and unconscious,.encompassing the goals and processes of normal and abnormal thinking. In the writings of Klein (1970), for example, a psychoanalytic view of thought processes is presented; it is based on Freud, modified in the light of cognitive psychology and relevant to a broader range of individual behaviors than any of the purely intellectual theories. Modern psychoanalytic theory also offers a rich reservoir of concepts and observations concerning early development which, as Murphy (1973) has shown, are directly relevant to academic research in developmental psychology. In theoretical formulations concerning the dynamics of thinking and the development of the child, as in other specialized areas, contemporary psychoanalytic scholars are demonstrating the enduring vitality of the Freudian concern with the organization of cognition, affect, and behavior in the individual. These formulations represent a diversity of viewpoints but nevertheless provide the comparative investigator with unique and useful ways of conceptualizing individual development and adaptation. Three of these are illustrated below.

Developmental lines.　This is a concept elaborated by Anna Freud (1965) which frees psychoanalysis from its position as a single-sequence theory of developmental stages (oral/anal/genital) and explicitly posits multiple avenues of psychological ontogeny. When development along different lines fails to correspond within some optimal range, psychopathology can result. Gedo and Goldberg (1973, pp. 73–100) have attempted to reformulate the psychoanalytic theory of the development of psychic structure in terms of developmental lines. The possibilities for linkages with other theories of psychological ontogeny (e.g., that of Piaget) are enhanced by the use of this concept to guide research and theory.

Attachment.　The psychoanalytic theory of object relations has in recent years given birth to empirical research on infant–mother attachment, rooted in evolutionary considerations and investigated with objective methods, longitudinal as well as cross-sectional research designs, and quantitative analysis. As presented in the treatise by Bowlby (1969), this is perhaps the best example to date of psychoanalytic theory being used in conjunction with systems theory and Darwinian evolutionary biology to generate a specific line of developmental research. As initiated in the pioneering monograph by Ainsworth (1967), it is also our best example to date of developmental research carried on first in a non-Western society (the Baganda) and later in the West (Ainsworth, Bell, & Stayton, 1974). While attachment research in psychology has concentrated so far on short-term developmental effects of a limited scope that seems distant from the concerns of psychoanalysis, its longitudinal findings are only beginning to emerge, and its broader theoretical implications are matters for future exploration. Meanwhile, the investigations of Ainsworth and her colleagues and students provide a new model for the reduction of psychoanalytic concepts to empirical research, one that avoids the "black box" of earlier behavioristic reductions by operationalizing to a greater degree the intervening processes that mediate between the social environments of the young child and the child's overt social behavior.

The self.　Concepts of the self have long occupied a prominent place in social science theory and research, largely without reference to psychoanalysis. Freud's most explicit contribution in this direction was his article on narcissism (1914), but for many years psychoanalytic attention was focused on object relations. Erikson's formulations on ego identity (1959) represented a major turning point, especially in relating personality and social role, but their impact was greater in the social sciences, particularly history, than in psychoanalysis itself. In recent years, however, the self has become a major concern among Freudian theorists such as Kohut (1971; 1977), Schafer (1976), and Kernberg (1976). Their concepts differ, but their greater focus on the ways in which the individual experiences himself provides a bridge to phenomenological approaches in the social sciences (e.g., that of Hallowell, 1955) and promises joint theoretical development for the future.

The concepts of developmental lines, attachment, and the self refer to extensive theoretical and research literatures worthy of attention by students of comparative human development. Many other relevant topics are dealt with in contemporary psychoanalytic publications as covered by the articles and book reviews of the *Journal of the American Psychoanalytic Association,* the *International Journal of Psychoanalysis,* and the annual *Psychoanalytic Study of the Child*—e.g., the role of fantasies involving metaphorical images and symbolic representations of self and others in psychological development, relationships between psychopathology and normal development in children and adults. To locate formulations and observations of potential utility for comparative developmental research, the student must search diligently through volumes devoted largely to case histories and metapsychological essays, remain undiscouraged by the invocation of metapsychological terminology and concepts even in some of the more empirically oriented works, and seek guidance from someone well acquainted with the literature of contemporary psychoanalysis. The effort will be rewarded not with data but with depth—particularly the kind of insight that comes from exploring clinically and theoretically aspects of a problem that are not ready for empirical study.

How can psychoanalytic theory in its various contemporary forms contribute to comparative research on human development? To answer this question, I propose a view of cross-cultural research design that consists of three phases. In the first phase, the investigator conceptualizes an aspect of psychological development in terms that are universal to the human species, i.e., pancultural according to the best evidence available from diverse cultures. Insofar as this conceptualization goes beyond a description of anatomy, physiology, and overt behavior to involve psychological contents, it constitutes a hypothesis about the universal meanings of developmental events and processes. In the second phase, the investigator studies ethnographically the cultural meanings with which this aspect of development is endowed in a particular human society. This includes inquiry into its status in the beliefs and values of that society as they are formulated in folk systems of ideas and used by individuals in their public and private lives. Now the investigator is ready to embark upon the third phase, designing an empirical data collection program to test specific developmental hypotheses about the acquisition or modification of particular patterns of psychological organization, i.e., hypotheses about factors involved in the establishment and alteration of linkages between affective reactions, cognitive beliefs, and individual behavior in social situations.

That the first two phases are prerequisite to the third is one of the most reliable principles of cross-cultural methodology. When investigators attempt to study the development of complex psychological response patterns in other cultures without grounding their data collection methods in an empirical understanding of the meanings which form the universal and culture-specific contexts of development for the individuals they are studying, they invariably (and often unwittingly) substitute meanings derived from their own cultural backgrounds for those of their subjects. The results are thus ethnocentrically biased and misleading. Cross-cultural methodology has arisen to provide scientific solutions to this problem, and detailed attention to pancultural and culture-specific meanings and contexts is fundamental in those solutions.

Psychoanalytic theory can contribute substantially to the two phases of cross-cultural research design that precede the empirical testing of hypotheses with individual psychological data. It will be of greatest use to the investigator as a source of ideas concerning meanings and their psychological function in a developmental context. In the first phase, psychoanalytic theory provides conceptions of the universal meanings in terms of which developmental events are experienced and registered psychologically. Kluckhohn long ago articulated this point from the perspective of the anthropological field worker:

> When I began serious field work among the Navaho and Pueblo . . . , my position on psychoanalysis was a mixed one. I had been analyzed and was thoroughly convinced that Freudian psychology was the only depth psychology of much importance. On the other hand, I tended to believe that psychoanalysis was strongly culture bound. . . .
>
> Over the years, at least in certain crucially important respects, my position has steadily drawn closer to that of Roheim. I still believe that some of the cautions uttered by Boas and others on the possible extravagances of interpretations in terms of universal symbolism, completely or largely divorced from minute examination of cultural context, are sound. But the facts uncovered in my own field work and that of my collaborators have forced me to the conclusion that Freud and other psychoanalysts have depicted with astonishing correctness many central themes in motivational life which are universal. The style of expression of these themes and much of the manifest content are culturally determined, but the underlying psychologic drama transcends cultural difference.
>
> This should not be too surprising . . . for many of the inescapable givens of human life are also universal. Human anatomy and human physiology are, in the large, about the same the world over. There are two sexes with palpably visible differences in external genitalia and secondary sexual characteristics. All human infants, regardless of culture, know the psychological experience of helplessness and dependency. Situations making for competition for the affection of one or both parents, for sibling rivalry, can be to some extent channeled this way or that way but they cannot be eliminated, given the universality of family life. (Kluckhohn & Morgan, 1976, p. 120)

In the ensuing years, many other anthropologists (e.g., Fortes, 1977; Turner, 1978; Wilson, 1957) have found themselves "forced" by the facts uncovered in their field work to similar conclusions. This does not constitute formal validation of a psychoanalytic theory of personality development. It does show, however, that psychoanalysis has not outlived its usefulness for anthropologists interested in identifying the universal components of individual experience and development that are diversely elaborated in cultural symbols among peoples of differing traditions. Good examples of Freudian anthropology in this sense can be found in the works of Eggan (1949; 1952; 1961; 1966), Obeyesekere (1963; 1977a, b), Parsons (1969), and Kracke (1979). It is particularly noteworthy that while psychoanalytic conceptions of child development have changed and diversified greatly (as indicated above) since the time Kluckhohn was writing, psychoanalytic theory continues to be the primary reference point for researchers attempting to conceptualize how the invariants of man's biological heritage are translated into enduring mental representations. This is not only because psychoanalysis has more to say on this subject than other psychologies but because recent theorists such as Bowlby (1969), Mahler, Pine, and

Bergmann (1975), and Kohut (1977) have followed Freud in his concern with the universals of early experience as limits (evolved through natural selection) on normal psychological development beyond which pathogenesis occurs. These recent theorists differ from Freud and each other in what they claim to be most salient in early experience and how it relates to psychopathology, but they retain his focus on the biosocial basis of what is normal and pathological in development.

In the first phase, then, the investigator draws from psychoanalytic theory a preliminary version of what is universal in the psychological content of a developmental event, process, or transition and examines this in the light of ethnographic evidence from around the world. The theoretical conception is revised to fit this evidence until it can be formulated as a plausible universal of development like infant–mother bonding or attachment, the Oedipus complex in its generalized form (Parsons, 1969), or the phases of mourning the loss of a loved one (Pollock, 1961).

In the second phase, this universal or *etic* category is the subject of ethnographic inquiry in a specific culture. The aim of this *emic* inquiry is to discover its public and private meanings in that culture, beginning with a semantic exploration of the indigenous categories in terms of which the universal is experienced by native speakers of the local language. This includes the metaphors available to them for representing the developmental events in speech. The central activity of this phase, to which psychoanalytic theory can contribute heavily, is what I term person-centered ethnography. It is most generally an investigation of representations of self and other in cultural forms and individual experience. At the cultural level, the focus of the inquiry is on how individuals are presented and represented in the conventionalized dramas of social life: routine encounters between persons, public events containing an implicit or explicit narrative text (ceremonies, games, aesthetic presentations), and autobiographical reports (also containing a narrative text). In all three of these dramatic forms, the appearances of individuals (including the self) are presented in accordance with a normative script. The sequences of action in these scripts express collective ideals in metaphors of individual behavior and reflect collective standards of concealment and revelation of the self. From this ethnographic material, inferences can be made concerning culturally constituted defense mechanisms (Hallowell, 1955).

At the individual level, the focus of person-centered ethnography is on how individuals experience the collective dramas in which they participate as actors and spectators. Informed by a psychoanalytic perspective, the enthnographer assumes that individuals are capable of varying reactions to the normative environment around them. They may visibly conform to it and manage a public appearance of affective endorsement while deviating from it privately in clandestine deed and conscious or unconscious thought. If they support it privately as well as publicly, it may be not only because the culture's ideals and standards have become their own but also because the normative prescriptions of those collective dramas fulfill defensive functions for them, e.g., legitimizing the concealment of aspects of themselves (from their own or others' view) that are inconsistent with their sense of well-being after events that made them feel anxious, vulnerable, or incompetent.

The ethnographer collects biographical case material on how particular individuals use the representational resources of their social conventions and cultural forms to attain salient personal goals through social behavior. Obeyesekere (1977a) has called the developmental exploration of such biographical material "psychocultural exegesis;" it seeks to understand in psychoanalytic terms the social and personal background factors in an individual's life that have led him or her to adopt a particular culturally constituted defense in the management or resolution of a personal crisis in adulthood. Almost inevitably, depth explorations of this kind involve indigenous patterns of healing and require close attention to ethnomedical and religious beliefs and practices.

One of the finest published examples of how a developmental event in adulthood can be clarified by person-centered ethnography guided by psychoanalytic concepts is the study by Obeyesekere (1963) of Sinhalese pregnancy cravings. He shows with convincing ethnographic detail how the life situation of Sinhalese married women, including their indigenous stigmatization as impure and their heavily burdened work routines, motivates them toward envy of males and hostility toward their unborn children. The cultural complex called *dola-duka* makes their cravings for certain foods during the first and second trimesters of pregnancy socially acceptable and expectable. Obeyesekere shows that the foods they choose are symbolically associated with men, with the penis, with a desired regression to childhood indulgence, and with dangers to survival of the fetus, and that their cravings put them in an unusual and gratifying position of dominance and attention to their personal needs at one significant period in their lives. The investigator's intimate knowledge of his native culture and language makes this analysis particularly effective and indicates the rich possibilities of Freudian ethnography focused on developmental events, transitions, and crises.

Thus in person-centered ethnography, psychoanalytic theory, particularly in its psychodynamic aspects, helps the ethnographer move from the sociocultural functionalism of standard ethnography to a perspective in which social participation can be seen as fulfilling psychological functions for the individual players of social roles. One result of this is a more detailed and accurate description of what the universal developmental category of interest means to the individuals of a particular culture, not only in terms of collective beliefs and values but also in the context of their personal lives.

With ethnographic information on the cultural meanings in terms of which individuals experience an aspect of development, the investigator is ready to conduct empirical research on individual differences in development in that population. Phases one and two have given the investigator information on the stimulus equivalence (and nonequivalence) of that aspect of development—at a gross level for all cultures and in fine detail for one culture other than the investigator's own. With this information the investigator is in a position to design a developmental study in that setting, construct instruments for data collection, and interpret quantitative results, with a measure of validity that would otherwise be unattainable outside of the researcher's own culture. It is the combination of psychoanalytic concepts and ethnographic data in both phases that makes it possible to study the growth of psychological organization in a drastically different culture with a minimum of ethnocentrism. When this has been done in a number of settings, cross-cultural comparison will be called for.

SUMMARY

In this chapter I have sought to present in brief outline what psychoanalytic theory has to offer the comparative study of human development. Psychoanalytic theory has been changing in recent years, but it remains the one psychology with a conception of psychological organization encompassing the affective as well as cognitive, the abnormal as well as normal, the unconscious as well as conscious, the developmental as well as functional. Its greatest promise and appeal is that it will help eliminate from cross-cultural research on personality development the black box between environmental conditions and overt behavior on which interpretations of earlier findings have clashed and foundered. This promise gains support from recent psychoanalytic formulations that have built new (and largely unused) bridges between psychoanalysis and the research disciplines concerned with human development. References and examples are provided. The use of psychoanalytic concepts in developmental psychology, while still controversial, is indispensable for investigators interested in mental processes that vary cross-culturally. To define the place of psychoanalytic theory in comparative research on development, a three-phase view of research design is proposed in which psychoanalysis contributes as a source of theory about the universal meanings of development and about the psychological functions of collective representations in specific cultural contexts.

REFERENCES

Ainsworth, M. D. S. *Infancy in Uganda: Infant care and the growth of love.* Baltimore: John Hopkins University Press, 1967.

Ainsworth, M. D. S., Bell, S. M. V., & Stayton, D. J. Infant-mother attachment and social development: Socialization as a product of reciprocal responsiveness to signals. In M. P. M. Richards (Ed.), *The integration of a child into a social world.* Cambridge, Engl.: Cambridge University Press, 1974.

Bowlby, J. *Attachment and Loss* (Vol. 1), *Attachment.* New York: Basic Books, 1969.

Eggan, D. The significance of dreams for anthropological research. *American Anthropologist,* 1949, *51,* 177–198.

Eggan, D. The manifest content of dreams: A challenge to social science. *American Anthropologist,* 1952 *54,* 469–485.

Eggan, D. Dream analysis. In B. Kaplan (Ed.), *Studying personality cross-culturally.* Evanston: Row, Peterson, 1961.

Eggan, D. Hopi dreams in cultural perspective. In G. von Grunebaum & R. Callois (Eds.), *The dream and human societies.* Berkeley: University of California Press, 1966.

Erikson, E. *Childhood and society.* New York: W. W. Norton, 1950.

Erikson, E. *Identity and the life cycle: Selected papers.* New York: International Universities Press, 1959.

Fortes, M. Custom and conscience in anthropological perspective. *International Review of Psychoanalysis,* 1977, *4,* 127–153.

Freud, A. *Normality and pathology in childhood.* New York: International Universities Press, 1965.

Freud, S. On narcissism: An introduction (1914). In *The standard edition of the complete psychological works of Sigmund Freud* (Vol. 14). London: Hogarth Press, 1961, pp. 73–102.

Gedo, S., & Goldberg, A. *Models of the mind: A psychoanalytic theory.* Chicago: University of Chicago Press, 1973.

Hallowell, A. I. *Culture and experience.* Philadelphia: University of Pennsylvania Press, 1955.

Holzman, P. S. *Psychoanalysis and psychopathology.* New York: McGraw-Hill, 1971.

Hull, C. L. *Essentials of behavior.* New Haven: Yale University Press, 1951.

Kernberg, O. *Object relations theory and clinical psychoanalysis.* New York: Jason Aronson, 1976.

Klein, G. S. *Perceptions, motives and personality.* New York: Knopf, 1970.

Klein, G. S. *Psychoanalytic theory: An exploration of essentials.* New York: International Universities Press, 1976.

Kluckhohn, C., & Morgan, E. Notes on Navajo dreams. In G. Wilbur & W. Muenster-berger (Eds.), *Psychoanalysis and culture.* New York: International Universities Press, 1951.

Koch, S. Language communities, search cells, and the psychological studies. *Nebraska Symposium on Motivation, 1975.* Lincoln: University of Nebraska Press, 1975.

Kohut, H. *The analysis of the self.* New York: International Universities Press, 1971.

Kohut, H. *The restoration of the self.* New York: International Universities Press, 1977.

Kracke, W. *Force and persuasion: Leadership among the Kagwahiv Indians of Brazil.* Chicago: University of Chicago Press, 1979.

LeVine, R. *Culture, behavior and personality.* Chicago: Aldine Publishing, 1973.

Mahler, M., Pine, F., & Bergmann, A. *The psychological birth of the human infant: Symbiosis and individuation.* New York: Basic Books, 1975.

Murphy, L. B. Some mutual contributions of psychoanalysis and child development. In B. B. Rubinstein (Ed.), *Psychoanalysis and contemporary science* (Vol. 2). New York: MacMillan, 1973.

Obeyesekere, G. Pregnancy cravings (dola-duka) in relation to social structure and personality in a Sinhalese village. *American Anthropologist,* 1963, *65,* 323–342.

Obeyesekere, G. Psychocultural exegesis of a case of spirit possession in Sri Lanka. In V. Garrison & V. Crapanzano (Eds.), *Case studies in spirit possession.* New York: John Wiley & Sons, 1977 (a).

Obeyesekere, G. *Hair, or the connection between a symbol and a symptom.* Paper presented at the meeting of the American Anthropological Association, Houston, 1977 (b).

Parsons, A. *Belief, magic and anomie.* New York: Free Press, 1969.

Pollock, G. Mourning and adaptation. *International Journal of Psychoanalysis,* 1961, *42,* 341–361.

Rapaport, D. The structure of psychoanalytic theory: A systematizing attempt. In S. Koch (Ed.), *Psychology: A study of a science* (Vol. 3). New York: McGraw-Hill, 1959.

Schafer, R. *A new language for psychoanalysis.* New Haven: Yale University Press, 1976.

Turner, V. W. Encounter with Freud. In G. Spindler & L. Spindler (Eds.), *The Making of psychological anthropology.* New York: Holt, Rinehart & Winston, 1978.

Wilson, M. H. *Rituals of kinship among the Nyakyusa.* London: Oxford University Press, 1957.

4

Child Rearing versus Ideology and Social Structure as Factors in Personality Development

David C. McClelland

BASIC PERSONALITY STRUCTURE

In the 1930s, under the leadership of an anthropologist, Ralph Linton, and a psychoanalyst, Abram Kardiner (1939; 1945), personality development came to be viewed as the product of environmental conditions and early childhood experiences. Such a view owed an intellectual debt to Darwin, to Marx, and to Freud. The idea was that the economic conditions under which a culture has to live produce a pattern of social adaptation which enables it to survive. These adaptive primary institutions or "maintenance systems" in turn lead the culture to develop appropriate childrearing practices which produce the basic personality structure of members of the culture, and basic personality structure laid down in early childhood ultimately shapes all adult beliefs and practices.

Thus, for example, Kardiner observed in an ethnographic account of DuBois (1944) that it was appropriate, even necessary, for the Alorese to live by gardening in their habitat on an island in the Pacific. Furthermore, it was adaptive for the women to do most of the gardening that fit the environmental niche. The result was that when a new baby was born, the mother had to leave the infant with other caretakers during the day, often for long periods, while she worked in the garden. Thus the newborn child experienced regularly periods of abundance and deprivation, so that eventually it came to feel that people are not to be trusted: sometimes they provide and sometimes they don't. This very early learning in turn shaped adult Alorese interpersonal relationships and their values, which Kardiner called "projective systems" because they were supposed to be projections of largely unconscious emotional drives and conflicts acquired in early childhood. Kardiner, along with others of this line of thinking, was quite explicit in arguing that a complex value system like Christianity had no independent status as a causal factor in culture history but was itself a product of basic personality structure and could be accepted only where unconscious forces favored it.

Such a view proved attractive and was soon widely accepted. It was simple and straightforward. It was, at least in theory, testable. Above all, it was in tune with

73

major trends in American intellectual history at the time. It viewed personality as an adaptation to the environment, in accordance with social Darwinism. Even more, it treated the economic environment as a primary determinant of the human response, as the Marxists had been contending It accepted the Freudian—and also the New England Puritan—position that the early years in a child's life are all-important; that "as the twig is bent, so grows the tree." It fit the American behaviorist emphasis on the importance of early learning. In relegating values to a very secondary role, it satisfied the antireligious sentiments of a generation of social scientists still in revolt against the Christian worldview. Finally, it explained a phenomenon that almost all Americans at that time had experienced for themselves, namely, the way second-generation Americans could think, talk, and act just like everyone else even though their parents continued to talk and act in "funny ways" for the rest of their lives in America. Second-generation Americans were able to talk and think without an accent, so to speak, because they had spent the early years of their lives here; their "basic personality structures" were American.

The model was very influential. It shaped the culture and personality movement for a generation. Although some were skeptical (Orlansky, 1949), more argued for its plausibility and attempted to test it. The first paper I published in psychology (1942) marshalled the evidence then available to show that early learning differed in ways that make it more influential in adult personality development than later learning. Cognitively oriented psychologists influenced by Watson and the American behaviorist school (Kagan & Moss, 1962) were also ready to believe in the importance of early learning. The focus on childhood had enormous social consequences in the 1960s, when the Federal Government, under the promptings of public opinion, was trying in every way it could to alleviate poverty, crime, and racial and social disadvantages. Many policy makers felt that to try to change behavior in later life was impractical and expensive. Rather, it was crucial to reach people in the first few years of life if they were to have satisfactory adult personalities. Thus millions of dollars were spent for intervention programs aimed at the preschool years—to improve family life and to develop day care centers, nursery schools, or head-start programs. Word got around through the ill-starred Moynihan report (1965) that one could not expect well-socialized behavior from many adult blacks because they had had unfortunate childhood experiences which produced faulty basic personality structures, brought on through broken families, poverty, and discrimination. The only way to produce a social change was to get at people in the very earliest years.

What is the evidence today, a generation later, for so influential a model? It has had its critics all along, of course, but for the most part they simply reacted emotionally. They laughed at such notions as believing that swaddling could influence the basic personality structure of the great Russians so as to lead them, as some contended, to devise a repressive political system. Such efforts to dismiss the model as ridiculous often revealed only the fact that the critics were ignorant of the growing body of systematic evidence, collected chiefly by Whiting and Child and their associates, which connected child rearing practices with a variety of adult behaviors.

The purpose of this paper is to review some of these findings from the inside, as it were, as someone who was sympathetic with the notion of basic personality structure from the outset and who has contributed to its development over the years. To tip my hand in advance, as I have worked with empirical findings in this area over the years, I have gradually come to the view that the model, in its simplest form, is often wrong in putting such heavy, almost exclusive, emphasis on economic adaptation and early childhood. Rather, under many conditions, values and social structure are far more important in determining adult personality.

THE CROSS-CULTURAL APPROACH

Much of the evidence in support of the model comes from cross-cultural studies of correlates of variations in child rearing. Typical is the early landmark study by Whiting and Child (1953) of the association between various types of socialization anxiety and theories of disease. For example, they found that societies which are low in oral indulgence and wean early and severely are more apt also to give oral explanations for illness. Their interpretation is that the anxiety the child feels over eating extends into adult life and leads people to believe that if they don't feel well it must be due to something they ate. Analogously, if they have been severely punished for sexual activity as children, the resultant sexual anxiety is likely to persist into adulthood and be given as a reason for feeling poorly at that time. They recognize, of course, that the difficulty with all such correlational studies is that the causation may go the other way. Why isn't it just as reasonable to assume that adults who have sexual explanations for illness are likely to punish their children for sexuality so that they won't get sick? The answer they give is that such a reverse causation is indeed plausible for sexuality but that they did *not* find a significant association between the childrearing variable and theory of disease in the sexual area, whereas in the case of orality they did find a significant association; yet it is hard to understand why adults worried about eating would wean their children *earlier*. In other words, while the correlation does not mean causation, in some instances it is more reasonable to infer that the relationship goes one way rather than the other. Many cross-cultural correlations of this type have been published by the Whitings and their associates and challenged by others as to the direction of causation involved. LeVine (1970) has reviewed much of this literature and concludes, "In the welter of multiple connections exhibited by cultural variables, it is all too easy to find support for simple causal hypotheses, by limiting one's investigations to a few variables rather than looking at the larger structure of relations in which they are embedded" (p. 597).

In other words, a multivariate approach is desirable in which it might be possible to check the unique contribution of child training variables as opposed to other determinants of adult personality behaviors. In connection with the research on cross-cultural variations in drinking practices reported in *The Drinking Man* (McClelland, Davis, Kalin, & Wanner, 1972), we generated a large matrix of cross-cultural correlations which should permit just such an analysis. Furthermore, the area provides a good opportunity to test the basic personality model because few would argue that the adult behavior involved—namely, drinking—would cause variations in child training practices, method of earning a living, etc., rather than the other way around. It was in the course of working with this large correlation matrix over a period of years that my most serious doubts arose over the special importance of child training practices. For these reasons, it is worth focusing more closely on this particular set of relationships (see Chapter 24 in this volume).

Bacon, Barry, and Child (1965) had reported that various measures of child rearing practices were significantly related to measures of alcohol consumption in some 60–65 cultures. For example, childhood pressure toward achievement is significantly related to frequency of drunkenness ($r=0.28$, $p<0.05$) although not to general consumption of alcohol ($r=0.01$), and overall indulgence during infancy is negatively correlated with general consumption ($r=-0.36$, $p<0.01$) but not with frequency of drunkenness ($r=-0.08$). In preparing the results published in *The Drinking Man,* we decided to focus on a combined drinking rating which was the sum of the general consumption and frequency of drunkenness measures because we were not interested in *how* people drank but in some overall estimate of their alcohol consumption. The two measures used by Child, Bacon, and Barry (1965) were included in our overall correlation matrix, but unfortunately the computer printout and the cards on which it was based have since been lost, and all that is available at the present time is an extract from it which includes only the combined drinking measure. Thus the argument which follows is not as compelling as it might be. All that can be said in its defense is that it is internally consistent and that so far as I can remember, multivariate analyses of the constituent drinking measures yielded similar conclusions. It is worth recording that I started working with these data firmly convinced of the basic personality structure model and ended believing in an alternative model.

The first surprise in our correlation matrix was that none of the Bacon, Barry, and Child training variables correlated significantly with the combined drinking rating, and they included compliance versus assertion training, childhood indulgence, general press for and anxiety over responsibility, nurturance, self-reliance, achievement, obedience, and independence. The actual correlations varied between 0.10 and −0.15 for about 50 cultures. Our sample was slightly different from theirs, but it is unlikely that this is the explanation for the results. A close examination of their tables shows that if they had combined their drinking ratings too, in no case would the resulting correlation with the child training variable have been likely to reach significance. In fact, the correlation we found of +0.10 between the pressure for achievement in childhood and adult drinking is about what one would expect from averaging their two correlations for the same two variables. In view of the wide variations from one drinking measure to another, one might be permitted to wonder if some of their correlations might be due to chance. Bacon, Barry, and Child certainly correlated a large number of variables with the two drinking measures, and one would not expect the correlations to be so different in view of the fact that the two drinking measures themselves are highly intercorrelated ($r=+0.64$ in their sample and +0.77 in ours). Furthermore, for the *adult* variables in their matrix, the correlations tended to be high with *both* measures of alcohol consumption. For instance, instrumental dependence in adulthood correlates −0.37, $p<0.01$ with general consumption and −0.48, $p<0.01$ with frequency of drunkenness. At the very least, this suggests that adult variables are more consistently related to alcohol consumption than childhood training variables.

The second surprise was that the child training variables were generally unrelated also to social structural and ideologic or motivational variables, which, however, *were* related to adult drinking. Figure 4–1 shows the general pattern of relationships among variables related to child rearing, the economy, ideology, social structure, and adult drinking. Arrows have been included to show the most likely direction of causal relationships. The figure illustrates a typical pattern of relationships found in the overall correlation matrix. It includes only one particular child rearing variable found previously to relate to adult drinking, but the results for others are similar. It also includes just one variable relating to the economy—namely, dependence on

FIGURE 4–1. Cross-cultural relationships of child rearing, the economy, ideology, and social structure to adult drinking.

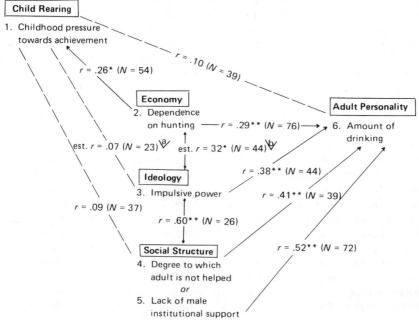

Note: Correlation of dependence on hunting with degree to which adult is not helped, 0.26* (*n*=50).

1. Childhood pressure toward achievement (Bacon, Barry, & Child, 1965).
2. Degree of dependence on hunting (Murdock, 1967).
3. Folktale code consisting of tags loading in high-power/low-inhibition quadrant (McClelland, Davis, Kalin, & Wanner, 1972).
4. Instrumental independence in adulthood (extent to which an adult's varied needs are met by independent actions rather than by help or cooperation of others; Bacon et al., 1965).
5. Factor Score from Wanner, given by McClelland et al. (1972): lack of male initiation, male solidarity, etc.
6. Sum of ratings for General Consumption and Frequency of Drunkenness (Child, Bacon, & Barry, 1965).
   a. Estimate based on correlations of 0.02, –0.02, and 0.24 with the three main components of this score.
   b. Estimate based on correlation of socioeconomic simplicity scale (which includes degree of dependence on hunting) with impulsive power factor score (from Wanner, given by McClelland et al., 1972).

*p <0.05; **p <0.01.

hunting—plus one variable drawn from content analysis of folktales and one social-structural variable measured somewhat differently by Bacon, Barry, and Child, and by Wanner (1972). These other variables have been chosen because of their firm relationship to amount of drinking; that is, dependence on hunting, impulsive power concerns in folktales, and lack of male institutional support are strongly related to drinking even when other factors are controlled. Thus even though, for example, childhood pressure toward achievement or some other value might not relate to adult drinking directly, it could influence either ideology or social structure, which in turn does relate to drinking. But this is not the case here, and it is generally not the case for other variables. For example, only one of the eight child training variables in the matrix is near significantly related to a variable such as belief in high gods (Murdock, 1967), namely, pressure for nurturance, $r=-0.37$, $n=30$, $p=0.05$); nor are any of the 24 correlations between child rearing variables and the three motive measures in folktales (n Power, n Achievement, or n Affiliation) significant in this sample. One can certainly not make a strong case here for child training being responsible for adult fantasies or beliefs, nor are the child training variables significantly related to such structural variables as the couvade, postpartum sex taboo, local jurisdiction hierarchy, class stratification, instrumental dependence in adulthood (lack of male institutions), and so forth. Overall one gets the impression the child training variables are not powerfully interrelated with either social-structural variables or with ideologic variables as represented in the many content analyses made of folktales and reported elsewhere (McClelland et al., 1972).

An alternative view is that child rearing variables reflect what is important for the culture although by themselves they may have little unique influence on adult personality development. For example, in Figure 4–1, it is clear that childhood pressure toward achievement is greater in societies which depend more on hunting, as one would logically expect to be the case. Thus whenever child rearing does turn out to be correlated with an adult personality variable, it may be because it is reflecting some more general factor which has a direct effect on adult personality—in this case the structural-ideational matrix, which leads to drinking because it insists a man must display his power largely on his own without help in hunting. Thus even if one starts with the Bacon, Barry, and Child correlation of 0.28 between achievement training and frequency of drunkenness, one could estimate that the relationship exists because of the correlation of both variables with a common variable—namely, hunting—and that a partial correlation would be reduced to insignificance if it were corrected for the size of these interrelationships of the magnitudes shown in Figure 4–1.

Wanner (1972) has tested the relative importance of social-structural variables and early-childhood variables in an analogous multivariate manner, as represented in

TABLE 4–1　Cross-cultural Relationship Between Father Distance, Male Groups, and the Combined Drinking Score (From Wanner, 1972)

	Percentage of Societies Above Median Combined Drinking Score	p Level
Father distance—distant (29)		
Male groups strong (17)	23.5%	
Male groups weak (12)	41.7	
Father distance—close (27)		
Male groups strong (6)	16.7	
Male groups weak (21)	61.9	$p < 0.10$
Male groups—strong (23)		
Father distance—distant (17)	23.5	
Father distance—close (6)	16.7	
Male groups—weak (33)		
Father distance—distant (12)	41.7	
Father distance—close (21)	61.9	$p < 0.50$

Number of cases in parentheses.

Table 4–1. His father-distance variable includes a long postpartum sex taboo, exclusive mother-baby sleeping arrangements, and large mother–father sleeping distance. His male groups variable includes presence of male initiation plus clear initiation impact plus strong male solidarity. The analysis shows that strong supportive male groups suppress adult drinking even when father distance is controlled as either distant or close, but the reverse is not true. Father distance—a key early childhood variable—makes no consistent contribution to variance in adult drinking across differences in male solidarity. In other words, an adult institutional variable is more important in influencing the amount of drinking than an early-childhood experience. Wanner also showed that living in a cooler, drier climate was more strongly associated with drinking than the two social variables listed in Table 4–1. One clear implication to be drawn from his analysis is that continuous environmental variables like climate and male social support are more important for determining adult personality than a discontinuous early-childhood experience such as sleeping with the mother for the first 2 years of life. Thus as far as these data are concerned the traditional model of the determinants of adult personally would appear to need revision along the lines shown in Figure 4–2. In the new model, child rearing does not occupy the center of the stage, responding on the one hand to economic and social conditions and determining on the other hand adult personality via its influence on infant personality. Rather, ideology—or norms and values combined with maintenance systems—is viewed as the central determinant of adult personality and also of child rearing practices. Child rearing influences child personality but is not seen as having any special importance for adult personality except as it reflects the more general norms or social structures which continue to influence the individual throughout his or her lifetime. Longitudinal studies have demonstrated, for example, that if a mother is hostile to her children in the preschool years they will be aggressive in return. However, her treatment at this time period does not seem to have any impact on their adult personality (see Kagan & Moss, 1962, appendix 12). But if, as we shall see in a moment, the mother's hostility represents something resembling rejection of the sex of the child, there can be impact on the adult personality because the mother's feelings will continue to influence her interaction with the child throughout the entire period the child is growing up.

FIGURE 4–2.   Schematic relationships of determinants of adult personality.

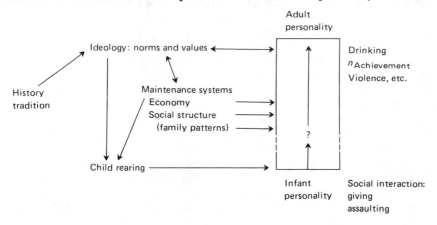

The new model also rescues norms and values or "shared cognitive systems" from the scrapheap of "projective systems" and places them squarely in the center of the matrix determining adult personality. In other words, beliefs about what is important are not simply post hoc rationalizations for economic institutions or early-childhood experiences. Rather, they should be considered as independent social determinants with a life of their own which can be traced in history and tradition. Sometimes they are responsible for changing social institutions, as we shall see, and always they shape the response to social institutions of adults. The wonder is that even for a time, they got relegated to such a secondary role. Probably one of the reasons was that it was thought cultural facts such as household type or mother–infant sleeping arrangements were more objective or more easily identifiable than values such as stress on impulsive assertiveness or the need for achievement. However, now that the methodology has been well developed for objective coding of myths and folktales for such values, there is no longer an excuse for ignoring them. In fact, one of the ironies of the basic personality structure model was that it was excessively psychological; it filled the gap between two externally associated variables such as hunting and drinking with all sorts of assumptions as to what was going on in the heads of the people involved, based on psychoanalytic theory for the most part.

But there is no need to guess; one can examine collective fantasies directly to see if the assumed themes are actually observable. This is just what we did in trying to discover the psychological mechanisms underlying variations in drinking behavior across cultures. Horton (1943), for example, had argued persuasively that subsistence anxiety explained the connection between hunting and drinking, but we could find no evidence of subsistence anxiety in the thought patterns of heavy drinking tribes (McClelland et al., 1972). Instead we found strong evidence of signs of impulsive assertiveness, which we interpreted as a value celebrated in song and story that strongly supports the institution of hunting. I hope that some day thematic analysis of collective fantasies or interpretations of cultures will become as routine and objective an approach to cultural analysis as classification of household types is now.

DEFENSIVE MASCULINITY: A TEST CASE

Perhaps no hypothesis deriving from the basic personality structure model has been more influential or more carefully investigated empirically than the view that mother–son sleeping arrangements are responsible for adult delinquency and crime. Bacon, Child, and Barry (1963) demonstrated that polygynous mother-child households were associated cross-culturally with a greater incidence of theft and personal crimes. The Whitings (see B. Whiting, 1965) interpreted this relationship as meaning that the young boy identified at first with his mother because she controlled all the resources and the father was largely absent. Thus the little boy will want to be like his mother. "If, later in life, he is involved in a world that is obviously dominated by men, a world in which men are perceived to be more prestigeful and powerful than women, he will be thrown into conflict. He will develop a strong need to reject his underlying female identity. This may lead to an over-determined attempt to prove his masculinity, manifested by a preoccupation with physical strength and athletic prowess or attempts to demonstrate daring and valor, or behavior that is violent and aggressive" (B. Whiting, 1965, pp. 126–127). This behavior is usually referred to as "protest masculinity." My purpose here is not to review all the evidence which has been collected to support the theory or the attacks that have been made on it (see LeVine, 1970). Rather, I want to use it as illustration of the difference between the traditional basic personality structure model and the new one, shown in Figure 4–2 (see Chapter 18 in this volume).

The "protest masculinity" hypothesis has been used to explain the greater incidence of crime and delinquency among black males as compared with white males in the United States. It is known that at least among urban lower-class black families the father is often missing. Thus it could be inferred that infant black boys identify more with their mothers and then learn as they grow older that they must be tough and assertive in the ghetto and hence develop a hypermasculine response in defense against their unconscious feminine identification. What are we to make of such a theory? Let us overlook the fact that Hendrick (1970) could find no evidence of primary feminine identification in young black boys; perhaps her measures were inadequate. The most extraordinary thing about the explanation is that it totally ignores the social conditions under which adult black males live, including racial discrimination and unemployment, and it also ignores values in the black family.

Glaser and Ross (1970) have reported some results that shed quite a different light on the determinants of delinquency among young black males. They were trying to find out how some young men grew up successfully in impoverished ghetto areas in which crime was rampant. Thus they located and interviewed a group of successful and unsuccessful (i.e., delinquent) black and chicano young men, all from very disadvantaged backgrounds. As one might expect, they found that absence of the father was more common in the background of the black than the chicano young men. Fifty-eight percent of the former, as contrasted with thirty-two percent of the latter, reported that there had been no fathers in their homes for a year or more ($\chi^2=3.51$, $p < 0.05$ in the predicted direction). It should be stressed, of course, as Billingsley has noted (1968), that father absence is by no means characteristic of all types of black families: it is just more common in urban impoverished areas.

TABLE 4–2 Characteristics of Successful and Unsuccessful Black and Chicano Males Aged 21–30 Years From Disadvantaged Backgrounds (After Glaser & Ross, 1970)

	Chicanos		Blacks	
	Successful ($n = 17$) percent	Unsuccessful ($n = 20$) percent	Successful ($n = 15$) percent	Unsuccessful ($n = 18$) percent
Behavioral				
Failing grades in school	35	67[*]	40	72
Charged as a juvenile	30	50	36	93[†]
Background				
Father decision maker	59	25	27	33
Mother decision maker	29	50	73	39
χ^2 Father versus mother, successful men = 5.23, $p < 0.05$				
Mother most influential				
person in his life	41	55	80	22
χ^2 for unsuccessful men = 3.00, $p < 0.10$				

[*]$p < 0.05$.
[†]$p < 0.01$.

If we compare the backgrounds of the successful and unsuccessful young men as summarized in Table 4–2, there is a rather startling difference between the blacks and chicanos. Since the young men were selected according to similar criteria, they are similar in terms of their failures in school or in being in trouble with the law. However, the two ethnic groups differ markedly in terms of whether the mother or the father is the most important influence in their life. Among the successful young men, the father was much more often the decision maker in the chicano families and the mother in the black families. Among the *unsuccessful* men, the mother was more influential among the chicanos but not among the blacks. So as far as black men are concerned, it is not those without strong fathers who show defensively masculine, delinquent behavior. The delinquents seemed to have neither a strong mother nor a strong father. It seems more reasonable to interpret the results as meaning that black families are traditionally matrifocal, whereas chicano families are patrifocal, as many studies suggest (see Kluckhohn & Strodtbeck, 1961). Boys are more likely to grow up successfully if the family pattern is normal, either father dominated if chicano or mother dominated if black, rather than if it is deviant for the culture. It is the *meaning* of father absence in the culture rather than the fact itself which influences adult behavior. Clearly a missing father is more important for producing delinquent behavior among chicanos than among blacks.

Focusing on meaning suggests that there may be a conflict for boys growing up in a culture which simultaneously stresses the importance of nurturance (mother values) and assertiveness (father values), but there is no reason to conclude that this value conflict influences an individual only or primarily in the early years through a complex cross-sex identification process which shapes adult personality. Rather, the two themes are often present throughout the lifetime of the individual.

In another connection, I have discussed (McClelland, 1975) a somewhat different interpretation of the explanation of higher personal violence in some of the six cultures studied by the Whitings and their associates than in others. B. Whiting explains the higher frequency of personal violence in Nyansongo (Kenya) and Khalapur (India) on the grounds that the young boys are much more exclusively with their mothers in those cultures than in Taira (Okinawa), Tarong (Philippines), and Orchard Town (U.S.), the cultures with lower incidences of personal violence. However, Mexican culture is a bit of a problem for this analysis because, as is generally agreed, there is a high incidence of personal crimes in Mexico. In fact, the term "macho" has come to be identified with a form of Mexican masculine assertiveness. If this is true, the Mexican case is clearly an exception to the "protest masculinity" hypothesis because the father is regularly present when the children are growing up. However, I argue that it is not really an exception. What is at fault is the misplaced reliance on father absence in *early* childhood as the primary determinant of "protest masculinity." Rather, in traditional Mexican culture, "the holy mother–holy child image has a strong hold on the imaginations of even the poorest Mexican" (McClelland, 1975, p. 191) and is strongly supported by the symbol systems of the culture in myth, song, and story. Furthermore, unambivalent identification with a strong father image is difficult because it is connected with the Spanish conquerors who raped native women. Thus Mexican boys may strongly identify with the strong nurturant female image and worry about being the "bad guy" male while at the same time wanting to be bold and conquering just like him. This may sound like the "protest masculinity" hypothesis all over again, but there is a crucial difference: here the emphasis is on the ambivalence in the value structure of the society rather than on a particular experience of the child in early life that has a lasting effect on him. Instead, the value conflict according to this model is present always in the life of the individual and continues to evoke conflict-ridden behavior in adulthood. Perhaps this explains the otherwise confusing results reported by Harrington (1970), who found that delinquent boys in this culture in fact showed more unconscious feminine characteristics in the Franck test, although there was no evidence of greater father absence in their backgrounds. The new model argues that value conflicts between nurturance and assertiveness can occur and arise from many sources but need not be traced to a single type of early experience.

In all of this, we have still said little about the importance of the structural or economic conditions in which adults find themselves. The new model clearly insists that that must be taken into account. Thus to return to the case of the greater incidence of crime among poor blacks, the model would insist that unemployment and discrimination arouse the need for power, which in turn leads to violence if there are no acceptable outlets for it. With such massive incitements to violence in the contemporary scene, it seems unlikely that experiences in early childhood would have much to contribute to the variance in adult crime behavior.

CULTURAL CHANGE

As Whiting and Child (1953) observed long ago, there is something unsatisfying about pitting alternative explanations like these against each other. Either or both can be made to seem plausible. How can one decide definitively between them? As they point out, studies of historical change ought to provide the best method of teasing out causal relationships. For example, if a visiting nurse introduced a change in child training practices for an native American tribe, it ought over generations to have an effect on adult personality if the basic personality structure model is correct —assuming, of course, that other changes did not also occur. Have there been documented cases of such changes in the time since they wrote? Not really. In a few historical instances people have argued that changes could easily have been explained by alterations of child rearing practices, but it is hard to be sure. For example, I used this approach to explain why achievement motivation declined in ancient Greece following its period of greatest affluence (McClelland, 1961). It seemed reasonable to infer from the historical record that as Greek families grew wealthier, they were able to support more slaves, including even the pedagogue, who literally walked the children to school. The presence of so many caretaking adults surrounding their children seemed likely to undermine the kind of independence training which has been associated with the development of achievement motivation. While such an interpretation of events seems plausible enough, it will have to remain speculative in view of our inability to measure directly the crucial assumed decline in independence and self-reliance training. All other accounts of historical changes in child rearing and their effects involve similar plausible reconstructions of the sequence of events. Thus the traditional basic personality model has not been demonstrated definitively by this method.

On the other hand, the importance of the variables stressed in the new model (Figure 4–2) has been amply demonstrated by historical studies. Religious movements such as Christianity, Islam, or Buddhism have repeatedly swept through populations, changing adult values, changing ways of earning a living, changing social institutions and adult personality structure. One of the clearest weaknesses of the traditional model is that it starts with the environment as the ultimate determinant of human behavior, yet historical evidence provides dozens if not hundreds of instances in which groups have changed their environment, not always for economic reasons. The Puritans came to New England and the Quakers to Pennsylvania primarily for ideologic and not economic reasons. The Quakers, at least, developed a church governing system and ultimately a political system which was quite different from that which they had left behind and that clearly derived from their value system. Whether or not all this influenced their child rearing practices we do not know—if anything, they do not seem to have been especially different from the practices of other Puritans—but they did develop a rather distinctive entrepreneurial adult personality type which was markedly successful in business.

Probably the best semicontrolled study of the impact of religious change on adult personality in a culture is reported in *The Achieving Society* (McClelland, 1961). In it the achievement motivation of children in school was compared in two Mexican villages alike in every aspect except that one had been totally converted to a Protestant form of fundamental Protestant Christianity about 7 or 8 years previously. The conversion had changed adult behavior directly in many ways: men did not drink any more; the citizens removed all images from their church and whitewashed the walls; they sang hymns together; and their children in school showed signs of higher achievement motivation than those in the traditional village. It is certainly not necessary nor even possible to explain all these changes in the time available as due to the impact of child rearing on basic personality structure. The events here seemed to recapitulate in miniature what happened historically much earlier in Europe when the Protestant Reformation promoted certain values which led to an increase in achievement motivation and ultimately entrepreneurship.

On the other hand, much evidence has accumulated showing that religious labels such as Protestant Christianity are not good proxies for the values they supposedly represent. Protestants in the United States do not score higher in achievement motivation than Catholics, nor do children who go to Protestant schools in India score higher than those who go to Hindu schools, which presumably would be less oriented toward self-reliant achievement. Nor do Yoruba Christians score higher in need for achievement than Muslim Yoruba in Nigeria (LeVine, 1966). What appears to be crucial in such historical instances is the value placed on reform, on resistance to and independence from traditional authority. It is during these periods that need for achievement in adult personality appears to be changed, and not later, when the reforms have become the new establishment. This helps to explain why communism as a reform movement in Russia increased the general level of achievement motivation in popular literature markedly from 1925 to 1950 and in China between 1925 and 1960, or why newly independent nations generally have higher levels of need for achievement (McClelland, 1961).

If one sticks to value orientations coded in popular literature, as opposed to religious labels, there is ample empirical evidence for the influence of changes in values on such national behaviors as rate of economic growth or whether or not a country gets involved in social reform movements or wars (McClelland, 1975). Many of these changes occur much too rapidly for the chain of influence to have gone through child training practices to infant personality and thence to adult behavior. For instance, there was a lag of only a few years between the assessed levels of need for achievement in children's textbooks in 1950 and changes in the rate of economic growth 6 or 7 years later (McClelland, 1961).

The influence of social and economic factors on adult personality has also been amply demonstrated, although it is less controversial and not really an issue between the two models. LeVine (1966) has demonstrated, for example, that higher achievement motivation among the Ibo in Nigeria seems clearly traceable to an open status mobility system which preceded their conversion to Christianity. In this system an Ibo was encouraged to rise socially by personal efforts and could be recognized publicly for doing so, which contrasts to the traditional client system characteristic of the Hausa in Nigeria, in which an individual's success comes from attaching oneself to a more powerful person. Similarly, opportunity structure and encouragement to "get ahead" are generally higher in the middle class in Western societies, as is n Achievement—which is exactly what one would expect if social structure and ideology were determining adult personality. In most such instances it is difficult to separate out which is more influential or which came first—the values and norms or the social structures with which they are associated. They usually go together, but because contemporary social science tends to emphasize the overwhelming importance of economic and social factors, it is worth stressing that ideologic factors can be more important. As a kind of type case, one can contrast the effectiveness of U.S. aid to India after World War II to Russian aid to China. U.S. aid was designed largely to change economic and social conditions in order to promote more rapid economic growth in India. Russian aid to China, at least in the beginning, was almost wholly ideologic in nature: its goal was to convert people to communism, which in turn led to other social-structural changes in social structure and even child rearing (Solomon, 1971). On the whole, the communist change in ideology seems to have been more effective in changing Chinese personality structure than the American attempt to make changes in economic and social conditions, which in turn are supposed to shape personality structure.

THE INDIVIDUAL APPROACH

While the major empirical method of checking up on the basic personality structure model has been cross-cultural, it is also possible to attempt to determine its validity through the study of individuals. Typical of this line of investigation is the evidence that parents, particularly mothers who stress independence and achievement at the appropriate age, tend to have sons who score higher in n Achievement, and that cultures which stress independence training tend to produce a higher proportion of successful entrepreneurs (McClelland, 1961). Since entrepreneurs tend to be higher in n Achievement, it has been inferred that an early child rearing practice—independence training—has some far-reaching effects on an adult personality characteristic (n Achievement). However, there are three flaws in this chain of reasoning so far as the traditional basic personality model is concerned. First, the child training experience does not occur very early but rather somewhere between the ages of 6 and 9 years, after the crucial period of child development postulated by Freud. Second, no one has yet shown that the independence training mothers provide is not simply a *response by them* to the greater n Achievement of their sons. In order to establish causation, one would have to test maternal attitudes toward child rearing when the mothers were pregnant and then wait to see if the sons of those who favored independence training grew up to have higher need for achievement. Third, there is as yet no definite evidence that a critical early period exists when, and only when, independence training leads to higher n Achievement. The reason n Achievement appears to be associated with attitudes toward independence in the years 6–9 is that the investigators chose to ask the mothers about tasks that children would be in the process of mastering at those ages. Feld (1967), in fact, demonstrated that the mothers who expected more independence and mastery 6 years later for more complex tasks also had sons with higher n Achievement. Thus it is entirely possible that higher n Achievement may be the consequence of mother's pressure for independence and mastery at any age or continuously.

To test the model properly and to avoid these difficulties, it is necessary to show that some critical life experience in the early years, and only in the early years, has a long-range effect on adult characteristics. J. Whiting had realized this and encouraged at least two studies which appear to have demonstrated just such an effect. One showed a connection between early infant stress and greater adult stature (Landdauer & Whiting, 1964), the other a link between father absence in the first 2 years and a number of characteristics of young males, such as a higher verbal than mathematical scholastic aptitude test score (Carlsmith, 1973). In both instances the same events occurring somewhat later in early childhood did not have the same effect. The studies have not gone uncriticized (see LeVine, 1970); furthermore, Santrock (1972) has reported that the meaning of father absence—whether it occurs through divorce or through death in the early years—may significantly alter its impact on the son's cognitive development. Thus it may be how the mother feels about and interprets the absence over time that is the crucial variable in the son's development. Obviously the relationships are complex and need to be investigated further, but at least the way remains open for believing that some early experiences have unique long-term effects (see Chapter 10 in this volume).

Methodologically speaking, the best evidence for or against the traditional model should come from longitudinal studies such as those carried out at the Fels Institute. Some relevant data given by Kagan and Moss (1962) are summarized in Table 4–3. At first glance they seem to support the hypothesis that early-childhood experiences can be quite decisive in adult personality formation. The maternal treatment variables in this study were actually recorded in home visits when the children were at

TABLE 4-3 Correlations Between Maternal Treatment and Adult Interview Behaviors (After Kagan & Moss, 1962)

	Adult Interview Variables			
	Achievement Behavior		Intellectual Needs	
Maternal Treatment	Males (n = 45)	Females (n = 44)	Males (n = 45)	Females (n = 44)
Age 0–3 years				
Hostility	−0.56[†]	0.59[‡]	−0.52[†]	0.53[‡]
Protection	0.27	−0.50[†]	0.42[*]	−0.42[†]
Age 3–6 years				
Hostility	0.00	0.18	−0.17	0.05
Protection	0.01	0.08	0.30[*]	0.19

[*] $p < 0.10$.
[†] $p < 0.05$.
[‡] $p < 0.01$.

various ages. The adult characteristics were obtained from interviews with the individuals after they had grown up and were in their mid-20s. The correlations in Table 4-3 indicate that mothers who treated their sons in a hostile manner in the first 2 or 3 years of life tended to have adult sons who were rated low in achievement behavior and intellectual needs. In contrasting fashion, if the mothers were nice and protected their infant sons, the boys tended to grow up to be more intellectual and achievement oriented; that is, they were presumably pursuing higher-level careers more vigorously. However, the hostility of the mothers to their sons when they were between the ages of 3 and 6 years did not seem to have any long-term effect on their achievement behavior or intellectual needs. What could be clearer evidence of the unique impact of a very early child rearing variable on adult personality characteristics?

Unfortunately, the asymmetry of the relationships between the same variables in girls raises some suspicions. Mothers who were harsh and underprotected their girls in the early years, but not later, tended to turn out daughters who as young women were achievement oriented and intellectual, presumably pursuing careers more vigorously. Why should the same set of child rearing variables have opposite effects for males and females? Perhaps some explanation can be worked out in terms of cross-sex identification. Little girls who are mistreated by their mothers may fail to identify with them, identify with their fathers instead, and behave in a more masculine manner by becoming more oriented toward pursuing intellectual careers. But then why is it that little boys who are protected by their mothers do not identify with them but also grow up being oriented around intellectual careers? It is difficult to see how these results can be interpreted according to a model which argues that it is the impact of such behaviors *on the child at the time* that matters. A simpler explanation might be that the hostility–protection dimension in the very earliest years provides a more accurate index of the mother's acceptance–rejection of the sex of the child, which affects the child continuously up to adulthood. If she is hostile to the male baby, it means that she doesn't like little boys or wishes she hadn't had a boy. If we make the further assumption that achievement and intellectual behavior are somewhat sex-typed in our society as being more appropriate for career-oriented males, we can infer that the little boy is reminded continuously that he is the wrong sex, so to speak, so that he fails to develop sexually appropriate career behavior as he grows up. The reverse is true of young girls. If the mother rejects them from the beginning, she is signifying that she doesn't like little girls; her daughter picks that up over the years and develops achievement and intellectual behavior appropriate to career-oriented males rather than the domestic female role which is apparently despised by her mother. According to such an interpretation, the reason that the same child rearing variables at ages 3–6 years do not seem to have the same effect on the child is that mother's treatments at later ages do not reflect so directly her prejudices. Her behavior later should be more conditioned by what the child does and by social norms as to how one should behave publicly towards boys and girls. However, in the first years of the child's life we get a more direct indication of the feeling she has about the sex of the child—a feeling that will continue to influence the child's orientation even though it no longer "shows," so to speak, in her overt behavior. Such an interpretation of the results, while speculative, seems to fit the facts better than the basic personality structure model, which would argue that it is the impact on the child up to age 3 years and not later that makes boys and girls treated the same way turn out so differently.

INDIVIDUAL CHANGE

As in the case of the cross-cultural approach, a good test of the importance of early childhood ought to be whether or not major change introduced during this period has important long-range effects on adult personality. Since psychologists and policy makers generally believed in the crucial importance of the early years, many large-scale programs were tried out in the 1960s in an attempt to facilitate cognitive and personality development among disadvantaged children. The effect of these preschool projects has been extensively evaluated by White, Day, Freeman, Hartman, and Messenger (1972). Their summary view, based on a thorough study of the evidence, may be simply stated:

> There is an immediate increase in IQ score for most preschool projects . . . [but] the effects of most preschool projects do not persist beyond the second or third grade. Immediate improvements in performance are found on achievement tests from preschool projects which focus on specific skills. In some cases, they persist longer than IQ increases but typically, they decline in a manner parallel to that of IQ scores. Data on non-cognitive effects of preschools are extremely limited, generally unreliable and of dubious validity. . . . Although there has been a general belief that the success of preschool projects would be increased if the age of intervention were lowered, there is currently little concrete support for this belief. (pp. 108–109)

In short, young children can be stimulated to learn more, but they also forget rapidly what they have learned unless there is some continuing support for the new learning. This should not be a surprise to anthropologists, since it is well known that young children who are transported from one culture to another readily learn the language and behaviors appropriate to the new culture, but if they go back to the original culture they just as rapidly lose the new language and customs they have learned. To put it succinctly, my son spoke fluent 2-year-old French at the age of 2 years without an accent, we were told, because he was exposed daily to a French-speaking housekeeper who spoke no English. She left soon afterwards, and today, in his 20s, my son does not speak French. Presumably he could relearn it faster, and perhaps without an accent, although even that has not been conclusively demonstrated. The wonder is that in the light of such evidence psychologists and policy makers have persisted so long in their belief that the experiences in the early years have permanent long-range effects on adult personality.

In contrast, attempts to change older children or adults seem to have somewhat longer-range effects. Adult businessmen who have undergone achievement motivation training lasting for about 50 hours over a 5-day period are still behaving in a more entrepreneurial fashion some 4 years later (Miron, 1976). Children receiving "origin training" in the sixth and seventh grades were still showing significantly improved cognitive and motivational development 1½–2 years later (deCharms, 1976). These empirical studies also confirm the widely observed fact that individuals who undergo a "religious" conversion, whether to Christianity or to communism, often stay converted throughout the rest of their lifetimes, and their adult behavior changes in many dramatic ways. Certainly the ideologic conversion of a small group of Chinese adults to communism had a much more powerful impact in the long run on Chinese society than centuries of traditional early-childhood training that produced quite different adult Chinese personality types (see Solomon, 1971). The weight of the evidence suggests that ideologic conversion has a greater impact on individuals in adulthood than exposure to various child rearing practices in early childhood. This is not to argue, of course, that all attempts to change adults are effective. Most are not (see McClelland & Winter, 1969). Those which are seem to be the ones that stress ideologic conversion plus social supports of the sort described by McClelland and Winter.

A similar case can also be made for the great importance of changes in social-structural or economic conditions on adult personality formation. For example, social scientists are still picking up attitudes among older U.S. adults which were shaped by the experience of the Great Depression in the 1930s. It would be difficult indeed to demonstrate that for most of these people what happened to them in the first year or two of life was more significant for their adult personality formation than the experience of deprivation they had during the 1930s, during young adulthood.

Are we to conclude that the basic personality structure model is wrong? Not really. It is impossible to disprove entirely so general a model, and there remains some good evidence that certain early experiences are uniquely important for shaping such adult characteristics as stature and perhaps cognitive orientation. The conclusion is rather that the importance of the early years in shaping adult personality has been greatly exaggerated in the light of the evidence which has so far been accumulated to support such a conviction. Most of the studies in the area admit of other interpretations, usually in terms of continuous ideologic or social-structural determinants of adult personality. At the very least, the weight of the evidence indicates strongly that what happens later in life is more important. Child rearing affects child personality, but children learn quickly and forget easily. It has proven very difficult to trace definitively adult personality characteristics which can be uniquely attributed to early childhood experience, to connect childhood learnings with adult characteristics. In contrast, the effects of values and social structure on adult personality are large, easily observed, and longer lasting. Thus while the basic personality structure model remains appealing for social-historical reasons, it deserves to be replaced by a model which stresses the importance of continuity in the concrete life situation in human development.

REFERENCES

Bacon, M. K., Barry, H., III., & Child, I. L. A cross-cultural study of drinking: II. Relations to other features of culture. *Quarterly Journal of Studies on Alcohol, Supplement 3*, 1965, *26*, 29–48.

Bacon, M. K., Child, I. L., & Barry, H., III. A cross-cultural study of correlates of crime. *Journal of Abnormal and Social Psychology*, 1963, *66*, 291–300.

Billingsley, A. *Black families in America*. Englewood Cliffs, N.J.: Prentice-Hall, 1968.

Carlsmith, L. K. Some personality characteristics of boys separated from their fathers during World War II. *Ethos*, 1973, *1*, 466–477.

Child, I. L., Bacon, M. K., & Barry, H., III. A cross-cultural study of drinking: I. Descriptive measurements of drinking customs. *Quarterly Journal of Studies on Alcohol, Supplement 3*, 1965, *26*, 1–28.

deCharms, R. *Enhancing motivation change in the classroom*. New York: Irvington-Halsted-Wiley, 1976.

DuBois, C. *The people of Alor*. Minneapolis: University of Minnesota Press, 1944.

Feld, S. C. Longitudinal study of the origins of achievement strivings. *Journal of Personality and Social Psychology*, 1967, *7*, 408–414.

Glaser, E. M., & Ross, H. *A study of successful persons from seriously disadvantaged backgrounds*. Los Angeles: Human Interaction Research Institute, 1970.

Harrington, C. *Errors in sex-role behavior in teen-age boys.* New York: Columbia Teachers College Press, 1970.

Hendrick, S. J. *Gender identity and belief in invariance of gender among boys with gender identity alienated fathers.* Unpublished doctoral dissertation, Harvard University, 1970.

Horton, D. The functions of alcohol in primitive societies. A cross-cultural study. *Quarterly Journal of Studies on Alcohol,* 1943, *4,* 199–320.

Kagan, J., & Moss, H. A. *Birth to maturity.* New York: John Wiley & Sons, 1962.

Kardiner, A. *The individual and his society.* New York: Columbia University Press, 1939.

Kardiner, A. *The psychological frontiers of society.* New York: Columbia University Press, 1945.

Kluckhohn, F. R., & Strodtbeck, F. L. *Variations in value orientations.* Evanston, Ill.: Row, Peterson, 1961.

Landauer, T. K., & Whiting, J. W. M. Infantile stimulation and adult stature. *American Anthropologist,* 1964, *66,* 1007–1028.

LeVine, R. A. *Dreams and deeds: Achievement motivation in Nigeria.* Chicago: University of Chicago Press, 1966.

LeVine, R. A. Cross-cultural study in child psychology. In P. H. Mussen (Ed.), *Carmichael's manual of child psychology.* (Vol. 2, 3rd ed.). New York: John Wiley & Sons, 1970.

McClelland, D. C. Functional autonomy of motives as an extinction phenomenon. *Psychological Review,* 1942, *49,* 272–283.

McClelland, D. C. *The achieving society.* New York: Van Nostrand, 1961.

McClelland, D. C. *Power: The inner experience.* New York: Irvington-Halsted-Wiley, 1975.

McClelland, D. C., Davis, W. N., Kalin, R., & Wanner, E. *The drinking man.* New York: Free Press, 1972.

McClelland, D. C., & Winter, D. G. *Motivating economic achievement.* New York: Free Press, 1969.

Miron, D. *The economic effects of achievement motivation training on entrepreneurs in three sample populations.* Unpublished doctoral dissertation, Graduate School of Education, Harvard University, 1976.

Moynihan, D. P. *The Negro family: The case for national action.* Washington, D.C.: U.S. Department of Labor, Office of Planning and Research, 1965.

Murdock, G. P. Ethnographic atlas: A summary. *Ethnology,* 1967, *6,* 109–236.

Orlansky, H. Infant care and personality. *Psychological Bulletin,* 1949, *46,* 1–48.

Santrock, J. W. Relation of type and onset of father absence to cognitive development. *Child Development,* 1972, *43,* 455–469.

Solomon, R. H. *Mao's revolution and the Chinese political culture.* Berkeley: University of California Press, 1971.

Wanner, E. Power and inhibition: A revision of the magical potency theory. In D. C. McClelland, W. N. Davis, R. Kalin, & E. Wanner (Eds.), *The drinking man.* New York: Free Press 1972.

White, S. H., Day, M. C., Freeman, P. K., Hantman, S. A., & Messenger, K. P. *Federal programs for young children (Vol. II). Review of evaluation data for Federally sponsored projects for children.* Washington, D.C.: U.S. Government Printing Office, 1972.

Whiting, B. B. Sex identity conflict and physical violence. A comparative study. *American Anthropologist,* 1965, *67,* 123–140.

Whiting, J. W. M., & Child, I. L. *Child training and personality.* New Haven: Yale University Press, 1953.

5

Uses and Limitations of Ethnographic Descriptions

Herbert Barry, III

The development of children constitutes an especially important aspect of culture. The survival of the society depends on training appropriate characteristics in each new generation. Stability of the culture is maintained with the help of traditional methods of child training. Adjustment of the culture to new conditions is often mediated by appropriate changes in treatment of children.

Information on child development may be especially useful for studying differences among societies. Many attributes of child training show wide variations in a world sample of societies. Cultural differences in many attributes of adult behavior develop partly from corresponding differences in the behavior learned during the formative years of early childhood. Accordingly, child training practices have been related to various attributes of culture in several studies of large samples of diverse societies.

This chapter summarizes the contributions of these studies. Limitations and uncertainties of the conclusions must be emphasized because of shortcomings of the ethnographic data and the inherent ambiguities of correlational studies. The correspondence between ethnographic reports and quantitative codes is demonstrated for two societies. Consideration of the deficiencies in prior research leads to recommendations for future research with the help of recent improvements in the quality of ethnographic data.

ETHNOGRAPHIC INFORMATION

Written descriptions constitute the raw material for the cross-cultural studies. Most of these descriptions are by professional ethnographers, reporting their personal observations and information received from selected members of the society. The societies vary greatly with respect to adequacy of the information on childhood. The profession of anthropology has developed techniques and traditions that ensure at least the attempt to include an adequate description of childhood.

The users of these ethnographies should be aware of some deficiencies prevalent in the descriptions of childhood. In spite of the shortcomings, however, valid information is available on diverse attributes of childhood in a large number of societies, representing all areas of the world that are inhabited by humans. The use of this information is helped by the Human Relations Area Files, which make widely available the ethnographies and a system of topical categories for a large number of societies.

Historical Trends

Part of the cultural heritage of Western European civilization is to ignore childhood as an important portion of the culture and as a formative stage of life. Accordingly, children have been excluded from most adult activities and from most written accounts of the culture.

Information on childhood is very meager in the written descriptions of the ancient precursors of Western European civilization, such as the ancient Egyptians, Babylonians, Hebrews, Greeks, and Romans. This deficiency applies also to the early accounts of exotic cultures written by explorers and missionaries. For example, there is almost no information on childhood among the aboriginal American tribes east of the Mississippi River because these aboriginal cultures disappeared prior to the modern development of interest in describing childhood.

Western European civilization changed greatly during the 19th century. One of the important changes was the development of a strong and widespread interest in the training of children. Several diverse influences contributed to this. The philosophy of John Locke included the doctrine that the individual's development is shaped primarily by learning rather than by hereditary predispositions. The Utilitarian philosophers emphasized the perfectibility and rationality of human behavior, and they dramatized the efficacy of child training by the example of one of their members, John Stuart Mill, trained as an intellectual prodigy from an early age by his father. The doctrine of behaviorism in psychology, publicized most effectively by John B. Watson and B. F. Skinner, emphasizes the diversity of learning and the strength of habits that have been learned. Consequently, the initial learning experiences during infancy and early childhood are especially important.

The most important influence on the increasing interest in child training was the psychoanalytic theory of Sigmund Freud. Early experiences were identified as the sources of both pathologic and adaptive behaviors throughout later life. The effects of the child's social environment were given special emphasis by Alfred Adler, originally an adherent and subsequently a rival of Freud.

The profession of anthropology has developed high standards for ethnographic field work as a comprehensive, objective account of all aspects of culture. Under the influence of Freud and Adler and their followers, ethnographic descriptions routinely include information on infancy and childhood. In many cases the information on childhood is meager. Most ethnographers are males, who may not be allowed to observe the relationships of mothers with their infants and young children in the privacy of their homes.

The prominence of childhood in ethnographic descriptions has been advanced effectively by influential female ethnographers who were receptive to psychoanalytic theory. Cora DuBois (1944) emphasized pathologic aspects of mother–child relationships among the Alorese. Margaret Mead (1978) concentrated heavily on child development in her descriptions of the Arapesh, Balinese, Manus, and Samoans. In addition to stimulating more extensive reports on children by subsequent ethnographers, these exemplary descriptions have been important in cross-cultural research because their excellent information on childhood has caused these societies to be included in most samples used for relating coded childhood measures to other cultural attributes.

An important further development in anthropologic field work is the technique of observing or testing a sample of individuals. In addition to providing information on individual differences, this technique allows an accurate measurement of the average or typical behavior and of the extent and frequency of deviations. Samples of children in two age categories have been studied in a comparison among six cultures (B. Whiting & Whiting, 1975). The *Journal of Cross-Cultural Psychology* publishes reports on measurements of individuals in various cultures. Some of these studies are on children.

Evaluation of Ethnographic Descriptions

Most of the ethnographic descriptions used in cross-cultural studies were written by anthropologists subsequent to 1930. Their field work benefited from a well-established tradition of comprehensive, objective observations, with recognition of childhood as an important aspect of culture. Most of these descriptions also suffer from some prevalent deficiencies.

The ethnographic accounts are predominantly unsystematic and anecdotal. They emphasize the public and conspicuous aspects of culture, such as outdoor work and ceremonies. Instances of children's behavior and interactions with adults are reported in detail, but it is uncertain whether they are selected because they are typical or easily visible or unusual. Instances of behavior are described but usually not classified or counted. Ethnographers have access only to small samples or second-hand accounts of the life in the home, which is the principal environment of infants and young children.

Some ethnographies include detailed autobiographic accounts by informants. These provide useful information, but it is doubtful whether these individuals are typical of the society members. Also, the information on childhood obtained from these adult informants consists of their own reminiscences, subject to distortions of memory, or descriptions of their behavior toward their own children. Although ethnographers report many unusual and bizarre incidents of adult life, their descriptions of childhood generally emphasize the normal and typical behavior. Children probably sometimes exhibit deviant and pathologic behaviors in most societies, but such instances are seldom included in ethnographic descriptions. There is a general tendency for ethnographers to emphasize the normal, prevalent patterns of behavior. This is enhanced in descriptions of children by selectively greater access to children in public settings, when deviant and emotional expressions are strongly inhibited.

A traditional concern in evaluating ethnographic accounts is the effect of the ethnographer's ethnocentric bias. Much of the ethnographic information about childhood consists of general conclusions by the observer, such as the degree of indulgence toward children or the personality traits of children. Such general statements may be especially susceptible to distortion by the ethnographer's expectation or personal cultural background. Detailed examples and specific observations of child behavior are meager in many ethnographies because of limited access to the homes, especially among male ethnographers.

The effects of ethnocentric bias are probably small, however, because anthropologists are trained to be aware of this danger. Observers of exotic culture show a prevalent desire to report accurately and objectively what they see and what their informants tell them. Even before the emergence of anthropology as a professional discipline, the 19th century explorers and missionaries showed an ability to distinguish their observations from their prejudices. Most of them believed that "to spare the rod is to spoil the child." Numerous observers commented that they observed an appalling lack of punishments applied to the children but that in spite of this neglect of parental duties the children were surprisingly well behaved, affectionate, and cheerful.

Even these early observers appear to have given accurate descriptions of the customs in spite of their judgmental attitudes. It is likely, however, that the descriptions are influenced subtly by their ethnocentric biases. For example, an observer who is accustomed to harsh treatment of children might be expected to exaggerate the degree of permissiveness in a more indulgent society. The descriptions by trained anthropologists also are probably influenced to varying degrees by such biases.

New techniques are remedying some of the shortcomings of ethnographic descriptions. Some field work has been done by male and female couples, thereby avoiding a sex bias in access to information and in point of view. This procedure was used for several of the ethnographies in a comparison of six cultures (B. Whiting, 1963). Samples of individual children have been studied systematically by some ethnographers, notably in the comparison of six cultures (B. Whiting & Whiting, 1975). These important improvements in ethnographic techniques have been applied to only a few societies, but they can be expected to become more prevalent in the future.

Availability of Information

Ethnographic descriptions constitute an accumulating fund of information about cultural customs. The value of the information is enhanced especially by multiple, independent descriptions of the same society. Some accounts of specialized topics provide information on important aspects of childhood, such as schooling, occupational training, naming ceremonies during infancy, adolescent initiation ceremonies, and social organization of the nuclear family. A comprehensive study of available information must include many brief articles or monographs on specialized topics in addition to the extensive monographs that attempt to describe all aspects of the culture.

The Human Relations Area Files provide a uniquely valuable compilation and classification of the available ethnographic information on a large sample of societies. The Files attempt to reproduce all the important ethnographic literature on each society included, with translation of foreign-language sources into English. In addition to making available all the sources on the society, the Files include a system of topical categories that bring together in the same location the information from each ethnographic source on the specified topic for the society. For example, under the general topical section Socialization, the Files contain the following topical categories in which the relevant information is collected: techniques of inculcation; weaning and food training; cleanliness training; sex training; aggression training; independence training; transmission of cultural norms; transmission of skills; transmission of beliefs.

The user who desires information about one or more of these topical categories can find it collected in the designated location. Other information on childhood is available in various other topical categories, notably in the topical sections on Infancy and Childhood, Education, Family, and Living Standards and Routines.

The Files include a wide variety of societies and nations. Because of a project for the U. S. Government done after World War II, there is extensive information on several nations important in world politics, such as Afghanistan, China, Czechoslovakia, India, Indochina, Iran, Korea, Malaya, and Thailand. Most large samples of societies that have been studied include a large proportion available in the Files. It is advantageous for researchers to select societies that are in the Files not only to make the ethnographic information more easily available for themselves but also because of the greater uniformity and availability of the information for other researchers. Samples in future studies may increasingly be selected among the societies included in the Files. A world "probability sample" of societies in the Files has been specified (Lagacé, 1976). An alternative sample of 60 different societies is being prepared.

The files are available in the form of paper slips at more than 20 institutions and in the form of microfiche at more than 200 institutions. Further information about the Files is given by Barry (in press) and in a booklet (Lagacé, 1974) published by HRAF, Inc., Box 2054 Yale Station, New Haven, CT 06520.

ETHNOGRAPHIC DESCRIPTIONS OF TWO SOCIETIES

Following is a reproduction of extracts from the ethnographic descriptions of the Ganda and Azande. These two societies, located in Central Africa, are the same in many features of environment and historical antecedents. They are both Bantu tribes, with the same language family (Niger-Congo). Their similarities allow a more precise study of the differences between them.

Both of these societies are available in the Human Relations Area Files and are included in the HRAF probability sample of 60 societies (Lagacé, 1976). The full ethnographic information is therefore available at all institutions with either the paper or microfiche version of the Files.

The extracts reproduced here constitute all the information found by the present author on the topics of obedience and responsibility during childhood, in the sources used for the codes published in Barry, Josephson, Lauer, and Marshall (1976, 1977). These extracts also provided important portions of the information used for additional codes, notably on self-reliance and on agents and techniques for child training. The sources are numbered in order of progressively decreasing importance for the codes on childhood, although not necessarily for the particular codes selected as examples in the present chapter.

Selected Information on Ganda
Standard Sample: Number 12. HRAF No. FK7.
Source No. 1: The Rev. J. Roscoe. The Baganda; An account of their native customs and beliefs. London: MacMillan, 1911 (HRAF Source No. 2).

9. . . . Girls and boys . . . picked themselves up when they woke in the morning, going off at once to play.
15. Children had free scope to enjoy life to the full, because there were many of them to herd the large flocks of goats and sheep which belonged to the communities, and to play as they herded them. . . . The children were free to do as they liked; when tired they would . . . sleep, and then go off to play again.
44. It was considered rude for a boy or girl to keep silent when called, and any chief would punish severely either a boy or girl for such a breach of good manners.
60–61. . . . Children were taken away from their mother after they had been weaned and had little, or nothing to do with her afterwards. Still, children, as they grew up, had some regard for their parents; the father was at least feared and respected, while there was something approaching love shown towards the

mother. No mother ever thought of kissing her child. . . . She might hug it, and pat it, when it was small, when it was cross or had been hurt. . . .

61. Children . . . were taken away to some member of the father's clan. They had, however, a warmer feeling for their mother than for their father.

75–76. Both boys and girls were careless about bathing during their minority; custom obliged them to wash their hands before meals, but they seldom did more than that. . . . Boys were sent to herd goats and sheep, and assist generally in such duties as they were able to perform. . . . About ten, they were expected to perform light duties such as carrying their relative's beer and mat, or going messages for him.

77. Boys had a free and happy life while the time of herding lasted; they met together daily, and while the animals browsed, they had ample time for all kinds of games.

79. Girls were taught to cook and to cultivate as soon as they could hoe. . . . Peasant girls were frequently sent to herd the goats, when there was no boy available to do it. . . .

80. Girls seldom played games; they were kept busy for the whole day, and were taught to make mats and baskets to occupy their leisure time; they also drew water and brought in fire-wood.

267. Petty theft and disobedience on the part of a child was often punished by burning the child's hand or cutting off his ear. The punishment of children was usually far in excess of the fault; and little mercy was shown when the child was a slave or an orphan.

416. Peasants sent their boys to herd any cows they possessed, but girls and women were forbidden by custom to do this work. . . .

418. If the calf was unhealthy, and his fellow-herdsmen considered that the boy was to blame, they [be]rated him soundly and even flogged him.

419. Boys sometimes boiled milk on the sly, and even cooked meat in it, but this practice was considered to be fraught with serious danger to the cows.

435. A child was left to watch the fire. . . .

438. . . . One of the maids or a boy poured water over the hands of the guests, as they washed them. . . .

Source No. 2: L. P. Mair. An African people in the twentieth century. London: Routledge, 1934 (HRAF Source No. 1).

21. Work begins in the Baganda household at dawn—children sweep the yards . . . ; girls go to the well for water; women set out with their hoes, taking with them children old enough to help. . . . The midday meal is prepared, though this is sometimes done by the children left behind.

22. The children carry out the remains [of the meal]. . . .

25. Children, especially girls, are taught to dance from their earliest infancy; even babies who cannot stand are held upright by their mothers and jerked in the appropriate movement in time to the music.

64–66. The education of children in the old days consisted mainly in learning the various household activities in practice, by imitating their elders but without the help of much deliberate explanation. In case of girls, one can still observe it. At the age of three they are given small hoes and go out to work with their mothers, and at little more handed a knife and told to peel plantains. By the time they are seven or eight, they are as quick at this as a grown-up person.

They are also given a calabash to scoop out. Next they are taught how to wrap up food and set it on the fire. I have seen three children, of whom the eldest was not more than six, quite competently preparing a meal with no supervision. . . . At about seven they begin raffa-work . . .

Boys in the pre-school era had to get up early and sweep the yard in front of the house to be neat by the time the head of the household was ready to go out, then to fetch the goats and tie them up in the yard till the dew was off the grass, when they went off to herd them. In most cases the only work for which they needed actual instruction was barkcloth-making; this they learnt by working with the father. Specialists, such as smiths and potters, taught their sons their crafts . . .

Etiquette is still an important element in education. Children begin to be taught the phrases of greeting and farewell almost before they can speak, and they are drilled in the correct gestures—to kneel and put their hands in the stranger's. Refusal to do this is one of the few reasons for which I have seen a child beaten. . . . Girls, in particular, begin as soon as they can sit without support at all to be taught to sit decorously. . . . Their mothers take hold of their feet and tuck them in place. The obligation to make presents to a guest is impressed very early on small children.

Such general information and advice as children received was imparted in the main by fathers to sons and mothers to daughters. . . .

Both boys and girls received a certain amount of general advice on conduct. 67–68. Girls' education was definitely orientated towards marriage, and in the performance of each household task they were reminded that this was work which they would later have to do as wives. . . .

Of all the relatives among whom the child grew up the one whom he was taught to treat with most respect was the father's sister. . . . It would be very rare for her potent curse to be used against a young child . . . but, at any rate in the old days, the child knew that he had it to fear and behaved accordingly. 122. Boys herded goats until they were old enough to help with barkcloth-making. . . . Older boys and girls or slaves fetched wood and water.

Source No. 3: M. Southwold. The Ganda of Uganda. In J. L. Gibbs, Jr. (Ed.) Peoples of Africa. New York: Holt, Rinehart & Winston, 1965, pp. 81–118 (HRAF Source No. 15).

107. Once the child can talk, parents take pains to teach it good behavior, especially respect toward adults; toddlers kneel before a visitor and timidly squeak out the formal greetings, and thereafter sit quietly on the floor until dismissed to play or work. As soon as it is able, the child is given tasks to do, taking small pans to fetch water from the spring, or cultivating its own small garden with a miniature hoe. Girls of five or six also help their mothers in the kitchen, and are sometimes able to do most of the work of preparing and cooking a meal. In the old days boys of six or seven began to go out herding the goats.

108. Ganda believe in bringing up children strictly, and I was told that they are frequently beaten if they are naughty—though I never witnessed this, partly perhaps because Ganda family life is conducted largely in privacy. Children, though extremely well behaved, do not usually appear to be cowed; and the strictness of discipline is mitigated by the obvious fondness of most parents or guardians for their children.

Selected Information on Azande

Standard Sample Number 28 (HRAF No. F07)
Source No. 1: C.-R. Lagae. Les Azande ou Niam-Niam. . . . l'organization Zande, croyances religieuses et magiques, coutumes familiales (The Azande or Niam-Niam. . . . Zande organization, religious and magical beliefs, familial customs). Bruxelles: Vromant, 1926 (HRAF Source No. 3).

76. The precept of respect and obedience due parents is admitted by all.

88. Among many of the chiefs, the *benge* [ceremonially collected root] is entrusted to the care of a small group of young boys.

157. The husband takes care of the heavy clearing, aided by his wives and sons.

164. The boys aid their father with various jobs of building, clearing, and hunting. The daughters aid their mother in the agricultural work assigned to the women, as well as in the work of the kitchen.

174. Until the age of six, only the mother occupies herself with the child. She is extremely devoted. In the beginning she covers the child with caresses. The father also fondles the child from time to time, but this is rare, since the mother lives largely apart in her own dwelling. The entire early education is left to the mother.

861. Very gently, when the child already knows how to reason all alone, a new manner of discipline appears, depending on the sex of the child. The mother will send the boy to amuse himself near his father, but keeps the girl near her. Yet it is the mother who gives to the child the little tasks which its age permits it to execute. She is very severe. All formal disobedience is immediately punished by corporal punishment. All Azande children know the effect of the *gbwangbwaki*, a kind of horse whip.

When the child is about six years old, the father commences to initiate him into various sorts of work: cutting wood, light agricultural work, carrying water, etc. The boy accompanies his father on the hunt and carries the snares (filets). When his father goes visiting, the small son follows him carrying a small chair for him. He himself sits on the ground. He listens to all conversations and learns much. The woman continues to teach her daughter all women's work, until ready for marriage.

198–200. If the girl is still small, she continues to live with her mother, but when she can cook without aid, she is taken to her husband. . . . The mother. . . . addresses the daughter, advising her. . . .

Source No. 2: P. T. W. Baxter & A. Butt. The Azande, and related peoples of the Anglo-Egyptian Sudan and Belgian Congo. London: International African Institute, 1953 (HRAF Source No. 56).

17. . . . One of the employments given to small sons is to carry [tobacco pipes] for their fathers when the latter go on a visit.

47. Children are set to perform useful tasks as soon as they are old enough, though, except for the older girls, work is combined with play, is often performed in company, and is not tedious. The child, suckled and petted until it is three or four, is then trained to help with little household chores and encouraged to be a help rather than an encumbrance to its mother. Between six and seven a boy will gradually leave his mother's protection and come under the tutelage of his father, carrying his stool and pipe when he pays visits, accompanying him

to the fields, to hunting expeditions, and even to court. By the time he is 10 or 11 years old a boy is expected to be a real help to his father; a girl at the same age is already expected to be shaping into a competent housewife. If she shows vigour and culinary skill she will be considered ready for betrothal. . . . A boy will stay at home assisting his father until he himself contemplates marriage. . . .

68. Parents are very affectionate towards their children and have considerable authority over them. . . . A daughter was completely under her father's control and infant betrothals were frequent. . . .

   A certain deference is accorded to the eldest brother. . . .

Source No. 3: E. E. Evans-Pritchard. Witchcraft, oracles and magic among the Azande. Oxford: Clarendon Press, 1937 (HRAF Source No. 2).

16. Family life is characterized by inferiority of women and authority of elders.

78. When a girl smashes her water-pot or a boy forgets to close the door of the hen-house at night they will be admonished severely by their parents for stupidity. The mistakes of children are due to carelessness or ignorance and they are taught to avoid them while they are still young. People do not say that they are effects of witchcraft. . . .

Source 4: C. C. Reining. The Zande scheme. Evanston, Ill.: Northwestern University Press, 1966 (Not in HRAF).

53. The administration forbade men to punish their wives or children by the more extreme means that had been used before. . . . A man could get into trouble if he beat or otherwise physically punished a wife or child.

Source not listed: C. G. Seligman & B. Z. Seligman. Pagan tribes of the Nilotic Sudan. London: George Routledge & Sons, 1932, pp. 495–539 (HRAF Source No. 1).

505. . . . Boys received their education in the chief's court. . . . Lads and adolescents from perhaps 10 to 25 acted as pages. . . . and as servants. . . . Discipline was strictly observed.

512. As the girl grows she will be taken from time to time by her mother to visit her betrothed. . . . three or four visits, each lasting a month or two. . . . She is trained in household routine and the duties of a wife.

514. For a girl . . . even in childhood her life and training is coloured by the fact that she is already promised in marriage. Her early training in marriage at her mother-in-law's house is somewhat in the nature of education at a boarding school, from which she returns for the holidays to her own parents. . . . As boys hope to marry they must be obedient and work for their fathers. . . .

Comments on the Descriptions

The foregoing extracts demonstrate the unsystematic and anecdotal nature of most ethnographic descriptions. Many specific incidents are described vividly but without indication of why these were selected for the ethnographic account. It is uncertain whether the ethnographic information is limited to the typical and frequent events or includes descriptions of unusual or abnormal occurrences. The ethnographers make some general conclusions, such as about emphasis on obedience and attitudes of adults toward children, but there is no systematic compilation of the information on which these conclusions are based.

Some of the information gives contradictory impressions. For example, the Ganda children are characterized as being free to enjoy themselves most of the time (Roscoe, 1911), but the same ethnographer also describes drastic punishments (burning the child's hand or cutting off an ear). More details would be needed, such as the incidence of the punishments and the degree to which the typical child is made to fear them, in order to determine which contradictory information should be given greater weight in a quantitative scale of degree of indulgence or permissiveness toward children. Another example of ambiguity due to insufficient information is the statement by another ethnographer (Southwold, 1965) that he was told that the Ganda children were frequently beaten but that he had never witnessed this. Deficiency of the information is acknowledged by this ethnographer's comment on his limited access to the privacy of family life.

In spite of some deficiencies, the ethnographic descriptions provide a large amount of diverse information. Measures of childhood obedience toward adults and responsibility for tasks can be coded on the basis of several items of information, including specific observations and general conclusions by the ethnographer. An important advantage is the availability of different ethnographies on both of these societies. For the Ganda, the principal source of information on childhood (Roscoe, 1911) was an early missionary. The HRAF has designated a professional ethnographer (Mair, 1934) as the principal source of general ethnographic information. These two diverse sources, along with a third, give a generally consistent portrayal of childhood while contributing different items of information and expressing different points of view.

The five sources on the Azande include a fairly early French ethnographer (Lagae, 1926) and a much later description by two English ethnographers (Baxter & Butt, 1953). The descriptions of Azande childhood in these and the other three sources are consistent with each other, and the aggregate provides much more information than any one of the sources. The ethnographic material on this society, as on the Ganda, contains contradictory impressions. Lagae (1926) describes the Azande mother as being extremely affectionate but also severely punitive.

In general, the ethnographic information is better on the Ganda, perhaps because of differences between the two societies in childhood environment. The Ganda children spend much of their time away from their parents. The ethnographers may thereby be better able to observe the children, and the descriptions of behavior both with and away from the adults provide a wide range of information. The Azande children spend most of their time with their parents. The ethnographic descriptions give only a few examples of the parent–child interactions, and most of the information on children is limited to the occasions when they are with their parents or other adults.

CODES ON THE TWO SOCIETIES

Effective cross-cultural comparisons require more condensed and standardized information than is provided by the ethnographic descriptions. Therefore the material reproduced above has been translated into codes that measure various attributes of childhood. The same codes have been applied to large world samples of societies, including the Ganda and Azande. Comparisons can be made among different codes for the same society. Each code separately can be used for comparing these two societies with each other and with the other members of the sample.

Various Comparisons

The principal purpose of the codes is to enable comparisons among different societies. The first step, however, is to assess the correspondence of the codes with the ethnographic descriptions by summarizing the pattern of relationships among the codes for the same society.

The left-hand column of numbers in Tables 5–1, 5–2, and 5–3 shows the quantitative scores assigned to the Ganda. The codes in Table 5-1 indicate that the Ganda are trained most strongly in obedience and most weakly in responsibility. For each type of behavior, the positive learning is consistently stronger than the anxiety over nonperformance. Comparison between the sexes shows that girls are trained to be more responsible, boys to be more self-reliant. In Table 5–2 a separate study again shows that the children are trained most strongly in obedience and most weakly in industry, which is similar to responsibility. Sex differences are slight for the measures in Table 5–2, but Table 5–3 shows that nonparents are much more important caretakers and authority figures for boys than for girls. Ganda children of both sexes are trained most frequently by example (imitation and instructions) and least frequently by corporal punishment.

The second column of numbers in Tables 5–1, 5–2, and 5–3 shows the codes for the Azande. The codes in Table 5–1 indicate that the children are trained most strongly in obedience and most weakly in self-reliance. For obedience, the quantitative scores for anxiety over nonperformance equal or exceed the scores for positive learning. Girls are trained to be more responsible, boys to be more self-reliant. A separate study (Table 5–2) likewise shows that the children are trained most strongly in obedience and most weakly in self-reliance. A further characteristic shown in Table 5–2 is a higher degree of affection than permissiveness toward the children. In Table 5–3 the parents are the exclusive authority figures and the predominant caretakers. Corporal punishment is the most frequent training technique.

TABLE 5–1 Quantitative Codes on Child Training Practices (Barry et al., 1967) for Two Societies, and Summaries for the Entire Sample

	Sex	Ganda	Azande	Total Sample		
				Mean	SD	n
Obedience						
Positive learning	Boys	14	12	10.1	2.5	100
	Girls	14	13	10.6	2.4	98
Anxiety over nonperformance	Boys	13	13	8.9	3.1	102
	Girls	13	13	9.0	3.0	99
Responsibility						
Positive learning	Boys	9	9	8.6	2.6	107
	Girls	11	11	9.7	2.3	106
Anxiety over nonperformance	Boys	7	8	6.6	3.2	103
	Girls	7	10	6.7	2.9	101
Self-reliance						
Positive learning	Boys	12	9	11.0	2.1	107
	Girls	10	6	8.7	2.1	105
Anxiety over nonperformance	Boys	8	5	7.5	2.3	106
	Girls	5	4	5.5	2.0	104

Each code is based on a scale from 2 (extremely low) to 14 (extremely high).

Comparisons between the two societies for each code show selected differences. Ganda children are trained more strongly to be obedient and self-reliant (Tables 5–1 and 5–2). Azande children receive more affection (Table 5–2). Nonparent caretakers and authority figures are much more important among the Ganda (Table 5–3). The most frequent technique for child training is by example (imitation and instructions) among the Ganda and corporal punishment among the Azande.

The Ganda and Azande were included in a sample of 110 societies for the codes shown in Table 5–1 (Barry, Bacon, & Child, 1967) and a partially different sample of 186 societies for the codes shown in Tables 5–2 and 5–3 (Barry, Josephson, Lauer, & Marshall, 1976; 1977). Each of the three tables includes summaries for the samples, showing for each code the mean, standard deviation (SD), and number of societies coded (n). These summaries permit comparisons of the Ganda and Azande with the samples of which they were two representatives.

TABLE 5–2 Quantitative Codes on Traits Inculcated (Barry et al., 1976) and on General Attitudes Toward Children (Barry et al., 1977) for Two Societies, and Summaries for the Entire Sample

	Ganda	Azande	Total Sample		
			Mean	SD	n
Obedience					
Boys	8	5	4.9	2.2	160
Girls	8	5	5.2	2.2	161
Industry					
Boys	2	3	2.8	1.4	166
Girls	3	3	3.3	1.5	165
Self-reliance					
Boys	5	1	4.0	2.0	155
Girls	5	1	3.5	1.8	153
Permissiveness					
Boys	5	5	6.2	1.9	169
Girls	4	5	5.8	1.8	167
Affection					
Boys	4	6	5.9	1.6	155
Girls	4	6	5.7	1.7	155

Each code is based on a scale from 0 (extremely low) to 10 (extremely high).

In Table 5–1 obedience training is much stronger for both the Ganda and Azande than for the mean of the sample. In Table 5–2 permissiveness is weaker for both of these societies than for the mean of the samples. These are the only measures in which these two societies differ in the same way from the mean. They differ in opposite directions from the sample mean with respect to self-reliance (Tables 5–1 and 5–2), importance of nonparental caretaker and authority figure for boys (Table 5–3), and the techniques of training children by example (imitation and instructions) and by corporal punishment (Table 5–3). In general, the comparisons with the total sample indicate that the codes in which the Ganda and Azande differ from each other are more numerous than the codes in which they resemble each other.

TABLE 5-3 Quantitative Codes on Importance of Nonparental Agents and Frequency of Different Techniques for Child Training (Barry et al., 1977) for Two Societies, and Summaries for the Entire Sample

		Ganda	Azande	Total Sample		
				Mean	SD	n
Importance of nonparent						
Caretaker:	Boys	6	2	3.7	1.8	179
	Girls	3	2	3.7	1.8	180
Authority figure:	Boys	5	1	3.1	1.8	175
	Girls	3	1	3.0	1.8	176
Techniques						
Imitation and instructions		9	5	7.4	1.4	152
Lecturing and exhortations		6	5	5.6	2.0	137
Corporal punishment		3	6	3.8	2.1	145

Importance of nonparent is based on a scale from 1 (exclusively parent) to 7 (exclusively nonparent). Each technique is based on a scale from 0 (extremely low) to 10 (extremely high).

Evaluation of the Codes

The numerical values for the Ganda and Azande, shown in Tables 5-1, 5-2, and 5-3, fulfill a necessary function for cross-cultural research. The diverse and extensive ethnographic descriptions are summarized by several quantitative scores. These codes facilitate comparisons between the two societies and are especially important for comparisons among many societies.

Each individual code in Tables 5-1, 5-2, and 5-3 provides a meager portion of the detailed and vivid ethnographic descriptions, but the combination of all the codes gives an accurate summary of the principal characteristics. The codes indicate that the Ganda train children to be independent with the help of predominance of nonparental agents of socialization, whereas the Azande children receive a high degree of affection but also corporal punishment, predominantly from their parents. Both societies treat children severely rather than permissively, with strong emphasis on obedience training.

Each of the codes in Tables 5-1, 5-2, and 5-3 is defined as a generalized, abstract attribute of child training. The score for each society takes into account all the pertinent ethnographic information. For example, positive learning of obedience (Table 5-1) and inculcation of obedience (Table 5-2) are influenced by each specific instance and the ethnographer's conclusions concerning obedience. Some information that does not specify obedience nevertheless is relevant and influences the scores assigned, such as frequency of contact with authority figures and severity of punishments for transgressions in general. The coders can also adjust the scores to compensate for cultural contexts or peculiar attributes that modify the effects of specific behaviors. For example, the ethnographic description of the Ganda children as being "free to do what they liked" (Roscoe, 1911) implicitly but not explicitly refers only to the portion of their time spent away from the surveillance of the elders. Even the codes that are potentially specific measures of single attributes are defined in a general way. Thus corporal punishment is defined as any pain-inflicting treatment rather than a specific technique such as whipping or spanking, it takes into account the degree to which pain is inflicted for the purpose of punishment, and it is on a quantitative scale of frequency rather than as absent or present.

The sensitivity of generalized codes to all the relevant, valid information also makes the scores susceptible to errors. The ethnographer's generalizations may be distorted by ethnocentric assumptions or other sources of bias. Such ethnographic errors affect generalized codes but not codes that are based on objective, specific items of information. Another source of error is the coder. The generalized codes depend on the coder's judgment concerning which items of information are relevant and how heavily to weight each relevant item in determining the quantitative score. Some human judgments are inevitably erroneous. The definitions of the codes cannot specify the full range of information to be taken into account, and the coders are usually not fully aware of all the factors that influence the score assigned to a particular society. Among the great variety of ethnographic descriptions, the coder overlooks some relevant items and ascribes excessive importance to some other items.

The codes are especially susceptible to errors when the information is contradictory or meager. For example, in Table 5–1 the Ganda score of 13 on a scale of 2–14 for anxiety over nonperformance of obedience takes into account both the low frequency and the extreme severity of punishments. The quantitative score could be influenced substantially by small changes in the ethnographic descriptions or in the coder's judgments. The same score of 13 for the Azande on the same measure is primarily inferred from the close contact with the parents and the frequent corporal punishment rather than being based on reports of punishments specifically for disobedience. When the information is meager, a difficult and potentially erroneous judgment by the coder is whether or not the society should be given a quantitative score. In addition to the measures shown in Table 5–2, the societies were coded on degree of inculcation of responsibility (Barry, Josephson, Lauer, & Marshall, 1976). The Azande were not given a score on this measure, which is defined as "regular performance of duties or economic activities without continual supervision." The ethnographic descriptions do not specify whether or not the Azande children perform tasks without supervision. Table 5–2 shows that the Azande were given a score on the closely related measure of industry, which is defined as "the demand that the child keep busy on activities which involve responsibility or obedience." Therefore the Azande score on industry is based on information about obedience rather than responsibility.

In contrast to the danger of spurious, inferential scores, some of the codes are insensitive to differences that are described in the ethnographies. For example, boys and girls are given the same score in most of the codes shown in Table 5–2, although sex differences are evident in the corresponding codes in an earlier study (Table 5–1) and in the ethnographic descriptions. One reason for the lower frequency of sex differences in Table 5–2 is a narrow range of scores, indicated by the smaller SD values for the total sample in Table 5–2 than in Table 5–1. A further reason may be that the codes in Tables 5–2 and 5–3 are limited to the early stage of childhood (Barry, Josephson, Lauer, & Marshall, 1976; 1977), whereas the codes in Table 5–1 do not differentiate between these stages. Sex differences are generally smaller in early childhood. Also, the differences are generally greater between the two stages than between boys and girls. The differential codes for the two stages (Barry, Josephson, Lauer, & Marshall, 1976; 1977) may have obscured the sex differences.

Relationships to Other Cultural Attributes

In most cross-cultural studies, measures of child training have been coded for the purpose of relating the childhood codes to other cultural attributes. Such relationships can be tested for the two societies (Ganda and Azande) for which ethnographic extracts and codes have been reproduced. This sample of two societies is obviously insufficient for demonstrating statistical significance, but it can provide indications testable with larger samples.

The childhood codes for these two societies differ from the sample mean by showing stronger obedience training (Table 5–1) and less permissiveness (Table 5–2). The societies resemble each other in many other cultural attributes, summarized in the Ethnographic Atlas codes (Murdock, 1967). Both have primarily agricultural economy, polygynous marriage, patrilineal descent, social stratification, and political integration beyond the local community. They are at a medium level of cultural complexity (Murdock & Provost, 1973). They also share some characteristics that seem to indicate high levels of stress. Food shortages are frequent or annual and the amount of protein intake is low in both societies (M. G. Whiting, as given by Textor, 1967), and both societies are classified as showing extreme bellicosity and emphasis on military glory (Slater, as given by Textor, 1967).

The principal differences between these two societies in the childhood codes (Tables 5–1, 5–2, and 5–3) consist of greater independence from elders and especially parents but stronger training in obedience for the Ganda children and more affection but more frequent corporal punishment by parents toward the Azande children. These differences in child training suggest more severe conflict over submission to social rules among the Ganda and more severe conflict over emotional feelings toward other people among the Azande.

Theories of illness (Murdock, Wilson, & Frederick, 1978) indicate differences consistent with these different types of conflict. Among the Ganda, important theories include mystical retribution due to violation of taboos and aggression by spirits of deceased ancestors or kin. These seem to express guilt and conflict over obedience. Among the Azande, the predominant theory is witchcraft, use of the evil eye by people with special malevolent powers. The evil eye is an expression of envy and indicates conflict over the desire to be special and superior.

Other cultural attributes indicate characteristic expression of conflicts in the form of group actions by the Ganda and in the form of individual actions by the Azande. A code by Murdock and Wilson (1972) shows that the most prominent community ceremonial emphasizes cannibalism, human sacrifice, or ceremonial killing among the Ganda, whereas it emphasizes music, dancing, games, or drama among the Azande. On the other hand, a code by Slater (given by Textor, 1967) shows that emphasis on killing, torturing, or mutilating the enemy, and also extreme boastfulness and sensitivity to insult, characterize the Azande but not Ganda.

Behavior during adolescence indicates emphasis on groups among the Ganda and on individualism among the Azande. Adolescent youths form peer groups among the Ganda (Harley, as given by Textor, 1967). Premarital sex behavior is freely permitted for boys and girls among the Azande (Broude & Greene, 1976).

Differential environmental stressors are also consistent with these other differences. Population density is more than 100 people per square mile among the Ganda but only 1–5 people per square mile among the Azande (Murdock & Provost, 1973). Chronic scarcity of food characterizes the Azande but not the Ganda (M. Whiting, as given by Textor, 1967).

The similarities of these two societies in many attributes set limits on the generality of the differences between them. For example, the relationships indicated between childhood codes and other cultural attributes might apply only to other societies with low childhood indulgence, agricultural economy, and polygynous marriage. The purpose of cross-cultural research on socialization, however, is not to generalize to a larger sample of similar societies but to use the information on specific societies to determine the general ways in which child training relates to other features of culture. The comparison between two societies that resemble each other in many respects is advantageous because the differences are made more conspicuous and consistent by holding constant many of the cultural variables. The relationships of the childhood codes to other cultural attributes might be obscured if tested in a world sample of diverse societies.

STUDIES OF WORLD SAMPLES

Several studies have tested relationships of childhood measures to other cultural attributes in large world samples of societies. The codes on various measures of childhood constitute a valuable and accumulating research resource. The findings have contributed to our understanding of culture as an integrated system. There is vast scope, however, for more and better research by scientists in the future.

Available Codes

The first major cross-cultural study of child training was by J. Whiting and Child (1953), who used a world sample of 75 societies. They reported quantitative scores on satisfaction potential and socialization anxiety for each of five systems of behavior: oral, anal, sexual, dependence, and aggression. Barry, Bacon, and Child (1967), using a sample of 110 societies, reported quantitative scores on infancy indulgence and on several types of behavior trained in children. Some of the childhood measures are shown in Table 5-1. A carefully defined world sample of 186 societies (Murdock & White, 1969) has been used for new, more extensive sets of codes on infancy and early childhood (Barry & Paxson, 1971) and on early and late stages of childhood (Barry, Josephson, Lauer, & Marshall, 1976; 1977). Some of the codes in the latter two articles are shown in Tables 5-2 and 5-3. Several measures of parental and child behavior (Rohner, 1975) have been applied to a world sample of 101 societies.

Most of these measures of childhood are quantitative scores for general, abstract attributes, relying largely on the interpretations and conclusions by the ethnographers and on the judgments of the coders. Some specific, objective measures are also available. The codes on infancy reported by Barry and Paxson (1971) include specifications of the usual carrying devices and carrying position. (See chapter 7 in this volume.) This information is often obtained from photographs. A similar but independently coded measure of infancy carrying practices (Ayres, 1973) was applied to a sample of 54 societies. Sleeping arrangements during infancy were coded by Barry and Paxson (1971) and independently by Munroe, Munroe, and Whiting (1973) on a sample of 74 societies. Relationships of children with their parents are affected by husband-wife sleeping arrangements, which were coded by J. Whiting and Whiting (1975) on the same sample of 186 societies as used by Barry and Paxson (1971) and for the codes in Tables 5-2 and 5-3. Codes on adolescent initiation ceremonies for males (Whiting, Kluckhohn, & Anthony, 1958), applied to a sample of 55 societies, included presence or absence of genital mutilations and several other specific features.

Reviews by Barry (1969b; 1979) describe several other codes on childhood. Most of them constitute a limited range of measures, applied to a small sample of societies. The Ethnographic Atlas (Murdock, 1967), applied to a very large world sample of more than 1000 societies, includes a few codes on childhood. These are duration of post partum sex taboo, age of male genital mutilations, segregation of adolescent boys, and norms of premarital sex behavior of girls. A wide range of measures of sex behavior (Broude & Greene, 1976; see Chapter 19 in this volume) has been applied to the same sample of 186 societies as the codes in Tables 5–2 and 5–3.

The codes on childhood can be related to numerous available codes on various other cultural attributes. The Ethnographic Atlas (Murdock, 1967) includes a wide range of codes on more than 1000 societies. Improved and expanded versions of most of these codes, and many additional measures, have been applied to a carefully selected sample of 186 societies (Murdock & White, 1969) in a series of articles in *Ethnology* (most recently Murdock et al., 1978). Various other codes are identified in a review by Barry (in press). Further codes are available in some of the studies cited by a bibliography (O'Leary, 1973), which also cites earlier bibliographies. A source of special interest may be Textor (1967), providing many diverse codes on the first 400 societies in the Ethnographic Atlas, because it includes several otherwise unpublished codes. Some of these have been identified earlier in the present paper as examples of cultural attributes of the Ganda and Azande.

Most of the codes are in numerical form or can easily be converted from alphabetical characters into numbers in order to facilitate statistical analyses. Many of the codes are suitable for parametric measures, such as mean, standard deviation, product-moment correlation coefficients, and factor analysis. Computer programs for statistical analyses of cross-cultural data are available from HRAF (Naroll, Michik, & Naroll, 1976). Some codes, in the form of punched cards that can be entered into most computer systems, are also available from HRAF. These include the Ethnographic Atlas (Murdock, 1967), the childhood codes (of which Tables 5–2 and 5–3 show a small sample), and most of the codes on the same sample of 186 societies reported in articles cited by Barry, Josephson, Lauer, & Marshall (1976; 1977).

Cultural Role of Childhood

Childhood is one part of the individual's lifespan and one component of the social system. Each of the attributes of society mutually adapt to each other in a continuous process of cultural evolution. J. Whiting and Whiting (1978) portray the interrelationships of child training with other aspects of culture.

In most cross-cultural studies, childhood has been interpreted as a causative agent. Cultural variations in child training are assumed to cause corresponding variations in adult personality. Selected cultural attributes, which presumably are expressions of adult personality, are interpreted as consequences of childhood experiences if they are correlated with the measures of child training. In the initial major cross-cultural study, J. Whiting and Child (1953) suggested that cultural variations in theories of illness are consequences of cultural variations in child training practices. Likewise, variations in art style (Barry, 1957), frequency of crime (Bacon, Child, & Barry 1963), frequency of drunkenness (Bacon, Barry, Buchwald, Child, & Snyder, 1965), and attitudes toward supernatural beings (Lambert, Triandis, & Wolf, 1959; Rohner, 1975) have been interpreted as consequences of variations in child training. These are only a small sample of the studies reviewed by Barry (in press) and cited in a bibliography by O'Leary (1973) and in his earlier bibliographies.

A frequent theme is to interpret irrational or pathologic cultural customs as consequences of pathologic childhood experiences, such as harsh treatment. This point of view is emphasized in a review by Barry (1969b) and in a book by Rohner (1975). The value of this explanation is limited by the fact that most ethnographies contain very little information on pathologic conditions or responses during childhood. Extremely harsh treatment of children is reported for a few societies (Barry, 1969b), but this is either rare or usually not reported by ethnographers.

Some cross-cultural studies have emphasized the adaptive function of child training, contributing to the transition from childhood behavior to the demands of adult life. Child training has thus been interpreted as a preparation for adult sex role (Barry, Bacon, & Child, 1957) and for participation in the subsistence economy (Barry, Child, & Bacon, 1959). Such adaptive functions are probably more prevalent than pathologic effects of childhood experiences. The adaptive functions may be more difficult to identify as causative influences, however, because they are well integrated in the total cultural pattern.

A general limitation to the correlational findings is that they do not specify the direction or agent of causation. For example, Barry, Child, and Bacon (1959) suggested that agricultural or herding societies train children in compliance in order to develop the traits necessary for the adult activities. An alternative plausible explanation, suggested by Barry (1969a), is that societies with strong compliance training may choose to develop agriculture or herding. Likewise, J. Whiting (1964) reported evidence that cultural variations in diet and social structure may cause cultural differences in some attributes of child training.

Our understanding of adaptive cultural functions may be increased by identifying close relationships between child training practices and other cultural attributes in large world samples of societies. Since each society in the samples is studied at a single time, the data are not suitable for determining which attributes are the causes and which are the consequences. Cultural evolution involves changes in many attributes. Most of the changes probably constitute concurrent adaptations, with no clear distinction between causes and consequences.

Recommendations for Researchers

Ethnographic descriptions and codes on childhood and on other attributes of culture are accumulating and improving in quality. These progressive changes can be expected to increase the value and scope of cross-cultural research. Future studies should be done systematically and carefully, in accordance with a list of suggestions by Rohner, Naroll, Barry, Divale, Erickson, Schaefer, and Sipes (1978).

The comparison between the Ganda and Azande, in the present chapter, demonstrates the value of studying societies that resemble each other in some respects. Barry (1969a) reported a study of 12 pairs of closely related societies. This technique can be applied to comparisons within the same society, such as different regions or occupational groups. Comparisons between different time intervals for the societies might be especially useful. Characteristics of children should be related more closely to characteristics of adults in the next generation than in the same generation. Sequences of cultural changes might help to distinguish between the causes and consequences. A further important dimension of research within each society is the study of differences among individuals, such as the systematic study of samples of children in each of six societies (B. Whiting & Whiting, 1975).

Further codes on childhood are needed, especially measuring conflicts between different motivations and attitudes, such as dependency versus independence. Most ethnographies do not give direct information on conflicting motives in children, but some behavioral expressions, described in many societies, might provide valid measures of conflict. For example, children might express severe conflict by highly variable behavior or by frequent behavior that is contrary to the cultural norms.

Whenever feasible, coding should be done independently by two people. The records should include the source and page number used for each code. This procedure helped the present author to locate the pertinent passages in the ethnographies on the Ganda and Azanda for the present chapter. When two people code a society, they should subsequently discuss their discrepancies and specify a set of consensus codes. This procedure improves the codes by correcting oversights or other errors by one of the people and also by helping both people to develop and maintain more consistent criteria for coding.

Data analyses should be both thorough and selective. Extensive statistical tests are made possible by the many codes available on most samples of societies and by computer programs. A critically important part of the research, however, is to identify and select the most important measures for detailed analyses and for communicating the results to other scientists. Important findings can usually be summarized clearly and simply.

Interpretations should be cautious. Culture is a complex system, involving interactions among many individuals and the pressures of adaptive changes conflicting with adherence to enduring traditions. In each cross-cultural study the codes on childhood and other attributes provide measures of only a small portion of the culture. Relationships between cause and effect are usually ambiguous. In spite of these limitations, however, the cross-cultural studies may be expected to increase our understanding of the role of human development in culture.

REFERENCES

Ayres, B. Effects of infant carrying practices on rhythm in music. *Ethos*, 1973, *1*, 387–404.

Bacon, M. K., Barry, H., III, Buchwald, C., Child, I. L., & Snyder, C. R. A cross-cultural study of drinking. *Quarterly Journal of Studies on Alcohol, Supplement 3*, 1965.

Bacon, M. K., Child, I. L., & Barry, H., III. A cross-cultural study of correlates of crime. *Journal of Abnormal and Social Psychology*, 1963, *66*, 291–300.

Barry, H., III. Relationships between child training and the pictorial arts. *Journal of Abnormal and Social Psychology*, 1957, *54*, 380–383.

Barry, H., III. Cross-cultural research with matched pairs of societies. *Journal of Social Psychology*, 1969, *79*, 25–33 (a).

Barry, H., III. Cultural variations in the development of mental illness. In S. C. Plog & R. B. Edgerton (Eds.), *Changing perspectives in mental illness*. New York: Holt, Rinehart & Winston, 1969 (b), pp. 155–179.

Barry, H., III. Description and uses of the Human Relations Area Files. In H. C. Triandis (Ed.), *Handbook of cross-cultural psychology* (Vol. 2). Boston: Allyn & Bacon, in press.

Barry, H., III, Bacon, M. K., & Child, I. L. A cross-cultural survey of some sex differences in socialization. *Journal of Abnormal and Social Psychology*, 1957, *55*, 327–332.

Barry, H., III, Bacon, M. K. & Child, I. L. Definitions, ratings, and bibliographic sources for child training practices of 110 cultures. In C. S. Ford (Ed.), *Cross-cultural approaches*. New Haven: HRAF Press, 1967, pp. 293–331.

Barry, H., III, Child, I. L., & Bacon, M. K. Relations of child training to subsistence economy. *American Anthropologist,* 1959, *61,* 51–63.

Barry, H., III, Josephson, L., Lauer, E. M., & Marshall, C. Traits inculcated in childhood: Cross-cultural codes 5. *Ethnology,* 1976, *15,* 83–114.

Barry, H., III, Josephson, L., Lauer, E. M., & Marshall, C. Agents and techniques for child training: Cross-cultural codes 6. *Ethnology,* 1977, *16,* 191–230.

Barry, H., III, & Paxson, L. M. Infancy and early childhood: Cross-cultural codes 2. *Ethnology,* 1971, *10,* 466–508.

Baxter, P. T. W., & Butt, A. *The Azande, and related peoples of the Anglo-Egyptian Sudan and Belgian Congo.* London: International African Institute, 1953.

Broude, G. J., & Greene, S. J. Cross-cultural codes on twenty sexual attitudes and practices. *Ethnology,* 1976, *15,* 409–429.

DuBois, C. *The people of Alor.* Minneapolis: University of Minnesota Press, 1944.

Evans-Pritchard, E. E. *Witchcrafts, oracles and magic among the Azande.* Oxford: Clarendon Press, 1937.

Lagacé, R. O. *Nature and use of the HRAF files: A research and teaching guide.* New Haven: HRAF Press, 1974.

Lagacé, R. O. Sixty cultures: A guide to the HRAF probability sample files. New Haven: HRAF Press, 1976.

Lagae, C.-R. *Les Azande ou Niam-Niam. . . . l'organization zande, croyances religieuses et magigues, coutumes familiales (trans. by HRAF, Inc.).* Bruxelles: Vromant, 1926.

Lambert, W. W., Triandis, L. M., & Wolf, M. Some correlates of beliefs in the malevolence and benevolence of supernatural beings: A cross-cultural study. *Journal of Abnormal and Social Psychology,* 1959, *58,* 162–169.

Mair, L. P. *An African people in the twentieth century.* London: Routledge, 1934.

Mead, M. The evocation of psychologically relevant responses in ethnological field work. In G. D. Spindler (Ed.), *The making of psychological anthropology.* Berkeley: University of California Press, 1978, pp. 89–139.

Munroe, R. L., Munroe, R. H., & Whiting, J. W. M. The couvade: A psychological analysis. *Ethos,* 1973, *1,* 30–74.

Murdock, G. P. *Ethnographic atlas.* Pittsburgh: University of Pittsburgh Press, 1967.

Murdock, G. P., & Provost, C. Measurement of cultural complexity. *Ethnology,* 1973, *12,* 379–392.

Murdock, G. P., & White, D. R. Standard cross-cultural sample. *Ethnology,* 1969, *8,* 329–369.

Murdock, G. P., & Wilson, S. F. Settlement patterns and community organization: Cross-cultural codes 3. *Ethnology, 1972, 11,* 250–295.

Murdock, G. P., Wilson, S. F., & Frederick, V. World distribution of theories of illness. *Ethnology,* 1978, *17,* 449–470.

Naroll, R., Michik, G. L., & Naroll, F. *Worldwide theory testing.* New Haven: HRAF Press, 1976.

O'Leary, T. J. Bibliography of cross-cultural studies: Supplement II. *Behavior Science Notes,* 1973, *8,* 123–134.

Reining, C. C. *The Zande scheme.* Evanston, Ill.: Northwestern University Press, 1966.

Rohner, R. P. *They love me, they love me not: A study of the world-wide effects of parental acceptance and rejection.* New Haven: HRAF Press, 1975.

Rohner, R. P., Naroll, R., Barry, H., III, Divale, W. T., Erickson, E. E., Schaefer, J. M., & Sipes, R. G. Guidelines for holocultural research. *Current Anthropology,* 1978, *19,* 128–129.

Roscoe, J. *The Baganda: An account of their native customs and beliefs.* London: MacMillan, 1911.

Seligman, C. G., & Seligman, B. Z. *Pagan tribes of the Nilotic Sudan.* London: George Routledge & Sons, 1932, pp. 495–539.

Southwold, M. The Ganda of Uganda. In J. L. Gibbs, Jr. (Ed.) *Peoples of Africa*. New York: Holt, Rinehart & Winston, 1965, pp. 81–118.

Textor, R. B. *A cross-cultural summary*. New Haven: HRAF Press, 1967.

Whiting, B. B. (Ed.) *Six cultures: Studies of child rearing*. New York: Wiley, 1963.

Whiting, B. B., & Whiting, J. W. M. *Children of six cultures: A psycho-cultural analysis*. Cambridge, Mass.: Harvard University Press, 1975.

Whiting, J. W. M. The effects of climate on certain cultural practices. In W. H. Goodenough (Ed.), *Explorations in cultural anthropology: Essays in honor of George Peter Murdock*. New York: McGraw-Hill, 1964, pp. 511–544.

Whiting, J. W. M., & Child, I. L. *Child training and personality*. New Haven: Yale University Press, 1953.

Whiting, J. W. M., Kluckhohn, R., & Anthony, A. The function of male initiation ceremonies at puberty. In E. Maccoby, T. M. Newcomb, & E. L. Hartley (Eds), *Readings in social psychology* (3rd ed.). New York: Henry Holt, 1958, pp. 359–370.

Whiting, J. W. M., & Whiting, B. B. Aloofness and intimacy of husbands and wives: A cross-cultural study. *Ethos*, 1975, *3*, 183–207.

Whiting, J. W. M., & Whiting, B. B. A strategy for psychocultural research. In G. D. Spindler (Ed.), *The making of psychological anthropology*. Berkeley: University of California Press, 1978, pp. 41–61.

6

The Study of Minority Groups in Complex Societies

Alan Howard • Robert A. Scott

It is now commonly recognized that social scientists have often inappropriately applied concepts derived from observations of dominant groups in society to minority populations whose behavior patterns, lifestyles, and values differ. Although some critics have questioned the motives of the scholars involved, more often the practice is seen as the result of an unthinking bias toward middle-class values. Despite a growing awareness, we believe the full implications of such a bias remain to be explored.

In this chapter we examine a number of issues posed to social science by the study of minority populations. Our main contention is that a strong middle-class bias has resulted in a body of research findings that focuses on alleged deficiencies in minority groups, and that this has led to faulty understanding and weak theory. We use the label *deficiency formulations* to characterize studies carried out in this fashion. The proposition we advocate is that the purposes of social science would be much better served by naturalistic studies focusing on prevailing characteristics within minority groups than by studies focusing on deficits.

There are two main types of deficiency formulation, although in practice they are frequently combined. The first focuses upon attributes socially valued by mainstream groups that are observed to be absent or weakly represented within particular minorities. At the group level this type is indicated by the use of such terms as "disorganized," "normless," and "unstable," while individuals are described as "ego deficient," "immature," or "lacking in motivation," "self-control," "the ability to delay gratification," and so on. The second type focuses upon attributes socially devalued by mainstream groups that are supposedly characteristic of certain study populations. Descriptions of families as "matricentric" and individuals as "prone to violence," "hedonistic," or "present oriented" are indicative of this type. Such conceptualizations are concerned primarily with specifying forms of deviation from valued attributes. They imply a failure or inability to behave in an appropriate way and so imply social and personal deficits. The first type is essentially vacuous with regard to information about the groups under investigation. It calls attention to the ways that people do not behave rather than how they act, and to ways they do not organize themselves rather than how they order their social lives. The second type yields more information, but of a highly selective kind. By focusing on deviations from mainstream norms, it turns attention away from alternate social forms and organizational principles that may be of central importance within the group. To the extent that these differ from those of mainstream groups, such an approach leaves an informational void.

If identification of attributes absent or indicative of weakness is one feature of deficiency formulations, efforts to explain deficits by relating one to another is a second. Deficiency explanations assume a characteristic form in that they attempt to account for deficits in one area of life by pointing to deficits in another. Thus hedonistic behavior, for example, may be attributed to lack of internalized control; underachievement to lack of motivation; lack of respect for property to a poor self-image; or social ineptitude to immaturity. Grander theories are sometimes proposed linking an entire array of deficiencies, such as, for example, when economic deprivation is used to explain the failure of men to assume appropriate roles in the family, which in turn is held responsible for family instability, which purportedly produces pathology in children who are unable to cope, are uneducable, and unable to obtain gainful employment as adults, leading to a repetition of the cycle.

Deficiency formulations are themselves deficient in some fundamental ways. Most obvious is the distortion that comes from using concepts that have derived their substantive meaning from normative patterns within one group to characterize patterns in a group whose norms may be quite different. This leads observers to misconstrue the meaning and significance of social acts and to overlook important features of cultural and personal organization. Less obvious is the fact that such an approach necessarily leads to weak theory that is ill suited for designing remedial programs. By focusing on ways in which minority groups deviate from mainstream norms, such theory fails to provide systematic information about the more normal, everyday aspects of social life and how they are organized. Furthermore, preoccupation with deficits and deviations leads observers to ignore intragroup variability in favor of intergroup comparisons between minority and mainstream groups. As a result, deficiency formulations lead to highly fragmented and unsystematic accounts of minority groups; they generally contain far more information about the values and presuppositions of the dominant groups in which the concepts were developed, tested, and substantiated. The situation is somewhat analogous to examining fish solely in terms of the ways they differ from birds. While it may be of some interest to learn that fish cannot fly because they lack wings and appropriate breathing apparatus, there is a lot more we would want to know about fish if we were to theorize about their particular adaptive forms. We would want to know, for example, how they do propel themselves and breathe. If we did not, we would be prone to make some fatal mistakes when attempting to construct benign environments for them to flourish. The point is not that deficiency formulations are necessarily false or inaccurate, only that they are of limited informative value and therefore provide a poor basis for generating theory and developing helpful action programs.

What we want to emphasize is that a central objective of social science research must be to provide a clear sense of how the social life of a group is ordered. Even though profound frustrations exist, minority group members pursue various goals and sometimes achieve them; they actively engage in interpersonal relations from which they derive satisfaction; and they organize their activities in ways that are meaningful to themselves and those with whom they associate. A major flaw of deficiency formulations is that they neglect to document such behavior and activities and thereby fail to provide a firm basis for understanding the nature of social life among minority populations.

We hasten to add that although deficiency formulations tend to be disparaging, social scientists who employ them do not necessarily regard the people so described as inferior. We are convinced that the vast majority of social scientists are sympathetic toward the people they describe and that the tenaciousness of the deficiency bias in the face of a social ethic that has come to tolerate if not encourage ethnic and cultural diversity reflects deeply rooted epistemologic presuppositions that have shaped Western thought. Therefore in addition to illustrating the problem of deficiency formulations through examples, we will briefly explore some of the presuppositions that have informed empirical research with minority groups. We then discuss several recent attempts to confront the issues raised by deficiency formulations, followed by a contrasting of the naturalistic with the deficiency approaches to the study of minority populations. Finally, we explore some of the pragmatic implications of these alternative perspectives.

THE TROUBLE WITH THEM IS . . .

A major portion of the encyclopedic social science literature on minority populations is devoted to detailing alleged deficiencies in their cultural repertoires, family life, and personal capacities and to providing explanations for them. We do not propose to review all of this research here, but rather to draw selectively from certain works, all of them acknowledged to be significant contributions to the social science literature. Our object is not to condemn these studies, for there is much of value in each of them, but merely to point out the impact of one intellectual strand among many on characterizations of minority populations.

We have organized the discussion around three levels of analysis accentuated in the literature—culture, the family, and personality. Since the prototype of deficiency is poverty, we focus upon the literature on lower-class populations, bringing in ethnic variations where they have been emphasized by the respective scholars. It has been among the lower classes—the economically marginal members of society—that the Western elite has looked most searchingly for, and found, its "social problems." However, since black Americans have been particularly victimized by deficiency formulations, we have included a special section concerning their characterization in the social science literature.

The "Culture of Poverty"

The basic premises for treating the poor as deficient were clearly articulated by Oscar Lewis in his conceptualization of the "culture of poverty," which he saw as both an adaptation to and a reaction of the poor to their marginal position in a class-stratified, highly individuated capitalistic society. He described the major characteristics of the culture of poverty as follows:

> It represents an effort to cope with feelings of hopelessness and despair which develop from the realization of the improbability of achieving success in terms of the values and goals of the larger society. Indeed, many of the traits of the culture of poverty can be viewed as attempts at local solutions for problems not met by existing institutions and agencies because the people are not eligible for them, cannot afford them, or are ignorant or suspicious of them. (Lewis, 1966, p. xliv)
> . . . On the family level the major traits of the culture of poverty are the absence of childhood as a specially prolonged and protected stage in the life cycle, early initiation into sex, free unions or consensual marriages, a relatively high incidence of the abandonment of wives and children, a trend toward female- or mother-

centered families and consequently a much greater knowledge of maternal relatives, a strong predisposition to authoritarianism, lack of privacy, verbal emphasis upon family solidarity which is only rarely achieved because of sibling rivalry, and competition for limited goods and maternal affection.

... On the level of the individual the major characteristics are a strong feeling of marginality, of helplessness, of dependence and of inferiority. (Lewis, 1966, p. xlvii)

... Other traits include a high incidence of material deprivation, of orality, of weak ego structure, confusion of sexual identification, a lack of impulse control, a strong present time orientation with relatively little ability to defer gratification and to plan for the future, a sense of resignation and fatalism, a widespread belief in male superiority, and a high tolerance for psychological pathology of all sorts. (Lewis, 1966, p. xlviii)

Lewis held that the culture of poverty was perpetuated through the socialization experiences of children:

The culture of poverty ... is not only an adaptation to a set of objective conditions of the larger society. Once it comes into existence it tends to perpetuate itself from generation to generation because of its effect on the children. By the time slum children are age six or seven they have usually absorbed the basic values and attitudes of their subculture and are not psychologically geared to take full advantage of changing conditions or increased opportunities which may occur in their lifetime. (Lewis, 1966, p. xlv)

Nowhere has the basic premise of deficiency formulations been more clearly stated than by Lewis when he wrote that "it would be helpful to think of the subcultures of poverty as the zero point on a continuum which leads to the working class and middle class (Lewis, 1969, p. 190).

Many other accounts of lower-class culture echo Lewis' characterization. In her thorough review of the social science literature on the lower classes in America during the 1960s, Keller notes that researchers describe lower-class culture as involving "a simplification of the experience world" (Keller, 1970, p. 21). She notes that much of the research deplores the presence of certain values, such as traditionalism, authoritarianism, ethnocentrism, antiintellectualism, person rather than object orientation, and an excessive love of power, that differ from values held by members of higher classes. Weakly adhered to or entirely absent are said to be the middle-class virtues of "a stress on career, planning one's life into a series of achievable stages, creative self-development, a love of ideas and of possessions" (p. 27). The culture of the lower class is characterized as unintegrated and inconsistent. Keller asserts that "if consistent moral values are necessary for the development of an integrated image of one's self and the world, there is reason to assume that this consistency and the integration it fosters is weak or absent in lower-class environments" (p. 30). She also reports that social scientists bemoan "an aversion to planning and to thinking about the future except with anxiety and fear, a short-range time perspective, a live-for-today attitude, a pervasive suspicion and distrust of the larger world, and a lesser emphasis on self-reliance than dependence on outsiders" (p. 72).

Distinguishing between the upper-lower and lower-lower classes, she reports that economic and educational deprivations among the latter "seem to foster characteristic attitudes of suspicion, distrust, fear of the future, and concern with immediate gratifications not found as extremely in the higher classes" (Keller, 1970, p. 9). Members of the lower-lower class are described as living in a "disordered deprived environment" in which "every moral epithet in the community is levelled against them as a group—incest, drinking, dirt, vulgarity, laziness, criminality, and lack of desire to better themselves" (Keller, 1970, p. 21; see also Blake, 1955).

The Lower-class Family

Keller remarks that we remain ignorant about lower-class families as a result of too heavy reliance on concepts reflecting real or imagined features of middle-class life. She reminds us that lower-class families are more than just "inadequate versions of the middle class"; instead, they are "fundamentally different in their organization and lifestyles" (Keller, 1970, p. 71). The picture that emerges from Keller's review is almost entirely negative. She reports that lower-class households are described by social scientists as "normless, alienated, chaotic," and as "less stable and cohesive" and "more . . . strife ridden than . . . other classes" (p. 31). She also notes that lower-class families are typically portrayed as being unable to educate their children, cure their ills, provide them with jobs, or effectively control their behavior (p. 5).

The tendency to characterize lower-class family life negatively is particularly evident in research done on two specific areas: relations between the sexes and patterns of child rearing. Relations between the sexes are described as "specialized," "impersonal," and "segmental," with intimacy at a minimum (Keller, 1970, p. 32). The result is said to be "great emotional distance between the sexes" and relations that are "unstable and fraught with mutual recrimination and difficulties" (pp. 32–33). In that part of the lower class termed "rough," husband–wife relations are seen as "filled with suspicion and hostility," the women defensively independent, the men defensively masculine, and sex role differences, at least in their middle-class form, absent. The sexes are described as "going past each other. . . . The men want to be mothered, nurtured, and taken care of but they also want to be free and dominant. The women want to be loved and protected and yet be in control. There is fear, hostility, and rejection as well as need on both sides" (Keller, 1970, p. 35).

Relations between parents and children are described as "distant," stressing only overt, formal aspects of relationship while minimizing affectional and emotional components (Keller, 1970, p. 38). Lower-class parents are described as being unaware of and unconcerned about their children's activities at school and at play and as lacking in appreciation for "the significance of the unique personality and the unique potential of each individual child" (p. 43). Parents are said to rely completely on "negative techniques of child rearing, especially deprivation or pain" (p. 43), while "enjoining proper conduct by means of threats and punishments, and by using physical rather than psychological techniques" (p. 46).

The conclusions drawn from this type of analysis are that the lower-class family is "a poor negative of the ideal-type middle-class family;" that it is "less effective as a transmitter of cultural values . . . [than] the middle-class" family (Keller, 1970, p. 75); and that its "significance . . . for personality development is in doubt" (p. 54).

Lower-class Personality

Descriptions of lower-class people are replete with terms denoting characterologic defects. The poor are described as "authoritarian," "intolerant," "hard," "tough," "cynical," "distrustful," and "preoccupied with material possessions" (Keller, 1970, p. 21). They are also seen as haunted by fear of loneliness, lacking in self-confidence, and tending toward passivity. According to Keller, in such research they emerge as self-centered; "interested in little outside of their own narrow circle, they have few ideas and are preoccupied with creature comforts" (Keller, 1970, p. 60). One study characterizes them as "reluctant to meet people or to initiate interaction" (Cohen & Hodges, 1963), another as suffering from pervasive anxieties about physical safety, dependable income, and emotional satisfaction (Rainwater, 1960). It is also reported that "pity and preoccupation with the unfortunate are their most readily experienced emotions" (Keller, 1970, p. 34).

Few are spared in the social scientists' search for pathology. Lower-class men are portrayed as feeling inadequate as husbands and fathers, leading Rainwater, for example, to interpret their tendency to bluster and aggression as a cover up for inferior feelings (Rainwater, 1960). It is said that they "want badly to he mothered" and that they are preoccupied by "the powerful temptation to escape the intolerable burden of being only half a man by being a woman" (Keller, 1970, p. 37). Children are seen as exposed to an incoherent and fragmented view of a world governed by opposing principles; as a result, they tend to compartmentalize values and actions, a process deemed to have "dubious merit for moral development" (p. 29).

Banfield succinctly sums up much of the literature on the character of lower class persons when he writes

> The lower-class individual lives from moment to moment. If he has any awareness of the future, it is of something fixed. . . . Impulse governs his behavior, either because he cannot discipline himself to sacrifice a present for a future satisfaction or because he has no sense of the future. He is therefore radically improvident: what he cannot consume immediately he considers valueless. His bodily needs (especially for sex) and his taste for "action" take precedence over everything else —and certainly over any work routine. (Banfield, 1970, p. 53)

The conclusions to which such deficiency formulations inevitably lead are that lower-class culture, social organization, and personality are all problematic. We are asked to think of lower-class culture as "the zero point on a continuum" (Lewis, 1969, p. 190) and are told that in the lower class "the family as such . . . does not exist in its conventional form" (Keller, 1970, p. 75). Lower-class persons, as a result of being subjected to such a putatively vacuous environment, are portrayed as an accumulation of pathologic deficits.

Afro-American Subculture
Of all the ethnic groups that have been subjected to this type of analysis, Afro-Americans have undoubtedly been the most intensive targets. A deeply rooted social science tradition has condemned the majority of them, by implication if not accusation, to an array of categories denoting deviance. As Ladner has eloquently put it,

> Blacks have always been measured against an alien set of norms. As a result they have been considered to be a deviation from the ambiguous white middle-class model, which itself has not always been clearly defined. This inability or refusal to deal with blacks as part and parcel of the varying historical and cultural contributions to the American scene has, perhaps, been the reason sociology has excluded the black perspective from its widely accepted mainstream theories.
> Mainstream sociology, in this regard, reflects the ideology of the larger society, which has always excluded black lifestyles, values, behavior, attitudes, and so forth from the body of data that is used to define, describe, conceptualize, and theorize about the structure and functions of American society. Sociology has in a similar manner excluded the totality of black existence from its major theories, except

insofar as it *deviated* from the so-called norms. (Ladner, 1973, p. xxiii; italics in original)

Attempts to prove blacks inferior go back to early efforts to justify slavery. Following the Civil War, the racial inferiority of blacks was asserted as an explanation for (and justification of) the squalid conditions under which they lived. Thus John Van Ervie, in a book entitled *White Supremacy and Negro Subordination,* published in 1870, asserted that "the Negro isolated by himself, seems utterly incapable of transmitting anything whatsoever to the succeeding generation" (cited by Jones, 1973, p. 121). Assaults on the integrity of the black family also appeared early in the social science literature. Howard Odom's characterization was typical. He stated that relations between husband and wife often set a poor example for the children, that blacks liked to crowd together and were not content unless several were sleeping in one room, that the interior of the house was not kept in good repair, that disorder and filth were characteristic, that basic supplies and provisions were not purchased, and that there was an absence of literature in the home. He attributed these failings to the inherent inability of most blacks to grasp the basic principles of family and home life (Odom, 1910).

More recent social science accounts of Afro-Americans continue to focus on negative traits but explain them differently, i.e., in terms of oppression. Pettigrew's widely cited synthesis of research on black Americans (Pettigrew, 1964) is a prime example of this tendency. For Pettigrew, the overwhelming fact of life for all black people is oppression, and the key to understanding their behavior is how they react to it. Indeed, it is fair to say that reactions to oppression and black personality are virtually synonymous in his view (see also Kardiner & Ovesey, 1951). He writes, "The socially-stigmatized role of negro is the central feature of having dark skin in the United States.... At the personality level, such enforced role adaptation ... divides the individual negro both from other human beings and from himself" (Pettigrew, 1964, p. 4). "Imagine, then, the depth of the effect of having to play a role which has such vast personal and social significance that it influences virtually all aspects of daily living. Indeed, the resulting confusion of self-identity and lowering of self-esteem are two of the most serious 'marks of oppression' upon negro American personality" (Pettigrew, 1964, p. 6). He then goes on to describe reactions to the hostile environment such as the "oppression phobia" experienced by many Afro-Americans—an expectation of violent mistreatment combined with a feeling of utter helplessness (from Cayton, 1951, p. 276). He cites McClelland's work to the effect that slavery in all its forms has sharply lowered the need for achievement, and asserts that slavery has vitiated family life. He goes on to state that "being a negro in America is less of a racial identity than a necessity to adjust to subordinate social roles. The effects of playing this 'negro' role are profound and lasting. Evaluating himself by the way others react to him, the negro may grow into a servile role; in time the person and the role become indistinguishable" (Pettigrew, 1964, p. 252; see also Brazziel, 1964; Grossack, 1957a, b; Guba, Jackson, & Bidwell, 1959).

Pettigrew attributes the matricentric family pattern reported in the literature to slavery and asserts that both poverty and migration act to perpetuate the pattern. Poverty renders a healthy family life unattainable through dilapidated housing, crowded living conditions, restricted recreational facilities, and direct contact with the most corrupting elements of urban disorganization; it also makes the ideal American pattern of household economics practically impossible. As evidence of family instability he cites the following data:

Over a third of all non-white mothers with children under six years of age hold jobs as compared with less than a fifth of white mothers with children under six; only three-fourths of all non-white families have both the husband and wife present in the household as compared with nine-tenths of white families; and only two-thirds of non-whites under eighteen years of age live with both of their parents as compared with nine-tenths of such whites. (Pettigrew, 1964, pp. 16–17)

He then goes on to discuss the personality effects on children living under these conditions, that is, living "in a disorganized home without a father" (Pettigrew, 1964, p. 17). He cites a study that reveals that 8- and 9-year-old children whose fathers are absent seek immediate gratification far more than children whose fathers are present in the home and then adds, "This hunger for immediate gratification among fatherless children seems to have serious implications. Regardless of race, children manifesting this trait also tend to be less accurate in judging time, less 'socially responsible,' less oriented toward achievement and more prone toward delinquency. Indeed . . . psychologists maintain that the inability to delay gratification is a critical factor in immature, criminal and neurotic behavior (Pettigrew, 1964, p. 17; see also Antonovsky & Lerner, 1959, pp. 132–138).[1]

Pettigrew follows with an analysis of sex roles. He cites a finding that 5–14-year-old black youths without fathers experience unusual difficulty in differentiating between male and female roles, and then he reviews a large body of literature concerning the effect of father absence on a young boy's sex identity. Noting that black males scored higher than white males on a measure of femininity in some studies, he concludes that "these findings reflect not only the effects of family disorganization but also the effeminate aspects of the 'negro' role many of these men must play in adult life. Servility is often required, and most low-pay service occupations typically open to unskilled negro males—for example, cook, waiter orderly, dishwasher—generally carry a connotation in American culture of being 'women's work.' Thus, the sex-identity problems created by the fatherless home are perpetuated in adulthood" (Pettigrew, 1964, p. 21).

Pettigrew is not alone in painting a negative composite view of the Afro-American lifestyle. Bernard, for example, describes children reared in black families as "humanly destroyed" (Bernard, 1966, p. 144), explaining that "in their world, physical gestures, grunts, facial expressions and tones of voice constitute the major means of communication. These, of course, are inadequate and greatly restrict the child's ability to learn. Socialization under these circumstances is enormously handicapped. Whatever socialization takes place in such circumstances is almost wholly inadequate, even accidental. People react, when they do, on the emotional level; few abstractions enter the relationship" (Bernard, 1966, pp. 143–144). This constitutes a state of deprivation so severe, she claims, that "the mental and emotional capacity [is] irredeemably lost" (Bernard, 1966, p. 144).

An illuminating example of the tendency to focus on personal deficiencies of Afro-Americans is Rohrer and Edmonson's study of southern blacks, *The Eighth Generation Grows Up*. Their research, which involved extensive interviews with a subsample of black adults in New Orleans who, as children, had been subjects in Davis and Dollard's (1940) *Children of Bondage* study, has been widely cited to buttress claims about the devastating consequences oppression and discrimination can have. The subjects of this research, all "ordinary people," employed, living with their families, and in no apparent difficulty with the law, are described almost entirely in terms of weakness and deficits. One subject, for example, is diagnosed as "confused about his sexual identity," "inadequate in his occupational world," "fearful in his relations with others," and generally prone to "paranoid delusions" (Rohrer & Edmonson, 1960, p. 95). A woman is characterized as having "only a hazy awareness of altruism" and as being dependent on "magical thought processes" (pp. 95, 135). Another is termed "a beaten-down paranoid" who is "passive and submissive," with defenses of "repression, avoidance, denial, pain, dependency and use of rationalization" (pp. 152–153). A young man in their study is labeled a "hedonistic, impulsive man in conflict with a depriving world," unable to understand why the world should not grant his "infantile wishes" (p. 183). About him they write,

> It is clear that [his] behavior is not antisocial so much as it is dyssocial. He has grown up in an environment that has manifest disregard for the usual social code. He has lived all his life in this abnormal moral atmosphere and he has adhered to the values of his predatory and criminal group. He was deprived of any real love in his childhood. The result of this pathological rearing is that [he] has only a stunted capacity for joy, love or hope. It is doubtful that he feels much inner conflict or acceptance, either, since chronic depression is one of his recognizable personality characteristics. Underneath he must feel himself to be a failure even in terms of his own social values and moral codes . . . He is hedonistic, has a poorly developed conscience, and lacks the judgment or ability to learn from experience or from punishment. He is manipulative and extortionistic, and continually uses the primitive techniques of hit and grab. He has violent emotions, and lacks ability to form lasting ties with other people. . . . In his heart of hearts he knows himself to be a failure[,] . . . weak, nameless and criminal, and he is unhappy. (Rohrer & Edmonson, 1960, p. 185)

Another subject, a professional man, is described as "marginal" and "pretty sick," lacking in any apparent need for "acceptance and recognition common to many, perhaps most professional people." The authors add that there is a "regressive quality to this lack" (Rohrer & Edmonson, 1960, p. 271). Their analysis is littered with other terms denoting deficiency and weakness such as "rebellious little hoyden," "fearful passive little girl," "desperate and embattled petty thief," and "fearful isolated old maid" (pp. 295–296).[2]

Explanations for Deficiencies

In most of the studies discussed above, some attempt is made to account for the patterns described. What we find is an unmistakable tendency to find explanations for deficits in one area of life by relating them to deficits in other areas, thereby suggesting that the absence of one attribute accounts for the absence of another. Pettigrew, for example, argues that "employment discrimination has traditionally made it more difficult for the poorly educated negro male to secure employment than the poorly educated negro female . . . [and] when the unskilled negro male does manage to secure a job, he generally assumes an occupation that pays barely enough to support himself—much less a family" (Pettigrew, 1964, p. 16). This failure by the men to provide for their families is said to give rise to a number of problems, including family instability, personal pathology on the part of men, heightened conflict between husband and wife, and a failure of the family unit to fulfill its main social functions. Pettigrew is particularly concerned with the effects on children's personality of being reared in a father-absent home. He cites a study showing that 8- and 9-year-old children whose fathers are absent seek immediate gratification far more than children whose fathers are present in the home. This inability to delay gratification, according to Pettigrew, is in turn correlated with an inability to "judge time, a diminished social responsiveness, diminished orientation toward achievement, proneness to delinquency, and to immature, criminal and neurotic behavior" (Pettigrew, 1964, p. 17). He continues, "Family disorganization upsets the normal socializing influence of the home and creates the potential for juvenile delinquency" (p. 21). A person reared under such conditions is "psychologically vulnerable," "crippled by weak ego development," and "more likely to fall prey to mental illness, drug addiction or crime, depending on his particular life history. He has few personality resources to withstand the gale winds of discrimination that strike him full force in adolescence. Thus, segregation has its most fundamental influence on negro personality in the manner in which it affects negro family functioning" (pp. 22–23).[3]

Perhaps the work that stimulated the most controversy over this type of explanation was Daniel Moynihan's essay, "Employment, Income and the Ordeal of the Negro Family," published in 1965. Moynihan held that opportunity for the large mass of black workers in the lower range of training and education has not been improving and that in many ways the circumstances of these workers relative to the white work force had grown worse. This, he maintained, "has led to, or been accompanied by, a serious weakening of the negro social structure, specifically of the negro family" (Moynihan, 1965, p. 747). The cumulative result of unemployment, low income, and excessive dependence upon the income of women created a crisis in the black family, in Moynihan's view, "and raises the serious question of whether or not this crisis is beginning to create conditions which tend to reinforce the cycle that produces it in the first place" (p. 755).

Moynihan's line of reasoning is as follows: Poor families, suffering the strains of marginal incomes and unemployed fathers, are likely to break under the responsibilities imposed by many children, and as a result of diminishing opportunities. Blacks are more likely to find themselves in these circumstances than whites. HEW estimates are that approximately 60 percent of black children in the United States are growing up in poverty-stricken families. The fundamental problem is the position of the husband/father, who is faced with unemployment and/or menial, low-paying jobs. This leads to the break up of the family, an increase in welfare dependency, and the tangle of pathology—the complex of interrelated disabilities and disadvantages that feed on each other and seem to make matters steadily worse for the individuals and communities caught up in it (Moynihan, 1965). The effect of this "pathology" on children is held to be disastrous, since a high proportion begin their lives with no father present and have no stable male figure available as a model. Their mothers have to begin working early and remain employed if they are to stay off welfare, weakening their socializing influences through both absence and diminished educational opportunities. Moynihan concludes that at the heart of the deterioration of the fabric of black society is the deterioration of the family (Moynihan, 1965; for an even more extreme view of the presumed pathologic effects of black family structure see the work by Etzkowitz & Shaflander, 1969, p. 14).

The importance of economic deficiencies is also stressed by Keller, who writes that "in the middle class, the existence of economic security does not necessarily make for a happy life, but it does permit the family to exercise the main social functions (of biological reproduction, maintenance, socialization and status placement)," and research on the poor gives the impression that "the absence of economic security leaves lower-class family cohesion to the workings of personal need and affection, bonds that have generally proved too tenuous to make the institution either very stable or very permanent" (Keller, 1970, p. 5).

Conflict and strife within the lower-class family are likewise traced to economic failures. For example, Cohen and Hodges suggest that a challenge for the lower-class male is to evolve a way of life that will reduce his insecurity and enhance his power in ways that do not depend upon achievement in the labor market. One way to do this is to establish close relationships with kinsmen; another is to participate in high-solidarity friendship groups. The obligations incurred by males in meeting the commitments involved conflict with conjugal obligations, resulting in husband–wife clashes (Cohen & Hodges, 1963). Pettigrew states that "the negro wife . . . can easily become disgusted with her financially-alienated husband, and her rejection of him further alienates the male from the family life" (Pettigrew, 1964, p. 16), thereby increasing marital conflict.

Various character defects among lower-class men are traced to economic incompetence as well. Thus Rainwater attributes the "bluster and aggressiveness" of lower-class men to feelings of inadequacy arising from their inability to provide properly for their families (Rainwater, 1960), and Keller states that many feel that this "intolerable burden of being only half a man" generates deep-seated temptations to become a woman. The logic behind this temptation is that "if he were a woman his inadequacies and failures would not exist, for he could escape the tests and trials that beset his life." This temptation to abandon the male role is then cited to explain the "exaggerated emphasis on masculinity, ridicule of homosexuality, the need to prove one's self [sic] a man, to domineer over women, and to be chronically unfaithful" (Keller, 1970, p. 37).

While these examples may be considered extreme by some, the logic behind them is commonplace—poverty causes family disorganization, which in turn causes socialization failures, which cause character defects, which perpetuate poverty. The form of this analysis has structured social scientific accounts of a wide range of minority groups in contemporary societies, including native Americans, Puerto Ricans, Filipino-Americans, Mexican-Americans, the Irish in England, the Maoris in New Zealand, and the Aborigines in Australia, to name but a few. One reason for the widespread acceptance of these premises is that they have an appeal for those social scientists who are committed to a sympathetic explanation for the social problems they see plaguing these groups. Superficially, at least, the blame is placed on poverty and the solution is a redistribution of opportunity and/or access to resources. The implicit assumption is that if conditions were so altered, the behavior patterns of these ethnic groups would coincide with those who constitute the cultural mainstream. The presupposition is that cultural differences between these groups, and between each group and the mainstream, are insignificant. In short, the position implies that the most important behavior patterns among these peoples are those *in reaction to* external contingencies. But this has the effect of denying the validity of each group's unique cultural heritage and the positive ways culture structures behavior. Our central point is that a sound theoretical basis for the study of cross-cultural human development requires just the opposite—that the cultural logic underlying each subculture be placed at the heart of description and explanation. This does not require that external contingencies, including access to resources, be ignored; what it does require is that significant group differences in beliefs, values, and worldview be recognized so that judgments of competence can be made against relevant criteria.[4]

The Question of Evidence

In evaluating the material presented in this section, it is important to examine the empirical evidence upon which some of these claims are based, for when we do this we discover the preoccupations with deficiencies are often so pervasive that almost anything is regarded as indicative of incompetence or pathology. Pettigrew, for example, supports his characterization of black youths as "anxious" and "hyperactive" by citing a study (Caldwell, 1959) indicating that black youths are more likely than whites to give an affirmative answer to the MMPI item "I work under a great deal of tension." As evidence for the split between true self and public role of black, which results in a shy, dependent personality, he cites the finding that black students score *higher* than whites on an MMPI item having to do with "organizing their work and lives systematically," and lower on an item dealing with "interest in the opposite sex" (Pettigrew, 1964, p. 301). Nowhere does he indicate the relevance of the items to the conclusions drawn. Elsewhere he interprets as evidence of a strong "anti-white prejudice" a poll (*Newsweek*, 1963, pp. 15–34) that shows 56 percent of low-income blacks agree with the statement, "Most white men are out to keep us down" (Pettigrew, 1964, p. 40; also see Cothram, 1951, McDaniel & Babchak, 1960). As evidence for sex role confusion among black males he cites their high score on two items that he interprets as indicative of femininity, "I would like to be a singer," and "I think I feel more intensely than most other people" (Pettigrew, 1964, p. 29). Finally, while claiming that blacks drink to excess, he acknowledges that the data of several studies do not support his contention but dismisses this information on the grounds that drinking is a more serious problem among blacks than other groups because "they have, as a group, more from which to escape" (Pettigrew, 1964, p. 53).

Rohrer and Edmonson show the same inclination in their research. In one case history they describe a subject's "antiwhite prejudice" and cite as evidence an episode in which a bus conductor threatened to have a woman moved because she was sitting in front of the screen separating white from black passengers. The subject expressed pleasure over the fact that a policeman refused to support the bus conductor's threat (Rohrer & Edmonson, 1960, p. 118). Another subject was described as showing "rebellious touchiness" because "he told his white boss during an argument 'don't holler at me . . . Just talk to me like I'm people' " (p. 160). A third subject was said to have a "serious confusion" about racial identity because he had said, "We are perfectly willing to accept the 'desired' and 'forthcoming' integration as negroes. Our fight, however, is for the 'integration of opportunity' and not the complete loss of identity and absorption of a race that we happen to be proud of" (p. 236). Earlier we noted that these authors had described a subject as a "beaten-down paranoid;" the sole evidence for this diagnosis was the fact that a psychiatrist had commented on the possible presence of a paranoid tendency in her Rorschach protocol, yet in the course of numerous interviews with her the investigators encountered no feelings of persecution or rage. This led them to conclude that her paranoia was concealed, hence their characterization of her as a "beaten-down paranoid." The same subject, we are told, resorts to the "use of ritual" as a main mechanism of psychological defense, as evidenced by the fact that "she sleeps with a bible under her pillow and says prayers before she goes to bed" (Rohrer & Edmonson, 1960, pp. 152–153). Another subject is described as "suspicious" and "sullen" because he wanted to know what the researchers planned to do with the tape recordings made of his conversations with them. Still another is cynically described as "unrealistic" because he claims that "he can obtain anything he wishes to," yet the researchers add that "to be sure, he has obtained many of these things" (p. 203). One feels that they are stretching their generosity when they admit that a mother of six children who, while holding a full-time job, completed a regular 4-year degree in a local college by attending night school "may yet become a winner" (p. 297).

Equally noteworthy is the failure of many social scientists to consider evidence for stability and competence. An example is supplied by Rosow's essay on the elderly in American society, in which he reports that studies show elderly members of ethnic minorities are better off and better adjusted than the middle-class aged (Rosow, 1965). In none of the studies we have cited are findings such as these mentioned.

Findings

It may be instructive to pinpoint more precisely what it is about minorities that elicits the negativism of deficiency formulations. Surely one factor is what might be termed the "objective conditions of poverty" which are endemic to the lower classes. In our opinion observers are correct and justified in pointing out the detrimental consequences of unemployment, poor housing, overcrowding, poor health care, poor schooling, and a multitude of other conditions that stem from abject poverty. These deprivations, we believe, involve real costs to people regardless of their values and cultural preferences, and we have no quarrel with those whose research has centered on this aspect of the situation. But in most of the studies cited above the objective conditions of material deprivation are not the focus of concern. More often the primary interest is in social institutions and personal characteristics that are assumed to result from living in an environment that is considered to be *socially* and *culturally* impoverished. That is, what catches the social scientist's eye are such things as speech behavior, expressions of emotion, and patterns of social interaction. It is from selective judgments of these kinds of data, rather than from economic conditions, that statements are derived concerning instability, disorderliness, and incohesiveness of family life; attitudes indicative of suspicion and distrust of others; disinterest in the future and concern for immediate gratification; a tendency to express emotions, particularly anger and rage, in an uninhibited fashion; lack of sexual restraint; reliance on gesturing rather than words for communication; reliance on punishment, and particularly physical punishment, in rearing children; an absence of a clear division of labor in the family; lack of forceful control of children by parents; disregard for the significance and potential of each individual; pervasive attitudes of traditionalism, authoritarianism, intolerance, ethnocentrism, antiintellectualism, hedonism, self-centeredness, and concern for creature comforts; disregard for self-reliance; lack of altruism; reliance on fantasy and a tendency toward unrealistic life planning; self-pity; lack of self-confidence and a passive approach to life; and a lack of selfhood. Aside from the fact that this partial list of deficiencies attributed to the poor is often contradictory (they are said to be self-centered, yet lacking in a sense of self; the family is said to destroy the humanness of children during socialization at the same time that it is said to have little influence on them; men are described as both passive and overly aggressive), one is struck by the fact that what is being described in the form of character traits, institutional patterns, and behavioral deviations involves little more than modes of conversation, thinking, and behaving that offend the values of middle-class moralists. The point is that the locus of the problem is centered within the poor and their institutions—*they* are regarded as pathologic. Material conditions then become one mechanism by which the pathology can be explained. At issue is whether assessments of deficiency and pathology are justified in the first place, or whether a more objective accounting would not cast an entirely different light on the issue.

Theoretical and Methodologic Issues

The deficiencies attributed to minority groups cluster around five basic themes: control and mastery; rationality; orientation toward the future and long-term planning; self-development; and a sense of order based upon clearly bounded, corporate groups. We shall comment on each of these briefly.

Control and Mastery

In the research we have reviewed, people are described pejoratively as being passive, reactive, dependent, submissive, apathetic toward the outside world, insulated from it, fatalistic about their lot in life, and resigned to accepting it. They are called escapists, persons who avoid direct confrontation by letting things slide by. Many are termed "dissociative" or reliant on repression in their affective lives. They are said to feel inferior, helpless, and powerless, to lack self-control, self-reliance, and self-confidence. These characterizations imply an unwillingness or inability on the part of lower-class people to seize the initiative in attacking their "problems." The implicit assumption is that through acts of willpower people *can* control their own destinies, and that it is "normal" to attempt to do so. It is further assumed that the impetus to take control comes from within the individual, or at least from within individuals who have not been damaged by faulty socialization. Lack of concern for control is therefore treated as symptomatic of personal incompetence. Despite the fact that the poor lack resources to exercise realistic control, they are nevertheless viewed as deficient because they often verbally reject the premise involved, which implies, of course, that they are responsible for their own poverty.

Rationality

A second source of concern centers on the place that reason plays in people's lives. This is the value base from which accusations of antiintellectualism are made. The poor are described as exhibiting little concern for ideas, as displaying evidence of cognitive simplification, and as having difficulties in handling abstractions. They are accused of being authoritarian in temperament, intolerant toward others, and reliant upon magical thought processes in their personal lives. It is held that they try to socialize their children by recourse to physical force and that they rely upon such forms of nonverbal communication as grunts and physical gestures to communicate with children. Thus the priority of reason as a basis for action is affirmed as normal; what is problematic is emotionalism. This assumption articulates with the concern for control inasmuch as it is based on the premise that emotion is inherently disruptive and requires strong cerebral checks for an orderly social life to exist.

Future Orientation

A third key value underlying deficiency formulations concerns the absence of an orientation toward the future and long-term planning. Lower-class persons are described as fearing the future, and they are faulted for failing to plan their lives in a series of achievable steps, especially occupationally. They are said to be averse to planning and to have little orientation toward achievement. They are also accused of having a short-range time perspective and of being concerned only with gaining immediate gratification. They are described as focusing on the tangible here-and-now rather than orienting toward abstract goals. What is regarded as remarkable and pathologic is the absence of apparent concern for the future in organizing the present, a character trait explained as the product of a deficient upbringing. This type of analysis betrays the assumption that it is "normal" for human beings to forgo current gratifications for potential future rewards and that people who choose otherwise are defective. Planning for the future is, of course, instrumental for achieving control over one's life and environment, and to be effective such planning must be related in a utilitarian manner to the goals set forth, i.e., it must be "rational." Thus the value placed on planning for the future is an integral part of a total worldview in which rationality and control are equally significant components (see Horton, 1970, for a discussion of this point).

Self-development
Still another component of this worldview is the value placed on self-development, the idea that people should strive to develop themselves to their "fullest potential." Lower-class persons are described as lacking self-confidence and filled with self-hate or in more clinical terms, as having a poorly differentiated sense of self or as suffering from weak ego structure. Lower-class parents are accused of showing little concern for the development of their children, of being apathetic about education, of using techniques of discipline that are suppressive rather than oriented toward training and development. A crucial aspect of self-development, important because it provides a standard upon which judgments can be based, is self-awareness, particularly the degree to which individuals verbalize images of themselves. Because lower-class persons verbalize their self concepts less completely, less often, and with less assertiveness than middle-class individuals, the degree of their self-development is regarded as suspect.

Corporate Boundaries
All of the values mentioned thus far deal with personal qualities that so-called "normal" individuals are supposed to possess and that members of the lower class, or members of ethnic minorities, are said to lack. When these values are extended to social institutions they call for rationally structured, clearly bounded corporate organizations as the basis for an orderly social life. This is most obvious in studies of the family, which social scientists traditionally regard as the cornerstone of a stable society and the natural unit for socializing children. The great variation in family forms among lower-class groups makes them appear disorganized, unstable, uncoordinated, unintegrated, and inconsistent to those using concepts based upon dominant group values. Lower-class family life is portrayed as uncohesive and unstable, tending toward a chaotic, alienated, normless set of relationships. The composition of the family seems uncertain, its boundaries continually shifting as people come and go, its roles blurred. Parents are seen as having little control over their children, as being inadequate socializers. The presence of caretakers other than parents is often used as evidence to support such an assertion, and the pattern of using older children to care for younger ones may be regarded as tantamount to parental rejection or abandonment. An apparent high level of overt conflict within the nuclear family unit, low levels of communication between family members, and the diversion of resources outside the nuclear unit constitute the types of evidence that support interpretations of the lower-class family as pathologic or deficient.

Middle-class Values and Minority Group Research
Perhaps the most interesting yet disconcerting fact about deficiency formulations is that they appear so frequently in the works of scholars who explicitly caution against adopting middle-class standards and values when doing research with minor-

ity groups.[5] Thus despite an expressed desire to be sympathetic and fair to such groups, many investigators unwittingly lapse into a theoretical stance in which these standards serve as measuring rods against which the behavior of lower-class people is described and explained. That this occurs among researchers who explicitly caution against it should alert us to the likelihood that the problem is more than just a matter of biased attitudes. Indeed, to cast the issue in attitudinal terms implies a false distinction between researchers who presumably misperceive reality because of value biases and those who supposedly are engaging in a value-free social science (and therefore presumably perceive reality correctly). It is our view that many social scientists are led to see lower-class people and institutions as deficient not so much because they are blinded by personal and/or class prejudice but because so much of the conceptual apparatus of social science is infused with the value assumptions discussed above.

It is beyond the scope of this essay to discuss in detail the ways in which the cluster of values we have identified were woven into the assumptive fabric of social scientific paradigms, but the issue is so basic that it requires some exposition. The matter is essentially an historical one; the values at issue played an important role in the industrial revolution and the modernization of the West. Quite obviously, stressing mastery and control, rationality, future time orientation, and a social order based on corporate responsibility are highly serviceable principles in a society undergoing industrialization. For the emerging middle-class entrepreneur, rational long-term planning coupled with new technology helped greatly to create unique opportunities for controlling resources and using them to further specific ends. In this pursuit, self-development became an important motivating force, providing a justification and rationale for personal strivings. It became linked with such pragmatic needs as the acquisition of knowledge through formal education, the application of long-term planning to careers as well as to industry, and the capacity to assert oneself in shaping personal relationships to achieve one's ends. Rational control over self in the interest of future accomplishments became an integral part of the developing cultural paradigm, at the same time that control over one's children's fate as an extension of one's own career led to the sanctification of the nuclear family.

It seems clear that these and associated values implicit in social science have historical roots that run deep in Western culture, and that by the time social scientists began to formulate theories they were widely accepted as part of the natural scheme of things. Consequently, what became problematic were deviations from these accepted standards and not the standards themselves. Indeed, the social problems associated with conditions such as poverty were defined in relation to them.[6] The possibility that there might be alternative values of equal or greater merit, while explicitly entertained by a few social thinkers, never seriously shook these axiomatic underpinnings.

The theoretical consequences of this equation of basic values with a natural social order have been enormous. Identifiable segments of the population, particularly the poor, and especially the ethnic poor, came to be regarded as social problems in that they manifested greater statistical deviations than "normal" from key indicators of these values in the form of divorce, school dropouts, crimes of passion or aggression, and so on. Applied social science then concerned itself largely with identifying the conditions leading to these deviations and attempted to use research findings to formulate programs for correcting them. Rarely was consideration given to patterns of behaving and thinking that were viable but different from the mainstream norms.

As a result, programs were almost invariably "remedial" and practically never constructionist.

The tendency to regard certain social forms as normal and to question deviations from them is well illustrated by work done on the family in American society. Until quite recently most social scientists have assumed that permanent monogamous marriage is natural and proper, or at least highly "functional," within our society. The view derives from the sanctification of the nuclear family and its alleged suitability for carrying out basic tasks in modern industrial society. Indeed, it is often treated as the primary anchor in an otherwise unstable social system—the very basis for stability itself. Therefore divorce and separation are made to appear problematic, while permanent conjugal bonds are taken for granted. The basic question has always been, "Why do couples 'fail' to make their marriages work?"—a question that ignores entirely the difficult problem of understanding how it is possible for two people, who may be of differing backgrounds and undergoing constant change, to live together compatibly for a lifetime. To take a second example, social science perspectives have always regarded attachments within the nuclear family as "naturally" more important than relationships outside of it, even to the extent of labeling them as "primary." If, for example, a man spends his income to maintain friendships at the expense of his family, he is likely to be labeled as "irresponsible," and reasons are sought for his deviation. Yet there are cultures in which this value priority is not accepted, cultures in which peer group ties are recognized as equal in importance to family relationships (see, for example, Howard, 1974). The point we are trying to make here is that what has come to be regarded as problematic in social science research on the family is shaped largely by implicit conceptions of what a normal family is, and that these conceptions are deeply rooted in the specific historical circumstances of industrial development in Western society. Conceptions of what is normal and natural are in fact culture and class specific; minority groups who deviate from them have borne the brunt of labels that make them out to be abnormal and unnatural.

This basic orientation toward groups whose values and lifestyles are at variance with those of the dominant culture are strongly buttressed by certain assumptions of physical science that many social scientists have come to accept as axiomatic. Imputed to social phenomena are the same qualities and characteristics other disciplines impute to the physical universe. Most basic of all is the assumption that the goal of science is to reveal "the truth" about "reality." This assumption fosters the idea of convergent explanation, which holds that when alternative interpretations are provided for a phenomenon it is necessary to clearly choose between them or to synthesize them into a single, "truer" proposition. It is germane to the present discussion because it supports the underlying premise upon which all deficiency formulations rest—namely, that every scientific statement can be placed along a scale of correctness and by virtue of its correctness, of value.[7] When extended to "social reality," this perspective fosters a consensus view of society, the notion that the social fabric is held together by common commitment to a set of shared beliefs and values and that deviations from them are disruptive, disorganizing, and threatening to an orderly social life. In other words, one view of society is accepted as indicative of social reality, and the genuine diversity of perspectives is downplayed or ignored. The presumed consensus is invariably defined in terms of mainstream activities (economic, political, legal) that incorporate such specific value premises as control, rationality, self-development, and corporateness. Observers whose theoretical formulations stem from a consensus viewpoint are thus led to interpret all behavior in terms of universally applied standards derived from but one segment of the population. Minority groups are then placed in the position of being described and evaluated against a set of standards that is to a greater or lesser extent alien to them.

The effects of a commitment to convergent explanation are reflected in many methodologic procedures employed by social scientists, procedures that are effectively recipes for producing deficiency formulations. One example is the procedure of deducing a hypothesis from a theory prior to collecting data. Since few social scientists have had first-hand experience with the daily lives of minority group members, hypotheses have tended to focus on propositions derived from observations of mainstream groups. As a result, the hypotheticodeductive method has served sometimes as a straitjacket, hampering the recognition of alternate perspectives and the development of theories based on the discovery of previously undiscerned patterns.

By defining their task in terms of discovering the nature of social reality, after the model set by the physical sciences, social scientists have frequently been led to give short shrift to their subjects' own perceptions and interpretations of their condition. This tendency to disregard the actor's viewpoint as invalid, naive, and simplistic has had the effect of diverting social scientists from seriously attempting to ascertain the beliefs and values of their subjects except insofar as they diverge from the presumed consensus. As a result, behavior is often portrayed in mechanistic terms, depriving it of the meaning it has for the actor. The emphasis on parsimony in the construction of theory further exaggerates this tendency; the quest to limit explanations to a few "significant" propositions or laws leads naturally to a narrowing of the scope of investigation, on the one hand, and a strong tendency toward simplification, on the other. The natural complexity and diversity of human behavior is thus sacrificed for elegance of theoretical structure.

Finally, the emphasis on quantification, in conjunction with the consensus view of society, has led to an exaggeration of intergroup differences and a failure to give due consideration to intragroup variability. Perhaps the most pernicious effect of this overreliance on central tendency comparisons has been the temptation to treat marginal differences between groups as representative of qualitative difference, despite considerable overlap. Prototypical has been the use (and abuse) of intelligence and aptitude testing in which statistically marginal differences between groups have been interpreted by some as indicative of racial inferiority. The way in which this use of statistics can mislead is illustrated by the data on Afro-American family structure, which, it will be recalled, has been described in terms of disorganization in contrast to the white family. Yet when we examine the data cited by Pettigrew and others as indicative of instability we find that three-quarters of black families are "complete"—they contain both husband and wife. Thus according to this indicator the vast majority are in fact stable; the judgment of instability is made only in relation to white families, of which nine-tenths contained both parents. Thus a difference of approximately 15 percent is translated into a qualitatively different characterization of black family as unstable, white family as stable. If the comparison group had been upper-class families, among which divorce rates are relatively high, the black family would have appeared unremarkable or even relatively stable.

These data regarding the alleged instability of the black family raise a further point indicative of the prejudicial premises from which many social scientific accounts proceed. The data most often cited in connection with family instability are drawn from studies conducted during the 1950s and 1960s when white families were especially cohesive. This is less true today, as rates of divorce, desertion, and separation have risen sharply. It is interesting to note how social science perspectives have changed in response to this shift. When these rates were substantially higher among poor and black groups, research centered around efforts to discover personality deficiencies that correlate with family "disorganization," implying that there was something wrong with people who formed unstable unions and that their personal deficits were responsible. But when the rates of family dissolution among middle-class whites began to escalate rapidly the basic research question changed to one focusing on whether or not the nuclear family is still a viable social institution, thereby implying that middle-class marital problems are due to institutional breakdown and not the failure of individuals.

Even this brief discussion should make it clear that we are not accusing social scientists of being blindly ethnocentric. Rather, we believe the epistemologic assumptions that underlie most research have made it almost inevitable that poor people, and the ethnic poor in particular, be portrayed as deficient. As a result, even sympathetic, well-intentioned researchers have often been trapped into treating minorities as unfortunate deviations from implicit norms. What is required now is that minority populations be studied with proper attention to their own perceptions of social reality, that their purposes be understood, and that their patterns of behavior be described in terms of what they are rather than what they are not. In essence, we are suggesting that the present emphasis on convergent explanation be supplemented with, if not supplanted by, an emphasis on divergence. This will require a research strategy that encourages the study of minority groups as potentially unique cultural systems. The task would then be to discover the values, organizational principles, and cultural logic that provide the basis for their particular ordering of social reality.

REACTIONS AND CORRECTIVE TENDENCIES

Although we have stressed an apparent preoccupation with deficiencies in social science research on minority groups, there are some notable exceptions. Reactions have come from many quarters—academic, political, and the victims themselves. In this section we discuss some of these responses, particularly those that have direct implications for theory and method and those raising vital issues and questions about possible directions for future research.

One set of reactions has focused on the "culture of poverty" concept. Critics have pointed out that the concept of "culture," as currently used by anthropologists, presumes that human beings are more than passive reactors to environmental contingencies, even though it is recognized that such contingencies can have a powerful patterning effect. That is, it presumes that people develop plans and pursue goals. Therefore to project a people's lifeway as a mere shadow image of middle-class patterns is to abdicate the essence of the scientific task, which is to discover what those goals are, what types of plans are formulated in pursuit of them, and how behavioral patterns relate to them. Only then can the real impact of circumstances imposed upon them from the outside be assessed. Reflecting the behavior of minorities against middle-class norms as the primary way of comprehending it is tantamount to denying the possibility of subcultural variations and has the result of personalizing the "blame" for economic deprivation. Charles Valentine makes this point in his book *Culture and Poverty:*

> The culture-of-poverty notion and related ideas contradict all important positive aspects of the culture concept. This thesis of contradiction extends not only to the essential meaning of the idea of culture but also to its major implications for theory and method in the human sciences, philosophical issues, public attitudes and public policies. While one assumes that the purposes of the authors involved were quite otherwise, the presentation and particularly the popularization of these notions have had one outstandingly important effect. That is, these formulations support the long-established rationalization of blaming poverty on the poor. Nothing could be further from the meaning, the spirit, or the ideological implications of the original concept of culture. (Valentine, 1968, p. 15)

Another set of reactions against deficiency formulations has come from the Afro-American community. The rise of the Black Power movement in the 1960s spearheaded an increased sense of ethnic awareness and a search for self-definition that could be rooted in valued aspects of one's heritage. Ethnic pride required a comprehension of the uniqueness of black experience, of the strengths of black people and black institutions, and an affirmation of those values and beliefs upon which the achievements of black people were based. This triggered a reassessment among social scientists of existing data on Afro-American behavior patterns and their cultural underpinnings. For example, using the same data base as Moynihan, Robert Hill employed criteria developed from a black perspective and produced a book entitled *The Strengths of Black Families* (Hill, 1972). Hill maintained that black and white norms differ with respect to family structure and that the data should be interpreted in the context of black norms. He identified the following characteristics that he regards as functional for survival in a hostile environment: (1) strong kinship bonds, (2) strong work orientation, (3) adaptibility of family roles, (4) strong achievement orientation, and (5) strong religious orientation. He notes:

> Although these traits can be found among white families, they are manifested differently in the lives of black families because of the unique history of racial oppression experienced by blacks in America. In fact, the particular forms that these characteristics take among black families should be viewed as adaptations necessary for survival and advancement in a hostile environment. (Hill, 1972, p. 4)

One of the realizations this new perspective generated was that accounts of Afro-American institutions were conceptually oversimplified, that the complexities and variations had been overlooked as a result of their being reflected against a limited, stereotypic set of middle-class norms. This realization is reflected in Billingsley's reinterpretation of the black family, in which he explores the sources of strength in black families that have enabled some not only to survive in the face of adversity but to move beyond survival to stability and social achievement (Billingsley, 1968).

A key issue that developed in academic circles in response to black nationalism was whether or not there *is* a distinctive Afro-American culture (see, for example, Berger, 1970; Blauner, 1970; Hannerz, 1970; Schorr, 1963; Seeley, 1959). A number of social scientists held the position that the behavior patterns of blacks could be accounted for almost entirely by social class and involved no distinctive cultural features. It was therefore a challenge to those who believed otherwise to demonstrate the existence of a unique black culture. The core concept around which the effort was made is "soul," which was first introduced into the social science literature by Charles Keil in *Urban Blues* (Keil, 1966).

Keil asserts that the social definition of blacks—the fact that they have been treated as outcasts—has almost hidden the fact that they have a culture. He argues that social scientists neglected that special domain of black culture wherein black people had proved and preserved their humanity:

> This domain or sphere of interest may be broadly defined as entertainment from the white or public point of view and as ritual, drama, or dialectical catharsis from the Negro or theoretical standpoint. By this I mean that certain Negro performances, called "entertaining" by Negroes and whites alike, have an added but usually unconscious ritual significance for Negroes. The ritualists I have in mind are singers, musicians, preachers, comedians, disc jockeys, some athletes, and perhaps a few Negro novelists as well. These entertainers are the ablest representatives of a long cultural tradition—what might be called the soul tradition—and they are all identity experts, so to speak, specialists in changing the joke and slipping the yoke. An analysis of the Negroes' situation in America today, if it is to be thorough and constructive, must take these strategic figures into account. (Keil, 1966, p. 15)

Keil considers the entertainment component of black culture significant in at least four basic respects. First, it is the one area in black life that was not obliterated by slavery, the rituals having an indisputable West African foundation. Second, unlike other immigrant traditions that have almost completely dissolved in America, the cultural legacy linking black Americans to Africa has not only survived but has thrived on adversity and grown stronger through the years. Third, it is now a full-fledged tradition in its own right. Fourth, and most important, "the entertainers are masters of sound, movement, timing, the spoken word. One can therefore find in their performances the essentials and defining features—the very core in fact—of Negro culture as a whole" (Keil, 1966, p. 16).

Keil goes on to contrast cultural modes of expression in white and Black America:

> The unique and full status of Negro culture is only partly dependent on the basic institutional elements, such as Church and family, that do not fit white American specifications. On another and perhaps more fundamental level, the shared sensibilities and common understandings of the Negro ghetto, its modes of perception and expression, its channels of communication, are predominantly auditory and tactile rather than visual and literate. Sensibilities are of course matters of degree, and the sense ratio or "ratio-nality" of a particular culture can't be measured precisely. Nevertheless, the prominence of aural perception, oral expression, and kinesic codes or body movement in Negro life—its sound and feel—sharply demarcate the culture from the irrational white world outside the ghetto. Negro and white Americans share the same general language (superficially a good argument for those who would relegate the Negro to a subcultural corner in homogenized America), but their attitudes toward that language are polarized. In white America, the printed word—the literary tradition—and its attendant values are revered. In the Negro community, more power resides in the spoken word and oral tradition—good talkers abound and the best gain power and prestige, but good writers are scarce. It is no accident that much of America's slang is provided by Negro culture. Nor is it strange that Negro music and dance have become America's music and dance. (Keil, 1966, pp. 16–17)

Keil particularly takes aim at those psychiatric and social scientific characterizations that interpret the behavior of black males as signifying acute sexual identity problems (deficient masculinity), which presumably derive from being raised in households lacking fathers or other stable male figures. He points out that some patterns interpreted by white students as feminine (e.g., falsetto singing) come directly from Africa, where they are regarded as the very essence of masculine expression. Keil asserts that "any sound analysis of Negro masculinity should first deal with the statements and responses of Negro women, the conscious motives of the men themselves, and the Negro cultural tradition. Applied in this setting, psychological theory may then be able to provide important new insights in place of basic and unfortunate distortions" (Keil, 1966, p. 28).

Keil's contribution was to shift the description of Afro-American behavior away from those aspects that could be construed as deviations from middle-class norms to aspects that are positive affirmations of black culture and identity (see also Liebow, 1967: Ellison, 1964). No longer are black people seen only as inadequate whites; they are now seen as people whose behavior conforms to a cultural logic of their own, as well as to circumstances. As a result they emerge as actors instead of mere reactors, as *persons* actively engaged in living in a culturally rich and complex environment instead of passive vessels who are empty of substance because they are economically and culturally deprived. Keil's "positive" ethnography has helped shift the theoretical focus for social scientists concerned with Afro-Americans. Instead of trying to account for deviations from middle-class norms, the emphasis has changed to one of trying to describe and explain what the patterns of black culture and behavior *are* in other areas of life: What are the variations *within* the Black community, and what structures them? What positive functions are served by Afro-American institutions, given the circumstances of black people? What are the lives of "normal" or "average" blacks like? This refocusing is evident in the work of Ladner (1971), who has studied young black women in a St. Louis slum. She describes the questions that concerned her as follows:

> What is life like in the urban Black community for the "average" girl? How does she define her roles, behaviors, and from whom does she acquire her models for fulfilling what is expected of her? Is there any significant disparity between the resources she has with which to accomplish her goals in life and the stated aspirations? Is the typical world of the teen-ager in American society shared by the Black girl or does she stand somewhat alone in much of her day-to-day existence? (Ladner, 1971, pp. 12–13)

Ladner spent four years interviewing, testing, observing, and "hanging out" with the girls she studied, and she spent a considerable amount of time in their homes with them and their families, at church, parties, dances, in the homes of their friends, shopping, in her own apartment, and in various other situations. The field work carried her into the community at irregular hours and involved her in intensive relationships with her subjects and frequently with their mothers. She used open-ended interviews and took life histories, taping them to ensure accuracy in recording so that she would be able to present their views in their own language. The picture that emerges is infinitely richer than accounts based on survey and census data or on short-term observations. More importantly, it forces a theoretical reorientation toward a wide range of issues associated with the nature of the Afro-American family and its developmental consequences for children.

Two other recent studies of Afro-American families that have taken a substantive approach are Carol Stack's *All Our Kin* (1974) and Joyce Aschenbrenner's *Lifelines* (1975). Both are based on intensive ethnographies and support the viewpoint that there is an identifiable Afro-American culture that structures family life and behavioral patterns. Both emphasize that family life must be understood in a broader context of kin, friendship, and other relationships. From this perspective the various forms of the black family emerge as expressions of value commitments as well as responses to economic and social pressures. When they are seen in this light, and not merely as reactive aberrant forms of the "normal" nuclear family, it becomes possible to ask a set of substantive questions concerning the significance of these patterns for the development of children born into them.

This shift from a deficiency to a substantive framework requires a reformulation of theory and method alike, as illustrated by the work of Howard and Gallimore on a Hawaiian-American community located near Honolulu. The research was stimulated by a report surveying the status of Hawaiian-Americans during the early 1960s (Liliuokalani Trust, 1962). The report stated that this segment of Hawaii's diverse ethnic population was statistically overrepresented in virtually every category of "social problem" and greatly underrepresented on most standard indicators of social and economic success. Before doing fieldwork the researchers sought information from a number of social agencies in order to orient their investigation; predictably they found Hawaiian-Americans portrayed almost entirely in terms of deficit. Families were characterized as disorganized, parents as irresponsible and uninterested in their children's education, students as unmotivated and lacking in self-control, and so forth. All of the jargon in the social science literature on the poor was applied. As with Afro-Americans, it was argued by some and accepted by most that traditional Hawaiian culture had been destroyed years ago and that the behavior of their predominantly mixed-breed offspring could be explained as a reaction to poverty. What the agencies wanted to know was how to break the poverty cycle so as to draw Hawaiian-Americans into the cultural mainstream.

The study began with a year-long ethnographic investigation of a Hawaiian homestead community in rural Oahu called Aina Pumehana (a pseudonym). The researchers found that although almost all the formal, overt trappings of Hawaiian culture had disappeared, including the language, at the level of social interaction traditional Polynesian patterns were very much in evidence. Specifically, they found a strong emphasis on affiliation and a deemphasis of individualized competitive achievement. This pervasive value commitment affected a wide range of structural features and behavior patterns and cast quite a different light on them than had been cast by deficiency formulations.

In the area of family structure, for instance, the observed marginality of husbands/fathers in a large proportion of households (from the middle-class perspective), interpreted as irresponsibility from a deficiency standpoint, could be understood as the positive expression of important affiliative bonds outside the nuclear family. Particularly for men, and more specifically young men, commitments to peers and workmates often superseded those to spouses and perhaps even children. Only if one makes sacred the nuclear family and assumes that it is "natural" for commitments to the family of procreation to take precedence over all others can this pattern be seen as deficient or pathologic. In social relations the key question for understanding Hawaiian-Americans turned out to be, "How do people invest resources, time, and effort in social relations?" rather than "How does poverty affect the nuclear family?" Significantly, the more income people had at their disposal, the more they invested in social capital by expanding their interpersonal networks (Howard, 1971; 1974). In other words, even those who had the resources tended to pattern their behavior in accordance with the local value of affiliation rather than the middle-class virtue of investing in material accumulation.

Using the ethnographic data as a starting point, Howard and Gallimore began a series of social psychological experiments with school children that resulted in a theoretical shift from a deficiency model toward a substantive one. Working back and forth between the experiments and their ethnographic materials, the researchers found that achievement *behavior* among Hawaiian-American children was associated with need Affiliation rather than need Achievement. By refocusing their methods and theoretical constructs to accommodate this discovery they were able to recast patterns described previously strictly in terms of deficit into a substantive description of the coping strategies employed by Hawaiian-Americans in everyday life (see Howard, 1974; Gallimore, Boggs, & Jordan, 1974; Chapter 21 in this volume). The research strategy employed by Howard and Gallimore illustrates the value of using ethnographic and experimental techniques in tandem when studying developmental processes within minority populations (for another example of this approach, see Levinger, 1965).

N. Graves and Graves (1974), working among the Polynesian Maori minority in New Zealand, have likewise reacted against the deficit model and have employed substantive methods to describe developmental patterns. Careful ethnographic observation of children and adults in schools and play areas led them to conclude that the Maori socialization pattern leads to an interactive style that is "inclusive" (group oriented), while the Pakeha (white) pattern is "exclusive" (individually or dyadically oriented). The individualistic, competitive bias in New Zealand schools generally favors the Pakeha pattern, leading educators to see Maori children as low achievers; however, as the Graves point out, the cooperative-inclusive pattern of problem solving is often more effective when the context allows.

In a subsequent paper N. Graves (1976) uses data acquired from Cook Island Polynesians to challenge the Piagetian notion that sociocentric behavior develops through a "decentering" process out of "adualism," a state of complete self-centeredness. True social communication and cooperation are held by Piaget to require the conceptual differentiation by the child of self from others. Social exchange behavior prior to this decentering process, which is supposedly completed around age 9 years, is considered to be "precooperative" (Piaget & Inhelder, 1969). Graves challenges these formulations and suggests that in Cook Island society the fact that separation of self from others is not culturally encouraged actually hastens true sociocentrism at an early age. "As long as a child is mapped into a functioning, face-to-face system which is socially and economically interdependent, little happens to hinder the growth and development of a basically human sociocentrism" (N. Graves, 1976, p. 12).

Research among Mexican-Americans by Madsen and his associates has also traced deficiency characterization of school children to the cooperative style (Madsen, 1967; Madsen & Shapira, 1970; Kagan & Madsen, 1971). In these studies an experimental reward system was arranged so that competitive behavior was maladaptive, leading to failure. These investigators found that a tendency toward irrational competition appears to develop with age among Anglo-Americans, and to a lesser extent among Mexican-American children. In Mexico they found that rural children and lower-class urban children behaved in a much more cooperative manner on an experimental task than did urban middle-class children. They infer from these findings that the developmental milieu in the United States, and in middle-class environments in general, rewards competition to such an extent that children generalize it to situations in which it is maladaptive. Their studies show, by the way, how easy it is to reverse deficiency formulations when alternative values are imposed. From the rural Mexican or Polynesian standpoints Anglo-Americans are deficient in their capacity to share and cooperate.

The Mexican-American case differs from both that of Afro-Americans and Hawaiian-Americans in one important way. Whereas the latter groups were seen from a deficiency standpoint as being cultureless, the Mexican-Americans were seen as having a culture, but one that is damaging. As Ramirez and Castaneda (1974) point out:

> The "damaging-culture" assumption as it has been applied to Mexican-Americans has consistently led to the conclusion that the culture of Mexican-Americans socializes individuals to become lazy, resigned, passive, fatalistic, nongoal-oriented, docile, shy, infantile, criminally prone, irrational, emotional, authoritarian, unreliable, limited in cognitive ability, untrustworthy, lax, priest-ridden, and nonachievement-oriented. (Ramirez & Castaneda, 1974, p. 9)

These authors assert that despite aspirations to objectivity, the damaging-culture assumption has been pervasive in social science studies of Mexican-Americans, and that such studies have contributed to a view of Mexican-American children as products of a culture dominated by values that make learning difficult (Ramirez & Castaneda, 1974, p. 9). They also point out that the concentration on such variables as economic status and educational achievement has obscured the highly diverse and heterogeneous character of the Mexican-American population in many other important spheres of life, and claim that social scientists have neglected to describe the diversity of child socialization practices in the Mexican-American population and the effects of these practices on personality development and behavior (Ramirez & Castaneda, 1974, p. 13).

Ramirez and Castaneda trace the presumed learning difficulties of Mexican-American school children to substantive value conflicts:

> Mexican-American children experience difficulty in school because their culture is not given recognition in the classroom and because school personnel are not aware of differences between traditional Mexican-American and mainstream American middle-class cultures. The sociocultural system of traditional Mexican-American culture is composed of four major value clusters: (1) identification with family, community, and ethnic group: (2) personalization of interpersonal relationships: (3) status and role definition in family and community: and (4) Mexican Catholic ideology. Mainstream American middle-class values most often represented in schools can be categorized under the value cluster: (1) sense of separate identity: and (2) individual competitive achievement. (Ramirez & Castaneda, 1974, p. 56)

Drawing upon a body of research literature that relates cognitive and motivational styles to different cultural values and associated socialization practices (Beman, 1972; Cohen, 1969; Lesser, Fifer, & Clark, 1965; Ramirez, 1973; Ramirez & Price-Williams, 1974; Stodolsky & Lesser, 1967; Witkin, 1967), Ramirez and Castaneda focus their research on field dependence/field independence as a key variable for comprehending the distinction between Mexican-American and middle-class Anglo-

American learning patterns. They find that the traditional Mexican-American value system fosters a field-dependent cognitive style, characterized by a high degree of sensitivity to the interpersonal environment and a relational style responsive to those forms of reward that offer personalized support, recognition, or acceptance. In contrast, the middle-class Anglo-American value system fosters a field-independent cognitive style, characterized by responsiveness to aspects of the impersonal environment and an aggressive, direct, and analytic learning style.

Cultural Deprivation

It was perhaps inevitable that the logic of deficiency formulations would be applied to education. The documentation that the children of the poor, and particularly the ethnic poor—Afro-American, Mexican-American, native American, Puerto Rican, Hawaiian-American, etc.—do poorly in school is extensive and compelling. By virtually every measure of academic achievement, including test scores, grades, and years of schooling completed, children from these backgrounds fall below the norm, increasingly with age. Earlier attempts to explain these "failures" relied on genetic explanations. The poor were less intelligent (otherwise they would not be poor), and they transmitted their inferior genes to their children. The position is not dead, of course, having been resurrected by Arthur Jensen and his associates (Jensen, 1969). The genetic position is unacceptable to most social scientists, but many of them have latched onto the notion that economic deprivation leads to "cultural deprivation," a condition resulting in an inadequate environment for normal development. The idea is that lower-class homes lack books, toys, and other articles that stimulate learning and cognitive development and that lower-class parents speak substandard English, do not verbalize sufficiently, do not encourage educational activities such as reading, and fail to generate motivation to succeed. In extreme cases, it has been hypothesized, these conditions may lead to "sociogenic brain damage" (Montagu, 1972; for a discussion of this issue in relation to minority groups, see the article by C. Valentine & Valentine, 1975).

Thus lower-class children are presumed to arrive at school without the basic cognitive, motivational, and social skills necessary to master the curriculum and with a negative self-image that leads them to give up easily (Deutsch, 1960; 1963; Deutsch et al., 1967; Riessman, 1962; Stott, 1966). However, a number of scholars have pointed out that the concept of "cultural deprivation" serves as a rationalization for failures by educators in dealing with lower-class children (see, for example, Clark, 1965; Mackler & Giddings, 1965). The concept has also been criticized for overgeneralization and oversimplification, for the way in which it encourages the glossing over of individual and group differences. As Clark and Potkin put it, "The hard realities and complexities of analyzing differences in environment are avoided by substituting a global explanatory term, cultural deprivation" (Clark & Plotkin, 1972, p. 66). Closely related to the stereotyping that accompanies the concept is, according to Clark and Plotkin, an almost total lack of measurement of environmental variables. They point out that our catalogue of tests of individual differences is extensive, whereas our measurement of environmental differences is restricted to a few techniques dealing with social class and economic status (Clark & Plotkin, 1972, p. 67). In lieu of the absence of sophisticated measurement techniques, social scientists frequently rely on superficial indices based on middle-class ideals and focus on what is absent (e.g., books) rather than facing the much more complex task of describing what is present.

"Intelligence"

At the heart of the cultural deprivation perspective is the notion that growing up in a lower-class environment reduces, or fails to develop, "intelligence." Since much of the evidence that supports this position comes from intelligence testing, it is important to examine some of the assumptions that lie behind it. Ginsburg, in a book critically reviewing the data on poor children's intellect and education (1972), discusses four "myths" concerning the IQ test and the "intelligence" that it presumably measures.

First is the myth that the IQ Test measures an intelligence which is a unitary mental ability. According to this perspective, individuals differ in the extent to which they possess the entity or ability of intelligence, and the IQ score reflects this difference. But, as Ginsburg points out, performance on an IQ test involves complex acts of perception, comprehension, and memory, all of which must be translated into a response. Thus, although consistent differences between social classes occur on IQ tests, what those differences indicate is not clear.

The second myth is that differences in IQ scores reflect fundamental differences in intellect. The underlying assumption is that the tests measure those abilities that are central to intellect, and that what the tests do not measure is unimportant. However, at least some research has shown the relationship between IQ and various measures of creativity to be questionable (Getzels & Jackson, 1962), and in fact most IQ tests appear to focus on relatively passive, conventional verbal skills, ignoring or glossing over nonverbal aspects of intelligence regarded as central to development in psychological theories such as Piaget's. Furthermore, Ginsburg asserts, IQ testing by its very nature is oriented toward measuring *differences;* it therefore tends to focus on measuring abilities on which children differ rather than on those possibly more fundamental capacities on which they are alike.

The third myth is that IQ tests measure intellectual competence, that a test score reflects the upper limit of a person's mental capabilities. This assumption presumes that those who take the test are motivated to do their best, but we know that children from different backgrounds respond differently to test situations. For some children test situations are routine, for others they are a source of anxiety and apprehension, while others may be indifferent. A study by Hertzig et al. (1968) of Puerto Rican children in New York is revealing of subcultural differences. The researchers kept behavioral records of a sample of working-class Puerto Rican and middle-class Anglo children during IQ test performance. As expected, the middle-class children scored significantly higher. In general, the middle-class children were friendly, interested in the test situation, followed instructions, and worked persistently. The Puerto Rican children were also friendly, but were easily distracted, were somewhat less verbal, did not follow instructions well, and did not focus attention on the task. Even when IQ test scores were equivalent, the Puerto Rican children were less task oriented than the middle-class Anglos. Hertzig et al. interpret their results as a reflection of cultural orientation. They describe Puerto Rican families as sociable and relaxed, not pressuring children toward achievement and not persistently trying to "educate" their children with toys and by other means. They characterize the cultural milieu as "person oriented" rather than " problem oriented." The result is low motivation to perform on impersonal tasks such as intelligence tests. The investigators are careful to point out that their results are indicative of different lifestyles rather than any deficiency on the part of Puerto Rican culture (although note that their description focuses on the way Puerto Rican parents do *not* behave).

The fourth myth is that the IQ test measures an innate ability which is relatively unaffected by experience. This assumption, Ginsburg clearly shows, is contradicted by a wealth of empirical evidence showing that IQ scores are not constant throughout the lifespan and that they are responsive to environmental events and emotional experiences.

Ginsburg acknowledges that IQ scores are moderately accurate predictors of academic achievement but holds that the reason for this is not necessarily that the tests measure "intelligence" or profound intellectual abilities. Instead, he conjectures, it may be because both schools and IQ tests emphasize verbal skills, mental drudgery, and a certain docility of character. Also, teachers may develop expectancies concerning student performance based on IQ scores and may act in ways unintentionally calculated to bring reality in line with prophecy. After reviewing all the data regarding class differences in relation to intelligence, Ginsburg draws three conclusions:

First, social-class differences in IQ should not be taken too seriously. The numerical difference is relatively small—10 or 20 points—and does not necessarily indicate fundamental intellectual differences between middle-class and lower-class children, or between blacks and whites.

At most, the IQ test may indicate that poor children possess to a lesser degree than do middle-class children certain intellectual and motivation skills which current schools approve and reward.

Second, the IQ test fails to teach us much of a positive nature about the intellect of poor children. It indicates that they are slightly deficient in skills that middle-class children possess and current schools favor. But what are the unique capabilities of the poor? What intellectual skills have they developed to cope with their environment? The IQ test is not designed to discover the answer to such questions.

Third, the relatively high correlation between IQ and academic achievement is not immutable. The correlation shows that poor children's skills are not well matched with the demands of schools *as currently constituted.* But drastic reform of the schools could change the situation. If schools nurtured, encouraged, and utilized the skills which poor children possess, then the IQ might be irrelevant for predicting academic achievement. (Ginsburg, 1972, p. 57; emphasis in original)

Language and Cognition

Another critical area implicated by the concept of cultural deprivation is language. The basic position held by deprivation theorists is that because poor children are not exposed to elaborated language forms during their formative years their intellectual abilities are impaired. The grounds for this viewpoint were spelled out by Bernstein (1961), whose work among English populations led him to distinguish between "elaborated codes" utilized by middle-class parents and "restricted codes" employed by the poor. Characteristically, the restricted codes of the poor were described in deficiency terms. Their main features were said to be short, simple sentences which are often incomplete and syntactically weak; simple and repetitive use of conjunctions such as "so," "then," "and," "because;" few subordinate clauses; limited and repetitive use of adjectives and adverbs; and confusion of reason and conclusions so as to produce categoric statements. These features render restricted codes a poor vehicle for thought in Bernstein's view, leading to further deficiencies. They are held to be incapable of communicating complex ideas or relationships, of not being able to deal with logical implication in other than a crude way, in being so limited in generalization and abstraction that thought is forced into stereotyped channels, and so on. Bernstein's formulation elaborated and documented what many educators had already taken for granted, that the children of the poor spoke substandard dialects and that their speech patterns were essentially an accumulation of errors or deviations from Standard English.

Critics of this perspective have pointed out that the notion of error obscures the richness and complexity of speech patterns employed by various groups. Some have shown, for example, that certain dialects elaborate connotative codes far more than Standard English (Howard, 1970). Others, such as Labov, Cohen, Robins, & Lewis (1968), have demonstrated that dialects such as those spoken by black ghetto children are systematic and can be described in terms of their own rules rather than as mere deviations from the norms of Standard English. The task, according to these critics, is to accurately describe and understand the language patterns in use among various minority populations. Only then can comparisons be made.

Another proposition advanced by cultural deprivation theorists is that the conceptual abilities of poor children are impaired by the environments in which they are raised. Ironically, as Ginsburg points out, one view holds that the homes of poor children lack sufficient stimulation to facilitate conceptual learning, while another asserts that such environments contain too much stimulation for proper learning to occur. After criticizing both positions on the grounds that they lack any convincing supporting evidence, Ginsburg queries the basic premises underlying the notion of conceptual retardation:

> After all, what kind of environment does a child—any child—need for normal intellectual development? What sort of raw material does he require for the construction of knowledge? The answer depends on the kind of knowledge involved. In the case of language, what a child needs is to hear other people speak, and every poor family does that. In the case of form perception, what the child needs is shapes to see and to explore. Would anyone maintain that the poor child's world is formless? In the case of object permanence, what the child needs is an environment containing things which continue to exist even when unobserved. Surely the poor child's world is no different from ours in this respect. In the case of the "concepts" *up, down, behind, in front of,* and all the rest, what the child needs is again a world of real things, and there can be no doubt that he has it.
>
> I maintain, in short, that the poor child's environment is in many respects adequate for intellectual development. He is active and wants to make sense of the world. He lives in a rich and stimulating environment, not in an institution. And the interaction between the active child and his world inevitably produces knowledge—the cognitive universals. (Ginsburg, 1972, pp. 184–185)

The reason that poor children do poorly in school, according to Ginsburg, is that they often lack certain *specific* cognitive skills, such as reading and writing, but to postulate a general conceptual retardation is unwarranted.

The research reviewed in this section is a small but representative sample of recent work by social scientists who are endeavoring to supplant deficiency formulations with more meaningful analyses of the social life of minority groups and its implications for child development. Although such research is increasing in quantity and quality, a great deal more work needs to be done on minority populations before social scientists will legitimately be in a position to claim a special understanding of them. In concluding our discussion of this research we wish to reiterate a point stated earlier—that the impetus for deficiency formulations derives less from prejudiced attitudes on the part of social scientists than from the epistemologic underpinnings that have informed their research.

DEFICIENCY VERSUS SUBSTANCE: CONSIDERATIONS FOR FUTURE RESEARCH

In this chapter we have described two different approaches to social science research on minority groups—deficiency formulations that derive from comparisons with mainstream groups and substantive accounts that are the product of naturalistic observations of behavior in its cultural context. We now discuss some key contrasts between them in the hope that by clarifying them we may help to alert future researchers to the pitfalls that have ensnared otherwise sympathetic researchers into portraying culturally distinctive minorities as incompetent versions of mainstream groups.

Descriptions of Behavior

A main purpose of description is to provide content for analysis. Whenever we describe the characteristics of events or persons, we inevitably utilize labels and categories to specify what we perceive as distinctive about them. In deficiency formulations, concepts are typically constructed by reference to a prescribed configuration of traits or significant features. Observations are then made in terms of the presence or absence of these defining features, or their relative strength. The concept of "self-control" provides an example. Persons are labeled as "having self-control" if they react calmly to frustration and provocation, if they choose to maximize long-term interests rather than short-term gains, if they persist at designated tasks no matter how boring they are, and so on. Such concepts imply the existence of a scale from "all defining characteristics present, and in full strength" to "all defining characteristics absent." Contrasts are made along such a scale, with the degree of differentiation dependent on the purposes of the person doing the describing. Concepts of this type lead us to search for order (which is the essence of the scientific task) by looking for a high density of the defining characteristics and, where they are of low density, to discover apparent disorder. For example, if the concept of "family" requires certain behavioral patterns from husbands and wives, the absence of these patterns is an indication of chaos, or "disorganization."

There are a number of advantages to employing such "ideal-type" definitions that have made them attractive to social scientists. Ideal types provide a basis for abstraction and hence comparison, thereby facilitating the formulation of universally applicable theory (which always involves comparison). They also lend themselves to quantification, allowing precise operations to be performed on their informational content. However, these very capabilities can lead to disembodied descriptions of people, transforming them into objects composed of bundles of traits in greater or lesser degree. Those with a high density of the defining characteristics can be described substantively, but those with a low density emerge as vacuous, shadow figures whose outlines are prescribed by the characteristics of others. Deficiency formulations thrive on such conceptualizations, and when strong positive value loadings are placed on the defining characteristics and the sense of order they imply, people who do not possess them are inevitably portrayed as social pariahs.[8]

When a naturalistic approach is adopted, concepts are derived differently. The commitment of naturalism is to remain as true as possible to phenomena and their nature. Its loyalty is to the experiential world (Matza, 1969, pp. 1–10). The aim of naturalistic accounts is to describe a phenomenon in a manner that maintains the phenomenon's integrity rather than the integrity of a particular theoretical viewpoint. A basic assumption of the naturalistic approach is that human behavior is purposeful, and that persons participate in defining social reality in an active way. For this reason humans are seen as transcending the physical realm in which conceptions of cause, force, and mechanical reactivity are readily applicable. When approaching the study of humans, therefore, naturalism compels the adoption of a subjective view and consequently requires supplementing more rigorous scientific methods with the distinctive tools of humanism—personal experience, intuition, and empathy. The descriptive aim of naturalism is a faithful rendition of human activity, even though only an approximation of that ideal is ever actually possible.

Naturalistically oriented social scientists attempt to learn how characteristics cluster together empirically through the development of substantive accounts. They assume that order exists and define their task as that of identifying the characteristics and distinguishing features that are the basis of that order. Concepts are then generated out of the various ways in which these distinguishing features are observed to combine in ordinary circumstances or under experimental conditions. The previously discussed polarity "field independent/field dependent" used by Ramirez and Castaneda (1974) provides a simple example. Each concept describes a set of perceptual habits that contrast with one another. As additional correlated perceptual or behavioral characteristics are observed in natural or experimental settings, the concepts can be given additional substance so that each contains a high density of information. Neither is defined in terms of the absence of features characterizing the other.

Social scientists are able to generate concepts with a high density of information about the people they are describing through efforts to reconstruct social reality from the perspective of the actors who are their subjects. One obvious way is to employ concepts used by the people themselves. An example is Rodman's study of lower-class family life in Trinidad, in which he employs the local terms "friending" (a quasimarital relationship in which the couple resides separately) and "living" (a relationship based on common residence without legal marriage) as a means of describing patterns of male–female alliances rather than relying on vacuous and uninformative statements about deviations from legal marital norms (Rodman, 1971). Keil's exploration of the term "soul" in the black community is another example (Keil, 1966).

Whether or not they utilize terms employed by the people they describe, social scientists with substantive concerns require a good deal of input from their subjects before arriving at descriptive categories. Their concern is that the categories contain a high density of information, rich in meaning for the people being studied. To be suitable vessels for describing how people manage their lives, such concepts must necessarily take into account the principles by which those persons organize the information they acquire about the world in which they live. It is important for the naturalist to know what contrasts in the overall stream of events are meaningful to those being described, so that an excessive amount of information is not lost at conceptual boundaries. To do this requires intensive interaction with the subjects of study, the use of open-ended questions, and opportunities to observe people in natural settings.

Naturalistic accounts require a relaxation of the rules of scientific method as these have traditionally been applied in the physical sciences. Where substantive knowledge is unavailable about a minority group, or a specific segment of it, it is necessary to arrive at a description that can serve as a source of hypotheses for further research; to do so requires free reign for intuition and interpretation of qualitative data and the freedom to manipulate quantitative data to check the credibility of emerging understandings. That is, the goal of such research is to generate grounded theory (Glaser & Strauss, 1967) or, ethnographically, to develop a theory of the culture being studied (Goodenough, 1957). This contrasts with the hypothesis-testing emphasis in the physical science model of inquiry, where a body of substantive knowledge informs theory construction and data collection. As Howard and Gallimore have shown, there is a role for experimentation in substantive research with minority groups (Howard, 1974; Gallimore et al., 1974; see also Bronfenbrenner, 1976), but it is used more for generating hypotheses than for testing them. By planning experiments on the basis of extensive substantive accounts, researchers are able to distinguish usual from unusual behavior during experiments. The research done by Cole and associates among the Kpelle in Africa provides an excellent example of the value of experimentation in conjunction with ethnography for researching cognition in a culturally different group (Cole, Gay, Glick, & Sharp, 1971). Their approach would serve well as a model for research among minority populations in complex societies.

Deficiency formulations stem from a tradition that emphasizes generality and attempts to explain behavior by recourse to abstracted forms. Naturalistic accounts, in contrast, are as much concerned with the context of behavior as with its forms. There are two main reasons for this. First, the meaning of behavior to people cannot be ascertained without taking into account the circumstances under which it occurs, since context partly determines the meaning actions have for individuals. Second, the naturalists' commitment to treating people as subjects (actors) rather than objects (reactors) requires that their purposes and goals be understood, a task that necessitates relating behavior to the circumstances in which it occurs. To ignore context, as deficiency formulations are prone to do, has the effect of treating behavior as the product of mechanical forces and of reducing individuals to the status of physical objects. They are thereby deprived of their humanity, inadvertently justifying manipulative intervention in their lives without serious consideration being given to their wants, leading to a situation in which social scientific information is used *against* the poor rather than *for* them, as Hampden-Turner persuasively argues (Hampden-Turner, 1974).

A related characteristic of deficiency formulations, which further dehumanizes those who are studied, is the tendency to focus on intragroup regularities and intergroup contrasts, thereby leading to the development of stereotypic images. By contrast, the naturalistic approach includes a manifest concern for intragroup variability. Social scientists of this persuasion attempt to identify significant social and economic differences within a minority group, as well as variant patterns on subcultural themes that may not be shared with the mainstream groups. The theoretical importance of paying attention to intragroup variation is illustrated by the research of Howard and Gallimore, which showed that intragroup differences in achievement behavior among Hawaiian-Americans are accounted for by different variables than those that explain between group differences (Howard, 1974; Gallimore et al., 1974).

There are two aspects of context that should be of particular concern for students of human development researching minority groups in complex societies. One is the context of developing capabilities, the other the context of performance. We have emphasized the importance of the family literature precisely because the family provides such an important part of the context of human development. When the family is conceived as disorganized and malfunctioning, researchers are almost invariably led to look for pathology in development. When family life is looked upon as healthy and constructive, the tendency is to see development in similar terms. For this reason it is important to have substantive descriptions of family structure and functioning among the groups we study. To take the issue still further, the context of family life within the broader ethnic community is necessary to assess the impact of the family as an institution on human development. Where extensive affiliation is valued among kin, the boundaries of the nuclear family may be porous and socialization functions diffused. To call families disorganized under such conditions because individuals spend much of their time and resources away from "home" is to look for organization at the wrong level, in the wrong place. Among groups that stress even broader affiliative values—inclusive of neighbors, peers, and workmates —the travesty is even greater. Thus an appreciation of the organizational principles that do in fact operate in people's lives is necessary for comprehending the context of development. Likewise, grasping the significance of an individual's performance, whether under experimental or "natural" conditions, requires an appreciation for the way in which those conditions fit into the broader context of an individual's experience. Substantive ethnographic knowledge of a group's sociocultural system is a minimum necessity for making a relevant assessment.

Lest the naturalist viewpoint be mistaken for one of extreme cultural relativism, we wish to make it clear that we are not advocating descriptions that are so highly individualized that comparisons are impossible or that portray everyone, every-where, as paragons of virtue. To insist that content as well as form is required for adequate description, and that context is necessary for understanding behavior, is not to deny the importance of comparison. It is, however, a position that makes comparison more complex and more difficult; this we perceive as a challenge to be met rather than as a deterrent. The important point is that the types of oversimplifi-cation resulting from deficiency formulations have led to inadequate description and have therefore retarded productive comparisons. Likewise, the highly pejorative descriptions that characterized deficiency accounts have had a pernicious effect on our understanding of developmental processes by narrowing the focus of research concerns to limited and, from some standpoints, trivial questions. For example, such questions as, How much intelligence do people have? Who has more and who has less? How much intelligence is normal? and so on are far less interesting from a substantivist viewpoint than how people use the intelligence they have, what condi-tions pattern perception and cognition, and so on. From this latter point of view, the idea that people lack motivation is incomprehensible. Just to stay alive requires motivation; the questions of importance concern what types of motivation exist and how they are patterned. While it is true that such a perspective tends to reduce the value judgments implicit in deficiency research, it does not obviate the possibility of evaluation. What it does do is open the door to a wider range of premises for making evaluative judgments. Whereas deficient intelligence is a "problem" vis-à-vis high intelligence, the question of whether achievement or affiliation is a superior motive, or whether field independence is a more suitable cognitive mode than field depen-dence, leaves greater room for debate.

Explanation

One of the most frequent objections to deficiency research is that it implies that the problem lies *within* the group or the individuals who compose it. Thus the Moynihan Report implies that something is wrong with the black family; so too the concepts of "cultural deprivation" and "culture of poverty" have the effect of blaming the victim. Although the ultimate explanation may be sought in economic deprivation, racism, or some other sociocultural condition, the immediate cause of the presumed deficiency is the failure of the family to perform its designated functions satisfactorily, particularly socialization. It is the family that needs to be changed if the deficits are to be removed. As critics have pointed out, this not only adds insult to injury, it creates a charter for intervention into the lives of people, often against their will. The overall paradigm parallels the medical model. Behavioral "symptoms" indicate the presence of "pathology," which indicates a defect within the organism that must be corrected to restore "health." While some critics have turned this around, locating pathology within the dominant group or power elite (providing a charter for revolutionary change), we would argue that a more satisfactory explanatory position is that behavior can be meaningfully regarded as pathologic only in the context of a system of relations. From this perspective, pathology must be located in the *relationships* that generate and support the behavior patterns involved, not within individual actors or groups of actors (Bateson et al., 1956). Pathology from this standpoint is best conceived as an ailment of the (social) system, not of the component subsystems or individual components, except in extreme cases, i.e., cases in which no possible reorganization would adaptively integrate the components involved.

When we adopt such a position it obliges us to portray culturally distinctive populations from a perspective that treats the values of the dominant group as problematic, rather than accepting them as "normal." To the extent that these values contribute to the genesis and maintenance of relationships that are maladaptive for component subsystems (such as ethnic groups), they are part of, and significant causes of, the pathology. To imply that *people* are pathologic because they deviate from such values is, from this standpoint, a paradoxic absurdity.

Finally, deficiency formulations have a built-in limitation that at best results in weak theory. Thus the basic form of deficiency formulations relies on propositions that distinguish A from $not\ A$ (normal from not normal). The burden of explanation is to identify conditions (e.g., economic differences) that differentiate one from the other, but since $not\ A$ may be a class that contains an enormous amount of internal variation, a wide range of additional variables may be at work that can be ignored. Substantive theory, in contrast, requires a form that distinguishes A from $B, C, D, E, \ldots$ The burden of such theory is to explain the manner in which each group is alike and different from each other group in a contrastive set. It is therefore more genuinely comparative and better suited for the generation of a cross-cultural theory of human development—one that will take into account significant variation within complex social systems as well as between them.

CONCLUSION

Quite clearly, deficiency theory and substantive theory have very different implications for action programs aimed at improving the lot of minority groups and at reducing inequality within modern societies. The implications of deficiency theory are quite clearcut. The current macrosystem is taken for granted, mainstream norms are accepted as valid, and the solution suggested is to generate conditions that will make it possible for minority populations to assimilate in the sense of achieving a reasonable level of economic success and social respectability. The strategies called for are remedial, involving the removal of deficits by correcting inappropriate organizational patterns, attitudes, and behaviors. Appropriate cognitive skills and motives are to be instilled so that performance levels can be raised to acceptable standards. The tactics called for vary, depending on the specific deficits at issue and their presumed causes as well as upon pragmatic assumptions concerning what is practicable, but the goals are inherent in the perspective itself.

From a substantive viewpoint the issues are far more complex. The current structure of the macrosystem and its mainstream norms are regarded as problematic. Indeed, the perspective calls into question the viability of such a system over the long run, and at least one significant issue it poses concerns alternative macrosystemic structures that would reduce inequality and nurture cultural pluralism. Many believe such a radical restructuring to be prerequisite to any lasting solution to the problem of minority groups, although there is considerable difference of opinion as to what a viable structure would be like, and how it could be evolved.

But even if the current system is accepted as given, the substantivist position entails a different view of the issues and is suggestive of a different set of strategies and tactics. Whereas failure to perform adequately according to mainstream norms is interpreted as an indication of general incompetence from a deficiency standpoint, from the substantivist point of view it is evidence, at most, of an inability or unwillingness to perform under specific conditions. From the latter perspective, general statements concerning competence can be inferred only after performance has been examined in a range of contexts that duplicates the variety of circumstances in which people ordinarily behave. This means taking into account an actor's subculture and the way it defines situations and standards for determining the adequacy of performance. In other words, poor performance in one cultural milieu does not necessarily preclude the possibility of competence—the ability to produce adequate performances—in another. This view presumes that complex societies are multicultural by nature and that minority group members are likely to be bicultural (or multicultural) in at least some senses.

If we accept the proposition that competence in the dominant culture is desirable for everyone, on the grounds that failures in the public domain are costly for the individuals involved as well as for society at large, then the strategy suggested by the substantivist perspective calls for identifying those areas of competence people have developed in their subcultures and building upon them. Instead of dwelling upon deficits, this calls for focusing upon their strengths. The assumption is that it is easier to build upon existing competencies and motives—e.g., interpersonal sensitivities, affiliative motives, etc.—than it is to deny them or attempt to eradicate them.

Perhaps the ultimate conclusion to which one is drawn is that the deficiency perspective, by labeling people as incompetent, tends to generate remedial structures that perpetuate powerlessness and dependence, thereby validating the initial judgments. It is hoped that the developing substantivist perspective will lead to structural arrangements that will not only recognize but actively reinforce alternate competencies and, by so doing, optimize conditions in which all parties can increase the scope of their adaptive repertoires.

NOTES

1. For other studies reporting this view, see Lott and Lott, 1963; Rosen, 1959.

2. For similar statements about black culture, see Glazer and Moynihan, 1963, as cited in Blauner, 1970, p. 132; and Frazier, 1957, p. 301.

3. Clark echoes this view, stating, "The child without a secure family is often forced either into aggression and delinquency or into apathy and despair" (Clark, 1965, p. 47). Moynihan (1965) makes essentially the same argument.

4. An interesting variation on deficiency explanations is provided by Gans in his study of lower-class Italian-Americans. He describes his subjects as "operating without a self-image" (Gans, 1962, p. 98). They "develop a deficient 'me' with a different type of 'generalized other' [leading to] a lack of inner self" (Gans, 1962, p. 98). He explains this as a consequence of person-oriented values: "The person-oriented type develops a monastic self, which makes it difficult for the individual to differentiate between his own and others' view[s] of him. The lack of a clear self-image encourages and requires display. Thus the communication process between the 'I' and other people is limited as much as possible to routine behavior among intimately known people. When the process is disturbed, the individual becomes selfish (p. 101). At the same time Gans explains their custom of bringing gifts of food when visiting as a result of their lack of self-image: "While they give of themselves as freely as other people, they cannot conceive of themselves doing so. . . . The West Ender cannot conceive of the self that he gives. Therefore he brings gifts when he goes visiting" (p. 99; see also Miller & Swanson, 1960).

5. See Keller's admonitions concerning descriptions of lower-class families (Keller, 1970, p. 71), noted in the opening pages of this chapter. Also see Jessie Bernard, who writes that her "deliberate and purposive exclusion of control data on the white population is based on the assumption that such comparisons usually turn out to be studies of the white population with emphasis on nonwhite data as representing deviations from a white norm" (Bernard, 1966, p. vii), and Oscar Lewis, who states in his introduction to *La Vida* that "in writing about multiproblem families . . . social scientists often stress the instability, the lack of organization, lack of direction and lack of order. Certainly there are many contradictory attitudes and inconsistencies expressed in these autobiographies. Nevertheless, it seems to me that their behavior is clearly patterned and reasonably predictable. Indeed, one is often struck by the inexorable repetition and the iron entrenchment of these behavior patterns" (Lewis, 1966, p. xxviii). He advises that "middle class people, and this would certainly include some social scientists, tend to concentrate on the negative aspects of the culture of poverty. . . . They tend to assign negative values to such traits as present-time orientation and concrete versus abstract orientation. . . . Yet some of the positive aspects which may flow from these traits must not be overlooked" (Lewis, 1966, p. li).

6. For a discussion of this point, see Mills, 1943.

7. The idea of a singular, universal truth is a basic element that pervades Western thought. Perhaps the most fundamental manifestation of this idea is monotheistic belief in a single, omniscient, omnipotent God.

8. See Glaser and Strauss, 1967, for a discussion of this point. For an excellent discussion of this problem as it relates to social science research on deviant behavior, see Matza, 1969.

REFERENCES

Antonovsky, A., & Lerner, M. Occupational aspirations of lower class negro and white youths. *Social Problems*, 1959, *7*, 132–138.

Aschenbrenner, J. *Lifelines: Black families in Chicago.* New York: Holt, Rinehart & Winston, 1975.

Banfield, E. *The unheavenly city.* Boston: Little, Brown, 1970.

Bateson, G., Jackson, D. D., Haley, J., & Weakland, J. H. Toward a theory of schizophrenia. *Behavioral Science*, 1956, *1*, 251–264.

Beman, A. Piagetian theory examined cross-culturally. Unpublished doctoral dissertation, Rice University, 1972.

Berger, B. Black culture or lower-class culture? In L. Rainwater (Ed.), *Soul.* Chicago: Aldine, 1970.

Bernard, J. *Marriage and the family among Negroes.* Englewood Cliffs, N.J.: Prentice-Hall, 1966.

Bernstein, B. Social structure, language and learning. *Educational Research*, 1961, *3*, 163–176.

Billingsley, A. Black families in white America. Englewood Cliffs, N.J.: Prentice-Hall, 1968.

Blake, J. Family instability and reproductive behavior in Jamaica. In *Current Research in Human Fertility.* New York: Milbank Memorial Fund, 1955.

Blauner, R. Black culture: Lower-class result or ethnic creation? In L. Rainwater (Ed.), *Soul.* Chicago: Aldine, 1970.

Brazziel, W. Correlates of southern Negro personality. *Journal of Social Issues*, 1964, *20* (2), 46–53.

Bronfenbrenner, U. The experimental ecology of human development. Unpublished position paper, Foundation for Child Development, Cornell University, 1976.

Caldwell, M. Personality trends in the youthful male offender. *Journal of Criminal Law, Criminology and Police Science*, 1959, *49*, 405–416.

Cayton, H. The psychology of the Negro under discrimination. In A. Rose (Ed.), *Race, prejudice and discrimination.* New York: Knopf, 1951.

Clark, K. *Dark Ghetto.* New York: Harper & Row, 1965.

Clark, K., & Potkin, L. A review of the issues and literature of cultural deprivation theory. In *The Educationally Deprived.* New York: Metropolitan Applied Research Center, 1972.

Cohen, A. K., & Hodges, H., Jr. Characteristics of the lower-blue-collar class. *Social Problems*, 1963, *10*, 303–334.

Cohen, R. A. Conceptual styles, culture conflict and nonverbal tests of intelligence. *American Anthropologist*, 1969, *71*, 828–856.

Cole, M., Gay, J., Glick, J. A., & Sharp, D. W. *The cultural context of learning and thinking.* London: Methuen, 1971.

Cothram, T. C. Negro stereotyped conceptions of the white liberal. *Arkansas Academy of Science Proceedings*, 1951, *4*, 123–129.

Davis, A., & Dollard, J. *Children of bondage.* Washington, D.C.: American Council of Education, 1940.

Deutsch, M. Minority groups and class status as related to social and personality factors in scholastic achievement. *Monographs of the Society for Applied Anthropology*, 1960, *2*.

Deutsch, M. The disadvantaged child and the learning process. *Integrated Education*, 1963, *1*, 11–12.

Deutsch, M., et al. *The disadvantaged child.* New York: Basic Books, 1967.

Ellison, R. *Shadow and act.* New York: Random House, 1964.

Etkowitz, H., & Shaflander, G. *Ghetto crisis: Riots or reconciliation?* Boston: Little, Brown, 1969.

Frazier, F. *The Negro in the United States.* Chicago: University of Chicago Press, 1957.

Gallimore, R., Boggs, J., & Jordan, C. *Culture, behavior and education: A Study of Hawaiian-Americans.* Beverly Hills: Sage, 1974.

Gans, H. *The urban villagers.* New York: Free Press, 1962.

Getzels, J. W., & Jackson, P. W. *Creativity and intelligence.* New York: John Wiley & Sons, 1962.

Ginsburg, H. *The myth of the deprived child: Poor children's intellect and education.* Englewood Cliffs, N.J.: Prentice-Hall, 1972.

Glaser, B., & Strauss, A. *The discovery of grounded theory.* Chicago: Aldine, 1967.

Glazer, N., & Moynihan, D. *Beyond the melting pot.* Cambridge: MIT Press & Harvard Press, 1963.

Goodenough, W. Cultural anthropology and linguistics. In P. Garvin (Ed.), *Report of the seventh annual round table meeting on linguistics and language study.* Monograph Serieš on Language and Linguistics. Washington, D.C.: Georgetown University, 1957.

Graves, N. Egocentrism and cultural deprivation: Empirical evidence for the ethnocentrism of Piagetian theory. *South Pacific Research Institute Report No. 12,* Auckland, New Zealand, 1976.

Graves, N., & Graves, T. Inclusive versus exclusive behavior in New Zealand school settings: Polynesian-Pakeha contrasts in learning styles. *South Pacific Research Institute Report No. 5,* Auckland, New Zealand, 1974.

Grossack, M. M. Group belongingness and authoritarianism in southern Negroes— A research note. *Phylon,* 1957, *18,* 261–266. (a)

Grossack, M. M. Some personality characteristics of southern Negro students. *Journal of Social Psychology,* 1957, *46,* 125–131. (b)

Guba, E. G., Jackson, P., & Bidwell, C. Occupational choice and the teaching career. *Educational Research Bulletin,* 1959, *38,* 1–12, 27–28.

Hampden-Turner, C. *From poverty to dignity: A strategy for poor Americans.* Garden City, N.Y.: Anchor, 1974.

Hannerz, U. The significance of soul. In L. Rainwater (Ed.), *Soul.* Chicago: Aldine, 1970.

Hertzig, M. E., Birch, H. G., Thomas, A., & Mendez, O. A. Class and ethnic differences in the responsiveness of preschool children to cognitive demands. *Monographs of the Society for Research in Child Development,* 1968, *33* (117).

Hill, R. *The strength of black families.* New York: National Urban League, 1972.

Horton, J. Time and cool people. In L. Rainwater (Ed.), *Soul.* Chicago: Aldine, 1970.

Howard, A. *Learning to be Rotuman.* New York: Columbia Teachers College, 1970.

Howard, A. *Households, families and friends in a Hawaiian-American community* (Working Paper No. 19). Honolulu: East-West Population Institute, 1971.

Howard, A. *Ain't no big thing.* Honolulu: University Press of Hawaii, 1974.

Jensen, A. How much can we boost IQ and scholastic achievement? *Harvard Educational Review,* 1969, *39,* 1–123.

Jones, R. Proving blacks inferior: The sociology of knowledge. In J. A. Ladner (Ed.), *The death of white sociology.* New York: Random House, 1973.

Kagan, S., & Madsen, M. Cooperation and competition of Mexican, Mexican-American, and Anglo-American children of two ages under four instructional sets. *Developmental Psychology,* 1971, *5,* 32–39.

Kardiner, A., & Ovesey, L. *The mark of oppression.* New York: Norton, 1951.

Keil, C. *Urban blues.* Chicago: University of Chicago Press, 1966.

Keller, S. *The American lower class family.* Albany: New York State Division for Youth, 1970.

Labov, W., Cohen, P., Robins, C., & Lewis, J. *A study of the nonstandard English of Negro and Puerto Rican speakers in New York City* (2 Vols.). (Final Report, Cooperative Research Project No. 3288). Washington, D.C.: U.S. Office of Education, 1968.

Ladner, J. *Tomorrow's tomorrow: The black woman.* Garden City, N.Y.: Doubleday, 1971.

Ladner, J. Introduction. In J. Ladner (Ed.), *The death of white sociology.* New York: Random House, 1973.

Lesser, G. S., Fifer, G., & Clark, D. H. Mental abilities of children from different social-class and cultural groups. *Monographs of the Society for Research in Child Growth and Development,* 1965, *30* (4).

Levinger, G. Marital cohesiveness and dissolution: An integrative review. *Journal of Marriage and the Family,* 1965, *27,* 19–28.

Lewis, O. *La vida.* New York: Random House, 1966.

Lewis, O. Review of C. Valentine, *Culture and poverty: A critique and counter-proposals. Current Anthropology,* 1969, *10,* 189–192.

Liebow, E. *Tally's corner.* Boston: Brown, Little, 1967.

Liliuokalani Trust. *A survey of the socio-economic status of the Hawaiian people today.* Honolulu, 1962.

Lott, A. J., & Lott, B. E. *Negro and white youth.* New York: Holt, Rinehart & Winston, 1963.

McDaniel P., & Babchuk, N. Negro conceptions of white people in a Northeastern city. *Phylon,* 1960, *21,* 7–19.

Mackler, B., & Giddings, M. G. Cultural deprivation: A study in mythology. *Teachers College Record,* 1965, *66,* 608–613.

Madsen, M. Cooperative and competitive motivation of children in three Mexican subcultures. *Psychological Reports,* 1967, *20,* 1307–1320.

Madsen, M., & Shapira, A. Cooperative and competitive behavior of urban Afro-American, Anglo-American and Mexican village children. *Developmental Psychology,* 1970, *3,* 16–20.

Matza, D. *Becoming deviant.* Englewood Cliffs, N.J.: Prentice-Hall, 1969.

Miller, D., & Swanson, G. *Inner conflict and defense.* New York: Holt, Rinehard & Winston, 1960.

Mills, C. W. The professional ideology of social pathologists. *American Journal of Sociology,* 1943, *49,* 165–180.

Montagu, A. Sociogenic brain damage. *American Anthropologist,* 1972, *74,* 1045–1061.

Moynihan, D. P. Employment, income and the ordeal of the Negro family. *Daedalus,* 1965, *94,* 745–770.

Newsweek. The Negro in America. *Newsweek,* July 29, 1963, pp. 15–34.

Odum, H. Social and mental traits of the Negro. New York: Longmans, Green, 1910.

Piaget, J., & Inhelder, B. *The psychology of the child.* New York: Basic Books, 1969.

Pettigrew, T. *Profile of the Negro American.* Princeton: Van Nostrand, 1964.

Rainwater, L. *And the poor get children.* Chicago: Quadrangle Books, 1960.

Ramirez, M. III. Cognitive styles and cultural democracy in education. *Social Science Quarterly,* 1973, *53,* 895–904.

Ramirez, M., III, & Castaneda, A. *Cultural democracy, biocognitive development, and education.* New York: Academic Press, 1974.

Ramirez, M., III, & Price-Williams, D. Cognitive styles of children of three ethnic groups in the United States. *Journal of Cross-Cultural Psychology,* 1974, *5* (2).

Riessman, F. *The culturally deprived child.* New York: Harper & Row, 1962.

Rodman, H. *Lower-class families: The culture of poverty in Negro Trinidad.* New York: Oxford University Press, 1971.

Rohrer, J., & Edmondson, M. *The eighth generation grows up.* New York: Harper & Row, 1960.

Rosen, B. Race, ethnicity and the achievement syndrome. *American Sociological Review,* 1959, *24,* 47–60.

Rosow, I. And then we were old. *Trans-Action,* 1965, *2,* 21–26.

Schorr, A. The nonculture of poverty. *Proceedings of the American Orthopsychiatric Society Meetings,* 1963, p. 74.

Seeley, J. The slum. *Journal of the American Institute of Planners,* 1959, *25,* 7–14.

Stack, C. *All our kin.* New York: Harper & Row, 1974.

Stodolsky, S. S., & Lesser, G. Learning patterns in the disadvantaged. *Harvard Educational Review,* 1967, *37,* 546–593.

Stott, D. H. *Troublesome children.* New York: Humanities Press, 1966.

Valentine, C. *Culture and poverty: A critique and counter-proposals.* Chicago: University of Chicago Press, 1968.

Valentine, C., & Valentine, B. Brain damage and the intellectual defense of inequality. *Current Anthropology,* 1975, *16,* 117–150.

Witkin, H. A. Cognitive styles across cultures. *International Journal of Psychology,* 1967, *2,* 233–250.

Part II

Early Experience and Growth

❧ 7 ❧

Environmental Constraints on Infant Care Practices

John W. M. Whiting

This chapter deals with the first two steps in the model for psychocultural research (J. Whiting, 1973) which can be summarized as follows:

(1) Features in the history of any society and in the natural environment in which it is situated influence
(2) the customary methods by which infants are cared for in that society, which have
(3) enduring psychological and physiologic effects on the members of that society, which are manifested in
(4) the cultural projective–expressive systems of the society and the physiques of its members.

Some of the effects of variations in the manner in which infants are cared for (steps 2–4 in the model) have been summarized and reviewed in other chapters. Broude (Chapter 19 in this volume) presents evidence that the proportion of the day that an infant is held or carried is related to the cultural rules governing premarital sex. Brown (Chapter 17 in this volume) reports the relationship of the relative salience of the mother and father during infancy to female initiation ceremonies. Munroe, Munroe, and Whiting (Chapter 18 in this volume) present evidence that the salience of the father in infancy affects male sex role resolution. Landauer and Whiting (Chapter 10 in this volume) present evidence that stress during infancy affects the rate of physical growth.

Since the consequences of variations in infant care practices are, as indicated above, discussed extensively elsewhere in this volume, this chapter will focus on a detailed exploration of the variations in infant care by region, an analysis of the way in which they are patterned and how they are constrained by climate. The following world tour through the ethnographic reports describing infant care practices will make more meaningful scales to be used in the formal analysis.

In Africa, infants after the lying-in period and before they become active toddlers[1] spend most of their waking hours during the day on someone's back—usually the mother's, sometimes an older sister's. They are held in place by a shawl or animal skin, the ends of which are either passed diagonally over one of the carrier's shoulders and tied in front or passed under both arms and tied above the mother's breasts. The former method permits the infant to be brought around to the side to be held astride the carrier's hip rather than on the back.

Konner (1976) described the use of the sling by the !Kung San Bushmen of the Kalahari Desert in Botswana:

155

From the earliest days of life and throughout the first year, three positions characterize infant posture: (1) awake, held sitting or held standing in the lap of the mother or other caretaker (since there are no chairs, adults are typically sitting on the ground); (2) awake or asleep, in the infant sling at the mother's side; (3) asleep, lying on a cloth on the ground beside the mother is added to these three. Infants are rarely permitted to lie down while awake. Mothers consider that this is bad for motor development. . . .

The sling merits specific description because it differs in important ways from carrying devices in many other non-technological societies. . . . It is maximally non-restrictive, leaving the arms and legs moving freely. It allows constant skin-to-skin contact between mother and infant. And it keeps the infant on the mother's side (hip) rather than on her back or front. The side position has the following noteworthy features: (1) the infant sees what the mother sees, thus sharing her view of the social world and the world of objects, especially a close view of work in the mother's hands and eye-level contact with children, who take considerable interest in babies; (2) the infant has constant access to the mother's breasts, which are uncovered, and after the development of visually directed reaching feeds himself [or herself] whenever he likes (more or less continually); (3) the infant has constant access to cosmetic and decorative objects hanging around the mother's neck, and often occupies himself in playing with them. (Konner, 1976, pp. 220–222)

While awake, typical African infants spend most of their time in body contact with someone. Super (n.d.) reports for the Kipsigis, a back- and shawl-carrying culture, that in 70 percent of 593 spot observations of 25 infants under 1 year old, they were in body contact with a caretaker, and in only 4 percent were they out of the caretaker's reach (beyond 1 meter). Leiderman and Leiderman (1973) report very similar data for 67 Kikuyu infants observed during their first year (972 observations). They were in contact with the mother or another caretaker in 68 percent of the observations. Konner (1976) also reports similar findings for the !Kung San. In this case also, spot observations showed that infants were in physical contact with their mothers approximately 79 percent of the time at 10 and 20 weeks.

It should not be supposed that infants spend all their contact time in slings or shawls. This is particularly true during the first few months of life, since it is believed in many cultures that to stretch an infant's legs apart to the degree that they must be in the shawl on the back position would be harmful to the small infant. That this belief is acted on is indicated by Super's data. No infant was observed on the mother's back during the first or second month, and in only 4 of 55 observations were the infants observed on the back during the third and fourth months. During the next 6 months, Kipsigis infants spend 80 percent of their contact time on a caretaker's lap, in a shawl on their back, or on their hip without a sling.

Kipsigis infants who were asleep when observed ($n = 188$) were on their mother's back 16 percent of the time, but their usual position was lying on a rug or blanket —75 percent of the observations. Thus an infant who falls asleep on the caretaker's back is often permitted to remain there, but the infant on someone's lap or held in the arms is usually put down in a prone position.

Although not reported in detail in Super's Kipsigis study, most African societies use a mat or rug as the infant's napping place. Special baskets for carrying, napping, and resting are reported for some on the North African societies, particularly those situated in the Sudan savannah. These include the Nuer, the Shilluk, and the Shonghai. Huffman (1931) describes the Nuer basket:

A basket made of branches of a pliable wood is used as a baby-basket. A piece of animal skin which has had the hair scraped off smooth is put in the basket for the baby to lie on. If the mother has a piece of cloth she may cover the baby with it. Then a large woven grass mat is placed on top of the basket, being rolled up at each side until it just covers the top of the basket and also keeps an active baby from sitting while being carried. The Ahaggaren Tuareg in addition to such a basket use a hammock stretched between the poles of their tent as a resting place, and use a sling to carry the infant.

Before the advent of Christian missionaries, most infants in sub-Saharan Africa wore no clothes, and the mother, except for the carrying shawl, was topless. Thus while being carried the infant was in skin contact with the mother. Nowadays, infants are sometimes dressed in a short cotton shirt, and the mothers wear a thin blouse or dress.

Except in modern families, diapers are not used, but the infant is "held out" when the caretaker anticipates upcoming urination or defecation. A method that may have been widely used, although it is not reported in the literature, is described by deVries and deVries (1977) for the Giriama of Kenya. The mother sits on the edge of a porch with her legs outstretched and slightly apart. Arms outstretched, she holds the infant astride her legs just above the ankles. deVries reports that infants quickly learn that this is a signal to defecate.

Finally, African infants typically sleep next to their mothers on a sleeping mat or platform. Since night clothes are usually not worn by either mother or infant, prolonged skin-to-skin contact is again the rule.

The typical pattern for infant care for Africa has been described above. Exceptions and variations will be noted when the data from all regions are pooled and compared.

Infant care in Eurasia is quite different from the pattern described for Africa. Only in a few societies is the infant carried in a sling or shawl. Elsewhere, it is moved about in a transportable cradle (in which the infant may be moved about in the house and carried to the field where the mother is working). Where reindeer, horses, or camels are used for transport or travel, the infant is bound to the cradle, which is either lashed to the saddle of the transport animal or to the sled or wagon or is held by a riding caretaker. In most instances, cradles are too heavy for the mother to carry handily on her back or side, but the Lapps use a light hollow trough with a hood which the mother may strap to her back. Colinder (1949, p. 68) reports,

On journeys, the mother carries the cradle with the baby in it on her back if she walks or goes on skis. On longer trips, the cradle is often hung on one side of a pack reindeer, with an adequate counterpoise on the other side.

The baby carriage or cradle on wheels is the common method of carrying infants in Western Europe. According to Jelliffe (1975), perambulators were first made in England in the early 18th century.

As might be expected if a transportable cradle is used as a carrying device, it is also used as a place for the infant to rest and nap during the day and to sleep in at night. In every instance of a Eurasian cradle culture in which such a judgment could be made from the ethnographic evidence, the infant was held or carried by the mother or other caretaker less than half the time. Lewis and Ban (1977, p. 340) report the results of systematic home observations of mothers and infants in Yugoslavia—a cradle culture. Eighteen 3-month-old infants and their mothers were observed for 1 hr during the day while they were awake (eyes open). Whether or not the infants were being touched or held by the mother was recorded for each 10-sec interval. By this measure, the Yugoslav infant was in direct contact with the mother 27 percent of the time. This compares with 70 percent reported above for the shawl-carrying Kipsigis.

Even when the infant is held or carried in the cradle cultures of Europe and Central Asia, the infant is separated from the mother by thick clothing. Many of the societies, particularly in Eastern Europe, practice swaddling. This is described by Lee (1953, p. 97) for the Greek peasants as follows:

> Traditionally, the baby is swaddled all over, until it is a stiff bundle. Each knee is straightened out; in many regions, each leg is wrapped separately, and then the two are wrapped together; the arms are pressed to the sides and then the swaddling cloth is wrapped tightly over all.

Although this was not systematically coded, most cradles were either provided with rockers or built so that they could be suspended from a beam in the house or sometimes the limb of a tree. In some cultures, particularly in the Middle East, hammocks were used in place of or sometimes in addition to cradles. All of these devices permitted the infant to be rocked or swung, and this was reported to be done both to comfort the child and to put the child to sleep. In sling and shawl cultures, walking with the infant on the back or carrying out rhythmic domestic chores such as pounding grain with mortar and pestle serves the same function.

The disposal of urine and feces in climates where the temperature can fall below freezing creates a problem which peoples living in the tropics do not have to face. Adjustment to extreme cold is illustrated by the Chuckchee, who live in Eastern Siberia, just below the Arctic Circle. According to Sverdup (1938, p. 24),

> The children . . . as babies . . . are put in a fur bag with four extra bags for arms and legs, and with a big flap between the legs. The flap is filled with dry moss, which is changed everytime the baby cries. . . . When a child is to be taken out for an airing, the bag with the four smaller bags is put into a larger one which is rarely carried, but is dragged along the ground. The baby is propped up against a tree and is happy and comfortable even if the temperature goes far below zero.

Odulok (1954, p. 43) describes an episode in which a Chuckchee family with an infant shifted camp. The move was made on sleds pulled by reindeer. The baby in his fur bag rode on one of the sleds. The trip was long and the baby wet himself but could not be changed until the long trip was over. When they arrived at their destination, the mother removed the baby from his fur bags and found that the inner bag and moss were frozen to the baby's back and buttocks so that when it was removed some of the baby's skin came off with it. The wound was licked by a dog and anointed with grease. This episode illustrates the problem of urine disposal in cold countries. The use of disposable diapers of moss is also reported for the Lapps, whereas washable diapers were used in Western Europe. A unique solution is reported for a large group of societies in Central Asia. This is the urine tube reported for the Kurds, Afghans, Georgians, Armenians, Crimeans, and Kirghiz. The Kurdish version is described by Hansen (1961, pp. 100–101) as follows:

> In both the wooden base [of the cradle] and the mattress, there is a hole near the center. . . . A pipe-shaped wooden object is put vertically down through the hole. . . . If for a male child there is a circular opening at the head of the pipe, if

for a female, an oval one. This urinating tube is carefully wound round with rags in order that it shall not be uncomfortable when pressed up between the baby's legs. The child lies outstretched on its back with a cylindrical pillow . . . under the neck, and its arms extended along the body. In this position, it is bound fast. This is done with two padded bandages. At the end of these bandages there are straps through which is pulled a heavy woolen cord that is stretched out along the side of the cradle underneath from leg to leg.. . . One bandage is passed over the child's arms and chest, the other across the abdomen and legs, holding the urine discharge pipe in position.. . . A small rag is placed under the baby to absorb any excrement, urine being taken by the pipe.. . . A bottle could be hung under the cradle . . . in the winter . . . but in the summer . . . in rooms without carpets, liquids [were allowed to] run on the ground or floor.

According to Thomas Barfield (personal communication), a modern version of the urine tube is being sold in Kabul, Afghanistan. For boys, this has a plastic tube extension that fits over the penis. The pipe leads over the side of the cradle rather than between the infant's legs and out the bottom.

The shawl replaces the cradle as a carrying device in Korea, Japan, Okinawa, and Southern China as well as in some of the societies in Southern India. The family bed or sleeping platform provides a place where the infant rests, naps, and sleeps. In some of the societies in Southeast Asia a sling is used to carry an infant, but the infant rests and sleeps in a hanging cradle.

Sling or shawl as a carrying device and a mat as a napping place is, as in sub-Saharan Africa, typical of societies in islands of the Indian and Pacific Oceans. Infants are more often carried on the hip than on the back, and a higher proportion of the cases than in Africa report no carrying devices at all. The following description by Firth (1936) of infant care in Tikopia describes the most commonly occurring patterns in this region of the world:

> It is laid to sleep on a bed of bark-cloth, padded with many thicknesses, in the middle of the floor, and a little sheet of some soft material is laid over the top to protect it from flies or dust . . . A short supplementary piece of this stuff [bark cloth] is kept underneath its body and changed when necessary. (p. 139)
>
> As the child grows and its body gains strength it is carried round in the arms of the women of the household.. . . A sling of bark-cloth is used for an infant old enough to be held upright but unable to support itself, and in this it is set and carried on the back or on the side of its nurse. A broader piece of bark-cloth is also usually held as a shield over the head and side of the babe to protect it from the sun, since at this stage its skin is pale and delicate. Older children are held on the hip without the sling or carried pick-a-back fashion, and one of the common sights of the village in the early morning or evening is to see quite young boys and girls from about four years of age upwards, acting as carriers for younger brothers and sisters in this way, neither of the pair wearing a stitch of clothing. (p. 141)
>
> By the women of the house, who of course are clothed in the bark-cloth skirt, a curious method of supporting the child is in vogue: its stands upright at the back of its nurse, using her waistbelt as a foothold, digging in its small toes and grasping her shoulders with its hands. (p. 140)

There are some variations that should be mentioned. The Aranda of Australia are reported to sometimes place infants in a shallow wooden trough used otherwise for carrying vegetables. Since there is no indication that the infant is bound in this trough, it is unlikely that the infant spends much time in it. A wicker basket is used as a carrier and resting device in Ifaluk, a Micronesian atoll. This was presumably introduced by a Christian missionary. In New Guinea and some of the nearby islands, a net bag called a bilum in Pidgin English is used as a portable hammock. It is a large, completely flexible, tightly woven net bag which, when being used as a carrying device, hangs over the mother's back, reaching to her buttocks. Hogbin (1943, p. 298) describes its use by the Wogeo as follows:

> At night the baby sleeps enfolded in its mother's arms on the floor, but in the daytime, when not actually nursing it, she puts it into a basket [net bag] which is then hung on a convenient rafter near where she is working. This receptacle, though generally new and always lined carefully with soft green leaves, is of the ordinary type for carrying vegetables from the garden, and as it is fully fifteen inches deep and no effort is made to keep the top open, the inside must be both dark and stuffy. The child rarely makes any objection, nevertheless, and usually lies quiet even when awake.. . . It is always removed and carried about when really irritable, but an attempt is usually made to still its cries first by rocking the basket gently to and fro, or by scratching the outside.

The New Guinea Fore, who use the net bag in much the same manner as the Wogeo, are not reported to convert it into a hammock by hanging it up. During my field work among the Kwoma, who also use the bilum for carrying infants, I never saw an infant hung up in a bag. The infant, when not being carried, was usually held in the lap or arms.

Thus in general infants are cared for in the insular Pacific in much the same way as they are in Africa. They are in skin-to-skin contact with their caretaker most of the day and night.

Infant care in North America is similar to that in Eurasia. All societies between latitudes 32° and 55° N use the cradleboard. Although there are minor variations in its construction, the general form was similar to that described by Morgan (1901, p. 57) for the Iroquois when he observed them (1844–1850):

> The baby-frame . . . is an Indian invention. It appears to have been designed as a convenience to the Indian mother for the transportation of her infant, rather than, as has generally been supposed, to secure an erect figure. The frame is about two feet in length by about fourteen inches in width, with a carved footboard at the small end, and a hoop or bow at the head, arching over at right angles. After being enclosed in a blanket, the infant is lashed upon the frame with belts of bead-work, which firmly secure and cover its person, with the exception of the face. A separate article for covering the face is then drawn over the bow, and the child is wholly protected. When carried, the burden-strap attached to the frame is placed around the forehead of the mother and the [baby-frame] upon her back. This frame is often elaborately carved, and its ornaments are of the choicest description.

Although their infants are similar to Eurasian infants in that they are heavily swaddled and bound to a cradle, Iroquois and other native Americans use cradleboards that differ in that they are constructed of light material so that they can be carried more easily, and they lack legs or rockers which are common in the Eurasian model. When carried, the cradleboard is strapped to the mother's back with the infant facing backward, away from the mother. Whenever possible, the cradle is kept upright by being leaned against some object or being hung in an upright position from the branch of a tree or tent pole. The Eurasian cradle, by contrast, is generally in a horizontal position even when it is suspended from a rafter.

Whatever the psychological effect of an upright versus a prone position might be, the problem of urine disposal is solved more efficiently by the native American cradleboards than by the Eurasian horizontal cradles. A disposable diaper of dry moss or the like and a hole at the end of the cradle suffices.

The Eskimo and most native tribal groups in the Northern polar region do not use a cradleboard. Infants are carried on the mother's back under her parka, which is belted at the waist and loose at the shoulders, thus forming a sort of rucksack. The infant faces the mother and is in close contact, but since both wear undergarments skin-to-skin contact is not achieved. When not being carried, Eskimo infants are laid on the sleeping platform inside the igloo or tent.

South of the Rio Grande, the sling or shawl (rebozo) or the arms replace the cradleboard as a carrying device, but a boxlike cradle is reported as a resting place in several cultures in this area. A hammock or mat, however, is more commonly used for this purpose. Infants also usually sleep in their mother's bed, though in some cultures baby hammocks are used for sleeping.

This pattern spreads all the way south to Patagonia, where the cradleboard reappears. Constructed in a way quite similar to the North American cradle board, it is used both as a carrying device and for sleeping and resting.

From this brief world survey, two things become evident. First, societies in the same region generally have similar methods of infant care which, quite probably, they have borrowed from one another. This is particularly clear for the more elaborately constructed cradles of Eurasia, the cradleboards of North America, and the net bags of New Guinea. The sling or shawl is such a simple idea that it may well have been reinvented frequently. It is also clear that the diffusion of infant care practices is neither random nor in concentric circles from some point of origin. The spread of these customs is constrained by rather rigid boundaries that seem to be closely related to climatic isotherms.

The relationship of various infant care practices to climate for world samples of cultures has been previously reported (J. Whiting, 1964). Where the winter climate is hot or mild (the average temperature for the coldest month is $\geq 10°C$ [50°F]), mothers and infants sleep in the same bed or on the same mat in 85 percent of 91 cases. By contrast, where the winter climate is cool or cold (the average temperature for the coldest month falls below 10°C), only in 29 percent of 45 cases do mother and infant sleep together; in the remainder infants sleep separately in a crib or cradle.

Since in many cultures sleeping arrangements are a private affair, specific ethnographic reports are often lacking and judgments are often made inferentially or cannot be made at all. In studies by Ayres (1973) and J. Whiting (1971) which focused on carrying and resting devices, sleeping arrangements were also coded. Of 135 societies, ratings could be made in but 44 percent of the cases. Barry and Paxson (1971) also coded sleeping arrangements on the standard sample (Murdock & White, 1969) with virtually the same results. They were able to rate with confident judgments only 46 percent of the cases. Furthermore, of the 114 cases that were rated in both studies, there was but 75 percent agreement.

Whether or not cradles were used as a carrying device was also coded in these studies. By contrast, judgments could be made in 84 and 83 percent, respectively, of the cases, and the agreement on the 78 overlapping cases was 91 percent. This contrast between the inference level of sleeping arrangements and carrying devices is not suprising. Infants on a mother's back, in her arms, or bound in a cradleboard are a favorite subject for illustrative photographs appearing in the ethnographic accounts, and low-inference judgments can be made from them. Furthermore, how an infant is cared for during the day is more often described in detail than where the infant sleeps at night.

Where a child rests when not being carried was also coded in the Ayres–Whiting work. The available ethnographic data for coding this variable permitted judgment on 65 percent of the sample—better than sleeping arrangements but not as good as carrying devices. Since there was no variable that corresponded exactly to resting devices in the Barry and Paxson study, a reliability check could not be made.

The proportion of the day that an infant was held or carried, however, was coded in these studies. This was also apparently a high-inference variable. Only 56 percent of the Ayres and Whiting sample and 35 percent of the Barry and Paxson sample could be coded confidently. Furthermore, the coding agreement was only 73 percent on the 26 cases that were rated in both studies.

Fortunately, all these variables are strongly related to one another and most importantly to the carrying devices, which is the most codable and most highly reliable datum and which requires the least inference from available ethnographic material. If cradles are used for carrying infants, they are also usually used as a resting device ($\phi = 0.79$) and as a place for the infant to sleep ($\phi = 0.51$). Furthermore, infants are carried and held less if there is a cradle to carry them ($\phi = 0.64$), and infants are heavily swaddled in cradle cultures ($\phi = 0.54$). Carrying devices can therefore be used as the best single index of the amount of physical contact between mother and infant.

For the above reasons it was decided to concentrate our analysis on carrying devices. First the Ayres and Whiting sample was combined with the Barry and Paxson sample. The few cases (14 percent) in which there was coding disagreement were either omitted or a judgment was made by referring again to the ethnographic literature. (The Barry and Paxson scores were judged to be correct in eight of the cases and Ayres and Whiting in nine, and appropriate changes were made.)

Although the Ayres and Whiting sample and the standard sample were both drawn with some regard for "Galton's problem" (see Naroll, 1970) and thus to reasonably assure an equitable coverage of the ethnographic universe, when they were combined it was evident that certain regions of the world and certain language families, such as the Niger-Congo–speaking peoples of sub-Saharan Africa and the Malayo-Polynesian–speaking peoples of Oceania, were grossly overrepresented and that other regions and languages, such as Eurasia and Indo-European, underrepresented. Rather than reducing the overrepresented regions and languages, it was decided to increase the underrepresented. In this search information only on carrying and resting devices was sought.

From the evidence presented thus far it can be presumed that the closeness of contact between mother and infant is influenced both by climate and by history. Before attempting to estimate the independent influence of these two factors, the effect of the climate alone upon the measures of mother–infant contact for this extended sample will be presented.

To accomplish this, data on winter temperatures was taken from two sources. The scores published by J. Whiting (1964) derived from those of Finch, Trewartha, Robinson, & Hammond (1957). Additional cases were derived from Parkins' "Map of Surface Temperatures" published in *Goode's World Atlas* (Espenshade, 1957). Both Finch et al. and Parkins used the following classification for surface temperature:

Hot: 20°C (above 68°F)
Mild: 10°–20°C (50°–68°F)
Cool: 0°–10°C (32°–50°F)
Cold: 0°C (below 32°F)

As mentioned above, in the earlier study it was found that mothers and infants slept in the same bed in societies with hot and mild winter temperatures but slept apart in societies with cool and cold temperatures. As shown in Table 7–1, the same distribution between mild and cool also applies to the use of cradles for carrying (or resting) infants.

These results indicate that societies situated in a region where the winter temperature falls below 10°C tend to use cradles for infants, whereas those where the winter temperature remains above 10°C usually do not. Thus 10°C (50°F) seems empirically to constitute an isotherm which has a determining effect on infant care practices.

Such an isotherm is not intuitively meaningful. Why should a temperature of 10°C be critical? A definitive answer to this question awaits further research, but the following information suggests that the possibility of the temperature falling below freezing may be the critical factor: Detailed data from weather stations situated within or near the territory of a society was available for a small number of cases in the present sample. These data came from the Klima Atlas (Walter & Leith, 1967) and were coded by John Sodergren. Data on the mean daily minimum of the coldest month was available for 13 of the 59 cases coded as cool (0°–10°C). For 5 of these cases the daily minimum fell below freezing. It is therefore possible that the discontinuous environmental effect of the temperature when it falls below freezing—water becomes ice, rain becomes snow or sleet, plants wilt, etc.—required many lifestyle adjustments, one of which may be the method of caring for infants.

Thus far "Galton's problem" has been neglected for the pooled sample. The cases are by no means independent of one another. It could be that the correlations reported above are regional artifacts. If most of the cradle cultures were situated in North America, which has cool or cold winter temperatures, most of the cultures lacking cradles were situated in Africa, which has mild or hot climates, and the presence or absence of cradles was randomly distributed with respect to climate in Eurasia and South America, a historical explanation rather than a functional explanation would be appropriate.

A number of methods have been used to estimate the historical relatedness of cultures. The culture area concept developed by Wissler (1923) and Kroeber (1939) for the Amerindians of North American is the most well known. This is essentially an intuitive grouping of cultures based on a combination of proximity and the number of shared cultural elements. This method was developed originally for the

TABLE 7–1 Proportion of Cases Using Cradle for Carrying Infants as Related to Winter Temperature

	Cradles Used for Carrying
Cold (under 0°C)	66 (61)
Cool (0°–10°C)	67 (39)
Warm (11°–20°C)	7 (57)
Hot (over 20°C)	8 (92)

Number of cases in each cell is indicated in parentheses.

reconstruction of history. Recently it has been used by Driver (1966) to estimate the relative contribution of historical and functional interpretations of kin avoidances. The culture area concept has also been the basis of Murdock's (1968) attempt to draw world samples of reasonably independent cases.

Naroll (1970) and Naroll and D'Andrade (1963), assuming that a people are more likely to borrow from a neighboring group than from those at a distance, have used geographic proximity as a method of correcting for historical influences when testing a functional hypothesis.

Since the independent variable climate is not subject to diffusion and is constant over large regions, methods described above for controlling the effects of diffusion are inappropriate. The world has been divided into three sections, each representing regions in which widespread borrowing of carrying devices is known to have taken place. For convenience the major regional classification used in the Ethnographic Atlas (Murdock, 1967) has been chosen:

A. *Africa,* exclusive of Madagascar and the northern and northeastern portions of the continent.

C. *Circum-Mediterranean,* including Europe, Turkey and the Caucasus, the Semitic Near East, and Northern and Northeastern Africa.

E. *East Eurasia,* excluding Formosa, the Philippines, Indonesia, and the area assigned to the Circum-Mediterranean, but including Madagascar and other islands of the Indian Ocean.

I. *Insular Pacific,* embracing all of Oceania, as well as areas like Australia, Indonesia, Formosa, and the Philippines.

N. *North America,* including the indigenous societies of this continent as far south as the Isthumus of Tehuantepec.

S. *South America,* including the Antilles, Yucatan, and Central America, as well as the continent itself.

These regions taken separately do not permit adequate variation in winter temperature—Africa, Insular Pacific, and South America lie mostly in warm or hot climatic zones, whereas Circum-Mediterranean, East Eurasia, and North America are largely in cool and cold zones. In order to give full range to winter temperature and still retain the regional component, regions that are proximate on a north–south axis were combined. Thus three world sections were formed:

I   Africa and Circum-Mediterranean.
II   East Eurasia and Insular Pacific.
III   North and South America.

The hypothesis may now be rephrased as follows: The 10°C isotherm acts as a barrier across which infant-carrying devices tend not to be borrowed. Borrowing, however, is expected to occur within the warm and hot and within the cool and cold regions of each section, but it is predicted to be minimal between sections even when the climate is similar. Thus carrying devices can be widely diffused within each segment of a section in which there is a constant climate, but minimally so, if at all, between sections even if the winter temperature is similar. Thus the societies in the warm climates of sub-Saharan Africa can and probably do borrow the back shawl as a method of carrying infants, but is is unlikely that they borrowed this idea from either the Insular Pacific or South America. Similarly, the cradles of Europe are widely diffused throughout the cold climate of this region, but it is improbable that the cradles used in North America or Patagonia were borrowed from this source. In fact, they are quite different from one another. Although borrowing may have taken place between Europe and East Eurasia, in fact, the typical cradle of Central Asia is quite different from that used in Europe. (See Figures 7–1 and 7–2.)

Thus if the 10°C isotherm is an effective barrier to the borrowing of infant-carrying devices in each of the three world sections, the hypothesis will be confirmed with a reasonable control for the effects of diffusion.

As can be suspected from the data already presented, the hypothesis is supported in each world section. It is clear from Table 7–2 and Figure 7–2 that the isotherm indicated in Table 7–2 is operative in each section of the world and that the association between carrying devices and climate is thus both general and robust.

It should be noted, however, that no attempt was made in drawing the sample to ensure the independence of the cases chosen. In fact, as stated above, many were known to belong to the same culture area and to be closely related. A test of the statistical significance of the associations is therefore inappropriate and was not made.

Although the effects of diffusion were controlled by the method of dividing the world into sections, this procedure provides no control for the possible effect of common origins. In tabulating the cases for the relevant tables, it was evident—and this is the case in many cross-cultural studies—that the Niger-Congo–speaking peoples of sub-Saharan Africa and the Malayo-Polynesian peoples of the Insular Pacific were heavily overrepresented. There were 35 reports in the former category and 27 in the latter—representing over 20 percent of the total sample. These and other cases of sets of societies speaking a language in the same phylum represent cultures of common origin, and thus a historical rather than a functional interpretation of the course of their choice of infant-carrying devices is plausible. If all or most of the societies assigned to a language phylum fall in a single cell in a χ^2 table—and this is generally the case—the effect of climate on carrying devices independent of common origins is overestimated.

To correct for this, the language phylum of each case was obtained for columns 64 and 65 of the Ethnographic Atlas (Murdock, 1967) and the cross-tabulations presented in Table 2 were recalculated based on the number of independent language phyla rather than the number of societies in each cell of the table.[2] The results of this recalculation are presented in Table 7–3.

A comparison of Tables 7–2 and 7–3 indicates that the ϕ value of the association drops from 0.65 to 0.43 for section I, from 0.55 to 0.47 for section II, and from 0.75 to 0.65 for section III.

A comparison of the two sets of tables also permits an estimate of the amount of variance contributed by common origins and by climate. To do this an estimate of variance contributed by climate as measured by independent languages was calculated by adjusting the ϕ^2 value obtained in Table 7–3[3] and subtracting it from the adjusted ϕ^2 obtained in Table 7–2. The results are shown in Table 7–4.

These results are enlightening. In section I the amount of variance that can be attributed to the effect of common origins (0.19) is nearly as great as that estimated for the effect of climate, whereas the ratio is 1 : 3 for section III. Section I is characterized by expansionist cultures such as the Niger-Congo–, Indo-European–, and Afro-Asiatic–speaking peoples who occupy most of the region—the 83 societies in the section represent but 16 independent languages. By contrast, the New World—section III—is characterized by a multitude of diverse independent languages. In this case, the 91 societies in the sample represent 54 independent languages. This fact should be taken into account in future cross-cultural research testing functional hypotheses.

FIGURE 7-1. Infant-carrying practices in Europe, Africa, and Asia.

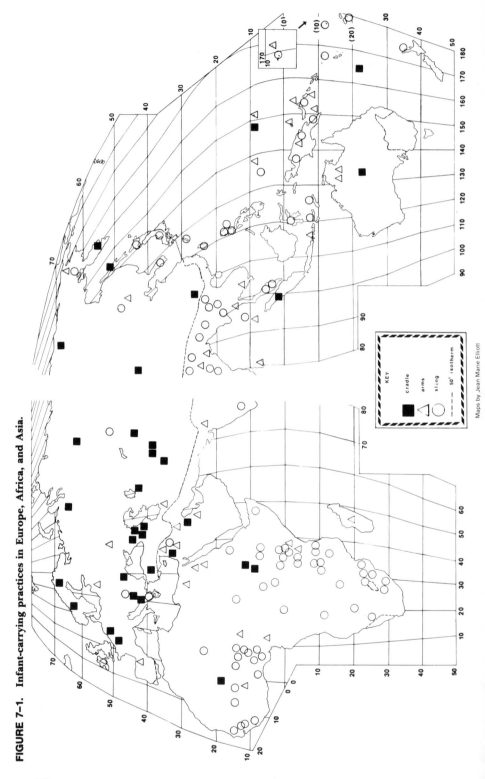

Maps by Jean Marie Elliott

KEY
cradle
arms
sling
50° isotherm

FIGURE 7-2. Infant-carrying practices in North and South America.

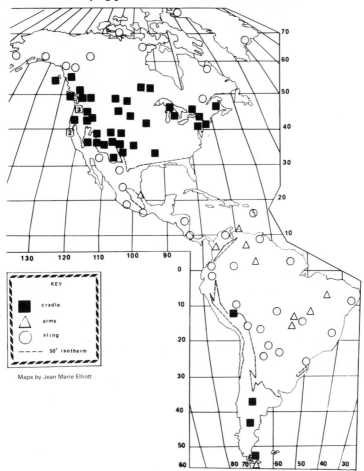

Maps by Jean Marie Elliott

TABLE 7-2 Association Between the 10°C Isotherm Based on the Mean Temperature for the Coldest Month and the Use of Cradles as a Carrying Device for Infants

		Winter Temperature					
		Cool & Cold	Warm & Hot	Cool & Cold	Warm & Hot	Cool & Cold	Warm & Hot
Cradles used as a carrying device for infants:	Yes	13	5	12	4	43	2
	No	5	60	9	51	15	31
		$n = 83$		$n = 76$		$n = 91$	
		$\chi^2 = 34.6$		$\chi^2 = 22.7$		$\chi^2 = 50.7$	
		$\phi = 0.65$		$\phi = 0.55$		$\phi = 0.75$	
		$\phi^2 = 0.42$		$\phi^2 = 0.30$		$\phi^2 = 0.56$	
Section		I (A, C)		II (E, I)		III (N, S)	

The tests are calculated separately for three sections of the world: I, Africa and Circum-Mediterranean; II, East Eurasia and Insular Pacific; III, North and South America.

TABLE 7-3　Association Between the 10°C Isotherm and the Use of Cradles as Carrying Devices for Infants Using Independent Language Phyla as Cases in Each Cell

		Winter Temperature					
		Cool & Cold	Warm & Hot	Cool & Cold	Warm & Hot	Cool & Cold	Warm & Hot
Cradles used as carrying devices for infants:	Yes	5	3	9	2	20	2
	No	2	8	15	14	8	12

$n = 19$	$n = 29$	$n = 54$
$x^2 = 3.37$	$x^2 = 6.43$	$x^2 = 22.6$
$\phi = 0.43$	$\phi = 0.47$	$\phi = 0.65$
$\phi^2 = 0.19$	$\phi^2 = 0.22$	$\phi^2 = 0.42$
Section	I (A, C)	II (E, I)	III (N, S)

The tests are presented separately for each section of the world: I, Africa and Circum-Mediterranean; II, East Eurasia and the Insular Pacific; III, North and South America.

It had been intended to further test the hypotheses by using the method of controlled comparison (Eggan, 1954). Does the association hold true within language phyla as well as across them? To carry out this test, variation in the independent variable is required. Some of the societies belonging to a single phylum must be located on each side of the isotherm. Surprisingly, although there were 35 language phyla with two or more exemplars, in only one of them—the Indo-European —was this the case. Exemplars of the previously mentioned Niger-Congo and Malayo-Polynesian languages were, in each case, all on the warm and hot side of the winter temperature isotherm. Thus 10°C is apparently an isotherm which acts as a barrier to migration as well as to the choice of carrying devices.

However, the Indo-European–speaking peoples who are an exception to the above rule permit one controlled comparison test of the hypothesis (Table 7–5). The ϕ value obtained is very similar to the values reported in Table 7–3 and indicates that climate has the predicted effect even within a language phylum.

In all the tests presented above, the absence of the cradle in mild and hot climates is more striking than the presence in cool and cold climates. Cradleboards and baby carriages are clearly not the only adaptive method for carrying infants in a cold climate. The Eskimo technique of carrying an infant in a sling under a parka is one that is frequently used in the polar regions of North America and Siberia. The Greek method of carrying a heavily swaddled infant in a sling is another alternative. A more important exception to the use of cradles in cold climates is the modern revolution

Table 7-4　Variance as Measured by Adjusted ϕ^2 That Can be Attributed to Climate and to Common Origins

	Section		
	I	II	III
a.　Total variance (adjusted ϕ^2/all cases)	0.42	0.30	0.56
b.　Variance due to climate (adj. ϕ^2/languages)	0.23	0.22	0.42
c.　Variance due to common origins (line a minus line b)	0.19	0.08	0.14

Table 7-5 Controlled Comparison of the Effect of Winter
Temperature on the Use of Cradles as Carrying Devices for
Infants for Societies Speaking an Indo-European Language

Use of Cradles as Carrying Devices	Winter Temperature	
	Cool & Cold	Mild & Hot
	(n = 10)	(n = 0)
Present	Gheg	
	Dutch	
	Norwegians	
	French	
	Serbs	
	Osset	
	Armenians	
	Hazara	
	Tajik	
	Yankees	
	(n = 4)	(n = 6)
Absent	Bulgarians	Greeks
	Lithuanians	Kurd
	Irish	Bhil
	Iranians	Vedda
		Uttar Pradesh
		Saramacca

$\chi^2 = 7.47; \phi = 0.61; \phi^2 = 0.37.$

in infant-carrying techniques. Since the ethnographic present in none of the cases in the sample used in this study was later than 1960, this trend was not reflected. This trend is reported in a paper by Jelliffe (1975) on recent trends in infant carrying. He reports that slings are being widely used in Sweden, Great Britain, Canada, the United States, New Zealand, Australia, and Japan. Numerous firms are advertising products with brand names such as "Sling-cuddler," "Snugli," "Rebozo," "Meh Tai," and "Kodomo." One firm prominent in the field has estimated roughly "that approximately 1.5 million soft carriers (either sling, front or back) are used . . . , and possibly 2 to 2.5 million frame carriers." "Soft carriers" would be classified as slings in this study and "frame carriers" as carrying cradles; thus it is evident that within the 15 years since this trend began the sling has replaced the baby carriage in many localities where the winter temperature falls below 10°C.

Evidence is lacking as to whether the crib or cradle as a resting or sleeping device is also being replaced, but it is not likely, if there has been a change, that it is as dramatic as that for carrying devices.

The recent change in carrying devices in cold climates is an important lesson for cross-cultural research. Although winter temperature may control 50 percent of the variance in predicting carrying devices before 1960, such a relationship is not immutable.

Despite the above condition, any cross-cultural study that uses the amount and closeness of mother–infant contact should take account of the possible effect of winter temperature.

As indicated above, the type of infant-carrying device used by a society was chosen as a variable because it was a low-inference and highly codable index of the amount of body contact with a caretaker that an infant experienced. Societies that use a cradle as a carrying device tend to use it also as a place for the infant to rest and nap during the day and sleep at night. Infants also tend to be heavily clothed or swaddled in these societies and are also infrequently held in the arms or on the lap of the caretaker. By contrast, in those societies in which slings are used as a carrying device, infants generally wear little or no clothing, are in close body contact with their caretaker during most of their waking hours, and sleep next to their mothers in the same bed at night. In societies with no carrying device, infants have more contact with their caretakers than those with a cradle but less than those with a sling. There is thus wide variation over the world in the closeness and duration of body contact between infants and mothers or other caretakers. Does this make any difference?

There is some controversy today as to whether events in early infancy have any lasting effects. Following Freud, it was taken for granted that the relationship established by infants with others, particularly their mothers, was a primary factor in the development of their personalities. Freud assumed that either deprivation or overindulgence in any of the stages of psychosexual development—oral, anal, or phallic —would lead to fixation at that stage. Erikson posited that a mother's treatment of a child led to trust if she was responsive and consistent and to distrust if she was aloof or inconsistent. Ainsworth (1963) and Bowlby (1969) have developed a theory of attachment based upon the nature of mother-infant relationships. Borrowing from ethology as well as psychoanalysis, they posit that a close and stable relationship of infant to mother during infancy is a prerequisite to establishment of healthy social relationships in later life. Psychologists such as Sears, Maccoby, and Levin (1957) and Miller and Dollard (1941) have used the principles of learning to explain how overdetermined dependent and aggressive behavior can result from the interaction of mother and infant.

Developmental psychologists of the Piagetian school, however, are more interested in invariant and irreversible sequences that change with age than in environmental effects. They are also more concerned with how children cognize their physical environment that with their socioemotional status. They therefore tend to treat Freudian, neo-Freudian, and learning theory with some skepticism.

Kagan (1973), an outspoken critic of the assumption that events in infancy have a lasting effect, cites evidence of radical changes in the abilities of children as their immediate environment becomes more or less supportive.

Many of the cross-cultural studies reported in other chapters of this monograph are based on the assumption that customary events in infancy and childhood have a lasting effect on the modal personality of a culture which is measurably manifested in some feature of the projective-expressive system of that culture. The justification for such a strategy is detailed by J. Whiting and Child (1953, pp. 35 ff) and by J. Whiting (1973). The positive and statistically significant findings of these studies cannot all be dismissed because they are correlational rather than experimental and thus subject to alternative explanations. McClelland's argument (Chapter 4 in this volume) that variations in magicoreligious beliefs cause predictable variations in child rearing practices may account for some but hardly all of the reported findings.

It should be noted here that most of the dependent variables shown in the cross-cultural studies to be related to events occurring in infancy and childhood are features of the projective-expressive system of a culture. They include rituals such as male and female initiation rites, the couvade, theories of disease, sex taboos, and beliefs about the nature of supernatural beings. It is assumed that these represent culturally approved defenses against intrapsychic conflicts. The assumed mechanisms include projection, displacement-introjection, fixation, and identification. The conflicts include guilt, anxiety about sex, aggression, and dependency, and cross-sex identity. The events in infancy and childhood are assumed to be stressful, such as mother-infant separation, low infant indulgence, shifts in the salience of father and mother, and severity of socialization.

There is no cross-cultural evidence that any of these or other child rearing practices affect the competence of the adults in the society. There is no evidence that any customs of infant care or child socialization produce cognitive deficits that persist to adulthood and thus characterize a society as being intellectually deficient. Thus there is no contradiction between the above findings supporting Freudian theory and Kagan's (1973) position that early events have no lasting effects. His position concerns cognitive abilities, not emotional conflicts that are unconscious and persistent.

Nevertheless, the cross-cultural evidence in support of the "Freudian" position remains tentative. In many of the studies the samples are small and are not properly controlled for historical effects. Most of the early cross-cultural studies assumed a simple linear relationship between childhood and projective systems, where a multivariate approach would have been more appropriate. Finally, the tests reported have seldom been replicated, and until this is done the findings should be considered as very tentative.

Some of the effects of the amount of body contact between infant and caretaker were reported at the beginning of this chapter. These studies should be replicated on new samples if possible, and winter temperature and region should be controlled for. Also, the differential effects of a single measure, such as carrying devices, or a combined measure, using carrying devices, resting devices, swaddling, and sleeping arrangements, should be explored.

It would be very valuable if there were more field studies with accurate time samples of the amount and type of contact between infants and caretakers like those carried out by Super (nd.), Konner (1976), Leiderman and Leiderman (1973), and Lewis and Ban (1977). Those who plan to study infants in other cultures, please take note.

A brief review of some of the hypotheses that have been proposed concerning the effects of variations in infant care practices will suggest some of the research that needs to be done.

Interest in the effects of swaddling originate from Watson's theory that infants react to restraint with rage. Although this theory was based on his observation of infants reported in 1917 (Watson & Morgan, 1917), it appeared as an established truth in many of his later works and in the psychological and educational textbooks. In fact, the hypothesis influenced pediatric practice in the swaddling cultures of Central and Eastern Europe to the degree that mothers were strongly advised to give up the practice.

Later, more careful research by various psychologists carried out on various groups of infants in the United States, including whites, Pueblo, and Navaho, indicated that Watson had overstated the case. This evidence is reviewed by Dennis (1940). Violent reactions could be induced by any strong stimulus, and it was unclear if these responses should be classified as "rage." Furthermore, Dennis reported that the Hopi and Navaho gave no indication that being swaddled in a cradleboard was frustrating.

In 1939 the "frustration-aggression hypothesis" (Dollard, Doob, Miller, Mowrer, Sears, Ford, Hovland, & Sollenberger, 1939) in which frustration was defined as "any interference with an ongoing (instigated) response" was formulated. This hypothesis would also predict that infants would be frustrated by swaddling only if they were instigated to move, and the effect of swaddling could be either comforting or frustrating depending on the infant's expectations.

Greenacre (1944, pp. 97–98), a psychoanalyst, reviewed the literature on infant restraint and, although she admitted that Watson's original hypothesis was over-stated, reported clinical evidence that restraint during infancy might have a lasting effect on personality:

> Prolonged restraint may be a factor in producing . . . chronic negativism, stub-bornness, blocking, or lack of good and sustained concentration. In extremely severe cases it may produce a condition resembling the functional deterioration of chronic psychotic states. . . . The tendency for such early restraint to increase the sado-masochism is clear, but the exact pattern cannot be well established. . . . From a few observations on patients in the course of psychoanalytic treatment, I have thought that prolonged early restraint, producing a condition in which stimu-lation to the body far exceeded possible motor discharge, also resulted in an increasing body erotization and was a factor augmenting the problems generally associated with this condition.

The possible effect of swaddling was also considered by a group—including Ruth Benedict, Margaret Mead, Geoffrey Gorer, and John Rickman (Mead & Metraux, 1953; Gorer & Rickman, 1962)—concerned with the study of national character. To explain the national character of the Great Russians they developed the "swaddling hypothesis." The most extreme position was taken by Gorer and Rickman, who write

> When human infants are not constrained they move their limbs and bodies a great deal, especially during the second six months of life; it seems probable that much of this movement is physiologically determined, as an aspect of biological matura-tion. Infants tend to express emotion with their whole body and not merely their face, for example arching their back or thrashing about or hugging. They also explore their own body and the universe around them with their hands and their mouth, gradually discovering what is edible and what inedible, what me and what not-me. While swaddled in the Russian manner, Russian infants can do none of these things; and it is assumed that this inhibition of movement is felt to be extremely painful and frustrating and is responded to with intense and destructive rage, which cannot be adequately expressed physically. . . . These feelings of rage and fear are probably made endurable, but also given emphasis, by the fact that the baby is periodically loosed from the constraints, and suckled and petted while unswaddled. This alternation of complete restraint continues for at least the first nine months of life. It is the argument of this study that the situation outlined in the preceding paragraphs is *one* of the major determinants in the development of the character of the Great Russians. (1962, pp. 123–124).

The consequences of this pattern of infant care suggested by Gorer and Rickman include optimism, ability to endure privation, and the love of orgiastic feasts.

Aware of the fact that swaddling is practiced by many societies that have different national characters, Gorer and Rickman suggest that differences in the method of swaddling should be taken into account. They list the following variables as potentially important: the amount of body swaddled, the length of time swaddled, the presence or absence of hunger or other unpleasant internal sensations, the degree to which handling is personal or impersonal, and whether or not babies are unswaddled for nursing.

Benedict takes the position that swaddling practices are a consequence rather than a cause of cultural beliefs. She writes (1949),

Any . . . student of comparative studies must press his [or her] investigation to the point where he can describe *what is communicated* by the particular variety of the widespread technique he is studying. In the case of swaddling, the object of investigation is the kind of communication which in different regions is set up between adults and the child by the procedures and sanctions used. (p. 43)

Swaddling is tightest and is kept up longest in Great Russia. The baby's arms are wrapped close to its sides and only the feet emerge. After tight wrapping in the blanket, the bundle is taped with criss-cross lashings till it is, as Russians say, "like a log of wood for the fireplace". . . . The swaddling in Russia is explicitly justified as necessary for the safety of an infant who is regarded as being in danger of destroying itself. In the words of informants, "It would tear its ears off. It would break its legs. It must be confined for its own sake and for its mother." (p. 344)

Benedict emphasizes her point by describing Polish beliefs about the nature of infants. "The Polish version of swaddling is quite different from the Russians. The infant is regarded not as violent but as exceedingly fragile. It will break in two without support given by the bindings. . . ." Swaddling is conceived as a first step in a long process of "hardening" a child. She characterizes the national character of the Russians as having a strong component of impersonal violence, whereas "the Poles characteristically tend to prove their own worth by their sufferings" (1949, p. 343).

Margaret Mead (1953, p. 644) takes a position similar to that of Benedict. "The prolonged and very tight swaddling to which infants are subjected in Russian child-rearing practice is one of the means by which Russians communicate to their infants a feeling that a strong authority is necessary." She goes on to say that this value is mediated by Russian culture, which is determined by its history.

Mead and Benedict thus view swaddling and presumably other infant care practices as a component of the expressive aspect of a culture. The way in which infants are cared for is an index of cultural belief about human nature and values concerning the ideals of national character. Unlike Gorer and Rickman, and Greenacre, they carefully avoid committing themselves to the Freudian assumption that salient events in infancy may have lasting effects. They thus implicitly reject the model for psychocultural research presented at the beginning of this chapter.

Little has been written on the 'swaddling hypothesis" since the early 1960s. Whether the Watson and Morgan (1917) and Gorer and Rickman (1962) assumption that swaddling induces rage in the infant or the Dennis position that an infant adapts to swaddling and finds it comforting rather than frustrating is correct has not been satisfactorily resolved. Even more importantly, is the psychoanalytic view expressed by Greenacre and Gorer and Rickman that the infantile experience has an enduring effect on personality viable, or is the Mead-Benedict position that infant care practice is an expression of national character rather than a cause of it the more correct hypothesis? These questions are worthy of further research.

A quite different hypothesis about the effects of swaddling was that it inhibits motor development. Several studies carried out in cultures that practice swaddling indicated that any such effects were evanescent. Danziger and Frankl (1934) compared ten Albanian infants who were heavily swaddled during the first year of life with a group of Viennese infants who were not swaddled. The Albanian infants were indeed retarded as long as they were still swaddled, but they caught up soon after they were taken out of their swaddling clothes. Dennis (1947, p. 43) reported similar results for Hopi and Navaho infants. "In spite of the enforced extension of the limbs, the young Indian infant when freed from his [or her] bindings for the bath or for the change of bedding, takes the usual flexed position. Although his hands are held downward perhaps 23 hours in 24, when he is at liberty he puts them to his mouth and carries objects to his mouth as do white children. He reaches for his toes and puts his toes in his mouth. Sitting, creeping and walking follow in the usual sequence." These results support the Kagan (1973) hypothesis that events in infancy which retard motor and cognitive development do not have lasting effects.

There has been some speculation about the possible effects of how infants are held or carried (see Chapter 8 in this volume). Konner (1976) has suggested that infants who spend more time in an upright than in a prone position should be more alert, more aware of what is going on around them, and hence cognitively precocious. This hypothesis, to my knowledge, has not been tested cross-culturally.

Possible effects of the orientation of the infant to the carrier have also been speculated about. Does being carried facing backward and seeing the environment recede have a different effect from riding astride the hip and looking forward?

It is a matter of folk wisdom that frightened infants can be comforted by body contact. A vivid illustration of this phenomenon is reported by Sorenson (1976). While photographing infants among the Fore of New Guinea he accidentally got between two toddlers and their parents and older siblings. He reports that the toddlers were frightened, started to cry, and immediately approached and embraced one another for mutual comfort. His picture vividly affirms his interpretation. If this assumption is correct, the probability of delay in being comforted by body contact should be much greater in societies that use cradles than for those that use slings. Thus infant stress is minimized in those societies with close and continuous body contact. The consequences of infant stress on physical growth are discussed by Landauer and Whiting in Chapter 10 of this volume.

In an earlier, brief version of this chapter (J. Whiting, 1971) it was suggested that the contrast between cradle and sling cultures involved differences not only in physical contact between mother and infant but also in the nature of their social interaction.

In the close contact cultures it is as though the infant is not yet born. He is, to all intents and purposes, still a part of his mother. He has a piggy-back view of his mother's role which has, as a consequence, what I would like to call *symbiotic identification*. This period of *symbiotic identification* with the mother should lead to an initial identification with the female role, the consequences of which, particularly for the boy, will be discussed later.

The crib and cradleboard infants are separated from their mothers at birth. If they need help they often need to cry for it. They are at once helpless and in dominant control of their caretakers if they make the proper instrumental responses. But they never can be sure how soon their mothers will come. In other words, crib or cradle infants, rather than continuing in a symbiotic relation to their mothers, have one of ambivalent dependency. (Whiting, 1971, pp. 5–6)

It can be said that cradle babies are detached from their mothers at birth, whereas sling babies are not detached until they are weaned from their mother's back and bed. Thus cradle babies are completely helpless when they are detached, whereas sling babies—if they are weaned from the back and bed when a younger sibling is born—usually when they are 2 years old—are more mature and capable of considerable autonomy. It has been frequently reported in the ethnographic literature that an infant's response to being weaned from the back is one of rage and violent temper tantrums. I observed such a case among the Kwoma when a mother for the first time refused to take her infant to the garden with her.

One morning Kum's mother put on her net bag to go to the swamp to collect sago. Kum, observing her, said "Mother, I want to go too." "No," she replied, "you must stay at home." Kum repeated his request more vigorously, but his mother did not heed him. Then he began to cry, but still without success. His crying increased in intensity until he was screaming. His mother, having finished her preparations, started down the path. Kum ran after her and clasped her leg, trying to hold her back, and shrieking. When she disengaged her leg he threw himself on the ground and rolled over and over in the grass. (J. Whiting, 1941, p. 34)

Such a response is not surprising. For 2 years the sling-carried infant has communicated kinesthetically with the mother, and wiggles have generally led to immediate reinforcement. At weaning the communication system with the mother is completely taken away; wiggles are no longer meaningful. Thus weaning from the back of the mother should enhance her value. She becomes for the first time a scarce resource. At the same time she is to blame for rejecting him. It is argued by Munroe, Munroe, and Whiting (Chapter 18 in this volume) that this set of conditions is one of the factors leading to cross-sex identity conflict.

The early life history of those infants in cradle cultures who are detached at birth is quite different. Their communication is distal rather than proximate, verbal rather than kinesthetic. They are on a schedule of delayed and aperiodic reinforcement. Whiting (1978) has argued that these conditions are one of the factors that produce "dependency hangup" in which independence and self-reliance are highly valued and at the same time dominant dependent behavior is subtly rewarded. This conflict contrasts with the "cross-sex identity hangup" of the sling culture.

It has also been suggested (J. Whiting, 1971, p. 34) that "the high gods of Judaeo-Christian religion and the belief in the guardian spirits which characterizes many of the North American Indians both flourish in cradle cultures and represent the kind of a dependent relationship between men and the supernaturals that might be theoretically expected."

SUMMARY AND CONCLUSIONS

In sum, then, the manner in which infants are cared for during their waking and sleeping hours is to a considerable extent constrained by the physical environment, the temperature of coldest month of the year being the most important factor.

In cold climates infants tend to be carried in a cradle, swaddled, and put in a cradle to rest and nap during the day and to sleep at night. In warm climates they are usually carried in a sling or shawl, often nap on their caretaker's back, sleep next to their mother at night, and are clothed lightly or not at all. Central heating and "backpack culture" make it possible for warm climate methods to be used in cold climates, and the prestige value of cribs and baby carriages may impel peoples in warm climates to use them. Nevertheless, it is evident that infant care practices are not distributed randomly over the cultures of the world.

Whether or not these variations in methods of infant care have any enduring effects is a more important question. The evidence needed to answer this question is not yet in. From what we know thus far it seems that practices which inhibit or delay motor and cognitive development are not enduring and "catching up" in these domains is possible given a favorable environment in later life. Styles of social interaction and early learned defenses against emotional conflict are much more resistant to change. Hypotheses detailing the predicted consequences of early learned techniques of persuasion and modes of avoiding conflict should be the most promising to develop and test.

NOTES

1. Most ethnographies refer simply to babies or infants, but when ages are given we have focused on the second through the eighth months.

2. I wish to acknowledge the suggestions of Lawrence Baldwin, Thomas Landauer, Michael Burton, and Stephen Fjellman for developing the method used here for estimating the effect of common origin.

3. Since the ϕ^2 value cannot be as high as 1.0 if the rows and columns in the table from which it is derived are skewed, it cannot be taken as an estimate of variance without adjustment. This is done by setting the smallest cell in the table at 0, changing the values in the other three cells so that the marginals remain the same, and recalculating ϕ^2. This yields the maximum value of ϕ^2 with the given marginals. The adjusted ϕ^2 is then obtained by dividing the original ϕ by ϕ max and squaring the results. This procedure was suggested by Michael Burton (1965).

REFERENCES

Ainsworth, M. D. S. The development of infant-mother interaction among the Ganda. In B. M. Foss (Ed.), *Determinants of infant behavior* (Vol. 2). London: Methuen, 1963.

Ayres, B. Effects of infant carrying practices on rhythm in music. *Ethos,* 1973, *1,* 387–404.

Ayres, B., & Whiting, J. W. M. *Code of infant care practices.* Unpublished manuscript, 1970.

Barry, H., & Paxson, L. Infancy and early childhood: Cross cultural codes 2. *Ethnology,* 1971, *10,* 466–508.

Benedict, R. Child rearing in certain European countries. *American Journal of Orthopsychiatry,* 1949, *19,* 342–350.

Bowlby, J. Attachment and loss (Vol. 1). *Attachment.* New York: Basic Books, 1969.

Burton, M. *Cluster analysis of cross-cultural data.* Paper presented at the meeting of the Southwestern Anthropological Society, University of California, Los Angeles, April 1965.

Collinder, B. *The Lapps.* Princeton: Princeton University Press (for the American Scandinavian Foundation), 1949.

Danziger, L., & Frankl, L. Zum problem der funktionsreifung. *Zeitschrift fur Kinderforschung,* 1934, *43,* 219–225.

Dennis, W. Infant reaction to restraint: An evaluation of Watson's theory. *Transactions of the New York Academy of Sciences*, May 1940, pp. 202–217.

Dennis, W. Does culture appreciably affect patterns of infant behavior? In T. M. Newcomb & E. L. Hartley (Eds.), *Readings in social psychology*. New York: Henry Holt & Co., 1947.

de Vries, M. W., & de Vries, M. R. The cultural relativity of toilet training readiness: A perspective from East Africa. Unpublished paper presented at the Meeting of the Society for Research in Child Development, New Orleans, March 1977.

Dollard, J., Doob, L. W., Miller, N. E., Mowrer, O. H., Sears, R. R., Ford, C. S., Hovland, C. I., & Sollenberger, R. T. *Frustration and aggression*. New Haven: Yale University Press, 1939.

Driver, H. Geographical *versus* psycho-functional explanations of kin avoidances. *Current Anthropology*, 1966, *7*, 131–182.

Eggan, F. Social anthropology and the method of controlled comparison. *American Anthropologist*, 1954, *56*, 743–763.

Erikson, E. *Childhood and society* (2nd ed.). New York: W. W. Norton & Co., 1963.

Espenshade, E. B., Jr. (Ed.). *Goodes's world atlas*. Chicago: Rand McNally, 1957.

Finch, V. C., Trewartha, G. T., Robinson, A.H., & Hammond, E. H. *Physical elements of geography* (4th ed.). New York: McGraw-Hill, 1957.

Firth, R. W. *We, the Tikopia: A sociological study of kinship in primitive Polynesia*. London: Allen & Unwin, 1936.

Gorer, G., & Rickman, J. *The people of Great Russia*. New York: W. W. Norton & Co., 1962. (Originally published in 1949)

Greenacre, P. Infant reactions to restraint: Problems in the fate of infantile aggression. *American Journal of Orthopsychiatry*, 1944, *14*, 204–218.

Hansen, H. *The Kurdish woman's life: Field research in a Muslim society, Iraq*. Copenhagen: National Museum, 1961.

Hogbin, H. I. A New Guinea infancy, from conception to weaning in Wogeo. *Oceania*, 1942–43, *13*, 285–309.

Huffman, R. *Nuer customs and folklore*. London: Oxford University Press (for the International Institute of African Languages and Cultures), 1931.

Jelliffe, E. F. Recent trends in infant carrying. *Environmental Child Health*, 1975.

Kagan, J. Cross-cultural perspectives on early development. *American Psychologist*, 1973, *28*, 947–961.

Konner, M. Maternal care, infant behavior and development theory among the !Kung. In R. Lee & I. De Vore (Eds.), *Kalahari hunter-gathers: Studies of the !Kung San and their neighbors*. Cambridge, Mass.: Harvard University Press, 1976.

Kroeber, A. L. *Cultural and natural areas of native North America*. Berkeley: University of California (Publications in American Archaeology and Ethnology, Vol. 38), 1939.

Kroeber, A. L. (Ed.). *Anthropology today: An encyclopedic inventory*. Chicago: University of Chicago Press, 1953.

Lee, D. D. Greece. In M. Mead (Ed.), *Cultural patterns and technical change*. Paris: UNESCO, 1953.

Leiderman, P. H., & Leiderman, G. F. Familial influences on infant development in an East African agricultural community. Unpublished data. In Cultural and Social Influences in Infancy and Early Childhood, Burg Wartenstein Symposium No. 57.

Lewis, M., & Ban, P. Variance and invariance in the mother-infant interaction: A cross-cultural study. In P. H. Leiderman, S. R. Tulkin, & A. Rosenfeld (Eds.), *Culture and infancy*. San Francisco: Academic Press, 1977.

Mead, M. National character. In A. L. Kroeber (Ed.), *Anthropology today*. Chicago: University of Chicago Press, 1953.

Mead, M., & Metraux, R. (Eds.). *The study of culture at a distance.* Chicago: University of Chicago Press, 1953.

Miller, N. E., & Dollard, J. *Social learning and imitation.* New Haven: Yale University Press, 1941.

Miller, N. E., Sears, R. R., Mowrer, O. H., Doob, L. W., & Dollard, J. The frustration-aggression hypothesis. *Psychological Review,* 1941, *48,* 337–342.

Morgan, L. H. *League of the Ho-de-no-sau-nee or Iroquois* (H. M. Lloyd, Ed. and annotator) (Vol. 1). New York: Dodd, Mead, 1901.

Murdock, G. P. Ethnographic atlas: A summary. *Ethnology,* 1967, *6,* 109–236.

Murdock, G. P. World sampling provinces. *Ethnology,* 1968, *7,* 305–326.

Murdock, G. P., & White, D. R. Standard cross-cultural sample. *Ethnology,* 1969, *8,* 329–369.

Naroll, R. Galton's problem. In R. Naroll & R. Cohen (Eds.), *A handbook of method in cultural anthropology.* Garden City, N. Y.: Natural History Press, 1970.

Naroll, R., & D'Andrade, R. G. Two further solutions to Galton's problem. *American Anthropologist,* 1963, *63,* 708–731.

Odulok, T. *Snow people (Chuckchee)* (J. Cleugh, trans.). New Haven: HRAF Press, 1954.

Sears, R. R., Maccoby, E., & Levin, H. *Patterns of child rearing.* Evanston, Ill.: Row, Peterson, 1957.

Sorenson, E. R. *Edge of the forest.* Washington, D. C.: Smithsonian Institution Press, 1976.

Super, C. Unpublished fieldnotes, n.d.

Sverdup, H. *Hos tundrafolket.* Oslo: Gyldendal Norsk Forlag, 1938.

Walter, H., & Lieth, H. *Klimachagramm-weltatlas.* Jena: Gustav Fischer, 1967.

Watson, J. B., & Morgan, J. J. B. Emotional reactions and psychological experimentation. *American Journal of Psychology,* 1917, *28,* 163-174.

Whiting, B. B. The dependency hang-up and experiments in alternative life-styles. In S. Cutler & M. Yinger (Eds.), *Major social issues: A multidisciplinary view.* New York: Free Press, 1978.

Whiting, J. W. M. *Becoming a Kwoma.* New Haven: Yale University Press (for the Institute of Human Relations), 1941.

Whiting, J. W. M. Effects of climate on certain cultural practices. In W. Goodenough (Ed.), *Explorations in cultural anthropology.* New York: McGraw-Hill, 1964.

Whiting, J. W. M. *Causes and consequences of the amount of body contact between mother and infant.* Paper presented at the Annual Meeting of the American Anthropological Association, New York, 1971.

Whiting, J. W. M. *A model for psycho-cultural research.* Distinguished Lecturer Address presented at the Annual Meeting of the American Anthropological Association, New Orleans, 1973.

Whiting, J. W. M., & Child, I. L. *Child training and personality.* New Haven: Yale University Press, 1953.

Wissler, C. *Man and culture.* New York: Thomas Y. Crowell, 1923.

ETHNOGRAPHIC BIBLIOGRAPHY

Most of the ethnographic sources will be found in the bibliographies of the Human Relations Area Files, the Ethnographic Atlas (*Ethnology,* 1962–1967), and works by J. Whiting (1964), Murdock and White (1969), and/or Barry and Paxson (1971). Additional sources are listed below.

Chard, C. The Kamchadal: A synthetic sketch. In *Kroeber Anthropological Society Papers,* Nos. 8–9. Berkeley: University of California Press, 1953.

Dennis, W., & Dennis, M. G. Cradles and cradling practices of the Pueblo Indians. *American Anthropologist,* 1940, *42,* 107–115.

Fischer, J. L., & Fischer, A. The New Englanders of Orchard Town, U. S. A. In B. Whiting (Ed.), *Six cultures: Studies of child rearing.* New York: John Wiley & Sons, 1963.

Hitchcock, J. T. *The Magars of Banyan Hill.* New York: Holt, Rinehart & Winston, 1966.

Hollos, M. *Growing up in Flathill: Social environment and cognitive development.* Bergen and Oslo: Scandinavian Universities Press, 1973.

Lee, R. B., & DeVore, I. (Eds.). *Kalahari hunter-gatherers: Studies of the !Kung San and their neighbors.* Cambridge, Mass.: Harvard University Press, 1976.

Levin, M. G., & Potapov, L. P. *Peoples of Siberia.* Chicago: University of Chicago Press, 1956.

Murray, E. Kirghiz of Tekes Valley: With the nomads of Central Asia, a summer's sojourn in the Tekes Valley, plateau paradise of Mongol & Turkic tribes. *National Geographic Magazine,* 1950.

Nydegger, W., & Nydegger, C. Tarong: An Ilocos barrio in the Philippines. In B. Whiting (Ed.), *Six cultures: Studies of child rearing.* New York: John Wiley & Sons, 1963.

Passantino, J. E. Kunming, southwestern gateway to China. *National Geographic Magazine,* 1946, *90,* 137–168.

Shirokogoroff, S. M. *Social organization of the northern Tungus.* Commercial Press, 1929.

Whiting, J. W. M., & Murdock, G. P. *The development of the individual in Tenino culture.* Unpublished manuscript, 1935.

Wylie, L. *Village in the Vaucluse.* Cambridge, Mass.: Harvard University Press, 1974.

∼❧ 8 ❧∼

Behavioral Development in Infancy

Charles M. Super

Infancy has long held a special place in theories of human development: the emerging blend of biology and psychology is rapid and salient, the roots of the psyche are said to be formed, the nearly certain potential of the small and vulnerable creature is awesome, and babies are cute. For a long period in the history of the social sciences, the infant was seen as a tabula rasa, if not necessarily for the environment to scribble upon at will, then as a medium for spelling out the theoretician's views. The dramatic progress in our understanding of the importance and the dynamics of infancy over the past few decades reflects primarily the collection and interpretation of a large body of facts about normative development and its relationship to various social and biological influences. The focus on infancy in the comparative human literature shares many theoretical concerns with psychology, as well as providing a point of convergence for anthropological theories of culture and personality.

Infancy could not gain serious attention within anthropology until the theories became "individualized" (Harris, 1968), and Margaret Mead's early work, which marks the emergence of culture and personality as a field of study, can thus be identified as initiating anthropological interest in the first two years of life (Mead, 1930; Bateson & Mead, 1950; 1952; 1954). Ethnographic description of infant care remained the anthropological datum until J. Whiting and Child's (1953) landmark quantitative work. Psychology has been inherently more individualistic and infants received early scrutiny within Western culture (Tiedemann, 1787, cited by Kessen, Haith, & Salapatek, 1970). Psychological research in this century has of course been marked by quantitative methods, but psychologists have tended to remain in their own culture, if not their own laboratory. Erik Erikson (1950) ranks as one of the first psychologists professionally to observe infant life outside the Western European tradition. The first truly quantitative, culturally comparative, behavioral study of infancy cited in this review, which is intended to be reasonably comprehensive, was published in 1940 (Dennis); the great majority have been carried out in the last decade. In short, the field is itself young, young enough for only portions of what is needed to have been worked on. Still, there is an emerging outline of the common thrust of infancy, its variations, and their evolutionary and developmental significance.

This chapter is directed primarily toward assembling reports of infant behavioral development in non-Euro-American societies, especially in the first year of life, and considering what they can tell us about infancy. The behavioral review is organized into five topical domains: the newborn infant and motor, cognitive, social, and state behavior in the subsequent 2 years. Following this central presentation is a discussion of the patterning of infant care and development, that is, of how infant life is integrated into larger cultural systems. Finally, there is a brief consideration of how comparative research might best contribute in the future to our understanding of infancy.

The concept of "geographic race" (Garn, 1965) is useful in organizing some of the sections and subsections below because it overlaps with cultural groupings in a gross sense and because we usually lack more specifically relevant background information. Occasionally, as in the newborn case, the theoretical question is a genetic one, but it should be evident that "race" is not considered here to be a generally useful variable for causal analysis.

INFANT BEHAVIOR

Status at Birth

There is a frequent assumption in cross-cultural research generally, not often made explicit, that all cultural and ethnic groups are identical at the population level in genetically transmitted dispositions of behavioral or psychological significance. While this assumption may be correct, it has been challenged in the past few years with sufficiently intriguing data to warrant serious review. With the exception of Jensen's predominantly psychometric argument (which in the end also turns to the newborn findings: Jensen, 1969, p. 86), these challenges are usually based on alleged differences in the first hours and days after birth, comparisons which supposedly preclude any environmental effects. The logic of arguments based on neonatal data does not match their simple elegance, however, for two reasons. First, there is no reason to believe that all or even any major portion of behaviorally significant, genetically controlled differences will be evident at birth. Sex difference which do not appear until puberty provide an obvious example. Null results at birth therefore do not themselves rule out genetic differences. Second, differences at birth do not imply genetic differences, since neonatal status is not free of environmental effects. Maternal nutrition, health, and psychological state have been operative factors for 9 months. There are, in addition, powerful perinatal and postnatal factors that rapidly affect performance, and most newborn assessment is not carried out until several days have elapsed.

The behavioral and neurological assessment of newborns is a difficult and still emerging enterprise, and before reviewing the comparative work in detail it is worth considering what questions it does and does not address. Comparing newborns of unmedicated, malnourished mothers from a developing country to those of middle-class American mothers in excellent health but who were heavily anesthetized, for example, can yield an accurate picture of newborns in those groups as they actually are under the prevailing circumstances. This may prove useful in understanding parental or professional responses to the babies or for following their subsequent development, but it can tell us nothing about inherent, genetically determined differences because the important nongenetic factors of maternal health and medication are not controlled.

Fifteen years ago R. Bell (1963) outlined six factors that require careful control in studies of neonatal behavior because they are known sources of significant variation in performance. Research since that time and consideration of the nature of the comparative enterprise suggest five other factors requiring attention in the interpretation of newborn test results. The first two factors are characteristics of the subject. (1) Both *gestational and postnatal age* are important, the former determining the developmental maturity of the organism, at least within a range of variation (Fantz, Fagan, & Miranda, 1975; Tilford, 1976), and the latter reflecting physiological stabilization (Prechtl & Beintema, 1964; Rosenblith, 1961; Yang, 1962) and interacting with perinatal drugs (Brazelton, 1961), maternal hormones transmitted in utero (Migeon, Bertrand, & Wall, 1957; Migeon, Keller, Lawrence, & Shephard, 1957), and postnatal experience.

(2) *Parity* has important correlates with maternal hormone production and status of the uterus (see discussion by R. Bell, 1963), and subsequent effects on infant and maternal behavior (Thoman, Turner, Leiderman, & Barnett, 1970; Waldrop & Bell, 1966). It can affect at least one index of autonomic nervous functioning (basal skin conductance) such that laterborns appear more mature than firstborns (Weller & Bell, 1965); according to one source, parity has a similar effect on skeletal maturity at birth (Christie, Dunham, Jenss, & Dipple, 1941). Unfortunately, most research on parity focuses on firstborns versus laterborns (i.e., second and third), since that is the major contrast in the Western subcultures where the work has been done. Cross-cultural work more often includes a range of ten or more births per mother, and there is no good study of this difference.

There is in addition a large number of environmental conditions which influence newborn behavior. (3) *Complications and conditions of pregnancy and delivery* constitute the largest category. Physiological complications can of course lead to temporary or permanent abnormality, and the incidence of complications varies even among subgroups in Western society (Pasamanick & Knobloch, 1957/58). There are enormous cultural differences in attitudes toward pregnancy and childbirth: their public and private salience and their sexual implications; themes of achievement and atonement; whether they are seen as secular or supernatural, clean or defiling, normal or "sick" (Newton & Newton, 1972). These differences are reflected in obstetric management and psychological state of the mother, and they can in turn affect the course of pregnancy and delivery and the behavior of the newborn (Dart, 1977; Davids, Holden, & Gray, 1963; Dlugokinski & Jones, 1978; Escardo & de Coriat, 1960; Ferreira, 1960; Grimm, 1967; Newton, 1970; J. Rosenblatt, 1967; C. Smith & Steinschneider, 1975). In general, psychological characteristics of the mother, such as anxiety level or attitudes toward pregnancy, have been linked to suboptimal behavioral dispositions in the infant, such as irritability or muscular hypertension. Behavioral effects of obstetric procedures, aside from drugs and the question of risk, have not been well researched. Recent claims for beneficial effects for the infant of "birth without violence" (Leboyer, 1975) are not adequately supported by data (Odent, 1976; Rapoport, 1975/1976). Diet, spacing of pregnancies, and maternal age may also affect newborn status and behavior, as does, apparently, even the season of the year (Ignat'eva, 1969; McDonald, 1966).

(4) The pervasive effects of *medication* deserve special mention. The tragic consequences of some kinds of medication during pregnancy are well known; it is not known whether or not other substances, modern or traditional, have nonpathogenic effects that are more subtle. Maternal medication during labor and delivery is well documented as causing variations in infant behavior (Bowes, Brackbill, Conway, & Steinscheider, 1970; Moreau & Birch, 1974), although questions remain about type

and dosage effects and possible interactions with ethnicity (Horowitz, Ashton, Culp, Gaddis, Levin, & Reichman, 1977).

A variety of postnatal procedures affect infant behavior rapidly enough to show up in neonatal assessment. (5) *Method of feeding* is important for several reasons: some maternal drugs and immunities can be transmitted in breast milk, and the personal olfactory cues may play a role in early communication (MacFarlane, 1975). There are several reports of greater activity or arousal in breastfed infants, in most cases within the first few days (R. Bell, 1966; Bernal & Richards, 1970; Davis, Sears, Miller, & Brodbeck, 1948; Hoefer & Hardy, 1929), although the causes are not clear (Bernal & Richards, 1970). Physical growth effects of demand versus scheduled feeding have been experimentally demonstrated in the first week of life in at least one population (Salber, 1956). (6) *Other routines* with demonstrated early effects on arousal or social behavior are swaddling (Giacoman, 1971; Lipton, Steinschneider, & Richmond, 1965), covering (deVries & Super, 1979), bathing (Whitner & Thompson, 1970), visual stimulation (Boismier, 1977), maternal intervention and vocalization (Thoman, Korner, & Beason-Williams, 1977), and circumcision (Richards, Bernal, & Brackbill, 1976).

Finally, there are important issues in test procedures. (7) *Controlling the infant's state of arousal* is now recognized as critical (Brazelton, 1973; Korner, 1972; Prechtl & Beintema, 1964). (8) *The physical and social setting* for the examination plays a role, as does the timing of the examination with regard to the baby's activity and prandial cycles (Ashton & Connolly, 1971; deVries & Super, 1979; Schmidt & Burns, 1971). (9) There are probably *tester differences* in the ability to elicit certain kinds of behavior (Osofsky, 1976), even though testers can be trained to score reliably the same observed behaviors. (10) Since effects of *tester expectations* have been demonstrated in far more objective situations (Rosenthal, 1966), one must assume that they can operate here (see Kaye & Tronick, 1977, concerning reports of sex differences). This is especially important because most researchers active in the area are working from a particular theoretical point of view, formulated in advance of much of their empirical investigation. (11) The final procedural point concerns *sampling.* Neonatal studies, with very few exceptions, are carried out in Western-style hospitals, in part to provide a standard setting and in part because hospitals, like other formal institutions, are routes of access for outside researchers. The portion of a population that delivers at a hospital can vary from virtually all (urban America) to virtually none (rural Africa), and may be biased toward high-risk cases (e.g., Britain) or in other ways. Cross-cultural researchers are not always attentive to differential sampling, and some are less careful than others about generalizing to an entire ethnic or racial group.

No single cross-cultural or cross-ethnic study of newborns has adequately controlled for even a majority of these factors, and there is, alas, no simple way to do so. A few, such as state and medication, are now almost routinely taken into account, but if one controls for parity, medication, and setting, for example, it is not possible to have similar sampling in many groups. Tester differences and expectations involve equally knotty problems. Really firm conclusions therefore ultimately rest on replication of results, replication by different scientists working under a variety of circumstances and theories.

Despite this pantheon of methodological problems, the evidence reviewed below makes it apparent that even in the first few days of life infants of various groups and subgroups may differ in their typical patterns of behavior. It is also evident, however, that it is difficult at present to describe, interpret, and draw theoretical conclusions from these differences. The fragility of even the essential findings reported here is a sure marker of the need for more and better research.

Studies of African Newborns

The most widely known study of group differences at birth is that by Geber and Dean (1957a), although there is considerable disagreement over what, if anything, was demonstrated and over its interpretation. They report, after examining a large number of predominantly Baganda newborns in hospitals in Kampala, Uganda, that these African babies were "at a more advanced state of development than newborn European children." The precocity was most evident in a lesser degree of flexion in muscle tone, by a "remarkable control of the head," and by "the frequent absence of primitive reflex activity." This latter characteristic is the most important from the point of view of the behavioral scientist because the primitive reflexes, such as Moro, Babinski, and grasping reflexes, normally disappear in Euro-American samples only after 6–10 weeks of age, presumably as a function of important neurological maturation in the higher, cortical areas of the brain (Peiper, 1963). To find that one racial or ethnic group was dramatically advanced in such a basic aspect of development would have profound implications. The typical newborn in their sample, Geber and Dean reported, was at a level of maturity comparable to the average 4–6-week-old European infant.

There are enough internal flaws in this work to have suggested caution in accepting it, but it has been widely quoted, it is reprinted in at least one introductory reader, and it has remained virtually unchallenged in the literature until fairly recently. The shortcomings are of two sorts. First, the analysis and reporting of results are inadequate. No average scores are presented, and no statistical analyses are performed. Comparison groups of European and Asian newborns are briefly mentioned but are not described, and no actual data are provided. In short, these results of potentially great import are "presented by scarcely more than verbal assurance," to borrow Warren's (1972) apt phrase. There are in addition several internal contradictions in the reporting of this work, ranging from the relatively unimportant (the number of infants examined is given once as 107 [Geber & Dean, 1957a], and again as 113 [1957b]) to the major theme: the typical plantar response is described variously as both extensor (Geber & Dean, 1957a) and flexor (Geber & Dean, 1964).

The second shortcoming derives from technical aspects of the examination procedures. Geber and Dean used an examination developed by André-Thomas, Chesni, and Saint Anne-Dargassies (1960) for the detection of neurological risk, that is, for distinguishing the normal newborn from the one who has suffered, or may have suffered, neurological damage. Its usefulness for identifying important differences among normal individuals is not clear. In addition, the majority (78 percent) of Geber and Dean's African subjects were under 2 days of age, when newborn behavior may not have stabilized adequately even for reliable medical screening (Beintema, 1968; Prechtl & Beintema, 1964). This is all the more critical because no control was exercised, apparently, over the infant's state of arousal during the attempted elicitations.

Research since Geber and Dean's newborn report is consistent in contradicting the claim of remarkable neural maturity in African infants at birth. In conjunction with studies of somatic development carried out both before and after 1957, the literature presents a somewhat more complicated answer with regard to other aspects of African neonatal precocity, one that might be summarized for the student of behavior as a modest "no."

Neurological status. The question of neurological advancement is directly addressed by several reports from Africa. J. Griffiths (1969) examined Bantu newborns in Johannesburg, focusing on the Moro, plantar, and abdominal reflexes. She shows that the Moro response persisted and then receded over the first few months at a rate very similar to that reported for white babies in Boston (Paine, Brazelton, Donovan, Drorbaugh, Hubbell, & Sears, 1964). Similarly, the plantar reflex progressed from flexion to extension as reported in Europe (Brain & Wilkinson, 1959). Technical problems prevented a quantitative comparison of groups with regard to the abdominal reflex, but Griffiths states that the Bantu infants responded similarly to whites.

Konner (1972) used Prechtl and Beintema's (1964) neurological examination on a limited sample of babies of the !Kung San hunter–gatherers in the Kalahari desert of Botswana and reported the normal presence of neonatal reflexes. Super (unpublished data) has found normal responses among agricultural Kipsigis in Kenya, as did Keefer, Dixon, Tronik, and Brazelton (1978) among their neighbors the Gusii. In Zaire, Vincent and Hugon (1962) found that 61 percent of newborns over 3 kg in a hospital sample demonstrated the standing reflex. This figure is somewhat low by Euro-American standards, but no details are provided concerning perinatal procedures or testing factors such as the control of state. Only 16 percent of the infants responded with the automatic walking reflex, but the authors note that this response was "capricious" on repeated testing.

A thorough study was carried out by Warren and Parkin (1974) in Kampala, the site of Geber and Dean's original work. In examining 104 African and 52 European infants from the same hospitals, they failed to replicate several of Geber and Dean's findings. All African (and European) babies demonstrated the "doll's eye" reflex, compared to the earlier report of complete absence. Of 19 other classic reflexes tested (excluding for the moment the Moro reflex), three showed significant racial differences, two being stronger in the Europeans and one in the Africans.

Warren and Parkin did find racial differences on the Moro reflex, 5 of the 6 differences being statistically significant. On both the "drop" and "thump" methods of elicitation, Ugandan neonates had higher thresholds and less extention and adduction of the arms. These differences relate in some sense to the notion of weaker Moro responses although by no means to the claim of near absence. Equally important, Warren and Parkin go on to pursue the logical significance of their result, and they conclude that the greater extent of response would correspond to greater maturity for the Europeans. None of their Moro measures correlates with gestational age (that is, presumably, maturation) as estimated by external characteristics (Farr, Mitchell, Neligan, & Parkin, 1966), but they cite a more accurate study based on calculations from the last menstrual period (Finnström, 1971) which indicates that within the newborn period stronger Moro responses are positively correlated with maturity ($r = 0.71$). The analogy with decline over 3 or 4 months therefore is not valid, and this analogy is the core of Geber and Dean's logic.

Sertel, De Sosa, and Moosa (1976) directly measured the speed of conduction in two peripheral nerves (ulnar and posterior tibial), a procedure which reflects the state of maturity of the peripheral nervous system and, one might imagine, the central nervous system as well. Newborns of English, West Indian (predominantly

African), and Turkish ancestry were compared, and the West Indian infants were not faster (more mature) than the other groups. They were, in fact, slower than the English infants, but this effect was significant for males only, and there is some reason to think that conduction in the English males in this sample was unrepresentatively fast. No differences were found at 3 months of age.

There are three other relevant reports, all claiming African neonatal precocity, but for various reasons they are difficult to evaluate or cannot be given much weight. Freedman (1974) reports that in a predominantly Hausa sample from a Northern Nigerian hospital the Babinski and Moro reflexes were "relatively muted," while the automatic walking response was especially "brisk." Because the data are analyzed in a multigroup comparison and the African sample size is relatively small, it is not possible to assess the statistical significance of the apparent Caucasian–African difference. In any event, data on the two weak reflexes do not corroborate Geber and Dean's more dramatic claim, as Freedman points out. Freedman relates the stronger walking reflex to later motor precocity, a topic which is reviewed below, and clearly puts it in the domain of strength and muscle tone rather than neurological maturity (as the term "briskness", rather than "ease of elicitation," implies). Unfortunately, no information is given about perinatal medication or postnatal care for his groups, factors which could play a role in the results.

Electroenecephalographic ("brainwave") records were taken from eight Bantu newborns in Johannesburg by Nelson and Dean (1959), who found some suggestion (unspecified) of "a degree of maturity greater than that usually found in European newborn children." The authors conclude, however, that these preliminary results from a small sample should be "treated with reserve." In the same article they imply clear differences in later infancy, but a more detailed report of the same study (Nelson, 1959) states that normal African infants had dominant frequencies "similar to [those of] normal American children."

Finally, Vouilloux (1959a) reports a replication of the rapid diminution of two neonatal reflexes in a sample from Cameroon, and this is occasionally cited as confirmation of Geber and Dean's newborn findings. On examination, however, the evidence is problematic and probably contradictory. No data are given for the Moro reaction because the number of subjects was insufficient; Vouilloux states only that the trend was similar to that for the plantar extensor response, which "diminishes much more quickly [with age] than for European infants" (p. 14). There are three difficulties in accepting this statement at face value. First, the median number of subjects at each age is below nine, which seems small for reliable estimates given the instability of the response documented by Touwen (1971). Second, the procedural details are scanty, and the reader has little information, for example, about the infants' states or the particular stimulus used. For a response as complex and as difficult to score as the plantar reflex, such details are critical. In the newborn period it is not difficult to confuse elicitation of the Babinski extension with the plantar grasp (flexion) response (Prechtl & Beintema, 1964, p. 36). In later months the receptive field for the extensor reflex diminishes dramatically (Brain & Wilkinson, 1959), as flexion becomes predominant with stimulation in some areas. State of arousal also becomes influential (Waggoner and Ferguson, 1930). Third, and most critically, no quantitative comparison with European data is presented, and the basis of Vouilloux's conclusion is therefore not clear. His data for the neonatal period are in fact identical to those from European reports—all infants show extension. The diminution occurs later in the first year, when, as Vouilloux points out, experiential effects could be present. In any case, the figures he gives are not obviously different from published European data, granted the methodologic shortcomings. Forty-eight percent of Vouilloux's subjects gave an extensor response at 6 months, for example. Schlesinger (1927) reports a shift from extension to flexion at 6 months; Waggoner and Ferguson (1930) found 1–72 percent extension, depending on the strength of the stimulus and how one scores extension of the big toe combined with flexion of the other toes. They give figures of 88–96 percent full flexion for infants 12 months old, compared to Vouilloux's 91 percent.

In short, there is no reliable corroboration of Geber and Dean's claim of neurological precocity in African newborns. Substantial contradictory evidence now exists, as well as doubt about the original methodology.

Physical maturity.   There is an older and more complex line of inquiry, however, concerning black–white differences in physical development at birth. The evidence considered below substantiates several such differences, but it would appear to be inaccurate to draw from them any conclusion regarding a generalized somatic precocity. A number of points must be reviewed in demonstrating this conclusion, and along the way it will be useful to keep in mind Tanner's statement that "since different body systems do not all mature at the same rate, different measures of maturity give different results" (Tanner, 1974, p. 88). Dental and skeletal development, which figure importantly in the racial difference literature, are two systems which show particular independence at the individual level (Tanner, 1962, p. 84). Once the notion is put aside that black and white babies grow according to fundamentally different clocks, it will be evident that the specific and limited racial differences are probably of no importance to the behavioral and social scientist.

The issue is best introduced with the data of Vincent and Hugon (1962). Working in a hospital in Leopoldville (now Kinshasa), they noted that the classic Euro-American definition of prematurity (birthweight under 2.5 kg) did not yield the expected clinical results. By that criterion 28 percent of their patients were premature, compared to European figures of about 8 percent. They suggest a criterion for Africa of 2.1 kg, on the grounds that French and Zairois results are then approximately equal for (1) percent of sample defined as premature, (2) mortality rates, (3) radiographic analysis of skeletal development, and (4) the recovery of birthweight. The authors invoke a racial factor to explain this state of affairs because nothing else, in their words, can explain how infants could be born "more mature, with smaller birth weights, after a shorter period of growth."

Are African babies in a more mature bodily state after a shorter gestation? The answer depends on what data one accepts as more reliable and how one goes about sorting out the interactions of birthweight and maturity. Unitl recently many American physicians concluded simply that blacks had a higher rate of prematurity (i.e., a greater percentage of births under 2.5 kg). Vincent and Hugon's data clearly indicate that more is involved, and some scientists summarize the facts by standardizing on birthweight: "Low birth weight African infants," write Grantham-McGregor and Back (1971, p. 86) of the Leopoldville study, were "more mature in the developmental processes than European infants of the same weight." However, one could equally well standardize on developmental processes and conclude that Africans weigh less than European infants of the same developmental status.

To try to achieve some resolution on this issue, let us first review the evidence for each of the three characteristics mentioned (birthweight, gestation period, maturity) and then return to the logic of interpretation. Most relevant studies report lower average birthweights for infants of African as compared to European ancestry (e.g., Anderson, Brown, & Lyon, 1943; Crump, Carell, Masuoka, & Ryan, 1957; Meredith, 1952; Warren & Parkin, 1974). Although this has not been demonstrated with rigorous sampling and control over maternal health and nutrition, prenatal care, and parity, the finding has been repeated under so many circumstances, sometimes including apparently healthy, well-nourished black mothers, that the evidence is reasonably convincing. The "true" difference is probably considerably smaller than what is reported in most of these studies, however, since the gap is narrowed in samples selected under relatively optimal circumstances (Scott, Jenkins, & Crawford, 1950).

There is conflicting evidence on the second question, whether black babies undergo a shorter or equal gestation. Anderson, Brown, and Lyon (1943) estimated on the basis of maternal recall of the last menstrual period that black singletons in Cincinnati had a mean gestational period of 274.0 days, compared to 279.5 for white singletons. (The difference is statistically significant even when low-birthweight and therefore possibly premature infants are excluded.) Hotelling and Hotelling (1932) report figures of 276.3 (black) and 281.4 (white) days from a California clinic. Similar results (276.9 and 279.8 days) are given by Meyer (1915). Schachter, Kerr, Wimberly, and Lachin (1975), on the other hand, found means of 277.2 and 276.5 days, respectively, a nonsignificant difference in the opposite direction. Unfortunately, none of these studies controls for parity, a factor that might bias toward shorter gestation in whichever group had more children (Hotelling & Hotelling, 1932, found a small, nonsignificant effect of parity on gestational age.) Simply on the grounds of recency, the results of Schacter et al. may be less confounded with maternal health and nutrition.

It is difficult, of course, to obtain reliable information on the last menstrual period, and in many populations it is impossible. The only alternative for calculating gestational age, however, is problematic for the present purposes: it involves estimation on the basis of physical and/or neurological signs of maturity (e.g., Dubowitz, Dubowitz, & Goldberg, 1970) and therefore is not an independent measure. The results are nevertheless relevant in their own right to our third question, regarding somatic maturity. The more strictly neurologic results have been reviewed above. Using the Dubowitz, Dubowitz, and Goldberg (1970) procedures, which emphasize somatic signs such as skin texture and flexibility of joints, Brueton, Palit, and Prosser (1973) examined 640 predominantly Yoruba newborns in Nigeria. The regression equation they derived for estimating gestational ages was not significantly different from the one found by Dubowitz (1972) for white babies, and they conclude that there is "no evidence of advanced development."

Parkin (1971) has reported in detail the results of similar examinations of Ugandan and British newborns. The Ugandan infants showed a significant advance in skull hardness, lanugo hair, and nail texture, the last not significant if only subjects between 24 and 36 hours are included. There are nonsignificant trends for the Africans to be advanced in skin texture, breast size, and nail length. Parkin presents three possible interpretations: that the obtained differences are artifactual, that they are unimportant *specific* differences, and that they represent a true dimension of general somatic maturity.

Parkin rejects the possibility that there are no "real" racial differences on the grounds that his procedures and controls are adequate. Despite a few unexplored possibilities such as maternal nutrition, the conclusion seems reasonable.

Second, Parkin suggests, there might be only two highly specific real racial differences, in body hair and osseous development, with no implications for overall maturity. Here we need to consider for a moment the logic of inferring greater maturity for a group on the basis of a few indices, since the problem is central to many group comparisons. Suppose that a certain characteristic has been shown to progress from state A to state B in the process of maturation, and that group 1 has been shown to have "more" of state A at birth than group 2. It does not follow that group 1 is less mature than group 2, since there may be sources of variance other than maturity. Consider, for example, skin color. All newborns darken somewhat in the first weeks of life, presumably on exposure to higher levels of sunlight than exist in utero. It is also true that Africans have darker skin than whites in the first days. This does not constitute evidence for greater maturity, however, because race is itself associated with differences in pigmentation. The differences persist throughout life, and their significance at birth is debatable, since whatever analogy is used could apply equally later with no clear sense: Can group 1 be less mature at age 20 years, or 60? Does group 2 have a shorter lifespan?

The reliable differences in Parkin's data are ones that persist and appear to be true racial differences in their own right, as Parkin points out. In the first case, it is a common observation, supported by more organized inquiry, that whites tend to have more body hair in adulthood than do Africans (Garn, 1951; Seligman, 1966, p. 122).

The evidence regarding osseous development is more complex. There are many reports of advanced skeletal development in African infants, both in Africa (Beresowski, & Lundie, 1952; Falkner, 1957; Jones & Dean, 1956; Kagwa, 1970; Massé & Hunt, 1963) and in the New World (Christie, Dunham, Jenss, & Dippel, 1941; Dunham, Jenss, & Christie, 1939; Hess & Weinstock, 1925; Kelley & Reynolds, 1947). The advancement generally consists of a higher proportion of black infants than white with identifiable presence of certain centers of epiphysial growth at birth (other centers show no racial differences: Beresowski & Lundie, 1952). The sizes of centers that are present in a high proportion of all infants, such as the distal end of the femur, do not show significant racial differences (Thompkins & Wiehl, 1954). Despite occasional notes of caution in interpretation (Kagwa, 1970) and some technical procedures such as equating on birthweight that might introduce a bias (e.g., Christie et al., 1941), the basic finding seems firm.

Studies of skeletal maturity beyond early childhood are fewer and rest on different measures, but Todd (1931), Malina (1970), and Marshall, Ashcroft, and Bryan (1970) are in general agreement that American blacks show modest evidence of relative advancement at some points in middle and late childhood. In Malina's report, especially, the data are equivocal for males, probably because of sexual asymmetry of the influx of white genes. Massé and Hunt (1963) found a reversal of relative skeletal maturity in childhood, but this is probably due to nutritional factors. The picture is further complicated by the fact that racial variations in mean velocity of skeletal growth are more marked in the long bone centers. This is presumably related to blacks' longer extremities at maturity (Garn, 1965, p. 27; Laska-Mierzejewska, 1970; cf. Satgé, Debroise, Dan, Cros, Coly, Rayboud, & Villoud, 1968), but its implication for the infant data, which concern the carpals and tarsals almost exclusively, is not clear. These round bone centers have low predictive efficiency in

American white children (Garn, Silverman, & Rohmann, 1964) and show "considerable variability in the assessment of skeletal age later in the growth period" (Malina, 1970, p. 387).

It is well established that some of the permanent teeth (e.g., the third molars) erupt earlier in African children (as well as in other groups) than among Europeans (e.g., Carothers, 1947; Chagula, 1960; Shourie, 1946; Steggerda & Hill, 1942; Suk, 1919). Data on the second molar are more equivocal (see Hiernaux, 1970). The precocity reports have occasionally been related to the separate skeletal work, but there is no reason to think the two domains are necessarily and particularly linked in their timing (Tanner, 1962, p. 84). There is no racial difference in the development of deciduous dentition, which appears to vary in timing independently of skeletal and bodily maturity (Tanner, 1962, pp. 71, 85). It may be that a small difference in hormonal functioning in the last trimester of pregnancy could account for some of this patterning of racial contrasts in dentition (Tanner, 1966), but in any event we are again prompted to avoid a comparison in terms of generalized maturity.

In short, there seem to be three possibilities among which one can make no certain choice but none of which argues for overall skeletal precocity. First, the variety of reported differences in osseous development could possibly be environmentally caused (Massé, cited by Hiernaux, 1970). Second, there may be some possibly inter-related racial differences in skeletal maturation up to adolescence, at which point a host of other factors enter and after which the relevant questions, if there are any, seem not to have been asked. The skeletal differences therefore might be classified as a long-term racial difference and not indicative of general precocity at birth. Finally, one could reject the childhood data as equivocal and isolate the infant differences as a special case unrelated to any overall skeletal maturity. In this interpretation, too, the evidence would not suggest advanced development in general in utero.

Although Parkin acknowledges the possibility of this sort of argument, he rejects it in the end on two grounds in favor of a generalized racial difference. Geber and Dean, he points out, found substantial neurological and behavioral advancement, which supports the advanced maturity position. But as reviewed above, later work, to which Parkin made a major contribution, has failed to support the Geber and Dean report. Parkin's second reason was that allowing specific racial differences in hair and bone does not explain the nonsignificant trends for nail texture and length, breast size, and skin texture. It seems quite possible, however, that these phenomena can be explained, too, without recourse to overall maturity. There are probably lifelong racial differences in skin texture, as at least some obstetricians have noticed regarding the incidence of tearing of the perineum during delivery (Robertson-Glasgow, personal communication). In both the maternal and infant cases, the difference is smoother, more flexible skin in blacks. As for the African newborns' more advanced breast development, it is possible that the absence of control for parity could play a role, since parity is known to affect levels of at least some hormones in both mother and fetus (see R. Bell, 1963). There is no obvious explanation for differences in nail length and texture, but there might be some uncontrolled factor such as parity involved, or it, too, might be a specific racial difference.

One can note, in addition, that there are other indices not traditionally examined in this context but which nevertheless would imply white precocity, following the same flawed logic. The greater birthweight of whites is one. Schachter, Kerr, Wimberly, and Lachin (1974) report another: higher resting heart rate (in sleep) in a sample of black American newborns than in whites, not attributable to birthweight, gestational age, degree of motor activity, amount of crying, or percentage REM (rapid eye movement) sleep. Since resting heart rate declines with age, this finding would be evidence for relative immaturity of blacks.

There are bodily racial differences at birth, as there are at other ages. The relevant questions here are, (1) Do any of these differences indicate differences in level of maturity at birth? (2) Do any of these differences have implications for behavioral or psychological development, aside from the question of maturity? The answer to the first question appears, on the basis of the evidence reviewed above, to be no; there is no convincing argument that the differences imply overall precocity at birth. It seems likely that the notion of level of maturity at birth, borrowed from medical concerns with pathology and risk, is not relevant to the complex pattern of specific somatic black–white differences.

As for the second question, none of the differences cited above has any direct or obvious relevance to behavior. The only study seeking an empirical relationship between selected anatomical and behavioral variables in newborns (Crowell, 1962) was unsuccessful. Furthermore, even if one were to dismiss the entire discussion of specific racial differences and accept the black–white newborn data at face value as evidence of black precocity, the typical difference amounts to 4–5 days (Parkin, 1971; Anderson, Brown, & Lyon, 1943). This compares to an error of prediction from physical and neurological signs of about 17 days and a standard for behavioral and medical significance of about 14 days either side of term. The obtained difference, in other words, would have no practical or probably even normally detectable significance.

Newborn behavior. There are several studies which directly assess the behavior of African and black newborns. Reliable behavioral differences would obviously be of considerable importance in understanding culturally patterned methods of infant care and their consequences, but in general the evidence concerning African neonates is negative. There may be an exception in the realm of muscle tone or motor response, although the reports are not in full agreement and there is at present no adequate basis for explaining the difference.

Geber (1973) followed up her Ugandan work in several other African countries, primarily Zambia, where she examined 90 newborns from subsidized and fee-for-service wards in an urban hospital. Without making any specific quantitative comparison, she reports that the infants from lower-class homes suffered from edema, dry skin, and poor pigmentation, indicative of poor maternal health and nutrition. In their behavior, she found the babies to show a high degree of flexion and to be relatively quiet and unresponsive. The 10 babies from middle-class homes appeared much healthier and thus comparable to the infants she examined in Uganda. There is no mention, however, of neurological precocity. (In this report Geber also notes that 11 of the 90 Zambians and 14 of the 113 Ugandans were born with one or more extra fingers, an incredible figure.) Geber examined, in addition, small numbers of newborns in Zaire and Senegal, where she was impressed with the infants' development, and in South Africa, where she was not.

Brazelton, Koslowski, and Tronick (1976) also examined Zambian infants, all of lower-class parents, and they are in substantial agreement with Geber concerning the general state of health at birth. Their comparison with 10 American infants is quantitative and explicit. Using the Neonatal Behavioral Assessment Scale (NBAS) developed by Brazelton and his associates (Brazelton, 1973), they found the Zambian newborns low on activity and attentiveness and relatively irritable. Their generally poor state was attributed to a physiologically inadequate intrauterine environment caused by several closely spaced births and poor nutrition. The American sample showed no evidence of dysmaturity and behaved more adequately on the first day. Ten days later the American babies had changed relatively little from their original level, while the Zambians, both recovering from dehydration and undernutrition and benefiting from close maternal contact, the authors infer, improved rapidly. By day 10 they excelled in consolability, social interest, and alertness.

More recent work by the Brazelton group (Keefer, Dixon, Tronick, & Brazelton, 1978) in Kenya found Gusii infants equivalent to a low-risk white American sample in all NBAS items except for motor maturity and general tone. They characterize the difference to be greater control of muscle tone by the Gusii infants, both in their natural movements (e.g., smoother arcs) and in response to the examination procedure (e.g., strong but not hypertonic). This is partially reminiscent of Geber and Dean's report (1957a) of lesser flexion and hypertonicity in Ugandan neonates, a finding which was not replicated by Warren and Parkin (1974). It also resembles the contrast drawn by Escardo and de Coriat (1960) between Argentine infants delivered by standard obstetric procedures and those whose mothers had prepared for "natural childbirth."

deVries and Super (1979), in a primarily methodological paper, present some results from testing several Kenyan groups with the NBAS in varying environments, including traditional homes and modern hospitals. They conclude that physical context (e.g., amount of light), social context (who is present and what they believe about the infant's hardiness, comfortable home or impersonal hospital, etc.), and patterns of care (swaddling, rubbing with oil, rhythms of feeding) all affect the newborn's behavior on the examination and that this properly reflects the way the infant and family are actually adapting to each other. These effects can be seen in the newborn period, on day 5, for example, when the NBAS is commonly used. Because of these factors, as well as the primarily medical ones outlined by R. Bell (1963), the authors point out the immense difficulties in trying to tease out innate group differences from such behavioral data, even in the newborn exams.

The Kenyan and Zambian results, then, provide useful pictures of the actual status of certain samples of infants—how they are behaving and what the parents are therefore responding to—but, as several of the authors indicate, the variations reflect at least in part known environmental differences and are not strong evidence for innate differences.

Three studies report on behavioral examinations of black infants outside Africa. Coll, Sepkoski, and Lester (1977; submitted) report data from black and white American infants (as well as Puerto Rican babies) in northern Florida. The infants were examined relatively early (within 2 days of birth) and were carefully screened for risk factors. Black–white comparisons are not specifically calculated, but apparently a significant difference occurred for only one of their eight a priori summary measures (which were designed to highlight Puerto Rican–white differences): The black babies scored higher on defensive movements when a cloth was put on the face and on hand to mouth activity.

Hopkins (1976) tested black West Indian and white English infants in London. He found the West Indian neonates superior in general tonus and postural control on day 3. After 1 month the same patterns were clearer, probably abetted by differences in postnatal experience such as handling procedures. In addition, the correlation of items had changed, such that some temperament items (e.g., irritability) correlated with motor items for the English infants but not for the West Indians. Hopkins suggests the West Indian babies are "preadapted" for the motor behaviors, but not enough information is provided on perinatal and postnatal treatment to conclude this with any certainty.

Graham, Matarazzo, and Caldwell (1956) also included American babies of African ancestry in their research, using a set of items which were later incorporated, in part, into the NBAS and the Graham/Rosenblith test. There were no race differences on pain threshold, irritability, or muscular tension, but on the maturation scale blacks did score higher. The maturation scale is a summary of several items reflecting motor reflexes (e.g., head turn, grasp), perceptual orienting (e.g., response to bell), and the vigor and persistence of defensive reactions to cotton or paper being placed over the nose. These items are not reported separately, nor is adequate background information given about the two groups; thus it is difficult to evaluate this finding.

The predominant conclusion of these behavioral studies of African and black infants is, in one sense, that of equivalence with white samples, despite chronic failure to control for maternal functioning during pregnancy, parity, medication, perinatal care, and other relevant nonracial variables. Given these confounds, the only repeated finding of differences concerns black superiority in some aspect of motor or muscular behavior, although this term variously includes hand-to-mouth activity, general tonus, postural control, and briskness of the walking reflex. Most of the specific findings are not replicated from one study to another. Brazelton, Koslowski, and Tronick (1976) did not find any such results, although their Zambian subjects were at an obvious environmental disadvantage. It is not yet possible, in short, to reach a satisfactory answer with regard to black–white neonatal differences in an ill-defined domain of motor or muscular strength, activity, or threshold. Whatever differences there might be are apparently slippery and not easily assessed with current techniques, and several explanations would be possible. There is no evidence of differences in any other behavioral domain.

Predictive studies.   Racial differences in the relationship of newborn measures to later behavior are reported by Rosenblith (1974) and Serunian and Broman (1975). Both studies included a full range of neonates, including those at high risk, and report weaker relationships between neonatal and later measures for blacks than for other groups. The latter authors examined black, white, and "Colored Portugese" (a cultural and genetic mixture of West African and Portugese) babies born in the Northeastern United States. Apgar scores, which are a gross estimate of viability immediately after birth, were predictive of Bayley scores at 8 months for the Colored Portugese and the combined sample but not for the black or white groups alone. Rosenblith (1974), using the Graham/Rosenblith procedures, found fewer newborn to 8-month relationships for blacks than for whites, but mental development at 8 months was marginally more related to newborn motor scores, specifically, for blacks than for whites. While these studies do not speak to innate differences in initial level of behavior, they do raise the possibility, as does Hopkins (1976), of different organizational predispositions. In all three studies, however, the amount of intervening experience between the two points of observation is substantial, and in the absence of any coherent theory of structural differences it seems simplest to assume the results reflect unspecified effects of care and environment. Such an assumption, of course, is fragile, and exploring its validity would be a worthwhile direction for research.

Studies of Oriental Newborns

As with African babies, there is a claim in the scientific literature of behavioral differences between infants of Oriental and Euro-American background. In the Oriental case the claim is more precise, less cluttered with poor reports, and freer of occasional racist overtones. The accuracy of the claim, however, is still open to some question and interpretation.

Differences in temperament. Freedman and Freedman (1969) made the original report. Chinese-American and European-American babies averaging 33 hours old were tested using the Cambridge Neonatal Scales, a preliminary version of the NBAS. The subjects were sampled primarily from a single hospital in San Francisco and tested by the same tester during the same period of time. There were several minor background differences between the groups—for example, in parity and more critically in maternal medication (the Chinese were more likely to receive systemic drugs). These differences were found to be unimportant by means of an unspecified statistical treatment, but the value of procedures often used for such purposes is uncertain, for example, when group membership is not randomly assigned (e.g., Woodward & Goldstein, 1977). The two groups were "essentially equal" in sensory development, CNS maturity, motor development, and social responsivity, but the Chinese-American babies scored reliably lower on a number of items that have been characterized as excitability or irritability. Their states of arousal during the examination changed less often, as did their coloring, and they showed less activity and upset when placed on their stomachs (face down) or had a cloth cover the nose. They habituated more rapidly to at least one stimulus (a light in the eyes while sleeping), and were more consolable and self-quieting when they did get upset. While one might wonder about some background and treatment variables not discussed by the authors, the results are fairly convincing on their own terms. One external consideration that makes them particularly believable is the correspondence of the obtained differences to dimensions of temperament that have their own history of research and evidence as biologically influenced personality variables (e.g., Torgersen, 1973).

Freedman has augmented and replicated this work with data from Japanese-American infants in Hawaii, an additional Chinese-American sample in Chicago (working with Kuchner), and a group of Navajo, who, he argues convincingly, are closely related genetically to the other Oriental groups (Freedman, 1974). The importance of this inherited disposition toward behavioral passivity or imperturbability, Freedman theorizes, is its role in the regulation of early child care practices and, eventually, in the culture as a whole. "While it must be true that different cultural practices differentially reward babies' behavior, it is equally likely that biological predispositions effect what become the cultural norms" (Freedman, 1971, p. 228).

Evaluation of a thesis with the clarity and bold sweep of Freeman's requires attention to several different levels of argument. It is unfortunately difficult to review alternative interpretations from internal evidence in Freedman's reports because they are generally written with a broad scope of theory, not with the procedural and analytic detail to support intense scrutiny. This aspect, combined with the occurrence of factual errors in some publications, may give pause to some readers, even though the errors are largely trivial (see McCoy, 1976). Nevertheless, there are two independent reports that are consistent with Freedman's characterization of Oriental infants.

Chisholm (1978) replicated the Navajo–Caucasian differences in irritability. Compared to a working-class sample in London, the Navajo infants were less active and irritable and better at self-quieting when upset. Second, Kagan, Kearsley, and Zelazo (1978) report that older Chinese infants showed less heart rate variability than Caucasian babies while looking at visual stimuli, were more often inhibited in an uncertain social situation, and were often less fussy in the laboratory.

Conflicting reports.   Other reports call into question the accuracy of the temperamental contrast. Two of them parallel discordant findings by Freedman that are not central in his presentation of temperament differences, and they therefore point up difficulties in the generality of that presentation. In their large-scale study of ethnic Chinese children in Hong Kong, Field and Baber (1973) used the Brunet-Lézine scale (1965), a French test inspired by Gesell's work. The "Napkin Test," an item administered at months 5–9, is similar to the test for defensive movements on the Cambridge (and NBAS) procedures: a napkin is placed over the face. This procedure, write Field and Baber, was "not satisfactory for Chinese children. They resented the napkin being placed on their heads to such an extent that they refused to cooperate for the rest of the test. Many of them would not attempt to remove the napkin even if we suspected that they could do so, but lay underneath it with arms held rigidly by their sides' screaming" (p. 103). While Freedman (1974, pp. 163ff.) notes a possibly related observation that Japanese-American babies react more strongly and negatively to immunization and to later pediatric visits, the characterization of temperament suggested by the Hong Kong study is not consistent with the newborn work. To the same effect, M. Takahashi (1973a) reports data on Japanese infants which, when compared to Korner's (1969) American study, confirm Freedman's findings of greater tremulousness and startle in Japanese newborns (Freedman, 1974, p. 163). This fact, too, is difficult to integrate with the irritability differences.

Rosenblith and her associate Anderson-Huntington present primarily contradictory evidence (Rosenblith, 1978, personal communication; Rosenblith & Anderson-Huntington, 1975). The Graham/Rosenblith Scale includes a Tactile-Adaptive score (TA) based on the infant's strongest response to thrice-repeated (1) occlusion of the nares with a piece of loose cotton and (2) covering the nose and mouth with a piece of cellophane. Comparing 46 Hawaiian-born babies of Hawaiian or Japanese descent to a large sample of infants born in Providence, R.I., from mixed racial and economic backgrounds, Rosenblith and Anderson-Huntington found no difference on TA scores. The Hawaiian-borns, however, were not as consistent in their objections to the procedure. The Japanese babies scored 4.18 on a "Low TA" score which represents the infant's weakest reaction, compared to 5.01 for the Providence sample (the ethnic Hawaiians scored 2.86). Ethnic Hawaiians (and Samoans), they also report, have an unusually high incidence of sudden infant death syndrome (SIDS), deaths that are caused by an unknown factor or factors that apparently include apneic spells (pauses in breathing). In contrast, Oriental groups in Hawaii, including Filipino, Japanese, and Chinese, have low SIDS rates compared to Caucasians.

Rosenblith's Hawaiian-born subjects were also more upset during the examination than those in the Providence sample. When ratings are adjusted for the "suitability" of fussing, that is, to compenseate for example for greater hunger resulting from breastfeeding, the Hawaiian-born babies appear more like the mainland ones but still not less irritable. In addition, their muscle tone was more tense. With the possible exception of the small Japanese–Rhode Island difference in Low TA score, these results are not consistent with Freedman's conclusion. It is difficult to evaluate the consistency of the Low TA result, since the Cambridge Scales are intended generally to reflect a baby's optimal response (Brazelton & Freedman, 1971).

In Chisholm's study (1978) of Navajo infants mentioned above, there were several minor discrepancies from Freedman's report, beyond the general similarity. Chisholm did not replicate any sample differences in the automatic walking reflex or reaction to being pulled up to a sitting position. He also found no differences in defensive movements to a cloth on the face (Freedman does not explicitly report this item for the Navajo sample). Of more theoretical importance, Chisholm located some intriguing correlates of irritability more specific than ethnicity: maternal age, parity, problems in previous pregnancies, and (negatively) length of the first stage of labor. The most powerful predictor ($r = 0.67$) was maternal blood pressure in the second trimester of pregnancy. Chisholm, Woodson, and DaCosta-Woodson (1978) replicated this finding using maternal blood pressure 24 hours before delivery in a sample of Malay, Chinese, and Tamil infants in Malaysia. Chisholm et al. interpret their results to indicate the role of a physiological depletion or stress factor in neonatal irritability, possibly independent of ethnicity.

In summary, several studies following Freedman's discoveries have complicated the factual picture to a point where it is difficult to draw together all the findings. The little information available on proximate correlates of irritabiltiy does not particularly point to the genetic theory proposed by Freedman. Despite these problems, however, there is enough evidence of Oriental–Caucasian differences during the newborn period to suggest that further research should be fruitful. Careful and specific replication by different investigators using a variety of procedures will be necessary to clarify the puzzle of inconsistent reports.

Studies of Newborns in the New World
Beyond the Navajo work cited above, studies of nonimmigrant New World neonates are restricted to Central and South America. These reports do not address the question of genetic differences, and they provide no really relevant data. They do present a useful picture of the status of newborns in several ecologies, however, and include fine documentation of the effects of some deplorable conditions.

Two reports on Mexican newborns appeared in 1969. Cravioto, Birch, De Licardie, Rosales, and Vega (1969) published the first report of their longitudinal study in a preindustrial community, including some comments and data on newborns. Despite serious community health problems, the babies appeared in good condition at birth, and the authors even report that their average level of maturity at that time corresponds to about 12 days in Euro-American populations. The basis of this claim is not specified, however, and it is difficult to see how such a claim could be made with their procedures. No comparative data were collected and the investigators seem to make their statement on the basis of comparison with Gesell's classic work in New Haven. This work, however, does not provide adequate norms for comparison (that is, means and standard deviations on a carefully drawn sample).

Furthermore, the youngest age for which key behaviors are given is 4 weeks. It is interesting, nevertheless, that their newborn scores, however derived, correlate with only one background variable (parental economic status) out of a large set.

Brazelton, Robey, and Collier (1969; also Brazelton, 1972; 1977) studied infant development in a more isolated group of Mayan farmers, the Zinacantecos of the southern Mexican highlands. Five newborns were examined several times within the first week of life, and the scores are compared to three white babies in Boston born of unmedicated mothers. The Zinacantecan neonates, delivered at home in dark, smoky huts, appeard similar initially to the American babies in most elicited behaviors such as pull-to-sit but were both more "fluid" and quiet in spontaneous movements and activity. In addition, they adapted more quickly to repeated stimulation and were less irritable and excitable. These impressions stand in some agreement with both the Navajo results and the kind of differences deVries and Super (1979) found could result from contextual factors.

There are three reports from Guatemala concerning the same rural villages and possibly involving overlapping data. In the first, Sellers, Klein, Sellers, Lechtig, and Yarbrough (1971) present the results of testing 36 newborns with the NBAS. By visual comparison with data collected in Kansas by Horowitz, the authors find no differences in some items contributing to the now familiar irritability dimension, such as lability of skin color and consolability. The Guatemalan infants were less responsive, however, on many other items, including alertness and orientation.

In a quantitative analysis of 157 newborns from the same villages, but ranging in age up to 28 days old, Brazelton, Tronick, Lechtig, Lasky, and Klein (1977) illustrate the importance of several background variables (also see Lasky, Lechtig, Delgado, Klein, Engle, Yarbrough, & Matorell, 1975). Two substantially overlapping clusters of items, selected a priori to represent "good performance which might elicit optimal caretaking" and integrity of motor organization, are found to be related to birthweight, gestational age, maternal height (interpreted as an index of maternal nutrition), and birth interval (with the unexpected result that unusually long intervals, presumably indicative of reproductive difficulty, were associated with low performance). A socioeconomic index also correlated with the motor organization factor as well as with several other items. All the infants were light at birth, somewhat dysmature in the clinical sense described by Clifford (1954), and judged to be limp, lacking in vigor and interest in stimulation, and trembly in their movements compared to the researchers' conception of clinically normal. They attribute this state of affairs to the poor nutritional status of the mothers and suggest similarities with "small for date" infants in Boston who later show a high incidence of feeding, sleeping, temperament, and pediatric disorders. They conclude by suggesting that "in Guatemala the underdemanding infants might act synergistically with a nutritionally depleted caretaker and in a stressed environment to make chronic malnutrition such as kwashiorkor an almost certain outcome." While this conclusion may seem to omit consideration of parental expectations and the hardiness of most human development, there is circumstantial evidence that such a sequence of events can precede chronic childhood malnutrition (e.g., Pollitt, 1973).

Coll, Sepkoski, and Lester (1977; 1978) compare results from Puerto Rican newborns in San Juan to black and white babies in Florida. The Puerto Rican sample showed greater orientation and alertness, less motor maturity and tone, greater state control, fewer startles, and mixed differences on four other summary scales. The subjects were carefully selected for comparable normal medical status, and it is therefore of particular interest that the correlation of neonatal status with physicomedical indices (e.g., Apgar scores, ponderal index) was significant only in the Puerto Rican group. Since little information is given on other background and contextual variables, however, it is difficult to know what factors are contributing to the differences in average score and to the differences in their correlates.

Lastly, data from Montevideo, Uruguay have been reported by Horowitz, Aleksandrowicz, Ashton, Tims, McCluskey, Culp, and Gallas (1973). They find substantial differences from a Kansas sample, but interpretation is difficult because of differences in level of medication. In a later and more appropriate comparison with Israeli newborns, the Uruguayan subjects were less attentive and appeared more excitable on a few items (Horowitz, Ashton, Culp, Gaddis, Levin, & Reichmann, 1977). The authors, in focusing on drug effects, do not directly interpret this finding, and indeed it would be difficult to do so without more detailed background information.

In summary, the thrust of the literature on newborns of New World populations is to document how early the tragedies of poverty begin. In addition to the purely medical issues, the infant's behavioral disposition can be distorted to his or her immediate disadvantage in interacting with the new environment. Other reports raise interesting and important questions about obtained sample differences but contain few hard clues to suggest answers.

Other Studies of Newborns

There are a few other relevant, more isolated studies of newborns. Brazelton, Tryphonopoulou, and Lester (1977) examined three Greek samples using an early version of the NBAS. They found that orphanage babies, who probably did not fare well in utero, were low on state and interactive measures compared to their lower-class compatriots with similar medication. Middle-class subjects scored relatively low on physiological measures probably because of substantial levels of perinatal medication. Differential recovery over 10 days was seen in the three groups, presumably reflecting medical, caretaking, and possibly intrinsic differences.

Horowitz, Ashton, Culp, Gaddis, Levin, and Reichman (1977) examined Israeli newborns with the purpose of exploring the effects of perinatal medication, and after comparison with data from other samples they suggest that ethnic groups may differ in their sensitivities to medication, at least in consort with psychological factors. This speculation is based on the observation that their Israeli infants, like a sample from Uruguay, showed fewer drug/no-drug effects than newborns in Kansas, but they also point out that a critical cut off point for drug effects could produce similar results, since the Kansas group tended to have higher levels of medication.

Freedman (1974) reports two samples in addition to those already mentioned. He tested 17 Australian Aboriginal neonates in a Darwin hospital. They scored relatively high on motor items, but the most interesting result is a suggestion of a different correlational structure in this sample: the infants started out in an unusually high initial state but were low on visual and auditory attention. Freedman also mentions an unpublished finding in conjunciton with Strieby of "the most motorically precocious group yet seen" among the Punjabis of northern India. The Punjabis are a Caucasian group, and Freedman concludes that sample differences are likely to be local adaptations, not related to more general, phylogentic trends.

Discussion

It is clear that newborn babies are not the same the whole world over. At birth, and increasingly in the days after, infants of different cultural and ethnic groups may vary in their spontaneous and/or elicited behavior. Some of this variation can be understood with the same conceptual tools applied to individual variation within Western society. Several investigators have speculated about how parents in other cultures might react to these various types and levels of behavior, but these guesses have rarely, if ever, been verified in the appropriate culture contexts.

The cross-cultural literature, in conjunction with European and American Studies, provides ample evidence of how environmental forces can produce differences in neonatal behavior. Whether or not there is, in addition, a genetic basis for some of the ethnic and racial differences remains open to question. Most of the interesting possibilities are difficult to replicate exactly for reasons that are not always clear. Others have been more amenable, in the end, to other interpretations. Considering the variety of methodological difficulties which converge on the cross-cultural study of newborns, we should not expect all the questions to be sorted out in the immediate future—a great deal more work, probably with some new procedures, needs to be done.

For the moment, there are three major questions for the student of newborn reports. The first is how to characterize those discrete findings which seem reliable. Grand generalizations such as "precocity" and "irritability" carry far too much excess meaning to be useful at our current level of knowledge. One of the pitfalls of such generalization is illustrated by the fact that essentially the same contrast with American infants—subdued but well-organized reflexes such as the Moro and grasp —is characterized as either precocity or temperament depending on whether the sample is from Africa or the New World. More technically, there are enough exceptions to the broad generalities to suggest that they overstate the facts. For example, the imperturbable, nonirritable Navajo neonates are unusually labile in their skin color during examination (Freedman, 1974), and this bears some resemblance to Wolff's research on Caucasian–Oriental differences in "flushing" (Wolff, 1977). In the end, perhaps firm conclusions can be made only at the level of relatively discrete behaviors: the regularity, style, or strength of certain reactions to certain kinds of stimulation under certain circumstances.

The second questions concerns the hypothesized cause of differences. There is good evidence that the kinds of variation reported can result, at the individual level, from environmental influences, be they pre-, peri-, or postnatal. There is also evidence for genetic involvement in some related individual differences. Because environment and ethnicity are confounded in the real world and because the necessary evaluation of independent variables is extremely costly in time and money, conclusive evidence about group differences is elusive. It may remain elusive for other reasons as well. If there are inherent ethnic, racial, or mating group differences at birth, they are unlikely to be "main effects" in the analysis of variance sense. Rather, they may appear only in certain kinds of interactions with environmental factors. To illustrate with speculation, group differences in newborn irritability might be directly related to maternal stress during pregnancy, but groups of mothers may react differently to some environmental stressors, and fetuses in their response to intrauterine ones. In all present research there are possible group differences in the types and levels of stressors.

Finally, we arrive at the matter of what theoretical importance to attach to cultural variation in newborn behavior, whatever the characterization and cause. The theory that newborns elict caretaker behavior, and that different infant behavior might therefore elicit different care, is potentially very powerful. Attributing cultural traits to subtle newborn differences is risky, however, since the reasoning is inherently post hoc and too often limited in perspective. Why, after all, should a Japanese mother respond to a quiet baby with more quieting? Had the results been otherwise, we might have argued mothers naturally try to quiet more excitable infants. Similarly, the interpretation that Navajo imperturbability explains their use of the cradleboard neglects the fact that up until recent times most European mothers also swaddled their babies (Lipton, Steinschneider, & Richmond, 1965). John Whiting's preceding chapter in this volume makes a convincing argument that environmental factors (such as climate) account for much of the worldwide variation in the use of swaddling and cradles. Ideological forces, such as the Enlightenment with its concern for both children and freedom, have played a role in changing Euro-American caretaking, and their role is continuing (Jelliffe, 1975). Other economic and ideological factors have altered Japanese use of the ejiko cradle (Sofue, Suye, & Murakami, 1957). The perspective of culture change does not alter the newborn results, of course, and in fact could return us to the question of prenatal influences and a population's range of reaction to environmental conditions, but it does suggest that understanding the importance of group differences in newborn behavior is no simpler than verifying their existence or establishing their cause.

Motor Development after the Newborn Period

The possibility of different rates of motor development (age at first walking, etc.) in various cultural and ethnic groups is closely related to the question of neonatal precocity, both logically and historically. Unlike the newborn case, the evidence for group differences is strong. The literature suggests environmental factors to be the predominant and possibly exclusive cause.

The "baby tests" developed by American psychologists in the early part of this century were soon used outside middle-class white groups. Early studies of black and white infants in the American South indicated generally retarded motor development in black babies, resulting, it was thought, from poor nutrition and health care (e.g., McGraw, 1931). Ironically, in view of later developments (Jensen, 1969), some saw the poor performance as evidence of innate inferiority. These few group comparisons did not figure predominantly in the literature, however, even though the complementary roles of biology and environment were a central and hotly debated focus of developmental concern for several decades, especially with reference to motor development (e.g., Gesell & Thompson, 1929; McGraw, 1935).

African Infant Precocity

The traditional pattern. Marcelle Geber focused attention on the issue of group differences in her reports from Uganda (Geber, 1956; 1958a, b, c; 1960; 1961; 1962; 1973; 1974; Geber & Dean, 1957b; 1958; 1964). These reports, along with other African studies, have been reviewed with varying degrees of thoroughness and critical attitude by Dasen (1972), Super (in press), Warren (1972), Werner (1972), Wober (1975), and Zempléni and Rabain-Zempléni (1972), and it is unnecessary to recount all the history and details here. In brief, Geber reports that Ugandan children (her samples are predominantly from the Baganda tribe) show advanced development in the first year or two of life, obtaining DQs (developmental quotients, homologous to intelligence quotients) well above the theoretical Western average of 100. This relative precocity is said to occur in all areas of development, but most dramatically and reliably with regard to motor skills. The Ugandan babies could walk and sit, for example, a month or two earlier than American norms. The precocity diminishes in the second year of life, and in the third year average performance drops below that of American infants. It was further observed that "a few children who were being brought up in the European way . . . did not show . . . precocity after the first month" (Geber, 1958c, p. 194) and that children who went to nursery school did not decline in performance in the second and third years (Geber, 1956).

At least partial replications of this general picture, especially the early precocity, have been reported in various degrees of detail for other African samples in Uganda (Ainsworth, 1967; J. Kilbride, Robbins, & Kilbride, 1970; J. Kilbride, 1976); Senegal (Bardet, Massé, Moreigne, & Senecal, 1960; Faladé, 1955, 1960; Lusk & Lewis, 1972; Moreigne, 1970; Valantin, 1970), the Ivory Coast (Dasen, Inhelder, Lavallée, & Retschitzki, 1978), Zambia (Goldberg, 1972; 1977), Madagascar (Ramarasaona, 1959), Botswana (Konner, 1976; 1977), Kenya (Leiderman, Babu, Kagia, Kraemer, & Leiderman, 1973; Leiderman & Leiderman, 1974a, b; 1977; Ssengoba, 1978; Super, 1973a, b, 1976; in press), South Africa (Liddicoat, 1969; Liddicoat & Griesel, 1971), Nigeria (Durojaiye, personal communication; Mundy-Castle & Okonji, 1976; Poole, 1969), the Republic of Guinea (Naidr, 1975), Tanzania (Varkevisser, 1973), and Cameroon (Vouilloux, 1959a, b). Only Falmagne (1959; 1962) and Theunissen (1948), both of whom worked in South Africa, report overall similarity of rate of development. Motor scores for Miller's (1976) South African infants, in the second year of life, were essentially "average" (e.g., 104).

The empirical basis for the claim of infant precocity has not always been as firm as it might appear, however, and the procedural inadequacies that plagued the first decade and a half of research are probably in part responsible for the long period of ignorance about causal factors. The early reports were so flawed, in fact, that when Warren (1972) reviewed the literature up to about 1970, he was not able to conclude with any certainty that there was in fact such a phenomenon as "African infant precocity."

There are five major shortcomings in this body of literature. First, most of the samples are not representative of any general population. Geber's main sample, for example, was explicitly chosen for its stability, thus probably overestimating the population's health and rate of development (Geber, 1974; Geber & Dean, 1957b).

Second, the data are often problematic. Early reports tended to use the Gesell scales (Gesell & Amatruda, 1947), which are not satisfactory for such work. The reliability of scoring has been questioned (Werner, 1965), and examiners not carefully trained in the original techniques tend to score items at too advanced a level (Knobloch, 1958; Knobloch & Pasamanick, 1958). An occasional observer (e.g., Varkevisser, 1973) in fact did no testing, relying instead on maternal reports of motor milestones. Even when the testing appears reliable, very few studies have accurate birthdates for their rural subjects, for whom the precocity is greatest. In at least one rural sample where birthdates were recorded at the time and could be compared to maternal recall later, discrepancies of a month or more were not uncommon after a year's interval (Super, unpublished data).

These problems are compounded by the third shortcoming: most studies have used published norms for comparison rather than collecting their own comparative data. The Gesell and Amatruda figures are not adequately standardized as population norms and in any event appear to underestimate present values (J. V. Hunt, 1976; Knobloch & Pasamanick, 1976). The various sets of "norms" for European and American children differ, in fact, among themselves due to subtle differences in definition of the specific test items and perhaps due also to true sample differences. When does the average baby sit? Bayley (1969) reports 6.6 months ("steadily"), Gesell and Amatruda (1947) 28 weeks ("erect"), and Griffiths (1954) 8 months ("alone for a short time"). Similar definitional discrepancies are found for other items such as fine finger–thumb prehension (9.3 or 11 months). Even among Western European samples on an identical item, true sample differences can be found: the average age of walking is a month later in Zurich than in Stockholm (Hindley, Filliozat, Klackenberg, Nicolet-Meister, & Sand, 1966). Dutch infants sit 6 weeks later than English ones (Touwen, 1971; cf. Neligan & Prudham, 1969). The degree of African precocity, then, depends on the Western norms used for comparison. Ganda babies, as the finding is often cited, walk at "eleven rather than fourteen months" (Lavatelli & Stendler, 1972, p. 73), but the best normative data (Bayley, 1969) give 11.7 months as mean age of walking in the United States. If instead of relying on published averages the cross-cultural investigator collects data from all groups to be compared, this problem can obviously be avoided. It is on this basis more than any other that Warren (1972) questioned the existence of African precocity: the two studies he reviewed that did make their own comparisons failed to find overall African–European differences (Falmagne, 1962; Theunissen, 1948). A closely related problem is the use of different testers for the groups to be compared. This is of course the case when norms are used, but it can also occur in collaborative projects. With very few exceptions, most items on infant motor tests have enough ambiguity in their definition, and are dependent enough on the tester's ability to coax out the desired behavior, to make the use of different testers undesirable.

Fourth, many reports do not present the samples, procedures, and results with enough detail. Statistical evaluation, even simple quantitative comparisons, are absent in some cases. Geber (1958c), in her report best known to American scholars, reports simply that, for example, "at ten months [the Ganda child] could walk," and offers photographic illustrations (actually from Senegal: Wober, 1975), without indicating the basis of that presumably average measure or its variation within the sample.

Finally, there has been a curious inattention to the nature of the specific behaviors being measured, to both their theoretical coherence as measuring "motor development" over the first few years of life and their empirical relationships with the hypothetically controlling forces. This has resulted in a global view of the phenomenon adequately summarized by the common term African infant precocity. "African" (the independent variable) infants are precocious in "motor development" (the dependent variable). None of the major reports has offered an item analysis of the developmental scales used or a similar "unpacking" (B. Whiting, 1976) of the independent variable.

There is to date no formally published study which satisfies all these points. Nevertheless, the public literature, together with some unpublished works and preliminary analyses, offers a clearer picture than was available to any of the previous reviewers. First, there is little doubt now that there are often group differences in motor development. The more recent studies have been carried out and reported with enough attention to sampling, testing, analysis, and reporting to be thoroughly convincing. Those by Leiderman, Babu, Kagia, Kraemer, & Leiderman (1973) and J. Kilbride (1976; Kilbride, Robbins, & Kilbride, 1970) stand out in this regard. Like their less convincing companions, they demonstrate high developmental quotients (e.g., 130) for motor development in the first year or two of life.

The explanations that have been offered for this state of affairs have included genetics (Geber, 1956; Geber & Dean, 1957b; Jensen, 1969; Brackbill & Thompson, 1967), maternal psychological state during pregnancy (Geber, 1958c), and several aspects of infant care such as backcarrying (Geber & Dean, 1957b; 1958; Goldberg, 1977) and the intimate mother–infant relationship (Geber & Dean 1957b). Several reports have noted the possibility of different development in African groups of varying social class, but the initial reports by Geber (1956; 1958a) were followed by a diversity of confirming, contradicting and complicating studies (to be cited here).

The most detailed theory presented to date rests on the patterning of discrete behavioral differences, viewed with reference to specific, theoretically relevant environmental experiences. African infants, according to this approach, are relatively advanced in behaviors which (1) they are specifically taught and (2) they can practice often. They achieve other milestones at the same time or later than infants from other cultures, again depending on the specific environmental encouragement and support. In addition, there may be a general accelerative effect of the high levels of physical contact or handling. Intimations of this view can be found in several early works (e.g., Ainsworth, 1967; Falmagne, 1962; Geber & Dean, 1957b; Vouilloux, 1959a, b), and it has been explicitly formulated, in whole or part, by Hopkins (1976), the Kilbrides (J. Kilbride, 1976; P. Kilbride & Kilbride, 1975), Konner (1972; 1976; 1977), and Super (1973a, b; 1976; in press).

Skills related to sitting and walking are the ones in which African infants are found to be most reliably and most dramatically advanced. One or both skills are deliberately taught by most, if not all, traditional African cultures on which we have relevant information: the Baganda of Uganda (Ainsworth, 1967; P. Kilbride & Kilbride, 1975; Welbourn, 1963); the Acholi of Uganda (Ocitti, 1973; Apoko, 1967); the Sara of Chad (Patterson, personal communication); the Luhyia (Lijembe, 1967), Gusii (LeVine & LeVine, 1966), and Kamba of Kenya (Ssengoba, 1978); the Sukuma of Tanzania (Varkevisser, 1973); the Wolof of Senegal (Faladé, 1955); and the Yoruba, Ibo, and Hausa of Nigeria (Bakare, personal communication; Durojaiye, personal communication; S. LeVine, personal communication; Mundy-Castle & Okonji, 1976). Super (1976; in press) found that the great majority of mothers specifically taught these skills in several East African groups: Kipsigis, Pokot, Masai, Teso, Duruma, Somali, Boran, Luhyia, Luo, Kiga, Baganda, and Gikuyu. The teaching is a deliberate, culturally explicit practice and reflects the value adults place on early development of these skills ("Baby Sets a New Record," 1976; P. Kilbride & Kilbride, 1975; Konner, 1972; Super, 1976). It may become more frequent or intense as a baby passes what is considered the normal age for the skill in question, but it is generally initiated several months before this expected age, at least in the one sample where detailed data are available (Super, 1976). The teaching may take place every day over this period. For sitting, the most common procedure involves propping up the infant in a circle of cloths or towels or placing the infant in a shallow hole. In both cases, the lower back is given support and the baby is left in this position for a short period of time. Standing and walking are usually taught just as they are tested in the Bayley procedures: hoisting the baby to the upright position and slowly withdrawing support, or holding the baby's hands and slowly "pulling" him or her forward. A less common procedure apparently used by the Ibo, and possibly other groups, is to construct a wooden railing or walker for the infant to practice on.

In addition, many African babies cared for in traditional or rural environments receive considerable exercise in these behaviors in the normal course of everyday life. Babies in Super's Kipsigis sample spend over 60 percent of their waking time in the sitting position, even in the first months of life, half again as much as an American sample. Similarly, the frequency of riding on the caretaker's back and hip can be assumed to strengthen and coordinate the trunk, buttock, and inside thigh muscles involved in both walking and sitting.

Zelazo, Zelazo, and Kolb (1972) have provided experimental evidence that practice of the walking reflex in newborns can lead to maintenance of the reflex beyond the second month, when it is usually seen to abate, and to significantly earlier walking. The experimental practice in their study lasted 12 min/day for the second through eighth weeks, a much smaller amount than most African babies apparently receive (see Super, 1976). Zelazo (1976) has argued that the neonatal reflexes become incorporated into the hierarchy of voluntary behavior while still retaining their identity, and observations among the Kipsigis are consistent with this. There is no experimental evidence so specifically relevant to sitting skills within the normal range of experience (cf. J. McV. Hunt, Mohandessi, Ghodssi, & Akiyama, 1976; Sayegh & Dennis, 1965), but the inference that the deliberate and incidental practice received by the African babies directly contributes to their precocity seems reasonable at both the muscular and neural levels.

Prone behaviors—lifting the head, turning over, crawling—are not particularly valued or encouraged in most African groups, although there is some variation. The Acholi (Ocitti, 1973), Teso, and Somali (Super, 1976; in press) of East Africa, for example, actively teach crawling by putting the baby down in a crawling position, tempting with attractive objects, and demonstrating (usually by a sibling). This is uncommon, on the other hand, among the Boran, Luo, and Kipsigis (Super, 1976, in press). In addition, most rural African babies have little opportunity to practice prone behaviors on their own, since they are rarely put down while awake. Super (1976) reports a figure of lying down 10 percent of the time for rural Kipsigis, compared to over 30 percent for an American sample, and this seems to be true for a number of groups. The !Kung San of Botswana believe that lying down is bad for the infant and retards motor development (Konner, 1976). Using these two measures of environmental encouragement (maternal reports of teaching and observations of time lying down), Super (1976) found that he could predict average age of crawling in six East African groups with a multiple correlation of 0.97. In those cases where little practice is available, the average age of crawling is behind Bayley's norms for American babies by about a month. A delay in crawling is also reported by Kilbride (1976) for her Baganda sample and by Konner for the !Kung San (Chang, 1976). Delays in other prone behaviors, especially the early items for turning over, are reported by Kilbride (1976) in Uganda, Falmagne (1962) in South Africa, and Super (1976; in press) and Leiderman (personal communication) in Kenya. As with walking, there is experimental support for a causal relationship between deliberate teaching of crawling and acceleration of development (Lagerspetz, Nygård, & Strandvik, 1971).

Toilet training is not usually considered in the realm of motor behavior, but the cultural variations in training, and their apparent effectiveness, prompt mention in this context. Most of the examples concerning the strictness of training are contained in ethnographic sources; J. Whiting and Child (1953) present a brief summary of these variations. An interesting review of American opinion over the decades and a case study of the Digo of Kenya are given by deVries and deVries (1977). The Digo begin training in the first week of life, using a particular postural position. Through nurturant conditions and attentiveness to the infant when carried, daytime dryness is achieved by 5 or 6 months.

The "modernizing" pattern.   Comparisons of ethnic groups differing in the encouragement and support they offer for various motor skills also include, of course, variation in genetic background. Studies of socioeconomic effects, on the other hand, tend to be done within a given ethnic group and might therefore offer a more rigorous analysis of environmental effects. Unfortunately, most such analyses use only very gross measures such as rural/urban residence, parental education, occupation, religion, or "modernization" as indices of possible variations in infant care. The actual, relevant aspects of infant care are usually not measured, which probably accounts for the confusing set of results. Most reports indicate greater precocity in more traditional groups (Geber, 1956; 1958a; Geber & Dean, 1958; Ramarasaona, 1959; Super, 1976; Varkevisser, 1973; Vouilloux, 1959a, b). Poole (1969) and Kilbride (1972), however, found no reliable relationship in their samples from Nigeria and Uganda. Finally, Akim, McFie, and Sebigajju (1956), Janes (1975), Leiderman, Babu, Kagia, Kraemer, and Leiderman (1973), and Geber (1961) all report the opposite relationship: the more modern families had the more precocious infants ($r = 0.45$ in the superior Leiderman et al. study).

The central problem in interpreting these reports is that each considers a different range and quality of variation in modernization or social class, and there is little reason to expect a uniform relationship between the gross socioeconomic indices and the critical aspects of infant care. This is illustrated by Super (1973b; 1976), who found that infants of highly educated families in Nairobi from the same ethnic stock as his rural Kipsigis sample performed approximately midway between their rural compatriots and Bayley's American infants and that they also recieved an intermediate level of environmental encouragement and support. He then replicated his measures of deliberate teaching and incidental practice in the Gikuyu village studied by Leiderman, Babu, Kagia, Kraemer, and Leiderman (1973) and found them to correlate with economic modernization as theory would predict, given the Leiderman et al. findings. For example, infants who were deliberately taught to sit and walk came from substantially wealthier families than those who were not. Why this should be is not clear, but it nevertheless adds support to the environmental explanation and suggests that results from the previous reports concerning socioeconomic variations are merely different, not contradictory.

Beyond the patterning of motor development.   On the Bayley Scale of Motor Development only three clusters of items in the first year contain more then four individual items: progress in sitting and walking each contain six, as does a set with the infant vertical in the examiner's arms. Over the first 12 months items which involve a vertical position take up half the test, compared to one quarter for the prone and supine positions and one quarter for grasping and manipulative behaviors. In short, the Bayley test, like the other scales in common use, overrepresents those domains of skill, such as sitting, in which African infants tend to excel. Those in which they often do poorly compared to American or European norms, such as crawling, may be represented by a single item. It is not easy to interpret this fact, since testing for sitting momentarily and again for sitting 30 sec is not inherently more reasonable than testing for crawling 1 inch and for crawling 9 inches, but it does explain why the particular patterning of precocity, equivalence, and delay consistently yields high overall scores.

Is the discrete patterning of items based on environmental factors the only element in these ethnic differences? It can be noted that the amount of advance (in progress to sitting and walking, for example) is often, although not always, larger and more reliable than the relative delay (e.g., in crawling and turning over). There are two interpretations of this fact. It might be that infant care in America and Europe is not optimal for motor development compared to the species' inherent potentials. Short of overwhelming deprivation of the kind documented for some institutional care in these cultures, it would be difficult, in this view, to be less supportive, while there is plenty of room for improvement. There is something to be said for this hypothesis. On the other hand, it is also possible that the patterning of advance and delay described above is imposed on a more general African advancement, this general precocity being inadequate to overcome serious environmental neglect of a particular skill.

Such a pervasive precocity could have environmental and genetic roots. The environmental possibility is indicated by the similarity between cultural differences in daily infant care and experimental manipulations known to produce nonspecific acceleration of development in a variety of species, including humans. The beneficial effects of "handling" and other mild stresses on infant rats are well known (see Thompson & Grusec, 1970), although recent work suggests strongly the possibility of artifact with respect to the findings of advancement in general physical maturity (King, 1969; Stein & Labarba, 1977). Experimental studies of levels of environmental stimulation (e.g., Rosenzweig, Krech, Bennett, & Diamond, 1968) and maternal behavior (Butler, Suskind, & Schanberg, 1978) seem more robust, but in any case the present argument need not rest on interspecies inference. Gunders and Whiting (1968) provide evidence that early maternal–infant separation may affect physical growth in humans. Relatively small amounts of tactile or vestibular stimulation (e.g., 5 min each hour for 10 days) has been shown to significantly improve the physical, neurological, gross motor, and sensorimotor development not only of institutionalized (Casler, 1965) and premature infants (Rice, 1977; Solkoff, Yaffe, Weintraub, & Blase, 1969; White & Labarba, 1976) but also normal ones. (Casler, 1975, and Kramer, Chamorro, Green, & Knudtson, 1975, report some failures to replicate, however.) The most striking demonstrations with normal infants are those of Porter (1972), who used a fairly vigorous, passive exercise, and Clark, Kreutzberg, and Chee (1977), who effected advancement in reflexive and gross motor behavior with 80 min of moderate spinning in a swivel chair over the course of a month. The exact mechanisms for such effects are not clear, although adrenal mediation is involved in the stress studies (cf. Butler et al., 1978). Sperry (1951, p. 237), among others, has pointed to an apparent reciprocity between myelination and funtion of nerve fibers in the immature organism. Not only does the development of function in various systems correlate with their rate of myelination, but functioning seems also to stimulate and facilitate myelinization.

There are a few reports of correlations between kinesthetic measures, such as

FIGURE 8–1. Percentage of observations in which infant and caretaker were seen to be in physical contact, Cambridge (U.S.) and Kokwet (Kenya). Number of observations per point is approximately 15 in Cambridge, 35 in Kokwet. See Super (1976) for a description of methodology.

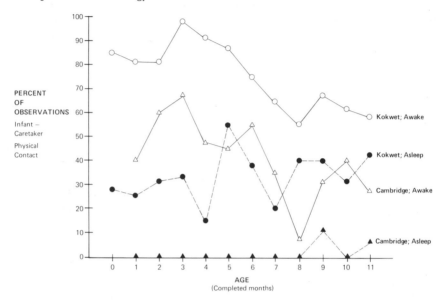

amount of physical handling, and a number of indices of development within American groups (e.g., Yarrow, Rubenstein, & Pedersen, 1975), and the cross-cultural comparisons are dramatic. Hopkins (1976) has reported deliberate stretching, massaging, and exercising in Nigeria and Uganda and argues for its role in enhancing development. Many rural African babies also receive substantial amounts of incidental physical contact and handling. J. Kilbride (1976) and Konner (1976) provide quantitative evidence for the Baganda and !Kung San. Figure 8–1 compares the amount of physical contact experienced by infants in Kokwet (a rural Kenyan community) and Cambridge, Mass. Even when awake, the African babies are being held or carried or are sitting in someone's lap two or three times as much as the American children. This measure of physical contact, derived from several hundred "spot observations" in each sample, presumably reflects tactile, vestibular, and muscular stimulation. It is a small inference from the experimental evidence that this kind of variation in daily experience could produce a pervasive and possibly substantial advancement in motor development.

There are a number of cultural and ecological influences on how much incidental physical stimulation an infant receives: J. Whiting's analysis in this volume (Chapter 7) explores one major constraint, the ambient temperature. Two other reports relate motor development to climate. M. Smith, Lecker, Dunlap, and Cureton (1930) found in comparing infants from Hawaii, California, Iowa, and New York that a warmer climate was associated with earlier walking. In contrast, the data reported by Hindley et al. (1966) yield a correlation of approximately –0.78 between latitude of their European samples and age of walking (df = 3, $p = 0.11$). Since the direction of this correlation is opposite to that reported by Smith et al., a hypothesis of generalized physiological mediation is problematic, and one is left to speculate about different cultural patterns of indoor versus outdoor carrying, bundling, and exercise.

The possibility of a genetic contribution to a generalized African motor precocity has been considered by a number of writers, varying to all extremes in their acceptance of the idea. The present review of the African and experimental literature suggests that a genetic explanation is neither adequate nor necessary to explain the published findings. Nevertheless, since there are obviously some genetically controlled differences between the so-called black and white races, the question of a genetic difference in rate of motor development is an obvious one. Curiously, there have been no genetically oriented studies that can address the question of group differences. The literature reviewed here may be compatible with a genetic factor, but it lends no particular support to the hypothesis. Wilson (1972b) has demonstrated in his work with twins that in the apparent absence of relevant environmental variation, genetic similarity is associated with similarity in the spurts of development as measured by the Bayley Scales. While this demonstrates the theoretical possibility of genetically based group differences by affirming a biological component in individual development, it does not speak to whether this possibility is in fact manifest.

The suggestion by Keefer, Dixon, Tronick, and Brazelton (1978) that African newborns may have more responsive motor tone raises the possibility of a genetically influenced racial difference of this specific sort, patterned in subsequent months by the environmental factors discussed above. Stambak's (1963) finding of no relationship between neonatal tone and later motor development suggests caution in accepting this hypothesis, but the supporting environment for motor development is divergent enough in rural Africa to make the parallel a weak one. In any case, there are problems in drawing genetic conclusions from neonatal results, as has already been discussed.

Studies of Africans living in Europe and America.   Research with black populations living outside Africa could, in theory, provide a test of the genetic approach (leaving aside the problem of admixture), and it is commonly asserted that American blacks show a similar precocity, if not quite so large, without the environmental encouragement found in traditional African groups. There is some doubt, however, about both halves of this claim.

The motor precocity of black infants outside Africa is not as soundly established as one might expect for a genetically based effect. Bayley's (1965) analysis of her carefully collected normative American data does reveal significant black advancement on the motor scale at most points between 3 and 14 months. The differences occur primarily in the areas of standing, sitting, turning side to back, head control, combining cubes at midline, and playing pat-a-cake, a pattern similar but not identical to the African results. Brown and Halpern (1971) and King and Seegmiller (1973) also report predominantly superior motor performance by black Americans in the first year or 18 months of life. Curti, Marshall, and Steggerda (1935), Grantham-McGregor and Back (1971), and Grantham-McGregor and Hawke (1971) report similar results for black Jamaican infants, as do Hood, Oppé, Pless, and Apte (1970) for infants of black West Indian immigrants in England.

On the other hand, Pollak and Mitchell (1974) found West Indian immigrant babies superior to English babies only in extension at 1 month, not in other motor skills at 3 or 9 months, nor in age of walking. Walters (1967) controlled for SES and prenatal care in black and white samples from Florida and found race differences in Gesell motor scores only at 12 weeks, not at 24 or 36 weeks of age. Rhodes (1937), using older children (2.5–5 years), found no black–white differences in motor skills. No differences in overall Bayley motor scores appeared in Broman, Nichols, and

Kennedy's (1975) large scale study (assessment at 8 months). Scott, Ferguson, Jenkins, and Culter (1955) found no differences up to 30 weeks between black and white American infants on several neuromuscular items when SES was controlled, and Solomons and Solomons (1964) report no overall motor difference at 4 months. The early work of McGraw (1931) showing a white superiority on many (but not all) items was mentioned above, but there are probably serious health and nutritional differences between her groups. Adler (1973) found in a sample of speech-defective children in Knoxville that white babies were reported by their mothers as walking earlier than the black babies. Finally, Knobloch and Pasamanick originally reported that black babies in New Haven scored significantly above Gesell's white norms on motor development (Pasamanick, 1946; Knobloch & Pasamanick, 1953), but when they ran their own large-scale comparison ($n = 500$) in Baltimore, they found nearly identical scores for black and white babies: DQ at 40 weeks was 115 for white babies, 113 for black, and 114 and 115 at 3 years (Knobloch, 1958; Knobloch & Pasamanick, 1958).

These studies, like the African ones, also report a number of correlations with socioeconomic indicators, but again the picture is complicated, presumably because the directly relevant variables bear no inherent relationship to parental education, occupation, or income. Williams and Scott (1953), in their well-known study, found black infants of lower SES in Washington, D.C. to be more advanced in motor development (Gesell test) than those of higher SES. They attribute this result to fewer restrictions in the lower group on an infant's behavior and a more permissive attitude toward nonapproved behaviors. The correlation of parental attitude and infant performance was replicated within each SES level (see also Blank, 1964). Similarly, Scott, Ferguson, Jenkins, and Culter (1955) found black babies in a clinic population, but not those who could afford private consultations, to be precocious relative to previously published data from white subjects. Other investigators have found the inverse relationship: Walters (1967) in a Florida town, Brown and Halpern (1971) among rural families in the Mississippi delta, and Curti, Marshall, and Steggerda (1935) in Jamaica. In these cases, the effect can be attributed to serious health and nutritional problems in the lower economic groups. Grantham-McGregor found no correlation between motor development and parents' SES in lower-class and lower-middle-class black samples in Jamaica (Grantham-McGregor & Back, 1971; Grantham-McGregor & Hawke, 1971). Bayley (1965), as noted above, found no correlation with SES in her large-scale study, nor did Adler (1973).

While the findings of a correlation between motor development and parental attitudes are consonant with the environmental thesis derived from the African work, these studies of black infants in Britain and the New World do not provide the specific information about teaching, incidental practice, and stimulation one would need for an adequate test. Is there any reason to think that any of these aspects of traditional care continue outside the African continent? Herskovits (1941) has argued cogently for substantial continuity in many domains, but there are only a few scattered hints about infant care. Hopkins (1976) reports that his West Indian mothers massaged, stretched, and actively exercised their infants in a manner quite similar to that in Nigeria. He also cites a report from a single Jamaican mother who lived in the U.S. for 4 years that she had seen no such formal handling there. But the only ethnographic material from America sounds very reminiscent of the African studies. In a Georgia town in the early 1960s, writes Young (1970), babies were "held and carried most of the time" and "jumped generously [on laps] when they want to flex and stiffen their muscles." They are kept from crawling on the floor but are "urged to precocious . . . walking" and are often given walkers (although primarily to restrict travel!). There is apparently no published information about these matters for other samples of Afro-Americans.

It is difficult to draw any strong conclusion from the work on motor development in African peoples outside of Africa because there is no quantitative description of the directly relevant environmental variables. It seems possible to make a tentative statement, however, to the effect that these studies pose no threat to the environmental point of view and offer no support for the genetic theory. Like the African research, they do not actually refute the genetic hypothesis, but the few clues available point toward an environmental cause in that portion of the literature where racial differences have been found.

The decline of precocity. The decline of precocity toward the end of infancy is primarily the result of a change in what is being tested rather than a relative decay in skills that were previously advanced. The later Bayley Motor Scale items, for example, focus on tricky variations in walking such as walking on a thin board or a line, hopping on one foot, and walking backwards. One-third of the Bayley items falling after 16 months involve the use of stairs. It seems likely that the opportunity and encouragement for these skills vary considerably from culture to culture, and they appear not to be considered significant by most African parents. Most babies in rural Africa or Jamaica (Grantham-McGregor & Hawke, 1971) have little experience with squeezing a doll or drinking from a cup. Clapping hands while singing may be a frequent game, as among the Duruma (Super, in press), or virtually absent, as in the Kamba (Ssengoba, 1978). In the poorer samples, nutrition or health may also play an increasingly important role as breastfeeding decreases (Bardet, Massé, Moreigne, & Senecal, 1960; Geber, 1956; Moreigne, 1970; Ssengoba, 1978), even though weaning trauma was probably overestimated in much early work (see Wober, 1975, or Zempléni & Rabain-Zempléni, 1972, for reviews of this topic). Infants from reasonably healthy samples may not drop below Western norms for several years, when the tests become even more obviously separate and culture bound (J. Kilbride, Robbins, & Kilbride, 1970; Ssengoba, 1978; Vouilloux, 1959a, b), especially if the children are from relatively Europeanized families and attend nursery school (e.g., Geber, 1956).

Patterns of Development in Other Groups
While we lack the kind of coordinated detail concerning infant care and motor development in other areas of the world that is available for Africa, the picture for much of the rest of the non-Western world appears to be similar. As Werner pointed out in her 1972 review, which still covers most of the available literature, traditionally reared infants in preindustrial Asia and Latin America are usually precocious on motor tests in the first year of life, followed by a relative decline; they also receive intimate, unscheduled care in the context of a large family unit; they often experience large amounts of tactile and vestibular stimulation; and infants in "Westernized" families show little of the advance or later decline in psychomotor scores. The overall picture is consistent with the African analysis of environmental factors and changing content of the tests. In some samples relatively quiet, passive caretaking is linked with motor development that is initially similar to North American norms but that begins to fall behind after several months. It is difficult to draw two distinct

patterns, however, because among those cases where we have adequate data to see the whole fabric of development there seems to be a gradient of the time at which relative decline occurs, anywhere from 3 to 12 months or more. At the worst extreme, several studies illustrate the retarding effects of poor nutrition and other debilitating factors. It should be noted, however, that many of the reports that follow suffer from the same methodological problems outlined for the African literature.

Normal variations in timing. The best set of data (outside Africa) indicating early precocity is from India, and incidental encouragement through daily care appears to be an important factor. Phatak (1969; 1970a, b) studied a large sample of infants from upper and lower socioeconomic levels in Baroda, along with a rural sample. Although the upper-class infants scored higher on the Bayley Scales overall during the first 30 months, the lower-class and rural groups were superior in fine and gross motor performance in the first 6 months. All groups scored above Bayley's American norms. The Indian babies then slowly lost their initial advantage, but at different rates for the three samples. By the end of the first year the rural and lower-class urban infants had dropped below the upper-class urban group, and by the end of the second year all were below U.S. norms. Patel and Kaul (1971) and Das and Sharma (1973) report average scores above American values, especially among infants from richer families, but Patel and Kaul found a slightly different pattern of urban–rural differences. The infants in all samples were apparently carried around by their mothers for substantial amounts of time, but were also free to explore the house and courtyard on their own. The mothers were said to put little emphasis on motor skills and did not particularly encourage their development. However, Hopkins (1976) and Leboyer (1976) suggest that formal massage and exercise are common in India. The subsamples are not adequately differentiated with quantitative evidence on patterns of child care to relate them to the divergent patterns of test performance.

Indian infants also tend to be lighter at birth than whites; thus there may be confusion about precocity relative to birthweight, as in the African literature (Saigal & Srivastava, 1969). Phatak's (1970) data, however, do not support the theory that low birthweight is causally linked to motor precocity (Fernando & Gomes, 1961).

Several less substantial studies replicate the general picture of strong early motor development for other samples in India, but there is one report of clear delay. Venkatachar (cited by Phatak, 1970a) found babies from economically advantaged homes in Mysore to excel in pursuit and manipulative behaviors on the Gesell test in the first 6 months but subsequently to perform at normative levels. Abhichandani's (1970) New Delhi sample performed better than American norms on some Bayley items. Two reports do not indicate any significant advance but are difficult to evaluate. Jha (1969) found no precocity in the first year among babies in the poorest section of Bombay, followed by motor retardation. The nutritional and medical status of these infants must have been quite poor; thus performance at Bayley's norms is in fact fairly impressive. Uklonskaya, Puri, Choudhuri, Dang, and Kumari (1960) studied a lower-class sample in New Delhi and found the infants performing at the average Russian level until about 7 months, and less well thereafter. Since the Russian standards are not given and no formal comparison is presented, it is difficult to relate this report to the other literature. However, the Soviet project used for comparison was specifically oriented toward facilitation of motor development, and the Indian babies were likely to be medically and nutritionally disadvantaged; thus the comparison is still striking. Kandoth, Sonnad, and Athavale (1971), in contrast, report that a group of infants from very low economic background were delayed in motor skills assessed by the Gesell procedures.

Early precocity and later decline in summary measures of motor development have also been reported for two general groupings, Mestizo and Indian babies in Mexico (Robles, 1959; G. Solomons & Solomons, 1975; H. Solomons, 1978) and Guatemala (Wug DeLeon, De Licardie, & Cravioto, 1964), and Israeli kibbutz-reared infants (Kohen-Raz, 1968; Rabin, 1958). In Guatemala, sitting and prehension appeared particularly advanced, while later locomotion was delayed. The Solomons found a similar picture in their three Mexican samples, which showed no group differences, and they commented on the patterning. The Mestizo and Mayan infants were especially advanced in fine motor coordination, which is heavily weighted in early sections of the Bayley test. Walking, on the other hand, was considerably delayed. The authors attribute this to the fact that the babies are almost always carried around while awake. Because floors are either dirt or cold tile in these communities, the babies are rarely put down, the authors note, but are instead carried around in the arms or on the hip.

Dennis (1940) and Dennis and Dennis (1940) also report delayed walking among Hopi and Tewa groups in the American Southwest but no difference between those infants who were bound to a cradleboard more or less often. This set of findings among native Americans might suggest a genetic trait, and Freedman (1974) relates it to weak leg responses in newborn tests. Since late walking often occurs with early precocity in other groups, however, the results are equally consistent with a hypothesis of environmental patterning. Except for the Solomons' comment, we have no detailed information about such a possibility.

The slight (not significant) superiority of Israeli infants in group care in a kibbutz is usually explained with reference to a particularly rich environment. Their relative decline near the end of the first year is associated with a lack of freedom to explore, inappropriate social interaction, and possibly the disruption of transfer from mother to metapalet and Infant House to Toddler House (Golan, 1958; Kohen-Raz, 1968; Rabin, 1958).

A number of other reports from Israel focus on the effects of ethnic background. Palti, Gitlin, and Zloto (1977) indicate that children of immigrants from Western countries perform better on the Bruet-Lézine test than those from Eastern countries. Since this group effect is not found in second-generation children, an initial difference in child rearing patterns followed by acculturation is proposed to explain the results. Ivanans (1975) reports a substantial positive correlation of Bruet-Lézine scores with maternal education, and also an effect of ethnicity: Jewish infants of North African background were advanced when compared to those of European background, even controlling for maternal education. Children of Kurdistani immigrants who are carried in the traditional cradle (as opposed to a crib) appear precocious on a few measures (e.g., sitting and walking), but little information is given concerning other child care correlates (Block, 1966).

McLaren and Yatkin (1973) report on a sample of Lebanese children from a poor economic background. Developmental Quotients on the Griffiths motor scale averaged above 100 and remained fairly constant in the first year. Little background description is provided.

Werner and associates (Werner, Bierman, & French, 1971; Werner, Simonian, & Smith, 1968) found minor differences in Cattell scores among various ethnic groups in Hawaii (Japanese greater than Portugese- and Anglo-American, which were greater than Filipino and Hawaiian). They interpret these differences as reflecting cultural expectations and practices concerning the encouragement of activity, independence, and specific motor skills, but the relevant variations in infant experience were not measured.

Japanese and some groups of Latin-American infants do not score substantially above U.S. levels on motor tests. Arai, Ishikawa, and Toshima (1958) found Japanese infants to perform like American subjects on the Gesell motor scale from 1 to 3 months but then to show a general decline in the rate of fine and gross motor development. The authors attribute this deceleration to the relatively low level of maternal stimulation. They similarly account for another slowing down near the end of the first year with reference to the restrictions on locomotor practice imposed by frequent carrying on the mother's back. No specific evidence is offered to support this interpretation, however. Some observers find that Japanese parents typically place a relatively low value on precocious development (Kitano, 1961; Kojima, personal communication).

Brazelton describes a related pattern of interaction and development for the Zinacantecos of Southern Mexico (Brazelton, 1972; Brazelton, Robey, & Collier, 1969). Infant care is oriented toward keeping the baby quiet and calm through motor restraint and frequent nursing. The babies' faces are often covered with a cloth when they are not feeding, and they are never "propped up to look around, talked to or stimulated . . . , nor are they put on the floor to explore on their own" (Brazelton, Robey, & Collier, 1969, p. 276). Motor development is generally delayed by a month or more. A similar picture of extremely low levels of stimulation and delayed development appears in an isolated Mayan sample in highland Guatemala (Kagan & Klein, 1973) and for a Ladino group (Tolbert, n.d.). In Peru, Abelove (1978) reports that babies of the Shipibo Indians achieve the major motor milestones in the first 6 or 9 months at about the same time as American babies (based on observation, not testing). They appear to walk rather late, however, and Abelove suggests this is related to the techniques of carrying and active discouragement of walking.

Finally, there is an interesting series of reports on British and American babies concerning the possible consequences of sleeping position. Holt (1960) noted that American babies generally crawl before British babies and are better in lifting their heads in the prone position. This was attributed to their relatively greater frequency of being put down in the prone position, while British babies, said to be more often supine, were found to excel in being pulled to sit from that position. Francis-Williams & Yule (1967) make the same argument to explain their finding of British superiority in eye–hand coordination and midline skills. Modlin, Hawker, and Costello (1973), however, encountered difficulty in trying to make generalizations about sleeping position from actual observations: the variations and instabilities were large. Summarizing as best they could, they found no significant differences, other than what one might expect by chance, between 7-month-old babies who were predominantly prone or supine, either awake or asleep. The original observations of trans-Atlantic skill differences thus remain unexplained.

There are a few scattered references to the deliberate encouragement of motor skills in various cultures, but we lack comparative information about performance. Mead reports that the Manus of New Guinea and the Balinese teach their infants to walk and provide them with special walking rails (Bateson & Mead, 1950; Mead, 1932; Mead & McGregor, 1951). In Bali, at least, crawling is explicitly discouraged because it is seen as animallike. A baby's feet may never touch the ground before a ceremony at 7 months. Mead and McGregor (1951) also illustrate how these and other considerations lead to a slightly different sequence of upright behavior: the Balinese child learns to squat as part of a progression from a flexible "all-fours" locomotion, to sitting, then squatting, and standing. The typical American child learns to squat only after standing. L. Thompson (1940) reports that parents in Fiji take particular interest in early milestones such as crawling and standing. A baby late in learning to stand will be given brief daily practice by burial up to the chest in sand for support in a standing position. Hopkins (1976) finds evidence that formal procedures of massaging and exercising infants may be common outside Africa, particularly in the Indian subcontinent.

Deprivation and retardation. A number of studies illustrate the existence and causes of tragically retarded development, larger than that seen in the normal variations described above, and resulting from different conditions. Malnutrition can be a potent factor, interfering with behavioral as well as physical growth. This has been demonstrated by research in Mexico, Brazil, Peru, Chile, and Guatemala (Chavez, Martínez, & Yachine, 1975; B. Schmidt, Maciel, Boskovitz, Rosenberg, & Cury, 1971; Pollitt & Granoff, 1967; Mönckeberg, 1968; Klein, Lasky, Yarbrough, Habicht, & Sellers, 1977; Lasky, Lechtig, Delgado, Klein, Engle, Yarbrough, & Matorell, 1975). Dennis, working with orphanage babies in Beirut and Teheran, has shown that development can be severely slowed (Cattell quotients of 63, for example) when staff ratios are so poor as to deprive the infants of "normal" stimulation (Dennis & Najarian, 1957; Dennis, 1960). Kohen-Raz (1968) obtained similar results in Israel, and they are in agreement with American and British reports.

Mental Development
Traditional Psychometric Tests
Mental development in infancy, as evaluated by the traditional psychometric tests such as the Bayley and Gesell, is not so easily differentiated from other domains of development as the labels for scales and subscales might imply. While a theoretical distinction is essential to some views (e.g., Kagan, Kearsley, & Zelazo, 1978; cf. Piaget, 1952), the mental and motor scales of the Bayley procedures, for example, overlap substantially during the middle portion of the first year ($r = 0.78$ at 6 months, declining to 0.24 in the second year). The psychological core underlying tests of infant intelligence has been variously described as sensory-motor alertness (Hofstaetter, 1954) or psychobiological intactness and maturity (Crano, 1977). Stott and Ball (1965) argue for the intellectual nature of motor manipulations early in the first year of life and thus that the old motor–mental dichotomy is inappropriate at that time.

It does not follow, however, that there is a unitary psychological entity such as intelligence reflected in all items even within a particular mental scale. McCall, Hogarty, and Hurlburt (1972), using American data, have presented evidence against a unitary factor in infant mental tests. In addition, the covariance of items that does occur in American samples may result partly from commonalities in the unique structure of American infants' experience.

The two important themes of research around the world using traditional tests of infant development reflect this theoretical uncertainty about the grouping of infant test items into scales or factors. On one hand, developmental quotients from mental, adaptive, language, or other scales show cultural variation somewhat similar to the picture described above for motor scales. At the same time, there is enough variation in the exact patterns of item performance to make such a broad generalization unsatisfactory. Fortunately, there are scattered clues to the causal connections between specific environmental conditions and performance on particular items, even though the literature as a whole suffers from the same methodological weaknesses as outlined earlier for motor development.

Test results.   Many of the research projects in Africa cited above have also reported the results of one or another of the standardized tests of infant mental development. The Gesell Schedules, used by many early investigators, cover areas other than motor skills, such as adaptive, language, and personal–social behavior. Faladé (1955) found her Senegalese subjects advanced in all spheres. Geber (1958b) reports Ugandan precocity in the social and verbal areas. Ainsworth (1967) and Liddicoat and Koza (1963) also report advances in language development on Gesell items in Uganda and South Africa. Others, however, report performance at or below Gesell norms for other African samples, at least in the verbal–vocal domain (Massé, 1969; Ramarasaona, 1959; Theunissen, 1948; Vouilloux, 1959a, b).

Using Bayley's procedures, Lusk and Lewis (1972) found Senegalese infants to have mental quotients significantly over 100, while Leiderman, Babu, Kagia, Kraemer, and Leiderman (1973) and J. Kilbride (1976) make similar reports from Kenya and Uganda. These studies, like virtually all others, find advances on mental scales to be noticeably less than those for motor performance. Some researchers do not report unusually high scores in African samples on items like those on the Bayley mental scale. More of Falmagne's (1962) perceptual and sensorimotor items indicate relative European advancement than South African black (22 versus 15). In Senegal, Valantin (1970) found little precocity in the manipulation of objects and coordination of hands.

A number of studies of infants of African background living in Western nations yield a similar mosaic of differences and equalities in scale scores in comparison with American and British performance, primarily on the Gesell schedules. Walters' (1967) sample of Afro-American infants in Florida, from a range of socioeconomic groups, performed slightly (not significantly) better than matched Caucasian controls on the adaptive, language, and personal–social scales at 12 weeks and at comparable levels at 24 and 36 weeks. There are minor limitations to this generalization at different socioeconomic levels. In Mississippi, Brown and Halpern (1971) found rural black children marginally advanced compared to the Gesell norms in all areas until the beginning of the second year, when DQs dropped below 100. Knobloch and Pasamanick's (1958) carefully validated report from Baltimore indicates no racial differences in Gesell scores. Curti, Marshall, and Steggerda (1935) report relatively poor performance by low-SES Jamaican babies, in comparison with the New Haven norms, on the nonmotor scales. More recently, Grantham-McGregor and Hawke (1971) found higher-SES infants performing better at 1 year than their less fortunate compatriots in the language (significant) and adaptive (not significant) domains. In England, infants from the West Indies obtained lower scores on adaptive language and personal–social scales than infants from Cyprus or native English babies at 9 months (Pollack & Mitchell, 1974). There were no differences in these areas at 1 or 3 months.

In Bayley's (1965) massive normative study in the U.S. there were no black–white differences on the summary mental scale. King and Seegmiller (1973) found first born black male infants in Harlem to score significantly above the national mental norms at 14 but not 18 or 24 months.

The use of standardized tests with other populations further documents their sensitivity to ethnicity, subculture, or culture construed in a general sense. Patel and Kaul (1971) and Venkatachar (cited by Phatak, 1970a) found upper-class Indian infants achieving many Gesell items earlier than the New Haven norms in the first year. Similar results are reported by Phatak (1969; 1970b) for the Bayley scales. Lower-SES Indian infants show few positive differences on mental items (Phatak, 1970; Uklonskaya, Puri, Choudhuri, Dang, & Kumari, 1960) and in some samples perform quite poorly (Athavale, Kandoth, & Sonnad, 1971; Kandoth, Sonnad, & Athavale, 1971).

In Israel, Kohen-Raz (1967; 1968) found relatively few differences on Bayley mental scores between kibbutz, home-reared, and institutionalized infants in the first 8 months of life, although the last did fall behind thereafter on items that seem to be particularly dependent on social interaction and differential environmental responsiveness (hidden objects, verbal imitation, verbal and vocal expression). The kibbutz and home-reared infants tended to have higher average scores than the American norms. Greenbaum and Landau (1977) report little difference in vocal development between middle- and lower-class and Bedouin samples until 11 months. Babies of Moroccan immigrants to Israel perform better than children of Western European background on many items of the Brunet-Lézine scale in the first 18 months, but not afterwards (Smilansky, Shephatia, & Frenkel, 1976). The education and ethnicity effects on motor development reported by Ivanans (1975) hold for the adaptive, language, and social scales as well.

In European samples, Rebelsky (1972) notes the relatively low scores obtained by Dutch babies on Cattell tests and argues that such results reflect adaptive differences in child rearing techniques and goals. Francis-Williams and Yule (1967) have identified several items of the Bayley mental scale on which English infants exceeded the American norms.

Arai, Ishikawa, and Toshima (1958) included all the Gesell scales in their large-scale study of Japanese infants. As was the case with motor development, the Japanese babies were at par with American norms for language-related behavior (i.e., babbling) until about 16 weeks and subsequently fell behind. This finding, too, is consonant with Caudill and Weinstein's (1969) description of national differences in patterns of maternal care. Koga (1967), on the other hand, found in a large-scale standardization of the Cattell Infant Intelligence Scale for the Japanese middle class that item placement differences were minimal in the first year, but subsequently there were more items placed earlier in Japan than the American standardization sample (15 versus 4). Several sampling factors may be involved in the Koga-Aria-Cattell differences.

Minor differences in Cattell DQs are reported among Japanese, Portuguese, Anglo, Filipino, and Hawaiian infants at 20 months (Werner, Bierman, & French, 1971). The authors attribute the variation to different cultural expectations and practices concerning independence, activity, and related behaviors.

Studies in Latin America primarily document again the tragic effects of malnutrition. Pollitt and Granoff (1967) illustrate retardation on the Bayley measures of mental development under conditions of severe malnutrition. The level of malnutrition in the Guatemalan research (Klein, Lasky, Yarbrough, Habicht, & Sellers 1977;

Lasky, Lechtig, Delgado, Klein, Engle, Yarbrough, & Martorell, 1975) is less severe but is nevertheless reflected in scores on items culled from several standardized tests of infant development.

Correlates of variation.   This brief cataloguing necessarily omits some interesting details and discussion of infant mental development, but even so it is easy for the reader to grow numb from the repeated demonstration of group differences on one set of items or another. There are, fortunately, at least a few attempts to document differences in experience and relate them to the patterning of test performance. At the simplest level, some authors take pains to point out cultural factors of obvious relevance to specific test items. Grantham-McGregor and Hawke (1971), for example, observe that in their Jamaican sample young babies are rarely given cups to drink from and have no experience in squeezing a doll, imitatively or otherwise; poor performance on these items therefore would not suggest the same psychological differences as it would in a group where these experiences are universal. Such items, in short, are culturally biased and may reflect group differences only in cultural experience, not mental development.

More empirically, Leiderman, Babu, Kagia, Kraemer, and Leiderman (1973) were among the first to document environmental–performance correlations in a non-Western sample, even though both sets of measures were atheoretical composites (i.e., modernization and mental DQ). As with their findings concerning motor development, high economic and educational status of the parents were associated with superior performance. In addition, infants who were often tended by more than one caretaker had significantly higher scores on the Bayley mental test than those with "monomatric" care (Leiderman & Leiderman, 1974a). The authors attribute this to the additional stimulation provided by a variety of caretakers and note that the effect was greatest for infants from the most impoverished backgrounds. Lusk and Lewis (1972) failed to find any relationship between infant performance and observed maternal interaction. This is not surprising, however, since their ten subjects varied in age from 2 to 12 months, and this surely was an overwhelming influence on behavior.

Recently the Kilbrides have related the specific pattern of mental development in Ugandan babies to their social and psychological environment. At the ethnographic level, they discuss Baganda family interaction and the value on social facility as they affect smiling, a behavior heavily weighted on Bayley's mental scale and included in most other tests (J. Kilbride & Kilbride, 1975). J. Kilbride (1976) demonstrated an empirical correspondence in a longitudinal sample between the pattern of specific item precocity and child care practices. Observed frequency of being in the supine position, for example, was related to grasping and manipulative behavior, a finding reminiscent of the English–American puzzle cited earlier. High scores on visual behavior were correlated with the frequency of being lifted to the caretaker's shoulder. These within sample differences generally correspond to American–Ugandan group differences in caretaking and performance, although this is less well documented, and they are also in agreement with research on individual differences within American and other samples (Sayegh & Dennis, 1965; White, 1968; Yarrow, Rubenstein, Pedersen, & Jankowski, 1972).

Miller's (1976) report on infants in the Entokozweni Early Learning Center near Johannesburg is also rich in an analysis of individual differences, some of which parallel European results. For example, high scores on the Bayley mental test in the second year were found to be related to frequent social contact. While single, positive correlations are rarely decisive in cross-cultural research (compared to the critical negative result), the accumulation of replications under varied circumstances is powerful, if more slow.

Despite these promising results, there remain many unexplored questions about mental development, however assessed, to which the "natural experiments" of cross-cultural work can make a unique contribution because they concern the effects of long-term differences in care of a sort one can not ethically or practically manipulate in true experiments.

Theoretically Based Tests: Piaget

The traditional baby tests reviewed above consist of often unrelated behavioral items, chosen primarily on the basis of their regular, ordered attainment at the group level by infants in a normative sample. In contrast, there are two relatively new schools of infant testing based on specific theoretical viewpoints. The major one is derived from the seminal work of Piaget; a smaller body of work has emerged from studies of infants' attention to familiar, novel, and changing stimuli as indicative of their cognitive functioning. While work with the older psychometric tests tends to point up group differences in rate of global development, the thrust of research from these newer perspectives emphasizes commonality in the process of development. In part this reflects the relatively small group variation found in most cases, but it derives as well from the universalist orientation of the scientists who have worked in these theoretical traditions.

Piaget's studies of the emergence of intelligence in infancy, particularly with reference to the actively growing understanding of physical existence and space, have inspired three closely related sets of assessment procedures: the Albert Einstein Scales of Sensorimotor Development (Escalona & Corman, 1967; Corman & Escalona, 1969); the Casati-Lézine test (Casati & Lézine, 1968; Lézine, Stambak, & Casati, 1969); and the scales developed by Užgiris and Hunt (1975). These tests have been used now in a number of non-Western samples and in general they replicate the Euro-American sequence of developmental steps. This result is of primary theoretical importance for, unlike the psychometric approach, the Piagetian model requires universals of a basic logical sequence of development. Even in these studies, however, several minor variations in the pattern of development can be identified, bearing a rough correspondence with the infants' cultural surround. There are in addition several reports of substantial group differences in timing of cognitive accomplishments, and while their import has not yet been fully explored, they warn against premature conclusions about the inevitability of normal cognitive growth rates.

Reports emphasizing similarities. The most thorough reports have come from the Ivory Coast (Bovet, Dasen, Inhelder, & Othenin-Girard, 1972; Dasen, 1973; Dasen, Inhelder, Lavallée, & Retschitzki, 1978; Dasen, Lavallée, Retschitzki, & Reinhardt, 1977). Infants (ages 5–31 months) from a rural village of the agricultural Baoulé people were tested with the Casati-Lézine procedures, which include scales for object permanence, use of intermediaries, exploration of objects, and combination of objects. The primary result, in the authors' words, was "the remarkable similarity between the behavior observed among the Baoulé babies and those described by Lézine [in France]" (Dasen, Inhelder, Lavallée, & Retschitzki, 1978, p.

125). In comparing the results to French norms, the test items fell primarily into two groups (Dasen, Inhelder, Lavallée & Retschitzki, 1978; cf. Bovet et al., 1972, where there may have been a difference in testers). The Baoulé children were found to be advanced, by a month or two, in attaining items involving use of an instrument or the combination of two objects (e.g. pulling a string or using a stick to retrieve an object). There was no difference from French norms in the exploration of objects or search for objects after displacements on the object permanence task. (The African babies were behind the French norms on one or two specific items, but there is no clear explanation for this.) These similarities and differences in subscale performance tended to occur at all levels within the subscale, that is, throughout the full age range tested.

The Ivory Coast project also compared the development of well-nourished infants to those who received only half the daily requirements of calories and protein. There were several small but reliable delays in the latter group on the cognitive tests, but the most striking consequence was lessened exploration of the environment and active manipulation of objects observed during a structured free play session.

Since the Casati-Lézine tests are not appropriate in the first part of the first year, Dasen and associates also used the prehension scale developed by Corman and Escalona. On the basis of a preliminary report (Dasen, 1973), the Ivorian babies appear to proceed through the early stages (1 to 2.3) at a similar speed to that of babies in New York.

Konner used the Einstein scales in his work with the !Kung San hunter–gatherers of Botswana. So far he has reported formally only on the prehension subscale (Konner, 1976; 1977). He found the !Kung infants to progress through the same sequences as European babies, and they passed items concerning simple object manipulation (e.g., grasping) at about the same ages as the Corman-Escalona sample. They generally started more complex behaviors involving the mutual regulation of schemata (e.g., visually guided reaching) about 2–3 weeks earlier than the New York babies. Konner relates this result to the physical and social stimulation and opportunities provided by frequent vertical posture. In a preliminary analysis with a very small number of subjects, D. Robinson (1976) compared Konner's !Kung data on the space subscale to American infants and found no reliable sample differences, although the !Kung babies were slightly younger in each stage than the Americans.

Urban Zambian infants were tested with the Einstein scales by Goldberg (1972; 1977). At the period of overlap with Konner's data, stage 3 or about 6 months, she reports the infants in Lusaka also to be advanced in prehension compared to American infants. They did not appear to be particularly advanced on the space or object permanence scales, however, or at later ages, although Goldberg expresses some reservations about the validity of results due to a frequent lack of cooperation on the infants' part. This was particularly troublesome for the repeated frustrations in testing object permanence, and this may account for the fact that the Zambian infants performed at higher levels on the space scale than they did on object permanence, a result opposite to the American picture. In trying to account for the overall pattern of results, Goldberg stresses the initially supportive and later restricting role of back carrying and presents an interesting intrasample analysis. In general, however, she found little statistical relationship among her experiential and performance measures.

In using Piagetian tests in India, Kopp, Khoka, and Sigman (1977) find another pattern of results. The procedures were a slight modification of the Casati-Lézine test, and the authors found a small but significant advance by American subjects, relative to infants in New Delhi, at 9–12 months, but not earlier. There were no SES or modernization effects within the samples, nor were there any overall differences in the understanding of object permanence, use of intermediaries, or exploration (the behaviors of interest at these ages). Instead, the American advance was restricted to two specific situations. These infants performed better on hidden objects because, it seemed, the U.S. caretakers were more likely to redirect the babies' attention back to an unsolved problem during testing, encouraging the child to "work on it." In New Delhi caretakers were more often seen to soothe or nurse the baby in the face of frustration. Although one can wonder about the possible effects of such interactional differences repeated day after day, the investigators were satisfied that behavior in the testing situation itself was adequate to explain the behavioral difference. More importantly, in their analysis, the Indian subjects performed less well on the use of tools in some intermediaries tasks, namely, use of cloth support and attached strings to obtain an object. This difference is attributed to a "subtle task demand which may be more difficult for infants whose gross motor explorations are temporarily limited by care-giving practices." The Indian babies are described as being held "almost constantly" and thus being at a disadvantage in operating in the horizontal plane, compared to the babies in Los Angeles, who are more frequently prone. While this explanation seems reasonable, the reader is left curious about the exact difference in horizontal experience, especially since other knowledgeable investigators working with samples which seem culturally and ecologically equivalent to the naive reader, report that while the babies are often carried, they are also free to explore.

K. Takahashi and Hatano (1976) used only the object permanence subscale from the Użgiris-Hunt tests with their Japanese subjects at 9 months. The babies were at a stage of development essentially the same as that reported for American samples. Takahashi and Hatano also report correlations between individual performance and several measures derived from observations of naturally occurring behavior in the home, primarily the mother's attentiveness to and "acceptance" of the baby and the "happiness" of the baby's behavior.

It is fitting in this context to point out several valuable observations of infants' play behavior, not only because the picture they present is similar to the formal Piagetian test results but also because the tests were originally derived from Piaget's rich observations of naturally occurring behavior. Dasen, Inhelder, Lavallée, and Retschitzki (1978) studied play with objects in both free and structured settings, and they were impressed with the structural similarity to play seen in European children. This was true for both conventional (i.e., appropriate) and symbolic use of objects. The timing of the developmental progression of play was the same as in French infants. This is particularly interesting because the authors report that adults do not emphasize play with objects and the Baoulé babies in fact have few, if any, official "toys." The environment, however, is rich in unstructured objects for play (e.g., sticks) and the children are allowed to explore the physical environment. Valantin (1970; 1973) and Zempléni-Rabain (1970) make similar observations on the fact that objects are not used to mediate social interaction and development in their Senegalese samples. Valantin indicates that prehension skills develop slowly in the children she observed, but she presents no quantitative data.

Fenson (personal communication) replicated in Guatemala some of the procedures used earlier in the U.S. to observe the developmental progression of manipulative play (Fenson, Kagan, Kearsley, & Zelazo, 1976). Babies in both samples were seen to combine two objects in an apparently deliberate and meaningful way at about 12 months. This kind of play marks an important development in the use of mental schemas.

Infants from different environments may use their similar underlying competence in various ways, and differences in the style of play have been reported. The Baoulé children in the Ivory Coast were seen to play quietly and with relatively restricted use of space. In Mexico, Finley and Layne (1971) found children at 1, 2, and 3 years of age to be significantly less active than an American sample in their play.

The major theme of these studies related to Piaget's work is one of commonality in both the sequence and timing of cognitive development, especially concerning the exploration of physical reality and the interactive construction of relevant schemata. The extrapolation of schemes for using objects to obtain a goal may be the most susceptible to experiential effects in the rate of development. This would be in rough accord with American studies (e.g., Wachs, Użgiris, & Hunt, 1971) and can be at least potentially related to the infants' everyday play experiences.

Large differences in development.   Reports of large group differences in the rate of development always have several possible interpretations, and the problems are pronounced when the absence of relatively simple behavioral responses is the basis for inference about cognitive competence. The studies reported below focus on object permanence and the difficulties of maintaining the infant's interest in the face of an unusual kind of repeated frustration have been commented on by Dasen, Inhelder, Lavallée and Retschitzki (1978), Kopp, Khoka, and Sigman (1977), and Goldberg (1977). While there is no particular reason to doubt the procedures in the studies below, caution is needed in interpreting delays among babies probably relatively unassertive and easily discouraged during testing. Nevertheless, the potential significance of these delays is great, and they suggest that a simple maturational interpretation of studies finding no group differences is premature.

The most striking delays in test performance (up to 2 years) are reported by Hunt and his associates, who worked with infants in orphanages in Iran (J. McV. Hunt, Mohandessi, Ghodssi, & Akiyama, 1976) and Greece (Paraskevopoulos & Hunt, 1971). In both cases it was found that increasing the amount of stimulation, or simply increasing the adult:child ratio, dramatically reduced the delay in attaining object permanence. More germane to the present review, home-reared infants in Athens are reported to lag about 6 months behind American babies on some of the more complex test items (Hunt, Paraskevopoulos, Schickendanz, & Użgiris, 1975). The authors point out that a large number of social class and cultural differences make difficult any clear understanding of this finding.

Work in Guatemala also emphasizes group differences in the development of cognitive abilities. The delays are smaller than in the Hunt studies but are still substantial. Kagan and Klein (1973) found Mayan infants in a remote village achieved object permanence about 3 months later than urban American subjects. They attribute this delay to the low level of stimulation and experience with variety in the first year. Later work includes a number of related findings (Kagan, Kearsley, & Zelazo, 1978; Kagan, Klein, Finley, Rogoff, & Nolan, in press). A separate study among lower-class Ladino babies reports test data which indicate substantial delays relative to Corman and Escalona's (1969) figures, but no explicit comparison is drawn (Lester, Kotelchuck, Spelke, Sellers, & Klein, 1974).

Theoretically Based Tests: Infant Attention
A third body of research on infant cognitive development in non-Western settings is derived from the extensive work over the past 15 years on patterns of attention shown by infants of different ages to a variety of stimuli. As with the Piagetian work, the cross-cultural evidence here is most persuasive with respect to similaries in the basic developmental process; but again some differences in the timing have been suggested.

One of the most reliable developments involves a decline with age in infants' visual attention to models of the human face, from 4 to about 10 months, and then an increase in interest in the second year. Kagan (1971) has argued that the initial decline results from the infant's increasing facility in assimilating the stimulus as a face, while the increase reflects a growing ability to try to understand the discrepancies between the models and actual faces. As evidence for this latter interpretation, Kagan notes that increase in attention is greatest if the face is distorted by having its features rearranged in an unnatural pattern.

This basic curvilinear relationship between age and attention to facial masks has been replicated with Mayan subjects in rural Mexico (Finley, Kagan, & Layne, 1972), !Kung San infants in Botswana (Konner, 1973), and Ladino babies in Guatemalan villages (Sellers, Klein, Kagan, & Minton, 1972). Data from the latter two studies are adequately spaced to place the low point of interest at approximately the same age as in American samples, but there may be some minor differences in the exact location of the low point. Differences in the relative power of the "scrambled" face hint at the possibility of subtle experiential effects among the samples, but the evidence is fragile.

M. Takahashi (1973b) has performed several related studies. The results are generally similar, indicating for example a peak of smiling at 3–4 months. The curvilinear relationship of looking and age in her Figure 3 appears the opposite of the previously reported pattern, that is, looking was greatest in the middle months of the first year. However, this is apparently an artifact of converting fixation scores to logarithms before averaging, combined with age related changes in the pattern of looking (e.g., fewer looks of longer duration in the latter half of the first year). Analysis of unconverted scores for length of first fixation per stimulus presentation reveals the expected inverted curve, but with a relatively early rise: mean duration at 3, 5, 7, 9, and 12 months (Experiment I) was 15.6, 4.6, 4.2, 4.4, and 5.6 seconds (M. Takahashi, personal communication).

Because these testing procedures have until recently yielded only group scores, not individual ones, no analysis of within sample variation was possible. Further, since testing was generally carried out at widely spaced intervals (e.g., 4 months), differences in the timing of this age pattern have to be quite large to show. Nevertheless, Kagan and his associates (Kagan, Kearsley, & Zelazo, 1978; Kagan & Klein, 1973; Kagan, Klein, Finley, Rogoff, & Nolan, in press) find some evidence for differences in the emergence of the ability to activate hypotheses about discrepancy among three groups of Guatemalan infants varying in the amount of stimulation and experience they receive. The greatest delays were found in an isolated village on Lake Atitlan. The Mayan babies there spend most of the first year of life in the "small, dark interior of [a] windowless hut," while they are "rarely spoken to or played with" and have access to no toys or playthings (Kagan & Klein, 1973, p. 949). The thrust of their work documents delays of a few months (generally 2–3) in a variety of cognitive landmarks: object permanence, stranger anxiety, separation distress, vacillation to discrepancy, inhibition to novelty, and relational and symbolic aspects of play. At the same time, they point out, all these phenomena do occur in the same general period as in America despite the marked variations in environmental stimulation, indicating the same critical developments in active memory retrieval. They further suggest that the pattern of intragroup variance also points to powerful control by biological maturational forces (Kagan, Klein, Finley, Rogoff, & Nolan, in press) (see Chapter 2 in this volume).

Lasky, Klein, and Martínez (1974) generally replicated the American evidence that 5- and 6-month olds can discriminate pictures of people differing in age and sex, except that they did not find any effect of the subject's (infant's) sex. Other work in Latin America illustrates the disruption of cognitive behaviors—weak orienting and little habituation—when the biology is stressed by malnutrition (Lester, 1975; Lester, Klein, & Martínez, 1975; Vuori, Christiansen, Clement, Mora, Wagner, & Herrera, 1979).

The major effects of stimulus novelty on the visual and manipulative exploration of 3–18-month-olds have been replicated in Japan by Yamada (1978): habituation to repetition and dishabituation to novelty. The Japanese infants showed a concordance of responsiveness in looking and reaching at 6 months, as has been reported for American infants.

Discussion

There is a tension in current discussions of the development of early intelligence between the concepts of plasticity and canalization. Psychologists who emphasize plasticity are impressed with the fact that "very small infants and young children are highly reactive to both enhancing and depriving conditions in their surroundings, as well as to highly specific teaching programs" (H. Robinson & Robinson, 1968, p. 38). They are concerned, by and large, with details of the patterning of development and especially with its rate, as indexed by various marker behaviors or achievements. There is often concern, implicit or explicit, that these differences are important for functioning in maturity. The opposing view—it is usually seen as opposing—focuses on the common thrust of early development in all human infants and appeals to evolutionary considerations in understanding this species-general pattern. Self-correcting responses to short-term deviations are emphasized. In one form, genetic forces are held to regulate even small details of individual fluctuations in development (Wilson, 1972a, b), although this view is disputed (McCall, 1972; Scarr-Salapatek, 1976; Wachs, 1972).

The cross-cultural results summarized above reflect this tension in perspective. They also contribute to a synthesis, however, by sketching a full range of human variation in environment and development. The complexity of results is itself an important kind of variation. Except for conditions of minimal stimulation and/or malnutrition, one cannot conclude that infants from a particular culture, or a particular kind of culture, show more rapid cognitive development in general than infants from other cultures. The literature includes examples of environmental influence on individual items, primarily instances in which infants in a particular setting have little experience with test materials or the kind of activity they call for. This is most common with standard psychometric tests, and their future use for the purpose of group comparison seems inefficient, at best, because of the enormous amount of detailed empirical work required to explain adequately the pattern of item differences. Only after this Herculean task has been finished can attention be turned to fundamental issues of experience and development.

The development of test procedures based on Piaget's theory is an important step forward because one can follow the emergence of critical cognitive structures (such as object permanence) through theoretically diagnostic behaviors. In addition, the constructionist approach moderates the two extremes identified above and therefore fits comfortably with the kind of cross-cultural commonality and variation that has been observed. There remains a problem of bias in the diagnostic items, however, even though it is less severe than with the traditional baby tests. For example, can breastfeeding facilitate the infant's bringing one or both hands to an object placed in the mouth without affecting the psychological structures assumed to underly stage 2.2 in the development of prehension schemes? Having dark-skinned hands (against a light background) probably encourages early and prolonged gazing at the hand (see White & Castle, 1964) and thus yields more advanced scores on the same scale, but it may be irrelevant to coordinated object manipulation. The result, even for Piagetian tests, appears to be a complex variety of blips and dips on age curves in different environments without easy generalization. It would seem that these small item differences can be accounted for by discrete experiential factors or aspects of the testing format itself.

It is difficult to go beyond the level of item analysis in the cognitive tests for two reasons. Unlike the motor scales, items on the mental tests are of less interest by themselves than for what they are thought to imply about internal competencies. After testing walking, one draws conclusions about the ability to walk. After testing an infant's eye–hand behavior one makes inferences about the infant's intelligence or cognitive structures. The central question for motor tests, then, when performance on particular criterion items has been accounted for, is whether or not it is meaningful or useful to smooth over or differentially weight positive and negative differences to arrive at a global summary of "motor development." There is no question about the reality of discrete differences, but for mental development, after noting experiential effects on particular items, the next question is, Are these effects "cultural bias," or are they "real differences" in cognitive development? That is, to what extent do the items reflect some hypothetical, internal characteristic of the baby?

Second, easily recorded physical aspects of the environment are usually irrelevant for cognitive development. Very different experiences may be functionally equivalent for certain aspects of mental growth. Użgiris (1977) has noted that if the opportunity to explore environmental variety is needed at one stage of development, for example, it can be provided by interaction with older siblings in a monotonous setting or by unrestricted access to a middle-class house. She argues that understanding the role of experience will require not only a taxonomy of the functional equivalencies in the environment but also coordination of this analysis with the functional requirements of the growing mind at the sequential stages of development. The problem is further complicated by the fact that infants, through attentional selection and cognitive assimilation, construct their own psychological environments from actual settings.

Careful study of infants' attentional strategies holds promise for minimizing comparative problems. First, it gets us a step closer to the psychological processes of theoretical interest by focusing on the dynamics of infant behavior rather than on particular behavioral milestones. Further, it is less restricted to motor acts, such as reaching and manipulation, than most test items. Finally, it permits the baby to show to the investigator the meaning and usefulness of objects and events from his point of view. These advantages seem particularly useful when working in other cultures.

They can be gained either through insightful observation during achievement testing (Dasen, Inhelder, Lavallée, & Retschitzki, 1978; Kopp, Khoka, & Sigman, 1977) or through the more formal procedures used, for example, by Kagan, Kearsley, and Zelazo (1978).

Kagan's and J. McV. Hunt's work showing cognitive delays prevents one from focusing only on minor environmental tinkering with particular test items; they illustrate the possibility that the entire process of mental development might occur at different rates under certain circumstances and that such circumstances can occur "naturally" in stable, viable home environments. One can only speculate on the roles of (1) discrete effects massive in size and number and (2) general effects environmental in origin but mediated by nutrition or hormonal or state responses to care, or by low levels of stimulation for neurological growth (Rosenzweig, Krech, Bennett, & Diamond, 1968). Nevertheless, one must be impressed with similarities in the sequence of development and in the resulting organism at infancy's close—in other words, with the developmental power of biologically regulated canalization. The term plasticity was originally used to characterize the *functional* openness of individual nerve cells during embryonic growth. While there is some variation in the timing of particular accomplishments, and possibly of particular developments, the basic cognitive outcome of infancy appears universal. The plasticity in infant mental development is less in the functional achievements and organization and more in the materials used and speed of travel during that journey.

Social Development

Social scientists have examined early social behavior in a variety of cultural contexts with the same complementary goals evoked for the study of early cognition: to trace the emergence of universal forms of social interaction and to describe the circumstances that differentially promote and shape this emergence. The two approaches to social behavior differ not so much in their methodology, as was the case for cognitive development, but in their theoretical emphasis on commonality and divergence and in their subsequent concern with long-term consequences. Workers from both perspectives have focused their attention on the frequency and patterning of naturally occurring behavior rather than on particular landmarks of competence. The standard baby tests such as the Bayley and Gesell include several items involving social interaction (such as playing "pat-a-cake") and an even larger number that depend on social imitation as a procedural base. With a few exceptions, such as P. Kilbride and Kilbride's (1974) analysis of smiling, however, such traditional test items have been passed over by those interested in social development in favor of other, more directed paradigms.

A large number of studies of diverse intellectual parentage have focused on the "natural history" of specific social behaviors in various populations. They are valuable for two reasons. First, a variety of internal dynamics are reflected at different stages in the development of any single response system, for example, the smile (Ambrose, 1961; Kagan, 1971). The studies reviewed here and in the context of cognitive development confirm in major outline the processes thought to be universal in the development of two important social responses, smiling and vocalization. Second, research in other cultures highlights both commonalities and divergences in the integration of such systems with each other and with the caretaker's repertoire of behaviors.

The best-documented instance of maturationally based transitions in infancy occurs around the third or fourth month, when association areas of the cerebral cortex, as well as limbic and other structures, are seen to begin a period of rapid myelinization (Yakovlev & Lecours, 1967). EEG measurements from visual areas of the brain show a more mature pattern at this time in amplitude, frequency, and latency (Beck & Dustman, 1975; Ellingson, 1967), and visual habituation becomes a frequent and reliable phenomenon (Jeffrey & Cohen, 1971). Immature patterns of sleep (Spitz, Emde, & Metcalf, 1970) and motor behavior (McGraw, 1946) are transformed. Changes in emotional (Spitz et al., 1970), language (Kagan, 1971), and intellectual (Piaget, 1952) behavior are evident.

Smiling

When comparable observations are made in non-Western settings, a similar picture of emerging behaviors is found. The case is clearest for the development of smiling. This response increases dramatically between the second and fourth months in American (Wolff, 1963; Ambrose, 1961) and Israeli (Gewirtz, 1965; Landau, 1977) samples. The Israeli data come from diverse groups, with kibbutz, lower- and middle-class Jewish, and Bedouin infants showing identical peaks of smiling at 4 months. (Institutionalized babies respond maximally a month later, as Ambrose [1961] previously reported for European institutionalized infants.) Konner (personal communication) found a strikingly similar 4-month peak in smiling among his !Kung sample. From Japan, M. Takahashi (1974) reports several important changes at this age. The month-to-month correlations for individual differences in rate of smiling stabilize (e.g., correlation from 3 to 7 months $= -0.15$; from 4 to 7 months, $r = 0.74$) and become reliably related to the rate of spontaneous smiling in the neonatal period (e.g., 0 to 3 months, $r = 0.31$; 0 to 4 months, $r = 0.62$). In addition, the amount of smiling to facial models becomes proportional to their similarity to a real face at this time.

These results are in accord with the evolutionary view of smiling as a response so important to successful functioning of individuals of the species as to be under strong biologic direction. A smile provokes similar interpretations by viewers of all cultures subject to study (Ekman, 1973). At the individual level, twin studies indicate a substantial hereditary role (Freedman, 1965), and even blind infants develop the response in a fashion distinctly parallel to normal children, although slightly delayed (Freedman, 1974).

The pervasive influence of a behavior with such human meaning can be illustrated by the data in Fig. 8–1. The rise in physical contact during the third month of life in both Kipsigis and American samples may reflect the infant's increased attractiveness to the caretaker as the baby displays maturationally governed flowering of smiling, mutual regard, and, possibly, contingent responsiveness (Lusk & Lewis, 1972). Greenbaum and Landau (1977) report a similar increase in the rate of maternal questions in their three home-reared samples.

Any genetically structured behavioral system matures, of necessity, through interaction with a particular environment. Piaget (1952) and Kagan (1971), along with others, have argued convincingly that an infant's smile is often an indication of particular cognitive events. Of parallel influence on the pattern of daily behavior, however, the rate of infant smiling has been shown to be responsive to at least short-term reinforcement effects.

Presumed environmental influences on the use of smiling are evident as soon as the general structures become functional. There is some dispute as to just when this occurs, but among the Baganda, who place considerable value on infant smiling, the emergence of smiling is no different from Bayley's norms (P. Kilbride & Kilbride, 1974). Certainly by 4 months, as the steep rise in smiling reaches its peak, substantial differences in absolute rate can be found, and only some of these differences can be attributed to procedural variations among the studies. Around this age, Kipsigis infants in rural Kenya smile at least once during 20 percent of their waking minutes (Super & Harkness, in press). A comparable figure for babies of American middle-class families can be derived from the data of Moss (1967) to be 10 percent. Prorating from different time bases and methodologies, one can further estimate an urban Zambian figure, under less naturalistic conditions, to be 14 percent (Goldberg, 1977); for Yugoslavia, 8 percent (Lewis & Ban, 1977); for rural Senegal, 6 percent (Lusk & Lewis, 1972); and for Navajo, 5 percent (Chisholm, 1978). These estimates rest on assumptions that are not entirely firm, but they serve to indicate what the range of variation might be. The developmental course in succeeding months may be even more diverse, although subsequent data points are available in only a few studies. Gewirtz (1965) demonstrates divergence after 4 months in kibbutz, home-reared, day nursery, and institutionalized infants in Israel. Landau (1977) does the same for kibbutz, Bedouin, and middle- and lower-class babies.

It is of theoretical interest—as well as human interest—to note that in contrast to population divergence in the rate of spontaneous smiling, mothers of all cultures may be equally competent in eliciting smiles from their infants when deliberately attempting to do so. Landau (1977) demonstrates this for her four Israeli samples. (Callaghan [1978a, b] found a similar equivalence of Anglo, Hopi, and Navajo mothers in success at getting their infants' attention, although they did so by culturally specific techniques.)

Vocalization
Vocalization, like smiling, serves as a unique channel of communication among humans and appears to undergo some regular maturational developments during infancy. The transitions around 3 or 4 months include an increase in the rate of naturally occurring vocalizations, but language is considerably more complex than smiling. Greenbaum and Landau (1977) present the most effective comparative developmental data, derived from the same four Israeli samples mentioned earlier, plus an institutionalized group, at 2, 4, 7, and 11 months. For the rate of vocalization of discrete consonants and vowel–consonant combinations the increase between 7 and 11 months is substantially larger than any other period. This probably reflects a number of growing competencies during the second half of the first year. Age changes in the rate of vowel production, however, are curvilinear with age, and there are significant sample effects. The lower- and middle-class urban infants, as well as the institutionalized babies and those reared in a kibbutz, all show essentially an inverted-U pattern from 2 to 11 months, even though there are substantial differences in absolute level of vocalization of vowels. The Bedouin infants, in contrast, decrease vowel production from 2 to 4 months, with a shallow increase thereafter. There is no ready explanation for this effect, although differences in the language environment would seem a likely place to look. The Bedouin environment, in general, is certainly supportive of verbal development, as reflected in their other measures.

The relationship of vocal development to maternal vocalization patterns is complex in these data, with no sample effects bearing obvious connection to differences in the maternal behavior until 11 months, when infants in the "richer" environments (kibbutz, middle class, and Bedouin) begin to use more complex utterances and words than do the other babies (lower class and institutionalized). "Richer," in this case, does not necessarily mean linguistically or verbally richer, to judge from the maternal measures. Early verbal development therefore seems responsive to other, unspecified environmental features as well as reflecting powerful maturational growth.

Reports from other cultures are less informative because they do not present the necessary age curves, but they appear also to show a few early variations which become more pronounced by the first birthday. In some cases there may be a qualitative relationship to adult vocalizations, but the picture is not simple. Rebelsky (1973) presents an interesting comparison of mother–infant vocalization in Holland and America. The American dyad increases the rate of mutual vocalization between 2 and 12 weeks, while in Holland it declines. At 3 or 4 months American infants spontaneously vocalize at least once during about 59 percent of their daytime waking minutes (calculated from Moss, 1967). Data from rural Senegal (calculated from Lusk & Lewis, 1972) and Kenya (Super & Harkness, in press) indicate rates of under 39 and of 27 percent, respectively. Prorating from Caudill and Weinstein's (1969) 1 sec/15 sec observations, the figure for urban Japanese infants is about 30 percent, and the derived figure for the Navajo is the same (Chisholm, 1978). Similarly, one can derive an estimate of about 52 percent from Lewis and Ban's (1977) Yugoslav observations (reported per 10-sec period). Despite widely differing rates of caretaker vocalization (from 20 to 60 percent), the infant data at this age are striking in their similarity, with the exception of the Western samples. If the estimates are reasonably accurate, the fact that American infants vocalize at about twice the rate of infants from a variety of other cultures may call into question the generalizability of American findings regarding the correlates of early vocal development: circumstances which produce such an extreme effect may also alter the dynamic relationships among variables.

We have fewer world samples for older infants. Three estimates are offered from rural Guatemalan infants, based on 10-sec time periods: 9 percent in one Ladino sample at 10 months (Tolbert, n.d.); 18 percent for another at 8 months (Klein et al., 1977); and 6 percent for Kagan and Klein's (1973) isolated Mayan village at 8–16 months. This compares to American figures of 23 percent for working-class and 25 percent for middle-class infants 10 months of age (Tulkin, 1977). More striking is Kagan and Klein's report that the amount of babbling does not increase significantly in their sample from 8 and 16 months, but no precise data are presented. Chisholm's Navajo sample shows a rate of vocalization in the last quarter of the first year similar to that of Anglo infants (26 versus 28 percent).

There are qualitative reports of high levels of verbal interaction in other samples —Uganda (P. Kilbride & Kilbride, 1974), Nigeria (Mundy-Castle & Okonji, 1976; Whitten, 1975), and Brazil (Sollitto, 1972). While the absence of adequate comparisons renders evaluation difficult, it may be noteworthy that these reports involve relatively urban families.

Social Interaction
When discrete social behaviors are integrated into a larger picture of the development of social interaction and affective relations, one can begin to address the major

qualitative issues of socialization and personality formation. Leaving aside for the moment the body of work on attachment theory, there are three clusters of reports in the domain of affective interaction, corresponding to geographical areas; the first two are major foci of comparative infant social development.

Oriental studies.   Caudill and his associates have carried out an intensive study of the first 6 years of life in Japan and America (Caudill, 1972; Caudill & Frost, 1973; Caudill & Schooler, 1973; Caudill & Weinstein, 1969). Through detailed observations of maternal and infant behavior, and with firm ethnographic understanding of the culture, they present the following picture of early development: One of the Japanese mother's goals is to help her infant become integrated into the fabric of social life in the family and, by anticipation, in the larger society. She therefore encourages a close and solicitous relationship with the purpose of rearing a passive and contented baby. In contrast, the American mother bears in mind the need to assist her infant's emerging independence, to facilitate individual activity, assertiveness, and self-direction.

There are two striking aspects of these divergent goals. One is their adaptive harmony with the "preferred patterns of social interaction at later ages" (Caudill & Weinstein, 1969) and with the larger patterns of social organization in the two societies. The other is the subtlety with which these goals are approached through both deliberate and probably unconscious techniques of infant care. The Japanese mothers were found to spend more time with their infants than did the American mothers, and provide more soothing, lulling, and rocking. The American infants, on the other hand, receive more stimulation, especially through verbal interaction or "chatting." Even at 3–4 months the infants in both groups had "learned to behave in different and culturally appropriate ways" (Caudill & Weinstein, 1969), with the American babies showing greater vocalization, activity, and physical play. These patterns of socialization are shown to continue in later years (Caudill & Schooler, 1973). Additional work (Caudill & Frost, 1973) found American mothers of recent Japanese descent, and their infants, to behave generally more like the earlier Euro-American group than the Japanese sample. In particular, the Japanese-American mothers were found to chat to their infants *more* than Euro-American mothers, and their babies did more "happy vocalizing" in return. There were also some discernible continuities between the Japanese and Japanese-American mother–infant pairs.

The elegance of this work is marred by the fact that analysis of individual differences within cultures does not replicate the cultural contrasts. This is not unusual in comparative research and could result from two conditions: error variance within cultures, which averages out for the full sample, or truly different sources of variance between and within groups. In the latter case, the discrepancy could be a genuine one or a differential artifact in the two substudies. Caudill and his associates went to unusual effort to minimize differences in the observers, but the simple presence of an observer may cause divergent reactions in America and Japan. Outside visitors to the home are relatively rare in Japan and might evoke substantial concern over the image presented by one's baby.

Kuchner (cited by Freedman, 1974) has looked at some related aspects of early interaction in Oriental-American families in Chicago, replicating many of the contrasts found in Caudill's reports. Notably, they appear in her earliest observations, at 2 weeks of age. Kuchner also replicated some of Freedman's (1974) newborn findings and suggests that temperament differences at birth may contribute to the later patterns of maternal interaction—for example, through differing frequency of changing state. The theoretical discrepancies between the work of Kuchner and that of Caudill and Frost (1973) cannot be resolved until the more recent study is published in detail.

African studies. A second body of work on early social interaction concerns Africa. In an openly speculative paper in which he tries to draw some common themes of personality development in agricultural African societies, LeVine (1973; see also 1974a) writes, "African mothers rarely lavish on their infants the kind of affectionate attention that we think of as 'instinctively maternal behavior' " (1973, p. 142) such as the mutual hugging, smiling, and kissing involved in expressive, stimulating interaction. At the time he wrote there were few quantitative studies that could speak to the issue, and his proposition was apparently based on his own extensive experience and on the work of Ainsworth (1967), who writes, "Ganda babies very rarely manifest any behavior pattern even closely resembling European affection" (p. 344).

Taking into account more recent work, there is a puzzle regarding to what extent and in what manner this description might be true. Preliminary results from the Gusii project directed by LeVine seem reasonably consonant. The Gusii of Kenya deemphasize, in their values, direct expression of intense affect, and they avoid face-to-face interaction. Home observations indicate relatively little overt affectionate behavior toward infants (LeVine, personal communication). Furthermore, the mothers display signs of embarrassment when specifically asked to talk and play with their baby positioned face-to-face in an American infant seat (Keefer, Dixon, Tronick, & Brazelton, 1977). There is preliminary evidence that the Gusii infants establish quite early a standard maneuver to ignore the threatening "impassive face" presented by the mother under instruction, whereas American infants, perhaps finding it more unusual, initially escalate their attempts to elicit a response, and then withdraw in a depressed fashion. Among both the Gusii and their neighbors the Luo the relatively traditional mothers are likely to think talking to a baby or toddler is "silly" and purposeless (LeVine, personal communication; Blount, 1969; 1972).

Goldschmidt (1975) presents a case for low affect toward infants among the Sebei of Uganda, using as data 27 photographs in which a mother appeared holding her infant but in which the pair was not central to the purpose of the photograph. This sample, Goldschmidt argues, is "representative . . . of the manner in which the mothers handle their infants when outside the home" (p. 160). In only one of the photos (3.7 percent) are the mother and infant looking at each other and interacting in a noninstrumental manner. In a second case the mother is seen to be looking at the child (7.4 percent). In short, Goldschmidt concludes that the Sebei mother, with "idle hands and absent eyes," sustains her infant's basic development but without engaging much satisfying emotional involvement. The low level of affect learned at this stage is consistent with the relatively distant relationships found among adults in this group.

It is difficult to evaluate Goldschmidt's claim of low affective interaction between mothers and infants relative to Western cultures because of the snapshot data base, the uncertain ages of his subjects, and the unusual sampling procedure. The figures that are available, however, do not necessarily appear grossly different from the Sebei data. Clarke-Stewart (1973) reports mutual regard in her sample of firstborn 11-month-old infants in American mother–infant pairs to occur in 7 percent of the observed 10-sec periods, and the instantaneous figure would doubtless be smaller. A figure of 11 percent of 1-min periods can be calculated from Moss and Robson's (1968) report on 3-month-olds, corrected for sleeping time from Moss (1967); prorating from other work (Super, unpublished data), this would suggest about 5 percent of 10-sec periods, and less for brief moments. Among Catholic and non-Catholic middle-class mothers of 10-month-olds, Tulkin found face-to-face interaction 3 and 5 percent of the time, respectively (10-sec periods). The comparison for maternal looking only is more suggestive of a difference: Clarke-Steward reports 39 percent, and Caudill and Weinstein, using 1-sec periods, found Japanese mothers looking at their 4-month-old infants 61 percent of waking time. However, given the differential requirements for looking when in physical contact or not (see Figure 8–1), it is not clear whether these differences represent affection or vigilance.

There are several qualitative reports of little affective interaction in African mother–infant pairs, but they are even more difficult to evaluate than Goldschmidt's study. Ainsworth's (1967) comments have already been noted, but her observations were not designed to be minimally disruptive: they "perhaps bore more resemblance to social visits than to scientific interviews" (Ainsworth, 1967, p. 39) and the need to entertain an important visitor probably biased against casual, affectionate play with the baby. R. H. Munroe and Munroe (1971, p. 11), in a study focusing on other aspects of infant care in a Maragoli sample, found high levels of attentiveness but incidentally remark on the low "amount of exchange of overt affectional responses."

Several reports from other African groups present a different picture. In contrast to Ainsworth's presentation, and reminiscent of Caudill's analysis, P. Kilbride and Kilbride (1974) point to continuities among the Ganda social order, adult values, socialization, and infant behavior. They report that "adults and children are frequently seen smiling at and talking to infants to coax smiles from them" (p. 305). The conscious emphasis on social behavior, according to the Kilbrides, is a reflection of status mobility in traditional and present-day Ugandan society. While no explicit comparison is offered, the infant observations presented by J. Kilbride (1976) would seem to support their view. Whitten (1975, p. 7) comments on the elaborateness of social interaction among Ibo families of Nigeria, in which the infant "is held in the eye-to-eye position and engage[s] in prolonged babbling conversations." Similarly, Mundy-Castle and Okonji (1976, p. 3), in describing several Nigerian samples, derive a set of attitudes and practices as "characteristically African [which] relate especially to the emotional and social support given to babies."

At a quantitative level, Super and Harkness (in press) present evidence that caretaker–infant interaction in their Kenyan sample may be richer than relevant American samples in smiling and mutual regard, equivalent in affectionate nuzzling and kissing, and lower only in infant (but not caretaker) vocalization. Lusk and Lewis' (1972) rural Senegalese data on maternal and infant smiling about equal American levels (Lewis & Ban, 1977), while Goldberg's (1977) measures from working-class urban Zambians appear two to three times greater. All these comparisons are technically flawed in one manner or another, but they seem sufficient to require caution in generalizing even about rural agricultural groups in sub-Saharan Africa.

Central American studies.   Reports from Central America lack the depth and breadth of the Asian and African work, but they have a certain coherence. Brazelton, Robey, and Collier (1969) have commented on the low levels of stimulation in early infancy in highland Mexico, and Guatemalan studies (Kagan & Klein, 1973; Kagan, Klein, Finley, Rogoff, & Nolan, in press; Tolbert, n.d.) repeat and extend this picture, as indicated above. Verbal interaction and play are relatively rare and impoverished, although there is some indication that the amount of reciprocal vocalization is about the same as in American working-class mother–infant pairs (Tolbert, n.d.).

Discussion. As this review demonstrates, it is exceedingly difficult to go beyond the tabulation of frequencies in observational data to illuminate the larger qualities of caretaker–infant interaction. A number of scientists have worked on this issue, with useful results, but integrating discrete quantitative measures with a deeper understanding of the nature of the interaction is not just a statistical procedure. Gaining and communicating such insight rests instead on the investigator's "clinical," ethnographic, and literary sensitivities. We have therefore a few gemlike case studies but little common ground, few overlapping dimensions, for comparison. Even the definition and analysis of second-order measures such as "reciprocal vocalization" or "maternal responsiveness to infant distress" are idiosyncratic enough to make comparison of different works nearly impossible. The very few reports that contain their own multicultural comparisons are therefore particularly valuable— those of Caudill and associates, Lewis and Ban, and a few others in progress—and their results are provocative. Lewis and Ban (1977), for example, found American and Yugoslav mothers to vocalize to their infants at about the same overall rate. American mothers were twice as likely, however, to respond with vocalization to their infants' vocalization. Yugoslav mothers, on the other hand, were more likely to initiate vocalization sequences with their babies. Caudill's (1972) analysis reveals very different patterns in the use of vocal communication in Japan and America.

The general pattern of communications through the various senses may be seen to diverge at the cultural level as well, as Landau (1977), Goldberg (1977), and others have noted. Lewis and Ban (1977) pursued this question in an ingenious manner by correlating the rank order, within each society, of maternal behaviors toward their infants in several societies, drawing on their own data as well as those of others. The maternal behaviors included were, in descending order of frequency for American mothers, hold, vocalize, look, touch, play, and smile. The correlations they derive, when subjected to hierarchic clustering analysis (Johnson, 1967), yield the following grouping: ((((Holland + Yugoslavia) + U.S.) + Zambia) + Senegal). In other words, the Dutch and Yugoslavian samples were most similar in the rank order of maternal behavior, then joined by U.S., then Zambia, and then Senegal. To the many ways that have been used to compare cultures, a full scale analysis of this sort would be a significant and potent addition.

It is at such higher levels of interaction and patterning that one can begin to see culture, mediated by caretaker behavior, as a major force in early interpersonal development. Alas, it is also at such higher levels that the comparative data run thin. To capture the variations in infant social interaction and to relate them both to social-structural variables and to personality development was the original spark of interest in comparative infant studies, and it will probably remain the flickering goal for years to come.

Attachment

Cultural variation has been put to quite different use by students of attachment theory (Bowlby, 1969), which is concerned with the universal dynamics of the ontogeny of interpersonal relations: in one sense, the growth of love. Bowlby cast this infant–caretaker bonding as a human evolutionary adaptation that promotes physical and emotional proximity and thus prevents accidents, predation, and abandonment. The process by which attachment behaviors (smiling, reaching, etc.) are elaborated and focused on a particular caretaker (or caretaker*s*, to foreshadow a theoretical concern) thus became of major interest for both theoretical and clinical purposes.

Cross-cultural research has contributed substantially to the force of several claims of attachment theory by replicating in a variety of settings observations concerning the appearance of particular behaviors and some aspects of their emotional dynamics. At the same time, the comparative literature raises questions about the importance of the socially defined context of attachment behaviors and about their underlying organization.

Emergence. The first question the culturally oriented researcher asks of a theoretical description of development claiming universality is, Do the defining behaviors emerge in similar ways and at similar times in widely differing settings? At a general level, ethnographic accounts describe infant attachments as very similar to those that Western psychologists are familiar with. More specific confirmation is also available, especially for a few diagnostic behaviors such as distress to the approach of a stranger or maternal departure.

Figure 8–2 presents the percentage of infants from five samples who cry when the mother departs in an experimental situation (adapted from Kagan, 1976). (Technically, the distress must be shown to be differentially elicited by the departure of the caretaker as opposed to others, but under the circumstances differentiation seems a reasonable inference here.) The samples are disparate: working-class Americans, Ladino and Mayan Guatemalans, !Kung San in the Kalahari Desert, and Israeli

FIGURE 8–2. **Percentage of children in five samples who cry when the mother leaves in an experimental study of "attachment." Adapted from Kagan (1976), who gives procedural details.**

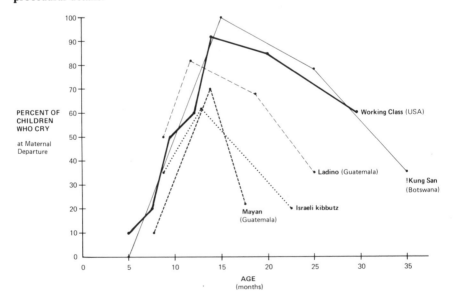

infants reared in baby houses in a kibbutz. There are some difficulties of comparison because the tests were not carried out on infants of exactly the same ages. Given this level of uncertainty, however, the most salient feature of Figure 8-2 is the similarity across samples in the growth of separation distress. Very few infants cry when the mother departs until about 7 or 8 months; the likelihood then rises steeply to a peak shortly after the first birthday and then declines.

This is an impressive demonstration of fundamental species similarity, but the best way to formulate the essential characteristics of this similarity is the subject of debate. The original theory posits the universality as a reflection of biologically influenced emotional dynamics, the attachment behaviors necessary for normal development homing in, if you will, on the primary caretaker, who is usually, of course, the mother. Kagan and associates (Kagan & Klein, 1973; Kagan, Kearsley, & Zelazo, 1978), however, have focused on the specific cognitive maturity necessary to support this process, and they see the distress experienced at maternal departure as essentially no different from related fears and distress to unfamiliar people, objects, and situations. It is because the infant can now appreciate discrepant situations and "activate hypotheses" about their cause and consequences that distress and inhibitions emerge so rapidly in the last quarter of the first year. It is not surprising from this perspective that Chisholm (1978) presents a "fear of strangers" curve for his Navajo subjects which is quite similar in form and placement to Figure 8–2. In the Ivory Coast project (Dasen, Inhelder, Lavallée & Retschitzki, 1978), the same rise, delayed by a few months, is seen in the percentage of infants initially refusing testing, a separate but related index. Stranger anxiety is relatively late in Kagan's remote Mayan sample, he explains (Kagan & Klein, 1973; Kagan, Kearsley, & Zelazo 1978), because the cognitive abilities develop more slowly there than in more stimulating environments. In fact, the various theories concerning the emergence of attachment behaviors are largely complementary rather than contradictory. It is evident that several relevant subsystems of the brain are undergoing functional changes in the latter part of the first year, including both the higher cognitive centers and the limbic system, often thought of as the central mediation area for emotions and their interconnections (Yakolev & Lecours, 1967).

Singularity of the bond. There are two features of attachment theory which distinguish it from other approaches to interpersonal development: the notion of monotropism and the hypothesized web of antecedent and consequent relationships.

The principle of monotropy was formulated by Bowlby (1969) to emphasize the "strong bias for attachment behavior to become directed mainly towards one particular person and for a child to become strongly possessive of that person" (Bowlby, 1969, p. 308). There is said to be a positive correlation between the strength of the primary attachment and the number of secondary attachments that can be formed. Such an observation, Bowlby notes, has been reported from both Scotland and Uganda (Schaffer & Emerson, 1964; Ainsworth, 1967).

The strength of the bias of monotropy, however, seems weaker in those settings where infant care is shared among several family members. A reanalysis of Ainsworth's Ugandan data indicates that the strength of attachment to the mother is negatively correlated with the number of persons in the household (R. L. Munroe, Munroe, & LeVine, 1972). This is difficult to reconcile with Ainsworth's original observation but in any case suggests that it may be partly the European infant's ecology that is monotropic. The Leidermans (1974a; 1977) have described in detail the sharing of infant care with older siblings that occurs in many East African families. They emphasize that while the mother remains "preferred by the infant, especially in times of stress" (1977, p. 432), the child-caretaker also has a central role, increasingly so after 5 months, when she may be in charge for a majority of the day. There are developmental correlates of "polymatric" care, some of them to the advantage of infants with sibling caretakers. On this basis, the Leidermans consider that theoretical models of infant socialization based on maternal centrality are not adequate. These comments are in general agreement with Rabin's (1958) classic work indicating the absence of dangerous effects of "multiple mothering" in the kibbutz setting. Fox (1977; 1978) has augmented this work and finds that except for some firstborn children, whose mothers treat them differently, most kibbutz infants are equally comforted by the mother and the caretaker. As more American infants come to share the world norm for plurality of caretakers, similarly healthy patterns of psychological development are being documented in this country (e.g., Caldwell, Wright, Honig, & Tannenbaum, 1970; Kagan, Kearsley, & Zelazo, 1978).

Caretaking by older siblings is common in many cultures (Weisner & Gallimore, 1977). A more unusual situation has been described for the Hausa of Nigera (R. LeVine, LeVine, Iwanaga, & Marvin, 1970). Among the families studied, marriage for the woman is arranged while she is still in her early teens, and the hostility and rejection which often occur are given formal outlet in a posture of avoidance toward the husband. This culturally constituted defense mechanism also extends to the firstborn child, especially if the child is male. The mother may experience shame or shyness toward the baby, and "is expected to behave toward it with great aloofness, looking at it only to a minimal degree, expressing no affection for it, and avoiding use of the baby's name" (p. 5). This expected pattern of maternal avoidance was found actually to occur in many cases, and in Ainsworth's "strange situation" the mothers were low on all scales of contact, availability, and acceptance (compared to Hausa mothers of laterborns). The maternal grandmother often played a complementary role for these mothers, and the infants could be characterized as attached to more than one caretaker. In their spontaneous behavior in the family compounds, the Hausa infants were observed to be attached to an average of three or four people, even though some babies directed a greater frequency of attachment behaviors to a single caretaker (Marvin, VanDevender, Iwanaga, LeVine, & LeVine, 1977). Whether or not the relationships described in the non-Western studies conflict with the proposition of monotropy depends on where one draws the limits of "*strong* bias" and "directed *mainly* towards one . . . person."

Antecedent and consequent relationships. The yeoman service of cross-cultural research is to help disentangle causal relationships by increasing the amount of naturally occurring variance in important variables and by decoupling variables that are confounded in any one society. One of the salient contributions of attachment theory has been the web of antecedent and consequent relationships it has drawn, primarily with respect to the promotion of emotional security in early childhood (e.g., Ainsworth, 1977; Sroufe & Waters, 1977). In this view, rapid and consistent responding to attachment behaviors does not increase the rate of their occurrence, as would be predicted by a simple conditioning paradigm, but rather creates a secure attachment in which later dependence is decreased, permitting confident exploration by the toddler. There is some evidence for this hypothesis in the Western literature (Ainsworth & Bell, 1977; Bell & Ainsworth, 1972; Maccoby

& Masters, 1970), although there are other interpretations of the data (Gewirtz & Boyd, 1977a, b).

The cross-cultural literature lends further evidence but raises the question of the role of other socializing agents that may facilitate exploration. Konner (1976) reports that comparison of British and !Kung San children in the first 5 years reveals both a closer infant–mother relationship and greater exploratory independence in early childhood among the !Kung. N'Dao (1972), in discussing modernization of mother–child relations in Senegal from a different perspective, also emphasizes the function of traditional mother–infant closeness in facilitating socialization into the larger social grouping. Observational studies of nonhuman primates, as reviewed by Konner (1976), also indicate this ontogenetic pattern. Finally, the Leidermans (1974a; 1977) report that Gikuyu infants reared with a single maternal figure were less negative to a stranger's approach or maternal departure than those with significant amounts of care by an older sibling. Unfortunately, all of these studies share a common problem of natural experiments, namely, a number of unspecified but possibly relevant factors are confounded with the measures of interest. In the African cases, for example, the social group to which the older infant transfers much interaction is often more supportive of exploration than the comparable European peer group, formally organized and supervised for a few hours a day.

A related contribution concerns the inherent link between physical contact and fear reduction. One of the critical indices of attachment is use of the mother as a base for exploring unknown objects or territories and as a source of emotional comfort in all fear-inducing conditions. The classic work of Harlow (e.g., H. Harlow & Harlow, 1965) and others (e.g., Mason, 1968) demonstrates that establishment of this bond in monkeys depends not on the feeding properties of a surrogate mother, for example, but on its tactile and kinesthetic (or cuddly) properties. Marvin, Van-Devender, Iwanaga, LeVine, and LeVine (1977) found attachment to various caretakers in their Hausa sample to be determined by the relative frequency of physical contact and interaction rather than by feeding. Related evidence in humans is provided by reports of "attachment" to blankets or stuffed animals in populations low in physical contact with caretakers. It is a common observation that infants and toddlers in traditional preindustrial settings do not use such "transitional objects," as Winnicott (1953) has termed them from a separate theoretical perspective. Gaddini (1970) quantified this observation on rural Italian children (4.9 percent developed such attachments), urban Italian children in Rome (31.1 percent) and foreign born children also living in Rome, primarily Anglo-Saxon in origin and upbringing (62.2 percent). Similarly, Hong and Townes (1976) report 54 percent of the children of American medical residents in a Seattle hospital used a "security blanket," compared to 34 percent of children of Korean medical residents training in America and to 18 percent of medical residents at Seoul National University Hospital. In both studies a number of variables indicating physical contact covary negatively with these group differences in attachment to cuddly objects: amount of breastfeeding, carrying, and sleeping with the mother. A possibly related instance is provided by Caudill and Weinstein's (1969) report that Japanese infants are (1) rocked more than Americans and (2) suck less on their fingers or pacifier.

Through a kind of intellectual triangulation, these studies lend support to the extension of related animal studies to humans. The evidence is by no means complete, but it appears to confirm the role of physical contact and its normal correlates in the development and use of certain stimuli for emotional security. In this regard, cultural comparisons indicate a possible mechanism for part of the developmental scheme provided by attachment theory.

Other investigations, however, suggest clusters of ontogenetic relationships which are not entirely consonant with those hypothesized on the basis of European and American research. Consider again the data on distress reactions to maternal departure presented in Figure 8-2. In addition to the similarities in timing of initial growth, there is substantial variation in the absolute amount of crying and, more significantly, in the decline of distress over the second and third years. The decline is much slower in the American and !Kung samples than in the Guatemalan or Israeli ones. Infant life in the former cases is characterized by almost exclusive salience of a single caretaker, the mother, with little assistance from other adults or children. This is not true in the latter samples, yet the American and !Kung infants are probably at opposite extremes in other dimensions, such as physical contact, which are said to facilitate secure attachment and, to judge from Konner's (1976) !Kung–British comparison, in concurrent dispositions to explore away from the mother.

Are the differences in decline of separation distress a function of the nature of attachment bonds formed under different rearing conditions, or can they be ascribed to differences in the psychological stimulus that results for toddlers of different cultures when their mothers depart? The question is even more relevant to the differences in absolute level of distress and may address the apparent contradiction between the Leidermans' data and Figure 8-2 concerning shared caretaking and departure distress. How often and under what circumstances does the mother leave in each setting? Is it a common event in which other known caretakers are always available, or is it highly unusual with unpredictable consequences? Kagan, Klein, Finley, Rogoff, and Nolan (in press), for example, report that separation distress occurs earlier in their remote Mayan sample than in a less isolated village because the act of maternal departure is vastly more unusual. Lester, Kotelchuck, Spelke, Sellers, and Klein (1974) make a similar interpretation of their American–Ladino (Guatemalan) comparison. Fear of strangers among Navajo infants is likewise related negatively to the size of their immediate community and to its closeness to the trading post (Chisholm, 1978). Of particular interest, Chisholm also reports a divergence in the decline of fear of strangers between Navajo and Anglo children, but not in its initial rise or peak.

The methodological dilemma is a familiar one in cross-cultural research. If absolutely identical stimuli are used to elicit responses that are interpreted with regard to underlying psychological structures, there is a risk that the stimuli will "mean different things" in two cultural contexts. Their ecologic validity and representativeness may vary, along with their ethical status (Kessel & Singer, 1973). On the other hand, equating stimuli for equivalent reactions is difficult work at best and may render meaningless the original question.

The dilemma for theory is more profound, but it can also be more productive if it leads to multiple evaluations directed toward a cluster of theoretical concepts. One shortcoming of the present cross-cultural literature on attachment is the paucity of measures concerning the quality of attachments that emerge. Current American research emphasizes individual differences in the nature of the maternal–infant relationship (see Ainsworth, Blehar, Waters, & Wall, 1978). Emotional responses at reunion, for example, can differentiate qualitative differences not seen in protest at separation (e.g., Fox, 1977). It seems reasonable to hypothesize cultural differences in the kinds of attachment as a function of cultural variations in care. The consequences in later childhood of qualitative differences in attachment are currently a major focus of inquiry and debate in the European and American literature. Whether or not the same consequences, whatever they turn out to be, necessarily follow the cultural variations has hardly been addressed at the research level but promises to be a fertile field of inquiry. The result could be a fractionation of the operational subsystems behind the complex construct of attachment. While it is far too early to tell, the empirical bits and snatches already reported suggest that comparative research may identify several relatively independent processes, such as fear reduction, security to explore, and acceptance of strangers.

In any event, it is clear that the immediate pattern of attachments and interpersonal behaviors varies with the pattern of care and that the pattern of care is intimately related to larger patterns of social organization. At a purely structural level, the nature of maternal care is mediated at least by the mere availability of other people; other people can provide not only supplementary care for the baby but also emotional support to the mother. Konner (1976) has commented on this for the !Kung San. The study by R. H. Munroe and Munroe (1971) relating caretaker responsiveness to household density among the Maragoli has already been mentioned. Minturn and Lambert (1964) found both between and within cultures that household density is positively related to measures of maternal warmth. Similarly, J. Whiting (1961; 1971) found in a larger world sample that "infant indulgence," a rough measure of physical attention, is related to the number of adults living in the household. It follows that societies organized around extended households are more likely to rate high on infant indulgence than, for example, those with a nuclear family structure (87 versus 42 percent of societies in each group).

Psychological aspects of culture are also critical, since patterns of attachment related behaviors may be more or less adaptive in varying social and physical circumstances. The value placed on early social behavior, for example, is not the same in all groups, and caretaker behavior necessarily reflects such values (e.g. P. Kilbride & Kilbride, 1974). In the Hausa case mentioned earlier, the grandmother's potential role in providing less ambivalent care than the mother may prove critical in future years by forging sound ties to the maternal kin to balance the father's family's greater legal claims. Strong fear of strangers will not be as adaptive in an urban setting as it is in an isolated Navajo campsite. Physical protection may require different strategies of restraint on exploration in different social and physical settings. The Western emphasis on infant–*mother* attachment, in short, has probably led us to ignore the larger pattern of social relationships in infancy (Landau, 1976). This may distort our understanding of social development in our neighbors' children as much as it does when we look farther afield.

Attachment to the infant.   There is, of course, another side to attachment, that of the mother to the infant. Klaus and Kennell (1976) and their associates have explored the possibility of there being a sensitive period in the first hour or so after birth during which time physical separation of mother and infant will impede her psychological bonding to her newborn. This hypothesis is derived from impressive experimental research on other species and several controlled evaluations in North and Central America and in Scandinavia.

For a number of methodological reasons, the sensitive period hypothesis remains highly controversial (e.g., Feldman, 1977). Nevertheless, the larger question of variations in perinatal arrangements is an important and largely neglected one.

Newton and Newton (1972) have reviewed the ethnographic literature and drawn the major dimensions of variation, outlined in the beginning of this chapter. Harkness (1977), working in a single Kenyan community, suggests that social management of the postpartum period plays a general role in maternal mood and functioning. It seems likely from this perspective that a variety of culturally defined institutions and attitudes would mediate maternal attachment to the infant.

Lozoff (1977) examined the Human Relations Area Files (HRAF) with the Klaus and Kennell thesis specifically in mind. She concludes that "contact in the first few hours has a significance for hospitalized women within the context of patterns of infant care in urban societies but not for the species as a whole" (p. 1). With particular attention to the possible model during our species' evolution, she points out that in 80 percent of world cultures the mother and infant are not put in immediate skin-to-skin contact and that nursing usually is not started until day 3. The intervention of providing early contact in urban hospitals, Lozoff concludes, may be effective in altering the developing relation primarily when the woman is removed from familiar surroundings and supports. While one might question the accuracy of many of the ethnographic descriptions in the Area Files regarding childbirth, as they were often written by male anthropologists whose primary interests and points of access to the culture lay elsewhere, Lozoff's general conclusion is consonant with several other bodies of work (e.g., Newton, 1970).

State Behavior

The regulation of state of arousal has been a topic of growing interest to developmental psychologists not only for its methodological importance in infant testing but also as a developmental phenomenon in its own right. The responsiveness of state to external manipulation, its power in mediating experience, its role in the rhythm of development, and its implications for physiological growth have all been foci of interest (e.g., Korner, 1972). Considerable research has been devoted to understanding its biological basis. The comparative human literature is quite small but is provocative enough to warrant separate discussion.

Given the strong biological perspective with which state behavior is usually viewed, one might reasonably expect its fundamental pattern of development to appear the same in diverse rearing environments. The precise aspects of behavior which fulfill this expectation can be only sketched faintly. The total amount of sleeping by rural Kenyan and urban American infants is virtually identical for the first few months and is not significantly different thereafter (Super, unpublished data; Parmalee, Wenner, & Shultz, 1964). The longest periods of sustained wakefulness, presumably reflecting maturation of the arousal system, also appear to follow a similar developmental course in the two groups, as does the overall day–night distribution of sleep. Early adaptations can be seen, however, in the maximum length of sleep periods; the Kipsigis infant, breastfed on demand and with little pressure to sleep through the night, averages about 4 hours as the longest period of sleep throughout the first 16 weeks, compared to an increase from 4 to 8.5 hours in America.

The pattern of feeding is intimately linked to regulation of state, and it is commonly observed in nonindustrial societies that nursing is frequent. In the Kenyan data sucking bouts number over 20 per day in the first 4 months of life. Konner's estimate (personal communication) for the !Kung hunter–gatherers is considerably higher. These data put in new perspective Gaensbauer and Emde's (1973) inference that an innate rhythm lies behind the 4-hour cycle of demand-fed American infants.

Frequent feeding has obvious implications for visceral activity. In addition, it is well established with American adults that short "naps" do not have the same internal structure of quiet and active sleep as do longer episodes, and it is also known that hormonal levels (especially human growth hormone) vary as a function of stage of sleep (Sassin, Parker, Mace, Gotlin, Johnson, & Rossman, 1969). It seems likely that the rural African pattern of infant sleep (and relatedly, feeding) is more common both today and historically than current Western practice. Whether or not this new pattern has any important physiological consequences is not known.

Certainly the familial negotiations surrounding night sleep are quite different in the two settings (mother and infant share a bed in the Kenyan sample, with the father in a separate room or house) and yield divergent strategies of transition. In Kenya, the infants usually fall asleep in someone's arms, both day and night, and the second most frequent method, on a caretaker's back, also involves close physical contact. It is not, in general, an area of conflict or anxiety on the mother's part. Caudill and Weinstein (1969) have described the Japanese mother's approach to state transitions, different from that in both America and Kenya. She is more likely than the American mother to let the infant fall asleep in her arms, but she then also spends more time repeating the task, since the infant wakes up when put down. The rural African infant often continues to sleep in body contact. The possibility of pervasive consequences of such differences is raised by the recent report of Ozturk and Ozturk (1977) that the way of falling asleep (left to fall asleep alone instead of falling asleep while sucking or being rocked) is the strongest antecedent of thumbsucking of several possibilities examined.

Long periods of vertical posture, while riding on the caretaker's back or hip, are probably conducive to greater calm and alertness than lying in a crib or playpen (Gregg, Haffner, & Korner, 1976; Korner & Thoman, 1970) and may recruit hormonal changes as well (Harper, 1972). A number of observers have commented on the possible role of this fact in the often precocious behavior of Third World infants, and there is some suggestion of such an effect even among American samples (Harper, 1972; Yarrow, Rubenstein, & Pedersen, 1975).

The pattern of social stimulation—its frequency and quality—also affects the pattern of arousal. Even in the opening days of life, cultures vary dramatically in the amount of stimulation provided or allowed (Brazelton, Tronick, Lechtig, Lasky, & Klein, 1977; Kagan & Klein, 1973), and the effects of such variation can be seen in newborn behavior (deVries & Super, 1979). The Japanese-American contrast in quieting and stimulating has already been mentioned (Caudill & Weinstein, 1969). Keefer, Dixon, Tronick, and Brazelton (1977) suggest a different picture of Gusii infants. While placed in infant seats watching their mothers trying to elicit their attention, the Gusii babies maintain a relatively steady state of arousal despite the mothers' rapid changes from intense stimulation to disengagement. American infants are more likely to follow their mothers' ups and downs. While the particular assessment procedure is strange in the Gusii context, Keefer et al. indicate that the contrast is an accurate one for naturally occurring behavior as well, and it is consonant with the picture of affective socialization they sketch.

State of arousal is an important mediator of the motor, cognitive, and social behaviors reviewed earlier, and it is more intimately involved in physiological and hormonal functioning. It is presumably subject to its own combination of maturational and environmental influences, although the behavioral sciences have only recently focused attention on them. Even as the field stands, however, it should be clear that the most basic tasks of self-regulation are learned in widely varying niches and that the underlying rhythms and flow of behavior taken for granted in Western research on infancy may be themselves among the most important strata of environmental influence.

INTEGRATION OF INFANCY AND THE LARGER CULTURE

The studies reviewed in the major section of this chapter have been concerned with the early ontogeny of motor, cognitive, social, and state behavior in non-Western cultures, but infancy does not exist in isolation. Just as some of these developments bear orderly relationships to certain environmental conditions, so also do the environmental conditions function within orderly patterns of culture. A full review of research on these larger patterns is beyond the scope of the present work, but two aspects require some discussion. They lead in opposite directions from the focus above—first, relating infant care to *its* cultural determinants, and, second, relating infant development to later functioning in adulthood.

Patterning of Care

The broad perspective of psychological anthropology provides the major insights into the patterning of child care. In the model developed by J. Whiting (1977; see also Chapter 7 in this volume) the physical environment and historical circumstances determine a society's maintenance systems, which include the social structure, economy, and household type. These maintenance systems, in turn, influence the number and identity of caretakers, children's tasks, techniques of discipline, etc.—in short, the child's learning environment. This environment then interacts with the universal, innate nature of human growth and development to produce the personality and skills of the adult. Finally, the adult personality influences the culture's projective–expressive systems (religious and magical beliefs, rituals, art, recreation, and so on).

LeVine (1969; 1974b; 1977) has paid special attention to parental values as mediators between culture and child care. With a strong emphasis on adaptive usefulness, he points out that culturally encoded attitudes may contain, either consciously or unconsciously, information that increases the chances of survival of both the children and the culture. They are part of the projective–expressive system in J. Whiting's model as well, and it is not possible to sort out simple, linear, causal sequences within the integrated network of influences.

Nevertheless, a large number of studies carried out from the anthropological perspective attempt to describe and explain, with varying degrees of success, the kinds of patterning that do exist. Starting at a most fundamental point, J. Whiting, Bogucki, Kwong, and Nigro (1977) relate the occurrence of infanticide to the economic base of a society: it is nearly seven times more likely in cultures that depend on hunting, fishing, and/or gathering than in pastoral and agricultural groups. The cross-cultural codes developed by Barry and Paxson (1971) allow other interesting illustrations of social-structural influences. The father's role and importance during infancy, for example, can be related to subsistence type (e.g., high when birds and small mammals, but not large game, are hunted; low when animal husbandry is important); geographic area (high in East Eurasia and the Insular Pacific, moderate in the Americas, low in Africa and Circum-Mediterranean); societal organization (high with bilateral or matrilineal descent and with monogamy or limited polygyny);

and other social features (low if adolescent boys are segregated or circumcised; high when responsibility and obedience training are lenient). There seems to be a negative correlation of "indulgence" of infants with level of economic organization (Prothro, 1966) and, not coincidentally, a positive one with household density (R. H. Munroe & Munroe, 1971; Minturn & Lambert, 1964), but it may be inappropriate to generalize too broadly about permissiveness toward infants as a single dimension of variation (Prothro, 1960). Case studies of economic change in developing countries have been able to trace some of the functional dynamics of such statistical associations concerning child care (Leiderman & Leiderman, 1977) and physical growth (Cravioto, Birch, De Licardie, Rosales, & Vega, 1969). Climatic factors, primarily temperature, have also been related to the physical closeness of infants to their mothers (J. Whiting, Chapter 7 in this volume).

More or less explicit cultural values concerning interpersonal relations and individualistic behaviors are clearly identifiable in many aspects of infant care (Caudill & Weinstein, 1969; J. Whiting, Chasdi, Antonovsky, & Ayres, 1966). The values can differ between groups not only in their content but also in their intercorrelational structure (Guthrie, 1966). Specific beliefs concerning the supernatural are often used to justify some practices, although other purposes may also be served. The Kwoma of New Guinea (J. Whiting, 1971) and Zinacantecans of Mexico (Brazelton, Robey, & Collier, 1969), for example, keep their infants close or private to avoid dangers of witchcraft. The Gusii of Kenya grease and cover their babies so that small particles will not collect on their skin, where they may be pressed in the body by the evil eye (LeVine, personal communication). A Mojave mother may substitute gruel for nursing after a particular encounter with a snake leads her to think her infant may be venomous (Devereux, 1968). Other beliefs, whatever their basis, are also influential. Parents may invoke cultural assumptions about the nature of the sexes (Condry & Condry, 1976; P. Rosenblatt & Skoogberg, 1974), the naturalness or distress-signal value of crying (Rebelsky, 1973), the fragility or heartiness of newborns (deVries & Super, 1979), or the purpose and efficacy of teaching various behaviors to babies (Blount, 1972; Harkness & Super, 1977; Super, 1976) and adjust their care accordingly. The changing attitudes that come with urbanization and modernization are powerful influences on methods of infant care, although the patterning of resistance and change is not fully understood (e.g., Maclean, 1965; 1966).

Consequences of Care

Western belief in the unique importance of early experience has motivated a large body of investigation. Some instances of early effects are persuasive (see W. R. Thompson & Grusec, 1970); others are the subject of debate (see Clarke & Clarke, 1976). The anthropological literature contains numerous qualitative interpretations of the consequences of care in infancy (and early childhood) for adult personality, often from a more or less psychoanalytic perspective (e.g., Du Bois, 1944; Roland, 1965; U Sein Tu, 1964). The difficulty of this kind of large-scale post hoc interpretation can be illustrated by two articles on personality development among the Hausa of Nigeria (Holthouse & Kahn, 1969; Salamone, 1969). Starting from the same ethnographic descriptions of infancy and early childhood, the authors derive discrepant "predictions" for adult functioning. The more etic, universalist interpretation by Holthouse and Kahn is that the traditional Hausa infant should have great difficulty in developing a sense of basic trust (Erikson, 1950). This psychodynamic characteristic, they say, is later adapted to making clever business arrangements, a behavioral characteristic for which the Hausa are commonly known. Salamone is more emic and, following Opler's (1969) criticism of Erikson's analysis of native American groups, tries to give theory more flexibility. Salamone argues that child care practices gain their meaning in part through the symbolic value given them by the larger society; thus the psychodynamics of being adopted by relatives are quite different in Hausa and European culture. It is therefore consistent, says Salamone, that Hausa adults are not meek and distrustful.

There is substantial quantitative investigation at the cultural level, and infant care and socialization has been related to the perceived nature of the gods (Spiro & D'Andrade, 1958; Lambert, Triandis, & Wolf, 1959); physical violence among adults (Prescott, 1975; Prescott & Wallace, 1976); common games (Barry & Roberts, 1972); the type of rhythms in music (Ayres, 1973); and a variety of aspects of adult mental functioning (J. Whiting & Child, 1953; Zern, 1970, 1972; R. L. Munroe, Munroe, & Whiting, 1973). LeVine (1970) and J. Whiting (1977) provide reviews of this cross-cultural approach.

The shortcomings of such studies in validating particular theories have been addressed by others, but their contributions to both the testing and generation of hypotheses have nevertheless been the major force behind the growth of the comparative study of human development. One task that remains to be tackled is a detailed consideration of the mechanisms that contribute to the associations that have been observed. That is to say, enough different kinds of relationships between infant care and adult functioning are now available to move beyond the testing of narrow hypotheses derived from particular theories and to look instead at how such associations fit into the larger picture of human development in the societies under study. Such an approach would take place at a higher level of analysis than the testing of static alternate hypotheses as usually construed in the more rigorous cross-cultural efforts and would take account of the growing recognition in the larger field of life span developmental psychology that the threads of human development can be and appear to be continuous or not depending in large degree on the particular patches of behavior they join.

Reviewing the kinds of associations that have been reported in the anthropological literature, it seems that several possible mechanisms need to be considered in a more general developmental approach, not all of them resident in the individual psyche. The persistence in an individual of the psychological dispositions acquired at particular periods has been the central model for the cross-cultural studies mentioned above. It also lies at the core of most psychological research in Western countries. Although there have been some attempts to integrate with this view later environmental influences that can maintain, or fail to maintain, the acquired dispositions (e.g., Kagan & Moss, 1962), no general model has been put forward.

One reason for this state of affairs may be exactly the kind of myopia that the cross-cultural lens can correct, the near blindness of more strictly developmental theories to larger social structural considerations. At the same time, the anthropological work, presbyopic in most cases, has not given adequate attention to the developmental course of life. Sorting out the continuities in culture and personality will require attention to the following possibilities:

1. There may be innate and stable dispositions, of genetic or prenatal cause, which vary with ethnic identity (e.g., Freedman, 1974).
2. Associations between infant socialization and adult personality might derive from the persistence of learned dispositions. Thus the Alorese may be affectionless and

suspicious as adults as a result of the basic character formation during the first few years of cold, even rejecting treatment (Du Bois, 1944), and twins may vary in the style of performing equivalent motor acts because of early training (McGraw, 1977).

3. There may also be lasting effects of early treatment resulting not from primarily psychological stability but rather from alterations in more general biological substrates, mediated, for example, by hormone levels (Landauer & Whiting, 1964).

4. As a final alternative at the individual level, early learning may have no essential lasting effects but may sensitize the organism to rapid relearning when similar conditions reoccur (Campbell & Spear, 1972).

5. It may also be true that early learning is no less modifiable and no more fundamental than learning at any other time (Kagan, Kearsley, & Zelazo, 1978) and that similarities in early and mature behavior result from similarities in the circumstances of their occurrence. The environment could have stable characteristics in its own right, or positive feedback loops could become established in which certain behavior patterns, whether social, cognitive, or whatever, modify the effective environment to elicit more of the same.

One can construct a companion list of possibilities leading toward discontinuity, including (1) maturationally controlled behavior transformations (e.g., at adolescence), (2) social pressure toward arbitrary behavioral standards (e.g., some aspects of sex roles), and (3) institutionally imposed efforts to alter the course of development, such as formal education or rites of passage (Super & Harkness, in press).

It would be unreasonable to expect the cross-cultural approach, working from a small data base and with severe analytic restrictions, to fully resolve issues that have proven so resistant in other paradigms. Nevertheless, a more sophisticated developmental outlook joined with the basic cross-cultural method should be productive for all parties.

LOOKING AHEAD

There may be a necessary sequence of stages as any one branch of the social sciences discovers that Americans and the British are not a random sample of humanity. The first is to seek variance in behavior, be it visual acuity, marriage arrangements, or linguistic structure. Comparative human development has been in that stage for a while, and the findings of variance and invariance have served well in stimulating thought on their causes. Even as recently as 1970, a focus on dependent behavioral variables was recommended as a fruitful strategy (LeVine, 1970). As our knowledge increases, however, there is a growing consensus that equal attention is required by causal and mediating variables (e.g., LeVine, 1977).

For this next, more theoretically directed stage (which is already under way) to be fruitful, several persistent difficulties in the research literature need to be remedied. While the problems exist in most areas of comparative research, they seem particularly salient after reviewing the infant literature. First, it should be clear that comparative infant studies must be quantitative. It is true for most societies that infancy is relatively indulgent and the transition to childhood is marked by the imposition of more severe socialization. Qualitative judgments of whether this is more or less so among the Arapesh, for example, than among Americans are nearly useless. Many of the classic ethnographic works were carried out by men with no child rearing experience, and the bases of their evaluations are unknown. A personal anecdote will illustrate the ease of misperception. LeVine's (1973) essay suggesting low levels of affective display in many rural African groups came to my attention shortly after I began my observations of infant–caretaker interaction in Kokwet. "It's true," I thought, "I haven't seen very much mutual smiling and kissing." A preliminary tabulation of the data confirmed this impression of low rates of smiling, for example. Comparison with American data, however, indicated the level was not *relatively* low in Kokwet, that is, smiling is not very frequent in either society. Some aspects of affectionate attention were found to be more frequent in Kokwet than America (Super & Harkness, 1974; in press). Although such interaction is a relatively low-frequency behavior in all cultures, it had high salience in my informal (and paternal) scheme for caretaker interaction. It follows from this incident that appropriate quantitative information must be available on both sides of the comparison.

To expect exactly comparable data as part of every study is unrealistic, especially if one wishes to escape the apparently unavoidable invidiousness of any two-group comparison. Yet the difficulties of using published data are often substantial, as the present discussion of social development illustrates. The stream of behavior is divided vertically into acts and horizontally into time units that vary from study to study. It would increase enormously the value of expensive and difficult field studies if a core of common measures were developed for inclusion in published reports whenever feasible.

Second, one must regretfully note that the general scientific quality of comparative research on human infancy is not high. Widely accepted canons of sample selection, reliability assessment, etc. are often neglected, sometimes for respectable reasons, other times not. At a more strategic level, a few discrete behaviors too quickly become an index of a much larger, unvalidated concept of temperament, cognitive ability, or attachment. Statistical tests which speak to the probability of replication are interpreted to confirm a general theory that is relevant but not identical to the obtained result. Too much explanation is post hoc, without adequate consideration of alternative hypotheses, and often dependent on unmeasured hypothetical antecedents.

Third, a great deal of the published research does not address any particular theoretical question. As indicated above, simply trying out a favorite test in a new culture, looking for variance in the dependent variable, is no longer the most desirable strategy. One reflection of this shortcoming of theory is the disproportion of work directed toward surface level behavior, such as reflexes and sitting, instead of underlying constructs more central to much social and scientific thought—for example, cognitive and social competence, skills, and dispositions. Research in our own culture does not share this disproportion. Similarly, the geographic distribution of the research literature appears to be more a consequence of the recent history of the British Empire, of ease of access and funding, than the result of strategic scientific choice. A final reflection of weakness in theory is the gross nature of independent variables so often used in analysis—ethnicity, socioeconomic status, etc. Lewis (1972) has argued that we need to break down such large indices into variables that will show us the process of development.

A fourth failure stems in part from the hiatus over the past 25 or 30 years in the once prominent dialogue between anthropology and psychology. For the past few decades they seem to have withdrawn from the interface, especially with regard to infancy, to tend their own theories. Very few of the studies reviewed here achieve, or even attempt, an integration of infant care and development on the one hand with functional and value characteristics of the larger culture on the other. Success in this direction requires both sound ethnographic knowledge of the culture as well as a quantitative baseline of information about the infants' daily lives.

Fortunately, this list of complaints about the existing literature also corresponds to the major trends emerging in comparative infant research—more emphasis on theoretically directed, quantitative studies for the exploration and testing of hypotheses, carried out with increased sensitivity to the social and cultural context of development. While much of the present literature may appear discouraging to the social scientist with a perceptive but critical eye, the trend of the last decade is encouraging. Infancy has shared in the increase in production and appreciation of the comparative developmental method.

There is, after all, no aspect of human life that is unaffected by culture in its social and physical aspects, nor is there any stage of life isolated from the humanly structured environment. The studies reviewed here sketch some major contours of infancy in this perspective. The common thrust of our biological heritage, the canalization of our species' early development, is the major dimension, occasionally as surprising as it is obvious. Our alleged hallmark of cognitive abilities is perhaps the least malleable by our cultural variety, although as with motor skills, there is a fine patterning in the timing of universal developments. The diversification of overt social behavior is more complex, variations entangling the core in ways we do not yet see.

The essential problem of research on infancy in other cultures is the same as that of comparative research in general and, in fact, as that in our own culture and subcultures as well: to sort out the functional relationships behind the statistical ones we find in natural experiments and our own occasionally unnatural ones. To use B. Whiting's (1976) felicitous phrase, we must begin to unwrap the packaged variables we use as background measures and also the behavioral packages which attract our initial attention. At the same time, infancy holds a unique place in the human sciences, for methodological reasons and because it approaches within a few months the endpoint of ontogenetic reductionism. Developing a firm empirical base concerning both the invariances and the variations will help us unwrap several packages.

ACKNOWLEDGMENTS
Original research reported here was made possible in part by funds granted by the William T. Grant Foundation and by the Carnegie Corporation of New York. A number of colleagues commented on an earlier version of this work, and I appreciate their helpful comments. I am especially indebted to Dr. Hideo Kojima for assistance in locating and understanding the Japanese literature cited here. Thanks go also to the many scientists around the world who responded to my appeal for papers that were unpublished or not widely known.

REFERENCES
Abelove, J. M. Pre-verbal learning of kinship behavior among Shipibo infants of eastern Peru. Unpublished doctoral dissertation, City University of New York, 1978.
Abhichandani, P. A study of growth and development in the first 18 months of life. Unpublished MD dissertation, All India Medical School, New Delhi, 1970.

Adler, S. Developmental patterns as a function of ethnicity. *Journal of Communication Disorders,* 1973, *6,* 184–192.

Ainsworth, M. D. S. *Infancy in Uganda: Infant care and the growth of love.* Baltimore: Johns Hopkins Press, 1967.

Ainsworth, M. D. S. Attachment theory and its utility in cross-cultural research. In P. H. Leiderman, S. R. Tulkin, & A. Rosenfeld (Eds.), *Culture and infancy: Variations in the human experience.* New York: Academic Press, 1977.

Ainsworth, M. D. S., & Bell, S. M. Infant crying and maternal responsiveness: A rejoinder to Gewirtz and Boyd. *Child Development,* 1977, *48,* 1208–1216.

Ainsworth, M. D. S., Blehar, M. , Waters, E., & Wall, S. *Patterns of attachment.* Hillsdale, N.J.: Earlbaum, 1978.

Akim, B., McFie, J., & Sebigajju, E. Developmental level and nutrition: A study of young children in Uganda. *Journal of Tropical Pediatrics,* 1956, *2,* 159–165.

Ambrose, J. A. The development of the smiling response in early infancy. In B. M. Foss (Ed.), *Determinants of infant behavior* (Vol. 1). London: Methuen, 1961.

Anderson, N. A., Brown, E. W., & Lyon, R. A. Causes of prematurity: III. Influences of race and sex on duration of gestation and weight at birth. *American Journal of Diseases of Children,* 1943, *65,* 523–534.

André-Thomas, Chesni, Y., & SaintAnne-Dargassies, S. *The neurological examination of the infant.* London: National Spastics Society, 1960.

Apoko, A. At home in the village: Growing up in Acholi. In L. K. Fox (Ed.), *East African childhood.* Nairobi: Oxford University Press, 1967.

Arai, S., Ishikawa, J., & Toshima, K. Développement psychomoteur des enfants Japonais. *Revue de Neuropsychiatrie Infantile et d'Hygiène Mentale de l'Enfance,* 1958, *6,* 262–269.

Ashton, R., & Connolly, K. The relation of respiration rate and heart rate to sleep states in the human newborn. *Developmental Medicine and Child Neurology,* 1971, *13,* 180–187.

Athavale, V. B., Kandoth, W. K., & Sonnad, L. Developmental pattern in children of lower socio-economic group below 5 years of age. *Indian Pediatrics,* 1971, *8,* 313–320.

Ayres, B. Effects of infant carrying practices on rhythm in music. *Ethos,* 1973, *1,* 387–404.

Baby sets a new record! *Daily Nation* (Nairobi), April 24, 1976, p. 3.

Bardet, C., Massé, G., Moreigne, F., & Senecal, M. J. Application du test de Brunet-Lézine à un groupe d'enfants Ouolofs de 6 mois à 24 mois. *Bulletin de la Société Médicale d'Afrique Noire de Langue Française,* 1960, *5,* 334–356.

Barry, H., III, & Paxson, L. M. Infancy and early childhood: Cross-cultural codes 2. *Ethnology,* 1971, *10,* 466–508.

Barry, H., III., & Roberts, J. M. Infant socialization and games of chance. *Ethnology,* 1972, *11,* 296–308.

Bateson, G., & Mead, M. *Karba's first years.* New York University Film Library, 1950.

Bateson, G., & Mead, M. *Childhood rivalry in Bali and New Guinea.* New York University Film Library, 1952.

Bateson, G., & Mead, M. *Bathing babies in three cultures.* New York University Film Library, 1954.

Bayley, N. Comparisons of mental and motor test scores for ages 1–15 months by sex, birth order, race, geographical location, and education of parents. *Child Development,* 1965, *36,* 379–411.

Bayley, N. *Manual for the Bayley Scales of Infant Development.* New York: The Psychological Corporation, 1969.

Beck, E. C., & Dustman, R. E. Changes in evoked responses during maturation and aging in man and macaque. In N. Burch & H. L. Altshuler (Eds.), *Behavior and brain electrical activity.* New York: Plenum, 1975.

Beintema, D. J. *A neurological study of newborn infants*. London: Spastics International Medical Publications, 1968.

Bell, R. Q. Some factors to be controlled in studies of the behavior of newborns. *Biologia Neonatorum*, 1963, *5*, 200–214.

Bell, R. Q. Level of arousal in breast-fed and bottle-fed human newborns. *Psychosomatic Medicine*, 1966, *28*, 177–180.

Bell, S. M., & Ainsworth, M. D. S. Infant crying and maternal responsiveness. *Child Development*, 1972, *43*, 1171–1190.

Beresowski, A., & Lundie, J. K. Sequence in the time of ossification of the carpal bones in 705 African children from birth to six years of age. *South African Journal of Medical Sciences*, 1952, *17*, 25–31.

Bernal, J., & Richards, M. P. M. The effects of bottle and breast feeding on infant development. *Journal of Psychosomatic Research*, 1970, *14*, 247–252.

Blank, M. Some maternal influences on infants' rates of sensorimotor development. *Journal of the American Academy of Child Psychiatry*, 1964, *3*, 668–687.

Block, A. The Kurdistani cradle story. *Clinical Pediatrics*, 1966, *5*, 641–645.

Blount, B. G. *Acquisition of language by Luo children.* Unpublished doctoral dissertation, University of California at Berkeley, 1969.

Blount, B. G. Parental speech and language acquisition: Some Luo and Samoan examples. *Anthropological Linguistics*, 1972, *14*, 119–130.

Boismier, J. D. Visual stimulation and wake-sleep behavior in human neonates. *Developmental Psychobiology*, 1977, *10*, 219–227.

Bovet, M. C., Dasen, P. R., Inhelder, B., & Othenin-Girard, C. Étapes de l'intelligence sensori-motrice chez l'enfant Baoulé: Étude préliminaire. *Archives de Psychologie*, 1972, *41*, 363–386.

Bowes, W. A., Jr., Brackbill, Y., Conway, E., & Steinschneider, A. The effects of obstetrical medication on fetus and infant. *Monographs of the Society for Research in Child Development*, 1970, *35*, (4, Serial No. 137).

Bowlby, J. *Attachment and loss, (vol. 1). Attachment.* New York: Basic Books, 1969.

Brackbill, Y., & Thompson, G. G. *Behavior in infancy and early childhood.* New York: Free Press, 1967.

Brain, R., & Wilkinson, M. Observations on the extensor plantar reflex and its relationship to the functions of the pyramidal tract. *Brain*, 1959, *82*, 297–320.

Brazelton, T. B. Psychophysiologic reactions in the neonate. II. Effect of maternal medication on the neonate and his behavior. *Journal of Pediatrics*, 1961, *58*, 513–518.

Brazelton, T. B. Implications of infant development among the Mayan Indians of Mexico. *Human Development*, 1972, *15*, 90–111.

Brazelton, T. B. *Neonatal Behavioral Assessment Scales.* London: Spastics International Medical Publications, 1973.

Brazelton, T. B. Implications of infant development among the Mayan Indians of Mexico. In P. H. Leiderman, S. R. Tulkin, & A. Rosenfeld (Eds.), *Culture and infancy: Variations in the human experience.* New York: Academic Press, 1977.

Brazelton, T. B., & Freedman, D. G. Manual to accompany Cambridge Newborn Behavioral and Neurological Scales. In G. B. A. Stoelinga & J. J. Van Der Werff Ten Bosch (Eds.), *Normal and abnormal development of brain and behavior.* Leiden: Leiden University Press, 1971.

Brazelton, T. B., Koslowski, B., & Tronick, E. Neonatal behavior among urban Zambians and Americans. *Journal of the American Academy of Child Psychiatry*, 1976, *15*, 97–107.

Brazelton, T. B., Robey, J. S., & Collier, G. A. Infant development in the Zinacanteco Indians of Southern Mexico. *Pediatrics*, 1969, *44*, 274–290.

Brazelton, T. B., Tronick, E., Lechtig, A., Lasky, R., & Klein, R. The behavior of nutritionally deprived Guatemalan infants. *Developmental Medicine and Child Neurology*, 1977, *19*, 364–372.

Brazelton, T. B., Tryphonopoulou, Y., & Lester, B. M. A comparative study of Greek neonatal behavior. *Pediatrics*, 1977.

Broman, S. H., Nichols, P. L., & Kennedy, W. A. *Preschool IQ: Prenatal and early developmental correlates.* Hillsdale, N.J.: Lawrence Earlbaum, 1975.

Brown, R. E., & Halpern, F. The variable pattern of mental development of rural black children. *Clinical Pediatrics*, 1971, *10*, 404–409.

Brueton, M. J., Palit, A., & Prosser, R. Gestational age assessment in Nigerian newborn infants. *Archives of Disease in Childhood*, 1973, *48*, 318–320.

Brunet, O., & Lézine, I. *Le développement psychologique de la première enfance.* Paris: Presses Universitaires de France, 1965.

Butler, S. R., Suskind, M. R., & Schanberg, S. M. Maternal behavior as a regulator of polyamine biosynthesis in brain and heart of the developing rat pup. *Science*, 1978, *199*, 445–446.

Caldwell, B. M., Wright, C. M., Honig, A. S., & Tannenbaum, J. Infant day care and attachment. *American Journal of Orthopsychiatry*, 1970, *40*, 397–412.

Callaghan, J. W. Anglo, Hopi, and Navajo infants and their mothers: A cross-cultural perspective. Paper presented at the International Conference on Infant Studies, Providence, R.I., 1978 (a).

Callaghan, J. W. Anglo, Hopi, and Navajo mothers' face-to-face interactions with their infants. Unpublished master's thesis, University of Chicago, 1978 (b).

Campbell, B. A., & Spear, N. E. Ontogeny of memory. *Psychological Review*, 1972, *79*, 215–236.

Carothers, J. C. Age and wisdom teeth in Africans. *East African Medical Journal*, 1947, *24*, 304–306.

Casati, I., & Lézine, I. *Lés etapes de l'intelligence sensori-motrice. Manuel.* Paris: Centre de Psychologie Appliquée, 1968.

Casler, L. The effects of extra tactile stimulation on a group of institutionalized infants. *Genetic Psychology Monographs*, 1965, *71*, 137–175.

Casler, L. Supplementary auditory and vestibular stimulation: Effects on institutionalized infants. *Journal of Experimental Child Psychology*, 1975, *19*, 456–463.

Caudill, W. Tiny dramas: Vocal communication between mother and infant in Japanese and American families. In W. P. Lebra (Ed.), *Transcultural research in mental health (Vol. 2 of Mental health research in Asia and the Pacific)* Honolulu: University of Hawaii Press, 1972.

Caudill, W., & Frost, L. A comparison of maternal care and infant behavior in Japanese-American, American, and Japanese families. In W. Lebra (Ed.), *Youth, socialization, and mental health (Vol. 3 of Mental health research in Asia and the Pacific).* Honolulu: University of Hawaii Press, 1973.

Caudill, W. A., & Schooler, C. Child behavior and child rearing in Japan and the United States: An interim report. *Journal of Nervous and Mental Disease*, 1973, *157*, 323–338.

Caudill, W. & Weinstein, H. Maternal care and infant behavior in Japan and America. *Psychiatry*, 1969, *32*, 12–43.

Chagula, W. K. The age of eruption of third permanent molars in male East Africans. *American Journal of Physical Anthropology*, 1960, *18*, 77–82

Chang, N. Y. Cross-cultural perspectives of motor development in infants. Unpublished undergradute thesis, Harvard University, 1976.

Chavez, A., Martínez, C., & Yaschine, T. Nutrition, behavioral development, and mother-child interaction in young rural children. *Federation Proceedings*, 1975, *34*, 1574–1582.

Chisholm, J. S. Developmental ethology of the Navajo. Unpublished doctoral dissertation, Rutgers University, 1978.

Chisholm, J. S., Woodson, R. H., & DaCosta-Woodson, E. M. Maternal blood pressure in pregnancy and newborn irritability. *Early Human Development*, 2(2), 171–178, 1978.

Christie, A. Prevalence and distribution of ossification centers in the newborn infant. *American Journal of Diseases of Children*, 1949, 77, 355–361.

Christie, A. U., Dunham, E. C., Jenss, R. M., & Dippel, A. L. Development of the center for the cuboid bone in newborn infants. *American Journal of Diseases of Children*, 1941, 61, 471–482.

Clark, D. L., Kreutzberg, J. R., & Chee, F. K. W. Vestibular stimulation influence on motor development in infants. *Science*, 1977, 196, 1228–1229.

Clarke, A. M., & Clarke, A. D. B. *Early experience: Myth and evidence*. New York: Free Press, 1976.

Clarke-Stewart, K. A. Interactions between mothers and their young children: Characteristics and consequences. *Monographs of the Society for Research in Child Development*, 1973, 38, (6–7, Serial No. 153).

Clifford, S. G. Postmaturity with placental dysfunction: Clinical syndrome and pathologic findings. *Journal of Pediatrics*, 1954, 44, 1–13.

Coll, C. H., Sepkoski, C., & Lester, B. M. Differences in Brazelton Scale performance between Puerto Rican and North American white and black newborns. Paper presented at the meeting of the Society for Research in Child Development, New Orleans, 1977.

Coll, C., Sepkoski, C. & Lester, B. M. Differences in Brazelton Scale performance between Puerto Rican and mainland black and Caucasian infants. Manuscript submitted for publication, 1978.

Condry, J., & Condry, S. Sex differences: A study of the eye of the beholder. *Child Development*, 1976, 47, 812–819.

Corman, H. H., & Escalona, S. K. Stages of sensorimotor development: A replication study. *Merrill-Palmer Quarterly*, 1969, 15, 351–362.

Crano, W. D. What do infant mental tests test? A cross-lagged panel analysis of selected data from the Berkeley Growth Study. *Child Development*, 1977, 48, 144–151.

Cravioto, J., Birch, H. G., De Licardie, E., Rosales, L., & Vega, L. The ecology of growth and development in a Mexican pre-industrial community report I: Method and findings from birth to one month of age. *Monographs of the Society for Research in Child Development*, 1969, 34, (5, Serial No. 129).

Crowell, D. H. Associations among anatomical and behavioral variables of full-term neonates. *Child Development*, 1962, 33, 373–380.

Crump, E. P., Carrell, P. H., Masuoka, J., & Ryan, D. Growth and development: I. Relation of birthweight in Negro infants to sex, maternal age, parity, prenatal care, and socioeconomic status. *Journal of Pediatrics*, 1957, 51, 678–697.

Curti, M. W., Marshall, F. B., & Steggerda, M. The Gesell schedules applied to one-, two-, and three-year-old Negro children of Jamaica, BWI. *Journal of Comparative Psychology*, 1935, 20, 125–156.

Dart, M. T. The effects of three prenatal psychological interventions on the course and outcome of pregnancy. Unpublished doctoral dissertation, Harvard University, 1977.

Das, V. K., & Sharma, N. L. Developmental milestones in a selective sample of Lucknow children: A longitudinal study. *Indian Journal of Pediatrics*, 1973, 40, 1–7

Dasen, P. Le développement psychologique du jeune enfant Africain. *Archives de Psychologie*, 1972, 41, 341–361.

Dasen, P. R. Preliminary study of sensori-motor development in Baoulé children. *Early Child Development and Care*, 1973, 2, 345–354.

Dasen, P. R., Inhelder, B., Lavallée, M., & Retschitzki, J. *Naissance de l'intelligence chez l'enfant baoulé de Côte d'Ivoire*. Berne: Hans Huber, 1978.

Dasen, P. R., Lavallée, M., Retschitzki, J., & Reinhardt, M. Early moderate malnutrition and the development of sensorimotor intelligence. *Journal of Tropical Pediatrics and Environmental Child Health,* 1977, *23,* 145–157.

Davids, A., Holden, R. H., & Gray, G. B. Maternal anxiety during pregnancy and adequacy of mother and child adjustment eight months following childbirth. *Child Development,* 1963, *34,* 993–1002.

Davis, H. V., Sears, R. R., Miller, H. C., & Brodbeck, A. J. Effects of cup, bottle, and breast feeding on oral activities of newborn infants. *Pediatrics,* 1948, *2,* 549–558.

Dennis, W. Does culture appreciably affect patterns of infant behavior? *Journal of Social Psychology,* 1940, *12,* 305–317.

Dennis, W. Causes of retardation among institutional children: Iran. *Journal of Genetic Psychology,* 1960, *96,* 47–59.

Dennis, W., & Dennis, M. G. The effect of cradling practices upon the onset of walking in Hopi children. *The Pedagogical Seminary and Journal of Genetic Psychology,* 1940, *56,* 77–86.

Dennis, W., & Najarian, P. Infant development under environmental handicap. *Psychological Monographs,* 1957, *71,* (7, Whole No. 436).

Devereux, G. L'image de l'enfant dans deux tribus: Mohave et Sendang et son importance pour la psychiatrie de l'enfant. *Revue de Neuropsychiatrie Infantile et d'Hygiène Mentale de l'Enfance,* 1968, *16,* 375–390.

deVries, M. W., & deVries, M. R. Cultural relativity of toilet training readiness: A perspective from East Africa. *Pediatrics,* 1977, *60,* 170–177.

deVries, M. W., & Super, C. M. Contextual influences on the Brazelton Neonatal Behavioral Assessment Scale and implications for its cross-cultural use. In A. Sameroff (Ed.), Organization and stability of newborn behavior: A commentary on the Brazelton Neonatal Behavioral Assessment Scale. *Monographs of the Society for Research in Child Development,* 1979, *43,* 5–6 (Serial No. 177).

Dlugokinski, E., & Jones, F. The relationship of stress during pregnancy to perinatal status and maternal readiness. Paper presented at the International Conference on Infant Studies, Providence, 1978.

Du Bois, C. *The people of Alor.* Minneapolis: University of Minnesota Press, 1944.

Dubowitz, L. M. Assessment of gestational age. Unpublished MD thesis, University of Sheffield, 1972.

Dubowitz, L. M., Dubowitz, V., & Goldberg, C. Clinical assessment of gestational age in the newborn infant. *Journal of Pediatrics,* 1970, *77,* 1–10.

Dunham, E. C., Jenss, R. M., & Christie, A. U. A consideration of race and sex in relation to the growth and development of infants. *Journal of Pediatrics,* 1939, *14,* 156–160.

Ekman, P. Cross-cultural studies of facial expression. In P. Ekman (Ed.), *Darwin and facial expression.* New York: Academic Press, 1973.

Ellingson, R. J. The study of brain electrical activity in infants. In L. P. Lipsitt & C. C. Spiker (Eds.), *Advances in child development and behavior* (Vol. 3). New York: Academic Press, 1967.

Erikson, E. H. *Childhood and society.* New York: Norton, 1950.

Escalona, S. K., & Corman, H. H. *Albert Einstein Scales of Sensorimotor Development.* New York: Albert Einstein School of Medicine, 1967.

Escardo, F., & de Coriat, L. F. Development of postural and tonic patterns in the newborn infant. *Pediatric Clinics of North America,* 1960, *7,* 511–525.

Faladé, S. *Le développement psychomoteur de jeune Africain originaire du Sénégal au cours de sa première anée.* Paris: Foulon, 1955.

Faladé, S. Le développement psycho-moteur de l'enfant Africain du Sénégal. *Concours Médical,* 1960, *82,* 1005–1013.

Falkner, F. The state of development of newborn African children. *Lancet*, 1957, *273* (2), 389.

Falmagne, J.-C. *Étude de certains aspects du développement du nourisson de 0 à 6 mois.* Unpublished doctoral dissertation, Université Libre de Bruxelles, 1959.

Falmagne, J.-C. Étude comparative du développement psychomoteur pendant les six premièrs mois de 105 nourrissons blancs (Bruxelles) and 78 nourrissons noirs (Johannesburg). *Mémoirs de L'Academie Royale des Sciences d'Outre-Mer. Classes des Sciences Naturelles et Médicales*, 1962, *13*, fasc. 5.

Fantz, R. L., Fagan, J. F., III, & Miranda, S. B. Early visual selectivity. In L. B. Cohen & P. Salapetek (Eds.), *Infant perception: From sensation to cognition* (Vol. 1). New York: Academic Press, 1975.

Farr, V., Mitchell, R. G. Neligan, G. A., & Parkin, J. M. The definition of some external characteristics used in the assessment of gestational age in the newborn infant. *Developmental Medicine and Child Neurology*, 1966, *8*, 507–511.

Feldman, S. S. The bonding bind. (Review of *Maternal–infant bonding*, by M. H. Klaus & J. H. Kennell). *Contemporary Psychology*, 1977, *22*, 486–487.

Fenson, L., Kagan, J., Kearsley, R. B., & Zelazo, P. R. The developmental progression of manipulative play in the first two years. *Child Development*, 1976, *47*, 232–236.

Fernando, P., & Gomes, W. J. The pattern of growth and development in infants in Colombo and factors affecting them. In S. K. Bose & A. K. Dey (Eds.), *Asian pediatrics: The scientific proceedings of the First All-Asia Congress of Pediatrics, New Delhi, 1961.* London: Asia Publishing House, 1961.

Ferreira, A. J. The pregnant woman's emotional attitude and its reflection on the newborn. *American Journal of Orthopsychiatry*, 1960, *30*, 553–561.

Field, C. E., & Baber, F. M. *Growing up in Hong Kong.* Hong Kong: Hong Kong University Press, 1973.

Finley, G. E., Kagan, J., & Layne, O., Jr. Development of young children's attention to normal and distorted stimuli: A cross-cultural study. *Developmental Psychology*, 1972, *6*, 288–292.

Finley, G. E., & Layne, O., Jr. Play behavior in young children: A cross-cultural study. *Journal of Genetic Psychology*, 1971, *119*, 203–210

Finnström, O. Studies on maturity in newborn infants: III. Neurological examination. *Neuropaediatrie*, 1971, *3*, 72–96.

Fox, N. A., Attachment of kibbutz infants to mother and metapelet. *Child Development*, 1977, *48*, 1228–1239.

Fox, N. A. The relationship of ordinal position to attachment behaviors on the Israeli kibbutz. Paper presented at meeting of the Society for Cross-Cultural Research, New Haven, Conn., 1978.

Francis-Williams, J., & Yule, W. The Bayley infant scales of mental and motor development: An exploratory study with an English sample. *Developmental Medicine and Child Neurology*, 1967, *9*, 391–401.

Freedman, D. An ethological approach to the genetical study of human behavior. In S. G. Vandenberg (Ed.), *Methods and goals in human behavior genetics.* New York: Academic Press, 1965.

Freedman, D. G. Genetic influences on development of behavior. In G. B. A. Stoelinga & J. J. Van der Werff Ten Bosch, *Normal and abnormal development of behavior.* Leiden: Leiden University Press, 1971.

Freedman, D. G. *Human infancy: An evolutionary perspective.* Hillsdale, N.J.: Earlbaum, 1974.

Freedman, D. G., & Freedman, N. C. Behavioral differences between Chinese-American and European-American newborns. *Nature*, 1969, *224*, 1227.

Gaddini, R. Transitional objects and the process of individuation. *Journal of the American Academy of Child Psychiatry*, 1970, *9*, 347–365.

Gaensbauer, T. J., & Emde, R. N. Wakefulness and feeding in human newborns. *Archives of General Psychiatry,* 1973, *28,* 894–897.

Garn, S. M. Types and distribution of the hair in man. In J. B. Hamilton (Ed.), The growth, replacement, and types of hair. *Annals of the New York Academy of Sciences,* 1951, *53,* 498–507.

Garn, S. M. *Human races* (2nd ed.). Springfield, Ill.: Charles C. Thomas, 1965.

Garn, S. M., Silverman, F. N., & Rohmann, C. G. A rational approach to the assessment of skeletal maturation. *Annals of Radiology,* 1964, *7,* 297–307.

Geber, M. Développement psycho-moteur de l'enfant africain. *Courrier,* 1956, *6,* 17–29.

Geber, M. L'enfant africain occidentalisé et de niveau social supérieur en Ouganda. *Courrier,* 1958, *8,* 517–523 (a).

Geber, M. Tests de Gesell et de Terman-Merrill appliqués en Uganda. *Enfance,* 1958, *11,* 63–67 (b).

Geber, M. The psycho-motor development of African children in the first year, and the influence of maternal behavior. *Journal of Social Psychology,* 1958, *47,* 185–195 (c).

Geber, M. Problèmes posés par le développement du jeune enfant Africain en fonction de son milieu social. *Travail Humain,* 1960, *23,* 97–111.

Geber, M. Développement psychomoteur des petits Baganda de la naissance à six ans. *Schweizerische Zeitschrift für Psychologie und ihre Anwendungen,* 1961, *20,* 345–357.

Geber, M. Longitudinal study and psychomotor development among Baganda children. In *Proceedings of the Fourteenth International Congress of Applied Psychology* (Vol. 3). Copenhagen: Munksgaard, 1962.

Geber, M. L'environnement et le développement des enfants africains. *Enfance,* 1973, *3–4,* 145–174.

Geber, M. La recherche sur le développement psychomoteur et mental à Kampala. In *Compte-rendu de la XII Réunion des Équipes Chargées des Études sur la Croissance et de développement de l'enfant normal.* Paris: Centre International de l'Enfance, 1974.

Geber, M., & Dean, R. F. A. The state of development of newborn African children. *Lancet,* 1957, *272* (1), 1216–1219 (a).

Gerber, M., & Dean, R. F. A. Gesell tests on African children. *Pediatrics,* 1957, *20,* 1055–1065 (b).

Geber, M., & Dean, R. F. A. Psychomotor development in African children: The effects of social class and the need for improved tests. *Bulletin of the World Health Organization,* 1958, *18,* 471–476.

Geber, M., & Dean, R. F. A. Le développement psychomoteur et somatique des jeunes enfants africains en Ouganda. *Courrier,* 1964, *14,* 425–437.

Gesell, A., & Amatruda, C. S. *Developmental diagnosis* (2nd ed.). New York: Hoeber, 1947.

Gesell, A., & Thompson, H. Learning and growth in identical infant twins. *Genetic Psychology Monographs,* 1929, *6,* 1–124.

Gewirtz, J. L. The course of infant smiling in four child-rearing environments in Israel. In B. M. Foss (Ed.), *Determinants of infant behavior* (Vol. 3). London: Methuen, 1965.

Gewirtz, J. L., & Boyd, E. F. Does maternal responding imply reduced infant crying? A critique of the 1972 Bell and Ainsworth report. *Child Development,* 1977, *48,* 1200–1207 (a).

Gewirtz, J. L., & Boyd, E. F. In reply to the rejoinder to our critique of the 1972 Bell and Ainsworth report. *Child Development,* 1977, *48,* 1217–1218 (b).

Giacoman, S. L. Hunger and motor restraint on arousal and visual attention in the infant. *Child Development,* 1971, *42,* 605–614.

Behavioral Development in Infancy 255

Golan, S. Behavioral research in collective settlements in Israel: 2. Collective education in the kibbutz. *American Journal of Orthopsychiatry*, 1958, *28*, 549–556.
Goldberg, S. Infant care and growth in urban Zambia. *Human Development*, 1972, *15*, 77–89.
Goldberg, S. Infant development and mother-infant interaction in urban Zambia. In P. H. Leiderman, S. R. Tulkin, & A. Rosenfeld (Eds.), *Culture and infancy: Variations in the human experience*. New York: Academic Press, 1977.
Goldschmidt, W. Absent eyes and idle hands: Socialization for low affect among the Sebei. *Ethos*, 1975, *3*, 157–163.
Graham, F. K., Matarazzo, R. G., & Caldwell, B. M. Behavioral differences between normal and traumatized newborns: II. Standardization, reliability, and validity. *Psychological Monographs*, 1956, *70* (21, Whole No. 428).
Grantham-McGregor, S. M., & Back, E. H. Gross motor development in Jamaican infants. *Developmental Medicine and Child Neurology*, 1971, *13*, 79–87.
Grantham-McGregor, S. M., & Hawke, W. A. Developmental assessment of Jamaican infants. *Developmental Medicine and Child Neurology*, 1971, *13*, 582–589.
Greenbaum, C. W., & Landau, R. Mothers' speech and the early development of vocal behavior: Findings from a cross-cultural observation study in Israel. In P. H. Leiderman, S. R. Tulkin, & A. Rosenfeld (Eds.), *Culture and infancy: Variations in the human experience*. New York: Academic Press, 1977.
Gregg, C. L., Haffner, M. E., & Korner, A. F. The relative efficacy of vestibular-proprioceptive stimulation and the upright position in enhancing visual pursuit in neonates. *Child Development*, 1976, *47*, 309–314.
Griffiths, J. Development of reflexes in Bantu children. *Developmental Medicine and Child Neurology*, 1969, *11*, 533–535.
Griffiths, R. *The abilities of babies*. London: University of London Press, 1954.
Grimm, E. R. Psychological and social factors in pregnancy, delivery, and outcome. In S. A. Richardson & A. F. Guttmacher (Eds.), *Childbearing—Its social and psychological aspects*. Baltimore: Williams & Wilkins, 1967.
Gunders, S., & Whiting, J. W. M. Mother-infant separation and physical growth. *Ethnology*, 1968, *7*, 196–206.
Guthrie, G. M. Structure of maternal attitudes in two cultures. *Journal of Psychology*, 1966, *62*, 155–165.
Harkness, S. Dreams and memories in pregnant and post-partum Kipsigis women. Paper presented at the meeting of the American Anthropological Association, Houston, 1977.
Harkness, S., & Super, C. M. Why African children are so hard to test. In L. L. Adler (Ed.), Issues in cross-cultural research, *Annals of the New York Academy of Sciences*, 1977, *285*, 326–331.
Harlow, H. F., & Harlow, M. K. The affectional systems. In A. M. Schrier, H. F. Harlow, & F. Stollnitz (Eds.), *Behavior of non-human primates* (Vol. 2). New York: Academic Press, 1965.
Harper, L. V. Early maternal handling and preschool behavior of human children. *Developmental Psychobiology*, 1972, *5*, 1–5
Harris, M. *The rise of anthropological theory*. New York: Crowell, 1968.
Herskovits, M. J. *The myth of the Negro past*. New York: Harper, 1941.
Hess, A. F., & Weinstock, M. A comparison of the evolution of carpal centers in white and Negro new-born infants. *American Journal of Diseases of Children*, 1925, *29*, 347–354.
Hiernaux, J. Interpopulational variation in growth, with special reference to sub-Saharan Africa. In J. Brozek (Ed.), Physical growth and body composition: Papers from the Kyoto Symposium on Anthropological Aspects of Human Growth. *Monographs of the Society for Research in Child Development*, 1970, *35* (7, Serial No. 140).

Hindley, C. B., Filliozat, A. M., Klackenberg, G., Nicolet-Meister, D., & Sand, E. A. Differences in the age of walking in five European longitudinal samples. *Human Biology*, 1966, *38*, 364–379.

Hoefer, C., & Hardy, M. Later development of breast-fed and artificially-fed infants. JAMA (*Journal of the American Medical Association*), 1929, *92*, 615–619.

Hofstaetter, P. R. The changing composition of "intelligence:" A study in T technique. *Journal of Genetic Psychology*, 1954, *85*, 159–164.

Holt, K. S. Early motor development: Posturally induced variations. *Journal of Pediatrics*, 1960, *57*, 571–575.

Holthouse, R. J., & Kahn, M. W. A study of the influence of culture on the personality development of the Hausas of Kano City. *International Journal of Social Psychiatry*, 1969, *15*, 107–119.

Hong, K. M., & Townes, B. D. Infants' attachment to inanimate objects: A cross-cultural study. *Journal of the American Academy of Child Psychiatry*, 1976, *15*, 49–61.

Hood, C., Oppé, T., Pless, L., & Apte, E. *Children of West Indian immigrants*. London: Institute of Race Relations, 1970.

Hopkins, B. Culturally determined patterns of handling the human infant. *Journal of Human Movement Studies*, 1976, *2*, 1–27.

Hopkins, B. The early development of black and white infants living in Britain. Paper presented at the meeting of the International Association for Cross-cultural Psychology, Tilburg, 1978.

Horowitz, F. D., Aleksandrowicz, M. K., Ashton, J., Tims, S., McCluskey, K., Culp, R., & Gallas, H. American and Uruguayan infants: Reliability, maternal drug histories, and population differences using the Brazelton Neonatal Scales. Paper presented at the meeting of the Society for Research in Child Development, Philadelphia, 1973.

Horowitz, F. D., Ashton, J., Culp, R., Gaddis, E., Levin, S., & Reichmann, B. The effects of obstetrical medication on the behavior of Israeli newborn infants and some comparisons with Uruguayan and American infants. *Child Development*, 1977, *48*, 1607–1623.

Hotelling, H., & Hotelling, F. A new analysis of duration of pregnancy data. *American Journal of Obstetrics and Gynecology*, 1932, *23*, 643–657.

Hunt, J. McV., Mohandessi, K., Ghodssi, M., & Akiyama, M. The psychological development of orphanage reared infants: Interventions with outcomes (Teheran). *Genetic Psychology Monographs*, 1976, *94*, 177–226.

Hunt, J. McV., Paraskevopoulos, J., Schickendanz, D., & Uzgiris, I. C. Variations in the mean ages of achieving object permanence under diverse conditions of rearing. In B. Z. Priedlander, G. Sterritt, & G. E. Kirk (Eds.), *The exceptional infant. II: Assessment and intervention*. New York: Brunner/Mazel, 1975.

Hunt, J. V. Something old, something new: A classic revisited (Review of *Gesell and Amatruda's developmental diagnosis*, 3rd revision and enlarged edition, by H. Knobloch & B. Pasamanick, Eds.). *Contemporary Psychology*, 1976, *21*, 16–17.

Ignat'eva, R. K. Effect of seasons on the physical development of newborn infants. *Zdravookhranenie Rossiiskoi Federatsii*, 1969, *13*, 20–22.

Ivanans, T. Effect of maternal education and ethnic background on infant development. *Archives of Disease in Childhood*, 1975, *50*, 454–457.

Janes, M. D. Physical and psychological growth and development. *Journal of Tropical Pediatrics*, 1975, *21*, 26–30 (Special Issue).

Jeffry, W. E., & Cohen, L. B. Habituation in the human infant. In H. W. Reese (Ed.), *Advances in child development and behavior* (Vol 6.). New York: Academic Press, 1971.

Jelliffe, E. F. Recent trends in infant carrying. (The demise of the perambulator— A silent revolution in infant carrying methods and their effect on somatic and cognitive development in infants). *Journal of Tropical Pediatrics*, 1975, *21*, 93–108.

Jensen, A. R. How much can we boost IQ and scholastic achievement? *Harvard Educational Review,* 1969, *39,* 1–123.

Jha, S. A longitudinal study of infants belonging to a sweeper community in Bombay City. I & II. *Pediatric Clinics of India,* 1969, *4,* 49–56, 57–60.

Johnson, S. C. Hierarchical clustering schemes. *Psychometrika,* 1967, *32,* 241–254.

Jones, P. R. M., & Dean, R. F. A. The effects of kwashiorkor on the development of the bones of the hand. *Journal of Tropical Pediatrics,* 1956, *2,* 51–68.

Kagan, J. *Change and continuity in infancy.* New York: John Wiley & Sons, 1971.

Kagan, J. Emergent themes in human development. *American Scientist,* 1976, *64,* 186–196.

Kagan, J., Kearsley, R. B., & Zelazo, P. R. *Infancy: Its place in human development.* Cambridge, Mass.: Harvard University Press, 1978.

Kagan, J., & Klein, R. E. Cross-cultural perspectives on early development. *American Psychologist,* 1973, *28,* 947–961.

Kagan, J., Klein, R. E., Finley, G., Rogoff, B., & Nolan, E. Cross-cultural study of cognitive development. *Monographs of the Society for Research in Child Development,* in press.

Kagan, J., & Moss, H. A. *Birth to maturity.* New York: John Wiley & Sons, 1962.

Kagwa, J. A. Estimation of maturity by roentgen studies of ossification centres in African newborn infants. *East African Medical Journal,* 1970, *47,* 557–561.

Kandoth, W. K., Sonnad, L., & Athavale, V. B. Milestones in lower socioeconomic group. *Indian Pediatrics,* 1971, *8,* 176–183.

Kaye, K., & Tronick, E. Discrimination among normal infants by multivariate analysis of Brazelton scores: Pooling, lumping, and smoothing. Unpublished manuscript, 1977. (Available from K. Kaye, University of Chicago, Chicago, Ill.).

Keefer, C. H., Dixon, S., Tronick, E., & Brazelton, T. B. A cross-cultural study of face to face interaction: Gusii infants and mothers. Paper presented at a meeting of the Society for Research in Child Development, New Orleans, 1977.

Keefer, C. H., Dixon, S., Tronick, E., & Brazelton, T. B. Gusii infants' neuromotor behavior. Paper presented at the International Conference on Infant Studies, Providence, 1978.

Kelley, H. J., & Reynolds, L. Appearance and growth of ossification centers and increases in the body dimensions of white and Negro infants. *American Journal of Roentgenology,* 1947, *57,* 477–516.

Kessel, F. S., & Singer, S. Day care and the attachment of disadvantaged "Coloured" South African infants: Results of a study that succeeded, ethical implications of a study that failed. Paper presented at a meeting of the Society of Research in Child Development, Philadelphia, 1973.

Kessen, W., Haith, M. M., & Salapatek, P. H. Human infancy: A bibliography and guide. In P. Mussen (Ed.), *Carmichael's manual of child psychology* (3rd ed., vol. I). New York: John Wiley & Sons, 1970.

Kilbride, J. E. The influence of socio-environmental factors on Ugandan infants' motor development. In M. C. Robins, P. L. Kilbride, & R. B. Pollnac (Eds.), *Nkanga.* Kampala: Makerere Institute for Social Research, 1972.

Kilbride, J. E. Mother-infant interaction and infant sensorimotor development among the Baganda of Uganda. Unpublished doctoral dissertation, Bryn Mawr College, 1976.

Kilbride, J. E., & Kilbride, P. L. Sitting and smiling behavior of Baganda infants: The influence of culturally constituted experience. *Journal of Cross-Cultural Psychology,* 1975, *6,* 88–107.

Kilbride, J. E., Robbins, M. C., & Kilbride, P. L. The comparative motor development of Baganda, American white, and American black infants. *American Anthropologist,* 1970, *72,* 1422–1428.

Kilbride, P. L., & Kilbride, J. E. Sociocultural factors and the early manifestation of sociability behavior among Baganda infants. *Ethos*, 1974, *2*, 296–314.

King, D. The effect of early experience and litter on some weight and maturational variables. *Developmental Psychology*, 1969, *1*, 576–584.

King, W., & Seegmiller, B. Performance of 14- to 22-month-old black, firstborn male infants on two tests of cognitive development: The Bayley Scales and the Infant Psychological Development Scales. *Developmental Psychology*, 1973, *8*, 317–326.

Kitano, H. Differential child-rearing attitudes between first and second generation Japanese in the United States. *Journal of Social Psychology*, 1961, *53*, 13–19.

Klaus, M. H., & Kennell, J. H. *Maternal-infant bonding: The impact of early separation or loss on family development*. St. Louis : C. V. Mosby, 1976.

Klein, R. E., Lasky, R. E., Yarbrough, C., Habicht, J.-P., & Sellers, M. J. Relationship of infant/caretaker interaction, social class and nutritional status to developmental test performance among Guatemalan infants. In P. H. Leiderman, S. R. Tulkin, & A. Rosenfeld (Eds.), *Culture and infancy*. New York: Academic Press, 1977.

Knobloch, H. Precocity of African children. *Pediatrics*, 1958, *22*, 601–604.

Knobloch, H., & Pasamanick, B. Further observations on the behavioral development of Negro children. *The Pedagogical Seminary and Journal of Genetic Psychology*, 1953, *83*, 137–157.

Knobloch, H., & Pasamanick, B. The relationship of race and socioeconomic status to the developmental of motor behavior patterns in infancy. *Psychiatric Research Reports*, 1958, *10*, 123–133.

Knobloch, H., & Pasamanick, B. A clarification of issues. *Contemporary Psychology*, 1976, *21*, 446–447

Koga, Y. *MCC baby test*. Tokyo: Dobunshoin, 1967.

Kohen-Raz, R. Scalogram analysis of some developmental sequences of infant behavior as measured by the Bayley Infant Scale of Mental Development. *Genetic Psychology Monographs*, 1967, *76*, 3–21.

Kohen-Raz, R. Mental and motor development of kibbutz, institutionalized, and home reared infants in Israel. *Child Development*, 1968, *39*, 489–504.

Konner, M. J. Aspects of the developmental ethology of a foraging people. In N. G. Blurton Jones (Ed.), *Ethological studies of child behavior*. Cambridge, Eng.: Cambridge University Press, 1972.

Konner, M. J. Infants of a foraging people. Unpublished doctoral dissertation, Harvard University, 1973. (a)

Konner, M. J. Newborn walking: Additional data. *Science*, 1973, *179*, 307. (b)

Konner, M. J. Maternal care, infant behavior and development among the !Kung. In R. Lee & I. DeVore (Eds.), *Kalahari hunter-gatherers*. Cambridge, Mass.: Harvard University Press, 1976.

Konner, M. J. Infancy among the Kalahari Desert San. In P. H. Leiderman, S. R. Tulkin, & A. Rosenfeld (Eds.), *Culture and infancy: Variations in the human experience*. New York: Academic Press, 1977.

Kopp, C. B., Khoka, E., & Sigman, M. A comparison of sensorimotor development among infants in India and the United States. *Journal of Cross-Cultural Psychology*, 1977, *8*, 435–52.

Korner, A. F. Neonatal startles, smiles, erections, and reflex sucks as related to state, sex, and individuality. *Child Development*, 1969, *40*, 1039–1053.

Korner, A. F. State as variable, as obstacle, and as mediator of stimulation in infant research. *Merrill-Palmer Quarterly*, 1972, *18*, 77–94.

Korner, A. F., & Thoman, E. B. Visual alertness in neonates as evoked by maternal care. *Journal of Experimental Child Psychology*, 1970, *10*, 67–78.

Kramer, M., Chamorro, I., Green, D., & Knudtson, F. Extra tactile stimulation of the premature infant. *Nursing Research*, 1975, *24*, 324–334.

Kuchner, J. A cross-cultural study of Chinese-American and European-American mothers and their infants. Paper presented at the International Conference on Infant Studies, Providence, 1978.

Lagerspetz, K., Nygård, M., & Strandvik, C. The effects of training in crawling on the motor and mental development of infants. *Scandinavian Journal of Psychology,* 1971, *12,* 192–197.

Lambert, W., Triandis, L., & Wolf, M. Some correlates of beliefs in the malevolonce and benevolence of supernatural beings: A cross-societal study. *Journal of Abnormal and Social Psychology,* 1959, *58,* 162–169.

Landau, R. Extent that the mother represents the social stimulation to which the infant is exposed: Findings from a cross-cultural study. *Developmental Psychology,* 1976, *12,* 399–405.

Landau, R. Spontaneous and elicited smiles and vocalizations of infants in four Israeli environments. *Developmental Psychology,* 1977, *13,* 389–400.

Landauer, T. K., & Whiting, J. W. M. Infantile stimulation and adult stature of human males. *American Anthropologist,* 1964, *66,* 1007–1028.

Laska-Mierzejewska, T. Morphological and developmental difference between Negro and white Cuban youths. *Human Biology,* 1970, *42,* 581–597.

Lasky, R. E., Klein, R. E., & Martínez, S. Age and sex discriminations in five- and six-month old infants. *Journal of Psychology,* 1974, *88,* 317–324.

Lasky, R. E., Klein, R. E., Yarbrough, C., & Matorell, R. The usefulness of anthropometry as a predictor of psychomotor performance in rural Guatemala. Paper presented at the meeting of the Society for Research in Child Development, New Orleans, 1977.

Lasky, R. E., Lechtig, A., Delgado, H., Klein, R. E., Engle, P., Yarbrough, C., & Matorell, R. Birth weight and psychomotor performance in rural Guatemala. *American Journal of Diseases of Children,* 1975, *129,* 566–569.

Lavatelli, C. S., & Stendler, F. *Readings in Child Behavior and Development* (3rd ed.). New York: Harcourt Brace Jovanovich, 1972.

Leboyer, F. *Birth without violence.* New York: Alfred A. Knopf, 1975.

Leboyer, F. *Loving hands: The traditional Indian art of baby massaging.* New York: Alfred A. Knopf, 1976.

Leiderman, P. H., Babu, B., Kagia, J., Kraemer, H. C., & Leiderman, G. F. African infant precocity and some social influences during the first year. *Nature,* 1973, *242,* 247–249.

Leiderman, P. H., & Leiderman, G. F. Affective and cognitive consequences of polymatric infant care in the East African Highlands. In A. D. Pick (Ed.), *Minnesota symposia on child psychology* (Vol. 8). Minneapolis: University of Minnesota Press, 1974. (a)

Leiderman, P. H., & Leiderman, G. F. Familial influences on infant development in an East African agricultural community. In E. J. Anthony & C. Koupernik (Eds.), *The child and his family: Children at psychiatric risk* (Vol. 3). New York: John Wiley & Sons, 1974. (b)

Leiderman, P. H., & Leiderman, G. F. Economic change and infant care in an East African agricultural community. In P. H. Leiderman, S. R. Tulkin, & A. Rosenfeld (Eds.), *Culture and infancy: Variations in the human experience.* New York: Academic Press, 1977.

Lester, B. M. Cardiac habituation of the orienting response to an auditory signal in infants of varying nutritional status. *Developmental Psychology,* 1975, *11,* 432–442.

Lester, B. M,. Klein, R. E., & Martínez, S. J. The use of habituation in the study of the effects of infantile malnutrition. *Developmental Psychobiology,* 1975, *8,* 541–546.

Lester, B. M., Kotelchuck, M., Spelke, E., Sellers, M. J., & Klein, R. E. Separation protest in Guatemalan infants: Cross-cultural and cognitive findings. *Developmental Psychology,* 1974, *10,* 79–85.

LeVine, R. A. Culture, personality, and socialization: An evolutionary view. In D. A. Goslin (Ed.), *Handbook of socialization: Theory and research.* Chicago: Rand McNally, 1969.

LeVine, R. A. Cross-cultural study in child psychology. In P. Mussen (Ed.), *Carmichael's manual of child psychology* (3rd ed., vol. 2). New York: John Wiley & Sons, 1970.

LeVine, R. A. Patterns of personality in Africa. *Ethos,* 1973, *1,* 123–152.

LeVine, R. A. Comment on the note by Super and Harkness. *Ethos,* 1974, *2,* 382–386. (a)

LeVine, R. A. Parental goals: A cross-cultural view. *Teachers College Record,* 1974, *76,* 226–239. (b)

LeVine, R. A. Child rearing as cultural adaptation. In P. H. Leiderman, S. R. Tulkin, & A. Rosenfeld (Eds.), *Culture and infancy: Variations in the human experience.* New York: Academic Press, 1977.

LeVine, R. A. & LeVine, B. B. *Nyansongo: A Gusii community in Kenya.* New York: John Wiley & Sons, 1966.

LeVine, R. A., LeVine, S., Iwanaga, M., & Marvin, R. Child care and social attachment in a Nigerian community: A preliminary report. Paper presented at meeting of the American Psychological Association, Miami Beach, 1970.

Lewis, M. Cross-cultural studies of mother-infant interaction: Description and consequence: Introduction. *Human Development,* 1972, *15,* 75–76.

Lewis, M., & Ban, P. Variance and invariance in the mother-infant interaction: A cross-cultural study. In P. H. Leiderman, S. R. Tulkin, & A. Rosenfeld (Eds.), *Culture and infancy: Variations in the human experience.* New York: Academic Press, 1977.

Lézine, I., Stambak, M., & Casati, I. *Les étapes de l'intelligence sensori-motrice.* Paris: Centre de Psychologie Appliquée, 1969.

Liddicoat, R. Development of Bantu children. *Developmental Medicine and Child Neurology,* 1969, *11,* 821–822.

Liddicoat, R., & Griesel, R. D. A scale for the measurement of African urban infant development: Preliminary report. *Psychologia Africana,* 1971, *14,* 65–75.

Liddicoat, R., & Koza, C. Language development in African infants. *Psychologia Africana,* 1963, *10,* 108–116.

Lijembe, J. A. The valley between: A Muluyia's story. In L. K. Fox (Ed.), *East African childhood.* Nairobi: Oxford University Press, 1967.

Lipton, E. L., Steinschneider, A., & Richmond, J. B. Swaddling, a child care practice: Historical cultural and experimental observations. *Pediatrics,* 1965, *35* (Suppl.), 519–567.

Lozoff, B. The sensitive period: An anthropological view. Paper presented at a meeting of the Society for Research in Child Development, New Orleans, 1977.

Lusk, D., & Lewis, M. Mother-infant interaction and infant development among the Wolof of Senegal. *Human Development,* 1972, *15,* 58–69.

Maccoby, E. E., & Masters, J. C. Attachment and dependency. In P. Mussen (Ed.), *Carmichael's manual of child psychology* (3rd ed., vol. 2). New York: John Wiley & Sons, 1970.

MacFarlane, J. A. In *Parent-infant interaction* (CIBA Foundation Symposium No. 33). Amsterdam: Associated Scientific Publishers, 1975.

Maclean, C. Tradition in transition: A health opinion survey in Ibadan, Nigeria. *British Journal of Preventive and Social Medicine,* 1965, *19,* 192–197.

Maclean, C. Yoruba mothers: A study of changing methods of child rearing in rural and urban Nigeria. *Journal of Tropical Medicine and Hygeine,* 1966, *69,* 253–263.

Malina, R. M. Skeletal maturation studies longitudinally over one year in American whites and Negroes six through thirteen years of age. *Human Biology,* 1970, *42,* 377–390.

Marshall, W. A., Ashcroft, M. T., & Bryan, G. Skeletal maturation of the hand and wrist in Jamaican children. *Human Biology*, 1970, *42*, 419–435.

Marvin, R. S., VanDevender, T. L., Iwanaga, M. I., LeVine, S., & LeVine, R. A. Infant-caregiver attachment among the Hausa of Nigeria. In H. McGurk (Ed.), *Ecological factors in human development*. Amsterdam: North Holland Publishing, 1977.

Mason, W. A. Early social deprivation in the non-human primates: Implications for human behavior. In D. C. Glass (Ed.), *Environmental influences*. New York: Rockefeller University Press, 1968.

Massé, G. Croissance et développement de l'enfant à Dakar. Paris: Centre International d'Enfance, 1969.

Massé, G., & Hunt, E. E., Jr. Skeletal maturation of the hand and wrist in West African Children. *Human Biology*, 1963, *35*, 3–25.

McCall, R. B. Similarity in developmental profile among related pairs of human infants. *Science*, 1972, *178*, 1004–1005.

McCall, R. B., Hogarty, P. S., & Hurlburt, N. Transitions in infant sensorimotor development and the prediction of childhood IQ. *American Psychologist*, 1972, *27*, 728–748.

McCoy, N. L. A rose by any other name . . . or evolution's the thing! (Review of *Human infancy: An evolutionary perspective* by D. G. Freedman). *Contemporary Psychology*, 1976, *21*, 270–271.

McDonald, R. L. Lunar and seasonal variations in obstetric factors. *Journal of Genetic Psychology*, 1966, *108*, 81–87.

McGraw, M. B. A comparative study of a group of southern white and Negro infants. *Genetic Psychology Monographs*, 1931, *10*, 1–105.

McGraw, M. B. *Growth: A study of Johnny and Jimmy*. New York: Appleton Century, 1935.

McGraw, M. B. Maturation of behavior. In L. Carmichael (Ed.), *Manual of child psychology*. New York: John Wiley & Sons, 1946.

McGraw, M. Theories and techniques of child development research during the 1930's. Address to the meeting of the Society for Research in Child Development, New Orleans, 1977.

McLaren, D. S., & Yatkin, U.S. Infant precocity. *Nature*, 1973, *244*, 587.

Mead, M. *Growing up in New Guinea*. New York: Morrow, 1930.

Mead, M. An investigation of the thought of primitive children, with special reference to animism. *Journal of the Royal Anthropological Institute*, 1932, *62*, 173–190.

Mead, M., & McGregor, F. C. *Growth and culture: A photographic study of Balinese childhood*. New York: Putnam, 1951.

Meredith, H. V. North American Negro infants: Size at birth and growth during the first postnatal year. *Human Biology*, 1952, *24*, 290–308.

Meyer, A. W. Fields, graphs, and other data on fetal growth. *Contributions to Embryology*, 1915, *4*, 55–68.

Migeon, C. J., Bertrand, J., & Wall, P. E. Physiological disposition of 4-C^{14}-cortisol during late pregnancy. *Journal of Clinical Investigation*, 1957, *36*, 1350–1362.

Migeon, C. J., Keller, A. R., Lawrence, B., & Shephard, T. H. Dehydro epiandrosterone and androsterone levels in human plasma: Effect of age and sex; Day to day and diurnal variations. *Journal of Clinical Endocrinology and Metabolism*, 1957, *17*, 1051–1062.

Miller, R. The development of competence and behavior in infancy. Unpublished doctoral dissertation, University of Witwatersrand, 1976.

Minturn, L., & Lambert, W. W. *Mothers of six cultures*. New York: John Wiley & Sons, 1964.

Modlin, J., Hawker, A., & Costello, A. J. An investigation into the effect of sleeping position on some aspects of early development. *Developmental Medicine and Child Neurology*, 1973, *15*, 287–292.

Mönckeberg, F. Effect of early marasmic malnutrition on subsequent physical and psychological development. In N. Scrimshaw & J. E. Gordon (Eds.), *Malnutrition, learning, and behavior*. Cambridge, Mass.: MIT Press, 1968.

Moreau, T., & Birch, H. G. Relationship between obstetrical general anesthesia and rate of neonatal habituation to repeated stimulation. *Developmental Medicine and Child Neurology*, 1974, *16*, 612–619.

Moreigne, F. Le développement psycho-moteur de l'enfant Wolof en milieu Dakarois de 6 mos à 6 ans. *Revue de Neuropsychiatrie Infantile et d'Hygiène Mentale de l'Enfance*, 1970, *18*, 765–783.

Moss, H. A. Sex, age, and state as determinants of mother-infant interaction. *Merrill-Palmer Quarterly*, 1967, *13*, 19–36.

Moss, H. A., & Robson, K. S. Maternal influences in early social visual behavior. *Child Development*, 1968, *39*, 401–408.

Moss, H. A., & Robson, K. S. The relation between the amount of time infants spend at various states and the development of visual behavior. *Child Development*, 1970, *41*, 509–517.

Mundy-Castle, A. C., & Okonji, M. O. Mother-infant interaction in Nigeria. Paper presented at a meeting of the International Association for Cross-cultural Psychology, Tilburg, 1976.

Munroe, R. H., & Munroe, R. L. Household density and infant care in an East African society. *Journal of Social Psychology*, 1971, *83*, 3–13.

Munroe, R. L., Munroe, R. H., & LeVine, R. A. Africa. In F. L. K. Hsu (Ed.), *Psychological anthropology* (new ed.). Cambridge, Mass.: Schenkman, 1972.

Munroe, R. L., Munroe, R. H., & Whiting, J. W. M. The couvade: A psychological analysis *Ethos*, 1973, *1*, 30–74.

Naidr, J. Psychomotorický vývoj afrických dětí. *Československá Pediatrie*, 1975, *30*, 173–176.

N'dao, S. Relation mère-enfant dans une société traditionnelle Africaine (Sénégal): Consequences psychologiques et socials. Paper presented at Colloquium on Civilisation de la Femme dans la Tradition Africaine, Abidjan, Ivory Coast, 1972.

Neligan, G., & Prudham, D. Norms for four standard developmental milestones by sex, social class, and place in family. *Developmental Medicine and Child Neurology*, 1969, *11*, 413–422.

Nelson, G. K. The electroencephalogram in Kwashiorkor. *Electroencephalography and Clinical Neurophysiology*, 1959, *11*, 73–84.

Nelson, G. K., & Dean, R. F. A. The electroencephalogram in African children: Effects of Kwashiorkor and a note on the newborn. *Bulletin of the World Health Organization*, 1959, *21*, 779–782.

Newton, N. The effect of psychological environment on childbirth: Combined cross-cultural and experimental approach. *Journal of Cross-Cultural Psychology*, 1970, *1*, 85–90.

Newton, N., & Newton, M. Childbirth in cross-cultural perspective. In J. G. Howells (Ed.), *Modern perspectives in psycho-obstetrics*. New York: Bruner/Mazel, 1972.

Ocitti, J. P. *African indigenous education (as practiced by the Acholi of East Africa)*. Nairobi: East African Literature Bureau, 1973.

Odent, M. À propos de l'expérience de la maternité de Pithiviers: "Le phenomène Leboyer." *Revue de Psychosomatique*, 1976.

Opler, M. K. Culture and child rearing. In J. G. Howells (Ed.), *Modern perspectives in international child psychiatry*. Edinburgh: Oliver & Boyd, 1969.

Osofsky, J. D. Neonatal characteristics and mother-infant interaction in two observational situations. *Child Development*, 1976, *47*, 1138–1147.

Ottinger, D. R., & Simmons, J. E. Behavior of human neonates and prenatal maternal anxiety. *Psychological Reports*, 1964, *14*, 391–394.

Ozturk, M., & Ozturk, O. M. Thumbsucking and falling asleep. *British Journal of Medical Psychology*, 1977. *50*, 95–103.

Paine, R. S., Brazelton, T. B., Donovan, D. E., Drorbaugh, J. E., Hubbell, J. P., & Sears, E. M. Evolution of postural reflexes in normal infants and in the presence of chronic brain syndromes. *Neurology*, 1964, *14*, 1036–1048.

Palti, H., Gitlin, M., & Zloto, R. Psychomotor development of two-year-old children in Jerusalem. *Journal of Cross-Cultural Psychology*, 1977, *8*, 453–464.

Paraskevopoulous, J., & Hunt, J. McV. Object construction and imitation under differing conditions of rearing. *Journal of Genetic Psychology*, 1971, *119*, 301–321.

Parkin, J. M. The assessment of gestational age in Ugandan and British newborn babies. *Developmental Medicine and Child Neurology*, 1971, *13*, 784–788.

Parmalee, A. H., Jr., Wenner, W. H., & Schulz, H. R. Infant sleep patterns: From birth to 16 weeks of age. *Journal of Pediatrics*, 1964, *65* (4), 576–582.

Pasamanick, B. A comparative study of the behavioral development of Negro infants. *The Pedagogical Seminary and Journal of Genetic Psychology*, 1946, *69*, 3–44.

Pasamanick, B., & Knobloch, H. Race, complications of pregnancy, and neuropsychiatric disorder. *Social Problems*, 1957/58, *5*, 267–278.

Patel, N. V., & Kaul, K. K. Behavioral development of Indian rural and urban infants in comparison to American infants. *Indian Pediatrics*, 1971, *8*, 443–451.

Peiper, A. *Cerebral function in infancy and childhood.* New York: Consultants Bureau, 1963.

Phatak, P. Motor and mental development of Indian babies from 1 month to 30 months. *Indian Pediatrics*, 1969, *6*, 18–23.

Phatak, P. Mental and motor growth of Indian babies (1–30 months). Final Report, Department of Child Development, M. S. University of Baroda, Baroda, India, 1970. (a)

Phatak, P. Motor growth patterns of Indian babies. *Indian Pediatrics*, 1970, *7*, 619–624. (b)

Piaget, J. *The origins of intelligence in children.* New York: International University Press, 1952. (Originally published in 1936.)

Pollak, M., & Mitchell, S. Early development of Negro and white babies. *Archives of Diseases of Childhood*, 1974, *49*, 40–45.

Pollitt, E. Behavior of infant in causation of nutritional marasmus. *American Journal of Clinical Nutrition*, 1973, *26*, 264–270.

Pollitt, E., & Granoff, D. Mental and motor development of Peruvian children treated for severe malnutrition. *Revista Interamericana de Psicológica*, 1967, *1*, 93–102.

Poole, H. E. The effect of Westernization on the psychomotor development of African (Yoruba) infants during the first year of life. *Journal of Tropical Pediatrics*, 1969, *15*, 172–176.

Porter, L. S. The impact of physical-physiological activity on infants' growth and development. *Nursing Research*, 1972, *21*, 210–219.

Prechtl, F. R. R., & Beintema, D. *The neurological examination of the full term newborn infant.* London: Spastics International Medical Publications, 1964.

Prescott, J. W. Abortion or the unwanted child: A choice for a humanistic society. *The Humanist*, 1975, *35* (2), pp. 11–15.

Prescott, J. W., & Wallace, D. Developmental sociobiology and the origins of aggressive behavior. Paper presented at the 21st International Congress of Psychology, Paris, 1976.

Prothro, E. T. Patterns of permissivness among preliterate peoples. *Journal of Abnormal and Social Psychology*, 1960, *61*, 151–154.

Prothro, E. T. Socialization and social class in a transitional society. *Child Development*, 1966, *37*, 219–228.

Rabin, A. I. Behavior research in collective settlements in Israel: 6. Infants and children under conditions of "intermittant" mothering in the kibbutz. *American Journal of Orthopsychiatry*, 1958, *28*, 577–584.

Ramarasaona, Z. Psychomotor development in early childhood in the Tananarive region. Report of the CSM Meeting of Specialists on the Basic Psychological Structures of African and Madagascan Populations. London: CCTA/CSA Publication No. 51, 1959.

Rapoport, D. "Pour une naissance sans violence": Resultats d'une première enquête. *Bulletin de Psychologie*, 1975–76, *39* (322), 8–13.

Rebelsky, F. First discussant's comments: Cross-cultural studies of mother-infant interaction: Description and consequence. *Human Development*, 1972, *15*, 128–130.

Rebelsky, F. G. Infancy in two cultures. In F. G. Rebelsky & L. Dorman (Eds.), *Child development and behavior* (2nd ed.). New York: Alfred A. Knopf, 1973. Reprinted from Nederlands Tijdschrift voor de Psychologie, 1967, *22*, 379–385

Rhodes, A. A comparative study of motor abilities of Negroes and whites. *Child Development*, 1937, *8*, 369–371.

Rice, R. D. Neurophysiological development in premature infants following stimulation. *Developmental Psychology*, 1977, *13*, 69–76.

Richards, M. P. M., Bernal, J. F., & Brackbill, Y. Early behavioral differences: Gender or circumcision? *Developmental Psychobiology*, 1976, *9*, 89–95.

Robinson, D. M. A cross-cultural study of cognitive development from six to eighteen months. Unpublished undergraduate thesis, Harvard University, 1976.

Robinson, H., & Robinson, N. The problem of timing in preschool education. In R. D. Hess & R. M. Bear (Eds.), *Early education: Current theory, research, and action.* Chicago: Aldine, 1968.

Robles, B. Influencia de ciertes factores ecológicos sobra la conducta del niño en el medio rural Mexicano. *IX Reunion de la Sociedad Mexicana de Investigation Pediatrica.* Cuernavaca: Morales, 1959.

Roland, J. L. Développement de la personnalité et incidences de l'environnement au Maroc. *Maroc Medical*, 1965, *44*, 269–271.

Rosenblatt, J. S. Social and environmental factors affecting reproduction and offspring in infra-human mammals. In S. A. Richardson & A. F. Guttmacher (Eds.), *Childbearing—Its social and psychological aspects.* Baltimore: Williams & Wilkins, 1967.

Rosenblatt, P. C., & Skoogberg, E. L. Birth order in cross-cultural perspective. *Developmental Psychology*, 1974, *10*, 48–54.

Rosenblith, J. F. The modified Graham behavior test for neonates: Test-retest reliability, normative data, and hypotheses for future work. *Biologia Neonatorum*, 1961, *3*, 174–192.

Rosenblith, J. F. Relations between neonatal behaviors and those at eight months. *Developmental Psychology*, 1974, *10*, 779–792.

Rosenblith, J. F. Newborn characteristics of infants who became victims of the sudden infant death syndrome (SIDS). *JSAS Catalogue of Selected Documents in Psychology*, 1978, *8*, 60. (ms. No. 1716.)

Rosenblith, J. F., & Anderson-Huntington, R. B. Defensive reactions to stimulation of the nasal and oral regions in newborns: Relations to state. In J. F. Bosma & J. Showacre (Eds.), *Development of upper respiratory anatomy and function: Implications for sudden infant death syndrome.* Bethesda: Department of Health, Education and Welfare Publication NIH 75–941, 1975.

Rosenthal, R. *Experimenter effects in behavioral research.* New York: Appleton Century Crofts, 1966.

Rosenzweig, M. R., Krech, D., Bennett, E. L., & Diamond, M. C. Modifying brain chemistry and anatomy by enrichment or impoverishment of experience. In G. Newton & S. Levine (Eds.), *Early experience and behavior.* Springfield, Ill.: Charles C. Thomas, 1968.

Salamone, F. A. Further notes on Hausa culture and personality. *International Journal of Social Psychiatry*, 1969, *16*, 39–44.

Salber, E. J. The effect of different feeding schedules on the growth of Bantu babies in the first week of life. *Journal of Tropical Pediatrics*, 1956, *2*, 97–102.

Saigal, S., & Srivastava, J. R. Anthropometric studies of 1000 consecutive newborns with special reference to determine criteria of prematurity. *Indian Pediatrics*, 1969, *6*, 24–33.

Sander, L. W., Stechler, G., Burns, P., & Lee, A. Change in infant and caregiver variables over the first 2 months of life: Integration of action in early development. In E. B. Thoman (Ed.), *Origins of the infant's social responsiveness*. Hillsdale, N. J.: Erlbaum, in press.

Sassin, J. F., Parker, D. C., Mace, J. W., Gotlin, R. W., Johnson, L. C., & Rossman, L. G. Human growth hormone release: Relation to slow-wave sleep and sleep-waking cycles. *Science*, 1969, *165*, 513–515.

Satgé, P., Debroise, A., Dan, V., Cros, J., Coly, F., Raybaud, N., & Villod, M. T. Croissance staturo-pondéral de l'enfant de 0 à 7 ans en zone rurale au Sénégal. *L'Enfant en Milieu Tropical*, 1968, *49*, 3–14.

Sayegh, Y., & Dennis, W. The effect of supplementary experiences upon the behavioral development of infants in institutions. *Child Development*, 1965, *36*, 81–90.

Scarr-Salapatek, S. An evolutionary perspective on infant intelligence: Species patterns and individual variations. In M. Lewis (Ed.), *Origins of intelligence*. New York: Plenum, 1976.

Schachter, J., Kerr, J. L., Wimberly, F. C., III, & Lachin, J. M., III. Heart rate levels of black and white newborns. *Psychosomatic Medicine*, 1974, *36*, 513–524.

Schachter, J., Kerr, J. L., Wimberly, F. C. III, & Lachin, J. M. III. Phasic heart rate responses: Different patterns in black and in white newborns. *Psychosomatic Medicine*, 1975, *36*, 326–332.

Schaffer, H. R., & Emerson, P. E. The development of social attachments in infancy. *Monographs of the Society for Research in Child Development*, 1964, *29* (3, Serial No. 94).

Schlesinger, J. Der Fusssohlenreflex biem Säugling *Klinische Wochenschrift*, 1927, *6*, 2384–2386.

Schmidt, B. J., Maciel, W., Boskovitz, E. P., Rosenberg, S., & Cury, C. P. Une enquête de pédiatrie sociale dans une ville brasilienne. *Courrier*, 1971, *21*, 127–133.

Schmidt, K., & Birns, B. The behavioral arousal threshold in infant sleep as a function of time and sleep state. *Child Development*, 1971, *42*, 269–277.

Scott, R. B., Ferguson, A. D., Jenkins, M. E., & Culter, F. F. Growth and development of Negro infants: V. Neuromuscular pattern of behavior during the first year of life. *Pediatrics*, 1955, *16*, 24–30.

Scott, R. B., Jenkins, M. E., & Crawford, R. P. Growth and development of Negro infants: I. Analysis of birth weights of 11,818 newly born infants. *Pediatrics*, 1950, *6*, 425–431.

Seligman, C. G. *Races of Africa* (4th ed.). London: Oxford University Press, 1966.

Sellers, M. J., Klein, R., Kagan, J., & Minton, C. Developmental determinants of attention: A cross-cultural replication. *Developmental Psychology*, 1972, *6*, 185.

Sellers, M. J., Klein, R. E., Sellers, E., Lechtig, A., & Yarbrough, C. Medición de infantos recién nacidos en una muestra rural de Guatemala usando la escala de Brazelton. Guatemala City: División de Desarrollo Humano, Instituto de Nutrición de Centro America y Panama, internal publication, 1971.

Sertel, H., De Sosa, M., & Moosa, A. Peripheral nerve maturation in English, West Indian, and Turkish newborn infants. *Developmental Medicine and Child Neurology*, 1976, *18*, 493–497.

Serunian, S. A., & Broman, S. H. Relationship of Apgar scores and Bayley mental and motor scores. *Child Development*, 1975, *46*, 696–700.

Shourie, K. L. Eruption age of teeth in India. *Indian Journal of Medical Research,* 1946, *34,* 105–118.

Smilansky, E., Shephatia, L., & Frenkel, E. *Mental development of infants from two ethnic groups* (Research Report No. 195). Jerusalem: Henrietta Szold Institute, 1976.

Smith, C. R., & Steinschneider, A. Differential effects of prenatal rhythmic stimulation on neonatal arousal states. *Child Development,* 1975, *46,* 574–578.

Smith, M., Lecker, G., Dunlap, J. W., & Cureton, E. E. The effects of race, sex, and environment on the age at which children walk. *Pediatric Seminars,* 1930, *38,* 489–498.

Sofue, T., Suye, H., & Murakami, T. Anthropological study of *Ejiko,* Japanese cradle for child: Its distribution and areal variations. *Journal of the Anthropological Society of Nippon,* 1957, *66,* 77–91.

Solkoff, N., Yaffe, S., Weintraub, D., & Blase, B. Effects of handling on the subsequent developments of premature infants. *Developmental Psychology,* 1969, *1,* 765–768.

Sollitto, N. A. Mother-child interaction in a natural situation. Unpublished doctoral dissertation, Catholic University of São Paulo, 1972.

Solomons, H. C. The malleability of infant motor development: Cautions based on studies of child-rearing practices in Yucatan. *Clinical Pediatrics,* 1978, *17,* 836–890.

Solomons, G., & Solomons, H. C. Factors affecting motor performance in four-month-old infants. *Child Development,* 1964, *35,* 1283–1296.

Solomons, G., & Solomons, H. C. Motor development in Yucatecan infants. *Developmental Medicine and Child Neurology,* 1975 *17,* 41–46.

Sperry, R. W. Mechanisms of neural maturation. In S. S. Stevens (Ed.), *Handbook of experimental psychology.* New York: John Wiley & Sons, 1951.

Spiro, M. E., & D'Andrade, R. G. A cross-cultural study of some supernatural beliefs. *American Anthropologist,* 1958, *60,* 456–466.

Spitz, R. A., Emde, R. N., & Metcalf, D. R. Further prototypes of ego formation: A working paper from a research project on early development. *Psycho-analytic Study of the Child,* 1970, *25,* 417–441

Sroufe, L. A., & Waters, E. Attachment as an organizational construct. *Child Development,* 1977, *48,* 1184–1199.

Ssengoba, C. M. E. B. The effects of nutritional status on the psychomotor development of rural Kenyan infants. Unpublished doctoral dissertation, University of Michigan, 1978.

Stamback, M. *Tonus et psychomotoricité dans la première enfance.* Neuchâtel: Delachaux et Niestlé, 1963.

Steggerda, M., & Hill, T. J. Eruption time of teeth among whites, Negroes, and Indians. *American Journal of Orthodontics and Oral Surgery,* 1942, *28,* 361–370.

Stein, C. K., & Labarba, R. C. Neonatal stimulation and accelerated maturation in BALB/c mice. *Developmental Psychology,* 1977, *13,* 423–424.

Stott, L., & Ball, R. S. Infant and preschool mental tests: Review and evaluation. *Monographs of the Society for Research in Child Development,* 1965, *30* (3, Serial No. 101).

Suk, V. Eruption and decay of permanent teeth in whites and Negroes, with comparative remarks on other races. *American Journal of Physical Anthropology,* 1919, *2,* 351–388.

Super, C. M. Infant care and motor development in rural Kenya: Some preliminary data on precocity and deficit. Paper presented at the 1st Pan-African Conference on Psychology, Ibadan, Nigeria, 1973. (a)

Super, C. M. Patterns of infant care and motor development in Kenya. *Kenya Education Review,* 1973, *1,* 64–69. (b)

Super, C. M. Environmental effects on motor development: The case of "African infant precocity." *Developmental Medicine and Child Neurology*, 1976, *18*, 561–567.

Super, C. M. Unpacking African infant precocity. In N. Warren (Ed.), *Studies in cross-cultural psychology* (Vol. 3). London: Academic Press, in press.

Super, C. M., & Harkness, S. Patterns of personality in Africa: A note from the field. *Ethos*, 1974, *2*, 377–381.

Super, C. M., & Harkness, S. Affectionate behavior in infancy and adulthood. In H. Stevenson & D. Wagner (Eds.), *Cultural perspectives on child development*. San Francisco: Freeman, in press.

Takahashi, K. Development of material bonding. Paper presented at the meeting of the Japanese Psychological Association, Nagoya, 1976.

Takahashi, K., & Hatano, G. Mother-child interaction and cognitive development. Paper presented at the meeting of the Japanese Psychological Association, Nagoya, 1976.

Takahashi, M. Smiling responses in newborn infants: Relations to arousal level, spontaneous movements, and the tactile stimulus. *Japanese Journal of Psychology*. 1973, *44*, 46–50. (a)

Takahashi, M. The cross-sectional study of infants' smiling, attention, reaching, and crying responses to the facial models. *Japanese Journal of Psychology*, 1973, *44*, 124–134. (b)

Takahashi, M. The longitudinal study of infants' smiling responses in relation to neonatal spontaneous smiles. *Japanese Journal of Psychology*, 1974, *45*, 256–267.

Tanner, J. M. *Growth at adolescence* (2nd ed.). Oxford: Blackwell Scientific Publications, 1962.

Tanner, J. M. Growth and physique in different populations of mankind. In P. T. Baker & J. S. Weiner (Eds.), *The biology of human adaptability*. Oxford: Oxford University Press, 1966.

Tanner, J. M. Variability of growth and maturity in newborn infants. In M. Lewis & L. A. Rosenblum (Eds.), *The effect of the infant on its caregiver*. New York: John Wiley & Sons, 1974.

Theunissen, K. B. A preliminary comparative study of the development of motor behavior in European and Bantu children up to the age of one year. Unpublished master's dissertation, Natal University College, 1948.

Thoman, E. B., Korner, A. F., & Beason-Williams, L. Modification of responsiveness to maternal vocalization in the neonate. *Child Development*, 1977, *48*, 563–569.

Thoman, E. B., Turner, A. M., Leiderman, P. H., & Barnett, C. R. Neonate-mother interaction: Effects of parity on feeding behavior. *Child Development*, 1970, *41*, 1103–1111.

Thompkins, W. T., & Wiehl, D. G. Epiphyseal maturation in the newborn as related to maternal nutritional status. *American Journal of Obstetrics and Gynecology*, 1954, *68*, 1366–1377.

Thompson, L. *Fijian frontier*. San Francisco: American Council, Institute of Pacific Relations, 1940.

Thompson, W. R., & Grusec, J. E. Studies of early experience. In P. Mussen (Ed.), *Carmichael's manual of child psychology* (3rd ed., Vol. 1). New York: John Wiley & Sons, 1970.

Tilford, J. The relationship between gestational age and adaptive behavior. *Merrill-Palmer Quarterly*, 1976, *22*, 319–326.

Todd, T. W. Differential skeletal maturation in relation to sex, race, variability, and disease. *Child Development*, 1931, *2*, 49–65.

Tolbert, M. K. Mothers and infants in rural Guatemala: A preliminary report. Unpublished manuscript, no date.

Torgersen, A. M. Temperamental differences in infants: Their cause as shown through twin studies. Unpublished doctoral dissertation, University of Oslo, 1973.

Touwen, B. A study of the development of some motor phenomena in infancy. *Developmental Medicine and Child Neurology*, 1971, *13*, 435–446.

Touwen, B. *Neurological development in infancy*. London: Spastics International Medical Publishers, 1976.

Tulkin, S. R. Social class differences in maternal and infant behavior. In P. H. Leiderman, S. R. Tulkin, & A. Rosenfeld (Eds.), *Culture and infancy: Variations in the human experience*. New York: Academic Press, 1977.

U Sein Tu. The psychodynamics of Burmese personality. *Journal of the Burma Research Society*, 1964, *2*, 263–286.

Uklonskaya, R., Puri, B., Choudhuri, N., Dang, L., & Kumari, R. Development of static and psychomotor functions of infant in the first year of life in New Delhi. *Indian Journal of Child Health*, 1960, *9*, 596–601.

Užgiris, I. Č. Plasticity and structure: The role of experience in infancy. In I. Č. Užgiris & F. Weizmann (Eds.), *The structuring of experience*. New York: Plenum Press, 1977.

Užgiris, I. Č., & Hunt, J. McV. *Assessment in infancy: Ordinal scales of psychological development*. Urbana, Ill.: University of Illinois Press, 1975.

Valantin, S. Le développement de la fonction manipulatoire chez l'enfant sénégalais au cours des deux premières années de la vie. Unpublished doctoral thesis, Université de Paris, 1970.

Valantin, S. Problems raised by observation of children in various cultural environments. *Early Child Development and Care*, 1973, *2*, 276–289.

Varkevisser, C. M. *Socialization in a changing society: Sukuma childhood in rural and urban Mwanza, Tanzania*. Den Haag: Center for the Study of Education in Changing Societies, 1973.

Vincent, M., & Hugon, J. L'insuffisance pondérale du prématuré africain au point de vue de la santé publique. *Bulletin of the World Health Organization*, 1962, *26*, 143–174.

Vouilloux, P. D. Étude de la psychomotoricité d'enfants africains au Cameroun: Test de Gesell et reflexes archaïques. *Journal de la Société des Africainists, 1959, 29*, 11–18. (a)

Vouilloux, P. D. Test moteurs et réflexe plantaire chez de jeunes enfants camerounais. *Presse Médicale*, 1959, *67*, 1420–1421. (b)

Vuori, L., Christiansen, N., Clement, J., Mora, J. O., Wagner, M., & Herrera, M. G. Nutritional supplementation and the outcome of pregnancy: II. Visual habituation at 1–3 days. *The American Journal of Clinical Nutrition*, 1979, *32*, 463–469.

Wachs, T. Similarity in developmental profile among related pairs of human infants. *Science*, 1972, *178*, 1004.

Wachs, T., Užgiris, I. Č., & Hunt, J. McV. Cognitive development in infants of different age levels and from different environmental backgrounds: An explanatory investigation. *Merrill-Palmer Quarterly*, 1971, *17*, 283–317.

Waggoner, R. W., & Ferguson, W. G. The development of the plantar reflex in children. *Archives of Neurology and Psychiatry*, 1930, *23*, 619–633.

Waldrop, M. F., & Bell, R. Q. Effects of family size and density on newborn characteristics. *American Journal of Orthopsychiatry*, 1966, *36*, 544–550.

Walters, C. E. Comparative development of Negro and white infants. *Journal of Genetic Psychology*, 1967, *110*, 243–251.

Warren, N. African infant precocity. *Psychological Bulletin*, 1972, *78*, 353–367.

Warren, N., & Parkin, J. M. A neurological and behavioral comparison of African and European newborns in Uganda. *Child Development*, 1974, *45*, 966–971.

Weisner, T. S., & Gallimore, R. My brother's keeper: Child and sibling caretaking. *Current Anthropology*, 1977, *18*, 169–190.

Welbourn, H. F. Custom and child health in Buganda: II. Methods of child rearing. *Tropical and Geographical Medicine*, 1963, *15*, 124–133.

Weller, G. M., & Bell, R. Q. Basal skin conductance and neonatal state. *Child Development*, 1965, *36*, 647–657.

Werner, E. E. Gesell Developmental Schedules, 1940 Series. *Sixth mental measurements yearbook*. Highland Park, N. J.: Gryphon, 1965, pp. 808–809.

Werner, E. E. Infants around the world: Cross-cultural studies of psychomotor development from birth to two years. *Journal of Cross-Cultural Psychology*, 1972, *3*, 111–134.

Werner, E. E., Bierman, J. M., & French, F. E. *The children of Kauai: A longitudinal study from the prenatal period to age ten*. Honolulu: University of Hawaii Press, 1971.

Werner, E. E., Simonian, K., & Smith, R. Ethnic and socioeconomic status differences in abilities and achievement among preschool and school age children in Hawaii. *Journal of Social Psychology*, 1968, *75*, 43–59.

White, B. L. Informal education during the first months of life. In R. Hess & R. Bear (Eds.), *Early education: Current theory, research, and action*. Chicago: Aldine, 1968.

White, B. L., & Castle, P. W. Visual exploratory behavior following postnatal handling of human infants. *Perceptual and Motor Skills*, 1964, *18*, 497–502.

White, J. L., & Labarba, R. C. The effects of tactile and kinesthetic stimulation on neonatal development in the premature infant. *Developmental Psychobiology*, 1976, *9*, 569–577.

Whiting, B. B. The problem of the packaged variable. In K. F. Riegel & J. A. Meacham (Eds.), *The developing individual in a changing world* (Vol. 1). The Hague: Mouton, 1976.

Whiting, J. W. M. Socialization process and personality. In F. L. K. Hsu (Ed.), *Psychological anthropology*. Homewood, Ill.: Dorsey Press, 1961.

Whiting, J. W. M. Causes and consequences of mother-infant contact. Paper presented at the meeting of the American Anthropological Association, New York, 1971.

Whiting, J. M. W. A model for psychocultural research. In P. H. Leiderman, S. R. Tulkin, & A. Rosenfeld (Eds.), *Culture and infancy: Variations in the human experience*. New York: Academic Press, 1977.

Whiting, J. W. M., Bogucki, P., Kwong, W. Y., & Nigro, J. Infanticide. Paper presented at the meeting of the Society for Cross-cultural Research, East Lansing, Mich., 1977.

Whiting, J. W. M., Chasdi, E. H., Antonovsky, H. F., & Ayres, B. C. The learning of values. In E. Z. Vogt & E. M. Albert (Eds.), *People of Rimrock*. Cambridge, Mass.: Harvard University Press, 1966.

Whiting, J. W. M., & Child, I. L. *Child training and personality*. New Haven: Yale University Press, 1953.

Whitner, W., & Thompson, M. C. The influence of bathing on the newborn infant's body temperature. *Nursing Research*, 1970, *19*, 30–36.

Whitten, A. Mother-infant interaction in Nigeria and Oxford: A pilot study (preliminary report). Unpublished manuscript, 1975.

Williams, J. R., & Scott, R. B. Growth and development of Negro infants: IV. Motor development and its relationship to child rearing practices in two groups of Negro infants. *Child Development*, 1953, *24*, 103–121.

Wilson, R. S. Similarity in developmental profile among related pairs of human infants. *Science*, 1972, *178*, 1006–1007. (a)

Wilson, R. S. Twins: Early mental development. *Science*, 1972, *175*, 914–917. (b)

Winnicott, D. W. Transitional objects and transitional phenomena. *International Journal of Psychoanalysis*, 1953, *34*, 89–97.

Wober, M. *Psychology in Africa*. London: International African Institute, 1975.

Wolff, P. H. Observations on the early development of smiling. In B. Foss (Ed.), *Determinants of infant behavior* (Vol. 2). New York: John Wiley & Sons, 1963.

Wolff, P. H. Biological variations and cultural diversity: An exploratory study. In P. H. Leiderman, S. R. Tulkin, & A. Rosenfeld (Eds.), *Culture and infancy: Variations in the human experience.* New York: Academic Press, 1977.

Woodward, J. A., & Goldstein, M. J. Communication deviance in the families of schizophrenics: A comment on the misuse of analysis of covariance. *Science,* 1977, *197,* 1096–1097.

Wug de Leon, E., De Licardie, E., & Cravioto, J. Operacion Nimiquipalq. VI: Desarollo psicomotor del niño en una poblacion rural de Guatemala. *Guatemala Pediatrica,* 1964, *4,* 92–106.

Yakovlev, P. I., & Lecours, A. The myelogenetic cycles of regional maturation of the brain. In A. Minkowski (Ed.), *Regional development of the brain in early life.* Oxford: Blackwell Scientific Publications, 1967.

Yamada, Y. Effects of stimulus novelty on visual and manipulative exploration in infancy. *Japanese Journal of Educational Psychology,* 1978, *1,* 41–51.

Yang, D. C. Neurologic status of newborn infants on first and third day of life. *Neurology,* 1962, *12,* 72–77.

Yarrow, L. J., Rubenstein, J. L., & Pedersen, F. A. *Infant and environment.* New York: John Wiley & Sons, 1975.

Yarrow, L. J., Rubenstein, J. L., Pedersen, F. A., & Jankowski, J. Dimensions of early stimulation and their differential effects on infant development. *Merrill-Palmer Quarterly,* 1972, *18,* 205–218.

Young, V. H. Family and childhood in a Southern Negro community. *American Anthropologist,* 1970, *72,* 269–288.

Zelazo, P. R. From reflexive to instrumental behavior. In L. P. Lipsitt (Ed.), *Developmental psychobiology: The significance of infancy.* Hillsdale, N.J.: Earlbaum, 1976.

Zelazo, P. R., Zelazo, N. A., & Kolb, S. "Walking" in the newborn. *Science,* 1972, *176,* 314–315.

Zempléni, A., & Rabain-Zempléni, J. Milieu Africain et développement. *Psychopathologie Africaine,* 1972, *8,* 233–295.

Zempléni-Rabain, J. L'enfant wolof de 2 à 5 ans (Sénégal): Échanges corporels et échanges mediatisés par les objets. *Revue de Neuropsychiatrie Infantile et d'Hygiène Mentale de l'Enfance,* 1970, *18,* 785–798.

Zern, D. The influence of certain child-rearing factors upon the development of a structured and salient sense of time. *Genetic Psychology Monographs,* 1970, *81,* 197–254.

Zern, D. The relationship between mother-infant contact and later differentiation of the social environment. *Journal of Genetic Psychology,* 1972, *121,* 107–117.

9

Body Size and Form among Ethnic Groups of Infants, Children, Youths, and Adults

Howard V. Meredith

In reference to body size and form of the human phenotype, an "ethnic group" can be defined as a small breeding population (tribe or localized race), living in a particular place, at a given time, under a specific complex of socioeconomic (nutritional, hygienic, and occupational) conditions.

A few examples will serve to illustrate why this definition, in addition to its genetic component, has geographic, temporal, and cultural components. Two samples of Quechua infants born during 1966 in Peru showed that birthweight was less at Cuzco, elevation 3.4 km, than at Lima, elevation 0.2 km (McClung, 1969). Two samples of Mayan children age 4 years reared during the early 1960s at Guatemalan villages of similar elevation showed that mean standing height was less at a village deficient in nutritional resources than at a village where children received food supplements and their parents were given professional advice on child nutrition (Guzmán, Scrimshaw, Burch, & Gordon, 1968). Two samples of Yoruba girls age 8 years measured between 1962 and 1970 at Ibadan gave means for head girth and arm girth that were higher for girls of well-to-do families than those of poor families (Janes, 1974). Samples of youths of Dutch ancestry living in Holland, Mich., gave means for height and weight that were higher in 1958 than 25 years earlier (Spurgeon, Young, & Meredith, 1959). Samples of Sara young men measured in Chad during 1968 gave means for shoulder width and hip width that were higher for residents of an agricultural area than for residents of Fort-Archambault (Crognier, 1969).

Most somatologic reports on ethnic groups make some reference to the ancestral gene pool and environmental setting of the group(s) studied. However, rarely is a group described in respect to each of the following: the intergrade and kinship boundaries of its genetic sources; the altitude, latitude, longitude, and population density of its habitat; the caloric and nutrient contents of its diet; the sanitary aspects, immunizaton provisions, and debilitating features of its health history; the energy expenditures and sorts of activity that typify its vocational and avocational pursuits; and the calendar year(s) during which it was studied. It follows that the available

271

reports on ethnic groups can be reviewed, and their findings systematized, only within the limits of the information they provide. Fortunately for the future of research, there is increasing cognizance of "the interaction of nutrition and genetics" (Garn, 1975), "the synergism of malnutrition and infection" (Scrimshaw, 1966), and the advances needed in assessing and reporting particulars on the genetic heterogeneity, adequacy of diet, health status, activity routine, and geographico-secular locus of each ethnic sample drawn for somatologic investigation (Garn, 1961; Gibbs, 1965; Malina, 1969; Meredith, 1976; Robson, 1975; Salzano, 1971).

The scope of the present chapter is constricted in several ways. There is ontogenetic constriction to birth and age 1 year in infancy, to ages 5 and 8 years in childhood, to ages 13 years (females) and 15 years (males) in adolescence, and, in adulthood, to young and elderly adults. There is anthropometric constriction, in infancy to body weight, vertex-soles length, body stem and lower limb components of total length, head circumference, and perimeter of thorax; and at later ontogenetic stages to standing height, sitting height, lower limb height, head width and depth, widths of shoulders and hips, girths of head, chest, arm, and calf, and body weight. Measures of body form include the cephalic index, skelic index, cephalothoracic index, shoulder–hip index, and limb girth index.

Except for occasional reference to early studies for historical or comparative purposes, there is secular constriction to data gathered between 1960 and 1970. In infancy and childhood, where it is known that sex differences in the variables under study are either small and systematic (males slightly larger than females) or lacking, findings are given for both sexes taken together. There is restriction to sample averages for body size and form, and there is statistical estimation of population differences in average size and form between ethnic groups. Studies reporting statistics on less than 20 subjects are not cited.

INFANCY

Body Weight and Length at Birth

Average body weight at birth has been determined on hundreds of human samples (Krogman, 1941; Martin, 1928; Meredith, 1950; 1970). Historical examples of birth-weight means, each computed from no less than 100 hospital delivery records, are as follows: 3.20 kg for 120 Irish infants born during 1785 at Dublin (Clarke, 1786), 3.31 kg for 712 United States white infants born between 1865 and 1872 at Philadelphia (Stockton-Hough, 1885), and 3.32 kg for 10,000 Australian white infants born during 1857–1887 at Melbourne (Fetherston, 1887). Early investigators of vertex–soles length at birth reported means of 48.6 cm on 400 Melbourne neonates (Fetherston, 1862), 48.7 cm on 2053 Edinburgh neonates (Duncan, 1864), and 48.8 cm on 721 Philadelphia neonates (Stockton-Hough, 1885). By 1890, findings from these and other studies had shown that for white ethnic groups, on average, newborn males were a little heavier and longer than females and firstborn neonates were a little lighter and shorter than those from later pregnancies. Fasbender (1878), for instance, from weight and length measures on 630 infants born in Berlin obtained means (1) higher for males than females by 0.10 kg and 0.5 cm and (2) lower for firstborn infants than those of later birth ranks by 0.17 kg and 0.5 cm.

Table 9-1 presents means for body weight and vertex–soles length at birth on ethnic groups of liveborn human infants on whom these measures were taken between 1960 and 1970. Before complementing the content of each row with an

TABLE 9-1 Mean Body Weight (kg) and Vertex–Soles Length (cm) for Liveborn Infants of Both Sexes Studied Between 1960 and 1970

Tag	Ethnic Group	Number Measured	Mean Weight at Birth	Mean Length at Birth
1	Hindu, Vārānasi	510	2.33	46.8
2	Lumi, New Guinea	63	2.40	—
3	Hindu, Calcutta	600	2.54	46.3
4	Lunda, Angola	2,342	—	47.0
5	Mayan, Guatemala	45	2.68	—
6	Hindu, Delhi	703	2.79	48.2
7	Hindu, Bombay	2,000	2.84	48.3
8	Ceylonese, Kandy	813	2.88	—
9	Colombian, Medellin	1,650	2.90	48.2
10	Mexican, rural Mexico	291	2.90	48.4
11	Javanese, Sumatra	1,584	2.90	48.7*
12	Ladino, Guatemala	47	2.98	48.0
13	Hindu, Surinam	2,756	3.02	48.0*
14	Black, Kampala region	570	3.03	48.6*
15	Bushnegro, Surinam	306	3.06	48.2*
16	Black, Baltimore	3,156	3.06	—
17	Quechua, Cuzco	100	3.07	—
18	Indonesian, Surinam	380	3.09	48.1*
19	Jamaican, Kingston	271	3.09	48.2
20	Black, New Orleans	200	3.11	49.2
21	Hopi, Arizona	682	3.15	—
22	Puerto Rican, Philadelphia	65	3.15	50.0
23	Chinese, Surinam	117	3.18	48.4*
24	English, Sheffield	106	3.19	48.4
25	Navajo, Utah to New Mexico	13,080	3.20	—
26	Brazilian, Bello Horizonte	1,860	3.20	49.6
27	Uzbek, Uzbekistan	1,867	3.22	52.1
28	Italian, Bologna	200	3.23	50.6
29	Creole, Surinam	4,292	3.25	48.4*
30	Russian, Yaroslavl	996	3.25	49.5
31	Kazakh, Kazakhstan	564	3.27	50.6
32	Maronite, Beirut	129	3.27	49.6
33	Druse, Israel	2,242	3.29	—
34	English, London	900	3.32	—
35	White, Massachusetts	10,848	3.34	—
36	White, Christchurch	1,174	3.35	—
37	Chilean, Chile	684	3.35	—
38	Aleut, Aleutian Islands	486	3.35	—
39	Tasmanian, Tasmania	1,114	3.36	51.5
40	Polish, Warsaw	1,297	3.37	51.5
41	Sioux, Northern Plains	4,388	3.40	—
42	Swedish, Malmö	4,124	3.45	50.5
43	Cree, James Bay	768	3.78	—

*With seven exceptions, sample size is the same for weight and length: in rows 11, 13, 14, 15, 18, 23, and 29, ns for length are 1492, 2348, 530, 282, 178, 85, and 3060 respectively. For body weight, standard error of mean approximates 0.10 kg where n = 45, 0.05 kg where n = 200, 0.03 kg where n = 500, 0.02 kg where n = 1500, and 0.01 kg where n = 3000. Corresponding values for body length are 0.30, 0.14, 0.09, 0.05, and 0.04 cm.

elaborating comment, it is relevant to note that (1) every mean represents liveborn neonates of both sexes, (2) the means for body weight are listed in ascending order of magnitude, and (3) a number is assigned to each row for use in referring to either the row or its complemental materials.

Tag 1. Consecutive liveborn infants weighing 0.5 kg or more (Tandon, Gupta, & Dikshit, 1971). At Kampur, another city in Uttar Pradesh, means of 2.49 kg and 47.5 cm were obtained for 1000 sequential live offspring of parents in the "lower economic strata"; 44 percent of these infants weighed less than 2.5 kg (Saigal & Srivastava, 1969).

Tag 2. Data from villages in the Sepik district located 0.5 km above sea level on foothill ridges of the Toricelli mountains. In these villages malnutrition was common and malaria holoendemic (Wark & Malcolm, 1969).

Tag 3. Liveborn offspring of "middle-class" parents (S. Das, Roy, Paul, & Chakraborty, 1975). Another sample of Bengali neonates born in Calcutta gave a mean birthweight of 2.67 kg for 3430 viable infants (Banerjee & Roy, 1962).

Tag 4. Offspring of "melanodermic aborigines of traditional civilization" living at villages in the northeast Lunda district, considered "a true negro type strongly influenced by pygmoid elements" (David, 1972).

Tag 5. Live births at a "Mayan village typical of preindustrial culture" located 37 km from Guatemala City at an elevation of 2.0 km (Mata, Urrutia, & García, 1967).

Tag 6. Viable infants weighing 0.4 kg or more born into "middle-class" families (Kukowski, London, Sutnick, Kahn, & Blumberg, 1972). From other analyses, 40 percent of 1000 liveborn Delhi infants weighed 2.5 kg or less (Walia, Khetarpal, Mehta, Ghai, Kapoor, & Taneja, 1963), 26 percent of 500 infants delivered at Agra weighed 2.5 kg or less (Kalra, Kishore, & Dayal, 1967), mean body length was 47.8 cm for 47 offspring of families of "lower-middle" socioeconomic status residing at Bhopal and Gwalior (Sharma, 1970), means were 2.83 kg and 46.9 cm for the 500 neonates delivered at Agra (Kalra et al., 1967), and means were 3.00 kg and 49.9 cm for 79 liveborn offspring of Delhi parents in the "professional-managerial" category (Banik, Krishna, Mane, Raj, & Taskar, 1970).

Tag 7. Liveborn offspring of "middle-class" parents (Udani, 1963). Other birth records gave means of 2.58 kg and 45.5 cm for 1000 neonates of "lower-class" families, 3.25 kg and 50.8 cm for 270 neonates of "upper-class" families (Udani, 1963), 2.60 kg for 2080 offspring of low-income families surviving beyond the third postnatal day (Jayant, 1964), and means lower by 0.9 kg and 4.8 cm for 38 infants weighing 2.5 kg or less than for 50 infants weighing more than 2.5 kg (Shiddhaye, Shah & Udani, 1972). Means of 2.76 kg and 48.1 cm were obtained on 200 neonates born at Poona to parents of "above-average" socioeconomic status (Limaye, Chouhan, Lakhani, & Phadke, 1974).

Tag 8. Viable neonates delivered at a "nonpaying" hospital (Amarasinghe, 1966). Of 1988 successive live births in Colombo, 21 percent weighed less than 2.5 kg (Soysa & Jayasuriya, 1975).

Tag 9. Infants of mixed white, black, and Amerind ancestry weighing between 2.0 and 4.0 kg. Although the parents were at "the lowest economic level," the infants "looked well nourished and in good physical condition" (Oberndorfer, Mejia, & Palacio del Valle, 1965). Means of 3.13 kg and 48.9 cm were secured from 63 offspring of the highest social classes in Bogotá (Luna-Jaspe, Ariza, Rueda-Williamson, Mora, & Pardo, 1970).

Tag 10. Progeny of families residing at a typical Mexican agricultural village, elevation 0.9 km, situated in a semitropical subhumid zone of southwest Mexico (Cravioto, Birch, de Licardie, Rosales, & Vega, 1969).

Tag 11. Offspring of Javanese immigrant parents of laboring status living on a north Sumatran rubber estate (Shattock, 1968).

Tag 12. Individuals of mixed Spanish and Amerind ancestry studied at four villages northeast of Guatemala City in the department of El Progreso (Yarbrough, Habicht, Malina, Lechtig, & Klein, 1975).

Tag 13. Individuals of Indian and Pakistani descent belonging to families residing in Surinam villages and towns (Kuyp, 1967).

Tag 14. Liveborn neonates. Their fathers were "small peasant farmers or slum-dwelling laborers . . . ; no mother appeared severely malnourished" (Jelliffe, 1967). Baganda subgroups gave means of 2.81 kg for 65 neonates where the maternal placenta was infected with malaria and 3.09 kg for 311 neonates where the placenta was not infected (Jelliffe, 1968). For other black groups studied in Africa, means were 2.95 kg for 8139 live infants born at Dar-es-Salaam into low-income families among whom "malnutrition was frequent and standards of health and hygiene very low" (Ebrahim & D'Sa, 1966); 3.11 kg and 51.5 cm for 525 infants weighing more than 1.7 kg. born at Khartoum and Omdurman (El-din-Ahmed & Abdalla, 1967); and 3.15 kg on 100 live infants, largely of the Mandinka tribe, born at a semirural village in the Kombo St. Mary district of Gambia (Marsden & Marsden, 1965). The Sudanese sample gave subgroup means of 2.99 kg for 187 firstborn infants and 3.32 kg for 275 infants of third and later birth ranks. See also tag 4.

Tag 15. Offspring of seminomadic descendants of African slaves residing in the interior of Suriman (Kuyp, 1967).

Tag 16. Live, singleton neonates. Thirteen percent weighed 2.5 kg or less; the 1542 offspring of mothers who did not use tobacco weighed 0.15 kg more than the 1614 offspring of mothers who, during pregnancy, regularly smoked cigarettes (Reinke & Henderson, 1966). A mean of 3.08 kg was found for infants weighing 1.0 kg or more born at Charleston, S.C., into families of low economic status; subgroup means were 2.98 kg for 260 progeny of mothers who smoked ten or more cigarettes daily during pregnancy and 3.13 kg for 1790 progeny of nonsmoking mothers (P. Underwood, Hester, Laffitte, & Gregg, 1965).

Tag 17. Liveborn offspring of Quecha and mestizo parents residing in Peru at an elevation of 3.4 km; a comparable group of 88 infants, elevation 0.2 km, gave a mean higher by 0.22 kg (McClung, 1969).

Tag 18. Offspring of immigrants of Indonesian lineage living in Surinam (Kuyp, 1967).

Tag 19. Liveborn, singleton neonates. Eleven percent weighed less than 2.5kg; more than 90 percent had predominantly black progenitors with "lower and low-middle socioeconomic backgrounds" (Grantham-McGregor, Desai, & Back, 1972). Benoist (1962) reported a mean birthweight of 3.01 kg for 171 viable offspring of black parents residing on Tortuga island, north of Haiti.

Tag 20. Viable offspring of low-income families. Eleven percent weighed less than 2.5 kg (Cherry, 1968).

Tag 21. Liveborn, singleton, Amerind infants delivered "in the United States Public Health Service medical facilities." An identical mean was secured on 853 infants of the Zuni tribe, and a mean of 3.17 kg was found for 2107 infants of the Apache tribe (Adams & Niswander, 1973).

Tag 22. Offspring of parents of low socioeconomic status (Johnson & Beller, 1976). A mean of 3.16 kg was obtained on 1848 neonates of Puerto Rican parentage delivered at several hospitals in the continental United States (Naylor & Myrianthopoulos, 1967).

Tag 23. Viable offspring of Chinese immigrants residing in Surinam (Kuyp, 1967). A mean of 3.13 kg was reported for 200 physically normal infants born into families of Chinese lineage and low to middle socioeconomic status living in urban areas of Hong Kong island (Chang, Lee, Low, Chui, & Chow, 1965).

Tag 24. Liveborn infants (Illingworth & Eid, 1971). Another sample of 708 Sheffield neonates gave a mean weight of 3.18 kg (Illingworth & Lutz, 1965).

Tag 25. Same source as for tag 21. An identical mean was found for 642 Pueblo infants and a mean of 3.29 kg for 267 neonates of the Paiute tribe.

Tag 26. Live deliveries. Subgroup means were 3.12 kg and 49.3 cm for 1068 neonates born into families of below-average economic status and, for 792 offspring of above-average families, 3.29 kg and 50.0 cm (Machado & Memoria, 1966). Means obtained on 524 infants born at Ribeirão Prêto were 3.18 kg and 49.5 cm; 7.8 percent of the infants weighed between 1.3 and 2.4 kg (Woiski, Romera, Corrêa, Raya, & Lima-Filho, 1965). On healthy infants with gestational ages largely between 35 and 43 weeks delivered at Porto Alegre, birthweight means were 3.27 kg for 1013 black neonates and 3.33 kg for 4724 white neonates (Araújo & Salzano, 1975).

Tag 27. Individuals of mixed Mongoloid-Caucasian ancestry born in the Uzbek Soviet Socialist Republic (Goldfeld, Merkova, & Tseimlina, 1965). The means shown are 0.9 kg and 0.5 cm lower than those reported: these adjustments were made on the assumption that the reported means represent neonates weighing 2.5 kg or more (Meredith, 1970; 1971; V. G. Vlastovsky, personal communication, 1969).

Tag 28. Viable infants supervised during their first postnatal year partly at a child welfare clinic and partly in private pediatric practice (Grandi, 1965). An identical mean weight was obtained on 746 liveborn Italian neonates of all social classes delivered at Genoa (Salvadori & Papadia, 1965).

Tag 29. Mixed black and mulatto members of families living "in Paramaribo, the Coronie district, and Para settlements". Their birthweights were 0.7 kg or more (Kuyp, 1967).

Tag 30. Adjusted means (see tag 27) for liveborn progeny of Russian parents residing at Yaroslavl. Other estimated means for newborn Russian infants unselected by bodyweight are 3.27 kg and 49.5 cm for 4762 infants born at Saratov and 3.29 kg and 51.4 cm for 2000 infants born at Volgograd (Goldfeld et al., 1965).

Tag 31. Adjusted means for Turko-Mongol liveborn neonates of the Kazakh Soviet Socialist Republic (Goldfeld et al., 1965).

Tag 32. Singleton, live offspring of parents in "the low socioeconomic stratum." For two other Beirut ethnic groups, means were 3.26 kg and 49.2 cm for 118 Sunni infants and 3.32 kg and 49.3 cm for 134 Armenian infants (Harfouche, 1966).

Tag 33. Viable infants, 6.4 percent weighing less than 2.5 kg. For other groups living in Israel, an identical mean was secured for 171,972 Jewish infants, 5.8 percent weighing less than 2.5 kg, and a mean of 3.32 kg was found for 41,245 Arabian infants of Arab descent, 5.1 percent weighing less than 2.5 kg (Grossman, Handlesman, & Davies, 1974).

Tag 34. Live, singleton neonates weighing 1.0 kg or more. Their mothers were under prenatal supervision and gave "little evidence of inadequate socioeconomic conditions" (Armitage, Boyd, Hamilton, & Rowe, 1967).

Tag 35. Subgroup means were 3.20 kg for 4889 offspring of mothers who, during pregnancy, smoked ten or more cigarettes daily and 3.46 kg for 5959 offspring of mothers who did not use tobacco (MacMahon, Alpert, & Salber, 1965). P. Underwood et al. (1965), from data collected at Charleston on white neonates weighing 1.0 kg or more, obtained a mean of 3.20 kg from progeny of 488 mothers smoking ten or more cigarettes daily and a mean 0.32 kg higher for progeny of 865 nonsmoking mothers.

Tag 36. Infants weighing 1.0 kg or more born into urban families of South

Island, New Zealand. Subgroup means were 3.41 kg for 717 offspring of nonsmoking mothers and 3.19 kg for 208 offspring of mothers who smoked ten or more cigarettes daily during pregnancy (Bailey, 1970).

Tag 37. Viable infants born in seven distributed geographic areas. The maternal diet was "somewhat deficient in calories, protein and vitamin A" (Berry, 1961).

Tag 38. The source was given in tag 21. Means reported for other ethnic groups were 3.32 kg for 2950 Eskimo and 647 Blackfoot, 3.34 kg for 1008 Alaskan and 970 Papago, and 3.39 kg for 2489 Cherokee, 700 Creek, and 136 Seminole neonates.

Tag 39. Viable infants. Subgroup values were 3.27 kg for 462 firstborn infants and 3.48 kg for 314 infants with birth ranks three and up (Coy, Lewis, Mair, Longmore, & Ratkowsky, 1973).

Tag 40. Subgroup means were 3.32 kg and 51.2 cm for newborn females and were higher by 0.11 kg and 0.7 cm for newborn males (Kurniewicz-Witczakowa, Miesowicz, Mazurczak, & Jarmolinska-Eska, 1972).

Tag 41. Means for other tribes were 3.40 kg for 676 Pima; 3.41 kg for 432 Crow; 3.42 kg for 1830 Chippewa, 362 Kiowa, 273 Comanche, and 128 Chickasaw; and 3.44 kg for 1385 Choctaw (Adams & Niswander, 1973).

Tag 42. Liveborn neonates (Kullander & Källén, 1971). An identical mean for body weight was obtained by Pettersson (1969) for 3490 Swedish infants born at Uppsala. Both studies found the progeny of maternal cigarette smokers had a lower mean weight at birth than the progeny of nonsmokers (see Meredith, 1975).

Tag 43. Canadian Amerind newborns weighing 0.7 kg or more. Their parents inhabited coastal settlements and the subarctic towns of Moosonee and Moose Factory (Partington & Roberts, 1969). Means above 3.45 kg obtained for United States tribes were 3.46 kg for 123 Winnebago, 3.47 kg for 119 Mohave, 3.48 kg for 535 Cheyenne, and 3.49 kg for 205 Omaha infants (same source as tag 41).

Among the comparative findings available from Table 9-1 and its supporting information, the following were selected for specification:

1. Means for liveborn neonates of ethnic groups studied between 1960 and 1970 varied from 2.33 to 3.78 kg in body weight and from 45.5 to 52.1 cm in vertex–soles length. For both measures, means were relatively low on Hindu infants, intermediate on black infants, and relatively high on white infants. The mean weight of Swedish neonates at Malmö and Uppsala was 48 percent higher than that for Hindu neonates at Vāranasi, and the mean length of Polish neonates at Warsaw was 11 percent higher than that for Hindu neonates at Calcutta.
2. The distribution of means for birthweight of Amerind tribes studied during the 1960s extended from 2.68 kg for Mayan infants to 3.78 kg for Cree infants. Intervening means were 3.07 kg for Quechua, 3.20 kg for Navajo, 3.40 kg for Sioux, and 3.49 kg for Omaha infants. The Cree average was higher than the Mayan average by 1.1 kg (41 percent) and higher than the Quechua average by 0.7 kg (23 percent).
3. Mean body weight at birth was 30 percent higher for Mandinka infants of Gambia than for Lumi infants of New Guinea; 18 percent higher for white neonates in Christchurch, New Zealand than Hindu neonates in Agra, Uttar Pradesh; 12 percent higher for Maronite offspring of low-income parents in Beirut, Lebanon than offspring of laboring parents at a Sumatra plantation; and, in reference to parents of above-average socioeconomic status, 19 percent higher for progeny at Bello Horizonte, Brazil than for progeny at Poona, India.

4. One-tail statistical tests at $p = 0.01$, using population standard deviations of 2.0 cm for vertex–soles length and 0.70 kg for body weight, warrant the following generalizations: in the period 1960–1970, (1) mean body length was less for Lunda neonates of Angola than Swedish neonates of Malmö by an amount likely exceeding 3.3 cm, and (2) mean birthweight was less for black offspring of low-income, poorly nourished mothers at Dar-es-Salaam, Tanzania than for black offspring of low-income, nonsmoking mothers at Charleston, S.C. by an amount probably exceeding 0.5 kg.

Head Girth, Chest Girth, and Cephalothoracic Index at Birth

Early studies of head circumference and thoracic perimeter were reported by Chapin (1894) and Holt (1897). From measures on 446 "fullterm infants" (new-borns weighing 2.5 kg or more) delivered at two New York hospitals, Holt obtained 35.0 cm for mean head girth, 33.7 cm for mean chest girth, and 96 percent for the thoracic mean as a percentage of the cephalic mean.

Assembled in Table 9-2 are statistics for several ethnic groups studied between 1960 and 1970 in Africa, America, Asia, and Europe. Many rows carry tags assigned in elaborating the content of Table 9-1; tags 44–53 are newly assigned.

Tag 44. Same as tag 12, except for reference (Malina, Habicht, Martorell, Lechtig, Yarbrough, & Klein, 1975).

Tag 45. Infants born into families residing in a rural community near Hyderabad (Swaminathan, Jyothi, Singh, Madhavan, & Gopalan, 1964).

Tag 46. Offspring born during the mid-1960s to parents of "all districts and social groups" in Lublin (Chrzastek-Spruch, 1968).

Tag 47. Infants of middle-class families living in metropolitan Delhi (Ghai & Sandhu, 1968).

Tags 48–53. Neonates born in Sassari province (Aicardi & Depperu, 1966), region of Sofia (Kadanoff, Mutafov, & Pandova, 1975), Friuli province (DeLuca, D'Andrea, Pelizzo, & Cozzi, 1965), cities in Peru (McClung, 1969) and the Soviet Union (Goldfeld et al., 1965), and Pnompenh and vicinity (Nouth-Savoeun, 1966).

Some investigators analyzed data collected during 1960–1970 for neonatal head girth but not chest girth: means reported were 32.2 cm for 600 infants in Calcutta (tag 3), 33.5 cm for 813 infants in Kandy (tag 8), 33.7 cm for 703 infants in Delhi (tag 6), 33.8 cm for 273 Jewish infants in Jerusalem (Palti & Adler, 1975), 33.9 cm for 331 English infants in London (Gampel, 1965), 34.0 cm for 525 Sudanese infants in Khartoum and Omdurman (tag 14), 34.5 cm for Swedish infants in Malmö (tag 42), and 35.4 cm for 47 Chilean infants (tag 37). On three stratified Ceylonese samples studied at Colombo, means for head girth were 30.3 cm for 159 infants weighing 2.25 kg or less, 32.7 cm for 143 infants weighing 2.25–2.50 kg, and 34.0 cm for 150 infants weighing 2.50 kg or more (Soysa & Jayasuriya, 1975).

Using findings based on 1960–1970 measures where sample size exceeded 100, three comparative statements are tenable:

1. Average head circumference at birth was between 32 and 34 cm for Hindu infants at Agra, Calcutta, Delhi, and Kampur; it was larger (between 34 and 35 cm) for European infants at Bologna, Lublin, Malmö, and Sheffield. The smallest and largest means were those for Hindu neonates at Varanasi and Russian neonates at Volgograd, respectively.

2. Average chest perimeter at birth was between 29 and 31 cm for Hindu infants at Agra, Delhi, and Kampur; it was larger (33 or more) for European infants at

TABLE 9-2 Mean Head Girth (cm), Chest Girth (cm), and Cephalothoracic Index on Neonates of Both Sexes Born Between 1960 and 1970

Tag	Ethnic Group	Number Measured	Mean Girth Head	Mean Girth Chest	Chest Girth X 100 / Head Girth
		Liveborn: disregarding birth weight			
24	English, Sheffield	106	34.3	30.9	90
1	Hindu, Vārānasi	501	31.8	29.1	92
1	Hindu, Kampur	1,000	32.8	30.2	92
6	Hindu, Agra	500	32.8	30.3	92
44	Ladino, rural Guatemala	40	33.3	30.8	92
20	Black, New Orleans	200	33.7	31.5	93
14	Black, Kampala region	402	33.0	31.7	96
26	Brazilian, Ribeirão Prêto	524	34.5	33.0	96
28	Italian, Bologna	200	35.0	33.7	96
		Birthweight 2.0 kg and up			
45	Hindu, rural	44	32.7	30.4	93
6	Hindu, Agra	435	33.5	31.1	93
46	Polish, Lublin	290	34.5	33.0	96
9	Colombian, Medellin	1,650	33.5	32.5	97
		Birthweight 2.5 kg and up			
47	Hindu, Delhi	111	33.7	31.1	92
7	Hindu, Bombay	50	35.5	32.9	93
17	Quechua, Cuzco	68	34.2	32.6	95
48	Sardinian, Sardinia	200	34.3	32.6	95
49	Bulgarian, Bulgaria	300	34.7	33.1	95
50	Italian, Friuli province	500	34.9	33.4	96
51	Quechua, Lima	85	34.2	33.2	97
52	Russian, Volgograd	2,000	35.7	34.5	97
53	Cambodian, Pnompenh area	~200	34.7	34.5	99

For head girth, standard error of the mean (sem) approximates 0.24 cm where $n = 40$, 0.15 cm where $n = 100$, 0.08 cm where $n = 400$, and 0.04 cm where $n = 1500$. Corresponding values for chest girth are 0.27, 0.17, 0.09, and 0.04 cm.

Bologna, Lublin, and Sheffield. Extreme values characterized the same groups as above.

3. For ethnic groups studied in Africa, Europe, India, North America, and South America, mean head girth at birth exceeded mean chest girth. Chest girth was between 92 and 93 percent of head girth on several Hindu groups and between 95 and 97 percent on European and South American groups.

Stem Length, Lower Limb Length, and Skelic Index at Birth

From measures amassed during 1865–1872 on 712 white infants born in Philadelphia, Stockton-Hough (1885) secured means of 32.0 cm for stem (vertex–rump) length, 16.8 cm for lower limb length (vertex–soles length minus vertex–rump length), and 52 percent for the skelic index (lower limb length X 100/stem length). Given in the same order, statistics derived from records accumulated since 1960 are 31.9 cm, 14.4 cm, and 45 percent for Hindu neonates at Calcutta (tag 3); 33.6 cm, 15.6 cm, and 46 percent for Jewish neonates at Jerusalem (Palti & Adler, 1975); 31.6

cm, 15.3 cm, and 48 percent for Hindu neonates at Agra (tag 6); 32.7 cm, 16.5 cm, and 50 percent for Quechua neonates at Cuzco and Lima (tags 17 and 51); 32.0 cm, 16.2 cm, and 51 percent for Jamaican neonates at Kingston (tag 19); 31.1 cm 16.4 cm, and 53 percent for Hindu neonates at Kampur (tag 1); 31.8 cm, 17.2 cm, and 54 percent for Hindu neonates at Delhi (Banik, Krishna, Mane, Raj, & Taskar, 1970); and 29.4 cm, 17.4 cm, and 59 percent for Hindu neonates at Vārānasi (tag 1). The differences among skelic index averages from contemporary Hindu studies (45 to 59 percent) suggest the need for improved standardization of procedures in measuring neonatal vertex–soles and vertex–rump distances (see Meredith, 1960). On the whole, the studies reviewed indicate that human body length at birth is about two-thirds the length of the body stem and one-third the length of the lower limbs.

Body Length and Weight at Age 1 Year
Table 9-3 displays, for age 1 year, means for vertex–soles length and body weight based on data collected in different parts of the world between 1960 and 1970; the means for body length are listed in increasing order of magnitude.

Tag 54. Considered a representative sample for East Pakistan in the early 1960s; about 70 percent rural residents; malnutrition was "widely prevalent" (Rosenberg & Reiner, 1966).

Tag 55. Individuals measured in the early 1960s at scattered villages. There were nutritional deficiencies in thiamine, riboflavin, and iodine (Berry, 1962a). From measures taken in the late 1960s at Bangkok, means higher by 6.0 cm and 1.76 kg were obtained on about 170 infants of the "middle and professional classes" lacking any sign of malnutrition or deficiency disease (Khanjanasthiti, Supachaturas, Mekanandha, Srimusikapodh, Choopanya, & Leesuwan, 1973).

Tag 56. Records obtained at villages in four regions of Java. There was "no evidence of growth retardation in infants with spleen and/or liver enlargement" (Bailey, 1962). Refer to tag 11: these families received "good rations" and free medical services; from data for body length of 100 infants and body weight of 1098 infants, means were 70.0 cm and 7.32 kg.

Tag 57. Members of the Bundi tribe living in the Madang district at villages from 0.6 to 2.2 km above sea level. Although overt signs of malnutrition were rare, diet was appraised as deficient in protein (Malcolm, 1970). For members of the Chimbu tribe living in villages at elevations from 1.5 to 2.4 km, means were 7.82 kg for 55 infants and 68.5 cm for 23 infants (Bailey, 1964). Means for body weight were 7.10 kg for 30 infants of the Lumi tribe (tag 2), and 8.00 kg for 317 infants of the Kaiapit tribe living in the Markhan valley, 128 km west of Lae at an elevation of 0.3 km (Malcolm, 1969b).

Tag 58. Individuals of Amerind, Spanish, and mestizo progenitors residing in eight departments. Their diet was frequently deficient in calcium, animal protein, riboflavin, vitamin A, and iodine (Fisk, 1964b).

Tag 59. Inhabitants of villages "in all directions around Poona." There was prevalent intestinal parasitism, marked vitamin A deficiency, and moderate insufficiencies in calories, calcium, protein, and vitamin C (Phadke & Kulkarni, 1971). For 87 infants living in a rural community near Hyderabad means were lower by 1.4 cm and 0.69 kg (Swaminathan et al., 1964), and for 30 infants residing at villages in the Lubhiana district means were 70.1 cm and 7.12 kg (Neumann, Shanker, & Uberoi, 1969); for both groups, socioeconomic status was low and there were "varying degrees of protein-calorie malnutrition."

Tag 60. Refer to tag 3, S. Das et al. (1975). Other urban means reported were 67.4 cm and 6.40 kg for 64 infants of lower-middle socioeconomic status measured at Bhopal and Gwalior, none showing signs of malnutrition or vitamin deficiency

TABLE 9-3 Mean Vertex—Soles Length (cm) and Body Weight (kg) on Ethnic Groups of Infants Age 1 Year Measured Between 1960 and 1970

Tag	Ethnic Group	Number Measured	Mean Length	Mean Weight
54	Pakistani, East Pakistan	125	66.1	6.92
55	Thai, Thailand	69	66.8	7.03
56	Javanese, Java	226	67.6	7.52
57	Bundi, New Guinea	80	67.9	7.71
12	Ladino, Guatemala	341	68.4	7.73
58	Bolivian, Southwest Bolivia	92	68.5	8.12
59	Hindu, rural region	~500	69.0	7.49
60	Hindu, Calcutta	174	69.4	7.37
61	Filipino, Bayambang	33	—	7.73
62	Tunisian, Chott el Djerid	138	69.9	7.95
63	Basotho, Lesotho	1,584	—	8.10
64	Ugandan, Namulonge	38	70.6	8.53
65	Eskimo, Alaska	287	71.2	10.07
66	Lebanese, Lebanon	51	71.4	8.20
67	Shona, Rhodesia	108	—	9.00
68	Sardinian, Sassari province	992	71.9	9.08
18	Indonesian, Surinam	48	72.0	7.98*
69	Australian aborigine	196	72.6	8.45*
70	Spanish, rural Spain	1,476	72.7	9.20
71	Nigerian, Lagos	107	72.8	8.63
72	Jamaican, rural Jamaica	190	72.8	8.87
73	Black, New Orleans	180	73.0	9.49
13	Hindu, Surinam	451	73.3	8.16*
74	Czech, Olomouc region	37	73.5	9.56
75	Russian, Minsk	268	73.6	9.82
76	Yemenite, Israel	122	73.6	9.54
77	Romanian, rural region	880	73.7	9.29
78	Chinese, Hong Kong	297	73.8	8.50
79	Brazilian, Guanabara	~170	73.8	9.39
80	Dominican, Santo Domingo	~80	73.8	9.10
81	Italian, Turin	~200	74.1	10.05
82	Colombian, Bogatá	64	74.1	9.51
29	Creole, Surinam	837	74.3	9.25*
83	Bulgarian, Sofia	612	74.4	9.84*
84	Turkish, Istanbul	457	74.9	9.81
85	White, Oakland	>1,000	75.1	10.00
86	Polish, Lublin	248	75.4	9.97
87	Finnish, Helsinki	214	75.8	10.25*
39	Tasmanian, Tasmania	1,114	75.9	10.54
88	Dutch, Netherlands	468	76.2	10.23

*With seven exceptions, sample size is the same for length and weight; body weight ns are 868 for tag 56, 135 for tag 18, 330 for tag 69, 931 for tag 13, 1185 for tag 29, 994 for tag 83, and 209 for tag 87.

For vertex—soles length, sem approximates 0.51 cm where $n = 35$, 0.36 cm where $n = 70$, 0.21 cm where $n = 200$, and 0.09 cm where $n = 1000$. Corresponding values for body weight are 0.43, 0.31, 0.18, and 0.08 kg.

(Sharma, 1970); 70.3 cm and 7.70 kg for 973 Delhi infants of all social classes (Banik et al., 1970); 70.9 cm and 9.04 kg for 77 Burla infants of "low-middle and low socioeconomic strata" (Mohanta, Panda, & Prahara, 1972); 72.0 cm and 8.30 kg for about 200 infants of Poona reared under "near-optimal" conditions of diet and health care (Limaye et al., 1974); 72.9 cm and 8.67 kg for 111 middle-class infants of Delhi (Ghai & Sandu, 1968); and 73.4 cm and 8.82 kg for 47 offspring of Delhi professional and managerial families (Banik et al., 1970).

Tag 61. Data gathered at Bayambang, Luzon Island (K. V. Bailey, personal communication, 1966).

Tag 62. Children of "Arab, Negro, and Berger" ancestry living at villages around this large lake bordering the Sahara desert. Their dietary staple was unfortified wheat; they were studied to provide a baseline before introducing a diet fortified with quality protein, vitamins, and iron (Boutourline, Tesi, Kerr, Stare, Kallal, Turki, & Hemaidan, 1972; 1973).

Tag 63. Progeny of parents residing at villages in the Maluti mountains 130 km east of Maseru, elevation about 2.1 km. They received irregular supplements of dried milk and wheat, were somewhat malnourished, and had few diseases other than gastroenteritis, whooping cough, and pneumonia (Cohen, Clayden, & King, 1976).

Tag 64. Rural infants enrolled for longitudinal study at a clinic 24 km from Kampala; they were selected as "not malnourished" (Rutishauser, 1974). An earlier analysis of data collected at the same clinic on healthy middle-class Baganda children making "satisfactory" gain in weight during the 6 weeks prior to measurement gave $n = 169$ and mean of 70.4 cm for length and $n = 606$ and mean 9.10 kg for weight (Rutishauser, 1965). Means for body length were 71.8 cm on 347 Lunda infants of Angola (tag 4), 69.5 cm on Shi infants of Zaire living along the western shore of lake Kivu, and 72.0 cm on Hutu infants of Rwanda living along the eastern shore of lake Kivu (Vis, 1969; H. L. Vis, personal communications, 1947, 1975).

Tag 65. Infants living at villages in southwest Alaska (Heller, Scott, & Hammes, 1967).

Tag 66. Individuals measured at widely distributed villages. They were predominantly Arabs and mainly from low-income homes; their diet was marginal in thiamine and calories and deficient in iron, riboflavin, vitamin A, and iodine (Berry, 1962b). For 33 infants studied at Arab communities in Israel, means were 71.7 cm and 8.39 kg (Zaizov & Laron, 1966), and for three Lebanese ethnic groups of low economic status residing at Beirut means were 73.7 cm and 9.13 kg for 103 Sunni infants, 74.1 cm and 9.50 kg for 94 Maronite infants and 74.4 cm and 9.61 kg for 104 Armenian infants (Harfouche, 1966).

Tag 67. Progeny of black parents of all socioeconomic levels living in the Mofakose township, 16 km from Salisbury. They were under health supervision at a child health clinic; their mothers were encouraged to start weaning 3 months after parturition, and dried skim milk was supplied from this time (Whittle, Whittle, & Wicks, 1970).

Tag 68. Offspring of native-born parents living in northwest Sardinia. Their mothers were given periodic advice on infant nutrition and health care (Aicardi & Depperu, 1966).

Tag 69. Progeny of "full-blood aborigines" studied at three coastal missions in Arnhem Land, Northern Territory. Their feeding was professionally supervised, but many had "intestinal and chest infections" (Kettle, 1966).

Tag 70. Measures amassed at 100 villages in eight provinces (Palacios-Mateos, Garcia-Almansa, Vivanco, Fernández, Garcia-Robles, & Moreno-Esteban, 1970).

Tag 71. Subgroup means of 70.9 cm and 8.00 kg were secured on 36 infants of low economic status and 75.6 cm and 9.85 kg on 26 infants of high status (Rea, 1971).

Tag 72. Offspring predominantly of black parents living in an agricultural region 24 km from Kingston. They were under pediatric guidance, and their mothers were periodically advised on infant care (Desai, Miall, & Standard, 1969). Thirty infants residing in a rural area 2.1–2.7 km northwest of Kingston gave means of 71.0 cm and 8.17 kg; these infants had few diseases or parasitic infections and showed no overt signs of malnutrition, but their diet was low in protein and calories (Ashcroft, Lovell, George, & Williams, 1965). Means of 73.9 cm and 9.21 kg were obtained on 256 predominantly black progeny of Kingston "working class" families (Grantham-McGregor et al., 1972).

Tag 73. Refer to tag 20. Other means on North American black groups were 74.1 cm and 9.28 kg for 533 "poverty area" infants studied in health care projects of the United States Children's Bureau (Mortison, 1969); 74.4 cm and 9.70 kg on about 100 healthy infants of Washtenaw County, Mich. (Robson, Larkin, Bursick, & Perri, 1975); 74.9 cm and 10.10 kg on more than 500 middle-class infants measured at Oakland (Wingerd, Schoen, & Solomon, 1971); 75.7 cm and 9.40 kg on 69 offspring of low-income families living in Washington, D.C. (Verghese, Scott, Teixiera, & Ferguson, 1969); and 9.78 kg for 52 healthy, well-nourished infants studied at Dallas (Fry, Howard, & Logan, 1975).

Tag 74. Progeny of parents living in a rural region near Olomouc (Holibková & Holibka, 1968). For body length, a mean 2.8 cm higher was obtained from measures taken on 500 infants representing "the normal population in Brno" (Gerylovová & Bouchalová, 1974).

Tag 75. Infants living in the capital of the Byelorussian S.S.R. Means from data collected at other cities in the Soviet Union were (n = 144) 73.7 cm, 10.01 kg at Astrakhan; (n = 257) 74.1 cm, 10.19 kg at Yaroslavl; (n = 129) 74.7 cm, 10.02 kg at Rostov-on-Don (Goldfeld et al., 1965); (n = 425) 75.1 cm, 10.11 kg at Moscow (Goldfeld et al., 1965; Kogan, 1969); (n = 207) 75.3 cm. 10.71 kg at Murmansk (Lapitskii, Belogorskii, Nemzer, Pogorely, Sinopalnikov, & Zolotareva, 1970). The Murmansk means exceed the Minsk means by 2 percent for length and 9 percent for weight.

Tag 76. Offspring of parents residing at Yemenite communities in Israel (Zaizov & Laron, 1966).

Tag 77. Means for about 700 urban infants were higher by 1.2 cm and 0.48 kg (Tănasescu, Chiriac, Stanciulescu, Domilescu, & Jelezneac, 1970).

Tag 78. Infants attending the Harcourt Health Center. Subgroup means for body length were 73.6 cm on 250 infants of low economic status and 74.8 cm on 47 infants of middle status (Low, 1971). From records on 210 infants living in the south-central part of Singapore Island, means of 73.9 cm and 8.70 kg were reported; about 68 percent of these infants had Chinese progenitors, and the remainder had mainly Malay and Hindu progenitors (Wong, Tye, & Quek, 1972).

Tag 79. Physically normal "white, negro, and brown infants" (Musso & Musso, 1964).

Tag 80. Progeny of the "underprivileged class" living in an urban suburb of Santo Domingo (Hernández, 1966).

Tag 81. Infants measured at consultation and outpatient clinics (Lanza & Bolgiani, 1965). Means from groups studied in other parts of Italy were 73.4 cm and 9.73 kg on about 70 infants living in the district of Novi Ligure (Lanzavecchia & Mazzarello, 1965), 74.1 cm and 10.15 kg on 58 infants residing in the province of Massa-Carrara (Venezia, Previtera, & Vignale, 1965), 75.0 cm and 10.02 kg on more than 100 infants residing in the province of Aquila (DeMatteis, Cantalini, Cinque, & Vesi, 1972), 75.1 cm and 9.94 kg on about 390 infants living at Bologna (Grandi, 1965; Tonelli & Marinelli, 1963) and 77.3 cm and 10.36 kg for 1286 infants living in the province of Grosseto (Terrosi, 1968).

Tag 82. Offspring of parents in the professional and managerial classes (Luna-Jaspe et al., 1970).

Tag 83. Data collected under the auspices of the Bulgarian Academy of Sciences (Yanev, 1965).

Tag 84. Progeny of Turkish parents (Soysal, Gürson, & Neyzi, 1960). A later Istanbul study gave means of 76.0 cm for 1748 progeny of well-to-do families and 71.2 cm for 85 offspring of parents living in "an underdeveloped area" (Neyzi, 1967).

Tag 85. Infants of middle-class families living under economic circumstances comparable with the Oakland black infants of tag 73. Other means secured from North American white samples were 74.6 cm and 9.57 kg for 213 "poverty area" infants (Systems Development Project Staff, 1968); 75.3 cm and 9.90 kg for about 140 healthy infants of Washtenaw County, Mich. (Robson et al., 1975); and, for 208 infants measured in states representative of the North-Central region, 75.9 cm and 10.20 kg (Fryer, Lamkin, Vivian, Eppright, & Fox, 1972).

Tag 86. Refer to tag 46. A sample of similar size studied at Warsaw gave means of 76.0 cm and 10.26 kg (Kurniewicz-Witczakowa et al., 1972; Wolanski, 1964).

Tag 87. Approximately 84 percent of the parents were Helsinki residents, and 16 percent resided in the vicinity of Helsinki (Bäckström & Kantero, 1971).

Tag 88. Data collected at infant centers; sample considered representative for the Netherlands as a whole (Wieringen, 1972).

For age 1 year, drawing from Table 9–3 and its complementary materials—all pertaining to averages for persons of both sexes taken together—the following are found:

1. In the period between 1960 and 1970, infants of the Netherlands were larger than their age peers of East Pakistan by 10 cm, (15 percent) in mean body length, and 3.3 kg (47 percent) in mean body weight.

2. Means for body length were near 68 cm for Bundi infants of New Guinea and Ladino infants of Guatemala; 70 cm for Tunisian infants at Chott el Djerid and Javanese infants at a Sumatra plantation; 72 cm for Sardinian infants and Lunda infants of Angola; 74 cm for Singaporian infants and Maronite infants of Beirut; and 76 cm for infants of Brno and Warsaw. In each instance, sample size was 80 or more.

3. Body weight means near 7.5 kg, 8.5 kg, 9.5 kg, and 10.5 kg were obtained on Javanese, Australian Aborigine, Yemenite, and Tasmanian infants respectively. Other means were near 7.0 kg for Lumi infants of New Guinea, 8.0 kg for Basotho infants of Lesotho and Kaiapit infants of New Guinea, 9.0 kg for Shona infants of Rhodesia and Baganda infants of Uganda, and 10.0 kg for infants of Astrakhan, Lublin, Oakland, and Rostov-on-Don.

4. Means for body length were 72.0 cm at Poona for infants reared under "near optimal" conditions of diet and health care and, for infants of upper-class families, 73.4 cm at Delhi, 74.1 cm at Bogotá, 75.6 cm at Lagos, and 76.0 cm at Istanbul. The Poona mean was 2.6 cm lower than the mean for "poverty area" white infants of the United States. The body weight mean for United States black infants living in poverty areas was 8 percent higher than that for Uganda village infants selected as "not malnourished."

5. Statistically evaluated at $p = 0.01$, using population standard deviations of 3.0 cm and 1.1 kg, 1-year-old Hindu rural infants of low economic status living in the vicinity of Hyderabad were shorter and lighter than their age peers of high economic status living at Delhi (by more than 4.0 cm and 1.3 kg). The same procedure indicated that infants lacking any overt sign of malnutrition were, on average, at least 4.0 cm longer and 1.9 kg heavier for Thai at Bangkok than for Hindu at Bhopal and Gwalior.

Cephalothoracic Index and its Components at Age 1 Year

Table 9–4 presents, for age 1 year, statistics for the same variables dealt with at birth in Table 9–2. As indicated in the first column and second footnote of Table 9–4 all but one of the ethnic groups represented were described earlier.

As at birth, some studies at age 1 year included findings for head girth but not for chest girth. Means reported for head girth were 41.0 cm on 174 Hindu infants of Calcutta (tag 60); 43.9 cm on 210 Singaporian infants (tag 78); 45.7 cm on 180 black infants of New Orleans (tag 73); and, at Oakland, 46.5 cm on more than 1000 white infants and 46.6 cm on more than 500 black infants (tags 73 and 85).

Selected findings, specific for the period 1960–1970, are as follows:

1. At age 1 year, means for head girth were near 41 cm on Hindu infants at Calcutta; 44 cm on Singaporian infants and Ladino infants of Guatemala; and 47 cm on Polish infants at Warsaw. Means near 44.5 cm, 46.5 cm, and 48.5 cm typified black infants at Washington, D.C., Polish infants at Lublin, and Russian infants at Murmansk, respectively. The value obtained at Murmansk was 7.8 cm (19 percent) larger than that at Calcutta.
2. The cephalothoracic index at age 1 year was below 100 on Hindu, Ladino, Tunisian, and U.S. black infants; it was above 100 on Italian, Bulgarian, Polish, and Sardinian infants. Part of the difference between any pair of index means

TABLE 9–4 Mean Head Girth (cm), Chest Girth (cm), and Cephalothoracic Index on Infants of Both Sexes Age 1 Year Studied Between 1960 and 1970

| | | Number | Mean Girth | | Chest Girth × 100 |
Tag	Ethnic Group	Measured	Head	Chest	Head Girth
45	Hindu, Hyderabad region	87	42.7	40.7	95
7	Hindu, Bombay	50	43.7	42.5	97
62	Tunisian, Chott el Djerid	138	44.3	43.0	97
75	Russian, Murmansk	207	48.8	47.2	97
12	Ladino, rural Guatemala	342	43.8	43.1	98
60	Hindu, Delhi	973	43.8	43.1	98
73	Black, Washington, D.C.	69	44.6	43.7	98
80	Dominican, Santo Domingo	~80	44.8	44.4	99
64	Ugandan, Namulonge	38	45.6	45.1	99
55	Thai, Bangkok	~130	44.7	44.7	100
53	Cambodian, Pnompenh area	~200	45.2	45.3	100
89	German, Hamburg & Kiel*	68	45.6	46.0	101
48	Sardihian, Sassari prov.	992	45.1	45.9	102
53	Italian, Aquila province	>100	45.7	46.4	102
30	Russian, Yaroslavl	257	46.5	47.5	102
86	Polish, Lublin	248	46.5	47.8	103
75	Russian, Minsk	268	46.5	47.7	103
86	Polish, Warsaw	~230	46.9	48.3	103
81	Italian, Grosseto prov.	1,286	47.6	49.0	103
83	Bulgarian, Sofia	565	46.0	47.4	103
81	Italian, Bologna	200	45.6	48.1	105

*Measured at infant homes and welfare clinics (Spranger, Ochsenfarth, Kock, & Henke, 1968). For head girth, standard error of the mean is near 0.16 cm where $n = 70$, 0.09 cm where $n = 200$, and 0.04 cm where $n = 1000$. Corresponding values for chest girth are 0.27, 0.16 and 0.07 cm.

(e.g., part of the difference between means for Minsk and Murmansk) may arise from systematic variation in the two studies regarding level of placement, or tension applied, in use of the measuring tape (see Meredith, 1946; 1970).
3. During infancy, chest girth relative to head girth increases. In eight instances, the same ethnic groups appear in Tables 9–2 and 9–4; the indices of these groups average 95 at birth (chest girth 95 percent of head girth) and 100 at age 1 year (thoracic and cephalic circumferences equal).

Skelic Index at Age 1 Year
As indicated previously, from studies reporting means for vertex–soles length and vertex–rump length it is possible to derive lower limb length and compute the skelic index (lower limb length X 100/stem length). Skelic indices for infants age 1 year were 65 on black infants at Washington, D.C. (tag 73), 61 on Tunisian infants at Chott el Djerid and Hindu infants at Delhi (tags 60 and 62), 59 on German infants at Hamburg and Kiel (tag 89), 58 on Jamaican infants at Kingston, Hindu infants at Calcutta, and Hindu infants inhabiting a rural area near Hyderabad (tags 19, 59, and 60), and 54 for Bulgarian infants at Sofia (tag 83).

Lower limb length relative to length of the body stem increases during infancy. Index values obtained at birth and age 1 year were 54 and 61 on infants at Delhi (Banik et al., 1970), 51 and 58 on Jamaican infants (tag 19), and, from earlier (1947–1957) data for other ethnic groups, 49 and 58 on black infants at Philadelphia (Kasius, Randall, Tompkins, & Wiehl, 1957), 50 and 55 on white infants of New Jersey (Kornfeld, 1954), and 51 and 56 on Japanese infants at Tokyo (Sato, 1957).

CHILDHOOD

Height of Rural Children at Ages 5 and 8 Years
Erect standing height in childhood has been studied since the 1760s (Scammon, 1927). A study in the early 1830s obtained averages of 95.2 cm at age 5 years and 112.7 cm at age 8 years on Belgian children from "all classes of society" living at Brussels (Quetelet, 1836). Averages secured from measures taken at Brussels during 1960–1961 were higher by 12.2 cm and 13.7 cm at ages 5 years and 8 years, respectively (Twiesselmann, 1969).

Displayed in Table 9–5 are statistics for standing height based on data gathered between 1960 and 1970 on groups of children inhabiting hamlets, villages, and small towns in rural regions of the earth. Groups not described previously are as follows:

Tag 90. Refer to tag 55 (Berry, 1962a). At age 5 years, a mean 9.5 cm higher (104.6 cm) was reported from measures on 243 healthy children of middle-class families residing at Bangkok (Khanjanasthiti et al., 1973).

Tag 91. Members of the Cakchiqual tribe living at villages in the highland mountains at elevations near 0.9 km. Their diet included few fruits and "little animal protein" (Méndez & Behrhorst, 1963; Sabharwal, Morales, & Méndez, 1966).

Tag. 92. Children with Malay or Chinese progenitors living in the Muar rural health district southeast of Malacca; a "low-income group" (Wadsworth & Lee, 1960).

Tag 93. Residents of a rural region and small town located at altitudes from 4.0 to 5.5 km. Their diet was evaluated as adequate in calories, protein, and iron (Frisancho & Baker, 1970). The parents were about 95 percent Quechua indigenes and 5 percent mestizos; they resided in the district of Nuñoa and were largely pastoralists or agriculturalists.

TABLE 9-5 Standing Height (cm) of Children of Both Sexes Measured Between 1960 and 1970 at Rural Locations in Different Parts of the World

Tag	Ethnic Group	Age 5 Years n	Age 5 Years Mean	Age 8 Years n	Age 8 Years Mean
57	Bundi, New Guinea	87	93.3	121	106.2
90	Thai, Thailand villages	78	95.0	57	111.3
91	Cakchiqual, Guatemala	—	—	55	111.8
92	Malayan, Muar district	—	—	51	112.3
93	Quechua, Peruvian Andes	24	95.2	73	115.3
2	Lumi, New Guinea	44	95.6	25	107.4
94	Hindu, Poona region	~800	95.7	100	113.8
4	Lunda, Angola villages	1,640	96.4	1,615	111.3
95	Zapotec, rural Mexico	—	—	43	113.1
96	Burmese, Burma villages	89	96.7	97	113.4
97	Trio & Wajana, Surinam	—	—	55	114.0
12	Ladino, Guatemala villages	294	97.8	—	—
98	Taiwan aborigine	—	—	355	114.7
99	Lufa, New Guinea	84	98.4	—	—
100	Bolivian, Bolivia	—	—	83	116.3
11	Javanese, Sumatra	100	99.7	100	116.4
101	Chuvash, Chuvashia	223	100.8	240	118.0
62	Tunisian, Chott el Djerid	92	100.8	—	—
102	Turkish, rural Turkey	—	—	~200	118.0
103	Galla, Ijaji	50	101.2	45	118.2
104	Nivkn, Sakhalin Island	43	102.3	48	116.1
105	Indonesian, rural Surinam	463	102.7	825	117.6
106	Puerto Rican, Puerto Rica	~70	102.9	~75	118.1
107	Tatar, rural Tatarstan	—	—	200	118.8
108	Kirghiz, Kirghiz S.S.R.	—	—	183	119.0
109	Tswana & Pedi, Transvaal	128	103.5	40	121.6
110	Spanish, rural Spain	10,470	103.8	14,506	120.4
111	Japanese, Kagawa prefecture	~2,700	103.9	~6,600	119.4
112	Eskimo, Quebec	—	—	33	119.7
66	Lebanese, Lebanon	88	103.9	165	121.5
113	Mexican, Colorado & Mexico	43	104.0	~200	116.9
114	Hindu, Surinam	1,516	104.3	2,203	119.8
115	Gypsy, Czechoslovakia	—	—	108	120.1
116	Moldavian, Moldavian S.S.R.	—	—	487	120.6
117	Black, east-central Jamaica	146	104.5	120	120.7
118	Polish, rural Poland	58	104.6	106	121.0
119	Australian aborigine	67	104.9	42	124.8
15	Bushnegro, Surinam	90	105.0	132	121.9
120	Bulgarian, Bulgarian villages	479	105.3	349	122.8
121	Lithuanian, Lithuanian S.S.R.	—	—	229	123.0
122	Fijian, Fiji Islands	178	105.7	145	123.8
123	Creole, Surinam	599	106.5	631	123.3
124	Russian, Komi S.S.R.	192	108.2	303	124.4
125	Cree, Quebec & Ontario	—	—	82	124.8
126	Maori, New Zealand	—	—	399	126.3
127	Amerind, Montana	57	108.8	127	126.8
128	Czech, Czechoslovakia	124	108.8	40	128.1

At age 5 years, standard error of the mean approximates 0.79 cm where $n = 40$, 0.50 cm where $n = 100$, 0.29 cm where $n = 300$, and 0.13 cm where $n = 1500$. At age 8 years, corresponding values are 0.95, 0.60, 0.35, and 0.15 cm.

287

Tag 94. Refer to tag 59. A mean of 112.4 cm was obtained on 785 children age 8 years living at villages in Palghar Taluk; nutritional status was rated poor or very poor for 13 percent of these children (Shah & Udani, 1968).

Tag 95. Rural residents of the Oaxaca Valley, considered to typify Zapotec-speaking pueblos of Mexico (Malina, Selby, & Swartz, 1972).

Tag 96. Inhabitants of several scattered villages in Burma. They showed no sign of caloric insufficiency, protein inadequacy, or deficiency of vitamins A, C, or D, but iodine, riboflavin, and thiamine intakes were low (Berry, 1963).

Tag. 97. Individuals of two Amerind tribes living in the tropical forest. They appeared "fit, well-nourished, and in good health" (Glanville & Geerdink, 1970).

Tag 98. Members of the Ami, Yami, Atayal, and Paiwan tribes. There were "frequent nutritional deficiency signs" (Chen, Chiang, Huang, & Chen, 1974).

Tag 99. Rural children residing in the Lufa subdistrict of the eastern highlands. A mean of 99.8 cm was obtained on 52 Melanesian children age 5 years living in villages on Karkar Island (Harvey, 1974; R. G . Harvey, personal communication, 1974).

Tag 100. Residents of rural communities and small towns located in west-central Bolivia at elevations from 0.2 to 4.1 km. Their parents were Aymara, people of Spanish lineage, or Spanish-Amerind hybrids; nutrition was poor and infection common (Omran, McEwen, & Zaki, 1967).

Tag 101. Chuvash (predominantly Turko-Tatar) people living on collective farms in the Kanashsky region of the Chuvash S.S.R. (Goldfeld et al., 1965).

Tag 102. Inhabitants of the Etimesgut area (Nashed & Bertan, 1968). A mean of 120.2 cm was obtained from data on 21,413 individuals measured in a school survey covering "each of the Egyptian governates" (McDowell, Taskar, & Sarhan, 1970).

Tag 103. Individuals measured at a typical Ethiopian highland agricultural village about 215 km west of Addis Ababa; mainly Galla, with some Amhara and Gourage; infections and "mild–moderate protein-calorie malnutrition" were common (Hofvander & Eksmyr, 1971).

Tag 104. Members of the largest ethnic group on this island off eastern Siberia, north of Japan (Arkhipova, 1967).

Tag 105. People of Indonesian descent living in agricultural areas (Kuyp, 1967).

Tag 106. A sample representative of Puerto Rican isolated rural communities. Diet was appraised as deficient in calories, calcium, vitamin A, riboflavin, and iron (Fernández, Burgos, Asenjo, & Rosa, 1969).

Tag 107. Turkic Tatar people living at rural villages in the northeast part of the Tatar S.S. R. (Goldfeld et al., 1965).

Tag 108. Rural residents of the Kirghiz S.S.R. drawn partly from settlements at elevations of 2.3 –2.8 km in the Osh district of the Pamir-Altai mountains and partly from villages at elevations near 0.7 km in the Kirov district of the Frunze region. Subgroup means were 119.4 cm for the low-altitude sample ($n = 121$) and 118.2 cm for the high-altitude group ($n = 62$); the high-altitude pastoral families were isolated from main transport routes (Miklashevskaya, Solovieva, & Godina, 1973).

Tag 109. At age 5 years, members of the Tswana, Nguni, and Shangaan tribes living in northeast and east Transvaal (B. D. Richardson, personal communication, 1974). Other reported means at this age were 97.5 cm on 367 Shi children of Zaire (tag 64); 99.2 cm on 56 children, largely of the Pare, Shambala, and Chagga tribes, living at highland and lowland villages in northeast Tanzania (Kreysler & Schlage, 1969); 100.3 cm on 34 children, "mostly Mandinkas," measured at hinterland villages about 160 km from Bathurst, Gambia (McGregor,

Rahman, Thompson, Billewicz, & Thomson, 1968); 101.1 cm on about 35 members of the Angus and Sura tribes "in good nutritional state" residing at villages in the Pankshin area of the Jos plateau, Nigeria (Collis, Dema, & Lesi, 1962); and 103.6 cm on 217 Hutu children of Rwanda (tag 64). At age 8 years, the tabled values were obtained on members of the Pedi tribe living at Kgolokoe's Location, Sekhukhuniland (Leary, 1968). In Tanzania, means secured at this age were 116.1 cm on 47 rural children residing in the Kilimanjaro and Tanga regions (Kreysler & Schlage, 1969); 117.4 cm on 22 members of the Nyakyusa tribe residing in the Rungwe district, elevation about 1.5 km, under "healthy and prosperous" conditions (Hautvast, 1971); and 118.8 cm on 22 members of the Kisi tribe living at isolated villages on the northeast shore of Lake Nyassa in an "unhealthy and poor" area (Hautvast, 1971). A mean of 122.6 cm was obtained in Ghana on about 180 black persons age 8 years measured at villages in the Tonu, Lower Volta district between Accra and Lome (Fiawoo, 1973).

Tag 110. Inhabitants of 136 villages in 48 Spanish provinces (Palacios-Mateos & Vivanco, 1965).

Tag 111. Individuals residing in agricultural areas of this prefecture (Kambara, 1969; T. Kambara, personal communication, 1973).

Tag 112. Persons living at four settlements on the east coast of Hudson Bay (Partington & Roberts, 1969).

Tag 113. At age 8 years, refer to tag 10. The data at age 5 years were collected in Colorado on children of migrant Mexican farm laborers (Chase, Kumar, Dodds, Sauberlich, Hunter, Burton, & Spalding, 1971). A mean of 105.1 cm at age 5 years was obtained on 96 private and public kindergarten children measured at Navojoa (Adriano & Sánchez, 1975).

Tag 114. Inhabitants of rural regions in Surinam whose progenitors came from India and Pakistan (Kuyp, 1967). On 595 Hindu-Guyanese children age 8 years living in rural settings typical of sugar and rice agriculture, a mean of 120.5 cm was secured. The ancestors of these children came largely from Uttar Pradesh and Bihar; overt signs of malnutrition or hookworm disease were rare (Ashcroft, Bell, & Nicholson, 1968).

Tag 115. Romi residing in Bohemian and Slovakian districts (Suchy & Malá, 1973).

Tag 116. Sample drawn from several rural areas (Goldfeld et al., 1965).

Tag 117. Persons "predominantly of West African ancestry" living in the Glengoffe rural region. Their diet was low in calories and protein, but they showed no overt sign of malnutrition or disease (Ashcroft et al., 1965). A mean of 121.4 cm at age 8 years was reported on 660 children of "predominantly African descent" living in typical rural areas of St. Vincent Island (Ashcroft & Antrobus, 1970).

Tag 118. Individuals residing in the Ostroleka and Suwalki districts at villages far removed from urban centers (Wolanski & Pyzuk, 1973). From rural data collected in the Lublin district, means were 105.6 cm ($n = 182$) at age 5 years and 122.8 cm at age 8 years ($n = 184$) (Chrzastek-Spruch & Dobosz-Latalska, 1973; H. Chrzastek-Spruch, personal communication, 1974). Other means reported for age 8 years were 122.5 and 122.9 cm on 162 and 137 inhabitants of the Puck and Nowy Targ districts, respectively; 122.9 and 125.4 cm on 1434 children measured in Brzeziny county, near Lodz and on 56 children living in the vicinity of Nowa Huta, respectively (Mackiewicz, Romejko, Mirota, Sejmicka, Szeszenia, & Swiderska, 1967; Pyzuk & Wolanski, 1968; Wojtowicz & Miaskiewicz, 1966).

Tag 119. The statistics at age 5 years were obtained at coastal missions on "full-blood" persons reared under "communal feeding . . . designed to provide extra nourishment" (Kettle, 1966). At age 8 years, people were measured at the Yuendumu settlement 290 km northwest of Alice Springs; and about 90 percent were Wailbri and 10 percent Pintubi (Brown & Barrett, 1971).

Tag 120. Inhabitants of representative Bulgarian villages (Yanev, 1965).

Tag 121. Village residents of the Moletsk area (Goldfeld et al., 1965).

Tag 122. Melanesian inhabitants of coastal villages in the Fiji Archipelago; about 3 percent showed borderline malnutrition (Hawley & Jansen, 1971).

Tag 123. Rural Creole (mixed black and mulatto) people living in the Coronie district and Para settlements (Kuyp, 1967). On 437 members of black families who typically cultivated crops on small farms in Guyana, a mean of 124.2 cm was obtained; there were few overt signs of malnutrition (Ashcroft et al., 1968).

Tag 124. Inhabitants of rural areas in the Udor region (Martirosian, 1973). Other means for rural Russians age 8 years were ($n = 320$) 119.3 cm, Buinak region; ($n = 211$) 121.2 cm, Ulyanovsk region; ($n = 207$) 121.4 cm, Moscow region; ($n = 203$) 121.6 cm, Kalinin region; ($n = 201$) 121.9 cm, Pskov region; ($n = 215$) 122.1 cm, Ryazan region; ($n = 211$) 122.5 cm, Stavropol territory; ($n = 368$) 122.8 cm, Altai territory; ($n = 219$) 123.1 cm, Vitebsk region; and, for native-born Ukrainians living in the Kiev region, ($n = 357$) 123.2 cm. (Goldfeld et al., 1965; Kerimov, 1968; Litichevskii, 1966; Morozova & Boldurchidi, 1965).

Tag 125. Amerinds living in the James Bay area at small towns and coastal settlements south of the treeline (Partington & Roberts, 1969). Johnston, McKigney, Hopwood, and Smelker (1978) obtained a mean of 125.5 cm on 81 Chippewa children age 8 years, measured in 1965 at the Red Lake reservation in northern Minnesota.

Tag 126. New Zealanders "having 50 percent or more Polynesian ancestry" (New Zealand Department of Health, 1971).

Tag 127. Members of the Assiniboine, Blackfoot, and Gros Ventres tribes residing on the Blackfoot and Fort Belknap reservations. At each reservation diet was appraised as inadequate in calories, protein, calcium, iron, and vitamins A and C (Fisk, 1964a; 1964c).

Tag 128. Findings at age 5 years on inhabitants of a rural region near Olomouc (Holibková & Holibkova, 1968) and, at age 8 years, on inhabitants of a rural region near Podebrady (Hrubcová, 1963).

When a sample from an ethnic group is measured, the objective is to gain knowledge regarding the group, or population, of which it is a part. Quantitative comparisons among the ethnic groups represented in, or associated with, Table 9–5 were derived as one-tail estimates at $p = 0.01$, using a population standard deviations 5.0 cm at age 5 years and 6.0 cm at age 8 years. Tenable generalizations for standing height in the period between 1960 and 1970 include the following:

1. Bundi children of New Guinea were shorter than their Amerind age peers of Montana by more than 12.5 cm at age 5 years and 18.0 cm at age 8 years.
2. Lunda children of rural Angola were shorter than their Creole age peers of rural Surinam by at least 9.0 cm at age 5 years and 11.0 cm at age 8 years.
3. At age 5 years, children living in the Udor rural region of the Komi Soviet Socialist Republic were taller than their age peers living in rural communities around Poona by more than 11.0 cm. At age 8 years, compared with Cakchiqual children of rural Guatemala, Cree children of eastern Canada were taller by at least 9.5 cm.
4. Village children of the Fiji Islands were taller than village children of Thailand by no less than 8.5 cm at age 5 years and 9.5 cm at age 8 years.
5. Average standing height at age 5 years was near 104 cm on Hindu children residing in rural areas of Surinam and on rural children of Kagawa prefecture, Lebanon, and Spain. At age 8 years, average height was near 118 cm on groups of rural Chuvash, Ethiopian, Turkish, and Puerto Rican children.

Height of Environmentally Privileged Children at Ages 5 and 8 Years

Brought together in Table 9–6 are means for erect standing height at two childhood ages on environmentally privileged ethnic groups of both sexes. As before, succinct row-by-row elaboration will precede extraction of comparative findings.

Tag 129. Children attending "preparatory schools in the wealthier suburbs of Kingston." Many were grandchildren of persons born in southern China (Ashcroft & Lovell, 1964).

Tag 130. Offspring of wealthy Hindu families. They were "well privileged" in respect to health care and good nutrition (Banik, Nayer, Krishna, & Raj, 1972).

Tag 131. Children of southern Chinese, mainly Kwangtung, ancestry. Their parents held "professional, managerial, or other leading positions" (Chang, Lee, Low, & Kvan, 1963; Low, 1971).

TABLE 9–6 Mean Standing Height (cm) of Groups of Environmentally Privileged and Moderately Privileged Children of Both Sexes Studied During 1960–1970

		Age 5 Years		Age 8 Years	
Tag	Ethnic Group	n	Mean	n	Mean
	Privileged: upper classes				
129	Jamaican Chinese, Kingston	27	105.9	30	121.8
130	Hindu, Delhi	46	106.7	—	—
131	Chinese, Hong Kong	—	—	364	123.2
9	Colombian, Bogotá	64	107.5	—	—
132	Turkish, Istanbul	>70	107.8	>70	124.6
133	Chilean, Santiago	~35	109.0	—	—
134	Jamaican white, Kingston	76	109.1	119	127.4
135	Russian, Petropavlovsk	186	109.4	—	—
136	Hindu elite, India	~34	109.7	982	125.3
137	Baganda, Uganda	—	—	283	126.0
138	Ghana black, Accra	—	—	~50	127.2
139	Yoruba, Ibadan	185	110.2	85	127.3
140	White, Guatemala City	35	111.5	81	127.7
141	Jamaican black, Kingston	—	—	36	127.9
142	Ghana white, Accra	—	—	~35	128.1
143	Dutch, Netherlands	50	112.9	36	131.4
	Moderately privileged: middle and upper classes				
144	Ethiopian, Addis Ababa	81	104.1	81	121.6
145	Thai, Bangkok	243	104.6	—	—
146	Bantu, Johannesburg	134	105.8	—	—
147	Liberian, Monrovia	—	—	~55	120.3
148	Hindu, Poona	~200	107.1	—	—
149	Chilean, Santiago	141	107.6	—	—
150	Armenian, Beirut	179	108.6	—	—
151	Sara, Fort-Archambault	63	109.0	52	123.8
152	Hindu, Kerala	~60	109.2	—	—
153	Spanish, Madrid	100	110.4	200	127.1
154	Puerto Rican, San Juan	—	—	138	128.1
155	White, United States	—	—	178	128.3

Tag 132. Children of the upper social classes living in the Nisantasi area. They were measured in private pediatric practice; their parents were judged to have "good educational and cultural standards" (Neyzi & Gürson, 1966).

Tag 133. Inhabitants of the best residential section of Santiago. They represented "a population where malnutrition was practically nonexistent" (Barja, La-Fuente, Ballester, Mönckeberg, & Donoso, 1965).

Tag 134. Offspring of "prosperous" families. They were measured at "fee-paying preparatory schools in the wealthier suburbs of Kingston;" most of them were born in Jamaica (Ashcroft & Lovell, 1964).

Tag 135. Children reared under superior environmental conditions (Neki-sheva, 1974). Besides tripartite classification on the basis of living conditions, the 554 children measured were classified in terms of family income; the mean for 122 progeny of high-income parents was 109.5 cm.

Tag 136. At age 5 years, persons of "the best socioeconomic group" in Bombay (Udani, 1963); at age 8 years, individuals of socially elite families measured at residential private schools in different parts of India (Raghavan, Singh, & Swaminathan, 1971).

Tag 137. Bantu girls, from well-to-do families, attending a private school near Kampala. They received excellent dietary and health care (Burgess & Burgess, 1964). Sex-specific means from large samples of Lunda and Creole children age 8 years were as high for females as for males (David, 1972; Kuyp, 1967).

Tag 138. Persons attending expensive private schools. Their parents were "wealthy or highly educated" (Fiawoo, 1973).

Tag 139. Yoruba children of well-to-do families (Janes, 1974; M. D. Janes, personal communication, 1975).

Tag 140. Persons predominantly of Spanish descent attending private schools in Guatemala City. They were born in Guatemala, reared in homes of upper and upper-middle socioeconomic status, and educated in an environment of sound nutrition, health care, and physical activity (Johnston, Wainer, Thissen, & Mac-Vean, 1976; Méndez & Behrhorst, 1963; Sabharwal et al., 1966).

Tag 141. Jamaican children of West African ancestry attending tuition preparatory schools in the wealthier suburbs (Ashcroft & Lovell, 1964).

Tag 142. Individuals attending the same private schools as the "privileged" group of tag 138. Their parents held "key positions . . . in government, education, commerce and diplomatic fields" (Fiawoo, 1973).

Tag 143. Offspring of Dutch parents in the professional and major managerial strata (Wieringen, 1972).

Tag 144. Children of upper- and middle-class families attending private schools and "living under relatively good socioeconomic conditions." They were largely Amhara, with some representation of Tigre, Galla, and Gourage (Eksmyr, 1971).

Tag 145. Healthy, well-nourished Thai children of "middle and professional class families" (Khanjanasthiti et al., 1973).

Tag 146. Children of the Tswana, Nguni, and Shangaan tribes attending nursery schools in Soweto. They ate two meals daily at school and were almost free of protein-calorie malnutrition (Richardson, 1973; B. D. Richardson, personal communication, 1974).

Tag 147. Healthy children belonging largely to middle and upper socioeconomic groups. Non-Liberian children were excluded (Davies & Vardy-Cohen, 1962).

Tag 148. Children living in homes of above average socioeconomic status. They were in good health and showed "no clinical signs of malnutrition" (Limaye et al., 1974).

Tag 149. Offspring of "high middle class" parents. They were measured at several preschools (Montoya & Ipinza, 1964).

Tag 150. Children of Armenian ancestry belonging to "upper- and middle-class" families (S. J. Karayan, personal communication, 1976).

Tag 151. Black children living mainly in homes of middle and upper socioeconomic status at the principal city in the province of Moyen-Chari, Chad. They were in good health and showed no signs of malnutrition (Hiernaux & Asnes, 1974).

Tag 152. Children from homes of "high and middle socioeconomic groups" inhabiting the Cochin-Ernakulam-Alwaye zone of Kerala. They were measured at a health guidance clinic (Gokulanathan & Verghese, 1969).

Tag. 153. Healthy, well-nourished individuals measured at two schools in Madrid. The reported mean at age 5 years was for girls only (García-Almansa, Fernández-Fernández, & Palacios-Mateos, 1969).

Tag 154. Progeny of parents predominantly of Spanish lineage and middle to upper socioeconomic status (Knott, 1963).

Tag 155. Members of white families with an income in the mid-1960s of $10,000 or more (Hamill, Johnston, & Lemeshow, 1973b).

Table 9–6 shows that in the period 1960–1970 different ethnic groups of environmentally privileged children of the upper socioeconomic stratum varied in average standing height through a range approximating 7.0 cm at age 5 years and 9.5 cm at age 8 years. Means at age 5 years were near 106, 110, and 113 cm for children of Chinese ancestry at Kingston, Yoruba children at Ibadan, and Dutch children of the Netherlands, respectively. At age 8 years, low and high means were near 122 and 131 cm for Jamaican Chinese and Dutch children, respectively, with intermediate values near 125 cm on Turkish children at Istanbul, 126 cm on Baganda children of Uganda, and 128 cm on black children at Kingston and white children at Accra and Guatemala City.

It is left for the reader to draw comparative findings from the portion of Table 9–6 pertaining to moderately privileged children.

Skelic Index and its Components at Age 8 Years

This index of body form was studied in 1880 on children of German ancestry living at Milwaukee, Wisc.; at age 8 years, averages obtained were 65.1 cm for erect sitting height, 53.9 cm for lower limb height (standing height minus sitting height), and 83 for the skelic index ($n = 620$) (Peckham, 1881). Comparable values secured seven decades later on 329 German children measured at Kiel were 70.0 cm, 59.1 cm, and 84 (Jürgens, 1960).

Exhibited in Table 9–7 are means for sitting height, lower limb height, and the skelic index on children of both sexes age 8 years studied between 1960 and 1970.

Tag 156. Children measured in the Murat district. Ninety-four percent "of the fathers were factory workers, most of them unskilled" (Neyzi, Tanman, & Saner, 1965).

Tag 157. Records amassed during 1970 under the auspices of the Japanese Ministry of Education (K. Kimura, personal communication, 1973).

Tag 158. Residents of urban districts. Their progenitors were largely from the province of Kwangtung (Chan, 1972).

Tag 159. Mainly individuals of British ancestry. The sample included small numbers of Chinese, Hindus, and non-Maori Pacific islanders (New Zealand Department of Health, 1971). Almost identical findings were obtained from a United States "probability sample" of 1049 noninstitutionalized white children; specific values were 68.0 cm for sitting height, 58.7 cm for lower limb height, and 86 for the skelic index (Malina, Hamill, & Lemeshow, 1974).

Tag 160. These findings were reported by Pietrangeli & DiStefano (1962).

TABLE 9–7 Mean Sitting Height (cm), Lower Limb Height (cm), and Skelic Index at Age 8 Years on Groups of Children of Both Sexes Measured Between 1960 and 1970

Tag	Ethnic Group	Number Measured	Sitting Height	Lower limb Height	Skelic Index
93	Quechua, Peruvian Andes	73	64.9	50.4	78
156	Turkish, Istanbul	104	64.3	50.8	79
91	Cakchiquel, Guatemala	55	62.4	49.4	79
157	Japanese, Japan	18,268	68.0	54.5	80
57	Bundi, New Guinea	121	58.5	47.7	82
158	Chinese, Hong Kong	2,000	66.2	54.7	83
120	Bulgarian, rural	349	66.3	56.5	85
83	Bulgarian, Sofia	413	67.9	57.7	85
126	Maori, New Zealand	399	68.4	57.9	85
140	White, Guatemala City	46	69.0	58.9	85
159	White, New Zealand	1,801	68.1	58.8	86
128	Czech, Czechoslovakia	40	68.8	59.3	86
160	Italian, Chieti province	120	65.3	56.8	87
161	Hungarian, Budapest	445	68.1	59.0	87
162	German, Kiel & vicinity	102	69.5	60.8	87
60	Hindu, Bhopal & Gwalior	35	62.9	55.1	88
163	White, Havana	53	65.5	58.4	89
164	Yoruba, Ibadan	38	65.3	58.1	89
97	Trio & Wajana, Surinam	55	59.9	54.1	90
60	Hindu, Burla	60	59.8	55.2	92
73	Black, Washington, D.C.	102	65.9	61.5	93
151	Sara, Fort–Archambault	52	63.9	59.9	94
165	Black, Havana	33	64.6	61.1	95
109	Kisi & Nyakyusa, Tanzania	44	59.9	58.2	97

Taking population standard deviations at 3.0 cm for sitting height, 3.5 cm for lower limb height, and 4 for the skelic index, standard error of the mean values are 0.47 cm, 0.55 cm, and 0.6 where n = 40; 0.15 cm, 0.18 cm, and 0.2 where n = 400; and 0.07 cm, 0.08 cm, and 0.1 where n = 1000.

Tag 161. Data gathered during 1968–1969 (Eiben, Hegedüs, Bánhegyi, Kiss, Monda, & Tasnádi, 1971).

Tag 162. North German children measured at Kiel and its environs (Spranger et al., 1968).

Tags 163 and 165. These findings pertain to Cuban white children and Cuban black children excluding mulattoes (Laska-Mierzejewska, 1967).

Tag 164. More than 90 percent Yoruba, a few Ibo and others (Jürgens, Allan, & Tracey, 1964).

The skelic index column of Table 9–7 indicates the following for age 8 years:

1. Amerind, Bundi, Chinese, and Japanese children studied between 1960 and 1970 had relatively short lower limbs; their lower limb height averaged about 80 percent of sitting height.
2. Black children studied in Chad, Cuba, Nigeria, Tanzania, Surinam, and the United States had relatively long lower limbs; their lower limb height averaged between 90 percent and 97 percent of sitting height.
3. Intermediate indices, those from 85 to 87, characterized white children studied in Bulgaria, Czechoslovakia, Guatemala, Hungary, Italy, and West Germany.

Examination of the columns in Table 9-7 pertaining to components of the skelic index shows the following:

1. Means for sitting height varied from 58.5 cm on Bundi children of New Guinea to 69.5 cm on German children living in the region of Kiel; they were near 68 cm on Japanese and Maori children and on white children at Budapest and Sofia.
2. Means for lower limb height varied from 47.7 cm on Bundi children through 55 cm on Hindu children at Bhopal, Burla, and Gwalior to 61.5 cm on black children at Washington, D.C.

Head Width, Head Depth, and Cephalic Index at Age 8 Years

The cephalic index is defined as maximum transverse head diameter X 100/maximum anteroposterior head diameter. Means for the index and its components are displayed in Table 9-8.

Tag 166. Progeny of middle-class agriculturalists residing in Punjab (Bansal, 1969).

Tag 167. Inhabitants of a small Sunda island (Glinka, 1972).

Tag 168. Persons living at Gondar and nearby villages. There was "about equal mixture" of Amhara and Tigrinian tribes (Dellaportas, 1969).

Tags 169-173. Samples of physically normal Dutch (Hautvast, 1967), Belgian (Twiesselmann, 1969), Sicilian (Correnti, 1969), Russian (Miklashevskaya, 1966; 1969), and Chinese (Chang, Chan, & Low, 1967) people each studied at the city specified.

Tag 174. Individuals of mixed Mongoloid-Caucasian ancestry residing in the Uzbek Soviet Socialist Republic (Miklashevskaya, 1966; 1969).

TABLE 9-8 Means at Age 8 Years for Maximum Transverse and Anteroposterior Head Diameters (cm) and Cephalic Index on Children of Both Sexes Measured During 1960-1970

Tag	Ethnic Group	Number Measured	Head Width	Head Depth	Cephalic Index
109	Nyakyusa, Tanzania	22	13.5	18.1	75
166	Hindu, Amritsar region	74	13.1	17.3	76
167	Palue islander, Indonesia	58	13.4	17.6	76
109	Kisi, Tanzania	22	13.6	18.0	76
164	Yoruba, Ibadan	38	13.8	18.0	77
60	Hindu, Burla	60	13.8	17.7	78
151	Sara, Fort-Archambault	54	13.8	17.4	79
168	Ethiopian, Gondar region	303	13.5	16.8	80
160	Italian, Chieti province	120	13.8	17.3	80
169	Dutch, Nijmegen	71	14.1	17.6	80
170	Belgian, Brussels	875	14.3	17.7	81
171	Sicilian, Palermo	209	14.1	17.4	81
97	Trio & Wajana, Surinam	55	13.9	17.0	82
172	Russian, Moscow	124	14.7	17.4	84
173	Chinese, Hong Kong	1,906	14.3	17.0	84
118	Polish, rural region	99	—	—	85
115	Gypsy, Bohemia	39	—	—	86
174	Uzbek, Tashkent	130	14.9	16.4	91

For head width, standard error of mean approximates .09 cm where n = 40, .05 cm where n = 120, and .02 cm where n = 800. Corresponding values are .11 cm, .06 cm, and .02 cm for head depth and, for the cephalic index, 0.6%, 0.4%, and 0.1%.

Subjection of statistics from Table 9–8 to one-tail significance tests at $p = 0.01$ leads to the following generalizations, each specific for age 8 years and the calendar span from 1960 to 1970:

1. Mean biparietal head width was larger on Uzbek children at Tashkent than on Hindu rural children of Punjab state by an amount likely between 1.5 and 2.1 cm.
2. Mean glabelloopisthocranial head depth was smaller for Uzbek children of Tashkent than for Yoruba children at Ibadan by an amount probably exceeding 1.2 cm.
3. It is unlikely that the average cephalic index of the population on Palue Island was greater than 78 or that the corresponding value for the Uzbek population at Tashkent was less than 90. Cephalic index averages were between 75 and 78 on groups of black children in Chad, Nigeria, and Tanzania; they were between 80 and 85 on groups of white children in Belgium, Italy, Netherlands, Poland, Russia, and Sicily.

Shoulder Width, Hip Width, and Shoulder–Hip Index at Age 8 Years

Table 9–9 presents means for age 8 years for biacromial shoulder width, biiliocristal hip width, and the index hip width X 100/shoulder width.

Tags 175 and 178. Statistics based on measures taken in 1964 at Tokyo and during 1963–1964 at Tainan City (Kimura & Tsai, 1968).

Tag 176. Individuals measured at a farm village on the north side of the Motobu peninsula (Kimura, 1975a).

Tag 177. Sassari inhabitants whose parents were born in the province of Sassari (DeToni, Aicardi, & Podestà, 1966c; DeToni, Aicardi, & Rovetta, 1966d).

Tag 179. Data collected at schools in the capital of the Estonian S.S.R. (Heapost, 1973).

Tag 180. Residents of this southeastern Polish city (Chrzastek-Spruch & Szajner-Milart, 1974).

Tag 181. Members of North American white families in "the managerial and skilled trade occupational groups." About 60 percent had resided in the tropics more than 4 years (Eveleth, 1968).

Tag 182. Residents of Moscow measured during 1960–1961 (Solovyeva, 1964).

Tag 183. Records obtained at villages of the Ostroleka and Suwalki districts (Wolanski & Lasota, 1964; N. Wolanski, personal communication, 1972).

Table 9-9 indicates the following for the period 1960–1970:

1. Mean biacromial shoulder width at age 8 years was near 25 cm on Cakchiquel children of rural Guatemala; near 26 cm on Japanese, Taiwanese, and Kirghiz children at Tokyo, Tainan, and villages in the region of Frunze; and near 28 cm for Pedi children on a reserve in Transvaal and white children of above-average socioeconomic status living in Brazil.
2. Mean biiliocristal hip width at age 8 years was less than 19 cm on Cakchiquel children and black children of Chad, Cuba, Nigeria, Tanzania, and Transvaal. Means between 20 and 21 cm were secured from large samples of white children at Brussels, Budapest, Moscow, Palermo, and Sofia.
3. On black children at Fort-Archambault, Havana, Ibadan, and Washington, D.C., mean biiliocristal hip width was approximately 70 percent of mean biacromial shoulder width. Other indices were 72 on Japanese at Tokyo; 73 on Belgians at Brussels, Hungarians at Budapest, and Sardinians at Sassari; 74 on Estonians at

TABLE 9-9 Means at Age 8 Years for Shoulder Width (cm), Hip Width (cm), and Shoulder–Hip Index for Groups of Children of Both Sexes Measured Between 1960 and 1970

Tag	Ethnic Group	Number Measured	Shoulder Width	Hip Width	Shoulder–Hip Index
109	Pedi, Transvaal	40	28.1	18.7	67
109	Kisi, Tanzania	22	26.1	17.8	68
164	Yoruba, Ibadan	38	26.4	18.3	69
151	Sara, Fort–Archambault	52	25.5	17.5	69
73	Black, Washington, D.C.*	102	27.3	18.8	69
165	Black, Havana	69	26.6	18.6	70
140	White, Guatemala City	46	27.6	19.5	71
109	Nyakyusa, Tanzania	22	25.4	18.0	71
175	Japanese, Tokyo	230	26.1	18.7	72
176	Okinawan, Nakijin	26	26.4	18.9	72
170	Belgian, Brussels	875	27.3	20.0	73
161	Hungarian, Budapest	445	27.5	20.0	73
177	Sardinian, Sassari	170	26.8	19.5	73
178	Taiwanese, Tainan City	109	26.0	18.9	73
163	White, Havana	106	26.4	19.3	73
179	Estonian, Tallinn	376	27.4	20.4	74
180	Polish, Lublin	123	26.9	20.0	74
91	Cakchiquel, Guatemala	55	25.0	18.5	74
181	White, Rio de Janeiro	30	27.9	20.6	74
182	Russian, Moscow	478	27.3	20.4	75
183	Polish, rural districts	146	26.7	20.0	75
171	Sicilian, Palermo	209	27.1	20.2	75
108	Kirghiz, Kirghiz S.S.R.	183	26.2	19.7	75
120	Bulgarian, rural areas	349	26.9	20.4	76
83	Bulgarian, Sofia	414	27.2	20.6	76

*A sample of 182 black children measured in scattered regions of the United States gave values of 27.9 cm, 18.2 cm, and 65; from 1049 white children values were 27.7 cm, 19.4 cm, and 70 (Malina et al., 1974).
For shoulder width, standard error of the mean approximates 0.28 cm where $n = 40$, 0.18 cm where $n = 100$, and 0.09 cm where $n = 400$. Corresponding values are 0.25, 0.16, and 0.08 cm for hip width and 0.6, 0.4, and 0.2 for shoulder–hip index.

Tallinn and Poles at Lublin; 75 on Russians at Moscow and Sicilians at Palermo; and 76 on Bulgarians at Sofia.

Arm Girth and Calf Girth at Age 8 Years

On different ethnic groups, averages for arm girth (also for calf girth) spread across a 4.0 cm range. Obtained means for arm girth were 15.3 cm on 101 Tutsi of Rwanda (Hiernaux, 1965; Petit-Maire-Heintz, 1963), 16.3 cm on 52 Sara (tag 151), 16.4 cm on 55 Cakchiquel (tag 91), 16.7 cm on 209 Sicilians at Palermo (tag 171), 17.0 cm on 31 Trio and Wajana (tag 97), 17.2 cm on 22 Kisi (tag 109), 18.2 cm on 414 Bulgarians at Sofia (tag 83), 18.3 cm on 182 United States blacks (Table 9-9, second footnote), 18.4 cm on 875 Belgians at Brussels (tag 170), 18.7 cm on 1049 United States whites (tag 159), and 19.3 cm on 46 white private school children at Guatemala City (tag 140).

Means for calf girth were 22.5 cm on 22 Kisi, 22.8 cm on 31 Trio and Wajana, 23.0 cm on 101 Tutsi, 23.7 cm on 52 Sara, 24.1 cm on 209 Sicilian, 24.8 cm on 182 United

States black and 25.2 cm on 1049 white children, 25.5 cm on whites at Rio de Janeiro (tag 181), and 26.5 cm on 138 white of above-average socioeconomic status at San Juan (tag 154).

ADOLESCENCE

In the sections on infancy and childhood it was parsimonious and biologically defensible to pool the sexes; this procedure becomes untenable beyond childhood. For measures such as standing height, sitting height, shoulder width, hip width, arm girth, leg girth, and body weight, (1) females precede males in velocity increases during early adolescence and (2) from late adolescence into early adulthood sex differences get progressively larger (Meredith & Boynton, 1937; Roche & Davila, 1972; Shuttleworth, 1939).

This section will focus on age 13 years for females and age 15 years for males. At these ages, the sexes typically are at similar stages of somatologic development (Meredith, 1967).

Secular Change in Standing Height of Female Youths Age 13 Years

The standing height of female and male youths was studied prior to 1840 in Belgium (Quetelet, 1836), England (Horner, 1837), and France (Scammon, 1927). Horner, from measures on youths of Lancashire and Yorkshire, reported averages of 134.8 cm for females age 13 years and 145.8 cm for males age 15 years. Averages from data collected 111 years later "in widely scattered parts of England" were higher by 16.3 cm on females age 13 years and 17.4 cm on males age 15 years (Sutcliffe & Canham, 1950).

Displayed in Table 9-10 are statistics at age 13 years for groups of female youths measured recently and comparable groups measured at earlier times, 22–126 years ago. Columns 3–6 give the times of data collection and the means obtained; column 7 expresses each change (increase) in terms of cm/decade.

Tag 184. Female progeny of white Australian-born parents. Each mean was computed from more than 1000 measures (Jones, Hemphill, & Meyers, 1973; Roth & Harris, 1908).

Tag 185. Both samples pertain to "all classes of society" residing at Brussels (Quetelet, 1836; Twiesselmann, 1969).

Tag 186 The recent mean was based on 472 measures taken in 23 states and the District of Columbia (Hamill, Johnston, & Lemeshow, 1973a), and the earlier mean on 5500 measures taken in 16 states and the District of Columbia (O'Brien, Girshick, & Hunt, 1941).

Tag 187. Canadian youths of "primarily British" ancestry. Sample size was more than 250 at London (Stennett & Cram, 1969) and 744 at Toronto (Boas, 1898).

Tag 188. Refer to tag 73. For the earlier sample, $n = 270$ (MacDonald, 1899).

Tag 189. Data collected 1965–1971 at several Swedish cities and towns ($n = 360$) (Ljung, Bergsten-Brucefors & Lindgren, 1974) and earlier at Stockholm ($n = 298$) (Key, 1885).

Tag 190. Düsseldorf ($n = 1509$) (Schulze & Wissing, 1969) and Freiberg ($n = 76$) (Geissler & Uhlitzsch, 1888).

Tags 191, 192, and 195. Each of these six samples was larger than 1000 (Brundtland, Liestöl & Wallöe, 1975; Japanese Ministry of Education, 1901; 1971; Schiotz, 1923; Suchy, 1972).

TABLE 9-10 Standing Height (cm) at Age 13 Years for Females Measured During 1960–1970 and Females of Similar Ancestry Measured 2–12 Decades Earlier

		Recent		Earlier		Increase (cm)
Tag	Ethnic Group	Time	Mean	Time	Mean	per Decade
184	Australian, Sydney	1970	153.9	1901–07	145.0	1.3
185	Belgian, Brussels	1960–61	153.6	~1834	137.8	1.3
186	White, United States	1966–70	156.9	1937–39	152.6	1.4
187	White, Ontario	1967–69	154.9	1892	144.7	1.5
188	Black, Washington, D.C.	1963–65	156.5	1896–98	145.8	1.6
126	Maori, New Zealand	1969	156.1	1934	150.5	1.6
189	Swedish, urban	1965–71	158.6	1883	143.0	1.8
190	German, urban	1967	157.8	1886	142.1	1.9
191	Czech, Bohemia & Moravia	1968–70	156.7	1894–95	141.2	2.1
192	Japanese, Japan	1970	150.3	1900	135.5	2.1
193	Southern Chinese	1961–65	149.7	1915–25	139.8	2.3
194	Sardinian, Sassari	1965	149.0	1930	140.3	2.5
195	Norwegian, Oslo	1970	158.4	1920	145.6	2.6
196	Kalmuck, Elista area	1964–65	148.9	1925	138.0	2.8
197	Georgian, Tiflis	1963–64	154.6	1936	147.1	2.8
198	Russian, Syktyvkar	1967	152.5	1927	138.6	3.5
199	Kirghiz, Kirghiz S.S.R.	1960–61	150.1	1928–29	137.2	4.0
200	Russian, Orel	1965	150.8	1943	141.8	4.1

Tag 193 Inhabitants of Kwangtung and Fukien provinces (Stevenson, 1925) and residents of Hong Kong whose progenitors came largely from Kwangtung (Chan, 1972).

Tag 194. The increase found in this comparison (Aicardi & Rovetta, 1965) was similar to that reported from 1950 and 1962 data on Italian females residing at Genoa (DeToni, Aicardi, & Castellano, 1965).

Tags 196–200. Studies in the Soviet Union on members of the Kalmuck tribe living in a rural region near Elista (Kasparov, 1967), Georgians at Tiflis (Tsabadze, 1965), Kirghizes (Afanasenko, & Mamyrov, 1965), and Russians at Syktyvkar (Shumakher & Sevelev, 1969) and Orel (Belousov, Kardashenko, Kondakova-Varlamova, Prokhorova, & Sgromskaia, 1968). A 10-year comparison at Sverdlovsk, Siberia gave an increase of 4.3 cm (Rozenblat & Mezenina, 1968).

Other findings over periods of less than 20 years were increases of 3.9 cm decade for Hungarians measured at Kaposvar in 1947 and 1962 (Véli, 1971) and for Spaniards measured at Madrid in 1954 and 1968 (Garcia-Almansa et al., 1969), and 2.6 cm on Jamaican black females of low socioeconomic status measured at the same six schools in 1951 and 1964 (Ashcroft & Lovell, 1965).

Table 9-10 yields the following findings:

1. Female youths measured between 1960 and 1970 were taller than their age peers measured 20–125 years earlier; each of 18 comparisons at age 13 years registered secular increase.

2. The magnitude of average increase in standing height for females age 13 years approximated 2.3 cm/decade. Where sample size exceeded 1000, paired groups measured in 1970 and 50–70 years earlier gave decadal increases (1) alike in average magnitude for Czech and Japanese females and (2) twice as large for Norwegian than Australian white females.

Previous publications, pertaining to males or both sexes (Meredith, 1963; 1976; Tanner, 1966), have dealt more completely with secular change in human body size during the last century. Ontogenetically, they have presented substantial evidence showing that secular increase in standing height and body weight occurred and became progressively greater at successive ages from infancy to midadolescence.

Height and Weight of Environmentally Privileged Females Age 13 Years

Brought together in Table 9-11 are means for standing height and body weight of contemporary female youths reared in privileged or moderately privileged conditions; data collection occurred between 1960 and 1970 in Africa, Asia, Europe, Central America, and the West Indies.

Tag 201. Female youths belonging to high-income families of the Punjabi population (Sikri, 1972).

Tag 202. Members of families in the "professional, major managerial, or high official" categories; persons of "Jewish, Greek, and Armenian minority groups" were excluded (Neyzi, Yalçindag, & Alp, 1973).

Tag 203. Female youths of above-average socioeconomic status (Souisa, 1969).

Tags 204–206. Female offspring of parents in the middle and upper social and economic strata (Ashcroft, Heneage, & Lovell, 1966).

The averages in the upper part of Table 9-11 show that at age 13 years (1) exceptionally privileged Baganda females were 7.0 cm shorter than Dutch females belonging to families of the professional and managerial classes and (2) upper-class females of Chinese ancestry at Hong Kong were 9.1 kg lighter than socioeconom-

TABLE 9-11 Standing Height (cm) and Body Weight (kg) at Age 13 Years of Environmentally Privileged and Moderately Privileged Females Studied Between 1960 and 1970

		Standing Height		Body Weight	
Tag	Ethnic Group	n	Mean	n	Mean
	Privileged: upper classes				
137	Baganda, Uganda	407	151.6	412	43.2
131	Chinese, Hong Kong	331	152.2	328	39.1
136	Hindu elite, India	226	152.2	226	43.8
140	Spanish-American, Guatemala	37	152.8	37	47.0
201	Arora Punjabi, Delhi	39	153.8	39	42.2
202	Turkish, Istanbul	53	155.6	53	48.2
143	Dutch, Netherlands	105	158.6	105	46.2
	Moderately privileged: middle and upper classes				
147	Liberian, Monrovia	~90	146.5	~90	42.6
203	Hindu, Hyderabad	266	148.5	266	36.3
204	Jamaican Chinese, Kingston	38	149.7	38	41.7
153	Spanish, Madrid	100	153.8	100	46.9
154	Puerto Rican, San Juan	71	154.8	71	48.9
205	Jamaican White, Kingston	85	155.5	85	45.3
206	Jamaican Black, Kingston	180	155.8	180	46.5

For standing height, standard error of the mean approximates 1.2 cm where $n = 37$, 0.7 cm where $n = 100$, and 0.4 cm where $n = 330$. Corresponding values for body weight are 1.5, 0.9, and 0.5 kg.

ically comparable Turkish females at Istanbul. Comparative examination of the lower part of Table 9-11 indicates that means representing the middle and upper classes were higher for Jamaican black females than for (1) Liberian age peers at Monrovia by 9.3 cm and (2) Hindu age peers at Hyderabad by 10.2 kg.

Raghavan et al. (1971), besides reporting averages for Hindu females attending elite residential schools (Table 9-11, tag 136), reported averages at age 13 years for 97 Hindu females of "low-income families" residing at Hyderabad; the well-to-do group, none of whom showed signs of malnutrition, exceeded the low-income group by 12.2 cm and 13.6 kg for mean standing height and mean body weight, respectively. At Istanbul, 50 Turkish females whose fathers were unskilled workmen gave averages below those of Table 9-11, tag 202 , by 7.7 cm and 6.2 kg; at Hong Kong, 429 females of Southern Chinese ancestry and low socioeconomic status gave averages lower than those of Table 9-11, tag 131, by 4.6 cm and 3.8 kg; and in the Netherlands, 920 Dutch females whose fathers were placed in the unskilled or semiskilled occupational categories gave averages lower than those of Table 9-11, tag 143, by 2.3 cm and 0.8 kg.

Trunk Widths and Shoulder–Hip Index of Females Age 13 Years

Means for biacromial shoulder width, biiliocristal hip width, and shoulder–hip index are assembled in Table 9-12.

Tag 207. Females measured between 1960 and 1965 at villages in the Ostroleka and Suwalki districts (Wolanski & Lasota, 1964; Wolanski & Pyzuk, 1973).

TABLE 9–12 Means at Age 13 Years for Biacromial and Biiliocristal Widths (cm) and Shoulder–Hip Index on Groups of Females Measured During 1960–1970

Tag	Ethnic Group	Number Measured	Shoulder Width	Hip Width	Shoulder–Hip Index
164	Yoruba, Ibadan	56	31.1	21.4	69
73	Black, Washington, D.C.	42	34.1	23.9	70
109	Nyakyusa, Tanzania	64	30.4	21.7	71
165	Cuban Black, Havana	34	32.7	23.1	71
175	Japanese, Tokyo	103	32.5	23.3	72
163	Cuban White, Havana	51	32.2	23.9	74
161	Hungarian, Budapest	390	33.0	24.7	75
207	Polish, rural areas	105	31.9	24.0	75
180	Polish, Lublin	104	32.4	24.2	75
178	Taiwanese, Tainan City	43	32.6	24.4	75
208	Romanian, rural regions	~1,150	31.6	24.0	76
209	Romanian, urban centers	~1,020	32.6	24.8	76
170	Belgian, Brussels	563	32.7	24.9	76
179	Estonian, Tallinn	236	32.8	25.0	76
210	Italian, Genoa	158	32.7	24.7	76
108	Kirghiz, low altitude	62	31.6	24.0	76
108	Kirghiz, higher altitude	33	30.7	23.3	76
177	Sardinian, Sassari	89	32.3	24.6	76
83	Bulgarian, Sofia	213	32.9	24.9	77
120	Bulgarian, rural areas	194	32.1	25.0	78
182	Russian, Moscow	203	32.9	25.5	78
171	Sicilian, Palermo	103	32.5	25.3	78

For shoulder width and hip width, standard error of mean approximates 0.3 cm where $n = 40$, 0.2 where $n = 100$, and 0.1 cm where $n = 400$.

Tags 208 and 209. Statistics secured by Cristescu (1969) from data amassed during 1963–1966.

Tag 210. Measurement of these females took place in 1962 (DeToni, Aicardi, Castellano, & Chessa, 1966a).

Table 9-12 yields the following findings on females age 13 years measured between 1960 and 1970:

1. Mean biacromial shoulder width varied from less than 31 cm on youths of the Nyakyusa tribe living in Tanzania to near 34 cm on United States black youths living at Washington, D. C. Averages clustered between 32 and 33 cm were obtained on urban females at Brussels, Budapest, Genoa, Lublin, Moscow, Palermo, Sofia, Tallinn, and Tokyo. In each instance, $n > 100$.

2. Mean biiliocristal hip width varied from less than 22 cm on members of the Yoruba tribe residing at Ibadan to more than 25 cm on Russian females residing at Moscow. Intermediate averages were near 23 cm for black females at Havana, 24 cm for Polish and Romanian rural inhabitants, and 25 cm for Estonian females at Tallinn and Bulgarian females living at scattered villages.

3. As at age 8 years, the average shoulder–hip index was comparatively low (hip width about 70 percent of shoulder width) for black groups in Africa, Cuba, and the United States. For groups largely of Mongoloid descent, average shoulder–hip indices were 72 (Japanese), 75 (Taiwanese), and 76 (Kirghiz). Indices on European white groups fell between 74 and 78.

Skelic Index and its Components on Male Youths Age 15 Years

Presented in Table 9-13 are means for sitting height, lower limb height, and the skelic index derived from data collected on male youths during the 1960–1970 calendar period.

Tag 211. Male youths "in utero at the time of the atomic bombing." Subgroup means were 84.3 cm, 71.8 cm, and 85 percent for offspring of mothers living within 2.0 km of the explosion site and 86.6 cm, 73.3 cm, and 85 percent for offspring of mothers who moved into the city later (Burrow, Hamilton, & Hrubec, 1965).

Tag 212. Members of middle-class "Punjabi-speaking Hindu Khatri" (Singh, 1970a).

Tags 213 and 216. Data collected in 23 states and the District of Columbia on a "probability sample" of United States youths, excluding persons confined to institutions, living in Hawaii, or residing on Amerind reservations (Hamill et al., 1973a).

Tag 214. Kashmiri Pandit youths of middle-class families. Individuals showing "symptoms of malnutrition" or having had "any major ailment" were excluded (Kaul, 1971).

Tag 215. Data collected at "villages in the Meerut Division" of Uttar Pradesh (Nath, 1972).

The means in Table 9-13 for sitting height and lower limb height show large differences among ethnic groups of males age 15 years studied between 1960 and 1970. Sitting height was near 87 cm for Maori youths of New Zealand and about 18 cm less for Bundi youths of New Guinea; lower limb height was near 84 cm on black youths of Washington, D.C. and about 22 cm less on Bundi youths. Estimating at $p = 0.01$, male youths of southern Chinese ancestry living at Hong Kong were larger than their Quechua age peers living in the Peruvian Andes by amounts likely within the fiducial zones of 6.9–11.1 cm for mean sitting height, and 6.6–10.8 cm for mean lower limb height.

TABLE 9-13 Means at Age 15 Years for Sitting Height (cm), Lower Limb Height (cm), and Skelic Index of Male Youths Measured Between 1960 and 1970

Tag	Ethnic Group	Number Measured	Sitting Height	Lower Limb Height	Skelic Index
211	Japanese, Nagasaki	88	85.3	72.5	85
93	Quechua, Peruvian Andes	44	76.7	67.2	88
158	Chinese, Hong Kong	1,622	85.7	75.9	89
57	Bundi, New Guinea	31	68.5	62.5	91
208	Romanian, rural regions	~360	81.0	74.9	92
83	Bulgaria, Sofia	180	85.7	79.2	92
126	Maori, New Zealand	151	87.1	79.9	92
140	Spanish–American, Guatemala	30	86.5	79.4	92
209	Romanian, urban centers	~320	84.5	79.0	93
212	Khatri, Delhi	50	81.3	76.0	93
213	White, United States	526	87.2	82.1	94
120	Bulgarian, rural areas	191	83.1	78.0	94
128	Czech, Poděbrady region	97	85.0	79.6	94
159	White, New Zealand	1,065	85.7	81.1	95
161	Hungarian, Budapest	231	84.9	81.3	96
163	Cuban White, Havana	56	82.5	79.2	96
214	Brahmin, Srinagar	39	78.2	75.0	96
114	Hindu, Guyana	34	77.5	77.6	100
215	Jat, Uttar Pradesh	50	80.4	81.4	101
216	Black, United States	86	83.7	84.4	101
73	Black, Washington, D.C.	61	83.7	84.4	101
165	Cuban Black, Havana	38	80.5	82.1	102
123	Black, Guyana	34	78.5	80.9	103
109	Nyakyusa, Tanzania	38	73.6	78.2	106

For sitting height and lower limb height, standard error of mean approximates 0.8 cm where $n = 40$, 0.3 cm where $n = 300$, and 0.1 cm where $n = 1600$. Corresponding values for skelic index are 0.8, 0.3, and 0.1.

From examination of the right-hand column of Table 9-13, comparison of Tables 9-7 and 9-13, and reference to the skelic index findings in infancy (above), the following observations can be made:

1. At age 15 years, the skelic index of males was relatively low (85–89) for Amerind, Chinese, and Japanese groups; relatively high (101–106) for black groups in Cuba, Guyana, Tanzania, and United States; and intermediate (92–96) for white groups in Bulgaria, Cuba, Czechoslovakia, Guatemala, Hungary, New Zealand, Romania, and the United States. A similar ordering of skelic index averages was found among ethnic groups age 8 years.

2. The skelic index increased with age between infancy and midadolescence. Increases were, for Quechua of Peru, from near 50 at birth to 88 at age 15 years; for Bulgarians of Sofia, from near 54 at age 1 year to 92 at age 15 years; for United States blacks, from 65 at age 1 year to 101 at age 15 years; for Chinese at Hong Kong, from 83 at 8 years to 89 at 15 years; for Maori of New Zealand, from 85 at 8 years to 92 at 15 years; and for Hungarians, from 87 at 8 years to 96 at 15 years.

Height and Weight of Males Age 15 Years Living in Rural Areas

Means for standing height and body weight on male youths age 15 years measured between 1960 and 1970 are brought together, and ordered for height, in Table 9-14.

Tag 217. Refer to tag 107. Means 2.7 cm and 2.4 kg higher were secured on about 60 Tatar youths residing in the Tumen district (Gur'ev, 1967).

Tag 218. Individuals living in the Ostroleka and Suwalki areas; 68 male youths measured at villages in the Lublin district gave means higher by 4.5 cm and 4.8 kg (see tag 118).

Tag 219. Similar means (155.1 cm for height and 39.7 kg for weight) were reported on 101 Guyana youths with progenitors from India and Pakistan (refer to tag 114).

TABLE 9-14 Height (cm) and Weight (kg) of Male Youths Age 15 Years Studied During 1960–1970 at Rural Locations in Different Parts of the World

Tag	Ethnic Group	Number Measured	Mean Height	Mean Weight
57	Bundi, New Guinea	35	131.0	30.9
91	Cakchiquel, Guatemala	20	142.7	39.5
93	Quechua, Peruvian Andes	44	143.9	38.5
64	Shi Bantu, Zaire	~90	146.9	38.6
4	Lunda & Tshokwe, Angola	845	149.0	—
11	Javanese, Sumatra	50	149.7	38.7
100	Bolivian, west–central Bolivia	52	149.9	46.1
101	Chuvash, Chuvashsk S.S.R.	112	150.3	41.1
10	Mexican, southwest Mexico	~100	150.5	42.2
109	Nyakyusa, Tanzania	38	151.8	43.6
54	Pakistani, East Pakistan	216	152.7	38.5
98	Taiwan aborigine	220	152.8	42.0
105	Indonesian, rural Surinam	158	153.1	42.9
217	Tatar, rural Tatarstan	100	153.8	44.1
218	Polish, rural districts	43	154.8	45.8
219	Hindu, rural Surinam	393	155.8	39.8
208	Romanian, rural areas	~360	155.9	46.5
220	Kirghiz, Frunze region	60	156.0	—
94	Hindu, Palghar Taluk	283	156.2	32.2
116	Moldavian, Moldavian S.S.R.	214	156.2	47.0
15	Bushnegro, Surinam	40	156.8	47.6
64	Hutu, Rwanda	~90	157.1	43.1
121	Lithuanian, Lithuanian S.S.R.	118	157.1	47.6
122	Fijian, Fiji Islands	49	157.2	45.0
66	Lebanese, Lebanon	58	157.9	50.2
111	Japanese, Kagawa prefecture	4,000	158.7	48.7
221	Russian, Vitebak region	175	159.0	48.9
222	Creole, rural Surinam	135	159.1	45.6
120	Bulgarian, rural villages	192	161.1	49.9
125	Cree, Quebec & Ontario	30	161.6	50.4
215	Jat, Uttar Pradesh	50	161.8	42.8
119	Australian aborigine (Wailbri)	23	163.3	—
128	Czech, Poděbrady region	68	164.6	57.7

For standing height, standard error of mean approximates 1.4 cm where $n = 35$, 1.0 cm where $n = 100$, 0.5 cm where $n = 350$, and 0.3 cm where $n = 800$. Corresponding values for body weight are 1.8, 1.1, 0.6, and 0.4 kg.

Tag 220. A mean lower by 2.7 cm was obtained on 43 Kirghiz youths residing in the Osh region at altitudes from 2.3 to 2.8 km (tag 108).

Tag 221. Inhabitants of rural areas in the Vitebsk region. Means from other rural samples of Russian males age 15 years were ($n = 98$) 156.8 cm and 47.9 kg, Ryazan area; ($n = 118$) 158.3 cm and 50.0 kg, Komi region; ($n \sim 60$) 158.6 cm and 48.5 kg, Tumen district; ($n = 95$) 158.8 cm and 48.8 kg, Ulyanovsk region; (n = 101) 159.0 cm and 50.7 kg, Kalinan area; and ($n = 76$) 160.5 cm and 52.1 kg, Pskov region (Goldfeld et al., 1965; Gur'ev, 1967; Martirosian, 1973).

Tag 222. Refer to tag 123. On 93 members of farm families in Guyana, means of 159.4 cm for height and 45.1 kg for weight were obtained.

From rural studies of standing height and body weight on males age 15 years measured during 1960–1970, comparative findings include the following:

1. Bundi youths living in the Madang district of New Guinea were smaller than Czech youths inhabiting a rural region near Podebrady by (1) obtained differences of 33.6 cm in mean height and 26.8 kg in mean weight and (2) population differences, one-tail estimation at $p = 0.01$, likely exceeding 27 cm and 19 kg for average height and weight, respectively.
2. Mean standing height was near 149 cm for Angola youths of the Lunda and Tshokwe tribes; 153 cm for Taiwan youths of the Ami, Atayal, Paiwan, and Yami tribes; 156 cm for Moldavian youths living in rural areas of the Moldavian Soviet Socialist Republic; and 159 cm for Japanese youths residing in agricultural areas of Kagawa prefecture. In each instance, sample size was greater than 200.
3. Body weight means were approximately 32 kg on Hindu youths residing at villages in Palghar Taluk; 39 kg on Shi youths inhabiting the western shore of Lake Kivu; and, on youths living in rural regions of Romania and Bulgaria, respectively, 46 and 50 kg. Sample size was 90 or more in each instance.

Height and Weight of Males Age 15 Years Living at Urban Centers

Table 9-15, like Table 9-14, pertains to standing height and body weight of males age 15 years measured between 1960 and 1970. The tables are dissimilar and complementary in that Table 9-14 focuses on rural studies and Table 9-15 draws exclusively from urban studies.

Tag 223. Male youths measured at a school in Koge, New Guinea (Morishita, 1969).

Tags 224, 226, 228, 230, 233, and 239. These samples are urban counterparts of the rural materials in tags 101, 105, 116, 107, 111, and 123, respectively.

Tag 225. The school population sampled represented socially favored youths of Tunisia (Beghin, Wachholder, Trabelsi, & Cantraine, 1975).

Tags 227, 231, 235, 237, 240, 242, 246, 248, 249, 256, and 257. These are representative ethnic samples of males age 15 years living at Lagos (Johnson, 1972), Cairo (Abdou & Mahfouz, 1967), Tainan City (Kimura & Tsai, 1967), Palermo (Correnti, 1969), Sassari (DeToni, Aicardi, & Rovetta, 1966d), Frunze (Imanbaev, Kim, & Sidorova, 1971), Montreal (Demirjian, Jenicek, & Dubuc, 1972), Amsterdam (Oppers, 1964), Riga (Goldfeld et al., 1965), Oslo (Brundtland et al., 1975) and Düsseldorf (Schulze & Wissing, 1969).

Tag 229. Iranian youths measured at the capital of Fars province (Forbes, Ronaghy, & Majd, 1971; A. P. Forbes, personal communication, 1972).

Tag 232. Youths living on the main island of Japan, at the major city of the Tohoku region (Takahashi, 1966; E. Takahashi, personal communication, 1966). Means higher by 1.4 cm and 0.8 kg were secured by Kambara (1969) on 10,659 males age 15 years living at urban centers in Kagawa prefecture.

TABLE 9-15 Height (cm) and Weight (kg) of Male Youths Age 15 Years Studied During 1960–1970 at Urban Centers in Different Parts of the World

Tag	Ethnic Group	Number Measured	Mean Height	Mean Weight
223	Chimbu, Koge	33	148.6	43.5
214	Brahmin, Srinagar	39	153.2	37.5
224	Chuvash, Cheboksar	76	155.1	44.7
225	Tunisian, Cap Bon	402	155.5	45.9
226	Indonesian, urban Surinam	51	156.0	43.6
227	Nigerian, Lagos[†]	~45	156.0	42.1
147	Liberian, Monrovia	~75	156.5	46.6
228	Moldavian, Kishinev	105	157.1	46.2
229	Iranian, Shiraz	85	157.2	46.0
212	Khatri, Delhi	50	157.3	41.6
230	Tatar, Kazan	253	157.9	48.4
231	Egyptian, Cairo	429	158.6	47.8
232	Japanese, Sendai	1,700	158.8	48.8
233	Hindu, urban Surinam	146	159.1	43.7
234	British, Newcastle–on–Tyne*	178	159.5	50.1
235	Taiwanese, Tainan City	70	159.8	47.1
236	Belgian, Courtrai	614	160.1	48.8
237	Sicilian, Palermo	115	160.3	49.9
158	Chinese, Hong Kong	1,622	161.6	45.8
163	Cuban white, Havana	56	161.7	51.0
238	Jamaican Chinese, Kingston	50	161.8	52.3
239	Creole, urban Surinam	425	162.3	48.2
165	Cuban black, Havana	38	162.6	50.0
240	Sardinian, Sassari	91	162.8	51.5
241	Russian, Kalinin	511	163.2	52.7
242	Kirghiz, Frunze	~90	163.4	50.3
209	Romanian, urban centers	~320	163.5	53.0
243	Polish, Lublin	~140	163.9	53.4
244	Turkish, Istanbul	162	164.5	56.3
245	Japanese–white hybrid, Japan	25	164.7	51.9
246	French–Canadian, Montreal	237	164.7	54.2
83	Bulgarian, Sofia	180	164.9	53.1
247	Jamaican black, Kingston	210	165.4	52.6
248	Dutch, Amsterdam	97	165.6	51.8
249	Latvian, Riga	114	165.7	53.5
250	Australian white, Sydney[†]	883	166.0	54.5
161	Hungarian, Budapest	231	166.2	54.3
251	French, Paris	64	166.4	54.0
252	Italian, Genoa	502	166.5	56.6
253	Ontario white, London	>250	167.6	56.3
254	Ohio white, Cincinnati	255	167.8	58.2
255	Ohio black, Cincinnati	90	168.1	58.1
189	Swedish, urban	380	170.1	55.6
256	Norwegian, Oslo	1,176	170.3	57.2
257	German, Düsseldorf	2,011	170.7	57.7

*Means higher by 6.5 cm and 3.8 kg were reported by Scott (1961) from measures taken in 1959 on 792 British males age 15 years attending schools in the county of London.

[†]Data collected in 1965 on male youths age 15 years attending schools at Lourenço Marques, Moçambique, gave means of 160.3 cm and 47.7 kg for 92 youths of black ancestry and, for 307 youths of white ancestry, 166.3 cm and 56.9 kg (Martins, 1968).

Tag 234. Individuals participating from birth in a longitudinal study of normal human development (Miller, Billewicz, & Thomson, 1972).

Tag 236. Statistics reported by Franckx (1969); means higher by 4.5 cm and 4.3 kg were obtained from 643 Belgian youths measured at Brussels (tag 170).

Tags 238 and 247. Male samples studied at the same time as the female samples of tags 204 and 206.

Tag 241. Two samples were pooled (Goldfeld et al., 1965; Ivanov, Frolova, & Nagornova, 1963). Means reported on youths residing at other cities in the Soviet Union: Pskov, $n = 100$, 158.5 cm, 48.8 kg; Vladivostok, $n = 174$, 159.0 cm, 48.5 kg; Ryazan, $n = 91$, 159.1 cm, 49.4 kg; Penza, $n = 236$, 160.3 cm, 50.0 kg; Kazan, $n = 368$, 160.5 cm, 51.3 kg; Syktyvkar, $n \sim 290$, 161.6 cm, 50.8 kg; Kansk, $n = 100$, 161.7 cm, 51.3 kg; Norilsk, $n = 135$, 161.0 cm, 54.0 kg; Gorki, $n = 121$, 162.1 cm, 51.1 kg; Chelyabinsk, $n = 298$, 162.2 cm, 52.1 kg; Vologda, $n = 233$, 162.3 cm, 50.9 kg; Barnaul, $n = 170$, 162.4 cm, 51.8 kg; Yaroslavl, $n = 178$, 162.4 cm, 51.0 kg; Monchegorsk, $n \sim 340$, 162.5 cm, 52.0 kg; Leningrad, $n = 317$, 163.1 cm, 52.0 kg; Kirovsk, $n = 140$, 163.4 cm, 52.2 kg; Lvov, n 337, 163.8 cm, 54.2 kg; Stavropol, $n = 158$, 163.9 cm, 52.5 kg; Moscow, $n = 211$, 164.0 cm, 53.2 kg; Kemerovo, $n \sim 250$, 164.2 cm, 53.2 kg; Rostov-on-Don, $n = 100$, 164.4 cm, 53.4 kg; Kuibyshev, $n = 137$, 164.6 cm, 54.0 kg; Sverdlovsk, $n = 131$, 164.8 cm, 54.4 kg; Tomsk, $n = 103$, 165.1 cm, 54.6 kg; Simferopol, $n = 118$, 165.5 cm, 53.4 kg; Kharkov, $n = 200$, 166.0 cm, 57.1 kg; Krasnodar, $n = 131$, 166.5 cm, 54.3 kg; and Frunze, $n \sim 90$, 167.2 cm, 56.3 kg (Filippova, 1965; Fingert, 1969; Goldfeld et al., 1965; Goppe, 1972; Kamaletdinov, 1969; Lapitskii & Pozorelyi, 1967; Lapitskii, Nemzer, & Belogorskii, 1969; Matovskii & Bulochnikova, 1966; Morozova & Boldurchidi, 1965; Orlik, 1967; Panasenko, 1967; Popova, 1968; Rozenblat & Mezenina, 1968; Shumakher & Sevelev, 1969; Solovyeva, 1964).

Tag 243. Refer to tag 180. Means lower by 1.9 cm. and 0.4 kg. were secured from measures on 70 Polish youths at Lodz (Debiec, Godzisz, Gasinska, Kamer, Lipiec, Niewodniezy, Przyluska, Stawiszynska, & Zielinska, 1973).

Tag 244. Refer to tag 202. The means in Table 9-15 are from all social classes.

Tag 245. Japanese-white hybrids living "under the same nutritional conditions and environments as the native Japanese" (Suda, Yamaguchi, Hoshi, Endo, & Eto, 1965).

Tag 250. White males whose parents were born in Australia (Jones et al., 1973). On 42 "second-generation Australians of British ancestry" measured at Melbourne during 1966–1968, means were 169.8 cm and 57.5 kg; these youths were enrolled in a longitudinal growth study (Bowden, Johnson, Ray, & Towns, 1976).

Tag 251. Youths of French nationality participating in a longitudinal study of human development (Sempé, Sempé, & Pédron, 1972).

Tag 252. Members of families long residing in Genoa (DeToni, Aicardi, & Podestà, 1966b).

Tag 253. Refer to tag 187. On 99 Saskatchewan boys living at Saskatoon and enrolled for several years in a study of strength development, means were 168.8 cm and 56.7 kg (Carron & Bailey, 1974).

Tag 254. A "randomized sample" of youths attending public and parochial schools in Cincinnati (Rauh, Schumsky, & Witt, 1967). Other studies reported means of 168.3 cm and 59.9 kg on 56 white males measured at Watertown, Conn. (Birdsall, 1966) and 168.9 cm and 60.7 kg on 111 white males measured at Iowa City (Knott & Meredith, 1963).

Tag 255. Statistics from the study cited above by Rauh et al. (1967). Means from measures taken at Washington, D.C. on 61 black youths were 168.1 cm and 56.3 kg (see tag 73).

Tables 9-14 and 9-15, together with their attached materials, yield the following rural–urban comparisons, each having reference to males age 15 years studied between 1960 and 1970:

1. In Romania, youths residing at urban centers were taller and heavier than those inhabiting rural regions. Similarly in Kagawa prefecture, youths living in urban communities were taller and heavier than those residing in agricultural districts. Obtained means differed by 7.6 cm and 6.5 kg for the Romanian youths ($n > 300$) and, for Japanese youths, by 1.5 cm and 0.9 kg ($n > 3900$).
2. In Surinam, youths of Hindu, Creole, and Indonesian ethnic groups living at urban centers were taller and heavier than their respective age peers residing in rural areas. Obtained means differed by 3.3 cm and 3.9 kg on Hindu youths, 3.2 cm and 2.6 kg on Creole youths, and 2.9 cm and 0.7 kg on Indonesian youths.
3. In Europe and Asia, youths were measured at several cities and nearby rural localities. Obtained means were higher by (1) 7.4 cm for Kirghiz youths at Frunze compared to those in the Kirov district, (2) 4.8 cm and 3.6 kg for Chuvash youths at Cheboksar compared to those in the Kanashsky region, (3) 4.6 cm and 2.8 kg for Polish youths at Lublin compared to those in the Lublin district, and (4) 4.2 cm and 2.0 kg for Russian youths at Kalinin compared to those in a neighboring rural zone.
4. Bulgarian youths at Sofia were taller and heavier than their age peers inhabiting widely scattered Bulgarian villages by 3.8 cm and 3.2 kg. For Tatar youths, obtained means at Kazan exceeded those from (1) villages in northeast Tatarstan by 4.1 cm and 4.3 kg and (2) villages of the Tumen district by 1.4 cm and 1.9 kg.
5. Rural–urban differences did not occur consistently in one direction. Obtained means were (1) almost identical for Japanese youths at Sendai and in agricultural areas of Kagawa prefecture, (2) lower by 2.0 cm for Russian youths at Pskov than those in an adjoining rural region, and (3) lower by 0.8 kg for urban compared to rural Moldavian youths.

On contemporaneous groups of urban males age 15 years, the following were found:

1. In the mid-1960s, Norwegian youths at Oslo were larger than Brahmin youths at Srinagar by amounts probably (one-tail estimates at $p = 0.01$) between 13 and 21 cm in standing height and between 15 and 24 kg in body weight.
2. Among samples where $N > 200$, mean standing height was near 158 cm for Tatar youths at Kazan, 160 cm for Belgian youths at Courtrai, 163 cm for Russian youths at Kalinin, 165 cm for Jamaican black youths at Kingston, 168 cm for United States white youths at Cincinnati, and 170 cm for youths living at Swedish urban centers.
3. Mean body weight approximated 46 kg on youths of southern Chinese ancestry at Hong Kong, 48 kg on Egyptian youths at Cairo, 50 kg on Russian youths at Penza, 54 kg on French-Canadian youths at Montreal and Russian youths at Kuibyshev, Lvov, and Norilsk, 56 kg on Turkish youths at Istanbul, 58 kg on United States white and black youths at Cincinnati, and 60 kg on United States white youths at Watertown and Iowa City.

ADULTHOOD

Secular Change in Standing Height of Young Adult Females

Assembled in Table 9-16 are means for standing height of female adults representing calendar dates from 18 to 126 years apart. The means pertain to young women measured at ages varying from 17 to 21 years, except where the following text stipulates otherwise.

TABLE 9-16 Mean Height (cm) of Adult Women Studied Between 1960 and 1970 Compared with Mean Height of Sex-Age Peers Studied 2-12 Decades Earlier

		Recent		Earlier		Increase (cm)
Tag	Ethnic Group	Time	Mean	Time	Mean	per Decade
258	Polish, Plonsk district	1964	155.4	1901–06	154.5	0.15
259	Polish, Przasnysz district	1962	152.4	1914	151.6	0.17
260	Tristan da Cunha islander	1962–68	162.1	1937	161.4	0.25
261	Filipino, Luzon	1960–65	150.8	c. 1908	149.4	0.26
262	White, lower classes	1968–70	159.7	1875–76	156.9	0.30
185	Belgian, Brussels	1960–61	161.5	c. 1834	157.4	0.33
194	Sardinian, Sassari	1965	155.5	1930	154.0	0.43
187	White, Ontario	1967–69	160.0	1892	156.5	0.46
263	White, upper classes	1966	162.6	1875–76	158.0	0.51
264	Black, United States	1966–70	162.3	1896–98	158.2	0.58
184	Australian, Sydney	1970	162.3	1901–07	158.4	0.59
186	White, United States	1966–70	162.9	1937–39	161.1	0.60
265	Skolt Lapp, north Finland	1967–68	149.7	1926–34	146.6	0.84
193	Southern Chinese	1961–65	156.1	1915–25	151.7	1.02
266	Czech, Bohemia & Moravia	1968–70	164.1	1951	162.1	1.11
195	Norwegian, Oslo	1970	167.3	1920	161.6	1.14
267	Black, California	c. 1965	163.9	1936–38	160.6	1.18
192	Japanese, Japan	1970	155.6	1900	147.0	1.23

Sample size is 40–90 in 13 instances, 100–200 in 12 instances, and >300 in 11 instances. Standard error of the mean standing height approximates 0.85 cm where $n = 50$, 0.49 cm where $n = 150$, and 0.32 cm where $n = 350$.

Tags 258 and 259. Data for each row collected at the same villages on females of "the native population aged 20 to 69 years" (Charzewska, 1968).

Tag 260. Women 18–39 years of age residing on this island, 2800 km west of Cape Town; their progenitors came from Europe and Africa (Marshall, Tanner, Lewis, & Richardson, 1971).

Tag 261. Records gathered in "Luzon and the Visayas" (Matawaran, Gervasio, & De Gala, 1966) and at Manila (Bobbitt, 1909).

Tags 262 and 263. White female residents of the United States. The recent statistics were obtained on women of "lower-income families" measured in eight states (United States Center for Disease Control, 1972) and women of "middle and upper classes" measured in Massachusetts (Dwyer, Feldman, & Mayer, 1967); Bowditch (1879) secured the earlier statistics from measures taken at Boston on women whose fathers were classified in either the "skilled and unskilled" or "professional and mercantile" occupational group.

Tag 264. The sources were specified in tags 186 and 188. A mean of 159.5 cm was reported on 276 black women ages 17–25 years measured during 1941 at New York City (Michelson, 1943); 28 years later a similar mean (160.0 cm) was obtained on 95 black women of low-income-status sampled in eight states (see tag 162).

Tag 265. Women between ages 20 and 49 years measured at Nellim, Pasvik, Sevettijärvi, and Suenjel (Lewin, Jürgens, & Louekari, 1970).

Tag 266. Representative samples at each time (Fetter, Prokopec, Suchy, & Sobová, 1963; Suchy, 1972).

Tag 267. Data collected at Berkeley and Los Angeles (Hampton, Huenemann, Shapiro, Mitchell, & Behnke, 1966; Lloyd-Jones, 1941).

The 18 secular comparisons in Table 9-16 gave a composite average increase of

0.6 cm/decade in standing height of young women. This is markedly less than the composite average increase of 2.3 cm/decade found at age 13 years. Tables 9-10 and 9-16—together with other findings on human females and males studied during the past several generations in Asia, Australia, Europe, and North America—allow the following generalization: magnitude of secular increase in human standing height has been greater at successive ages from infancy to midadolescence and smaller at successive ages from midadolescence into early adulthood (Marcusson, 1961; Meredith, 1963, 1976; Tanner, 1966; Vlastovsky, 1966; Wieringen, 1972).

Findings on the standing height of two Eskimo isolates are of tangential interest. In 1846, a mean of 149.4 cm was secured on 32 women ages 19–50 years measured at "Kinnooksook, Hogarth Sound, Cumberland Strait" (Sutherland, 1856). Measurements taken 116 years later on 20 "pure polar Eskimo" women ages 21–40 years living in the Thule district, Greenland, gave a mean of 150.8 cm (Gilberg, Jorgensen & Laughlin, 1975). Longitude of habitat was similar for the two groups (65°–68° W), with latitude near 65° N for the Baffin Island tribe and near 76° N for the Greenland tribe.

Averages for standing height of young women measured in the period 1960–1970 were distributed through a range of 25 cm. Means between 142 and 143 cm were reported on 38 Northern Pahira inhabiting slopes of the Ajodhya hills, West Bengal; 260 Yanomama living in northern Brazil and southern Venezuela; 156 Telefolmin residing in the Tekin Valley, New Guinea; and 91 Vailala (Kukukuku) inhabitants of the Menyamya subdistrict, New Guinea (Basu, 1969; MacLennan, Bradley, & Walsh, 1967; Malcolm 1969a; Spielman, Rocha, Weitkamp, Ward, Neel, & Chagnon, 1972). Among the Vailala people diet was suboptimal, especially in animal protein; among the Telefolmin people symptoms of malnutrition were rare, and no palpable spleens were found. As shown in Table 9-16, means approximated 150 cm for Filipino and Skolt Lapp women, 155 cm for Japanese and Sardinian women, 160 cm for Canadian women at London, and 167 cm for Norwegian women at Oslo.

Age Change in Male Standing Height During Adulthood

Early studies on change with age in average height of adult men were made in Belgium and Great Britain. About 1834, Quetelet (1836) took measurements on men of "all classes" living at Brussels; obtained means declined from 168.0 cm at age 25 years through 163.9 cm at age 60 years to 161.3 cm at age 80 years. Obtained means on British men measured a half century later were 172.7 cm for the age group 30–40 years and 1.5 cm less for the group 60–70 years (Galton, 1884; Hrdlicka, 1936).

Table 9-17 presents means for standing height secured from data collected during 1960–1970 on young adult men and men at later ages. Unfortunately, not all studies used the same age categories; younger age groups varied from 18 years to 35–44 years and older age groups from 30–60 years to 60–96 years.

Tag 268. Data collected on young adult males during 1968–1969 (Eiben et al., 1971) and on elderly males during 1965–1968 (Dezsö, Eiben, & Thoma, 1969).

Tag 269. Largely men living in the Tohoku region of the main island (Miyashita & Takahashi, 1971). Means obtained in the mid-1960s by the Japanese Ministry of Health and Welfare were 165.2, 161.3, and 157.9 cm for age groups 19–29, 40–49, and 60–69, respectively (Kimura, 1975b).

Tag 270. These means were secured in the early 1960s (Parízková & Eiselt, 1966; Prokopec, 1968). On Czech men ages 18–29 years and 50–64 years, respec-

TABLE 9-17 Standing Height (cm) of Men Studied During 1960-1970 in Early and Later Adulthood

		Early Adulthood		Later Adulthood		Decrease in
Tag	Ethnic Group	Age(s)	Mean	Age(s)	Mean	Mean Height
268	Hungarian, Budapest*	18	175.9	60-96	166.5	9.4
269	Japanese, farming areas[†]	18-29	166.1	50-69	158.2	7.9
18	Indonesian, Surinam[‡]	20-29	165.2	>49	157.6	7.6
270	Czech, Prague*	18	176.1	>65	169.3	6.8
271	Welsh, Glamorgan region*	28-42	171.1	63-77	164.9	6.2
272	White, United States[†]	25-34	175.5	65-79	169.4	6.1
273	East German*	20-39	172.5	>49	167.0	5.5
29	Creole, Surinam*	20-29	172.4	>49	167.1	5.3
274	Black, South Carolina[‡]	35-44	175.8	>64	171.2	4.6
13	Hindu, Surinam[‡]	20-29	167.3	>49	162.8	4.5
275	West German*	20-29	171.3	50-69	167.0	4.3
127	Amerind, Montana*	20-39	175.9	>44	171.6	4.3
276	White, New Zealand[‡]	20-39	174.3	>59	170.1	4.2
277	Slovak, Yugoslavia[†]	18-40	170.3	>50	166.3	4.0
15	Bushnegro, Surinam[‡]	20-29	165.8	>39	162.0	3.8
278	Wabag, New Guinea*	18-30	158.6	>49	155.1	3.5
279	Bulgarian[†]	20-39	170.6	>49	167.1	3.5
280	Polar Eskimo, Greenland[‡]	21-40	163.2	>40	159.7	3.5
23	Chinese, Surinam[§]	20-29	168.5	>39	165.6	2.9
261	Filipino*	20-29	162.5	60-65	159.6	2.9
106	Puerto Rican, rural*	20-39	165.4	>59	162.6	2.8
281	Rutherian, Yugoslavia[†]	18-40	168.9	>50	166.3	2.6
282	Chimbu, New Guinea*	20-39	157.5	>49	155.0	2.5
2	Lumi, New Guinea*	22-29	157.8	50-64	155.3	2.5
283	Hutterite, United States*	20-29	171.6	40-59	169.1	2.5
284	Hindu, rural India*	26-35	162.4	>46	160.3	2.1
285	Zapotec, rural Mexico[‡]	18-39	159.0	>39	156.9	2.1
286	Australian aborigine*	20-39	168.9	>39	166.9	2.0
287	Ecuadorian, Andes[‡]	25-44	156.4	45-64	154.6	1.8
288	Bantu, South Africa*	20-29	168.1	30-60	166.4	1.7
260	Tristan da Cunha islander[‡]	18-39	174.3	>39	173.5	0.8
57	Bundi, New Guinea*	30-39	156.5	>49	156.2	0.3
289	Venda, South Africa*	30-39	167.8	>49	167.6	0.2

* The smaller of the two *ns* falls between 60 and 170.

† For each age group *n* falls between 180 and 1000.

‡ The smaller of the two *ns* falls between 30 and 55.

§ *ns* are 40 for ages 20-29 years and 20 for ages above 39 years.

Standard error of the mean approximates 0.99 cm where *n* = 45, 0.61 cm where *n* = 120, and 0.38 cm where *n* = 300.

tively, other means were 176.2 and 167.6 cm at Brno and 173.1 and 168.7 cm at Ostrava (Lorencová & Benes, 1974).

Tag 271. Men residing in the Glamorgan coastal district west of Cardiff. Means on men living in Rhondda Fach, a coal mining valley, were 170.5 cm for ages 25-39 years and 6.5 cm less for ages 60-74 years (Miall, Ashcroft, Lovell, & Moore, 1967).

Tag 272. Records amassed in several parts of the continental United States. About 90 percent obtained on white males (Stoudt, Damon, McFarland, & Roberts, 1965). Means for height of white men measured in southwestern Ohio during 1965–1967 were 177.1 cm for ages 25–50 years and 6.0 cm lower for ages 65–87 years (Hertzog, Garn, & Hempy, 1969).

Tags 273–279. Data collected in East Germany (Möhr & Milev, 1972), Charleston county (Pollitzer, Boyle, Cornoni, & Namboodiri, 1970a), West Germany (Knussmann, 1968), Carterton (Evans, Prior, Davidson, & Morrison, 1968), the province of Vojvodina (Gavrilovic, Rumenic, & Stajic, 1966), villages near Mount Hagen (Wolstenholme & Walsh, 1967), and Bulgaria (Möhr & Milev, 1972).

Tag 280. Inhabitants of the Thule district, northwest Greenland, 63 percent "pure Eskimo" and 37 percent Eskimo hybrids (Gilberg et al., 1975).

Tag 281. Same reference as tag 277.

Tag 282. Measurements made at hamlets in the areas of Gumine, Mintima, and Wandi. Diet was deficient in protein, fat, and salt intake, and incidence of infections was high (Maddocks & Rovin, 1965). Small samples of Tolai residing in the Gazelle peninsula of New Britain gave means of 163.6 cm for 20 men ages 18–30 years and 2.3 cm less for 18 men ages 31–60 years (Champness, Bradley, & Walsh, 1963).

Tag 283. Data from colonies of the Schmiedenleut division of Hutterites residing "in the northern Plain States" (Howells, 1970).

Tag 284. Individuals living at villages about 32 km from Hyderabad (Jyothi, Dhakshayani, Swaninathan, & Venkatachalam, 1963).

Tag 285. Data collected on Zapotec-speaking villagers of the Oaxaca valley (Himes & Malina, 1975).

Tag 286. Men measured at Beswick, Haast's Bluff, Kalumburu, Maningrida, and Yalata (Abbie, 1967).

Tag 287. Randomly selected adults from "the parroquia of La Esperanza in the province of Pichincha," elevation 2.8 km. About 80 percent indigine and 20 percent mestizo or white; diet low in protein and iron; high prevalence of goiter (Greene, 1973).

Tag 288. Other means for white South Africans were no higher on 49 men ages 20–29 years than on 103 men ages 30–60 years (Wal, Erasmus, & Hechter, 1971).

Tag 289. Bantu males, about 55 percent living at Johannesburg and 45 percent in rural areas (Loots & Lamprecht, 1971).

For different rows of Table 9-17, the gap between the upper limit of the younger age group and the lower limit of the older age group varies from more than 40 years (tags 268 and 270) to 0 years (tags 260, 280, and 285–287). This influences the amount of difference between the means for standing height; decreases exceeding 6.5 cm are associated with age categories separated by 40 years and decreases of 3.5 cm or less with those from bipartite division of the adult age continuum. Average decrease of means is 4.8 cm for 11 rows where the age gap is 20 years and 2.7 cm for 11 rows where the gap is 10 years.

In tag 269, the Japanese rural comparison yields a decrease in mean height of 7.9 cm for a period of about 36 years and the more general comparison from the Japanese Ministry of Health and Welfare a decrease of 7.3 cm for a period of about 40 years. Taking the lower value of 7.3 cm for 40 years, what part of this might have been due to secular change and what part to age change? More than 100,000 Japanese young men ages 19 and 20 years were measured during each of the years 1922 to 1962 (Inoue & Shimizu, 1965); the mean for 1962 was 4.8 cm higher than that obtained 40 years earlier. Disregarding a possible relationship between height and longevity, it follows as a reasonable estimate that in the early 1960s Japanese men age 60 were shorter than Japanese men age 20 by about (1) 4.8 cm due to generational increase in average height of young men and (2) 2.5 cm due to ontogenetic decrease in average height of adult males with time.

In tag 272, means for white men of the United States yield a decrease of 6.1 cm for a period approximating 42 years ($n = 675$ and 337). Following the procedure of the foregoing paragraph, what portion of this decrease was likely due to secular change and what portion to age change? United States white men ages 17 and 18 years were measured during 1937–1939 in 16 states and the District of Columbia and, during 1966–1970, in 23 states and the District of Columbia (O'Brien et al., 1941; Hamill et al., 1973a). The mean from 2770 records representing the earlier time was 173.7 cm and that from 417 records at the later time 175.7 cm. This 30 year secular difference of 2.0 cm was adjusted to its equivalent of 2.8 cm for 42 years. Using 2.8 cm, 6.1 cm appears tenably apportioned as about one-half generational increase in average height of young adult white men and one-half decrease during adulthood in average height of white men.

Ethnic groups taller and shorter than any represented in Table 9–17 were measured between 1960 and 1970. A mean of 151.4 cm was obtained on 52 Vailala (Kukukuku) men ages 20–39 years living in the highlands of New Guinea (Malcolm, 1969a) and a mean of 181.6 cm on 279 Northern Dinka ages 18–45 years inhabiting the Upper Nile province of southern Sudan and "following their tribal way of life" (Roberts & Bainbridge, 1963). On average, these Northern Dinka young men in Africa were 30 cm (20 percent) taller than the contemporary Vailala young men in Oceania.

Table 9–17 includes one group each of young men in Ecuador and Mexico, and five groups in New Guinea, for whom standing height was below 160.0 cm (tags 2, 57, 278, 282, 285, and 287). Other means below 160.0 cm secured on young men measured during the 1960s were 153.2 cm for 316 Yanomama men of northern Brazil and southern Venezuela (Spielman et al., 1972); 156.3 cm on about 80 Quechua and mestizo men living at a Peruvian lowland village 15 km southwest of Nauta (Buck, Sasaki, & Anderson, 1968); 157.5 cm on 155 Twa men—none showing deficiency in calories, protein, vitamin A, or iodine—inhabiting a rain forest region near Lake Tumba, Zaire (Hiernaux, Crogneir, & Vincke, 1974); 159.3 cm on 964 Lunda male aborigines of Angola (tag 4); and 159.9 cm on 62 Quechua men residing at the Peruvian highland villages of Nuñoa and Ondores (Frisancho, Borkan, & Klayman, 1975).

Means below 160 cm for groups of adult males unselected by age were as follows: in New Guinea, 154.1 cm on 511 Maring men measured at villages in the Simbai valley located 0.9–1.5 km above sea level (Buchbinder & Clark, 1971), and 156.2 cm on 99 Bomai—Chimbu vegetarians—measured at isolated jungle hamlets in the Eastern Highlands (Barnes, 1965); in the Sarawak colony of Borneo, 156.5 cm on 137 men of the Kedayan, Land Dayak, and Melanau tribes, 157.9 cm on 209 men of the Iban, Kayan, and Kenyah tribes, and 158.7 cm on 91 Malay men (Kurisu, 1970); in India, 156.7 cm on 400 Khasi men, 100 each of the Bhoi, Khyngren, Pnar, and War divisions inhabiting the Khasi and Jaintia hills of Assam (Das, 1967); in Guatemala, 156.8 cm on 42 Cakchiquel agriculturists living at villages 1.8 km above sea level whose diet included few vegetables and little animal protein (Méndez & Behrhorst, 1963); in Taiwan, 156.9 cm on 265 men of the Bunan and Paiwan tribes, and 158.4 cm on 187 men of the Rukai and Saisiat tribes, all residing at villages 0.3–1.8 km above sea level (Chai, 1967); in Surinam, 157.3 cm on 190 men of the

Trio and Wajana tribes (tag 97); in New Britain, 157.7 cm on 347 Baining men inhabiting hamlets in the northwest section of the island (Kariks & Walsh, 1968); in Congo, 158.0 cm on 178 Bira men living in the rain forest (Sporcq, 1975); and in Peru, 158.2 cm on 123 male offspring of native parents residing at isolated towns on the north coast in the vicinity of Chiclayo (Lasker, 1962).

On men at adult ages under 45, means near 176 cm are shown in Table 9–17 for Czech and Hungarian groups in Europe and Amerind, black, and white groups in the United States (tags 127, 268, 270, 272, and 274). Other obtained means were 176.2 cm on 308 Sara men ages 20–30 years at Fort-Archambault (Crognier, 1969), 177.5 cm on 1230 Dutch men ages 19–25 years measured in a Netherlands survey (Wieringen, 1972), 177.7 cm on 135 Dutch men ages 19–21 years at Amsterdam (Oppers, 1964), and 181.0 cm on 724 Norwegian men ages 19–21 years at Oslo (Brundtland et al., 1975).

Means between 165 and 180 cm were secured from measures on several groups of young adult males: 165.5 cm on 240 nomadic or "half-nomadic" gypsies living at encampments or slums in Slovak districts of Czechoslovakia (Benes, 1974); 165.9 cm on 62 black males residing at Dar es Salaam (Davies, Mbelwa, Crockford, & Weiner, 1973); 166.8 cm on 106 Taiwan Chinese men at Tainan City (tag 178), about 65 mestizo men at a Peruvian village 21 km east of Moquegua (Buck et al., 1968), and 192 Pakistani men of middle and low socioeconomic status living in the region of Lahore (Underwood, Hepner, Gross, Mirza, Hayat, & Kallue, 1967); 167.9 cm on 113 Japanese men at Tokyo (Morita & Ohtsuki, 1973), 111 Hindu men at Hyderabad (Singh, 1964), and 1074 men of Chinese ancestry at Hong Kong (Chan, 1972); 168.5 cm on 370 Russian men at Chelyabinsk (Matovskii & Bulochnikova, 1966) and 174 Fadidja men measured at villages in the Egyptian Nubia resettlement area near Kom Ombo (Strouhal, 1971); 168.7 cm on 100 Ethiopian men at Gor_._.r (Dellaportas, 1969); 168.8 cm on 159 Egyptian men at Cairo (Abdou & Mahfouz, 1967); 168.9 cm on 476 Sardinian men at Sassari (tag 177); 169.3 cm on 915 young Turkish military men (Hertzberg, Churchill, & Dupertuis, 1963); 170.1 cm on 421 Italian men living in the province of Rovigo (Bussadori, 1965); 170.3 cm on 69 Cuban black men at Havana (tag 165); 170.5 cm on 117 Cape Verde Islanders measured at villages on São Nicolau (Florey & Cuadrado, 1968) and 1084 young Greek military men (Hertzberg et al., 1963); 170.6 cm on 58 Western Apache men living in east-central Arizona (Miller, 1970); 172.1 cm on 124 Italian men at Genoa (tag 252); 172.3 cm on 365 Russian men at Moscow (tag 182); 172.6 cm on 53 men of Cape Verdean heritage residing at Waterbury, Conn. and New Bedford, Mass. (Florey & Cuadrado, 1968); 172.9 cm on 201 British men at Newcastle-on-Tyne (tag 234); 173.5 cm on 154 Fijian men measured at coastal villages (tag 122) and 235 Sara men at the village of Ndila and nearby hamlets of Moyen-Chari (Crognier, 1969); 173.9 cm on 54 Italian men of Udine province (Cetorelli & Ferro-Luzzi, 1967); 174.0 cm on 105 Jamaican black men at Kingston (tag 206); 174.8 cm on 457 Norwegian men, including men of Lapp descent, living in the northern counties of Finnmark and Troms; and 179.3 cm on 262 Norwegian men in the southern counties of Aust-Agder and Vest-Agder (Udjus, 1964).

Measures for standing height of adult males, analyzed without regard to age, gave means of 163.8 cm on 215 Bantu men (about 100 of the Pare tribe) measured at highland and lowland villages in Tanzania (tag 109); 165.4 cm on 130 Cayapo men living at three isolated places in Mato Grosso and Pará, Brazil (Rocha & Salzano, 1972); 165.9 cm on 39 black men (Siddis) inhabiting isolated villages in the Gir forest of Gujarat, India (Bhattacharya, 1969); 166.3 cm on 104 Hakka Chinese inhabitants of Taiwan, 57 Japanese-Americans of Hawaii, and 43 Eskimo-Americans of northern Alaska (Froehlich, 1970; Jamison & Zegura, 1970; Kanda, 1974); 166.9 cm on 42 Torque Islanders (Benoist, 1962); 167.2 cm on 205 black men measured at villages in the Lower Shire area of southern Malawi (Burgess, Burgess, & Wheeler, 1973); 167.9 cm on 359 Fur men residing in the mountainous, hot, semiarid region of Sudan (Sukkar, 1976); 168.5 cm on 116 Dogon men measured at villages in the Sanga savanna area of Mali (Huizinga & Birnie-Tellier, 1966); 168.7 cm on 272 men living in the Savoie department, southwest France (Billy, 1975); 169.4 cm on 94 Seminole men of southern Florida (Pollitzer, Rucknagel, Tashian, Shreffler, Leyshon, Namboodiri, & Elston, 1970c); 169.5 cm on 2052 Sicilian men residing in the provinces of Agrigento, Palermo, and Trapani (Ridola, Nesci, Valenza, & Zummo, 1975); 169.7 cm on 25 Vatwa men of Angola (Weninger, 1965); 170.2 cm on 42 Xavante men of west-central Brazil and 56 Seminole men of Oklahoma (Niswander, Keiter, & Neel, 1967; Pollitzer, Namboodiri, Elston, Brown, & Leyshon, 1970b); 170.4 cm on Chilcotin and Nootka men of British Columbia (Birkbeck, Lee, Myers, & Alfred, 1971); 170.9 cm on 44 Samaritan men residing in Israel and 50 Melungeon men living in the Appalachian mountains "where eastern Tennessee and western Virginia join" (Bonné, 1966; Pollitzer & Brown, 1969); 171.0 cm on 107 Kurumba men living at a village in Upper Volta (Huizinga, 1968); 171.1 cm on 54 Chimba men of Angola (Weninger, 1965); and 172.9 cm on 74 natives of the Lau Archipelago living on the island of Vanua Mbalavu (Lourie, 1972).

Cephalic Index and its Components on Male Adults

Averages derived from data collected during the 1960s on adult males are displayed in Table 9–18 for the cephalic index and the maximum transverse and anteroposterior diameters of the head.

Tag 290. Men living in the Western Desert about 274 km south of the Mediterranean coast (Ibrahim, Kamel, Selim, Azim, Gaballah, Sabry, El-Naggar, & Hoerman, 1974).

Tag 291. Measures taken on a Tinguelin group living 45 km north of Garoua and a Kangu group living "more to the north" (Huizinga & Reijnders, 1974).

Tag 292. Bantu cattle farmers living in highlands of the Huila district about 170 km south of Sa da Bandeira. Corresponding statistics on 22 Vatwa men of an adjacent tribe were 14.3 cm, 19.1 cm, and 75 percent (Weninger, 1965). Values of 14.1 cm, 19.0 cm, and 74 percent were obtained on 36 Kurumba men living at the Upper Volta village of Roanga, north of Ouahigouya (Huizinga, 1968).

Tag 293. Males ages 18 years and up measured at the village of Simoes Lopes, Mata Grosso (Niswander et al., 1967). Averages for 130 Cayapo men residing at isolated locations in the states of Mato Grosso and Pará were 15.0 cm, 18.5 cm, and 81 (Rocha & Salzano, 1972). Note the effect on the cephalic index of the large tribal difference in anteroposterior distance from glabella to opisthocranian.

Tag 294. United States Air Force basic trainees measured in 1965. Averages for 400 white trainees measured at the same time were 15.3 cm, 19.5 cm, and 78 (Churchill, Robinow, & Erskine, 1973).

Tag 295. Largely men living on the reservations of Okombahe and Fransfontein (Knussmann & Knussmann, 1970). Averages of 14.5 cm, 19.0 cm, and 76 were secured on 84 Dogon men of Mali residing at traditional villages in the Sanga area of the thorn savanna belt (Huizinga & Birnie-Tellier, 1966).

Tag 296. Predominantly white men "with some Negroid influence;" village residents in the "New Nubia resettlement area near Kom Ombo" (Strouhal, 1971).

TABLE 9–18 Means for Transverse and Anteroposterior Head Diameters (cm) and Cephalic
Index on Groups of Adult Males Measured Between 1960 and 1970

Tag	Ethnic Group	Number Measured	Head Width	Head Depth	Cephalic Index
290	Egyptian, Siwa Oasis	34	14.1	19.6	72
291	Fali, north Cameroun	165	14.4	19.4	74
215	Jat, Uttar Pradesh	50	14.1	19.1	74
292	Chimba, southwest Angola	44	14.3	19.2	74
293	Xavante, west-central Brazil	42	14.9	20.0	75
109	Nyakyusa, southern Tanzania	40	14.6	19.4	75
294	Black, United States	383	15.1	19.8	76
295	Dama, southwest Africa	281	14.8	19.5	76
296	Fadidja, Egyptian Nubia	174	14.5	19.1	76
297	Bira, northeast Congo	378	14.5	18.9	77
298	Ami, rural Taiwan	192	14.5	18.8	77
299	Pahira, eastern India	185	13.9	18.1	77
300	Eskimo, northwest Greenland	31	15.1	19.7	77
301	White, Ontario	285	15.3	19.6	78
302	Black, Haiti area	229	14.9	19.1	78
303	Danish, Denmark	102	15.5	19.9	78
304	Land Dayak, Sarawak	47	14.5	18.5	78
305	Melungeon, Tennessee	36	15.0	19.3	78
170	Belgian, Brussels	441	15.4	19.4	79
171	Sicilian, Palermo	152	15.2	19.2	79
306	Yanomama, Brazil & Venezuela	316	14.8	18.4	80
173	Chinese, Hong Kong	432	15.2	18.8	81
307	Atayal, Taiwan	139	14.6	18.1	81
308	Seminole, Oklahoma	56	15.6	19.3	81
309	Samaritan, Israel	42	14.9	18.5	81
310	Greek, Greece	1,084	15.5	18.9	82
311	German, West Germany	778	15.8	19.3	82
312	Japanese, Japan	510	15.5	18.8	82
97	Trio & Wajana, Surinam	190	15.0	18.4	82
313	Bunun, Taiwan	120	14.8	18.1	82
172	Russian, Moscow	55	15.5	19.0	82
314	Chinese, Taiwan	325	15.4	18.6	83
315	Iban, Kedayan, & Malay	258	15.1	18.1	83
316	Polish, rural districts	159	15.8	19.1	83
317	Turkish, Turkey	915	15.7	18.6	84
318	French, Savoy region	280	16.1	19.2	84
313	Paiwan & Rukai, Taiwan	264	15.0	17.8	84
319	Romanian, Bucharest	244	15.6	18.5	84
320	Nordestino, Brazil	198	15.4	18.3	84
283	Hutterite, United States	105	15.8	18.7	84
321	Western Apache, Arizona	58	15.9	18.6	85
322	Peruvian, northwest Peru	123	15.7	18.2	86
323	Melanau, Sarawak	38	15.4	18.0	86
324	Uzbek, Tashkent	52	15.8	18.1	87

For head width, standard error of the mean approximates 0.09 cm where $n = 40$, 0.05 cm where
$n = 160$, 0.03 cm where $n = 300$, and 0.02 cm where $n = 900$. Corresponding values are 0.11,
0.06, 0.04, and 0.02 cm for head depth and 0.55, 0.28, 0.20, and 0.12 for cephalic index.

Tag 297. Bira men living in savanna (200) and forest regions (Sporcq, 1975). Similar values—14.6 cm, 18.8 cm, and 77—were secured on 37 Siddis measured at villages in the Gir forest, west-central India. These men were predominantly of Congoid descent; their average age was 33 years (Bhattacharya, 1969).

Tag 298. Data gathered during 1962–1963 on aborigines inhabiting villages at altitudes varying from sea level to 0.5 km (Chai, 1967). Corresponding values from measures taken in 1969 on 29 men of the same tribe were 14.7 cm, 18.9 cm, and 78 (Kanda, 1974).

Tag 299. Primitive, hamlet-dwelling men inhabiting slopes of the Djodhya hills, West Bengal (northern Pahira), and (southern Pahira) the Dalma hills and ranges westward across the Subarnarekha River, Bihar (Basu, 1969). Cephalic indices of 77 and 81 were obtained on 50 Punjabi-speaking men of northern India (tag 212) and 118 Newar men of the Shrestha and Jyapu castes living in the Katmandu valley, Nepal (Bhasin, 1971). Means for head width were identical on the Newar and Punjabi and were less on the Pahira by 0.8 cm; means for head depth were similar on the Newar and Pahira and were greater on the Punjabi by 0.8 and 0.9 cm. On 400 Khasi men residing in the Khasi and Jaintia hills of Assam, means were 14.4 cm, 18.7 cm, and 78 (Das, 1967).

Tag 300. Polar "Thule pure" Eskimos (tag 280). Corresponding statistics on other adult male samples were 15.2 cm, 19.2 cm, and 79 on 99 Greenland Eskimos at Augpilagtok (Jorgensen & Skrobak-Kaczynski, 1972); 15.4 cm, 19.2 cm, and 80 on 50 Greenland Eskimos at Upernavik (Drenhaus, Skrobak-Kaczynski & Jorgensen, 1974); and 15.5 cm, 19.0 cm, and 82 on 43 Alaska "Wainwright pure" Eskimos (Jamison & Zegura, 1970). Compared with the Thule means, the Wainwright means were higher by 0.4 cm for head width and lower by 0.7 cm for head depth.

Tag 301. Canadian white men measured at Trent University, Peterborough; 95 percent were permanent residents of Ontario (Helmuth, 1973).

Tag 302. Materials amassed at villages on the island of Grande Cayemites and at the mainland town of Pestel. About 80 percent of the men had black progenitors, some French, and fewer Amerind (Basu, Namboodiri, Weitkamp, Brown, Pollitzer, & Spivey, 1976). Averages of 14.7 cm, 18.7 cm, and 79 were secured from measures on 40 male inhabitants of Tortuga island, north of Haiti (Benoist, 1962).

Tag 303. Male dental students ages 20–30 years measured at Copenhagen (Solow, 1966). On 5765 Norwegian men age 20 years examined in 1962, averages were 15.3 cm, 19.4 cm, and 79 (Udjus, 1964).

Tags 304 and 323. Natives of Borneo living in this northern colony (Kurisu, 1970).

Tag 305. Preponderantly white men "with some Indian and possibly Negroid admixture" inhabiting the Appalachian mountains where eastern Tennessee and western Virginia join (Pollitzer & Brown, 1969).

Tag 306. Males ages 18–45 years living at villages in northern Brazil and southern Venezuela; members of "one of the largest and least acculturated tribes in South America" (Spielman et al., 1972).

Tag 307. Statistics from measures taken during 1962–1963 (Chai, 1967). On 32 men of the same tribe measured in 1969, averages were 14.7 cm, 18.5 cm, and 79 (Kanda, 1974). Averages were 14.6 cm, 18.3 cm, and 80 for 68 men of the Saisiat tribe and 14.8 cm, 18.3 cm, and 81 for 81 men of the Tsou tribe (Chai, 1967). All three groups inhabited villages at elevations from 0.5 to 1.8 km.

Tag 308. On 95 Seminole men residing in southern Florida, averages were 15.6 cm, 18.9 cm, and 83 (Pollitzer et al., 1970b; Pollitzer et al., 1970c). The Oklahoma Seminole values were closely matched by averages of 15.7 cm, 19.3 cm, and 81 on 47 men of the Lau Archipelago living at coastal villages on Vanua Mbalavu island (Lourie, 1972).

Tag 309. Men of Samaritan ancestry living in Israel (Bonné, 1966).

Tag 310 and 317. Greek and Turkish young military men (Hertzberg et al., 1963).

Tag 311. Data collected in Rhineland-Palatinate, northern Baden-Wurttemberg, and southern Hesse (Knussmann, 1968).

Tag 312. Men ages 18–29 years living in the farm areas and urban communities (Miyashita & Takahashi, 1971). Measures taken at Tokyo on 113 men age 20 years yielded averages of 15.9 cm, 18.9 cm, and 84 (Morita & Ohtsuki, 1973), and averages obtained on 57 Japanese-American men residing in Hawaii were 15.5 cm, 19.0 cm, and 82 (Froehlich, 1970).

Tag 313. Statistics reported by Chai (1967). From the same source, averages for 73 Puyuma men were 15.0 cm, 18.4 cm, and 82.

Tag 314. Hakka and Hoklo Chinese men residing on Taiwan (Kanda, 1974).

Tag 315. Men living in the Sarawak colony of Borneo. The same averages were found to represent the head size and form of each group (Kurisu, 1970).

Tag 316. Males at ages and places indicated in tags 258 and 259.

Tag 318. Adult male members of families long residing in the Savoy region of southeast France (Billy, 1975).

Tag 319. Male students age 20 years (Enachescu, Pop, & Georgescu, 1963). From data on 262 Hungarian men ages 60–96 years living at Budapest and environs, averages were 16.0 cm, 19.2 cm, and 83 (Dezsö et al., 1969).

Tag 320. Adult male phenotypes derived principally from a mixture of Portuguese whites, African blacks, and Brazilian Amerinds; they were immigrants to Sao Paulo from the north, where they lived under conditions of "poor nutrition and high rates of infection" (Eveleth, 1972).

Tag 321. Men ages 22–33 years living in east-central Arizona (Miller, 1970).

Tag 322. Descendants from indigene, black, and white mixtures over the last 400 years; third generation residents of three coastal towns (Monsefú, San José, and Mochumi) near Chiclayo City (Lasker, 1962).

Tag 324. Men ages 18–19 years; "a mixed Mongoloid-Caucasoid group with Caucasoid features predominating" (Miklashevskaya, 1966).

Comparative findings from Table 9–18 and its complemental materials are as follows:

1. Means for biparietal head width of adult males studied between 1960 and 1970 varied from 13.9 to 16.1 cm; the mean obtained on French men of the Savoy was 2.2 cm (16 percent) greater than that on Pahira men of Bihar and West Bengal. Intermediate means were 14.5 cm on Ami, Bira, Dogon, Fadidja, and Land Dayak men; 14.8 cm on Bunun, Dama, Tsou, and Yanomama men; 15.4 cm on Belgian, Melanau, Nordestino, and Taiwan Chinese men; and 15.8 cm on Upernavik Eskimo, German, Hutterite, Polish, and Uzbek men. For 14 of these 20 groups, sample size exceeded 100; where means from 100 measures on each of two groups differ by 0.3 cm, there is strong likelihood ($p = 0.01$) that the two population means also differ.

2. For glabelloopisthiocranial head depth, means were distributed from 17.8 cm on Paiwan men to 20.0 cm on Xavante men. One-tail fiducial estimates, at $p = 0.01$, indicated population means for head depth of Fali and Pahira men differed, the Pahira being smaller by at least 1.0 cm. Head depth means were similar (near 19.0 cm) on Bira, Dogon, Jat, Haiti black, Hawaiian Japanese, Kurumba, Polish, Russian, and Vatwa men.

3. Among different groups of adult males measured during 1960–1970, mean head width relative to mean head depth was less than 75 percent for some groups and more than 85 percent for others. Group-to-group increase in cephalic index was to an extent associated with rising head width and declining head depth: for groups with indices below 75 (Chimba, Egyptian of Siwa, Fali, Jat, Kurumba), near 80 (Atayal, Belgian, Cayapo, Chinese, Eskimo, Lau islander, Newar, Norwegian, Oklahoma Seminole, Saisiat, Samaritan, Sicilian, Tortuga islander, Tsou, Yanomama), and above 85 (Melanau, Peruvian, Uzbek), combined averages were 14.2, 15.1, and 15.6 cm for head width and 19.3, 18.8, and 18.1 cm for head depth.

Averages for the cephalic index were presented in Table 9–8 on children of both sexes age 8 years and in Table 9–18 on male adults. Several ethnic groups were characterized in both tables, namely, Chinese at Hong Kong, Belgian at Brussels, Nyakyusa in Tanzania, Russians at Moscow, Sicilians at Palermo, Trio and Wajana in Surinam, and Uzbek at Tashkent. Were it known that males and females of these groups did not differ appreciably in average cephalic index, direct comparison of indices at the two stages of ontogeny could be made. This comparison is possible: the report on each group gave statistics at several ages between early childhood and adulthood showing similarity of females and males in average cephalic index. Composite average indices for the five Chinese, Uzbek, and white groups common to Tables 9–8 and 9–18 declined from 84 at age 8 years to 82 in adulthood; for the other groups, there was no change. On Chinese, Uzbek, and several white groups, more exhaustive analyses afforded slowly declining index trends across the years from early childhood into adulthood (tags 170–173; Dokládal, 1959; Miklashevskaya, 1966; 1969; Wolanski & Pyzuk, 1973).

Shoulder–Hip Index and its Components on Adult Females

Table 9–19 displays averages for biacromial shoulder width, biiliocristal hip width, and shoulder–hip index (hip width expressed as a percentage of shoulder width). The averages characterize groups of adult women measured during the 1960s, except that the column at the far right lists averages (in parentheses) for the shoulder–hip indices of adult men.

Tag 325. Women ages 20–60 years residing in the province of Anta at an altitude of 3.3 km (Quevedo-Aragón, 1961).

Tag 326. Fuchen-Chinese measured during 1963–1964 (Kimura & Tsai, 1968). From a 1969 study in Taiwan, Kanda (1974) reported averages of 34.0 cm, 27.3 cm, and 80 on 82 Hoklo Chinese women and 34.5 cm, 27.7 cm, and 80 on 33 Hakka Chinese women; the shoulder–hip indices for males were 73 in each instance.

Tag 327. Statistics based on measures taken at the village of Ndila and nearby hamlets in the prefecture of Moyen-Chari (Crognier, 1969). For adult members of the Kurumba tribe measured at the village of Roanga, Upper Volta, corresponding values were 33.8 cm, 25.0 cm, and 74 on 131 women and 70 on 107 men (tag 292).

Tag 328. Students attending the University of Colorado (Kelso, Tinsman, Lewis, & Tully, 1972). Comparable values were 36.7 cm, 27.3 cm, and 74 on 61 German women attending the University of Hamburg (Zerssen, 1968); 36.0 cm, 27.8 cm, and 77 on 387 Canadian white women attending Trent University (Helmuth, 1973); and 36.4 cm, 28.1 cm, and 77 on 46 white female nurses, mean age 23 years, measured at Rochester, Minn. (Novak, 1970).

TABLE 9-19   Means for Biacromial and Biiliocristal Widths (cm) and Shoulder-Hip Index on Groups of Adult Females Studied During 1960–1970

Tag	Ethnic Group	Number Measured	Shoulder Width	Hip Width	Shoulder–Hip Index
325	Quechua, Peru	40*	33.2	22.9	69
326	Taiwanese, Tainan	119†	36.0	26.1	73 (67)
291	Fali, north Cameroun	62‡	34.1	24.9	73 (68)
109	Nyakyusa, south Tanzania	61*	33.7	24.7	73 (69)
327	Sara, southern Chad	269*	34.5	25.7	74 (68)
295	Dogon, rural Mali	48‡	33.4	24.7	74 (70)
267	Black, Berkeley	117§	36.2	26.8	74 (65)
165	Cuban black, Havana	66§	35.1	26.0	74 (67)
177	Sardinian, Sassari	357§	35.4	27.0	76 (72)
328	White, United States	180‡	35.9	27.3	76 (70)
170	Belgian, Brussels	598†	35.5	27.3	77 (72)
210	Italian, Genoa	212§	35.8	27.7	77 (72)
329	Atayal, Taiwan	174‡	33.7	26.1	77 (71)
330	Hungarian, Budapest	117§	34.7	26.7	77 (72)
331	Sicilian, Sicily	1,839‡	34.8	27.3	78 (71)
332	Paiwan, Taiwan	241‡	33.3	26.0	78 (71)
179	Estonian, Tallinn	202§	35.5	27.8	78 (72)
118	Polish, rural areas	100§	34.8	27.0	78
333	American-Japanese, Hawaii	53†	34.9	27.1	78 (71)
334	Filipino, United States	47†	34.4	26.7	78
335	White, Berkeley	245§	35.8	28.2	79 (71)
83	Bulgarian, rural & urban	494†	35.1	27.7	79 (73)
182	Russian, Moscow	411§	34.9	27.7	79 (73)
336	Ami, Taiwan	104‡	34.1	27.0	79 (74)
163	Cuban white, Havana	92§	34.0	26.8	79 (71)
108	Kirghiz, low elevation	57‡	34.2	27.0	79 (74)
337	Basque, north-central Spain	116‡	35.6	29.4	83 (76)
300	Wainwright Eskimo, Alaska	36‡	35.6	29.5	83 (77)

* Within age span 20–60 years.
† Within age span 18–30 years.
‡ Adults, lower age only given (20 years up) or age span not specified.
§ Ages between 17 years and 22 years.

For shoulder width and hip width, standard error of the mean approximates 0.28 cm where $n = 50$, 0.20 cm where $n = 100$, 0.11 cm where $n = 350$, and 0.08 cm where $n = 600$. Corresponding values for shoulder–hip index are 0.54, 0.38, 0.20, and 0.16, where the figures in parentheses are averages for shoulder–hip index of adult males.

Tag 329. Data collected during 1962–1963 (Chai, 1967). From other samples of this tribe measured between 1964 and 1969, averages were 33.8 cm, 27.6 cm, and 82 on 134 women (Hsü, 1970) and 33.7 cm, 27.1 cm, and 80 on 50 women (Kanda, 1974); shoulder–hip indices were 72 and 71, respectively, for 127 and 31 men.

Tag 330. Refer to tag 161. Corresponding values were 36.6 cm, 25.7 cm, and 70 on 179 women ages 18–22 years measured at Szombathely Teacher's College (Eiben, 1969).

Tag 331. Residents of the provinces of Agrigento, Palermo, and Tropani (Ridola et al., 1975). On 63 women ages 20–21 years, data collected at Palermo gave averages of 36.4 cm, 28.9 cm, and 79 (Correnti, 1969).

Tag 332. Chai (1967). Similar findings from other tribes studied by Chai were 34.5 cm, 26.6 cm, and 77 on 81 Tsou women; 33.3 cm, 26.1 cm, and 78 on 119 Puyuma women; and 33.3 cm, 25.9 cm, and 78 on 102 Rukai women. Male indices were 70, 71, and 71, respectively.

Tag 333. Grandchildren of emigrants from Japan and Okinawa; mostly university students (Froehlich, 1970). Corresponding values were 34.6 cm, 27.4 cm, and 79 on 112 women college students at Tokyo (Nagamine & Suzuki, 1964) and 35.1 cm, 27.3 cm, and 78 on 37 "Oriental" young women measured at Berkeley (Hampton et al., 1966).

Tag 334. Women taking advanced nurses training. None had lived in the United States more than 3 months (Novak, 1970).

Tag 335. Materials gathered about 1965 on high school seniors (Hampton et al., 1966). Refer to tag 328. Other averages were 36.0 cm, 28.0 cm, and 80 on 379 white women ages 25–35 years "employed in the San Francisco Bay area" (Steinkamp, Cohen, Gaffey, McKey, Bron, Siri, Sargent, & Isaacs, 1965) and 33.9 cm, 27.8 cm, and 82 on 446 white high school seniors of the "middle and upper classes" living in a Massachusetts suburban community (Dwyer et al., 1967).

Tag 336. Refer to tag 298. The averages from Kanda (1974) were 34.4 cm, 27.5 cm, and 80. For other tribes, averages were 33.7 cm, 27.0 cm, and 80 on 131 Bunun women and 34.1 cm, 26.9 cm, and 79 on 60 Saisiat women (Chai, 1967).

Tag 337. Women residing in Guipúzcoa province and adjacent regions (Marquer, 1963).

Statistics comprising and complementing Table 9–19 yield the following findings for the period 1960–1970:

1. Mean biacromial shoulder width was between 33 and 34 cm on ethnic groups of adult women studied in Mali (Dogon), Tanzania (Nyakyusa), Peru (Quechua), and Taiwan (Atayal, Bunun, Paiwan, Puyuma, and Rukui). For seven of the same tribes, means reported on adult males were higher by amounts between 2.5 and 3.5 cm.

2. Adult women for whom average biacromial diameter was near 36 cm included Fuchen-Chinese at Tainan, Italians at Genoa, and United States black and white groups at Berkeley. Averages from companion samples of men were higher by 3.2, 2.6, 3.9, and 4.2 cm, respectively.

3. Means for biiliocristal hip width of adult females approximated 23 cm on Quechua women; 25 cm on Dogon, Fali, and Nyakyusa women; and 29 cm on Basque and Alaskan Eskimo women. Averages for this width were near 27 cm on Ami, Bunun, and Saisiat women of Taiwan; Polish rural and German college women; Belgian, Hungarian, and Sardinian women at Brussels, Budapest, and Sassari; and women of Japanese ancestry residing in Japan, Hawaii, and California.

4. From data for biiliocristal diameter on ethnically paired groups of males and females, similar means were secured (1) near 26 cm on adults of the Atayal and Puyuma tribes, (2) near 27 cm on Ami, Bunun, Cuban white, and Kirghiz adults, and (3) near 28 cm on Estonian, Russian, and United States white adults at Tallinn, Moscow, and Berkeley. Means for the two sexes did not differ by more than 0.5 cm on Alaskan Eskimo, Basque, Bulgarian, California black, Cuban black, Fali, German, Italian, Paiwan, Rukai, Saisiat, Sicilian, and Tsou adults. For Belgian, Dogon, Hungarian, Sara, and Sardinian adults, means were higher for males than females by 0.6–1.2 cm.

5. The paired index values at the right of Table 9–19 consistently are higher for females than males; they average 77 and 71 on adult females and males, respec-

tively. Mainly, as shown in foregoing paragraphs, this sex difference resulted from similarity of the sexes in hip width and greater shoulder width of men than women. As at age 8 years (Table 9–9), hip width in percentage of shoulder width was less for black groups—Berkeley black, Dogon, Fali, Havana black, Nyakyusa, and Sara—than for Bulgarian, Estonian, Kirghiz, and Russian groups.

Tables 9–9 and 9–19 have nine groups in common (tags 83, 108, 109, 163, 165, 170, 177, 179, and 182). Taking these groups together, average shoulder–hip index for males decreased from 73 at age 8 years to 71 in early adulthood and for females increased from 73 at age 8 years to 77 in early adulthood.

Adult male indices were between 68 and 70 for the Dogon, Fali, Nyakyusa, and Sara rural groups in Table 9–19; similar clustering was found from 1960–1970 data on other adult groups of black males studied in Africa. Mean hip width relative to mean shoulder width was 68 percent for "308 young adult Sara Majingay males" measured at Fort-Archambault (Hiernaux, 1972) and 67 percent in each instance for 326 young adult Luba males reared in rural areas of the Congo, 148 Venda men largely at ages 26–55 years measured at Chiawelo Township, Johannesburg, and 142 Chewa men of the Lilongwe district, Malawi (de Villiers, 1972; Hiernaux, 1972; Nurse, 1972). On 47 adult male natives of the Lau Archipelago, Lourie (Tag 308) obtained an index of 73, the same as that shown in Table 9–19 for Bulgarian and Russian groups.

Comparisons for early and later segments of adulthood were made on Hutterite (tag 283), Venda (tag 289), and Perpo men (Lee, 1970). Age groups were 20–29 years and 40–59 years (Hutterite), 30–39 years and 50 years and up (Venda), and 20–39 years and 50–69 years (Perpo). In each instance there was no change in mean shoulder width and an increase in mean hip width. Similar results were obtained on Czech adult men below and above age 65 years (Parizková & Eiselt, 1966). Composite shoulder–hip indices from the four studies were 71 and 74 for the younger and older groups, respectively.

Cephalothoracic Index and its Components in Adulthood

Table 9–20 presents averages for head circumference, chest circumference, and cephalothoracic index (chest circumference as a percentage of head circumference).

Tag 338. Punjabi-speaking men of this caste measured "at Government Schools of Delhi" and "one of the campus colleges of Delhi University" (Singh, 1969; 1970b).

Tag 339. Men and women residing in the Morobe district at villages in the Kuper range with elevations from 0.9 to 1.5 km. Included were five male dwarfs having means of 54 and 75 cm for head and chest girths, 117 and 59 cm for standing and sitting heights and 22 and 25 cm for arm and leg girths (Malcolm & Zimmerman, 1973).

Tag 340. Young military men (White, 1964).

Tags 341 and 342. Surveys during 1961 of young men and women inhabiting the Slovak and Czech areas of Czechoslovakia (Prokopec, 1964).

Tag 343. Men and women ages 18–19 years; references as in tags 210 and 252. Corresponding statistics on 1358 Italian military men, mean age 26.5 years, were 56.5 cm, 95.0 cm, and 168 (Hertzberg et al., 1963).

Tag 344. Data collected in 1969 at two villages, principally Sikikun, in the northern region (Hsü, 1970).

From Table 9–20 and other analyses of measures for head girth and chest girth gathered during 1960–1970, findings are as follows:

TABLE 9–20 Means for Head and Chest Perimeters (cm) and Cephalothoracic Index on Adult Males Measured Between 1960 and 1970

Tag	Ethnic Group	Number Measured	Head Girth	Chest Girth	Chest Girth × 100 / Head Girth
338	Khatri, Delhi	100*	55.1	78.5	142
339	Baung, New Guinea	28†	55.3	82.0	148 (151)
340	Vietnamese, Vietnam	400*	54.2	80.8	149
299	Newar, Nepal	118†	54.1	81.9	151
319	Romanian, Bucharest	243*	55.6	84.4	152 (145)
177	Sardinian, Sassari	476*	56.3	86.1	153 (148)
73	Black, Washington, D.C.	48*	55.6	85.6	154 (128)
341	Slovak, Slovakia	~2,000*	56.0	88.1	157 (155)
342	Czech, Bohemia & Moravia	~2,000*	56.3	88.6	157 (161)
343	Italian, Genoa	1,037*	56.4	88.7	157 (156)
294	Black, United States	383*	56.2	90.1	160 (147)
171	Sicilian, Palermo	181*	56.1	90.2	161 (150)
83	Bulgarian, Sofia	144*	56.8	91.4	161 (145)
344	Atayal, Taiwan	127†	55.3	89.7	162 (157)
294	White, United States	400*	55.9	91.8	164 (154)
293	Xavante, rural Brazil	42†	57.0	93.2	164 (162)
309	Samaritan, Israel	42†	54.3	89.2	164
317	Turkish, Turkey	915‡	55.2	91.1	165
293	Cayapo, rural Brazil	81†	54.5	89.7	165 (155)
310	Greek, Greece	1,084‡	55.7	92.5	166
300	Wainwright Eskimo, Alaska	43†	55.7	94.2	169

* Ages between 17 years and 22 years.
† Denotes a wide spread of adult ages.
‡ Within age span 18–30 years.

For head girth, standard error of the mean approximates 0.27 cm where $n = 40$, 0.09 cm where $n = 400$, and 0.05 cm where $n = 1000$. Corresponding values for chest girth are 0.95, 0.30, and 0.19 cm. Values in parentheses are averages for cephalothoracic indices of adult females.

1. Average head girth of adult males varied from 52.8 cm on 186 Pahira men of eastern India (tag 299) through 55.3 cm on 432 men of Chinese ancestry at Hong Kong (tag 173) to 59.1 cm on 42 Tortuga islanders (tag 302). For 101 Pahira women and 358 Hong Kong Chinese women, averages were lower than those for males by 1.2 and 1.5 cm, respectively. Chest girth statistics were not reported on any of these groups.

2. On groups of young men, other than those represented in Table 9–20, means for chest girth at ages 17–18 years were 84.1 cm on 86 Kirghizians, 86.0 cm on 119 Russians at Barnaul, 86.9 cm on 195 Uzbeks, 88.4 cm on 269 Russians at Vologda, 89.0 cm on 140 United States blacks at Berkeley, and 90.7 cm on 774 East Germans (tag 108; Goldfeld et al., 1965; tag 267; Oehmisch, 1970). A mean of 85.4 cm was obtained on 280,778 Japanese men, ages 18–21 years, measured in 1962 (K. Kimura, personal communication, 1967). In Africa, on Luba young adults reared in rural Congo, means were 85.1 cm for 112 Luba-Katanga men and 86.9 cm for 214 Luba-Kasai men (Hiernaux, 1972). On Venda subgroups means were 83.4 cm for 199 rural men residing in Vendaland, Transvaal and 87.4 cm for 147 urban men measured at Chiawelo Township, Johannesburg (de Villiers, 1972). The Venda comparison is clouded: at ages either below 26 years or above

55 years there was 50 percent of the rural sample and less than 15 percent of the urban sample (see below). For "adult" men of Taiwan, means were 83.9 cm on 163 Ami, 86.4 cm on 119 Rukai, 86.6 cm on 145 Paiwan, and 91.7 cm on 120 Bunan; means for women of the same tribes were lower by amounts between 3.9 and 7.4 cm (Chai, 1967).

From measures on members of the Perpo (Siraya) tribe residing in a rural region of Taiwan, means were 85.3 cm on 187 men ages 20–29 years, 86.5 cm on 133 men ages 40–49 years, and 84.9 cm on 50 men ages 60–69 years (Lee, 1970); harmonizing with this trend, means rose from 94.7 to 103.8 cm on Hutterite men ages 20–29 years and 40–59 years (tag 283) and fell from 93.7 to 91.9 cm on Czech men ages below and above 65 years (Parízková & Eiselt, 1966). Hungarians at ages 60–69 years gave means of 97.3 and 91.4 cm on 263 men and 222 women, respectively (Dezsö et al., 1969).

3. Mean chest girth expressed as a percentage of mean head girth was (1) 149 on Vietnamese young men and 161 on Bulgarian young men and (2) 151 and 165 on Newar and Cayapo men, respectively. In the first comparison, there were substantial group differences in head girth and chest girth; in the second comparison, the index difference was produced largely by the means for chest girth.

4. From United States Air Force data, averages for the cephalothoracic index were (1) 164 on 400 young white men and 174 on 400 "older" men and (2) 154 on 400 young white women and 159 on 230 women ages 30 years and older (Churchill et al., 1973). For Hungarian men and women ages 60–96 years (study cited above) average indices were 173 and 168. These sex differences are consistent with the bulk of the sex differences in Table 9–20, and the materials reviewed on chest girth presage the index increase from early to middle adulthood shown for United States white men and women.

5. Reference to Tables 9–2, 9–4, and 9–20 shows that the cephalothoracic index increased with age from below 100 at birth to above 125 in early adulthood. Hindu studies reported indices of 93 or less on neonatal groups and 142 to 151 on young adult males. For United States black residents of Washington, D.C. (tag 73) respective averages at ages 1, 9, and 17 years were 98, 120, and 154 on males and 98, 116, and 128 on females. At ages 1, 5, 10, 15, 20, and 25 years, average indices of Bulgarians living in Sofia (tag 83) were for males 103, 109, 122, 142, 161, and 162; and for females 103, 108, 122, 140, 144, and 147.

Arm Girth, Calf Girth, and Limb-Girth Index of Adults

Exhibited in Table 9–21 are averages on adult males for arm and calf girths and averages on adults of both sexes of limb-girth indices (arm girth in percentage of calf girth).

Tag 345. Men of the Perpo tribe living on nonmechanized farms in the regions of Kaohsiung and Tainan (Lee, 1970). Subgroup averages on 375 men ages 20–39 years were 25.4 cm for arm girth, 34.0 cm for calf girth, and 75 for limb-girth index; corresponding values on 150 men ages 50–69 years were 25.0 cm, 32.9 cm, and 76.

Tag 346. Venda subgroup averages were 24.1 cm, 32.4 cm, and 74 on 199 rural men and 27.0 cm, 35.0 cm, and 77 on 148 urban men (de Villiers, 1972). Composition of the urban and rural samples, respectively, was 10 and 34 percent for men at ages below 26 years and, at ages above 55 years, 4 and 16 percent.

Tag 347. Statistics from data collected in 1966 at villages on the island of Vanua Mbalavu. Native Lau islanders were appraised for skin color as "lighter than Fijians and darker than Tongans" (tag 308).

TABLE 9–21 Means for Arm Girth (cm), Calf Girth (cm), and Limb Girth Index on Groups of Adult Males Studied During 1960–1970

Tag	Ethnic Group	Number Measured	Arm Girth	Calf Girth	Arm Girth × 100 ——————— Leg Girth
338	Khatri, Delhi	100*	22.7	30.7	74
345	Perpo (Siraya), Taiwan	671†	25.3	33.8	75
333	Japanese, college students	96‡	26.2	34.8	75 (69)
339	Buang, New Guinea	23†	25.5	34.0	75 (72)
344	Atayal, Taiwan	127†	26.4	35.2	75 (73)
331	Sicilian, three provinces	2,052†	26.6	35.0	76 (74)
346	Venda, Transvaal	347†	25.3	33.5	76
215	Jat, rural Uttar Pradesh	100*	24.1	31.9	76
317	Turkish, Turkey	915‡	27.2	35.5	77
97	Trio & Wajana, Surinam	23*	25.1	32.6	77 (77)
297	Bira, northeast Congo	378†	25.5	32.3	79
310	Greek, Greece	1,084‡	28.4	36.1	79
347	Lau islander	72†	30.9	38.9	79
343	Italian, Italy	1,358‡	29.2	36.5	80
348	Luba, Congo	326‡	26.8	33.4	80
291	Fali, north Cameroun	165†	26.0	32.2	81 (83)
300	Thule Eskimo, Greenland	31†	27.8	34.0	82 (78)
296	Fadidja, Egyptian Nubia	175†	26.7	32.6	82
109	Nyakyusa, south Tanzania	40†	26.3	31.9	82 (84)
333	Oriental, Berkeley	35*	29.2	35.1	83 (76)
283	Hutterite, United States	105‡	28.9	34.9	83
302	Tortuga Islander, West Indies	42†	28.4	34.3	83 (78)
328	German, college students	61‡	31.3	37.2	84 (75)
300	Wainwright Eskimo, Alaska	42†	29.2	33.9	86 (88)
335	White, Berkeley	224*	30.5	35.6	86 (76)
267	Black, Berkeley	140*	31.6	35.1	90 (78)

* Ages between 17 years and 22 years.
† Denotes a wide spread of adult ages.
‡ Within age span 18–30 years.
For arm girth and calf girth, standard error of mean approximates 0.40 cm where $n = 40$, 0.25 cm where $n = 100$, 0.13 cm where $n = 400$, and 0.08 cm where $n = 1000$. Corresponding values for limb-girth index are 0.74, 0.47, 0.24, and 0.15, where values in parentheses are averages for limb-girth indices of adult females.

Tag 348. Young adult males reared in rural areas of the Congo. Subgroup averages were 26.3 cm, 32.9 cm, and 80 for 112 Luba-Katanga and 27.0 cm, 33.7 cm, and 80 for 214 Luba-Kasai (Hiernaux, 1972).

Means for arm girth were less than 25 cm on men studied in India, Kenya, New Guinea, Peru, and Zaire. Besides the Table 9–21 statistics on Jat and Khatri men (tags 215 and 338), obtained means were 20.1 cm on 62 Quechua men ages 20–40 years measured at Peruvian highland villages (Frisancho et al., 1975); 23.7 cm on 454 Maring men residing at villages in the Simbai valley, New Guinea (Buchbinder & Clark, 1971); 24.1 cm on 155 Twa men living near Lake Tumba, Zaire (Hiernaux et al., 1974); 24.2 cm on 27 Maasai men, mean age 23 years, inhabiting "Narok, Amboseli, and the Loita Hills" of rural Kenya (Day, Carruthers, Bailey, & Robinson, 1976); and 24.9 cm on 99 Bomai men, mean age 28 years, measured at scattered jungle hamlets in the Chimbu Subdistrict, New Guinea (Barnes, 1965). Other means were 25.4 cm on 205 Malawian men ages 20 years and up inhabiting villages in the Lower Shire region (Burgess et al., 1973); 25.7 cm on 127 Yongamuggl men, mean age 29 years, living in the Chimbu Subdistrict (Barnes, 1965); and 27.7 cm on 308 young adult Sara men residing at Fort-Archambault (Hiernaux, 1972). Means for 390 Malawian women, 452 Maring women, and 64 Bomai women were less than corresponding means for men by 0.2 cm, 3.3 cm, and 5.1 cm.

Measures of arm girth on Hutterites ages 20–29 years gave means of 28.9 cm for 105 males and 25.3 cm for 149 females; corresponding values representing ages 40–59 years were higher by 2.5 and 4.9 cm for 81 males and 80 females, respectively (tag 283). Chimbu means at ages 20–39 years were 25.0 cm on 127 males and 21.3 cm on 72 females; at ages 50 years and up, means on 82 males and 44 females were lower by 2.4 and 1.1 cm (tag 282). Sizes of samples and means for arm girth at ages 18–24 years, 35–44 years, 55–64 years, 65–74 years, and 75–79 years, respectively, were (1) on United States men—about 10 percent nonwhite—411 and 30.0 cm, 703 and 31.5 cm, 418 and 30.2 cm, 265 and 29.5 cm, and 72 and 27.7 cm, and (2) on United States women 534 and 25.9 cm, 784 and 29.0 cm, 443 and 30.2 cm, 299 and 29.2 cm, and 70 and 27.9 cm (Stoudt, Damon, McFarland, & Roberts, 1970).

Averages for calf girth from measures taken during the 1960s were 29.3 cm on 316 Yanomama men ages 18–45 years (tag 306); between 30 and 33 cm on Bira, Fadidja, Fali, Jat, Khatri, Nyakyusa, Trio, and Wajana men (Table 9–21); 32.9 and 34.3 cm, respectively, on 260 Venda men of rural South Africa and 247 men of Johannesburg (tag 289); between 35 and 36 cm on Atayal, Greek, Italian, Turkish, and United States white men at Berkeley (Table 9–21); 35.4 and 35.2 cm on Czech men below and above age 65 years (Parízková & Eiselt, 1966); 36.1 cm on 42 Xavante men (tag 293); near 36.0 cm on United States black and white military men whose mean age was 19 years (tag 294); and 38.9 cm on Lau Islanders between ages 20 and 64 years (Table 9–21).

Female means for calf girth were 27.0 cm on 260 Yanomama ages 16–45 years (tag 306); 30.6 cm on 40 Quechua ages 20–60 years (tag 325); near 31 cm on 62 Fali, 61 Nyakyusa, and 24 Trio and Wajana (Table 9–21); near 33 cm on 24 Buang, 47 Filipino, 179 Hungarian, 1839 Sicilian, and 39 Xavante (tags 339, 334, 330, 331, and 293); and near 35 cm on 117 black and 245 white females living in California (tags 267 and 335).

Mean arm girth was 74–76 percent of mean calf girth on Atayal, Buang, Jat, Khatri, Perpo, and Sicilian men; 79–82 percent on Bira, Fadidja, Fali, Greek, Italian, Lau, Luba, Nyakyusa, and Thule Eskimo men; and 86–90 percent on Wainwright Eskimo men and United States black and white men (Table 9–21). Limb-girth indices were 68 on 40 Quechua women (tag 325); 69 on 112 Japanese college women (tag 333); 73 on 47 Filipino nurses (tag 334); 78 on Thule Eskimo, Tortuga Islander, and United States black women (Table 9–21); and between 83 and 88 on Fali, Nyakyusa, and Wainwright Eskimo women (Table 9–21).

Sitting Height, Lower Limb Height, and Skelic Index of Adults

Averages for sitting height, lower limb height, and the skelic index are brought together in Table 9–22.

Tag 349. Indigenes (Amerinds) measured at Ahousat, a Nootka reserve on Flores Island, off the west coast of Vancouver Island. On Amerinds measured at Anaham, a Chilcotin reserve west of Williams Lake, averages were 90.2 cm, 80.1

TABLE 9-22 Mean Sitting Height (cm), Lower Limb Height (cm), and Skelic Index of Adult Males Measured Between 1960 and 1970

Tag	Ethnic Group	Number Measured	Sitting Height	Lower Limb Height	Skelic Index
91	Cakchiquel, Guatemala	58*	85.0	71.7	84 (84)
349	Nootka, British Columbia	36*	92.3	78.1	85 (85)
350	Japanese, Japan	11,318†	90.2	77.6	86 (83)
158	Chinese, Hong Kong	1,074†	90.3	77.6	86 (84)
287	Ecuadorian, Andes	104*	83.2	72.5	87 (87)
351	Mestizo, rural Colombia	114‡	87.3	76.2	87 (85)
140	Spanish-American, Guatemala	97*	90.6	79.0	87 (89)
313	Puyuma, Taiwan	73*	85.6	74.4	87 (85)
306	Yanomama, Brazil & Venezuela	316‡	81.3	71.9	88 (88)
93	Quechua, Peruvian Andes	117‡	85.4	74.9	88 (80)
309	Samaritan, Israel	44*	90.7	80.2	88 (82)
299	Newar, Nepal	118*	85.1	75.8	89
352	Wainwright Eskimo, Alaska	41*	87.8	78.5	89 (86)
317	Turkish, Turkey	915‡	89.7	79.6	89
310	Greek, Greece	1,084‡	90.3	80.2	89
340	Vietnamese, Vietnam	400‡	85.3	75.8	89
337	Basque, north-central Spain	527*	89.6	80.4	90 (88)
353	Paiwan, Taiwan	145*	82.5	74.1	90 (87)
343	Italian, Italy	1,358‡	89.7	80.9	90
301	White, Ontario	286†	92.2	83.4	90 (89)
338	Khatri, Delhi	50†	87.9	80.0	91
163	Cuban White, Havana	103†	88.2	80.0	91 (89)
354	White, United States	1,086‡	91.2	83.9	92 (86)
288	White, South Africa	49‡	90.4	83.6	92 (93)
355	Atayal, Taiwan	234*	84.4	77.8	92 (88)
283	Hutterite, United States	106‡	89.4	82.2	92 (92)
83	Bulgarian, Sofia	285†	89.4	82.5	92 (89)
356	Norwegian, southern Norway	262†	93.2	86.1	92
357	Bundi, New Guinea	280*	81.1	75.1	93 (93)
259	Polish, Przasnysk district	79*	86.0	79.6	93 (90)
358	Hungarian, Budapest	71†	91.1	84.8	93 (90)
359	Chewa, Malawi	142*	86.2	79.8	93
347	Lau islander	74*	89.6	83.3	93
293	Xavante, west-central Brazil	42*	87.8	82.4	94 (92)
215	Jat, Uttar Pradesh	50†	89.5	85.0	95
296	Fadidja, Egyptian Nubia	174*	86.4	82.1	95
293	Cayapo, rural Brazil	130*	84.9	80.5	95 (93)
327	Sara, southern Chad	235‡	89.0	84.5	95 (94)
6	Hindu, Bhopal & Gwalior	55†	85.5	81.5	95 (92)
346	Venda, Transvaal	344*	84.7	82.0	97
320	Nordestino, Brazil	198*	82.0	79.6	97
97	Trio & Wajana, Surinam	190*	79.8	77.5	97 (95)
165	Cuban Black, Havana	69†	86.3	84.0	97 (96)
360	Black, United States	383†	88.2	86.7	98 (94)
291	Fali, north Cameroun	94*	85.6	83.6	98 (95)
73	Black, Washington, D.C.	48†	87.9	86.1	98 (97)
295	Dogon, rural Mali	82*	84.3	84.2	100 (97)
361	Kurumba, Upper Volta	79*	85.5	85.5	100 (98)

TABLE 9-22 (Continued)

Tag	Ethnic Group	Number Measured	Sitting Height	Lower Limb Height	Skelic Index
288	Bantu, South Africa	68‡	83.8	84.3	101 (96)
292	Chimba, southwest Angola	44*	84.4	86.7	103 (96)
109	Nyakyusa, southern Tanzania	40‡	79.8	83.5	105 (100)

*Denotes a wide, or unspecified, spread of adult ages.
†Between ages 17 and 22 years.
‡Within the age span 18–49 years.
For sitting height and lower limb height, standard error of the mean approximates 0.63 cm where n = 40, 0.40 cm where n = 100, 0.20 cm where n = 400, and 0.10 cm where n = 1000. Corresponding statistics for the skelic index are near 0.68, 0.43, 0.22, and 0.14, where values in parentheses are averages for skelic indices of adult females.

cm, and 89 for 36 men and 83.6 cm, 72.9 cm, and 87 for 55 women (Birkbeck et al., 1971).

Tag 350. Source specified in tag 157. Corresponding statistics on Japanese-Americans residing in Hawaii (tag 333) were 57, 89.3 cm, 77.0 cm, and 86 (84).

Tag 351. Descendants of Spanish immigrants and Chibcha Amerinds; measured at Tenza, a subsistence farming community in the Department of Boyaca (Himes & Mueller, 1977).

Tag 352. Refer to tag 300. For other groups of adult men, statistics were 86.0 cm, 74.2 cm, and 86 on 50 Greenland Eskimos at Upernavik; 84.5 cm, 75.6 cm, and 89 on Greenland Eskimos at Augpilagtok; and, on 31 Greenland Eskimos at Thule, 84.9 cm, 76.3 cm, and 90. Averages for 33 "Thule pure" women were 79.1 cm, 71.1 cm, and 90.

Tag 353. See tag 313. On the Rukai, Saisiat, and Tsou tribes, respectively, comparable values were 119, 83.3 cm, 74.9 cm, 90 (86); 68, 83.5 cm, 75.2 cm, 90 (89); and 81, 86.0 cm, 78.0 cm, 91 (88).

Tag 354. These statistics were for ages 18–34 years (tag 272). For ages 55–79 years, corresponding values were 755, 88.7 cm, 81.7 cm, 92 (85). Averages on young air force personnel (tag 294) were 400, 91.3 cm, 83.7 cm, 92 (89) and, for personnel over age 30 years, 400, 91.5 cm, 84.3 cm, 92 (89).

Tag 355. Composite averages from measures taken during 1962–1963 (Chai, 1967) and in 1969 (Hsü, 1970). Statistics from Chai (1967) were 120, 81.9 cm, 75.3 cm, 92 (88) on the Bunun tribe and 163, 85.4 cm, 79.2 cm, 93 (91) on the Ami tribe. For findings on other aborigines of Taiwan, see tags 313 and 350.

Tag 356. Statistics from measures taken in 1962 on Norwegian men age 20 years residing in the counties of Aust-Agder and Vest-Agder (Udjus, 1964).

Tag 357. Source of Bundi study given in tag 57. On members of the Buang tribe, averages were 80.5 cm, 78.3 cm, and 97 for 23 physically normal men; 59 cm, 58 cm, and 98 for 5 male dwarfs; and 76.5 cm, 73.5 cm, and 96 for 24 normal women (Tag 339).

Tag 358. Refer to tag 161. Other findings were 84.6 cm, 75.2 cm, and 89 on 179 young women attending a teachers' college (tag 330); 85.4 cm, 76.3 cm, and 89 for young women attending a physical education college at Budapest (Eiben, 1969); and, on Hungarians over age 60 years, 86.1 cm, 80.4 cm, and 93 for 262 men and 79.6 cm, 72.9 cm, and 92 for 222 women (Dezsö et al., 1969). For Czechs living at Prague, averages were 90.3 cm, 79.6 cm, and 88 on 75 men at or below 65 years and 89.3 cm, 80.0 cm, and 90 on 95 men above age 65 years (Parízková & Eiselt, 1966).

Tag 359. Men examined during 1970 in recruitment as mine laborers; considered to represent the Chewa adult male population in the Lilongwe district (Nurse, 1972).

Tag 360. See tag 294. From the same military source, measures on 146 young adult black females gave averages of 83.0 cm, 78.4 cm, and 94. Similar averages of 83.1 cm, 77.2 cm, and 95 were obtained from a civilian sample of 83 United States black females age 17 years (tag 216).

Tag. 361. Records for this study were gathered during 1966–1967 at the village of Roanga, north of Ouahigouya (Huizinga, 1968).

Some of the findings for 1960–1970 that can be drawn from Table 9–22 and its supporting materials are as follows:

1. Means of sitting height of adult males were near 80 cm on Trio and Wajana in Surinam and Nyakyusa in Tanzania; other means below 85 cm represented groups in Africa (Chimba, Dogon, South African Bantu), New Guinea (Bundi, Buang), Taiwan (Atayal, Bunun, Paiwan, Rukai, Saisiat), and South America (Nordestino, Yanomama). Means were near 92 cm on white college men of Ontario and Nootka Amerinds of British Columbia; other sample means at or above 90 cm characterized groups of Chinese, Japanese, Greek, Hungarian, Samaritan, South African white, and United States white men. Statistical estimation of population differences (one-tailed, at $p = 0.01$) indicated that average sitting height of Nootka men residing on Flores Island was greater than that of Trio and Wajana men inhabiting the tropical forest of Surinam by an amount probably exceeding 10 cm (12 percent). The corresponding minimum estimate was 11 cm (13 percent) for the extent to which sitting height of men in southern Norway surpassed that of Nyakyusa in Tanzania.

2. For lower limb height of adult males, derived averages varied from near 72 cm on Cakchiquel and Yanomama in Central and South America to between 85 and 87 cm on Chimba in Angola, Jat in India, Kurumba in Upper Volta, Norwegian in southern Norway, and American black in the United States. At $p = 0.01$, it can be inferred that average lower limb height (subischio–soles distance) for men of the Chimba tribe exceeded that of their Yanomama sex-age peers by at least 12 cm (16 percent). Intermediate sample means were near 75 cm for Bundi, Bunun, Quechua, Rukai, and Saisiat men and near 80 cm for Basque, Cayapo, Czech, Greek, Hungarian, Khatri, Nordestino, Samaritan, and Turkish men.

3. Averages for the skelic index in adulthood were 86 on Chinese and Japanese men; 86–90 on Eskimo men in Greenland and Alaska; 87–93 on male aborigines of Taiwan; 89–95 on Jat , Khatri, and Newar men in India and Nepal; and 93–105 on black groups in Africa, Cuba, and the United States. Averages obtained on Amerind groups were widely dispersed—from 84 on Cakchiquel men through 88 and 94 on men of the Yanomama and Xavante tribes to 97 on Trio and Wajana men.

4. Skelic indices on both sexes were available for ten black groups and eight tribes of Taiwan aborigines (Table 9–22 and text for tags 350 and 352). The average sex difference was three percentage points in each instance; specifically, composite indices were 91 and 88 for men and women of the Taiwan tribes and, for men and women of the black groups, 99 and 96. Of the 38 paired index values in Table 9–22, there were eight instances where the female index equaled or exceeded the male index: they included a wide assortment of ethnic groups—Bundi, Cakchiquel, Ecuadorian, Hutterite, Nootka, South African white, Spanish-American, and Yanomama.

From research on white males and females, it has been known for several decades that the skelic index increased during the period between infancy and midadolescence and then decreased from midadolescence to early adulthood (Meredith & Knott, 1938). Previous sections of this chapter have cited analyses of measures taken during 1960–1970 on white and nonwhite groups yielding average skelic indices between 45 and 59 at birth, between 51 and 65 at age 1 year, and upwards from 78 at age 8 years. Tables 9–13 and 9–22 have 12 ethnic male groups in common, with composite average indices of 96 at age 15 years and 93 in adulthood. Nine groups —Chinese, Hindu, black, and white—showed decline, while Bundi, Quechua, and one white group did not.

Skelic index averages were accessible at annual ages from 9 to 17 years on several groups of females: at ages 9, 13, and 17 years respective averages were 78, 84, and 81 for Andean Quechua (tag 93); 81, 84, and 83 for native Japanese (tag 157); 83, 87, and 84 for Chinese at Hong Kong (tag 158); 83, 85, and 83 for Guatemala Cakchiquel (tag 91); 87, 89, and 86 for Bulgarian females at Sofia (tag 83); 88, 96, and 93 for Hindu females at Bhopal and Gwalior (tag 60); 89, 92, and 89 for Hungarian females at Budapest (tag 160); 91, 93, and 91 for white females at Havana (tag 163); 96, 99, and 97 for black females at Washington, D.C. (tag 73); 97, 100, and 98 for black females at Havana (tag 165); and, not showing a decrease from midadolescence to early adulthood, 88, 91, and 91 for Bundi females of New Guinea (tag 57). For males, respective averages at ages 10, 15, and 20 years were 81, 88, and 86 on Guatemala Cakchiquel (the adult average in Table 9–22 was secured for ages 20–35 years); 86, 89, and 86 on Chinese at Hong Kong; 89, 92, and 87 on Spanish-American males; 91, 100, and 95 on Hindu males at Bhopal and Gwalior; 92, 96, and 91 on white males at Havana; and, not registering a late-adolescent decline, 83, 91, and 93 on Bundi males and 88, 92, and 92 on Bulgarian males of Sofia (tags 57, 60, 83, 91, 140, 158, 163, and 165). Generalizing, during the 1960s it was established for several diverse ethnic groups that the lower limbs elongated faster than the body stem from early infancy to midadolescence and more slowly than the body stem during the late adolescent years.

CONCLUSIONS

The reader is alerted to the fact that this chapter, although appearing fairly broad in outline, is considerably circumscribed in content. Changes in body size and form between ages 2–4 years and 9–12 years are not discussed; the large research literature on size and form of the face is excluded; and sparse reference is made to the hundreds of somatic investigations published in the period from 1930 to 1960.

Had the chapter dealt comprehensively with research on external size and form of the human body, several facets of somatic variation among ethnic groups would not have come within its scope. These include chondrification, ossification, and epiphyseal union; formation, eruption, and attrition of teeth; thickness and distribution of adipose tissue; form, pigmentation, and amount of hair; and biologic differences between ethnic groups in other organs, tissues, and cells.

What has the chapter done? One of its principal tasks has been to document and systematize differences and similarities among contemporary ethnic groups in *mean magnitude* of 17 somatic measures of external size and form. Intercomparison of studies conducted between 1960 and 1970 has shown the following:

1. At birth, body weight of Swedish neonates delivered at Malmö was more than 40 percent higher than that of Indian neonates delivered at Vārānasi. Among native American tribes, body weight of the Cree exceeded that of the Maya by 40 percent. Vertex–soles length was 4 cm greater for Polish neonates at Warsaw than Lunda neonates of northeast Angola.

2. At age 1 year, infants of the Netherlands surpassed those of East Pakistan by fully 40 percent in body weight and about 10 cm in vertex–soles length. Total length was 4 cm greater for infants of Turkish upper-class families at Istanbul than for their Indian age peers nurtured at Poona under "near optimal" conditions of nutrition and health care. Head girth was more than 4 cm larger for Russian infants at Murmansk than Ladino infants of rural Guatemala.

3. At age 5 years, Bundi children of New Guinea were shorter than their Amerind age peers of Montana by more than 12 cm. Children of wealthy Hindu families in which there was "well-privileged" nurture were shorter than children of Dutch parents in the managerial and professional strata by an amount likely between 3 and 9 cm.

4. At age 8 years, Thai children residing at villages in Thailand were fully 12 cm shorter than their Czech age peers inhabiting a rural region near Podebrady. The cephalic index was below 80 for Indonesian children of Palue Island and above 90 for their Uzbek age peers at Tashkent. Lower limb height was 80 percent of sitting height for children of Japan and near 95 percent for black children of Chad, Tanzania, and Cuba. Hip width was less than 70 percent of shoulder width on Yoruba children at Ibadan and more than 75 percent on Bulgarian children at Sofia.

5. At age 13 years, female youths of Dutch families in the professional and managerial strata were 5 cm taller and 6 kg heavier than those of Chinese (Hong Kong) families in the same socioeconomic categories. In turn, the Chinese female youths of upper-class Hong Kong families were 4 cm taller and 3 kg heavier than their age-sex-city peers belonging to families of low socioeconomic status.

6. At age 15 years, Bundi male youths living in the Madang district of New Guinea were 25 cm shorter than their Jat age-sex peers inhabiting villages in Uttar Pradesh; Chuvash youths at Cheboksar were 12 cm shorter and 9 kg lighter than German youths at Düsseldorf. Aligned with male youths residing at urban centers, those living in rural areas were 7 cm shorter in Romanian and Kirghiz comparisons, 4 cm shorter in Chuvash and Tatar comparisons, and 2 cm taller in a comparison of Russians at Pskov and in an adjoining rural region. Lower limb height was less than 90 percent of sitting height for male youths of Quechua ancestry in the Peruvian Andes and more than 100 percent for those of Afro-black ancestry in rural Guyana.

7. On adults, standing height of female groups varied from below 145 cm for South Americans of the Yanomama tribe to above 165 cm for Norwegians at Oslo; among male groups, variation was from below 155 cm for Vailala of New Guinea to above 180 cm for North Dinka of Sudan. Lower limb height was 84 percent of sitting height on Cakchiquel men and women and, on Nyakyusa men and women, 105 and 100 percent. Male cephalic indices were spread from below 75 on Chimba, Egyptian, Fali, Jat, and Kurumba groups to above 85 on Melanau, Peruvian, and Uzbek groups. For Taiwanese adults, hip width relative to shoulder width was 73 percent on females and 67 percent on males, with corresponding

values for Basque adults of 83 percent on females and 77 percent on males; the sex differences arose from similarity of males and females in hip width, and wider shoulder of males. For Khatri women of Delhi, arm girth was near 23 cm and calf girth near 31 cm; for Lau women on Vanua Mbalavu, arm girth was near 31 cm and calf girth near 39 cm. Arm girth relative to calf girth varied from 70 to 85 percent among female groups and from 75–90 percent among male groups.

A second task of the chapter has been to reveal somatic changes with time common to a number of ethnic groups. It has shown the following:

1. Female youths and adult women measured between 1960 and 1970 were taller than their age peers measured 2–12 decades earlier. Comparisons, 18 at each of the two ontogenetic levels, included groups of Chinese, Filipino, Japanese, Kirghiz, Lapp, Maori, and mulatto females, along with white females in Australia, Europe, and the United States. Average increases were 2.3 cm/decade for females age 13 years and 0.6 cm/decade for adult women.
2. The standing height of men measured during 1960–1970 was greater at early adult ages than at late adult ages: this was found for each of 33 ethnic groups studied in Africa, Asia, Australia, Europe, Greenland, North and South America, Oceania, and the West Indies. Comparisons based on a gap of 20 years between "early" and "later" adulthood gave an average decrease of 4.8 cm. Estimates from studies on Japanese and United States white males indicated that about 3 cm of this decrease was due to decline in height during ontogeny, while the remainder arose from differential secular increase represented in the simultaneous measurement of young and older adults.
3. Chest girth was less than head girth at birth and became increasingly larger than head girth from infancy to adulthood. For 21 neonatal groups, chest girth was between 92 and 99 percent of head girth; on 21 groups of adult males, it was between 142 and 169 percent. Lower limb height relative to sitting height increased between infancy and midadolescence and then decreased slightly in late adolescence: skelic index averages were 51 on 8 groups studied at birth, 87 on 24 groups studied at age 8 years, 95 on 24 male groups studied at age 15 years, and 92 on 46 adult male groups. Nine ethnic groups studied at age 8 years and in early adulthood gave averages for hip width relative to shoulder width that decreased from 73 to 71 percent on males and increased from 73 to 77 percent on females.

As a third task, both implicitly and explicitly the chapter has given methodological and problem-centered leads for future research. For example:

1. Standing height and body weight have been studied on many more ethnic groups than have measures of the head, trunk, and limbs. Future studies on external body size should afford a better balance of findings for overall and segmental measures. It is proposed that studies commonly include measures of arm girth, calf girth, and distance from vertex to the infraischia plane.
2. In many of the 1960–1970 studies, sample size was below 50 for at least some of the measures taken or subgroups formed. There should be greater awareness that samples are drawn for the purpose of estimating characteristics of populations, and small samples yield crude estimates. Future studies in which socioeconomic, dietary, age, and other subgrouping is planned call for consideration of subgroup specificity and adequacy of subgroup size. Particularly in designing childhood

studies, it should be recognized that measures on 90 children at one age, as an alternative to measures on 30 children at each of three consecutive ages, provide more valuable statistics for both descriptive and comparative use. This is especially so in regard to variability and correlation statistics.

3. A few of the studies cited were concerned with relationships between somatic variables and variables such as altitude and latitude of habitat, type of health supervision, or amount of calcium and animal protein in the diet. Far more substantial knowledge is needed on most relational problems. Future investigators should endeavor to define nonsomatic variables objectively, measure somatic variables reliably, avoid confounding in index derivation and data analysis, and explore group modifications under different conditions of genetic admixture, climatic milieu, and health facilitation.

ACKNOWLEDGMENTS
Gratitude is expressed to the persons who assisted with literature search, reference procurement, provision of unpublished material, language translation, verification of statistics, and manuscript typing: C. J. Alber, K. V. Bailey, P. T. Baker, A. Birdsall, S. Cecere, K. C. Chan, H. Chrzastek-Spruch, B. Debiec, E. DeToni, O. Eiben, R. Eksmyr, A. P. Forbes, J. E. Goettsch, R. G. Harvey, M. D. Janes, D. L. Jones, T. Kambara, S. J. Karayan, K. Kimura, V. B. Knott, L. A. Malcolm, N. N. Miklashevskaya, F. J. Miller, M. A. Neel, O. Neyzi, M. V. Phadke, M. Prokopec, K. A. Rageth, J. L. Rauh, B. D. Richardson, K. P. Sabharwal, M. Sempé, J. Spranger, M. Steffens, D. A. Stewart, M. C. Swaminathan, E. Takahashi, A. M. Thomson, H. L. Vis, V. G. Vlastovsky, J. Wingerd, N. Wolanski, and S. Y. Zukeran. Appreciation for generous departmental support is tendered to Dean Warren K. Giese and Professors John H. Spurgeon, Steven N. Blair, and Roger G. Sargent, all of the College of Health and Physical Education, University of South Carolina. Special recognition is due E. Matilda Meredith for invaluable helpfulness in many ways.

REFERENCES
Abbie, A. A. Skinfold thickness in Australian aborigines. *Archaeology and Physical Anthropology in Oceania,* 1967, *2,* 207–219.

Abdou, I. A., & Mahfouz, A. H. Heights and weights of school children in Cairo as indications of their nutritional status. *Journal of the Egyptian Public Health Association,* 1967, *42,* 114–124.

Adams, M. S., & Niswander, J. D. Birth weight of North American Indians: A correction and amplification. *Human Biology,* 1973, *45,* 351–357.

Adriano, A. G., & Sánchez, A. La somatometría en los preescolares de Navojoa, Sonora, en 1966 y 1974. *Salud Publica de Mexico,* 1975, *17,* 517–523.

Afanasenko, P. P., & Mamyrov, B. M. Changes in physical development in the Kirghizian S.S.R. *Gigiena i Sanitariya,* 1965, *30,* 115–117.

Aicardi, G., & Depperu, E. Lo sviluppo del bambino nei primi due anni di vita in provincia di sassari. *Minerva Pediatrica,* 1966, *18,* 2264–2270.

Aicardi, G., & Rovetta, D. G. La dinamica dell'accrescimento staturo-ponderale delle femmine sassaresi durante 35 anni. *Studi Sassaresi,* 1965, *6,* 567–577.

Amarasinghe, A. A. W. Head circumference of the newborn Ceylonese baby. *Archives of Disease in Childhood,* 1966, *41,* 556–557.

Aráujo, A. M., & Salzano, F. M. Parental characteristics and birthweight in a Brazilian population. *Human Biology,* 1975, *47,* 37–43.

Arkhipova, G. P. Physical development of children and adolescents of the minority nationalities of Sakhalin Island. *Gigiena i Sanitariya*, 1967, *32*, 107–109.

Armitage, P., Boyd, J. D., Hamilton, W. J., & Rowe, B. C. A statistical analysis of a series of birthweights and placental weights. *Human Biology*, 1967, *39*, 430–444.

Ashcroft, M. T., & Antrobus, A. C. K. Heights and weights of schoolchildren in St. Vincent. *Journal of Biosocial Science*, 1970, *2*, 317–328.

Ashcroft, M. T., Bell, R., & Nicholson, C. C. Anthropometric measurements of Guyanese schoolchildren of African and East Indian racial origins. *Tropical and Geographical Medicine*, 1968, *20*, 159–171.

Ashcroft, M. T., Heneage, P., & Lovell, H. G. Heights and weights of Jamaican schoolchildren of various ethnic groups. *American Journal of Physical Anthropology*, 1966, *24*, 35–44.

Ashcroft, M. T., & Lovell, H. G. Heights and weights of Jamaican children of various racial origins. *Tropical and Geographical Medicine*, 1964, *4*, 346–353.

Ashcroft, M. T., & Lovell, H. G. Changes in mean size of children in some Jamaican schools between 1951 and 1964. *West Indian Medical Journal*, 1965, *14*, 48–52.

Ashcroft, M. T., Lovell, H. G., George, M., & Williams, A. Heights and weights of infants and children in a rural community of Jamaica. *Journal of Tropical Pediatrics*, 1965, *11*, 56–68.

Bäckström, L., & Kantero, R-L. Cross-sectional studies of height and weight in Finnish children aged birth to 20 years. *Acta Paediatrica Scandinavica*, 1971, *220* [Suppl.], 9–12.

Bailey, K. V. Rural nutrition studies in Indonesia: VII. Field surveys in Javanese infants. *Tropical and Geographical Medicine*, 1962, *14*, 110–120.

Bailey, K. V. Growth of Chimbu infants in the New Guinea highlands. *Journal of Tropical Pediatrics*, 1964, *10*, 3–16.

Bailey, R. R. The effect of maternal smoking on the infant birth weight. *New Zealand Medical Journal*, 1970, *71*, 293–294.

Banerjee, A. R., & Roy, S. K. Preliminary study on the quantitative genetics in man: The effect of parity of the mother on the birth weight of the offspring. *Journal of the Indian Pediatric Society*, 1962, *1*, 89–98.

Banik, N. D. D., Krishna, R., Mane, S. I. S., Raj, L., & Taskar, A. D. A longitudinal study of physical growth of children from birth up to 5 years of age in Delhi. *Indian Journal of Medical Research*, 1970, *58*, 135–142.

Banik, N. D. D., Nayar, S., Krishna, R., & Raj, L. The effect of nutrition on growth of pre-school children in different communities in Delhi. *Indian Pediatrics*, 1972, *9*, 460–466.

Bansal, I. J. S. Head dimensions of Punjabi boys and girls aged 6–15 years. *Indian Journal of Pediatrics*, 1969, *36*, 263–270.

Barja, I., LaFuente, M. E., Ballester, D., Mönckeberg, F., & Donoso, G. Peso y talla de pre-escolares chilenos urbanos de tres niveles de vida. *Revista Chilena de Pediatria*, 1965, *36*, 525–529.

Barnes, R. Comparisons of blood pressures and blood cholesterol levels of the New Guineans and Australians. *Medical Journal of Australia*, 1965, *1*, 611–617.

Basu, A. The Pahira: A population genetic study. *American Journal of Physical Anthropology*, 1969, *31*, 399–416.

Basu, A., Namboodiri, K. K., Weitkamp, L. R., Brown, W. H., Pollitzer, W. S., & Spivey, M. A. Morphology, serology, dermatoglyphics, and microevolution of some village populations in Haiti, West Indies. *Human Biology*, 1976, *48*, 245–269.

Beghin, D., Wachholder, A., Trabelsi, M., & Cantraine, F. La taille et le poids des ecoliers du Cap Bon, Tunisie. *Annales Societe Belge de Medicine Tropicale*, 1975, *55*, 341–358.

Belousov, A. Z., Kardashenko, V. N., Kondakova-Varlamova, L. P., Prokhorova, M.

V., & Sgromskaia, E. P. Dynamics of the physical development of children and adolescents in the city of Orel. *Sovetskoe Zdravookhranenie*, 1968, *27*, 25–28.

Benés, J. On the physical anthropology of the Gypsies in Czechoslovakia. *Scripta Faculta Prírodovedecká Ujep Brunensis*, Biologia 2, 1974, *4*, 83–90.

Benoist, J. Anthropologie Physique de la population de l'Ile de la Tortue (Haiti): Contribution a l'étude de l'origine des noirs des Antilles Françaises. *Bulletins et Mémoires de la Société d'Anthropologie de Paris*, 1962, *3*, 315–335.

Berry, F. B. *Chile: Nutrition survey, 1960.* (Report, Interdepartmental Committee on Nutrition for National Defense.) Washington, D.C.: United States Government Printing Office, 1961.

Berry, F. B. *Kingdom of Thailand: Nutrition survey, 1960.* (Report, Interdepartmental Committee on Nutrition for National Defense.) Washington, D.C.: United States Government Printing Office, 1962. (a)

Berry, F. B. *Republic of Lebanon: Nutrition survey, 1961.* (Report, Interdepartmental Committee on Nutrition for National Defense.) Washington, D.C.: United States Government Printing Office, 1962. (b)

Berry, F. B. *Union of Burma: Nutrition survey, 1961.* (Report, Interdepartmental Committee on Nutrition for National Defense.) Washington, D.C.: United States Government Printing Office, 1963.

Bhasin, M. K. Group differences among Newars of Nepal for somatometry. *Zeitschrift für Morphologie und Anthropologie*, 1971, *63*, 192–214.

Bhattacharya, D. K. Anthropometry of a negro population in India: Siddis of Gujarat. *Zinruigaku Zassi*, 1969, *77*, 254–259.

Billy, G. Anthropometric evidence of exogamy related to secular changes in present-day populations. *Journal of Human Evolution*, 1975, *4*, 517–520.

Birdsall, A. Normal foot length of children. Unpublished master's thesis, New York University, 1966.

Birkbeck, J. A., Lee, M., Myers, G. S., & Alfred, B. M. Nutritional status of British Columbian Indians: II. Anthropometric measurements, physical and dental examinations at Ahousat and Anaham. *Canadian Journal of Public Health*, 1971, *62*, 403–414.

Boas, F. The growth of Toronto children. *Report, United States Commissioner of Education*, 1898, *2*, 1541–1599.

Bobbitt, J. F. The growth of Philippine children. *Pedagogical Seminary*, 1909, *16*, 137–168.

Bonné, B. Genes and phenotypes in the Samaritan isolate. *American Journal of Physical Anthropology*, 1966, *24*, 1–20.

Boutourline, E., Tesi, G., Kerr, G. R., Stare, F. J., Kallal, Z., Turki, M., & Hemaidan, N. Nutritional correlates of child development in southern Tunisia: I. Linear growth. *Growth*, 1972, *36*, 407–424.

Boutourline, E., Tesi, G., Kerr, G. R., Stare, F. J., Kallal, Z., Turki, M., & Hemaidan, N. Nutritional correlates of child development in southern Tunisia: II. Mass measurements. *Growth*, 1973, *37*, 91–110.

Bowden, B. D., Johnson, J., Ray, L. J., & Towns, J. The height and weight changes of Melbourne children compared with other population groups. *Australian Paediatric Journal*, 1976, *12*, 281–295.

Bowditch, H. P. The growth of children: A supplementary investigation. *Tenth Annual Report, Massachusetts State Board of Health*, 1879, 35–62.

Brown, T., & Barrett, M. J. Growth in Central Australian aborigines: Stature. *Medical Journal of Australia*, 1971, *2*, 29–32.

Brundtland, G. H., Liestöl, K., & Walløe, L. Height and weight of school children and adolescent girls and boys in Oslo 1970. *Acta Paediatrica Scandinavica*, 1975, *64*, 565–573.

Buchbinder, G., & Clark, P. The Maring people of the Bismarck ranges of New Guinea. *Human Biology in Oceania*, 1971, *1*, 121–133.

Buck, A. A., Sasaki, T. T., & Anderson, R. I. *Health and disease in four Peruvian villages: Contrasts in epidemiology*. Baltimore: Johns Hopkins Press, 1968.

Burgess, A. P., & Burgess, H. J. L. The growth pattern of East African schoolgirls. *Human Biology*, 1964, *36*, 177–193.

Burgess, H. J. L., Burgess, A., & Wheeler, E. F. Results and appraisal of a nutrition survey in Malawi. *Tropical and Geographical Medicine*, 1973, *25*, 372–380.

Burrow, G. N., Hamilton, H. B., & Hrubec, Z. Study of adolescents exposed in utero to the atomic bomb, Nagasaki, Japan: II. Growth and development. JAMA (*Journal of the American Medical Association*), 1965, *192*, 357–364.

Bussadori, G. Valori antropometrici con riferimenti auxologici degli alunni delle scuole medie inferiori e superiori della provincia di rovigo. *L'Arcispedale S. Anna di Ferrara*, 1965, *18*, 711–728.

Carron, A. V., & Bailey, D. A. Strength development in boys from 10 through 16 years. *Monographs of the Society for Research in Child Development*, 1974, *39* (4, Serial No. 157).

Cetorelli, L., & Ferro-Luzzi, A. Lo spessore delle pliche cutanee in un gruppo di soggetti Italiani. *Quaderni della Nutrizione*, 1967, *27*, 293–315.

Chai, C. K. *Taiwan aborigines: A genetic study of tribal variation*. Cambridge, Mass.: Harvard University Press, 1967.

Champness, L. T., Bradley, M. A., & Walsh, R. J. A study of the Tolai in New Britain. *Oceania*, 1963, *34*, 66–75.

Chan, B. S. T. Sex differences in the growth of stature and its component segments of Hong Kong Chinese children. *Zeitschrift für Morphologie und Anthropologie*, 1972, *63*, 323–340.

Chang, K. S. F., Chan, S. T., & Low, W. D. Head growth in Chinese children in Hong Kong. *Far East Medical Journal*, 1967, *3*, 314–319.

Chang, K. S. F., Lee, M. M. C., Low, W. D., Chui, S., & Chow, M. Standards of height and weight of Southern Chinese children. *Far East Medical Journal*, 1965, *1*, 101–109.

Chang, K. S. F., Lee, M. M. C., Low, W. D., & Kvan, E. Height and weight of Southern Chinese children. *American Journal of Physical Anthropology*, 1963, *21*, 497–509.

Chapin, H. D. A plan of infantile measurements. *Medical Record*, 1894, *46*, 649–651.

Charzewska, J. Zmiany wybranych cech morfologicznych u ludnosci wiejskiej z powiatów przasnysz i plonsk w latach 1900–1964. *Prace I Materialy Naukowe, Istytut Matki I Dziecka*, 1968, *11*, 7–34.

Chase, H. P., Kumar, V., Dodds, J. M., Sauberlich, H. E., Hunter, R. M., Burton, R. S., & Spalding, V. Nutritional status of preschool Mexican-American migrant farm children. *American Journal of Diseases of Children*, 1971, *122*, 316–324.

Chen, M. L., Chiang, C. H., Huang, C. S., & Chen, J. S. A study on the nutritional status and physical growth of Chinese children and young adults. *Journal of the Formosan Medical Association*, 1974, *73*, 374–386.

Cherry, F. F. Growth from birth to five years of New Orleans underprivileged Negro children. *Bulletin of Tulane University Medical Faculty*, 1968, *24*, 233–240.

Chrzastek-Spruch, H. Badania ciagle nad rozwojem fizycznym niemowlat, lubelskich. *Prace I Materialy Naukowe, Instytut Matki I Dziecka*, 1968, *11*, 65–104.

Chrzastek-Spruch, H., & Dobosz-Latalska, C. Ocena rozwoju fizycznego dzieci wiejskich z województwa lubelskiego. *Medycyna Wiejska*, 1973, *8*, 93–102.

Chrzastek-Spruch, H., & Szajner-Milart, I. Badania nad rozwojem fizycznym dzieci i mlodziezy szkolnej miasta lublina. *Przeglad Pediatryczny*, 1974, *4*, 121–133.

Churchill, E., Robinow, D., & Erskine, P. Factor analysis of anthropometric data for fifteen race-age-national origin specific groups. Paper presented at the IXth International Congress of Anthropological and Ethnological Sciences, Chicago, 1973.

Clarke, J. Observations on some causes of the excess of the mortality of males above that of females. *Philosophical Transactions of the Royal Society of London*, 1786, *16*, 122–130.

Cohen, N. M., Clayden, A. D., & King, B. Cross-sectional-type weight reference values for village children under five years in Lesotho. *Growth*, 1976, *40*, 107–121.

Collis, W. R. F., Dema, I., & Lesi, F. E. A. Transverse survey of health and nutrition, Pankshin Division, Northern Nigeria. *West African Medical Journal*, 1962, *11*, 131–154.

Correnti, V. L'Accrescimento da 6 a 20 anni nella popolazione palermitana. *Revista di Antropologia*, 1969, *55* [Suppl.], 1–210.

Coy, J. F., Lewis, I. C., Mair, C. H., Longmore, E. A., & Ratkowsky, D. A. The growth of Tasmanian infants from birth to three years of age. *Medical Journal of Australia*, 1973, *2*, 12–18.

Cravioto, J., Birch, H. G., Licardie, E. de, Rosales, L., & Vega, L. The ecology of growth and development in a Mexican preindustrial community. *Monographs of the Society for Research in Child Development*, 1969, *34* (5, Serial No. 129).

Cristescu, M. *Aspecte ale cresterii si dezvoltarii adolescentilor din Rupblica Socialista Romania*. Bucharest: Editura Academiêi Republicii Socialiste Romania, 1969.

Crognier, E. Données biométriques sur l'état de nutrition d'une population africaine tropicale: Les sara du tchad. *Société de Biométrie Humaine Revue*, 1969, *4*, 37–55.

Das, B. M. Étude des charactèrs anthropométriques des Khasi de l'Assam, Inde. *Anthropologie*, 1967, *71*, 97–134.

Das, S. R., Roy, M., Paul, A., & Chakraborty, R. A growth study of Indian infants: non-relationship with placental alkaline phosphatose genotypes. *Human Biology*, 1975, *47*, 219–230.

David, J. H. S. Height growth of melanodermic natives in northeastern Lunda (Angola). *South African Journal of Medical Science*, 1972, *37*, 49–60.

Davies, A. M., & Vardy-Cohen, D. The health of schoolchildren in Monrovia. *West African Medical Journal*, 1962, *11*, 207–214.

Davies, C. T. M., Mbelwa, D., Crockford, G., & Weiner, J. S. Exercise tolerance and body composition of male and female Africans aged 18–30 years. *Human Biology*, 1973, *45*, 31–40.

Day, J., Carruthers, M., Bailey, A., & Robinson, D. Anthropometric, physiological and biochemical differences between urban and rural Maasai. *Atherosclerosis*, 1976, *23*, 357–361.

Debiec, B., Godzisz, J., Gasinska, A., Kamer, B., Lipiec, J., Niewodniezy, G., Przyluska, E., Stawiszynska, A., & Zielinska, W. Changes of body weight and height in the school children in the Widzew district of the city of Lodz. *Pediatria Polska*, 1973, *48*, 51–58.

Dellaportas, G. J. Growth of schoolchildren in Gondar area, Ethiopia. *Human Biology*, 1969, *41*, 218–222.

DeLuca, G., D'Andrea, S., Pelizzo, M. T., & Cozzi, M. Auxologia del neonato friulano. *Minerva Pediatrica, Monograph Series*, 1965, 210–211.

DeMatteis, F., Cantalini, C., Cinque, T., & Vesi, G. Rilievi biometrici ed auxologici su 6,981 bambini della provincia de l'aquila dalla nascita a 14 anni. *Minerva Pediatrica*, 1972, *24*, 159–192.

Demirjian, A., Jenicek, M., & Dubuc, M. B. Les normes staturo-pondérales de l'enfant urbain canadien français d'âge scolaire. *Canadian Journal of Public Health*, 1972, *63*, 14–30.

Desai, P., Miall, W. E., & Standard, K. L. A five-year study of infant growth in rural Jamaica. *West Indies Medical Journal*, 1969, *18*, 210–221.

De Toni, E., Aicardi, G., & Castellano, A. S. Variazioni dell'accrescimento somatico nelle femmine dell'Italia Settentrionale durante dodici anni. *Minerva Pediatrica, Monograph Series,* 1965, 261–265.

De Toni, E., Aicardi, G., Castellano, A. S., & Chessa, M. Nuovo contributo sul comportamento auxologico di 2,066 femmine dell'Italia Settentrionale di età dai 10 ai 19 anni. *Minerva Pediatrica,* 1966, *18,* 1–7. (a)

De Toni, E., Aicardi, G., & Podestà, F. Aggiornamento dei valori auxologici e biometrici dei maschi dell'Italia Settentrionale. *Minerva Pediatrica,* 1966, *18,* 2158–2165. (b)

De Toni, E., Aicardi, G., & Podestà, F. Valori auxologici e funzionali delle femmine sassaresi da 6 a 21 anni. *Minerva Pediatrica,* 1966, *18,* 1335–1342. (c)

De Toni, E., Aicardi, G., & Rovetta, D. G. Valori auxologica e funzionali dei maschi sassaresi da sei a ventun anni. *Minerva Pediatrica,* 1966, *18,* 1323–1332. (d)

de Villiers, H. A study of morphological variables in urban and rural Venda male populations. In D. J. M. Vorster (Ed.), *The human biology of environmental change.* London: International Biological Programme, 1972.

Dezsö, G., Eiben, O., & Thoma, A. Metrikus testalkati jellegek eloszlása egy időskorú mintában. *Anthropologiai Közlemények,* 1969, *1,* 31–37.

Dokládal, M. Growth of the main head dimensions from birth up to twenty years of age in Czechs. *Human Biology,* 1959, *31,* 90–109.

Drenhaus, U., Skrobak-Kaczynski, J., & Jorgensen, J. B. Über den säkularen trend der akzeleration bei grönländischen Eskimos aus dem nördlichen bezirk von Upernavik. *Zeitschrift für Morphologie und Anthropologie,* 1974, *65,* 293–304.

Duncan, J. M. On the weight and length of the newly-born child in relation to the mother's age. *Edinburgh Medical Journal,* 1864, *10,* 497–502.

Dwyer, J. T., Feldman, J. J., & Mayer, J. Adolescent dieters: Who are they? Physical characteristics, attitudes and dieting practices of adolescent girls. *American Journal of Clinical Nutrition,* 1967, *20,* 1045–1056.

Ebrahim, G. J., & D'Sa, A. Prematurity in Dar es Salaam. *Journal of Tropical Pediatrics,* 1966, *12,* 55–58.

Eiben, O. Általánosított korrdináták antropológiai alkalmazása. *Anthropologiai Közelmények,* 1969, *13,* 103–120.

Eiben, O., Hegedüs, G., Bánhegyi, M., Kiss, K., Monda, M., & Tasnádi, I. *Budapesti óvodások és iskolások testi fejlettsége (1968–1969).* Budapest: Eötvös Loránd University, 1971.

Eksmyr, R. Anthropometry in Ethiopian private school children: CNU report No. 40. *Nutrition and Metabolism,* 1971, *13,* 7–20.

El-din-Ahmed, N., & Abdalla, L. Some physical measurements and haematological studies in the Sudanese newborn baby. *Journal of Tropical Medicine and Hygiene,* 1967, *70,* 271–274.

Enachescu, T., Pop, S., & Georgescu, V. Dimorfismul sexual al nou-nascutului in relatia sa ontogenetica cu adultul. *Probleme de Anthropologie,* 1963, *7,* 57–76.

Evans, J. G., Prior, I. A. M., Davidson, F., & Morrison, R. B. I. The Carterton Study: Height, weight and skinfold measurements in a sample of town-dwelling New Zealand Europeans. *New Zealand Medical Journal,* 1968, *68,* 318–322.

Eveleth, P. B. Physical growth of American children living in the tropics. *Revista de Antropologia,* 1968, *16,* 13–25.

Eveleth, P. B. An anthropometric study of northeastern Brazilians. *American Journal of Physical Anthropology,* 1972, *37,* 223–232.

Fasbender, H. Mutter- und Kindeskörper. *Zeitschrift für Geburtshülfe und Gynäkologie,* 1878, *3,* 278–297.

Fernández, N. A., Burgos, J. C., Asenjo, C. F., & Rosa, I. R. Nutrition survey of five rural Puerto Rican communities. *Boletin de la Asociacion Medisa de Puerto Rico,* 1969, *61,* 42–52.

Fetherston, G. H. A statistical report of the Melbourne Lying-in Hospital for a period of thirteen months, May 31, 1861, to June 30, 1862. *Australian Medical Journal,* 1862, *7,* 276–278.

Fetherston, R. H. Weight of Victorian infants. *Australian Medical Journal,* 1887, *9,* 495–496.

Fetter, V., Prokopec, M., Suchy, J., & Sobová, A. Vyvojová akcelerace ü mládeze podle antropometrickych vyzkumu z let 1951 a 1961. *Ceskoslovenská Pediatrie,* 1963, *18,* 673–677.

Fiawoo, D. K. Physical growth and the social environment—A West African example. Paper presented at the IXth International Congress of Anthropological and Ethnological Sciences, Chicago, 1973.

Filippova, A. G. Physical development of Vladivostok school children. *Gigiena i Sanitariya,* 1965, *7,* 122–124.

Fingert, S. S. Physical development of school children of Pskov. *Zdravookhranenie Rossiiskoi Federatsii,* 1969, *13,* 32–36.

Fisk, S. C. *Blackfeet Indian Reservation: Nutrition survey, 1961.* (Report, Interdepartmental Committee on Nutrition for National Defense, and Division of Indian Health, United States Public Health Service.) Washington, D.C.: United States Government Printing Office, 1964. (a)

Fisk, S. C. *Bolivia: Nutrition survey, 1962.* (Report, Interdepartmental Committee on Nutrition for National Defense.) Washington, D.C.: United States Government Printing Office, 1964. (b)

Fisk, S. C. *Fort Belknap Indian Reservation: Nutrition survey, 1961.* (Report, Interdepartmental Committee on Nutrition for National Defense, and Division of Indian Health, United States Public Health Service.) Washington, D.C.: United States Government Printing Office, 1964. (c)

Florey, C. du V., & Cuadrado, R. R. Blood pressure in native Cape Verdeans and in Cape Verdean immigrants and their descendants living in New England. *Human Biology,* 1968, *40,* 189–211

Forbes, A. P., Ronaghy, H. A., & Majd, M. Skeletal maturation of children in Shiraz, Iran. *American Journal of Physical Anthropology,* 1971, *35,* 449–454.

Franckx, H. Lengte en gewicht bij scholieren uit het kortrijkse. *Archives Belges de Medecine Sociale, Hygiene, Medecine du Travail et Medecine Legale,* 1969, *27,* 109–114.

Frisancho, A. R., & Baker, P. T. Altitude and growth: A study of the patterns of physical growth of a high altitude Peruvian Quechua population. *American Journal of Physical Anthropology,* 1970, *32,* 279–292.

Frisancho, A. R., Borkan, G. A., & Klayman, J. E. Pattern of growth of lowland and highland Peruvian Quechua of similar genetic composition. *Human Biology,* 1975, *47,* 233–243.

Froehlich, J. W. Migration and the plasticity of physique in the Japanese-Americans of Hawaii. *American Journal of Physical Anthropology,* 1970, *32,* 429–442.

Fry, P. C., Howard, J. E., & Logan, B. C. Body weight and skinfold thickness in black, Mexican-American, and white infants. *Nutritional Reports International,* 1975, *11,* 155–160.

Fryer, B. A., Lamkin, G. H., Vivian, V. M., Eppright, E. S., & Fox, H. M. Growth of preschool children in the north central region. *Journal of the American Dietetic Association,* 1972, *60,* 30–37.

Galton, F. Report of the Anthropometric Committee. *British Association for the Advancement of Science,* 1884, 253–306.

Gampel, B. The relation of skinfold thickness in the neonate to sex, length of gestation, size at birth, and maternal skinfold. *Human Biology,* 1965, *37,* 29–37.

Garcia-Almansa, A., Fernández-Fernández, M. D., & Palacios-Mateos, J. M. Patrones de crecimiento de los niños españoles normales. *Rivista Clinica Espanola,* 1969, *113,* 45–48.

Garn, S. M. *Human races.* Springfield, Ill.: Charles C. Thomas, 1961.

Garn, S. M. Symposium on nutrition in physical anthropology: Introduction. *Yearbook of Physical Anthropology,* 1975, *19,* 154–157.

Gavrilovic, Ž., Rumenic, L., & Stajic, N. Prilog proucavanju telesnog razvoja i stanja uhranjenosti slovaka i rusina iz vojvodine. *Revue de la Société Anthropologie Yougoslave,* 1966, *3,* 41–53.

Geissler, A., & Uhlitzsch, R. Die grössenverhältnisse der schulkinder im schulinspektions bezirk Freiberg. *Zeitschrift des Koniglich-Sächsischen Statistischen Burea's,* 1888, *34,* 28–41.

Gerylovová, A., & Bouchalová, M. The relationship between children's and parents' heights in the age-range 0–6 years. *Annals of Human Biology,* 1974, *1,* 229–232.

Ghai, O. P., & Sandhu, R. K. Study of physical growth of Indian children in Delhi. *Indian Journal of Pediatrics,* 1968, *35,* 91–108.

Gibbs, J. L., Jr. (Ed.). *Peoples of Africa.* New York: Holt, Rinehart & Winston, 1965.

Gilberg, R., Jorgensen, J. B., & Laughlin, W. S. Anthropometrical and skinfold thickness measurements on the polar Eskimos, Thule District, North Greenland. *Meddelelser om Gronland,* 1975, *203,* 1–23.

Glanville, E. V., & Geerdink, R. A. Skinfold thickness, body measurements and age changes in Trio and Wajana Indians of Surinam. *American Journal of Physical Anthropology,* 1970, *32,* 455–462.

Glinka, J. Das Wachstum von Kopf und Gesicht bei Kindern und Jugendlichen von 7-17 Jahren auf der Insel Palue (Kleine Sunda-Inseln). *Zeitschrift für Morphologie und Anthropologie,* 1972, *64,* 20–28.

Gokulanathan, K. S., & Verghese, K. P. Socio-cultural malnutrition: Growth failure in children due to socio-cultural factors. *Journal of Tropical Pediatrics,* 1969, *15,* 118–124.

Goldfeld, A. Y., Merkova, A. M., & Tseimlina, A. G. *Materials on the physical development of children and adolescents in cities and rural localities of the U.S.S.R.* Lenigrad: Meditsina, 1965.

Goppe, D. I. Some indices of the physical development of Kemerovo school children (data collected 1969–1970). *Zdravookhranenie Rossiiskoi Federatsii,* 1972, *16,* 27–29.

Grandi, F. Confronto fra l'accrescimento nel primo anno di vita del bambino allevato in istituto (I.P.I. di Bologna) e del bambino di privata consultazione, su di una base di eguale condotta dietologica e terepeutica. *Minerva Pediatrica, Monograph Series,* 1965, 178–182.

Grantham-McGregor, S. M., Desai, P., & Back, E. H. A longitudinal study of infant growth in Kingston, Jamaica. *Human Biology,* 1972, *44,* 549–561.

Greene, L. S. Physical growth and development, neurological maturation and behavioral functioning in two Ecuadorian Andean communities in which goiter is endemic. *American Journal of Physical Anthropology,* 1973, *38,* 119–134.

Grossman, S., Handlesman, Y., & Davies, A. M. Birth weight in Israel, 1968–70: I. Effects of birth order and maternal origin. *Journal of Biosocial Science,* 1974, *6,* 43–58.

Gur'ev, V. I. Physical development of school children of Russian and Tatar nationality in the rural areas of the Tumen district. *Nauchnye Trudy Kazanskogo Meditsinskogo Institut,* 1967, *24,* 31–32.

Guzmán, M. A., Scrimshaw, N. S., Bruch, H. A., & Gordon, J. E. Nutrition and infection field study in Guatemalan villages, 1959–1964: VII. Physical growth and development of preschool children. *Archives of Environmental Health,* 1968, *17,* 107–118.

Hamill, P. V. V., Johnston, F. E., & Lemeshow, S. *Body weight, stature, and sitting height: White and Negro youths 12–17 years.* (Vital and Health Statistics, Series 11, No. 126,

DHEW Pub. No. HRA-74-1608.) Washington, D.C.: United States Government Printing Office, 1973. (a)

Hamill, P. V. V., Johnston, F. E., & Lemeshow, S. *Height and weight of children: Socioeconomic status.* (Vital and Health Statistics, Series 11, No. 119, DHEW Publ. No. HSM-73-1601.) Washington, D.C.: United States Government Printing Office, 1973. (b)

Hampton, M. C., Huenemann, R. L., Shapiro, L. R., Mitchell, B. W., & Behnke, A. R. A longitudinal study of gross body composition and body conformation and their association with food and activity in a teen-age population: Anthropometric evaluation of body build. *American Journal of Clinical Nutrition,* 1966, *19,* 422–435.

Harfouche, J. K. *The growth and illness patterns of Lebanese infants: Birth–18 months.* Beirut: Khayats, 1966.

Harvey, R. G. An anthropometric study of growth and physique of the populations of Karkar Island and Lufa subdistrict, New Guinea. *Philosophical Transactions of the Royal Society of London,* Series B, 1974, *268,* 279–292.

Hautvast, J. G. A. J. *Growth changes in the human head, face, and stature.* Nijmegen: Thoben Offset, 1967.

Hautvast, J. Physical growth and menarcheal age in Tanzanian schoolchildren and adults. *Human Biology,* 1971, *43,* 421–444.

Hawley, T. G., & Jansen, A. A. J. Height and weight of Fijians in coastal areas from one year till adulthood. *New Zealand Medical Journal,* 1971, *73,* 346–349.

Heapost, L. Tallinna kooliopilaste somatomeetriliste tunnuste ja kehaproportsioonide kujunemine. *Eesti Nsu Teaduste Akadeemia Toimetised Bioloogia,* 1973, *22,* 287–301.

Heller, C. A., Scott, E. M., & Hammes, L. M. Height, weight and growth of Alaskan Eskimos. *American Journal of Diseases of Children,* 1967, *113,* 338–344.

Helmuth, H. Anthropometry of university students: Trent University, Peterborough, Ontario. *Zeitschrift für Morphologie und Anthropologie,* 1973, *65,* 174–185.

Hernández, L. E. Crecimiento y desarrolo normal del niño pobre dominicano. *Boletín de la Oficina Sanitaria Panamericana,* 1966, *61,* 27–39.

Hertzberg, H. T. E., Churchill, E., Dupertuis, C. W., White, R. M., & Damon, A. *Anthropometric survey of Turkey, Greece, and Italy.* New York: Macmillan, 1963.

Hertzog, K. P., Garn, S. M., & Hempy, H. O. III. Partitioning the effects of secular trend and aging on adult stature. *American Journal of Physical Anthropology,* 1969, *31,* 111–115.

Hiernaux, J. La croissance des écoliers Rwandais. *Académie Royale des Sciences d'Outre-Mer, Classe des Sciences Naturelles et Médicales.* 1965, *16,* 1–204.

Hiernaux, J. A comparison of growth and physique in rural, urban and industrial groups of similar ethnic origin. In D. J. M. Vorster (Ed.), *The human biology of environmental change.* London: International Biological Programme, 1972.

Hiernaux, J., & Asnes, D. Le croissance des enfants Sara de 3 and 10 ans a Fort-Archambault (Républigue du Tchad). *Bulletin et Mémoires de la Société d'Anthropologie de Paris,* 1974, *13,* 427–453.

Hiernaux, J., Crogneir, E., & Vincke, E. A comparison of the development of the upper limb in two African populations living in contrasting environments. *International Journal of Ecology and Environmental Sciences,* 1974, *1,* 41–46.

Himes, J. H., & Malina, R. M. Age and secular factors in the stature of adult Zapotec males. *American Journal of Physical Anthropology,* 1975, *43,* 367–370.

Himes, J. H., & Mueller, W. H. Aging and secular change in adult stature in rural Colombia. *American Journal of Physical Anthropology,* 1977, *46,* 275–280.

Hofvander, Y., & Eksmyr, R. Anthropometry of children in a typical rural district and an urban slum area in Ethiopia. *Courrier,* 1971, *21,* 1–4.

Holibková, A., & Holibkova, V. Die körperliche entwicklung der kinder der Olomoucer ländlichen. *Acta Universitatis Palackinae Olomucensis Facultatis Medicae*, 1968. *51*, 127–138.

Holt, L. E. *The diseases of infancy and childhood.* New York: Appleton, 1897.

Horner, L. Practical applications of physiological facts. *Penny Magazine*, 1837, *339*, 270–272.

Howells, W. W. Hutterite age differences in body measurements. *Papers, Peabody Museum of Archaeology and Ethnology*, 1970, *52* (2), 1–123.

Hrdlicka, A. Growth during adult life. *Proceedings, American Philosophical Society*, 1936, *76*, 847–897.

Hrubcová, M. Somatische untersuchung der schuljugend sowie der heranreifenden jugend in der gegend von Podebrady. *Anthropos*, 1963, *7*, 115–127.

Hsü, W. C. Anthropological studies of the Sikikun Atayal. *Nagasaki Igakkai Zassi*, 1970, *45*, 46–67.

Huizinga, J. New physical anthropological evidence bearing on the relationships between Dogon, Kurumba and the extinct West African Tellem populations. *Proceedings, Koninklijke Nederlandse Akademie van Wetenschappen*, 1968, *71*, Series C, 16–30.

Huizinga, J., & Birnie-Tellier, N. F. Some anthropometric data on male and female Dogons. *Proceedings, Koninklijke Nederlandse Akademie van Wetenschappen*, 1966, *69*, Series C, 675–695.

Huizinga, J., & Reijnders, B. Skinfold thickness and body fat in adult male and female Fali (North Cameroon). *Proceedings, Koninklijke Nederlandse Akademie van Weten-schappen*, 1974, *77*, Series C, 496–503.

Ibrahim, W. N., Kamel, K., Selim, O., Azim, A., Gaballah, M. F., Sabry, F., El-Naggar, A., & Hoerman, K. Hereditary blood factors and anthropometry of the inhabitants of the Egyptian Siwa Oasis. *Human Biology*, 1974, *46*, 57–68.

Illingworth, R. S., & Eid, E. E. The head circumference of infants and other measure-ments to which it may be related. *Acta Paediatrica Scandinavica*, 1971, *60*, 333–337.

Illingworth, R. S., & Lutz, W. Head circumference of infants related to body weight. *Archives of Disease in Childhood*, 1965, *40*, 672–676.

Imanbaev, S. I., Kim, N. I., & Sidorova, V. S. Physical development of school children in Frunze. *Sovetskoe Zdravookhranenie Kirgizii*, 1971, *6*, 14–17.

Inoue, T., & Shimizu, M. *Physical and skeletal growth and development of* Japanese chil-dren. Tokyo: Japan Society for the Promotion of Science, 1965.

Ivanov, K. A., Frolova, N. A., & Nagornova, E. P. Apropos of the physical develop-ment of school children in Kalinin. *Sovetskoe Zdravookhranenie*, 1963, *20*, 30–34.

Jamison, P. L., & Zegura, S. L. An anthropometric study of the Eskimos of Wain-wright, Alaska. *Arctic Anthropology*, 1970, *7*, 125–143.

Janes, M. D. Physical growth of Nigerian Yoruba children. *Tropical and Geographical Medicine*, 1974, *26*, 389–398.

Japanese Ministry of Education. *Report for 1900.* Tokyo: Ministry of Education, 1901.

Japanese Ministry of Education. *Report for 1970.* Tokyo: Ministry of Education, 1971.

Jayant, K. Birth weight and some other factors in relation to infant survival: A study on an Indian sample. *Annals of Human Genetics*, 1964, *27*, 261–270.

Jelliffe, E. F. P. Placental malaria and foetal growth failure. In G. E. W. Wolsten-holme & M. O'Connor (Eds.), *Nutrition and infection.* Boston: Little, Brown, 1967.

Jelliffe, E. F. P. Low birth weight and malarial infection of the placenta. *Bulletin, World Health Organization*, 1968, *38*, 69–78.

Johnson, T. O. The physique of urban Nigerians in the adolescent period. *Journal of Tropical Pediatrics and Environmental Child Health*, 1972, *18*, 134–138.

Johnston, F. E., & Beller, A. Anthropometric evaluation of the body composition of black, white, and Puerto Rican newborns. *American Journal of Clinical Nutrition*, 1976, *29*, 61–65.

Johnston, F. E., McKigney, J. I., Hopwood, S., & Smelker, J. Physical growth and development of urban native Americans: a study of urbanization and its implications for nutritional status. *American Journal of Clinical Nutrition*, 1978, *31*, 1017–1027.

Johnston, F. E., Wainer, H., Thissen, D., & MacVean, R. Hereditary and environmental determinants of growth in height in a longitudinal sample of children and youth of Guatemalan and European ancestry. *American Journal of Physical Anthropology*, 1976, *44*, 469–476.

Jones, D. L., Hemphill, W., & Meyers, E. S. A. *Height, weight and other physical characteristics of New South Wales children: Part 1. Children aged five years and over.* Sydney: New South Wales Department of Health, 1973.

Jorgensen, J. B., & Skrobak-Kaczynski, J. Secular changes in the Eskimo community of Augpilagtok. *Zeitschrift für Morphologie und Anthropologie*, 1972, *64*, 12–19.

Jürgens, H. W. Über sexualdifferenzierte Proportionsveränderungen beim Wachstum des Menschen. *Zeitschrift für Morphologie und Anthropologie*, 1960, *50*, 210–219.

Jürgens, H. W., Allan, N. C., & Tracey, K. A. Über Beziehungen zwischen sichelzellmerkmal und Körperform in Sud-Nigeria. *Zeitschrift für Morphologie und Anthropologie*, 1964, *56*, 142–163.

Jyothi, K. K., Dhakshayani, R., Swaminathan, M. C., & Venkatachalam, P. S. A study of the socio-economic, diet and nutritional status of a rural community near Hyderabad. *Tropical and Geographical Medicine*, 1963, *15*, 403–410.

Kadanoff, D., Mutafov, S., & Pandova, B. Körpeliche entwicklung und wachstumstumpo der kinder im alter von O bis 3 jahren. *Aerztliche Jugendkunde*, 1975, *66*, 11–16.

Kalra, K., Kishore, N., & Dayal, R. S. Anthropometric measurements in the newborn: A study of 1,000 consecutive livebirths. *Indian Journal of Pediatrics*, 1967, *34*, 73–82.

Kamaletdinov, A. Z. Shifts in the physical development of pupils of Ukranian schools of L'vov from 1958 to 1967. *Sovetskoe Zdravookhranenie*, 1969, *28*, 32–36.

Kambara, T. Studies on growth and nutritional intake of school children in Kagawa prefecture: Regional differences in growth. *Shikoku Igaku Zasshi*, 1969, *25*, 570–582.

Kanda, S. Anthropological studies on the inhabitants in Formosa: Somatometries on the Hoklo and Hakka Chinese and the Atayals and Amis. *Journal of the Anthropological Society of Nippon*, 1974, *82*, 269–288.

Kariks, J., & Walsh, R. J. Some physical measurements and blood groups of the Bainings in New Britain. *Archeology and Physical Anthropology in Oceania*, 1968, *3*, 129–142.

Kasius, R. V., Randall, A., Tompkins, W. T., & Wiehl, D. G. Maternal and newborn nutrition studies at Philadelphia Lying-In Hospital: Newborn studies, V. Size and growth of babies during the first year of life. *Milbank Memorial Fund Quarterly*, 1957, *35*, 323–372.

Kasparov, E. L. The physical development of Kalmuck children in the dynamics of the past 40 years. *Zdravookhranenie Rossiiskoi Federatsii*, 1967, *2*, 30–32.

Kaul, S. S. Physical growth and development (human): A study based on Kashmiri Pandit boys of school-going age in Srinagar, Kashmir. Unpublished doctoral dissertation, Panjab University, 1971.

Kelso, A. J., Tinsman, J. H., Lewis, A. S., & Tully, M. S. Some monofactorial phenotypes and anthropometric variation. *Human Biology*, 1972, *44*, 15–28.

Kerimov, M. K. Physical development of children of school age in the Buinak region of the Daghestan A.S.S.R. *Sovetskoe Zdravookhranenie*, 1968, *27*, 28–33.

Kettle, E. S. Weight and height curves for Australian aborigines infants and children. *Medical Journal of Australia*, 1966, *1*, 972–977.

Key, A. *Läroverkskomiténs underdaniga utlatande och förslag.* Stockholm: Kongl, 1885.

Khanjanasthiti, P., Supachaturas, P., Mekanandha, P., Srimusikapodh, V., Choopanya, K., & Leesuwan, V. Growth of infants and preschool children. *Journal of the Medical Association of Thailand*, 1973, *56*, 88–100.

Kimura, K. Comparative studies on the physical growth and development of the children in Okinawa. *Journal of the Anthropological Society of Nippon*, 1975, *83*, 151–171. (a)

Kimura, K. Growth studies of the Japanese. In S. Watanabe, S. Kondo, & E. Matsunaga (Eds.), *Anthropological and genetic studies on the Japanese*. Tokyo: University of Tokyo Press, 1975. (b)

Kimura, K., & Tsai, C. M. Comparative studies of the physical growth in Formosans: I. Height and weight. *Zinruigaku Zassi*, 1967, *75*, 11–18.

Kimura, K., & Tsai, C. M. Comparative studies of the physical growth in Taiwanese: II. Biacromial breadth and bicristal diameter. *Zinruigaku Zassi*, 1968, *76*, 193–204

Knott, V. B. Stature, leg girth, and body weight of Puerto Rican private school children measured in 1962. *Growth*, 1963, *27*, 157–174.

Knott, V. B., & Meredith, H. V. Body size of United States schoolboys at ages from 11 years to 15 years. *Human Biology*, 1963, *35*, 507–513.

Knussmann, R. Neue normtabellen anthropometrischer merkmale für die erbbiologische gutachterpraxis. *Anthropologischer Anzeiger*, 1968, *30*, 272–279.

Knussmann, R., & Knussmann, R. Die Dama—Eine Altschicht in Südwestafrika? *Journal of South West African Scientific Society*, 1970, *24*, 9–32.

Kogan, R. B. Assessing the high level of physical development of young children. *Zdravookhranenie Rössiiskoi Federatsii*, 1969, *13*, 29–32.

Kornfeld, W. Neuere Durchschnittswerte für die anthropometrische Analyse von Körperbau und Entwicklung. *Österreichische Zeitschrift für Kinderheilkunde und Kinderfursorge*, 1954, *10*, 71–88.

Kreysler, J., & Schlage, C. The nutrition situation in the Pangani basin. In H. Kraut & H-D. Cremer (Eds.), *Investigations into health and nutrition in East Africa*. München: Weltforum Verlag, 1969.

Krogman, W. M. Growth of man. Den Haag: Tabulae Biologicae, 1941.

Kukowski, K., London, W. T., Sutnick, A. I., Kahn, M., & Blumberg, B. S. Comparison of progeny of mothers with and without Australia antigen. *Human Biology*, 1972, *44*, 489–499.

Kullander, S., & Källén, B. A prospective study of smoking and pregnancy. *Acta Obstetricia et Gynecologica Scandinavia*, 1971, *50*, 83–94.

Kurisu, K. Multivariate statistical analysis on the physical interrelationship of native tribes in Sarawak, Malaysia. *American Journal of Physical Anthropology*, 1970, *33*, 229–234.

Kurniewicz-Witczakowa, R., Miesowicz, I., Mazurczak, T., & Jarmolinska-Eska, H. J. Wskazniki rozwoju fizycznego dzieci warszskich w wieku od O od 36 miesiaca zycia. *Problemy Medycyny Wieku Rozwojowego*, 1972, *2*, 45–61.

Kuyp, E. van der Body weights and heights of the Surinam people. *Voeding*, 1967, *28*, 435–469.

Lanza, I., & Bolgiani, M. P. Rilievi sull'accrescimento staturo-ponderale durante i primi due anni di vita del bambino torinese. *Minerva Pediatrica, Monograph Series*, 1965, 184–185.

Lanzavecchia, C., & Mazzarello, G. Valori auxologici normali del bambino della prima infanzia del Novese (Circondario di Novi Ligure). *Aggiornamento Pediatrico*, 1965, *16*, 131–136.

Lapitskii, F. G., Belogorskii, V. Y., Nemzer, M. P., Pogorely, I. A., Sinopalnikov, O. V., & Zolotareva, M. P. Basic indices of physical development of children in the second and third years in Murmansk. *Zdravookhranenie Rossiiskoi Federatsii*, 1970, *14*, 28–31.

Lapitskii, F. G., Nemzer, M. P., & Belogorskii, V. I. Some data on the physical development of school children at Kirov in 1965. *Zdravookhranenie Rossiiskoi Federatsii,* 1969, *13,* 11–13.

Lapitskii, F. G., & Pozorelyi, I. A. The physical development of school children in Monchegorsk in 1964. *Zdravookhranenie Rossiiskoi Federatsii,* 1967, *11,* 28–32.

Laska-Mierzejewska, T. Desarrollo y maduración de los niños y jóvenes de la Habana. *Revista Cubana de Pediatria,* 1967, *39,* 385–447.

Laska-Mierzejewska, T. Morphological and developmental difference between negro and white Cuban youths. *Human Biology,* 1970, *42,* 581–597.

Lasker, G. W. Differences in anthropometric measurements within and between three communities in Peru. *Human Biology,* 1962, *34,* 63–70.

Leary, P. M. The body measurements of Pedi schoolchildren. *South African Medical Journal,* 1968, *42,* 1314–1322.

Lee, L. On the physical changes by living environments of the farmers of the Perpo (Siraya) tribe in Taiwan. *Kureme Medical Association Journal,* 1970, *33,* 591–621.

Lewin, T., Jürgens, H. W., & Louekari, L. Secular trend in the adult height of Skolt Lapps. *Arctic Anthropology,* 1970, *7,* 53–62.

Limaye, C., Chouhan, C. N., Lakhani, S. M., & Phadke, M. V. Optimal growth standards from Poona. *Indian Pediatrics,* 1974, *11,* 673–676.

Litichevskii, P. O. Physical development of rural schoolchildren in the Kiev region. *Gigiene i Sanitariia,* 1966, *31,* 117–119.

Ljung, B-O, Bergsten-Brucefors, A., & Lindgren, G. The secular trend in physical growth in Sweden. *Annals of Human Biology,* 1974, *1,* 245–256.

Lloyd-Jones, O. Race and stature: A study of Los Angeles school children. *Research Quarterly,* 1941, *12,* 83–97.

Loots, J. M., & Lamprecht, D. V. Anthropometric evaluation. *South African Medical Journal,* 1971, *45,* 1284–1288.

Lorencová, A., & Benes, J. Vyska tela moravské prumyslové populace. *Scripta Prírodovedecká Fakulta Ujep Brunensis, Biologia 2,* 1974, *4,* 47–54.

Lourie, J. A. Anthropometry of Lau islanders, Fiji. *Human Biology of Oceania,* 1972, *1,* 273–277.

Low, W. D. Stature and body weight of southern Chinese children. *Zeitschrift für Morphologie und Anthropologie,* 1971, *63,* 11–45.

Luna-Jaspe, H., Ariza, J., Rueda-Williamson, R., Mora, J. O., & Pardo, F. Estudio seccional de crecimiento, desarrollo y nutricion en 12,138 niños de Bogotá, Colombia: II. El crecimiento de niños de dos clases socio-económicas durante sus primeros seis años de vida. *Archivos Latino-Americanos de Nutricion,* 1970, *20,* 151–165.

MacDonald, A. Experimental study of children. *Annual Report, United States Commissioner of Education,* 1899, *1,* 985–1204.

Machado, J. P., & Memoria, J. M. P. Pêso de recém-nascidos em hospitais de Belo Horizonte. *O Hospital,* 1966, *69,* 393–402.

Mackiewicz, M., Romejko, A., Mirota, Z., Sejmicka, K., Szeszenia, N., & Swiderska, Z. Somatic development of school children in Brzeziny county near Lodz. *Zdrowie Publiczne,* 1967, *1,* 37–43.

MacLennan, R., Bradley, M., & Walsh, R. J. The blood group pattern at Oksapmin, Western Highlands, New Guinea. *Archaeology and Physical Anthropology in Oceania,* 1967, *2,* 57–61.

MacMahon, B., Alpert, M., & Salber, E. J. Infant weight and parental smoking habits. *American Journal of Epidemiology,* 1965, *82,* 247–261.

Maddocks, I., & Rovin, L. A New Guinea population in which blood pressure appears to fall as age advances. *Papua and New Guinea Medical Journal,* 1965, *8,* 17–21.

Malcolm, L. A. Determination of the growth curve of the Kukukuku people of New

Guinea from dental eruption in children and adult height. *Archaeology and Physical Anthropology in Oceania,* 1969, *4,* 72–78. (a)

Malcolm, L. A. Growth and development of the Kaiapit children of the Markham Valley, New Guinea. *American Journal of Physical Anthropology,* 1969, *31,* 39–52. (b)

Malcolm, L. A. Growth and development of the Bundi child of the New Guinea Highlands. *Human Biology,* 1970, *42,* 293–328.

Malcolm, L. A., & Zimmerman, L. Dwarfism amongst the Buang of Papua New Guinea. *Human Biology,* 1973, *45,* 181–193.

Malina, R. M. Exercise as an influence upon growth. *Clinical Pediatrics,* 1969, *8,* 16–26.

Malina, R. M., Habicht, J-P., Martorell, R., Lechtig, A., Yarbrough, C., & Klein, R. E. Head and chest circumferences in rural Guatemalan Ladino children, birth to seven years of age. *American Journal of Clinical Nutrition,* 1975, *28,* 1061–1070.

Malina, R. M., Hamill, P. V. V., & Lemeshow, S. *Body dimensions and proportions, white and negro children 6–11 years.* (Vital and Health Statistics, Series 11, no. 143, DHEW Publ. No. HRA-75-1625.) Washington, D.C.: United States Government Printing Office, 1974.

Malina, R. M., Selby, H. A., & Swartz, L. J. Estatura, peso, y circunferencia del brazo en una muestra transversal de niños zapotecos de 6 a 14 años. *Anales de Antropologia,* 1972, *9,* 143–155.

Marcusson, H. *Das wachstum von kindern und jugenlichen in der deutschen demokratischen republic.* Berlin: Akademie-Verlag, 1961.

Marquer, P. Contribution a l'étude anthropologieque du peuple Basque et au problème de ses origines raciales. *Bulletins et Mémoires de la Société Anthropologie de Paris,* 1963, *4,* Series 11, 1–240.

Marsden, P. D., & Marsden, S. A. A pattern of weight gain in Gambian babies during the first eighteen months of life. *Journal of Tropical Pediatrics,* 1965, *10,* 89–99.

Marshall, W. A., Tanner, J. M., Lewis, H. E., & Richardson, M. A. Anthropometric measurements of the Tristan Da Cunha islanders 1962–1968. *Human Biology,* 1971, *43,* 112–139.

Martin, R. *Lehrbuch der anthropologie.* Jena: Gustav Fischer, 1928.

Martins, D. da C. Dinâmica do crescimento e desenvolvimento da criança em Moçambique. Dissertation, Universidade de Coimbra, 1968.

Martirosian, R. B. Physical development of preschool and school children of rural regions of the Komi A.S.S.R. *Zdravookhranenie Rossiiskoi Federatsii,* 1973, *17,* 25–26.

Mata, L. J., Urrutia, J. J., & García, B. Effect of infection and diet on child growth. In G. E. W. Wolstenholme & M. O'Connor (Eds.), *Nutrition and infection.* Boston: Little, Brown, 1967.

Matawaran, A. J., Gervasio, C. C., & DeGala, A. B. Preliminary report on the average height and weight of some Filipinos. *Philippine Journal of Nutrition,* 1966, *19,* 29–49.

Matovskii, I. M., & Bulochnikova, V. V. Comparative data on the physical development of adolescents of Chelyabinsk. *Zdravookhranenie Rossiiskoi Federatsii,* 1966, *10,* 17–19.

McClung, J. *Effects of high altitude on human birth.* Cambridge, Mass.: Harvard University Press, 1969.

McDowell, A. J., Tasker, A. D., & Sarhan, A. E. *Height and weight of children in the United States, India, and the United Arab Republic.* (Vital and Health Statistics, Series 3, No. 14, PHSP Publ. No. 1000.) Rockville: United States National Center for Health Statistics, 1970.

McGregor, I. A., Rahman, A. K., Thompson, B., Billewicz, W. Z., & Thomson, A. M. The growth of young children in a Gambian village. *Transactions, Royal Society of Tropical Medicine and Hygiene,* 1968, *62,* 341–352.

Méndez, J., & Behrhorst, C. The anthropometric characteristics of Indian and rural Guatemalans. *Human Biology,* 1963, *35,* 457–469.

Meredith, H. V. Physical growth from birth to two years: II. Head circumference, a review and synthesis of North American research. *Child Development*, 1946, *17*, 1–61.

Meredith, H. V. Birth order and body size: II. Neonatal and childhood materials. *American Journal of Physical Anthropology*, 1950, *8*, 195–224.

Meredith, H. V. Methods of studying physical growth. In P. H. Mussen (Ed.), *Handbook of research methods in child development*. New York: John Wiley & Sons, 1960.

Meredith, H. V. Change in the stature and body weight of North American boys during the last 80 years. In L. P. Lipsitt & C. C. Spiker (Eds.), *Advances in child development and behavior*. New York: Academic Press, 1963.

Meredith, H. V. A synopsis of puberal changes in youth. *Journal of School Health*, 1967, *37*, 171–176.

Meredith, H. V. Body weight at birth of viable human infants: A worldwide comparative treatise. *Human Biology*, 1970, *42*, 217–264.

Meredith, H. V. Growth in body size: A compendium of findings on contemporary children living in different parts of the world. In H. W. Reese (Ed.), *Advances in child development and behavior* (Vol. 6). New York: Academic Press, 1971.

Meredith, H. V. Relation between tobacco smoking of pregnant women and body size of their progeny: A compilation and synthesis of studies. *Human Biology*, 1975, *47*, 451–472.

Meredith, H. V. Findings from Asia, Australia, Europe, and North America on secular changes in mean height of children, youths, and young adults. *American Journal of Physical Anthropology*, 1976, *44*, 315–326.

Meredith, H. V., & Boynton, B. The transverse growth of the extremities: An analysis of girth measurements for arm, forearm, thigh, and leg taken on Iowa City white children. *Human Biology*, 1937, *9*, 366–403.

Meredith, H. V., & Knott, V. B. Changes in body proportions during infancy and the preschool years: III. The skelic index. *Child Development*, 1938, *9*, 49–62.

Miall, W. E., Ashcroft, M. T., Lovell, H. G., & Moore, F. A longitudinal study of the decline of adult height with age in two Welsh communities. *Human Biology*, 1967, *39*, 445–454.

Michelson, N. Investigations in the physical development of Negroes: Stature. *American Journal of Physical Anthropology*, 1943, *1*, 191–213.

Miklashevskaya, N. N. Growth of the head and face in boys of various ethnic groups in the U.S.S.R. *Human Biology*, 1966, *38*, 231–250.

Miklashevskaya, N. N. Sex differences in growth of the head and face in children and adolescents. *Human Biology*, 1969, *41*, 250–262.

Miklashevskaya, N. N., & Solovieva, V. S., & Godina, E. Z. Process of human growth in the conditions of high altitudes. Paper presented at the IXth International Congress of Anthropological and Ethnological Sciences, Chicago, 1973.

Miller, F. J. W., Billewicz, W. Z., & Thomson, A. M. Growth from birth to adult life of 442 Newcastle-upon-Tyne children. *British Journal of Preventive and Social Medicine*, 1972, *26*, 224–230.

Miller, P. S. Secular changes among the Western Apache. *American Journal of Physical Anthropology*, 1970, *33*, 197–206.

Miyashita, T., & Takahashi, E. Stature and nose height of Japanese. *Human Biology*, 1971, *43*, 327–339.

Mohanta, K. D., Panda, T. N., & Prahara, K. C. Anthropometric measurements of children of Western Orissa. *Indian Journal of Pediatrics*, 1972, *39*, 12–14.

Möhr, M., & Milev, N. Ein ländervergleich über die ernährungssituation und den körperzustand der bevölkerungen in der VR Bulgarien und der deutschen demokratischen republik. *Die Nahrung*, 1972, *16*, 259–275.

Montoya, C., & Ipinza, M. Peso y estatura de pre-escolares santiaguinos pertenecientes a dos estratos sociales diferentes. *Revista Chilena de Pediatria,* 1964, *35,* 269–277.

Morishita, H. Physique and physical performance of the primary school children in the central highland of New Guinea. *Archaeology and Physical Anthropology in Oceania,* 1969, *4,* 123–128.

Morita, S., & Ohtsuki, F. Secular changes of the main head dimensions in Japanese. *Human Biology,* 1973, *45,* 151–165.

Morozova, T. V., & Boldurchidi, P. P. The physical development of children and adolescents in Stavropol and Stavropol territory. *Zdravookhranenie Rossiiskoi Federatsii,* 1965, *9,* 8–11.

Mortison, J. *Low birth weight study: Height and weight tables and charts.* (Systems Development Project, Study Series No. 9–3–4a.) Washington, D.C.: United States Children's Bureau, 1969.

Musso, A., & Musso, L. K. O crescimento de criança no primeiro ano de vida no estado da guanabara. *Boletin Instituto de Puericultura e Pediatria,* 1964, *21,* 161–180.

Nagamine, S., & Suzuki, S. Anthropometry and body composition of Japanese young men and women. *Human Biology,* 1964, *36,* 8–15.

Nashed, S., & Bertan, M. Growth and physical development of primary schoolchildren in Etimesgut, Turkey. *Turkish Journal of Pediatrics,* 1968, *10,* 101–115.

Nath, S. A study of age-changes of different biological variables in the Jat boys of Meerut (U. P.). Unpublished doctoral dissertation, University of Delhi, 1972.

Naylor, A. F., & Myrianthopoulos, N. C. The relation of ethnic and selected socioeconomic factors to human birth-weight. *Annals of Human Genetics,* 1967, *31,* 71–83.

Nekisheva, Z. I. Effect of certain social factors on the physical development of preschool children attending kindergartens. *Gigiena Sanitariya,* 1974, *2,* 58–61.

Neumann, C. G., Shanker, H., & Uberoi, I. S. Nutritional and anthropometric profile of young rural Punjabi children. *Indian Journal of Medical Research,* 1969, *57,* 1122–1149.

New Zealand Department of Health. *Physical development of New Zealand school children 1969.* (Health Services Research Unit, Special Report No. 38.) Wellington: Government Printer, 1971.

Neyzi, O. Somatik gelisme indekslerinin tatbiki degeri. *Haseki Tip Bülteni,* 1967, *5,* 1–41.

Neyzi, O., & Gürson, C. T. *Physical measurements on two groups of Istanbul children: Normal and undernourished.* Stockholm: Swedish Medical Research Council, 1966.

Neyzi, O., Tanman, F., & Saner, G. Preliminary results of a child health survey in an underdeveloped area of Istanbul. Unpublished manuscript, University of Istanbul, 1965.

Neyzi, O., Yalçindag, A., & Alp, H. Heights and weights of Turkish children. Unpublished manuscript, University of Istanbul, 1973.

Niswander, J. D., Keiter, F., & Neel, J. V. Further studies on the Xavante Indians. *American Journal of Human Genetics,* 1967, *19,* 490–501.

Nouth- Savoeun. Contribution à l'étude de la croissance physique des enfants cambodgiens de la naissance à 14 ans. Unpublished doctoral dissertation, Universite Royale de Phnom-Penh, 1966.

Novak, L. P. Comparative study of body composition of American and Filipino women. *Human Biology,* 1970, *42,* 206–216.

Nurse, G. T. The body size of rural and peri-urban adult males from Lilongwe district. In D. J. M. Vorster (Ed.), *The human biology of environmental change.* London: International Biological Programme, 1972.

Oberndorfer, L., Mejia, W., & Palacio del Valle, G. Anthropometric measurements of 1,650 newborn in Médellin, Colombia. *Journal of Tropical Pediatrics,* 1965, *2,* 4–13.

O'Brien, R., Girshick, M. A., & Hunt, E. P. *Body measurements of American boys and girls for garment and pattern construction.* (Bureau of Home Economics, Department of Agriculture, Publ. no. 366.) Washington, D.C.: United States Government Printing Office, 1941.

Oehmisch, W. *Die entwicklung der körpermasse bei kindern und jugendlichen in der c ̃utschen demokratischen republik: Ergebnisse einer repräsentativen untersuchung in den jahren 1967/68.* Berlin: Deutschen Akademie für Arztliche Fortbildung, 1970.

Omran, A. R., McEwen, W. J., & Zaki, M. H. *Epidemiological studies in Bolivia.* New York: Research Institute for the Study of Man, 1967.

Oppers, V. M. Groeidiagrammen van amsterdamse kinderen. *Op Grond van Cijfers,* 1964, *2,* 51–65.

Orlik, I. M. The physical development of adolescents in Kharkov over the 40-year period 1923–1964. *Gigiena i Sanitariia,* 1967, *32,* 35–39.

Palacios-Mateos, J. M., García-Almansa, A., Vivanco, F., Fernández, M. D., García-Robles, R., & Moreno-Esteban, B. El crecimiento de los niños españoles desde el nacimiento hasta los cinco años. *Revista Clinica Espanola,* 1970, *118,* 419–424.

Palacios-Mateos, J. M., & Vivanco, F. Datos de talla y peso de 128,000 niños españoles. *Revista Clinica Espanola,* 1965, *99,* 230–238.

Palti, H., & Adler, B. Anthropometric measurements of the newborn, sex differences, and correlation between measurements. *Human Biology,* 1975, *47,* 523–530.

Panasenko, K. D. Physical development of elementary school children in Krasnodar in 1964–1965. *Zdravookhranenie Rossiiskoi Federatsii,* 1967, *2,* 23–27.

Parízková, J. & Eiselt, E. Body composition and anthropometric indicators in old age and the influence of physical exercise. *Human Biology,* 1966, *38,* 351–363.

Partington, M. W., & Roberts, N. The heights and weights of Indian and Eskimo school children on James Bay and Hudson Bay. *Canadian Medical Association Journal,* 1969, *11,* 502–509.

Peckham, G. W. *The growth of children.* Sixth Annual Report of the Wisconsin State Board of Health, 1881, pp. 28–73.

Petit-Maire-Heintz, N. Croissance et puberté féminines au Rwanda. *Mémoires Académie Royale des Sciences d'Outre-Mer, Classe de Sciences Naturelles et Médicales,* 1963, *12,* 1–146.

Pettersson, F. Smoking in pregnancy: Retrospective study of the influence of some factors on birth weight. *Acta Socio-Medica Scandinavica,* 1969, *1,* 13–18.

Phadke, M. V., & Kulkarni, H. D. Growth and development in the under-privileged sections of the Bombay area. *Indian Journal of Medical Research,* 1971, *59,* [Suppl.], 164–176.

Pietrangeli, E., & DiStefano, F. Rilievi biometrici sulle bambine di età scolare in provincia di chieti. *Annali Isnardi,* 1962, *9,* 135–144.

Pollitzer, W. S., Boyle, E., Cornoni, J., & Namboodiri, K. K. Physical Anthropology of the Negroes of Charleston, S. C. *Human Biology,* 1970, *42,* 265–279. (a)

Pollitzer, W. S., & Brown, W. H. Survey of demography, anthropometry, and genetics in the Melungeons of Tennessee: An isolate of hybrid origin in process of dissolution. *Human Biology,* 1969, *41,* 388–400.

Pollitzer, W. S., Namboodiri, K. K., Elston, R. C., Brown, W. H., & Leyshon, W. C. The Seminole Indians of Oklahoma: Morphology and serology. *American Journal of Physical Anthropology,* 1970, *33,* 15–29. (b)

Pollitzer, W. S., Rucknagel, D., Tashian, R., Shreffler, D. C., Leyshon, W. C., Namboodiri, K., & Elston, R. C. The Seminole Indians of Florida: Morphology and serology. *American Journal of Physical Anthropology,* 1970, *32,* 65–81. (c)

Popova, L. S. Physical development of school children of Rostov-on-Don. *Zdravookhranenie Rossiiskoi Federatsii,* 1968, *12,* 35–37.

Prokopec, M. Studies of child growth in Czechoslovakia. *Indian Pediatrics,* 1964, *1,* 100–111.

Prokopec, M. Growth and socioeconomic environment. Paper presented at the Kyoto Symposium on Anthropological Aspects of Human Growth, Kyoto, 1968.

Pyzuk, M., & Wolanski, N. Niektóre wlasciwosci fizjologiczne dzieci i mlodziezy jako wynik adaptacji do róznych warunków srodowiskowych: Doniesienie II. *Prace I Materialy Naukowe, Instytut Matki I Dziecka,* 1968, *11,* 129–151.

Quetelet, M. A. *Sur l'homme et le développment de ses facultes.* Paris: Bachelier, 1836.

Quevedo-Aragón, S. A. Antropologia del indigena cuzqueno. *Revista Universitaria,* 1961, *50,* 159–270.

Raghavan, K. V., Singh, D., & Swaminathan, M. C. Heights and weights of well-nourished Indian school children. *Indian Journal of Medical Research,* 1971, *59,* 648–654.

Rauh, J. L., Schumsky, D. A., & Witt, H. T. Heights, weights, and obesity in urban school children. *Child Development,* 1967, *38,* 515–530.

Rea, J. N. Social and economic influences on growth of pre-school children in Lagos. *Human Biology,* 1971, *43,* 46–63.

Reinke, W. A., & Henderson, M. Smoking and prematurity in the presence of other variables. *Archives of Environmental Health,* 1966, *12,* 600–606.

Richardson, B. D. Growth standards: An appraisal with special reference to growth in South African Bantu and white pre-school children. *South African Medical Journal,* 1973, *47* [Suppl.], 699–702.

Ridola, C., Nesci, E., Valenza, V., & Zummo, G. Rivievi biomorfologici sull'uomo siciliano della provincia de palermo, provincia de agrigento, y provincin di trapani. *Bollettino, Societa Italiana di Biologia Sperimentale,* 1975, *51,* 781–799.

Roberts, D. F., & Bainbridge, D. R. Nilotic physique. *American Journal of Physical Anthropology,* 1963, *21,* 341–366.

Robson, J. R. K. Problems in assessing nutritional status in the field. *Yearbook of Physical Anthropology,* 1975, *19,* 158–165.

Robson, J. R. K., Larkin, F. A., Bursick, J. H., & Perri, K. D. Growth standards for infants and children: A cross-sectional study. *Pediatrics,* 1975, *56,* 1014–1020.

Rocha, F. J. da, & Salzano, F. M. Anthropometric studies in Brazil Cayapo Indians. *American Journal of Physical Anthropology,* 1972, *36,* 95–102.

Roche, A. F., & Davila, G. H. Late adolescent growth in stature. *Pediatrics,* 1972, *50,* 874–880.

Rosenberg, I. H., & Reiner, M. L. *Nutrition survey of East Pakistan.* (Report, Ministry of Health, Government of Pakistan, with University of Dacca, and Nutrition Section, Office of International Research, National Institutes of Health.) Washington, D.C.: United States Government Printing Office, 1966.

Roth, R. E., & Harris, M. *The physical condition of children attending public schools in New South Wales.* Sydney: Department of Public Instruction, 1908.

Rozenblat, V.V., & Mezenina, L. B. The dynamics of physical development of adolescents of the Ural region in the past and present. *Sovetskoe Zdravookhranenie,* 1968, *27,* 25–30.

Rutishauser, I. H. E. Heights and weights of middle class Baganda children. *Lancet,* 1965, *2,* 565–567.

Rutishauser, I. H. E. A longitudinal study of growth of Ugandan preschool children. *East African Medical Journal,* 1974, *51,* 659–674.

Sabharwal, K. P., Morales, S., & Méndez, J. Body measurements and creatinine excretion among upper and lower socio-economic groups of girls in Guatemala. *Human Biology,* 1966, *38,* 131–140.

Saigal, S., & Srivastava, J. R. Anthropometric studies of 1,000 consecutive newborns with special reference to determine criteria of prematurity. *Indian Pediatrics,* 1969, *6,* 24–33.

Salvadori, B., & Papadia, S. Aumento ponderale del peso alla nascita espressione dell'accelerazione dell'accrescimento umano? *Minerva Pediatrica, Monograph Series,* 1965, 116–118.

Salzano, F. M. (Ed.) *The ongoing evolution of Latin American populations.* Springfield, Ill.: Charles C. Thomas, 1971.

Sato, H. Growth pattern in the Japanese infant studied by longitudinal observation. *Kaibo Gaku Zashi,* 1957, *32,* 455–481.

Scammon, R. E. The first seriatim study of human growth. *American Journal of Physical Anthropology,* 1927, *10,* 329–336.

Schiotz, C. *Physical development of children and young people during the age of 7 to 18–20 years.* Christiania: Jacob Dybwad, 1923.

Schulze, H., & Wissing, W. Körperlänge and körpergewicht der düsseldorfer jugend. *Oeffenthche Gesundheitswesen,* 1969, *31,* 250–267.

Scott, J. A. *Report on the heights and weights (and other measurements) of school pupils in the county of London in 1959.* London: County Council, 1961.

Scrimshaw, N. S. The effect of the interaction of nutrition and infection on the preschool child. In *Pre-school child malnutrition: Primary deterrent to human progress.* Washington, D.C.: National Academy of Science—National Research Council, Publ. No. 1282, 1966.

Sempé, P., Sempé, M., & Pédron, G. *Croissance et maturation osseuse.* Paris: Théraplix, 1972.

Shah, P. M., & Udani, P. M. Medical examination of rural school children in Palghar Taluk. *Indian Pediatrics,* 1968, *5,* 343–361.

Sharma, J. C. *Physical growth and development of the Maharastrians.* Lucknow: Ethnographic and Folk Culture Society, 1970.

Shattock, F. M. Heights and weights in a Javanese labour population of a north Sumatra rubber estate. *Tropical and Geographical Medicine,* 1968, *20,* 147–158.

Shiddhaye, S., Shah, P. M., & Udani, P. M. Physical growth and development of pre-term children during the first five years of life: Longitudinal study. *Indian Pediatrics,* 1972, *9,* 282–289.

Shumakher, R. Z., & Sevelev, I. P. Physical development of school children of the Komi A.S.S.R. during the past 40 years. *Sovetskoe Zdravookhranenie,* 1969, *28,* 34–36.

Shuttleworth, F. K. The physical and mental growth of girls and boys age 6 to 19 in relation to age at maximum growth. *Monographs of the Society for Research in Child Development,* 1939, 4 (3, Serial No. 22).

Sikri, S. D. A comparative study of height and weight of government and public school children of Panjabi population. *Indian Journal of Medical Research,* 1972, *60,* 491–500.

Singh, R. *Nutritional somatometric study of adult males with special reference to skinfold measurements and intercorrelations.* Paper presented at Dalhousie Summer School in Anthropology, Punjab, India, 1964.

Singh, R. Growth in the head dimensions of the Punjabi boys aged 11 to 18 years. *Acta Medica Auxologica,* 1969, *1,* 203–211.

Singh, R. A cross sectional study of growth in five somatometric traits of Punjabi boys aged eleven to eighteen years. *American Journal of Physical Anthropology,* 1970, *32,* 129–138 (a).

Singh, R. Growth in arm girth and other anthropometric parameters of the Punjabi boys aged 11–18 years. *Zeitschrift für Morphologie und Anthropologie,* 1970, *62,* 166–171 (b).

Solovyeva, V. S. Material on the sexual development of Moscow school pupils and students. *Voprosy Antropologii,* 1964, *17,* 35–61.

Solow, B. The pattern of craniofacial associations. *Acta Odontologica Scandinavica,* 1966, *24* [Suppl.], 1–46.

Souisa, H. M. Growth studies of children. Unpublished master's thesis, Osmania University, Hyderabad, 1969.

Soysa, P. E., & Jayasuriya, D. S. Birth weight in Ceylonese. *Human Biology*, 1975, *47*, 1–15.

Soysal, S. S., Gürson, C. T., & Neyzi, O. Istanbul çocuklarinda fizik gelisme normlari. Onaltihci Milli Türk Tip Kongresi, 1960.

Spielman, R. S., Rocha, F. J. da, Weitkamp, L. R., Ward, R. H., Neel, J. V., & Chagnon, N. A. The genetic structure of a tribal population, the Yanomama Indians. *American Journal of Physical Anthropology*, 1972, *37*, 345–356.

Sporcq, J. The Bira of the savanna and the Bira of the rain forest: A comparative study of two populations of the Democratic Republic of the Congo. *Journal of Human Evolution*, 1975, *4*, 505–516.

Spranger, J., Ochsenfarth, A., Kock, H. P., & Henke, J. Anthropometrische normdaten im kindesalter. *Zeitschrift für Kinderheilkunde*, 1968, *103*, 1–12.

Spurgeon, J. H., Young, N. D., & Meredith, H. V. Body size and form of American-born boys of Dutch ancestry residing in Michigan. *Growth*, 1959, *23*, 55–71.

Steinkamp, R. C., Cohen, N. L., Gaffey, W. R., McKey, T., Bron, G., Siri, W. E., Sargent, T. W., & Isaacs, E. Measures of body fat and related factors in normal adults: II. A simple clinical method to estimate body fat and lean body mass. *Journal of Chronic Diseases*, 1965, *18*, 1291–1307.

Stennett, R. G., & Cram, D. M. Cross-sectional percentile height and weight norms for a representative sample of urban, school-aged, Ontario children. *Canadian Journal of Public Health*, 1969, *60*, 465–470.

Stevenson, P. H. Collected anthropometric data on the Chinese. *China Medical Journal*, 1925, *34*, 855–898.

Stockton-Hough, J. Statistics relating to seven hundred births (white) occurring in the Philadelphia Hospital (Blockley) between 1865–1872. *Philadelphia Medical Times*, 1885, *16*, 92–94.

Stoudt, H. W., Damon, A., McFarland, R., & Roberts, J. *Weight, height, and selected body dimensions of adults.* (Public Health Service, Publ. No. 1000, Series 11, No. 8.) Washington, D.C.: United States Government Printing Office, 1965.

Stoudt, H. W., Damon, A., McFarland, R. A., & Roberts, J. *Skinfolds, body girths, biacromial diameter, and selected anthropometric indices of adults.* (Public Health Service, Publ. No. 1000, Series 11, no. 35.) Washington, D.C.: United States Government Printing Office, 1970.

Strouhal, E. Anthropometric and functional evidence of heterosis from Egyptian Nubia. *Human Biology*, 1971, *43*, 271–287.

Suchy, J. Trend of physical development of Czech youth in the 20th century. *Review of Czechoslovak Medicine*, 1972, *18*, 18–27.

Suchy, J., & Malá, H. The development of Gypsy children in changing living conditions. Paper presented at the IXth International Congress of Anthropological and Ethnological Sciences, Chicago, 1973.

Suda, A., Yamaguchi, B., Hoshi, H., Endo, B., & Eto, M. Longitudinal observation on the stature and body weight of Japanese-American hybrids from 6 to 15 years of age. *Zinruigaku Zassi*, 1965, *73*, 54–63.

Sukkar, M. Y. Skinfold thickness and body fat in adult Fur men and women of western Sudan. *Human Biology*, 1976, *48*, 315–321.

Sutcliffe, A., & Canham, J. W. *The heights and weights of boys and girls.* London: John Murray, 1950.

Sutherland, P. C. On the Esquimaux. *Journal of the Ethnological Society of London*, 1856, *4*, 193–214.

Swaminathan, M. C., Jyothi, K. K., Singh, R., Madhavan, S., & Gopalan, C. A semi-longitudinal study of growth of Indian children and the related factors. *Indian Pediatrics*, 1964, *1*, 255–263.

Systems Development Project Staff. *Height and weight charts and tables on poverty area children*. (Systems Development Project, Study Series No. 8–9.) Washington, DC.: United States Children's Bureau, 1968.

Takahashi, E. Growth and environmental factors in Japan. *Human Biology*, 1966, *38*, 112–130.

Tanasescu, G., Chiriac, I., Stanciulescu, E., Domilescu, M., & Jelezneac, I. Nivelul dezvoltarii fizice a copiilor de 0-3 ani din republica socialista romania. *Pediatria*, 1970, *19*, 97–108.

Tandon, L., Gupta, S. P., & Dikshit, S. K. Anthropometric criteria for assessing prematurity by gestation. *Indian Pediatrics*, 1971, *8*, 321–330.

Tanner, J. M. The secular trend towards earlier physical maturation. *Tijdschrift voor Sociale Geneeskunde*, 1966, *44*, 524–539.

Terrosi, F. Indagine auxometrica nel bambino della provincia de grosseto. *Archivio Italiano di Pediatria e Puericultura*, 1968, *26*, 148–160.

Tonelli, E., & Marinelli, M. Resultati dell'applicazione di un metodo statistico al controllo auxologico dei bambini di 6–36 mesi. *Igiene e Sanità Pubblica*, 1963, *19*, 453–480.

Tsabadze, V. M. Physical development and its dynamics in school children in Tiflis. *Soobshcheniya Akademii Nauk Gruzinskoi S.S.R.*, 1965, *20*, 447–454.

Twiesselmann, F. *Développement biométrique de l'enfant à l'adulte*. Bruxelles: Presses Universitaires de Bruxelles, 1969.

Udani, P. M. Physical growth of children in different socio-economic groups in Bombay. *Indian Journal of Child Health*, 1963, *12*, 593–611.

Udjus, L. G. *Anthropometrical changes in Norwegian men in the twentieth century*. Oslo: Universitetsforlaget, 1964.

Underwood, B. A., Hepner, R., Cross, E., Mirza, A. B., Hayat, K., & Kallue, A. Height, weight, and skin-fold thickness data collected during a survey of rural and urban populations of West Pakistan. *American Journal of Clinical Nutrition*, 1967, *20*, 694–701.

Underwood, P., Hester, L. L., Laffitte, T. Jr., & Gregg, K. V. The relationship of smoking to the outcome of pregnancy. *American Journal of Obstetrics and Gynecology*, 1965, *91*, 270–276.

United States Center for Disease Control. *Ten-state nutrition survey 1968–1970: III. Clinical, anthropometry, dental*. (Department of Health, Education and Welfare, Publ. No. HSM-72-8131.) Washington, D.C.: United States Government Printing Office, 1972.

Véli, G. Menarche, growth and development in Hungary. *Acta Paediatrica Academiae Scientiarum Hungaricae*, 1971, *12*, 209–221.

Venezia, A., Previtera, A., & Vignale, A. M. Indagine auxologica sul lattante della provincia di masse-carrara. *Lattante*, 1965, *36*, 906–939.

Verghese, K. P., Scott, R. B., Teixeira, G., & Ferguson, A. D. Studies in growth and development: XII. Physical growth of North American Negro children. *Pediatrics*, 1969, *44*, 243–247.

Vis, H. L. Protein deficiency disorders. *Postgraduate Medical Journal*, 1969, *45*, 107–115.

Vlastovsky, V. G. The secular trend in the growth and development of children and young persons in the Soviet Union. *Human Biology*, 1966, *38*, 219–230.

Wadsworth, G. R., & Lee, T. S. The height, weight, and skinfold thickness of Muar schoolchildren. *Journal of Tropical Pediatrics*, 1960, *6*, 48–54.

Wal, B. W. van de, Erasmus, L. D., & Hechter, R. Stem and standing heights in Bantu and white South Africans. *South African Medical Journal*, 1971, *45*, 568–570.

Walia, B. N. S., Khetarpal, S. K., Mehta, S., Ghai, O. P., Kapoor, P., & Taneja, P. N. Observations on 1,000 liveborn infants. *Indian Journal of Child Health*, 1963, *12*, 243–249.

Wark, L., & Malcolm, L. A. Growth and development of the Lumi child in the Sepik District of New Guinea. *Medical Journal of Australia*, 1969, *2*, 129–136.

Weninger, M. Chimba und Vatwa, bantuide viehzüchter und nicht-bantuide wild-beuter. *Mitteilungen Anthropologischen Gesellschaft in Wien*, 1965, *95*, 180–190.

White, R. M. Anthropometric survey of the Armed Forces of the Republic of Vietnam. United States Army Natick Laboratories, Natick, Massachusetts, 1964.

Whittle, H., Whittle, A., & Wicks, A. The weights of young African children in a township of Rhodesia. *Central African Journal of Medicine*, 1970, *16*, 1–5.

Wieringen, J. C. van *Seculaire groeiverschuiving: Lengte en gewicht surveys 1964–1966 in Nederland in historisch perspectief*. Leiden: Netherlands Instituut voor Praeventieve Geneeskunde TNO, 1972.

Wingerd, J., Schoen, E. J., & Solomon, I. L. Growth standards in the first two years of life based on measurements of white and black children in a prepaid health care program. *Pediatrics*, 1971, *47*, 818–825.

Woiski, J. R., Romera, J., Corrêa, C. E. C., Raya, L. C., & Lima-Filho, E. C. Indices somaticos dos recem-nascídos normais no hospital das clinicas de ribeirao preto. *Rivista Paulesta di Medicena*, 1965, *66*, 12–23.

Wojtowicz, E., & Miaskiewicz, C. Somatic development of children in Nowa Huta. *Folia Medica Cracoviensia*, 1966, *8*, 339–347.

Wolanski, N. Ocena rozwoju fizycznego dziecka w wieku do trzech lat. *Prace i Materialy Naukowe, Instytut Matki I Dziecka*, 1964, *2*, 95–124.

Wolanski, N., & Lasota, A. Physical development of countryside children and youth aged 2 to 20 years as compared with the development of town youth of the same age. *Zeitschrift für Morphologie und Anthropologie*, 1964, *54*, 272–292.

Wolanski, N., & Pyzuk, M. (Eds.). *Studies in human ecology*. Warsaw: Polish Academy of Sciences, 1973.

Wolstenholme, J., & Walsh, R. J. Heights and weights of indigenes of the Western Highlands District, New Guinea. *Archaeology and Physical Anthropology in Oceania*, 1967, *2*, 220–226.

Wong, H. B., Tye, C. Y., & Quek, K. M. Anthropometric studies on Singapore children: Heights, weights and skull circumference on pre-school children. *Journal of Singapore Paediatric Society*, 1972, *14*, 68–89.

Yanev, B. *Physical development and fitness of the Bulgarian people from birth to age twenty-six*. Sofia: Bulgarian Academy of Sciences Press, 1965.

Yarbrough, C., Habicht, J-P., Malina, R. M., Lechtig, A., & Klein, R. E. Length and weight in rural Guatemalan Ladino children: Birth to seven years of age. *American Journal of Physical Anthropology*, 1975, *42*, 439–448.

Zaizov, R., & Laron, Z. Body length and weight at birth and one year of age in different communities in Israel. *Acta Paediatrica Scandinavica*, 1966, *55*, 524–528.

Zerssen, D. Habitus und geschlecht: Eine korrelationsstatistische analyse. *Homo,* 1968, *19*, 1–27.

❧ 10 ❧
Correlates and Consequences of Stress in Infancy

Thomas K. Landauer • John W. M. Whiting

During the 1950s there were a number of reports that early handling of infant rodents could have enduring consequences. Early-handled animals usually, although not always, were tamer, less emotional, and physically larger as adults. Experiments by Denenberg (e.g., Denenberg and Karas, 1959), Levine (e.g., 1957; 1960; 1962) and many others found the same sorts of effects when very young rats were subjected to a wide variety of different treatments (see Daly, 1973, Denenberg, 1969, Levine, 1960, and Thompson & Grusec, 1970, for reviews). Apparently effective treatments included stroking with a brush, briefly removing the pup from the nest, and administration of painful electric shocks. Based on fairly convincing evidence from these studies it was generally concluded that the common causative factor was exposure of the immature animal to potential physiological stressors—events or agents that in an adult animal would induce an endocrine stress reaction. It was also observed that the effect depended strongly on the time when the treatment was applied. Generally, effects were growth facilitative only if the treatments occurred in the first few weeks of a rat's life. A variety of different sequelae were identified. They included superior avoidance learning, lower "open field" anxiety, increased resistance to stress-related pathology, and directly measured changes in adrenal cortex functioning (but see Daly, 1973, for a review of conflicting evidence).

The mechanism by which early stress has its effects has never been clearly established. Perhaps the best guess at present is that an acute stress-inducing stimulus in early life, while the endocrine system is still labile, changes the response to stress encountered later in life (Levine, 1962). Nevertheless, the occurrence of dramatic, long-lasting effects of stressful experiences in early life was, by the late 1950s, a reasonably well-documented phenomenon in laboratory mammals.

At about that time we set out to determine whether or not evidence could be found of such an effect in humans as well. We knew that many preindustrial societies around the world customarily subjected infants to rather rigorous and potentially stressful rituals, often believing them to be beneficial to physical growth, while other cultures believed that infants should be carefully protected from all strong stimulation. Consequently cross-cultural research offered an attractive method for attacking the problem.

355

In the remainder of this chapter we will review in detail the cross-cultural work on the effects of early stress in humans. We will also summarize converging evidence from intraculture correlational studies and confirming experimental results. We will not review the animal research further because we regard this as having been primarily a stimulus for the cross-cultural research rather than a necessarily integral part of the overall evidential picture.

We first describe the cross-cultural research showing a correlation between early stress and physical growth. Second, we describe a variety of control analyses that have been performed to investigate whether or not the correlation could be due to a spurious association with some other causative agent. Next, we summarize converging evidence from sources other than cross-cultural research, and in particular an experimental study of early smallpox vaccination. Finally, we review studies that have investigated other possible consequences of early stress.

CROSS-CULTURAL STUDIES OF THE RELATION BETWEEN EARLY STRESS AND GROWTH

As mentioned above, the initial studies begun in 1959 were stimulated by a desire to see whether the results that had been reported in the animal literature might be reflected in an association between apparently stressful infant care practices with humans and any of the characteristics of development that seem to have been affected in the animal research. Procedures like scarification, tattooing, circumcision, and ear piercing were performed on infants in many places around the world. Preliminary examination of the materials in the Human Relations Area Files (HRAF) suggested that it would be possible to identify quite a large number of potentially stressful infant care practices, ranging widely in severity.

In order to identify the infant care variables that should be studied, an initial exploratory study was conducted. Descriptions of child care practices were excerpted from relevant portions of the Human Relations Area Files and from other ethnographic sources. The excerpts were performed "blind" by research assistants whose instructions were solely to get all information that bore on how young children were treated. These assistants did not know the purpose of the study or values of the other variables being sought. A list of customs initially rated as potential stressors is given in Table 10-1, in descending order of intuitively judged severity. At the same time, information on growth in the same societies was independently

TABLE 10-1 **Definitions of Potentially Stressful Infant Care Practices (After Landauer & Whiting, 1964)**

Circumcision
Piercing of nose, lips or ears
Scarification by cutting or burning
Vaccination
Molding by forceful stretching or shaping (not passive pressure as in a headboard)
Extremes of temperature: hot or cold baths
Internal agents: emetics, irritants, or enemas
Abrasion: rubbing with sand or scraping with shell or other hard object
Extraordinarily intense stimulation: massaging, annointing, exposure to loud noises
Binding: swaddling or other severe restriction of movement

excerpted. Only adult stature of males yielded sufficient quantitative data for analysis. Following this, ratings were made of the infant care practices for each society on the basis of how stressful they appeared to be and how often they occurred. The raters again worked without knowledge of physical growth data. A summary score was formed to indicate the amount of stress during the first 2 weeks of life. For the 62 societies with both kinds of data, the correlation between this rough overall index and adult stature was .30 and statistically significant. Thus with only crude measures and little attempt at quality control, but careful attention to the avoidance of bias, a reliable correlation was found. It should be noted that the index used here made no discrimination among possible potential stressors but rather counted anything that the raters, graduate students in child development, intuitively felt was a likely physiological stress agent.

The next step in the research was an attempt to refine the measures somewhat. The physical growth measure initially used included many unsubstantiated statements of "average height" whose validity was at best questionable. To improve upon this, we limited the sample to those groups for whom at least 25 actual measurements of stature had been made. The problem of refining the index of stress was more difficult. One might have liked adrenal steroid response assays, but this was obviously out of the question. Moreover, what was really of interest was not the specific hypothesis that physiologic stressors lead to changes in development but rather that there are experiences that happen in early human infancy that have such effects. Thus the approach that we took was merely to discard practices that appeared uncorrelated with stature and also appeared, on reconsideration, to be unlikely stress stimuli. This left only circumcision, piercing, scarification, vaccination, and molding. (As we will see later, molding should probably also have been eliminated.) The animal research results and as much analysis as was possible in the preliminary data had suggested that the effect might have a thresholdlike quality, that is, one stressor seemed about as good as another, and one seemed about as good as two or more. Consequently, the reanalysis utilized only two levels of stress, present or absent.

In addition, the age criterion for "early" stress was changed from 2 weeks to 2 years. This choice was essentially arbitrary but was prompted by the fact that 2 years was the average age of weaning in primitive societies and appeared to provide the best division of cases in the preliminary data.

Analyzed in this way, the association between the presence of an early stress and stature was quite strong. The adult males in the 17 societies with stressful infant care practices as thus defined averaged 2.5 inches taller than those in the 18 comparison societies without such practices, 65.2 versus 62.7 inches, respectively ($t = 3.72$, p <0.002). Of course, these results could have been somewhat inflated by the fact that the antecedent measures used had been selected to some extent on the basis of their observed correlation with the consequent measure. Therefore it was desirable to replicate these findings using a new and independent sample where the identification of the effective variables, age criteria, and so forth were not confounded with the statistical test of their effects.

The next step, then, was to obtain a new and independent sample of societies. We managed to find another 30 societies for whom there were appropriate data. Once again, the child-rearing and stature data were obtained independently by raters who were ignorant of the other information and of the purpose of the study as a whole. The results were nearly identical to those in the original data; there was a statistically significant 2.6 inch difference in mean adult stature favoring those with early stress practices ($t = 4.68$, $p < 0.001$).

These results make it quite clear that the differences were not due simply to a selection of variables that had a fortuitous relation to adult stature.

Because the initial and replication data were so closely similar, they were combined in order to yield a larger sample for more refined control and exploratory analyses. One of these was an analysis of the effect of age at which the stress occurred. The combined data allowed a rough division according to whether the first customary stress occurred in the first 2 weeks, between 2 weeks and 2 years, between 2 and 6 years, between 6 and 15 years, or not at all. The average adult male stature for these five subgroups was 65.4, 65.9, 63.6, 61.7, and 63.0 inches, respectively, suggesting that the assumption of a sensitive period of the first 2 years was correct. However, the discovery of additional effective stress experiences—to be reviewed below—alters certain features of this analysis slightly; thus we will return to its discussion later.

In order to determine whether the association of early stress with stature might be due to chance association of early stress variables with other factors that might be conducive to greater growth, a number of control analyses were performed. The logic of these analyses was as follows: First, for a "third variable" to be responsible for the observed association, it would have to be correlated both with the infant stress measure and with adult male stature. Second, if any such variable existed, if the sample were then divided into subsets within which there was a relatively restricted range of values on that variable, the relation between infant stress and stature within each subset should be attenuated. For example, *suppose* that cross-culturally there were an association between the amount of protein in the diet and terminal stature (although, in fact, we were unable to find such a correlation in the sample of societies studied). Suppose further that by chance the societies with stressful infant care practices have more protein than those without (although, again, we did not find this to be true). Such chance associations would produce a spurious correlation between stress and growth. To investigate the possibility, one can divide the total sample of societies into those with relatively great amounts of protein and those with relatively little. Within each of these subsets, the total effect of differences in amount of protein would have to be smaller, because the range of differences is smaller. If the effect of stress were due to an association with such differences, its apparent effect would also have to be reduced within such subsets.

The control factors that were studied and reported by Landauer and Whiting (1964) were measures of nutrition, climate, and a combination of genetic, geographic, and historical differences. Ratings of the nutritional value of the diet were obtained for a subset of our societies for which sufficient information was available. M. Whiting, a nutritionist, provided the new data in conjunction with a doctoral dissertation at the Harvard School of Public Health (M. Whiting, 1958). Without knowledge of stress or stature data, she estimated the quantity and quality of several different aspects of diet, including total calories and protein calories. While her data did show a marginally significant association between some aspects of diet and stature in a sample that partially overlapped with ours, in our sample all correlations between dietary measures and stature were essentially zero. Moreover, there was no discernible association between any of the estimated dietary factors and the presence of early stress. Consequently, insofar as we were able to determine, the association between stress and stature could not have been due to a common association with differences in diet. Similar negative results with climatic and geographic factors added additional confidence to this conclusion, since these factors would normally be expected to influence the quality and quantity of diet as well.

Cohen (1966) has suggested that a dietary factor might still be involved if stressed children ate more or better than unstressed children as a reaction to stress. There is no way to reject this possibility entirely, since there is no way of observing such things in available cross-cultural data. Indeed, even the randomized experiment that we will report later cannot rule out involvement of this kind of variable, one that is an effect of infant stress itself and is the "real" cause of changes in growth. In one sense, such a hypothesis is not a denial that stress causes an increase in growth but simply a guess as to its mechanism. Finding that infant stress caused a change in adrenal response that is in turn responsible for increased growth would be a mediational hypothesis of a similar sort. No one, of course, believes that stress itself, directly, with no intervening mechanism, leads to increased stature.

Further control analyses for genetic, geographic, economic, climatologic, and dietary factors were performed on these data without modifying the conclusions. However, rather than reviewing these analyses here, we will report the results of new analyses recently completed that utilize additional data and take some more recent relevant findings into account. First, let us introduce the new evidence.

ANOTHER EFFECTIVE EARLY STRESS: SEPARATION OF THE INFANT FROM ITS MOTHER

Gunders (1961), having noted that a common feature of most of the animal studies of infant stress included separation of the infants from their mothers (cf. Koch & Arnold, 1972; Russell, 1973), studied the matter in humans cross-culturally. She found a significant correlation between the custom of removing an infant from its mother and greater adult male stature. Gunders and Whiting (1968) refined and extended this study. They obtained ratings on a variety of aspects of the care of newborn infants. The results indicated that almost all societies can be classified into one of two contrasting patterns. In some societies, infants are rarely separated from physical contact with their mothers or some other caretaker. Prior to weaning the infant is held in the arms or carried close to the caretaker's skin almost constantly, and the treatment of the infant is uniformly protective. In the other category of societies, infants are often segregated from their mothers for the first 24 hours and at other times as a customary ritual. They may also be heavily swaddled and placed in a crib (see chapter 7 in this volume). Gunders and Whiting hypothesized that the deprivation of warmth and contact comfort might itself constitute a stress stimulus for the newborn, or that other potential stressors that are ordinarily neutralized by contact comfort (Harlow, 1960) have strong effects on the separated infant. They found a significant association between separation from the mother at birth and greater adult male stature. Gunders and Whiting performed control analyses similar to those described above. In this case, too, the association between the presence of the infantile stress and adult stature was independent of estimates of genetics, geography, and diet. They did find in their sample of societies a significant relation between the presence of dairy herds and stature, but holding this variable constant statistically did not reduce the separation–stature association.

PHYSICAL AND SEPARATION STRESSORS: ALONE AND IN COMBINATION

Many of the societies with separation customs also engage in other forms of infant stress. A tabulation to illustrate some separate and joint effects of various experiences is shown in Table 10–2. For this purpose we have combined data from Landauer and Whiting (1964), Gunders and Whiting (1968), and a small number of newly rated cases. Although the numbers are not very large for some variables, the pattern of results suggests some interesting conclusions.

Several different kinds of stressors, when they occur in isolation—that is, in the absence of other stress—are significantly associated with greater adult stature. These include piercing (of ears, nose, or lips), scarification (by cutting or burning), and separation. By contrast, molding, one of the originally rated physical stressors, does not appear to lead to greater stature by itself. This fact probably went unnoticed in earlier analyses because most societies that practice molding also practice separation or some other form of physical stress.

The data with respect to vaccination are also of special interest. It turns out that of the five societies in the original sample that practiced infantile vaccination, three also practiced separation, and the remaining two lacked information on separation. Thus although we reported earlier (J. Whiting, Landauer, & Jones, 1968) that adult male stature is significantly greater in societies practicing infantile vaccination than in ones with no stress, it is impossible to tell whether or not the association is actually with vaccination per se. The available cross-cultural data unfortunately do not provide a test of the effect of vaccination in isolation.

The next question addressed by the data in Table 10–2 concerns how the incidence of various stressors are related and how their effects combine. It is reasonably apparent that combinations of two or more stressors are not associated with greater stature than are single stressors. Also, it can be seen that physical and separation stress have a tendency to appear together. The relation is statistically significant

TABLE 10–2 Stressful Practices in Isolation and Combination

Stressful Practice (Before Age 2 Years)	Adult Male Height (inches)				
	n	Mean	SEM*	t versus None	
1. Piercing only	4	64.9	1.14	1.66	$p < 0.10$
2. Scarification only	2	67.2	0.35	2.72	$p < 0.01$
3. Molding only	6	63.8	0.31	1.11	—
4. Circumcision, plus 3, or plus 2 and 3	2	65.5	0.50	3.72	$p < 0.01$
(Any physical stress)	14	64.9	0.45	2.97	$p < 0.01$
Separation only	10	65.3	0.90	2.42	$p < 0.03$
Both physical and separation stress	23	65.4	0.65	3.07	$p < 0.01$
None	18	62.8	0.54		

This table contains data only for societies on which information about the presence or absence of both physical and separation stress in infancy was available; p values are one-tailed; n is the number of societies, each counted as a single case. The actual number of individuals measured to yield the source data was more than 20,000.

*Standard Error of the Mean

($\chi^2 = 4.46$, $p < 0.05$) and of some importance to the overall interpretation of the cross-cultural evidence. One of the things that seemed most surprising about the initial results was that intentional stress in infancy could have a dramatic effect over and above the variety of natural experiences that children have. If events like scarification and piercing can cause acceleration of growth, would not all children in all cultures normally be exposed to events of sufficient stress potential? Suppose, as the data we have just reviewed suggest, that the effect is essentially all-or-none, that one sufficiently severe type of stress is enough. Then, in order for the correlations we have observed to have arisen, there must be many children in the nonstress societies who, during the sensitive period, are not subjected to any such stressors.

Gunders and Whiting's observation that many societies have very protective attitudes and customs regarding young infants may provide at least part of the answer. If the nonstress societies in the sample are able to give sufficient protection to their infants that a fair proportion of them live their first 2 years free of severe stress, the apparent paradox would be resolved. Reexamination of the societies in the initial study shows that most of the nonstress groups that were rated by Gunders and Whiting were rated as highly protective. Thus the actual dimension tapped was more than whether or not a stressful care practice was customary—rather whether the society was one which carefully protected infants during their first few years or one that did not and in addition arranged for intentional stresses. Given this observation, it becomes quite plausible that the proportion of children subjected to effective stress experiences in infancy does differ between cultures.

A final important point to note in the results shown in Table 10-2 concerns the apparent equivalence of various physical and separation stresses as antecedents of increased stature. Several different customs are significant predictors in isolation. While, as just observed, the occurrence of physical and separation stress is correlated to a nonchance degree, they are not identically distributed. The cultural, ecological, and historical factors that determine the presence of one practice do not necessarily evoke others. For the association of stress and stature to be a spurious result of stress being itself associated with some third variable that is the actual cause of increased stature, that third variable would have to occur cross-culturally in conjunction both with several different customs of physically stressful infant care and with customs of infant separation. It is certainly possible that all of these kinds of customs are expressions of a common influence that also is somehow related to stature. Nevertheless, the a priori unlikelihood of such a situation increases our confidence that the important common element is what originally led them to be considered together, their potential to induce a physiological stress reaction.

However, now that we have somewhat better defined the range and nature of the stress variable, we are ready to address the problem of possible alternative explanations in a more direct way.

NEW CONTROL ANALYSES

In earlier reports (Landauer & Whiting, 1964; Gunders & Whiting, 1968), control analyses utilized either physical stress or separation, never both. While these earlier analyses failed to show any involvement of "third variables," it is clearly more pertinent to examine the relation between such factors and the presence of stress of either kind.

The factors we wish to consider are genetics, climate and nutrition. These are the main candidates we know of for potent causes of differences in stature, and include all those for which we have been able to find any significant association with stature in cross-cultural data.

The method of analysis, as described above, is to hold one or more of such variables relatively constant either statistically or by examining differences within relatively homogeneous subsets of the total sample. If the apparent effect of stress is not attenuated, it cannot be wholly a result of its association with the other variables. In what follows, a society is classified as having stressful infant care practices if it is known to have used infantile circumcision, piercing, scarification, molding, separation, or any combination of these. It is classified as lacking infant stress only if information is available to determine that it practiced neither physical nor separation stress on infants under the age of 2 years.

To make comparisons in the sizes of various effects meaningful, we have used a common set of 75 societies for which all the needed information is available as the basis of these analyses. In this set of data the average height of adult males is 63.0 inches for societies without stress and 65.4 inches for societies with stress, an overall difference of 2.4 inches (significant beyond the 0.001 level by t test).

Table 10–3 displays the results of an analysis designed to examine the influence of genetic factors. The total sample was divided into societies in four different regions of the world—Africa, America (indigenes only), Insular Pacific, and Eurasia. Within each grouping, the societies are relatively homogeneous, as compared to the overall sample, with respect to genetics, culture, history, and geography.

Within each subset there is a significant or nearly significant association between infant stress and adult stature. The size of the difference between those with and without stress varies somewhat from region to region, but the average difference within regions, weighted by number of cases per region, is about 2.4 inches. Thus partialling out major genetic and geographic differences has no effect on the size of the stress–stature relation. Thus it can be safely concluded that the observed association is not an accident of cultural history having placed all societies that practice infant stress in a common, genetically tall subgroup or in a part of the world where growth is facilitated by the environment.

The data shown in Table 10–3 also answer partially questions about climatic influences in that the various geographic areas vary considerably in climate. To study the matter more directly we examined climatic differences, such as longitude, alti-

TABLE 10–3 Control Analysis for Genetic-Geographic Factors:
Mean Adult Male Stature in Inches

Genetic-Geographic Region	Infant Stress				
	Total	Absent	Present	Diff.	n
Africa	65.8	64.4	66.4	2.0[†]	7, 16
Eurasia	64.4	62.0	65.3	3.3[†]	4, 11
Oceania	63.9	62.1	65.5	3.4*	6, 7
America (indigene)	64.1	62.7	64.5	1.8*	5, 19
	$F = 3.27*$				
	(3, 71)				

Difference significant at 0.05* or 0.01[†] level by one-tailed t test.

TABLE 10–4 Control Analysis for Rainfall: Mean Adult Male Stature in Inches

Mean Annual Rainfall (Inches).	Infant Stress				
	Total	Absent	Present	Diff.	n
< 48	65.5	63.6	65.9	2.3*	7, 31
≥ 48	63.8	62.7	64.6	1.9*	15, 22
Difference	1.62*				

*Difference significant at 0.01 level by one-tailed t test.

tude, location in various ecological zones—deserts, rain forests, seacoasts, etc.—and amount of rainfall and sunlight. Of these, only average rainfall was correlated significantly with adult stature. A cross-analysis of this variable with infant stress is shown in Table 10–4. The average difference between stress and nonstress groups within high- and low-rainfall subdivisions is about 2.1 inches. Thus the stress effect appears to be largely, if not entirely, independent of rainfall. We have found it hard to account for the effect of rainfall on stature, particularly in the absence of a relation to direct measures of received sunlight (cf. Landauer & Whiting, 1965). One possibility is that rainfall is actually a better measure of sunlight received on the skin because it is not only inversely correlated with sunshine but also determines the extent to which people live in shelters and wear clothes. Sunshine on the skin may lead to accelerated growth through its relation to vitamin D. This, however, is speculation. At any rate, it appears unlikely that this variable mediates the stress–growth relation.

The last control variable to be considered is diet. We have already mentioned our failure to find a dietary factor associated with stature in the original physical stress study, despite the use, among other indices, of direct nutritional estimates. However, Gunders and Whiting (1968) found a significant association between stature and the presence of herds of milking animals (cattle, goats, or reindeer). A control analysis using this variable is shown in Table 10–5. The average stress versus nonstress difference within groups homogeneous with respect to the possession of milking herds was about 2.4 inches. The effect of stress is thus not attenuated at all by holding constant the only "dietary" variable we have been able to show to be associated with stature cross-culturally.

We can only speculate on the basis of the association of greater stature with the presence of milking herds. Four possibilities come to mind—additional dietary protein, calcium, or vitamin D or, just possibly, stress resulting from vaccinia (cowpox)

TABLE 10–5 Control Analysis for Presence of Milking Herds

Milking Herds	Infant Stress				
	Total	Absent	Present	Diff.	n
Absent	64.1	62.2	64.8	2.6*	14, 33
Present	65.7	64.2	66.3	2.1*	8, 20
Difference	1.6*				

*Difference significant at 0.01 level by one-tailed t test.

TABLE 10–6 Intercorrelation Among Variables in Cross–Cultural Study of Stress and Stature (n = 75) (See Text for Definition of Variables)

	Height	Stress	Milk	Rain
Stress	0.480			
Milk	0.331	0.002		
Rain	-0.436	-0.126	-0.333	
Region	0.332	-0.011	0.517	-0.316

infection. Protein seems an unlikely candidate in light of our failure to find associations with direct estimates of protein in the diet. It is interesting that the only reports of successful facilitation of growth with experimental diet supplements have been those that used milk (see Malcolm, 1970; Mathews, MacKay, Tucker, & Malcolm, 1974). In the study by Malcolm, the children were reported to have had other adequate sources of calcium, and it is not stated whether or not the dry skim milk preparation used was fortified with vitamin D. The vaccinia stress hypothesis seems at odds with the Malcolm results but is compatible with the effects of smallpox vaccination (to be discussed below). The vitamin D hypothesis is related to our conjecture that the effect of rainfall differences is due to sunlight. However, as we shall see below, the presence of dairy herds is very closely associated with genetic-geographic differences, and in such a manner as to raise a suspicion as to whether or not the presence of dairy herds is itself of direct significance in determining stature.

Further statistical analyses were performed to explore the relation among, and joint effects of, the four variables that have been found to be related to stature cross-culturally: stress, presence of dairy herds, rainfall, and genetic-geographic group. These analyses were performed by stepwise multiple linear regression techniques. Stress was represented as a two-valued variable—one if either any physical stress or separation was practiced, zero if neither was present. Rainfall was entered as number of inches per year, attempts to find transformations that would increase its correlation with stature having failed. A single ordered variable representing genetic-geographic group was constructed by taking as its value for each society the mean stature of the subgroup, as shown in Table 10–4, of the region in which that society fell.[1]

Coefficients of the first-order intercorrelations among the variables are shown in Table 10–6. Results of the stepwise multiple linear regression analysis are shown in Table 10–7. The variables are listed in the order in which they "entered" the analysis

TABLE 10–7 Results of Stepwise Multiple Linear Regression Analysis of Adult Male Stature as a Function of all Cross–Cultural Variables With Which it is Known to be Associated (n = 75) (See Text for Definition of Variables)

Order of Entry	Variable	F ratio	Beta Weight
1	Stress	24.18	0.45
2	Rain	7.96	-0.28
3	Region	2.59	0.17
4	Milk	1.94	0.15

(chosen by an algorithm that picks that variable that will maximize the variance acounted for at each step) along with their final beta weights and associated F ratios. The multiple regression accounts for 44 percent of the variance in stature across cultures.

First note, in Table 10–6, that stress is essentially uncorrelated with any of the other three predictor variables, while the latter are all correlated with each other. Stress by itself accounts for about 23 percent of the cross-cultural variance in stature. When the other three variables were used alone, in an analysis not shown, they accounted together for 27 percent of the variance. In the stepwise regression analysis, the beta weight for stress was 0.48 before the other variables were entered and fell only to 0.45 when all variables were included. Thus it is clear that the relation between stress and stature is not mediated by any one of the other variables or by any linear combination of them.

Of the variables in the stepwise multiple regression analysis, only the presence of milking herds failed to enter the equation with a significant incremental effect. This suggests that milking herds do not have an independent effect on height. However, when the stepwise analysis was performed in a different order, with stress not allowed to enter the prediction equation until last, milking herds entered first with a strong weighting and it was the genetic-geographic group variable that failed to make a significant contribution (stress and rainfall contributions remained essentially unchanged).

Thus genetic-geographic group and possession of milking herds are largely redundant in predicting stature. To gain some further insight into the relation between these two variables we applied the same kind of control analysis that we had to combinations of other variables with stress. The results are shown in Table 10–8. Essentially, milking herds are found only among African and Eurasian societies in our sample. These subgroups are also the tallest of the four. From this aspect of the data one cannot distinguish between the contributions of milking herds and genetic-geographic region. However, within the Eurasian group alone there is a significant effect of milking herds. Therefore this variable must have at least some independent influence on stature.

A NEW ANALYSIS OF THE EFFECT OF AGE AT FIRST STRESS

The finding that physical and separation stress appear equivalent also prompted reanalysis of the effects of variation in the age at which customary stressors are applied. Unfortunately, when either physical or separation stress is counted, the

TABLE 10–8 Control Analysis for the Combined Effects of Genetic-Geographic Region and Presence of Milking Herds: Mean Adult Male Stature in Inches

Genetic-Geographic Region	Milking Herds				
	Total	Absent	Present	Diff.	n
Africa	65.8	65.0	66.2	1.2	7, 16
Eurasia	64.4	62.6	65.4	2.8*	5, 10
Oceania	63.9	63.9	—	—	13, 0
America	64.1	64.2	63.3	–0.9	2, 22

*Difference significant at 0.01 level by one-tailed t test.

TABLE 10–9 Relation Between Mean Adult Male Stature (inches) and Age at Which
First Customary Stress (Either Physical or Separation) Occurred

Age at First Stress	n	Mean	SEM*
2 weeks or less	20	65.4	0.31
2 years or less	33	65.3	0.40
2–6 years	4	63.4	0.55
6–15 years	5	61.1	0.92
Not until after 15 years	13	63.5	0.56

*Standard Error of the Mean

number of cases in which the time of first stress can be well specified decreases, and in particular the number of cases in which there is a first stress after the age of 2 years becomes rather small. Nevertheless, the data, as shown in Table 10–9, are quite interesting. The second category, under 2 years, probably includes many cases in which the first stress occurs at various times other than the first 2 weeks. The mean stature for this group is the same as that for the first category, where stress is applied in the first 2 weeks. This suggests that the whole first 2 years constitutes a sensitive period in which stress has growth enhancing effects. The fact that the means for categories 3 and 4, those between 2 and 15 years, are not greater than that of category 5, those not customarily stressed at all before maturity, suggests that stress any time after age 2 years does not enhance growth. The especially low value for category 4, those first stressed between 6 and 15 years, is intriguing. The mean is actually significantly lower than that for societies with no stress ($t = 2.30$, $p < 0.05$, two-tailed). It is conceivable that the low value reflects a negative effect of stress on growth during this period of rapid maturation.

Other evidence related to this effect is apparently supplied by Rohner (1975, p. 111). In a cross-cultural study of parental attitudes and behavior toward children between the ages 2 and 6 years it was "found that adult males the world over are taller in societies where young children are accepted than in societies where they are rejected ($r = 0.38$; $p = 0.021$)." However, when the presence of infant stress is controlled for in the 34 overlapping cases, the early childhood rejection–acceptance effect disappears. For societies with no infant stress the mean adult male stature is 63.0 ($n=6$) inches for the societies low on childhood acceptance and 63.1 ($n=6$) for those high on this variable. For societies in which infant stress occurs the respective means are 66.0 ($n=6$) and 66.5 ($n=16$). The effect reported by Rohner apparently results from a positive relationship between infant stress and parental acceptance during early childhood.

OTHER GROWTH VARIABLES: AGE OF MENARCHE AND FEMALE STATURE

All of the data reviewed so far used average adult male stature as the dependent variable. J. Whiting (1965) searched for other possible cross-cultural measures of growth. He was successful in finding a number of societies in which information was available on age of menarche in girls. His finding was that the presence of infant stress was significantly correlated with age at first menstruation.

J. Whiting's (1965) results were based on stress indices that were not strictly comparable to those reported in the preceding paragraphs. Accordingly, we have reanalyzed the age of menarche data as a function of the presence of either physical stress before age 2 years or mother–infant separation. Overall, girls in societies with either kind of infant stress had an average menarcheal age of 12.8 years, while those in societies without infant stress had an average menarcheal age of 13.6 years. This difference is not statistically significant ($t = 1.19$). However, the age of menarche estimates are based on undocumented ethnographic assertions. In an attempt to improve the data quality we considered only those cases in which average adult female stature is also reported. There are 15 such cases available for examination, 9 with and 6 without stressful infant care practices. The mean menarcheal age is 12.2 and 14.1 years, respectively, for the stress and nonstress groups ($t = 2.39$, p <0.025).

J. Whiting (1965) also reported a difference in adult female stature associated with infant stress. This difference was found using the combined physical and separation stress variables as well. The mean adult stature of females was 61.3 and 57.3 inches, respectively, for those with and without stress ($t = 2.84$, p <0.01).

CONVERGING AND CONFIRMATORY EVIDENCE

Since the focus of this book is on cross-cultural studies, we will not go into as much detail on the other sources of evidence regarding the stress–growth association. However, since it is our belief that one of the chief values of cross-cultural research is to provide an initial test of an hypothesis that should also be tested by other means, and that the stress–growth research has provided a rather good example of the possibility of convergence of differing lines of evidence, we will review such evidence briefly.

Following the original cross-cultural study, sources of evidence were sought in which differential mortality could be held constant and data on parental stature obtained. Many careful longitudinal studies of physical growth have been conducted in which these requirements are met. Unfortunately, for most of them there were no readily identifiable variations in early stress. However, two studies were located that had been conducted during the 1930s, before infantile vaccination for smallpox became universal in Western countries. In both the Fels Institute growth study (Garn, 1962; Kagan, 1964) and the Berkeley Guidance Study (MacFarlane, 1938) some of the children had been vaccinated for smallpox or other diseases before their second birthdays and others had not. With the cooperation of the Fels and Berkeley Guidance Study personnel, J. Whiting, Landauer, and Jones (1968) reexamined these data. In both cases, careful medical histories had been taken, and it was possible to assert that there was no selective mortality or morbidity. That is, there was no difference in survival rate or in rated amount of illness between early- and late-vaccinated children. Analysis was performed on terminal stature data for males and females, statistically adjusted for the best prediction of their height on the basis of that of their parents.[2] In all four groups—males and females from the Berkeley and Fels studies—those vaccinated early were taller, on the average, than those vaccinated later or not at all (see Table 10–10). The overall difference was statistically significant ($p < 0.02$).

An intraculture study of the effect of infant separation was performed by Gunders and Whiting (1964), who studied infants born in a relocation camp in Israel. In this camp only some of the children were born in a hospital (primarily determined by the location of dwelling units with respect to the hospital tent). The cultural custom of the people inhabiting the camp was of the protective sort. In the hospital, by

TABLE 10-10 Mean 18 Year Stature Adjusted for Parental Stature of Children With and Without Early Immunization

Sample and Sex	Immunization Treatment Before 24 Months	n	Adjusted (and Raw) Mean 18 Year Stature (cm)	F
Berkeley Guidance Study				
Male	1 or more	38	180.31 (180.66)	1.073
	None	42	179.05 (178.74)	
Female	1 or more	48	166.61 (167.00)	2.116
	None	42	164.97 (164.52)	
Fels Growth Study				
Male	1 or more	52	178.51 (178.73)	6.161
	None	25	175.99 (175.53)	
Female	1 or more	45	165.45 (166.35)	1.107
	None	25	164.08 (162.46)	

From Whiting, Landauer, and Jones (1968), with permission.

contrast, "modern" practices were observed in which the infant was taken from its mother at birth and placed in a nursery. Followup weight but not height records were available for these children at ages 1–4 years. The children born in the hospital were significantly heavier than those born at home.

To return momentarily to the longitudinal results on vaccination, as shown in Table 10–10, the hospital birth finding provides a possible clue to the small effect of vaccination seen here as compared to effects seen cross-culturally. We do not know what proportion of the children in the Fels Study were hospital born, although most of them probably were; all of those in the Berkeley Study were. We have observed before that the effects of multiple stressors are usually not additive. Since most of the longitudinal study children presumably were subject to separation stress, one would expect, as observed, that in these groups the difference in stature attributable to vaccination would be much smaller than in the worldwide sample where comparison groups had no identifiable stress.

Certain other observations have appeared in the literature that taken alone seemed puzzling and fortuitous but that are easily accounted for if there is a causal relation between early stress and growth. Graham and her collaborators (Graham, Ernhart, Thurston, & Craft, 1962; Corah, Anthony, Painter, Stern & Thurston, 1965) found that children who had suffered mild anoxia at birth were significantly advanced in physical development over control infants at the ages of 3 and 7 years.

The increased average stature of people in Western societies over the last 100 years or so (which despite popular belief has never been adequately explained) is historically associated with the introduction and increasing popularity of infanti;e vaccination for smallpox and other diseases. To get more information on the question, we reexamined data from the Fels Growth Study (Landauer, 1973). Children studied in this project were born over a considerable historical period, from 1928 to 1944. Of those born during the early part of this period, before 1938, only 42 percent were vaccinated before the age of 2 years, while of those born during the later part of the period 93 percent were vaccinated early. Moreover, for these children there was an increase in average terminal stature of about 1 cm per birth-decade, but the increase turned out to be almost totally attributable to the changing proportion of vaccination. When only early-vaccinated children are considered, there is almost no secular trend, and the same is true if only those who were not vaccinated early are considered. This is best shown by comparing children with their parents. The early-vaccinated children averaged 2.4 cm taller than their parents, while among those not vaccinated before age 2 years the difference was only 0.1 cm.

The final and most compelling source of evidence comes from a systematic, controlled experiment on the effects of early vaccination that we initiated in Kenya in 1968. In connection with a more general comparative developmental research project, we established a child health clinic in one panel community.[3] We discovered that many children beneath the age of 4 years had not been given smallpox vaccinations or any other kind of immunization, although almost all older children and adults in the community, and those in surrounding communities, had been vaccinated. We undertook the vaccination of the younger children in stages, vaccinating a randomly chosen portion of them before the age of 2 years and postponing vaccination for the rest until after that time. The procedure was as follows: We first made a census of the community to identity children under the age of 4 years and to obtain vaccination histories for them. Then, in 1968 and 1970 we invited all children in this age range to attend a general-purpose clinic. Vaccination histories were taken again, and all children were weighed and measured and given a brief physical examination and a treatment for worms. Of those not previously vaccinated and not found to have counterindicating symptoms, a random 5/13 were vaccinated for smallpox, and in some cases given BCG, polio, and/or DPT vaccinations as well. The rest were vaccinated after they reached 2 years of age. In 1973, the first of a series of planned followup measurements as made. The children were then 3–7 years old, with an average age of about 5½ years. The measurements were obtained by trained medical students who were not aware of the vaccination histories of the children. The data were analyzed by first finding each child's status on a particular anthropometric variable relative to the norm for his or her age and then correcting these values by the statistical best prediction of the child's status relative to other children on the basis of weight measurements taken before assignment to the experimental or control group.[4] Thus the data used were adjusted for both the age of the child at the time of measurement and for relative growth status before entering the study. The results, shown in Table 10–11, were that the children vaccinated before the age of 2 years had grown more in the intervening years than those who had not been vaccinated. The advantage was significant for overall stature and head circumference and in the same direction but not statistically reliable for sitting height and for weight. An index of leg length derived by subtracting sitting height from standing height was most reliably associated with early vaccination. Since most differences in terminal stature are attributable to leg length, this finding is not surprising.

In 1968 (J. Whiting, Landauer, & Jones, p. 65) we said "no single definitive test of this hypothesis has been made, nor is one likely to appear in the future, because the experimental study of the effect of early stress is not possible with human subjects as it has been with laboratory animals." We must recant that prophecy. The vaccination study gave us the opportunity to perform the required experiment. While at the most recent measurement the children were only between 3 and 7 years old so that we cannot yet make any final judgment about the effects of early stress on terminal stature, the initial results nonetheless are perfectly consistent with what

TABLE 10-11 Effect of Age at First Vaccination on Growth During
Early Childhood—Mean (and Standard Errors) of Deviations from
Normative Values (Weight in kg, other measures in cm)

Group (n)	Height	Sitting Height	Leg Length	Head Circumference	Weight
Early vaccination (101)	0.87	0.19	0.69	0.29	0.09
	(0.50)	(0.27)	(0.34)	(0.13)	(0.20)
Later vaccination (177)	−0.40	−0.14	−0.26	−0.13	−0.06
	(0.31)	(0.16)	(0.21)	(0.10)	(0.11)
	*			†	†

Difference significant at 0.025* or 0.01† level by one-tailed t test.

the cross-cultural and other data indicated. Indeed, the effect on stature at mean age 5 years is approximately 1.3 cm, which is about what one would expect if the children are destined to achieve the same terminal statures as vaccinated and unvaccinated Americans. In addition, the difference between the randomly assigned vaccination group and the randomly assigned control group was of the same magnitude as that between the stature of those who had been vaccinated "naturally" before we started our study and those of comparable ages who were not vaccinated. Thus the direct, randomized, and controlled experiment appears to be producing results equivalent to those given by the cross-cultural and longitudinal correlational methods applied earlier.

OTHER EFFECTS OF EARLY STRESS

As previously mentioned, animal research on early stress has found a number of sequelae other than accelerated growth, all being at least plausibly manifestations of a change in endocrine function. The effects have included increased boldness in an open field test, improved learning ability where an aversive motivator is involved, a change in adrenal response to stress, and increased resistance to certain stress-related diseases. None of these consequences lends itself easily to direct measurements in cross-cultural research. Nevertheless, a few attempts have been made to relate early stress to cultural variables that might indirectly reflect differences in boldness, emotionality, and the like.

We have not seriously pursued this problem but can report some preliminary explorations. These are based on variables used in other cross-cultural studies that used samples that overlapped with ours. We chose those that might by any stretch of the imagination reflect temperamental differences relating to differences in endocrine functioning. On the assumption that boldness might be related to warlikeness, we chose *collective pugnacity* (Slater & Slater, 1965). On the hypothesis that adults might be more anxious if they were not stressed in infancy, we chose the *fear of ghosts and witches* (Whiting & Child, 1953) and whether the society indulged in heavy drinking (Bacon, Child, Barry, & Snyder, 1965). Finally, on the assumption that the boldness reported in the animal studies might be related to risk taking, we correlated infant stress with the reported presence of games of chance (Roberts, Arth, & Bush, 1959). As might be expected with variables not explicitly designed for the purpose of measuring temperament, the results were essentially negative. Only games of chance showed a statistically significant positive relationship ($\chi^2 = 5.4$, $p < 0.05$). Perhaps greater readiness to take risks is a consequence of infant stress.

Another nonanthropometric correlate of infant stress is reported by Ayres (1968). In a cross-cultural study of music, folk songs were scored as to their range and accent. On the assumption that a preference for music with a wide range and heavy accent indicates temperamental boldness, she tested the relationship between our scores and the Lomax scores and found that societies that practiced infant stress had a wider range ($p < 0.005$) and a more forceful accent ($p = 0.025$) than those that did not stress their infants.

Games of chance and singing styles are rather indirect measures of possible differences in endocrine response, and the case cannot be made from such evidence. These findings do suggest that there may well be a measurable temperamental effect of infant stress and that this should be seriously explored.

Intraculture and experimental studies have also contributed some relevant observations. Included in the longitudinal data available from the Berkeley Guidance Study were regular periodic medical histories. On the basis of these, ratings were made of the frequency and duration of disease or injury episodes that were likely to be accompanied by physiological stress reactions. There were, contrary to expectation, no differences in these ratings either before or after the age of 2 years between early-vaccinated and not-early-vaccinated children. (It is also worth noting that the amount of disease so measured was not correlated with stature.)

In the experiment on the effects of vaccination going on in Kenya, the 1973 followup measurements included an assessment of cognitive development with an IQ-like test battery for all children over the age of 4 years, developed in collaboration with L. A. Streeter. There were two reasons for thinking there might be differences in such a measure. First, if there are differences in growth rate, they might generalize to neurological and thus intellectual development rates as well. Second, if there are differences in boldness, they might mediate more beneficial interaction with the environment and yield more rapid intellectual growth. The results did indicate an approximately 4 month acceleration in cognitive development of the early-vaccinated over the late-vaccinated group, an acceleration of comparable magnitude to that in stature. However, given the larger variance and a smaller sample, children under 4 years not being testable, this difference was not statistically reliable.

We would summarize the results to date on consequences other than physical growth as far from conclusive but certainly intriguing. None of the studies so far has shown a strong and easily interpretable effect. On the other hand, there have been positive correlations, and they are such that with some imagination they can be seen as parts of an emerging overall picture of general effect of early stress on development.

SUMMARY AND DISCUSSION

Investigation of a possible relation between early stress and development in humans began almost 20 years ago. Laboratory research with lower mammals, mostly rats, had shown that acute stressors administered very early in life had lasting consequences. Perhaps the most reliable of these was an acceleration of physical growth. It was of obvious importance to find out, if possible, whether or not such an effect occurred in humans, but it seemed at the time equally obvious that one could not stress human infants experimentally. However, it was common knowledge among ethnologists (and a considerable source of puzzlement as well) that many primitive societies around the world customararily subjected infants to a variety of different stressful-appearing practices. Thus the cross-cultural method offered an opportunity to observe the results of a "natural experiment" that might provide evidence on the question. Such a study was conducted, and there was found a striking and significant 2½ inch difference in adult male stature between societies with stressful infant care practices and those without. Further analyses showed that the association occurred independently in four widely different historical-geographic-genetic groupings of the world's cultures and that it was independent of the best available estimates of diet and climate. The data suggested that the stress must occur before the age of 2 years to have a positive effect on growth and that two or more different stressors occurring in the same population produced little, if any, greater effect than one alone. There were enough data available to show that certain stressors alone, like piercing, scarification, and separation of infant from mother, had stature-enhancing effects. It was also found that most societies in which none of the effective forms of stress was institutionalized were characterized by protective child care regimens, so that it appears plausible that a high proportion of infants in such societies are in fact never exposed to any severe stress. Cross-cultural results also showed that another index of growth rate, age of menarche, was associated with early stress. Other more tenuous cross-cultural results have indicated that there may be differences in emotionality or timidity that follow from early stress as well.

Meanwhile, other sources of evidence were adduced to confirm the relation between early stress and growth. This was made possible largely by the observation in the cross-cultural data that a generally benign procedure—smallpox vaccination—appeared to have the same effect as other stressors. This factor could be profitably studied in Western cultures and, eventually, experimentally. Reexamination of data from longitudinal studies found a positive relation between early vaccination and adult stature under circumstances where differential parental stature and factors of mortality and morbidity could be shown to be irrelevant. Another study showed that hospital birth also was associated with more rapid growth. Finally, an ongoing prospective study of physical growth that included a random assignment of smallpox vaccination either before 2 years of age or later has produced initial evidence that the vaccinated children are growing faster.

Taken together, the evidence leaves little room for doubt that early stress leads to accelerated growth. The experimental study establishes the relation as causal, but even previously the causal inference was reasonably secure. A number of unusual and fortunate aspects of the data in this case has made the application of the cross-cultural method remarkably successful. First, data on both antecedent and consequent variables were available from a large number of societies widely distributed around the world. This made it possible to do control analyses to investigate whether the relation was merely the result of a common association of both stress and stature with some third variable that was actually the causative agent. It proved possible to examine most known or suspected factors that might influence growth and no evidence was found that any third factor could account for the results. Another unusual aspect of the problem that turned out to be quite important was that the antecedent and presumably causal factor—infant stress—could be manifested in a variety of forms. The fact that accelerated growth was associated with several forms of early stress, rather than with just one particular cultural practice, made it much more likely that the effect was due to the hypothesized causative factor rather than to chance association with some other factor or historical accident.

Thus we believe that a very strong case for causal relation between early stress and physical growth could have been made on the basis of cross-cultural evidence alone. Not every question to which the cross-cultural method is relevant will turn out to have the fortuitous combination of features that makes a strong causal argument possible. However, we believe that the stress-growth research constitutes an existence proof that convincing evidence, even if not perfect proof, on causal matters can be derived from the method.

We still do not know why infant stress leads to accelerated growth. The research reviewed here was designed to find out if the one led to the other, not why. Indeed, if, as some of the animal researchers suspect, the effect is mediated by a change in the pituitary-adrenal system, the research methods used here would have little to contribute. This also means that it would be presumptuous of us to offer further speculation as to the mechanisms.

However, there are other kinds of questions that these results lead to that could be attacked by cross-cultural research. For example, if it is taken as established that growth is accelerated in societies with infantile vaccination or other stressful occurrences, then a very-large-scale "natural experiment" in developmental psychology is at hand. Nature or culture has given us two classes of societies in one of which physical development proceeds more rapidly and to a greater extent than in the other. There are any number of questions to be asked about what other features of development go along with more rapid physical growth, what consequences faster growth has for the individual and for society (e.g., larger people with earlier menarche are likely to make greater demands on food production), and what ecological or cultural factors have led some societies to the "discovery" that stressful infant care practices are "desirable."

NOTES

1. This procedure necessarily overestimates the relation between the genetic-geographic variable and stature because random as well as systematic variations between subgroups contribute to the correlation. The overall multiple r is also somewhat inflated as a result. Nonetheless, the resulting pattern of intercorrelations and the multiple regression analysis based on them serve to expose the interrelationships among the variables.

2. The adjustment was made by first deriving predictions for each child's height from a pooled within-group linear regression on stature of both parents. Residuals from these predictions were then added to sex-by-sample means to yield the adjusted values shown.

3. This study was carried on under the auspices of the Child Development Research Unit of the University of Nairobi, Kenya. The medical aspects of the study were under the supervision of Dr. J. M. Kagia, then chief medical officer of the nearest major government hospital. It should be noted that there were no cases of smallpox disease reported in the study community or the surrounding area either during or after the period in which our vaccination program was conducted.

4. Children in the late-vaccination group were provided vaccination opportunities at later project programs and elsewhere. Means and standard deviations of actual ages at first vaccination were 11.1 ± 5.8 and 47.2 ± 12.2 months for early- and late-vaccination groups, respectively.

Of the measurements taken, only weight was available on all children at the earliest age seen. Preexperimental weight-for-age served as an unbiased control variable in that it was almost identical, on the average, for the two groups and that its correlation was approximately the same with each of the dependent variables (including later weight). The statistical method was to first compute age-dependent growth measures as deviations from a linear prediction from age and then adjust again on the basis of individual deviations from a fitted growth function relating preexperimental weight to age. Preexperimental weight probably reflects both genetic and environmental influences on growth, and its statistical control thus reduces the contribution of chance differences in such factors to both intergroup differences and experimental error.

Weight before entering the experiment was approximately equal, 270 and 183 g below age norms for those assigned early, and late-vaccination, respectively. Background data available for subsamples of the two groups disclosed no appreciable differences in social, economic, or demographic factors such as father's occupation, amount of land, or number of cows owned.

REFERENCES

Ayres, B. Effects of infantile stimulation on musical behavior. In A. Lomax (Ed.), *Folksongs, style and culture.* Washington, D.C.: American Association for the Advancement of Science, 1968.

Bacon, M. K., Child, I. L., Barry, H., III, & Snyder, C. R. A cross-cultural study of drinking. *Quarterly Journal of Studies on Alcohol, Supplement 3,* 1965, *26.*

Cohen, Y. A. An alternative view of the individual in culture-and-personality studies. *American Anthropologist,* 1966, *68,* 355–361.

Corah, N. L., Anthony, E. J., Painter, P., Stern, J. A., & Thurston, D. Effects of perinatal anoxia after seven years. *Psychological Monographs,* 1965, *79* (596).

Daly, M. Early stimulation of rodents: A critical review of present interpretations. *British Journal of Psychology,* 1973, *64,* 435–460.

Dennenberg, V. H. Animal studies of early experience: Some principles which have implications for human development. In J. P. Hill (Ed.), *Minnesota Symposia on Child Psychology* (Vol. 3). Minneapolis: University of Minnesota Press, 1969.

Dennenberg, V., & Karas, G. G. Effects of differential infantile handling upon weight gain and mortality in rat and mouse. *Science,* 1959, *130,* 629.

Garn, S. M. Genetics of normal human growth. In L. Gedda (Ed.), *De genetica medica.* Rome: Gregor Mendel, 1962.

Graham, F., Ernhart, C. B., Thurston, D. S., & Craft, M. Development three years after perinatal anoxia and other potentially damaging newborn experiences. *Psychological Monographs,* 1962, *76* (522).

Gunders, S. M. The effects of periodic separation from the mother during infancy upon growth and development. Unpublished doctoral dissertation, Harvard University, 1961.

Gunders, S. M., & Whiting, J. W. M. The effects of periodic separation from the mother during infancy upon growth and development. Paper presented at International Congress of Anthropological and Ethnological Science, Moscow, August 1964.

Gunders, S. M., & Whiting, J. W. M. Mother-infant separation and physical growth. *Ethnology,* 1968, *2,* 196–206.

Harlow, H. F. Primary affectional patterns in primates. *American Journal of Orthopsychiatry, 1960, 30,* 676–684.

Kagan, J. American longitudinal research on psychological development. *Child Development,* 1964, *35,* 1–32.

Koch, M. D., & Arnold, W. J. Effects of early social deprivation on emotionality in rats. *Journal of Comparative and Physiological Psychology*, 1972, *78*, 391–399.

Landauer, T. K. Infantile vaccination and the secular trend in stature. *Ethos*, 1973, *4*, 499–503.

Landauer, T. K., & Whiting, J. W. M. Infantile stimulation and adult stature of human males. *American Anthropologist*, 1964, *66*, 1007–1028.

Landauer, T. K., & Whiting, J. W. M. Reply to comments of Hunt and Jackson. *American Anthropologist*, 1965, *67*, 1000–1003.

Levine, S. J. Infantile experience and resistance to physiological stress. *Science*, 1957, *126*, 405.

Levine, S. J. Stimulation in infancy. *Scientific American*, 1960, *202*, 80–86.

Levine, S. J. Psychophysiological effects of infantile stimulation. In E. L. Bliss (Ed.), *Roots of behavior*. New York: Paul B. Hoeber, 1962.

Macfarlane, J. Studies in child guidance. I. Methodology of data collection and organization. *Monographs of Society for Research in Child Development*, 1938, *3* (19).

Malcolm, L. A. Growth retardation in a New Guinea boarding school and its response to supplementary feeding. *British Journal of Nutrition*, 1970, *24*, 297–305.

Mathews, J. D., MacKay, I. R., Tucker, L., & Malcolm, L. A. Interrelationships between dietary protein, immunoglobulin levels, humoral immune responses and growth in New Guinean schoolchildren. *American Journal of Clinical Nutrition*, 1974, *27*, 908–915.

Roberts, J. M., Arth, M. J., & Bush, R. R. Games in culture. *American Anthropologist*, 1959, *61*, 597–605.

Russell, P. A. Effects of maternal disturbance on offspring growth and behavior in rats. *Journal of General Psychology*, 1973, *88*, 127–133.

Rohner, R. P. *They love me, they love me not*. New Haven: Human Relations Area Files, 1975.

Slater, P. E., & Slater, D. A. Maternal ambivalence and narcissism: A cross-cultural study. *Merrill-Palmer Quarterly of Behavior and Development*, 1965, *11*, 241–259.

Thompson, R. W., & Grusec, A. Early environmental experiences. In P. Mussen (Ed.), *Carmichael's manual of child psychology*, New York: John Wiley & Sons, 1970.

Whiting, M. G. A cross-cultural nutrition survey of 118 societies representing the major cultural and geographic areas of the world. Unpublished doctoral dissertation, Harvard School of Public Health, 1958.

Whiting, J. W. M. Menarchael age and infant stress in humans. In F. A. Beach (Ed.), *Sex and behavior*. New York: John Wiley & Sons, 1965.

Whiting, J. W. M., & Child, I. L., *Child training and personality: A cross-cultural study*. New Haven: Yale University Press, 1953.

Whiting, J. W. M., Landauer, T. K., & Jones, T. M. Infantile vaccination and adult stature. *Child Development*, 1968, *39*, 59–67.

Part III

Cognitive and Moral Development

11

The Development of Language in Children

Ben G. Blount

The most recent renascence of child language studies began in the early 1960s, catalyzed by a series of interesting new discoveries about children's acquisition of grammar. Working independently, researchers at three institutions found that children's speech exhibited a characteristic structure at the two-word stage (Braine, 1963; Brown & Fraser, 1963; Miller & Ervin-Tripp, 1964). Children's two-word utterances were patterned, indicating that they were rule governed. That opened the possibility that children were employing a grammar at a very young age, before they were 2 years old. Moreover, the grammar appeared not to be merely a reduced, simplified version of adult grammar but to possess characteristics of its own. A grammar unique to children and not derived from an adult model was an exciting possibility and laden with importance for child development research. Stimulated by the idea of a relatively autonomous child grammar, numerous research projects were initiated during the 1960s. The dominant research questions were (1) What are the formal properties of early child grammar? (2) What types of grammatical rules can best account for the competence that children display in their multiword constructions?

Several descriptive and analytic approaches have been utilized to address the question of how children order their words in multiword utterances. The major proposals will be reviewed here, with two objectives in mind. One is to show how the conception of children's language has progressed from an overriding concern for linguistic form to an emphasis on meaning and context. The second objective is to underscore the importance of cross-linguistic and cross-cultural research in child language. The history of child language research reveals clearly that whatever the theoretical orientation of the research is, investigations have turned inevitably to comparisons of languages and cultures to clarify questions about the relative roles of language structure, cognition, and social environmental influences.

THE PIVOT GRAMMAR HYPOTHESIS

Renewed interest in child language was based on the discovery of patterned word order in child speech. Brown and associates at Harvard University found that children's utterances resembled "telegraphic speech" (Brown & Fraser, 1963). Their utterances contained content (or nounlike) words and functor (or verblike) words, but they did not contain words like "the," "a," "in," "for," words that are essential for English grammar but whose meanings are more relational than contentive. Adjectives, demonstratives, and adverbs can often be omitted without completely impairing the meaning of a sentence, as in a telegram, and it appeared that children were using only the words that were most essential for meaning. In effect, they appeared to be applying rules that selected and ordered their utterances. The structure of children's two-word utterances resulted from their acquisition of content and functor words and their application of positional rules to order those words sequentially. The evidence for the grammar constituted by those rules was the distribution of the surface—i.e., spoken—forms.

At the University of California at Berkeley, Miller and Ervin-Tripp found structures in protocols of children's speech identical to "telegraphic speech" (1964). Content words and functor words were characteristic of two-word utterances, such as "that'sa dog," "gimme cookie," and "more milk." Miller and Ervin-Tripp suggested that children had two categories of words, an open class consisting of noun-like content words and an operator class containing verblike words that perform some function or "operate" in relation to an open class word. The operator class contains two subcategories, operators that tend to appear in the initial slot of a two-word utterance and those that tend to occur in the second slot. Examples are "more" (more milk, more cookie, more ball) and "off" (shoes off, clothes off, kitty off). Children's two-word utterances were a combination of those two classes. Frequent combinations were *operator* + *open* (e.g., gimme milk) and *open* + *operator* (e.g., daddy do). *Open* + *open* constructions (e.g., baby shoe) were infrequent, and *operator* + *operator* (e.g., more off) almost never occurred. Children's knowledge of the two word classes, operator and open, was considered to be the basis for word order in their two-word utterances. That knowledge was attributed to the children, again, on the basis of distributional evidence.

Braine of Walter Reed Army Hospital made similar discoveries about the structure of children's two-word utterances (1963). He found that children appeared to have two word classes, one containing a large number of content words and the other, with more restricted membership, made up of function, verblike words. These classes are essentially the same as Brown's *content* and *functor* and Miller and Ervin-Tripp's *open* and *operator*. Braine's terminology was slightly different; he labeled them *open* and *pivot* classes, respectively, and the grammar they produced was termed pivot grammar. The most frequently occurring construction was *pivot* + *open*, followed by *open* + *pivot, open* + *open*, and very infrequently *pivot* + *pivot*. Braine suggested that children were using distributional rules themselves to produce the ordered sequences. Pivots were the key to this process. A given *pivot* word, such as "allgone," "off," or "more," almost always occupied the same position in a two-word construction, e.g., "allgone ____," "____ off," and "more ____." Word order, theoretically, was built around the pivot. Once a given pivot was selected, the remaining slot would be filled by an *open* class word.

The pivot grammar answer to the question of what accounts for the patterned order of children's two-word constructions can be readily summarized. At the onset of the two-word phase (approximately 18–24 months), children begin to add functor words to their linguistic system, and they use these as pivot words in conjunction with content, or open class, words. The pivots operate on the open class words, and the children use their knowledge of word classes, word positions, and their distributional properties to generate grammatical utterances.

The children in the three studies were from different areas of the United States.

Social environmental influences were therefore thought to be insignificant, since the socialization processes would not likely be the same across families. The remarkable similarities of the pivot grammars were considered to be the consequence of something more fundamental than socialization, perhaps similar cognitive functioning, or even the expression of a phylogenetic component of language. Each of those possibilities was an interesting question, and each required cross-cultural research. If pivot grammars were found among children in non-Western societies, with radically different child-rearing practices, their status as a universal would be enhanced.

Prior to making claims about a universal, it was necessary to consider the dominant word order in the adult usage of a language. That word order might play a determinant role in the word order of children's utterances. English is a strict word order language. Grammatical relations are indicated by the dominant word order, subject–verb–object. The strict word order of pivot grammar, then, could possibly be derived from the English adult model. A test case would be provided by the existence of a pivot grammar in a free word order language, one in which grammatical relations would be shown by inflection rather than word order. Russian is a language with relatively free word order, and a pivot—i.e., strict word order—grammar in Russian would mean that the claim for universal status would be strengthened. Children learning to speak Russian, it was found, did produce pivot grammars, almost identical to those in English (Slobin, 1966). Additional research in non-Western languages, notably Samoan (Kernan, 1969) and Luo (Blount, 1969), revealed more pivot grammars, again almost identical to those in English. Pivot grammars can easily be translated across languages. The adult model language was, it appeared, not a significant or perhaps not even a contributing factor to the observable structure of children's early grammars, and it seemed that pivot grammars might, indeed, be universal.

CHILD LANGUAGE AND TRANSFORMATIONAL GRAMMAR

Pivot grammar was tentatively accorded the status of a universal in children's language acquisition, but questions to the contrary soon began to be raised. One early criticism was that the process of contextual generalization (word order defined in relation to pivots), supposedly responsible for the word order in pivot grammar, could not possibly be the major process by which grammar is acquired (Bever, Fodor, & Weksel, 1965). English grammar cannot be adequately described on the basis of the distributional properties of grammatical categories alone. A speaker could not learn the grammar of English through successive generalizations about word order from the contexts in which words appear. Bever et al. rejected Braine's proposals for contextual generalization, contending that they were inadequate and based on a false assumption. The psychological unity of phrases (or pivot grammars) cannot be attributed solely to the associative bonds between the words in a phrase. A higher-order structure is required. Bever et al. argued for transformational generative grammar as a better and more tenable system.

The merit of the Bever et al. criticism was that it seriously questioned the usefulness of word association and contextual generalization as concepts in child language. They did not demonstrate, contrary to later claims about their work, that pivot grammar could not possibly be an acquisition strategy by children. An obvious implication of their arguments, however, was that children could not rely heavily or for long on an associative grammar, such as a pivot grammar, because that alone would not lead them to the adult grammar of the language. A consequence of their article and of the rapidly expanding acceptance of Chomskyan linguistics was a turn to transformational grammar as the dominant research tool for child language.

An early advocate of the transformational approach was McNeill. He argued that children acquired their grammar as part of a maturational process (1966). According to this view, children progressed linguistically through a differentiation of the pivot categories into other grammatical categories, arriving eventually at the categories of their adult language. Grammar emerged in each child because he or she was endowed with a language acquisition device (LAD), a species-specific capacity that emerged in children as they matured. The LAD, originally hypothesized by N. Chomsky (1965), consisted of linguistic universals (noun phrases, verbs), a hierarchy of grammatical categories (noun phrase, noun, determiner), and basic grammatical relations (subject-of, predicate-of, etc.).

If one accepted this nativist position, then a primary task of research was the identification of the properties and rules of grammar for specific languages and a description of the emergence of those grammatical components in child grammar. The overall goal was the discovery of emergent linguistic competence, stated in formal, linguistic terms. To accomplish that, one wrote formal grammars of children's utterances. As children progressed, successive generative grammars would reveal the emergence of linguistic competence, in effect, the ordered output of the LAD and its modification in accordance with the specific properties and requirements of each language.

Several studies in the late 1960s and the 1970s were conducted in the generative grammar framework. One of the more successful was the Klima and Bellugi study of negative words and *"wh"* words (1966). They found that children acquiring English went through specific stages of development and that these led in a stepwise progression to the syntactic structure of English as spoken by adults. Menyuk (1969) and C. Chomsky (1969), among others, also found regularities in children's acquisition of syntax.

The most comprehensive study of children's early grammar from a Chomskyan framework was carried out by Bloom (1970). She described the emergence of grammar in three children, following their development over a period of 3–8 months. Her goal was to write grammars "to account for the children's sentences by specifying the relationship of the surface structure of obtained utterances to inferred underlying structure" (1970, p. 32). The underlying, or deep, structure of children's utterances represents their linguistic competence, and that is what the grammars are intended to describe.

Bloom did find regularities in the grammar of the three children. One finding, in particular, was that constraints operated to restrict the length of the children's utterances. Bloom attributed the constraints to (1) cognitive limitations, i.e., to the fact that the cognitive systems of the children were immature, and (2) the nature of the languages they were acquiring. Part of this "nature" was a reduction transformation, which basically was a set of rules that deleted a portion or portions of the underlying sentence to prevent it from appearing at the surface level. A common reduction transformation is a subject deletion transformation, in which a subject noun (or pronoun) in the underlying structure is deleted and thus does not appear in the surface structure. A standard example is the deleted "you" in commands.

What specifically does Bloom's use of a Chomskyan grammatical model attribute to children in terms of knowledge they use to acquire their language? A grammar formalizes the knowledge that children have of the constituent structure of sentences, namely, that a sentence divides into hierarchically ordered subwholes. Further, a grammar expresses the knowledge that children have of grammatical relations, such as subject-of and object-of. The grammar also describes the knowledge that children have of subcategorization, i.e., that some words belong to the same part of speech or category and that although words belonging to the same class have similar privileges of occurrence, they do not have exactly the same privileges. Not all nouns can occur with all verbs. This latter point implies that the semantic roles associated with a given noun or verb are distinguished in the grammar, but it leaves open the question of how selectional restrictions are to be implemented in child language.

Despite the emphasis on transformational grammar and its widespread impact on all aspects of language study, its success in child language research was limited as an account of how children begin to acquire grammar. The basic problem was the power of transformational grammar. Much of the theoretical discussion about transformational grammar is directed at the problem of how its generative power, the power to produce ordered strings of lexical items, is to be limited. The constraints on generative power are specific to each language, but restrictions must be set so that only some strings can be generated—specifically, only those that are grammatical.

Child grammar poses special problems in relation to the power of transformational grammar. If one applies the basic hierarchical relation S → NP + VP to children's sentences, then the comparatively simple structure of children's utterances requires complex reduction constraints. An utterance such as "see doggie" requires a subject deletion transformation. "More cookie" necessitates a subject and verb deletion. The majority of children's two-word utterances require at least one reduction transformation. Within this framework children must be attributed a competence that surpasses what they actually produce at the surface level in their utterances. That procedure may be appropriate at the adult language level, but it is unnecessarily complex for the onset of child grammar and an unproductive way for research to proceed. The relatively simple syntactic expressions of early child grammar are not well described by a transformational grammar.

Transformational grammar, understandably, proved to be of limited utility in cross-cultural child language research. A transformational model has been used for languages other than English—for example, Japanese (McNeill & McNeill, 1968), German (Park, 1970a), Korean (Park, 1970b), Luo (Blount, 1969) and Finnish (Bowerman, 1973). The relative successes of those studies are contingent in large part on two factors. A transformational approach gives better results when applied to the speech of older children (where the problem of restricting generative power is less acute), and a grammar of the adult language facilitates greatly an understanding of child grammar. Transformational grammars are not available for most non-Western languages, and the enormous effort required to describe even superficially the syntax of a language was beyond the scope of research in child language. Without a model of adult syntax, the study of child syntax poses severe methodological difficulties.

Transformational grammar is inappropriate for child language research not only in the ways specified above but also in another fundamental way. In describing formal syntactic relations, semantic properties are assigned to children's competence only within the framework of what is necessary for syntax. The syntactic requirements were allowed to constrain the semantic definition of children's utterances. In some instances, particularly at the two-word utterance stage, that procedure assigned more knowledge than was necessary, and in other instances it failed to represent adequately the semantic distinctions that children were making in their speech. In effect, syntactic approaches to early child language, including first grammars, do not adequately describe the semantics that children employ in their speech. This limitation is discussed in detail below.

SEMANTICS AS A BASE FOR GRAMMAR

Several individuals recognized the semantic inadequacy of syntactic approaches soon after the framework began to be used in child language studies. The first reactions were to the role of the LAD. In an insightful article, Kernan argued that while children have knowledge of word classes (one of the components of the LAD), they do not rely solely on grammatical relations (the second component) to produce strings of words (1970). Rather, they acquire semantic relations such as possession, attribution, and modification, and they use that knowledge to produce word sequences. Two-word utterances are generated by children on the basis of their knowledge that words differ in function and content, that words are sequenced to express semantic relations, and that the order of words in a string is regulated by the semantic relation that is expressed.

Although Bloom's analyses of child speech (1970) were made in a transformational framework and were intended to illustrate the primacy of that approach, she presented strong evidence for a semantic interpretation of child language. To begin with, Bloom used the apparent meaning of children's utterances as a guide to syntactic analyses. Children's development of sentence negation, for example, was better analyzed when the semantics of negation were taken into account. A child's use of the morpheme "no" might have one of several possible meanings. Bloom found that it was necessary to distinguish among nonexistence, rejection, and denial as different meanings represented by "no" in the surface structure (1970, pp. 172–173). In the underlying structure the semantic interpretations for each kind of negative require different syntactic structures. The overall effect of this approach was to shift the burden of analysis to semantics, since a syntactic description was dependent on the identification of children's semantic categories.

In addition to Kernan's form classes and Bloom's semantic categories, two other proposals emphasized the primacy of semantics in the study of children's language acquisition. Each was formed within a grammatical framework—i.e., in terms of how grammar is derived, or produced, by semantic categories or relations—but neither was tied directly to a Chomskyan perspective. Fillmore's case grammar (1968) and Schlesinger's intention markers (1971) both are focused on the semantic relations in children's early multiword utterances. Their first priority is to account adequately for semantic categories and their relational function in multiword strings.

Schlesinger's framework attributes to children knowledge of semantic categories and relations, such as *agent + action, agent + object,* and *action + object.* His concern is how children might use these rules to generate regular, consistent word order in their sentences. The answer he provides is that children have intention markers (I markers) that designate both semantic relations and their relative sequential positions of the concepts that define the relations. In effect, the rules that children apply to produce word order are conceptual in origin but are specifiable in terms of ordering semantic relations, and Schlesinger was primarily interested in the latter.

Fillmore also chose to make semantic relations the central process of underlying sentence formation (1968). Each noun in the underlying sentence has a definitive relationship with a verb, and those relations, called *case* by Fillmore, are limited and recurrent. For example, agentive is the case in which a noun is the agent of the action specified by the verb, whereas the dative case includes possession and possessor or the person affected by the verb's action. A case grammar, then, orders nouns and verbs in sentences in terms of their case relations. Ontogenetically, the case relations are acquired as semantic concepts and relations, and the relations become ordered as children increase their use of multiword sequences. Fillmore himself was not primarily concerned with the question of how children acquired case grammars. His interest was in constructing a theory of syntax in which semantics was the central process. His case grammar did, however, appear useful as a way of investigating child grammar. Kernan's work on Samoan (1969; 1970) utilized some of Fillmore's ideas on case grammar.

Bowerman also utilized Fillmore's case grammar in her studies of children acquiring Finnish (1973). She was particularly interested in comparing a case grammar approach with a Chomskyan tranformational grammar, and she provided alternative analyses of Finnish-speaking children's utterances. Although she found each approach to have deficiencies, she found that case grammar was superior in accounting for the children's early sentence structures. She also used cross-cultural data, illustrating her claims for the superiority of a semantic approach with data on child speech from English (Brown & Bellugi, 1964; Brown & Fraser, 1963) and Luo (Blount, 1969).

In recent years, two excellent studies have documented the progress of child grammar studies during the past decade, and through cross-cultural comparisons they have defined new research problems and issues. The first of these (Braine, 1976) adheres to a linguistic approach to child language. The second (Brown, 1973) goes beyond linguistics to questions about cognitive bases of language. Braine's summary and new directions are reviewed here, Brown's in the following section.

Braine collected from the literature available corpora of children's two-word utterances and reassessed the grammars written for the individual children. Two methodological procedures, generally absent in the original studies, were employed consistently in the analyses, since in a small corpus their inclusion could alter significantly the formal properties of the grammar, and the corpora of all the children in a given study were analyzed collectively, not as individual grammars (as early studies had tended to do). Using those procedures and working with speech corpora from English (Braine, 1963; 1974; Brown, 1973), Finnish (Bowerman, 1973), Samoan (Kernan, 1969), Hebrew (Braine, 1974), and Swedish (Lange & Larsson, 1973), Braine found recurrent patterns of two-word utterances in all of the corpora.

Not all of the children had the same patterns, but there were sufficient parallels for Braine to identify three types of two-word combinations. Relying on surface distributional evidence, he found that some of the children's utterances could be described as *constant + variable*, akin to the *pivot + open* concept, and these appeared frequently in the children's speech. Another, less frequent pattern was what Braine called "groping patterns." In this case, the two words, or components, are at first unordered; then, as a child acquires a rule to order the components, a stable order emerges. Braine views that process as central to the formation of stable word order in children's two-word utterances. Children acquire a number of positional formulae that map components of meaning into a stable surface structure, and each formula expresses a specific range of relational conceptual content. Braine refers to these as limited-scope formulae and to the structures as positional productive patterns, the third type of two-word structure.

What is important about Braine's findings is the demonstration that the rules, or formulae, are defined in semantic terms and are derived from conceptual relations, and that the formulae are not rules of the kind that occur in transformational or in case grammars. Not only is the NP and VP of a transformational model too broad a characterization of children's competence at the two-word stage, but the concepts noun and verb in case grammar are too general as well. The relations marked by children's two-word combinations are specific and limited. The import of these claims is that the motivation for children's grammar is to be found in their conceptual system, which would include semantic categories, semantic relations, and rules that apply to specific categories and relations. Nouns and verbs are later developments in child language, and noun phrases and verb phrases occur perhaps still later.

COGNITIVE BASES OF GRAMMAR

Throughout the past decade, the research focus has shifted from a concern with form to the meaning of children's utterances, and a corresponding development has been a move from syntax to semantics as the way to account for children's utterances. It has been increasingly recognized that grammatical categories and rules of an adult language are not suitable for analysis of children's first multiword utterances. It is now beginning to be clear that the same criticism can be applied to semantic approaches that are designed primarily to account for early grammatical output. Semantics alone cannot suffice as an explanation of how word order appears developmentally. Two consequences of that realization require discussion. One is that research has, from approximately 1970, turned more and more to the question of what underlies the semantic categories that children use in their speech. The most common answer is cognition. Concepts and their relationships, it is held, are available to a child before he or she can express them adequately with severely limited linguistic systems. Cognitive development has consequently become a leading research area in the study of child language. The second point, and one that has been the object of relatively less organized research, is the question of the relative weight that must be assigned to cognition, semantics, and syntax as determinants of acquisition. Although cognition may be a major factor and syntax a minor one in the earliest stages of multiword development, older children do rely on syntactic devices, they do acquire transformations, and they can at the age of 8 years or so provide grammaticality judgments. One would expect that syntax would play a major role in acquisition of language by older children. If, however, research focuses on grammatical development at ages 3–4 years, when the syntactic system is relatively simple, acquisition would be less determined by syntactic properties. In either case, one must view as problematic the relative importance attached to cognitive, semantic, and syntactic explanations and treat as an empirical question the relative determinant weight of case.

In his classic work, *A First Language,* Brown compared speech corpora from English (Brown & Bellugi, 1964; Brown & Fraser, 1963; Bloom, 1970), Finnish (Bowerman, 1973), German (Park, 1970a), Samoan (Kernan, 1969), and Luo (Blount, 1969). His findings paralleled those of other studies. The majority of two-word utterances, regardless of the particular language, can be classified according to semantic function such as *possession, agent + action, action + object,* etc., and a relatively brief list of functions (eight in Brown's study) will include the vast majority of utterances. Acquisition of those relationships characterized what Brown called stage I of grammatical development.

Particularly significant for the present discussion is Brown's account of the source of semantic relations. He views them as outgrowths of sensorimotor patterns acquired by children in interaction with their environment. Children acquire concepts that are expressed first in behavior patterns and later as sensorimotor morphemes. The knowledge that children use, then, to produce ordered sequences of morphemes must be described initially in nonlinguistic terms. Moreover, Piagetian psychology appears particularly appropriate as an investigative framework. Brown noted that speech in stage I could be characterized by three operations of reference —nomination, recurrence, and nonexistence—and these are all operations that children learn during the first 18 months, the developmental period Piaget describes as sensorimotor intelligence.

Brown also reported on his extensive investigations of child speech at stages beyond the two-word period. He was particularly interested in the word order that children used in longer sequences. From the Harvard data on three English-speaking children, he found that 14 morphemes whose functions were essentially grammatical were acquired in a highly similar development order.[1] To take some examples, the three children acquired the present progressive, the plural, and past irregular early in the grammatical morpheme stage of development. Uncontractible auxiliary ("is," "am," "are"), contractible copula (-s, -z, -m, -r, as in "Ruth's," "he's," "I'm," and "we're"), and contractible auxiliary (-s, -z, -m, -r) were acquired later in development (1973, p. 274).

Each grammatical morpheme was analyzed according to semantic complexity and syntactic complexity in an effort to identify determinants of acquisition. The more semantic features a morpheme includes and the more transformations are required in syntax, the more complex the grammatical morpheme is, and the later it should be acquired. A general difficulty with this approach is that there is no well-developed theory of semantic complexity, and differing interpretations of syntactic complexity are possible (see Crystal, 1974, for a review of Brown's work on these grounds). Even with these inherent problems, however, Brown was able to draw important conclusions:

> Our conclusion must be that there is evidence that transformational complexity is a determinant of the order of acquisition but that, except for the simple plurals and the predicate nominative plurals, this evidence can be alternatively interpreted as demonstrating that semantic complexity is a determinant of the order of acquisition. Whether it will some day be possible to separate the two kinds of complexity remains to be seen. Advances in semantic theory yielding a general definition of complexity that could be applied to the elementary meanings in our set of morphemes may be made. More refined notions of grammatical complexity may eventually re-order some constructions or order some that are presently unordered. Ths study of languages not historically related to English may break down the semantic–grammatical confounding found in the one language and show where the real determinants lie. There is an approximately invariant order of

acquisition for the 14 morphemes we have studied, and behind this invariance lies not modeling frequency but semantic and grammatical complexity. (1973, p. 379)

Brown's innovative work in determinants of language acquisition provides an excellent model for cross-cultural research. His discovery of the regular order of grammatical morphemes is particularly challenging for studies across languages. If children acquiring languages other than English portray either an unstable or, what is more likely, a different order of grammatical morphemes, then the determinants should reflect cognitive and linguistic dimensions. A language with a past tense system highly regular compared to English would likely have an acquisitional order reflecting that fact, and, as Brown noted, research with non-Western languages should provide evidence to clarify the relative status of semantics and grammar.

In recent years, some child language researchers have turned their attention to syntactic development in older children. This important topic was neglected in the early years of research in large part because the assumption was made that children had already acquired the basics of their grammar by the age of 5–6 years. Recent studies have revealed that assumption as without good foundation. In one important study, Ingram found that most of the transformations of English are acquired between the ages of 6 and 12 years (1975). Working with a sample of children ranging in age from 2 to 12 years, Ingram observed that up to age 4 years, most of the children's sentences were simple structures. From 4 to 6 years, some complex structures appeared, complex in that one sentence was embedded in another. The full development of transformations necessary for embedding and complexity occurred between the ages of 6 and 12 years.

Ingram noted that the acquisition of transformations is predicted by Piaget's theory of cognitive development (1975; pp. 118–119). Once the developmental period of concrete operations is underway, at approximately the age of 7 years, a child has the ability to perform reversible operations. Without that ability, a child cannot transformationally relate two propositions. Ingram illustrated that point by citing data from experiments on language and cognition conducted by Ferreiro and Sinclair (1971). In those experiments, only children who had acquired the capacity for reversible operations could encode actual sequences of events and transform them sententially in other sequences.

Ingram's major conclusion was that children can relate one proposition with another only after they can perform concrete operations (1975; p. 124). Cognitive development is thus a prerequisite for aspects of syntactic development. Tremaine, in some recent experimental studies, has carried the cognitive-syntax relationship one step further. Citing results of Kessler's studies on English-Italian bilingual acquisition (1971) and her own work on English-French acquisition, Tremaine showed that children's comprehension of each language increased sharply after they acquired the ability to perform concrete operations (1975). Comprehension in English-French bilingual children was measured on 11 syntactic subtests, and 62 of 65 independent analyses of variance supported the hypothesis that children classified as operational would perform significantly better than those classified as nonoperational. Tremaine concluded that the same abilities are involved in the comprehension of syntax and in operational thought (1975; pp. 260–261).

If operational intelligence and syntactic comprehension are not isomorphic but form an identity, then some interesting theoretical issues are posed. What, for example, are the cognitive abilities that account for the identity? Tremaine suggests that an explanatory model will be based not on formal similarities between syntax and logicomathematical concepts but in a learning process that underlies both of those (1975; p. 265). Following Piaget (1971), she suggests that a cybernetic model is necessary and that syntactic acquisition proceeds in two phases. The first can be characterized as a serial, loop feedback process involving trial and error and probabilistic learning. With the onset of concrete operational thought, the second phase of syntactic acquisition begins, characterized by complete reversibility in the equilibration process (1975; p. 264).

Tremaine's suggestions are interesting in broad outline, and they should provide impetus for more research in this promising area. There are numerous questions to raise. Much more needs to be known about what aspects of cognition are involved in the acquisition of syntax. When does the first phase of syntactic development begin, in relation to phase 1, above? Can that development really be described as probabilistic? What evidence is acceptable as a first indication of syntactic acquisition, or, to ask the question a different way, what criteria do we use to ascertain that children have acquired concepts such as nouns, verbs, subject-of, object-of, etc. as opposed to some developmentally prior generative base such as semantic relations? Some aspects of early syntactic development may appear to be probabilistic only because they are viewed from a syntactic framework. Assessment from another perspective may reveal a more systematic psychological and linguistic acquisitional base, as has been described in other sections of this review.

ONE-WORD GRAMMAR?

The search for formal properties of child grammar has turned not only to the speech of older children but to the utterances of children before they are in an observable grammatical stage of development at all. It has long been observed that children's single-word utterances are not restricted to referential meaning but act as a phrase or even a sentence. Especially during the part of the one-word stage of development, when children are approximately 18–20 months old, they use single words to represent larger units of meaning. A child who says "book," for instance, may mean "that's a book," "gimme (the) book," "my book," and so on, according to the particularities of any given situation.

Single-word utterances that seem to function like sentences have been called holophrases, indicating that children command a language competence that is more complex than what is directly manifested in speech. A description of a child's competence must allow for this holophrastic or one-word grammar capacity. The characteristics of one-word grammar are of particular interest to psycholinguists, since the formal properties should shed some light on the emergence of two-word grammars. The central idea is that one-word grammars would be continuous developmentally with two-word grammars; conversely, if no continuity was found, then two-word grammar would represent a qualitatively new development.

Whether there actually is continuity between a one-word grammar and a two-word grammar has been a matter of some dispute (see Dore, 1975; Greenfield & Smith, 1976). Resolution of the issue depends in large part on what aspects of a child's language competence one bases a search for continuity. Four recent discussions of the problem of continuity from single-word grammars to multiword grammars are presented below. They represent historically the research on children's holophrastic development and, at the same time, reflect the trend in child language research as described in this paper, a progression from syntax to semantics to cognition and social interaction as the units and determinants of language acquisition.

One recent description of children's holophrastic development was made by Ingram (1971). Recognizing that children use gesture, intonation, and single words to convey a variety of holophrastic messages, Ingram proposed a model of language based on Fillmore's case grammar (1968), but he replaced Fillmore's category of verb with the concept of semantic transitivity. To explain, every utterance, or propo-VERB with the concept of semantic transitivity. To explain, every utterance, or proposition, communicates about either an act or a state. If it communicates about an act, then not only is an action (or potential action) involved, but there must be some relationship between an agent or cause and the action. Where there is a realization of that relationship, semantic transitivity obtains. When a proposition communicates about a state, no action is realized, and the proposition is characterized by semantic intransitivity.

Children show in their communicative acts that they are aware of the distinction between action and state and of the notion of cause or agent before they have any concept of VERB. A model of their language development must reflect that knowledge. Moreover, semantic transitivity represents an important aspect of grammatical development. It is ontogenetically prior to the development of syntactic components such as NOUN and VERB.

The particular value of Ingram's model, however, is that the concept of semantic transitivity relates semantic features of lexicon to a higher-order linguistic structure, namely, sentences. For a one-word utterance to be a sentence—that is, to make the claim that some conceptual apparatus underlies and generates something more complex than a label or name—there must be a specification of semantic features such as ± definite, ± human, ± animate, etc. for the single "word," and an incorporation of those features into a higher-order, a more abstract structure. Ingram suggests that children who produce holophrases have sentences because they distinguish semantic features and systematically differentiate action and stative predication according to those features. One cannot, for example, have semantic transitivity if there is not an action or potential action and an agent. Children are aware of those concepts and the semantic features that define them. By acquiring vocabulary, children learn and utilize semantic features, and undoubtedly semantic features play an important role in grammatical development, especially at the one-word stage.

Ingram's model is suggestive but far from comprehensive. He dealt with only two grammatical cases, Agent and Object, and he worked with a limited corpus of published data (from Leopold, 1939–1949). To mention another problem, it is not clear from his model how one is to distinguish between linguistic and psychological components of sentence production. Are children's utterances limited to one word because of linguistic constraints, psychological constraints, or some combination of both? That question is addressed directly in another study, carried out by Bloom (1973).

Bloom analyzed the speech of her daughter and three other children when they were in the later stages of the one-word utterance period. She identified a sequence of stages in the children's development, culminating in grammar. The first stage was chained successive single-word utterances, "chained" because the utterances were linked by action. The second stage occurred when a child was able to hold a whole event in mind, and the stage was designated as "holistic successive single-word utterances." Third, the children began to develop semantic categories of words by acquiring an awareness of the meaning relations between words. In the fourth stage the children became aware of the relative order between semantic categories for coding the meaning relations (1973; pp. 122–123).

At stage 4 the children had knowledge of semantic categories, and it was also necessary for them to have grammatical relationships that ordered the categories. Moreover, the order is a linguistic representation of the cognitive or conceptual categories that are a part of any given successive single-word (or multiword) utterance. Bloom makes a sharp distinction between linguistic structure and cognition, and she opts for linguistic structure as the limiting factor in children's single-word utterances. Children don't use longer utterance units because they lack the ability to encode beyond single words the sequences of phenomena on which they report or comment.

The separation of linguistic and cognitive aspects of children's speech leads Bloom to conclude that the one-word stage lacks continuity with later language development. It is clear that the complex syntactic system that children later acquire does not have a full range of antecedent or incipient structural components at the one-word stage, but that does not preclude continuity in some aspects of grammar. The constraints on utterance length may in some cases be due to linguistic inability, but to assign the constraints primarily to linguistic factors is to overemphasize the importance of syntax, and there is no reason to assume that syntactic rules are the structural principles which direct and guide children's language development. A more accurate interpretation is that rules of word order follow from other aspects of language development, and once acquisition of an aspect of syntax is underway, that aspect interacts with other features of language development.

From the early stages of language development, children encode some aspect of action scenes for which they have a word or words available, and they select the aspect to be verbalized according to saliency and to interactional and semantic criteria. This is the conclusion of several recent studies of child language and communication (Bates, 1976; Blount, 1972; Braine, 1974; Bruner, 1975; Dore, 1975; Greenfield & Smith, 1976). In his review of the available corpora of children's two-word utterances, Braine concluded that a semantic interpretation was superior to a syntactic one for children's language at that stage (1974). Children's multiword utterances were guided by a limited set of semantic relationships that specified word order of the two morphemes and the nature of the utterance in relation to the environment (e.g., *agent-action, action-object, possession,* etc.).

Braine also presented a strong argument for "holophrastic lexical insertion" as a productive process at the two-word stage. The formal definition of the concept is the insertion of a word into a higher mode of the rule system than can be done appropriately in adult language (1974; p. 79). At the one-word stage, a single word is inserted into the S (sentence) mode to become a holophrase. At the two-word stage, a holophrase can be inserted into the action mode of a sentence, as in *agent -action* sentences. Word choice is thereby not restricted to a referential function nor dictated by syntactic rules. Word choice is determined pragmatically, according to the action mode of a sentence and its relationship to the action event in which the utterance is produced.

A similar conclusion was reached by Greenfield and Smith in their study of children's early language development (1976). One of their major accomplishments was to demonstrate that children distinguished at the one-word stage referential from sentential meaning. Children used single-word utterances for standard naming identification, but they also used them for larger units of meaning. These larger units are not necessarily sentences. In fact, they probably are not sentences at all but communicative acts of which the single word is but one part of the structure. Children even at the one-word stage are sensitive to the informational structure of an event, and Greenfield and Smith showed that children encode the aspects of an act or event that are most uncertain or that can least be assumed to be known within the event. In effect, a communicative event has a structure, and a child names some aspect of that structure, according to principles, and allows the unnamed part of the structure to complement and support the meaning of the child's utterance. Adults use conversational structures in the same way, although they have a greater linguistic repertoire and more skill in negotiating the relative communicative load that the linguistic form will carry in relation to the load of the supportive context. As children progress linguistically toward the adult model, they use more complex linguistic structure to encode and verbalize selected aspects of the communicative structure.

To illustrate Greenfield's and Smith's claims more fully, we can consider their treatment of presupposition. Every sentence has a presupposition or presuppositions, conditions that obtain such that a sentence makes literal sense. Children's utterances have presupposed, assumed elements. These, by definition, are not verbalized but are nevertheless required for the utterances to be meaningul. The presuppositions tend to be those elements that are evident or "certain." For instance, when children have acquired the semantic functions *action/state* and *object*, presuppositions can be used to predict when each of the functions will be the one expressed:

1. When the *object* is securely in the child's possession and while it is undergoing its process or *state* change, it becomes relatively certain and the child will first encode *action/state*.
2. In such a situation, the only exception occurs when an adult question changes focus to the *object* by presupposing its *action* or *state*. Then the child will express *object* rather than its *action-state*.
3. When the *object* is *not* in the child's possession, it becomes more uncertain, and his first utterance will express the *object*.
4. Once the most uncertain or informative element in the situation has been encoded, be it *object* or *action-state*, it becomes more certain and less informative. At this point, then, if the child continues to encode the situation verbally, he or she will switch to expressing verbally the other aspect, heretofore unstated. (1976, p. 188).

In summary, Greenfield and Smith conclude that although the one-word period may be static in syntactic form, it is a period of considerable language development. Children advance in their communicative development by acquiring semantic functions such as *agent, action/state,* and *object* and the ability to encode those functions so that their utterances are meaningful. Children's dialogues in the one-word stage resemble two-person sentences. Through verbal interaction with adults, children are able to construct their utterances so that they are understood. They use words, presuppositions, and context in increasingly rule-governed ways, enabling them to encode more and more of the situation linguistically and ultimately syntactically.

In an incisive review of previous work on holophrases, Dore identified several theoretical dilemmas that have resulted from the various findings and conclusions (1975). One of these dilemmas is the research question that has motivated much of the study of child language, namely, how to explain the acquisition of syntax. If syntax is not a specifically innate capacity, as is unlikely, then one should be able to discern the processes of acquisition. That task has proven extremely difficult and elusive.

Another dilemma concerns the question of the relative weights that can be attributed to syntactic, semantic, and conceptual components in a child's acquisition of language, an issue that was raised, as we have seen, for the two-word stage of development by Brown (1973). That issue complicates the study of child language but places it in a more theoretically promising perspective. Stated simply, a search for determinants of language acquisition has shifted focus relatively from linguistic determinants to social and psychological ones. Children clearly acquire specific linguistic features, such as subject-of, object-of, noun, and verb, but they are not solely the product of earlier linguistic development. Other factors are also responsible. Exactly which factors and what their relative contributions are have become the current issues in research in this complex area of inquiry.

How has the redirection of research interests affected the study of holophrases? We have seen that one effect was the elevated importance of lexical semantic features. A second effect has been an interest in children's speech acts, as expressed and emphasized by Dore (1973; 1975). One of the shortcomings of earlier work on holophrases was that analyses began with the concept of sentence, forcing the accounts into a linguistic framework. Dore proposed, instead, that children employ primitive speech acts, such as labeling, repeating, answering, and requesting (action or answer) (1975; p. 31).

A primitive speech act contains a rudimentary referring expression, which children learn through vocabulary acquisition, and a device to indicate "primitive force." This latter concept is derived from the concept of elocutionary force (Searle, 1969), the meaning in which an utterance or proposition is to be taken, as, for example, a promise, question, or demand. In the one-word stage, children's utterances have a similar force, although the force is not integrated with a linguistic system in the same way it is with adults. The force is more primitive. The principal way that primitive force is expressed is through prosody, in particular, intonation and stress.

A speech act mode of acquisition is consistent with much of what is known about children's pregrammatical development. They gain communicative control of prosody before they acquire lexicon, which in turn appears before true grammar is acquired. Using the same word form, a child can express different meanings by changing intonation, stress, volume, or duration. The prosodic pattern indicates the intention a child has in the communicative act, and it is well established that different intentions are present during the one-word stage and earlier. A second way in which a speech act approach is appropriate, as Dore points out, is that contextual features do not have to be reduced to, or encoded entirely in, lexical semantic features (1975 p. 32). A child's knowledge of and utilization of the immediate context does not have to be expressed in purely linguistic terms. That does not mean that no environmental features are mapped onto linguistic form, but it does introduce more flexibility into the interpretation. Not only is it unnecessary to posit sentences and syntactic relations as part of the child's competence, it is not even necessary at this stage to posit categorically case (semantic) relationships and lexical semantic features. Linguistics has not been entirely omitted, but the role of linguistic determinants has been considerably reduced. In effect, the role of a semiautonomous grammatical component in acquisition has been reevaluated. The notions of sentence and syntax are of questionable utility in evaluating children's single-word and early multiword utterances. As language acquisition proceeds, syntax does become important, even beyond the ages of 5–6 to 10–12 years or more. At the earlier, pregrammatical stages, however, semiautonomous syntax has been supplanted as a descriptive and explanatory device by perception and cognition on the one hand and language socialization on the other. The following two sections will be devoted in turn to aspects of lexical semantics and perception and to aspects of socialization.

VOCABULARY AND LEXICAL SEMANTICS

Numerous recent studies of child language have emphasized the importance of lexical semantics. The semantic features of the first words that children learn are important clues as to what perceptual strategies underlie acquisition of vocabulary and, later, semantic relationships. Discovering what their early lexical semantic features are, however, is a challenging research task. It is difficult to ascertain what children's words mean even in referential terms. They do not always have the same referential set or range that the same words in adult language have, and the meanings are frequently unstable, changing as the children advance in their vocabulary development.

Pioneer research in lexical acquisition has been carried out by Clark. In a summary article (1973), she surveyed diary records of children's early vocabulary usage and developed a perceptual model of acquisition. Children regularly overextend the meanings of words. They select some perceptual attribute of an object and extend that attribute to other objects which they label with the same, original term. The word "doggie," used initially to refer to a particular dog, may in time be used to name any animal with four legs. The perceptual attribute is shape, although size may also be involved. By examining the overextensions of children's words, Clark was able to identify several perceptual bases that children relied on regularly and consistently. The most frequent property was *shape,* and the other common ones were *movement, size, sound, texture, taste,* and *function* (1973). One, or sometimes more, of these properties would be selected by a child in relation to a lexical item, and the property would serve as the meaning of the child's use of that term for both the original item and others to which the term would be extended.

In more recent research, Clark has shown that not all of the overextensions in children's vocabulary are full overextensions (1975). Many of the extensions are "partial," meaning that children pick only some of the criterial properties that have been identified with the meaning of a word and that the properties selected vary with context. That finding complicates research on lexical acquisition, since children's selection and application of particular perceptual categories become more problematic. Form of objects still predominates over function in perceptual and semantic importance, but which formal criteria apply in which cases becomes more a question that requires empirical observation. That condition applies even more strongly in relation to growth of vocabulary and a consequent resorting and "reanalysis" by children of the criterial properties that define the meanings of terms. The domain of objects to which a lexical form applies changes as children acquire more vocabulary and invoke different combinations and orders of perceptual categories.

Perceptual bases of semantic features are a prime area for research in child language development, particularly cross-culturally. One would expect that variation as to kinds of categories would be minimal, but the selection of particular categories by children and their variation according to context are likely to be culturally sensitive. When context and variability become more important in acquisition, as they do throughout early vocabulary development, the input of culturally based differences can have a greater impact on acquisition. These cultural differences may be of several types, ranging from the semantic particularities of the language to characteristics of caretaker-child interaction and patterns of socialization.

Relatively little cross-cultural research has been done in this important area of lexical semantics. Some of the earlier work in semantic relationships—for example, Kernan's study of Samoan (1969, 1970)—noted the importance of lexical semantic features even though they were not central to the analyses. One early study that focused explicitly on lexicon was Stross's study of a Mayan language, Tzeltal (1969). Stross described the acquisition of botanical terms by Tzeltal-speaking children, discovering that the children differed considerably as to which perceptual attributes they used in their acquisition. Some children selected a single attribute such as size, generalizing the associated lexical item to other plants, and then acquiring new terms by adding new perceptual bases within the same general domain, e.g., size. Other children used the opposite strategy, applying distinctive attributes to specific terms and then constructing larger sets. In the first instance children moved developmentally from general to specific, and in the second they moved from specific to general.

Lexical acquisition in non-Western societies has been a neglected topic. A data base for cross-cultural comparisons is sorely needed, and it is to be hoped that considerably more research will be done in the future. A vital link in the acquisition of vocabulary, the interdependence of language and perception, is relatively unexplored across languages.

THE SOCIAL ENVIRONMENT AND LANGUAGE ACQUISITION

Several avenues of research have emerged recently that have promise for clarifying some of the complex questions about determinants of language acquisition. One of these avenues concerns the social environment of children in general and parental speech in particular. The role of parental speech in fostering language acquisition has long been an issue in child language studies, but its importance was called into question during the ascendancy of the innatist perspective on language development. The role of the social environment was viewed as passive, merely a reservoir of information from which children drew according to their particular stages of language development. Current views attribute considerably more importance to parental speech, but exactly how and to what degree aspects of parental speech addressed to children influence their language acquisition is still a subject of controversy.

The dominant question in language acquisition studies—how children accomplish grammar—has conditioned inquiries about the role of parental speech. Basically, does the speech of caretakers have a directive influence on the emergence of grammar? In 1965, Cazden reported on an experimental study of expansion training. Children's utterances such as "doggie run" were expanded by their adult interlocutors to standard syntax, e.g., "yes, the dog is running." Cazden attempted to measure the effect of expansions on child grammar, but she did not find any evidence that they were effective in acquisition. In Brown's study, an effort was made to measure the influence of parental speech in terms of the first 14 grammatical morphemes acquired by children. Examining parental speech profiles for frequency of the 14 morphemes, he found that the three sets of parents had remarkably similar and stable profiles. When these were matched with the acquisition order of children, however, the rank order correlations did not prove to be significant (1973, pp. 361–368). Brown concluded that frequency in parental speech was not a significant variable in acquisition of the grammatical morphemes.

In a recent study, Newport, Gleitman, and Gleitman (1975) found that well-formedness and syntactic complexity in mother's speech do not correlate significantly with the rate of child language growth. They did find, however, that features of maternal speech affected language acquisition when they interacted with the learning strategies of children. When deictic utterances (those that point to an object and name it) were presented to children more frequently, their vocabulary size increased and noun phrases became more elaborated (1975, p. 114). Newport et al. conclude, in support of a claim by Ervin-Tripp (1973), that children process speech in conjunction with nonlinguistic events. More specifically, the claim is that referentiality—the coincidence of maternal utterances with their referential events—promotes language acquisition.

The embedding of parental speech in concrete—i.e., referentially explicit—situations appears to be more critical than parental linguistic structure itself in fostering language acquisition. Increasingly, this idea is being adopted in child language studies (see Blount, 1972; Brukman, 1973; Bruner, 1975; Cross, 1975; Garnica, 1977; Wells, 1974; Wills, 1977). It seems eminently reasonable that children will attend to parental speech in terms of referentiality and that they will discover the formal properties of language by experiencing it situationally in structured parent –child activities. Wells suggested that the ideal situation "would be a shared activity with an adult in which the adult gave linguistic expression to just those meanings in the situation which the child was capable of attending and to which he was, at that particular moment, paying attention" (1974, p. 167). In exploratory studies, Cross investigated the ability of mothers to tailor their speech in increments according to children's linguistic and communicative capabilities (1975). Her focus was interactive, viewing language acquisition as a product of complex interactions between a child's capacity and the mother's sensitivities to them. Her major findings were that the following variables would likely be important in fostering language in children: (1) opportunities for children to engage in conversations with "sensitive" adults; (2) a mother's responsiveness to a child; and (3) the status of a child as interlocuter (1975, pp. 130–131).

There can be little doubt that parents tailor their speech for young children. The phenomenon of "baby talk" is most likely a universal speech register, language structure patterned according to use. It has been described in several dimensions. Drawing from descriptions of baby talk in 15 different languages, Ferguson (1975) has recently described and summarized many of its structural properties and processes (e.g., simplification and reduction of phonologic structures). Baby talk can be viewed from several perspectives. It can be regarded as the linguistic input stimulus to infants (Ferguson, 1975), as a speech register (Weeks, 1971), and as accommodative language (Ervin-Tripp, 1977). In the last sense, features of baby talk are accommodated to the adult expectations regarding a child's comprehension and capacity to respond, and it is this perspective that is particularly well suited for studies of language acquisition determinants.

An accommodative framework was adopted in a recent project on parent-child social interaction in English-speaking and in Spanish-speaking families (Blount &

Padgug, 1977). The adults' utterances to young children were analyzed for parental speech features, those aspects of the adult utterances that marked the speech as especially appropriate for talking to young children. Thirty-four paralinguistic, prosodic, and interactional features of that type were identified and described.

The children in this study ranged developmentally from the late babbling stage (9–10 months) to the onset of the two-word utterance stage (20–22 months). Only a small percentage of the children's utterances contained more than one word, and measures of the effects of parental speech on child grammar were not attempted. What the study reveals, however, is that the parental speech profiles show a shift in frequency of feature usage according to the age of the children. There is a marked tendency for the youngest children to receive speech with a comparatively high frequency of speech features that mark affect, features such as falsetto, high pitch, and exaggerated intonation. Slightly older children, those 14–16 months old, receive relatively higher percentages of features that are instructional in nature, features that direct a child's attention to an activity or to some aspect of an activity in which the child is a participant. Still another shift in frequency is seen in the speech features of children who are 18–22 months old. Parents begin to interpret the children's utterances as semantically meaningful, and they use more features in their speech to show that children's utterances are treated as meaningful, even when they may be nonsensical (Blount & Kempton, 1976).

The general conclusion of the Blount and Kempton study was that patterned aspects of parental speech relate to a telescoped version of developmental social interaction (1976, p. 273). The distribution of parental speech features demonstrates a pragmatic approach to acquisition requirements of children. Those requirements are that younger children must learn that speech is to be attended to, that their own speech and that of their parents warrant attention, and that the exchange of speech is meaningful. Parental speech patterns establish the groundwork for language socialization by providing children with the fundamental behavior pattern for discovering their language and its appropriate use.

Studies of parental language use in two East African societies also show accommodation to children's limited communication skills. Luo parents modify their babytalk to capitalize on infants' interactional capacities and thereby foster social interaction (Blount, 1972). Harkness found in a study of Kipsigis maternal speech that mothers adjusted the complexity of their speech as a function of their children's language development (1977). She also found that older children who served as nursemaids used different frequencies of sentence types than adults did. Mothers tended to use a large number of questions in their speech to young children, whereas older children tended to use more statements than questions. Harkness suggests that these differences may optimize the opportunity of young children to learn two styles of language, one being a question-answer style, and the other a sociable peer group style.

Interactional accommodation by parents to children's lesser communicative skills relies on affective bonds in the early stages of communicative development. Affectively based interaction serves as the medium through which language is acquired by the progressive mapping of language features onto aspects of the environment. Communicative contexts are created largely by parents in the early primitive interactions with their infants, either by calling an infant's attention to aspects of the environment or by capitalizing on an infant's attentiveness to the environment to establish interaction. This finding is likely a universal aspect of mother-infant interaction. Several studies in different languages have described this aspect of parental direction in prelinguistic conversations. It has been noted among Luo speakers (Blount, 1971, 1972), Spanish speakers (Blount & Kempton, 1976; Blount & Padgug, 1977), and English-speaking families (Freedle & Lewis, 1977; Lewis & Freedle, 1973; Stern, 1971; 1974).

Freedle and Lewis (1977) provide an excellent summary of developmental mother-infant interaction. The hypotheses of their study warrant repeating in full, since they constitute useful summary statements of discussions in the preceding pages of this review.

Hypothesis 1. Linguistic behavior has its origins in a general social communication system to which a formal lexicon and grammar are ultimately added.

Hypothesis 2. The mother-infant interaction patterns, which consist of both vocal and sensorimotor components, constitute a social system designed to facilitate the growth of communication.

Hypothesis 3. Of the various elements which compose the primitive communication system, the vocalization behaviors form a subsystem which is more important than the paravocal behaviors.

Hypothesis 4. Prelinguistic behaviors are situationally bound, even at a very early age. It is from such constraints that semantics can potentially emerge. (1976, p. 158)

Hypothesis 4 predicts later language development in children that is consistent with the results of recent studies cited and reviewed here. Children learn to contextualize the environment themselves as part of their interactional strategies as they acquire vocabulary and interactional proficiency. Children's use of context continues throughout acquisition of their language and their communicative skills. Different speech styles and speech registers have their genesis in variant contexts. Children learn to alter their speech in relation to characteristics of the individuals they address, as Harkness suggests (1977). Children, for instance, learn to use baby talk to younger siblings, and they themselves may be addressed by adults with language designed to socialize, the "language of socialization" (Berko-Gleason, 1973).

The social characteristics of the interlocuters are only one aspect of the environment that may become context. What was said earlier in a discourse of an interlocuter can be part of the context, and the utterance that immediately precedes a child's turn in the discourse can have a large role in the direction that discourse takes. If a "socially active" notion of context is adopted, following the recommendations of Cook-Gumperz and Gumperz, then the study of child language acquisition includes the way in which "children use talk to create and act out social activities" (1976, p. 5). Acquisition of a given aspect of language is thus viewed in social interactional terms in which the linguistic features are part of the process of contextualization. Learning a language requires learning how to contextualize; both are necessary for communication.

Examination of specific communicative requirements in a given context reveals how linguistic features are dependent on contextualization for their meaning and for their acquisition. Cook-Gumperz demonstrates that point in her work on the language socialization of school-age children, showing that children learn to use a variety of devices (e.g., direct imperatives, imperatives containing pronominals) to sequence and guide interaction in which they are engaged (1977). To take one more example, Mitchel-Kernan and Kernan (1977) examined the pragmatics in children's use of directives in role playing, finding that children 7–12 years of age were sensitive to the interpersonal functions of directives. The children recognized that choices among the ways that directives were issued and responded to had forceful social status implications.

CONCLUDING REMARKS

Parents structure their interaction with young children according to the children's abilities to participate. Accommodation to a child's perceptual, cognitive, and communicative skills provides the framework through which a child can discuss the relevant dimensions of his or her language; this applies to phonology, lexicon, and grammar. This general claim must be viewed in terms of another principle. The role of parents in structuring the communicative and learning environment of a child is relative to the capacities of the child. Also, as a child advances in communicative skills, she or he assumes a greater role in structuring the interaction. Pressures to communicate effectively are the likely sources for motivating changes in a child's language, and those sources are social in nature. The search for determinants of the order in child language must include accounts of children's communicative routines, including their organization and the expectations that parents apply to the children's behavior, the verbal and nonverbal communicative capacities of the children, and the interaction of the linguistic properties that describe a child's language at a particular stage of development.

The task of identifying the order in which children acquire aspects of their language can proceed primarily within a linguistic framework, but if one wants to discover the determinants of a particular aspect of development, then cognitive and communicative prerequisites must be investigated. Mastery of language by children is part of the process of socialization, including learning how to communicate, which in turn requires learning how to contextualize. Furthermore, when one becomes engaged in a search for developmental universals, cross-cultural studies are essential, since the communicative requirements of children vary across societies. Differences in communication pressures and interactional requirements mean that the types and frequencies of interactions in which children discover the relevant dimensions of their language will vary. A cross-cultural, interactional perspective will undoubtedly increase in importance as language acquisition studies proceed.

ACKNOWLEDGMENTS

Helpful comments and criticisms have been made by Karen Smith and especially by Elise Padgug. Editorial and substantive comments have also been provided by Ruth H. Munroe, Robert L. Munroe, and Beatrice B. Whiting.

NOTE

1. The mean order of acquisition of 14 morphemes across the three children in the Harvard study is (1) present progressive; (2, 3) in, on; (4) plural; (5) past irregular; (6) possessive; (7) uncontractible copula; (8) articles; (9) past regular; (10) third person regular; (11) third person irregular; (12) uncontractible auxiliary; (13) contractible copula; (14) contractible auxiliary (Brown, 1973, p. 274).

REFERENCES

Bates, E. *Language and context: The acquisition of pragmatics.* New York: Academic Press, 1976.

Berko-Gleason, J. Code switching in children's language. In T. E. Moore (Ed.), *Cognitive development and the acquisition of language.* New York: Academic Press, 1973.

Bever, T. G., Fodor, J. A., & Weksel, W. Theoretical notes on the acquisition of syntax: A critique of "Contextual Generalization." *Psychological Review,* 1965, *72,* 467–482.

Bloom, L. *Language development: Form and function in emerging grammars.* Cambridge, Mass.: MIT Press, 1970.

Bloom, L. *One word at a time: The use of single word utterances before syntax.* The Hague: Mouton, 1973.

Blount, B. G. *Acquisition of language by Luo children.* Working Paper No. 19, Language-Behavior Research Laboratory, University of California, Berkeley, 1969.

Blount, B. G. Socialization and the pre-linguistic system of Luo children. *Southwestern Journal of Anthropology,* 1971, *27,* 41–50.

Blount, B. G. Aspects of Luo socialization. *Language in Society,* 1972, *1,* 236–248.

Blount, B. G. & Kempton, W. Child language socialization: Parental speech and interaction strategies. *Sign Language Studies,* 1976, *12,* 251–277.

Blount, B. G., & Padgug, E. Prosodic, paralinguistic and interactional features of parent-child speech: English and Spanish. *Journal of Child Language,* 1977, *4,* 67–86.

Bowerman, M. *Early syntactic development: A cross-linguistic study with special reference to Finnish.* Cambridge, Engl.: Cambridge University Press, 1973.

Braine, M. D. S. The ontogeny of English phrase structure: The first phase. *Language,* 1963, *39,* 1–14.

Braine, M. D. S. Length constraints, reduction rules, and holophrastic processes in children's word combinations. *Journal of Verbal Learning and Verbal Behavior,* 1974, *13,* 448–456.

Braine, M. D. S. *Children's first word combinations. Monographs of the Society for Research in Child Development,* 1976, *41* (1).

Brown, R. *A first language: The early stages.* Cambridge, Mass.: Harvard University Press, 1973.

Brown, R., & Bellugi, U. Three processes in the acquisition of syntax. *Harvard Educational Review,* 1964, *34,* 133–151.

Brown, R., & Fraser, C. The acquisition of syntax. In C. N. Cofer & B. Musgrave (Eds.), *Verbal behavior and learning: Problems and processes.* New York: McGraw-Hill, 1963.

Brukman, J. Language and socialization: Child culture and the ethnographer's task. In S. T. Kimball & J. H. Burnett (Eds.), *Learning and culture: Proceedings of the American Ethnological Society.* Seattle: University of Washington Press, 1973.

Bruner, J. S. The ontogenesis of speech acts. *Journal of Child Language,* 1975, *2,* 1–19.

Cazden, C. *Environmental assistance to the child's acquisition of grammar.* Unpublished doctoral dissertation, Harvard University, 1965.

Chomsky, C. *The acquisition of syntax on children from 5 to 10.* Cambridge, Mass.: MIT Press, 1969.

Chomsky, N. *Aspects of the theory of syntax.* Cambridge, Mass.: MIT Press, 1965.

Clark, E. V. What's in a word? On the child's acquisition of semantics in his first language. In T. E. Moore, (Ed.), *Cognitive development and the acquisition of language.* New York: Academic Press, 1973.

Clark, E. V. Knowledge, context, and strategy in the acquisition of meaning. In D.

P. Dato (Ed.), *Development psycholinguistics: Theory and applications.* Washington, D. C.: Georgetown University Press, 1975.

Cook-Gumperz, J. Situated instructions: Language socialization of school age children. In S. Ervin-Tripp & C. Mitchell-Kernan (Eds.), *Child discourse.* New York: Academic Press, 1977.

Cook-Gumperz, J., & Gumperz, J. Context in children's speech. In J. Cook-Gumperz & J. J. Gumperz (Eds.), *Papers on language and context.* Working Paper No. 46, Language-Behavior Research Laboratory, University of California, Berkeley, 1976.

Cross, T. Some relationships between motherese and linguistic level in accelerated children. *Papers and reports on child language development,* Stanford University, 1975, No. 10.

Crystal, D. Review of Roger Brown, *A first language: The early stages. Journal of Child Language,* 1974, *1,* 289–307.

Dore, J. *The development of speech acts.* Unpublished doctoral dissertation, City University of New York, 1973.

Dore, J. Holophrases, speech acts and language universals. *Journal of Child Language,* 1975, *2,* 21–40.

Ervin-Tripp, S. Some strategies for the first two years. In T. E. Moore (Ed.), *Cognitive development and the acquisition of language.* New York: Academic Press, 1973.

Ervin-Tripp, S. A psychologist's point of view. In C. E. Snow & C. A Ferguson (Eds.), *Talking to children: Language input and acquisition.* Cambridge, Engl.: Cambridge University Press, 1977.

Ferguson, C. Baby talk as a simplified register. *Papers and reports on child language development,* 1975, *9,* 1–27.

Fillmore, C. The case for case. In E. Bach & R. T. Harms (Eds.), *Universals in linguistic theory.* New York: Holt, Rinehart & Winston, 1968.

Ferreiro, E., & Sinclair, H. Temporal relations in language. *International Journal of Psychology,* 1971, *6,* 39–47.

Freedle, R., & Lewis, M. Prelinguistic conversations. In M. Lewis & L. A. Rosemblum (Eds.), *Interaction, conversation and the development of language.* New York: John Wiley & Sons, 1977.

Garnica, O. *Nonverbal concomitants of language to children: Clues to meaning.* Ohio State University Working Papers in Linguistics, No. 22, 1977.

Greenfield, P. M., & Smith, J. H. *The structure of communication in early language development.* New York: Academic Press, 1976.

Harkness, S. Aspects of social environment and first language acquisition in rural Africa. In C. E. Snow & C. Ferguson (Eds.), *Talking to children: Language input and acquisition.* Cambridge, Engl.: Cambridge University Press, 1977.

Ingram, D. Transitivity in child language. *Language,* 1971, *47,* 888–910.

Ingram, D. If and when transformations are acquired by children. In D. P. Dato (Ed.), *Developmental psycholinguistics: Theory and application.* Washington, D. C.: Georgetown University Press, 1975.

Kernan, K. T. *The acquisition of language by Samoan children.* Working Paper No. 21, Language-Behavior Research Laboratory, University of California, Berkeley, 1969.

Kernan, K. T. Semantic relationships and the child's acquisition of language. *Anthropological Linguistics,* 1970, *12,* 171–187.

Kessler, C. *The acquisition of syntax in bilingual children.* Washington, D. C.: Georgetown University Press, 1971.

Klima, E., & Bellugi, U. Syntactic regularities in the speech of children. In J. Lyons & R. J. Wales (Eds.), *Papers in psycholinguistics.* Edinburgh: University of Edinburgh Press, 1966.

Lange, S., & Larsson, K. Syntactic development of a Swedish girl Embla, between 20 and 42 months of age. *Report No. 1, Project Child Language Syntax.* Institutionem for nordiska sprak, Stockholms Universitet, 1973.

Leopold, W. *Speech development of a bilingual child (3 vols.).* Evanston, Ill.: Northwestern University Press, 1939–1949.

Lewis, M., & Feedle, R. O. Mother-infant cycle: The cradle of meaning. In P. Pilner, L. Kramer, & T. Alloway (Eds.), *Communication and affect: Language and thought.* New York: Academic Press, 1973.

McNeill, D. Developmental Psycholinguistics. In F. Smith & G. Miller (Eds.), *The genesis of language: A psycholinguistic approach.* Cambridge, Mass.: MIT Press, 1966.

McNeill, D., & McNeill, N. B. What does a child mean when he says "no?" In E. Zale (Ed.), *Proceedings of the conference on language and language behavior.* New York: Appleton-Century-Crofts, 1968.

Menyuk, P. *Sentences children use.* Cambridge, Mass.: MIT Press, 1969.

Miller, W., & Ervin-Tripp, S. The development of grammar in child language. In U. Bellugi & R. Brown (Eds.), The acquisition of language. *Monographs for the Society for Research in Child Development,* 1964, *29*, 9–33.

Mitchell-Kernan, C., & Kernan, K. T. Pragmatics of directive choice among children. In S. Ervin-Tripp & C. Mitchell-Kernan (Eds.), *Child discourse.* New York: Academic Press, 1977.

Newport, E., Gleitman, L. R., & Gleitman, H. A study of mother's speech and child language acquisition. *Papers and reports on child language development,* Stanford University, 1975, No. 10.

Park, T.-Z. *The acquisition of German syntax.* Unpublished paper, University of Bern, Switzerland, Psychology Institute, 1970. (a)

Park, T.-Z. Language acquisition in a Korean child. Unpublished paper, University of Bern, Switzerland, Psychology Institute, 1970. (b)

Piaget, J. *Biology and knowledge: An essay on the relations between organic regulations and cognitive processes.* Chicago: University of Chicago Press, 1971.

Schlesinger, I. M. Production of utterances and language acquisition. In D. Slobin (Ed.), *The ontogenesis of grammar.* New York: Academic Press, 1971.

Searle, J. *Speech acts: An essay in the philosophy of language.* Cambridge, Engl.: Cambridge University Press, 1969.

Slobin, D. I. The acquisition of Russian as a native language. In F. Smith & G. Miller (Eds.), *The genesis of language: A psycholinguistic approach.* Cambridge, Mass.: MIT Press, 1966.

Stern, D. N. A micro-analysis of mother-infant interaction. *Journal of the American Academy of Child Psychiatry,* 1971, *10*, 501–517.

Stern, D. N. Mother and infant at play: The dyadic interaction involving facial, vocal, and gaze behaviors. In M. Lewis & L. Rosenblum (Eds.), *The effect of the infant on its caregiver.* New York:John Wiley & Sons, 1974.

Stross, B. *Language acquisition by Tenejapa Tzeltal children.* Working Paper No. 21, Language-Behavior Research Laboratory, University of California, Berkeley, 1969.

Tremaine, R. Piagetian equilibration processes in syntax learning. In D. P. Dato (Ed.), *Developmental psycholinguistics: Theory and applications.* Washington, D. C.: Georgetown University Press, 1975.

Weeks, T. Speech registers in young children. *Child Development,* 1971, *42*, 1119–1131.

Wells, G. Learning to code experience through language. *Journal of Child Language,* 1974, *1*, 243–269.

Wills, D. D. Participant deixis in English and baby talk. In C. E. Snow & C. A Ferguson (Eds.), *Talking to children: Language input and acquisition.* Cambridge, Engl.: Cambridge University Press, 1977.

Concrete and Formal Operations

Douglass Price-Williams

This chapter is concerned with cross-cultural material that bears directly on those periods in the cognitive development of the child that Piaget has called concrete and formal operations. A good deal of the substance that will be covered here has previously been considered by prior reviews. It will expedite our own treatment to discuss first some of these previous reviews.

Dasen (1972) was careful to distinguish three different interpretations of the Piagetian stages. There is first the question of the successiveness of the stages. Then there is the question of the successive acquisition of operations that bear on different contents but are assumed under identical structural principles. This is the problem of the so-called horizontal décalages. Then there is a third question regarding the sequence of substages with any particular task. The bulk of Dasen's review was devoted to the first problem determined by the simple fact that the actual studies that he reviewed had been concerned only with that point. Furthermore, most studies were focused on the concrete operations stage, so that Dasen's review was devoted almost exclusively to the precise question of the age of children who had achieved the point where concrete operations had been attained.

In a survey chapter preliminary to a study on the development of thought in Eskimo children, Feldman, Lee, McLean, Pillemer, and Murray (1974) emphasized theoretical problems germane to the assessment of results in the cross-cultural Piagetian field. They point out, for instance, that there is a decided difference in perspective according to whether the researcher adopts a theory-oriented or a subject-oriented experiment. By this distinction the authors have in mind either an experiment that directly tests an element of Piagetian theory or an experiment that through the use of Piagetian methods is primarily interested in the responses from varying populations. They exemplify the point by reference to the findings of previous work in Nigeria (Price-Williams, 1961) and in Senegal (Greenfield, 1966). Both studies had tested the age at which the notion of conservation had been attained. The Nigerian children had attained it by at least the age of 8 years; the Senegalese children had not completely grasped it by the age of 11 years. Feldman et al. (1974) make the following point:

> Price-Williams (1961), for example, modifies the standard procedure until the between-culture differences are removed. Hence he generally blames obtained differences on the task. Greenfield (1966), on the other hand, accepts her results as, for example, indicating non-conservation in Wolof children. Here differences

are attributed to the children and confidence is placed in the task. These choices are also tied up with an implicit view of Piagetian theory, and so the issues are not simple. Price-Williams, having eliminated differences, can say that he has validated Piagetian theory, at least the universality of conservation. Greenfield will argue that she has provided evidence that the theory is wrong and that culturally variable conditions affect such abilities as conservation. (p. 26)

Connected with this distinction is another one, namely, a universalistic versus a relativistic perspective. Feldman et al. consider the relativistic approach to assume that culturally correlated differences in test results reflect differences in the abilities that the test is designed to measure. Universalists, on the other hand, are reluctant to infer from the poor performance of some cultural group that they are indeed incompetent relative to the population on which the test was standardized. In general, Feldman et al. stress the ambiguity between the test as such and the subjects on whom the test is applied, so long as cross-cultural work is focused on the people tested and not on the theory that is tested thereby.

We might in passing mention the review by Glick (1975), who leaned pretty much on the previous review by Dasen, as we ourselves will need to do, and notes that the findings with respect to age attained for the various stages remain inconclusive.

Ashton (1975) produced a very thoughtful survey of the field. She noted, as had others before her, that the literature had pretty much focused on two points: verification of the succession of stages and identification of the various cultural factors thought to have influenced attainment or nonattainment of these stages. She reminds us of the previous work of Wohlwill (1968), who had noted that these two points by themselves contain doubtful relevance to the essentials of Piagetian theory. Ashton (1975) makes the following important point:

> Verification of the fundamentals of genetic epistemology is clearly necessary before researchers will be able to draw any robust inferences regarding age trends and stage transition trends in cognitive growth or environmental factors influencing the rate of cognitive growth. (p. 478)

Ashton points out, accurately enough, that what is really needed is a longitudinal research to resolve the notion of invariance across the major Piagetian stages, and this is precisely what is lacking in the cross-cultural literature. In the same article Ashton identifies a number of social factors that have been thought to influence cognitive growth, and we will need to follow her when we arrive at that point below.

Greenfield (1976), in her survey, subtitled her chapter "Paradox and Progress," which indicates her assessment of the state-of-the-art. She was mainly concerned with tasks pertinent to the concrete operations period. She made a point, which we will encounter elsewhere, to the effect that a major criticism of Piaget's theory of development when it is applied to cultures other than our own is that the notion of development inherent in the theory is simply the development of a Western scientist. Greenfield quotes a passage from Gardner (1973), who says that "Western scientific thought, however crucial it may seem today, does not represent with any fidelity or comprehensiveness, the form of thought valued in other cultures or during other periods" (p. 202). Other review articles we can note include those of Kohlberg (1968), Carlson (1976), and Ohuche and Pearson (1974). We pass now onto the review made by Piaget himself (1976; originally published in 1966).

The contribution of his chapter lies less in the consideration of data, collected to 1966, than in the relevance of cross-cultural work to his own theory. Since it is after all the imprimatur of the theorizer whose theories we are discussing, we will follow his schema assiduously with our own review.

Piaget determines four sets of factors that underpin his stage theory and upon which he believes the cross-cultural method can throw light. The first set comprises biologic factors. Here the question of the occurrence of sequential stages is fundamental. Uniformity as seen by a similar sequence of the stages across cultures would indicate, for Piaget, the dominance of the biologic factors. On the other hand, "inversions in the succession of stages, or major modifications of their characteristics, from one milieu to another, would mean that these basic biologic factors do not intervene in the cognitive development of individuals" (Piaget, 1976, p. 260). A second set of factors constitutes the notion of equilibration. For Piaget this means "activities specific to behavior in general, in its psychobiologic as well as sociocultural aspects" (p. 261). We may need to pursue this definition of equilibration further at a later point, since its translation to cross-cultural work is in need of amplification. The third set is social factors of interpersonal coordination. Piaget tends to distinguish *general* from *specific* social interactions. This latter is connected with the fourth set of factors, education and cultural transmission, and also includes the role of language.

It is doubtful if cross-cultural Piagetian researchers have ever paid close attention to this basis of classification in its practical aspects, although some other reviewers of the subject have noted it (e.g., Glick, 1975). As a matter of fact it is doubtful if a post hoc attempt, such as we are embarking on now, can follow the scheme sufficiently. The difficulty is the distinction among some of these factors in order to determine that particular research falls into one division rather than another. It may be noted that when he comes to actually specifying the cross-cultural researchers, Piaget himself groups the four factors into two sets of two each. The biologic and equilibration factors are taken together, and the general and specific social factors are likewise taken as a unit. Although it may still be difficult to make a completely confident judgment with any particular research as to whether or not, for example, it falls into the "equilibration" group, nevertheless we feel justified that the necessity for tying in the cross-cultural work with the actual theory is accomplished thereby.

GENERAL DESCRIPTION OF THE TWO STAGES

We will need to be reminded that the concrete operation period emerges in the child's development from the previous stage that is called by Piaget preoperational. In chronologic terms, and taking the data culled from Europe and North America as the point of reference, the concrete operation period is entered at the age of 7 years and lasts through the age of 11 years. Even within the subject population that is taken as the point of reference, one is forced to add the caveat "plus or minus." As Piaget himself tells us, there is an allowance in the theory itself for a margin of lag in years both within and between cultures. Substantively, however, the period of concrete operations can be described as the full comprehension of distinct psychological processes. These include the following processes:

Hierarchic classification. At the concrete operational stage the child is able to construct a hierarchic taxonomy and thus able to comprehend the notion of inclusion (e.g., able to include the class of fruit under the higher rubric of food). This also means that the child is able to deal simultaneously with the relationship between a whole and its parts.

Relations.　Now the child can manipulate ordinal relationship, which would further entail such notions as transitivity, and the grasp of the idea of a one-to-one relationship.

Number.　This can also include the one-to-one relationship point, but more importantly from the point of view of what has actually been done in the cross-cultural field this includes the idea of conservation. In turn, this entails the grasp of certain other factors, such as reciprocity, negation, and identity.

Imagery.　As Ginsberg and Opper (1969) best summarize this process:

> Until the age of approximately seven years, the child is only able to produce correct mental images of static situations. He concentrates on states, rather than transformations. After the age of about 7 years, the child becomes capable of correct kinetic and transformational imagery. (p. 161)

In general there are at least two basic differences between concrete and the succeeding formal operational thinking. We should remember that for Piaget, the term operations refers to internal actions, actions, that is, which are performed mentally. One such operation lies in the capacity for combinatorial properties, the capacity to combine elements into all possible combinations. The child at the level of concrete operations will understand that the element A might be included in B, that in turn B is included in C, and so on. The child at this stage, however, still has difficulty in comprehending that A can be included in C, or that both A and B might be included in D. At the formal operations stage, the child—or adolescent, as she or he is now—is able to utilize properly a model of operations that successfully allows him or her to comprehend this last statement. The model in question is called the INRC group (identity, negation, reciprocity, correlativity). This is a total system and not just the summation of these four factors. Together with another model, that of the 16 binary operations, which is a special case of the larger system of the total combinatorial system, the INRC system constitutes the content of the formal operations stage of development. Specific kinds of tests, such as those of introductory scientific concepts which would include, for example, the pendulum experiment (described in detail by Ginsberg and Opper, 1969, pp. 182–202), provide the means of probing the characteristics germane to this stage. On the aspect of imagery, the formal operations period is characterized by the ability to purely imagine operations as a basis for their application in action and that are subsequently to be tested by experience. In other words, the ability to hypothesize and check is built into the formal operations reasoning. One important element in this reasoning is the organizing of the concept of reversibility into the system. At the concrete operations stage the child can manipulate two aspects of reversibility, negation and reciprocity, but it is only when the child is immersed in the formal operations reasoning that he or she is able to combine these factors into a system by using negation in classification and reciprocity in relations.

BIOLOGIC AND EQUILIBRATION FACTORS

We will adopt Piaget's own division of cross-cultural material (1976, pp. 259–268) and proceed to discuss the material by taking his four factors as two pairs. Under the above section heading Piaget is concerned with two questions:

1. Does one always find the same stage of development?
2. Do the stages always occur at the same average age?

Before we even set about attempting to answer these questions, we need to determine what is meant by equilibration and how we might interpret it from the cross-cultural data. Piaget himself sees equilibration as meaning autoregulation, which generates a general coordination of actions. These actions relate to behavior in general. In his cross-cultural article Piaget tends to be ambiguous as to the source of equilibration; for him it could be either psychobiologic or sociocultural. Indeed, he inverts the definition somewhat by asking of the cross-cultural data a check on whether it is independent of the social environment or not. This specification will run us into difficulties unless we can further explicate the matter. The equilibration process is well described by Ginsberg and Opper (1968, pp. 174–175). Their definition is that the equilibration process is the "mechanism by which the child moves from one state of equilibrium to another," and that therefore "equilibration is a process of intellectual development ... whereby periods of incomplete understanding of reality are followed by periods of greater understanding." The progression is carried out by means of strategies. Ginsberg and Opper exemplify the process by reference to the conservation of continuous quantities problem. When water is poured from a tall glass to a shorter glass, for example, the child first focuses on the respective heights of the two containers; he or she focuses on the levels of the two liquids. When this strategy fails, she or he may focus on another strategy: say, paying attention to the width of the two containers. When this in turn fails he or she may try to form an impression of both height of liquid and width of container. After some juggling with these two indices, the child may see them as interactions and thus eventually grasp the notion of conservation.

Now, if we follow Ginsberg and Opper and identify the process of equilibration through the identification of strategies, there still remains the other problem of identifying them in the cross-cultural literature, where the strategies are not always noted obviously. Apparently Piaget himself encountered difficulty in doing this. He took as his chief example of cross-cultural data the study by Mohseni (1966) in Iran. One of Mohseni's findings had been that there was a discrepancy between conservation tests with performance tests, that is, tests in which the role of language is minimized. In comparing Iranian city and country children, there was a greater delay with the country children on performance tests than on the conservation tests. Piaget took this to mean that there is a difference between the general coordinations necessary to the proper working of the operational structures—characterized by the conservation tests—and the specific acquisitions that are related to the performance tests. Piaget considers that such a demonstration enables us to separate equilibration factors from social factors. Although this equilibration factor is still difficult to interpret from the cross-cultural material, we can say with some confidence that what we are looking for in the information provided to us from the studies are cases where there is a clear interplay with the geographic and ecologic environment as distinct from those cases marked by factors of social value, motivation, and so on, which can be labeled clearly "social."

In point of fact, something of the kind has already been outlined in the cross-cultural literature. Furby (1971), in her analysis of the cultural data pertinent to conservation, identified two kinds of explanation. One distinction was whether the culture was Western or non-Western, which incorporated the distinction of whether a culture relied on empirical testing or on magical reasoning. This distinction would clearly be called "social" in the Piagetian scheme we have adopted. Incidentally, Furby's reasoning has been criticized by Bovet (1974) on logical grounds, but at the moment we are not concerned with that aspect. Furby's other distinction is between those societies that are manually oriented and those that are machine oriented. Although this distinction in turn has been attacked on empirical grounds by Skanes (1976), who found no evidence to support Furby's thesis that this in fact correlated with success in conservation, the point is that dividing aspects of certain cultures' experience this way appears to approximate fairly well what is meant by equilibration. Also, there happens to be a fair number of studies relating to Piaget's theory, which include skills and interaction with the environment as a significant variable. We therefore feel confident in recognizing the equilibration factor in this way, and we apply it accordingly to the available literature.

We come now to the question of the successiveness of stages, and then to the related question of the ages at which the stages are attained.

In his 1972 article Dasen already had sufficient material to plot a series of ogives relating to the attainment of concrete operations. There were four types of curves that could be specified. First, the situation where a concept develops at the same rate as with European and American children. Second, the concept actually develops earlier. A third case is that the concept lags behind the norm of Europeans and Americans but eventually reaches it. Lastly, there is the case where the curve is flattened out at the higher age groups and where it appears that even some adults fail to attain the concept in question. Since Dasen (1972) has supplied richly documented studies to support his statements, it would be redundant to go over the material again. Suffice it to state that for the time when he was reviewing the evidence it seemed clear that although each of the four conditions had supporting studies the majority of studies fell into the third group, the one in which there was a time lag. However, there did seem to be a substantial number of cases that fell into the fourth class, the one in which many adults in the group never reached the concrete operation stage at all. The 3 or 4 years subsequent to Dasen's review have failed to force us to reorganize his pattern; thus we are obliged to ask, What does this mean? We can ask what this means both in its wider pragmatic sense and in the narrower sense of relation, to the evaluation of Piaget's stage theory. With respect to the first question, and taking off from the fourth class of cases that Dasen identified, Cole (1975) was provoked to give a somewhat skeptical response:

> I am left wondering about the cognitive status of people who do not conserve. Consider, for example, research done among people who live in semiarid locations where severe water shortages occur from time to time and natives' abilities to find scarce water are legendary (e.g., aborigines). Are we to believe that aborigine adults will store water in tall thin cans in order to "have more water"; do they think they lose water when they pour it from a bucket into a barrel? I am tempted to believe that they would have disappeared long ago were this the case. I also find it difficult to believe that they cannot think through an action and its reverse. Yet if we have to extrapolate the interpretations of poor performance from Genevan children to aborigine adults (note I am not quarreling with the *fact* that many aborigine adults fail to make conservation responses in experimental situations) what else can we conclude? (p. 170)

Cole's concern might be met with the distinction that Bruner (1966, p. 325) made between conservation in action and conservation as a linguistic judgment, yet it does behoove the reviewer to ask what these results mean with relation to experience at large and not just the arena of laboratory-type studies.

With respect to what the data mean to the Piagetian model of the basic stages, we are still left with a certain amount of ambiguity. We must remember that the majority of studies—indeed, there are very few exceptions—do not examine subjects with the margin of ages sufficient to span more than a single operational stage. We can of course *assume* that because a child from any given culture successfully responds to tests in the concrete operational range he or she has thus successively passed through the former two stages, but in point of fact there are few studies indeed that have addressed themselves to the purely successiveness aspect of Piaget's theory. Among the few are Otaala's work in Uganda (1973) and Feldman's work, now to be considered.

The work of Feldman and her associates (1974) is of importance because the studies that they employed on Alaskan Eskimos, and to a certain extent on children in rural Kentucky and Hawaii, were relevant to three stages—preoperational, concrete operations, and formal operations. The main tests consisted of the following tasks: The employment of colored blocks—these tested the relationship between items and the comparison of objects in terms of their component dimensions. A machine test that had to be arranged in certain ways to turn on a small light—this probed aspects of the combinatorial ability to children. Then there was a board test that was capable of expressing proportion in terms of orientation, and a formal test built of wooden cubes that specified the four logical operations of identity, reciprocity, correlation and negation. Feldman et al. indicated that the colored blocks test was developed to test directly the crucial point of the successiveness of the three global stages (1974, pp. 94–95). Their results indicated that a clear invariant sequence was manifest through the age periods in question. To be more precise, the hypothesis of an invariant sequence accounted for three-quarters of the variance. The remaining 25 percent could be accounted for by the hypothesis of familiarity of task material. When animal analogs—a more familiar set of items—were substituted for the blocks with the Alaskan Eskimos, then the researchers achieved 100 percent success on their tasks. The idea of familiarity is one to which we will need to return later in the chapter.

There is another aspect to the successiveness of stages questions, which is the question of the so-called décalage horizontale, that is, the order of acquisition of operations within different contents. The easiest example of this is the order of acquisition of the concepts of quantity, weight, and volume, all of which are examples of the notion of conservation. In original studies within Europe and North America the progression of achievement of these concepts is in this precise order— quantity first, then weight, and, later in age, volume. All are achieved, however, within the span of concrete operations. In one of the first cross-cultural studies in this subject (Hyde, 1970; originally reported in a doctoral thesis, 1959), this progression was found not to be the case. Since Hyde's time some studies have shown that the exact progression of quantity, weight, and volume holds; on the other hand, further studies have found that one or another concept is more difficult to attain in certain societies. Other studies note that the order itself is different. Dasen concluded that "it should be noted, however, that Piaget's theory does not [yet] predict or explain particular horizontal décalages. Cross-cultural variations thus cannot be seen as contradicting the theory" (1972, p. 32).

Anomalies of psychological processes operating at the same level of thought tend to persist in cross-cultural work. Very early Goodnow (1962) found that tests of conservation and tests of combinatorial reasoning failed to correlate and indeed seemed to be opposed to one another in her sample. Heron (1971) failed to find with his Zambian sample any connection at all of conservation task performance with the regular school competence. Presumably this finding would not jar very much with Piaget, since the performance quality of Mohseni's Iranian children relative to their conservation ability failed to worry him as being pertinent to the underlying theory.

With respect to the age question, and as we have already noted briefly in passing, the preponderance of the evidence goes in the direction of a developmental lag relative to Euro-American norms. As a matter of fact, in less developed regions within Western countries, the lag is manifested. Peluffo (1967), for example, found that only a quarter of his rural sample of children from Sardinia, and only a fifth of his illiterate adult sample from the same area, were capable of tasks reflecting combinatorial reasoning. In the non-Western world Philp and Kelly (1974) reported from New Guinea that they could not find any evidence at all of formal operational thinking in their groups. Further cross-cultural work on this point needs to distinguish carefully different levels of formal thinking, notably the distinction made by Inhelder and Piaget (1958) between level A—knowing some properties of formal relations—and level B—knowing the group properties of this operational stage and thus knowing all formal operations.

Although differing age attainments of the different stages and the substages within these can be found in the cross-cultural literature, one needs to ask whether or not the precise chronologic age is that relevant to the theory. Quite apart from the inherent flexibility of the four-factor model itself, which would tolerate differing age attainments on a global basis without doing injustice to the theory, there is the fact of differential maturation rates in different cultures. As Feldman et al. (1974) have specified, "different populations may differ in their rate of maturation. Thus, cross-cultural differences in the age of appearance of cognitive abilities [are] not impossible; in fact it is to be expected" (p. 87).

Before leaving the biologic and maturational aspects, we can raise in passing the question of possible genetic factors. This had hardly been raised in the cross-cultural literature for the present context. An exception was the study by De Lemos (1969), who suggested that the poor performance of his full Aboriginal subjects, compared to part Aborigine and to European subjects, might be due to genetic reasons. Dasen (1974) countered this argument also with respect to Australian Aborigines. The only other reference to genetics is a negative instance provided by Prince (1968). In his New Guinea sample, he noted that Highland people were genetically very different from the Melanesian population, yet both groups did equally poorly in the conservation tasks given.

We can interpret the first two factors in this fourfold scheme as counterbalancing agents. Undoubtedly there are purely biologic, maturational factors that strongly persuade the development of thought. However, these are modified by experiential factors—the equilibration factors—which will vary from one culture to another and indeed will have variance within the same culture. From the point of view of cross-cultural perspective we need to be able to identify these experiential factors. In another survey of the cross-cultural literature on cognitive process in general (and not just those identified with the Piagetian scheme) the present reviewer has labeled these experiential factors as examples of "interaction with the environment" (Price-Williams, 1976). One particular subset of interactions with the physical environment that has special relevance to Piagetian tasks is the role of skills. Many studies have indicated that the particular skills of the culture groups concerned tend to influence task performance. Most of the studies concerned have to do with conservation, although not all. Bovet (1974) in Algeria indicated that conservation of weight ability was correlated with experiential abilities of the people of that culture. Price-Williams, Gordon, and Ramirez (1969) matched up the skills of pottery-making children with the conservation task of substance (clay) in Mexican children. Dasen (1974) showed that Australian Aboriginal children excelled in spatial tasks that were related to their ecologic ability of terrain exploration. Not all the evidence is that positive, however. Greenfield and Childs (in press) found that experience in weaving skills with Zinacanteco girls failed to correlate with pattern representation when it was embedded in tasks to test this ability. Steinberg and Dunn (1976) replicated the above-mentioned pottery-making study with a Tzeltal-speaking group in Chiapas, Mexico and failed to find any influence at all of this early experience with conservation tasks. On the other hand, Adjei (1977, p. 248), working with Ghanaian children and mothers, reported that "on the whole the quantitative data on both Ghanaian age groups largely support the facilitative effects of the pottery-making experience" noted in the Price-Williams, Gordon, & Ramirez (1969) study. Once again we appear to grapple with contradictory evidence. The difficulty for the cross-cultural method lies in the disentangling of complex variables. Thus in the weaving study the authors suggested that what may be crucial here is less the factor of familiarity—raw experience at the manual level—than the more complex social variables with which it may be connected. Greenfield and Child specified the knowledge that comes from economic transaction (of pottery or weaving products) as a key element. In the Tzeltal-speaking group study, the authors pointed out that language may play an important role—a point to which we will need to return later.

A factor related to that of skills is the role of familiarity of task materials (reviewed by Price-Williams, 1976; Glick, 1975). Here again the evidence is not clearcut. Many studies have suggested that familiarity with the test material has undoubtedly assisted in the performance of the Piagetian tasks of conservation and classification. On the other hand, it has to be said that other studies do not show this. Unfortunately, it is not at all simple to know why some studies point in this direction and others do not. The meaning of what is meant by familiarity in the first place needs to be sorted out (Greenfield, 1974; Price-Williams, 1975). Glick (1975) has pointed out that while it is reasonable to use materials with known properties in our cross-cultural work, "too much familiarity may not allow the psychologist to distinguish between the formal and empirical aspects of the cognitive operations under study. Too little familiarity, on the other hand, may threaten comparability as well" (p. 606). From the point of view of Piagetian theory, however, it seems incumbent on the experimenter that he or she *need* deal with the experiential world of the subject in order to tap the equilibration factor. There may be other ways of translating this into experimental designs other than choosing familiarity as the paradigm. It does need, though, to be tapped.

GENERAL AND SPECIFIC SOCIAL FACTORS

We need to look back once more at our defining source (Piaget, 1966) and ask what exactly it is that falls under the heading of social factors. Piaget, as we have seen, divided the social dimension into two separate factors, social factors of interpersonal coordination and factors of educational and cultural transmission. The latter includes linguistic factors and seems pretty clear, but the former division is a little more difficult to understand. From our reading of Piaget it appears that what is intended here is an emphasis on the interpersonal and informal aspects of social life. For example, it would include informal exchanges between a child and its peers, and a child and its elders. What loosely comes under the heading of socialization would qualify for entrance under this heading. Now, in order to proceed further and relate this general social factor to the cross-cultural evidence, we need to spell out exactly what we are looking for. The prime difficulty, once again, is specifying those social variables that are tied in with cognitive variables. Let us take some examples. The rural-urban distinction has been referred to as a meaningful parameter with some cross-cultural Piagetian tasks (Ashton, 1975). Pursuing this further, Weisner (1976) has shown that there are at least two meaningful aspects of this distinction to cognitive material. One is the finding that urban children were more flexible and had less of an experimental "set" than their comparative group of rural children. The other aspect is that rural children are more authority oriented and more compliant than their urban peers. Now it is possible that these two aspects may be related in any one culture, that compliant children are those that are inflexible in the cognitive sense. We should also be alert to the fact that there may be degrees of flexibility within the same compliant children. The point is, however, that we are able to relate here a social and a cognitive variable. It is the *relationship* that makes the named social variable a meaningful one.

We often find purely *cognitive* or experiential distinctions that are made in the cross-cultural literature; we discussed some of these above. Such distinctions can be detected in the magical versus empirical reasoning noted by Greenfield and Bruner (1969) in their work among the Wolof. Bovet (1974) from another part of Africa—Algeria—while finding fault with this distinction, favors the distinction of a logical versus intuitive mode. In either case, what we need to establish is the social unit that goes along with these various distinctions. As a matter of fact, it was Bovet, in another publication (1976), who pointed succinctly to the direction which one needs to follow. Bovet found with her Algerian children that there was a discrepancy between the development of the acquisition of matter conservation and that of the development of length conservation. She noted further that the day-to-day life of children's activities with the two types of task appear to be quite different. She speculated that there may be distinct cultural differences in handling food and of distributing goods that could be of direct relevance in this connection. She notes that children are very often present when adults buy and sell things and when they discuss questions of price and quantity. Bovet further remarks that in different societies, bargaining is often based on quite different value judgments. As she puts it, the earliest concepts of quantity are influenced by the way a society regulates the distribution of goods:

> Moreover, inside the structure of the family, food may be distributed in different ways—authoritatian, egalitarian, subject to discussion, etc. If the situation is such that the mother distributes, in an authoritarian way, food which is not plentiful, and if moreover, containers of various shapes and sizes (bowls, plates, etc.) are used, it is possible that the child pays far more attention to the initial authoritarian act of distribution than to the perceptual indices i.e. the appearance of the food in the container. (1976, p. 275)

This quotation from Bovet specifies the linkage between an identifiable social unit (authoritarian in this case) and a cognitive experience (lack of perceptual distinctions) that in this case is related to food accumulation. It is to be noted in passing that Berry (1975) and Dasen (1975) have stressed the food accumulation cum ecology model as a meaningful parameter for an entirely different array of cognitive variables than the one we are discussing here. The same intention of linkage can be detected with Greenfield and Bruner's (1969) distinction between societies that are collectivist in outlook and those that are individualistic. These two writers maintained that the cognitive act of separating thought from the object of thought is more strongly reinforced by societies with an individualist value than those with a collectivist value. The intervening link here is that individualistic cultures encourage a more diversified cognitive set so as to inculcate recognition from different points of view than its own. A collectivist culture that enforces a mental attitude that does not separate thought from its object would of course be impoverished in imaginal productions, without that ability to shuffle representations in the head that Goodnow (1969) has considered to be crucial for certain cognitive tasks.

The same kind of reasoning has been applied to explain sex differences in Piagetian tasks when these crop up in the literature. Za'rour (1971), for instance, found that Lebanese boys are far more competent in tasks to do with weight conservation than Lebanese girls. He attributes this to the fact that in the traditional Lebanese culture boys are the ones that are encouraged to explore outside the home, to go and buy things at the stores, and often to check the weight of that which is bought.

When it comes to identifying specific social factors, the problem of locking these in to cognitive variables still remains. The actual task of specifying these specific social factors, on the other hand, has been easier to detect from the literature. Once again, previous reviews have tillaged the material. Dasen (1972), Ashton (1975), and Price-Williams (1976) have all discussed specific social agents that have been attributed to performance in the two Piagetian stages we are discussing. Westernization and acculturation, schooling, social class, and linguistic distinctions constitute the chief four factors under this heading. It has been remarked previously that these four factors are often intertwined. Dasen (1972), for example, had already noted from his survey of studies that Westernization was linked with the urban-rural difference, with social class, and with the advantage of acquiring an European language. Price-Williams (1976) had remarked that the notion of the Westernization variable was pretty vague. Furby (1971) did try to provide a matrix in which the various factors of schooling, Westernization, and urbanization could be disentangled, and it seems clear from Dasen's (1972) analysis that when these are sorted out the factor of Westernization nevertheless seems influential. It had been noted before (Price-Williams, 1976) that the Westernization influence had appeared so influential in a classification task with Australian Aborigines that the author (deLacey, 1970) felt that it would be to the advantage of Aboriginal children to be placed in the proximity of European influence. Such an evaluation really makes a reviewer consider to what extent is the Piagetian framework loaded in the direction of Western thought in the first place. We are reminded of Greenfield's (1976) point mentioned earlier in this chapter.

Schooling has been given considerable attention in the literature. We find, again, that the evidence is equivocal. Once again we need to return to the initial review by Dasen (1972), who evaluated the impact of formal schooling on Piagetian tasks. He noted that at least six studies showed cause to doubt the direct relationship of schooling to the development of concrete operations, but that there were four studies pointing in the opposite direction. In another survey Lloyd (1972) was forced to conclude that the evidence for the influence of schooling was debatable. If one goes from the generalized to the specific, the data are still ambiguous. Ashton (1975) noted in her survey that while there was evidence that some types of schooling promoted acquisition of conservation, other data indicated that other types of schooling did not. Type of schooling, of course, is a mandatory bit of information that is needed in this field, as was pointed out previously (Price-Williams, 1976). We need to have fairly detailed knowledge about curricula taught in the various schools concerned in these studies, perhaps information about teaching styles, and the general pervasiveness of the school ambience for the surrounding population. Cole and Scribner (1974) have in fact preferred to posit this question in terms of continuity versus discontinuity relative to the home environment. Also, we may need to delineate more specifically the type of mental operation thought to be more directly influenced by schooling. While it appears that there may be doubt about the effect of schooling on the conservation tasks, Ashton (1975) considers that it has far more relevance to the development of formal thought processes.

Very recently some new information has surfaced that throws further light on the question. Super (1977) has reported some findings from a study in Kenya evaluating the consequences of one year of school for children of an age range from 7 through 9 years, in other words, through the early part of the concrete operations period. While the data were not focused on Piagetian tasks, the findings are of note. On the positive side, Super found that schooling had a bearing on the child's test-taking ability and on those measures which were either implicitly or explicitly practiced in school, such as memory and visual analysis. However, on more fundamental aspects of information processing and neurologic development, Super found little effect of schooling. In another study reported in the same symposium (Nyiti, 1977) and which *was* directly focused on a Piagetian task—conservation—there was reported no difference between schooled and nonschooled Tanzanian (Meru) children on tasks of conservation related to substance, weight, and volume. This latter study would be in phase with other, similar studies that test conservation. A third study in the same symposium, done with Moroccan children (Wagner, 1977), suggests that the problem is a little more complicated. Wagner has followed the thesis that there are two main features of memory—structure and control processes. The literature has suggested that the structural features of memory may be less variable across cultures and across lifetime experiences than the control process feature of memory, which is known to vary with chronologic age. It is to this latter aspect that the influence of schooling is thought to be relevant. Wagner's study indeed did show with these Moroccan children that while the structural features of memory were invariant by age or by experiential background, the control process features were found to be a function of age only when it was coupled with schooling and to a lesser extent with urban environment. Undoubtedly, further research will help to clarify the issues involved with schooling and narrow down the exact relationship of type of schooling to kind of cognitive process.

Turning now to the area of social class or socioeconomic differences, we can first note that there are a number of articles that relate this to Piagetian test performance (Almy, Chittenden, & Miller, 1966; Gaudia, 1972; Peluffo, 1962; 1967; Tuddenham, 1970; Vernon, 1969). As with the material on the influence of Westernization, criticisms have been raised that the Piagetian theory has an intrinsic bias of a socio-economic nature built into it. Buck-Morss (1975) maintains that the structure of cognition with which Piaget is concerned reflects the structure of "an industrialized society with abstract, formal relations of production and exchange" (p. 45). There have been some hints from China in this direction. While this perspective needs to be kept in mind, we are still left with the empirical question of exactly what is being influenced by socioeconomic variables, and what are the interlocking variables. Case (1975) has made a step in this direction by arguing there is a strong probability that the reason for the lag in test performance by lower socioeconomic classes does not lie in their basic maturational schedules of development but rather in "the absence of the specific operative and figurative schemes whose coordination is required by Piagetian problems, and to the higher-order executive schemes responsible for accessing, monitoring, and coordinating the specific schemes" (p. 257).

Coming now to the linguistic variable, our first impression is that this has not been sufficiently studied systematically. In his own cross-cultural article Piaget (1976) opened the door to the influence of linguistics by citing a French study on the type of language used at the operational stage. This study found that there was a decided difference between conservers and nonconservers on the language used in the tasks of this nature. Conservers used vectoring language: "more," "less," etc. Nonconservers used absolute terms such as "big" and "small." Whereas conservers employed binary oppositions, such as "this one is longer and thinner" the nonconservers invoked a more cumbersome quaternary mode of expression, such as "this one is thick and the other one is thin; this one is long and the other one is short." Although Piaget's position is that thought leads to the structuralization of language, and not the reverse, he is nevertheless moved to speculate on the role of a language unlike French. For instance, he wondered what kind of results there would be with Turkish, where apparently there is only one vector available, corresponding to the English word "still." Exploring this suggestion of Piaget, we turn to examples from other languages where something of the sort might pertain. Unfortunately, there is not much material of this kind. At an earlier stage of the chapter the Chiapas study by Steinberg and Dunn (1976) was quoted as providing negative findings on the issue of pottery-using to conservation ability. Steinberg and Dunn (1976) did find, however, that language played a crucial role:

> Our research has led us to the conclusion that the Tzeltal language and culture influenced the children's conceptions of the demands of the testing situation and their assumptions about the strategies appropriate to solving conservation problems. (p. 22)

Now the Tzeltal language lacks the linguistic comparative. As Steinberg and Dunn indicate, things are not good or bad, or more or less—they are simply different. Specifically with respect to the idea of the conservation of substance, when a piece of clay is transformed from a ball to a sausage, the material is simply reclassified in the Tzeltal language. In the Australian Aborigine study previously cited, De Lemos (1969) noted that precise terms expressing number, comparison, and measurement were lacking in the Aboriginal language and wondered whether or not this might not account for the performance of this group. It is items of this kind which are relevant to Piaget's early concern with the role of language and indicate the direction in which further research can go.

Another direction concerns the formulation of questions for Piagetian tasks, a problem which exists with our own culture as well. For example, Mermelstein and Schulman (1967), who worked with samples of blacks in Virginia who had various degrees of schooling, found that the formulation of the question was basic to the understanding of the Piagetian tasks. In other cultures, this problem has from time to time been brought up. Greenfield (1966), for example, raised this early in regard to her Wolof subjects. Nevertheless, as mentioned before, more work needs to be done with the role of language. It may be that its role in Piagetian tasks may prove not to be crucial. On another part of the cognitive spectrum, with problems not in the Piagetian format, Glick (1975) made the assessment that "linguistic factors may have served to limit the degree to which a communicable reason could be ˌven for some performance, but that performance itself was relatively unaffected by the linguistic factor" (p. 629).

There is a wider sense in which language is important. The values and goals of both institutions and social groupings are encoded in language. Heron and Simonsson (1969) point out that in those areas where two languages operate—the indigenous one and a Western language in the school and administrative strata—it is important to know whether the two are congruent with one another or whether they embody quite different values. Incidentally, in the same article Heron and Simonsson report a nonverbal method of assessing conversation ability, a method which was repeated in Papua at a later date (Heron & Dowel, 1973). Findings related to nonverbal applications of Piagetian techniques are needed so as to assess by contrast the role of language.

ASSESSMENT AND FUTURE RESEARCH

Piagetian researches in the cross-cultural field have proved to be popular in the past and undoubtedly will prove to be popular in the future. Their popularity depends partly on their ease of presentation to diverse populations and partly on their direct pertinence to a valid developmental theory. The emphasis, however, has been on cross-sectional research, with relatively few tasks demanded of subjects. There have been few innovational attempts at trying out the Piagetian principles in domains outside the conventional laboratory trials that we have become accustomed to with Western populations. When one considers the advantages and disadvantages of further work along this line, a few salient points immediately arise. First, it seems clear that most cultures progress along the sequence of stages considered by Piaget (outside of a few exceptions that do not appear to have progressed to the formal operations stage and some that have advanced not even to the concrete operations stage). The rate of the progression, on the other hand, varies widely from one culture to another. The findings are supported even when Western nations are part of the composition of the populations studied. Goldschmid, Bentler, Debus, Rawlinson, Kohustamm, Modgil, Nicholls, Reykowski, Strupczewska, and Warren (1973) used the Concept Assessment Kit across the ages of 4–8 years in Australia, Holland, England, New Zealand, Poland, and Uganda, for both boys and girls. They found that age trends are consistent from culture to culture for both sexes, although the rate of conservation acquisition varies. Bergling (1974), comparing Swedish with Indian 10–11-year-olds found that the development of thought goes through a sequence of stages in both countries, although again the rate is different. One wonders if yet another study implementing these findings will add to our knowledge. What seems to be very much needed is a longitudinal study, tracking the same individual over time—a demand which Ashton (1975, p. 498) also articulates. If such a longitudinal study, for economic and pragmatic reasons, is difficult to mount, then one would like to see studies that focus on the overlapping of the Piagetian stages —studies aimed at the transition between preoperational and concrete operations, or between concrete operations and formal operations. At any rate, what is now required are studies that span quite a few years and not just those that concentrate on a limited span with limited tasks. These latter have undoubtedly done yeoman work; we certainly cannot disparage these efforts. But we need now to go on.

Another point which stands out is that Piagetian theory is complex and very often subtle. It is not always simple to follow the original arguments, and not easy to translate them into experimentation. To do these things in an area where there is already a difficult task of translation—the cross-cultural area—compounds the difficulties. It would do well, Feldman et al. have advocated, to be as sensitive as one can to Piagetian theory when one is working with his tasks. There are occasions, however, when this is extremely difficult to simulate. LeVine and Price-Williams (1974), for example, found, in investigating relational concepts among the Hausa by taking kinship as the domain, that the cultural situation introduced difficulties with the traditional form of questioning. The assumption that sibling relationships are symmetric and the assumption that there is a nuclear family unit of unambiguous reference were found to be tied into the Western family and were just not relevant to the Hausa situation. Thus questions from the Piagetian lexicon, based as they are on the Western family model, could not be invoked with this society. This type of difficulty is upsetting only if one demands the letter of Piagetian law and not the spirit. The principles underlying Piagetian theory can be dealt with successfully with quite complicated kinship situations, as can be seen with later work along this direction with the Zinacantecos of southern Mexico (Greenfield & Childs, 1977) and with rural Hawaiians (Price-Williams, Hammond, Edgerton, & Walker, 1977). As a matter of fact, an argument could be made for pursuing Piagetian studies into domains that, although more complex than the traditional pouring-of-water-into-containers, embody richer cultural connections. For example, Dempsey (1971) has pursued with Anglo, Mexican-American, and native American groups the idea of conservation in the domain of time, a domain that has obvious cultural complexities.

While those questions related to the very first Piagetian factor—the biological— appear to have run their course, the remaining three factors require far more elucidation. It is not just a matter of mere research; what is required is an examination of what is required in the first place.

The three factors need to be pared down to operational significance. The equilibration factor, for example, needs to be operationalized into distinct variables with which cross-cultural researchers can work. This factor needs to be carefully distinguished from the last two factors. When we come to the third factor, that of "general social," we need to be able to specify less enveloping variables than has been done to the present. Ashton (1975) again has our support when she complains that distinctions such as urban versus rural or schooling versus nonschooling are too gross to utilize after the very first identification.

Ballparks are no doubt important to specify where the game is played, but after that has been done we need to know who the players are. In our above discussion of this subject, we hope we have made suggestions for proper specifications.

There is also the problem of the relationship *among* the four factors. Few if any investigators have considered this problem. Okonji (1971) is one of the few who have formulated the question as a testable proposition. In terms of the Piagetian model, he speculated on the relationship between a "pure" experiential factor—the second factor—and the type of schooling, an element of the fourth factor:

> If the cultural environment properties for the development of a certain concept are adequate, the effect of schooling experience will definitely be minimal, but if they are not, the effect of schooling experience is bound to be more pronounced, to the extent that if it is missed at some critical ages, this deprivation may result in a permanent lack of acquisition of some conservation concepts. (p. 127)

This suggestion can be formulated in the perspective of relative *weighting* of the four factors. What type of social intervention can facilitate the neural developmental sequence? Are some experiential factors so dominant that they completely outweigh formal schooling? Are certain kinds of languages inimical to proper conceptual achievements? And so forth. The list of questions could be increased. They are all aimed at the degree of interdependence of the four factors.

The emphasis on experiential factors mentioned above brings into question the relevance of the idea of the ecologic validity of cues that might influence the various Piagetian schemata. A number of studies cited in this chapter have emphasized the relevance of the everyday working world of the subjects. A theoretical approach to thinking about this lies in the concept of ecologic cue validity, which has a formal basis in psychological studies (Brunswik, 1956; Segall, Campbell, & Herskovits, 1966).

A last point concerns the relationship of some of these Piagetian tasks to each other and to other cognitive measures. We note that at least with some populations there is a question regarding the formal unity of tasks within concrete operations (Heron & Dowel, 1974). The same senior investigator has questioned the relationship of the conservation group to psychometric measures (Heron, 1971). Given the fact that so many investigators measure with only one type of task, we do not yet know to what extent the unity of the stages may hold up.

Cross-cultural Piagetian studies have proliferated to the extent that a newsletter has been formed to keep up with the surge of interest.[1] Two recent compendiums have been published that are directly relevant (Dasen, 1977; Modgil & Modgil, in press). Anticipating the trend to continue, it is to be hoped that new investigators pay careful attention to the past, seeing where—at what theoretical points—further attention needs to be paid, inspecting what type of cultural variables need be explored, avoiding further redundancy, and keeping always the theoretical framework in mind.

ACKNOWLEDGMENTS

The author wishes to acknowledge support from the University of California, and Grant No. HD-04612, Mental Retardation Research Center, University of California, Los Angeles.

NOTE

1. The newsletter is called "Inventory of Cross-Cultural Piagetian Research." The first number came out in April 1969, and by September 1976 there had been six issues. The editors are Dr. Pierre R. Dasen, Bureau of Educational Research, Univer-

sity of Nairobi, P.O. Box 30197, Nairobi, Kenya and Professor Gavin N. Seagrim, Department of Psychology, Australian National University, P.O. Box 4, Canberra, A.C.T. 2600, Australia.

REFERENCES

Adjei, K. Influence of specific maternal occupation and behavior on Piagetian cognitive development. In P. R. Dasen (Ed.), *Piagetian psychology: Cross-cultural contributions.* New York: Gardner Press, 1977.

Almy, M., Chittenden, E., & Miller, P. *Young children's thinking: Studies of some aspects of Piaget's theory.* New York: Teachers College Press, 1966.

Ashton, P. T. Cross-cultural Piagetian research: An experimental perspective. *Harvard Educational Review,* 1975, *45,* 475–506.

Bergling, K. *The development of hypothetico-deductive thinking in children.* New York: John Wiley & Sons, 1974.

Berry, J. W. An ecological approach to cross-cultural psychology. *Nederlands Tijdschrift Voor de Psychologie,* 1975, *30,* 51–84.

Bovet, M. C. Cognitive processes among illiterate children and adults. In J. W. Berry & P. R. Dasen (Eds.), *Culture and cognition.* London: Methuen, 1974.

Bovet, M. C. Piaget's theory of cognitive development and individual differences. In B. Inhelder & H. H. Chipman (Eds.), *Piaget and his school: A reader in developmental psychology.* New York: Springer-Verlag, 1976.

Bruner, J. S. An overview. In J. S. Bruner, R. R. Olver & P. M. Greenfield (Eds.), *Studies in cognitive growth.* New York: John Wiley & Sons, 1966.

Brunswik, E. *Perception and the representative design of psychological experiments.* Berkeley: University of California Press, 1956.

Buck-Morss, S. Socio-economic bias in Piaget's theory and its implications for cross-culture studies. *Human Development,* 1975, *18,* 35–49.

Carlson, J. Cross-cultural Piagetian research: What can it tell us? In K. Riegel & J. Meacham (Eds.), *The developing individual in a changing world.* The Hague: Mouton, 1976.

Case, R. Social class differences in intellectual development: A neo-Piagetian investigation. *Canadian Journal of Behavioural Science,* 1975, *7,* 244–261.

Cole, M. An ethnographic psychology of cognition. In R. W. Brislin, S. Bochner, & W. J. Lonner (Eds.), *Cross-cultural perspectives on learning.* New York: John Wiley & Sons, 1975.

Cole, M., & Scribner, S. *Culture and thought: A psychological introduction.* New York: John Wiley & Sons, 1974.

Dasen, P. R. Cross-cultural Piagetian research: A summary. *Journal of Cross-Cultural Psychology,* 1972, *3,* 23–40.

Dasen, P. R. The influence of ecology, culture and European contact on cognitive development in Australian Aborigines. In J. W. Berry & P. R. Dasen (Eds.), *Culture and cognition: Readings in cross-cultural psychology.* London: Methuen, 1974.

Dasen, P. R. Concrete operational development in three cultures. *Journal of Cross-Cultural Psychology,* 1975, *6,* 156–172.

Dasen, P. R. (Ed.) *Piagetian psychology: Cross-cultural contributions.* New York: Gardner Press, 1977.

de Lacey, P. R. A cross-cultural study of classificatory ability in Australia. *Journal of Cross-Cultural Psychology,* 1970, *1,* 293–304.

De Lemos, M. M. The development of conservation in Aboriginal children. *International Journal of Psychology,* 1969, *4,* 255–269.

Dempsey, A. D. Time conservation across cultures. *International Journal of Psychology,* 1971, *6,* 115–120.

Feldman, C. F., Lee, B., McLean, J. D., Pillemer, D. B., & Murray, J. R. *The development of adaptive intelligence: A cross-cultural study.* San Francisco: Jossey-Bass, 1974.

Furby, L. A theoretical analysis of cross-cultural research in cognitive development: Piaget's conservation task. *Journal of Cross-Cultural Psychology,* 1971, *2,* 241–255.

Gardner, H. *The quest for mind: Piaget, Lévi-Strauss and the structuralist movement.* New York: Alfred A. Knopf, 1973.

Gaudia, G. Race, social class, and age of conservation on Piaget's task. *Developmental Psychology,* 1972, *6,* 158–165.

Ginsberg, H., & Opper, S. *Piaget's theory of intellectual development: An introduction.* Englewoods Cliffs, N. J.: Prentice-Hall, 1969.

Glick, J. Cognitive development in cross-cultural perspective. In F. G. Horowitz (Ed.), *Review of child development research,* (Vol. 4). Chicago: University of Chicago Press, 1975.

Goldschmid, M. L., Bentler, P. M., Debus, R. L., Rawlinson, R., Kohustamm, D., Modgil, S., Nicholls, J. C., Reykowski, J., Strupczewska, B., & Warren, N. A cross-cultural investigation of conservation. *Journal of Cross-Cultural Psychology,* 1973, *4,* 75–88.

Goodnow, J. J. a test of milieu effects with some of Piaget's tasks. *Psychological Monographs,* 1962, *76* (36, Whole No. 555).

Goodnow, J. J. Cultural variation in cognitive skills. In D. R. Price-Williams (Ed.), *Cross-cultural studies.* Harmondsworth, Engl.: Penguin, 1969.

Greenfield, P. M. On culture and conservation. In J. S. Bruner, R. R. Olver, & P. M. Greenfield (Eds.), *Studies in cognitive growth.* New York: John Wiley & Sons, 1966.

Greenfield, P. M. Comparing dimensional categorization in natural and artificial contexts: A developmental study among the Zinacantecos of Mexico. *Journal of Social Psychology,* 1974, *93,* 157–171.

Greenfield, P. M. Cross-cultural research and Piagetian theory: Paradox and progress. In K. Riegel & J. Meacham (Eds.), *The developing individual in a changing world* (Vol. 1). The Hague: Mouton, 1976.

Greenfield, P. M., & Bruner, J. S. Culture and cognitive growth. In D. A. Goslin (Ed.), *Handbook of socialization theory and research.* Chicago: Rand McNally, 1969.

Greenfield, P. M., & Childs, C. Understanding sibling concepts: A developmental study of kin terms in Zinacantan. In P. R. Dasen (Ed.), *Piagetian psychology: Cross-cultural contributions.* New York: Gardner Press, 1977.

Greenfield, P. M., & Childs, C. Weaving, color terms, and pattern representations: cultural influences and cognitive development among the Zinacantecos. *Interamerican Journal of Psychology,* in press.

Heron, A. Concrete operations, "g" and achievement in Zambian children. *Journal of Cross-Cultural Psychology,* 1971, *2,* 325–336.

Heron, A. & Dowel, W. Weight conservation and matrix-solving ability in Papuan children. *Journal of Cross-Cultural Psychology,* 1973, *4,* 207–219.

Heron, A., & Dowel, W. The questionable unity of the concrete operations stage. *International Journal of Psychology,* 1974, *9,* 1–9.

Heron, A., & Simonsson, M. Weight conservation in Zambian children: A non-verbal approach. *International Journal of Psychology,* 1969, *4,* 282–292.

Hyde, D. M. G. *Piaget and conceptual developments.* London: Holt, Rinehart & Winston, 1970.

Inhelder, B., & Piaget J. *The growth of logical thinking from childhood to adolescence.* New York: Basic Books, 1958.

Kohlberg, L. Early education: a cognitive-developmental view. *Child Development,* 1968, *39,* 1013–1062.

LeVine, R. A., & Price-Williams, D. R. Children's kinship concepts: Cognitive development and early experience among the Hausa. *Ethnology,* 1974, *13,* 25–44.

Lloyd, B. B. *Perception and cognition: A cross-cultural perspective*. Harmondsworth, Engl.: Penguin, 1972.

Mermelstein, E., & Shulman, L. S. Lack of formal schooling and the acquisition of conservation *Child Development*, 1967, *38*, 39–52.

Modgil, S., & Modgil, C. *Piagetian research: Compilation and commentary (Vol. 8). Cross-cultural studies*. Windsor, Engl.: NFER Publishing Company, in press.

Mohseni, N. La comparaison des reactions aux epreuves d'intelligence en Iraq et en Europe. These d'universite, Universite de Paris, 1966.

Nyiti, R. M. Schooling and conservation in Tanzania: A lack of effects. Paper presented at the meeting of the Society for Research in Child Development, New Orleans, March 1977.

Ohuche, R. O., & Pearson, R. E. Piaget and Africa: A survey of research involving conservation and classification in Africa. In *Final report. Seminar on the development of science and mathematics concepts in African countries*. Nairobi: UNESCO UNICEF, 1974.

Okonji, M. O. Culture and children's understanding of geometry. *International Journal of Psychology*, 1971, *6*, 121–128.

Otaala, B. *The development of operational thinking in primary school children*. New York: Teachers College Press, 1973.

Peluffo, N. Les notions de conservation et du causalite provenent de differents milieux physiques et socioculturels. *Archives de Psychologie*, 1962, *38*, 275–291.

Peluffo, N. Culture and cognitive problems. *International Journal of Psychology*, 1967, *2*, 187–198.

Philp, H., & Kelly, M. Product and process; some comparative data on the performance of school age children in different cultures. *British Journal of Educational Psychology*, 1974, *44*, 248–265.

Piaget, J. Need and significance of cross-cultural research in genetic psychology. In B. Inhelder & H. H. Chipman (Eds.), *Piaget and his school: A reader in developmental psychology*. New York: Springer-Verlag, 1976 [Originally published in French in the *International Journal of Psychology*, 1966, *1*, 3–13.]

Price-Williams, D. R. A study concerning concepts of conservation of quantities among primitive children. *Acta Psychologica*, 1961, *18*, 293–305.

Price-Williams, D. R. *Explorations in cross-cultural psychology*. San Francisco: Chandler & Sharp, 1975.

Price-Williams, D. R. Cross-cultural differences in cognitive development. In V. Hamilton & M. D. Vernon (Eds.), *The development of cognitive processes*. London: Academic Press, 1976.

Price-Williams, D. R., Gordon, W., & Ramirez, M. Skill and conservation: A study of pottery-making children. *Developmental Psychology*, 1969, *1*, 769.

Price-Williams, D. R., Hammond, O. W., Edgerton, C., & Walker, M. Kinship concepts among rural Hawaiian children. In P. R. Dasen (Ed.), *Piagetian psychology: Cross-cultural contributions*. New York: Gardner Press, 1977.

Prince, J. R. Science concepts in New Guinean and European children. *Australian Journal of Education*, 1968, *12*, 81–89.

Segall, M. H., Campbell, D. T., & Herskovits, M. J. *The influence of culture on visual perception*. New York: Bobbs-Merrill, 1966.

Skanes, G. R. Conservation and environment. *Canadian Journal of Behavioural Science*, 1976, *8*, 243–250.

Steinberg, B. M., & Dunn, L. A. Conservation competence and performance in Chiapas. *Human Development*, 1976, *19*, 14–25.

Super, C. M. The cognitive consequences of one year of school on 7, 8, and 9 year old rural Kenyan children. Paper presented at the meeting of the Society for Research in Child Development, New Orleans, March 1977.

Tuddenham, R. A "Piagetian" test of cognitive development. In D. Dockerell (Ed.), *On intelligence.* Toronto: Ontario Institute for Studies in Education, 1970.

Vernon, P. E. *Intelligence and cultural environment.* London: Methuen, 1969.

Wagner, D. A. The effects of schooling and environment on memory development. Paper presented at the meeting of the Society for Research in Child Development, New Orleans, March 1977.

Weisner, T. S. Urban-rural differences in African children's performance on cognitive and memory tasks. *Ethos,* 1976, *4,* 223–250.

Wohlwill, J. F. Piaget's system as a resource of empirical research. In I. E. Sigel & F. E. Hooper (Eds.), *Logical thinking in children.* New York: Holt, Rinehart & Winston, 1968.

Za'rour, G. I. Conservation of weight across different materials by Lebanese school children in Beirut. *Science Education,* 1971, *55,* 387–394.

Cognitive Consequences of Cultural Opportunity

Sara Beth Nerlove • Ann Stanton Snipper

A prominent concern in cognitive psychology has been the assessment of cognitive skills as present or absent, high or low. Individual differences have often thus been the endpoint rather than the starting point of the investigation. More recently, psychologists sensitized to context by a cross-cultural perspective have emphasized universals. They have reacted to the rather hasty and crude conclusions about fundamental deficits based primarily on two-culture comparisons fraught with a Westernized, industrialized, modernized, middle-class bias (e.g., Cole & Bruner, 1971; Cole & Scribner, 1974; Ginsburg, 1972; Goodnow, 1976; Pick, 1974). These psychologists have concentrated largely on differences in performance as arising from the testing situation and measurement error and as reflecting no differences in competence. Rosch (1978) cautions that by manipulating content and context of a test until it can be demonstrated that the people in culture X indeed have a given ability, one may end up learning little about basic human processes in the desire to defend their universality. The endpoint of these investigations is the discovery of similarities. One solution is to look beyond the testing situation to the cultural experiences which *affect* those circumstances and under which similarities in performance (or skilled performance) are produced. Only then will we begin to understand the link between experiences and the performance of skills.

A view more characteristic of, although certainly not exclusive to, anthropologists engaged in cross-cultural studies is that differences in performance may arise from different experiences and different phenomenology. The guiding question of this chapter is what sociocultural factors, including interactions with the social environment, permit or encourage the *performance* of various cognitive skills. In some sense, cognitive development is a reciprocal process between a culture and its members, and therefore, to some degree, we too believe that we cannot "know the dancer from the dance" (Rosenberg, 1977). Our ultimate aim is to gain in understanding the choreography, the cognitive demand characteristics of diverse cultural experiences, and to see these as providing "opportunities" to learn, to practice, and to be challenged to use the requisite skills and thus as having implications for cognitive development.

This approach does not challenge a notion of human universals in the existence of all cognitive processes or capacities. However, the distinction between process (competence) and performance is not a neat one. Performance can have an effect on the process itself. Olson (1976), whose point of view is akin to ours, speculates about a relationship between process and performance—namely, that intelligence, when considered in terms of underlying abilities, is that set of abilities required to master the tools, artifacts, and technologies of the culture. When considered in terms of skilled performance, it is the set of competencies achieved by the mastery of those technologies. Nevertheless, readers should be warned that our whole endeavor may be premature. Glick (1975) argues that much more needs to be known about the relationship between performance and cognitive competence before rational arguments about the etiologic factors in cognitive development can be pursued.

Cross-cultural studies have always attempted to take advantage of the diversity of social and cultural organization as a sort of "laboratory" in order to pinpoint sources of influence which have important effects on development. Unfortunately, much of the work that concerns itself with the relationship between cultural opportunities and cognitive consequences concerns itself only with careful measurement of the consequences and assumes differences in cultural opportunities, often using sample selection alone to provide the basis of variation. For example, even the elegant study of Holtzman, Diaz-Guerrero, and Swartz (1975) did better at choosing samples than it did in specifying the crucial cultural differences between the United States and Mexico. This concern with cognitive outcomes derives in part from the emphasis on them in cognitive psychology. In the last decade or so, however, cross-cultural studies have been increasing in sophistication in a way which Hunt (1961) had called for earlier. Instead of merely dichotomizing the traditional indices of intellectual environment, remote and multifaceted packaged variables of cultural experience (e.g., urban–rural, traditional–modern), an attempt has been made to specify—but less often to measure—the crucial aspects of experience more precisely and trace the processes involved. On the whole, we have tried to emphasize in our discussion those papers and bodies of work which specify and measure or attempt to measure not only cognitive outcomes but the "cultural opportunity" side of the equation as well.

METHODOLOGICAL ISSUES

Our interests involve us in all the problems and issues of cross-cultural studies (for recent reviews of these, see, e.g., Ember, 1977; Goodnow, 1976). Three of the largely methodological problems have been selected for discussion here because they are problems which are themselves rooted in differential cultural opportunities.

Selectivity

Perhaps the most fundamental problem in the study of the effects of cultural opportunity is the nonrandom nature of selection for most of those opportunities. Among the frequently overlooked factors affecting the selection process of both nontraditional and traditional cultural pathways are native theories of intelligence or ideas about suitability for certain roles in society. The investigation of primary causes becomes a dilemma in the face of the inextricability of certain parameters which cause the person to be channeled into a particular cultural pathway and the cognitive consequences of following that pathway. Super (1977) has made the point cogently for selection for schooling, emphasizing that cross-cultural studies, although providing a tantalizing increase in the range of variation, *cannot* be looked at as a panacea for the examination of Western universals. In their work on the effects of bilingualism, Lambert and his associates (cf. Lambert & Tucker, 1972) made careful pretest and posttest assessments, but preexperiment sampling equivalence was impossible to achieve. The sample children were those whose families volunteered to participate in the special program. Regarding the effects of literacy among the Vai of Liberia, where writing is learned outside of formal schools, Scribner and Cole (1977a) leave us with some selectivity questions; for example, who were the Vai adults who opted to learn Vai script and why did they choose to do so?

Testing Situation

In considering the problem of the testing situation, we are emphasizing "who" the parties involved are and "in what manner" the testing is carried out. It is difficult to test children from traditional societies. Harkness and Super (1977) pointed out that verbal production is the basis of much cognitive testing. Data from a Kipsigis group in Kenya showed that compared to middle-class Americans, Kipsigis children do not commonly practice the type of talking necessary for responding to psychological tests. Conversation with adults is not framed as teaching and learning, and the most important language skill is comprehension, not production. Furthermore, the norms of communicative competence are silence in the presence of older or high-status people; the discouragement of verbal expressiveness begins at age 2 or 3 years. The behavior thus required of children in traditional settings fits with cultural values of obedience and respect, which, in turn, may be related to the extended family structure which is characterized by social distance between children and adults (Whiting & Whiting, 1975). Thus the failure of African children to respond may have as much to do with how tasks get defined for different groups of subjects as with differences in cognitive skill.

Cultural experience may also hinder Westerners' ability to understand how to elicit thoughtful responses (Price-Williams, 1975). Mundy-Castle (1975) has raised the issue of a divisive notion of intelligence that is technological on the one hand and social on the other. He argues that they constitute differing strategies of adaptation involving distinctive patterns of culturally determined skills. In the developed nations these are biased toward technology, while in the underdeveloped nations they are more socially oriented. Moreover, he asserts that the roots of the difference lie in early experience; the development of a notion of social intelligence can be traced to the pattern of caretaking (Mundy-Castle & Anglin, 1974; Mundy-Castle & Okonji, 1976). This work implies that research on cognitive processes in isolation may be more justifiable in some cultures than in others. Indeed, there has been a lack of consideration of social, motivational, and affective factors as important contributors to cognitive growth. Cohen (1969), Gallimore, Tharp, and Speidel (1978), Harkness (1975), Istomina (1975), LeVine and Price-Williams (1974), and Weisner (1976) represent some of the counterexamples to this tendency among Western researchers.

Familiarity

The importance of familiarity, apart from the testing situation itself, was emphasized long ago (in 1916) by Binet and Simon (1916), who pointed out that familiarity with the task has to be constant in order to make reasonable comparisons between individuals performing that task. Cross-cultural studies not only rediscovered this idea, but they also have broadened and deepened our understanding of how the problem of familiarity affects comparisons among individuals from different cultures. Sometimes differential familiarity has been taken as the somewhat disappointing endpoint of the research, that is, the conclusion reached is that lack of familiarity accounted for the differences. A comprehensive treatment of this problem is given by Glick (1975), who warns us that there is a danger in the uncritical use of *familiar* materials in cross-cultural testing—what is automatic habit or well-practiced skill cannot be treated as if it were a challenging problem. He enumerates different bases of familiarity such as modes of representation, familiarity of materials and dimensions, familiarity of the application of a dimension to a domain, and the relationship between material and dimensions (cf. Fjellman, 1971). In addition, not only the materials but the activity itself, apart from the test situation, may be differentially familiar (Cole, Gay, Glick, & Sharp, 1971; Dube, 1977). The problem of familiarity is further complicated by schooling and other experiences which may make *novelty* more familiar.

SUBSTANTIVE ISSUES

If cognitive consequences are neither generalizable nor long term, they are clearly of less scientific importance. Thus transfer effects and permanence are two of the many largely substantive issues germane to the consideration of the cognitive consequences of cultural opportunity.

Transfer Effects

If a culture provides a particular experience which fosters learning or provides practice in a particular skill, how generally across situations does the skill manifest itself? Scribner and Cole (1977a, b), Cole, Sharp, and Lave (1976), and Lave (n.d.) are examples of recent work which indicate there is less generalizability of skills fostered and manifested in a particular context than has been formerly assumed. These studies provide data for Cole's (1975) earlier argument against viewing schooling, literacy, and acculturation as providing people with new cognitive processes, new abilities, and new intellectual tools. Cole (1975) implies that one must look not simply at particular experiences but at configurations of experiences when he states that some cultural institutions promote the widespread use of one particular process (e.g., abstraction) while others promote its application in only a few selected situations, as is the case among Gladwin's (1970) navigators. Similarly, he proposes that there should be emphasis on the examination of differences in the application of cognitive skills to different domains of activity within a given culture.

Price-Williams' (1975) notion of a graduating-steps design is aimed at the question of transfer. He proposes a design in which the baseline for study is the human organism in its natural ecology in order to assess experiments which can be conceived as graduating steps that lead away from the usual habitat:

> We need to find out within any culture the extent to which its population thinks outside of its accustomed experience. We cannot properly assess this ability if we adhere only to their usual world. Nor can we assess it if we give subjects tasks that only are exemplars of unaccustomed experience. We need to provide both instances and to connect them in a manner which allows for systematic variation. (p. 39)

Permanence

If a culture provides a particular experience which fosters learning practice in a particular skill, to what degree does the timing of the opportunity make a difference and to what degree does an acquired cognitive competence remain constant throughout the life cycle?

One position that has been taken is that cognitive competence is inevitable and that, in the main, experiential factors influence only the time of emergence but not the final level of intellectual capacity. Kagan and Klein (1973) draw such a conclusion based on comparative observations of United States and Guatemalan children. Guatemalan infants were judged to lead relatively socially isolated lives in non-stimulating environments—namely, small, dark, windowless huts in which movement was restricted. However, 11-year-old Guatemalans did not differ from United States 11-year-olds on various cognitive measures. Unfortunately, the authors do not provide a careful delineation of daily routines of Guatemalan families; thus there is no way to judge the relative amount of time infants spend under nonstimulating conditions. The possibility of this methodological artifact and ceiling effects on the cognitive tests administered to the 11-year-olds call their findings into question.

It should be emphasized that cultural opportunities may be *shifting* and *may continue* to make a difference rather than that their effects are either ephemeral or permanent. The cognitive-learning trend in psychotherapy (see Mahoney, 1977, for a review of this literature) is predicated on the assumption that after cognitive competence has presumably already "emerged" in adulthood, change may still occur. The work of Denney 1974a, b) also supports the notion that cognitive change occurs throughout the life cycle.

NATIVE CONCEPTIONS OF INTELLIGENCE

Mundy-Castle (1975) and Price-Williams (1975) have expressed concern and doubts about viewing intelligence as a monolithic concept, and Charlesworth (1976) has emphasized intelligence as a natural everyday behavioral phenomenon that is sensitive to context. These concerns point to an area which has not yet received much attention in the literature: native theories of intelligence. Native theories of intelligence are critical if one assumes that cultural environments somehow actively shape their members according to certain goals, values, and beliefs about important and necessary qualities. Seldom have investigators thought to ask or otherwise elicit from members of the culture what they themselves consider to be the defining criteria of intelligence and then tried to link these ideas with measures of how children and adults actually behave. Even in the United States nonpsychologists' views on the area have remained essentially untapped. In undertaking an examination of native theories of intelligence, a number of fundamental questions need to be considered. Among them are the following:

1. To what degree is there consensus on what members of the community value?
2. If there is community consensus, can it be measured?
3. What experiences in the child's environment provide opportunities for learning and practicing those capabilities? The answer to this question may ultimately allow us to make statements about the degree of fit between the valued capabilities and the opportunities that are provided in the form of tasks, games, interactive situations, and other activities, the degree to which cultural experiences serve to develop or foster adult capabilities deemed important and desirable in that society.
4. How and to what degree can community members spot intelligence in children and effectively "track" them, thereby making use of the talent available in the community needed for various special roles?

5. What is the relationship between indigenous theories of intelligence and Western theories of intelligence? Translated into performance terms, what is the relationship between a child's rating on indigenously valued capabilities and his or her performance on our Western tasks?

In this relatively uncharted area, some researchers have directly addressed one or more of the above questions, but our picture for any one society is fragmentary at best. The descriptions that follow will include greater detail on the few existing studies in this area.

A systematic attempt to understand native concepts of intelligence was made by Wober (1974), who investigated the concept of intelligence by mapping its network of connotations using a version of Osgood's Semantic Differential. He reported that the very concept of intelligence itself differed more clearly between groups of dissimilar education within the Baganda culture than it did between groups of similar education from two different but related cultures. Apparently, Western education may influence not only cognitive performance but also ideas about intelligence in the direction of Western values. If there are congruences between theories of intelligence and the development of particular cognitive skills, then this finding is notable in showing a rarely discussed way in which Western education may be exerting its effect. Serpell (1977), however, points out that a number of aspects of the study make such an interpretation difficult. For example, African subjects' responses to three different words for intelligence, including the English word "intelligence," are being compared, and, moreover, the respondents' interpretation of the task rather than their values is what may have shifted—partly as a result of cross-language semantic interference. In short, Serpell expresses doubts that the study really reveals information about the defining criteria of the Kiganda concept of intelligence.

It is not surprising that the question involving the relation between indigenous and Western assessments has received the most attention. It is the "IQ problem" of cross-cultural research. Some evidence of congruence has been shown between aspects of cognitive performance on Western tests and native conceptions of intelligence. Klein, Freeman, and Millet (1973) compared cognitive test performance of preschool boys from a rural Guatemalan village with estimates of their "intelligence" by adult community members acquainted with the subjects. A high degree of congruence among the rankings of the various judges was reported, and the ranking which represented the group's judgments was found to be correlated with a test of analytic ability, the Embedded Figures Test. Again, Serpell (1977) has served as a critic; he states that there is no reliable way to decide whether to attribute those correlations that were low to discrepancy between the meaning of the English and the indigenous word, poor ratings by the judges, or discrepancy between the tests and indigenous concepts of intelligence.

Klein, Freeman, Spring, Nerlove, and Yarbrough (1976) replicated the 1973 study in two Guatemalan villages and one United States community and found trends suggesting that popular conceptions of intelligence are partly congruent with aspects of cognitive performance on tests adapted from batteries originally developed in the United States, tapping language, memory, and analytic ability. They point out that it is impossible for judges to rate a child and not know her or his social background. Since tests also are sensitive to social status differences, it is unclear whether or not congruence is due to both judges' and tests' sensitivity to social differences valued in the two communities. They suggest that it is possible that both processes occur. Rather than considering this a confusion, one might also argue that social status differences are often a dimension of the assessment of intelligence.

Further evidence of congruence between tests and native theories is shown by Dube (1977). He conducted an investigation of native concepts of intelligence among Botswana villagers. For this phase of his study he chose adult judges who had shown themselves to be articulate and clear about the Botswana concept of intelligence. These judges were asked to rate nonliterate village children, classifying them into groups of high, medium, and low on the basis of the word "bothale," representing the most generalized concept of intelligence. His work supports the hypothesis that "intelligence" rating by community members is predictive of subjects' performance on a memory task. The memory task was a particularly appropriate one here because it matched the cognitive requirements of naturally occurring activities in the culture.

In contrast to the findings of Dube (1977) and of Klein et al. (1973; 1976), the results of a study by Serpell (1974) do not show congruence between test performances and native conceptions of intelligence. In this study, Serpell had adult community members assess children with whom they were familiar. These adults were asked which child they would choose to take responsibility in various situations and were later asked to directly rank the children in intelligence. The reliability for a given informant across these two assessment tasks was significantly high. The degree of concordance among informants for each assessment task, however, was low, making the attempt to relate those judgments to test scores and game ranks based on children's assessments of playing ability impossible to interpret. Further, the study indicated that it may not be possible to assess the fit between cultural experiences and desired capabilities by using mere modifications of extent cognitive tests because, for example, a cultural definition of intelligence might include an emphasis on the qualities of cooperation, as it does among the Chewa of Zambia whom Serpell was investigating. Considerations of social aspects of intelligence raise the issue of whether or not the characteristics desired of children remain constant through adulthood.

Serpell (1977) proposes a reason in addition to research caveats for the discrepancies in congruence between test performances and native conceptions of intelligence. He suggests that the larger village communities of Guatemala may evaluate intelligence in a manner more consonant with the modern American ethos than do the village communities of Zambia—but what, then, about Dube's (1977) findings from Botswana? Perhaps there is another aspect we should be thinking about in considering these discrepant findings. It is possible that there may simply be large cross-cultural differences in the degree to which consensus in community judgments of intelligence exists. Such cross-cultural differences can, of course, be uncovered only if similar assessment procedures are used. One study (Nerlove & Walters, 1977) was specifically concerned with developing a measure of community consensus on intelligence, a measure which is applicable to consensus on other topics as well, that could be used across different cultures. It dealt with the fundamental problem of assessing an adequate degree of consensus of native judgments prior to a composite rank ordering of such judgments in relation to other data. The study showed strong consensus among judges on ranked intelligence of boys and girls, taken separately, in two Guatemalan villages. The contrast in the findings of Nerlove and Walters (1977) as against those of Serpell (1974) may, in part, be due to variations, respectively, in stabilities in judgments achieved via greater sample size, the greater number of judges, the ranking technique, and the more restricted range of ages and sex of the judges. It is clear that Serpell (1974) was faced with severe demographic constraints in the choice of the judges and the judged. The two studies taken together raise an issue which merits further consideration, that is, who are the judges —the socializers, those in power, etc., what differences in native theories might there be in different subgroups, and what implications might these differences have for cognitive development?

Using the composite rank ordering derived from the work of Nerlove & Walters (1977), Nerlove, Roberts, & Klein (1975) found an association between children's scores on a formal test of language ability and community judgments of the children's smartness which were collected 2 years after the test data had been collected. In addition, a new kind of association was found between observed behavior and the application of native theory, namely, that between a "natural indicator," the observed frequency of children's participation in self-managed sequences (defined as work or play activities entailing the following of an exacting series of steps [Nerlove, Roberts, Klein, Yarbrough, & Habicht, 1974]), and community judgments of smartness collected 2 years after the observational data had been collected. The mechanism producing this association may be that the natural indicator is identified by the adult as illustrative of the acquisition or manifestation of cognitive skill classified as "smart," or it simply may be that smart children do smart things (according to categories of Western investigators), do well on tests, and are seen as smart by community judges. Although the work is at an early stage, the points of articulation of the three types of data are nonetheless of interest.

The associations found were most dramatic for the girls from one of the two villages. The circumstances that may contribute to this successful prediction through time from formal tests and behaviors to community judgments are discussed. For example, if observable skills are a defining factor and there is a key behavior which is both highly observable—that is, localized and public—and which is in an emergent state so that its mere occurrence is in and of itself meaningful at the time of the observations, prediction from behavior to judgments may be facilitated.

"FAMILY EFFECTS" AS CULTURAL OPPORTUNITIES

The first environment that the neonate encounters is the family. As an organizational device, we will follow Bronfenbrenner's (1977) ordering of the components of the ecology of human development in which the family is seen as one system nested in a set of systems which together constitute the developing person's ecologic environment. His conceptions draw extensively on the theories of Kurt Lewin (1935; 1936; 1948; 1951). The family is an example of a microsystem; that is, a complex of relations between the developing person and the environment in an immediate setting containing that person. The family is embedded in mesosystems, examples of which include interactions among family, school, and peer group. An exosystem (e.g., neighborhoods, the world of work) is an extension of the mesosystem embracing other specific social structures, both formal and informal, that do not themselves contain the developing person but impinge upon or encompass the immediate settings in which that person is found and thereby influence, delimit, or even determine what goes on there. Macrosystems refer to the overarching patterns of the culture or subculture, such as the economic, social, educational, and political systems which are carriers of information and ideology and which explicitly or implicitly endow meaning and motivation to micro-, meso-, and exosystems and their interrelations. This outline both focuses on the developing person and explicitly recognizes different classes of variations in "family effects" which may operate either directly or indirectly upon the developing person. We begin with the studies which investigate direct effects and variation on the microsystem level and continue with studies involving more indirect effects, with variations in meso-, exo-, and macrosystems.

The Mother–Child Dyad: Maternal Teaching Strategies

Underlying the research on maternal teaching strategies is the assumption that the learning which occurs within the family environment includes more than the socialization of drives and needs. Parents not only transmit values and attitudes but also act in specific ways that may foster or inhibit intellectual development.

Although many studies done in the United States have demonstrated an association between children's cognitive performance and parental status (usually social class), only in the last decade or so have researchers investigated the processes by which cognitive socialization occurs (Streissguth & Bee, 1972). These studies, which generally compared lower- and middle-class subjects, have demonstrated differences in language environments (Lewis & Wilson, 1972; Tulkin & Kagan, 1972) and in maternal teaching strategies (Bee, Van Egeren, Streissguth, Nyman, & Leckie, 1969; Hess & Shipman, 1967, 1968). Generally, middle-class mothers talked to their infants more, believed infants to be capable of learning, and, with older children, used more positive and less negative reinforcement and used different behavioral styles in orienting children to problem-solving tasks.

Cross-cultural investigations of cognitive socialization have conceptualized the problem similarly and followed the same general research strategies as these United States studies; however, they are also susceptible to the same problems. Although the basic premise holds that parents influence their children's cognitive development, difficulties arise in specifying exactly which parental behaviors are important and how they operate. For example, the maternal behaviors studied have been as grossly defined as verbal versus nonverbal communication or as specifically as usage of finger and hand movements. But how does the researcher know if the behavior of choice is an important one? In a study in the Philippines (Salvador-Burris, 1977), mothers were interviewed in great detail about child-rearing beliefs and practices, including many specific cognitive socialization behaviors. Despite the inclusiveness of the interview, no relationship was established between maternal behavior and children's performance on an IQ test. It could be that the nature of maternal influence remains unknown because of a focus on irrelevant maternal behaviors or because of the unreliability of maternal reports. This ambiguity leads to the next point. The measurement context in these studies has been problematical. Most investigators have used observation in a semistructured laboratory situation in which mothers were asked to teach their children a specific task. Although far from ideal for generalization purposes, Rogoff's (1977) experience—recording only six instances of maternal teaching in 1800 naturalistic observations—indicates that such a procedure may be necessary. Finally, there are the theoretical problems of establishing the mechanisms by which parental behaviors are linked to specific cognitive outcomes of children and of establishing direction of causality.

Harkness' (1975) work points out some further hazards of using United States research results uncritically in setting up cross-cultural studies. She assessed the language environment of 1½–3½-year-old rural Spanish-Speaking Guatemalan children. Unlike that of middle-class American mothers, Guatemalan mothers' speech to their children did not include expansions or "baby talk" and was characteristically rapid, repetitive, and delivered in a monotone. Additionally, the Guatemalan children were exposed to many more language socializers than American children, including a high proportion of children. Research in Guatemala (and presumably in other cross-cultural settings) which assumes that children's language environments approximate the American model could be adversely affected.

There are some interesting convergences in the findings of cross-cultural research on maternal teaching strategies, although to date few studies have been done. For example, mothers' use of the verbal as opposed to the nonverbal mode of communication is associated with their children's higher scores on cognitive tasks. Jordan (1977) observed Hawaiian mother–child dyads as the 4- and 5-year-old children copied designs, solved a puzzle, and built objects with Tinkertoys. Mothers were permitted to help their children. The videotaped sessions were coded every 12 seconds for maternal teaching behavior judged to be either verbal or nonverbal in nature. The children's prior scores on the WPPSI and Metropolitan Achievement Tests of reading and mathematics were also obtained. Those mothers who used the verbal mode either exclusively or predominantly had children who scored higher on both the WPPSI and in reading and mathematics. Rogoff (1977) found a similar relationship between mothers' verbal style and children's memory performance. A group of 31 children were chosen on the basis of their memory performances on tests of visual recognition and recall and verbal recognition and recall. This sample of children and their mothers were observed in their homes as the mother helped the child construct a model of an object that only she could see. The mothers who used verbal instruction had children who performed better on verbal memory tasks. Those mothers who used nonverbal demonstration techniques had children with lower performance on verbal memory. Neither maternal style was related to the visual memory tasks.

Two pieces of research specify further the aspect of verbal instruction which might be operating. Kirk (1977) administered two Piagetian conservation tasks and a perspectives task to 5-year-old Ga children. The mother–child dyads were then observed as each mother taught her child to assemble a puzzle. Forty-seven indices of maternal behavior were used in coding the mother–child interaction. The article lacks details on the construction and components of various composite indices of maternal behavior, making those results difficult to interpret. However, an interesting relationship emerges between a simple index of maternal behavior and the child's performance. The frequency with which the mother speaks about relationships among parts of the puzzle (termed "communicative specificity") was related to the child's aggregate score on the conservation tasks. It can be inferred that the mother heightens the child's attention to interrelationships, a strategy which may generalize to other problem-solving situations. Conservation tasks serve as an appropriate measure of the child's deployment of attention because in order to achieve conservation the child must attend to two dimensions simultaneously and notice complementary shifts between the two.

Feshbach (1973) observed middle- and lower-class 4-year-olds and their mothers in the United States, England, and Israel. Again, mothers taught their children to put together a puzzle. The research concentrated on the tone of the interaction, assuming that the type of reinforcement that the mother used in the laboratory was characteristic of her response style across many different child-training situations.

Results indicate that middle-class mothers in all three countries used more positive reinforcements than did lower-class mothers. The cross-cultural studies included no direct measures of children's cognitive output, but the author cites United States research which linked children's low cognitive performance with frequent use of maternal negative reinforcement (Bee et al., 1969; Hess & Shipman, 1967; 1968) as support for the hypothesis that maternal style influences children's cognitive development. In the current study, Feshbach (1973) relates reinforcement style to cognitive performance by observing United States middle-class mothers, each teaching her own child and two nonrelated children, one a problem reader and one a successful reader. For each of the three children, mothers of problem readers used more negative reinforcement, were more directive and intrusive, and appeared to be less patient than mothers of successful readers. Although maternal negative reinforcement co-occurred with children's lower performances, no causative statement can be made on the basis of this study. Mothers may develop negative styles at least partially in response to children who were and are relatively nonattentive. For example, mothers of problem readers did not give significantly more negative reinforcements to successful readers than did mothers of successful readers. This finding could be due to the fact that the performance of successful readers affords less opportunity for any type of correction. The questions that this study leaves unanswered highlight the importance of considering the mother-child dyad as a system instead of concentrating on maternal input alone.

In an interesting shift away from language-mediated effects, Kirk and Burton (1977) focused on mother's nonverbal behavior. Mother-child interaction involving the mother teaching her child a puzzle was filmed and coded for four aspects of nonverbal behavior. Mother's nonverbal specificity was positively related to children's performance on spatial tasks, including the Embedded Figures Task, Bender Gestalt, and conservation of area. The results are especially intriguing in light of Kirk's (1977) already cited results linking verbal communication specificity to cognitive performance. Both verbal and nonverbal specificity, assessed separately, were associated with higher cognitive performance. It would be interesting to see if and how they operate together. This exploratory work should certainly be pursued, paying more attention to theoretical concerns, both in choosing cognitive outcome procedures and in specifying how the nonverbal communication might influence cognitive development. Jordan (1977) and Rogoff (1977) reported that mothers tended to use one style to the exclusion of the other, but they measured only broad verbal versus nonverbal differences. Perhaps in the matter of specificity, mothers use both verbal and nonverbal cues or perhaps only one mode is preferred in this aspect of behavior.

The Family: Variations in Role, Membership, and Size

Child Care Arrangements

All of the studies reviewed to this point concentrate on mother-child interactions, although most children in other cultures are not cared for exclusively by their mothers (Barry & Paxson, 1971; Weisner & Gallimore, 1977; Whiting & Whiting, 1975) and thus may be exposed to many more potential "teachers." What effects do multiple caretaking arrangements have on the child's cognitive development? R. H. Munroe and Munroe (1975) addressed this question by conducting a followup study of 12 Kenyan children initially observed as infants and subsequently as 5-year-olds.

Some of the mothers of these children had begun sharing child care responsibilities when their infants were 5 months old, while others remained the sole caretakers until the infant was 16 months old or more. Outcome measures included a serial learning task, an embedded figures task, and a perseverance measure based on how long children worked on an extremely difficult jigsaw puzzle. Mothers who shared infant care early had 5-year-olds who learned faster on the learning task and scored as field independent on the Embedded Figures task. The children of mothers who remained their exclusive caretakers until late infancy were less proficient on the above tasks but persevered longer on the jigsaw puzzle. The authors interpret their results as an indication that early loss of the mother as the child's sole source of gratification fosters independence in the child, specifically, an independent problem-solution style.

Leiderman and Leiderman (1974) focused their study on sibling caretaking. Subjects were Kikuyu infants cared for exclusively by their mothers (monomatric) or tended by older siblings for long periods daily (polymatric). The Bayley Scales were used to assess the infants' level of cognitive development. All infants from families at a higher economic level and the polymatric infants of families from a lower economic level scored similarly. Monomatric infants from families at the lower economic level scored significantly lower on cognitive development, especially on those subscales relevant to social responsiveness and vocalization. In accounting for the difference between monomatric and polymatric families at the lower economic level, observations indicated that polymatric infants from lower economic levels received 2.5 times more social activity than did their monomatric peers. Presumably this heightened stimulation cushioned the infants from the detrimental effects usually associated with lower economic status.

These two studies (Leiderman & Leiderman, 1974; R. H. Munroe & Munroe, 1975) indicate that infants do not necessarily suffer and may benefit from caretaking arrangements where mothers share infant care responsibilities with others. Being exploratory in nature, neither study speaks to the processes by which multiple caretaking exerts its effects. Results from the low economic Kikuyu group hint that quantity of stimulation may emerge as more important than identity of caretaker where quality of attention to infants is not high. Yet another explanation may be that quality of maternal attention to the infant is affected by sharing responsibilities. For example, Gewirtz and Gewirtz (1965) found that group-reared kibbutz children received more of their parents' undivided attention than did children raised in nuclear family settings. Alternatively, the infant may experience more diversity when she or he has more than one caretaker and hence be more stimulated to explore his or her environment. In brief, multiple-caretaking may either affect the child directly, by adding something to her or his environment that is otherwise not present or by increasing something already there, or indirectly, by influencing the child by affecting the quality of the mother-infant relationship.

Father Absence

Similarly, the father's impact on his child's cognitive development may be direct, indirect, or both. Much research on fathers' contributions to cognitive development concentrates on measuring the impact of father absence. However, as Herzog (1974) points out, most of the research associating father absence with lower intellectual ability and poorer school performance of boys has failed to control for race, social class, cultural attitudes, and timing and duration of father absence. Herzog conducted a careful study, controlling for race and social class, in Barbados, where illegitimacy is common and not negatively viewed. The duration and timing of father absence from birth through the time of the study was ascertained for each of 119 schoolboys aged 6½ to 15½ years. The boys were tested on a battery of IQ and school-related achievement tests and were rated by their teachers for attitudes and behavior in school. The results were an interesting mix of direct and indirect effects. Father-present boys scored higher on the school's own arithmetic test and were judged to be quiet and cooperative and trying hard at schoolwork. They seemed to conform better to school routine. Father-absent boys did better on the novel tests which were only indirectly related to school curriculum. Teachers judged them to be "troublesome." By examining demographic data and field observation notes, Herzog showed that father absence had a different meaning at different times in the son's life. Father-absent boys' superiority on novel tests was accounted for by birth order, with firstborns excelling. Herzog hypothesized that firstborn boys were more likely to have frequent and intense interchanges with their mothers as infants because of the frequent pattern in Barbados of women giving birth to their first child while unmarried and living in their parents' homes. Barbados fathers are traditionally responsible for discipline and are quite stern. The conformity of father-present boys, suggests Herzog, is a direct effect of their fathers' heavy hands:

> In Barbados it is good for a boy to have his father away during the earliest years of his life because of what this is likely to mean for his relationship with his mother; it is equally good to have Dad return home after age 2 or 3, because this usually means he has regular employment and will provide a needed input of discipline and economic support. (Herzog, 1974, p. 81)

Family Size
Without specifying whether effects are direct or indirect, Zajonc (Zajonc, 1976; Zajonc & Markus, 1975) generated the following model to suggest how family size and membership might influence children's cognitive development: Cognitive growth is assumed to be a function of the individual's intellectual environment, with the family constituting the immediate intellectual environment. Each family member, including the child in question, contributes to the efficacy of that environment. The child's own contribution is zero at birth but increases as he or she matures, to a maximum of "30 points" at adulthood. The model predicts that birth order and agespacing between siblings will affect the cognitive development of an individual child.

Data gathered in testing the model consist of intellectual test performances of large populations of students in the United States, Netherlands, France, and Scotland. In all four countries, cognitive performances declined with family size, independently of SES, which is consistent with the assertion that the intellectual stimulation level for any one child is lower in large families. In the Dutch and American samples, with small age gaps between successive siblings, test performances declined appreciably with birth order, as predicted by the model. The model also accounts for recent declines in SAT scores in the United States among current high school seniors, who are much more likely to come from larger families and be of later birth order; it predicts the reversal of the downward trend in 1980–1981, because children born in 1963 who will be taking the tests will be from smaller families and of earlier birth orders; it accounts for the typically low IQ scores of twins and triplets, who simultaneously contribute zero to the intellectual environment;

and it predicts lower intellectual performance by children from single-parent homes that have only one adult contributing to the child's intellectual environment.

Streeter, Whiting, and Landauer (1977) tested the Zajonc and Markus model on 218 Kikuyan children aged 4–8 years. The cognitive measures—an animal-naming test, body parts identification, auditory integration, and Embedded Figures Test— were used to create an age-adjusted cognitive development quotient. Contrary to the findings of Zajonc (Zajonc & Markus, 1975; Zajonc, 1976), there was no linear relation between cognitive development scores and family size. Instead, a curvilinear relation was found, with firstborns and lastborns scoring higher than middleborns on the cognitive measures. This different pattern of results in a non-Western research setting could be due to the special status of the lastborn in Kikuyu culture or due to the effects of different household arrangements. It could also be related to the rapid social change being experienced by this group as reflected in the fact that some older siblings are more highly educated than their parents and thus may offer a relatively greater contribution to the intellectual environment of their youngest siblings. Finally, this pattern of results could derive from an interaction between family size and modernization in the case of the youngest child appearing when the family is well into the child-bearing cycle, when the family may be more prosperous and/or acculturated.

Although not cross-cultural, the study by Grotevant, Scarr, and Weinberg (1977) deserves mention for testing Zajonc's model. With individual IQ scores available for both parents and children, only 2% of the variance in children's intellectual performance was explained by parental intelligence, intelligence of siblings, and spacing between siblings. The authors point out that the aggregate data used by Zajonc and Markus (1975) to test their model masks sources of variation within families. They suggest that the Zajonc and Markus model may be more appropriate for predicting population trends than for explaining variance within individual families.

Impact of Family Variations on Social Cognition
The studies described above have focused on the importance of the size and composition of family membership and the child's position in the family group as potential influences on her or his cognitive development. Children's social cognition —their knowledge of others' attributes, feelings, and intentions—could also be affected by these family variations. Development of social cognition (cf. Shantz, 1975) is a relatively new area of research endeavor which could profit from cross-cultural work. LeVine and Price-Williams (1974) have ventured onto this ground in their study of children's understandings of kinship terms. They interviewed Hausa children aged 4–11 years, asking them about the identity and relationship to themselves of various residents of their compounds. Children's knowledge was qualitatively different at different ages in a fashion parallel with structural differences in logicomathematical cognitive development. More interesting for our purposes was the finding that in this culture children's knowledge was shaped by the social norms and customs of their milieu, such as norms of social distance between the sexes and the emotional salience of grandmothers for young children.

Larger System Variation

Ecological variables
Studies which attempt to link cognitive consequences to ecological variables derive, for the most part, from two theoretical frameworks. One is the Whiting and

Whiting (1975) theory, a current representation of the culmination of their thinking over the last two decades. In the model, physical environmental variations influence the history and maintenance systems of a culture. These, in turn, shape the child's learning environment. Different learning environments produce different cognitive outcomes. Witkin's theory of psychological differentiation is the second theory (see Chapter 14 in this volume). Ecological variables such as population density and subsistence patterns influence the direction of cultural adaptations in such areas as stratification and socialization techniques, which in turn affect the level of psychological differentiation achieved by individual children.

Findings converge nicely. Working out of the Witkin tradition, investigators have shown that child-rearing techniques which emphasize conformity and social dependency produce children who are more likely to score as field dependent (less able to disembed part of a field from the whole), whereas child-rearing techniques encouraging exploration and autonomy tend to produce children who score as field independent (Berry, 1966; Dawson, 1967; Okonji, 1969; Witkin, Price-Williams, Bertini, Christiansen, Oltman, Ramirez, & Van Meel, 1974). Working out of the Whiting tradition, R. L. Munroe, Munroe, & Daniels (1976) made indirect links between subsistence systems and cognitive outcomes. They demonstrated that cognitive performances other than field independence or dependence are affected by compliance training. Agriculturally based societies are somewhat less likely to emphasize compliance than are pastoral societies. In view of this association, the finding that children from an agriculturally based society scored better than children from a herding society on a conservation of mass task is suggestive of a link between compliance training and cognitive outcomes.

In another study, among the Logoli of Kenya (R. L. Munroe & Munroe, 1977), the impact of the subsistence system on children's cognitive performance was traced. Large homestead size predicted mothers' workloads, which in turn predicted mothers' responses on a semiprojective test of how harshly the mothers would punish children for misbehavior. The children themselves were administered a conservation of mass problem. Children whose mothers stressed harsh punishment performed less well than those whose mothers recommended milder forms of punishment. Pursuing the same general questions, although in another cultural setting, R. H. Munroe and Munroe (1978) observed Kikuyu children's naturally occurring behavior with attention to whether their activities had been initiated by another person or were spontaneous in origin. Children who were self-directed scored higher on the WISC digit-span test of short-term memory than did those children who were other-directed.

Another group of studies, tied to neither the Witkin nor the Whiting and Whiting tradition, uses setting differences as indicators that differences exist in the child's learning environment. Posner (1978) studied children from two Ivory Coast tribes to assess the effect of cultural environment on mathematical competence. One group (Dioula) was composed predominantly of merchants; the other (Baoulé) was primarily an agricultural tribe. It was predicted that children from the commercial environment would show superior performance on problems of mathematical reasoning. Children aged 5–10 years were given a series of tests including elementary perceptual judgments about relative quantity, conservation of number, and problems requiring counting and arithmetic solutions. On the most basic tasks children did not differ, which the author interprets as an indication that fundamental quantitative notions may be universal. On more advanced tasks, the unschooled children from the commercial Dioula tribe performed significantly better than unschooled Baoulé children and did not differ from the schoolchildren of both tribes. In addition, problem-solving strategies differed along tribal lines, with the Dioula children relying on number facts (e.g., "knowing" that $7 + 5 = 12$) and the Baoulé children using counting procedures.

Hollos (Hollos, 1975; Hollos & Cowan, 1973) used settings as indicators of the children's level of exposure to verbal-social interaction. In both Norway (Hollos & Cowan, 1973) and Hungary (Hollos, 1975), farm children were isolated from other children and verbal communication within the family was brief and sparse in detail. Village children in both cultures experienced frequent interaction with peers and families engaged in more verbal interaction. Children from towns spent even more time with peer groups and interacted with a larger variety of adults in more different social settings compared to village children. These studies found that isolated farm children performed as well as (Hollos & Cowan, 1973) or better than (Hollos, 1975) children who lived in villages and towns. This is evidence that lack of verbal stimulation does not interfere with the acquisition of logical operations, and the opportunity to spend time alone may actually accelerate development in this area. Farm children in both cultures scored lower than village and town children on role-taking tasks, however. Village and town children did not differ significantly. The authors hypothesize that a minimal level of social stimulation is necessary for acquisition of role-taking skills but that beyond that level additional social stimulation has no measurable effect. West's (1974) study in three Israeli settings supported this threshold hypothesis by finding no difference among boys' role-taking abilities from three settings differing in amount of peer interaction.

Urban–Rural

Exosystems such as urban and rural contexts may be associated with nutritional and health status differences, differential accuracy of age reporting, educational differences, and acculturation differences, among others. Thus special care is needed in specifying and measuring attributes of the environment thought to influence cognitive development. We will provide some examples of innovative efforts to overcome these difficulties (see Weisner, 1976, for a literature review).

Weisner's (1970; 1973; 1974) work on urban-rural differences is to be commended for careful sample selection, sensitivity to the situational aspects of urban-rural differences, and demonstration of an interaction between the testing situation and the milieu. The sample used consisted of a rural-urban kin network with fathers matched for age, education, and kin status. These rural and urban families kept in close contact with one another, and there was frequent movement back and forth between the two environments. The urban sample of men owned property in the rural area which was worked by their wives, and they sent their children to school in the rural areas. Thus the children in this sample are similar with respect to culture, acculturation level, and likelihood of migration (Weisner, 1973). Documenting the impact of the settings on children's lives, Weisner (1974) found that children in the urban setting lived in more crowded space, were exposed to more adults, including relatively unoccupied mothers, did fewer chores, and experienced more verbal stimulation, including multilingualism. The children's behavior was also different by setting, with the urban children showing more aggressive, less sociable, and less cooperative behavior with peers, and being more verbal with adults compared to the rural children. Weisner (1976) hypothesized that the different patterns of rural and urban life made different demands on the children and thus would be associated with differential cognitive performances by urban and rural children. The hypothesis was confirmed. Rural children were superior on experimental tasks when they were required to show compliance and deference to the experimenter, a finding that was linked to rural children's chore performance and the heavy compliance demands placed upon them. Urban children excelled on exploratory-manipulative tasks which required children to be assertive and self-reliant. This result was linked to Weisner's (1974) earlier findings that urban children were more talkative, exploratory, and assertive.

Fjellman (1971) criticized research which depicts rural children as more "concrete" thinkers than urban children on the grounds that the testing situation itself and the materials used were differentially familiar to the urban and rural children. She constructed a classification test based on the native taxonomic system, specifically, the domain of animals. On this classification test, urban children were the ones who gave perception-oriented responses, which have been considered to be more "primitive," and the rural children gave abstract responses based on inferential attributes. On a classification task using geometric forms, however, the pattern was reversed, with urban children, specifically urban boys, using form, which has been considered to be more "advanced," rather than color as a basis for sorting. The inclusion of both test contents provides a nice illustration of Fjellman's point that differential familiarity with materials, some of which is related to the urban-rural dimension, may mask children's ability to think abstractly.

Modernization

Shifting our focus to a macrosystem perspective, some cognitive consequences of modernization can be examined. Dealing with a rural Kipsigis community in western Kenya, Harkness (1975) considered relationships between one dimension of modernization, that is, change in personal values, and the area of child language socialization and development. She identified three social and linguistic environmental factors which correlated with personal modernization: mothers in the more modern families expressed more interest in promoting their children's language development, they maintained more sociable, less dominant relationships with their children, and they demanded less work of them. The children's rate of vocabulary development was related to the mother's language teaching values, particularly to the mothers' report that they had taught the names of objects to the children. Mothers' dominance had a significant negative relationship to the proportion of questions children asked. The children's rate of general language development as measured by mean length of utterance was significantly related to the amount of time children spent doing chores. Thus the study showed that personal modernization represents a shift in values toward those of Western, middle-class society, with its emphasis on individual development and parent-child intimacy at the expense of the child's contribution to the economic maintenance of the household. Harkness calls attention to the fact that in the Kipsigis community studied this shift was associated with negative as well as positive consequences for children's language development; thus it would appear that the behavioral consequences of values may vary in different cultural settings. The work of LeVine, Klein, and Owen (1967) suggests to us that changes in language socialization and development may be amplified by the even more dramatic shift in the father-child relations associated with modernization.

Societal Complexity

The even broader context within which modernization may be taking place is societal complexity. Berlin and Kay (1969, p. 16) stated that the total vocabularies of languages spoken by peoples possessing relatively simple technologies tend to be smaller than those of highly complex civilizations. Witkowski (1976) proposed an "unequal inventory" hypothesis asserting that a *majority* of, although not all, nonspecialist domains will tend to increase in semantic complexity concomitantly with increases in societal complexity. He notes, however, that semantic dimensions of kinship do not increase in complexity with an increase in societal complexity (Witkowski, 1972) and believes that kinship is not an isolated case but that there are other nonspecialist domains for which the association does not hold. For modern complex societies, Witkowski (1976) posits university education and the influence of mass media as the sources of the differences in semantic complexity, and for societies of more moderate complexity he tentatively suggests that specialist distinctions may be adopted into general usage.

For color nomenclature, a strong association exists between overall societal complexity and number of terms. Berlin and Kay (1969) suggested that the sequence of elaboration of color lexicon is evolutionary, accompanying, and perhaps a reflex of, increasing technologic and cultural advancement. Further, they pointed out that an increase in the number of basic color terms may be seen as part of a general increase in vocabulary, a response to an informationally richer cultural environment about which speakers must communicate effectively. Naroll (1970) confirmed Berlin and Kay's (1969) hypothesized association by making a formal comparison of societal complexity and number of color terms.

Harkness (1973), drawing on Chafe's (1970) model of "idiomatization," proposes a mechanism for how societal complexity relates to an increase in the number of color terms. She points out that the use of general or abstract terms becomes necessary when speakers do not share the same sociocultural background. She gives the specific cultural example of marketplaces where people come from various areas to sell things to each other, a situation which might encourage expansion of basic color term repertoires. Further, she conjectures that basic color terms may be developed mainly to describe manufactured articles which are not universally known.

For taste and touch nomenclature, there is also an association between societal complexity and number of terms (Deutch, Perkins, Hays, Schneiderman, & White, n.d.). C. Brown's (1977) work showed that the amount of diversity in botanical species influences the size of life form (e.g., tree, bush) lexicons only in simple societies. Increasing societal complexity encourages proliferation of life form terms, while severe lack of diversity in botanical species tends to *constrain* the growth of life from lexicons. C. Brown (1977) suggested that it may be of considerable value to retain and to add life form categories in complex societies, since the variety of involvement with the natural world is minimal and results in learning fewer specific and generic names and their referents.

DAILY LIFE

The circumstances of daily life are important sources of cultural variation which have implications for cognitive development. What tasks do the children do and with whom do they spend their time?

Cultural norms may determine not only what responsibility consists of but also the age when children can be assigned a more mature social, sexual, or cultural role. The results of a cross-cultural survey on 50 societies in the Human Relations Area Files (Rogoff, Sellers, Pirrotta, & White, 1975), however, suggest that modal cultural assignment of social responsibility falls in the 5–7-year-old range. Our attention, then, might best be focused on the interplay between universal constraints on the age of assignment and the cultural particulars of what responsibilities are assigned. Nonetheless, there are noticeable numbers of cultures whose shifts to the assumption of various new responsibilities do not fall in the modal period. In explaining these outlying cultures and the broad age ranges in some variables, Rogoff et al. suggest that there may be systematic differences between the cultures which accelerate or decelerate the integration of the child into society. Rogoff (cited by Rogoff et al., 1975) attempted without success to document these differences. We suggest a different analysis, which would not be possible on the basis of Human Relations Area Files data, focusing on the variability of the cognitive demands of the task or responsibility as realized in a particular culture.

A few studies have called attention to cognitive differences associated with characteristics of daily life. Among the Logoli of Western Kenya, children who went a greater distance from home in their free time had greater ability to perform spatial tasks (R. L. Munroe & Munroe, 1971). The researchers excluded directed activities from the calculation of their measure of distance from home on the grounds that the environmental experience gained by being away from home was very limited when children were doing chores—their movement was involuntary and they were following only a mechanical, unvarying route. Nerlove, Munroe, and Munroe (1971) did a replication of this study among the Gusii of Southwestern Kenya. The results of testing the relationship both among the Gusii and between the Logoli and the Gusii also suggest that distance from home may be an appropriate index of experience contributing to differential intellective task performances. In the second study, however, not all directed activities were excluded from the calculation of the measure of distance from home. Herding cattle, unlike trudging to the river to get water, both permits and inextricably involves environmental exploration:

> Not only may the child spend long hours in different places but also his [or her] route is only as unvarying as his cattle's meandering. Furthermore, upon reaching an open place where his cattle may settle down to placid grazing, he has ample opportunity for exploration and games. (Nerlove, Munroe, & Munroe, 1971, p. 5)

This study provides evidence that what is important is not simply experience in space but the nature of the activity which in turn shapes the nature of environmental experience.

In a study of Guatemalan children, Nerlove, Roberts, Klein, Yarbrough, and Habicht (1974) suggested that the relationship between distance and spatial tasks for the Kenyan children might be better described as one between self-managed activities (either voluntary or directed) and analytic ability, where self-managed activities entailed following an exacting series of steps. Notable among the activities contributing to the measure of self-managed sequences among the Guatemalan children were clotheswashing, work in the maize fields, role play, and rule games (mainly jacks and marbles). In contrast to the Guatemalan children, the "at home" behavior of the Kenyan children is characterized by simple tasks or passive behavior, by few playthings, and by a marked absence of role play; thus distance from home in the Kenya case was a good index of performance of self-managed sequences.

A clearer link between daily activities and cognitive growth is provided by Price-Williams, Gordon, and Ramirez (1969), whose work was followed up by Adjei (1977). This link was also studied by Greenfield and Childs (in press). Price-Williams et al. (1969) showed that pottery-making children learn by doing; they attained conservation earlier in substance (clay is the medium used in the test). Familiarity not only with the material but with the manipulation of the material is suggested as a necessary prerequisite in the attainment of conservation. Adjei (1977) studied conservation performance on the concepts of quantity, weight, and volume among Ghanaian children and illiterate adult women. On the whole, both her quantitative and qualitative data support the facilitative effects of the pottery-making experience as found by Price-Williams et al. (1969). In addition, the urban elite Ghanaian child also excelled on these tasks.

Greenfield and Child's (in press) study in Mexico showed that learning to weave failed to have a generalized effect. They studied whether or not learning to weave one of the three traditional Zinacantecan cloth patterns influenced a general ability to represent patterns. Cole's (1975) interpretation of their data rests on the notion that in order for problem-solving skills to be generalized, they must be learned through engaging in a variety of *different* problems of the same type. He asserts that three patterns simply are not enough. There is insufficient information to challenge the capacity of the mind, which can readily overlearn a small and constant amount of information. Price-Williams (1975) invokes quite a different line of reasoning to interpret Greenfield and Child's findings. He notes that the correspondence of weaving skill to cognitive ability is highly specific and that the task involving continuing on one line using sticks to form the pattern was not the appropriate match for the skill involved in weaving. The test should have been related to an appreciation of coordinates, since the essence of weaving craft lies in lacing materials at right angles to each other.

Another task with important associations with cognitive development is caretaking. Snipper (1978) observed child caretaker–infant interactions and found that caretakers' quality of thought was associated with the quality of their social behavior. Girls who scored high on four tests of conservation ability were also more likely to exhibit attentiveness toward their infant charges and were less likely to engage in active exchange with the infants. These results were explained by the increasing ability of children at the level of concrete operations to attend simultaneously to relevant dimensions of a problem and children's increasing ability, as they move toward formal operations, to think problems through without actively manipulating concrete objects. Rate of caretakers' cognitive development, however, was unaffected by the participation in caretaking. Caretakers and noncaretakers did not differ on tests of conservation ability and social cognition. The thrust of Snipper's findings, then, seems to be the impact of cognition on task rather than task on cognition.

Experience in child caretaking may also be associated with classroom attentiveness and industriousness, necessary although not sufficient conditions for learning to read. Gallimore et al. (1978) found that Hawaiian boys with experience in sibling caretaking systems were more generally attentive to peer tutors and teachers, but his study also suggested some evidence for the transfer of sibcare experience to peer tutoring beyond the effects of general responsibility training. He concluded, however, that to match secondary socialization practices of public schools to primary family socialization patterns in order to achieve gains in intellective functioning is not a productive approach for policy makers.

Snipper's (1978) study considers the implications of caretaking for caretakers, the Gallimore et al. (1978) study refers to experience in a sibcaretaking system not specifying the role, and William's (1969) study of the Dusun considers the implications of caretaking from the point of view of the charge. Although Williams provides no cognitive measures, the presentation of the multiple-branched pathways through life with respect to being given care, or taking care of, gives us insights into important differences. An individual's fate is largely shaped by demographic accident with regard to experiencing these alternative cultural opportunities. Their cognitive consequences should be explored. Who cares for the child—a 3–6-year-old, a 7–10-year-old, a grandparent, or a mother—and what is that care like? The nature of the care is related to the world of the caretaker, which in turn may reflect native theories of competence during different life stages.

There are other works which describe important patterns of difference in daily life but which do not present any cognitive measures. They are included here because they point to important areas of further research. For example, Barker and Schoggen (1973) have grouped behavior settings into habitats and have examined within those habitats such variables as attendance in them by children and their benefits to and from children. They have used these variables in an effort to validate in a novel way differences in childrearing systems between a town in the midwestern United States and one in northern England. Stephens (1976) discussed the importance for children's development of competence of their being engaged in natural graded series of tasks within the context of work which is largely observable and comprehensible.

What, then, is the distribution of a child's time across people and behavior settings? When and under what circumstances is he/she in mixed groups of all ages or is he/she in age- (and sex-)graded groups and what effect does this have on his/her growth and development? In the course of considering the nature of the interpenetration of settings and subgroups of people, one ultimately comes to the question of whether or not, in a given society, children are encouraged or indeed provided with any opportunity to be alone. Altman (1976; 1977) has portrayed privacy as crucial to the functioning of most cultures yet as sufficiently flexible to reflect major cultural differences. In Piaget's (1964) discussion of logicomathematical experience, in which knowledge is drawn from the action effected upon objects, he gives an example of how such knowledge may be discovered:

> When he was four or five years old . . . a small child . . . was seated on the ground in his garden and he was counting pebbles. Now to count these pebbles he put them in a row and he counted them one, two, three up to ten. Then he finished counting them and started to count them in the other direction. He began by the end and once again he found ten. He found this marvelous that there were ten in one direction and ten in the other direction. So he put them in a circle and counted them that way and found ten once again. Then he counted them in the other direction and found ten once more. So he put them in some other arrangement and keep counting them and kept finding ten. There was the discovery he made. (Piaget, 1964), p. 12)

Freedom from interruptions and the solitude which provides the opportunity for a person to assimilate experiences and information and to examine possible future relationships with others may be required for such discoveries.

Nerlove et al. (1974) attempted to identify congruences between experimental task requirements and structural features of disparate daily activities in cultural context. Participation in certain activities served as "natural indicators" of specific aspects of cognitive skill. Fundamental to the study is the idea that common, identifiable, structural features of adaptive and intelligent behavior can be defined cross-culturally. Serpell (1977) maintains that the study implies a causal relationship between participation in certain types of observed work and play activities and performance on intelligence tests. Indeed, the results of the Nerlove et al. study do not rule out intelligence as the underlying variable and thus suggest intelligent children as both exhibiting complex or crucial behaviors and performing well on formal tests.

In the light of this issue of whether participation in cultural experiences is formative or only reflective, Istomina's (1975) study on the development of voluntary memory in preschool-age children is of great importance. It lends support to the idea that behaviors of daily life are important not only with regard to the manifestation of cognitive skills but also to their *formation*. She found considerable differences in the complexity of the children's memory processes depending on the type of experiment—make-believe, in which the task presented to the child flowed intrinsically from the content of the activity, or laboratory, in which the task was imposed externally by adults. It was easier for a child consciously and explicitly to set the goal of remembering or recalling and for the child's memory processes to become purposeful processes in the play experiment as compared to the laboratory experiment. The transformation of the memory processes into purposeful specific strategies thus depends very intimately on the motivation for the child's activity as a whole. In the situation in which there is motivation for the activity as a whole, it appears that the production deficiency gap—between what children "can do" and what they "will do" —that A. Brown (1977) discusses in her work on strategies for remembering and their purposeful use is lessened. In this study, Istomina (1975) has made an important link between the socioemotional and cognitive aspects of behavior. In addition, she was able to interpret the changes she observed in both test situations as ones of actual formation of the operations of voluntary remembering and recalling rather than merely the transfer of the operations from one set of conditions to another.

Building upon this observed formation of memory operations, her next step was most exciting. She examined the influence of memory efficiency in the play situation on memory efficiency in the test situation. Practice in the make-believe situation caused not only a greater improvement in memory performance in the test situation than vice versa but also than in the make-believe situation itself. The school experience, as discussed in a subsequent section, contributes to freeing the individual from embeddedness in thinking; it may, however, be crucial to have diverse experiences in the form of embedded or contextually meaningful work activities or role-playing tasks to make a child truly ready for the disembedding process. This finding echoes Piaget's notion of linguistic or educational transition, which he describes as a fundamental but insufficient factor for structural development because the child can receive the information via language but to receive the information she or he must have a structure enabling assimilation of this information. Or, as Price-Williams et al. (1969) have said, a skill embodies a set of operations with a recognizable end; thus the role of skills, so defined, in cognitive growth may be very important.

FORMAL EDUCATION AND ITS EFFECTS

Schooling

A large body of research has now accumulated which demonstrates cognitive performance differences in formally schooled as compared to nonschooled children in such diverse cultures as Wolof, Zulu, Kpelle, and Mayan. For example, in various studies of classification ability, school-children were more likely to categorize by form or function as opposed to color (Evans & Segall, 1969; Greenfield, 1966; Luria, 1971; Schmidt & Nzimande, 1970; Serpell, 1969),[1] were able to reclassify an array in a new way (Fjellman, 1971; Sharp, 1971; Sharp & Cole, cited by Cole & Scribner, 1974), and were more adept at verbalizing the principles behind their categories (Fjellman, 1971; Scribner, 1974).[2] Additionally, in tasks of verbal reasoning, individuals with formal schooling were able to suspend everyday practical realities and treat syllogisms as purely logical problems (Luria, 1971; Scribner, 1978). Differences favoring educated subjects have also been found in the areas of picture perception (Hudson, 1960; Miller, 1973) and memory skills (Cole et al., 1971; Meacham, 1975; Wagner, 1974, 1977). Scribner and Cole (1973) summarize the differences between schooled and unschooled individuals as follows: (1) persons with formal education are more able to abstract and apply general rules to various specific problems, and (2) they are more adept at verbalizing their actions and explaining reasons for their behavior. Results from memory tasks suggest that they are also more likely to apply spontaneously cognitive skills to novel situations. In addition, the findings of cross-national research in Canada and the United States, where schooling is nearly universal, showed that years of education predicted performance on questions of fact and knowledge of current events regardless of the respondents' socioeconomic level or age (Hyman, Wright, & Reed, 1975).

In contrast, another group of studies concerned with acquisition of conservation has not shown differences due to schooling (Goodnow, 1962; Goodnow & Bethon, 1966; Kamara, 1975; Mermelstein & Shulman, 1967; Nyiti, 1976; Price-Williams, 1961). Piaget's theory provides an explanation for these findings, namely, that the child's own actions upon the world are critical in attaining concrete operations and that social transmission, including teaching by others, is of secondary importance (Piaget, 1964). The research cited above supports the contention that everyday environmental experience is sufficient for attaining conservation at the concrete operational level. It may be, however, that the testing situation contributes to successful performance on conservation tasks. Testing for conservation ability classically includes the presence of objects and materials which the subject may manipulate and the use of a clinical interview technique in which each subject is probed about his or her own responses rather than the dependence on a standardized interview format. This testing situation may be especially effective in eliciting successful performances when familiar materials are used (Price-Williams, 1961; Price-Williams et al., 1969) and where subjects approach the questions in a more intuitive, nonverbal fashion (Bovet, 1974).

Goodnow's (1962) work is instructive in showing the limitations of practical experience as contributing to intellectual development. Although illiterate Hong Kong boys performed as well as schooled boys on various conservation tasks, they performed poorly on combinatorial tasks which required them to think the problem through *before* manipulating the objects. This finding suggests that Piagetian tasks which require mental manipulation and hypothetical thinking will distinguish between schooled and unschooled subjects. In a review of cross-cultural Piagetian research, Dasen (1972) concluded that the hypothetical thinking characteristic of formal operations is not universally required. Formal operational tasks require complex mental manipulations. Piaget's mental imagery tasks require simpler mental manipulations; in Western subjects, proficiency on these tasks is attained at approximately the same age as acquisition of concrete operations. Youniss and Dean (1974) administered both concrete operations tasks and mental imagery tasks to Korean and Costa Rican urban and rural subjects. All individuals performed the conservation tasks adequately, but rural subjects were less successful with the mental imagery tasks. Following this same procedure with samples of schooled and unschooled subjects would clarify Goodnow's argument that schooling affects ability to solve problems mentally.

How does the schooling experience produce differences, even after only 7 months of formal education (Greenfield, 1966) and where schools are of poor quality (Cole et al., 1971; Scribner, 1978)? Some effects are undoubtedly related to what some investigators (Hess & Shipman, 1968; Precourt, 1975) refer to as the hidden curriculum of schools—namely, the repeated practice in dealing with unfamiliar adults, in being presented with a variety of puzzles and problems, and in being expected to persevere in solving them. The demands implicit in a testing situation are often similar if not identical—i.e., interaction with a strange experimenter, presentation of novel tasks, and the need for motivation and perseverance. Thus the structural features of the testing situation are probably more familiar to the schoolchild. Super's (1977) findings that 1 year of schooling dramatically increased testability of children confirms this supposition, as does the study by Irwin, Schafer, and Feiden (1974). Contrary to expectations, illiterate Mano farmers were only marginally superior to United States college students in sorting rice. These results are consonant with the position that the educated United States subjects were more familiar with testing in general and with classification tasks in particular. The fact that there were fewer poor sorters among educated United States subjects suggests an additional effect of schooling: school may serve as a kind of homogenizer, raising everyone to a level of minimal competence. Fjellman (1971) also provides evidence of homogenization. Nonschooled children provided more functional (i.e., nonabstract) reasons for sorting when items fell in the domain associated in their culture with their own sex; e.g., farming for boys and cooking for girls. This effect was minimal among schoolchildren.

Relatively little attention has been paid to differences between schools, although there are indications that quality of schools influences cognitive outcomes. For example, Goodnow (1962) found that conservation scores were depressed in a school which deemphasized everyday experience and which had a poor science program. Pollnac and Jahn (1976) found that schoolchildren from a rural school which emphasized daily prayer recitations performed significantly better on tests of recall, compared to urban and neighboring rural schoolchildren. Holtzman et al. (1975) found that young Mexican and United States children had similar levels of cognitive abilities but that they diverged considerably after several years of schooling.

In searching for those features of formal education which promote intellectual development, several investigators have proposed that school provides a special kind of learning experience different from that encountered in the course of everyday socialization (Greenfield & Bruner, 1969; R. L. Munroe & Munroe, 1975; Neisser, 1976; Scribner & Cole, 1973) The school experience is characterized as disconnected from everyday life in a traditional society. Informal learning in the traditional setting usually revolves around a specific task or skill which is transmitted by demonstration to the child by a person who has social and emotional ties to her or him. Classroom learning, in contrast, may have little immediate relevance to the child's daily life. The teacher, a stranger unconnected to the child's social world, transmits knowledge largely through language. Much energy is devoted to teaching and drilling the student in the use of abstract symbol systems—letters and numbers. These school experiences theoretically provide opportunities for the child's thought to be freed from the immediate social context. Children are taught to remove themselves from the material, a capacity which enables them to consider problems in a hypothetical fashion, imagining alternative situations and solutions and evaluating them with no concern for everyday practicalities. They are likewise able to consider many different situations and search for underlying similarities. In sum, the school experience encourages children to analyze, conceptualize, and generalize. They gain the ability to apply concepts to variety of problems, across many situations.

This interpretation has recently come under attack, however. Super (1977) questions it upon methodological grounds, showing how selectivity operates in determining which children attend school and which do not. School attendance in a Kipsigis community was linked to parental educational level, family adoption of Christianity, and parental judgments of children's maturity. Thus schoolchildren may have been more mature, intelligent, and Westernized than the nonschooled children even before entering school. Super further points out that analyses of effects of schooling must distinguish between cognitive abilities which emerge independent of special training and those abilities fostered especially by schools. Kipsigis children, for example, developed the following abilities around age 7 years without benefit of schooling: increased testability, increased analysis and construction of visual stimuli (e.g., Bender-Gestalt Test), increased speed of processing simultaneous information in visual and auditory modes, increased organization and functioning of semantic aspects of language, and use of logical responses on Piagetian tasks. Another example, Posner's (1978) study, found that unschooled Dioula children from a commercial tribe used even more sophisticated problem-solving strategies than their schooled peers. The school was teaching "new math," but it was the *unschooled* Dioula children who most frequently evidenced use of complex combinatorial strategies. For example, when the task called for adding $5 + 7 + 6$, the unschooled child might answer, "$5 + 7 = 10$ and 2 left plus 6 is 18."

Wagner (1974; 1977) has approached the problem of pinpointing schooling effects by attempting to show that structural features of memory (i.e., echoic store, short-term store, and long-term store) are universal capacities but that control processes (i.e., memory strategies such as rehearsal, clustering, etc.) are more affected by environmental variations. In both Mexico (Wagner, 1974) and Morocco (Wagner, 1977) formal schooling was found to affect memory strategies, with verbal rehearsal, for example, used only by older schooled subjects. He suggests that the control processes are "culture-specific, or a function of the particular experiences that surround each growing child" (1977, p. 11). Indeed, he asserts that "the present data indicate that without formal schooling, [higher mnemonic strategies] may not develop at all" (1974, p. 395).

While acknowledging that education *may* enable people to process information more efficiently, Cole et al. (1976) remain skeptical. They believe that effects of schooling may not transfer as widely as has been supposed but appear to transfer only because the cognitive tasks employed by researchers are so similar in form and content to school tasks. They also advance a more complex model of the effects of familiarity on performances:

Subjects who fail to produce what we consider a good performance may do so because they are unfamiliar with the required assemblage of subskills: *at least* three sources of unfamiliarity must be seriously considered when failures of performance occurs—at the level of stimuli, operations, and their assemblage, which is organized by knowledge of what constitutes adequate performance. (1976, p. 229)

Current research has moved beyond the description of illiterates as "concrete" thinkers and educated persons as "abstract" thinkers to an analysis of situational demands and subjects' resultant cognitive performances. School is presumed to make demands upon the child which necessitate the use of abilities such as inducing general rules and reasoning about hypothetical situations. Illiterate villagers do not exhibit these abilities because their environment does not require it of them. They are more likely to encounter a limited set of specific problems which can be resolved in traditional ways (R. L. Munroe & Munroe, 1975). When a problem requires a complex solution involving hypothetical thought, such as navigation without instruments, illiterate persons' use of hypothetical thought may not generalize to other situations or domains of reasoning (Gladwin, 1970). On the other hand, schooled persons' problem-solving skills acquired in classrooms may not generalize to situations of "mundane" intellectual demands (Cole et al., 1976).

This "environmental pressure" interpretation of differential performance is supported by Denney (1974a, b). Both young children and elderly adults tended to classify objects using complementary criteria—that is, the grouping of objects sharing functions or otherwise related, such as car and garage—as opposed to the more abstract similarity criteria—that is, grouping similar objects into hierarchic systems, such as car and train being means of transportation. Denney argues that children and the elderly are capable of classifying according to similarity but are under no special pressure to do so and so prefer the more "natural" complementary mode. Schools and occupations are examples of systems which create pressures to use similarity criteria. Denney (1974b) demonstrated that adult men and women aged 25 to 69 years who hold professional positions gave more similarity responses than a nonprofessional control group of adults who were matched for age.

Although reliable differences have been found between schooled and nonschooled groups, schooling is an example of a "packaged variable" (Whiting, 1976). There are many different aspects of schooling which might contribute to its effects, either independently or in combination with one another. A distinct advantage of cross-cultural studies has always been the opportunity to separate the effects of chronological age and the duration and type of schooling. However, only recently have investigators begun "unpacking" the variable of schooling itself in order to assess the impacts of its various components. One such component, literacy, will now be reviewed.

Literacy

The ability to read and write is almost inevitably a product of school experience. Several authors, however, have asserted that literacy has distinctive cognitive consequences separable from other cognitive consequences gained from the schooling experience. Goody (1973) and Goody and Watt (1962) trace the consequences of the invention of writing. Historically, access to easy systems of writing meant that eventually literate societies accumulated a recorded past which was permanent and unchanging. The capacity to store and retrieve information about the past made historical inquiry possible, which in turn encouraged an attitude of skepticism. Essentially, the authors argue that a revolution in thinking occurred. Received ideas of all kinds became subject to scrutiny. Alternative explanations could be compared and tested more easily. Logic itself, especially in the form of the syllogism, depended on writing—a system whereby speech could be recorded and subsequently analyzed.

Greenfield (1968) is another advocate of this viewpoint, albeit on the individual level. She reasons that writing has the effect of freeing the individual's thought from the immediate situational context. Once a thought is written down, it is more tied to linguistic than to situational context, and linguistic contexts are more easily manipulable. Thus the use of writing promotes and is in a sense equated with symbolic manipulation and conceptualization. Mundy-Castle (1975) and Farrell (1977) provide more examples of the assertion that reading and writing in and of themselves stimulate cognitive restructuring, resulting in heightened ability to think abstractly. Since both reading and writing are operations which can be applied across different situations and are used for different purposes, they are focal examples of "common operations . . . applied to a multitude of tasks" which Scribner and Cole (1973) described as encouraging rule generalization.

While such hypotheses are fascinating and plausible, they have remained at the level of speculation because literacy is so intertwined with formal schooling. Thus the recent Scribner and Cole (1977a) report of research carried out among the Vai of Liberia is particularly welcome. For generations, Vai society has utilized a phonetic writing system which is unrelated to the formal education system. The Arabic and Roman alphabets are also used in the society. The investigators estimated that about 30 percent of the adult male population was literate in at least one of the three scripts. Their extensive research program included detailed analyses of the functions of writing in the society, describing how literacy skills are learned, what the skills consist of, and how they are used. This information was based upon interviews with 700 men and women. Various psychological tasks were administered to groups of subjects who were illiterate or who were literate in Vai, Arabic, or English, although the number of subjects and the manner of selection for each group was not specified. The findings, like the research plan itself, were rich in detail and complex. A major finding of interest here was the overall *failure* of writing ability to predict increased performance on tests of general conceptual ability. In all cases, nonliterates were compared to persons literate in Vai and who had no formal schooling; those literate in Arabic who had been taught to write by rote in Koranic schools; and those literate in English who had learned to write English in formal schools. On a communications task—where subjects were taught a simple board game and then were asked to explain the game to someone unfamiliar with it in the absence of the board—groups were ranked in order from highest to lowest mean scores as follows: high school students, Vai literates, Arabic literates, and nonliterates. The authors explained the high scores of Vai literates as being linked to the specifically communication-serving function of the Vai script in the society. On a verbal learning task, which was designed to be similar to the Koranic teaching method, the groups were ranked in order from highest to lowest mean scores as follows: high school students, Arabic literates, Vai literates, and nonliterates. However, no differences were found between literates and nonliterates on tasks calling for the subject to remember and repeat a story and a free recall task. Finally, a language task—where Vai sentences were read very slowly syllable by syllable and had to be reconstructed and comprehended by the subject—favored Vai literates. The investigators link this finding to their observations of Vai literates' phonetic methods of reading. A test where sentences were read slowly word by word did not distinguish among literates, but all literates performed better than nonliterates. Vai and Arabic literates did not differ from nonliterates in performances on classification tasks and logic problems. The authors conclude:

> The consequences of literacy that we identified are all highly specific and closely tied to actual practices with particular scripts;. . . Vai literates and Arabic literates showed different patterns of skills, and neither duplicated the performance of those who had obtained literacy through attendance at Western-type English schools. (1977a, p. 27)

Another hypothesis about effects of literacy is the argument that the technology of writing has weakened dependence on memory so that memory skills should be heightened among nonliterate people. The studies reported below speak to this issue. While suggestive, they do not separate literacy from schooling nor from urban versus rural residence, making clearcut interpretation difficult.

Doob (1964) provides interesting data and anecdotal evidence of eidetic imagery as a means of storing information in the absence of writing. Subjects were rural and urban Ibo children and adults. Eidetic imagery is found in most or all children in Western societies but disappears with age, a phenomenon often attributed to schooling and learning to read. The urban Ibos followed this same pattern: more children than adults were eidetikers. In the rural population, however, an astounding 79 percent of adults reported eidetic images. Although the eidetic images lasted no more than 4 minutes, some subjects reported in interviews that they were able to revive images at will, and, for example, "replay" the events of a day. However, as Gray and Gummerman (1975) point out, variability of results in subsequent research by Doob and others is so great that it is impossible to reach any conclusions regarding cultural or schooling effects on eidetic imagery.

A few empirical investigations have attempted to assess the effect of literacy on short-term memory. Cole and Gay (1972) reported studies of memory skills employing such techniques as using items which were taxonomically related, cueing subjects' recall in various ways, and embedding items to be recalled in stories. Where clusterable and nonclusterable items were presented randomly, neither nonliterate nor schooled children categorized by taxonomic relations. However, when the situation was structured for the subjects such as presenting clusterable items together in a block, literate children clustered the items upon recall, and their ability to recall improved with practice. Nonliterate subjects showed no such tendency. Where the items to be recalled were embedded in a story, a "naturally occurring" situation in this culture, nonliterates performed well. Only Kpelle high school students, however, proved capable of spontaneously using clustering to organize their recall performances. This research supports the view that formal education encourages certain abilities, such as rule generalization and search for structure, which enable literate subjects to perform better than nonliterates (Cole & Scribner, 1974).

Dube (1977) used a story recall method to investigate the relation between literacy and memory. Nonliterate African adolescents, African junior high students, and rural United States junior high students were presented with one African folktale and one European fairy tale. They were asked to recall the stories in as much detail as possible immediately after the presentation, 1 and 5 weeks later. Each group of literate subjects included individuals who were rated low, medium, and high on intellectual achievement measures which were assumed to index intelligence. The illiterate subjects were judged to be high, medium, or low in intelligence by tribal elders. The African students performed better than the Americans on the story recall, with no significant difference between the nonliterate and literate African groups. The best performance was that of nonliterate Africans judged to be high in intelligence. Nonliterate subjects as a group also showed less forgetting over time than the other two groups. However, they were not superior to literate subjects in serial recall, that is, passing the story orally from one person to another. Neither the formal schooling explanation nor the technology hypothesis—that nonliterate cultures develop superior memory skills because they are compelled to rely solely on memory—is supported by this research. Nonliterates performed well on the task, but there was no difference in the performance of nonliterate and literate African subjects. The author suggests that familiarity of the task is the crucial factor. Although familiar with the stimulus material of stories, American youngsters had little practice in oral recall of stories. Story telling was a familiar activity for all the African students. This distinction between stimulus material and task requirement is a useful one. The studies of Cole and his associates (Cole & Gay, 1972; Cole et al., 1971), for example, used familiar objects and native taxonomies. However, the task requirement of recalling discrete items and spontaneously imposing a structure upon them was probably unfamiliar to unschooled persons.

BILINGUALISM: A DOUBLE-CULTURAL OPPORTUNITY

The most celebrated hypothesis of the consequences of language for thought is the Sapir-Whorfian hypothesis of linguistic relativity. We will consider at some length a related question, the effect of bilingualism on thought. We were drawn to this topic by Vygotsky's (1962) assertion that foreign language learning constitutes a special kind of "cultural opportunity." He believed that learning a foreign language enables the child to be free from the situation in which there is a "fixed relation" between the world and the linguistic expression of the world. In understanding that her or his language is one among many, the child is more likely to search out the formal systems underlying languages. Vygotsky quotes Goethe in saying, "he who knows no foreign language does not truly know his own." Leopold (1939–1949) concurs, stating that bilingualism "frees the mind of the tyranny of words." The child who speaks two languages need not tie ideas to words in a one-to-one correspondence and thus may be more flexible in thought.

There is empirical support for the idea that bilinguals are more aware of the properties of language and approach language itself more analytically. Ianco-Worrell (1972) tested 4–6-year-olds who were Afrikaaner-English bilinguals, Afrikaaner monolinguals, and English monolinguals. The bilingual children were advanced in their ability to attend to meaning rather than sounds.[3] They were also more aware of the arbitrary nature of object-word correspondence than were the monolingual controls. These results were supported by Cummins' (1978) Irish-English sample and Ben-Zeev's (1977) study of Hebrew-English bilinguals. Interestingly, Hebrew-English bilinguals had a more analytical grasp of syntax than monolinguals despite not differing from them in their grasp of basic rules of grammar (such as pluralization, formation of past tense and superlatives, etc.) and actually scoring lower than monolinguals on a vocabulary test.

Seeking to explain bilinguals' superior performance, Ben-Zeev (1977) hypothesizes that bilinguals experience an unusual amount of cognitive conflict as they learn a second language, which forces them to acquire an advanced understanding of the language system. Cummins' (1978) research, however, fails to support the hypothesis. His study included a group of language learners (children enrolled in an immersion language-learning program) as well as monolinguals and fluent bilinguals. The groups were matched for IQ, SES, sex, and age. Language learners and monolinguals did not differ and bilinguals performed significantly better on a test of sensitivity to surface and underlying structural ambiguities. Elsewhere, Cummins speculates that the process of objectification may explain bilingualism's effect on cognitive development (Cummins & Gulutsan, 1975). Objectifying refers to the ability to attend to a concept apart from its context. Exposure to two languages is said to stimulate comparisons between the languages, which then accelerates the attainment of objectification. Cummins proposes that the objectification process then operates "to direct the child's attention both to conceptual features of his environment and to the operations he [or she] performs with his two languages themselves" (Cummins & Gulutsan, 1975, p. 93).

Bilingualism has also been associated with increased mental flexibility and creativity. In a classic study, Peal and Lambert (1962) describe their bilingual French-Canadian subjects as possessing more mental flexibility than monolingual control subjects, a conclusion based on the bilinguals' superior performances on subtests requiring symbolic manipulation and on a factor analysis which showed bilinguals to have a more diversified intellect structure. Scott (1973, cited by Lambert, 1975) examined the relationship of bilingualism and divergent thinking, following over a period of 7 years a group of English-Canadian children enrolled in a French immersion program and a control group enrolled in a conventional English-language program. Bilinguals performed better than monolinguals, and their advantage increased over the 7 year period. Other studies where bilinguals performed better than monolinguals on measures of divergent thinking include those of Carriger (1974), Cummins and Gulutsan (1974), and Landry (1974).

Investigations seeking to show an effect of bilingualism on general reasoning abilities have usually failed to demonstrate convincing links. Ianco-Worrell (1970) tested bilinguals and monolinguals on tasks which were directly tied to theories of mental development (Kendlers' optional shift task and Piagetian classification tasks) and found no differences between the two groups. Ben-Zeev (1977) reports that her bilingual and monolingual subjects scored similarly on intelligence tests. The key study in this regard was carried out by Barik and Swain (1976), who followed the same children for 5 years. One group attended a French immersion school program, while the control group of monolinguals attended a standard English-language program. When initial IQ differences between the two groups were statistically controlled, no differences in IQ were found between the groups for the period through the third grade for which comparable data were available. Although some investigators have found that bilingual subjects score higher on both verbal and nonverbal tests of intelligence than do monolinguals (Cummins & Gulutsan, 1974; Liedtke & Nelson, 1968; Peal & Lambert, 1962), all the bilinguals in these instances were enrolled in special school programs. It seems likely that their higher scores were not due to bilingualism alone but also to the selection factor of choosing to be schooled in a second language.

Only recently have researchers begun to grapple with the construction of theory and questions of process. Previously most investigations involved purely empirical questions such as the existence of interference and transfer effects between the two languages (Keats & Keats, 1974; Lambert, Ignatow, & Krauthamer, 1968) or the consequences of the social context in which each language was acquired (Diebold, 1968; Lambert, 1969). But MacNamara (1970) points out that what is really required to explore either of these questions, and certainly to assess the impact of bilingualism on cognitive development, is a theory of semantics which relates the child's language production and interpretation to cognitive development and functioning. In addition, Lambert (1975) points out the need for attention to investigating *processes:* does the phenomenon—assuming it is reliable—operate because of better storage of information by bilinguals, because of the ability to separate linguistic symbols from their referents, or because bilingual contrasts of linguistic systems aid in the development of general conceptual thought?

Working out of the Piagetian theoretical tradition developed by Sinclair-De-Zwart (1969; 1973), Tremaine (1975) has moved in the suggested direction, demonstrating a concomitant acquisition by bilingual children of concrete operations and syntactic structures of the same order of complexity in both English and French. Other recent efforts include those of Bain (1975) and Dulay and Burt (1972; 1974a, b).

The research reviewed to this point has concerned subjects who were carefully screened to ensure that they were "balanced" bilinguals, fluent in both of their languages. Many speakers, however, more commonly have a dominant and a weaker language. Lambert (1975) has introduced a useful distinction between additive and subtractive bilingualism. Additive situations occur when both languages have social value and respect in each setting. In this case, the bilingual has added to or enriched her or his repertoire and is not replacing one language with another. These individuals are eventually more likely to become balanced bilinguals. In contrast, subtractive situations occur when one language is less valued and where there is pressure for members of the minority language group to accept the more prestigious language and drop their own. The outcome for these individuals is likely to be a dominant and a weaker language. Cummins (1977) suggests that the studies that found detrimental effects of bilingualism on cognitive development had subjects who were in a subtractive situation.

One group of studies has been concerned with nonbalanced bilinguals' cognitive competence in each of their languages. Ciborowski and Choy (1974) assessed free recall among Hawaiian Creole speakers as compared to Standard English speakers. Both groups were middle class in origin. Although teachers of Creole speakers judged them as having only marginal control of Standard English, their performance in recalling eight items in each language were nearly identical: 7.2 items recalled when the items were embedded in a Creole story and 6.3 recalled when the stories were English. These results indicate that the subjects were bidialectic in their use of languages for memory tasks, although perhaps a difference would have arisen if more than eight items had been presented for recall.

Lemon (1975) assessed the conceptual domains of Tanzanian secondary students in both Swahili, the students' second language, and English, their third language, the language of the school. The students were presented with a series of three names of countries and another series of three names of persons and were asked to explain how two of the items were similar and together differed from the third. Then each student was asked to rate pairs of countries and pairs of persons which he or she had previously rated as polar opposites on various dimensions. Both tasks were performed in both English and Swahili. The domain of "countries" was considered to be a school subject and hence more tied to English, the language of the school, while that of "people known personally" was tied to Swahili, the language of social discourse. As expected, the students' categorizations were more sharply defined and their concepts more differentiated when using English for the conceptual domain of countries and Swahili for the domain of personal acquaintances. The research suggests that nonfluent speakers, as in the case of students who receive instruction in a foreign language, may not automatically transfer the kinds of categorizations and discriminations made in one language and situation to a different language and situation.

Rubenstein (1977) reported similar findings from Belize. Standard English is the language of instruction in schools, but most children speak Spanish or Creole as their first language. Children aged 5–17 years were given a nonverbal test of cognitive development and a Semantic Strategies Test (SST), which consisted of a nonverbal sorting task and a verbal task designating which two of three objects go together. On the basis of the verbal SST, the child was rated as using a global, concrete, functional, or abstract strategy. Children who were given the SST in their first language demonstrated verbal strategies commensurate with their nonverbal level of cognitive development. When Spanish-speaking children were tested in English, however, their English semantic strategies lagged one level behind their nonverbal levels of development.

The implications of these and similar findings for both theory and application are currently being debated. MacNamara (1966) proposes a balance effect hypothesis—that development of skills in the new language is compensated for by loss of mother-tongue skills—that is little more than descriptive. Cummins (1977) advances an interdependence hypothesis—when two languages are learned sequentially, the optimal period for exposure to the second language occurs when the mother tongue is adequately developed, "the period between 6 and 9 years . . . when language starts to become functionally important in the child's cognitive processing and [she or] he becomes capable of representing his operational intelligence in a symbolic or abstract mode" (Cummins, 1977, p. 14). However, Cummins fails to make clear why sequential language learning should differ so widely from the early simultaneous learning of two languages: Ianco-Worrell's (1970; 1972) subjects, for example, learned a different language from each parent and did not suffer cognitively. Neither does Cummins take into account the recent research on language acquisition which shows language and thought to be interdependent from a very early age (Bates, Benigni, Bretherton, Camaioni, & Voletera, 1977). We suspect that other situational factors contribute to nonbalanced bilinguals' language competence. For example, a nonoptimal language-learning environment in the home and a high degree of divergence between the two languages may be a different and powerful factor in creating a nonbalanced and perhaps even *detrimental* bilingual situation.

There are no simple prescriptions for educating nonbalanced bilinguals. The Hawaiian results (Ciborowski & Choy, 1974), in concert with the finding that Hawaiian Creole speakers comprehend stories equally well in Creole and English (Au & Speidel, 1976), indicate that instruction for dialect speakers need not be confined to their own dialect. In fact, these researchers found that general language facility rather than language community origin was more related to early reading achievement (Au, 1976). The conclusion is supported by the results of a large-scale study comparing reading achievement in lower-class blacks taught with Standard English books. There was no appreciable difference found between the groups. Lemon's (1975) and Rubenstein's (1977) studies suggest that concepts learned in school may not readily transfer to nonschool settings and vice versa. The discrepancy may be due to differences in language competence in the majority language, as Cummins (1977) would suggest, or it may be accounted for by the degree of similarity between the child's native tongue and the language of instruction. Hawaiian Creole, for example, is quite similar to Standard English—indeed, Standard English speakers performed well on recall tests in Creole (Ciborowski & Choy, 1974). Programs which have achieved success using "readers" written in the children's first language involved Philipino Hiligaynon speakers switching to English (Orata, 1953), Pitean speakers switching to Swedish (MacNamara, 1966), and Chiapas Indians switching to Spanish (Modiano, 1973), in each case a jump to a new language family.

In general, school programs which have emphasized the majority language and discouraged all use of minority language have been characterized by the failure of many minority children (Cummins, 1977). Few of the school programs advocating this "direct method" have included adequate teaching of the second language *as* a second language to the students as they enter school. Instead, the introduction to the second language is often brief and inadequate, and instruction then proceeds in the second language. The generally poor educational quality of the language instruction is frequently coupled with, and exacerbated by, the disadvantaged social status of children who are required to learn the second language. Therefore, a good test of this direct method of instruction for teaching the second language has not yet been made, and current programs are frequently unsuccessful (Engle, 1976).

One response to this problem has been the institution of school programs which begin school instruction in the child's native tongue and only gradually shift to the standard language of instruction over 2–3 years time (e.g., MacNamara, 1966; Modiano, 1973; Orata, 1953). The experimental groups surpassed control groups, taught in the dominant language from the outset, on tests of language skills and reading comprehension in the dominant language.

Fishman (1977) terms the above programs transitional and finds them wanting because of their philosophy of assimilation. Two other types of programs include maintenance programs and immersion programs. Maintenance programs attempt to maintain the child's home language while promoting a high level of competence in the majority language. Cummins (1977) argues that children from minority language groups will achieve additive bilingualism with respect to the majority language only if their home language is highly developed and reinforced in the school situation.

Perhaps most intriguing in the realm of education are those programs which promote bilingualism in all children, speakers of the dominant language as well as minority group members. In Florida (Richardson, cited by John & Horner, 1970) and Texas (Pryor, cited by John & Horner, 1970), Spanish-speaking and English-speaking children were instructed in both languages. They were found to be adept at learning in both languages and scored better than control groups taught in English only on a variety of measures. The most ambitious such program, termed the St. Lambert project, has been carried out in Montreal (Bruck, Lambert, & Tucker, 1973; Bruck, Lambert, & Tucker, in press; Lambert & Tucker, 1972). Children from English-speaking homes were schooled entirely in French from kindergarten through seventh grade. Their cognitive development, language skills, mathematical abilities, and attitudes were assessed annually. Highlights of the suggestive findings of this project include the fascinating finding that children taught to read and compute in French exhibit these abilities almost simultaneously in English, with no special tutelage required. Thus no interference or confusion between languages occurred in these realms. By grade 2 and beyond, the experimental group performed as well as, and sometimes better than, English-instructed control groups on English language skills such as vocabulary, reading, and writing; they performed equally well on mathematical achievement tests. In addition, the experimental subjects showed remarkable ability to comprehend, study, and learn in the French language. Deficits were few. In the lower grades their French accents and language production skills were somewhat weak, and their comprehension of highly complex material suffered slightly in the upper grades. The experimental group was also consistently higher than control groups on various measures of creativity. This long-range project demonstrates that education in a second language need not be detrimental and may have significant cognitive advantages. Note, however, that the participating students were majority-group members, were solidly middle class in origin, and, moreover, volunteered to participate in the program. Thus the education in a second language could serve only to enrich their already stimulating environment. Recently the province of Quebec has declared French its official language. It would be interesting to study the effects of schooling on English-speaking students whose parents have not volunteered to place their children in schools where French is the language of instruction.

THINKING IN CROSS-CULTURAL CONTEXT: CLASSIFICATION

Concept behavior is a central part of the treatment of cognition; it deals with the ability of man to override the diversity of the environment and its detected features by organizing this diversity into categories (Glick, 1975):

> The category of concept describes an organizational feature of cognitive process whereby objectively discriminable stimuli are treated as being similar. This has the adaptive consequence of reducing the amount of complexity that must be dealt with and the psychological consequence of involving a level or organization that overrides and organizes discriminative abilities. (Glick, 1975, p. 596)

Considering the relation between cultural experience and classification, the universalistic approach may be more useful for perceptually based categories such as color and form, whereas a particularistic approach, which allows consideration of the impact of cultural opportunity, may be more useful for those categories which are not perceptually based. For example, if we know the number of basic color terms in a society, we can predict which colors they are (Berlin & Kay, 1969), whereas if we know the number of disease terms in a society, we can predict neither the categories nor, in our present state of knowledge, the dimensions in the domain.

There are several different foci for thinking about the relationship between cultural experience and classification. Among them are the following:

1. Classification itself as a cultural experience, which in turn has implications for cognitive processes.
2. Classifying behavior and concept attainment.
3. Natural classification systems.

Classification as Cultural Experience

One manner in which classification itself can be viewed as cultural experience with implications for cognition is exemplified by the work of Stefflre, Vales, and Morley (1966), a cross-cultural replication of a study by Lantz and Stefflre (1964). Stefflre and his associates subscribe to the idea that the organization of experience is reflected in linguistic behavior. Communication accuracy, a direct measure of codability, is linguistic behavior in which an item is described by an encoder so that another person, a decoder, will be able to pick it out from an array. Communication accuracy was found to affect memory rather than perception. They viewed memory as intrapersonal communication, a process that can be approximated by interpersonal communication, communication at two points in time using the brain as a channel, the "success" of which is measured by communication accuracy. They showed that both Mayan and Spanish speakers could accurately remember colors about which they could accurately communicate and that there were cultural differences as to which colors each group found easier to communicate about and hence easier to remember. What we do not know from their work is how communication accuracy related to the basic color categories in the two groups. It was suggested, however, in the earlier study (Lantz & Stefflre, 1964) that naming norms could perhaps be used in some way to predict *which* items will be easy to communicate and easy to remember for speakers of different languages as they communicate about different arrays of stimuli.

Rosch's (1973a) work among the Dani and the work of Cole et al. (1971) among the Kpelle provide other examples of work in which classification itself is viewed as cultural experience. In these studies, however, classification as cultural experience had implications for the *study* of cognition. Rosch took advantage of the absence of hue and form concepts among the Dani to test, via a learning experiment, her notion about natural prototypes (see discussion below for more about Rosch's work). Cole et al. (1971) investigated the validity of their concept categories for Kpelle culture to guard against ethnocentric bias in the definition of clusters. When the stimulus material and its organization proved meaningful they turned their attention to other conditions of the experimental situation. Thus they see an understanding of basic categories as necessary for the interpretation of concept learning and memory experiments.

Classifying Behavior and Concept Attainment

The investigation of classifying behavior—that is, of the attributes of objects that people select for classification—and concept attainment have been prominent concerns of Western cross-cultural psychologists. With some exceptions (e.g., Cole et al., 1971), most formal experiments have ignored natural categorizations, concepts designable by verbal behavior in natural languages. Instead, these experiments have involved artificial categories based on an experimenter's arrays of stimuli which are not related to the person's everyday environment, such as the geometric figures employed in much concept formation research. It is therefore not surprising that the work in this area is discussed in the sections of this chapter in which Westernization is an integral part of the variation of interest, e.g., formal schooling and rural–urban differences.

Natural Classification

Cultural variability in natural classification and descriptions of elements and dimensions in various domains (e.g., kinship, numeral classifiers, flora, and fauna) has been copiously documented by anthropologists (see Conklin, 1972, for a topically arranged bibliography on folk classification); important work continues in this area (e.g., Special Issue on Folk Biology, *American Ethnologist*, 1976). The work is on the whole nonempiric and noncomparative, involving neither cross-cultural nor intracultural comparisons. Interpretations have been made relating features of culture to classification, but not much empirically based attention has been given to understanding the way in which cultural experiences may influence naturally occurring categorization behavior. Rather, the tendency in anthropology during the last decade has been to treat segmentation of the world as originally arbitrary, although there has been work which has viewed cultural variation as a kind of natural cognitive experiment (Nerlove & Romney, 1967).

A series of highly suggestive papers about the classification of concrete objects have been written by Rosch (1973a, b; 1975a, b, c, d; 1976; 1977, 1978) and her associates (Mervis, Catlin, & Rosch, 1975; Rosch & Mervis, 1975; n.d.; Rosch, Mervis, Gray, Johnson, & Boyes-Braem, 1976). Although Rosch is also known for her earlier work on the Dani of New Guinea (e.g., Heider, 1971; 1972; Heider & Olivier, 1972) and although it is clear that her own cross-cultural perspective has influenced her more recent work, the work to be described is not cross-cultural. It is included here, however, because it presents fruitful ideas for which cross-cultural exploration is critical. Central to this work, are the following notions: (1) *basic level objects,* defined as categories of concrete objects at the level of abstraction which maximizes their validity—that is, they have the greatest family of resemblances to each other, the most attributes common to the members of the category, and the least attributes shared with members of other categories—and (2) *prototypes,* best examples within those categories, "the most valid of the valid." These ideas are somewhat similar to those of Berlin (1972) and other ethnobiologists.

To develop these concepts, Rosch and her associates have done an extensive series of experiments which have included looking at clusters of co-occurring attributes common to the category, sequences of motor movements common to typical use or interaction with the object, object similarity in the shape of the object, and identifiability of an average shape of objects in the class. Although they hold that the principle of category formation is universal, basic level objects for an individual, subculture, or culture must result from an *interaction* between the potential structure provided by the world and the particular emphases and state of knowledge of the people who are categorizing. However, the environment places constraints on categorizations. Human knowledge cannot provide correlational structure for concrete objects where none exists. Humans can only ignore or exaggerate correlational structures.

Rosch, then, eschews the notion still held by many anthropologists of categories as logically bounded entities in which membership is defined by the items' possession of a simple set of criterial features and in which all instances have a full and equal degree of membership. Rosch's hypothesis offers a framework for the comparison of categories across cultures and a basis for prediction of changes with culture change. Tversky (1977) proposes a new set-theoretical model for similarity that relates these concepts within a unified framework. In this model objects are represented as a collection of features; similarity is described as a feature-matching process. Thus in a formal, explicit manner he offers an explication of prototypicality and family resemblance in terms of similarity. Note, however, that neither Rosch nor Tversky has dealt with concepts whose relationship to empirical knowledge is uncertain. Socially constructed reality (e.g., of religious and logical systems) deals with the organization of thoughts with respect to each other and does not derive in any direct way, at least, from empirical knowledge.

Cross-cultural variation which may occur in the structure of the environment and the interest in and knowledge of attributes should be examined, for it is these aspects which, according to Rosch, prevent the *content* of categories from being universal. We need to know what is included in the culture's natural inventory in order to examine whether or not differences between prototypes for corresponding natural categories across cultures really represent differences in actual central tendencies of the categories. Examples of parameters of objects which could be investigated are the degree to which motor patterns are of dominant importance, the implications of knowledge for survival, the order of exposure, the frequency of encounter, and the time spent with objects per day.

Rosch's work provides us with a contrast to the efforts of many cross-cultural psychologists not only because she is concerned with natural categories but also because she is concerned with theory building. In the main, studies concerned with the importance of familiarity with objects (e.g., Irwin & McLaughlin, 1970; Irwin et al., 1974; Okonji, 1971) for performance in various sorting and classification tasks have not contributed to a theory, although they have furthered the now obvious but still important realization of how unsatisfactory it is to use Western materials and Western modes of representation to "test" Third World peoples. Rosch et al. (1976) discuss familiarity with a domain in their concern with expertise. Although the area awaits systematic study, they point out that the expert's knowledge is an exception which seems to confirm the rule of the existence of basic level objects, for expert knowledge is probably often confined to specific parts of a taxonomy, thereby creating unevenness in the categorization of that taxonomy.

With this presentation of the work of Rosch and her associates, we have a theoretical framework within which to think about some studies that have indeed addressed themselves to the issue of how cultural experiences affect natural classification. Geoghegan (1976) has demonstrated that the overall degree or tendency toward polytypy, a biological concept that refers to the systematic internal diversity of plant and animal taxa, is influenced by such factors as salience and agricultural practices, both of which have to do with motor programs and implications of knowledge for survival.

Fjellman's (1971) work addresses the relation of the order and degree of exposure to classification. She shows that among the Akamba of South Central Kenya, for a familiar sphere, that of domestic animals, children first learn the internal structure, while for a less familiar sphere, that of wild animals, they learn just the general labels. What is cognitively "unmarked," and therefore more difficult to verbalize about, is learned first. Thus, among the Akamba the class "domestic animals" provides the norm or baseline for the entire class of animals. These animals are not labeled "domestic" initially, since young children have nothing to contrast them with, not yet having knowledge of wild animals. In learning the adult cultural terminology, the children's reference point shifts. They learn the label for animals in its focal sense, first applying it only to wild animals. Only later do they extend this label to include domestic animals. In the process, wild animals become the "focal type," and thus the markedness of domestic animals is learned as a direct result of this "shift of reference." Learning higher-level features for less familiar categories enhances the development of corresponding covert terms for more familiar categories. This process was reflected in the children's performance on tasks administered by Fjellman. She found that in the familiar sphere of animals (domestic), children group by "midlevel" attributes and are unable to state higher-level common attributes, whereas in the less familiar sphere of animals (wild), the learning of features is from the top down.

Thus cultural experience alternatively may be situational in nature rather than simply cumulative. Changes in classification may occur as the life cycle progresses and yet still depend on the cultural situation which determines what gets learned first. The work of Denney (1974a, b), although not cross-cultural, goes one step further in this regard by showing that the shift need not be irreversible. She found a tendency to categorize according to functional as opposed to taxonomic criteria among young children and elderly adults, who do not experience much pressure for categorizing in any particular way. Their situation is contrasted to that of older children experiencing pressures of education and working adults experiencing pressures of occupation. She maintains that under circumstances of low pressure, functional categorization would be the most natural, since complementary items are grouped naturally in time and space.

Super, Harkness, and Baldwin (1977) suggest a validation of Denney's (1974a, b) notion that functional categorization is more natural. At the same time, their work speaks to the issue that Cole (1975) raised when he asked if an important dimension of cultural differences might rest on the variability of tasks and tools that people must deal with. The work of Super et al. relates to motor patterns which in turn relate to the structure of the environment, which is described not only by what is in that environment (nature and diversity) but also how many things are in it (quantity). The nature of experience in natural arrangements is proposed by Super et al. as a factor contributing to the results of formal experiments on categorization behavior. They present persuasive insights about two domains of experience: how people arrange physical objects in normal daily life and whether they encounter the objects as exemplars or particulars. They argue that people organize objects in order to maximize ease of both retrieval and maintenance. When there are many identical or functionally interchangeable members of a category, several related classes, and a need for choosing varying combinations of items selected from these classes, the most efficient organization of objects is by taxonomic class, such as in the standard American kitchen. Otherwise, grouping things that will be used together in physical proximity is more efficient. One example is the grouping together of tea utensils among the Kipsigis in Kenya. These utensils are always used at the same time and in the same place, and they are never used in combination with anything else:

> Cultures or subcultures that are materially simple will rarely require categorical organization, but when the immediate context does make it more efficient one will see rapid adoption, in that context, of the taxonomic grouping. Western cultures, with their vast number of things, more often require taxonomic organization for efficient functioning. (Super et al., 1977, p. 6)

It is precisely the materially simple populations which give "functional" responses on cognitive tests. In addition, the way in which these people encounter objects (i.e., frequent encounters with the same objects or with objects strongly embedded in a stable context) can be related to episodic rather than semantic storage. The psychology of test taking, which we know is affected by schooling, is joined by other cultural factors to produce the societal contrasts in test behavior and performance.

CONCLUSIONS

We should like to end, as we began, with some thoughts about the state-of-the-art of the investigation of the cognitive consequences of cultural opportunity and the directions in which we would like to see it move. First, however, it may be worthwhile to reflect on the advantages of looking across cultures in examining different opportunities rather than confining research to the various experiences extant within one culture. Cross-cultural research allows the investigator to test hypotheses in settings where there are variations in social settings, both in the extent of potential experiences and the organization of those experiences, that may never be encountered in the investigator's society. Many therefore have referred to cross-cultural research as a sort of natural laboratory. It cannot be considered a panacea, however, as we pointed out earlier, particularly with regard to the matter of selectivity discussed in the opening pages. To restate briefly, those who "take advantage" of various opportunities may constitute a select group, making it impossible to evaluate whether cognitive outcomes are due to opportunities or are mirroring a priori factors which channeled certain individuals into certain opportunity pathways. This dilemma, in different forms, pertained to many of the investigations reviewed here. For example, do children's chore performances accelerate their cognitive development in certain ways, or do mothers assign specific children to specific chores, having detected these children's prior aptitudes? Are urban children more articulate and better able to reason abstractly compared to rural children, or are their families of origin already different, as evidenced by their having chosen to migrate, in ways that would encourage children's development in just those ways? Does school affect children's intellectual abilities in specific ways, or do parents only choose to send bright, mature youngsters to school? Super (1977) has attacked the problem of selectivity in schools by attempting to measure such background variables of schooled versus non-schooled children as degree of Westernization and parental educational level. He also instituted a short-term longitudinal study, testing the "treatment" group of schooled children and the "control" group of nonschooled children periodically over the course of the first year of treatment. The documentation of cognitive improvements at various stages *along* an opportunity pathway provides a powerful argument that the changes are related to having followed that pathway. This strategy was also followed by Scribner and Cole (1977b), who showed that memory for sentences of *advanced* Vai literates far exceeded that of Vai literacy *beginners.*

We began our literature search with the intention of considering only those studies which attempted to measure the "cultural opportunities" side as well as the "cognitive consequences" side of the question. In general we have been encouraged by the large and increasing body of research which reflects efforts in that direction. Especially noteworthy are Herzog's (1974) and Weisner's (1970; 1973; 1976) sample selection procedures, Super's (1977) large-scale study of schooling effects, and the Scribner and Cole (1977a) research on effects of literacy. These studies illustrate a point we wish to emphasize: the importance of providing a precise and full description of the cultural experience of interest in its social context. Only with detailed knowledge about components of activities and how they fit together in a particular society will it be possible to assess whether or not specific cognitive skills were stimulated, enhanced, or encouraged and hence to make specific matches between "cultural opportunities" and "cognitive consequences." This knowledge is especially relevant for studies in the areas of schooling effects and daily activities.

Scribner and Cole's (1977a) research on effects of literacy utilized anthropological techniques of description to achieve this purpose. They assembled essentially an ethnography of literacy as it was acquired and used among the Vai. In so doing, they were able to design measures of cognitive consequences that "fit" with the abilities fostered by each distinct literacy tradition.

Future researchers might also want to consider adapting the methods of investigators whose work is in the psychological tradition. For example, White and Watts (1973) were concerned with conceptualizing and measuring the cognitive demands implicit in the young child's everyday environment and social interactions. They began their work having already identified two groups of preschoolers who were rated as having attained very high levels of competence or lower than average levels of competence. The corresponding "successful" and "unsuccessful" families were then observed over 26 months in natural settings as the mothers interacted with infant siblings of the preschoolers. From these naturalistic observations, dimensions of interactive competence of mothers and cognitively stimulating aspects of the environment were induced. Despite problems involving the use of middle-class observers, this research is an interesting effort to conceptualize and measure the full range of children's social experiences and experiences with the environment which might stimulate cognitive development.

The insights and methods of psychological ecologists (e.g., Barker & Gump, 1964; Barker & Schoggen, 1973; Barker & Wright, 1955) could potentially contribute both to the measurement of the interplay between micro-, meso-, exo-, and macrolevels and to the understanding of cognitive demands inherent in different settings. A good example of the latter would be the concept of *maintenance circuits* of behavior settings. Maintenance circuits generate pressures on individual actors to ensure that the essential roles of a behavior setting will be filled. Thus small schools, for example, were characterized as "undermanned" compared to large schools with a corresponding increase in the amount and diversity of responsibilities of each inhabitant in the small school and, potentially, a greater cognitive demand on her or him as well (Barker & Gump, 1962). Devereux (1977), however, sounds a note of caution in pointing out that the analytical techniques employed in the book *Qualities of Community Life* (Barker & Schoggen, 1973), which was intended to be a culmination of the previous work of Barker and his associates, obliterate the interrelations among mesosystems within a habitat.

Another effort currently underway is explicitly concerned with cross-cultural applicability but may be limited in use to an important, but insufficient, group of countries—the Westernized, modernized, industrialized nations (Nerlove, Bronfenbrenner, Blum, Robinson, & Koel, 1977). The goal of their "transcultural" code is a framework for the analysis of molar activities of children and their caretakers in natural contexts. Such a framework should provide clues to the kind of abilities, both cognitive and sociocognitive, that people might be expected to display.

"Cognitive consequences," the dependent variable in this review, also deserves critical attention. We have already discussed some of the issues of measurement, namely, the testing situation and differential familiarity with testing materials. It appears that consciousness has been raised and progress has been made with regard to these issues; however, we should like to point out a problematic tendency among researchers investigating cognition cross-culturally: their choice of measures of cognitive development. Two especially unsatisfactory approaches include the "shotgun technique," whereby a variety of cognitive measures which are seemingly unrelated to one another are administered, and the "grab bag technique," in which a particular cognitive skill is measured with little or no attempt to specify an appropriate match between the independent variable being considered and a corresponding cognitive consequence. Too often researchers seem willing to use a measure because it has been reliable in other settings. In addition, they tend to assume that because certain cognitive skills are "basic" they should be affected by whatever " cultural opportunity" is under investigation.

Both the "shotgun" and the "grab bag" approaches reflect the exploratory nature of the work in this area and its frequent lack of theoretical underpinnings. One avenue for bringing in theoretical concerns is to attend to native conceptions of intelligence. By considering native theories, we become sensitive to the definition of intelligence as an adaptation to real life problems and hence as multilithic. The position taken by A. Brown (1977) and Serpell (1977) is that "one cannot sensibly specify intelligence outside of the culture with which it is interacting" (Brown, 1977). In looking to native theories for guidance, however, one must beware of taking an extreme position of cultural relativism and thereby losing the ability to make comparisons across cultures. It is our belief that there are some common features of human adaptive behavior even across diverse living conditions or at the very least that one may be able to make large groupings of societies having such common features. Then, too, we may be interested in describing and comparing the interrelations between beliefs and behavior within a culture. Ultimately, perhaps, the "goodness of fit" between specified characteristics of intelligence and the cultural opportunities to acquire and practice the requisite skills could be compared crossculturally.

A second avenue for achieving theoretical relevance is to move beyond describing differences or demonstrating similarities in cognitive abilities and to consciously set oneself the goal of theory building. One step in this direction is to focus on questions of *process*. Research in the area of bilingualism has moved in that direction, with investigators designing studies to illuminate what mechanisms are involved in the association of the acquisition of a second language and increased mental flexibility. Research in the area of cognitive socialization hypothesizes that attributes of maternal teaching styles shape children's cognitive outcomes, with maternal behavior the process being investigated. As pointed out earlier, however, this research has yet to include the child as a member of the mother–child dyad or to consider that dyad as a system.

A recent, intriguing paper from Price-Williams (1977) attempts to lay out a program of research which would also be a systematic effort at theory building. Price-Williams calls for cross-cultural studies in the area of metacognition, a relatively new and exciting problem tackled by psychologists (e.g., A. Brown, 1977). He attempts to draw points of articulation between metacognition and concerns of ethnoscience, thus creating a new area of ethnopsychology. The focus of research would be to find out "what various cultural groups know about their own knowing, how they form deliberate strategies of memorizing, how they deliberately learn, how they instruct children to pay attention to, and so on." (1977, p. 7).

To summarize, mere documentation of cultural differences needs to be replaced by a thoughtful, substantive attempt to more accurately specify what is causing those differences. The "shotgun" and "grab bag" approaches need to be replaced by theories about process. In a word, more cognitive effort needs to be expended on research in cross-cultural cognition.

ACKNOWLEDGMENTS

We want to thank W. W. Lambert for inspiring us with his boldly innovative thoughts on this topic and for suggesting references. We also wish to thank Ronald Gallimore, Ruth and Robert Munroe, Marion Potts, and Thomas Weisner for their careful reading and thoughtful comments on this chapter.

NOTES

1. But see Fjellman (1971) for evidence that this is an artifact of testing; also Rosch and Mervis (n.d.) for discussion of the unnatural demands made by artificial arrays used in testing classification abilities.

2. Since color is immediately perceivable information, classification using color as the sorting basis is considered to involve less complex mental "work" than classification based on other attributes such as function, which must first be abstracted from the array. Similarly, ability to reclassify arrays and verbalize principles indicates mental flexibility.

3. Indeed such a phenomenon may account for the relative success of a whole-word versus a phonics approach to learning to read found among Hawaiian Creoles (Au, 1976).

REFERENCES

Adjei, K. Influence of specific maternal occupation and behavior on Piagetian cognitive development. In P. R. Dasen (Ed.), *Piagetian psychology*. New York: Gardner, 1977.

Altman, I. Privacy: A conceptual analysis. *Environment and Behavior,* 1976, *8,* 7–29.

Altman, I. Privacy regulation: Culturally universal or culturally specific? *Journal of Social Issues,* 1977, *33,* 66–84.

Au, K. H. *keep reading research: 1972–1975* (Technical Report No. 57). 1976.

Au, K. H., & Speidel, G. E. *Hawaii Creole speakers' listening comprehension abilities in Standard English and Hawaiian Creole* (Technical Report No. 53). Honolulu: Kamehameha Schools, Kamehameha Early Education Program, 1976.

Bain, B. C. Towards an integration of Piaget and Vygotsky: Bilingual considerations. *Linguistics,* 1975, *160,* 5–20.

Barik, H. C., & Swain, M. A longitudinal study of bilingualism and cognitive development. *International Journal of Psychology,* 1976, *11,* 251–263.

Barker, R. G., & Gump, P. V. *Big school, small school.* Stanford, Calif.: Stanford University Press, 1964.

Barker, R. G., & Schoggen, P. *Qualities of community life.* San Francisco: Jossey-Bass, 1973.

Barker, R. G., & Wright, H. F. *The midwest and its children.* New York: Harper & Row, 1955.

Barry, H., III, & Paxson, L. M. Infancy and early childhood: Cross-cultural codes. *Ethnology,* 1971, *10,* 466–508.

Bates, E., Benigni, L., Bretherton, I., Camaioni, L., & Voltera, V. From gesture to the first word: On cognitive and social prerequisites. In M. Lewis & L. A. Rosenblum (Eds.), *Interaction, conversation, and the development of language.* New York: John Wiley & Sons, 1977.

Bee, H. L., Van Egeren, L. F., Streissguth, A. P., Nyman, B. A., & Leckie, M. S. Social class differences in maternal teaching strategies and speech patterns. *Developmental Psychology,* 1969, *1,* 726–734.

Ben-Zeev, S. The influence of bilingualism on cognitive development and cognitive strategy. *Child Development,* 1977, *48,* 1009–1018.

Berlin, B. Speculations on the growth of ethnobotanical nomenclature. *Language in Society,* 1972, *1,* 51–86.

Berlin, B., & Kay, P. *Basic color terms: Their universality and evolution.* Berkeley: University of California Press, 1969.

Berry, J. W. Temne and Eskimo perceptual skills. *International Journal of Psychology,* 1966, *1,* 207–299.

Binet, A., & Simon, T. *The development of intelligence in children* (E. S. Kite, trans.). New York: Arno, 1973 [Originally published in 1916].

Bovet, M. C. Cognitive processes among illiterate children and adults. In J. W. Berry & P. R. Dasen (Eds.), *Culture and cognition: Readings in cross-cultural psychology.* London: Methuen, 1974.

Bronfenbrenner, U. Toward an experimental ecology of human development. *American Psychologist,* 1977, *32,* 513–531.

Brown, A. *Knowing when, where, and how to remember: A problem of metacognition* (Technical Report No. 74). Urbana-Champaign: University of Illinois, 1977.

Brown, C. Folk botanical life forms: Their universality and growth. *American Anthropologist,* 1977, *79,* 317–343.

Bruck, M., Lambert, W. E., & Tucker, G. R. *Cognitive and attitudinal consequences of bilingual schooling: The St. Lambert project through grade six.* Unpublished manuscript, 1973.

Bruck, M., Lambert, W. E., & Tucker, G. R. Bilingual schooling through the elementary grades: The St. Lambert project at grade 7. *Language Learning,* in press.

Carringer, D. C. Creative thinking abilities of Mexican youth: The relationship of bilingualism. *Journal of Cross-Cultural Psychology,* 1974, *5,* 492–584.

Chafe, W. L. *Meaning and the structure of language.* Chicago: University of Chicago Press, 1970.

Charlesworth, W. R. Human intelligence as adaptation: An ethological approach. In L. Resnick (Ed.), *The nature of intelligence.* Hillsdale, N.J.: Erlbaum, 1976.

Ciborowski, T., & Choy, S. Non-standard English and free recall: An exploratory study. *Journal of Cross-Cultural Psychology,* 1974, *5,* 271–281.

Cohen, R. Conceptual styles, culture conflict, and nonverbal tests of intelligence. *American Anthropologist,* 1969, *71,* 828–855.

Cole, M. An ethnographic psychology of cognition. In R. Brislin, S. Bochner, & W. J. Lonner, (Eds.), *Cross-cultural perspectives on learning.* New York: Halsted Press, 1975.

Cole, M., & Bruner, J. S. Cultural differences and inferences about psychological processes. *American Psychologist,* 1971, *26,* 867–876.

Cole, M., & Gay, J. Culture and memory. *American Anthropologist,* 1972, *74,* 1066–1084.

Cole, M., Gay, J., Glick, J. A., & Sharp, D. W. *The cultural context of learning and thinking.* New York: Basic Books, 1971.

Cole, M., & Scribner, S. *Culture and thought.* New York: John Wiley & Sons, 1974.

Cole, M., Sharp, D. W., & Lave, C. The cognitive consequences of education: Some empirical evidence and theoretical misgivings. *Urban Review,* 1976, *9,* (4), 218–223.

Conklin, H. C. Folk classification: A topically arranged bibliography of contemporary and background references through 1971. New Haven: Yale University, Department of Anthropology, 1972.

Cummins, J. *Educational implications of mother tongue maintenance in minority language groups.* Paper presented at Conference on Second Language Acquisition, College Universitaire St. Jean, University of Alberta, September 1977.

Cummins, J. Metalinguistic development of children in bilingual education programs. In M. Paradis (Ed.), *The Fourth LACUS Forum.* Columbia, S.C.: Hornbeam Press, 1978.

Cummins, J. & Gulutsan, M. Bilingual education and cognition. *Alberta Journal of Educational Research,* 1974, *20,* 259–269.

Cummins, J., & Gulutsan, M. Set, objectification and second language learning. *International Journal of Psychology,* 1975, *10,* 91–100.

Dasen, P. R. Cross-cultural Piagetian research: A summary. *Journal of Cross-cultural Psychology,* 1972 *3,* 23–29.

Dawson, J. L. M. Cultural and physiological influences upon spatial-perceptual processes in West Africa; Part I. *International Journal of Psychology,* 1967, *2,* 115–125.

Denney, N. W. Classification criteria in middle and old age. *Developmental Psychology,* 1974, *10,* 901–906. (a)

Denney, N. W. Evidence for developmental changes in categorization criteria for children and adults. *Human Development,* 1974, *17,* 41–53. (b)

Deutch, L. E., Perkins, R. D., Hays, D. G., Schneiderman, E. I., & White, M. J. *Taste and touch: In search of basic terms.* Unpublished manuscript, State University of New York at Buffalo, n.d.

Devereux, E. C. *Psychological ecology: A critical analysis and appraisal.* Unpublished manuscript, 1977.

Diebold, R. A. The consequences of early bilingualism in cognitive development and personality formation. In E. Norbeck, D. Price-Williams, & W. M. McCord (Eds.), *The study of personality: An interdisciplinary appraisal.* New York: Holt, Rinehart & Winston, 1968.

Doob, L. Eidetic images among the Ibo. *Ethnology,* 1964, *3,* 357–363.

Dube, E. F. *A cross-cultural study of the relationship between "intelligence" level and story recall.* Unpublished doctoral disseration, Cornell University, 1977.

Dulay, J., & Burt, M. Goofing: An indicator of children's second language learning strategies. *Language Learning,* 1972, *22,* 235–252.

Dulay, J., & Burt, M. Natural sequences in child's second language acquisition. *Language Learning,* 1974, *24,* 37–53. (a)

Dulay, J. & Burt, M. A new perspective on the creative construction process in child's second language acquisition. *Language Learning,* 1974, *24,* 253–278. (b)

Ember, C. Cross-cultural cognitive studies. In B. J. Siegel (Ed.), *Annual review of anthropology* (Vol. 6). Palo Alto: Stanford University Press, 1977.

Engle, P. L. The language debate: Education in first or second language? In P. Sanday (Ed.), *Anthropology and the public interest.* New York: Academic Press, 1976.

Evans, J. L., & Segall, M. H. Learning to classify by color and by function: A study of concept-discovery by Ganda children. *Journal of Social Psychology,* 1969, *77,* 35–53.

Farrell, T. J. Literacy, the basics, and all that jazz. *College English,* 1977, *39,* 443–459.

Feshbach, N. D. Cross-cultural studies of teaching styles in four-year-olds and their mothers. In A. Pick (Ed.), *Minnesota symposia on child psychology* (Vol. 7). Minneapolis: University of Minnesota Press, 1973.

Fishman, J. A. Bilingual education: The state of the social science inquiry. In *Bilingual education: Current perspectives* (Vol. 1). *Social Sciences.* Arlington: Center for Applied Linguistics, 1977.

Fjellman, J. C. *The myth of primitive mentality: A study of semantic acquisition and modes of categorization in Akamba children of South Central Kenya.* Unpublished doctoral disseration, Stanford University, 1971.

Folk biology. Special issue, *American Ethnologist,* 1976, *3,* (3).

Gallimore, R., Tharp, R. G., & Speidel, G. E. The relationship of sibling caretaking and attentiveness to a peer tutor. *American Educational Research Journal*, 1978, *15*, 267–273.

Geoghegan, W. H. Polytypy in folk biological taxonomies. *American Ethnologist*, 1976, *3*, 469–480.

Gewirtz, J. L., & Gewirtz, H. B. Stimulus conditions, infant behaviors, and social learning in four Israeli child-rearing environments: A preliminary report illustrating differences in environment and behavior between the "only" and the "youngest" child. In B. M. Foss (Ed.), *Determinants of infant behavior* (Vol. 3). New York: John Wiley & Sons, 1965.

Ginsburg, H. *The myth of the disadvantaged child.* New York: Prentice-Hall, 1972.

Gladwin, T. *East is a big bird.* Cambridge, Mass.: Harvard University Press, 1970.

Glick, J. Cognitive developments in cross-cultural perspective. In F. D. Horowitz (Ed.), *Review of child development research* (Vol. 4). Chicago: University of Chicago Press, 1975.

Goodnow, J. J. A test of milieu differences with some of Piaget's tasks. *Psychological Monographs*, 1962, *76*, (36, Whole No. 555).

Goodnow, J. J., & Bethon, G. Piaget's tasks: The effects of schooling and intelligence. *Child Development*, 1966, *37*, 573–582.

Goodnow, J. J. The nature of intelligent behavior: Questions raised by cross-cultural studies. In L. B. Resnick (Ed.), *The nature of intelligence.* Hillsdale, N.J.: Erlbaum, 1976.

Goody, J. Evolution & communication. *British Journal of Sociology*, 1973, *24*, 1–12.

Goody, J., & Watt, I. The consequences of literacy. *Comparative Studies in Society and History*, 1963, *5*, 304–345.

Gray, C. R., & Gummerman, K. The enigmatic eidetic image: A critical examination of the methods, data, and theories. *Psychological Bulletin*, 1975, *82*, 383–407.

Greenfield, P. M. On culture and conservation. In J. Bruner, R. Olver, & P. Greenfield (Eds.), *Studies in cognitive growth.* New York: John Wiley & Sons, 1966.

Greenfield, P. M. *Oral or written language: The consequences for cognitive development in Africa and the United States.* Paper presented at the meeting of the American Education Association, Chicago, February 1968.

Greenfield, P. M., & Bruner, J. Culture and cognitive growth. In D. Goslin (Ed.), *Handbook of socialization theory and research.* Chicago: Rand McNally, 1969.

Greenfield, P. M., & Childs, C. Weaving, color terms, and pattern representation: Cultural influences and cognitive development among the Zinacantecos. *Interamerican Journal of Psychology*, in press

Grotevant, H. D., Scarr, S., & Weinberg, R. A. Intellectual development in family constellations with adopted and natural children: A test of the Zajonc and Markus model. *Child Development*, 1977, *48*, 1699–1703.

Harkness, S. Universal aspects of learning color codes: A study in two cultures. *Ethos*, 1973, *1*, 175–200.

Harkness, S., & Super, C. Why are African children so hard to test? In L. L. Adler (Ed.), Issues in cross-cultural research. *Annals of the New York Academy of Sciences*, 1977, *285*, 326–331.

Harkness, S. Cultural variation in mothers' language. *Child Language*, 1975, *27*, 495–498.

Heider, E. R. "Focal" color areas and the development of color names. *Developmental Psychology*, 1971, *4*, 447–455.

Heider, E. R. Universals in color naming and memory. *Journal of Experimental Psychology*, 1972, *93*, 10–20.

Heider, E. R., & Olivier, D. O. The structure of the color space in naming and memory for two languages. *Cognitive Psychology*, 1972, *3*, 337–354.

Herzog, J. D. Father absence and boys' school performance in Barbados. *Human Organization,* 1974, *33* (1), 71–83.

Hess, R. D., & Shipman, V. C. Early experience and the socialization of cognitive modes in children. In J. P. Hill (Ed.), *Minnesota symposium on child psychology* (Vol. 1). Minneapolis: University of Minnesota Press, 1967.

Hess, R. D., & Shipman, V. C. Maternal influences upon early learning: The cognitive environments of urban preschool children. In R. D. Hess & R. M. Baer (Eds.), *Early education.* Chicago: Aldine, 1968.

Hollos, M. Logical Operations and role-taking abilities in two cultures: Norway and Hungary. *Child Development,* 1975, *46,* 638–649.

Hollos, M., & Cowan, P. A. Social isolation and cognitive development. Logical operations and role-taking abilities in three Norwegian social settings. *Child Development,* 1973, *44,* 630–641.

Holtzman, W. H., Diaz-Guerrero, R., & Swartz, J. D. *Personality development in two cultures.* Austin: University of Texas Press, 1975.

Hudson, W. Pictorial depth perception in sub-cultural groups in Africa. *Journal of Social Psychology,* 1960, *52,* 183–208

Hunt, J. M. *Intelligence and Experience.* New York: Ronald Press, 1961.

Hyman, H. H., Wright, C. R., & Reed, J. S. *The enduring effects of education.* Chicago: University of Chicago Press, 1975.

Ianco-Worrell, A. *Bilingualism and cognitive development.* Unpublished doctoral dissertation, Cornell University, 1970.

Ianco-Worrell, A. D. Bilingualism and cognitive development. *Child Development,* 1972, *43,* 1390–1400

Irwin, H. M., & McLaughlin, D. H. Ability and preference in category sorting by Mano school children to adults. *Journal of Social Psychology,* 1970, *82,* 15–24.

Irwin, H. M., Schafer, G. N., & Feiden, C. P. Emic and unfamiliar category sorting of Mano farmers and U.S. undergraduates. *Journal of Cross-Cultural Psychology,* 1974, *5,* 407–423.

Istomina, Z. M. The development of voluntary memory in preschool-age children. *Soviet Psychology,* 1975, *13,* 5–64.

John, V. P., & Horner, V. M. Bilingualism and the Spanish-speaking child. In F. Williams (Ed.), *Language and poverty.* Chicago, Markham, 1970.

Jordan, C. *Maternal teaching, peer teaching and school adaptation in an urban Hawaiin population.* Paper presented at meeting of the Society for Cross-Cultural Research, Michigan State University, East Lansing, February 1977.

Kagan, J., & Klein, R. E. Cross-cultural perspectives on early development. *American Psychologist,* 1973, *28,* 947–961

Kamara, A. *Cognitive development among Themne children of Sierra Leone.* Unpublished doctoral dissertation, University of Illinois at Urbana-Champaign, 1975.

Keats, D. M., & Keats, J. A. The effect of language on concepts acquisition in bilingual children. *Journal of Cross-Cultural Psychology,* 1974, *5,* 80–99.

Kirk, L. Maternal and subcultural influence on cognitive growth rate: The Ga case. In P. R. Dasen (Ed.), *Cross-cultural Piagetian psychology.* New York: Gardner Press, 1977.

Kirk, L., & Burton, M. Maternal kinesic behavior and cognitive development in the child. *Annals of the New York Academy of Sciences,* 1977, *285,* 326–331.

Klein, R., Freeman, H. E., & Millet, R. Psychological text performance and indigenous conceptions of intelligence. *Joournal of Psychology,* 1973, *84,* 219–222.

Klein, R. E., Freeman, H. E., Spring, B., Nerlove, S. B., & Yarbrough, C. Cognitive test performance and indigenous conceptions of intelligence. *Journal of Psychology,* 1976, *93,* 273–279.

Lambert, W. E. Psychological studies of the interdependencies of the bilingual's two languages. In J. Puhvel (Ed.), *Substance and structure of language*. Berkeley: University of California Press, 1969.

Lambert, W. E. culture and language as factors in learning and education. In A. Wolfgang (Ed.), *Education of immigrant students*. Toronto: Ontario Institute for Studies in Education, 1975.

Lambert, W. E., Ignatow, M., & Krauthamer, M. Bilingual organization in free recall. *Journal of Verbal Learning and Verbal Behavior*, 1968, *7*, 207–214.

Lambert, W. E., & Tucker, G. R. *Bilingual education of children: The St. Lambert experiment*. Rowley, Mass.: Newburg House, 1972.

Landry, R. G. A. A comparison of second language learners and monolinguals on divergent thinking tasks at the elementary school level. *Modern Language Journal*, 1974, *58*, 10–15.

Lantz, D., & Stefflre, V. Language and cognition revisited. Journal of Abnormal and Social Psychology, 1964, *69*, 472–481.

Lave, J. *Cognitive consequences of traditional apprenticeship training in West Africa*. Unpublished manuscript, n.d.

Leiderman, P. H., & Leiderman, G. F. Affective and cognitive consequences of polymatric infant care in the East African highlands. In A. Pick (Ed.), *Minnesoata symposia on child psychology* (Vol. 8). Minneapolis: University of Minnesota Press, 1974.

Lemon, N. Linguistic development and conceptualization: A bilingual study. *Journal of Cross-Cultural Psychology*, 1975, *6*, 173–188.

Leopold, W. F. *Speech development of a bilingual child* (4 vols.). Evanston, Ill.: Northwestern University Press, 1939–1949.

LeVine, R. A., Klein, N. H., & Owen, C. R. Father-child relationships and changing life-styles in Ibadan, Nigeria. In H. Miner (Ed.), *The city in modern Africa*. New York: Praeger, 1967.

LeVine, R. A., & Price-Williams, D. R. Children's kinship concepts: Cognitive development and early experience among the Hausa. *Ethnology*, 1974, *10*, 25–44.

Lewin, K. *A dynamic theory of personality*. New York: McGraw-Hill, 1935.

Lewin, K. *Problems of topological psychology*. New York: McGraw-Hill, 1936.

Lewin, K. *Resolving social conflict*. New York: Harper, 1948.

Lewin, K. *Field theory in social science*. New York: Harper, 1951.

Lewis, M., & Wilson, C. D. Infant development in lower-class American families. *Human Development*, 1972, *15*, 112–127.

Liedtke, W. W., & Nelson, L. D. Concept formation and bilingualism. *Alberta Journal of Educational Research*, 1968, *14*, 225–232.

Luria, A. K. Towards the problem of the historical nature of psychological processes. *International Journal of Psychology*, 1971, *6*, 259–272.

MacNamara, J. *Bilingualism and primary education: A study of Irish experience*. Edinburgh: Edinburgh University Press, 1966.

MacNamara, J. Bilingualism and thought. In J. E. Alatis (Ed.), Report of the twenty-first annual meeting on linguistics and language studies. *Georgetown Monograph Series on Language & Linguistics* (Vol. 23). Washington, D.C.: Georgetown University Press, 1970.

Mahoney, M. J. Reflections on the cognitive-learning trend in psychotherapy. *American Psychologist*, 1977, *32*, 5–13.

Meacham, J. A. Patterns of memory ability in two cultures. *Developmental Psychology*, 1975, *11*, 50–53.

Mermelstein, E., & Shulman, L. Lack of journal schooling and the acquisition of conservation. *Child Development*, 1967, *38*, 39–53.

Mervis, C., Catlin, J., & Rosch, E. Development of the structure of color categories. *Developmental Psychology*, 1975, *11*, 54–60.

Miller, R. J. Cross-cultural research in the perception of pictorial materials. *Psychological Bulletin,* 1973, *80,* 135–150.

Modiano, N. *Indian education in the Chiapas Highlands.* New York: Holt, Rinehart & Winston, 1973.

Mundy-Castle, A. C. Social and technological intelligence in Western and non-Western cultures. In I. Pilowsky (Ed.), *Cultures in collision.* Adelaide: Australian National Association for Mental Health, 1975.

Mundy-Castle, A. C., & Anglin, J. Looking strategies in infants. In L. J. Stone, H. T. Smith, & L. B. Murphy (Eds.), *The competent infant.* London: Tavistock, 1974.

Mundy-Castle, A. C., & Okonji, M. O. *Mother-infant interaction in Nigeria.* Paper presented at Third International Association of Cross-Cultural Psychology Congress, Tilburg, Holland, July 1976.

Munroe, R. H., & Munroe, R. L. Infant care and childhood performance in East Africa. Paper presented a the biennial meeting of the Society for Research in Child Development. Denver, April 1975.

Munroe, R. H., & Munroe, R. L. Compliance socialization and short-term memory in an East African society. *Journal of Social Psychology,* 1978, *104,* 135–136.

Munroe, R. L., & Munroe, R. H. Effect of environmental experience on spatial ability in an East African society. *Journal of Social Psychology,* 1971, *83,* 15–22

Munroe, R. L., & Munroe, R. H. *Cross-cultural human development.* Monterey, Calif.: Brooks/Cole, 1975.

Munroe, R. L., & Munroe, R. H. Land, labor and the child's cognitive performance among the Logoli. *American Ethnologist,* 1977, *4,* 309–320.

Munroe, R. L., Munroe, R. H., & Daniels, R. E. Relation of subsistence economy to a cognitive task in two East African societies. *Journal of Social Psychology,* 1976, *98,* 133–134.

Naroll, R. What have we learned from cross-cultural surveys? *American Anthropologist,* 1970, *72,* 1227–1288.

Neisser, U. General, academic, and artificial intelligence. In L. Resnick (Ed.), *The nature of intelligence.* New York: Erlbaum, 1976.

Nerlove, S. B., Bronfenbrenner, U., Blum, K., Robinson, J., & Koel, A. *Transcultural code of molar activities of children and caretakers.* Paper presented at Conference on Research Perspectives in the Ecology of Human Development, Ithaca, N.Y., August 1977.

Nerlove, S. B., Munroe, R. H., & Munroe, R. L. Effect of environmental experience on spatial ability: A replication. *Journal of Social Psychology,* 1971, *84,* 3–10.

Nerlove, S. B., Roberts, J. M., & Klein, R. E. Dimensions of *listura* ("smartness"): Community judgments of rural Guatemalan children. In P. Draper (Chair), Experiential correlates of cognitive abilities. Symposium presented at the biennial meeting of Society for Research in Child Development, Denver, April 1975.

Nerlove, S. B., Roberts, J. M., Klein, R. E., Yarbrough, C., & Habicht, J. P. Natural indicators of cognitive ability. *Ethos,* 1974, *2,* 265–295.

Nerlove, S., & Romney, A. K. Sibling terminology and cross-sex behavior. *American Anthropologist,* 1967, *69,* 179–87.

Nerlove, S. B., & Walters, A. S. Pooling intracultural variation: Toward empirical statements of community consensus. *Ethnology,* 1977, *16,* 427–441.

Nyiti, R. M. The development of conservation in the Meru children of Tanzania. *Child Development,* 1976, *47,* 1122–1129.

Okonji, M. O. Differential effects of rural and urban upbringing on the development of cognitive styles. *International Journal of Psychology,* 1969, *4,* 293–305.

Okonji, M. O. The effects of familiarity on classification. *Journal of Cross-Cultural Psychology,* 1971, *2,* 39–49.

Olson, D. R. Culture, technology, and intellect. In L. Resnick (Ed.), *The nature of intelligence.* Hillsdale, N.J.: Erlbaum, 1976.

Orata, P. T. The Iloilo experiment in education through the vernacular. In *Monographs on Fundamental Education VIII.* Paris: UNESCO, 1953.

Peal, E., & Lambert, W. E. The relation of bilingualism to intelligence. *Psychological Monographs,* 1962, *76* (27, Whole No. 546).

Piaget, J. Development and learning. In R. E. Ripple & V. N. Rockcastle (Eds.), *Piaget rediscovered.* Ithaca, N.Y.: Cornell University Press, 1964.

Pick, A. D. *The games experimenters play: A review of methods and concepts in cross-cultural studies of cognition and development.* Unpublished manuscript, University of Minnesota, 1974.

Pollnac, R. B., & Jahn, G. Culture & memory revisited: The example from Buganda. *Journal of Cross-Cultural Psychology, 1976, 7,* 73–86.

Posner, J. K. *The development of mathematical knowledge among Baolé and Dioula children in Ivory Coast.* Unpublished doctoral dissertation, Cornell University, 1978.

Precourt, W. E. Initiation ceremonies and secret societies as education institutions. In R. W. Brislin, S. Bochner, & W. J. Lonner (Eds.), *Cross-cultural perspectives in learning.* New York: Halsted Press, 1975.

Price-Williams, D. R. A study concerning concepts of conservation of quantities among primitive children. *Acta Psychologica.* 1961, *18* 297–305.

Price-Williams, D. R. *Explorations in cross-cultural psychology.* San Francisco: Chandler & Sharp, 1975.

Price-Williams, D. R. *An approach to the study of deutero-cognition.* Paper presented at the 76th Annual Meeting of the American Anthropological Association, Houston, November 1977.

Price-Williams, D., Gordon, W., & Ramirez, M. Skill and conservation: A study of pottery-making children. *Developmental Psychology,* 1969, *1,* 769.

Rogoff, B. *Mother's teaching style and child memory: A Highland Guatemala study.* Paper presented at the biennial meeting of the Society for Research in Child Development, New Orleans, March 1977.

Rogoff, B., Sellers, M. J., Pirrotta, N. F., Fox, N., & White, S. H. Age of assignment of roles and responsibilities to children: A cross-cultural study. *Human Development,* 1975, *18,* 353–369.

Rosch, E. H. Natural categories. *Cognitive Psychology,* 1973, *4,* 328–350.(a)

Rosch, E. On the internal structure of perceptual and semantic categories. In T. Moore (Ed.), *Cognitive development and the acquisition of language.* New York: Academic Press, 1973. (b)

Rosch, E. Universals and cultural specifics in human categorization. In R. Brislin, S. Bochner, & W. Lonner (Eds.), *Cross-cultural perspectives on learning.* New York: Halsted Press, 1975. (a)

Rosch, E. Cognitive reference points. *Cognitive Psychology,* 1975, *1* 532–547. (b)

Rosch, E. Cognitive representations of semantic categories. *Journal of Experimental Psychology: General,* 1975, *104,* (3), 192–233. (c)

Rosch, E. The nature of mental coders for color categories. *Journal of Experimental Psychology: Human Perception & Performance,* 1975, *1,* 303–322. (d)

Rosch, E. Human categorization. In N. Warren (Ed.), *Advances in cross-cultural psychology* (Vol. 1). London: Academic Press, 1977.

Rosch, E. Principles of categorization. In E. Rosch & B. Lloyd (Eds.), *Cognition and categorization.* Hillsdale, N.J.: Erlbaum, 1978.

Rosch, E., & Mervis, C. B. Family resemblances: Studies in the internal structure of categories. *Cognitive Psychology,* 1975, *7,* 573–605

Rosch, E., & Mervis, C. B. *Children's sorting: A reinterpretation based on the nature of abstraction in natural categories.* Unpublished manuscript, n.d.

Rosch, E., Mervis, C. B., Gray, W., Johnson, P., & Boyes-Braem, P. Basic objects in natural categories. *Cognitive Psychology,* 1976, *8,* 382–439

Rosenberg, M. *The dancer from the dance: An investigation of the contributions of microanalysis to an understanding of parental socialization effects.* Paper presented at Conference on Research Perspectives in the Ecology of Human Development, Ithaca, N.Y., August 1977.

Rubenstein, R. H. *Personal communication,* January 4, 1977.

Salvador-Burris, J. *Childrearing factors related to children's cognitive performance in urban Philippines.* Paper read at the 6th Annual Meeting of the Society for Cross-Cultural Research, East Lansing, Michigan, February 1977.

Schmidt, W. H. O., & Nzimande, A. Cultural differences in color/form preference and in classificatory behavior. *Human Development,* 1970, *13,* 140–148

Scott, S. *The relation of divergent thinking to bilingualism: Cause or effect?* Unpublished research report, McGill University, 1973.

Scribner, S. Developmental aspects of categorized recall in a West African society. *Cognitive Psychology,* 1974, *6,* 475–494.

Scribner, S. Modes of thinking and ways of speaking: Culture and logic reconsidered. In R. O. Freedle (Ed.), *Discourse production and comprehension.* Norwood, N.J.: Ablex, 1978.

Scribner, S., & Cole, M. Cognitive consequences of formal and informal education. *Science,* 1973, *182,* 553–559.

Scribner, S., & Cole, M. *Unpackaging literacy.* Paper prepared for NIE Conference on Writing, Los Angeles, June 1977. (a)

Scribner, S., & Cole, M. *Cognitive consequences of literacy.* Paper presented at 76th annual meeting of the American Anthropological Association, Houston, Texas, November–December 1977. (b)

Serpell, R. Cultural differences in attention preference for color over form. *International Journal of Psychology,* 1969, *4,* 1–8.

Serpell, R. *Estimates of intelligence in a rural community of eastern Zambia* (Report No. 25). University of Zambia, Human Development Research Unit, 1974.

Serpell, R. Strategies for investigating intelligence in its cultural context. The Quarterly Newsletter of the Institute for Comparative Human Development, 1977, *1* (3), 11–15.

Shantz, C. U. The development of social cognition. In E. M. Hetherington (Ed.), *Review of child development research* Vol. 5. Chicago: University of Chicago Press, 1975.

Sharp, D. W. *Discrimination learning and discrimination transfer as related to dimension dominance and dimensional variation among Kpelle children.* Unpublished doctoral dissertation, University of California, Irvine, 1971.

Sinclair-de-Zwart, H. Developmental psycholinguistics. In D. Elkind & J. H. Flavell (Eds.), *Studies in cognitive development.* New York: Oxford University Press, 1969.

Sinclair-de-Zwart, H. Language acquisition and cognitive development. In T. E. Moore (Ed.), *Cognitive development and the acquisition of language.* New York: Academic Press, 1973.

Snipper, A. S. *Child-caretaking in Mexico: An observational study.* Unpublished doctoral dissertation, Cornell University, 1978.

Stefflre, V., Vales, V. C., & Morley, L. Language and cognition in Yucatan: A cross-cultural replication. *Journal of Personality and Social Psychology,* 1966, *4,* 112–115.

Stephens, W. N. *Work opportunities for youth. Part I. Work for children and adolescents.*

Research Report for Strategic Planning and Research Division, Manpower and Immigration, Ottawa, 1976.

Streeter, L. A., Whiting, J. W. M., & Landauer, T. K. *Factors related to cognitive development in a changing African culture.* Paper presented at the biennial meeting of the Society for Research in Child Development, New Orleans, March 1977.

Streissguth, A. P., & Bee, H. B. Mother-child interactions and cognitive development in children. In W. W. Hartup (Ed.), *The young child: Reviews of research* (Vol. 2). Washington, D.C.: National Association for the Education of Young Children, 1972.

Super, C. M. *Who goes to school and what do they learn?* Paper presented at the biennial meeting of the Society for Research in Child Development, New Orleans, March 1977.

Super, C. M., Harkness, S. & Baldwin, L. M. *Category behavior in natural ecologies and in cognitive tests.* Paper presented at the meeting of the Society for Cross-Cultural Research, Michigan State University, East Lansing, February 1977.

Tremaine, R. V. *Syntax and Piagetian operational thought.* Washington, D.C.: Georgetown University Press, 1975.

Tulkin, S. R., & Kagan, J. Mother-child interaction in the first year of life. *Child Development,* 1972, *43,* 31–41.

Tversky, A. Features of similarity. *Psychological Review,* 1977, *84,* 327–352.

Vygotsky, L. S. *Thought and language.* Boston: MIT Press, 1962.

Wagner, D. A. The development of short-term and incidental memory: A cross-cultural study. *Child Development,* 1974, *45,* 389–396.

Wagner, D. A. *The effects of schooling and environment on memory development.* Paper presented at the biennial meeting of the Society for Research in Child Development, New Orleans, March 1977.

Weisner, T. S. *One family, two households: Rural-urban kin networks in Nairobi.* Paper presented at the meeting of the American Anthropological Association, San Diego, 1970.

Weisner, T. S. The primary sampling unit: A non-geographically based rural-urban example. *Ethos,* 1973, *1,* 546–559.

Weisner, T. S. *Urban-rural differences in sociable and disruptive behaviors of Kenya children.* Paper presented at the meeting of the American Anthropological Association, Mexico City, November–December 1974.

Weisner, T. S. Urban-rural differences in African children's performance on cognitive and memory tasks. *Ethos,* 1976, *4,* 223–250.

Weisner, T. S., & Gallimore, R. Child and sibling caretaking. *Current Anthropology,* 1977, *18,* 169–180.

West, H. Early peer-group interaction and role-taking skills: An investigation of Israeli children. *Child Development,* 1974, *45,* 1118–1121.

White, B., & Watts, J. *Experience and environment.* Englewood Cliffs, N.J.: Prentice-Hall, 1973.

Whiting, B. B. Unpackaging Variables. In K. F. Riegel & J. A. Meacham (Eds.), *The changing individual in a changing world.* Chicago: Aldine, 1976.

Whiting, B. B., & Whiting, J. W. M. Children of six cultures. Cambridge, Mass.: Harvard University Press, 1975.

Williams, T. R. *A Borneo childhood: Enculturation in Dusun society. New York: Holt, Rinehart & Winston, 1969.*

Witkin, H. A., Price-Williams, D. R., Bertini, M., Christiansen, B., Oltman, P. K., Ramirez, M., & Van Meel, J. Social conformity and psychological differentiation. *International Journal of Psychology,* 1974, *9,* 11–29.

Witkowski, S. Guttman scaling of semantic distinctions. In P. Reining (Ed.), Kinship studies in the Morgan centennial year. Washington, D.C.: Anthropological Society of Washington, 1972.

Witkowski, S. *Semantic complexity and societal complexity*. Paper presented at meeting of the Society for Cross-Cultural research, New York, February 1976.

Wober, M. Towards an understanding of the Kiganda concept of intelligence. In J. W. Berry & P. R. Dasen (Eds.), *Culture and cognition. London: Metheuen, 1974.*

Youniss, J., & Dean, A. Judgement and imaging aspects of operations: A Piagetian study with Korean and Costa Rican children. *Child Development*, 1974, *45*, 1020–1031.

Zajonc, R. B. Family configuration and intelligence. *Science*, 1976, *192*, 227–236.

Zajonc, R. B., & Markus, G. B. Birth order and intellectual development. *Psychological Review*, 1975, *82*, 74–88.

14

Developmental Issues in the Comparative Study of Psychological Differentiation

J. W. Berry

Recent theoretical and empirical statements relating to the theory of psychological differentiation (Witkin, Dyk, Faterson, Goodenough, & Karp, 1962) have focused attention upon its use across cultures. In particular, literature reviews by Witkin and his colleagues (Goodenough & Witkin, 1977; Witkin & Berry, 1975; Witkin & Goodenough, 1976; 1977) and by others (e.g., Serpell, 1976; Okonji, 1979), and empirical studies (Dawson, 1975; Berry, 1976) have served to extend, elaborate, and qualify the original theory. This chapter will serve to draw out some of the issues and themes which have emerged in this recent flurry of activity and will focus on those which have specific developmental import. Only the broad outlines of the current state of the theory will be provided here: readers who are unfamiliar with the history and background of the theory are urged to consult the work of Witkin et al. (1962) and Witkin and Goodenough (1976), and those unfamiliar with its cross-cultural use should consult the work of Witkin and Berry (1975).

The notion of differentiation refers to a process of change in a system toward greater specialization; this change occurs over time and constitutes a development in the system. Relatively undifferentiated systems are in a homogeneous state, not internally separated in structure or function; relatively differentiated systems have greater structural complexity—they have more parts, and they are more elaborately integrated. Differentiation is a feature of a system as a whole; it refers to the overall structure of, and within, all its component parts.

In cultural systems, the notion of differentiation is historically associated with the concept of evolution. For example, Spencer (1864, p. 216) defined evolution as "a change from a state of relatively indefinite, incoherent homogeneity to a state of relatively definite coherent heterogeneity, through continuous differentiations and integrations." In this definition, the term differentiation refers to the separations and distinctions, while the term integration refers to their tying together.

In psychological systems, as the term is employed by Witkin, differentiation takes on a more inclusive meaning, and in addition to referring to separations it also

475

implies a corresponding elaborate degree of integration. Furthermore, just as there is progressive change in cultural systems, there is development in psychological systems. Just as general differentiation pertains to the whole system, psychological differentiation is considered to characterize the total individual organism. That is, evidence for psychological differentiation may be sought in all areas of behavioral functioning—perceptual, cognitive, neurophysiologic, social, and affective. This evidence should indicate roughly similar levels of differentiation in each behavioral domain.

The literature reviews referred to earlier generally provide support for all of these basic expectations: psychological differentiation does increase with chronologic age; evidence for differentiation can be found in a variety of behaviors; and individual difference correlations tend to support the organismic interpretation. However, as Witkin et al. (1962, p. 389) anticipated, continuing research would provide new kinds of evidence which should lead to elaborations and refinements in the development of the theory itself. We now turn to the current conceptualization, and present it schematically in Figure 14-1; the model and its discussion follows closely a tentative proposal by Witkin and Goodenough (1976).

The model is pyramidal in structure, with the highest order construct (psychological differentiation) at the top and the most specific constructs at the base. It resembles models which are derived from factor analyses, although it is at present based only partly upon factor analytic evidence. In general, empirical observations are most often concentrated at the base, and inferences are required to ascend the pyramid. In contrast, theoretical interpretations flow from an apex downward.

An obvious feature of the model is its separation, at one level down from differentiation, into three sectors: segregation of psychological functions; segregation of neurophysiological functions, and autonomy or independence of the perceptual and social fields. The first refers to the specialization of functions—the separation of one

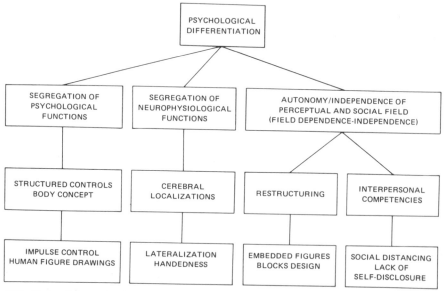

FIG. 14-1. Schematic diagram of hierarchical conception of psychological differentiation and lower order constructs and measures.

behavioral domain from another and the separation of functions within each domain. The second refers to neurophysiological specificity, and includes both localization of functions and lateralization. The third refers to the separation of the self from its environment or the field, leading to the use of the terms field dependence and field independence. It focuses on two areas of psychological functioning: perceptual-cognitive and social. The first is termed "restructuring" and includes such behaviors as disembedding and analysis. For example, on a test involving the identification of a simple figure embedded in a larger, organized context (the Embedded Figures Test, EFT), a person who is able to do the task quickly and accurately is considered to be displaying an ability to restructure the visual display being presented. In another test (the Portable Rod and Frame Test, PRFT), a person attempts to adjust a rod to the vertical in the context of a tilted frame surrounding it; the accuracy with which a person is able to set it to the vertical is taken as an indication of restructuring ability.

The second, "interpersonal competencies," includes social sensitivity and attention to social cues at one end and social distancing and autonomy at the other. For example, attention to social cues, a preference for "being with" people and even being physically close to them, and revealing more about one's feelings and ideas to others is taken as evidence for greater interpersonal competence. Taken together, these perceptual-cognitive and social components are designated by Witkin as a field-dependent to field-independent *cognitive style;* those at the field-dependent end of the dimension tend to rely on external referents, while those at the field-independent end tend to function autonomously of external referents. There is now fairly impressive evidence (at least within Western cultural settings) that those who are field independent on perceptual-cognitive tasks are also socially autonomous and distant in interpersonal relations.

One imporant implication of this relationship is that the dimension is bipolar with respect to conventional valuation; there are no clear "high" or "low," "good" or "bad" poles. For example, individuals who are high on restructuring competence tend to be low on interpersonal competencies, and vice versa (Witkin & Goodenough, 1977). The emergence of this relationship has led to a conceptualization of psychological development as proceeding "along different pathways" (Witkin & Goodenough, 1976). Those who are field independent employ internal referents in the development of restructuring skills but do not particularly develop social sensitivity or interpersonal skills. On the other hand, those who are field dependent employ external referents leading toward the development of interpersonal competencies but not particularly toward cognitive restructuring skills.

Cross-cultural use of the theory has been extensive in recent years. As in the case of most cross-cultural research, there have been three goals to this enterprise. First, there has been an interest in checking the transcultural generality of the theory, both in terms of relationships among behaviors and some of the antecedents (primarily socialization) to the development of differentiation. Second, there has been a search for new examples of differentiated behavior and new antecedents (primarily ecological and sociocultural). Third, there have been some attempts to extend and elaborate the theory to make it more nearly universal in scope; the recent theoretical formulations that we have just examined illustrate this process of theory development.

A number of models have been developed within which a variety of independent variables have been examined in relation to psychological differentiation. An ecological and cultural model has been developed by Berry (1966; 1971; 1975), and this was employed by Witkin and Berry (1975) and by Berry (1976) in their integrative treatments of the topic. A biosocial model has been developed by Dawson (1967; 1969; 1975) which deals more with some biologic varibles. Stewart-van Leeuwen (1978) has incorporated both approaches in her attempt to deal specifically with the origin of sex differences. In this chapter, variables which have been examined cross-culturally will be structured primarily according to the Berry (1975; 1976) model, supplemented by biosocial and sex-related variables developed by Dawson and by Stewart-van Leeuwen.

The schematic model presented in Figure 14-2 incorporates the main features which will be discussed; Tables 14-1 and 14-2 then outline the specific variables thought to be involved. These variables are presented as poles of a dimension; in each case the behavioral expectation is that high psychological differentiation will follow from the variables listed at the left-hand side, while lower differentiation will follow from those at the right-hand side of the dimension.

Looking firstly at the overall structure of Figure 14-2, there are five blocks of variables viewed as a system. Although feedback (bidirectional) relationships are illustrated, the general flow in the system is from ecology and acculturation (as exogenous, independent variables) through cultural and biologic adaptations to psychological differentiation (considered as a cluster of dependent variables).

It should be noted that the two input variables of ecology and acculturation are relatively independent of each other; for that reason, they are separated in Tables 14-1 and 14-2. It should also be noted that within Table 14-1, all variables within a column (left or right) are to be considered to be more or less "packaged" (Whiting, 1976); that is, they represent a cluster of features often found together in the respective subsistence groups. Finally, it is necessary to emphasize that these variables are considered to operate only for societies that are at (or near) subsistence level, where ecological press is a day-to-day force. Although some of the variables may be important factors in more complex societies, they are sufficiently removed from ecological press to require their treatment as a separate issue.

Turning to the constituent elements in Tables 14-1 and 14-2, we begin with the ecological variables. An ecological approach asserts that interactions between an organism (in pursuing satisfaction of its primary needs) and its habitat (with a definable set of environmental characteristics) will generate characteristic patterns of economic, demographic, sociocultural, and biologic adaptations. The relationships in such a system are probabilistic rather than deterministic, and the characteristics are to be viewed as likely adaptations rather than as guaranteed productions. One pervasive set of adaptations has been that of the "nomadic style" (Lee, 1968),

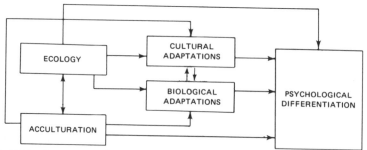

FIG. 14–2. Schematic model linking psychological differentiation to its adaptive context.

TABLE 14-1 Antecedent Variables to Psychological Differentiation: Ecological, Cultural, and Biological Adaptation

	Prediction of Psychological Differentiation	
	High	Low
Ecology (interactions among human organisms/ groups and their physical environment)		
Subsistence pattern	Hunting, gathering	Agriculture
Settlement pattern	Nomadic	Sedentary
Population density	Low	High
Cultural adaptations (learned group patterns adaptive to ecological press)		
Role diversity	Low	High
Stratification	Low	High
Socialization emphases	Assertion	Compliance
Biological adaptations (innate or acquired somatic characteristics adaptive to ecological press)		
Protein intake	High	Low
Hormone balance	Balanced	Imbalanced
Genetic selection	For differentiation	Against differentiation

and incorporates a nomadic settlement pattern, a low concentration of population, and a hunting and gathering subsistence base. An adaptation in sharp contrast to this may be termed a "sedentary style," and it includes a sedentary settlement pattern, a higher population concentration, and an agricultural economic base. Other subsistence activities, such as herding and fishing, have variable relationships to these demographic elements (see Berry, 1976, p. 119). This basic contrast in settlement styles is evident in much of the background literature of studies of cultural ecology (see, for example, Murdock, 1969; Murdock & Morrow, 1970).

In adaptation to these contrasting settlement styles are a set of cultural variables. In those societies with a nomadic style, there is likely to be relatively low levels of

TABLE 14-2 Antecedent Variables to Psychological Differentiation: Acculturative Influences

	Prediction of Psychological Differentiation	
	High	Low
Acculturation (cultural and behavioral changes induced by contact)		
Education	High	Low
Wage employment	High	Low
Urbanization	High	Low

role diversity and sociocultural stratification; these have been termed "loose" by Pelto (1968). In contrast, those with a sedentary style are likely to have higher levels of role diversity and stratification and have been termed "tight" by Pelto. Essentially the dimension being outlined is one of "cultural complexity" (Murdock & Provost, 1973). Also lying along the dimension are the characteristic socialization practices examined by Barry, Child, and Bacon (1959). In their classical analysis, they were able to demonstrate that those societies with a nomadic style (essentially low in "food accumulation," to use their terms) tended to foster "assertion" during child rearing, while those with a sedentary style (higher in food accumulation) tended to foster "compliance." The importance of these contrasting socialization emphases is that Dyk and Witkin (1965), Witkin (1969), Witkin et al, (1962) and Goodenough and Witkin (1977) have shown such emphases to be systematically related to the development of psychological differentiation among individuals within Western society. In the Western studies reviewed by Goodenough and Witkin (1977), socialization practices which emphasize strict rules and overprotection tend to foster low levels of psychological differentiation. In contrast, those practices which encourage separation from parental control tend to foster the development of higher levels of psychological differentiation. In the cross-cultural studies reviewed by Witkin and Berry (1975) a similar relationship was evident. In addition, there is strong evidence that differences in the broader societal pressures emanating from tight and loose structures may reinforce such specific socialization emphases.

Also in potential adaptation of the contrasting sets of ecological pressures are some biologic variables. Dawson (1969; 1975) has proposed that protein intake levels are likely to vary across the ecological dimension; hunters and gatherers (if successful) maintain high intake levels, while agricultural peoples would maintain lower levels. In addition to the general effects of protein intake level on human development, Dawson (1966) argues that low protein intake may alter the hormonal balance between androgens and estrogens. Inadequate levels (evidenced by the appearance of kwashiorkor) are associated with androgen imbalance, and such hormonal changes are considered predictive of lower psychological differentiation. More recent studies (Dawson, 1972; 1977) have pursued this relationship among protein intake, hormone balance, and spatial skills in laboratory rats. His results tend to confirm the relationship, although generalization from these animal studies is extremely difficult.

Related to this concern for protein intake and hormonal action is the common (but not universal) sex difference found in psychological differentiation, females tending to be more field dependent than males. Waber (1976) has argued that late maturation is associated with both high spatial skills and field independence. She later (Waber, 1977) added a complex set of genetic, endocrinologic, and neurologic factors to the model. Essentially the argument is that the presence of sex differences in field dependence points to the role of the biologic factors which are known to characterize male–female physical differences, and that they should be considered along with the sociocultural emphasis in the Witkin and Berry (1975) review.

Another biologic variable is the long-term adaptation to habitat of the gene pool in subsistence-level living. If there is a genetic base for psychological differentiation (as suggested by Goodenough, Gandini, Olkin, Pizzamiglio, Thayer, & Witkin, 1977), then there may be a selective advantage in some habitats. For example, disembedding is clearly demanded of hunters and gatherers in their daily economic activity, while it is less so for farmers. Genetic selection for disembedding and perhaps other aspects of differentiation may be ecologically adaptive. Similar arguments are also being made for spatial skills (e.g., Bock & Kolakowski, 1973; Yen, 1975), which may be related to restructuring.

A final set of variables (in Table 14-2) deals with the impact of other cultures on both the traditional culture and individuals in it. These acculturative influences include education (very often of a Western type), a shift from traditional economic activity to wage employment, and an increase in settlement size and population density (urbanization). It is considered that both education and wage employment often encourage the analytic activity which is measured in studies of psychological differentiation. Thus an increase is likely in most test performances.

In summary, we have proposed a model and some constituent elements which are theoretically linked to both individual and group differences in the development of psychological differentiation. This outline has necessarily painted a broad picture rather than treating any feature in detail. With this as background we will be able to confront many of the basic developmental issues in the cross-cultural patterning of differentiation. These concern its ontogenetic development, its patterning in relation to cultural complexity, some sources of development, and the question of the nature of development. Finally, the difficult question of the "value" of differentiation will be raised in relation to the cross-cultural evidence which is reviewed.

Following the discussion of these issues, some future directions for the cross-cultural study of psychological differentiation will be outlined.

ONTOGENETIC DEVELOPMENT

A fundamental difficulty facing the use of developmental theories which deal with the growth of individual differences is that when employed across cultures they suggest ethnocentric conclusions. In an early caution against such conclusions, entitled "The Child, the Savage and Human Experience," Hallowell (1939/1955) argued against drawing general parallels between ontogenetic development and both phylogenetic development and cultural evolution. Ranging widely over psychoanalytic and Piagetian psychology (e.g., Piaget, 1928, p. 256) and over the works of Lévy-Bruhl (1966), and Bühler (1930), he cited numerous examples of the equating of child thought with "primitive thought." He took great exception to such parallelisms and demonstrated them to be possible only if one accepted Haeckel's biogentic law (that "ontogeny recapitulates phylogeny"), and if one extended it by analogy to cultural evolution. Hallowell reviewed the evidence available within biology and concluded that the status of the biogenetic law was uncertain. Then turning to its cultural extension, he thoroughly discredited the anthropological and psychological assertions then being made. Essentially the problem lies in the use of analogy to close the gap between levels of analysis—between species and cultures as *groups* on the one hand and developing *individuals* on the other. To cap his arguments, Hallowell noted the paradox that "the children of savages are often less childlike in some respects than children in occidental society. Yet when these same children mature, their adult mentality often has been equated with the mentality of occidental children at the earliest levels of development" (1955, p. 31).

These general historical arguments set the stage for the contemporary debate surrounding the cross-cultural use of developmental theories and, more broadly, of psychological descriptions of any kind. At the outset, it should be made clear that no claim can be found in the current literature that "savages are childlike." Thus it is only by implication that such a charge may be leveled; it is possible to find that "fault" only if the critic chooses that interpretation. That is, such interpretations of cross-cultural differences are based upon the same faulty parallelisms discounted by Hallowell nearly 40 years ago.

It is clear that group differences in psychological differentiation are reported in the literature (e.g., Witkin & Berry, 1975; Berry, 1976). There is now also an interpretation of these differences as "the ascription of childlike status to adults" in the Third World (Cole & Scribner, 1977, p. 372); this charge is also leveled at the findings of cross-cultural Piagetian research (e.g., at those of Dasen, 1974; 1977). A response to such a view can be made at three levels. First, as we have already argued, the view rests upon *faulty parallelisms inherent in the criticisms,* not in the works criticized. Second, although psychological differentiation is claimed to be an ontogenetic developmental concept, *it does not claim to constitute development;* individuals develop psychologically in ways which are independent of the concept of psychological differentiation. Third, as we have already noted in the exposition of the theory, the emphasis is upon *different pathways of development* which are essentially value-free: there is a bipolarity and a multilinearity which neutralize such charges.

Returning to the first issue, the parallelisms which concerned Hallowell, we may begin the discussion by briefly reviewing evidence presented by Witkin and Berry (1975). In that review, two points came to the fore: there is *no single* "developmental status of various Third World peoples" (to use the phrase of Cole and Scribner, 1977); and the one apparent trend in these cross-cultural differences runs *counter to* the assumptions which underlay the earlier "evolutionary" research criticized by Hallowell. Taking the first point, we find virtually the whole range of differentiation task performance which can be observed developmentally within Western samples to be exhibited cross-culturally. Of course, we reject the false parallel between individual developmental differences and cross-cultural group differences, but even if we were to accept that comparison as legitimate, the evidence would not indicate any general developmental status for non-Western peoples. Some individual and group scores reach both the extremes of the performance range. Thus the "savage" is not "childlike" in the data of psychological differentiation, even if one insists upon drawing such parallels.

Turning to the second aspect (relating ontogenetic development to cultural evolution), we face another false parallel. As we shall argue below, cultures cannot be ranked as more or less developed in any absolute sense; the cultural development must be judged in relation to the adaptive problem. Again, if we were to accept such comparison as legitimate, the lay of the data suggests different pathways, with relatively greater psychological differentiation in the "less developed" hunting and gathering band societies than in the "more developed" agricultural societies. Thus contrary to early assumptions about relations between ontogenetic development and cultural evolution, if the comparison is forced, the "more savage" peoples are not the "more childlike." In summary, with Hallowell we reject the parallelisms which critics of developmental theories wish to draw. Even when such parallelisms are drawn, the cross-cultural data support neither a childlike status for non-Western peoples nor the assumed identity between the savage and the child.

Our second argument is that ontogenetic development is not equated with psychological differentiation. It is claimed to be a dimension of development, but not the whole of it. Individuals may exhibit development in many behavioral characteristics which do not correlate empirically or tie in theoretically with psychological differentiation. These include inter alia general intelligence (to be discussed in a later section) and effectiveness of integration.

Thus it is not possible to claim a "developmental status" for a cultural group on the basis of mean scores on tasks of psychological differentiation; other developmental dimensions are independent of it. Such claims, of course, have not been made by those working within the differentiation framework. Those who wish to advance such a claim run afoul of the data. Ontogenetic development is more than psychological differentiation, even though the latter constitutes one developmental dimension.

Turning to our third argument, we note that the general value position upon which such charges are based is that "childlike" characteristics are somehow not as valuable as adultlike characteristics. However, the value-free exposition of the theory of psychological differentiation argues that individuals (and groups) make their main developmental investments in different psychological domains, resulting in growth along different pathways. Possessing social sensitivity and interpersonal skills is not inherently less valuable than possessing cognitive restructuring skills.

In summary, we have argued that the old parallelisms among phylogenetic, cultural, and ontogenetic development have been sufficiently discredited by Hallowell (and, of course, many others) that assertions of any kind—whether they be propositions or criticisms—which are based upon them cannot stand on logical grounds. We have also argued that even if one ignores these logical flaws and proceeds to make criticisms on the basis of them, the empirical data and theoretical formulations do not allow such criticisms, at least with respect to psychological differentiation (Dasen, Berry, & Witkin, 1979).

CULTURAL DEVELOPMENT

As the preceding section illustrated, there are great difficulties inherent in advancing general statements about relationships *across* developmental domains. At the present time, *within* domains, trends along the phylogenetic (species) dimension are relatively free from serious dispute, as are individual trends along the ontogenetic dimension. However, in sharp contrast, the discussion of trends along a dimension of cultural development is fraught with contention. Early in the language of debate such terms as "savage" and "primitive" tended to be used; recently, these terms have been eliminated in favor of more descriptive and less evaluative adjectives such as "subsistence-level," "traditional," or "folk" societies. An implicit developmental dimension in early anthropological discourse was that societies evolved through stages (one after another, rather than within a single generation) from a state of primitiveness to the present state of civilization. The reaction within anthropology against such ethnocentrism led to the virtual dismissal of the concept of evolution from all discussion. However, an important distinction was introduced by Sahlins and Service (1960) between "specific evolution," in which new societal forms emerge in adaptation to new situations, and "general evolution," in which "progress" is involved: "higher forms arise from and surpass lower" forms (p. 13). Given the position of ecological functionalism which is espoused in this chapter and of "radical cultural relativism" espoused earlier (Berry, 1972), it should be clear that no general or absolute criteria of cultural development are being advanced here. Indeed, as Sahlins and Service (1960, p. 15) argue, "Adaptive improvement is relative to the adaptive problem; it is so to be judged and explained. In the specific context each adapted population is adequate, indeed superior, in its own incomparable way."

Most contemporary writers espouse a version of cultural evolution which is free of some absolute and universally valued endpoint. Consistent with such a perspective, this section will be concerned with the attempt to link specific cultural variables to performance on psychological differentiation tasks, even though most of the cultural variables may be viewed as components of one dimension of cultural evolution—that of "cultural complexity."

In our introductory display of the model we employed the terms "tight" and "loose" (Pelto, 1968) to indicate this dimension of cultural complexity. We may now inquire into the historical changes which have taken place in this particular variable. To begin, many early theoretical and empirical statements (see Freeman & Winch, 1957) promoted the idea that the historical movement has been a linear one, from the relatively simple to the relatively complex. Empirical analyses have indeed shown that Guttman scales can be developed to account for widespread differences in cultural or societal complexity. For example, Freeman and Winch (1957) and Pelto (1968) have produced such scales with a high degree of internal consistency. Although neither scale is explicitly tied to historical movement or to cultural evolution, their demonstration of a continuous linear arrangement provided an empirical base for such an interpretation.

Three subsequent studies have made important extensions to this work (Blumberg & Winch, 1972; Lomax & Berkowitz, 1972; Murdock & Provost, 1973). These studies raise questions about the linearity of the earlier findings, that is, about whether or not all cultural features usually included in measures of tightness or complexity move in a continuous way.

Essentially, they propose that some features of culture do not scale linearly but that a point of inflection is reached after which less complexity is more in evidence. A specific example is that in many generally complex societies, family type tends to become (again, as in most hunting societies) more nuclear. In the study by Blumberg and Winch (1972, their tables 1 and 5), there is evidence that "familial complexity" (basically an index of polygyny versus monogamy) increases in frequency across subsistence categories and political complexity up to a point of inflection and drops thereafter. In terms of subsistence economy, familial complexity increases from a low frequency in hunting and gathering groups through incipient agriculture to a high in extensive agriculture, but in those societies with more intensive agriculture (with irrigation), familial complexity drops in frequency. Similarly for political complexity, those societies with fewest levels in the political hierarchy have the lowest familial complexity, and this increases through one to two levels in the political hierarchy; but again there is a drop in familial complexity in those societies with three or four levels. They conclude that the relationship between general societal complexity and familial complexity is curvilinear, with lowest levels at the hunting–gathering and urban-industrial extremes and highest levels in agricultural societies.

Such a curvilinear relationship has been found for other variables as well. In the Murdock and Provost (1973, Table 5) study, evidence is provided that descent rules (in particular, the frequency of bilateral descent) display a curvilinear relationship to an index of general cultural complexity. Lomax and Berkowitz (1972, Figure 4) illustrate how a "cultural integration" factor (based upon such elements as the division of labor, the organization of groups, and levels of cohesiveness) displays a curvilinear relationship with subsistence categories (termed "evolutionary culture scale" in their study).

Across these three studies, there is a clear indication that over a broad range of cultures a number of cultural elements arrange themselves in a curvilinear relationship to the ecological dimension.

An alternative to this curvilinearity is a proposal by Boldt (1978), who speculates that the dimensions "tight-to-loose" and "complex-to-simple" are independent of each other. In this typology, hunting and gathering societies are simple and loose and agricultural societies are simple and tight, while modern pluralistic democratic societies are complex and loose and modern totalitarian societies are complex and tight. Such a conceptualization is plausible but at present lacks empirical evidence to support it. However, it may prove to be a valuable alternative approach to comprehending the varieties of societal contexts in which differing cognitive styles are developed.

In the review by Witkin and Berry (1975) and the monograph by Berry (1976), a broad set of evidence was produced which demonstrated some degree of inverse covariation between the development of psychological differentiation and a cultural group's position on the ecological dimension. However, most of the evidence available was derived from subsistence-level societies representative of those ecological adaptations in the middle range. Largely missing are data from African and Australian hunters and gatherers (who are often identified as early cultural adaptations). Some evidence exists for Australian groups (Berry, 1971; 1976), where the Central Australian Arunta sample were scored somewhat lower on many differentiation tasks than had been expected on the basis of their ecocultural position. Current work with Pygmy and forest Bantu groups in Central Africa may shed more light on this end of the scale, but clearly a much greater research emphasis is required here before any definitive statements can be made.

At the other end of the dimension, the available evidence from urban-industrial societies (and from subsistence-level societies undergoing acculturation to urban-industrial life) is that psychological differentiation is generally higher than among agriculturally based societies (Witkin & Berry, 1975).

If we incorporate such a curvilinear relationship into the ecocultural model, a common criticism (see e.g., Okonji, 1979)—that the ecological model cannot account for observed levels of psychological differentiation over the whole range of human cultural adaptations—tends to disappear. In Okonji's view, if cross-cultural psychology is serious about developing a universal psychology, it should not be limited to the examination and explanation of the behavior of subsistence-level peoples alone. The use of a curvilinear cultural predictor would allow the model to accommodate the psychological evidence now available from urban and industrial societies (see Berry, 1976, pp. 222–225).

In this section we have examined the general evidence for relationships between psychological differentiation and the cultural variable, defined variously as tightness or complexity. We have argued that a curvilinear cultural scale constitutes a "best fit" to both the theoretical and empirical features of the model proposed earlier. Over the middle range of subsistence patterns (hunting or agricultural ecological adaptations), cultural complexity increases while levels of psychological differentiation decrease. In the change to intensive agriculture and urban-industrial activity, the observed levels of complexity (particularly familial complexity) decline, while levels of psychological differentiation increase. In the earliest ecological adaptations (African and Australian hunter–gatherers) at least one cultural indicator suggests moderate levels. Thus returning to a major argument of the preceding section, there is no single "developmental status" of subsistence-level peoples; those relationships which do appear between cultural "development" and psychological development are curvilinear and over the middle range run contrary to the assumptions which underlie such concerns.

SOURCES OF DEVELOPMENT

In the schematic model outlined in Figure 14-2 and elaborated in Tables 14-1 and 14-2 a number of contextual variables were presented as being theoretically antecedent to the development of psychological differentiation. This section will be concerned with the relative power of each class of variables as a contributor to psychological differentiation. At the outset, it should be noted that there are systematic interactions among the ecological, cultural, biologic, and acculturational elements. Further, within each element there are systematic relationships among the specific variables which make up each of the four elements. Thus we are faced with a situation which should not be tackled from an "either–or" point of view. Rather, the perspective should be one from which these relationships are themselves taken into account and examined as interacting elements in the broad ecological context in which development takes place.

As the structure of the model was presented, although it is considered to be an interacting *system,* there is a clear flow from left to right: psychological differentiation is viewed primarily as a "product" of the systems, while two main "inputs" are nominated as ecology and acculturation. Intermediate in status are humankind's two adaptive systems, the cultural and the biologic. Finally, both the ecological engagement and acculturative experience of the individual are considered to be also directly influencing the development of differentiation. We can turn now to the examination of the basis for expecting relationships with the contextual elements in the model.

First, the ecological setting establishes an individual learning situation which may have direct behavioral consequences for the developing individual. These "ecological demands" (Berry, 1966) vary from one setting to another but clearly pose more frequent and more important visual discrimination, disembedding, analytical and restructuring problems to hunters and gatherers than to agriculturalists. Such functional analyses lead to the prediction that field independence will be more characteristic of those engaging the environment through nomadic hunting and gathering activity than through sedentary agriculture. Similarly, the lower-population-density demographic ecology of nomadic band societies suggests that the development of individual autonomy, independence, and self-reliance will be more prevalent than in larger agriculture-based demographic units. Thus on the basis of the ecological context alone, variations in the development of psychological differentiation are predictable.

Turning to the set of cultural adaptations, we find that the cluster of variables outlined in the model (Table 14-1), and which tend to characterize cultural life at the differing positions on the ecological dimension, are also predictive of varying levels of development. In particular, the lesser tightness and greater socialization for assertion which characterize most hunting and gathering societies both are predictive of generally greater psychological differentiation. In contrast, the greater tightness and emphasis upon compliance during socialization in agricultural societies both are predictive of lesser psychological differentiation. Similarly, it may be suggested that in societies where there is little role diversity and specialization, individuals will have to learn a more diversified set of behaviors; in contrast, where role diversity and specialization are higher, individuals may actually learn fewer kinds of behaviors. Although no evidence is available to relate individual role variability to the development of differentiated behaviors, it stands as a plausible hypothesis, one which is particularly suited to cross-cultural investigation.

Third, the biologic adaptive system may also play a role. There are two components essentially: genetic selection and protein/hormone variation. With respect to the role of genetic selection, we need to be able to demonstrate some genetic focus for psychological differentiation and then some evidence that these genes are distributed differentially across human groups. Neither has conclusive evidence, but both have enough support to propose that they may account for some of the cross-cultural variation. With respect to genetic locus, an X-chromosome model has been proposed by Goodenough et al. (1977), who cite some evidence in its support. With respect to the differential distribution of genes across groups, there are many examples in areas unrelated to differentiation (e.g., Beals & Kelso, 1975), but all are based upon a traditional Darwinian model of adaptive selection. There is no reason to suppose that once a gene locus is established for psychological differentiation it would not follow the conventional process of genetic selection where it has an adaptive advantage. However, in the view of Goodenough and Witkin (1977) cultural factors are the more potent. It is interesting to note in this context that one reason for the predominance of cultural over genetic factors may be that the cultural setting establishes the adaptive rules: early in human development genetic selection may have been for field independence, given the dominance of loose, hunting cultural forms, while later it may have been for field dependence, given the requirements for tighter group living.

A second biologic factor has been suggested by Dawson (1966; 1972) and derived from studies which show that androgen hormone imbalance often follows a reduction in protein intake. Dawson has also argued that gynecomastic human males and androgen balance-reduced rats, exhibit lower performance on tasks related to field independence. Thus a link between protein reduction and lower levels of psychological differentiation has been proposed.

In both these biologic arguments it can be seen that hunters and gatherers may exhibit greater differentiation than agricultural peoples. First, on the hunt, those lacking the appropriate cognitive style may not return to camp and maintain their presence in the breeding population. Second, among hunters there is evidence to suggest that their diet is not only adequate but protein rich (Lee & DeVore, 1968). Both observations suggest that biologic adaptation should be taken seriously as a variable in the cross-cultural distribution of cognitive style.

A fourth element in Figure 14-2 (and elaborated in Table 14-2) is that of acculturation. Expectations about the effects of acculturation on psychological differentiation derive from the deliberate analytical training received during Western-style education and from the new skills and techniques often learned from wage employment. Both these factors suggest that greater differentiation will result from acculturation. This may be particularly evident among hunting peoples, when some traditional ecological engagement persists (for example, on weekends or during vacations); this may be termed a "double dose" of experience fostering differentiation.

As we noted earlier, both in the opening pages and in our discussion of the curvilinearity of the cultural complexity variable, urbanization contributes many changes to the lives of people, not all of them consistently predictive of a directional change in psychological differentiation. Okonji (1969) proposed two factors that may be important: the loosening of tight socialization practices and the weakening of polygyny in urban areas in Africa. To this may be added the widespread increase in the prevalence of nuclear families noted earlier and the general decline in the strength of societal norms (Berry, 1967) which often accompany the move to the city or settlement. These four specific changes all are predictive of increasing differentiation with urbanization. However, in contrast, the accompanying greater population densities and new agents of social control which may "tighten" the social surround are possible contributors to lower levels of differentiation. On balance, though, these analyses suggest a positive contributing role for the package of new experiences which accompany urbanization.

We may now turn to the evidence which is available for each of these four contexts as antecedents of psychological differentiation. One study has included three of the variables (Berry, 1976), and this is a reasonable place to begin. The study examined the levels of field independence in 17 subsistence-level samples ranging from hunting and gathering to agricultural ecological engagements and from small-scale band groups to complex stratified social units. They also ranged from a low degree of acculturation to highly Westernized and fairly modern communities.[1] This range of background societal variation permitted the examination of the covariation of ecological, cultural, and acculturational variables with psychological differentiation.

Each of the three contextual variables was quantified [2] (into an ecological index, a cultural index, and an acculturational index) and relationships with test performance calculated. At the level of simple correlation, all three variables were predictive. For example, for Kohs Blocks, across 17 samples, the ecological index correlated $+0.83$, the cultural index correlated $+0.68$, and the acculturational index correlated $+0.65$; the multiple correlation achieved was $+0.92$. Across 793 individuals in the samples, the respective correlations were $+0.69$, $+0.60$- and $+0.47$, with the multiple correlation reaching $+0.72$. Thus whether taking mean sample performance or individual scores all three variables were consistent and significant in their prediction of task performance.

As the model is structured, the cultural index should be highly related to the ecological index. Indeed, at $+0.84$ the correlation across the 17 samples was sufficiently high to combine the two variables into an ecocultural index, drawing on each original index equally. When the ecocultural index and acculturational index were then examined for their relative contributions, it was found that the former was more highly related than the latter for all task performances at both the sample and individual levels. For example, again with Kohs Blocks, beta weights were 0.657 and 0.562, respectively, for ecocultural index and acculturational index at the sample level of analysis and 0.560 and 0.354, respectively, across the 793 individuals in the samples. We may conclude that the long-term ecological and cultural adaptation of the samples was a more potent factor than relatively recent acculturation in the distribution of field-independence scores.

Since the ecological and cultural experiences are often "packaged," it would not be an easy matter to tease out their respective contributions. However, the relative level of simple correlations in that study suggests a marginally stronger prediction from the ecology element to differentiation than from the culture element to differentiation. Thus direct ecological engagement, unmediated by cultural systems, appears to be the single most important variable. However, in the Berry (1976) study, no estimate of the biologic variables was made, and we are left with an unknown which in principle could mask the level of prediction already attained.

Other studies support the contributions of these variables to differentiation task performance. In the Witkin and Berry (1975) review, each variable was examined in turn, and virtually all studies reviewed provided evidence for the role of all four variables. However, since no other study has attempted a systematic examination of the relative contribution of the four variables, it is not possible to check the conclusions of the Berry (1976) study, and it is difficult to draw statistical evidence from data across these other studies. Clearly what is required is a replication and extension of work based upon broad sampling strategies and more precise sampling to systematically vary the background factors so that the "package" can be unwrapped and analyzed.

NATURE OF DEVELOPMENT

In this section we are concerned with the nature of development from the point of view of differentiation theory and the cross-cultural evidence relating to it. As we saw in the opening pages of this chapter, differentiation theory views development as an organism-wide process, as moving in all behavioral domains at more or less the same rate; this will be referred to as the issue of self-consistency. One aspect of this issue is the relationship between perceptual and cognitive restructuring and social autonomy in interpersonal relations, as diagrammed in Figure 14-1. Another aspect of this issue is the relationship of visually based field independence to differentiation in other sensory modalities ("sensotypes:" Wober, 1966). We also saw that a large sector of the differentiation model (including both restructuring and social autonomy) has been termed the area of "cognitive style." Questions have been raised in the literature (e.g., Serpell, 1976; Vernon, 1972) about the distinctiveness of such a concept from some others, such as "general ability." These three issues constitute the focus of this section.

Few developmental theories attempt to construct a comprehensive view of organism-wide change. For example, theories of perceptual development usually do not attend to personality development, and theories of cognitive development do not bother with social development. A broader task for large-scale theory builders is to show not only age-related changes within domains but also the self-consistency across domains. An early emphasis in the work of Witkin and his colleagues was on perceptual and, to a lesser extent, on cognitive tasks. This led to a tendency by many to identify differentiation as primarily a perceptual–cognitive developmental dimension. The two issues we are concerned with in this section both derive from this early misidentification.

Recent efforts by many researchers (reviewed by Witkin & Goodenough, 1977) have been devoted to the demonstration of wider covariation of behaviors beyond the perceptual and cognitive to the social and affective domains. Their review points out that whichever developmental pathway is followed, there is evidence of covariation between cognitive restructuring and social autonomy, and that evidence for consistency is now widespread. For example, in a large range of studies (but mainly within Western cultural settings) individuals who have been found to be field dependent on perceptual–cognitive tasks tend to use external social referents under ambiguous conditions, are more attentive to social cues, prefer to be physically close to other people, and are emotionally "open" to others during interpersonal exchange. In contrast, field-independent individuals tend to have an impersonal orientation and exhibit both physical and social distancing from other people during encounters. Additionally, field-dependent individuals tend to "get on" better and possess interpersonal skills not characteristic of field-independent persons. In summary, a fairly clear picture has emerged in which indicators of psychological differentiation from a number of domains tend to cluster in ways predictable from the original theory, and which now support the differentiation model presented in Figure 14–1.

In the cross-cultural area, not much work has yet been done. As in the case of the early work in Western settings, the initial effort was concentrated on perceptual and cognitive tasks. These constituted the bulk of the materials reviewed by Witkin and Berry (1975). However, some attempts have been made to assess social and affective functioning within differentiation theory. With respect to social behaviors, Berry (1967; 1972; 1976; 1979; Berry & Annis, 1974) has developed a modified Asch-type (Asch, 1956) line judgment task to assess the degree of independence exhibited when an individual is confronted with a suggested (false) group norm. Expectations were that in hunting and gathering-societies relative independence of group norms would prevail, while at the other end of the ecocultural dimension, lesser independence would be evident. In a summary analysis (Berry, 1976; 1979) the distribution of sample means on this task strongly supported the expectation and was taken as evidence in favor of the general ecological model. However, individual difference correlational analyses within each sample generally did not display consistent or significant relationships between perceptual tests of field independence and social independence. Although mostly positive in sign, the patterns of relationships constitute no evidence in favor of self-consistency.

A second approach (by Berry & Annis, 1974) has been to assess the degree of "reserve" in taking a Jourard-type (Jourard, 1968) self-disclosure test. Self-rated willingness to reveal personal information to either a parent or a friend tended to be lower in nomadic hunting samples than in more sedentary and stratified samples; this group difference is in keeping with the ecocultural model. Once again no evidence of self-consistency was apparent at the individual difference level.

These two examples employed tasks which on theoretical analysis should show relationships with field independence and which should contribute to a wider pattern of covariation. Within Western settings, the Jourard-type test covaries with other differentiation tasks (Sousa-Poza & Rohrberg, 1976; Sousa-Poza, Rohrberg, & Shulman, 1973), but it is now clear that Asch-type tasks do not relate to differentiation in the absence of actual interpersonal interaction in the test situation (Witkin & Goodenough, 1977). Thus although behavior across groups shows the expected covariation with the ecocultural dimension, a methodological problem has made it impossible to comment on the issue of self-consistency. Clearly, before this issue can be clarified more empirical evidence is required at both individual and group levels.

The second aspect of the self-consistency issue is less broadly based; all the discussion and data lie within the perceptual domain, but in this case they derive from differing sensory modalities. The original notion of "sensotypes" presented by Wober (1966) suggested that different cultural groups engage their environment in ways which emphasize different sense modalities. For example, the strong visual emphasis in Western societies may not be characteristic of other societies, where an auditory or proprioceptive emphasis might be stronger. If this were the case, then it may be that psychological differentiation in the perceptual domain (restructuring) would not proceed at similar rates or to similar extents in all modalities. Driving the argument further, this should lead to the prediction both of differing levels of differentiation task performance and low individual difference correlations across tasks employing different sense modalities.

Despite the attractiveness of this argument, there are both analytical and empirical difficulties in it. At the empirical level, Wober (1975, p. 118) himself has concluded that the sensotypes hypothesis is "still lacking respectable empirical support." Witkin and Berry (1975) have outlined the serious problems which have plagued most studies that have attempted to evaluate it. For example, the body-tilted version of the Rod and Frame Test employed by Wober (1966) introduces effects which do not exist in the body-upright version. Moreover, the size of his Rod and Frame apparatus was only one-third the size of those normally used. Despite these two differences, he directly compared his data to published norms and interpreted the differences in relation to the notion of sensotypes.

In addition to these experimental problems, there has not been any satisfactory measurement of the sensory ecologies which could lead to specific predictions; at best, stereotypic evidence (such as the frequent use of dance and song in African cultures) has been used to classify samples and to make predictions. Nor has there been any evidence presented to support the postulate that differential sensory experience affects development in that modality alone; indeed, contrary evidence is available (Gibson & Levin, 1975) to suggest that more general (or central) developmental consequences flow from experimental variations of experience in one particular modality.

At the analytical level, it is not clear why there should be a reduced level of correlation across modalities when examining for self-consistency. Although the predicted differences in extent of differentiation follow analytically, this is unrelated to the question of covariation. Since much of the evidence which is claimed to relate to the sensotypes hypothesis is of a correlational nature (see Witkin & Berry, 1975; Wober, 1975), the evidence is irrelevant to the proposition. It must be concluded, then, that analytical difficulties, experimental problems, and a lack of relevant data all conspire to render the "sensotypes" notion untested at the present time.

The third issue to be examined in this section is confined to an even narrower range of behaviors than the sensotypes issue—perceptual and cognitive behaviors predominantly based on the visual modality. This limited range is ironic because the alternative formulation is often phrased in terms of "*general* ability" (which surely requires a very broad behavioral base on which to make inferences); it is restrictive because counter-arguments in favor of the differentiation interpretation must be based, as we have seen in this section, on the covariation of behaviors beyond perceptual and cognitive functioning.

Essentially the issue concerns whether the evidence should be conceived of as a broad *style* (the "how" of behavior) or as a broad *ability* (the "how much").[3] As a style (or "cognitive style"), psychological differentiation is proposed as the characteristic way an individual interacts with his physical and social environment. In Figure 14-1, the right-hand portion of the construct illustrates this style. As we have seen, there are two major components: restructuring, which deals primarily with the physical environment, and interpersonal competencies, which is concerned more with the social environment. Individuals are said to be more differentiated if they characteristically exhibit more restructuring (including an analytical approach) and lesser interpersonal competencies (including social sensitivity).

Alternative views have been expressed that psychological differentiation is really only "intelligence," "general ability," "spatial ability," "perceptual skills," etc. (see, e.g., Zigler, 1963; Witkin et al., 1963; Cronbach, 1970; Vernon, 1972; Serpell, 1976). These views tend to classify the construct as one of *competence* and to limit it to the *perceptual and cognitive domain.* To claim otherwise (that it is a *style and is characterized by a broad set of behaviors*) we must demonstrate that it has no "high" or "low" ends, essentially a value question, and that behavioral covariation extends beyond this narrow ability domain. Here we will tackle the second issue and leave the value question to the next section of the chapter.

In part, the present question is one of convergent and discriminant validity. To what extent do tasks which are conceptually part of the differentiation construct actually covary? To what extent is the construct empirically separable from these alternative conceptualizations? An answer to these questions may be sought first within Western evidence and then in the cross-cultural arena.

The Western evidence is being interpreted in many ways, to a large extent directed by theoretical preferences. The self-consistency within perceptual and cognitive task data is impressive (Vernon 1972, p. 379; Witkin & Goodenough, 1976); and between these and social behaviors, it is also substantial (Witkin & Goodenough, 1977). This self-consistency also appears to be stable over time (Witkin, Goodenough, & Karp, 1967). When this Western evidence is viewed as a whole, it is difficult to avoid the conclusion that there is indeed a convergence, a patterning of behaviors, a stylistic approach which can be adequately covered by the construct of psychological differentiation.

Arguments against such a conceptualization propose either lower- or higher-order constructs as alternatives. Vernon (1972), for example, proposed an interpretation of task relationships in terms of both general intelligence (g) and spatial ability (s) factors. Cronbach (1970, p. 297) had earlier proposed an interpretation in terms of "general adaptive ability." But these and other proposals are based primarily on factor analytic studies; the factors which emerge are to a large extent influenced by the tests which are included in a test battery. When reference tests of g and s constitute a large element in the test battery *and* when few tests from social or affective domains are included, it is highly probable that a differentiation factor will not emerge—indeed, cannot emerge.

In the one factor analytic study conducted by Witkin's group (Goodenough & Karp, 1961), they were able to distinguish a factor which loaded a number of tasks requiring the overcoming of disembedding. They argued that relationships obtained between measures of field independence and standard tests of general intelligence are based upon this factor.

We can interpret these and the other findings in a hierarchic way: at the lowest level of Figure 14-1, perceptual, cognitive, and interpersonal *abilities* are being tapped, while at the higher level a characteristic *style* can be inferred. In a sense the style is being expressed in a range of abilities. The alternative conceptualization, that of a general ability, is both a more comprehensive concept (it includes many intellectual functions) and a less comprehensive concept (it does not include social and affective functioning).

Turning to the cross-cultural arena, the issue is even more difficult because of a number of problems which have not yet been solved. In particular, three questions need answering: Are constructs (such as differentiation or spatial ability) meaningful in other cultural settings? Is it logically possible to assess general intelligence in other cultural settings? Do we have sufficient data from enough cultures to make any judgments at the present time?

Transporting psychological constructs across cultures is fraught with difficulty. The construct must be defined conceptually and then assessed with both "imposed etic" and "emic" (Berry, 1969) measures, after which conceptual and empirical analyses must be brought to bear upon the data. In the case of most constructs now represented in the cross-cultural literature, only original, or slight modifications of, Western-based tests have been employed often enough to provide a reasonable basis for discussion, but "emic" analyses remain an urgent goal in cross-cultural research. Within this constraint, MacArthur (1975) has been able to draw out some common factors from Canadian and Greenlandic Inuit (Eskimo), Zambian Nsenga, and Eurocanadian samples. His factor analyses generally distinguish spatial, inferential, and verbal-educational clusters in all samples. Two points are important here: (1) *common* factors are appearing across divergent cultural groups, and (2) the inferential factor (based to a large extent on tests designed to measure g) is empirically separable from other constructs.

In MacArthur's (1975) study, differentiation tasks load on the same factor as spatial tasks. This finding is consistent with other evidence (e.g., Sherman, 1967) and is now being viewed by Witkin and Goodenough (1976) in hierarchic terms: although disembedding and spatial factors are separable as first-order factors, they come together at the level of restructuring.

In the cross-cultural arena, we may conclude that there is some usefulness in the "imposed etic" assessment of these constructs: they appear to make sense empirically. Beyond this argument, Berry (1976) has noted that all of the hypothesized antecedents to psychological differentiation (ecological engagement, social stratification, socialization) are universal features of human social life (cf. Aberle et al., 1950) and constitute a valid pan-human basis for expecting the differentiation construct to be a sensible one. Although we conclude that they make sense (in response to our question of appropriateness in other cultures), we must also conclude (in relation to our question of data bulk) that there is simply insufficient data at the present time to support any or some of the competing constructs.

To return to the second question, we may ask if it is logically possible to study the construct of "general intelligence" cross-culturally. For a number of reasons a position of "radical cultural relativism" (Berry, 1972) has been advocated with respect to the concept of general intelligence. One obvious problem is that any construct claiming to be a "general" one must be inferred from all possible relevant behaviors. This criterion is perhaps not met in its assessment within Western samples, and it is certainly not met in cross-cultural testing. With only "imposed etic" tests of general intelligence at our disposal, and with little sign that "emic" tests are about to be developed, the construct of general intelligence must be regarded as unmeasurable in the cross-cultural arena. Given this judgment, it must be regarded as an inappropriate alternative conceptualization of the cross-cultural work in differentiation, and indeed, of any psychological work.

In this section we have attempted to show that competing interpretations, such as some more limited abilities and skills, or a more comprehensive "general intelligence," do not fit with the data or with analytical requirements any better than the construct of psychological differentiation. Moreover, within Western samples, these alternatives can reasonably be rejected in favor of differentiation. Cross-culturally, although "general intelligence" is considered an inappropriate alternative, empirical data are insufficient at the present time to favor one concept over any other.

THE VALUE OF DIFFERENTIATION

Throughout this chapter, but in particular in the previous section, we have been confronted with value questions. Is being differentiated good or bad, primitive or civilized, smart or stupid, advanced or retarded? Of course, these are extreme phrasings of the question, but some aspects of each pair of terms underlie the issues we have been discussing. The answer which is proposed is that psychological differentiation is inherently value-free and that such questions make little sense within the framework of an ecological model.

To illustrate the validity of this assertion, we will examine two areas where group differences in psychological differentiation have conventionally been held to confirm its value-laden nature: these are the areas of cultural group and sex differences. With respect to such group differences in psychological differentiation, we have already argued for an *ecological* perspective and for an *adaptation* perspective. Inherent in both of these perspectives is the notion that the distribution and origins of a particular phenomenon can be sought, and found, in the nature of the developmental context. No phenomenon may be judged in relation to absolute criteria; rather, each developmental context must be seen as a unique milieu, posing a unique pattern of adaptive requirements, and questions of value can be judged only relative to these requirements. With this perspective and position as background, it should be clear that differences can be judged only as differences—they are inherently neither good nor bad. Only the particular ecological, sociocultural, or political context renders any evaluation.

With respect to the cultural group differences which have been described here and elsewhere (Witkin & Berry, 1975; Berry, 1976), a reasonable argument may be advanced that each group develops psychological differentiation as a general population characteristic to the extent necessary to meet the problems in its particular context. In a nutshell, given the ecological and cultural features which typically surround a hunter and a farmer, we are unlikely to find a successful low-differentiated hunter or a successful high-differentiated agriculturalist. A perceptually field-dependent hunter who also lacks some degree of social autonomy would be a burden on the group and a failure in adaptive terms; in such a case either physical environmental forces or social and political forces would likely attend to such a deviant case. Similarly, an independent agriculturalist who does not observe the norms of structured control would also be dealt with by the social and political forces of his group.

In essence the argument being made is that the group differences which can be detected can be satisfactorily accounted for (that is, in their distribution and origin) only in relativistic terms—only in relation to their adaptive ecological context. As we have argued, it is unnecessary, and even perverse, to jump between levels of analysis and attempt to explain (or imply an explanation of) such group phenomena in terms of individual and ontogenetic developmental differences. Of course, even if such jumps are made, we have further argued that differentiation and development are not synonymous: in those who are relatively undifferentiated, development has continued in the area of social sensitivity and interpersonal relations. Only an incomplete reading of the current differentiation literature permits the incorrect identification of the construct with development and in particular with perceptual and cognitive development.

A parallel argument may be made with respect to another set of differences which have appeared in the literature. In Western settings a common finding is that males tend to be more differentiated than females, and this had led to a value interpretation. That such differences are not always found was pointed out by Berry (1966), who observed that in one cultural group (the Baffin Island Inuit) no sex differences in differentiation were found. An interpretation was offered in terms of general social role dependency: "In societies where women assume a dependent role, they will have more field-dependent perceptual characteristics than the men, but in societies where women are allowed independence, sex differences will disappear" (p. 228). This lack of difference and the role-dependency interpretation was supported by MacArthur (1967) with other Inuit samples and by Berry (1971) with a broader set of cultural groups. Overviews of the cross-cultural evidence (Stewart-van Leeuwen, 1978; Witkin & Berry, 1975) indicate that indeed sex differences in differentiation are not universal; they tend not to be present in nomadic hunting and gathering societies but tend to be present in sedentary, stratified, usually agricultural societies. Interpretations of this pattern have been offered in terms of the ecological context. Berry (1966; 1971; 1976) and Witkin and Berry (1975) base the argument on both the lack of stratification or social tightness and the equal economic partnerships in marriage usually observed among hunting and gathering peoples. Stewart-van Leeuwen (1978) makes an attempt to separate the numerous factors which are packaged in such an ecological context; specifically, the economic factors are conceptually separated from the tightness or conformity factors, and both are distinguished from the biologic (hormonal/genetic) factors.

All of these interpretations of sex differences are made in terms of the various ecological contexts and their economic, cultural, and biologic implications. It is argued that such sex differences, like cultural group differences, are inherently neither good nor bad but should be seen as either successful or unsuccessful adaptations to ecological requirements. Once again, only the context can render an evaluative judgment.

In the case of both cultural group and sex differences, rapid changes in the context can bring about quick reevaluations. Acculturation, with imported values placed firmly upon skills leading to success in Western education or in industrial employment, may devalue a population very rapidly; the old ecological context is no longer the basic adaptive arena. Similarly, social change has overtaken Western societies' traditional allocation of sex roles and has established, through advocacy, a new set of allocation rules. There appears to be no longer (and perhaps has not been for more than a generation) an ecological context which requires a continuation of clear sex role distinction in Western society, but in keeping with the relativistic position it is probably not the case that such release from ecological demands on differential sex role allocation has occurred, or indeed will occur, soon, for many contemporary societies.

SOME FUTURE DIRECTIONS FOR COMPARATIVE RESEARCH ON PSYCHOLOGICAL DIFFERENTIATION

At least three goals have been outlined for cross-cultural psychology (Berry & Dasen 1974, p. 14). One is to transport our current Western-based theories and generalizations to other cultural arenas to test their validity. From this point of view a lot has been accomplished by differentiation workers, but much still needs to be attempted. For example, cross-cultural studies which examine the life span development of differentiation have yet to be conducted. In particular there have not been any longitudinal studies of the crucial ages from birth through young adulthood so that stability may be assessed, nor have there been any definitive cross-cultural studies of the role of socialization which Witkin and his colleagues have so closely observed in Western settings. Perhaps more importantly, we lack studies of the social and affective behaviors which are required in order to complete the picture of differentiation as a style, with regularities across a number of behavioral domains.

A second goal for cross-cultural psychology has been to explore other cultural systems for new variables (both cultural and behavioral) which may relate to the Western-based construct and its antecedents. In the case of psychological differentiation, a start has been made in this direction by taking socialization, viewing it as one element in a broader context of sociocultural stratification, and then further extending these antecedents to the ecological context to which cultural systems are adapting. Much, however, remains to be accomplished. We need to seek out more variations in ecological and cultural settings in order to obtain a more comprehensive view of the covariation of culture and differentiation and in order to unwrap the ecocultural package which frequently confounds our attempts to find more specific relationships. We also need to look more closely at the effects of acculturation and the mechanisms by which these effects occur.

A third goal has been proposed as the integration of data and theory derived from both our Western-based work and the cross-cultural enterprise. Through comparing and sifting, perhaps more general (even universal) laws may one day emerge. In the case of work on psychological differentiation, some integrative work has been accomplished; for example, the perspective of the ecological context in relation to cultural group and sex differences is now influencing interpretations of findings intraculturally. But so much of the cross-cultural data derives from subsistence–level societies where ecological press is substantial, while Western-based data come from societies which are responding to different-sourced pressures. This makes explicit comparison and integration difficult, as Okonji (1979) has pointed out. More comprehensive schemata are required if we are to bring together the numerous and valuable empirical sources and theoretical insights which have been generated in the last decade of work on psychological differentiation.

ACKNOWLEDGMENTS

Thanks are due to those who provided comments on and criticisms of an earlier draft: Jan Van de Koppel, H. A. Witkin, and the editors of this Handbook.

NOTES

1. These 17 samples were drawn from ten cultural groups: Temne of Sierra Leone, Telefol and Motu of New Guinea, Arunta and Koonganji of Australia, Inuit (Eskimo) of Arctic Canada, and Cree, Ojibway, Carrier, and Tsimshian of northern Canada.

2. These indices were constructed by employing the relevant variables listed in Tables 14-1 and 14-2. Each variable was coded and quantified, and an index was produced by standardizing the summation of the quantified codes.

3. In a hierarchic model such as the one proposed in Figure 14-1, there is no necessary contradiction between these two conceptualizations. At the lower levels

of the model there can be evidence of a variety of abilities (such as disembedding and analytical or spatial ability), while at the higher levels of the model their patterning can be evidence of a particular style.

REFERENCES

Aberle, D. F., Cohen, A. K., Davis, A. K., Levy, M. J., & Sutton, F. X. The functional prerequisites of a society. *Ethics*, 1950, *60*, 100–111.

Asch, S. E. Studies in independence and conformity. 1: A minority of one against a unanimous majority. *Psychological Monographs*, 1956, *70* (416).

Beals, K. L., & Kelso, A. J. Genetic variation and cultural evolution. *American Anthropologist*, 1975, *77*, 566–579.

Barry, H., Child, I., & Bacon, M. Relation of child training to subsistence economy. *American Anthropologist*, 1959, *61*, 31–63

Berry, J. W. Temne and Eskimo perceptual skills. *International Journal of Psychology*, 1966, *1*, 207–229.

Berry, J. W. Independence and conformity in subsistence-level societies. *Journal of Personality and Social Psychology*, 1967, *7*, 415–418.

Berry, J. W. On cross-cultural comparability. *International Journal of Psychology*, 1969, *4*, 119–128.

Berry, J. W. Ecological and cultural factors in spatial perceptual development. *Canadian Journal of Behavioural Science*, 1971, *3*, 324–336.

Berry, J. W. Radical cultural relativism and the concept of intelligence. In L. J. Cronbach & P. Drenth (Eds.), *Mental tests and cultural adaptation*. The Hague: Mouton, 1972.

Berry, J. W. Differentiation across cultures: Cognitive style and affective style. In J. Dawson & W. J. Lonner (Eds.), *Readings in cross-cultural psychology*. Hong Kong: University of Hong Kong Press, 1974.

Berry, J. W. An ecological approach to cross-cultural psychology. *Nederlands Tijdschrift voor de Psychologie*, 1975, *30*, 51–84.

Berry, J. W. *Human ecology and cognitive style: Comparative studies in cultural and psychological adaptation*. Beverly Hills: Sage/Halsted, 1976.

Berry, J. W. A cultural ecology of social behaviour. In L. Berkowitz (Ed.), *Advances in experimental social psychology*. New York: Academic Press, 1979.

Berry, J. W., & Annis, R. C. Ecology, culture and psychological differentiation. *International Journal of Psychology*, 1974, *9*, 173–193.

Berry, J. W., & Dasen, P. R. (Eds.). *Culture and cognition*. London: Methuen, 1974.

Bock, R., & Kolakowski, D. Further evidence of sex-linked major gene influence on human spatial visualizing ability. *American Journal of Human Genetics*, 1973, *25*, 1–14.

Boldt, E. D. Structural tightness and cross-cultural research. *Journal of Cross-Cultural Psychology*, 1978, *9*, 151–165.

Bühler, K. *The mental development of the child*. New York: Harcourt Brace & Co. 1930.

Blumberg, R. L., & Winch, R. Societal complexity and familial complexity: Evidence for the curvilinear hypothesis. *American Journal of Sociology*, 1972, *77*, 898–920.

Cronbach, L. J. *Essentials of psychological testing* (3rd ed.). New York: Harper & Row, 1970.

Cole, M., & Scribner, S. Developmental theories applied to cross-cultural cognitive research. *Annals of the New York Academy of Sciences*, 1977, *285*, 366–373.

Dasen, P. The influence of ecology, culture and European contact on cognitive development in Australian Aborigines. In J. W. Berry & P. R. Dasen (Eds.), *Culture and cognition*. London: Methuen, 1974.

Dasen, P. (Ed.). *Piagetian psychology: Cross-cultural contributions*. New York: Halsted, 1977.

Dasen, P., Berry, J. W., & Witkin, H. A. The use of developmental theories cross-culturally. In L. Eckensberger, Y. Poortinga, & W. Lonner (Eds.). *Cross-cultural contributions to psychology*. Amsterdam: Swets & Zeitlinger, 1979.

Dawson, J. L. M. Kwashiorkor, gynaecomastia and feminization processes. *Journal of Tropical Medicine and Hygiene*, 1966, *69*, 175–179.

Dawson, J. L. M. Cultural and physiological influences upon spatial perceptual processes in West Africa. Parts 1 and 2. *International Journal of Psychology*, 1967, *2*, 115–128, 171–185.

Dawson, J. L. M. Theoretical and research bases of bio-social psychology. *University of Hong Kong Gazette*, 1969, *16*, 1–10.

Dawson, J. L. M. Effects of sex hormones on cognitive style in rats and men. *Behavior Genetics*, 1972, *2*, 21–42.

Dawson, J. L. M. *Psychological effects of biosocial change in West Africa*. New Haven: HRAflex FC1-001, 1975.

Dawson, J. L. M. B. Developmental effects of different levels of protein and environmental stimulation on growth, endocrines, brain and spatial/activity skills. In Y. Poortinga (Ed.), *Basic problems in cross-cultural psychology*. Amsterdam: Swets & Zeitlinger, 1977.

Dyk, R., & Witkin, H. A. Family experiences related to the development of differentiation in children. *Child Development*, 1965, *36*, 21–55.

Freeman, L. C., & Winch, R. F. Societal complexity: An empirical test of a typology of societies. *American Journal of Sociology*, 1957, *62*, 461–466.

Gibson, E. J., & Levin, H. *The psychology of reading*. Cambridge, Mass.: MIT Press, 1975.

Goodenough, D. R., & Karp, S. A. Field dependence and intellectual functioning. *Journal of Abnormal and Social Psychology*, 1961, *63*, 241–246.

Goodenough, D. R., Gandini, E., Olkin, I., Pizzamiglio, L., Thayer, D., & Witkin, H. A. A study of X-chromosome linkage with field dependence and spatial-visualization. *Journal of Behavior Genetics*, 1977, *7*, 373–387.

Goodenough, D. R., & Witkin, H. A. The origins of field-dependent and field-independent cognitive styles. *ETS Research Bulletin*, 1977, RB-77-9.

Hallowell, A. I. The Recapitulation Theory and Culture. In A. I. Hallowell (Ed.), *Culture and experience*. Philadelphia: University of Pennsylvania Press, 1939/1955, pp. 14–31.

Jourard, S. M. *Disclosing man to himself*. New York: Van Nostrand, 1968.

Lee, R. B. What do hunters do for a living, or how to make out on scarce resources. In R. B. Lee & I. DeVore (Eds.), *Man the hunter*. Chicago: Aldine, 1968.

Lee, R. B., & DeVore, I. Problems in the study of hunters and gatherers. In R. B. Lee & I. DeVore (Eds.), *Man the hunter*. Chicago: Aldine, 1968.

Lévy-Bruhl, L. *How natives think*. New York: Washington Square Press, 1966.

Lomax, A., & Berkowitz, N. The evolutionary taxonomy of culture. *Science*, 1972, *177*, 228–239.

MacArthur, R. S. Sex differences in field dependence for the Eskimo: Replication of Berry's finding. *International Journal of Psychology*, 1967, *2*, 139–140.

MacArthur, R. S. Differential ability patterns: Inuit, Nsenga and Canadian whites. In J. W. Berry & W. J. Lonner (Eds.), *Applied cross-cultural psychology*. Amsterdam: Swets & Zeitlinger, 1975.

Murdock, G. P. Ethnographic atlas: A summary. *Ethnology*, 1967, *6*, 109–236.

Murdock, G. P. Correlations of exploitive and settlement patterns. In D. Damas (Ed.), *Ecological essays*. National Museum of Canada Bulletin No. 230, Anthropological Series No. 36, 1969.

Murdock, G. P., & Morrow, D. O. Subsistence economy and supportive practices: Cross-cultural codes 1. *Ethnology*, 1970, *9*, 302–330.

Murdock, G. P., & Provost, C. Measurement of cultural complexity. *Ethnology*, 1973, *12*, 379–392.

Okonji, M. O. Differential effects of rural and urban upbringing on the development of cognitive styles. *International Journal of Psychology*, 1969, *4*, 293–305.

Okonji, M. O. Cognitive styles across cultures. In N. Warren (Ed.), *Studies in cross-cultural psychology* (Vol. 2). London: Academic Press, 1979.

Pelto, P. The difference between "tight" and "loose" societies. *Transaction*, 1968 (April), 37–40.

Piaget, J. *Judgement and reasoning in the child*. New York: Harcourt, Brace & Co. 1928.

Sahlins, M. D., & Service, E. (Eds.). *Evolution and culture*. Ann Arbor: University of Michigan Press, 1960.

Serpell, R. *Culture's Influence on Behaviour*. London: Methuen, 1976.

Sherman, J. A. Problem of sex differences in space perception and aspects of intellectual functioning. *Psychological Review*, 1967, *74*, 290–299.

Sousa-Poza, J. F., & Rohrberg, R. Communicational and interactional aspects of self-disclosure in psychotherapy: Differences related to cognitive style. *Psychiatry*, 1976, *39*, 81–91.

Sousa-Poza, J. F., Rohrberg, R., & Shulman, E. Field dependence and self-disclosure. *Perceptual and Motor Skills*, 1973, *36*, 735–738.

Spencer, H. *First Principles*. New York, Appleton, 1864.

Stewart-Van Leeuwen, V. M. A cross-cultural examination of psychological differentiation in males and females. *International Journal of Psychology*, 1978, *13*, 87–122.

Vernon, P. E. The distinctiveness of field independence. *Journal of Personality*, 1972, *40*, 366–391.

Waber, D. P. Sex differences in cognition: A function of maturation rate? *Science*, 1976, *192*, 572–574.

Waber, D. P. Biological substrates of field-dependence: Implications of the sex difference. *Psychological Bulletin*, 1977, *84*, 1076–1087.

Whiting, B. B. The problem of the packaged variable. In K. F. Riegel & J. A. Meacham (Eds.), *The developing individual in a changing world*. The Hague: Mouton, 1976.

Witkin, H. A. A cognitive style approach to cross-cultural research. *International Journal of Psychology*, 1967, *2*, 233–250.

Witkin, H. A. Social influences in the development of cognitive style. In D. A. Goslin (Ed.), *Handbook of socialization theories and research*. New York: Rand McNally, 1969.

Witkin, H. A., & Berry, J. W. Psychological differentiation in cross-cultural perspective. *Journal of Cross-Cultural Psychology*, 1975, *6*, 4–87.

Witkin, H. A., Dyk, R. B., Faterson, H. F., Goodenough, D. R., & Karp, S. A. *Psychological differentiation*. New York: John Wiley & Sons, 1962.

Witkin, H. A., Dyk, R. B., Faterson, H. F., Goodenough, D. R., & Karp, S. A. Reply to Zigler. *Contemporary Psychology*, 1963, *8*, 363–365.

Witkin, H. A., & Goodenough, D. R. Field dependence revisited. *ETS Research Bulletin*, 1976, RB-76-39.

Witkin, H. A., & Goodenough, D. R. Field dependence and interpersonal behavior. *Psychological Bulletin*, 1977, *84*, 661–689.

Witkin, H. A., Goodenough, D. R., & Karp, S. A. Stability of cognitive style from childhood to young adulthood. *Journal of Personality and Social Psychology*, 1967, *7*, 291–300.

Wober, M. Sensotypes. *Journal of Social Psychology*, 1966, *70*, 181–189.

Wober, M. *Psychology in Africa*. London: International African Institute, 1975.

Yen, W. Sex linked major gene influence on selected types of spatial performance. *Behavior Genetics*, 1975, *5*, 281–298.

Zigler, E. Review of H. A. Witkin [et al.], *Psychological Differentiation*. *Contemporary Psychology*, 1963, *8*, 133–135.

15

The Comparative Study of the Development of Moral Judgment and Reasoning

Carolyn Pope Edwards

In 1955, when Havighurst and Neugarten published their well-known study of native American and white children, they noted that methods for investigating moral development were much less advanced than methods for studying mental development. Such methods as they relied on (principally drawn from Piaget's 1932 pioneering work, *The Moral Judgment of the Child*) were not refined measuring instruments and had not been much used in comparative studies of child development. Today, over 20 years later, the situation is beginning to change. Nevertheless, moral development remains one of the least understood aspects of comparative human development, and this deficiency is still the result of difficulties in measuring developmental processes in moral affect, judgment, and behavior.

The recent acceleration in the cross-cultural study of moral development has been almost entirely devoted to investigation of judgment or reasoning, rather than affect and behavior, and this review will be restricted to what we have learned about the development of moral judgment. The focus on judgment has resulted from current general interest in the cognitive-developmental theories of moral development of Piaget (1932) and Kohlberg (1969; 1971a). The cognitive-developmental approach to morality can be characterized as primarily a search for stages of reasoning which have evident *structure* and *sequence*. A moral judgment stage (Kohlberg, 1969) can be described as a general schema with definable formal organization (a coherent and consistent whole) which acts as a basic program or plan for understanding moral ideas and making moral decisions. Stages constitute a hierarchic system: each stage represents a differentiation of the basic elements in the preceding stage and their reintegration into a new, more logically powerful structure. The hierarchic order of stages also gives the developmental sequence, that is, the theoretically universal and invariant order in which the stages appear in the developing person. Insofar as a person's moral judgment changes, it transforms from a lower stage to a higher stage —without skipping any intermediate stage. Individual differences in moral development are expected to occur only in the *rate* at which individuals progress and in their

501

final point of development; that is, how far along the stage sequence different individuals ultimately progress.

Both Piaget and Kohlberg have claimed that their stage systems are culturally universal, and it is this claim that makes their theories especially interesting to students of comparative human development. Moral values are known to vary so greatly from culture to culture that a universal sequence in development of moral reasoning is a provocative idea. The chapter will first briefly review the historical context of both Piaget's and Kohlberg's theories, then discuss the pioneering work of Piaget and the comparative research which followed from it, and finally consider the fuller formulation by Kohlberg and the comparative research which has tested Kohlberg's claims.

HISTORICAL BACKGROUND

At the turn of the century, influential Western philosophers, inspired by Darwin, presented what they called "genetic" (i.e., ontogenetic or phylogenetic) theories of societal and individual moral development. Herbert Spencer (1899), James Mark Baldwin (1899), L. T. Hobhouse (1906), and John Dewey and James Tufts (1908) were among the noted thinkers who argued that ethical thought can be ordered along a dimension from primitive to advanced. As human social organization developed progressively beyond simple hunting and food gathering, so, they argued, did the level of moral thinking which bound together the group through custom, law, and religion. Western European constitutional democracy represented, for these theorists, the highest stage yet developed of both societal and ethical evolution. Hobhouse elaborated the most detailed description of societal/ethical evolution; he based his theory of succession on a comparative analysis of social institutions (marriage, class relations, law, property, punishment, etc.) and ethical concepts concerning human obligations and rights. Baldwin presented the most theoretically rich account of individual (psychological) moral development; he argued that individual moral growth reflects dialectic processes of assimilation and accommodation and proceeds through three steps—the adualistic or objective stage, the prudential or dualistic stage, and the ethical or ideal stage.

The early evolutionism had a seeming oversimplicity and ethnocentric bias that caused it to be rejected. Most observers came to agree that there was no objective basis for judging value systems of different cultures as superior or inferior. Moreover, they came to believe that the most interesting and significant differences in moral orientation were not related systematically to level of societal complexity but rather to other dimensions of cultural variations, such as family structure (M. Mead, 1950) or social control systems (Whiting, 1959). Comparative studies of moral development conducted during the 1940s and 1950s investigated cultural variation in core values, socialization practices, and moral motivation (shame and guilt) from a value-neutral standpoint; that is, without any one set of values, motives, or behavior reflecting a higher level of moral development.

The return of the doctrine of social evolution and with it the controversy over its ethnocentric bias resulted from the shift of focus from moral affect and behavior to reasoning and judgment. This move toward study of the cognitive component of moral development is part of the general shift toward study of cognition which has occupied the recent history of developmental psychology. Piaget in 1932 published *The Moral Judgment of the Child,* drawing heavily on the theory of James Mark Baldwin.

Kohlberg in 1958 presented a doctoral dissertation which expanded and elaborated Piaget's scheme; in 1969 he published "Stage and Sequence," an essay which set forth the theoretical foundation of the modern cognitive-developmental study of moral/social development. Kohlberg's theory has parallels in modern stage theories of character and ego development (see Kohlberg, 1969, and Loevinger, 1976) and has roots in the work of Baldwin, Hobhouse, Dewey, George Herbert Mead (1934), and William McDougall (1908), as well as Piaget.

Piaget and Kohlberg assert that they are describing culturally universal sequences of development. They claim to study the universal underlying "structures" or formal bases of decision-making *processes* used by people, not the systems of moral norms and attitudes which are the culturally specific *products* of reasoning. Yet neither of them believes that all cultural groups are equally highly developed in their typical level of judgment. Specifically, both believe that the people in simpler societies do not attain the higher levels of judgment displayed by at least some people in advanced societies. The deficiency in the simpler cultures is not due to biologic inferiority of people but rather to a lack of specific social role-taking experiences that stimulate the higher stages of development.

COMPARATIVE STUDIES BASED ON PIAGET'S THEORY

Piaget's (1932) study of the moral judgment of the child established the cognitive-developmental perspective as a major modern approach to moral development. Two features of Piaget's approach have become standard parts of all current structural approaches to moral/social development, including that of Kohlberg. The two features include (1) a method, the flexible clinical interview, which allows the tester considerable freedom to probe the "whys" of the subject's beliefs to uncover the underlying level of structure, and (2) a theory about causation, that social experience stimulates development by encouraging processes of role taking (the coordination of perspectives of self and others as a basis for choosing).

Piaget described two childhood stages of moral reasoning or judging, basing his work on the study of 5–13-year-old children of the Genevan working class. The earlier stage (generally found in children under age 7 or 8 years) he called *heteronomous morality* or *morality of constraint.* This stage is characterized by the naive assumption that moral rules are external, absolute, and unchanging. A rule's validity is not measured against any broader social standard such as tradition, legality, utility, fairness, consensus, etc. Rather, a rule defines what is forbidden and punished, and its rightness derives simply from the awesome activity of those powerful persons who do the forbidding and punishing. The later stage Piaget called *autonomous morality* or *morality of cooperation.* This stage is characterized by an understanding that moral rules are different from physical laws and that they are not necessarily absolute or unchanging. Moral rules, in general and in particular, are defensible by some broader social justification having to do with the group life of human beings.

Piaget seemed to feel that his two moral stages had broader generality, beyond simply Genevan children, but he did not believe that all cultures show the same rate or ultimate extent of development. Rather, he hypothesized that children who grow up in cultures where diversity is low and the authority of tradition and the elders is high would not be likely to fully attain the autonomous stage.

The comparative research testing the cross-cultural universality of Piaget's sequence has focused on two of nine dimensions of judgment change described in his

1932 book. These two dimensions include objective versus subjective responsibility ("intentionality") and immanent versus naturalistic justice.

Objective versus Subjective Responsibility

According to Piaget, young children tend to regard right and wrong in an absolute, black-or-white way, without appreciating any extenuating circumstances which might modify their judgment. They tend to be concrete; that is, they focus on the most immediate and observable physical aspects and consequences of an act when evaluating its "badness" rather than considering nonobservable aspects (such as intention). Piaget argued that this "objectiveness" results from their general cognitive immaturity. They have trouble differentiating their own perspective from that of others—they cannot really handle the fact that every person has a different mind and subjective self—and so they focus on the overt and visible. Thus in assessing blame they tend to consider as most bad the act which does most damage rather than the one which has the worst or "naughtiest" intentions. After about age 6 or 7 years, however, inferred intentions tend to overrule consequences in considering wrong doing.

Many studies confirm Piaget's hypothesis that children shift from objective to subjective responsibility (see the excellent review by Lickona, 1976). Trends toward increasing intentionality during the years of middle childhood have been documented for children from the following industrialized societies: Switzerland (Lerner, 1937a), Great Britain (Loughran, 1967), Italy (Ponzo, 1956), Belgium (Caruso, 1943), Israel (Kugelmass & Breznitz, 1967), and the United States (Lerner, 1937b; McRae, 1954; Boehm, 1962; Johnson, 1962; Medinnus, 1962; Grinder, 1964; and others).

Only one study has examined intentionality in children from nonindustrialized cultures (Kohlberg, Havighurst, & Neugarten, unpublished; unfortunately this study is not generally available, but it is described by Lickona, 1976, p. 225). The investigation, conducted among Atayal children of Formosa and twelve Native American communities, found an increase in intentionality for all groups during the middle childhood years, 6–11. However, during the years 13–18 the children of one of the groups began to give more answers with a consequences (objective) orientation.

The comparative results thus suggest regular age changes in the development of intentionality for children of many societies, but the evidence from non-Western societies is scant and ambiguous. The non-Western evidence neither establishes the cultural universality of the intentionality dimension nor suggests any general lag in children of traditional versus modern culture. The available studies do not make it possible to accept or reject Piaget's ideas about the stimulating effect of certain cultural conditions, such as social diversity, nor do they provide much insight into a question which seemingly must be asked: what is the relationship of adult cultural rules (concerning guilt and blame, responsibility and punishment) to children's concepts of objective versus subjective responsibility? For example, in different cultures the kind of subjective intentions a defendant has when committing an act of adultery, assault, or murder may be more or less relevant to the determination of damages and penalties. In some cultures the subjective intent is the critical factor in determining responsibility and damages in, say, a homicide case, while in others it may be more or less irrelevant to the calculation. A comparative study which combined anthropological investigation into adult cultures with psychological research on developmental stages could add greatly to our understanding of how children acquire concepts of intentionality.

Immanent versus Naturalistic Concepts of Justice

Cross-cultural investigation has scrutinized more closely Piaget's notion of "immanent" versus "naturalistic" concepts of justice. Because young children have difficulty in differentiating the subjective from the objective, they think about the consequences of violating social rules in the same way that they think about cause and effect in the natural, physical world. Just as effect follows cause immediately and inexorably in the realm of natural events, so they think punishment follows wrong doing in the realm of moral events. Thus they are inclined to simplistic concepts of punishment—inherent or "immanent" justice—exemplified by these answers of a Ghanaian school boy to a story used by Jahoda (1958, pp. 242–243):

Tester: This is a story about two boys. These two boys named Kofi and Kwame were out walking and they came to a place where a woman was selling oranges. Each of them stole an orange and ran away from it. But the seller saw them and ran after them. She caught Kofi and punished him, but Kwame got away. The same afternoon Kwame was chopping some wood, and the cutlass slipped and cut his foot. Why do you think Kwame's foot was caught?

School Boy: Because he sinned.

Tester: If Kwame did not steal the orange, would he cut his foot?

School Boy: He would not cut his foot if he did not sin.

Tester: Did the cutlass know he stole the orange?

School Boy: Yes, the cutlass knew.

Piaget (1932) reported a steep decline in belief in immanent justice for Genevan children between ages 6 and 11–12 years, from 86 down to 34 percent. He attributed this to changes in children's understanding of the universe: as they grow older they no longer think that nature obeys laws "that are as much moral as physical and that are above all penetrated down to the last detail with an anthropomorphic or even egocentric finalism (p. 256)." Thus older children come to realize that the sun does not go down because they go to bed and that the moon does not follow them as they walk in order to take care of them. Experience teaches them that adult justice is not perfect and thereby accelerates their disbelief in universal and automatic justice. They come to understand that punishment is a social act and therefore not necessarily inevitable; they develop "naturalistic" concepts of punishment and justice.

Most subsequent studies of children in Western societies have found the predicted shift from immanent to naturalistic concepts of justice (for example, Caruso, 1943; Grinder, 1964; Johnson, 1962; Lerner, 1937; MacRae, 1954), although one study (Curdin, 1966) reported a curvilinear trend for immanent justice and another (Medinnus, 1959) found the expected decline with age on one test story but an increase on another.

Studies conducted in non-Western cultures have obtained different and more variable results, however. Dennis (1943) found that immanent justice responses decreased markedly with age (from 64 percent at ages 11–12 years to 9 percent at ages 16–17 years) in a sample of Hopi schoolchildren. In contrast, Havighurst and Neugarten (1955) claimed to find counterevidence for the decline of immanent justice in native American children. They studied children of six tribes (Hopi, Zia, Navaho, Sioux, Zuni, and Papago) living in ten communities and found that with age more, rather than fewer, children thought the injury in the test story resulted from wrongdoing rather than simple accident. Jahoda (1958), however, has called attention to a fundamental flaw in the way that Havighurst and Neugarten coded the children's responses. According to Jahoda, the immanent justice concept properly involves two parts—(1) a belief that the injury is punishment for the wrongdoing coupled with (2) an attitude that the punishment somehow follows simply and automatically from the wrongdoing, as if (in the test story above) "the cutlass knows" that Kwame stole the orange. Jahoda contends that Havighurst and Neugarten made the mistake of not using both criteria in scoring responses to be the immanent justice type. In his own study, conducted in Ghana, Jahoda classified as of the pure immanent type only punishment responses where the origin of the punishment was not specified. Responses which attributed the punishment to someone's magical curse or to divine intervention were scored as nonimmanent, as were naturalistic responses which attributed the injury to simple accident or Kwame's guilty conscience. Following this procedure, Jahoda found pure immanent responses to decrease from 45 to 8 percent from ages 6 to 18 years.

Jahoda's critique and proposed solution are important because of the high frequency of supernatural (curse and act of God) responses in his Ghanaian protocols, especially those of the older children. Najarian-Svajian (1966) and Loves (1957) have obtained similar results in their researches in Lebanon and Zaire (then the Belgian Congo), respectively. Piaget himself met a very few such answers in his Genevan work; his solution was to throw the answers out as unscorable because they masked the underlying structure of the children's thought.

The problem facing future researchers is to develop interviewing techniques and probing questions to uncover that underlying structure. What are children really thinking about when they say something happens by "fate," or as an "act of God," or through the "magic" of a curse? How are these answers different in structure from the pure immanence responses of the younger children? In what way do they reflect increased maturity and complexity of understanding? Piaget's solution, throwing out answers referring to the supernatural, cannot work when studying children who give such answers much more frequently than naturalistic explanations, yet further proof is needed that supernatural answers are more developed than those punishment answers for which the origin of the punishment is unspecified.

Loves (1957) used a more open-ended interview than did the other investigators, and his results offer a clue to how cross-cultural research on Piaget's moral theories might be improved. He told the students a story about a thief who is killed by a falling tree and simply asked them, "What do you think of this death?" Many students answered in terms of what would happen to the thief next, rather than in terms of why the tree fell. As the students got older, they were less and less likely to point to "certain Hell" and more likely to suggest he could be "saved" by God's mercy, a term in Purgatory, remorse, or desire to make restitution for the theft. All of these answers suggest that the tree falling was divine punishment, but the latter answers seem to suggest a more complex and mature understanding of both the thief's and God's motivations than does the "certain Hell" response. Future researchers might take a hint from these findings and question children about more aspects of the immanent justice test story than simply why the injury happened. Questioning children about both the causes and the consequences of the injury may reveal more about their understanding of causation in the natural and supernatural worlds.

Conclusions and Recommendations: Piagetian Research

Piaget's theory is tantalizing because it seems to offer a new way to study inter- and intraculture differences in beliefs about responsibility, punishment, and other moral dimensions. However, the comparative evidence to date is too incomplete to establish the universality of the developmental sequence. Moreover, it certainly does not suggest a pervasive fixation at heteronomy which Piaget predicted for children of primitive societies (especially those of the homogeneous, gerontocratic type). Comparative studies are needed which accomplish better the task of exploring the structure of children's reasoning. The studies should also include much more complete description of the "official" adult cultural beliefs toward which the children are moving. They should include much more careful attention to problems of sampling, interviewing, translation, etc. than any of the studies have shown so far. Finally, future studies should include systematic attention to independent variables such as degree of acculturation, schooling, and social heterogeneity which might give insight into experiential factors in individual development.

COMPARATIVE STUDIES BASED ON KOHLBERG'S THEORY

Kohlberg's (1958; 1969; 1971a) cognitive-developmental approach to moral development is much more elaborate than Piaget's with respect to both theory and method. As a result, it has attracted much more attention from educators and psychologists. The approach has not only served as the subject for an extensive amount of research but has also generated a number of intervention projects in schools, prisons, and the like.

Kohlberg's theory is based on a system of six moral judgment stages, which are secondarily grouped into three levels. A summary of this system is presented in Table 15-1. Kohlberg's moral judgment system differs from Piaget's in that it makes much stronger claims about the nature of the stages in its sequence. Whereas Piaget explicitly disclaims that his moral judgment stages are true stages in the same sense as, say, the concrete and formal operational cognitive stages, Kohlberg asserts that his moral stage sequence does constitute a true stage system satisfying the requirements of qualitative change, invariant sequence, structured wholeness, and hierarchic integration (Kohlberg, 1969, pp. 352–353). Moreover, Kohlberg emphasizes more strongly the philosophic and ethical implications of his system. For example, he claims that his system represents a hierarchy of increasing logical and ethical adequacy of moral judging (Kohlberg, 1971a; Boyd & Kohlberg, 1973). Kohlberg's greater interest in the moral philosophy of his system may result from the fact that his sequence culminates in a principled level which can be achieved only through meta-ethical reflection (Gibbs, 1977). That is, this highest level requires from the individual an ability to conceptualize justice and virtue in an abstract, generalized mode, such as one encounters in most distilled form in the writings of moral, religious, and political philosophers. These two stages are rarely seen in the general population and appear, if they develop at all, only after adolescence (Kohlberg, 1973).

Kohlberg's approach not only makes more theoretical claims than Piaget's, but it also involves a considerably extended and elaborated methodology. Piaget rather unsystematically investigated a number of moral areas (immanent justice, intentionality, the origin of rules, etc.), and he documented a broad set of loosely related changes in children's moral orientation. Kohlberg, in contrast, developed a tighter research strategy. His method is intended to be a reliable measure of individual behavior and an organized description of the central structure of moral judgments. The procedure involves a standard set of moral dilemmas and probing questions

TABLE 15-1 Definition of the Moral Stages

I. *Preconventional Level*

At this level the child is responsive to cultural rules and labels of good and bad, right or wrong, but interprets these labels in terms of either the physical or the hedonistic consequences of action (punishment, reward, exchange of favors) or in terms of the physical power of those who enunciate the rules and labels. The level is divided into the following two stages:

Stage 1: The punishment and obedience orientation. The physical consequences of action determine its goodness or badness regardless of the human meaning or value of these consequences. Avoidance of punishment and unquestioning deference to power are valued in their own right, not in terms of respect for an underlying moral order supported by punishment and authority (the latter being stage 4).

Stage 2: The instrumental relativist orientation. Right action consists of what instrumentally satisfies one's own needs and occasionally the needs of others. Human relations are viewed in terms such as those of the market place. Elements of fairness, of reciprocity, and of equal sharing are present, but they are always interpreted in a physical pragmatic way. Reciprocity is a matter of "you scratch my back and I'll scratch yours," not of loyalty, gratitude, or justice.

II. *Conventional Level*

At this level, maintaining the expectations of the individual's family, group, or nation is perceived as valuable in its own right, regardless of immediate and obvious consequences. The attitude is not only one of *conformity* to personal expectations and social order, but of loyalty to it, of actively *maintaining*, supporting, and justifying the order, and of identifying with the persons or groups involved in it. At this level, there are the following two stages:

Stage 3: The interpersonal concordance or "good boy–nice girl" orientation. Good behavior is what pleases or helps others and is approved by them. There is much conformity to stereotypical images of what is majority or "natural" behavior. Behavior is frequently judged by intention—"he (or she) means well" becomes important for the first time. One earns approval by being "nice."

Stage 4: The "law and order" orientation. There is orientation toward authority, fixed rules, and the maintenance of the social order. Right behavior consists of doing one's duty, showing respect for authority, and maintaining the given social order for its own sake.

III. *Postconventional, Autonomous, or Principled Level*

At this level, there is a clear effort to define moral values and principles that have validity and application apart from the authority of the groups or persons holding these principles, and apart from the individual's own identification with these groups. This level again has two stages:

Stage 5: The social-contract legalistic orientation, generally with utilitarian overtones. Right action tends to be defined in terms of general individual rights and of standards that have been critically examined and agreed upon by the whole society. There is a clear awareness of the relativism of personal values and opinions and a corresponding emphasis upon procedural rules for reaching consensus. Aside from what is constitutionally and democratically agreed upon, the right is a matter of personal "values" and "opinion." The result is an emphasis upon the "legal point of view," but with an emphasis upon the possibility of changing law in terms of rational considerations of social utility (rather than freezing it in terms of stage 4 "law and order"). Outside the legal realm, free agreement and contract is the binding element of obligation. This is the "official" morality of the American government and constitution.

Stage 6: The universal ethical principle orientation. Right is defined by the decision of conscience in accord with self-chosen ethical principles appealing to logical comprehensiveness, universality, and consistency. These principles are abstract and ethical (the Golden Rule, the categorical imperative); they are not concrete moral rules like the Ten Commandments. At heart, these are universal principles of *justice*, of the *reciprocity* and *equality* of human *rights*, and of respect for the dignity of human beings as *individual persons*.

From Kohlberg, 1971a, pp. 164–165.

which are challenging for all levels of people. (Since these dilemmas turn out in practice to be rather difficult to use with young children and other respondents not prepared to verbalize logical reasoning about social issues, Piaget's rather than Kohlberg's method still is often used in studies of moral development in young children.) To illustrate what is asked of the respondent, Table 15-2 shows Kohlberg's best-known dilemma with its accompanying probing questions.

Kohlberg's dilemmas elicit a rich sample of reasoning from the average respondent, and the answers are coded to give a moral judgment score to the respondent. That is, a single measurement is obtained of the overall level of the respondent's moral judging. The scoring can be done in several ways, all requiring judgment and training on the part of the scorer. Procedures known as "sentence" and "global" scoring used to be followed (Kohlberg, 1958; Porter & Taylor, 1972), but they have now been replaced by "structural" and "standard" methods (Kohlberg, 1976; Gibbs, Kohlberg, Colby, & Speicher-Dubin, 1976). Trained scorers using all of these methods have typically achieved interrater reliability levels of 0.85–0.90, quite satisfactory by usual scientific standards.

As could be expected, Kohlberg's work has generated considerable controversy. Some authors have called for more evidence concerning the relationship of moral judgment to behavior (Burton, 1976). Others have wondered if the development of moral reasoning should be placed at the center of moral education projects (Aron, 1977; Hamm, 1977). In a major critique, Kurtines and Greif (1974) asked for better documentation of scoring methods and inter story and test–retest reliability. They also noted the lack of data to fully confirm some of Kohlberg's claims, such as the tendency of people to "prefer" advanced modes of reasoning to less advanced modes. Many of these criticisms were responded to by Broughton (1978). Here I shall leave aside a general critique of Kohlberg's cognitive-developmental approach

---

TABLE 15-2 The Dilemma of Heinz and the Drug

In Europe, a woman was near death from a special kind of cancer. There was one drug that the doctors thought might save her. It was a form of radium that a druggist in the same town had recently discovered. The drug was expensive to make, but the druggist was charging ten times what the drug cost him to make. He paid $200 for the radium and charged $2000 for a small dose of the drug. The sick woman's husband, Heinz, went to everyone he knew to borrow the money, but he could only get together about $1000, which is half of what it cost. He told the druggist that his wife was dying, and asked him to sell it cheaper or let him pay later. But the druggist said, "No, I discovered the drug and I'm going to make money from it." So Heinz got desperate and broke into the man's store to steal the drug for his wife.

1. Should Heinz steal the drug? Why or why not?
2. If Heinz doesn't love his wife, should he steal the drug for her? Why or why not?
3. Suppose the person dying is not his wife but a stranger. Should Heinz steal the drug for the stranger? Why or why not?
4. (If you favor stealing the drug for a stranger:) Suppose it's a pet animal he loves. Should Heinz steal to save the pet animal? Why or why not?
5. Is it important for people to do everything they can to save another's life? Why or why not?
6. It is against the law for Heinz to steal. Does that make it morally wrong? Why or why not?
7. Should people try to do everything they can to obey the law? Why or why not? How does that apply to what Heinz should do?

and instead focus on those portions of the work most problematic for the comparative study of human development.

Among the many studies designed to test or elaborate portions of Kohlberg's cognitive-developmental theory have been a number of investigations conducted in non-Western cultures. In the pages which follow I shall review and critique these studies, as well as briefly review relevant European and American studies. I will consider the following three issues: (1) the cross-cultural validity of Kohlberg's states of moral judgment; (2) methodologic issues in applying the system cross-culturally; and (3) the contributions of the cross-cultural research to understanding antecedent variables in moral development (an area in which comparative research is expected to be particularly valuable).

The Cross-cultural Validity of Kohlberg's Stages

Two of Kohlberg's most important claims are that the stages are universal and that their sequence is invariant. This means that the stages should be found in all cultures and groups and that they should develop in the same fixed order for everyone everywhere. Development should always proceed in a forward direction, from a lower stage to the next higher stage, without skipping any intermediate stage.

Cross-cultural evidence thus bears directly on the main issue: the universality of the stages and their sequence. Kohlberg (1969) presented the earliest comparative findings using his stages. He offered graphs of cross-sectional age trends in the United States, Taiwan, Mexico, Turkey, and Yucatan. These graphs showed the mean percentage of children's responses at each moral stage, for three age groups (10, 13, and 16 years). The graphs indicate age trends in the expected direction, at least with respect to stages 1–4, which were the only ones commonly used by the different groups. The findings would seem to support the notion that the stages (or some of the stages) can be found in other than American culture. Moreover, they would seem to suggest that each higher mode of judgment is indeed more difficult than each lower one. However, Kohlberg's (1969) paper contains at least three major weaknesses which have caused the cross-cultural findings to be questioned by critics (see, for example, Kurtines and Greif, 1974; Simpson, 1974). First, the published report includes absolutely no information about sample sizes or characteristics, testing methods, scoring procedures, and response variance, and therefore the findings lack credibility. Second, as Kohlberg himself fully recognizes, cross-sectional age trends give supportive but not conclusive evidence of invariant sequence. Hard proof of sequentiality can only come from longitudinal studies. Finally, Kohlberg does not adequately address the issue of different rates and ultimate extent of development in the five groups. Are these differences the consequence of social experience, as Kohlberg maintains, or are they an artifact of bias in testing or scoring?

Later researchers fortunately have provided work making it more possible to assess the claims for universality of stage and sequence. To assess the sequence issue, we have two reports of longitudinal research (White, Bushnell, & Regnemer, 1978; Turiel, Edwards, & Kohlberg, 1978). White and his colleagues studied school children aged 8–17 years on the island of Eleuthera in the Bahamas. Their data include a 3–7 year longitudinal sample, a series of 2–7 year longitudinal samples, three cross-sectional samples, and a series of sequential samples consisting of different cohorts at the same ages. The findings indicate a general pattern of upward stage change over time. In all subsamples, more respondents advanced than regressed.

The longer the time interval between subsequent testings, the more likely a subject was to have advanced rather than regressed. White et al. (1978) reasonably argue that their findings suggest the following pattern: moral judgment stages develop sequentially, but shortterm fluctuations either up or down may often take place in the context of long-term progression. Turiel et al. (1978) present age trends in moral judgment for urban and village respondents from three locales in Turkey. The longitudinal data, on a small number of males aged 10–25 years, from the village, fit the pattern discussed above. Most of the respondents either advanced or did not change between testings, but in a few cases regressions were observed. Clearly, these two sets of findings do not support a position that change goes forward only, never backward. However, they do support a modified position that could be accommodated by cognitive-developmental theory. As White et al. (1978) suggest, a Wernerian pattern of spiraling rather than linear progress may best describe the course of structural developmental change. (For recent discussions of this issue using American longitudinal data, see Kuhn, 1976b, and Holstein, 1976.)

The Bahamian and Turkish studies contain at least two limitations which should be addressed by future longitudinal studies conducted cross-culturally. First, they have the limitation that their evidence for sequentiality applies only to Kohlberg's lower stages (primarily stages 1–3) because these were the stages most used by the respondents. Second, they present no evidence on whether or not a person may ever bypass any stage in the process of development (for example, go directly from stage 2 to stage 4 without ever using stage 3 modes of thought). This issue is an exceedingly difficult one to investigate because it involves showing that a certain state of affairs never in fact occurs. No such demonstration has been accomplished even for American respondents. Nevertheless, this issue is an important one which should be investigated in more than one cultural setting.

Other comparative studies, those that are cross-sectional in design, provide evidence as to the universality of the stages, if not the universality of the sequence. The studies were conducted in a variety of different cultures and on a broad range of age groups: Kenyan secondary students, university students, and adults (Edwards, 1975a, b; 1978); Kenyan Kipsigis adults (Harkness, Edwards, & Super, 1977); Bahamian elder adults (White, 1977); Honduran Carib children aged 10–16 years (Gorsuch & Barnes, 1973); Indian secondary students and their parents (Parikh, 1975); Nigerian Muslim secondary students Maqsud, 1976; 1977a, b); Israeli students aged 13–17 years (Bar Yam, Reimer, & Kohlberg, 1971; Kohlberg, 1971b): Thai adults (Batt, 1975a, b); British secondary students (Simon & Ward, 1973; Simpson & Graham, 1971); Canadian elementary, secondary, and university students (Sullivan, McCullough, & Stager, 1970; Sullivan & Quarter, 1972; Sullivan, 1975): and New Zealand elementary students (Moir, 1974). Most of these studies were designed to test hypotheses about correlates of moral judgment rather than to establish the existence of the stages.

The studies consistently find at least some of Kohlberg's stages to be modes of judging that are easily elicited in other cultural settings. However, the highest stages (either 5 and 6, or 4, 5, and 6, depending on the particular study) have been found in only some groups studied, the less traditional cultures. Regarding these observed cultural differences in use of the highest stages, any of the following four positions might be taken:

1. The cultural differences observed result from poor testing procedures. They would disappear if people in traditional cultures were tested in ways that captured

their best, most advanced reasoning. (Simpson [1974] seems to vacillate between this position and number 4, below.)

2. The cultural differences result from a bias built into the definitions of the stages. They would disappear if the stage definitions were somehow revised to be more content-free. (Lee [1976] takes this position. He argues that the present stages are defined around a core value of fairness as reciprocity, equality, and individuality. This core value is appropriate for Western respondents but not for other peoples. For example, the core moral value of the Taiwanese is filiality. Different moral judgment scales, all based on social role taking, could be developed around different core values.)

3. The cultural differences result from variations in social experience. The differences can be interpreted in ways that do not involve invidious comparisons (see Edwards, 1975a, and Harkness et al., 1977), or they can be interpreted to rank order cultural groups on a hierarchy of moral adequacy (Kohlberg [1969; 1971b] takes this position).

4. The cultural differences result from a misguided attempt to capture multidimensional cultural variation on a unidimensional scale. They represent a distortion and oversimplification of reality. Stage sequences have no proper place in the study of cultural variation in normative thought (Simpson [1974] concludes her paper with this argument).

Which of these four positions is the correct one is by no means settled. However, the recent experience suggests that despite problems (to be discussed further below) Kohlberg's approach remains a fertile one. Hypothesis testing and theory building based on comparative research should continue for the following reasons: First, most critiques of Kohlberg's stages (including mine [Edwards, 1975a]) have not been aimed at the whole stage sequence but rather only at the higher stages. The first three or four stages seem to be relatively well established as a genuine developmental sequence (Gibbs, 1977). These early stages are the ones that are closely tied to the psychological stages of role taking (Selman, 1976), stages that are very likely to be culturally universal. Second, moral dilemma interviewing is different from many kinds of Western psychological testing in its ability to actively engage people from traditional societies. Respondents act as if they know exactly what to do with a task that requires them to reflect aloud about the rights and wrongs of a moral situation. If the dilemmas are well adapted to the cultural setting, they appear to arouse great interest in almost all respondents. Thus the procedure seems to tap into some part of an evaluative process, a process of "moral considering," which is central to the thought of human beings in a great variety of cultural settings. Support for this point comes from the finding that in one traditional culture, the Kipsigis of Kenya, moral judgment scores correlated highly with the people's own ratings of one another's moral integrity (Harkness et al., 1977).

Finally, moral judgments may be especially interesting cognitive processes for students of culture. The interest results from the fact that the moral judgment stages or structures appear to reflect people's conceptions of social structures and organization. That is, people's moral judgments tell us a good deal about what they think conflict is all about and what general procedures should be followed in resolving disputes. In contrast, other stage systems proposed recently in the burgeoning field of social cognition reflect differing aspects of children's thought—aspects not so closely related to children's conceptions of the formal or institutional framework of society (e.g., stages of role taking [Flavell, Botkin, Fry, Wright, & Jarvis, 1968]; stages of concepts of interpersonal relations [Selman, 1976]; stages of social mores, customs, and conventions [Turiel, 1975]). In the past, moral development research has not seemed to contribute much to our understanding of culture, but perhaps comparative studies of moral judgment would be more productive if they were not conducted in isolation from anthropological methods of studying cultural values and conflict resolution processes. For example, the analysis of transcripts of disputes, or "trouble cases," has proved worthwhile in modern legal anthropology and might be combined with a probing of the elders' reasoning in the moral judgment interview style about why they made the choices they did or urged certain solutions.

These arguments for continued comparative research using Kohlberg's methods rest on the presupposition that it can be conducted in a valid way, i.e., so that the procedures measure, with foreign respondents, a true equivalent to what they measure with United States respondents. The adequacy of past research, and suggestions to improve future research, will be considered in the following section.

Methodological Issues in Applying Kohlberg's System Cross-culturally

Regarding methodology, comparative research based on Kohlberg's system can be judged against three criteria. First, dilemmas must be "real" for the cultural group involved; that is, they must raise issues and pit values important to the respondents. This criterion requires adaptation of Kohlberg's original dilemmas or creation of new dilemmas to obtain dilemmas appropriate for other cultures. Second, interview procedures must be adequate to the sensitive task of eliciting respondents' "best" and most reflective reasoning. Especially pertinent here is the choice of oral versus written interviews. Third, dilemmas and probing questions must be translated in the best possible way into the native language of the respondents, and respondents' answers must be translated without distortion back into English for moral stage scoring. These criteria have in common that they assume thorough cultural knowledge of any people studied. Not all of the comparative studies discussed above were equally informed by this knowledge. The studies are uneven in quality according to the three criteria.

Most authors used Kohlberg's original stories in their studies rather than creating entirely new dilemmas situations. To suit the stories to the circumstances of the groups studied, minor changes were introduced—for example, the names of the characters in the stories. (The importance of changing the characters' names is indicated by Maqsud's 1977 study in which Nigerian Muslim adolescents were tested on stories differing only in the use of Muslim versus non-Muslim names. The adolescents scored significantly higher when tested with stories using Muslim names for the characters.) The decisions to use Kohlberg's original stories and the adaptations of these stories were in some cases based on thorough familiarity with the culture studied. For example, Parikh (1975) and Maqsud (1976; 1977a, b) were members of the groups that they investigated, and Harkness (Harkness et al., 1977) lived for 3 years as an anthropologist with the culture that she reported upon. In a few cases, however, the researchers were not so well informed.

Only two sets of authors—myself (Edwards, 1975a, b; 1978) and White et al. (1978)—have experimented with creating completely new dilemmas to use in conjunction with adapted original dilemmas. By far the most original approach has been taken by Lee (1973; 1976) in his work with Taiwanese aged 6–60 years. Lee broke away entirely from the original dilemmas and developed a series of situations centered around the moral issue of "filiality," or parent-child obligations. On the basis of the responses he received, he constructed a five-stage system for scoring the filiality judgments.

Most but not all of the cross-cultural studies have been based on oral rather than written interviews. An accepted part of the folklore of moral judgment research is that oral interviews generally yield somewhat higher scores for respondents than do written interviews because they are more motivating. In consequence, when evaluating certain aspects of the studies—for example, findings on the highest stage of reasoning found in non-Western samples—those studies based on oral interviews (e.g., Parikh, 1975; Gorsuch & Barnes, 1973; White, 1977; Harkness et al., 1977; Edwards, 1975; 1978) should receive greater weight than those studies based on written interviews (e.g., Batt, 1975b; Maqsud, 1977a).

Translation, finally, is one issue of methodology which no moral judgment researcher has yet adequately addressed. Some report that they were careful to use interviewers both conversant in the native language and trained in moral judgment interviewing. However, none explain how they actually solved the problems of translating difficult moral terms like "obligation," "conscience," and "responsibility." These terms are found not in the dilemma situations themselves but rather in the probing questions attached to the dilemmas. How the person responds to these questions determines in part how he or she scores on the test. Future researchers should give much more explicit consideration to issues of language and translation. Batt (1975a) presented extensive discussion of the denotative and connotative meanings of core moral terms in Thailand, the culture he studied. Eckensberger, Eckensberger, and Reinshagen (1975–1976) pbulished a set of translated inverview protocols and scoring manuals created for their ongoing research projects in Germany. Continuation of these kinds of efforts, coupled with systematic attention to issues of translation (e.g., using methods of backtranslation), would make a major contribution to the literature on moral judgment development.

Antecedent Variables for Moral Judgment Development

Comparative research, as discussed above, is essential for testing key assumptions of Kohlberg's theory of moral development. A second area for which its contribution is critical concerns antecedent variables in moral judgment development. Comparative research is needed to check generalizations about sources of development made on the basis of American studies. Of equal or greater importance, research can take advantage of the great range of natural variation in social life worldwide to generate and test new hypotheses. As we shall see, the available studies offer examples of both types of approaches to investigating antecedent variables.

Age as a Predictor of Moral Judgment Level

Any perusal of the U.S. and the cross-cultural literatures on moral development indicates that chronologic age is a very strong predictor of moral judgment level. Theoretically, moral development is a product of two factors—social experience, which stimulates moral and social problem solving, and cognitive development, which provides increased capacity to think operationally about all types of problems, including moral and social ones. Since age is a good proxy for both factors, the widely observed age level correlation is hardly surprising. However, recent research has gone beyond merely documenting age trends and has tried to determine the precise nature of the relationships between moral judgment and both cognitive development and social experience.

Moral and Logical Stage Relationships

One group of researchers has examined the relationship between moral judgment and logical cognition level (Lee, 1971; Byrne, 1973; Tomlinson-Keasey & Keasey, 1974; Keasey, 1975; Parikh, 1975; Cauble, 1976; Kuhn, Lauger, Kohlberg, & Hahn, 1977). This research is important because both Piaget (1932) and Kohlberg (1969; 1973) have asserted that moral development depends on cognitive development. According to the theory, the dependency is a specific rather than a general relation: particular cognitive transformations are necessary (although not sufficient) antecedents of particular moral transformations. In other words, moral judging at any given level requires at least a certain degree of cognitive maturity. While the empirical research provides some support for the notion of specific dependency, it does not present a consistent picture of what cognitive stage is a necessary precursor for every moral judgment stage. The one area of agreement concerns the relationship between concrete operations and moral judgment stage 2. Theory and empirical evidence strongly suggest that several characteristics of the concrete operational system (its flexibility, coordination, and reversibility) are required for an advance from moral judgment stage 1 to the "instrumental relativist" orientation of stage 2. The greatest controversy arises with respect to the logical cognition stage of formal operations. Kohlberg (1973) has hypothesized that the earliest manifestations of formal thinking (relations involving the inverse of the reciprocal) are necessary for moral judgment stage 3, while full formal operational thought (including combinatorial thinking) is required for moral stages 5 and 6. Others, such as Keasey (1975), do not make this distinction and seem to claim that formal operations are necessary only for the principled moral stages 5 and 6. The data presented by two of the empirical studies (Kuhn et al., 1977; Lee, 1971) would seem to suggest that attainment of formal operations precedes attainment of stages 4 and above but not stages 1–3.

The issue of the relationship between formal operations and moral judgment is important to understanding moral development cross-culturally, yet only one of the comparative studies to date has measured both the moral judgment and the logical cognition stage of respondents. This study, conducted in India by Parikh (1975), found that formal operational adolescents were more likely to be at moral stages 3 or 4, whereas concrete operational adolescents were more likely to be at stages 1 or 2. Parikh's finding cannot be explained simply by IQ differences between the two groups because she found no statistically significant relationship between IQ and moral judgment.

The question of moral and logical stage relationships deserves more study of a comparative type because of recent formulations concerning the formal operational stage. Several observers—for example, Neimark (1974), Buck-Morss (1975), Kuhn (1976a), and Bart (1977)—have suggested that formal reasoning is a mode of thought connected to the educational experiences and work roles of the middle and upper classes of technologically advanced societies. For example, Bart (1977) has said that formal reasoning is an adaptation to sociocultural demands which are "symbolically transmitted, abstractly presented, and often posed by distant social groups and institutions" (p.2). Hence he suggests that formal reasoning would not be expected to occur among the peoples of preindustrial societies or in deprived sectors of technological societies, since such peoples have minimal access to higher education and technological/scientific culture. If such theorizing is correct, and if formal reasoning is a necessary precondition for certain (as yet undetermined) of the higher moral judgment stages, then those higher moral stages would not be expected in every cultural setting. Comparative theory and research are vitally needed to clarify these issues. Studies should be done of the precise relationship of work roles, logical abilities, and moral reasoning of adults in different kinds of cultural contexts, both traditional and modern. Such research would greatly increase our understanding of the development and adaptive function of both formal reasoning and the higher moral judgment stages.

Social Experience and Moral Judgment Development

American research on the role of social experience in facilitating moral judgment development has proceeded more quickly than the work on logical and moral stage relationships. The goal of this research has been to find reliable ways to increase children's level of moral judgment. Work has taken one of two forms, either the educational intervention program or the controlled experiment. Both types of work (reviewed by Lickona, 1976; Sullivan, 1975; Rest, 1974; Turiel, 1972) have been based on theoretical notions about role-taking experiences and cognitive disequilibrium as the critical mental processes in moral stage transition. In the educational programs and the controlled experiments, participants are exposed to concentrated doses of moral ideas (through discussion groups, from teachers, films, or stories, in role-taking training, etc.). The studies have been designed to discover precisely what kinds of prearranged experiences effect demonstrable changes in participants' tested levels of moral judgment. They have not been designed to discover how these experiences correspond to the ordinary events of growing up.

In fact, only a small number of American research studies have related moral judgment development to real-life experiences with parents, peers, and the wider community (see review by Edwards, 1978). This paucity is probably the result of the focus on controlled experiments and intervention programs. As Lickona (1976, p. 239) has noted, experiences of change such as peer interaction "do not readily lend themselves to being telescoped into a brief experimental session." Despite this shortage of data, cognitive developmental theorists (Kohlberg, 1963; 1969; Turiel, 1974; Piaget, 1932) have speculated about the ways in which parents, peers, and secondary reference groups normally foster the development of moral judgment. Whereas Piaget stressed the impact of peer cooperation and reciprocity, the later authors put an equal emphasis on parent–child relations and the role of secondary institutions. Cognitive-developmental theory starts from a different position on moral socialization than do the social learning and psychoanalytic theories. The chief difference is that it does not place identification with parents at the center of moral development, nor does it consider the child's relationship with nurturing, disciplining caregivers to be a unique and direct source of conscience formation. Rather, moral judgment development fundamentally involves the successive restructuring of modes of role taking, and parents are only one set of social agents promoting this developmental process in the child. According to the theory, each stage of moral judgment represents a new framework for deciding what is fair and not-fair, good and not-good, in situations that involve conflicts of claims. Each stage involves a new way of conceptualizing conflict through taking the perspective of others toward the self and the self toward others. The social stimulus for moral development therefore can be defined as any kind of role-taking opportunity—that is, as an experience which encourages the child to take a social perspective in a better-balanced and coordinated ("more reciprocal") way. Role-taking opportunities become available to the child through participation in the family group, the peer group, and eventually the wider society. In Kohlberg's theory, participation in either family or peer group-ings is considered sufficient to advance the child through the early moral stages, but for the emergence of the higher stages the child must have the opportunity to take the perspective of society as a whole.

Studies on Parent Influences

It follows from what has been said that parents can be expected to play an impor-tant (if not unique) role in moral development. They help their children to learn to take the perspective of others, and they motivate their children to want to do so. Parents might accomplish these tasks in a myriad of ways, but in the literature to date only two behavior patterns have received much attention—induction (reasoning with the children about the consequences of their actions), and warmth and affection (motivating the children to care about others). Induction and affection are consid-ered important in other theories of moral development too, but in cognitive-developmental theory they are considered useful because they promote role-taking processes.

Studies conducted with United States samples have indeed found positive correla-tions between moral judgment level in children and parental affection and encour-agement of discussion about morality (Holstein, 1972; Schoffeitt, 1971; White, 1973; Denney & Duffy, 1974). Reading these studies, one gets a definite impression of the kind of parents believed most likely to have children at high moral judgment stages. The most successful parents are expected to be those verbal and overtly rational people who encourage warm and close relations with children and who promote a "democratic" style of family life. That is, they foster discussions oriented toward reasoned understanding of moral issues and toward a fair consideration of every-one's viewpoint. They conduct family life in a style obviously congruent with middle- and upper-class values in a bureaucratic, technological society.

In many non-Western societies, however, the intimate, rational, nonauthoritarian family is not the cultural ideal as it is in the middle and upper classes of the United States. This fact raises two critical questions for the comparative study of human development. First, do induction and affection predict high moral judgment devel-opment in societies different from our own? Second, what parental child-rearing behaviors correlate with moral judgment development other than those behaviors prominent in societies like the United States? That is, have some other societies evolved completely different strategies by which parents provide their children with role-taking opportunities? Do these strategies work as well as the strategies extolled by American psychologists, or is the type of family which is the cultural ideal in the United States the one best model for creating mature moral judgment?

The comparative literature provides two studies which address the first question. Parikh (1975) conducted a study of professional families living in the city of Ah-medabad, India. In her sample of upper-middle-class urban adolescents, stage of moral judgment was significantly correlated with the following factors: (1) extent of encouragement given by parents to children in the discussion of moral dilemmas; (2) extent of induction generally used by parents; and (3) extent of affection shown by parents. The first factor was measured by direct observation of parent-child discussions; the second and third were indirectly measured through parent and child reports. The three social environmental factors were much more strongly related to children's moral judgment stage than they were to their IQs or their logical cognition stage—a fact which suggests that the results were not simply the spurious result of an intervening relationship between child-rearing practices and intelligence. I (Edwards, 1974; 1978) studied secondary school students living in the Kenyan cities of Nyeri and Nairobi and found that students from more "modernized" backgrounds (as measured by parent education, occupation, and marriage type) showed higher stages of moral judgment than students from more "traditional" backgrounds, although they performed no better on an overall measure of academic ability (a standardized national achievement test). In Kenya modernization is associated with changing child-rearing practices: more modernized parents tend to negotiate disputes with their children and to allow children to interrupt and question their authority, whereas more traditional parents tend to expect obedience without prolonged discussion or negotiation. Thus the modernization dimension served as an indirect and approximate measure of the induction pattern of child rearing.

Both of these studies do suggest that some of the same kinds of family factors are conducive to moral judgment development in Western and non-Western societies, at least for children of urban or town settings. However, neither study investigates new hypotheses about child-rearing strategies different from those examined in the United States, yet ethnographic descriptions of socialization in nonindustrial societies (e.g., B. Whiting & Whiting, 1975; Middleton, 1970) could serve as a rich source of hypotheses. For example, it might be that parents provide role-taking opportunities to their children by arranging for them to care for their younger siblings and direct their work while the mother is absent. Further, parents may help their children take the perspective of a wider kin group by involving them in social processes such as storytelling, visiting, and ritual. Hypotheses like these must be investigated before we can claim to understand parental influences on moral judgment development from a universal human perspective.

Studies on Peer Influences

Relative to psychoanalytic theory, cognitive-developmental theory diminishes the role of parents in moral development. In fact, Piaget (1932), who studied working-class Genevan children, considered parents to be generally too authoritarian and constraining to contribute much to their children's moral judgment development. Instead, Piaget looked to interaction with peers for the kind of reciprocity and cooperation that he deemed essential for overcoming primitive childhood egocentrism and heteronomy. According to Piaget, peers are status equals and therefore must negotiate and bargain to achieve agreement. In that process, they learn to take one another's perspective. Kohlberg (1969), like Piaget, has stressed the role-taking opportunities inherent in peer group participation. However, Kohlberg has disagreed with Piaget on the necessity of peer group participation. Rather, he argues that the peer group simply serves as a good source for most children of general role-taking opportunities. Participation is partly a matter of sheer quantity of interaction with peers and partly a matter of leadership in the group: leadership positions require more complex, organized, and objective role-taking skills than do follower roles.

Researchers using American samples (Kohlberg, 1958; Keasey, 1971; Harris, Mussen, & Rutherford, 1976) have generally found that children who score higher on Kohlberg's scale are less likely to be socially isolated and more likely to be popular and highly regarded by peers (based on ratings by teachers, peers, or the self). Moreover, peer discussion groups and peer role-playing procedures have provided the framework for many experimental and educational interventions that have proved effective in changing participants' tested level of moral judgment (Maitland & Goldman, 1974; Sullivan, 1975; Blatt & Kohlberg, 1975; Arbuthnot, 1975; Saltzstein, 1975).

All of these American studies have considered one particular type of peer group only, that of schoolmates. Schools create groups of nonkin-related agemates whose experiences with one another occur primarily in an institutional setting under supervision of adults. These circumstances may be typical for peer groups in urban industrial society, but they do not necessarily obtain in other societies. In fact, the composition and functions of children's and adolescents' peer groups vary widely throughout the world, and this natural variation offers many possibilities for investigating the effect of peers on moral judgment development. Inter- and intrasociety variation provides a natural arena for discovering and testing hypotheses about particular dimensions of peer interaction which are stimulative of moral judgment development at particular stages of children's lives.

For example, on Israel kibbutzim children and adolescents experience greatly different amounts and kinds of peer interaction from their nonkibbutz counterparts. Bar Yam et al. (1971) have found kibbutz adolescents to show considerably less preconventional (stages 1 and 2) and more principled (stages 5 and 6) reasoning than city adolescents. Their sample is small and the study is not well controlled. Nevertheless, Kohlberg's (1971b) discussion of the data offers an excellent analysis of adolescent moral socialization on the kibbutz and how that socialization process might promote more mature moral reasoning in young adults. Rather than focusing just on the overall amount of peer group interaction, the analysis explains how the teacher forges a collective life for the adolescents which promotes identification first with the community and then with the society as a whole. Kohlberg's discussion stresses the specific characteristics of conventional and principled reasoning and how these two levels might be fostered by typical practices of kibbutz adolescent moral training.

In Africa two salient dimensions of intrasociety variation in peer interaction include the amount of cultural diversity and the extent to which schooling removes young people from traditional family life and parental authority. I (Edwards, 1974; 1978) have found that Kenyan university students attribute the greatest changes in their personal values to encountering ethnic and racial heterogeneity at school and to going away from home to live. Students felt that these experiences helped give them a social perspective on morality and also helped them to see themselves as moral agents. Both of these changes would be expected as part of the developmental change from preconventional to conventional morality. Indeed, the empirical evidence presented in the study (based on university and secondary samples) suggests that students attending culturally diverse (versus homogeneous) and residential (versus nonresidential) secondary schools advance more rapidly in moral judgment from the preconventional to the conventional level. Maqsud (1976; 1977a, b) obtained similar results on both dimensions with samples of Nigerian secondary students, except that he found students at semiresidential schools to score higher than students at either exclusively residential or nonresidential institutions.

These three studies are examples of how moral judgment development may be traced to natural peer influences. They present analyses of exactly what components of peer interaction might be critical influences on moral judgment. In this way they correct Piaget's unqualified statements about the value of peer interaction and suggest that sometimes peer interaction will have a positive effect and sometimes not, depending upon exactly what opportunities for role taking are provided by the peer contacts. Many other ideas about peer influences could well be explored through comparative studies. For example, numerous societies employ initiation rites to achieve abrupt status changes for girls or boys. Such sudden status transitions might be expected to provoke accelerated rates of change in the children's thinking about themselves and society, as measured by moral judgment stage. Another useful study might investigate children's natural play groups and the differential influence of mixed- versus same-aged grouping. The mixed-age group would be expected to include a wider range of developmental stages and might be very stimulating for the younger children involved—and perhaps also for the older ones, who experience the beneficial effects of being teachers. Other comparative work might focus on which types of peer groups act to retard rather than stimulate moral judgment development. Such studies would be interesting not only for learning about moral development but also for increasing knowledge of a little-understood area, the socializing function of peers.

Studies on the Influence of Wider Society: The Relation between Moral Stages and Social Structure

In one of his early papers, Kohlberg (1969) appears to make a distinction between primary and secondary reference groups in terms of their part in promoting role taking and hence moral development. Primary reference groups such as family and friends provide role-taking opportunities suitable for the types of interpersonal thinking involved in stages 1 and 2. However, primary reference groups are not sufficient to promote higher moral thinking because children must be able to take a generalized social perspective in order to attain moral stages 3 and above. For example, they must be able to think about roles and generalized social expectations for stage 3. For stage 4, they must elaborate this perspective into an organized "systems" conception and take the perspective of institutions such as government and the law. Thus social experiences that cause people to take a wider, societal view of morality are necessary precursors of moral stages 3 and above. The more people have such experiences (through work, education, and leadership roles), says Kohlberg, the more advanced they are likely to be in moral judgment. Hence in his view the characteristic moral stage of a cultural group reflects the "quality" of the social environment. Two types of groups he considered to be generally deprived are (1) the lower classes in complex, industrial societies and (2) people from traditional peasant and tribal societies. The former lack any real participation or control over the economic, political, and legal institutions of society and tend to become "fixated" at moral stage 2. The latter have a sense of participation in a village community but not in the national institutions and frequently become fixated at moral stage 3 (Kohlberg, 1969, pp. 401–402).

It is clear that Kohlberg believes that people in traditional cultures are not likely to achieve as developed moral reasoning as people in nontraditional societies. Moreover, these variations between cultures "are not morally arbitrary ... [because] there is a sense in which we can characterize moral differences between groups and individuals as being more or less adequate morally" (Kohlberg, 1971a, pp. 176–177).

Two aspects of this issue need to be examined. First, what does the comparative evidence indicate about the relationship between social structure and moral reasoning? Is there indeed evidence for a general difference in stage of moral judgment between members of simple versus complex societies? Second, does the comparative evidence suggest that cultural differences are reasonably interpreted as differences in *adequacy* of moral reasoning and of the social environment?

A review of the cross-cultural studies does suggest a general difference in performance on the moral judgment test by members of simple versus complex societies. Stages 4 and above do not seem to appear in the protocols of nonliterate or semiliterate adults or children who come from isolated peasant or tribal communities in Kenya, Turkey, the Bahamas, and British Honduras (Edwards, 1975a, b; Harkness et al., 1977; White et al., 1978; White, 1975; 1977; Gorsuch & Barnes, 1973). In contrast, stage 4 has been scored in the protocols of secondary or college educated adults and adolescents in Turkey, India, Thailand, Israel, Kenya, Nigeria, and Canada as well as in the United States (Turiel et al., 1978; Parikh, 1975; Batt, 1975b; Kohlberg, 1971; Edwards, 1974; 1975; 1978; Maqsud, 1977a; Sullivan, 1975). Thus stages 1–3 are found among groups of people whose frame of reference is a traditional face-to-face village community as well as people from modern or urban settings. Stages 4–6, in contrast, seem to be limited to educated adults whose frame of reference is a complex society such as a modern national state. A kind of boundary appears to exist between stages 3 and 4, corresponding to presence or absence of participation in the secondary institutions of a complex society. "Participation" seems to come about through education or engagement in modern work roles that foster taking a relatively abstract and general view of the national society (see Edwards, 1975).

While such differences between groups do exist, concepts of the adequacy of moral reasoning and the adequacy of the social environment appear to be the wrong way to think about them. Are simple, traditional societies less adequate social environments than complex, modern societies? Are forms of moral thought typically found in simple societies less adequate for them than the forms found in complex societies are for those systems?

The adequacy issue acts as a red flag and distracts our attention from the idea that moral judgment structures and social structures may have certain correspondences which are interesting in their own right. For example, an analysis of the structure of the stages suggests that built into the criteria of stages 3 and 4 are different assumptions about the nature of society and human relations (Edwards, 1975). Stage 3 definitions of authority, punishment, rules and law, guilt and blame, and individual liberty seem appropriate for the leadership and social control processes of a face-to-face community, while those of stage 4 correspond to a state or national system with formal institutions of government and law. Both stages involve generalized perspectives, but these perspectives are suitable for different types of social organization.

The stage 3 versus stage 4 distinction indicates one way in which individual moral development may be associated with wider social processes. That is, people living in complex societies may be more likely to develop moral stages 4 and above than are people living in noncomplex societies. If so, then it is clear that processes at the societal level (perhaps processes of leadership and conflict resolution, as argued above) somehow affect developmental processes at the individual level (moral reasoning). In a way, such a correspondence would not be surprising, since moral reasoning constitutes part of the person's mechanisms of *self*-control, whereas systems of leadership and conflict resolution constitute parts of the society's mechanisms of *social* control. Some psychological anthropologists have argued that self-control mechanisms of moral emotion (shame and guilt) correspond with societal mechanisms of social control (Benedict, 1946; J. Whiting, 1959; Levy, 1972). The hypothesis presented here simply builds on the approach of those psychological anthropologists and extends their argument to cover judgmental as well as emotional aspects of self-control. In both cases there is an assumption that morality is a product of adaptational forces (or processes of "equilibration," in Piagetian terms) that relate cultural, society-wide events with psychological, individual events. In cognitive-developmental theory, the functional fit is considered to arise because human intelligence strives for a match between interior mental structures and the organization of information in the environment. In the case of moral development, this would mean that human intelligence strives for a fit between most-used modes of moral judgment and the information about human nature and conflict resolution embodied in the social justice system.

Less evidence exists concerning the other moral stages and their possible relationship to social structure. Of potential interest are the stage 2 versus 3 and the stage 4 versus 5 distinctions.

The stage 2 to 3 transition marks the change from a concrete individual perspective to an ideal, group perspective on morality. One question is whether any cohesive society could exist without at least some of its adults functioning at moral stage 3. Harkness et al. (1977) found that culturally recognized moral leaders of a rural Kipsigis community in Kenya typically scored at stage 3. Nonleaders (matched for age, education, wealth, and religion with the leaders) scored significantly lower, predominantly at stage 2. Yet these findings do not prove that a viable stage 2 society could not exist. Stage 2 reasoning includes notions of reciprocity, exchange, and fairness that could conceivably serve as a basis for social order, especially in communities without formally designated authorities and without mechanisms of dispute settlement other than self-redress. Malinowski (1926) noted long ago that the major motivation for ordinary moral behavior in primitive (or any other) society is not the taboo but rather the knowledge that unless one keeps one's obligations to others, they will not keep theirs. People do right because they are bound into systems of reciprocal obligation on which their well-being depends. Such systems of exchange can conceptually be represented by any of the moral stages other than stage 1: for example, a stage 2 reasoner represents the system in terms of the instrumental exchange of concrete benefits. In only one of the adult samples studied so far, that of Bahamian elders investigated by White (1977), has stage 3 been found to be almost completely lacking. The question remains open whether or not stage 2 modes of thought can predominate in a viable social system and, if so, under what conditions.

The stage 4 to 5 transition marks a change from a "law-maintaining" societal perspective to a particular kind of "law-giving" perspective. Stages 5 and 6, the "principled" or "postconventional" stages, are theoretically based on the perspective of a rational person thinking about justice, equality, and social value abstractly and metaethically, free to go beyond the particular norms, laws, and rules of existing society. Very little of stages 5 and 6 reasoning has been scored thus far in the interviews of non-Western peoples—even the university-educated men and women. This scarcity of stages 5 and 6 may indicate that these people are less able to, or trained to, think metaethically about moral issues. On the other hand, and perhaps more likely, the scarcity may indicate that the current definition of stages 5 and 6 includes only two possible forms of postconventional reasoning—two particularly appropriate for capitalist societies of the constitutional type. As the philosopher Edel (1968) has noted, the question may be raised whether "these stages [5 and 6] should not be regarded as cultural specializations under determinable conditions, and in fact, whether the criteria in the whole third [principled] level—with an emphasis on contract, individual rights, and democracy, culminating in individual conscience—do not have a stress characteristic of the intense individualism of Western Europian culture in the last two centuries" (p. 19). Edel's hypothesis could easily be tested by interviewing adults from societies that are as complex as the Western industrial nations but are guided by different political and economic idologies (e.g., China). Such studies would show whether the most sophisticated moral reasoning in non-capitalist societies assumes the forms defined by Kohlberg as stages 5 and 6 or whether the people develop other reflective philosophies, at a metaethical plane of discourse, in leaving behind stage 4 forms of judgments and becoming postconventional (see Gibbs, 1977).

SUMMARY AND CONCLUSIONS: RESEARCH BASED ON KOHLBERG'S APPROACH

Cross-cultural research using Kohlberg's cognitive-developmental approach to moralization has proceeded further than research using Piaget's approach with respect to two major issues. The first issue is the validity of the developmental sequence in both traditional and modern cultures. The second involves sources of development —that is, antecedent variables for moral judgment change.

A number of longitudinal and cross-sectional studies provide preliminary support for cross-cultural validity—the universality of the stages and their sequence. The findings suggest that the first three moral stages (those most closely linked to the psychological stages of roletaking) are found in a wide variety of cultural settings. Furthermore, the longitudinal evidence suggests that these three stages are acquired in the expected order and that over time most respondents change in a forward, upward direction as predicted. The greatest problem arises with respect to Kohlberg's highest stages, which seem to be found much more commonly in complex than in simple societies. An explanation has been offered in terms of correspondences between moral judgment (psychological) structures and legal/political (societal) structures. Such an explanation derives from the cognitive-developmental theory of *equilibration,* which states that human adaptive intelligence leads to a fit between mental structures and the organization of information in the environment. Future research will tell whether or not this explanation is adequate.

The research on antecedent variables has provided most evidence about the influence of parents and peers on moral development during childhood and adolescence. A lesser amount of work has investigated the relation of moral development to cognitive development and the facilitative influence of wider society (through work, educational, and leadership roles) on moral development during later adolescence and adulthood. The studies have been intended to check generalizations about antecedent variables derived from American data and to test new hypotheses about the particular ways that development normally occurs in different cultures. This is a wide area for study, and although the research to date is promising it is still in a beginning stage on all the above topics. Furthermore, researchers have not addressed in a fully satisfactory way certain issues of methodology (especially translation). Nevertheless, the moral judgment interview has been demonstrated to actively engage the interest of respondents in a wide variety of cultures and to provide data which can be reliably and objectively scored. Studies using the technique have shown that they can provide new insight into human development.

REFERENCES

Arbuthnot, J. Modification of moral judgment through role playing. *Developmental Psychology*, 1975, *11*, 319–324.

Aron, I. Moral philosophy and moral education: A critique of Kohlberg's theory. *School Review*, 1977, *85*, 197–217.

Baldwin, *Social and Ethical Interpretations in Mental Development*. 1899. Reprint: New York: Arno Press, 1973.

Bar Yam, M., Reimer, J., & Kohlberg, L. Development of moral reasoning in the kibbutz. Unpublished manuscript, Harvard University, 1971.

Bart, W. M. A biosociological framework for the study of formal operations. Paper presented at the annual meeting of the Jean Piaget Society, Philadelphia, 1977.

Batt, H. W. Guilt, shame and the bureaucratic model: With specific reference to Thai public administration. Doctoral dissertation, State University of New York at Albany, 1975. [Ann Arbor: University Microfilms, 1975, 75–9462] (a)

Batt, H. W. Thai conceptions of justice on Kohlberg's moral development scale. Unpublished manuscript, 1975 (b).

Benedict, R. *The chrysanthemum and the sword*. Boston: Houghton Mifflin, 1946.

Blatt, M. M., & Kohlberg, L. The effects of classroom moral discussion upon children's level of moral judgment. *Journal of Moral Education*, 1975, *4*, 129–162.

Boehm, L. The development of conscience: A comparison of American children of different mental and socio-economic levels. *Child Development*, 1962, *33*, 575–590.

Boyd, D. & Kohlberg, L. The is-ought problem: A developmental perspective. *Zygon*, 1973, *8*, 358–372.

Broughton, J. The cognitive-developmental approach to morality: A reply to Kurtines and Greif. *Journal of Moral Education*, 1978, *7* (2), 81–96.

Buck-Morss. Socio-economic bias in Piaget's theory and its implications for cross-culture studies. *Human Development*, 1975, *18*, 35–49.

Burton, R. V. Assessment of moral training programs: Where are we going? Invited Address, annual meeting of the American Psychological Association, Washington, D.C., September, 1976.

Byrne, D. F. The development of role-taking in adolescence. Unpublished doctoral dissertation, Harvard Graduate School of Education, 1973.

Caruso, I. H. La notion de responsabilité et de justice immanente chez l'enfant. *Archives de Psychologie*, 1943, *29* (Whole No. 114).

Cauble, M. A. Formal operations, ego identity, and principled morality: Are they related? Developmental Psychology, 1976, *12*, 363–364.

Curdin, J. A study of the development of immanent justice. Unpublished doctoral dissertation, University of North Carolina at Chapel Hill, 1966.

Denney, N. W. & Duffy, D. M. Possible environmental causes of stages in moral reasoning. *Journal of Genetic Psychology*, 1974, *125*, 277–283.

Dennis, W. Animism and related tendencies in Hopi children. *Journal of Abnormal and Social Psychology*, 1943, *38*, 21–37.

Dewey, J., & Tufts, J. H. *Ethics*. New York: Henry Holt & Co., 1908.

Eckensberger, L. H., Eckensberger, U. S., and Reinshagen, H. Kohlbergs interview zum moralischen urteil Teil I—Teil IV. *Arbeiten der Fachrichtung Psychologie*, Nos. 31–34. Universitat des Saarlandes, Deutschland, 1975–1976.

Edel, A. Scientific research and moral judgment. Paper delivered at the Conference on the Acquisition and Development of Values, National Institute of Child Health and Human Development, 1968.

Edwards, C. P. The effect of experience on moral development: Results from Kenya. Doctoral dissertation, Harvard Graduate School of Education, 1974. [Ann Arbor: University Microfilms, 1975, 75–16860] (a).

Edwards, C. P. Societal complexity and moral development: A Kenyan study. *Ethos,* 1975, *3,* 505–527. (b)

Edwards, C. P. Social experience and moral judgment in Kenyan young adults. *Journal of Genetic Psychology,* 1978, *133,* 19–29.

Flavell, J. H., Botkin, P., Fry, C., Wright, J., & Jarvis, P. *The development of role-taking and communication skills in children.* New York: John Wiley & Sons, 1968.

Gibbs, J. C. Kohlberg's stages of moral judgment: A constructive critique. *Harvard Educational Review,* 1977, *47,* 1977, 43–61.

Gibbs, J., Kohlberg, L., Colby, A., & Speicher-Dubin, B. The domain and development of moral judgment: A theory and a method of assessment. In J. R. Meyer (Ed.), *Reflections on Values Education.* Waterloo, Ontario: Wilfrid Laurier University Press, 1976, pp. 19–46.

Gorsuch, R. L. & Barnes, M. L. Stages of ethical reasoning and moral norms of Carib youths. *Journal of Cross-Cultural Psychology,* 1973, *4,* 283–301.

Grinder, R. E. Relations between behavioral and cognitive dimensions of conscience in middle childhood. *Child Development,* 1964, *35,* 881–891.

Hamm, C. M. The content of moral education, or in defense of the "bag of virtues." *School Review,* 1977, 218–228.

Harkness, S., Edwards, C. P., & Super, C. M. Kohlberg in the bush: A study of moral reasoning among the elders of a rural Kipsigis community. Unpublished manuscript, 1977.

Harris, S., Mussen, P., & Rutherford, E. Some cognitive, behavioral, and personality correlates of maturity of moral judgment. *Journal of Genetic Psychology,* 1976, *128,* 123–135.

Havighurst, R. J., & Neugarten, B. L. *American Indian and white children: A sociological investigation.* Chicago: University of Chicago Press, 1955.

Hobhouse, L. T. *Morals in evolution: A study in comparative ethics.* London: Chapman & Hall, 1906.

Holstein, C. B. The relation of children's moral judgment level to that of their parents and to communications patterns in the family. In R. C. Smart & M. S. Smart (Eds.), *Readings in child development and relationships.* New York: MacMillan, 1972.

Holstein, C. B. Irreversible, stepwise sequence in the development of moral judgment: A longitudinal study of males and females. *Child Development,* 1976, *47,* 51–61.

Jahoda, G. Immanent justice among West African children. *Journal of Social Psychology,* 1958, *47,* 241–248.

Johnson, R. C. A study of children's moral judgments. *Child Development,* 1962, *33,* 327–354.

Keasey, C. B. Social participation as a factor in the moral development of preadolescents. *Developmental Psychology,* 1971, *5,* 216–220.

Keasey, C. B. Implicators of cognitive development for moral reasoning. In D. J. DePalma & J. M. Foley (Eds.), *Moral development: Current theory and research.* Hillsdale, N.J.: Lawrence Erlbaum, 1975, pp. 39–56.

Kohlberg, L. The development of modes of moral thinking and choice in the years ten to sixteen. Unpublished doctoral dissertation, University of Chicago, 1958.

Kohlberg, L. Moral development and identification. In H. W. Stevenson (Ed.), *Year-*

book of the National Society for the Study of Education. Part I. Child psychology. Chicago: University of Chicago Press, 1963, pp. 277–332.

Kohlberg, L. Stage and sequence: The cognitive-developmental approach to socialization. In D. Goslin (Ed.), Handbook of socialization. New York: Rand McNally, 1969, pp. 347–480.

Kohlberg, L. From is to ought: How to commit the naturalistic fallacy and get away with it in the study of moral development. In T. Mischel (E.), Cognitive development and epistemology. New York: Academic Press, 1971. (a)

Kohlberg, L. Cognitive-developmental theory and the practice of collective education. In M. Wolins & M. Gottesman (Eds.), Group care: An Israeli approach. New York: Gordon & Breach, 1971, (b).

Kohlberg, L. Continuities in childhood and adult moral development revisited. In Life span developmental psychology. New York: Academic Press, 1973, pp. 179–204.

Kohlberg, L. Moral stages and moralization: The cognitive-developmental approach. In T. Lickona (Ed.), Moral development and behavior. New York: Holt, 1976, pp. 31–53.

Kohlberg, L., Havighurst, R., & Neugarten, B. A. J. A further analysis of cross-cultural moral judgment data. Unpublished manuscript, Harvard University, 1967.

Kugelmass, S., & Breznitz, S. The development of intentionality in moral judgment in city and kibbutz adolescents. Journal of Genetic Psychology, 1967, 111, 103–111.

Kuhn, D. Relation of two Piagetian stage transitions to IQ. Developmental Psychology, 1976, 12, 157–161. (a)

Kuhn, D. Short-term longitudinal evidence for the sequentiality of Kohlberg's early stages. Developmental Psychology, 1976, 12, 162–166. (b)

Kuhn, D., Langer, J., Kohlberg, L., & Haan, N. S. The development of formal operations in logical and moral judgment. Genetic Psychology Monographs, 1977, 95, 97–188.

Kurtines, W., & Greif, E. B. The development of moral thought: Review and evaluation of Kohlberg's approach. Psychological Bulletin, 1974, 81, 453–470.

Lee, B., A cognitive-developmental approach to filiality development. Unpublished masters thesis, Committee on Human Development, University of Chicago, 1973.

Lee, B. Fairness and filiality: A cross-cultural cultural account. Paper presented at the annual meeting of the American Anthropological Association, Washington, D.C., November 1976.

Lee, L. C. The concomitant development of cognitive and moral modes of thought: A test of selected deductions from Piaget's theory. Genetic Psychology Monographs, 1971, 83, 93–146.

Lerner, E. The problem of perspective in moral reasoning. American Journal of Sociology, 1937, 43, 249–269. (a)

Lerner, E. Constraint areas and the moral Judgment of children. Menesha, Wisc.: Banta, 1937. (b)

Levy, R. I. Tahiti, sin, and the question of integration between personality and socio-cultural systems. In W. Muensterberger & S. Axelrad (Eds.), The psychoanalytic study of society (Vol. 5). New York: International Universities Press, 1972.

Lickona, T. Research on Piaget's theory of moral development. In T. Lickona (Ed.), Moral development and behavior. New York: Holt, 1976, pp. 219–240.

Loevinger, J. Ego development. Washington, D.C.: Jossey-Bass, 1976.

Loughran, R. A pattern of development in moral judgments made by adolescents derived from Piaget's scheme of its development in childhood. Educational Review, 1967, 19, 79–98.

Loves, H. Ancestral beliefs and Christian catechesis: Enquiry in 55 classes in Kwango, Belgian Congo. Lumen Vitae, 1957, 12, 353–376.

Maitland, K. A., & Goldman, J. R. Moral judgment as a function of peer group interaction. *Journal of Personality and Social Psychology*, 1974, *30*, 699–704.

Malinowski, B. *Crime and custom in savage society.* London: Routledge & Kegan Paul, 1926.

Maqsud, M. The effects of different educational environments on moral development of Nigerian children belonging to various tribes. Unpublished doctoral dissertation, University of London, 1976.

Maqsud, M. The influence of social heterogeneity and sentimental credibility on moral judgments of Nigerian Muslim adolescents. *Journal of Cross-Cultural Psychology*, 1977, *8*, 113–122. (a)

Maqsud, M. Social interaction and moral judgment in Northern Nigerian adolescents. Unpublished manuscript, Bayero University College, Kano, Nigeria, 1977. (b)

MacRae, D., Jr. A test of Piaget's theories of moral development. *Journal of Abnormal and Social Psychology*, 1954, *49*, 14–18.

McDougall, W. *An introduction to social psychology.* London: Methuen, 1908.

Medinnus, G. R. Immanent justice in children: A review of the literature and additional data. *Journal of Genetic Psychology*, 1959, *94*, 253–262.

Medinnus, G. R. Objective responsibility in children: A comparison with the Piaget data. *Journal of Genetic Psychology*, 1962, *101*, 127–133.

Mead, G. H. *Mind, self, and society.* Chicago: University of Chicago Press, 1934.

Mead, M. Some anthropological considerations concerning guilt. In M. L. Regmert (Ed.), *Feelings and emotions.* New York: McGraw-Hill, 1950, pp. 362–373.

Middleton, J. (Ed.). *From child to adult.* Garden City, N.Y.: Natural History Press, 1970.

Moir, D. J. Egocentrism and the emergence of conventional morality in preadolescent girls. *Child Development*, 1974, *45*, 299–304.

Najarian-Svajian, P. H. The idea of immanent justice among Lebanese children and adults. *Journal of Genetic Psychology*, 1966, *109*, 57–66.

Neimark, E. D. Intellectual development during adolescence. In *Review of Child Development Research (Vol. 4).* Chicago: University of Chicago Press, 1974, pp. 541–594.

Parikh, B. Moral judgment development and its relation to family environmental factors in Indian and American urban upper-middle class families. Unpublished doctoral dissertation, Department of Special Education, Boston University, 1975.

Piaget, J. *The moral judgment of the child.* 1932. [Reprint: New York: Free Press, 1965].

Ponzo, E. An investigation into the development of juridicial knowledge in children. *Education and Psychology*, 1956, *3*, 1–20.

Porter, N., & Taylor, N. *How to assess the moral reasoning of students.* Toronto: Ontario Institute for Studies in Education, 1972.

Rest, J. Developmental psychology as a guide to value education: A review of "Kohlbergian" programs. *Review of Educational Research*, 1974, *44*, 241–258.

Saltzstein, H. D. Role-taking as a method of facilitating moral development. Paper presented at the annual meeting of the Eastern Psychological Association, New York, 1975.

Selman, R. L. Social-cognitive understanding: A guide to educational and clinical practice. In T. Lickona (Ed.), *Moral development and behavior.* New York: Holt, 1976, pp. 299–316.

Schoffeitt, P. G. The moral development of children as a function of parental moral judgments and childrearing. Unpublished doctoral dissertation, George Peabody College for Teachers, Nashville, 1971.

Simon, A., & Ward, L. O. Variables influencing pupils' responses on the Kohlberg schema of moral development. *Journal of Moral Education*, 1973, *2*, 283–286.

Simpson, A. L., & Graham, D. The development of moral judgment, emotion, and behavior in British adolescents. Unpublished manuscript, University of Durham, England, 1971.

Simpson, E. L. Moral development research: A case study of scientific cultural bias. *Human Development,* 1974, *17,* 813–106.

Spencer, H. *The principles of ethics, Volume I.* New York: D. Appleton and Co., 1899.

Sullivan, E. V. *Moral learning: Some findings, issues, and questions.* New York: Paulist Press, 1975.

Sullivan, E. V., McCullough, G., & Stager, M. A. A developmental study of the relationship between conceptual, ego, and moral development. *Child Development,* 1970, *41,* 399–411.

Sullivan, E. V., & Quarter, J. Psychological correlates of certain postconventional moral types: A perspective on hybrid types. *Journal of Personality,* 1972, *40,* 149–161.

Tomlinson-Keasey, C., & Keasey, C. B. The mediating role of cognitive development in moral judgment. *Child Development,* 1974, *45,* 291–298.

Turiel, E. Stage transition in moral development. In R. M. Travers (Ed.), *Second handbook of research on teaching.* Chicago: Rand McNally, 1972.

Turiel, E. Conflict and transition in adolescent moral development. *Child Development,* 1974, *45,* 14–29.

Turiel, E. The development of social concepts: Mores, customs, and conventions. In D. J. DePalma & J. M. Foley (Eds.), *Moral development: Current theory and research.* Hillsdale, N.J.: Lawrence Erlbaum, 1975, pp. 7–38.

Turiel, Edwards, C. P. & Kohlberg, L. Moral development in Turkish children, adolescents, and young adults. *Journal of Cross-Cultural Psychology,* 1978, *9* (1), 75–86.

White, C. B. Moral judgment in college students: The development of an objective measure and its relationship to life experience dimensions. Unpublished doctoral dissertation, University of Georgia, 1973.

White, C. B. Moral development in Bahamian school children: A cross-cultural examination of Koblberg's stages of moral reasoning. *Developmental Psychology,* 1975, *11,* 535–536.

White, C. B. Moral reasoning in Bahamian and United States elders: Cross-national comparisons of Kohlberg's theory of moral development. Unpublished manuscript, University of Texas at Dallas, 1977.

White, C. B., Bushnell, N., & Regnemer, J. L. Moral development in Bahamian school children: A three-year examination of Kohlberg's stages of moral development. *Developmental Psychology,* 1978, *14,* 58–65.

Whiting, B. B., & Whiting, J. W. M. *Children of six cultures: A psychocultural analysis.* Cambridge, Mass.: Harvard University Press, 1975.

Whiting, J. W. M. Sorcery, sin, and the superego: A cross-cultural study of some mechanisms of social control. In M. R. Jones (Ed.), *Nebraska Symposium on Motivation.* Lincoln, Nebraska: University of Nebraska Press, 1959, pp. 187–193.

Part IV

Socialization and Outcomes

16

A Cross-cultural Perspective on Sex Differences

Carol R. Ember

Perhaps now more than ever people seem to want to understand how and why the sexes may be different. The current popular interest in sex differences has in one way been fortunate and in another way unfortunate. Fortunately, the current interest is likely to stimulate research on the nature and etiology of sex differences—an area often neglected in the past. In the future, even those researchers who are not explicitly studying sex differences may be more inclined to include girls and women in their studies. The unfortunate consequence of the current interest is that there is strong pressure to come to decisions about the "causes" of sex differences on the basis of the evidence now available. For some, this need to decide now may come from political considerations—there seems to be the feeling that if sex differences are shown to stem from "nurture," society will be unable to justify sexual discrimination. For others, the need to decide now may simply come from the desire for closure. Whatever the reason, I think that the pressure to decide now about the causes of sex differences is unfortunate because the available evidence does not warrant any strong conclusions, in my opinion.

I will try to do two things in the present review. One is to indicate what we know, as well as what we do not know, about which sex differences exist cross-culturally. (For another such survey, see Rosenblatt and Cunningham, 1976.) My second intention is to discuss theories that might explain the apparent sex differences. Because most cross-cultural research has been concerned with discovering sex differences, we know the most about how some sex differences are distributed cross-culturally. Since explicit theory-testing research has been less prevalent (both cross-culturally as well as intraculturally), we know relatively less about what might explain the particular sex differences that have been found. I devote a lot of space to what we do not know, or what we can only speculate about, because I think that to do so may serve a constructive purpose. It is only when we recognize that we cannot get very far on the basis of the available evidence that we can begin to design better research; it is only when we recognize that our theories are not specific enough to be testable that we have to revise our theories; and it is only when we speculate about why there are particular sex differences that we can generate new theories to test.

My review is organized around three classes of sex difference. The first consists of physical and physiologic differences (other than the obvious reproductive differences). The second consists of differences that are ethnographically described, with the exception of differences in socialization, which I reserve for the last section. The third class consists of psychological differences, i.e., those that are based on observations of individuals. I discuss socialization differences in this last section, rather than the second, because they may figure in the etiology of psychological differences between the sexes. Before turning to these three classes of sex difference I want to prepare the ground by discussing the relative value of the two kinds of cross-cultural research that have investigated sex differences—research designed explicitly to test theories and research designed to discover differences. [This review was prepared in the spring of 1977 and covers publications only through early 1977.]

EVALUATING THE RESEARCH ON SEX DIFFERENCES

As I have already indicated, relatively little cross-cultural research has been designed to test theories about why there are sex differences. In my view this is unfortunate; this is where I think cross-cultural research has the most value. One of the most difficult problems facing researchers who want to try to untangle the possible influences of biologic and social factors is that in any given society boys and girls are probably treated differently. It is precisely because biologic sex and social factors are not always confounded in quite the same ways in different societies that cross-cultural research has tremendous potential for helping us to test theories about the etiology of sex differences. For example, if we want to test a particular socialization theory, we can compare societies that differ on the *degree* to which boys and girls are differently treated and see if the size of the supposed sex-difference effect varies as expected.

Even biologic theories of sex differences may be tested cross-culturally if populations vary with respect to the *size* of some biologic difference between the sexes. Although we tend to think of sex as simply a dichotomous variable, human populations differ in the degree to which males and females are different in height, weight, and muscular strength. Populations may also differ in the degree to which hormone levels differ by sex. For example, Bushman males have been shown to have fairly high levels of estrogen (Tobias, 1966). If they are closer to females in levels of estrogen than are males in some other societies, the variation among human populations may help us test some theories about the effects of hormones on observed sex differences.

Most cross-cultural studies have devoted themselves to describing and documenting the nature of sex differences. Most frequently, the aim is to see if a particular sex difference is found consistently across cultures. Those interested in ethology have also sought to describe and document whether or not a particular sex difference is consistent across primates and other animal species.

Documenting the nature and the extent of sex differences across cultures is of some interest, but its value has, I think, been overestimated. Many researchers seem to assume that the pattern of sex differences (across cultures and across primates) can help us decide whether a particular sex difference is biologically based or a product of social learning. I must admit that I also thought so in the beginning and decided only after undertaking this review that such conclusions were unwarranted.

I came to this view because different people taking different sides of the "nature–nurture" controversy often point to the same distributional evidence to support their arguments. Since we know that the same evidence cannot support mutually contradictory theories, we can draw two conclusions—either the evidence is not particularly good, or the logic is not particularly compelling. I think that both are often true, as I shall try to show below.

A number of reasons are usually cited to make the case that a particular sex difference is probably biologically determined. I list these reasons and my objections to them.

A sex difference is consistent across cultures. Consistency may occur because most societies face similar life conditions and socialize for similar behaviors. Many things are consistent across cultures, but that does not necessarily make marriage, the incest taboo, restrictions on sexuality, division of labor by sex, or the presence of kinship terminologies biologically determined.

A sex difference appears in nonhuman primates as well as humans. It is entirely possible that some sex differences may be the result of differential socialization in nonhuman primates and humans. There is some evidence, for example, that rhesus mothers treat male and female infants differently. However, even if socialization differences or other differences in social learning cannot be linked to sex differences in other primates, it is possible that certain sex differences which have come under learned control in humans are under more genetic control in other primates. Inasmuch as humans are thought to have a higher proportion of their behavior profiles acquired through learning, there is no a priori reason why some sex differences may be learned in some primate species (e.g., humans) but not in others.

A sex difference has adaptive advantages. Even if a particular sex difference is argued to be generally adaptive for the human species and/or for all primates, that by no means implies that the difference is part of "nature." It should be clear that natural selection operates on the behavioral traits of individuals—it is irrelevant that those traits are acquired through learning or are genetically programmed.

A sex difference appears early in life. Unless we are talking about sex differences immediately after birth, socialization differences by sex may intervene to create some of the observed sex differences. As we will see, research in the United States does suggest some sex differences in the socialization of newborns. (The fact that we cannot as yet link a particular aspect of social learning or socialization to a particular sex difference is irrelevant—the absence of information, particularly when so little research has been done, does not warrant the conclusion that the cause must be biologic.) The converse of this proposition—that late-appearing sex differences are probably the result of socialization differences—does not make sense either. If, for example, a particular behavior is linked to changes in sex hormone levels, it may not begin to manifest itself until children are halfway through childhood.

Distributional evidence is also often used to argue that a particular sex difference is socially induced—a product of "nurture." Yet, as with the reasons given for biologic arguments, I would argue that the logic behind those distributional "reasons" is also not compelling. I list these reasons and my criticisms of them below.

A sex difference is not consistent across cultures.   Just as human populations differ in culture, they may differ in the frequency of certain physical traits. If certain biologic differences between the sexes (like hormone levels) are implicated in producing sex differences in behavior, then some populations might have more of a sex difference than others because of greater or less differences between the sexes in genetic makeup or in nutritional factors that may affect physiology. It is also possible that there is cross-cultural variability in sex differences because some societies seek to socialize *against* biologic predispositions. We cannot always assume that socialization will work to create differences—it may also be used to obviate them.

A sex difference is consistent across cultures, and socialization pressure in the direction of that difference is also consistent across cultures.   The assumption seems to be that if societies socialize boys and girls differently, and they behave differently, then socialization must have been responsible. Why should societies socialize differently if biology by itself would produce the difference? While it seems reasonable to think that social causation would be unnecessary on top of biologic causation, this argument is not that invulnerable to criticism. One could argue that societies might try to reinforce a biologic predisposition if a particular sex difference is useful or adaptive. Socialization pressure in the direction of a sex difference does not tell us anything about whether or not there are also biologic causes of that difference. Moreover, as I noted above, a consistent sex difference has been used to support biologic as well as social explanations. Cross-culturally consistent differences cannot by themselves warrant the conclusion that biologic or social causes are operating.

A sex difference appears only later in childhood.   The inference that appears to be made here is that the later a difference appears, the more it is likely to be due to socialization pressures. The argument, of course, takes on more plausibility if it can be shown that the sex difference appears only after the onset of a particular socialization practice that varies by sex of target. However, as I have pointed out earlier, late-appearing sex differences are not necessarily nonbiologic. If, for example, a particular trait is tied to hormonal control, then sex differences might very well not appear until boys and girls begin to differ in hormones.

In sum, I do not think that distributional patterns of sex differences can logically or empirically help us decide between a biologic explanation and a social explanation of a particular sex difference (or, for that matter, whether or not there is an interaction between them). Moreover, I think the collection of distributional evidence for answers to theoretical questions may hinder our attempt to understand the etiology of sex differences. Whenever we are blunted into looking at indirect evidence, we are not measuring the presumed "cause." Thus we do not have to specify *what exactly* about "nature" or "nurture" is presumed to affect a sex difference. With respect to "nature," are we talking about the influence of a specific sex-linked gene, the influence of hormones, or differences in neurologic organization between the sexes? With respect to "nurture," are we talking about differential reward and punishment for different behaviors exhibited by boys and girls, or other, more unconscious differences in social experience? It is only when we stop trying to find out if "nature" or "nurture" is the "cause," and start specifying what in particular we think is operating, that we can begin to design research to prove a theory false or discriminate between competing theories.

I by no means wish to imply that the distributional evidence (the patterning of sex differences) across cultures tells us nothing—it is just that it does not tell us as much as we would like. Distributional evidence can suggest whether a particular sex difference is a good candidate for a biologic or a cultural explanation. If, for example, a sex difference found in the United States hardly shows up in other cultural contexts, then probably there is something about the treatment of the sexes in the United States that creates the difference. (It would be unlikely, but not impossible, that some unique biologic characteristic of the U.S. is responsible for the U.S. sex difference.) If a sex difference is found in most cultures, we might suspect a pervasive biologic or social factor. If a sex difference appears mainly among sedentary agricultural and industrial peoples and seems lacking among hunters and gatherers (as, for example, with respect to field independence/dependence), then we might suspect or speculate about conditions (either biologic or cultural) that may differ in the different kinds of society. In short, distributional evidence may be provocative of interpretations, but they do not by themselves allow decisions about interpretations.

In my view, then, the establishing of distributional patterns of sex differences across cultures has limited value. At best, it can suggest only what sex differences may be candidates for a biologic or social learning interpretation. It cannot, as I have argued above, help us decide between alternative interpretations. However, cross-cultural research that is designed to test a theory can accomplish two goals at once. Not only does such research provide us with information about the patterning of particular sex differences in other cultural settings, but it obviously helps us say something more explicitly about the theory it is testing. If our goal is to understand sex differences, not just describe them, cross-cultural research must proceed in the theory-testing direction.

PHYSICAL AND PHYSIOLOGIC DIFFERENCES

In almost all animals that reproduce sexually, the two sexes are anatomically different (Wilson, 1975). While we expect differences in gonads and reproductive organs, it is not as clear why the male and female of many animal species—humans included —differ in other (secondary) sex characteristics. After examing some of the nonreproductive physical and physiologic traits that characteristically differ by sex, we will return to the question of what may account for human sexual dimorphism. This question has some importance because sexual dimorphism may partially account for male–female differences in social roles and expectations.

Differences in Adulthood

Probably the most documented male–female difference is in height. For any given human population, adult males are on the average taller than females. The caveat "for any given human population" is important, since if one compares across different human populations, males in some populations are not necessarily taller than the females in other populations (D'Andrade, 1966). Body weight, limb circumferences, bone weights, the proportion of fat and muscle, and physical fitness have been less often studied (Weiner, 1966). Nonetheless, the evidence from different human populations suggests that within a population males generally have heavier skeletons, greater bone densities, greater aerobic work capacities (greater maximum oxygen uptake during exertion), and a larger proportion of their total body weight in muscle (Andersen, 1966; Barfield, 1976; D'Andrade, 1966). Females have a generally larger proportion of fat (Barfield, 1976; D'Andrade, 1966) and a proportionately wider pelvis (Washburn, 1949).

Research conducted primarily in North America and northwestern Europe has documented other aspects of sexual dimorphism. Men have greater grip strength (Asmussen & Heeboll-Nielsen, 1956, cited by Hutt, 1972b), greater strength of arm pull, proportionately larger hearts and lungs, greater capacity for carrying oxygen in the blood (more hemoglobin), and a greater capacity for neutralizing the chemical products of exercise (Tanner, 1970). Assuming that these differences are found in other human populations, they indicate the relatively greater strength of males and their greater capacity for high-energy exertion. Hutt (1972a) suggests that males seem to be operating like an engine at higher levels of speed—both producing and requiring greater levels of energy.

Developmental Differences

Data from Western countries (and to a lesser extent from other countries) suggest that certain aspects of adult sexual dimorphism are negligible until puberty. Although newborn boys are slightly taller than newborn girls, there is generally no sex difference in height in childhood (Garai & Scheinfeld, 1968). Between the ages of 12 and 15 years (slightly varying in different populations), girls may temporarily be taller than boys (Hautvast, 1971a, b; Hiernaux, 1964), but the typical adult male pattern of greater height asserts itself later in adolescence. Males' greater hemoglobin, proportionately larger heart and lungs, and greater aerobic work capacity also may not appear until puberty (Andersen, 1966; Tanner, 1970).

Some aspects of dimorphism appear earlier than puberty. Studies in Western countries suggest that from infancy through adulthood boys have on the average larger and stronger muscles (except when girls have their adolescent growth spurt [Tanner, 1970]), higher basal metabolism, and higher caloric intake (Hutt, 1972a); girls have a larger proportion of fat (Reba, Cheek, & Leitnaker, 1968, cited by Barfield, 1976). Whether or not the cross-cultural data will indicate the same trends remains to be seen. Judging by some data on upper arm circumference, girls in other societies may temporarily exhibit the reversal noted above (Hautvast, 1971b; Stini, 1971). So perhaps, as with height, girls in some societies might temporarily have greater muscular strength than boys. Some studies indicate that at least by 5–8 years of age there is a greater proportion of fat in girls (Frisancho & Baker, 1970; Glanville & Geerdink, 1970).

The fact that some of the physical sex differences are not consistent at all ages might be due in part to the different rates of physical maturation in boys and girls. Girls appear to mature earlier than boys. In Western countries, it has been estimated that girls reach puberty about 1 year earlier than boys (e.g., Nicolson & Hanley, 1953), and reach their peak velocity of adolescent growth 2 years earlier (Tanner, 1970). Studies of embryonic and infant development (also conducted in Western countries) suggest that both in utero and among newborns females surpass males in physical development (Hutt, 1972b). Thus the precocity of girls may partly mask dimorphism in childhood.

Contrary to earlier opinion (e.g., Hutt, 1972a), the earlier physical maturation of girls does not appear to include earlier sitting, crawling, walking, and talking. There are two reasons for the change in opinion. First, recent studies show few sex differences in motor development in the United States (Bayley, 1969) and a few other cultures (J. Kilbride, 1973; G. Solomons & Solomons, 1975), and more recent studies show few sex differences in vocalization (Maccoby & Jacklin, 1974). Second, ages of sitting, crawling, walking, and talking may partly be functions of social learning. With respect to walking, Super (1976) and J. Kilbride, Robbins, and Kilbride (1970) have suggested that African children (as compared with Western children) may walk earlier because of greater encouragement by their mothers. If teaching affects age of walking, other maturational differences may also be affected by social learning. In other words, even if there are some motor differences by sex in childhood, which has yet to be shown, they may be products partly of differential social learning and therefore not really indicative of physical maturation alone.

Explanations of Sexual Dimorphism

Not all the physical differences we have discussed have been documented in a variety of human populations, but there seems little doubt that in any given human population adult males typically are taller, heavier, and have proportionately more muscle. What might account for these differences?

The physiologic reason males are bigger may be that typically they grow for a longer period of time. Bock et al. (1973) have suggested that growth curves for males and females are virtually the same prior to puberty but that during adolescence the growth period is longer for males. Although the mechanisms are not fully understood, the different growth period may be due in part to the different effects of androgen and estrogen on the formation of bone and muscle. Until they are about 8 years of age boys and girls do not differ in their hormone levels (Barfield, 1976). As androgen production increases in males around puberty, not only do the genitalia grow, pubic and facial hair increase, etc., but also formation of muscle and bone protein increases. This suggests that androgen facilitates the synthesis of proteins necessary for bone growth and muscular development. Androgen is also implicated in the increased production of red blood cells—a factor which may enhance aerobic work capacity. On the other hand, estogen production, which increases in girls around puberty and appears responsible for many of the sexual changes in girls, seems to have a different effect on growth—except for the pelvis, increased estrogen production appears to inhibit growth. It is around the time of puberty that linear growth stops in girls and the deposition of fat increases (Hutt, 1972a). If the sex hormones are largely responsible for sexual dimorphism, then such dimorphism is probably under genetic control.

Some degree of sexual dimorphism may also be influenced by social learning. Although it is hard to see how height might be affected (unless, for instance, male and female infants were differentially stressed—see Landauer and Whiting [1964] and Gunders and Whiting [1968] for the possible influence of stress), work and physical activity could certainly influence degree of muscular strength. It hardly needs documenting that exercise builds muscles. If males in a society typically engage in more physical activity (either through work or play), then their muscular strength may be enhanced. Aerobic work capacity may also be influenced by training. Andersen (1966) has shown that both male and female athletes show higher maximal oxygen uptake than nonathletes of comparable ages. Hunter–gatherers (who Andersen assumes work harder) have been shown to have higher aerobic capacities than representatives of more sedentary populations (Andersen, 1966). Although these data are suggestive, they do not really show that social factors are even partly responsible. We do not know if those who go in for athletics differ in muscular strength in the first place. Longitudinal data are needed here. We do not know if hunter–gatherers work harder, and we do not know if the different work capacities of different populations are not genetically controlled.

Even if sexual dimorphism is largely subject to genetic control, we still need to ask why natural selection should have favored it. There are two possible ways to view this question, (1) why should males be bigger? or (2) why should females be smaller? Stini (1971) has suggested that it would be adaptive for females to be fully developed skeletally in the birth canal by the time they could reproduce. If they were not, their chance of surviving childbirth would be greatly reduced. It is also possible that were the female to continue growing substantially after she began to reproduce, her fetus might have a reduced chance of surviving because of increased internal competition for nutrients. Natural selection, then, may have favored a growth time for females which ends shortly after puberty. But why should it be advantageous for males to continue to grow after puberty? A number of authors (Wilson, 1975, and references therein) have suggested that the greater size and strength of the males in many animal species relates to their aggressive behavior on the one hand and their low investment in the care of young on the other hand. The argument is that where male parental investment is low, males compete with each other for females. As a result, males that are bigger, stronger, and more aggressive have greater reproductive success. Where male investment in parenting is less, dimorphism is expected to be less. According to this theory, human males, who typically do not play as great a role in child care (as we shall see) as women, might also be expected to display this dimorphism. As for why dimorphic males invest so little parental care in their young, Wilson (1975) suggests that it is only in environments with abundant resources that males can afford to spend time and energy competing for females; in environments with scarce resources, greater parental investment by males as well as females is needed.

There may be another reason why males are typically larger. Aggressive behavior in animals is often displayed in the protection of territory and in competition for food (Wynne-Edwards, 1962). If such aggression is required, males are likely to be the aggressors (because females are less expendable for reproduction), and therefore selection may favor males who are larger and stronger.

What role might cross-cultural research play in evaluating the theories discussed above? Although those theories are addressed to the question of why males are generally bigger than females, we could see if cross-cultural variation in *degree* of sexual dimorphism is related to some of the presumed independent variables. For example, with regard to the "exercise" hypothesis, we can ask whether or not those societies with most equal work for boys and girls have the least sex differences in aerobic work capacities. We can ask if sexual dimorphism is greatest in societies where males invest little in parental care and intrasocietal fighting is frequent. We can even possibly bring some evidence to bear on the effect of hormones on sexual dimorphism. For example, if human populations vary in the degree to which males and females differ in hormone levels, we can ask if that variation corresponds to the degree of difference in height, weight, muscular strength, or work capacity. In other words, are populations with higher levels of estrogen in males less dimorphic? Intracultural comparisons in other cultural settings may also be useful. For example, if a society displays considerable variation in work assignment to boys and girls, one might be able to investigate whether or not girls who are asked to do boys' work (perhaps in families with no boys) have greater aerobic work capacities than other girls.

ETHNOGRAPHICALLY DESCRIBED SEX DIFFERENCES

Just as it is not obvious why males and females should look different (other than in their reproductive organs), it is not obvious why social institutions and social roles should structure themselves around sex. Yet men's and women's roles differ in most human societies, and most human societies emphasize one sex or the other in their social organization and status systems.

Women's and Men's Roles

Worldwide Patterns in the Division of Labor by Sex
Humans are unique among the primates in having a pronounced sexual division of labor in obtaining and processing food and other resources. It is only with respect to childcare, which is predominantly a female activity, and offense and defense, which are primarily male activities, that the human pattern follows the basic primate pattern.

Primary subsistence activities. Two cross-cultural surveys (Murdock, 1937; Murdock & Provost, 1973) have documented the subsistence activities that are characteristically performed by males or females across a worldwide sample of societies. Hunting, trapping, and catching large aquatic animals are almost exclusively men's activities. Men usually predominate in herding large animals, fishing, collecting honey, clearing land, and preparing the soil. Apparently there are no exclusively "feminine" subsistence activities, although women generally predominate in gathering wild plant foods. No sex consistently predominates in agricultural activities (other than clearing land and soil preparation, as mentioned), milking, and gathering small land or aquatic fauna (Murdock & Provost, 1973).

Crafts and manufacturing. A consistent sexual division of labor is also apparent in crafts. Men almost exclusively work with metal (mining, smelting, and working it), wood (including lumbering and making boats and musical instruments), stone, bone, horn, and shell (Murdock, 1937; Murdock & Provost, 1973). Men predominate in housebuilding, netmaking, and ropemaking, although these are not always exclusively their province. As with subsistence, there appear to be no craft and manufacturing activities which are exclusively "feminine" cross-culturally. One activity—spinning—is predominantly feminine, although men do more of it in a few societies. Some activities—weaving and making baskets, mats, clothing, and pottery—are usually women's work; but in many societies, particularly in some regions of the world, this is not so. The regional inconsistency may be due to the development of full-time craft specialization; Murdock and Provost (1973) hypothesize that men predominate when crafts become specialized. There is some statistical support for this hypothesis with respect to a few crafts. In noncommercial societies (Piatti, 1971) and in less complex societies (White, Burton, & Brudner, 1977), women are significantly more likely to make pots; the reverse is true in commercialized and complex societies. Hide preparation shows the same pattern (White et al., 1977).

Secondary subsistence activities. In most calculations of the relative contribution of each sex to subsistence (Brown, 1963; Divale, 1974; M. Ember & Ember, 1971; Heath, 1958; Sanday, 1973), only primary subsistence activities are included. In terms of such a measure, males in most societies seem to contribute more to subsistence (M. Ember & Ember, 1971). However, this type of computation may minimize women's contribution to subsistence, particularly if further preparation (e.g., cooking, grinding) is necessary for certain foods to be ingested. If we look at the contribution of women in the area of "secondary" subsistence activities, women seem to predominate in those activities. With the exception of butchering, which is predominantly a male activity, women consistently (in all regions of the world) predominate in the preparation of drinks, dairy production, preparation of vegetal food, and cooking. Although it is not consistent from region to region, in most socieites women are the ones that preserve meat and fish (Murdock & Provost, 1973). Thus women may make much larger contributions to subsistence than usually estimated, but by way of secondary subsistence activities.

Household tasks. With the exception of housebuilding, tasks necessary to the maintenance of the household and its activities are women's work in almost all societies (Murdock & Provost, 1973). Women usually gather fuel (for cooking and heat) and fetch water. Women usually do laundry.

Child care. The greater involvement of women in child care is one of the most characteristic sex differences in a variety of human cultures. Summarizing data coded by Barry and Paxson (1971), Weisner and Gallimore (1977) report that in most societies (77 percent) mothers are the principal caretakers of infants. The female role in caretaking is even more pronounced if we consider that in societes where children are the principal caretakers of infants, girls are usually assigned that role (Weisner & Gallimore, 1977).

Warfare. Although no systematic survey has documented male versus female participation in fighting, there is probably no need for such a survey. We cannot point to one society where females regularly participate in armed combat (M. Ember & Ember, 1971). Even in societies like Israel, where women are drafted into the army, they are rarely sent to the front lines.

Explanations of the Division of Labor by Sex
Most anthropologists agree that the sexual division of labor in getting food and processing it probably became characteristic of humans when meateating became a regular feature of the diet. Why this should be so, and why a sexual division of labor persists in the absence of hunting, is somewhat less agreed upon.

I will discuss three factors which are currently used to explain the more or less universal patterns in the division of labor by sex. Some authors (e.g., Murdock & Provost, 1973) suggest that these patterns can be explained in part by the superior strength of males and probably their superior capacity to mobilize strength in quick bursts of energy. Others stress the incompatibility between certain subsistence activities and childcare (this argument has been made most forcefully by Brown [1970a]; Murdock and Provost [1973]; and White et al. [1977] agree with it in part). Recently, it has also been suggested that economies of effort may play some role in explaining the performance by one sex of activities that are adjacent in the production sequence or physical location (White et al., 1977).

To support the "strength" hypothesis, Murdock and Provost (1973) point to the nature of men's versus women's work. Activities which require running (hunting, herding, warfare), the throwing of weapons (hunting, warfare), or lifting heavy objects (catching large animals, clearing land, working with stone, wood, and metals) appear to be consistently performed by men. The work more characteristically assigned to women—gathering, most secondary subsistence activities, most household tasks, and infant care—does not seem to involve the same degree of physical strength and quick bursts of energy. In spite of this consistency, a number of authors are critical of the "strength" argument (Brown, 1970a; White et al., 1977), citing evidence that women can and sometimes do perform heavy physical work. But given physical dimorphism, I do not see why it isn't most efficient for societies to assign a task requiring greater strength and bursts of energy to males. Undoubtedly, women do often perform heavy work—much agricultural work, for example, is quite heavy. But perhaps women undertake this work regularly only when men are engaged in warfare (or other long-distance activity) which interferes with their ability to do such work (M. Ember & Ember, 1971). Only when men cannot readily perform the heavy work may it be more efficient for women to do such work.

Brown (1970a) suggests that the traditional division of labor distinctions can be explained by the incompatibility of certain activities with child care. Activities which are not interruptible, which place a child in potential danger, and which take place far from home are viewed as incompatible with child care. It is assumed, of course, that the demands of nursing explain why child care is primarily women's work.

Brown's argument is an attractive one, although I am not sure that it is more parsimonious than the "strength" argument. It seems to me that most of the activities that are far from home and dangerous are the same ones that require greater strength and bursts of energy—hunting, herding, clearing land, mining, lumbering, fighting. Perhaps the "incompatibility" argument could better explain why men usually collect honey and fish (both of which are dangerous but generally do not require that much strength). The "incompatibility" argument probably could also explain why men usually engage in full-time craft specialization—producing large quantities of items for sale or exchange probably precludes interruption. The "strength" explanation, however, may better explain why men usually prepare soil, build boats and houses, and work stone, bone, horn, and shell.

As yet, there is no evidence that would allow us to choose between the "incompatibility" and the "strength" hypotheses. The problem is that support for both these interpretations is derived from the *same* distributional data. What we need are independent measures of the supposed predictors—strength and aerobic work capacity required, the danger involved, distance from home, and interruptibility. Then the competing interpretations could be tested against each other.

Certain work patterns do not seem to be predicted by either the "strength" argument or the "incompatibility" argument. For example, neither suggests why men should make musical instruments or nets or ropes. Furthermore, it is not clear why women should gather plants and do most secondary subsistence activities and housework just because they can! Perhaps a factor that needs to be explored further has to do with economies of effort. White et al. (1977) suggest, for example, that certain tasks may be performed because they are adjacent in the production sequence or because they are clustered in the same physical locations. The argument is that men may make nets and rope because they are needed for fishing (which men primarily do). Their argument also suggests, I might add, that musical instruments may be made by men because they lumber wood, that women primarily do secondary subsistence work and housework because men are often occupied in far-away contexts, and that economies of effort require women to do the work closer to home. In addition, men probably could not gather as well as hunt if the collected flora and fauna are located in different places.

It should be noted that White et al. (1977) support the "economies of effort" interpretation by appealing to the statistical associations between activities but do not actually measure their presumed independent variable. Thus to evaluate the predictiveness of this and the other two interpretations of division of labor we need to undertake research that measures all the presumed independent variables directly and independently.

Differential contribution to subsistence. Why do men usually contribute more to subsistence? Hunting, herding, and fishing are rarely predominant activities in most societies; thus male predominance in those activities cannot generally account for their generally greater contribution to subsistence. Most societies, as of recent times, depend on agriculture, but, as noted above, agriculture is not consistently the prerogative of one sex or the other.

As M. Ember and I (1971) have previously suggested, unless warfare interferes, males may generally do more toward subsistence than females because women are universally occupied with the demands of child care and other domestic chores. Although certain aspects of agriculture may be compatible with child care (Brown, 1970a), we do not see why women should usually do such work. It does not seem particularly convenient to bring infants or small children to the fields nor to arrange for others to watch them. It probably is not as work-efficient to be interrupted by children, even when there is no danger. However, if men cannot do the work because the timing of warfare interferes, it would be efficient for women to do it. There is marginal support for this hypothesis (see M. Ember & Ember, 1971)—women tend to contribute as much or more toward subsistence as men in those societies where men engage in warfare when work has to be done. If the timing or duration of warfare does not interfere with agricultural work in most societies (as I suspect is generally the case), this may explain partly why men generally contribute more to subsistence.

The warfare hypothesis may have been only marginally supported because it did not consider that certain activities, like herding and hunting, would be performed by men regardless of warfare or because it did not consider that men might be removed from subsistence work by other far-away activities such as long-distance trade (see M. Ember & Ember, 1971; see also Sanday, 1974). It also did not consider that gathering might have to be performed by women because men do the hunting. Such issues need to be clarified by additional research.

Sexual Behavior

There is some cross-cultural evidence that different behaviors are commonly expected from males and females in sexual activity. First, Ford and Beach (1951) report that a majority of societies believe that males should take the initiative in sex. Second, most societies are more concerned about women engaging in extramarital sex than they are concerned about men engaging in such sex (Broude & Greene, 1976; Ford & Beach, 1951). Third, if we can judge by the fact that premarital sex restrictions are coded cross-culturally only for females (Broude & Greene, 1976; Murdock, 1967), probably more societies are concerned about premarital sex in females than in males. Overall, then, there appears to be some tendency for societies to be more restrictive of female sexuality.

However, a consistent cross-cultural pattern is far from evident, and it would seem inadvisable to call "taking the initiative in sex" part of the male role or extramarital restraint part of the female role. These expectations are far from universal. For example, only 66 percent of a cross-cultural sample of societies have a double standard with regard to extramarital sex (Broude & Greene, 1976). Moreover, judging by the fact that extramarital sex is reported to be common for women in 57 percent of the cross-cultural sample, the double standard does not appear to be particularly effective. It would seem then that the appropriate question to ask about sexual roles is why some societies have a double standard while others do not. I am not aware of any theory or research on this question.

Cultural Emphasis on Males versus Females

Social Organization

Most societies favor one sex over the other in structuring social groups and access to resources. The Ethnographic Atlas (as summarized by Textor, 1967) shows that 89 percent of the societies in which married couples live with or near kin have a unilocal rule of residence (a rule stipulating that the couple lives with or near the kin of one sex); 85 percent of the societies with inheritance of real property have unilineal inheritance rules (only one sex inherits); 82 percent of societies with movable property have only one sex inheriting such property; and 89 percent of societies with lineal descent groups have unilineal groups (membership in such groups is passed through only one sex). Moreover, these social rules tend to be consistent, i.e., structured around the same sex.

Where one sex is chosen as the core of the residential group, as the core of the unilineal descent group, or as the inheritor of property, it *could* be either males or females, but by far most societies favor males (see also D'Andrade, 1966; Divale & Harris, 1976). Of the societies with unilocal residence, 81 percent have married couples living with the husbands' kin (patrilocal, virilocal, or avunculocal residence). Of the societies with unilineal descent, 73 percent have membership assigned through fathers (patrilineal descent). Of the societies with unilineal inheritance of real property, 87 percent assign it to male heirs. Of the societies with unilineal inheritance of movable property, 83 percent assign it to male heirs.

Why should most societies structure social groups and access to resources around one sex? And why is the structuring usually around males? Turning to the first question, it is not obvious why so many societies should make use of sex as a criterion for structuring groups. After all, some societies do have bilocal residence (where married couples live with either the husband's or wife's kin), some have ambilineal descent (membership can be acquired through one's mother or father), and some societies let both sexes or either sex inherit property.

Murdock (1949) suggests that postmarital residence changes are the key to understanding other changes in social organization. If so, to explain why social institutions are usually structured around one sex, perhaps it would be helpful to ask why most societies have unilocal residence rather than nonunilocal residence (neolocal or biolocal residence). To explain why institutions are usually structured around males, perhaps it would be helpful to ask why most unilocal societies have patrilocal residence.

The cross-cultural evidence suggests that nonunilocal residence appears only under special circumstances. Neolocal residence seems to be associated with the development of a money or commercial economy (M. Ember, 1967). Bilocal (multilocal) residence is predicted by sudden and unexpected losses of population, probably as a result of introduced European diseases (C. Ember & Ember, 1972). Rather than a choice, bilocal residence may represent a necessary departure from unilocal rules because so many people have died. Among hunter–gatherers, bilocal residence is also predicted by very small community size (50 or fewer people) and highly variable rainfall in a low-rainfall area (C. Ember, 1975). In these latter circumstances unilocality may also be difficult to maintain. Since the sex ratio is often skewed in very small groups just by chance, the rigid adherence to a unilocal rule might deplete or increase group size too much. With unreliable rainfall, unilocality might not allow sufficient adjustment of population to resources. Thus it would seem that noncommercial societies tend to adhere to a unilocal rule if they can.

Let us turn now to why most unilocal societies structure their social organization (fundamentally perhaps their rule of residence) around males. It was traditionally thought that pattern of residence (patrilocal, matrilocal, or bilocal) is a function of which sex (males, females, or neither, respectively) contributes the most to subsistence. However, as plausible as that interpretation seems, division of labor by sex in subsistence *does not* predict residence in a worldwide sample of societies (Divale, 1974; M. Ember & Ember, 1971), although it may partly explain residential variation among hunter–gatherers (C. Ember, 1975). Thus male or female contribution to subsistence cannot by itself explain why residence favors one sex or the other, nor can the generally greater contribution of males to subsistence account for the prevalence of patrilocality and related male-oriented institutions.

The role of men in warfare, however, may help explain the prevalence of patrilocality and related male-oriented institutions. One theory, suggested by M. Ember and me (1971), is that division of labor in subsistence may help explain residential patterns but that its effect is usually overridden by warfare considerations. Specifically, we suggested that if societies had internal warfare (within the language group and often between neighboring communities), families would prefer to have their married sons close to home to ensure themselves of a loyal fighting force, whether or not males contributed more to subsistence. Only if there was no war (which is rare in the ethnographic record), or if warfare was purely external (only outside the language group), might division of labor in subsistence determine residence. Patrilocality, then, would be most common in unilocal societies because internal warfare is frequent in the ethnographic record. Matrilocality would occur rarely because it is rare that warfare is purely external *and* women contribute substantially to subsistence. (For supporting evidence see M. Ember & Ember, 1971; see also C. Ember, 1974).

A second theory, proposed by Divale (1974), also implicates warfare as a predictor of residence, but as a consequence rather than a cause of residence. Based on its prevalence, Divale assumes that patrilocality is the "natural" form of residence. He suggests that matrilocality will be adopted (by a society that has recently migrated) in order to eradicate internal warfare, which would be maladaptive for such a society. Matrilocality is presumed to eradicate internal warfare because it breaks up fraternal interest groups. If this theory is correct, matrilocality may be rare because few societies have recently migrated. Divale's supporting evidence is in part the same as ours—a high association between patrilocality and internal war and between matrilocality and purely external war. Although his theory can be criticized on empirical grounds (C. Ember, 1974), suffice it to say here that it begs the question of why patrilocality is "natural" or what the mechanism would be that would cause people to adopt matrilocality (assuming that it is more adaptive for migrating societies). However, Divale and Harris (1976) suggest that the ubiquity of warfare, which gives a monopoly on weapons to men, accounts for the worldwide prevalence of male-oriented institutions.

It seems to me that the prevalence of warfare per se is not a compelling explanation of male-oriented institutions. If it is assumed that men will force the institutions their way because they have weapons, it is difficult to imagine why they should give up such power and switch to matrilocality on occasion. Matrilocal societies, just like patrilocal societies, usually have warfare. How then can the "monopoly of weapons" argument account for patrilocality?

Status

Different anthropologists have different definitions of what status means. Traditionally, anthropologists have defined status in terms of the degree to which a person has characteristics valued in a society (see references in the work by Sanday, 1973). Others have defined it in terms of the degree to which a person has control over himself or herself (Schlegel, 1972) or the degree to which a person has power and authority over others (Sanday, 1973; 1974). Others have assumed that customs of deference indicate relative status (Stephens, 1963). Since different authors mean different things, I will discuss the different aspects of status separately. The two basic questions here are, why do males generally have more power and authority? Under what circumstances do women have relatively higher status?

Power and authority. It does not need much documentation to note that women have rarely occupied superordinate positions in the political arena. (The domestic domain may be different and will be dealt with below.) Even in matrilineal societies, where women may have relatively more authority and influence, men usually occupy the political offices. For example, among the Iroquois, women seem to have relatively high status (women could influence the selection and deposing of ruling elders and influence decisions of the political council and had occasional power over the conduct of war), but women could not serve on the political council and could speak only through male speakers (Brown, 1970b).

Why have males almost always dominated the political arena? A few suggestions have been put forward, two of which emphasize the role of men in warfare. Sanday (1974) has offered a model of status suggesting that whenever warfare or long-distance activities are present, female status (in terms of power and authority in the public domain) will be low. Presumably warfare gives men more of a stategic position to control resources (although how they would do so is not clear). But even in the absence of war, Sanday suggests that males will still hold political power as long as they control production. As previously mentioned, Divale and Harris (1976) also suggest that the prevalence of warfare and male control over weapons may explain a whole complex of "male supremacist" institutions and attitudes—including higher male status.

Based on data from the !Kung Bushmen, Lee (1974) and Draper (cited by Kolata, 1974) have also suggested reasons for male dominance not involving warfare. Both cite the importance of mobility. Comparing nomadic !Kung bands with those recently settled down. Draper notes that in the latter women seem to have lost some of their influence in decision making. She suggests that the now sedentary women no longer have as much experience in the outside world and no longer contribute much to subsistence (both because they no longer gather); hence they have lost some of their political influence. Lee's (1974) theory about the origin of political power also stems from !Kung data, but in a much broader way. He asserts that the origin of male political power comes from the way early human society was constructed. Using !Kung bands as a model, he argues that bands were primarily based on mother–daughter bonds—sons-in-laws were recruited largely from outside. This gave males more power, he asserts, because they could forge alliances which were not based on kinship. As an explanation of male political power, this model seems highly far-fetched. First, we have to assume the !Kung form of residence was characteristic of early hunter–gatherers, but a recent survey of hunter–gatherers indicates that patrilocality is the predominant form (C. Ember, 1975). If patrilocality is more common, women, not men, are the ones who usually marry in! Second, marrying in does not seem to confer any political power, judging by the status of women in most patrilocal societies. Third, even if Lee's model of early human society were correct, it would be hard to argue how male supremacy would have persisted since early human society unless we postulate that male political power is built into their genes!

None of these theories has yet been systematically tested against data from the cross-cultural record; thus we do not know from empirical evidence how to evaluate these theories. All that we do know is that the contribution of each sex to subsistence *does not by itself* predict power and authority (Sanday, 1973). But the importance of male participation in warfare or the factor of male mobility have not yet been assessed. Even if one or both of these factors is predictive, I think some thought has to be given to why male participation in war or male mobility should enhance male political power. Do males hold political positions because of threat of force? Or do they hold such positions because communities may value their decision-making abilities with respect to war or because they have connections in other communities?

What of authority and power in the domestic sphere? As Sanday (1974) has pointed out, control in this sphere may be independent of control in the public domain. Nonetheless, it is likely that in many societies, particularly patrilocal ones, men also dominate in the domestic sphere. Many, if not most, matrilineal societies have male (husband or brother)-dominated households (Schlegel, 1972). One factor in such dominance may be that men are generally older than their wives (Rosenblatt & Cunningham, 1976).

Schlegel (1972) has addressed herself to predicting variation in household dominance in matrilineal societies; as yet we know little about domestic dominance in other societies. In matrilineal societies, Schlegel suggests that male dominance in the household declines (and women's dominance increases) where male power is dispersed—that is, where husbands and brothers have equal control. As might be expected, husbands have greatest domestic control in those matrilineal societies where residence is patrilocal or virilocal. This suggests what many suspect (but has not yet been demonstrated); that matrilocal residence in general may enhance women's authority.

Deference. In many societies women are expected to defer to their husbands, but rarely are men expected to defer to their wives (Stephens 1963). In Stephens's view, customs of deference indicate lesser power and privilege. Schlegel (1972) takes issue with this view; she suggests that "chivalrous" behavior by males should indicate greater power and privilege for women, but we know that women in Western societies (where "chivalrous" behavior is common) do not have greater power and privilege than men. It seems to me that not all deference behaviors equally indicate differential power. Walking behind another, keeping one's head lower, and keeping eyes downcast in the presence of another may reflect differential power and privilege, but "chivalrous" behavior may reflect only the belief that women are "delicate" and "fragile," not more powerful. Which "deference" behaviors are really associated with differential power and privilege could be investigated empirically (cf. Sanday, 1974).

PSYCHOLOGICAL DIFFERENCES

In this section I am concerned largely with nonphysical sex differences that are based on observations of individuals. I deal with behavior differences, differences in perception and cognition, differences in inferred personality, and differences in expressive behavior. At the end of each subsection, I discuss possible explanations of the particular differences described. Finally, I discuss some general psychological processes that may be involved in the whole area of psychological differences.

Behavior Differences In Infancy

Only a few researchers have observed infants in non-Western societies, and even fewer have looked for sex differences. Some sex differences, however, have been documented in the United States. Whether or not they appear elsewhere can be documented only by future research. To review those finding briefly, (1) there is some evidence that newborn females discharge their energy more in smiling and other facial movements, whereas male newborns discharge it more via total body activation (Korner, 1974; see also Freedman, 1972); (2) male infants (a few weeks to a few months old) may be more fretful than female infants (Moss, 1974); (3) in some studies, newborn girls show somewhat more tactile sensitivity than male newborns (Garai & Scheinfeld, 1968; Korner, 1974; Maccoby & Jacklin, 1974); (4) at about 1 year of age, girls look and vocalize more toward their mothers than fathers, whereas boys look and vocalize more toward their fathers than mothers (Lewis & Weinraub, 1974; Spelke, Zelazo, Kafan, & Kotelchuck, 1973); (5) in pictures and in play, male infants (10–18 months old) look more at other male infants, and female infants look more at female infants (Lewis & Weinraub, 1974).

Although not many sex differences have been described for infants, it is important for several reasons to know which of them may hold across cultures. The first reason is that universal differences appearing in newborns (without early differences in socialization) may very well represent biologic differences. Such differences could potentially condition parents to respond to boys and girls in different ways that may produce personality differences between the sexes. For example, if it turns out to be true that female infants smile more, parents might be apt to look at them more directly. As a matter of fact, research on parent–infant interaction in the United States suggests that mothers may hold female infants more face-to-face (Maccoby & Jacklin, 1974). Parents might also feel that females were more content and therefore spend less time attending to them. Research does suggest that parents spend more time handling, attending, and stimulating male infants (Korner, 1974; Maccoby & Jacklin, 1974; Moss, 1974).

The second reason to do cross-cultural research on sex differences in infancy is that it may clarify which differences are the result of differential socialization. For example, it is possible that the greater fretfulness of male infants in the U.S. is a result of a particular socialization practice—namely, routine circumcision within a few days after birth (Korner, 1974). Although research in the United States can help clarify the effect of circumcision, by comparing male infants that were not circumcised with those that were (see Korner, 1974), research in other cultures without circumcision would help even more.

A third reason for cross-cultural research on infancy is that such research may help us understand why parents may respond differently to male and female infants. If male infants are not universally more fretful, do parents still attend to them more? Does this vary with cultural preferences for boys versus girls or cultural ideas about whether boys or girls are more vulnerable? To some extent, statistical controls can help sort out the relative effects of infants' characteristics and of parents' behavior towards infants, as Moss (1974) has controlled for baby's irritability, but cultural variation may provide greater opportunities for sorting relevant factors.

Finally, the study of sex differences in infancy and differential parental reactions to infants is important because such early differences may affect sex differences later. For example, greater parental attendance to male infants might subtly reinforce egoistic behavior (which, as we shall see below, is generally more characteristic of boys). If so, one could investigate whether or not differential attending predicts cross-cultural (and intracultural) variation in the degree of egoism that boys and girls exhibit. It seems to me that, if the data are replicated, the tendency of infants to look and vocalize more to same-sex individuals has extremely important implications for understanding sex differences. These results may suggest very early cognitive gender identification in the infant. If by observing those of the same sex the infant is able to arrive at generalizations about expected behaviors even before verbal teaching and explicit socialization, the impact of society's social expectations may be more unconsciously experienced than we think.

Interpersonal Behavior in Childhood and Adulthood

We know somewhat more about cross-cultural sex differences in interpersonal behavior in childhood and adulthood, largely through observational studies of children in a number of different cultural settings. Most of the observational data comes from the *Six Cultures* project, in which children were observed in Nyansongo (Kenya), Juxtlahuaca (Mexico), Tarong (Philippines), Khalapur (India), Taira (Okinawa), and Orchard Town (United States). The sex differences observed have been summarized by B. Whiting and Edwards (1973) and by B. Whiting and Whiting (1975). We also have observations of sex differences in behavior in a number of other cultural settings: an Israeli kibbutz (Spiro, 1965); among the Logoli (R. L. Munroe & Munroe, 1971), Gusii (Nerlove, Munroe, & Munroe, 1971), and Luo of Kenya (C. Ember, 1973); among the !Kung Bushmen (Blurton-Jones & Konner, 1973; Draper, 1975); and in a comparative study of Swiss, U.S., and Ethiopian children (D. Omark, Omark, & Edelman, 1975). No observational study that I know of has systematically observed adult social behavior in other cultures, but Rohner (1976) has used ethnographers' reports to assess sex differences in adult levels of aggression.

A sex difference in aggression is perhaps the best-documented difference that seems to occur consistently across cultures. Boys usually (but not invariably) display more aggression than girls, and this difference seems to appear by 3 years of age. Fairly extensive research in the United States (as summarized by Maccoby & Jacklin, 1974; see also Rohner, 1976) concurs with the more limited number of studies conducted in other cultural settings (see B. Whiting & Edwards [1973] and B.

Whiting & Whiting [1975] for summaries of the *Six Cultures* data; see also Blurton-Jones & Konner [1973]; C. Ember [1973]; Omark et al. [1975]; Spiro [1965]). Using ethnographic reports on 101 societies, Rohner (1976) found that in 71 percent of those societies boys appear to be more aggressive than girls.

Whether males continue to be more aggressive in adulthood is not as clear. Experimental and projective research on adults in the United States (see Maccoby & Jacklin, 1974) suggests that the childhood sex difference continues into adulthood, but little comparable research has been done on adults outside Western countries. We have only Rohner's (1976) ethnographic survey, which shows no consistent sex difference in aggressive behavior among adults. When we have studies that measure adult behavior directly, we may know more about sex differences in aggression among adults.

In addition to aggression, there are other sex differences in childhood behavior which show consistency across a variety of cultures, but our conclusions must be more tentative because these features have not been studied as frequently as aggression. Tentatively, then, there seem to be some consistent cross-cultural sex differences in the areas of conformity, play behavior, and social distancing.

The evidence from the United States and elsewhere suggests that girls are somewhat more apt to conform to others, *particularly* to adults. In the United States, the clearest results on conformity come from studies of responses to adults' directions; in those studies (summarized by Maccoby & Jacklin, 1974) young girls are consistently more likely than boys to conform. In an analysis of the *Six Cultures* data, B. Whiting and Edwards (1973) found that girls were significantly more likely to conform to mothers than were boys. Research conducted in Israel and the U.S.S.R. is also suggestive of girls' somewhat greater orientation to adults, since girls that were brought up in collective settings were more likely than boys to shift responses in the direction of conventional moral standards (in contrast to mildly antisocial acts approved by peers) when threatened with social exposure (Shouval, Venaki, Bronfenbrenner, Devereux & Kiely, 1975).

In play, boys seem to show a preference for boys and girls show a preference for girls. This result was found by Omark, et al. (1975) in American, Ethiopian, and Swiss samples and by Blurton-Jones and Konner (1973) in London samples. (!Kung children showed no such same-sex preference, perhaps because they don't have that much choice of playmates [see Draper, 1975].) Omark et al. also report that boys and girls tend to play in different size groups. Boys are more likely to play in "swarms," girls in small groups of two or three.

Personal space (the space between individuals) also seems to differ by sex. Omark et al. (1975) report that boys maintain greater distance between themselves and other children. In an Israeli study, Lomranz, Shapira, Choresh, & Gilat (1975) found that children of both sexes stand significantly further from boys than from girls.

There are other sex differences in social behavior which show up in a variety of cultures, but not with the same degree of consistency. Let us turn first to those behaviors which show little or no sex difference in the United States but show sex differences fairly consistently elsewhere. There are two areas in which this pattern appears—nurturance and proximity to parents. As summarized by Maccoby and Jacklin (1974), research in the United States does not show greater nurturance on the part of females, nor does it show (in infancy or in childhood) a greater tendency for girls to stay closer to their parents.

Although data are not available from that many societies, the cross-cultural evidence *does* suggest that girls exhibit more nurturant behavior than boys. Data from the *Six Cultures* study indicate that 7–11-year-old girls are consistently (and significantly) more apt to offer help and support (B. Whiting & Edwards, 1973). Spiro (1965) finds that Kibbutz girls of 1–4 years of age are more apt to aid, assist, share, and cooperate. The age of onset of a sex difference in nurturance is not clear. Although Spiro observed differences among extremely young children (1–4 years), the *Six Cultures* data show no significant differences even among children 3–6 years of age.

The inconsistency between the U.S. findings and those in other cultures may reflect a cultural difference, or it could reflect a methodologic difference. The cultural possibility is that nurturant behavior may not be exhibited much by U.S. children altogether, so that sex differences may be minimal. However, since the *Six Cultures* study *did* find 7–11-year-old U.S. (Orchard Town) girls to be more nurturant, a more likely possibility is that the inconsistency is a product of research conducted in different settings and with children of different ages. Most studies of nurturance in the United States looked only at very young children. If a sex difference characteristically appears later, as the *Six Cultures* data suggest, then most studies in the United States may have missed some sex differences. Perhaps more important, most research in the United States was not conducted in the home. B. Whiting and Whiting (1975) have shown that different targets elicit different responses. Infants in particular seem to elicit nurturant behavior. If there are no infants or younger children around in the nursery school or laboratory, then nurturant behaviors may rarely be exhibited. Perhaps future studies in the United States may turn out to show a sex different in nurturance if older children are observed in the home.

Data from the United States also show no consistent tendency for female infants or for girls to stay closer to parents, other adults, or to home (Maccoby & Jacklin, 1974; B. Whiting & Whiting, 1975), although it appears that girls stay closer in other cultural settings where proximity behavior has been studied. Draper (1975) found among the !Kung that girls are more frequently nearer than boys to home and adults and that they more frequently interact with adults. In studies of playground behavior in three countries, Omark, et al. (1975) found that girls were significantly closer to teachers than boys. Although proximity to adults was not measured, data from the Logoli (R. L. Munroe & Munroe, 1971), the Gusii (Nerlove, Munroe, & Munroe, 1971; B. Whiting & Whiting, 1975), and communities in Mexico and India (B. Whiting & Whiting, 1975) also suggest this tendency, since boys were significantly further from home than girls.

Does the difference in findings from the U.S. reflect a cultural difference or a methodologic difference in research strategies? One factor that may have obscured a sex difference in proximity behavior in the U.S. is that the laboratory situations studied here are often stressful. Lewis and Weinraub (1974), who studied young children's attachment behavior, point out that when boys and girls first are put in a strange room with few toys no sex differences in proximity behavior appear, but after 15 min. girls show more attachment behavior to parents. Since most studies of proximity behavior in the United States have been conducted in the laboratory, this may account for the lack of a sex difference in proximity behavior. But there may be a real culture difference too. Even in the *Six Cultures* study, which employed natural observations, B. Whiting and Whiting (1975) found that older boys in Orchard Town were closer to home than girls. Is it possible that "outside the home" situations are in fact more worrisome for parents in the United States than in some other cultures so they restrict boys more because they fear boys will get into more trouble than girls? Maccoby and Jacklin (1974) present some evidence that parents are more restrictive of boys in the United States. Thus the difference between the U.S. findings and findings elsewhere with respect to proximity behavior may be explainable in two ways—(1) the difference in study settings, and (2) parental fear in the U.S. of dangers away from home and parents.

Some sex differences in social behavior have been noted in cross-cultural studies but have not been studied much in the United States. The cross-cultural studies suggest that boys are more apt to try to dominate others selfishly, whereas girls are more apt to try to dominate reponsibly (B. Whiting & Edwards, 1973; B. Whiting & Whiting, 1975; also C. Ember, 1973).

The few studies of dominance behavior in the United States generally show no sex differences, although when a difference was found the efforts to dominate tended to be more frequent in boys (Maccoby & Jacklin, 1974). However, little difference may have been found in most U.S. studies because researchers did not distinguish between the different styles of dominance. Dominance behavior may be thought of as attempting to exert influence to get others to do (or not do) something. In the *Six Cultures* project and in my study, a distinction was made between egoistic and prosocial dominance. Egoistic dominance is an attempt to get others to do things that satisfy one's own needs; prosocial dominance is an attempt to get others to do things that satisfy others' needs. Girls and boys, then, may both exhibit dominance but with characteristically different styles (B. Whiting & Edwards, 1973). If these styles are not distinguished, the sex differences may be obscured.

Sex differences in dependency behavior may also be obscured by not distinguishing among different modes of interaction. Looking at dependency behavior generally, most studies from the United States and other societies indicate little or no sex difference (Maccoby & Jacklin, 1974; B. Whiting & Edwards, 1973; B. Whiting & Whiting, 1975). (My Luo data, which show significantly more dependency behavior in boys, appear to be unusual [C. Ember, 1973].) However, girls and boys may exhibit different types of dependency behavior. The *Six Cultures* data and a reanalysis of my Luo data (Edwards & Whiting, 1974) suggest that after 7 years of age boys are significantly more apt than girls to *seek attention* and *material goods,* whereas in the 3–6-year-old age range girls are more likely than boys to seek *help* and *physical contact.*

In sum, the most consistent and most documented cross-cultural sex difference in interpersonal behavior appears to be that boys exhibit more aggression after age 3 years or so. More tentatively, girls appear to conform more to adults and to play in smaller same-sex groups than do boys. Girls also seem to stand closer to each other than do boys. Boys and girls may exhibit different styles of dominance and dependency behaviors. Boys seem to exhibit more egoistic dominance, girls more prosocial dominance (responsible behavior). As for dependency behaviors, boys may seek attention and material goods more; girls may seek help and physical contact more. Although it may be hazardous to generalize across the specific findings, these patterns suggest that girls are more oriented toward adults and behave in ways that are more socially acceptable; boys seem to be more oriented toward peers and behave more selfishly. Although there is no evidence that girls are more sociable, girls may engage in or seek closer, more intimate social contacts, whereas boys may be more extensively sociable yet more distancing.

There appears to be somewhat more cross-cultural variability in nurturance and proximity to parents. Data from the United States suggest little sex difference in those behaviors. However data from other cultures suggest that girls usually are more nurturant and are more likely to stay closer to home and adults. As discussed above, some of this discrepancy may result from different research techniques and may not reflect any real cultural difference.

How might we explain the apparent sex differences in interpersonal behavior? First, I will discuss some biologic explanations that have been suggested; then I will turn to some social learning interpretations.

Biologic Explanations

Many researchers and reviewers argue that the higher level of aggressiveness in males probably has a biophysical basis (Blurton-Jones & Konner, 1973; Hutt, 1972a; Maccoby & Jacklin, 1974; Rohner, 1976; Whiting & Edwards, 1973). Some researchers also think that dominance behavior (Omark et al., 1975) and the play and mobility patterns of males (Draper, 1975; Omark et al., 1975) may also be biologically determined. The consistency of these sex differences across cultures and across primate groups, and the early onset of a sex difference in aggressive behavior, are often cited in support of the biologic argument.

As I have argued earlier, these distributional patterns are not good reasons for accepting a biophysical hypothesis. Rather, we need evidence that links a particular behavior to a particular aspect of biology. Because there is some evidence that links hormonal changes to changes in aggressive behavior, the biophysical basis of aggression is rendered somewhat more plausible. Let us turn to this evidence first.

Androgen and aggression. Experimental research on nonhuman animals suggests that androgen, particularly if introduced during the critical time of sexual differentiation (prenatally in guinea pigs and primates, early in the postnatal period in rats [Phoenix, 1974; Hutt, 1972b]) may predispose an animal to exhibit more intraspecies aggression. Genetically female guinea pigs, rhesus monkeys, and rats which are androgenized during their critical periods show more aggressive behavior than control females (Phoenix, 1974). Conversely, early castration of male rodents (which reduces androgen) seems to lower aggression (Hutt, 1972b; Moyer, 1974).

Experimental research of this kind is not possible with humans, but prenatal androgenization of females has occurred in certain circumstances and its effect on behavior has been studied. (Some females seem to have a defective adrenal gland which releases too much androgen; other females become androgenized when their mothers are injected with progestin to prevent miscarriages.) As compared with either normal female controls or with their own normal siblings, fetally androgenized girls are reported to have a higher level of physical energy expenditure in rough outdoor play, are less interested in dolls, are more often identified as tomboys, and more often prefer boys to girls as playmates (Ehrhardt & Baker, 1974).

Although the results from these studies appear to be comparable to the nonhuman animal data, the two kinds of study differ in two important respects. First, the behaviors of the androgenized girls were assessed from interviews, not observation (as in the animal studies). Second, if prenatal androgenization increases aggressive behavior, androgenized girls should be reported to instigate fights more often—but, as noted by Ehrhardt and Baker (1974), that is not the case.

Some other studies have attempted to assess the relationship between circulating levels of androgen and levels of aggressive behavior in humans. As summarized by Mazur (1976), the results are equivocal—four of six studies showed no relationship between hormone level and aggressiveness. If, however, it is prenatal androgen that increases the propensity for aggression, these results are neither surprising nor particularly contradictory.

Although the data from humans are not particularly striking, the body of evidence taken as a whole does present a fairly plausible case that prenatal androgen may influence aggressive behavior. But plausibility does not mean that we have enough evidence to conclude that prenatal androgen affects aggression in humans—it means only that such a possibility should be explored further. There are alternative hypotheses which could account for the results that need to be ruled out before we can provisionally accept the "androgen" hypothesis.

As is possible with any experimental manipulation, some other factor that is correlated with the experimental manipulation of androgen might be the real factor operating to enhance aggression. Vande Wiele (1974), for example, has commented that a single injection of testosterone (an androgen) will usually alter an animal's steroid metabolism permanently. It therefore is possible that induced metabolic differences may create the differences in observed aggression, not the androgen per se. The finding that estrogen injections also increase aggression (Finney & Erpino, 1976) is perhaps consistent with that possibility. To rule it out, the effects of changes in metabolism have to be studied.

Another alternative hypothesis is that abnormal levels of prenatal androgen may alter the behavior of others toward the affected animal. Aggression may be enhanced not because the hormonally changed animal is predisposed to it but because altered treatment by others may arouse or inhibit aggression. There are a number of conceivable ways this could happen. First, mothers may treat an infant differently if she perceives it to be a male. (Androgenized females have masculinized genitalia.) Rhesus mothers do treat male infants more roughly (Mitchell & Brandt, 1970), and, as we shall see, human parents may also treat sons more roughly. A second possibility is that peers respond differently to an animal whose androgen level is changed (and whose appearance is altered). In some animals such as mice, olfactory cues may induce attack. If a castrated male, for instance, is treated with the urine of a more aggressive male, the castrated male will be attacked more often. This suggests that an endrocrine-dependent pheromone may elicit attack (Moyer, 1974). Even if olfaction is not a factor in other animals, peer behavior may still be altered by the appearance of the target. Do normal male juveniles engage in less rough-and-tumble play with castrated males and more with androgenized females by their own choice? If, as we shall discuss later, social behavior is in part determined by who is available for social interaction, the responses of peers could well affect social behavior.

Androgen and dominance.   There is another alternative interpretation of the above evidence, namely, the suggestion that androgen may enhance dominance behavior, which in some animals may be correlated with aggression (Mazur, 1976). In Mazur's view, this hypothesis better explains some of the inconsistencies in the research discussed above. First, Mazur (1976) notes that the relationships between circulating hormone levels and aggression levels are clearest for rodents and less clear for the higher primates (including humans). He suggests that this is because aggression and dominance behavior are clearly linked in rodents but not so clearly linked in higher primates. If androgen increases dominance behavior, hormone levels will be spuriously related to aggression in rodents, but there will be little or no relationship in higher primates. Second, Mazur notes that not all forms of aggression increase with increased androgenization, only intraspecific aggression. Third, Mazur points to some direct evidence from primate studies showing correlations between dominance behaivor and androgen level. These studies, by the way, suggest that the hormone–behavior relationship is not one-way: there is some evidence that androgen levels may change in response to (after) dominance encounters, as well as evidence that increased androgen precedes dominance behaivor. In short, before the androgen hypothesis about aggression is accepted, these and other alternative hypotheses need to be ruled out.

Let us now turn to some possible social explanations of some of the sex differences in interpersonal behavior that I have discussed.

Sociocultural Explanations

Probably most cultural or social anthropologists believe that sex differences are socially or culturally induced—a product of differential socialization. In spite of this belief, it is surprising how little attention in research has been paid to how particular socialization practices may affect sex differences.

Direct reward and punishment. Most people probably think of socialization in its most direct sense—the encouragement and discouragement of particular behaviors through reward and punishment by the socializing agents. It is usually assumed that the more parents and other adults pressure children to behave in a particular way, the more they will learn to behave in that way. For many behaviors, it seems plausible to argue that if societies exert differential pressure on boys and girls to behave differently, then socialization may account, at least partially, for sex differences in behavior.

Unfortunately, most of the cross-cultural studies that have investigated cross-cultural sex differences in socialization are not concerned with sex differences in behavior (Barry, Bacon, & Child, 1957; Barry, Josephson, Lauer, & Marshall, 1976), and those studies that are concerned with differences in behavior have not been concerned with sex differences in socialization. Therefore for most areas of behavior we cannot as yet say whether or not the societies that pressure the sexes most differently show the most sex differences nor even whether or not children who are most pressured in a particular direction actually learn to behave accordingly.

Although the cross-cultural evidence is largely indirect, is there any suggestion that differential socialization pressures on the sexes could account for some of the sex differences in behavior? What we need to look for are the areas in which *both* sex differences in socialization and actual sex differences have been cross-culturally observed, albeit usually in separate studies. Clearly, there are three such areas— aggression, nurturance, and responsibility. As noted above, the cross-cultural evidence generally indicates more aggressive behavior in males and more nurturant and responsible behavior in females. Data from Barry, Bacon, and Child (1957) and Barry, et al. (1976), as summarized in Table 16–1, suggest that, *where there are sex differences in socialization,* boys rather than girls are pressured to be aggressive, whereas girls rather than boys are pressured to be nurturant and responsible.

There are also two areas in which socialization pressures *may* correspond to behavioral differences. As already noted, boys are generally further from home and girls tend to comply more with adults' wishes. These two sex differences in behavior seem to correspond to two sex differences in socialization—that boys are pressured more to be self-reliant and girls are pressured to be more obedient.

There is some evidence then, indirect to be sure, that sex differences in socialization may correspond to some sex differences in behavior. But the data in Table 16–1

TABLE 16-1 Sex Differences in Socialization Pressure

| Area of Socialization | Stage | Percentage of Societies With Evidence of Sex Difference in Socialization in the Direction of: | | | |
		Boys	Girls	Neither	No. of Societies
Fortitude	Early childhood	18%	1%	81%	130
	Late childhood	28%	1%	71%	143
Aggressiveness	Early childhood	18%	2%	80%	116
	Late childhood	24%	3%	73%	125
Self-reliance	Early childhood	24%	3%	74%	151
	Late childhood	44%	2%	54%	151
(In 1957 study)	Combined	85%	0%	15%	82
Achievement	Early childhood	negligible differences			
	Late childhood	negligible differences			
(In 1957 study)	Combined	87%	3%	10%	31
Industriousness	Early childhood	2%	32%	65%	162
	Late childhood	4%	48%	47%	173
Responsibility	Early childhood	3%	24%	73%	147
	Late childhood	6%	38%	55%	154
(In 1957 study)	Combined	11%	61%	28%	84
Obedience	Early childhood	1%	14%	84%	159
	Late childhood	3%	13%	84%	158
(In 1957 study)	Combined	3%	35%	62%	69
Sexual Restraint	Early childhood	1%	23%	76%	152
	Late childhood	2%	45%	52%	160
Nurturance					
(In 1957 study)	Combined	0%	82%	18%	33

The data for this table come from two sources. Barry, Josephson, Lauer, and Marshall (1976) have provided coded cross-cultural data on socialization pressures for boys and girls in early and late childhood. I have tabulated the percentages of societies that show a difference (or no difference) between the pressures exerted on boys and girls for each type of behavior. Thus the top row indicates that 18 percent of the societies in that sample exert stronger pressure on boys to show fortitude; 1 percent exert stronger pressure on girls to show fortitude; and 81 percent show no differential pressure. The second set of percentages come from an earlier study (Barry, Bacon, & Child, 1957) which coded data for a different sample of 110 societies. In the earlier study, the percentages of societies showing a sex difference in socialization were already tabulated and are here reproduced.

suggest that sex differences in socialization pressures cannot possibly account for much of the variance in behavioral sex differences because most societies appear (at least in the Barry et al. [1976] study) to have *no* sex differences in socialization pressures in either early or late childhood. As Rohner (1976) pointed out with respect to aggression, a small percentage of societies pressuring boys to be more aggressive hardly seems to be able to account for cross-cultural consistency in greater male aggressive behavior. Nor, I might add, does the low percentage of societies pressuring boys to be more self-reliant and the low percentage of societies pressuring girls to be more responsible and obedient seem to be able to account for the cross-cultural differences in those behaviors.

But what about the percentages on sex differences in socialization pressures in the earlier Barry, Bacon, and Child (1957) study? Those percentages are a lot different from the corresponding ones in the Barry et al. (1976) study. For example, the earlier study suggested that most societies (85 percent) pressured boys to be more self-reliant, but the later study indicates that most societies (74 percent in early childhood and 54 percent in later childhood) do not differentially pressure boys and girls on self-reliance. The discrepancies between the later and earlier studies are extremely puzzling. It is hard to imagine why the early study shows such strong sex differences in socialization pressures while the later study does not (compare the numbers in Table 16–1 for the two studies with respect to self-reliance, achievement, responsibility, and obedience). Some of the discrepancies might be due to sample differences. Barry et al. (1976) report that the later sample includes more technologically advanced societies. If such societies have less differentiated socialization by sex (which we may suspect but do not know for sure), then the later sample might be expected to show fewer sex differences in socialization pressures. Until we understand why the discrepancies exist, we cannot assume that cross-culturally there are substantial sex differences in socialization pressures, at least as judged from ethnographers' reports.

There are several societies where investigators have looked at both socialization pressures and sex differences in behavior. The data from these societies also do not support the hypothesis that behavioral sex differences result from differential reward and punishment. For example, in the *Six Cultures* study, Minturn and Lambert (1964) report no differences in socialization pressure for boys and girls in the areas of responsibility, obedience, and aggression, despite the fact that there are behavior sex differences in those areas (B. Whiting & Whiting, 1975). On the basis of a number of studies, Maccoby and Jacklin (1974) similarly report no evidence in the U.S. of a greater tolerance of aggression in boys, despite the fact that boys display more aggression. In fact, there may be some tendency for parents in the U.S. to be more, rather than less, punishing of boys for aggression (Maccoby & Jacklin, 1974). Draper (1975) reports in her !Kung study that she also could find no socialization pressures that would account for girls being closer to home.

We must be cautious in interpreting these findings as contrary to the influence of direct socialization, because the Minturn and Lambert (1964) data and most of the data summarized by Maccoby and Jacklin (1974) are based on interviews with parents. B. Whiting and Whiting (1975) report a difference in task assignment to boys and girls, on the basis of observation, which was not picked up in mother interviews. This suggests that parents may be unreliable reporters of sex differences in socialization. If task assignment is reported by mothers as equal, when in fact it is not, then other interview data on sex differences in socialization may also be unreliable.

In sum, there is little that can be said about direct socialization as an explanation for cross-cultural sex differences in interpersonal behavior. Most problematically, socialization and sex differences usually have not been studied in the same societies; thus we do not generally know if differential pressures occur in the same societies in which behavioral sex differences appear. In the few societies where both have been studied, interview data suggest no socialization differences by sex. However, as I have pointed out, those data may not adequately reflect actual socialization differences. Nonetheless, because the evidence is largely indirect, we cannot conclude that direct socialization is irrelevant either! All we can say now is that there is no evidence yet to support the notion that differential socialization pressure produces sex differences in behavior. Only when studies are designed to test for such a direct effect will we be able to say anything more definite about it.

The socialization practices discussed above—the direct reward and punishment by caretakers of behaviors they want to establish—assumes a conscious effort on the part of parents and other caretakers to mold specific behaviors. But there are other ways in which caretaker behavior can shape child and adult social behavior. I turn here to a number of childhood experiences which may shape social behavior, but not necessarily because the socializers specifically intended to shape those social behaviors.

Task assignment. In many societies parents assign a great deal of work to their children. Such assignment probably parallels the adult division of labor by sex as much as possible, although, with the exception of herding, much men's work (either because it is dangerous or requires a lot of strength) probably cannot be done by boys. Consequently, in most societies in which there is work to be done by children, there is probably sexual differentiation in tasks assigned to children—either because boys and girls are assigned different work or because girls do more work than boys.

A number of different theoretical orientations would lead us to expect that sex differences in task assignment might produce sex differences in social behavior. First, learning theory would predict that behaviors learned in the course of task assignment would tend to generalize, either because of parental reward and punishment for appropriate task-related behavior or because of the indirect or intrinsic rewards of performing a task well (B. Whiting & Whiting, 1971; cf. Breer & Locke, 1965). Behavior may also be learned during the course of task assignment not so much because of what must be done to perform the task competently but because the social context of the task may require certain behavior. For example, if certain tasks place children in different social contexts, and different contexts require different social behaviors, then behavior habits may generalize from the social contexts of task performance (B. Whiting & Whiting, 1975). Second, identification and imitation theory would predict that a child might be likely to identify with and imitate the behaviors of the task model (B. Whiting & Whiting, 1971). Third, a "cognitive" theoretical orientation would suggest that children assigned sex-typed chores may behave in ways consistent with how they think others expect them to behave (C. Ember, 1973).

Regardless of the mechanism by which task assignment may exert its effect, let us review the evidence that links task assignment to social behavior.

A number of analyses from the *Six Cultures* study suggest linkages between task assignment and social behavior. Let us ignore sex differences for the moment: B. Whiting and Whiting (1971) have shown that in those societies in which herding is important boys score significantly higher on responsible social behavior as compared with societies in which herding is unimportant. B. Whiting and Whiting (1975) have also shown that in those societies in which children are assigned more chores (probably because their mothers' workload is greater) children exhibit social behavior profiles with more nurturant and responsible behavior. If we look now at sex differences in social behavior (particularly nurturant and responsible behavior), the *Six Cultures* data suggest that such differences may be explained in part by the unequal assignment of chores to boys and girls. Younger girls are significantly more often assigned responsible tasks of all kinds, and girls of this age show significantly more responsible social behavior (B. Whiting & Edwards, 1973). Older girls (as compared with boys) significantly more often care for infants, and they are significantly more likely than boys to offer support and help to others (B. Whiting & Edwards, 1973).

Thus data from the *Six Cultures* study suggest links between task assignment and social behavior, but some questions remain: Is there a relationship between task assignment and social behavior in particular individuals? (The *Six Cultures* data have been analyzed so far only in the aggregate.) Does the effect of task assignment generalize beyond the context of task performance itself? Do different kinds of tasks have different effects on social behavior?

Some preliminary answers to these questions come from a study that I conducted in a Luo community in southwestern Kenya (C. Ember, 1970; 1973). In that study I was able to investigate whether or not boys who were subject to the socialization pressures of tasks usually assigned to girls were more like girls in their social behaviors than boys not assigned such tasks. The assignment of "feminine" work to boys appeared not to be a function of self-selection, since such assignment could be predicted from demographic family factors. (If there was no older sister at home, the eldest boy was assigned such work.) Results from the study indicate that boys who were assigned "feminine" work (such as child care, housework, fetching water and firewood, milling flour—tasks that were considered culturally appropriate only for women and girls) were intermediate in their social behaviors between other boys and girls on a variety of social behaviors. They exhibited less overall egoism, less egoistic aggression, less egoistic dependency, and more prosocial behavior as compared with boys who did little "feminine" work. Further analysis suggested that different kinds of "feminine" work had very different effects. More specifically, "outside" feminine work (fetching water, firewood, going to market to mill flour) seemed to *enhance* rather than decrease overall eogism, egoistic dependency, and eogistic dominance—traits that are more "masculine." "Inside" feminine work (housework, cooking, and babytending) seemed to be the component of "feminine" work which was responsible for making boys' social behavioral profiles more "feminine." "Inside" feminine work was associated with decreased egoism, decreased egostic dependency, decreased egoistic dominance, and increased prosocial behavior. Of all the "inside" feminine tasks, babysitting seems to be most responsible for lowering levels of egoistic aggression. There is also some support for the generalization of social behavior outside the realm of task performance. Even when they were not performing tasks, boys high on feminine work in the home were intermediate in their social behavior between other boys and girls.

If task assignment does affect social behavior and boys and girls are assigned different kinds of tasks (or girls are simply assigned more), then differential task assignment may explain partly some of the cross-cultural sex differences in social behavior. But we still need research to resolve a number of issues, including the possible mechanisms by which task assignment may exert its effect and the relative effect of differential task assignment (as compared with other biologic and/or social factors) on sex differences in behavior.

Parenthetically, I should note that Rohner (1976) has used my Luo data to support the notion that task assignment cannot completely account for sex differences in aggression, since boys who did "feminine" work were only intermediate in their social behavior between other boys and girls. Such a conclusion is unwarranted, however, since boys who did "feminine" work did not do as much as girls; therefore the effect on them may not have been as great. In addition, it happened that boys who did "feminine" work were somewhat more likely to be "father-absent"—a factor which seems to increase aggressive behavior somewhat. When father absence was controlled for by looking only at father-present boys, boys who did "feminine" work were closer to girls than in the previous analysis (C. Ember, 1970). Thus if the amount of task assignment could be "prorated" and other variables controlled for in future research, it might be possible to assess the relative contributions of task assignment to sex differences in behavior.

Subtle sex differences in socialization.   As I mentioned at the outset, few studies have looked directly at connections between a particular aspect of socialization and a particular sex difference in behavior. Researchers have barely investigated the effects of direct socialization practices, much less indirect socialization effects. However, it may be the indirect or inadvertent socialization practices that turn out to have the most profound effects on social behavior. Since there is little theory or research bearing on this issue, what follows is highly speculative.

Data from the United States suggest a few early and subtle differences in socialization by sex which might play some role in enhancing egoistic behavior in males, including aggressive behavior. For example, U.S. parents spend more time attending to male infants in physical ways—holding them, touching them, stimulating them (Korner, 1974; Maccoby & Jacklin, 1974; Moss, 1974). In particular, parents are more apt to try to stress the musculature of boys to try to elicit "gross motor behavior" from their sons (Maccoby & Jacklin, 1974). As Maccoby and Jacklin interpret it, boy infants seem to be handled more roughly; girl infants seem to be treated as more fragile.

Could these socialization differences in handling and attention subtly reinforce the habit potential in boys of egoistic behavior? If parents attend more to boys when they fuss, might boys learn more than girls to seek attention and other satisfaction of their own needs? If parents are usually rougher with male infants, might this lead boys to be more prone to rough-and-tumble play—both to engage in it and to expect rough handling from others? If fathers in particular handle their male infants more roughly, such infants might be led to expect greater roughness from males in general. I think it is interesting in this connection that there is some evidence suggesting that boys stand further from each other (Lomranz et al., 1975: Omark et al., 1975) —which may be a response to early rough handling from males.

Of course, it is possible that parental reactions to infants may themselves be a response to biologic differences in male and female infants. Perhaps male infants are more fretful genetically, causing parents to attend to them more, or perhaps males are "rougher" (have greater grip strength), so that parents are "rougher" with them. Future research will have to try to control for the initial behavior of infants as well as initial parental reactions. However, even if male infants are more fretful and "rougher" with their parents than girls, this does not necessarily rule out the possibility that differential socialization may amplify genetic differences. Feedback effects and interaction effects between biologic factors and cultural factors are certainly possible and must be seriously considered in future research.

What other subtle sex differences in socialization may be present after infancy? Let me speculate for a moment about possible socialization influences on aggression. Maccoby and Jacklin's review (1974) suggests no greater parental tolerance of aggression in U.S. boys. As already noted, boys may receive more physical punishment and reprimands about aggression from about 2 years of age on. There is also some evidence of an interaction between the sex of the parent and the sex of the child with regard to the display of aggression toward the parent. A few studies suggest that fathers may be more permissive of aggression from girls and mothers may be more permissive of such behavior from boys. Of the 13 comparisions of tolerance of cross-sex aggression cited by Maccoby and Jacklin (1974), ten significantly indicate cross-sex permissiveness. Greater punishment of boys and cross-sex permissiveness could conceivably and unintentionally increase the aggressiveness of boys. The more severe physical punishment could generate increased anger, which may be displaced in the form of increased aggressive behavior to peers. The greater cross-sex permissiveness may unintentionally increase the habit potential of aggression in boys if mothers are the primary socializers—by tolerating aggression more from their sons than from their daughters, mothers may communicate that aggression is all right for boys. Although girls might receive such a communication from their fathers, they might receive it with much lesser frequency. Inadvertently, then, parents could enhance the aggressive potential of boys.

An extremely important factor which might influence differential socialization is the extent to which boys and girls may be around adults. Parents may have similar ideas about how boys and girls should behave; but if boys are not as often around, parents may have less of a chance to influence boys' behavior. Is it possible, then, that boys are less apt to learn to inhibit egoistic behavior (including aggression and dominance behavior), and are less apt to learn responsible and nurturant behavior, because adults simply do not see the boys' behavior often enough? If reward and punishment are successful in shaping social behavior, then differential exposure of boys and girls to parents might be a mediating influence between direct socialization and children's behavior.

More generally, it may be that the social context of learning contributes to the extent to which certain behaviors are learned. Girls, if they are more often around the home, will not only have adults around as overseers, they will also have a larger number of younger children around. Boys, if they are more often away from home, are probably more likely to have peers around. B. Whiting and Whiting (1975) have discussed how the targets of children's social interaction may affect the kinds of social behaviors which children exhibit: infants appear to evoke nurturance, parents appear to evoke touching behavior and seeking help, and peers appear to evoke aggression. Different targets also seem to minimize other behaviors: dominant or dependent behavior is rarely directed toward infants, aggression is rarely exhibited toward parents, and nurturance is rarely directed toward peers. Thus it seems that if a person is frequently interacting with a particular kind of target, different behaviors might become habitual. For this reason alone, boys (if they are more often around peers) might learn to exhibit more aggressive behavior and less nurturant behavior. Girls (if they are more often around adults and younger children) might learn to be nurturant toward younger individuals and seek help and physical contact from parents. They may also learn to inhibit aggression and dominance behavior.

Inadvertently, certain socialization practices might be responsible for the fact that boys spend more time than girls away from the home. For one thing, in many societies the differential assignment of tasks to boys and girls may be the reason, since girls' tasks are more frequently in or around the home while boys' tasks (like herding) are generally away from the home. (Also, if girls generally do more work than boys, as is probably often the case, then boys are probably freer to play and wander from home). A second reason that socialization may predispose boys to spend more time away from home is that mothers, at least in the U.S., seem to look more directly at female infants (Maccoby & Jacklin, 1974), which may predispose the girls later to spend more time with their mothers than boys do. Perhaps in this and other ways mothers are employing techniques to distance boys, possibly to prepare them for a life requiring more mobility. Consistent with this notion, Lewis and Weinraub (1974) report that by age 2 years, boys seem to change how they deal with their mothers (replacing proximity and touching behaviors with more distant looking and vocalizing), whereas girls at 2 years of age are still engaging in proximity and touching behavior. These and other inadvertent socialization practices, and their possible influence on sex differences in social behaviors, need to be explored further.

Father absence and conflict about identification.   Up until now I have focused largely on obvious or subtle things that parents do to children that might create some of the observed sex differences in social behavior. I mentioned only briefly the possibility that the child's identification with the task model might be responsible, at least in part, for the purported effect of task assignment on social behavior. Beyond that, the way in which boys and girls identify with their role models may affect their behavior generally. I will discuss later how gender identification in boys and girls may affect how they acquire cognitive skills, but for the moment let me speculate about some possible effects of identification on social behavior.

There is an extensive literature on the effects of father absence on males. Most of the research from Western countries, and to some extent the cross-cultural research, suggests that violent and aggressive behavior is characteristic of father-absent male adolescents and adults (Anderson, 1968; Bacon, Child, & Barry, 1963; Glueck & Glueck, 1950; Gregory, 1965; Siegman, 1966; B. Whiting, 1965). This association is widely interpreted as being part of a defensive attempt by some males to show or prove their "masculinity" because they unconsciously feel that they might be "feminine." If more aggression is exhibited by father-absent males, is it possible that males generally exhibit more aggression than females because males (in contrast to females) have their role models relatively absent? In other words, if fathers are relatively absent generally, might not boys in most societies exaggerate stereotyped masculine behavior (like aggression and dominance) in an attempt to demonstrate their masculinity? If so, could this explain why boys are generally more aggressive and dominant than girls?

Of course, this interpretation bypasses the issue of why boys should think that aggressive or dominant behavior is stereotypically part of the masculine role. However, if we realize that in most societies males participate in war and dominate the political arena, it is not too far-fetched to think that boys may generally associate "toughness," "aggressiveness," and "dominance" with the male role.

A more serious problem for this interpretation is that in seeming contrast to adolescents and adults, father-absent *boys* under about 10 years of age do not always exhibit more aggression. A number of studies in the United States and one in Norway have found less aggression in such boys (Bach, 1946; Sears, 1951; Stolz et al., 1954; Tiller, 1958) although one study reported more aggression (Lynn & Sawrey, 1959). However, most of the studies showing less aggression among father-absent boys measured doll-play rather than overt aggression (except for that of Stolz et al. 1954); thus we really do not know how father absence affects overt social behavior in U.S. and Norwegian boys. The effect of father absence on boys' overt social behavior has not been studied frequently in non-Western settings either, but tentatively the non-Western results suggest the originally predicted pattern. Although B. Whiting and Whiting (1975) did not directly examine the effects of father absence on social behavior in the *Six Cultures* project, they did find that in societies with patrilocal extended families—where husbands and wives were less intimate and where children interacted less with their fathers—children in general exhibited more authoritarian-aggressive behavior. In my own study in Kenya (C. Ember, 1970), father-absent boys were somewhat (but not significantly) more "masculine"—more egoistic, more aggressive, more dominant—than father-present boys (controlling for task assignment). Obviously, the precise effects of father absence have to be studied more extensively. In doing so, we may need to keep in mind that in some circumstances extreme father-absence could induce almost complete identification with the mother. If so, such boys would display "feminine" behavior. It may only be where the culture exerts strong social pressure on boys to identify with the male role—perhaps particularly in patrilocal, patrilineal societies—that boys may be inclined to exhibit masculine behavior defensively (Burton & Whiting, 1961; B. Whiting, 1965). In the United States and Norway (particularly in the middle-class families studied), boys may not be under that much pressure to display their "masculinity."

The hypothesis that boys may show more aggressive and dominance behavior because they are relatively deprived of their role model could be tested cross-culturally. One could rank order societies on the degree to which fathers were around as role models and then see if that rank ordering predicts degree of sexual differentiation in aggressive and dominance behavior. Intracultural tests (with individuals as the units of study) could similarly be conducted. Boys and girls should be more alike in aggressive and dominance behavior if both parents participate heavily in child care and be less alike if the father participates little in child care.

Perception and Cognition

Many researchers, particularly cross-cultural psychologists, have looked for differences in perceptual and cognitive abilities in a wide variety of cultures. Because the main concern has been cultural difference or similarity, sex differences largely have been ignored. However, there are two areas in which we know something about sex differences. My reading for a review of cross-cultural cognitive studies (C. Ember, 1977) suggests that cognitive development (in terms of Piagetian tests) generally shows no sex differences, but sex differences do appear both intraculturally and cross-culturally in measures of field independence/dependence and other visual–spatial abilities.

The terms field independence and field dependence refer to different perceptual styles and perhaps more broadly to different cognitive styles. Field independence refers to the "tendency for parts of the field to be experienced as discrete from the field as a whole;" field dependence refers to the parts being "fused with field, or experienced as global" (Witkin & Berry, 1975). Cross-culturally, perceptual style has been measured most frequently by the embedded figures test and by the Kohs block design test, less frequently by the rod and frame test.

The cross-cultural data (see Witkin & Berry, 1975, for a summary) and the data from the United States (Maccoby & Jacklin, 1974) generally provide a consistent picture. Males are more likely to be field independent while females are more likely to be field dependent, but in some places there are no sex differences. Sex differences have been reported in American adolescents and adults, Cree and Athapaskan adults, Temne mixed-age groups, Telefomin people of highland New Guinea, two Nigerian communities, traditional Tsimshian, older Nsenga Africans, Fijian schoolchildren, and Mexican schoolchildren. Using samples of college and university students, sex differences have also been found in Japan and India. No or few sex differences have been found among Eskimo and Arunta groups and among Zambian students. Witkin and Berry (1975) suggest that sex differences appear greatest in sedentary, agricultural societies and least in migratory, hunting societies. I discuss below why this may be true.

Few cross-cultural studies of field independence/dependence have included young children; thus it is difficult to judge whether or not a sex difference emerges at a particular age. There is some disagreement about the time of onset of a sex difference in the United States. Maccoby and Jacklin (1974) suggest that a sex difference does not emerge clearly until the beginning of adolescence, but Coates (1974), referring to recent studies which used specially developed tests for young children, suggests that there is a sex difference at about age 5 years. However, at this age there is a reversal—girls are more field independent! Whether or not this early sex difference is substantiated by further intra- and cross-cultural research remains to be seen. Even if girls are generally more field independent at this time, the effect seems to be short-lived—the difference disappears by 6 years of age (Coates, 1974).

Many researchers think of field independence/dependence as indicative of "analytical" ability—the ability to separate or disembed things from their contexts. However, Maccoby and Jacklin (1974) note that the few studies which use auditory stimuli or which require problem restructuring do not show superiority of males, and therefore it appeared to them that males are not clearly more "analytical." Rather, tests of field independence/dependence as currently constructed (relying heavily on visual–spatial tasks) may reflect merely a superior visual–spatial ability in males.

Whether or not field independence/dependence measures are merely measures of visual–spatial ability, do other measures of visual–spatial ability show superiority of males? Data from the United States do suggest male superiority in early adolescence and adulthood and even perhaps as early as the age of 8 or 9 years (Maccoby & Jacklin, 1974). Although the cross-cultural studies are few in number and the differences are not always significant, almost all samples show differences favoring males when there are sex differences. For example, Berry (1971) found significant sex differences only in one Temne community, but in five of seven of his other non-Western sample communities male scores exceeded female scores. In studies in Iran (Baraheni, 1974) and in Israel (Guttman, 1974), boys scored significantly higher. Using the Porteus maze test and a task involving reconstruction of a diagonal, Logoli (Kenya) boys performed significantly better than girls (R. L. Munroe & Munroe, 1971). Dawson, Young, and Choi (1974) found that Hong Kong boys scored significantly higher than girls on tests of three-dimensional pictorial perception. As with field independence/dependence, data from the U.S. suggest male superiority from 8 or 9 years of age. Since few studies have investigated young children in non-Western settings, we do not know if this age trend will be found cross-culturally. Dawson et al. (1974) did find that male superiority on three-dimensional pictorial perception emerged only after 8 years of age, but R. L. Munroe and Munroe (1971) found boys to be superior at some visual–spatial skills at ages 3–7 years. (It may be of interest that the graphs shown by Dawson et al. [1974] show some superiority of girls at ages 5–6 years; although this was not statistically evaluated, it is in line with Coates' [1974] suggestion that girls score higher on field independence/dependence at that age.)

With regard to verbal and quantitative abilities, sex differences in verbal and mathematical skills have been documented in the United States and Western countries, but little research has been done outside Western countries. In the United States and in other Western countries, girls appear to have superior verbal abilities which become noticeable after age 10 or 11 years (Maccoby & Jacklin, 1974). It had been thought that this superiority begins very early—from the time of the beginning of speech—but, as Maccoby and Jacklin point out, that conclusion was based on very early work with very small samples. Most of the recent work finds no sex differences before the age of 3 years or so in spontaneous vocalization, although when there is a difference it seems to favor girls. Perhaps, however, vocalization can be in the service of different things. I examined the summary of recent research on vocalization before 3 years of age (in the work by Maccoby & Jacklin, 1974), and it appears that three of the four studies that measured vocalization to the mother showed significantly greater vocalization by girls; in contrast, of the studies that measured overall frequency of vocalization before age 3 years (with the social target unspecified), none showed a sex difference favoring girls. Thus the data from the United States and other Western countries suggest a superiority in verbal skills after age 10 years or so in girls and (somewhat more tenuously) some superiority before the age of 3 years (which might be manifested particularly in greater vocalization to mothers).

While females in the United States and other Western countries seem to have the advantage in verbal skills, particularly after age 10 years or so, males seem to have the advantage on quantitative skills. Aside from girls seeming to do somewhat better earlier on some quantitative skills, such as enumeration (Maccoby, 1966; Maccoby & Jacklin, 1974), there is little differentiation in the preschool and early school years. After adolescence, boys clearly test superior to girls on quantitative skills. Whether or not these trends will show up in cross-cultural samples remains to be seen.

Biologic Explanations

Hormonal influences.   Dawson (1972) has presented a theory that "normal male cognitive style [higher spatial, numerical, and field-independence scores] is in part influenced by neonatal androgen programming of the brain and in part by the appropriate male socialization processes" (p. 22). Androgen, then, is presumed to account partly for greater visual–spatial abilities, just as it is believed by some to enhance aggression. In support of the hormonal part of his theory, Dawson cites evidence that West African males feminized by a kwashiorkor-induced endrocrine dysfunction (which increases estrogen) are significantly lower in spatial ability and significantly more field dependent than normal males. He also found that estrogen-treated male rats perform significantly less well on spatial maze tests than male controls (Dawson, 1972). Unfortunately, the androgen-treated female rats could not be studied because they did not survive the experimental manipulation; thus the rat data presented by Dawson do not bear directly on the presumed effects of androgenization.

Aside from the West African data, most of the other human data support the socialization part of the theory more than the hormonal part. In studies of human genetic abnormalities, hormonal imbalances do not appear to correlate with visual–

spatial performance; rather such performance seems to depend on whether the subject was thought to be (and reared) as a male or female. Genetic males with external female genitalia show a feminine pattern of scores if reared as females but a masculine pattern if reared as males (Masica, Money, Ehrhardt, & Lewis, 1969, cited by Dawson, 1972). Similar socialization effects are shown with Turner and Klinefelter syndromes (Dawson, 1972). Furthermore, girls and boys who had abnormally high levels of prenatal androgen did not do significantly better on spatial tests (Baker & Ehrhardt, 1974) as compared with their normal siblings and parents. Thus the case for hormonal differences in males and females as explaining male superiority in visual–spatial skills appears now to be equivocal at best.

Lateralization of the brain. There is evidence that the left cerebral hemisphere usually dominates verbal functions and the right cerebral hemisphere mostly but not as strongly dominates nonverbal functions (Buffery & Gray, 1972). Buffery (1970) has proposed that this supposedly innate "lateralization" develops earlier in girls than in boys and that the earlier lateralization in girls could account for the known sex differences in cognitive functioning—the superior linguistic ability in girls (which, as we have seen, is not yet documented cross-culturally) and the superior spatial and quantitative ability in boys. There is some evidence supporting some parts of this theory, but the evidence is not complete enough to support the notion that sex differences in cognitive skills result from differential lateralization. To be sure, some evidence supports the idea that girls lateralize earlier than boys (reviewed by Buffery & Gray, 1972), but we do not yet know if the early sex difference in lateralization produces the differences in linguistic and spatial skills. First, research has not yet shown that girls (or boys) who have earlier left hemisphere lateralization for verbal stimuli have better linguistic skills as measured by various school tests, nor has it been shown that boys (or girls) who lateralize more (versus less) on the right hemisphere for nonverbal stimuli have superior spatial skills. Second, as Buffery and Gray (1972) themselves point out, the research to date has not shown that lateralization occurs differently by sex *prior* to the emergence of speech. It is conceivable that greater lateralization does occur in girls, but *because* of their greater interest and facility in verbal activities rather than the other way around. Third, neither the sex difference in lateralization nor the linkage to cognitive skills has been shown in other cultures.

Social Explanations

"Tight" parental control and perceptual style. Witkin and his colleagues (Witkin, 1969) have suggested that the more a mother restricts her child and stresses conformity, the more likely that the child will not develop field independence. The presumption seems to be that perceptual style will follow from and perhaps be generalized from the nature of the mother–child relationship. The more controlling the parent, the less the child will be able to separate himself or herself socially as well as perceptually. Building on that theory and on supportive findings from the United States, Dawson (1967) postulates that people in societies with "stricter" child training should have more field dependence. Cross-cultural and intracultural comparisons (Berry, 1966; 1971; Dawson, 1967) have provided some support for this hypothesis.

It is assumed that this hypothesis might explain why girls are more field dependent in some societies (see, e.g., Witkin & Berry, 1975). The presumption seems to be that in some societies, particularly in sedentary agricultural societies, girls may be more controlled than boys. Perhaps in such societies girls do more work and are more often confined to the house, but these are just guesses. What we need to do is to rate societies on the degree to which girls are more "tightly controlled" than boys and see if this predicts the degree of sex difference in field independence/dependence.

Proximity to home and spatial ability.   Perhaps relevant to the idea of "tight" parental control affecting field independence is the suggestion by R. L. Munroe and Munroe (1971) that boys may be better at spatial skills because of their greater experience with movement through the physical environment. Consistent with that interpretation, Logoli boys were found to be significantly further from home in their free time than girls. Moreover, in age-matched boy–girl pairs the one that was more often farther away from home had significantly greater scores on two visual–spatial tasks. Essentially the same results were obtained in a replication among the Gusii (Nerlove, Munroe, & Munroe, 1971), except that a sex difference in environmental experience was significant only if time spent herding was added to free time.

Unfortunately, the above studies were not able to separate the effect of environmental experience from the possible effect of biologic sex—boys almost invariably had more environmental experience. It would be important to find some cultural situation where there was more variability in environmental experiences among boys and among girls so that the effect of environmental experience per se (apart from sex) could be studied. Some further but indirect support for the connection between experience and visual–spatial skills comes from a study of 5–8-year-olds in Guatemala. Nerlove, Roberts, Klein, Yarbrough, and Habicht (1974) found that both for boys and girls self-managed behavior (which includes activities some distance from home) correlates positively with performance on visual–spatial tests (the embedded figures test and a matching figures test.) Since environmental experience may be related negatively to degree of parental control, it would be important to try to design research that may sort out the possibly independent effects of these two factors.

Sex differences in achieving gender identification.   Lynn (1969) has suggested that some of the sex differences in perceiving and thinking may stem from basic differences in the ways boys and girls achieve their gender identifications. Lynn assumes that since the mother is usually the primary caretaker, children will identify with her first; boys not only have to shift their identifications later but also have to learn their masculine role more "abstractly" because their fathers are not as often around. Girls, on the other hand, have their role models—their mothers—more often in view and can learn their gender identification in a more direct way. Many of the supposed male-female cognitive differences (e.g., girls are better at rote memory, boys are more "analytical") which Lynn (1969) tries to explain with his theory are not clearly established as male–female differences (see Maccoby & Jacklin, 1974). However, Lynn's theory might explain the greater verbal fluency of girls in the United States and the relatively greater field independence of boys in some societies. Lynn suggests that girls may be more motivated to maintain a relationship with their mother as their role model and in the context of this personal relationship may acquire greater linguistic facility. Although Lynn does not explicitly mention field independence, he might say that boys' way of learning their gender role (constructing their identification indirectly) could generalize to a field-independent perceptual style.

Lynn's theory also suggests to me that male–female differences in cognition are likely to be greater in societies where fathers are hardly ever involved in caretaking or where the work that fathers do (in contrast to mothers' work) is rarely seen because it is dangerous or far away from home. In other words, sex differences in cognitive skills should be minimized where both parents are involved in child care, where both parents work close to home, or where the work of both parents is unseen.

Finally, Lynn's theory implies something about the effect of father absence—namely, that sex differences in cognitive skills would be greatest in those societies where father absence is a regular occurrence. It is possible, however, that father absence can reverse the process that Lynn proposes. A little bit of father absence, according to Lynn's theory, should create more difference between boys and girls with respect to cognitive style, but extreme father absence, I think, might make boys more similar to girls in cognitive style. If early identification with the mother persists because of the extreme absence of the father, boys may develop an identification similar to that of girls. Boys may switch later to a secondary masculine identification (because of societal pressures), but the habit patterns for cognitive style may already be set. Carlsmith (1964) found that men whose fathers were absent early had a "feminine" pattern with respect to SAT (college entrance examination) scores—such men were more likely than other men to have higher verbal than quantitative scores. Thus it may be that extreme father absence for boys creates an opposite effect from moderate father absence: extreme father absence may produce a "feminine" cognitive style.

Education.   In many parts of the world boys and girls are not given the same amounts or the same kinds of education. Since education may affect test performance on perceptual and cognitive skills (C. Ember, 1977), unequal education for males and females may account for some of the sex differences observed. For example, education is known to correlate positively with field independence (Berry, 1966; Dawson, 1967). One reason may be that Western-style education stresses "analytic" thinking (Cohen, 1969). A second reason may be that two of the tests for field independence/dependence (the embedded figures test and Kohs blocks test) depend on the ability of a person to deal with drawings and pictures—a facility that may be learned in school (C. Ember, 1977). I suspect that sedentary, agricultural societies may show more of a sex difference in field independence/dependence than hunter–gatherers because they have more unequal education by sex. Where education is voluntary, girls might be more often kept out of school when there is a great deal of work to be done around the house (probably more true for agriculturalists). Whether this is true or not, education certainly has to be controlled for in future cross-cultural research on sex differences in perception and cognition.

Inferred Personality Traits
Most of the psychological sex differences we have dealt with so far have been measured in a fairly direct manner—behavior differences have largely been studied by observation, perceptual and cognitive differences by reactions to standardized stimuli. But there are other aspects of personality that cannot be assessed in as direct or as objective a manner. If we want to know how people feel or what conflicts they

have, we must rely on people telling us what they feel inside or on projective tests which may reveal innermost feelings and conflicts.

Although projective testing was very much in vogue among anthropologists in the 1940s and 1950s, little attention was paid to sex differences. More attention has been paid to sex differences lately, but projective testing in other cultures has largely gone out of vogue. Thus we know relatively little cross-culturally about sex differences in what may be called "inferred personality traits." However, some research has been done on sex differences in anxiety, self-concept, and frequency of mental illness.

Anxiety

In an earlier review of sex differences, D'Andrade (1966) suggested that the cross-cultural projective test results indicated greater maladjustment and anxiety in males. Although projective testing has not been employed frequently of late, what has been done does not support that conclusion. In a fairly large comparative study of eight different East African communities, Edgerton (1971) found no such sex differences in Rorschach protocols. (The few sex differences he found suggested only that women had a more practical, particularistic approach to things and made less of an effort in responding.) Moreover, if we look at self-respect as a measure of anxiety, an opposite picture emerges—girls and women usually show up as more anxious. Self-report measures have been largely employed in the United States, although they have also been used in France, Japan, and Greece (Maccoby & Jacklin, 1974).

There are two discrepancies to explain here, (1) why the earlier studies show more projective anxiety in males while Edgerton's comparative study did not and (2) why the self-report studies (except among Japanese children) suggest an opposite pattern.

Assuming for the moment that both projective and self-report measures are tapping underlying anxiety, it is possible that both discrepancies may be due to cultural variability. It may be that in some cultural settings men have more role conflict; in others, women may have more. Women in Western societies may have more anxiety because traditional women's roles (i.e., housewife and mother) are no longer so valued—hence they may suffer from anxiety because of role conflict. (As we shall see later, role conflict may be related to higher rates of mental illness for women in some places.) Men may have more anxiety in other societies because they may be subject to another kind of role conflict induced by acculturation pressures. This latter possibility is suggested by Spindler's (1962) work among the Menomini. Women there show less projective anxiety than men; as Spindler points out, there are no pressing demands for change on them—they have maintained a greater continuity with traditional roles and values than men have. If role conflict is responsible for greater anxiety (either because of changing cultural evaluation or acculturation pressure), we should be able to establish it cross-culturally. Do societies with greater acculturation pressure on men have more anxious males? Do societies with recent changes in the role of women have more anxious females?

The cross-cultural discrepancy with regard to sex differences in anxiety could also be due to the use of different measuring devices in different cultural settings. Self-reports may give a totally different picture from projective tests. It may be that males are generally more anxious but less likely to admit weaknesses (Sarason, Hill, & Zimbardo, 1964). Only by employing both kinds of measures—self-report and projective tests—on the same individuals can we find out if both kinds of measure are tapping the same things.

Self-Concept
Little cross-cultural research has been done on how males and females feel about themselves. One particular aspect of the self-concept that has been cross-culturally studied is felt control over one's life. Using Rotter's internal/external "locus of control" scale, studies of college students in India (Sinha, 1972) and Japan (Mahler, 1974) generally concur with the picture from the United States (Maccoby & Jacklin, 1974) that males appear to feel they have more personal control over their lives than females do. Although this research is barely cross-cultural, in the sense that university students may generally have quite similar experiences in different countries and that all the countries studied are fairly developed, studies of the self-concept may be quite interesting. We might expect that ideas about oneself and one's potency may actually reflect reality—since males in most societies are more powerful, they may generally feel more personal control. The question arises as to whether the self-concept corresponds fairly directly to degree of cultural emphasis on one sex or the other. Do societies that are most strongly male dominated have the greatest discrepancy in male–female concepts of personal control? Do females feel more control in societies that are matrilocal and matrilineal or where they contribute substantially to subsistence?

Mental Illness
There is every reason to suspect that sex differences in the incidence of mental illness are variable across different cultural settings. Evidence from the United States (Gove & Tudor, 1973), from Eskimo groups (Bloom, 1975; Chance, 1965; Murphy, 1960, cited by Bloom, 1975), from two communities in Colombia (Angandona & Kiev, 1972), and from a city in Nigeria (A. Leighton, 1969) suggest that women have higher rates of mental illness than men, but psychiatric surveys in rural Ghana (referred to by Opler, 1967) and in Nigerian Yoruba villages (A. Leighton, 1969) find that men have higher rates of mental illness.

Role conflict and acculturation may affect rates of mental illness, and when the sexes are affected differently by these stresses different patterns of sex difference in mental illness may result.

Changing values may be one source of role conflict. In a comparative study of a few French-English communities, D. Leighton, Harding, Macklin, & Leighton (1963) report that women have lower rates of mental illness in the community where women are isolated from the sentiments of the larger society about changing women's roles, whereas women have higher rates of mental illness in the community where they are beset by conflicts about their roles. A similar pattern appears in Nigeria—rural women have lower rates of mental illness, urban women have higher (A. Leighton, 1969). Gove and Tudor (1973) point out that in the United States it is only among married persons that women are significantly more likely to be mentally ill. They suggest that this may be so because the "housewife" role no longer has much prestige, and married women who work have the burdens of two roles.

But changing values themselves may not be sufficient to produce role conflict. Perhaps it is really the result of a discrepancy between what one values and what one can achieve. For example, Chance (1965) in his studies of rural Eskimo communities found that women (who had higher rates of mental illness than men) had identified highly with Western culture but unlike men had no real contact with that culture; thus the conflict in women may have come from their inability to achieve what they wanted.

Expressive Behavior

If, as the cross-cultural data suggest, males and females have some characteristic personality differences, those differences ought to be reflected in a number of different expressive modes—in art, in music, in game preferences, and in dreams. This supposition follows from the theoretical model that expressive behavior reflects personality (e.g., J. Whiting & Child, 1953).

While sex differences in preferences for or in the performance of art, music, and games have not been explored much cross-culturally, some attention has been paid to sex differences in the content of dreams.

The bulk of the dream research has focused on the sex of the characters in males' and females' dreams. On the basis of dream data from the United States, from the Hopi, and from the Yir Yiront, Hall and Domhoff (1963) suggest that there is a "ubiquitous" tendency for males to dream more about males than females, whereas females tend to dream about the sexes equally. The same tendency is found by Grey and Kalsched (1971) in India and by Robbins and Kilbride (1971) in Uganda. The only contradictory evidence comes from Peru (Urbina & Grey, 1975). Obviously, data from more societies are needed to conclude that this pattern is "ubiquitous." However, assuming that it is, how might it be explained?

Hall and Domhoff (1963) theorize that the sex difference in dreams reflects males' greater unresolved problems with men. As partial support for their theory, they cite evidence that in men's dreams males have a higher proportion of aggressive interactions with males, whereas in women's dreams females divide aggression equally between both sexes. If this theory is correct, there should be a higher proportion of male characters in men's dreams in societies where child-rearing conditions exaggerate the Oedipus complex.

An alternative hypothesis is that dreams reflect real-life sex differences in interaction rather than in unconscious conflict. Grey and Kalsched (1971) cite some supportive evidence for this hypothesis from India. Pointing out that traditional Indian society is quite segregated by sex, they find that more traditional individuals (both males and females) have significantly lower numbers of opposite-sex characters in their dreams, and males who have more opposite-sex friends have a higher proportion of opposite-sex dream characters.

How would the "reality" hypothesis explain the apparent cross-cultural tendency of males to dream more about male characters? We have already noted the tendency for boys and girls to choose same-sex peers for play. Nonetheless, it may be generally true that girls who are more often at home see males and females in more equal proportions than boys do. The latter, who may be more often free to play, might spend more of their time in all-male groups. The greater tendency of males to have aggressive encounters with males in dreams may thus reflect a greater frequency of aggressive behavior in males. The "reality" hypothesis might be tested cross-culturally by looking to see if there is a relationship between observed sex differences in behavior and sex differences in dreams.

Some striking "reality" parallels are also suggested by a cross-cultural study of words in dreams (Colby, 1963) and a study of rural Chicano dreams in the American Southwest (Brenneis & Roll, 1975). Colby (1963) found in his study of dreams from 75 tribes that men were significantly more apt than women to mention weapons, death, animals, and coitus in their dreams. This tendency may reflect men's greater involvement in the occupations of hunting, herding, and war and perhaps their somewhat greater role in initiating sexual activity. Among the rural Chicano, men are more apt to mention large aspects of their dream setting (e.g., landscape), while women are more apt to describe interior settings and small spaces; men also are more apt to mention nonrelatives and aggressive and sexual encounters. Aren't such differences also consistent with the sex differences in behavior we have already noted? Males are more apt to work further from home and participate in political activities. Males are more likely to be aggressive and may somewhat more often take the initiative in sex. We expect then that the more male and female roles diverge, the more their (reports of their) dreams will diverge.

Although sex differences in drawing, song style, and games have not been explored cross-culturally, there is every reason to believe that sex differences will be found. Franck and Rosen (1949) have found in the U.S. that sex differences in drawing appear to reflect different body images that males and females have. After presenting college students with simple designs to complete, they found that men were significantly more likely than women to close designs, enlarge or expand designs upward, emphasize sharp or angular lines, etc. Women, on the other hand, were significantly more likely to leave designs open, elaborate designs internally, blunt or enclose sharp lines or angles, etc. Whether or not these differences occur cross-culturally, and why there might be varying degrees of difference, are problems for future research.

There is also reason to believe that cross-cultural sex differences will appear in games and song style. Cross-cultural research on games (Roberts & Sutton-Smith, 1962) and music (Ayres 1968; 1973; Lomax, 1968) suggests that different socialization practices in different societies may explain differing cultural preferences in games and music. Thus we might also expect sex differences in music and game preferences if boys and girls are socialized differently. For example, Roberts and Sutton-Smith (1962) found that in societies with strong pressure for obedience, games of strategy are preferred; in societies with strong pressure for responsibility, games of chance are preferred; and in societies that stress achievement, games of physical skill are preferred. Assuming that girls are more pressured to be responsible and obedient and boys more pressured to achieve, Roberts and Sutton-Smith predicted and found in a sample of U.S. schoolchildren that girls prefer games of strategy or chance while boys prefer games of physical skill.

Children's Acquisition of Sex-typed Behavior

Most of the explanations that I have dealt with in this section are rather specific —suggesting a particular biologic process or a particular overt or covert socialization practice that may be responsible for a particular sex difference. But we cannot ignore the possibility that children pick up sex-typed behavior on their own, either through imitation/identification with a same-sex model or through a more generalized acquisition of a conception of what persons of their gender do. If either or both of these processes operate, children may acquire sex-typed behavior as long as society has different sex roles and different emphases on one sex or the other. Even in the absence of direct teaching or more inadvertent differences in socialization, sex differences might continue to be acquired generation after generation.

Identification and Imitation

Theoretically, identification with and imitation of same-sex parents and other adults should play a large role in the acquisition of sex-typed behaviors. However, in a thoughtful review of the research, Maccoby and Jacklin (1974) are forced to the conclusion that there is little evidence indicating that these processes are important in the acquisition of sex-typed behavior. Research (primarily in the U.S.) on similarity to same-sex parents reveals few significant correlations, as does the imitation of same-sex adult models in experimental research.

Perhaps identification with the same-sex parent and modeling of same-sex adults is not very important in the United States but is of great importance in non-Western countries. This possibility seems likely to me in view of the fact that often the behavior which children in the United States observe may be perceived as irrelevant to their life or their future. After all, children in this country are rarely expected to do adult things—they play and go to school. As for their perceived futures, even if children in this country see their parents work (which is unusual), they may think that they will probably not do the same thing when they grow up. But this is not the case in more traditional societies. Identification with the same-sex parent and imitation of other same-sex adults might be more likely in such societies because children may want to acquire the skills they have to acquire. Whether or not this is the case remains for future research to decide.

Cognitive Acquisition of Gender Role

A possible way of understanding the acquisition of sex-typed behaviors without direct modeling of the parents comes from a cognitive view of gender identity (Kohlberg, 1966; Kohlberg & Ullman 1974; Lewis & Weinraub, 1974). In this view, children themselves, through their own cognitive development, acquire an understanding of their sexual identity, develop conceptions of appropriate behavior for their gender, and are motivated to act accordingly. Thus children may be influenced not by parents so much as by the generalized cultural expectations about what males and females are supposed to do.

There is some disagreement about the age at which children supposedly develop their gender identities. Kohlberg and Ullman (1974) assert that it is absent in the first 2 years of life and becomes stable only by age 6 or 7 years. Lewis and Weinraub (1974) believe that gender identity appears earlier in infancy. As supporting evidence, they cite data from their own and others' studies that infants prefer to look at same-sex parents and same-sex infants. They also cite the work of others on hermaphrodites who, when their genitals are altered to conform to their genetic sex, are reluctant (even at the age of 2 years) to change their sexual identity accordingly.

In sum, even very young children may know a lot more than we think they know about sex-typed behavior. For example, they may be quite aware that they will grow up to be men and women, and that men more often than women are away from home and more involved in aggressive and dominance activities, etc. Couldn't this early awareness be one of the factors that cause boys to behave differently from girls?

SUMMARY AND CONCLUSIONS

In assessing what we know and do not know about sex differences cross-culturally, it has become painfully obvious to me that we have a long way to go before we can be confident about the nature of sex differences and why they exist. Yet, in spite of our ignorance, there seems to be a great propensity to come to conclusions about which sex differences are biologically based and which are based on social learning. Most of these decisions are based on inferences from the patterning of sex differences across cultures. As I have argued, although the patterning of sex differences may be consistent with a biologic *or* social learning interpretation, such reasoning is too indirect. Most seriously, few cross-cultural studies (and even intracultural studies) have been designed to test an explanation of sex differences directly. If we want to understand sex differences, not just describe them, cross-cultural research should proceed in a theory-testing direction.

Lest I paint the picture too dimly, I should be quick to point out that cross-cultural studies present us with rare opportunities. Aside from presumed causes which do not vary across human populations (like supposed genetic predispositions which go back to early human history), almost any possible determinant probably varies cross-culturally in magnitude; therefore a cross-cultural study can be devised to test the explanation. We can also conduct intracultural tests in those societies which, for subcultural or other reasons, display variation in the determinants of interest to us.

Some theory-testing cross-cultural studies can be carried out with data already available. Ethnographic data can be used, at least as a start, for investigating some of the theories discussed in the sections on physical differences and on ethnographically described differences. As long as we can derive from a theory that some ethnographically described conditions should be predictive more or less of a particular sex difference, we should be able to design a cross-cultural test of that theory. To be sure, some research has already been conducted along those lines, but more is sorely needed. Existing psychological data can also be used if researchers who have collected data on similar variables in different cultural settings begin to pool their data to test hypotheses. This strategy is currently being employed by B. Whiting (in collaboration with other researchers) to examine sex differences in social behavior on the basis of observations conducted in 16 different cultural communities.

However, in order to test most of the hypotheses mentioned in this review, we need to collect new data from a variety of societies. Most notably in this regard, we know little about sex differences in newborns and infants in non-Western countries, nor do we know much about sex differences in linguistic skills, quantitative skills, self-concept, and expressive behavior. For all we know, there may be many sex differences not found in the United States which are prevalent elsewhere. But I think it is important not to continue to design research just to document the existence of a sex difference. Even if a researcher has the funds to study only one other cultural community, it would probably be possible to test at least one hypothesis (about the degree of variation among individuals there) that would have implications for understanding sex differences cross-culturally. If a researcher has funds to study more than one cultural community, then the prospects are more hopeful—then some preliminary attempt can be made to test predictions derived from an explanatory hypothesis both cross-culturally and among individuals within a culture.

Much more mileage can be gained from a theory-testing study if a researcher investigates the possible effects of more than one presumed cause at the same time —we need to assess the relative influences as well as the possible interactions among a number of factors. It is particularly important at this time to consider both biologic and social explanations in designing a study. In my opinion, choosing between "nature" and "nurture," particularly when we have so little evidence, is going to detract from our ability to understand sex differences. Even if we want to show that one or the other type of explanations is more important, we have to study both. If we fail to study both, we may never find out that biologic and social factors can sometimes interact with one another.

If we want to understand sex differences, we have a long way to go. But all we can lose is our ignorance.

REFERENCES

Andersen, K. L. Work capacity of selected populations. In P. T. Baker & J. S. Weiner (Eds.), *The biology of human adaptability.* Oxford: Clarendon, 1966, pp. 67–90.

Anderson, R. E. Where's dad? Archives of General Psychiatry, 1968, *18*, 641–649.

Angandona, M., & Kiev, A. *Mental health in the developing world: A case study in Latin America.* New York: Free Press, 1972.

Asmussen, E., & Heeboll-Nielsen, K. Physical performance and growth in children. *Journal of Applied Psychology,* 1956, *40*, 371–380.

Ayres, B. C. Effects of infantile stimulation on musical behavior. In A. Lomax (Ed.), *Folk song style and culture.* Washington: American Association for the Advancement of Science, 1968, pp. 211–221.

Ayres, B. C. Effects of infant carrying practices on rhythm in music. *Ethos,* 1973, *1*, 387–404.

Bach, G. R. Father-fantasies and father-typing in father-separated children. *Child Development,* 1946, *17*, 63–79.

Bacon, M. K., Child, I. L., & Barry, H., III. A cross-cultural study of correlates of crime. *Journal of Abnormal and Social Psychology,* 1963, *66*, 291–300.

Baker, S. W., & Ehrhardt, A. A. Prenatal androgen, intelligence, and cognitive sex differences. In R. C. Friedman, R. M. Richart, & R. L. Vande Wiele (Eds.), *Sex differences in behavior.* New York: John Wiley & Sons, 1974, pp. 53–76.

Baraheni, M. N. Raven's progressive matrices as applied to Iranian children. *Educational and Psychological Measurement,* 1974, *34*, 983–988.

Barfield, A. Biological influences on sex differences in behavior. In M. S. Teitelbaum (Ed.), *Sex differences: Social and biological perspectives.* Garden City, N.Y.: Anchor, 1976, pp. 62–121.

Barry, H., III, Bacon, M. K., & Child, I. L. A cross-cultural survey of some sex differences in socialization. *Journal of Abnormal and Social Psychology,* 1957, *55*, 327–332.

Barry, H., III, Josephson, L., Lauer, E., & Marshall, C. Traits inculcated in childhood: Cross-cultural codes 5. *Ethnology,* 1976, *15*, 83–114.

Barry, H., III, & Paxon, L. Infancy and early childhood: Cross-cultural codes 2. *Ethnology,* 1971, *10*, 466–506.

Bayley, N. *Bayley scales of infant development.* New York: The Psychological Corporation, 1969.

Berry, J. W. Temne and Eskimo perceptual skills. *International Journal of Psychology,* 1966, *1*, 207–229.

Berry, J. W. Ecological and cultural factors in spatial perceptual development. *Canadian Journal of Behavioural Science,* 1971, *3*, 324–336.

Bloom, J. D. Psychiatric problems and cultural transitions in Alaska. *Arctic,* 1975, *25*, 203–215.

Blurton-Jones, N. G., & Konner, M. J. Sex differences in behavior of London and Bushman children. In R. P. Michael & J. H. Crook (Eds.), *Comparative ecology and behaviour of primates.* London: Academic Press, 1973, pp. 690–750.

Bock, R. D., Wainer, H., Petersen, A., Thissen, D., Murray, J., & Roche, A. A parameterization for individual human growth curves. *Human Biology,* 1973, *45*, 63–80.

Breer, P. E., & Locke, E. A. *Task experience as a source of attitudes.* Homewood, Ill.: Dorsey Press, 1965.

Brenneis, C. B., & Roll, S. Ego modalities in the manifest dreams of male and female Chicanos. *Psychiatry*, 1975, *38*, 172–185.

Broude, G. J., & Greene, S. J. Cross-cultural codes on twenty sexual attitudes and practices. *Ethnology*, 1976, *15*, 409–429.

Brown, J. K. A cross-cultural study of female initiation rites. *American Anthropologist*, 1963, *65*, 837–853.

Brown, J. K. A note on the division of labor by sex. *American Anthropologist*, 1970, *72*, 1073–1078 (a).

Brown, J. K. Economic organization and the position of women among the Iroquois. *Ethnohistory*, 1970, *17*, 151–167 (b).

Buffery, A. W. H. Sex differences in the development of hand preference, cerebral dominance for speech and cognitive skill. *Bulletin of the British Psychological Society*, 1970, *23*, 233.

Buffery, A. W. H., & Gray, J. A. Sex differences in the development of spatial and linguistic skills. In C. Ounsted & D. C. Taylor (Eds.), *Gender differences: Their ontogeny and significance*. Edinburgh: Churchill Livingston, 1972, pp. 123–157.

Burton, R. V., & Whiting, J. W. M. The absent father and cross-sex identity. *Merrill-Palmer Quarterly*, 1961, *7*, 85–95.

Carlsmith, L. Effect of early father absence on scholastic aptitude. *Harvard Educational Review*, 1964, *34*, 3–21.

Chance, N. A. Acculturation, self-identification, and personality adjustment. *American Anthropologist*, 1965, *67*, 372–393.

Coates, S. Sex differences in field independence among preschool children. In R. C. Friedman, R. M. Richart, & R. L. Vande Wiele (Eds.), *Sex differences in behavior*. New York: John Wiley & Sons, 1974, pp. 259–274.

Cohen, R. Conceptual style, culture conflict and non-verbal tests of intelligence. *American Anthropologist*, 1969, *71*, 828–856.

Colby, K. M. Sex differences in dreams of primitive tribes. *American Anthropologist*, 1963, *65*, 1116–1122.

D'Andrade, R. G. Sex differences and cultural institutions. In E. E. Maccoby (Ed.), *The development of sex differences*. Stanford, Calif.: Stanford University Press, 1966, pp. 174–204.

Dawson, J. L. M. Cultural and physiological influences upon spatial-perceptual processes in West Africa—Part I. *International Journal of Psychology*, 1967, *2*, 115–128.

Dawson, J. L. M. Effects of sex hormones on cognitive style in rats and men. *Behavior Genetics*, 1972, *2*, 21–41.

Dawson, J. L. M., Young, B. M., & Choi, P. P. C. Developmental influences in pictorial depth perception among Hong Kong Chinese children. *Journal of Cross-Cultural Psychology*, 1974, *5*, 3–22.

Divale, W. T. Migration, external warfare, and matrilocal residence. *Behavior Science Research*, 1974, *9*, 75–133.

Divale, W. T., & Harris, M. Population, warfare, and the male supremacist complex. *American Anthropologist*, 1976, *78*, 521–538.

Draper, P. Cultural pressure on sex differences. *American Ethnologist*, 1975, *2*, 602–616.

Edgerton, R. B. *The individual in cultural adaptation*. Berkeley: University of California Press, 1971.

Edwards, C. P., & Whiting, B. B. Women and dependency. *Politics and Society*, 1974, *4*, 343–355.

Ehrhardt, A. A., & Baker, S. W. Fetal androgens, human central nervous system differentiation, and behavior sex differences. In R. C. Friedman, R. M. Richart, & R. L. Vande Wiele (Eds.), *Sex differences in behavior*. New York: John Wiley & Sons, 1974, pp. 33–52.

Ember, C. R. *Effects of feminine task-assignment on the social behavior of boys.* Unpublished doctoral dissertation, Harvard University, 1970.

Ember, C. R. Feminine task assignment and the social behavior of boys. *Ethos,* 1973, *1,* 424–439.

Ember, C. R. An evaluation of alternative theories of matrilocal versus patrilocal residence. *Behavior Science Research,* 1974, *9,* 135–149.

Ember, C. R. Residential variation among hunter-gatherers. *Behavior Science Research,* 1975, *10,* 199–227.

Ember, C. R. Cross-cultural cognitive studies. *Annual Review of Anthropology,* 1977, *6,* 33–56.

Ember, C. R., & Ember, M. The conditions favoring multilocal residence. *Southwestern Journal of Anthropology,* 1972, *28,* 382–400.

Ember, M. The emergence of neolocal residence. *Transactions of the New York Academy of Sciences,* 1967, *30,* 291–302.

Ember, M., & Ember, C. R. The conditions favoring matrilocal versus patrilocal residence. *American Anthropologist,* 1971, *73,* 571–594.

Finney, H. C., & Erpino, M. J. Synergistic effect of estradiol benzoate and dihydrotestosterone on aggression in mice. *Hormones and Behavior,* 1976, *7,* 391–400.

Ford, C. S., & Beach, F. A. *Patterns of sexual behavior.* New York: Harper & Row, 1951.

Franck, K., & Rosen, E. A projective test of masculinity-femininity. *Journal of Consulting Psychology,* 1949, *13,* 247–256.

Freedman, D. G. Genetic variations on the hominid theme: Individual, sex and ethnic differences. In F. J. Monks, W. W. Hartrup, & J. de Wit (Eds.), *Determinants of behavioral development.* New York: Academic Press, 1972, pp. 121–142.

Frisancho, A. R., & Baker, P. T. Altitude and growth: A study of the patterns of physical growth of a high altitude Peruvian Quechua population. *American Journal of Physical Anthropology,* 1970, *32,* 279–292.

Garai, J. E., & Scheinfeld, A. Sex differences in mental and behavioral traits. *Genetic Psychology Monographs,* 1968, *77,* 169–299.

Glanville, E. V., & Geerdink, R. A. Skinfold thickness, body measurements and age changes in Trio and Wajana Indians of Surinam. *American Journal of Physical Anthropology,* 1970, *32,* 455–462.

Glueck, S., & Glueck, E. Unraveling juvenile delinquency. Cambridge, Mass.: Harvard University Press, 1950.

Gove, W. R., & Tudor, J. F. Adult sex roles and mental illness. *American Journal of Sociology,* 1973, *78,* 812–935.

Gregory, I. Anterospective data following childhood loss of a parent. *Archives of General Psychiatry,* 1965, *13,* 99–109.

Grey, A., & Kalsched, D. Oedipus east and west: An exploration via manifest dream content. *Journal of Cross-Cultural Psychology,* 1971, *2,* 337–352.

Gunders, S., & Whiting, J. W. M. Mother-infant separation and physical growth. *Ethnology,* 1968, *7,* 196–206.

Guttman, R. Genetic analysis of analytical spatial ability: Raven's progressive matrices. *Behavior Genetics,* 1974, *7,* 273–284.

Hall, C., & Domhoff, B. A ubiquitous sex difference in dreams. *Journal of Abnormal and Social Psychology,* 1963, *66,* 278–280.

Hautvast, J. Growth in stature and head and face measurements in Dutch children aged 7 to 14. *Human Biology,* 1971, *43,* 340–343.

Hautvast, J. Physical growth and menarcheal age in Tanzanian schoolchildren and adults. *Human Biology,* 1971, *43,* 421–444.

Heath, D. B. Sexual division of labor and cross-cultural research. *Social Forces,* 1958, *37,* 77–79.

Hiernaux, J. Weight/height relationship during growth in Africans and Europeans. *Human Biology,* 1964, *36,* 273–293.

Hutt, C. *Males and females.* Harmondsworth, Engl.: Penguin Books, 1972.

Hutt, C. Neuroendocrinological, behavioural, and intellectual aspects of sexual differentiation in human development. In C. Ounsted & D. C. Taylor (Eds.), *Gender differences: Their ontogeny and significance.* Edinburgh: Churchill Livingstone, 1972, pp. 73–121.

Kilbride, J. E. *The motor development of rural Baganda infants.* Kampala: Makerere Institute of Social Research, Makerere University, 1973.

Kilbride, J. E., Robbins, M. C., & Kilbride, P. L. The comparative motor development of Baganda, American white, and American black infants. *American Anthropologist,* 1970, *72,* 1422–1428.

Kohlberg, L. A cognitive-developmental analysis of children's sex-role concepts and attitudes. In E. E. Maccoby (Ed.), *The development of sex differences.* Stanford, Calif.: Stanford University Press, 1966, pp. 82–173.

Kohlberg, L., & Ullman, D. Z. Stages in the development of psychosexual concepts and attitudes. In R. C. Friedman, R. M. Richart, & R. L. Vande Wiele (Eds.), *Sex differences in behavior.* New York: John Wiley & Sons, 1974, pp. 209–222.

Kolata, G. B. !Kung hunter-gatherers: Feminism, diet, and birth control. *Science,* 1974, *185,* 932–934.

Korner, A. F. Methodological considerations in studying sex differences in the behavioral functioning of newborns. In R. C. Friedman, R. M. Richart, & R. L. Vande Wiele (Eds.), *Sex differences in behavior.* New York: John Wiley & Sons, 1974, pp. 197–208.

Landauer, T. K., & Whiting, J. W. M. Infantile stimulation and adult stature of human males. *American Anthropologist,* 1964, *66,* 1007–1028.

Lee, R. B. Male-female residence arrangements and political power in human hunter-gatherers. *Archives of Sexual Behavior,* 1974, *3,* 167–173.

Leighton, A. H. A comparative study of psychiatric disorder in Nigeria and rural North America. In S. C. Plog & R. B. Edgerton (Eds.), *Changing perspectives in mental illness.* New York: Holt, Rinehart & Winston, 1969, pp. 179–198.

Leighton, D., Harding, J. S., Macklin, D. B., & Leighton, A. H. *The character of danger: Psychiatric symptoms in selected communities.* New York: Basic Books, 1963.

Lewis, M., & Weinraub, M. Sex of parent X sex of child: Socioemotional development. In R. C. Friedman, R. M. Richart, & R. L. Vande Wiele (Eds.), *Sex differences in behavior.* New York: John Wiley & Sons, 1974, pp. 165–189.

Lomax, A. *Folk song style and culture.* Washington, D.C.: American Association for the Advancement of Science, 1968.

Lomranz, J., Shapira, A., Choresh, N., & Gilat, Y. Children's personal space as a function of age and sex. *Developmental Psychology,* 1975, *11,* 541–545.

Lynn, D. B. *Parental and sex-role identification: A theoretical formulation.* Berkeley: McCutchan, 1969.

Lynn, D. B., & Sawrey, W. L. The effects of father-absence on Norwegian boys and girls. *Journal of Abnormal and Social Psychology,* 1959, *59,* 258–262.

Maccoby, E. E. (Ed.). *The development of sex differences.* Stanford, Calif.: Stanford University Press, 1966.

Maccoby, E. E., & Jacklin, C. N. *The psychology of sex differences.* Stanford, Calif.: Stanford University Press, 1974.

Mahler, I. A comparative study of locus of control. *Psychologia,* 1974, *17,* 135–139.

Masica, D. N., Money, J., Ehrhardt, A. A., & Lewis, V. G. I.Q., fetal sex hormones and cognitive patterns: Studies in the testicular feminizing syndrome of androgen insensitivity. *Johns Hopkins Medical Journal,* 1969, *124,* 34–43.

Mazur, A. Effects of testosterone on status in primate groups. *Folia Primatologica,* 1976, *26,* 214–226.

Minturn, L., & Lambert, W. W. *Mothers of six cultures: Antecedents of child rearing.* New York: John Wiley & Sons, 1964.

Mitchell, G., & Brandt, E. M. Behavioural differences related to experience of mother and sex of infant in the rhesus monkey. *Developmental Psychology,* 1970, *3,* 149.

Moss, H. A. Early sex differences and mother-infant interaction. In R. C. Friedman, R. M. Richart, & R. L. Vande Wiele (Eds.), *Sex differences in behavior.* New York: John Wiley & Sons, 1974, pp. 149–163.

Moyer, K. E. Sex differences in aggression. In R. C. Friedman, R. M. Richart, & R. L. Vande Wiele (Eds.), *Sex differences in behavior.* New York: John Wiley & Sons, 1974.

Munroe, R. L., & Munroe, R. H. Effect of environmental experience on spatial ability in an East African society. *Journal of Social Psychology,* 1971, *83,* 15–22.

Murdock, G. P. Comparative data on the division of labor by sex. *Social Forces,* 1937, *15,* 551–553.

Murdock, G. P. *Social structure.* New York: Macmillan, 1949.

Murdock, G. P. Ethnographic atlas: A summary. *Ethnology,* 1967, *6,* 109–236.

Murdock, G. P., & Provost, C. Factors in the sex division of labor. *Ethnology,* 1973, *12,* 203–225.

Murphy, J. *An epidemiological study of psychopathology in an Eskimo village.* Unpublished doctoral dissertation, Cornell University, 1960.

Nerlove, S. B., Munroe, R. H., & Munroe, R. L. Effect of environmental experience on spatial ability in an East African society. *Journal of Social Psychology,* 1971, *84,* 3–10.

Nerlove, S. B., Roberts, J. M., Klein, R. E., Yarbrough, C., & Habicht, J.-P. Natural indicators of cognitive development: An observational study of rural Guatemalan children. *Ethos,* 1974, *2,* 265–295.

Nicolson, A. B., & Hanley, C. Indices of physiological maturity: Derivation and interrelationships. *Child Development,* 1953, *24,* 3–38.

Omark, D. R., Omark, M., & Edelman, M. Formation of dominance hierarchies in young children. In T. R. Williams (Ed.), *Psychological anthropology.* The Hague: Mouton, 1975, pp. 289–315.

Opler, M. K. *Culture and social psychiatry.* New York: Atherton, 1967.

Phoenix, C. H. Prenatal testosterone in the nonhuman primate and its consequences for behavior. In R. C. Friedman, R. M. Richart, & R. L. Wiele (Eds.), *Sex differences in behavior.* New York: John Wiley & Sons, 1974, pp. 19–32.

Piatti, F. E. *The potters in noncommercial societies.* Unpublished master's thesis, Hunter College of the City University of New York, 1971.

Reba, R. C., Cheek, D. B., & Leitnaker, F. C. Body potassium and lean body mass. In D. B. Cheek (Ed.), *Human growth.* Philadelphia: Lea & Febiger, 1968, pp. 165–181.

Robbins, M. C., & Kilbride, P. L. Sex differences in dreams in Uganda. *International Journal of Cross-Cultural Psychology,* 1971, *2,* 406–408.

Roberts, J. M., & Sutton-Smith, B. Child training and game involvement. *Ethnology,* 1962, *1,* 166–185.

Rohner, R. P. Sex differences in aggression: Phylogenetic and enculturation perspectives. *Ethos,* 1976, *4,* 57–72.

Rosenblatt, P., & Cunningham, M. R. Sex differences in cross-cultural perspective. In B. B. Lloyd & J. Archer (Eds.), *Explorations in sex differences.* London: Academic Press, 1976, pp. 71–94.

Sanday, P. R. Toward a theory of the status of women. *American Anthropologist,* 1973, *75,* 1682–1700.

Sanday, P. R. Female status in the public domain. In M. Z. Rosaldo & L. Lamphere (Eds.), *Woman, culture, and society.* Stanford, Calif.: Stanford University Press, 1974, pp. 189–206.

Sarason, S. B., Hill, D. T., & Zimbardo, P. G. A longitudinal study of the relation of test anxiety to performance on intelligence and achievement tests. *Monographs of the Society for Research in Child Development,* 1964, *29* (No. 98).

Schlegel, A. *Male dominance and female autonomy.* New Haven: HRAF Press, 1972.

Sears, P. S. Doll play aggression in normal young children: Influence of sex, age, sibling status, father's absence. *Psychological Monographs,* 1951, *65* (No. 6).

Shouval, R., Venaki, S. K., Bronfenbrenner, U., Devereux, E. C., & Kiely, E. Anomalous reactions to social pressure of Israeli and Soviet children raised in family versus collective settings. *Journal of Personality and Social Psychology,* 1975, *32,* 477–489.

Siegman, A. W. Father absence during early childhood and antisocial behavior. *Journal of Abnormal Psychology,* 1966, *71,* 71–74.

Sinha, R. Internal versus external control of reinforcement as related to sex and achievement values among high school students in India. *Journal of the Indian Academy of Applied Psychology,* 1972, *9,* 1–8.

Solomons, G., & Solomons, H. C. Motor development in Yucatecan infants. *Developmental Medicine and Child Neurology,* 1975, *17,* 41–46.

Spelke, E., Zelazo, P., Kagan, J., & Kotelchuck, M. *Developmental Psychology,* 1973, *9,* 83.

Spindler, L. S. *Menomini women and culture change.* Washington, D.C.: American Anthropological Association, 1962 (Memoir 91).

Spiro, M. E. *Children of the kibbutz.* New York: Schocken Books, 1965.

Stephens, W. N. *The family in cross-cultural perspective.* New York: Holt, Rinehart & Winston, 1963.

Stini, W. A. Evolutionary implications of changing nutritional patterns in human populations. *American Anthropologist,* 1971, *73,* 1019–1030.

Stolz, L., Dowley, E. M., Chance, E., Stevenson, N. G., Faust, M. S., et al. *Father relations of war-born children.* Stanford, Calif.: Stanford University Press, 1954.

Super, C. M. A cross-cultural study of motor development. Paper presented at the annual meeting of the Society for Cross-Cultural Research, New York City, 1976.

Tanner, J. M. Physical growth. In P. H. Mussen (Ed.), *Carmichael's manual of child psychology* (3rd ed.). New York: John Wiley & Sons, 1970.

Textor, R. B. *A cross-cultural summary.* New Haven: HRAF Press, 1967.

Tiller, P. O. Personality development of children in sailor families. *Nordisk Psykologi's Monograph Series,* 1958, No. 9.

Tobias, P. V. The peoples of Africa south of the Sahara. In P. T. Baker & J. S. Weiner (Eds.), *The biology of human adaptability.* Oxford: Clarendon, 1966, pp. 111–200.

Urbina, S., & Grey, A. Cultural and sex differences in the sex distribution of dream characters. *Journal of Cross-Cultural Psychology,* 1975, *6,* 358–364.

Vande Wiele, R. L. Comment. In R. C. Friedman, R. M. Richart, & R. L. Vande Wiele (Eds.), *Sex differences in behavior.* New York: John Wiley & Sons, 1974, p. 78.

Washburn, S. L. Sex differences in the pubic bone of Bantu and Bushman. *American Journal of Physical Anthropology,* 1949, *7,* 425–432.

Weiner, J. S. Major problems in human population biology. In P. T. Baker & J. S. Weiner (Eds.), *The biology of human adaptability.* Oxford: Clarendon, 1966, pp. 2–24.

Weisner, T. S., & Gallimore, R. My brother's keeper: Child and sibling caretaking. *Current Anthropology,* 1977, *18,* 169–190.

White, D. R., Burton, M. L., & Brudner, L. A. Entailment theory and method: A cross-cultural analysis of the sexual division of labor. *Behavior Science Research,* 1977, *12,* 1–24.

Whiting, B. B. Sex identity conflict and physical violence: A comparative study. *American Anthropologist,* 1965, *66* (No. 6, part 2), 123–140.

Whiting, B. B., & Edwards, C. P. A cross-cultural analysis of sex differences in the behavior of children aged three through 11. *Journal of Social Psychology,* 1973, *91,* 171–188.

Whiting, B. B., & Whiting, J. W. M. Task assignment and personality: A consideration of the effect of herding on boys. In W. W. Lambert & R. Weisbrod (Eds.) *Comparative perspectives on social psychology.* Boston: Little, Brown, 1971, pp. 33–45.

Whiting, B. B., & Whiting, J. W. M. *Children of six cultures: A psycho-cultural analysis.* Cambridge, Mass.: Harvard University Press, 1975.

Whiting, J. W. M., & Child, I. L. *Child training and personality.* New Haven: Yale University Press, 1953.

Wilson, E. O. *Sociobiology: The new synthesis.* Cambridge, Mass.: Harvard University Press, 1975.

Witkin, H. A. Social influences in the development of cognitive style. In D. A. Goslin (Ed.), *Handbook of socialization theory and research.* New York: Rand McNally, 1969.

Witkin, H. A., & Berry, J. W. Psychological differentiation in cross-cultural perspective. *Journal of Cross-Cultural Psychology,* 1975, *6,* 4–87.

Wynne-Edwards, V. C. *Animal dispersion in relation to social behavior.* New York: Harper, 1962.

17

Cross-cultural Perspectives on the Female Life Cycle

Judith K. Brown

The female life cycle, demarcated by a series of physiologic events and divisible into discrete periods, readily lends itself to cultural elaboration. Such elaborations, whether in the form of a celebration or the imposition of a taboo, appear exotic to us, since no analogous practices are observed in our own society. For us, no celebration marks the attainment of puberty; no particular restrictions are imposed on menstruating women; and marriage need not be legitimized by the elaborate exchange of property. A body of research has attempted to explain the cross-cultural variation in such customs. Curiously, this work has received little impetus from recent interest in the anthropology of women, possibly because the anthropological studies of women have been at pains to prove that biology is not destiny. Yet the variety of customs which pertain to the female life cycle offers strong support for this very position by demonstrating that culture shapes the physiologic aspects of womanhood.

This review will be devoted to cross-cultural studies of customs which pertain to the female life cycle and to cross-cultural studies of customs relevant to time-limited events in the lives of women. An attempt will be made to interpret these observances from the female point of view. Material will be presented in approximately chronologic order within the life cycle, beginning with research dealing with girlhood and ending with research dealing with old age. Each study will be summarized and its findings will be reported. Significant, influential, and innovative research will be accorded more detailed treatment than lesser studies. Critical comments concerning hypotheses and methodology will follow each summary, and suggestions for further research will conclude most sections.[1]

There are several serious limitations which apply to the body of this research. First, the absence of a comprehensive developmental theory regarding the female life cycle has been reflected in the fragmentary nature of the cross-cultural studies. Each typically deals with only one specific aspect of the lives of women, such as initiation at puberty, menstrual observances, or the postpartum sex taboo. None views the female life cycle as a whole to discover the interrelationships among these practices.

Second, cross-cultural studies are limited to those research questions for which there are answers in a large number of available ethnographies. An innovative hypothesis often cannot be tested because an insufficient number of ethnographers have reported the relevant data. For example, little information is available concerning the lives of women in the mature years, and cross-cultural research reflects the uneven coverage of the female life cycle in most ethnographies. Furthermore, ethnographers rarely elicit the reactions of women to customs which apply only to them. Thus Richards (1956) never actually interviewed the girls whose initiation she reported in such elaborate detail.

Third, the problem of male bias is compounded in cross-cultural research (see Divale, 1976; Whyte, 1977); not only is the ethnographic data typically collected by men, but also the cross-cultural analysis is undertaken by men. Evidence of male bias appears in the choice of subject matter. For example, customs pertaining to pregnancy, birth, and lactation have not been studied nearly as fully as warfare. But male bias is perhaps most obvious in the cross-cultural studies of menstrual customs, which have been analyzed only in terms of the male response to the menses.

Finally, most cross-cultural research is restricted to an analysis of ethnographies published in English, a significant limitation (see Paige & Paige, 1973). For example, only German sources report the practice of female initiation rites that involve a genital operation for certain South American tribes (see Brown, 1962; 1971). English sources provide a limited and distorted view of the geographic distribution of this custom.

In sum, the cross-cultural research to be reviewed has been limited by the nature and the availability of ethnographic data and has so far failed to examine the interrelationships among the various customs which apply to the female life cycle.

GIRLHOOD AND MENARCHE

Whereas child rearing and child behavior have received considerable cross-cultural study (see Chapters 16, 19, and 20 in this volume), ceremonials for girls have not. Young (1965) rated "female childhood ceremonies" and "girlhood ceremonies" for the sample of societies used in his studies of initiation rites, but the ratings are not applied to the cross-cultural test of any hypothesis.[2] Only one study (Whiting, 1965) is concerned with menarche, suggesting that experiences of stress in early infancy result in decreased menarcheal age (see Chapter 10 in this volume).[3] Because of the near absence of cross-cultural research which focuses on the early years of the female life cycle, this review begins with a consideration of studies of initiation rites.

INITIATION RITES

The initiation of girls has been reported for societies on every continent except Europe.[4] These ceremonies vary in character, in timing, in complexity, and presumably also in purpose. Although the practice is widespread, it is not universal. Many early cross-cultural studies describe the varying character of the ceremonies and their geographic distribution (for example, Van Waters, 1913–1914; DuBois, 1932; Driver, 1941; Ford & Beach, 1951). Psychoanalytically oriented studies have concentrated on those relatively rare ceremonies that involve genital mutilation. Thus Bettelheim (1954), on the basis of clinical and very fragmentary cross-cultural evidence, suggests that genital mutilations are motivated by a universal, unconscious desire for the genitals of the opposite sex. If this motivation is indeed universal, why are these particular ceremonies for girls found in so few societies? Like many studies of female initiation rites, Bettelheim's work fails to account for the fact that these ceremonies are absent in many societies, including our own.

Perhaps the most widely cited and influential work on initiation has been that of Van Gennep (1909), which provides an analytical framework for the study of observances marking a variety of life cycle events. As individuals move from stage to stage, their status as well as their relationships to others are redefined. These transitions are marked by *rites of passage,* of which the initiation into adulthood is but one.

Turner (e.g., 1964; 1967; 1973) has drawn on the work of Van Gennep in his interpretation of initiation but has concentrated on the symbolism inherent in various aspects of the ritual. As the following excerpt demonstrates, Turner's intensive analyses defy brief summation:

> The mudyi tree, or milk-tree . . ., which is the focal symbol of the girls' puberty ritual of the Ndembu people of northwestern Zambia, at its normative pole represents womanhood, motherhood, the mother–child bond, a novice undergoing initiation into mature womanhood, a specific matrilineage, the principle of matriliny, the process of learning "women's wisdom," the unity and perdurance of Ndembu society, and all of the values and virtues inherent in the various relationships—domestic, legal, and political—controlled by matrilineal descent. Each of these aspects of its normative meaning becomes paramount in a specific episode of the puberty ritual; together, they form a condensed statement of the structural and communal importance of femaleness in Ndembu culture. At its sensory pole, the same symbol stands for breast milk . . ., mother's breasts, and the bodily slenderness and mental pliancy of the novice. (Turner, 1973, p. 1100)

Turner's provocative interpretations merit wider application (see, for example, Beidelman, 1964). Unfortunately, most descriptions of initiation rituals are not sufficiently detailed to make this possible.

Another major influence on the cross-cultural study of female initiation rites has been the research of Whiting and his co-workers (Whiting, Kluckhohn, & Anthony, 1958; Burton & Whiting, 1961; Whiting, 1964). These cross-cultural studies suggest that male initiation rites are a response to certain psychological conditions in the individual, which are in turn attributable to the child-rearing practices of some societies. Other societies in which such practices do not obtain do not celebrate initiation into adulthood. Whereas one cross-cultural study of initiation ceremonies for girls applies this approach to the data on female rites (Brown, 1962; 1963), two others challenge the approach and offer alternative interpretations (Young, 1965; Cohen, 1964a, b).

Harking back to the dictates of Durkheim, that social phenomena should not be explained by psychological factors, Young questions Whiting's "psychogenic" explanation of initiation rites. Young's alternative "sociogenic" hypothesis suggests that status dramatization at adolescence is related to the presence of solidarity groups, which are typical for societies at a midrange level of complexity. Although such solidarity groups abound for men, Young has difficulty in translating his hypothesis to accommodate the data on initiation rites for girls because only four societies in his sample had solidarity groups for women. Many more practiced female initiation rites. Young was forced to redefine solidarity groups as they apply to women. Female domestic work groups did not solve the problem. A variety of indicators was required: households which are bounded by walls and barriers, the presence of a household focus such as a shrine or a household crest, plus "multifemale household organization" (an index which combines polygynous with extended households). The variable which subsumed female initiation rites was trichotomized as follows: undramatic sex role recognition, individualized dramatization, and (most elaborate) group dramatization. Young's table which presents the relationship between the three levels of sex role dramatization to the indices of female solidarity is not tested for statistical significance. The frequencies appear to have a nearly random distribution. Similarly, another table which presents the relationship between the levels of sex role dramatization and "community–nation articulation level" is not tested for statistical significance and appears equally unpromising. Young's tables do not enumerate the societies which fall in each of the cells. Their placement must be deduced from the ratings reported for each society in the appendix. Although Young's sample of 54 societies is drawn from all the major culture areas (with Eastern Eurasia underrepresented), the possible effects of diffusion are difficult to detect because the tables do not identify societies. Young's polemic stance and the absence of tests for statistical significance serve only to accentuate the lack of support for his hypothesis concerning initiation rites for girls. This hypothesis appears to be an afterthought; initiation rites for males are Young's chief concern.

Cohen's (1964a, b) studies of initiation rites suggest a complex interrelationship among aspects of social structure, child-rearing practices and legal systems. According to Cohen, although socialization takes place primarily within the nuclear family, some societies stress the emotional anchorage of the individual in a descent group, whereas other societies stress emotional anchorage only within the nuclear family. In the former instances, socialization is carried out by the nuclear family as well as by members of the descent group; in the latter instances, socialization is carried out by the nuclear family as well as by other adults. The legal systems of the former are characterized by several (individual) and joint (group) liability. The legal systems of the latter stress several liability.

Cohen suggests that the period of late childhood is one of great individual vulnerability. The preadolescent experiences great hormonal activity, yet there are no external indicators of this internal stress. At puberty, on the other hand, the external signs of change are dramatic, but the individual is less vulnerable. Societies which stress emotional anchorage of the individual outside the nuclear family will mark the earlier period with brother–sister avoidance and/or with extrusion (i.e., children will no longer be allowed to sleep with their own families but will be sent to sleep with relatives or in a dormitory for young people). Such measures to wean children away from their nuclear families and to compel them to make emotional ties with their descent groups are considered traumatic by Cohen, since they befall the individual at a time of great vulnerability. These practices are followed by initiation rites once puberty is reached. Although initiation rites may appear dramatic to the Western observer, Cohen suggests that they do not have the tremendous emotional impact of the earlier measures. Societies in which the emotional anchorage of the individual continues to be within the nuclear family will not practice brother–sister avoidance, extrusion, or initiation rites.

Cohen tested these hypotheses on a sample of over 60 societies, representing all the major culture areas. The following results were statistically significant: the relationship between agents of socialization with extrusion and/or brother–sister avoidance ($p<0.001$); the relationship of agents of socialization with extrusion ($p<0.001$);

the relationship of the structure of the descent group with agents of socialization ($p<0.02$); the relationship of the structure of the descent group with extrusion and/or brother–sister avoidance ($p<0.02$); the relationship of agents of socialization with initiation rites ($p<0.001$); the relationship of the structure of the descent group and initiation rites ($p<0.01$); the relationship of experiences in growing up and concepts of legal liability ($p<0.001$).

The study raises a number of questions. First, since observances for girls and boys differ markedly, how does Cohen justify pooling these customs? Second, the practice of initiation rites seems redundant, since extrusion and/or brother–sister avoidance supposedly achieve the same results earlier in life, and more traumatically; what necessitates such duplication of effort? Third, in reporting instances of joint and several liability, Cohen refers almost entirely to evidence concerning crimes committed by men; how do these aspects of legal systems apply to women? Fourth, in the numerous societies practicing patrilocality, why should a girl's emotional anchorage be established with such effort in a descent group she typically leaves at marriage? Finally, Cohen's sampling procedures detract from the persuasiveness of his findings: The Circum-Caribbean and the Island Pacific area are overrepresented, whereas Eastern Eurasia is underrepresented. Only three societies are drawn from the Circum-Mediterranean area, and two of these are from Eastern Europe. All but one of the sub-Sahara African societies typically appear on one side of his dichotomized distribution, whereas the South American societies appear on the other. This suggests that some of the findings might be attributable to diffusion. Thus although Cohen's hypotheses are provocative and receive statistically significant support, they can be accepted only with caution.

The third study to be considered here is my own research (Brown, 1962; 1963),[5] which attempts to explain not only why some societies initiate girls whereas others do not but also suggests that rites which vary in character serve different purposes. Those few societies which practice ceremonies in which the initiate is subjected to extreme pain (typically in the form of a genital operation) are those which observe similar rites for males ($p<0.001$) and are those whose child-rearing arrangements generate what Whiting has termed "sex identity conflict" (Burton & Whiting, 1961). The painful rites appear to be an attempt to resolve this conflict ($p<0.02$). The more typical and more numerous rites are observed in those societies in which women make a major contribution to subsistence. The purpose of the ritual appears to be to assure the initiate and the community of her competence ($p=0.05$). Such ceremonies are also celebrated in those societies in which the girl does not leave the household of her mother at marriage ($p<0.001$). The rite serves to announce her adult status to those around her, since she will remain in the same household for life. In patrilocal or neolocal societies such ceremonies are not necessary, since the girl becomes part of a different household at marriage, a household she enters as an adult. The hypotheses were tested on a sample of about 70 societies drawn from all the major culture areas (with South America somewhat overrepresented).

The hypothesis concerning the relationship between initiation ceremonies for girls' and women's contribution to subsistence received the least strong support, yet it is this aspect of female initiation rites which is emphasized in a subsequent paper (Brown, 1978). Stressed in a number of ethnographic reports of girls' initiations (e.g., Frisbie, 1967; Kloos, 1969; 1971; Richards, 1956), the relationship is difficult to test cross-culturally owing to the nature of the available ratings on the role of women in subsistence activities (see Brown, 1969a; 1970a). Yet the relationship is an important one. In all probability, the observance of initiation ceremonies which stress tests for and magical assurances of female competence are a means of identifying societies in which women make a major contribution to the economy. Since assessment of the latter variable is complicated, whereas the practice of initiation rites is readily ascertained, such ceremonies may provide a cross-cultural index of women's economic role.

In a recent study by Paige and Paige (in press),[6] "menarche ceremonies" are given yet another interpretation. The authors provide an elaborate scenario in which the father of the girl is the central actor. As his daughter reaches menarche, his major object is to arrange a marriage which is as advantageous as possible. When the father has the backing of a strong kin group who can support him with military force if necessary, his right to bargain and the terms he sets forth are protected. However, when the kin group of the father is dispersed and weak, such protection is not available. The onset of menarche poses the threat that his daughter might be seduced or might elope, obviating the formation of a profitable marriage alliance. In such societies the father must rely on alternatives to political power: menarche ceremonies. The celebration is a means to achieve at least factional community support of his bargaining position and to provide some protection of his daughter's value until a suitable match can be arranged.

Using a sample of 114 societies, representing all the major culture areas, the authors tested the following hypotheses: First, menarche ceremonies will be celebrated in societies characterized by weak and dispersed kinship groups. Such ceremonies will not be observed in societies characterized by "fraternal interest groups." The latter term refers to male kin who live in the same community and who have the power to exert force as a group. To test this hypothesis, the authors used forms of postmarital residence to assess the presence or absence of fraternal interest groups. Societies characterized by patrilocal or avunculocal residence were considered to have fraternal interest groups and were found typically not to celebrate menarche ceremonies. On the other hand, such observances were practiced in societies characterized by matrilocal, bilocal, and neolocal residence—societies considered not to have fraternal interest groups ($p<0.001$).

The second hypothesis concerns the resources available to maintain the allegiance of the fraternal interest group. When fraternal interest groups are absent, "economic productivity" is unrelated to the celebration of menarche ceremonies. When fraternal interest groups are present but "economic productivity" is low, there are insufficient resources to support the fraternal interest group, and menarche ceremonies must be celebrated. "Low productivity" refers to the following subsistence activities: hunting, gathering, fishing, reindeer herding, hunting and raiding with horses, and shifting cultivation. "High productivity" refers to the subsistence activities of the following: African horticulturalists, tuber crop agriculturalists, pastoral nomads, and peasants. When high productivity characterizes the society with fraternal interest groups, menarche ceremonies are not observed ($p<0.001$). The authors suggest that there is interaction between the two antecedent variables.

A third hypothesis concerns the relationship of menarche ceremonies to the transfer of property at marriage. When marriage bargains include the payment of compensation to the wife's kin group, menarche ceremonies are not likely to occur. Such compensation can take the form of cattle, gifts, sister exchange and various forms of bride-price. When no such compensation takes place at marriage, or when only bride service is performed, menarche ceremonies typically are celebrated ($p<0.025$).

The interpretation provided by Paige and Paige for the celebration of menarche is innovative and well supported; nevertheless, a few criticisms are in order. First, using the ratings for residence forms to assess the presence of fraternal interest groups introduces some inaccuracy. Rules of exogamy and endogamy should also be considered (column 11 of the ratings devised by Murdock & Wilson, 1972, p. 262). Matrilocal, bilocal, and neolocal forms of residence, when combined with village endogamy, would not be characterized by dispersed groups of male kin. Second, high and low economic productivity dichotomizes subsistence activities in an unaccustomed manner, based in part on geography, in part on societal complexity. The classification as a measure of "productivity" seems arbitrary and requires justification. Finally, why does the father typically have such a minor role in a ceremony celebrated primarily to enhance his bargaining position? Some ethnographic evidence is needed to support what appears to be a highly etic explanation.

MENSTRUAL CUSTOMS

Until menopause, the passage of time in the life of an adult woman is marked by recurrent menstrual cycles, interrupted only by pregnancy and lactation. Women in many societies must observe specific customs at each menstruation. Although widespread, such practices are not universal. In our own society menstration is politely ignored and receives cultural elaboration only in a body of beliefs. Thus, for example, Ford (1945) reports "medical findings" which imply not only that the menstrual discharge is harmful to men but that even cut flowers will wither when handled by a menstruating woman. It is to the dangerous nature of the menstrual discharge that Ford ascribes the menstrual customs in his sample of over 60 societies—e.g., temporary seclusion in a special hut, prohibitions on sex and on food preparation (also see Coult, 1963; Wilson, 1964). These cumbersome customs are imposed in societies which have not devised an effective means for collecting menstrual blood. Only a few cases provided available data for testing this hypothesis, and the results were in the expected direction. Ford does not enumerate the societies in which menstrual customs are absent, but he suggests that where such observances are elaborate they contribute to the low prestige of women.

Ford's basic assumptions about the sinister nature of the menstrual discharge and the menstruant have gone largely unquestioned. However, according to Stephens (1961; 1962), the alleged danger inherent in the menstrual discharge is a mere rationalization for menstrual taboos. Like Roheim, Stephens asserts that the source of menstrual taboos is male castration anxiety. Cross-cultural variations in the elaborateness of menstrual taboos (which according to Stephens conform to a five-point Guttman scale) are ascribed to variations in the severity of castration anxiety. Since the latter is an intervening variable and can not be assessed directly, Stephens tested his hypothesis by regarding those child-rearing practices which are believed to exacerbate castration anxiety as his antecedent variables.

He found the following to be positively related to the elaborateness of menstrual taboos: intensity of sex anxiety ($p=0.01$); duration of the postpartum sex taboo ($p=0.02$); severity of punishment for masturbation ($p=0.01$); overall severity of sex training ($p=0.05$); severity of the socialization of aggression ($p=0.18$); importance of physical punishment as a technique of discipline ($p=0.07$); severity of punishment for disobedience ($p=0.18$); strictness of the father's obedience demands ($p=0.20$); and the father as the main disciplinarian ($p=0.20$). Using these variables, Stephens devised a "composite predictor score" to assess the intensity of castration anxiety.

Its relationship to the intensity of menstrual taboos was extraordinarily strong ($p=0.000001$), but the legitimacy of combining the antecedent variables is open to question. In addition, Stephens measured the relationship of the severity of menstrual taboos to the frequency of castration—suggestive incidents in folklore ($p=0.001$). Seventy societies were rated on the severity of their menstrual taboos. North America and the Island Pacific area are overrepresented, whereas Eastern Eurasia, the Circum-Mediterranean, and South America are underrepresented. However, on each of the many tests, smaller subsamples were used—subsamples with somewhat biased distributions. On the basis of sampling alone, Stephens' conclusions cannot be accepted without caution.

Stephens tested a variety of other explanations for menstrual taboos and found that none received cross-cultural confirmation. Thus, for example, he reexamined Ford's hypothesis that menstrual restrictions will be most severe in societies which have devised no adequate means for catching the menstrual discharge. On the basis of data from over 20 societies, the hypothesis was not supported. Stephens investigated the possibility that menstrual taboos are minimized in societies in which women make a major contribution to subsistence. Using Heath's (1958) ratings on the contribution of women to subsistence, Stephens found no relationship. However, since Heath's ratings are of questionable value (see Brown, 1963), this hypothesis is not necessarily disproved and bears reexamination. In addition, Stephens tested the hypothesis that menstrual taboos are minimized in societies in which marriage is monogamous and in which households are nuclear. He found "weak and ambiguous" support, but no exact figures are given. These relationships bear reexamination. Finally, he tested the hypothesis that severe menstrual taboos reflect the low position of women in society. Since no measure was available for assessing the status of women, Stephens used ratings of descent and postmarital residence. Accordingly, matrilineal and matrilocal societies should be characterized by less severe menstrual taboos than patrilineal and patrilocal societies. He found no relationship, but it is questionable that descent and residence provide a sensitive index to the relative status of women. The hypothesis remains essentially unsupported, like the other alternative hypotheses which Stephens attempted to test.

Young and Bacdayan (1965), in the manner of Young's study of initiation rites, suggest a "sociogenic" explanation for menstrual taboos. Using a revised form of Stephens' Guttman scale, they rated a subsample of Stephens' original sample on the severity of menstrual taboos. Their alternative hypothesis suggests that severe menstrual taboos are an index of discrimination against women in those societies in which men are dominant and tightly organized. Both male solidarity and severe menstrual taboos characterize societies high in "social rigidity." In such societies men and women are sharply separated and there is a lack of communication between them. Since the definition of social rigidity is not independent of the observance of severe menstrual taboos, the authors admit that the hypothesis is tautologic. Similarly, they admit that their Guttman scales for social rigidity and for male dominance are not independent. Both these scales are related to the scale for severity of menstrual taboos to a statistically significant degree ($p=0.01$). A test for Stephens' "psychogenic" hypothesis was recomputed for Young and Bacdayan's subsample and found to be of equal predictive value. The authors suggest that their hypothesis is nevertheless to be preferred because it is more parsimonious. Considering the methodologic infelicities of their study, this conclusion is not demonstrated. In a recent paper dealing with norms regarding premarital sex, Broude (1975) used a regression analysis to test the predictive value of a number of alternative hypotheses. Her results demonstrated that both psychological and structural variables are related to norms regarding premarital sex (the former to a greater degree than the latter). Broude's statistical analysis provides a support for her conclusions, which Young's and Bacdayan's combination of polemic and near replication can not match.

Both Montgomery (1974) and Bock (1967) have provided astute criticisms of Young's and Bacdayan's paper. Bock questions the validity of the Guttman scale for the severity of menstrual taboos, pointing out that it is physically impossible for a woman temporarily isolated to cook. He points out that the authors appear to be unaware of the possible effects of diffusion, demonstrating that the severity of menstrual taboos can be predicted with some accuracy simply by knowing the geographic location of a society. Bock enumerates possible biases in the ethnographic data used by Young and Bacdayan, and he suggests that Stephens' ratings should not have been reused without an examination of the ethnographic context of the facts upon which the ratings were based. Bock's comments, as well as those made more recently by Montgomery, suggest that Young's and Bacdayan's conclusions are unacceptable unless a better study can be designed to test them.

Montgomery's (1974) paper contains a full review of the previous literature on menstruation and suggests a hypothesis based on Bettelheim's (1954) concept of vagina envy. According to Montgomery, vagina envy will be reduced in those societies in which men are regarded as involved in the procreative function. However, in those societies in which vagina envy is exacerbated, men will feel the need to derogate the reproductive function of women and elaborate menstrual taboos will be imposed. A six-point scale modeled after that used by Young and Bacdayan was used to evaluate the elaborateness of menstrual taboos, and this scale was dichotomized to yield a high taboo score and a low taboo score. The low menstrual taboo score was then viewed in relationship to seven variables which assess male participation in procreation: male participation considered as integral to conception (no relationship, as this belief is nearly universal), involvement of men in the development of the fetus (no relationship), participation of men in prepartum taboos ($p<0.01$), participation of men in childbirth ($p<0.01$), participation of men in postpartum taboos ($p<0.01$), involvement of men in the ritual attainment of puberty by females ($p<0.001$), mythical reference to the importance of men in creation (no relationship). Montgomery's sample consisted of 44 societies drawn from every major culture area but the Circum-Mediterranean; the Americas and Eastern Eurasia were underrepresented. The author does not suggest that the relationships which she found explain the wide variation in menstrual customs; however, the findings suggest that an important aspect of the relationship between men and women in any society is the degree to which the process of procreation is viewed as mutual.

The glaring fault common to all the cross-cultural studies of menstrual customs is that these observances are viewed entirely from a male perspective. Montgomery notes that the attitudes of women toward menstruation have not been studied cross-culturally. A study by Skultans (1970), based on a small sample of Welsh women, gives some indication of the diversity of women's reaction to the menses. Some wanted to lose as much blood as possible, believing that this contributed to good health. Others feared losing blood, viewing it as debilitating. Varied as the responses may be, there is one universally recognized aspect of menstruation—the onset of each menstrual period indicates that pregnancy has not taken place. Menstruation may be eagerly welcomed or the cause of bitter disappointment. Beliefs and practices associated with menstruation must in some way reflect this meaning of menstruation in the lives of women. A cross-cultural study of menstrual customs from this point of view is needed.

A woman's interpretation is also needed for the actual observances associated with menstruation. Seclusion in a menstrual hut and prohibitions on food preparation, which previous studies have viewed as demeaning and restrictive, may actually constitute a welcome change from routine domestic responsibilities. Furthermore, such customs are possible only when household structure and subsistence activities are organized in such a way that each woman is dispensable for a brief period each month. In a sense, such observances are a luxury. Thus not only the customs themselves but their relationship to structural variables should be reexamined.

BETROTHAL

Only one cross-cultural study is concerned with betrothal. Rosenblatt, Fugita, and McDowell (1969) report that the custom is widespread, and they suggest the following hypothesis: rules governing the sexual behavior of the engaged couple become more restrictive in societies in which there is transfer of a considerable amount of property at marriage. Such restrictions are reduced during betrothal in societies in which little property is transferred at marriage. Since engagements tend to be of longer duration in societies in which marriage involves large transactions, the more stringent rules serve to protect the investment, which might be endangered by lovers' quarrels.

The hypothesis was tested on a sample of 27 societies, including only those which practice betrothal. Dowry, bride-price, and gift exchange at marriage represented the transfer of considerable property. Token gifts and the absence of gifts represented no such transfer. Bride service was not considered. Three categories were devised for changes in the restrictions on sexual behavior during betrothal: more restrictive than before betrothal, no change, and less restrictive than before betrothal. The hypothesis was confirmed by the findings. Societies which require a dowry, a bride-price, or gift exchange at marriage become more restrictive about sex during betrothal ($p < 0.01$); other societies institute no change or become less restrictive.

The sample used by the authors was small and vastly underrepresented the New World. A footnote reveals that restricting the sample to those societies that actually practice betrothal effectively eliminated a considerable number of New World and Island Pacific societies. Of those societies used to test the hypothesis, none of the five from the New World fell into the "more restrictive" category. These facts, which receive no comment from the authors, strongly suggest that diffusion may account for some of the findings. There is also ambiguity in the "no change" rating regarding restrictiveness, since it combines societies which are consistently restrictive with those which are consistently permissive. Finally, since this is the only cross-cultural study of betrothal, and since the custom is not universal, some comment should have been made regarding its prevalence and its distribution. A major question remains unanswered: Why do some societies practice betrothal, whereas others do not?

RITUAL DEFLORATION

To date, the custom of ritual defloration has remained unexplored cross-culturally. Neither Freud's provocative essay, "Contributions to the Psychology of Love. The

Taboo of Virginity" (1953), nor the recent analysis of ceremonial defloration among the Amhara by Reminick (1976), has inspired a cross-cultural test of the hypotheses proposed.

MARRIAGE

Betrothal, menstrual customs, and initiation rites for girls are not practiced universally, and cross-cultural studies of these customs must explain why these observances are found only in certain societies. Marriage, on the other hand, is conceded to be practiced universally, although anthropologists have not arrived at a consensus regarding its definition. Unlike cross-cultural studies of other customs, research on marriage is not required to explain its distribution. Nevertheless, the subject is so complex that cross-cultural studies of aspects of marriage continue to be fragmentary.

No cross-cultural study concerns itself with marriage as a rite of passage in the lives of women. This is extraordinary, since marriage ceremonials are generally well reported in the ethnographic literature and many of these rituals are rich in symbolism denoting status change. Other variables concerning marriage have been studied cross-culturally, but the analyses are not carried out from the point of view of women's lives. The following is a brief synopsis of cross-cultural research on marriage.

Stephens (1963) gives a descriptive overview of mate selection; Rosenblatt and Cozby (1972) have analyzed courtship; Minturn, Grosse, and Haider (1969) have examined arranged marriages; and Ayres (1972) has compared bride theft with raiding for women. Ford and Beach (1951) have examined forms of marriage (monogamy, polygyny, polyandry), and Osmond (1965) has suggested the interrelationship among them. Nag (1962) reviews the relationship of forms of marriage to fertility, and Ayres (1976) compares monogamy with polygyny in terms of reproductive success. Goody (1973b) examines the relationship of polygyny to the economic role of women in Africa and concludes that "the reasons behind polygyny are sexual and reproductive rather than economic and productive" (p. 189). The aloofness or intimacy between husbands and wives has been investigated cross-culturally by Whiting and Whiting (1975). Romantic love has been analyzed by Stephens (1963), Rosenblatt (1966; 1967), and Coppinger and Rosenblatt (1968). In a cluster analysis of a variety of sexual attitudes and behaviors, Broude (1976) has identified one cluster as "sexual exclusivity," in which she includes variables such as the husband's attitude concerning wife-sharing. Sweetser (1966) has examined in-law avoidances, and Murdock (1971) has analyzed a variety of customary behaviors between affines.

One recent study relates child-rearing practices to aspects of marriage. Barry (1976), using a sample of over 130 societies, found that those characterized by large sex differences in child-rearing practices during the middle years of childhood were also those in which virginity of the bride is demanded at marriage ($p < 0.01$). The practice of polygyny and the payment of a bride-price were also related to large differences in the ways boys and girls are reared ($p < 0.01$). According to Barry, these marriage customs imply prolonged parental control over girls. Such control is furthered by insistence upon "stereotyped femininity" in childhood and minimizes "the opportunity for expression of individual or rebellious attitudes" (Barry, 1976, p. 17).

Rosenblatt and Unangst (1974) suggest that societies in which there is a considerable transfer of property at marriage, in the form of a dowry, bride-price, or gift exchange, are likely to celebrate a marriage ceremonial, more particularly an elaborate marriage ceremonial. Marriage ceremonies will be minimal or absent in societies which practice bride service or token bride-price or in which no property is transferred at marriage. When tested on a sample of 43 societies, the hypothesis was supported ($p=0.05$). The authors note that all the New World societies are characterized by minimal property exchange at marriage. Thus diffusion may account for some of their results. Bride service seems to be misclassified. From the point of view of the groom, if the marriage fails, bride service is totally unrefundable and thus could be quite an expense indeed. Almost half of the societies in the sample are scored as "marriage ceremonials present," with no judgment on elaborateness. The relationship of this category to wealth transfer is ambiguous in terms of the hypothesis. The authors note that *both* the transfer of considerable property at marriage and the elaborateness of marriage ceremonials appear to be related to subsistence based on agriculture and herding. Are the two marriage variables simply another measure of societal complexity? Is it a coincidence that subsistence activities in which women make a minimal contribution are associated with elaborate marriage ceremonials? Rosenblatt and Unangst have made the only cross-cultural analysis of marriage ceremonials, but the study is merely suggestive at best.

Although other British social anthropologists have remained aloof from cross-cultural research, Goody has applied the method with considerable success in his studies of the dowry (1969; 1973a). Goody views the dowry as a form of premortem inheritance,[7] but it may also include gifts which pass from the groom directly to the bride and not to her kin group.[8] The dowry is one aspect of "divergent devolution" or the "woman's property complex," which refers to the transmission of property to children of *both* sexes. According to Goody (1969) this is in turn related to the following variables: Care is taken in arranging marriages, and the bride's virginity is insisted upon when women can control property ($p=0.001$). Various forms of endogamy are preferred in order that the property which women control does not pass from the group ($p=0.001$). Preference for father's brother's daughter marriage is a special example of such endogamous arrangements ($p=0.001$). Divergent devolution is also associated with monogamy ($p=0.001$), with polyandry, and with ambilocal or neolocal residence after marriage ($p=0.001$). Divergent devolution is typically associated with the intense use of resources, since this direct form of property transmission retains resources within the productive and reproductive unit. Thus societies practicing plough agriculture ($p=0.001$) or intensive agriculture ($p=0.001$), as well as large, stratified societies ($p=0.001$), tend to practice divergent devolution.

Goody's work is significant because it suggests that the dowry should not be viewed independently of inheritance rules. The concept of divergent devolution moves away from the fragmentation which characterizes so much cross-cultural research. Furthermore, Goody's findings suggest that the control of property by women is not without penalties. Where divergent devolution is practiced, women must accept greater control over their premarital sex lives and a reduced choice in marriage partners. Although the right to control property may seem to endow women with a certain amount of power, it appears to reduce some of their autonomy as well.

Goody's findings are provocative, yet they are open to question. First, it is highly unusual for so many cross-cultural tests to yield such uniformly significant results. Second, each table contains a slightly different sample, depending upon the availability of data, and each table contains a disturbingly large residual category of unascertainable cases. Furthermore, the particular societies which fall into the different quadrants of each table are not identified. It is therefore not possible to assess the influence of diffusion, nor would it be possible to replicate the tables.

A study by Michaelson and Goldschmidt (1971) which analyzes data from 46 peasant communities contradicts Goody's assertion that the control of property by women results in restrictions of a woman's premarital sex life and a lack of choice in her marriage partner. Michaelson and Goldschmidt found that "bilateral inheritance" is related to marriage by individual choice, not marriage by arrangement ($p<0.001$), and stress on premarital chastity is not particularly related to bilateral inheritance (no test of significance reported). There is, however, a curious convergence between the two studies. Michaelson and Goldschmidt suggest a relationship between bilateral inheritance and "machismo," whereas Goody suggests that preoccupation with family "honor" characterizes some societies practicing divergent devolution. The two male preoccupations are not synonymous, yet both studies seem to suggest that the right of women to control property appears in conjunction with male insecurity. It is a suggestion that merits further exploration.

In a later work, Goody (1973a) examines all types of transactions at marriage for a worldwide sample and concludes that the choice of dowry, bride-price, sister exchange, etc., is more strongly related to culture area than to descent (no test of significance is reported). The focus of this study is a detailed comparison between bride-price, found largely in Africa, and the dowry, found largely in Eurasia.[9] Goody concludes that "Dowry differentiates, just as bridewealth tends to homogenize" (1973a, p. 47). In other words, dowry and the control of property by women perpetuate stratification, whereas bride-price is typical of less complex, homogeneous societies.

The cross-cultural study of marriage has explored a great number of variables but has left us with many fascinating questions. Variation in the ages of women at marriage has not been explored, nor has the symbolism found in marriage rituals, the relationship among initiation, betrothal, and marriage, or that between various aspects of marriage and the ease and frequency of divorce.

DIVORCE

The cross-cultural study of divorce, a custom almost as universal as marriage, has typically been subsumed as part of other research. Thus Nag (1962) examines the relationship of divorce to fertility, with only tentative results. Stephens (1963) includes divorce in his descriptive study of the family. Minturn et al. (1969) rate the ease of divorce for men as part of a study of sexual attitudes and practices, and Goody and Buckley (1973) note the near absence of divorce among those African societies characterized by the "house–property complex."[10]

Using a sample of 40 societies, Murdock (1950) reports that more than half are characterized by a higher divorce rate than that of the United States. Unfortunately he does not specify the actual divorce rates he is comparing. He suggests that payment of a bride-price and the custom of arranged marriages are associated with a reduced incidence of divorce. Minturn et al. (1969) replicated the former finding, although the results were not significant ($p=0.10$); they failed to find support for the latter. Murdock asserts that in three-fourths of his sample divorce is initiated with equal ease by women or men, and that in one-tenth women "possess superior privileges as regards divorce" (1950, p. 196). These findings are extremely surprising and require replication.

Whereas Murdock's study is a largely descriptive attempt to identify some of the parameters which apply to the cross-cultural study of divorce, Ackerman (1963) sets out to test a hypothesis. He suggests that divorce will be low in those societies which embed marriage in "a network of conjugal affiliations" and high in those societies in which spouses "maintain disjunctive affiliations" (1963, p. 14). To test his hypothesis, Ackerman interpreted the practices of endogamy and cousin marriage as indications of conjunctive affiliations in societies practicing bilateral descent. Using a sample of 11 societies, he found the two variables associated with low divorce rates ($p=0.01$). For matrilineal and patrilineal societies and for societies practicing double descent, Ackerman interpreted the practice of the levirate as evidence for conjunctive affiliations. Using a sample of about 30 societies, he found the levirate to be associated with low divorce rates ($p=0.0002$). Ackerman's samples are small and poorly constituted. Furthermore, it is not clear why marriage arrangements are related to divorce rates in bilateral societies, whereas inheritance rules are related to divorce rates in lineal societies.

The cross-cultural study of divorce has left a number of major questions unanswered. Is it true, as Murdock asserts, that in most societies men and women can initiate divorce with equal ease? Is divorce more prevalent in matrilineal societies than in patrilineal societies, as has been suggested by Gluckman (1950), Gibbs (1964), and others? Are divorces more frequent in societies in which women make a considerable contribution to subsistence and less frequent in societies in which women depend upon a provider? Do the practices of trial marriage, the transfer of large amounts of property at marriage, or prolonged and costly marriage ceremonials reduce the rate of divorce? What is the relationship between divorce and rules of inheritance, a relationship alluded to by Ackerman (1963) and by Goody and Buckley (1973)?

CHILDLESSNESS

One factor which frequently leads to divorce, according to Murdock (1950) and Nag (1962), is childlessness. Only a few societies in Ford's (1945) sample recognize the possibility of male infertility. Typically a source of derision and contempt, childlessness is almost always blamed on the woman. In spite of Nag's caution that the data on childlessness from non-Western societies are meager and difficult to interpret, Rosenblatt and Hillabrant (1972) conducted a cross-cultural study of the relationship between divorce for childlessness and the penalties imposed on women for adultery. They found that where divorce for childlessness is not practiced penalties for a wife's adultery tend to be lax, whereas those societies that practice divorce for childlessness tend to punish a wife's adultery severely ($p<0.05$). The authors conclude that adultery may be a form of self-help in societies that have few means of coping with childlessness. This conclusion must be accepted with caution, since the sample on which the hypothesis was tested consisted of less than 20 societies. Furthermore, although the authors tested for the effects of diffusion, all the South American cases are clustered in one quadrant of the table.

In a subsequent study, Rosenblatt, Peterson, Portner, Cleveland, Mykkannen, Foster, et al. (1973) assert that childlessness is not accepted passively, and typically the first measures taken are of a "magico-religious-ethnomedical nature." The latter are viewed by the authors as less disruptive than divorce, adoption, or polygyny (adultery was not considered). Furthermore, as Ford originally pointed out, such measures also have the advantage of giving conception additional time to occur. The authors found that women are blamed for childlessness more frequently than men ($p < 0.001$) and suggest that this is "a result of the ubiquity of low status for women" (1973, p. 221). No attempt is made to document this assertion. It seems more likely, however, that women are held responsible for childlessness because this belief is consistent with a society's view concerning the role of the sexes in procreation and fetal growth. If the male's role in these processes is considered minimal, he can hardly be blamed for childlessness. Blame for childlessness should be reexamined in relationship to the variables identified by Montgomery (1974) in her study of menstrual customs. She noted that there is cross-cultural variation in the amount of mutuality between the sexes which is given recognition in beliefs regarding procreation.

PREGNANCY

Ford (1945) and Ford and Beach (1951) provide surveys of the customs associated with pregnancy. Young (1965) has analyzed pregnancy observances together with a variety of other customs, which he labels as "parenthood ceremonies" and which he believes conform to a Guttman scale. The scale combines practices involving the neonate, with those observed by the father and the mother both before and after birth. Such a combination seems questionable, but for Young's sociogenic interpretation all these customs indicate variations in the dramatization of parenthood. Young suggests that such dramatization will be stressed in societies characterized by a high-solidarity family, as manifested in the elaborateness of clan organization. Minimal recognition of parenthood, on the other hand, is associated with the absence of clan organization. The table he presents suggests that the findings are in the expected direction, but no test of statistical significance is reported.

More modest in scope but also more persuasive, Ayres's study (1954; 1967) provides a detailed examination of food and sex taboos in pregnancy. For Ayres these customs are related to the socialization experiences of the mother-to-be. Food taboos during pregnancy are extremely prevalent cross-culturally. Ayres found only 4 societies in her sample of 40 which imposed no food taboos, yet the observance of these taboos was only weakly related to aspects of oral socialization (Ayres, 1954). Ayres proposes the following model to explain food taboos: Pregnancy creates anxieties in the mother-to-be, anxieties which generate an increased need for nurturance and affection. This need is expressed in increased demands on the husband and other relatives in the form of food cravings.[11] The increased food consumption creates dangers for the mother and the unborn child (such as greater difficulty of delivery). Consequently, food taboos have the function of restricting the mother's intake of food, and this helps to assure the health and safety of the mother and baby. Ayres interprets food taboos as a response to the pregnant woman's dependency needs, needs which are established in childhood. Ayres found that societies with high indulgence for dependent childhood behavior also demand the observance of many food taboos during pregnancy ($p = 0.019$). Ayres hypothesized further that the severity of the sanctions concerning food taboos would be related to the extent of the unconscious anxiety which dependency needs arouse. The greater the unconscious anxiety concerning dependency, the more severe the sanctions on violations of food taboos. She tested this hypothesis and found that dependency socialization anxiety was indeed significantly related to the severity of sanctions regarding food taboos in pregnancy ($p=0.048$). (The samples used by Ayres to test her hypotheses contained about 30 societies and overrepresented the Island Pacific area and underrepresented South America.)

An alternative hypothesis suggests itself. Ayres reports that tabooed foods tend to be typical items of the diet, whereas the foods which are craved tend to be delicacies. It is possible that because certain foods are tabooed the pregnant woman craves unusual foods which provide the nutrients which she would otherwise obtain from foods now made inaccessible to her. To test this hypothesis, the nutritional properties of tabooed and craved foods would have to be analyzed.

Whereas food taboos are a response to realistic dangers, Ayres suggests that sex taboos in pregnancy are not. Indeed, in some societies frequent intercourse during pregnancy is considered necessary for the formation of the fetus. Only during the final weeks of pregnancy does intercourse pose any danger, yet most sex taboos during pregnancy are observed for a far longer period. According to Ayres, sex taboos during pregnancy are a response to sex anxiety generated in childhood. Ayres found a significant relationship between the extensiveness of sex taboos during pregnancy and the severity of the socialization of sexual behavior ($p<0.05$). (The sample used included about 30 societies and overrepresented the Island Pacific area.) Ayres suggests that a taboo on sex during pregnancy would be easier for men to observe in polygynous societies than in monogamous societies, a relationship which is confirmed. Since punishment for sexual behavior in childhood tends to be more severe in polygynous societies, Ayres examined the duration of the sex taboo in relationship to forms of marriage and to severity of sexual socialization. The results, although based on a small number of cases, suggest that polygyny does facilitate the observance of the taboo in societies where sex anxiety is present. Using yet another measure of sex anxiety—ratings of norms pertaining to premarital sexual behavior—Ayres found that societies which are restrictive concerning premarital sexual behavior tend to observe longer taboos on sex during pregnancy ($p<0.01$).

Ayres's study provides a convincing explanation for two types of pregnancy taboos. Although the samples used to test the hypotheses were small, a variety of measures provide consistent support for the basic relationship between pregnancy taboos and socialization practices. In conclusion, Ayres suggests that the food taboos which accompany other life cycle observances should be examined in terms of dependency needs, an interpretation which implies interrelationships among life cycle observances.

BIRTH PRACTICES

A variety of customs and beliefs concerning birth has been reviewed by Ford (1945) —e.g., the treatment of the newborn and the mother, the disposal of the afterbirth. One popular view, that giving birth is relatively painless in the non-Western world, is definitely not supported by the cross-cultural evidence presented by Ford and by Freedman and Ferguson (1950). Whiting and Whiting (1975) suggest that the presence of the father at the birth of his child provides one of several indications of husband–wife intimacy. Rosenblatt and Skooberg (1974) in a cross-cultural study of birth order found that firstborn children receive more elaborate birth ceremonies than those born later. Naroll, Naroll, and Howard (1961), studied the position of women in childbirth in 76 societies. Of the 104 reports of childbirth which they surveyed in collecting their data, only 6 were eyewitness accounts. The authors suggest that the upright position is advantageous, since it allows the force of gravity to aid the birth process. Although the authors were primarily interested in data quality control, their prediction was supported: the upright position in birth is more prevalent cross-culturally.

For Paige and Paige (1973), observances during pregnancy, at the time of birth, and in the postpartum period, whether they apply to the husband or the wife, are strategies concerning paternity rights. Observances which apply to the mother typically restrict her movements and activities and are practiced in societies characterized by fraternal interest groups (i.e., male kin who are able to act in concert and with force to support each other). Such groups act to enforce the bargain, often established by an exchange of wealth, which asserts paternal rights over the newborn. In the absence of an exchange of wealth and when no fraternal interest group is available to enforce a bargain, a husband's ritual involvement in the birth process represents an alternative effort to establish and/or defend paternity rights. The authors assert that in the arena of paternity negotiations "women are objects not actors" (1973, p. 668); thus the customs which pertain to pregnancy and childbirth are "part of a larger pattern of male control over women's activities" (p. 676).

The authors tested five hypotheses on a sample of 114 societies, which represented all the major culture areas. Two tests were performed on a subsample of more than 80 societies. First, the authors found that highly restrictive customs observed by the mother are associated with the presence of fraternal interest groups (considered present in societies with patrilocal and avunculocal residence), whereas such restrictiveness was not present in societies without fraternal interest groups (societies characterized by matrilocal, bilocal, and neolocal residence) ($p<0.001$). In societies characterized by fraternal interest groups, the father had little ritual involvement in the birth process, whereas his ritual participation was observed in societies without fraternal interest groups ($p<0.001$). Second, in societies in which wealth is exchanged at marriage (a bride-price, a substantial gift exchange, or sister exchange), maternal restrictions will be imposed. On the other hand, in those societies in which there is no transfer of property at marriage or in those in which the groom performs bride service, restrictions on the mother are not observed ($p<0.005$). (The dowry was not considered because it represents no exchange of wealth but rather wealth provided to the bride.) In societies with wealth exchange at marriage, ritual observances by the father are not practiced, whereas such customs pertain to societies with no exchange of property at marriage ($p<0.01$). The third hypothesis deals with compensation demands. When the bride-price must be returned or a gift must be presented in the case of abortion, infanticide, or barrenness, or when the latter three circumstances are grounds for divorce, leading to compensation demands, maternal restrictions will be observed. In societies without the custom of compensation demands, maternal restrictions will be low ($p<0.0005$). No statistically significant relationship was found between compensation demands and ritual observances by the father. As predicted, the authors found that wealth exchange, compensation demands, and the presence of fraternal interest groups were positively correlated to a statistically significant extent. The hypothesized negative relationship between maternal restrictions and paternal ritual involvement was supported only weakly. The authors attribute this to the fact that some societies observe both practices, whereas others observe neither—cases which are difficult to explain in terms of the authors' hypotheses. Finally, a path analysis of the relationships which were tested suggests that compensation demands are the most important determinant of maternal restrictions, whereas fraternal interest groups are the most important determinant of paternal ritual involvement.

The study by Paige and Paige is persuasive in its presentation, and more sophisticated methodologically than most cross-cultural research. Questions which remain are these: First, as in the study of menarche ceremonies (Paige & Paige, in press), the scoring for fraternal interest groups should have included ratings of rules of endogamy and exogamy. Second, judging from the ratings which appear at the end of their article the relationship between maternal restrictions and paternal ritual involvement is more complex than the authors suggest. The ethnographies of societies that practice both or neither custom should be examined to determine why these customs are not a simple reciprocal of each other. The extensive research by Munroe and Munroe (see, for example, Munroe, Munroe, & Whiting, 1973) should have been cited, since these authors have also suggested a relationship between forms of residence and the couvade. Finally, the authors claim that customs pertaining to birth, an event in which a woman is the chief actor, are to be explained as bargaining strategies among males; what ethnographic evidence suggests that such an interpretation is valid?

ABORTION AND INFANTICIDE

A large body of evidence supports the pervasive high valuation of parenthood implied by the beliefs and practices which pertain to pregnancy and childbirth. Marriage rituals and initiation ceremonies are rich in fertility symbolism and attempt to assure successful procreation through magical means. Childlessness is denigrated, and ethnographers become euphoric when describing how non-Western peoples cherish their offspring (see Stephens, 1963). Until recently, anthropologists seemed almost to overlook those customs which openly or indirectly serve to limit fertility.

Devereux's (1976) extensive study of abortion does not systematically test any hypotheses cross-culturally, although it presents data from many societies. Ford (1945) and Nag (1962) comment on abortion, and Whiting (1964) suggests that abortion in tropical South America serves the purpose of child spacing, which is achieved by means of the postpartum sex taboo in certain other societies (this was a subsidiary hypothesis and not a major focus of the study).

Similarly, until recently infanticide had not been studied systematically. Nag (1962) did not consider it as a variable in his omnibus work on factors affecting fertility, and Ford (1945) noted that the practice pertains to deformed babies, illegitimate babies, one or both twins, and babies of mothers who die in childbirth. Typically the neonate is killed before he or she is considered a member of society; consequently, infanticide is not viewed as murder. Yet infanticide is forbidden, and according to Ford the need for such prohibitions argues against a "maternal instinct" in humans. Ford fails to note whether or not the prohibitions on infanticide that he reports may have been the result of Western domination. Minturn and Hitchcock (1963) suggest that the introduction of Western laws forbidding female infanticide among the Rājpūts resulted in forms of malign neglect which achieved the same purpose.

Granzberg (1973) suggests a materialist explanation for infanticide practiced on twins, a custom which characterizes 18 of the 70 societies in his sample. (He notes that the sample overrepresents the New World and Africa.) Using a variety of measures to assess the work load of women and the amount of help available to them, Granzberg found that twin infanticide is practiced in societies in which it would be impossible for a mother to rear two infants simultaneously ($p<0.001$). Twin infanticide is not practiced in societies in which women have reduced responsibility for subsistence activities, in which women are not required to maintain continuous close contact with their infants, and in which kinship and settlement patterns are such as to provide women with potential helpers in raising their children.

The recent interest of anthropologists in the delicate balance that obtains between populations and the resources upon which they depend has given a new impetus to the study of customs which serve to limit fertility.[12] Divale and Harris (1976), in a recent controversial paper, view female infanticide and warfare as self-perpetuating measures which serve to regulate population in the face of limited resources. Artificially induced scarcity of women, combined with an ideology of male supremacy, is alleged to produce fierce warriors. Divale and Harris examined information from a sample of 561 localities representing 112 societies and suggested the Yanomamo as a "classical case" to illustrate the interrelationships among the variables.

Fjellman (1977) has examined the methodology of the Divale and Harris study and questions the combined use of locality and society as units in testing hypotheses cross-culturally. He also questions the use of the Yanomamo demographic data. Fjellman suggests that an unbalanced sex ratio does not necessarily imply the practice of infanticide, citing research by McKay (1977) and Whiting et al. (1977a) which reports that sex ratios in infancy are influenced by a variety of physiological and social factors. Divale's and Harris' study also invites criticism for its many unsupported, sweeping assertions, particularly in regard to "the existence of a pervasive institutionalized complex of male supremacy" (1976:521).

Additional cross-cultural findings regarding infanticide have been reported by Whiting, Bogucki, Kwong, & Nigro (1977b). In a sample of 99 societies, 84 were reported to practice infanticide. Whiting et al. suggest that infanticide practiced on deformed and illegitimate infants is probably universal but underreported. Infanticide practiced for "family planning," on the other hand, shows cross-cultural variation. Typically such infanticide involves one or both twins (as in East Africa) or the infant whose older sibling is not yet weaned or not yet able to walk. Whiting et al. suggest that this practice prevails among foragers (societies dependent upon hunting, gathering, and fishing) since their subsistence is unpredictable. The postpartum sex taboo functions to space births among cultivators. Of the accounts examined by Whiting et al., more than half report that it is the mother who commits infanticide before the neonate is named or considered a member of the group. (But is it the mother who also makes the decision that the child is to be killed?) Whiting et al. assert that the incidence of preferential female infanticide has been exaggerated. Of the 20 societies for which a sex preference was reported, 11 practice female infanticide and 9 practice male infanticide. For over 60 societies no sex preference is indicated.

Aside from abortion (which remains poorly studied cross-culturally) and infanticide (which has received considerable recent interest), various other customs have been reinterpreted as measures to limit fertility. Such reinterpretations apply to the following customs, among others: the practice of infibulation, as reported by Hayes (1975) for portions of northeast Africa; men's fear of female pollution, as reported by Lindenbaum (1972) for certain tribes in New Guinea; and men's fear of sex with women, studied cross-culturally by Ember (1978). What is needed is some understanding of the interrelationships among the various measures that limit fertility and what determines the choice of a particular practice.

LACTATION

Although a variety of cross-cultural studies have been concerned with the postpartum sex taboo and the feeding experience of the infant, lactation is typically not viewed from the point of view of the mother. Saucier suggests that the postpartum sex taboo "imposes a heavy burden on women" (1972, p. 249), and Nerlove speaks of nursing as "one aspect of a mother's caretaking which is particularly enervating and disruptive" (1974, p. 207). Such comments mask the fact that nursing might be enjoyable or fulfilling to the mother. Perhaps particularly in societies characterized by aloofness between husbands and wives (see Whiting & Whiting, 1975), the close physical relationship between mother and nursling must be highly pleasurable to the mother. Furthermore, when nursing is prolonged (2 years or more), as it is in many non-Western societies, the satisfactions it brings to the mother and the nursling go beyond the simple act of feeding and being fed. Data on the Navajo (cited by Stephens, 1962) suggest a strong erotic component in the nursing behavior of older, unweaned boys. Beyda (n.d.), reporting on a Mestizo community in Ecuador, describes the nursing behavior of boys in their second year as active and possessive.[13] This evidence suggests potential support for the assertion by Raphael that some mothers find nursing "so emotionally fulfilling that their femininity is enhanced and their sexual role as female is heightened" (1972, p. 254). Others report a lessened sex drive while lactating. These aspects of nursing have not been examined cross-culturally.

Nerlove (1974) investigated the relationship between supplementary foods in the infant's diet and the mother's involvement in subsistence activities. According to Nerlove, the introduction of supplementary foods is begun before the infant is 1 month old in those societies in which women make a substantial contribution to subsistence. In those societies in which women do not, supplementary food is introduced later. The hypothesis was tested on a sample of 83 societies, using two alternative test statistics ($p=0.02$ and 0.006). The sample excluded societies which depend upon gathering. Nerlove justified this omission, viewing gathering (unlike other subsistence activities) as highly compatible with nursing. However, minimal maternal involvement with subsistence activities is also compatible with nursing, yet such cases were included in the sample. The results of the study would have been more convincing if they had applied to the entire range of subsistence activities.

Nerlove suggests that her findings have demographic implications. Since recent evidence suggests that exclusive breastfeeding decreases the possibility of conception, the introduction of supplementary foods interferes with child spacing. Nerlove concludes that women's extensive contribution to subsistence "not only has implications for high morbidity and mortality, but may indeed foster higher fertility" (1974, p. 213).

Ford (1945) notes that the periodic feeding of infants typical in our own society is not practiced universally. He suggests that the more continuous nursing practiced in other societies may be better for the baby. A recent study by Konner (1972) describes !Kung infants as "continual feeders"—a pattern which Blurton Jones

(1972) suggests is particularly appropriate for human infants, when milk composition and sucking rates are compared for a variety of species. This feeding pattern assumes more continuous close body contact between mother and baby. Whiting (1971) has explored the implications of this closeness for the infant, but the implications for the mother remain to be investigated.

THE MATURE YEARS

Nursing and infant care comprise only a relatively brief period in the relationship of mother and offspring. Goodenough (1970) distinguishes three aspects of motherhood: physical motherhood, psychic motherhood, and jural motherhood, distinctions also observed by Barnes (1973) in his comparison of motherhood and fatherhood. Jural motherhood, which becomes more salient in a woman's relationship to her mature children, has not been studied cross-culturally.[14] In fact, very little cross-cultural research focuses on aspects of the lives of older women, a reflection of the paucity of ethnographic data on the subject. It is not known if menopause receives ceremonial recognition in any society, since there is almost no ethnographic information on menopause (see Ford, 1945). Nag's (1962) cross-cultural data suggest that the age at menopause is more variable than age at menarche. Skultans (1970) reports the reaction to menopause for a small sample of Welsh women. Applying the analytical framework suggested by Van Gennep for rites of passage, Skultans concludes that menopause lacks the final aspect of such rites: the incorporation into a new group. The data are simply not available for testing this formulation cross-culturally.

Unlike menopause, widowhood has been the subject of some cross-cultural research. Ackerman (1963) and Goody and Buckley (1973) have examined the practice of the levirate in relationship to the prevalence of divorce. Rosenblatt, Walsh, and . Jackson (1976) have examined remarriage after the death of a spouse in relationship to a number of "tie-breaking customs." The latter include fear of the ghost of the deceased, giving away personal property of the deceased, name taboos on the deceased, abandoning the dwelling of the deceased, and leaving the community of the deceased. The authors suggest that remarriage rates are positively associated with such customs and that the relationship is stronger in societies practicing the levirate or the sororate. The table which presents their findings suggests that the results are in the expected direction, and a number of the correlations reach statistical significance. However, the samples on which the correlations are based vary from merely 14 to 43 societies. Several of the tie-breaking variables are negatively correlated with each other, suggesting to the authors that such customs are functional equivalents of each other. The practice of polygyny is positively related to the remarriage of widows ($p < 0.05$) and to the practice of the levirate ($p < 0.05$). These two customs are negatively related to community size ($p < 0.025$, $p < 0.0005$). This scatter of findings using small samples suggests that aspects of widowhood bear further examination.

Apple's (1956) cross-cultural study of grandparenthood suggests that grandchildren and grandparents do not enjoy universally a relationship of friendly equality. Such a relationship prevails only in those societies in which grandparents do not continue to exercise authority over parents after the birth of grandchildren ($p < 0.001$). Relationships will be less friendly with those grandparents who are related to the child through the parent with greater household authority

(p=0.00005). The samples used (about 50 societies for the first test and about 20 societies for the second test) overrepresent Africa and underrepresent South America, as the author notes. Nevertheless, the universality of friendly equality between grandchildren and grandparents must be considered as unsupported by the cross-cultural evidence.

Simmons' (1945) ambitious cross-cultural study of the role of the aged suggests that marked sex differences obtain. Owing to the fragmentary ethnographic data on which the study is based, Simmons urges caution in the interpretation of his findings. No attempt is made to arrive at a cross-cultural definition of "aged," and active old age is not differentiated from decrepitude and senility. No demographic data are reported; hence one does not know the life expectancy for the members of the sample societies or if life expectancy varies by sex.

Simmons investigated a variety of aspects of aging: the assurance of food, property rights, status and prestige, general activities, political and civic involvement, the use of knowledge, magic, and religion, the relationship of the aged to their families, and societal attitudes about death and dying. To investigate these aspects of aging cross-culturally, over 50 items relating to the participation of the aged and their treatment were scored separately for old men and women. An attempt was made to relate these ratings to over 100 societal traits. The latter included habitat, subsistence activities, aspects of technology, the economy, aspects of social and political organization, and certain religious beliefs and practices. Using a sample of 71 societies, over 1000 correlations were calculated, but no tests of statistical significance are reported.

Simmons' findings suggest that in matrilineal and matrilocal societies, and in societies which depend upon hunting, gathering, and fishing, aged women are more likely to own property, to receive "respect," and to retain authority within the family. One outstanding activity of aged women in all types of societies is the practice of midwifery. Cross-culturally, aged women are less likely to marry young mates than are aged men. Matrilocality assures the services of a son-in-law, a form of support in old age which Simmons suggests is somewhat precarious. The abandonment of the dying and the killing or exposure of the aged are more likely to be practiced on aged women than on aged men. Simmons attributes this custom to the harshness of certain environments. Aged women, rather than aged men, are also more likely to be put to death in response to accusations of witchcraft and sorcery. This brief summary hardly does justice to Simmons' complex and ambitious study. It is remarkable that until recently this work stood alone as a cross-cultural study of the aged.

Maxwell and Silverman (1970) have reexamined some of Simmons' findings, using a sample of only 26 societies. The authors confirm that exposure or killing of the aged is related to ecologic factors and does not imply a lack of esteem for the elderly. They question the view that rules of descent result in sex differences in the treatment of the aged, agreeing, however that such sex differences are pronounced.

In a subsequent paper, Silverman and Maxwell (1978) report their preliminary findings concerning sex differences in deferential behavior experienced by the aged. For most of the six types of deference behavior identified by the authors, aged men receive substantially more than aged women. However, old women receive a large portion of that type of deferential behavior which subsumes custodial care. The findings are based on a sample of 34 societies and represent one-third of the data the authors are in the process of analyzing.

A large portion of the female life cycle, the mature years, has been but little explored cross-culturally. The jural role of the mother in relationship to her mature children, cultural responses to menopause and widowhood, the role of the midwife, and aspects of aging all invite further cross-cultural study.

CONCLUSION

Not only are there a number of events in women's lives which remain to be explored more fully by cross-cultural research, but many of the studies reviewed here require replication with larger and better-constituted samples. To achieve these ends additional apposite ethnographic data are needed, but there is more than a need for new information, a need for replication, and a need to investigate neglected aspects of women's lives.

First, psychological and sociocultural interpretations in cross-cultural research should not be viewed as competing but as complementary approaches, with equally legitimate explanatory values. In addition, all cross-cultural research should concern itself more fully with the geographic distribution of variables. As the study by Whiting (1964) suggests, geographic distribution can reveal far more about a variable than the effects of diffusion. Future cross-cultural research must integrate the psychological and the sociocultural approaches and should carefully assess and account for the geographic distribution of variables.

Second, a synthesis is needed for the cross-cultural study of practices and beliefs related to fertility, customs which strive to limit fertility, and customs which seek to enhance fertility. What is the relationship among such practices, and what determines the choice that any particular society will make among them?

Finally, the interrelationship among life-cycle observances needs to be explored. Customs which pertain to women's lives have too long been viewed in isolation from each other. The works of Paige and Paige, of Ayres, and of Goody suggest possible approaches for overcoming this fragmentation.[15] There are often similarities in the observances which occur at initiation, at marriage, and at the birth of a child. Do such practices supplement each other, or are they reiterative? Are some societies lavish in their ceremonial recognition of a variety of events in the lives of women, whereas other societies allow these same events to go unmarked? Does the repeated expenditure of time and goods on such rituals express anxious preoccupation with femininity, or does it represent an institutionalized recognition of the importance of women? If the latter could be demonstrated, ceremonies marking life cycle events would provide an index to the relative position of women in society. But the anthropology of women has been overly concerned with assessing the status of women (see Sacks, 1976). The present review seeks to demonstrate that there are more intriguing questions to ask regarding women's lives.

ACKNOWLEDGMENTS

My special thanks to Peter Bertocci for making available books and articles which would otherwise have remained inaccessible to me. I would also like to thank the following people for providing me with published and unpublished materials: Lauris Beyda, Carol Ember, Ruth McKay, Ruth and Lee Munroe, Raoul Naroll, Paul Rosenblatt, and John W. M. Whiting.

NOTES

1. The review will consider the following: When a study includes tests for the statistical significance of its findings, these are reported. The typical statistic is a

measure of correlation; however, the appropriateness of the test statistic is not evaluated. The validity of the ratings receives occasional comment, but the reliability of the ratings has not been checked, nor has the ethnographic context within which the variable is described been reexamined (see Bock, 1967). Such evaluations would be desirable but are beyond the scope of the present review. However, for each study the size of the sample is reported and the sample is checked for representativeness of the major culture areas identified in the *Ethnographic Atlas* (Murdock, 1967): sub-Sahara Africa, the Circum-Mediterranean, Eastern Eurasia, the Island Pacific Area, North America, and South America. (For an excellent evaluation of the regional distribution of a cross-cultural sample, see Paige and Paige [1973]). This constitutes only the crudest check on diffusion, yet samples used in a number of the studies to be reviewed are inadequate even by these criteria. Scarcity of appropriate ethnographic data often dictates the use of small and poorly constituted samples. Findings from such cross-cultural studies must be interpreted with great caution. Unfortunately, in the research to be reviewed methodologic elegance, particularly in sampling, is the exception rather than the rule.

2. Furthermore, it is difficult to determine what actual practices are included in each of Young's categories. One ritual for girls, infibulation, is an excruciatingly painful genital multilation practiced only among certain societies in Northeast Africa (Kennedy, 1970; Hayes, 1975). Is infibulation typical among girlhood ceremonials? Traditional Chinese foot binding provides still another example. As yet no cross-cultural study provides the needed overview.

3. Whiting's study was based on previous research which had suggested that various forms of infant stress result in increased adult stature (Landauer & Whiting, 1964; Gunders & Whiting, 1968), and Whiting found a strong negative relationship between adult female height and the onset of menarche ($p < 0.01$). This finding requires reexamination in the light of more recent research by Johnston, Malina, and Galbraith (1971) on American women—research which suggests a complex interrelationship among height, weight, and menarcheal age (see also Frisch & MacArthur, 1974). Some tentative evidence links late menarche with greater frequency of sterility (Nag, 1962). Should this relationship be verified, it would provide a rationale for the customs which appear to induce early menarche.

4. According to Winterstein (1928), there is evidence in fairy tales that female initiation rites were formerly practiced in Europe. For a full bibliography of materials relating to the initiation of girls, see Gray (1911) and Brown (1962; 1969b; 1975).

5. This study has raised considerable controversy; see Driver (1969; 1971; 1972), Brown (1970; 1971), and Opler (1972).

6. This study will comprise one chapter in a forthcoming book. I have worked from a draft copy of this single chapter, available to me for review. The reader should interpret my comments with caution, since neither the full book in manuscript nor the published version of this chapter can be consulted (Paige and Paige, in press).

7. This definition of the dowry has recently been disputed by McCreery (1976) on the basis of data from China, India, and Ceylon.

8. According to Goody, these gifts are sometimes mistakenly reported as bride-price payments. True bride-price payments, however, pass from the *kin group* of the groom to the *kin group* of the bride.

9. For an evolutionary interpretation of the geographic distribution of the dowry and bride-price, see Jackson and Romney (1973).

10. This refers to a system of inheritance practiced by certain polygynous, patrilineal African societies in which women make a considerable contribution to subsistence and in which sons inherit from their fathers those lands which their mothers cultivated and those cattle which their mothers cared for.

11. For a detailed and provocative study of food cravings during pregnancy among women in a Sinhalese village, see Obeyesekere (1963).

12. See, for example, Townsend (1971), Riches (1974), and Denham (1974).

13. Girls, on the other hand, are weaned at 8–9 months and never develop such behavior.

14. For example, Michaelson and Goldschmidt (1971) report that in certain of the peasant communities in their sample women gain increased domestic authority as the mothers of grown sons.

15. Published after the preparation of the present manuscript, a recent article by Zelman (1977) considers the interrelationship between the variables "female pollution-avoidance ritual" (which includes a variety of customs associated wtih menstruation and birth) and "male rituals associated with the female reproductive cycle." Zelman examines these customs in relationship to a number of variables such as the child care responsibilities of each sex, the role of women in the economy, and certain aspects of social structure, concluding that female pollution-avoidance rituals are associated with sex role distinctiveness or rigidity, whereas male ritual associated with the female reproductive cycle is associated with sex role flexibility.

REFERENCES

Ackerman, C. Affiliations: Structural determinants of differential divorce rates. *American Journal of Sociology*, 1963, *69*, 13–20.

Apple, D. The social strucutre of grandparenthood. *American Anthropologist*, 1956, *58*, 656–663.

Ayres, B. *A cross-cultural study of factors relating to pregnancy taboos.* Unpublished doctoral dissertation, Radcliffe College, 1954.

Ayres, B. Pregnancy magic: A study of food taboos and sex avoidances. In C. S. Ford (Ed.), *Cross-cultural approaches.* New Haven: HRAF Press, 1967, pp. 111–125.

Ayres, B. Bride theft and raiding for wives in cross-cultural perspective. Paper presented at the Meeting of the American Anthropological Association, Toronto, 1972.

Ayres, B. Marriage systems as reproductive strategies: Cross-cultural evidence for sexual selection in man. Paper presented at the meeting of the Society for Cross-cultural Research, New York, 1976.

Barnes, J. A. Genetrix: genitor: nature: culture? In J. Goody (Ed.), *The character of kinship.* New York: Cambridge University Press, 1973, pp. 61–73.

Barry, H., III. Cultural variations in sex differentiation during childhood. Typescript, 1976.

Beidelman, T. O. Pig (*Guluwe*): An essay on Ngulu sexual symbolism and ceremony. *Southwestern Journal of Anthropology*, 1964, *20*, 359–392.

Bettelheim, B. *Symbolic wounds.* Glencoe, Ill.: The Free Press, 1954.

Beyda, L. An investigation of the relationship between sex-role characteristics and the socialization of attention-getting behavior. Typescript. Ithaca: Cornell University, n.d.

Blurton Jones, N. Comparative aspects of mother-child contact. In N. Blurton Jones (Ed.), *Ethological studies of child behaviour.* Cambridge, Engl.: Cambridge University Press, 1972, pp. 305–328.

Bock, P. Love magic, menstrual taboos and the facts of geography. *American Anthropologist,* 1967, *69,* 213–217.

Broude, G. Norms of premarital sexual behavior: A cross-cultural study. *Ethos,* 1975, *3,* 381–402.

Broude, G. Cross-cultural patterning of some sexual attitudes and practices. *Behavior Science Research,* 1976, *11,* 227–262.

Brown, J. K. *A cross-cultural study of female initiation rites.* Unpublished doctoral dissertation, Harvard University, 1962.

Brown, J. K. A cross-cultural study of female initiation rites. *American Anthropologist,* 1963, *65,* 837–853.

Brown, J. K. Cross-cultural ratings of subsistence activities and sex division of labor: Retrospects and prospects. *Behavior Science Notes,* 1969, *4,* 281–290 (a).

Brown, J. K. Female initiation rites: A review of the current literature. In D. Rogers (Ed.), *Issues in adolescent psychology.* New York: Appleton-Century-Crofts, 1969, pp. 74–87 (b).

Brown, J. K. "Girls' puberty rites:" A reply to Driver. *American Anthropologist,* 1970, *72,* 1450–1451 (a).

Brown, J. K. Sex division of labor among the San Blas Cuna. *Anthropological Quarterly,* 1970, *43,* 57–63 (b).

Brown, J. K. Initiation rites for girls: A further reply. *American Anthropologist,* 1971, *73,* 1262–1263.

Brown, J. K. Adolescent initiation rites: Recent interpretations. In R. Grinder (Ed.), *Studies in adolescence: A book of readings in adolescent development.* New York: Macmillan, 1975, pp. 40–51.

Brown, J. K. The recruitment of a female labor force. *Anthropos,* 1978, *73,* 41–48.

Burton, R., & Whiting, J. W. M. The absent father and cross-sex identity. *Merrill-Palmer Quarterly of Behavior and Development,* 1961, *7,* 85–95.

Cohen, Y. The establishment of identity in a social nexus: The special case of initiation ceremonies and their relation to value and legal systems. *American Anthropologist,* 1964, *66,* 529–552 (a).

Cohen, Y. *The transition from childhood to adolescence.* Chicago: Aldine, 1964 (b).

Coppinger, R., & Rosenblatt, P. Romantic love and the subsistence dependence of spouses. *Southwestern Journal of Anthropology,* 1968, *24,* 310–319.

Coult, A. Unconscious inference and cultural origins. *American Anthropologist,* 1963, *65,* 32–35.

Denham, W. Population structure, infant transport, and infanticide among Pleistocene and modern hunter-gatherers. *Journal of Anthropological Research,* 1974, *30,* 191–198.

Devereux, G. *A study of abortion in primitive societies.* New York: International Universities Press, 1976 (Originally published in 1955).

Divale, W. T. Female status and cultural evolution: A study in ethnographer bias. *Behavior Science Research,* 1976, *11,* 169–211.

Divale, W. T., & Harris, M. Population, warfare, and the male supremacist complex. *American Anthropologist,* 1976, *78,* 521–538.

Driver, H. Girls' puberty rites in western North America. *University of California Anthropological Records,* 1941, *6,* 21–90.

Driver, H. Girls' puberty rites and matrilocal residence. *American Anthropologist,* 1969, *71,* 905–908.

Driver, H. Brown and Driver on girls' puberty rites again. *American Anthropologist,* 1971, *73,* 1261–1262.

Driver, H. Reply to Opler on Apachean subsistence, residence, and girls' puberty rites. *American Anthropologist,* 1972, *74,* 1147–1151.

Du Bois, C. *Girls' adolescence observances in North America.* Unpublished doctoral dissertation, University of California, 1932.

Ember, C. Men's fear of sex with women: A cross-cultural study. *Sex Roles: A Journal of Research,* 1978, *4,* 657–678.

Fjellman, S. A methodological critique of Divale and Harris: Male supremacy complex. Paper presented at the Meeting of the Society for Cross-Cultural Research, East Lansing, 1977.

Ford, C. S. *A comparative study of human reproduction.* Yale University Publications in Anthropology 32. New Haven: Yale University Press, 1945.

Ford, C. S., & Beach, F. *Patterns of sexual behavior.* New York: Harper Brothers, 1951.

Freedman, L., & Ferguson, V. M. The question of painless childbirth in primitive cultures. *American Journal of Orthopsychiatry,* 1950, *20,* 363–372.

Freud, S. Contributions to the psychology of love. The taboo of virginity. *Collected papers* (Vol. 4). London: Hogarth Press & the Institute for Psychoanalysis, 1953. *Originally published in 1918.*

Frisbie, C. J. *Kinaaldá: A study of the Navaho girl's puberty ceremony.* Middletown, Conn.: Wesleyan University Press, 1967.

Frisch, R., & McArthur, J. Menstrual cycles: Fatness as a determinant of minimum weight for height necessary for their maintenance or onset. *Science,* 1974, *185,* 949–951.

Gibbs, J. Social organization. In S. Tax (Ed.), *Horizons of anthropology.* Chicago: Aldine, 1964, pp. 160–170.

Gluckman, M. Kinship and marriage among the Lozi of northern Rhodesia and the Zulu of Natal. In A. R. Radcliffe-Brown & D. Forde (Eds.), *African systems of kinship and marriage.* London: Oxford University Press, 1950, pp. 166–206.

Goodenough, W. Epilogue: Transactions in parenthood. In V. Carroll (Ed.), *Adoption in eastern Oceania.* Association for Social Anthropology in Oceania Monograph 1. Honolulu: University of Hawaii Press, 1970, pp. 391–410.

Goody, J. Inheritance, property, and marriage in Africa and Eurasia. *Sociology,* 1969, *3,* 55–76.

Goody, J. Bridewealth and dowry in Africa and Eurasia. In J. Goody & S. J. Tambiah (Eds.) *Bridewealth and dowry.* Cambridge Papers in Social Anthropology 7. Cambridge, Engl.: Cambridge University Press, 1973, pp. 1–58 (a).

Goody, J. Polygyny, economy and the role of women. In J. Goody (Ed.), *The character of kinship.* New York: Cambridge University Press, 1973, pp. 175–190 (b).

Goody, J., & Buckley, J. Inheritance and women's labour in Africa. *Africa,* 1973, *43,* 108–121.

Granzberg, G. Twin infanticide—a cross-cultural test of a materialistic explanation. *Ethos,* 1973, *1,* 405–412.

Gray, L. Circumcision: Introduction. In J. Hastings (Ed.), *Encyclopaedia of Religion and Ethics.* New York: Charles Scribner, 1911, pp. 667–670.

Gunders, S. M., & Whiting, J. W. M. Mother-infant separation and physical growth. *Ethnology,* 1968, *7,* 196–206.

Hayes, R. O. Female genital mutilation, fertility control, women's roles, and the patrilineage in modern Sudan: A functional analysis. *American Ethnologist,* 1975, *2,* 617–633.

Heath, D. Sexual division of labor and cross-cultural research. *Social Forces,* 1958, *37,* 77–79.

Jackson, G., & Romney, A. K. Historical inferences from cross-cultural data: The case of dowry. *Ethos,* 1973, *1,* 517–520.

Johnston, F., Malina, R., & Galbraith, M. Height, weight and age at menarche and the "critical weight" hypothesis. *Science,* 1971, *174,* 1148.

Kennedy, J. Circumcision and excision in Egyptian Nubia. *Man*, 1970, *5*, 175–191.

Kloos, P. Female initiation among the Maroni River Caribs. *American Anthropologist*, 1969, *71*, 898–905.

Kloos, P. *The Maroni River Caribs of Surinam*. Assen, The Netherlands: Van Gorcum & Co., 1971.

Konner, M. J. Aspects of the developmental ethology of a foraging people. In N. Blurton Jones (Ed.), *Ethological studies of child behaviour*. Cambridge, Engl.: Cambridge University Press, 1972, pp. 285–304.

Landauer, T., & Whiting, J. W. M. Infantile stimulation and adult stature of human males. *American Anthropologist*, 1964, *66*, 1007–1028.

Lindenbaum, S. Sorcerers, ghosts, and polluting women: An analysis of religious belief and population control. *Ethnology*, 1972, *11*, 241–253.

Maxwell, R., & Silverman, P. Information and esteem: Cultural considerations in the treatment of the aged. *Aging and Human Development*, 1970, *1*, 361–392.

McCreery, J. Women's property rights and dowry in China and South Asia. *Ethnology*, 1976, *15*, 163–174.

McKay, R. Social factors affecting sex ratios. Paper presented at the Meeting of the Society for Cross-cultural Research, East Lansing, 1977.

Michaelson, E. J., & Goldschmidt, W. Female roles and male dominance among peasants. *Southwestern Journal of Anthropology*, 1971, *27*, 330–352.

Minturn, L., Grosse, M., & Haider, S. Cultural patterning of sexual beliefs and behavior. *Ethnology*, 1969, *8*, 301–318.

Minturn, L., & Hitchcock, J. The Rajputs of Khalapur, India. In B. Whiting (Ed.), *Six cultures: Studies of child rearing*. New York: John Wiley & Sons, 1963, pp. 203–361.

Montgomery, R. A cross-cultural study of menstruation, menstrual taboos, and related social variables. *Ethos*, 1974, *2*, 137–170.

Munroe, R. L., Munroe, R. H., & Whiting, J. W. M. The couvade: A psychological analysis. *Ethos*, 1973, *1*, 30–74.

Murdock, G. P. Family stability in non-European cultures. *Annals of the American Academy of Political and Social Science*, 1950, *272*, 195–201.

Murdock, G. P. *Ethnographic atlas*. Pittsburgh: University of Pittsburgh Press, 1967.

Murdock, G. P. Cross-sex patterns of kin behavior. *Ethnology*, 1971, *10*, 359–368.

Murdock, G. P., & Wilson, S. Settlement patterns and community organization: Cross-cultural codes 3. *Ethnology*, 1972, *11*, 254–295.

Nag, M. *Factors affecting human fertility in non-industrial societies: A cross-cultural study*. Yale University Publications in Anthropology 66. New Haven: Department of Anthropology, Yale University, 1962.

Naroll, F., Naroll, R., & Howard, F. Position of women in childbirth: A study in data quality control. *American Journal of Obstetrics and Gynecology*, 1961, *82*, 943–954.

Nerlove, S. B. Women's workload and infant feeding practices: A relationship with demographic implications. *Ethnology*, 1974, *13*, 207–214.

Obeyesekere, G. Pregnancy cravings (*Dola-Duka*) in relation to social structure and personality in a Sinhalese village. *American Anthropologist*, 1963, *65*, 323–342.

Opler, Morris E. Cause and effect in Apachean agriculture, division of labor, residence patterns, and girls' puberty rites. *American Anthropologist*, 1972, *74*, 1133–1146.

Osmond, M. W. Toward monogamy: A cross-cultural study of correlates of types of marriage. *Social Forces*, 1965, *44*, 8–16.

Paige, K., & Paige, J. The politics of birth practices: A strategic analysis. *American Sociological Review*, 1973, *38*, 663–676.

Paige, K., & Paige, J. *Politics and reproductive ritual*. Berkeley: University of California Press, in press.

Raphael, D. Comment on Polgar et al. *Current Anthropology*, 1972, *13*, 253–254.

Reminick, R. The symbolic significance of ceremonial defloration among the Amhara of Ethiopia. *American Ethnologist*, 1976, *3*, 751–763.

Richards, A. *Chisungu: A girl's initiation ceremony among the Bemba of northern Rhodesia.* New York: Grove Press, 1956.

Riches, D. The Netsilik Eskimo: A special case of selective female infanticide. *Ethnology*, 1974, *13*, 351–361.

Rosenblatt, P. A cross-cultural study of child rearing and romantic love. *Journal of Personality and Social Psychology*, 1966, *4*, 336–338.

Rosenblatt, P. Marital residence and the functions of romantic love. *Ethnology*, 1967, *6*, 471–480.

Rosenblatt, P., & Cozby, P. Courtship patterns associated with freedom of choice of spouse. *Journal of Marriage and the Family*, 1972, *34*, 689–695.

Rosenblatt, P., Fugita, S., & McDowell, K. Wealth transfer and restrictions on sexual relations during betrothal. *Ethnology*, 1969, *8*, 319–328.

Rosenblatt, P., & Hillabrant, W. Divorce for childlessness and the regulation of adultery. *Journal of Sex Research*, 1972, *8*, 117–127.

Rosenblatt, P., Peterson, P., Portner, J., Cleveland, M., Mykkanen, A., Foster, R., Holm, G., Joel, B., Reisch, H., Kreuscher, C., & Phillips. R. A cross-cultural study of responses to childlessness. *Behavior Science Notes*, 1973, *8*, 221–231.

Rosenblatt, P., & Skoogberg, E. Birth order in cross-cultural perspective. *Developmental Psychology*, 1974, *10*, 48–54.

Rosenblatt, P., & Unangst, D. Marriage ceremonies: An exploratory cross-cultural study. *Journal of Comparative Family Studies*, 1974, *5*, 41–56.

Rosenblatt, P., Walsh, P., & Jackson, D. Breaking ties with deceased spouses. In A. Bharati (Ed.), *The realm of the extra human: Agents and audiences.* Chicago: Aldine, 1976, pp. 217–231.

Sacks, K. State bias and women's status. *American Anthropologist*, 1976, *78*, 565–569.

Saucier, J. F. Correlates of the long postpartum taboo: A cross-cultural study. *Current Anthropology*, 1972, *13*, 238–249.

Silverman, P., & Maxwell, R. How do I respect thee? Let me count the ways. *Behavior Science Research*, 1978, *13*, 91–108.

Simmons, L. *The role of the aged in primitive society.* New Haven: Yale University Press, 1945.

Skultans, V. The symbolic significance of menstruation and the menopause. *Man*, 1970, *5*, 639–651.

Stephens, W. A cross-cultural study of menstrual taboos. *Genetic Psychology Monographs*, 1961, *64*, 385–416.

Stephens, W. *The Oedipus complex: Cross-cultural evidence.* Glencoe, Ill.: The Free Press, 1962.

Stephens, W. *The family in cross-cultural perspective.* New York: Holt, Rinehart & Winston. 1963.

Sweetser, D. Avoidance, social affiliation, and the incest taboo. *Ethnology*, 1966, *5*, 304–316.

Townsend, P. K. New Guinea sago gatherers: A study of demography in relation to subsistence. *Ecology of Food and Nutrition*, 1971, *1*, 19–24.

Turner, V. Betwixt and between: The liminal period in *Rites de passage*. In J. Helm (Ed.), *Symposium on new approaches to the study of religion. Proceedings of the American Ethnological Society.* Seattle: University of Washington Press, 1964, pp. 4–20.

Turner, V. *Mukanda*: The rite of circumcision. In V. Turner (Ed.), *The forest of symbols.* Ithaca: Cornell University Press, 1967, pp. 151–279.

Turner, V. Symbols in African ritual. *Science*, 1973, *179*, 1100–1105.

Van Gennep, A. *Les rites de passage.* Paris: Libraire Critique Emile Nourry, 1909.

Van Waters, M. The adolescent girl among primitive peoples. *Journal of Religious Psychology,* 1913–1914, *6,* 375–421; *7,* 32–40, 75–120.

Whiting, J. W. M. Effects of climate on certain cultural practices. In W. Goodenough (Ed.), *Explorations in cultural anthropology.* New York: McGraw-Hill, 1964, pp. 511–544.

Whiting, J. W. M. Menarcheal age and infant stress in humans. In F. Beach (Ed.), *Sex and behavior.* New York: John Wiley & Sons, 1965, pp. 221–233.

Whiting, J. W. M. Causes and consequences of the amount of body contact between mother and infant. Paper presented at the Meeting of the American Anthropological Association, New York, 1971.

Whiting, J. W. M., Bailey, R., Hartung, J., & de Zalchrono, B. Factors influencing sex ratio: Cross-cultural evidence. Paper presented at the Meeting of the Society for Cross-Cultural Research, East Lansing, 1977 (a).

Whiting, J. W. M., Bogucki, P., Kwong, W. Y., & Nigro, J. Infanticide. Paper presented at the Meeting of the Society for Cross-Cultural Research, East Lansing, 1977 (b).

Whiting, J. W. M., Kluckhohn, R., & Anthony, A. The function of male initiation ceremonies at puberty. In E. Maccoby, T. M. Newcomb, & E. L. Hartley (Eds.), *Readings in social psychology* (3rd ed.). New York: Henry Holt, 1958, pp. 359–370.

Whiting, J. W. M., & Whiting, B. B. Aloofness and intimacy of husbands and wives: A cross-cultural study. *Ethos,* 1975, *3,* 183–207.

Whyte, M. K. Cross-cultural studies of women and the male bias problem. Paper presented at the Meeting of the Society for Cross-Cultural Research, East Lansing, 1977.

Wilson, H. C. On the origin of menstrual taboos. *American Anthropologist,* 1964, *66,* 622–625.

Winterstein, A. Die pubertätsriten der mädchen mit deren spuren in märchen. *Imago,* 1928, *14,* 199–274.

Young, F. *Initiation ceremonies: A cross-cultural study of status dramatization.* New York: Bobbs-Merrill, 1965.

Young, F., & Bacdayan, A. Menstrual taboos and social rigidity. *Ethnology,* 1965, *4,* 225–240.

Zelman, E. C. Reproduction, ritual, and power. American *Ethnologist,* 1977, *4,* 714–733.

18

Male Sex-Role Resolutions

Robert L. Munroe • Ruth H. Munroe
John W. M. Whiting

Among the cultures of the world, there are two widespread institutions that deal with defining or affirming appropriate behavior for adult males—male initiation rites at puberty and the couvade. The type of male initiation to be considered in this chapter consists of a series of rites during which the initiate is transformed from a genderless child to an adult male. Ritual circumcision begins the sequence, followed by a period of exclusion from domestic life, and completed by a ceremony of reentry into the domestic and reproductive cycle. The couvade, sometimes termed "male childbed" because of the husband's involvement in the birth process, is a set of supernaturalistic observances on the part of the father of a newborn or to-be-born child. The observances in their intensive form (the focus of interest in this paper) require the father to deviate significantly from normal activities (Munroe, Munroe, & Whiting, 1973).

MALE INITIATION RITES

There are a number of initiation rites for males that, since they do not focus on sex gender, will not be considered in this chapter. Such rites may focus on the responsibilities of adult status (Schlegel & Barry, 1975; Granzberg, 1972; 1973); others are intended to introduce the novice to the supernatural world (Eliade, 1965); still others signal a transition from an ignorant child to an adult scholar. This chapter will be concerned with that set of rites that includes circumcision and that are defined by the culture as necessary for the attainment of adult *male* status.

The following case will serve to illustrate what we have defined as rites of induction into manhood:

The Masai are herders who inhabit southwestern Kenya and northwestern Tanzania. Although their culture has been somewhat modified by contact with Western society—Pax Britannica prohibits them from cattle raiding—they have resisted the adoption of Western schooling, cattle rather than shillings are still the most valued medium of exchange, and they continue to maintain an essentially pastoral economy. Initiation into manhood begins for a Masai youth when he is about 15 years old, when, together with his agemates from his own and neighboring kraals, he is ritually circumcised. When this ceremony is completed, he enters the status of junior warrior (*moran*). As morans they live with their agemates in a special kraal (*manyatta*), where, although they are responsible for guarding the herds assigned to them against animal and human predators, they spend much of their time grooming one another. They grow their hair long and paint their faces and bodies; thus made up, with spear in hand, small groups of them will visit the domestic kraals in the hope of setting up a secret tryst with one of the young married women. They may not marry during this period of moranhood, but in addition to the illicit philandering they may have affairs with young unmarried girls.

After a period of up to 15 years of moranhood, there is a changeover ceremony which marks the end of moranhood. Their heads are shaved. The elders make speeches to them emphasizing the responsibility of adulthood, and they return to the domestic kraal of their father, marry, and take on the responsibilities of adulthood.[1]

A serious consideration of male initiation rites in preindustrial societies dates from early in this century, when Arnold van Gennep (1909) published his *Rites de Passage*. In this monograph, he argued that initiation rites at puberty had characteristics in common with other ceremonies of transition from one status to another, such as birth, marriage, and death. He also noted that death and rebirth was a metaphor that was characteristic of the rite. He noted that since the rites generally did not correspond exactly in time to physiological puberty but might precede or follow this event by several years, they must be understood as socially rather than physiologically determined events. His most important contribution to our understanding of the ritual, however, was to point out that rites of passage were characterized by three phases: preliminal (separation), liminal (transition), and postliminal (incorporation). He emphasized the importance of the liminal phase, likening it to the no-man's-land at boundaries, and suggested its dangerous and sacred nature—a theme that has recently been developed by Douglas (1966) and Turner (1967).

The weakness of van Gennep's position is that he treated initiation rites as a universal phenomenon and did not consider variations in the form and emphasis they take in different societies or why this should be so—a problem that is the concern of most subsequent research on initiation rites and will be the focus of our discussion of them.

A number of authors have taken what Young (1965) refers to as a sociogenic as opposed to a psychogenic approach. These authors include Young himself, who argues that if the social system is characterized by male solidarity—that is, exclusive institutionalized male activities—sex-role recognition will be dramatized through male initiation rites (Young, 1965, p. 41). Cohen (1964) presents a similar sociogenic hypothesis. He assumes that rites would occur in societies with unilinear descent as a result of the functional need to separate children from their nuclear families and incorporate them into their lineage organizations. Both the Young and Cohen hypotheses are strongly supported by cross-cultural tests. Neither of these interpretations limits initiation rites to those involving circumcision and emphasizing manhood as opposed to adulthood.

A similar hypothesis is presented by Paige and Paige (in press). They emphasize the prevalence of circumcision as a component of many rites. They show that most societies that practice such rites have strong fraternal interest groups, i.e., bonds of related males with corporate interests. Maintenance of the male group's wealth and political and military power is dependent upon the continued loyalty of its members, and the possibility of fission represents a threat to the group's existence as a viable force:

Circumcision is intended as a demonstration of consanguineal allegiance in strong fraternal interest group societies and is required of every father by his close consanguines and lineage elders, who have the most to lose from a fission. . . . It is intended both to influence and to assess the opinions of important political allies or enemies and therefore is not primarily directed at the principal focus in the ritual, the son, at all, but rather at the father's consanguineal kin. (Paige & Paige, in press)

Status transition plays no part in the Paiges' hypothesis, which therefore differs from the previously discussed social interpretations in being completely non-child-centered. Also distinctive is their conceptualization of ritual as an alternative strategy to direct legal or political action—that is, as a strategy for asserting or defending rights in the absence of more potent sources of influence.

A number of psychological hypotheses concerning the meaning of initiation rites, particularly those involving circumcision, were proposed before any were put to the test. Sigmund Freud (1939) argued that circumcision represented a symbolic castration of the boy, thus preventing incest between mother and son and preserving the father's sexual rights over the mother.

Margaret Mead (1949) presented the "womb-envy" hypothesis, which holds that whereas women go through sharp discontinuous stages such as virginity, menarche, bearing of a child, and menopause, a male can achieve comparably dramatic sequences only by artificial social distinctions or by having something done to his body. Circumcision is one of the ways in which "members of his culture, armed with cultural tools, no longer following any clear rhythm of their biological inheritance, alter, deform, or beautify his body" (Mead, 1949, p. 140). Initiation cults, which often include circumcision and other body deformations, as well as various mysterious noise-making instruments, enable men to compensate for the fact that the most dramatic life stage of all is possessed by women: "By virtue of their ability to make children, [women] hold the secrets of life" (Mead, 1949, p. 84). But with initiation cults, men "can get the male children away from the women, brand them as incomplete, and themselves turn boys into men. Women, it is true, make human beings, but only men can make men" (Mead, 1949, p. 84).

The striking difference between Mead's hypothesis (and a similar one presented by Bettelheim, 1954) and the previously described sociogenic hypotheses is that the rites are assumed to satisfy intrapsychic needs of the individual rather than maintaining the structure of society. But these "psychogenic" hypotheses are, like the early sociogenic hypothesis of van Gennep, universalistic and make no specification of variation across cultures.

Mead (1949) was the first to propose a psychogenic hypothesis concerning initiation rites that could be tested cross-culturally. This was suggested by differences in seven societies in which she had done field work. She noted the following:

What we find within these seven societies is that those societies which have emphasized suckling, the most complementary relationship of all the bodily learning experience, there is the greatest symbolic preoccupation with the differentials between men and women, the greatest envy, over-compensation, ritual mimicry of the opposite sex, and so on. With the emphasis on the suckling relationship goes naturally enough a greater emphasis on the relationship between mother and child, or at least between lactating woman and nursling. The baby cannot be left too long in the charge of a father or a grandparent or a child-nurse; the tie to the breast is strong and central. When in addition male separateness from women has been developed into a strong institution, with a men's house and male intitiation ceremonies, then the whole system becomes an endlessly reinforcing one, in which each generation of little boys grows up among women, identified with women, envying women, and then, to assert their endangered certainty of their manhood, isolate themselves from women. Their sons again grow up similarly focussed on women, similarly in need of over-compensatory ceremonial to rescue themselves. (pp. 73–74)

Albert Anthony (1955), using the Whiting and Child (1953) child-rearing scores, set out to test the Mead hypothesis on a cross-cultural sample. He chose the duration of the nursing period as an index of what Mead referred to as an "emphasis on suckling" and found a statistically significant positive relationship between late weaning and the occurrence of male initiation rites.

Another finding of the Anthony study was that the duration of the postpartum sex taboo was even more strongly associated with initiation, especially if circumcision was part of the ritual. The ϕ value for the association between initiation and the age of weaning was 0.32 ($p < 0.05$), whereas the ϕ value of the association between the occurrence of initiation and the duration of the postpartum sex taboo was 0.62 ($p < 0.01$). Anthony also reported a positive relationship between the occurrence of male initiation rites with circumcision at puberty and patrilineal descent ($\phi = 0.31$, $p < 0.001$), and with polygyny ($\phi = 0.31$, $p < 0.05$).

These latter findings suggested that Freud's oedipal rivalry hypothesis might be more plausible than Mead's status envy hypothesis, particularly if a long postpartum sex taboo and polygyny could be taken as conditions that would intensify latent incestuous feelings between son and mother and hence rivalry between son and father.

A followup study was carried out by J. Whiting, Kluckhohn, and Anthony (1958) to test this interpretation. Exclusive mother–infant sleeping arrangements during the period when the postpartum sex taboo was in effect were taken as a set of conditions that might lead to unconscious seductive behavior of mother to infant son and thus exacerbate the incest problem. This interpretation was supported by a cross-cultural test.

Exclusive sleeping arrangements and a prolonged postpartum sex taboo were so strongly intercorrelated that their effects could not be independently estimated. Their associations with male initiation rites were both highly statistically significant ($p < 0.001$). The ϕ values were 0.57 and 0.60, respectively.

In reading the ethnographic descriptions of initiation during the course of this study, Whiting felt that the oedipal interpretation, even though it was apparently strongly confirmed in the above-reported study, was not satisfactory and was quite at odds with the interpretations given by native informants. Van Gennep's statement that initiation was a transition between sexless childhood and adult sexual manhood, and particularly Mead's interpretation that in societies with initiation rites boys initially envied women and were "in need of over-compensatory ceremonial to rescue themselves," corresponded much more closely to native theory. These theories held that the prepuce was a feminine adjunct which needed to be excised to permit complete masculine sexuality. In many societies practicing male circumcision, a girl's clitoris, which was considered masculine, was excised to permit her to become completely feminine (see Chapter 17 in this volume). Furthermore, in no instance did the father perform the operation—this was generally carried out by a specialist—and if the father played any role in the ceremony, it was as sponsor and supporter. Finally, hazing—generally carried out by members of the next older age grade rather than by the parental generation—occurred in the preliminal phase, while during the liminal phase initiates were often permitted sexual and aggressive license.

This reinterpretation of the meaning of the rites led to the assumption that the rites were a resolution of a conflict in sex identity rather than a resolution of the oedipal conflict. To square this interpretation with the empirical facts the status envy theory of identification was developed (J. Whiting, 1960). According to this theory, an infant or child tends to envy those perceived as controlling goods and resources and will, as a consequence, covertly practice the role of and identify with the envied person.

Exclusive mother–infant sleeping arrangements and a prolonged postpartum sex taboo were reinterpreted according to the above theory as providing the conditions under which the mother would be seen as the primary controller of goods and resources and hence the female role as the one to be envied and covertly practiced. For the boy, this would lead, according to this theory, to cross-sex identification.

In societies where an infant slept with both parents or more especially where she or he slept alone and the father and mother slept together, the parents of both sexes would be seen as controlling resources and generation–identity or dependence–independence conflict would be predicted. It could also be argued from this theory that the father, since he has the exclusive privilege of sleeping with the mother, would be envied. Thus oedipal rivalry would be more likely to occur in those societies that do *not* have exclusive mother–infant sleeping arrangements and a long postpartum sex taboo.

In order to arrive at a satisfactory explanation of male initiation rites from a cross-sex identity hypothesis, a further assumption must be made. There must be some countervailing force in the society that makes cross-sex identity unacceptable and instigates the adult males to ritually "rescue" the boys. The status envy theory suggests that such a condition would occur in those societies where the perceived source of power shifts from the mother to the father—from women to men—as the boy grows up. Societies with patrilocal residence fulfill these conditions. The father and his brothers have control of the resources. They own the land and/or the cattle, and they hold political power. The mother is a recent immigrant whose supporting kinsmen are distant and whose authority is limited to domestic affairs. When the boy is old enough to appreciate this state of affairs, the status to be envied is clearly male. If he has previously lived in mother–child households, perceived his mother to control resources, and formed a strong initial identification with her, this shift in the source of power as perceived by him should produce an intrapsychic conflict in optative gender identity. Is it better to be a girl or a boy, a woman or a man? The cross-sex identity conflict theory requires that male initiation rites will occur in societies where both these conditions obtain. The function of the rites, according to this hypothesis, is to solve the intrapsychic conflict by supporting the secondary desire to be a man through excision of the prepuce—a symbol of the boy's infantile desire to be a woman.

A cross-cultural study supported the above hypothesis. Initiation rites with circumcision were associated significantly with both patrilocal residence and exclusive mother–infant sleeping arrangements. Of a sample of 64 societies, 13 had initiation rites with circumcision; 12 of these 13 cases had both exclusive sleeping arrangements and patrilocal residence. One initiation case had exclusive sleeping arrangements but other than patrilocal residence. None of the cases with patrilocal residence and nonexclusive sleeping arrangements had initiation rites with circumcision. The full table was unfortunately not presented; thus the interaction between sleeping arrangements and residence cannot be reported (Burton & Whiting, 1961).

A further cross-cultural test of the cross-sex identity theory was made by Kitahara (1974). He argued that it was the distance of the infant from the father, rather than his closeness to the mother, that was the important factor. In a cross-cultural study, he showed that circumcision and/or the segregation of boys at adolescence was associated with whether or not the father was coresident with the mother–infant dyad. Secondary masculine identification was not considered in his formulation.

The sex-identity conflict interpretation of male initiation rites presumes that the rites serve to reduce the intrapsychic conflict. To be effective, the boy must be assured that he is a man and not a woman and be convinced that he wishes it to be so. The cross-cultural tests of the hypothesis reported above give no indication as to whether or not this is so. Furthermore, if there is a change in the self-image of a candidate for manhood, when and how does it occur?

Most ethnographic descriptions of male initiation focus on the rituals immediately surrounding the genital operations. Those who use van Gennep's formulation (for example, Turner, 1967) generally interpret circumcision as the preliminal or separation ritual, the period of seclusion (while the wounds are healing) as the liminal period, and the ritual termination of seclusion as the postliminal ritual. The whole sequence seldom lasts more than 2 or 3 months, and it is doubtful, no matter how dramatic and drenched with symbolism, that this sequence can effectively convince the novice that his identity has really been changed. A prolonged period of several years such as that described for the Masai moran at the beginning of this chapter is a more likely candidate for producing effective change. This period is clearly transitional and can appropriately be conceived of as liminal. The behavior expected of the moran is nondomestic. It might be conceived of as 15 years of practice in unchildish and unfeminine behavior.

A study by Herzog (1973) supports this interpretation. He gave a battery of masculine self-image tests to a group of 41 Kikuyu youths just before they were to be circumcised. The tests were repeated 4–5 months later. The scores were indeed more masculine on the second test, but the difference was not significantly greater than that for a control group of 42 boys a year younger who were tested at the same times as the experimental group.

Traditionally, after the ritual of circumcision, a Kikuyu joined an age-graded regiment of scouts (Muriuki, 1974) and lived a nondomestic liminal life similar to that of the Masai moran. Now that Christianity and schooling have been adopted, attending secondary school apparently has replaced scouting as a liminal status for most Kikuyu youth. In support of this hypothesis, Herzog found that when ages were matched, those of his subjects that were attending secondary school scored higher on his tests of masculine self-image than those who were still in primary school.

Thus it seems that a prolonged period during which a young man's life style sharply contrasts with the domestic sphere and the strong influence of his mother may effectively assure him that he is indeed not feminine and that at the end of this experience he can feel confident that he is and wants to be a man.

THE COUVADE

Before discussing the various theories that have been put forward to explain the couvade, we present a description of this institution as practiced by the Siriono:

> Except for being subject to certain food taboos, the normal life of a woman is little upset during pregnancy. . . .
> Some of these food taboos are generalized to the father, but not all of them. The only ones which he usually observes are the restrictions on eating the harpy eagle, anteater, and howler monkey, which in a strict sense are not pregnancy taboos, since these animals are never supposed to be eaten by anyone but an old person. However, these food taboos seem to be more carefully observed by the men when their wives are pregnant. . . .
> For about 3 days following childbirth the Siriono family undergoes a series of observances and rites. . . . These rites are designed to protect the life of the infant and to insure its good health. Not only is the infant believed to be extremely delicate during the period immediately following birth, and thus readily subject to disease and death, but it is thought still intimately to be connected with the parents and profoundly to be affected by their activities. Consequently the latter are restricted in various ways. Except for satisfying the calls of nature they do not move outside of the house. They stay close to their hammocks, and are subject to a number of food taboos. Neither jaguar nor coati is eaten lest the infant break out with sores all over its body; paca cannot be eaten lest the infant become a victim of diarrhea. . . .
> More important than the abstinence from certain foods is the carrying out of certain other practices that must follow the birth of every baby. On the day after the birth both parents are scarified on the upper and lower legs with the eye tooth of a rat or a squirrel. . . .
> Except during the scarification rite the parents stay close to their hammocks on the day following the birth, the father resting and the mother attending the infant. (Holmberg, 1950, pp. 66, 68–69)

Ceremonies for the purpose of terminating the couvade, held on the third day after birth, include a brief excursion into the forest, where the wife constructs a basket and the husband collects firewood, which he places in the basket. They then return home. Finally:

> Upon entering the hut the parents kindle a new fire with the wood carried back from the forest. The infant is then given a bath from the calabash of water which the mother took into and brought back from the forest. The period of couvade is then considered to be officially over, and the normal activities of life can be resumed. (Holmberg, 1950, p. 70)

As with male initiation rites, the earliest explanations for the couvade were sociogenic. Bachofen (1861) viewed the couvade as an attempt on the father's part to legalize his paternity in communities practicing "mother-right." Tylor (1889) concurred, but went further to posit that it was a precursor of the evolutionary change from mother-right to father-right. Tylor pointed out as well that the couvade expresses a physical bond between the father and his child whereby, on the principle of sympathetic magic, the father's behavior can affect the health of the child. Crawley (1902), Frazer (1910), and Karsten (1920) also attempted an explanation on the grounds of mystical connection between father and child.

Young (1964) proposes a somewhat different sociogenic hypothesis. He posits that "parenthood dramatization" is associated with social rigidity as measured by strongly corporate family structures (clans). Since these clans are not specified as being either patrilineal or matrilineal, this hypothesis is quite different from previous theories. Furthermore, his scale for parenthood dramatization includes seclusion of the mother; thus it is doubtful that it is, as he claims, a measure of the couvade as we have defined it.

Paige and Paige (1973) have elaborated and further specified the Bachofen hypothesis. They have taken the absence of fraternal interest groups as the variable which is associated with the couvade. They argue that in such societies the husband will be without strong kin support in asserting paternity claims. In contrast to the husband's lack of support, there are "the implicit claims of his wife's kinsmen dramatized by the wife's undeniable role in the birth" (Paige & Paige, 1973, p. 668). In order to offset these claims, and to assert his own paternity rights, the husband can be expected to involve himself ritually in the birth process—namely, by practicing the couvade. They support this hypothesis through a test based on the Standard Cross-Cultural Sample (Murdock & White, 1969).

A psychogenic theory is proposed by Reik (1953) and Spiro (1961). They interpret the couvade as an institutionalized method of defending against the father's latent hostility toward his offspring. In Spiro's words, "If we assume that fathers are initially hostile to their offspring of either sex (because they are competitors for his wife's affection, nurturance, and so forth), either repression of the hostility [through the couvade] or institutionalized avoidance (or some third functional equivalent) would serve to preclude the overt expression of the motive" (1961, p. 485). Spiro does not specify the sociocultural conditions which would lead to the couvade rather than the other two alternatives.

Bettelheim presents an alternative psychogenic theory. His interpretation is that "the man wishes to find out how it feels to give birth, or he wishes to maintain to himself that he can" (1954, p. 211). Although this is similar to the cross-sex identity theory to be presented below, Bettelheim, like Spiro, does not specify the sociocultural conditions that would lead a man to envy a woman's ability to bear children so strongly that it is institutionalized.

The present authors (Munroe, 1964; Munroe, Munroe, & Whiting, 1973) have proposed an explanation for the couvade which, like the explanation for circumcision rites presented above, is based on a theory of cross-sex identification. For the couvade, the theory posits that the salience of the father is perceived to be low by the son both during his infancy and later during his childhood. Such conditions are provided by exclusive mother–infant sleeping arrangements and matrilocal rather than patrilocal residence. Under these conditions, the mother and her siblings are perceived as controlling resources. The father is an interloper, and his supporting kin live elsewhere. A child brought up this way should be in much less conflict about his feminine identification and have no need for a ritual to help him reject it. On the other hand, a ritual—such as the couvade—which would serve to legitimize his envy of women would be appropriate.

A cross-cultural test supported this interpretation. The couvade was practiced in 70 percent of the societies with both exclusive mother–infant sleeping arrangements and matri-residence and in but 10 percent of the societies with neither of these practices ($\chi^2 = 9.26$, $\phi = 0.55$, $n = 31$). Those with one but not both independent variables present practiced the couvade in 35 and 25 percent of the cases, respectively. Taken separately, exclusive mother–infant sleeping arrangements were significantly associated with the couvade ($\chi^2 = 5.7$, $p<0.05$) but matri-residence was not $\chi^2 = 1.78$, NS). The combined effect of the two variables was reasonably robust ($\chi^2 = 17.81$, 6 df, $p<0.005$, $n = 74$ (Munroe, Munroe, & Whiting, 1973, p. 43).

If male initiation rites help to produce masculine sex identity and if couvade implies the presence of feminine sex identity, then the individual who participates in the first institution should have no need of the second. Circumcision ceremonies and the couvade ought to be mutually exclusive. Such an expectation is supported by the cross-cultural evidence and has been reported several times in the literature (Burton & Whiting, 1961; Munroe, 1961; J. Whiting, 1961). The results of an attempt to replicate the negative association between the institutions will be presented in a later section of this paper.

THE MEASUREMENT OF SEX IDENTITY

The cross-cultural findings deal only with inferred states of psychological functioning and thus remain indirect. But several studies have undertaken direct measurement of male sex identity and have thereby supplied evidence relevant to the sex-identity hypothesis. A single measure, male pregnancy symptomatology (the experience of femalelike symptoms by the husband during the wife's pregnancy) has proved valid within and across cultures: (1) male symptoms, including fatigue, food cravings, vomiting, headaches, and dizziness, have been reported as present in all societies in which they have been asked about systematically; (2) within seven different societies, "Men who have reported many symptoms have made more femalelike responses on various covert measures of sex role preference than men who have reported few or no symptoms" (Munroe & Munroe, 1973, p. 492); (3) among the seven societies, the incidence of male symptomatology is highest in "those societies that on theoretical grounds should have males with sex identity problems" (Munroe & Munroe, 1973, p. 492). Since the seven societies include several that practice circumcision and one that observes the couvade, the pertinence of male symptomatology to the issue of individuals and institutions should be apparent.

The Black Carib are a Central American society that practices the couvade, and the "Nilotes" are an East African society that theoretically should perform circumcision because of childhood-induced sex-identity conflict among the males but does not actually observe such a practice. In the African society, which is discussed here first, the early experience conditions of low male salience in infancy followed by high male salience in later childhood are present (Munroe & Munroe, 1973). These conditions, as discussed above, are associated with male circumcision rites on a cross-cultural basis, and they are further associated with circumcision in three societies that together surround the Nilotes geographically. Given that the Nilotes, unlike their neighbors, apparently have failed to "resolve" a sex-identity conflict through circumcision rites, their level of male symptomatology should be significantly higher than that found in the other three societies. This is the case, with the Nilotes averaging 4.7 symptoms per male and the neighboring groups averaging 0.9–1.5 symptoms. Moreover, the Nilote men frequently experienced something akin to labor pains during their wives' parturition: one man said that he usually had no troubles with his stomach but that when his wife was in labor he suffered severe pains; another said that he had severe pains in the lower part of his back and had to move gingerly; and another said that he had pain in his ribs and back and felt very cold during the period of labor. Symptoms during the labor process are not so much simulation of the female's pregnancy as of her actual travail and accordingly seem to be even more focally a symbol of the childbearing experience.

The Black Carib, through their couvade observances—taboos on various activities and on extramarital sexual behavior—are presumably expressing cross-sex identity and hence should also experience a high level of male pregnancy symptomatology. Their level, 5.0 symptoms per man, was in fact slightly higher than that of the Nilotes and included such phenomena as 77 percent of the men experiencing lassitude during all pregnancies of their wives, 47 percent experiencing vomiting in all pregnancies, and 56 percent experiencing toothache in all pregnancies (Munroe, Munroe, & Whiting, 1973). The possible significance of the pregnancy-related toothache, reported only infrequently by men in other societies investigated, is discussed in the following passage:

> A symbolic connection might be seen between the aching tooth and the growing fetus, both of which must be extracted before normality or balance is reachieved. One piece of evidence that would support such an interpretation came from a subject who had been working a few miles out of town during part of the time his wife was pregnant with his second child. While on the job one day, the subject began to have pains in his stomach. The pains were sufficiently severe that he had to be brought back into town to be treated. After treatment by the district physician, the pain ceased. On the following day, however, the subject was afflicted with a toothache, which bothered him through the night. In the morning, he went to have the tooth extracted. . . . The difficulties then ceased, and there were no more attacks of this kind. The subject told the story as one connected sequence when asked if he had had any toothaches during his wife's pregnancies. (Munroe, Munroe, & Whiting, 1973, p. 56)

The Black Carib mean of 5 symptoms per male is the highest yet reported where systematic questioning has been undertaken. Men in the four East African societies scored lower than the Carib (three of them significantly so), as did Mexican-American and Anglo-American men, for whom the means are less than 1 per male (Munroe & Munroe, 1975; Rubel & Spielberg, 1966). Furthermore, in the general ethnographic literature, where male symptomatology is sometimes reported incidentally (cf. Munroe & Munroe, 1971), there is only one society known to the authors to have a level at all comparable to that of the Carib (and the Nilotes). Among the Wogeo of New Guinea, males are as likely to suffer from morning sickness as their wives (Hogbin, 1943). The Wogeo also observe the couvade (Munroe, Munroe, & Whiting, 1973). Therefore the societies with certain institutional arrangements said to indicate the presence of male sex-identity problems are indeed those that exhibit prolific male symptomatology.

Does low father salience (or, more generally, low male salience) in the early years have a strong, long-term effect on male sex identity? As McClelland points out (Chapter 4 in this volume), enough studies fail to show effects of low male salience (Greenstein, 1966; Harrington, 1970; Hendrick, 1970) that the relationship must be seen as less sturdy than could be desired. Furthermore, it is difficult to demonstrate that, as McClelland puts it, "a particular experience of the child in early life . . . has a lasting effect on him or her." Low male salience is often confounded with several other experiential variables that may cumulatively produce the observed sex-identity outcome. But the overall evidence indicates that the relationship exists in many samples and across several cultures (cf. Biller, 1976; Hetherington & Deur, 1972;

Munroe & Munroe, 1975, pp. 122–124), that individual observance of the couvade is strongly associated with early low male salience among the Black Carib (Munroe, Munroe, & Whiting, 1973), and that male symptomatology is associated with early low male salience in three of the four societies in which it has been systematically asked about (Daniels, 1970; Munroe & Munroe, 1971). These findings, taken together with the original cross-cultural studies of circumcision ceremonies and the couvade, certainly must weigh heavily in any general evaluation of the effects of low male salience.

Defensive Masculinity

There is a factor that complicates discussions of cross-sex identity, and that is the fact that its manifestations often include defensive or protest masculinity. In displaying ultramasculine behavior, the male seems to be attempting to overcome some doubt or concern about his masculinity. But defensive masculinity appears only in some cases; in others, straightforward femalelike behavior is exhibited; and in still others, a mixture of the two appears. What determines the types of response the individual gives? One might expect that if there were no social pressures, a male whose identity was feminine would behave in a manner similar to that of females. However, a male's *attributed sex identity* (the status assigned a person by other members of his society) (Burton & Whiting, 1961) is almost always masculine, and it is likely that all societies exert pressures toward conformity to sex-role expectations. These pressures, though, depending on the values placed on sex-role differentiation, vary greatly from one society to another, and femalelike behavior on the part of males is more acceptable in some societies than others. Interacting with societal pressures is the degree of overtness of behavior. Since sex-typed behaviors that are relatively public are more easily scrutinized, the degree of overtness of a response gives a second basis for estimating the likelihood of its being subject to compensatory manipulation. No weighting system has been developed for integrating the contribution of cultural pressure on sex-role differentiation with that of the overtness of behaviors in order to predict when defensive masculinity will occur, but the available data can be inspected for clues.

A strong cultural value on sex-role differentiation can be found in the great majority of non-Western societies, which tend to be male dominated both in family organization and social structure (Murdock, 1967). B. Whiting (1965) showed that in the Six Cultures Project, the Nyansongans and the Khalapur Rajpūt, the two groups with a combination of low male salience in the early years and male-dominated family and social structure, possessed the highest rates of assault and homicide. Howe (1966) showed that in the Caymans early low male salience and later exclusive male associations were related to aggression and boisterous group drinking behavior. In the United States as well, subcultural groups with strong values on male dominance often breed adolescent gangs that display hypervirility. New Orleans black gang mambers, with frequent father-absent backgrounds, rejected middle-class values as "soft, effeminate, and despicable" (Rohrer & Edmonson, 1960, p. 163), and lower-class father-absent fifth-grade boys were more aggressive than father-present boys (Santrock & Wohlford, 1970).

Where the values on differentiated sex roles are weak, the social pressure for masculine behavior should also be weak, and the male with underlying cross-sex identity should exhibit femalelike behavior in a straightforward manner. Carlsmith (1973) showed such a pattern with upper-middle-class U.S. college males whose fathers had been absent in the early years of their lives. In comparison to a control group, these men showed a more feminine pattern of attitudes and interests, picked more feminine career choices, and described their ideal self as more like mother than father. On no measure did the father-absent males display hypermasculine behavior.

The second variable affecting manifestation of defensive masculinity, the overtness of the behavior, can be evaluated through data on male pregnancy symptomatology. For six societies in which male symptomatology has been formally investigated, there are data on everyday, publicly observable behaviors. The findings are highly consistent across five of the samples, with symptom-prone men approaching the image of the "tough male" in each. A partial list of the results is as follows: Among lower-middle-class whites in the United States, male symptoms were associated with a lower level of housekeeping activities (e.g., cooking, washing dishes, making beds), a higher level of decision making, and, on the "strong-weak" item of the semantic differential (D'Andrade, 1973; Osgood, Suci, & Tannenbaum, 1957), description of all-male roles (father, husband, brother, son) as stronger than all-female roles and description of self as closer to father than mother in strength (Munroe & Munroe, 1971). Among East African Nilotes, symptomatology was associated with drinking and with semantic-differential description of the self as strong (Munroe, Munroe, & Nerlove, 1973). Among two Bantu-speaking groups in East Africa, in one society symptoms were associated with drinking and with semantic-differential description of all-male roles as stronger than all-female roles and description of the self as closer to father than mother (Munroe & Munroe, 1971), and in the other society symptoms were associated with description of the self as closer to father (Munroe, Munroe, & Nerlove, 1973). Finally, among Black Carib males, symptoms were associated with cursing, drinking, gambling, and wife beating and with semantic-differential description of all-male roles as stronger than all-female roles (Munroe & Munroe, 1971). The Black Carib are of special interest because in practicing the couvade they are said to be directly expressing cross-sex identity, and Carib males who observed more intensive couvade practices displayed greater femalelike behavior on several covert measures of masculinity-femininity than did males observing less intensive couvade practices. Yet they also exhibited a pattern of hypermasculinity in everyday behavior: they drank more, they were considered braver men, and they tended to curse and gamble more frequently ($p < 0.10$) than nonintensive couvade males (Munroe, Munroe, & Whiting, 1973). Thus even in a society in which the tendency toward femalelike responses among males is very strong the most feminized males nevertheless strive to attain some ideal of hypervirility at the level of overt behavior.

It was noted above that males in one of the societies did not exhibit a pattern of defensive masculinity. These were Mexican-Americans in an urban neighborhood in the lower Rio Grande Valley of Texas (Rubel & Spielberg, 1966). Symptom-experiencing men in this group, prior to demonstration of their symptoms, had been adjudged by their male peers as "effeminate," "nonmacho," "henpecked," or "a homebody." These men did not participate, except occasionally and then peripherally, in the usual male verbal dueling behavior in cantinas, and when they left such places they were challenged—"Stay! Your wife won't scold you if you have another beer!" Rarely did the object of attack respond by challenging the other to a fight. After departing the cantina, the individual was the subject of discussion by those remaining: he was not given enough money by his wife, he was afraid of his wife, he was concerned that he was being cuckolded at that very moment.

The Mexican-American pattern for overt behavior is clearly the reverse of that in the other five societies. Why do the symptom-prone males fail to display protest masculinity? One possibility is the existence of the *machismo* syndrome among Mexican-American males (Garibay Patron, 1969). The pressures toward manliness are so strong in this subculture that they may be intimidating to the male with underlying cross-sex identity. In other words, we seem to have in this case an interaction between the two factors that determine the expression of defensive masculinity. The general tendency for the cross-sex identified male to be hypervirile in everyday life can be overridden if the pressures toward "tough maleness" are extreme. If the average male is already displaying hypervirility, then the symptom-experiencing male, as in this Mexican-American subculture, may be forced into overtly nonmasculine behavior.

The following general statements can be made about the overall findings, which fit together fairly coherently. In the majority of societies, males with unresolved sex-identity problems display covert femalelike behavior and overt hypermasculine behavior. But in two sets of circumstances, femalelike behavior will be found at not only the covert but also the overt level as well. These conditions are (1) where the values on sex-role differentiation are minimal and the pressures toward it are weak, or (2) where the pressures toward sex-role differentiation are extremely high, so high that the male population as a whole tends toward the "tough male" syndrome. Both of these sets of circumstances, as noted above, occur infrequently.

One conceptual distinction made in this paper has been without value. The Black Carib were said to be characterized by cross-sex identity and the Nilotes by unresolved conflict in sex identity. But the males in the two groups appear to have highly similar sex-identity profiles, i.e., femalelike at the covert level and hypervirile at the overt level. Unless further evidence is found to rejustify the distinction, the single term *conflict in sex identity* might be used to describe both cases.

SEX IDENTITY AND INSTITUTIONAL OUTCOMES

The cross-cultural studies of circumcision rites and the couvade have turned up a certain proportion of societies that fail to accord with prediction. The Nilotes, expected to practice circumcision but not doing so, represent one of these exceptional cases. What does it mean, in psychological terms, if a society "should" practice circumcision but does not? If the psychological data on the Nilotes are any kind of guide, they indicate that the commonly achieved cultural "solution" to early low salience is not necessary to either individual or sociocultural viability. Yet this is not to say that all outcomes are equivalent. We have seen that ostensibly because of circumcision ceremonies the three East African neighbors of the Nilotes exhibit a lower level of sex-identity concerns than the Nilotes themselves. Presumably the Nilote male must invest psychic energy in trying to establish what he can never be sure about, i.e., his maleness, and presumably the circumcised adult males in the neighboring societies need not invest much psychic energy in this matter.[2] Therefore, although systems can exist without the "appropriate" fit between psychological dispositions and institutions it is conceivable that the individuals in such systems operate at a lower level of adaptedness. This suggestion, obviously no more than a guess at present, could be investigated in future research.

Underlying the theoretical position advanced above is the idea that the psychological constellation of sex-identity conflict, if shared by a significant proportion of the males in a society, can create institutional outcomes that in some way reflect or "project" the originating psychological disposition. The evidence, while consistent with theoretical expectations, shows only that there is usually a fit between the individuals and the institutions. Still needed is some demonstration that the historical emergence or disappearance of a given institution can be linked to the proposed psychological determinant. While the social science and behavioral science literature provide little data that would allow the tracing of psychological factors and concomitant institutional changes through time, one exploratory approach has been to study the problem at the microcultural, or small-group, level (Munroe & Faust, 1976). It was assumed in this work that if strongly and similarly motivated individuals were brought together in an interactive situation, they would implement institutions that expressed their common motivational disposition. As predicted, three preselected male groups—one psychologically feminine, one average, and one masculine (according to the results of two standardized masculinity-femininity tests)—ordered themselves appropriately on two of three "instrumental-expressive" tasks. The instrumental-expressive dimension, which appears cross-culturally in male-female sex roles and in the family (Zelditch, 1955), as well as in small-group interaction (Parsons & Bales, 1955), is typically conceived as having a task-oriented or masculine pole and a social-emotional or feminine pole. On the first task, the allocation of a hypothetical county budget, the psychologically feminine males allotted relatively more to expressive than to instrumental budget categories (e.g., recreation programs as opposed to industrial expansion), and the psychologically average and masculine males allotted respectively less. On the second task, the composition of an essay whose topic was designed to elicit both expressive and instrumental responses, use of the putatively expressive concept of "cooperation" was significantly correlated with degree of psychological femininity of the male groups. (For both tasks, the expressive pole of the dimension was established through administration of the measures to a group of females.) The members of the groups, in either evolving or originating these patterned modes of behavior among themselves, were loosely realizing the core meaning of the institutionalization process (Goldschmidt, 1966), and therefore it can be said that psychological masculinity-femininity appears to have affected institutional outcomes at the microcultural level. While the relevance of laboratory research to natural institutions remains an open question, the findings in this exploratory work are consonant with theoretical models that do assume a critical role for individual motivation.

SOCIOGENIC VERSUS PSYCHOGENIC EXPLANATIONS: FURTHER FINDINGS

In the cross-cultural studies testing the sex-identity hypothesis (Burton & Whiting, 1961; Munroe, Munroe, & Whiting, 1973), the customary sleeping arrangements of mother, father, and infant were used as an index of conditions which should cause conflict in sex identity and therefore lead to either circumcision ceremonies or the couvade as a sex-role resolution. Although sleeping arrangements comprise a theoretically interesting index of the relative salience of the father and mother as perceived by an infant, a recent study (see Chapter 7 in this volume) of environmental constraints on infant care practices has shown that the relation of an infant to caretakers during the day is more often reported in the ethnographic literature and more reliably judged when it is reported. Various measures of closeness of contact between mother and infant made on a large cross-cultural sample included the use of a sling or the arms versus a basket or cradle for carrying the infant, the use of a crib, cradle, or hammock versus the lap as a resting place, and light or no clothing versus heavy swaddling as a means of temperature control. Of these measures, carrying devices were shown to be the most reliable and the most often reported. When a cradle is used for carrying infants, the same device is usually used for sleeping (see Chapter 7 in this volume) ($\phi = 0.51$), and carrying devices therefore can be used as a substitute for sleeping arrangements in measuring perceived salience of the mother to the infant.

Devices such as the cradleboard used by many of the North American tribes, or the European baby carriage, or the Kurdish crib that is carried like a suitcase, provide little or no opportunity for close contact between an infant and its carrier. On the other hand, the shawl or sling which holds the infant on the carrier's back or hip keeps the infant in close bodily contact. Those societies in which an infant is carried in the arms provide similar close contact. In the "cradle" societies, an infant communicates with its caretakers distally and verbally, whereas in the sling or arm societies the communication is proximal and tactile-motoric. Such close contact has been described as producing symbiotic identification between infant and carrier.

Since the period of infancy, for the purpose of coding carrying devices, is limited to the first 6–8 months of life, the mother is the primary caretaker and carrier in most cultures. Older siblings are usually not permitted to carry an infant until it is older. Although fathers are permitted to hold the infant in some cultures, they generally do so infrequently and for short periods of time. In none of the societies of the sample was the father the primary infant carrier. For these reasons, we have assumed that societies in which infants are carried in a sling, shawl, or in the arms provide the conditions for a stronger identification of an infant with its mother than societies that use cradles, cribs, and baby carriages.

To learn whether or not carrying devices are a valid predictor of sex-identity conflict and at the same time explore the interaction of the two dependent variables —couvade and male circumcision rites—a new cross-cultural test was carried out.

The cases were divided into two categories, based on the carrying device score— *mother–infant close,* those societies where the infant was reported to be carried in a sling, shawl, or in the arms, and *mother–infant distant,* those in which the infant was carried in a cradle, carriage, or crib. The score for the presence or absence of circumcision was taken from column 37 of the Ethnographic Atlas (Murdock, 1967), "Male Genital Mutilations." Ritual circumcision was coded as present if it occurred during childhood, adolescence, or early adulthood. Six societies representing three language families were coded as practicing circumcision during infancy. Since we felt it unlikely that sex-identity conflict would have developed at such an early age, we omitted these cases from our calculations. In fact, however, had they been included with the *circumcision present* category, the associations presented below would have been slightly strengthened. Three cases in which the age of circumcision was not ascertained, and one in which it occurred after age 25 years, were also omitted.

The couvade scores were taken from our previous study (Munroe, Munroe, & Whiting, 1973) with some new cases added. The following definition was used for the presence of couvade observances: if strong supernaturalistic observances were reported for the father, such that they involved his deviating from normal activities for more than half the time over a period of 1 day or longer, then a rating of intensive couvade observances was assigned. Societies coded as practicing a nonintensive couvade were classed with the couvade-absent cases.

The first hypothesis to be tested may be stated as follows: *societies in which mothers are highly salient to their infants as a consequence of being carried in close contact should also perform male circumcision rites or practice the couvade or both as a method of resolving or expressing sex-identity conflict.*

The sample used to test the above hypothesis consists of 96 societies on which data were available for all three of the variables to be used—infant carrying devices, male circumcision rites, and the couvade.

To ensure a reasonable degree of historical independence among the cases in our sample, we used the procedure described in Chapter 7 of this volume. Each society was coded as to its membership in a language family as given in the Ethnographic Atlas, columns 64–66 (Murdock, 1967). In the tables presented below, both the number of societies and the number of language families represented are indicated for each cell. This permits an estimate of the variance that can be attributed both to functional and to historical factors.

As indicated in Table 18-1, it is evident that close mother-infant contact is strongly associated with the occurrence of male sex-role resolutions, i.e., either ritual circumcision during childhood or adolescence, the practice of the couvade, or both. The value of $\overline{phi}^2$ based on the distribution of language families in the table, and thus of cases that are historically independent, indicates that 39 percent of the variance is accounted for.[3] Since language families can be assumed to be reasonably independent, a test of statistical significance appropriately can be made. The obtained value of χ^2 is 6.44, $p < 0.02$. It can also be seen that the residual variance attributable to common origins, 0.19, is substantial, although approximately half that is attributable to the functional hypothesis.

The second test pertains to the effect of postmarital residence as a variable that determines the type of sex-role resolution chosen. In previous studies we assumed that patrilocal residence would predict circumcision ceremonies and matrilocal residence the couvade. To test this hypothesis, we again used variables taken from the Ethnographic Atlas (Murdock, 1967)—column 16, "Marital Residence." In this code a distinction is made between two types of residence in which the couple reside with or near the husband's kin. If the husband's kin are structurally aggregated in local-

TABLE 18-1   Mother-Infant Contact and Male Sex-Role Resolutions

Mother-Infant Contact	Male Sex-Role Resolutions*	
	Absent	Present
Close	25 (19)	47 (19)
Distant	21 (19)	3 (3)

The numbers in parentheses indicate the independent cases in each cell, i.e., the number of different language families represented, $\overline{phi}^2$ all cases, 0.58, includes sets of societies speaking languages of the same family and hence closely related historically. $\overline{phi}^2$ independent cases, 0.39 ($p = 0.001$), includes but one exemplar from each language family and thus represents an estimate of the proportion of the variance contributed by mother-infant contact. $\overline{phi}^2$ residual, 0.19, represents an estimate of the variance contributed by migration and common origins. For a discussion of the derivation of $\overline{phi}^2$ see Note 3.

*Male circumcision rites or the couvade or both.

TABLE 18-2 Mother-Infant Contact, Marital Residence, and Male Sex-Role Resolutions

Mother-Infant Contact	Marital Residence	Male Sex-Role Resolutions			
		Circumcision		Couvade	
		%	(n)	%	(n)
Close	Patrilocal	56	(34)	14	(22)
	Virilocal	10	(21)	36	(11)
	Neutral	17	(18)	36	(11)
	Uxorilocal	7	(14)	78	(9)
	Matrilocal	11	(9)	100	(3)
Distant	Patrilocal	13	(15)	0	(4)
	Virilocal	0	(22)	13	(8)
	Neutral	0	(10)	0	(5)
	Uxorilocal	0	(5)	0	(2)
	Matrilocal	0	(8)	20	(5)

Percentage of cases that practice either male circumcision rites or the couvade in each of two conditions of mother-infant contact and five types of marital residence. The values in each cell are based on the number of independent cases—i.e., one exemplar from each language group. The numbers in parentheses indicate the total number of independent cases on which each cell-value percentage is based. Scores were available for a larger number of cases on the presence or absence of circumcision ceremonies than for the presence or absence of the couvade.

ized unilineal kingroups, the case is coded as *patrilocal* (P). If the husband's kinsmen are *not* structurally aggregated or localized, the case is coded as *virilocal* (V). A similar distinction is made (in cases where the couple reside with or near the bride's kin) between *matrilocal* (M) and *uxorilocal* (U). These distinctions have been retained. The remaining categories—avunculocal, neolocal, and ambilocal—imply no preference with respect to gender and have been combined into a *neutral* category. Since in Table 18-2 the highest percentage for circumcision ceremonies is in the group with patrilocal residence, and for couvade with matrilocal residence, our hypothesis seems to be supported. A closer look at Table 18-2, however, suggests that it should be modified. Considering the cases with close mother-infant contact, our hypothesis would suggest that virilocal residence would favor circumcision rather than couvade, whereas the opposite is the case. In fact, for those cases that have either patrilocal or virilocal residence and either one or the other of the sex-role resolutions, the association between virilocal residence and couvade is statistically significant (p <0.001). Also, even though the percentages are higher for the occurrence of couvade with uxorilocal or matrilocal than with virilocal or neutral residence patterns, this difference is not statistically significant.

Thus it seems from Table 18-2 that in societies with close mother-infant contact the couvade may be practiced in any society that lacks a corporate patrilineage, and male circumcision rites tend to occur only in societies with such a social organization. Our revised hypothesis then would be as follows: given close mother-infant contact which produces an initial feminine identity, this will tend to be ritually rejected by circumcision rites in societies with corporate patrilineages and tend to be ritually expressed by the practice of couvade when corporate patrilineages are absent. Table 18-3 presents a test of the revised hypothesis. The results are reasonably robust for the cases of close mother-infant contact and strongly similar for each type of male sex-role resolution. Furthermore, despite the fact that circumcision has a geographic focus in sub-Saharan Africa and the couvade is most commonly reported for South America, the residual values are surprisingly low.

Finally, it should be evident from the above tables that circumcision and couvade are apparently alternatives and should not occur in the same society. In fact, there were only 2 societies in our sample of 96 that were reported to have both practices. Either the two customs are not as incompatible as our theory suggests or there has been a coding error.

In sum, then, this study supports the position that neither a sociogenic nor a psychogenic theory alone can account for the phenomena we have labeled male sex-role resolutions. Patrilocal residence, the sociogenic variable that we have used to predict male circumcision rites, is conceptually similar to and empirically highly related to "male solidarity groups," suggested by Young, and particularly to the Paiges' "strong fraternal interest groups" that are characteristic of societies with corporate patrilineages. It differs from Cohen's unilinear descent group category in that his would include matriclans which, in our sample at least, are associated not with male circumcision rites but with couvade. Our data more strongly support the Paiges' position that the couvade is associated with the absence of patrilineages rather than uniquely with the "mother-right" variable suggested by Bachofen or the "parenthood dramatization" variable suggested by Young.

Despite this correspondence between our sociogenic variables and those specified by other theorists, our hypothesis specifies that these variables are effective only in societies where infants are brought up in close body contact with their mother. In other words, our theory requires the interaction between sociogenic and psychogenic variables to produce the predicted result.

The evidence presented above, especially in Table 18-3, clearly indicates that residence rules have a significant effect only in the *mother–infant close* group. For the *mother–infant distant* group, their effect is negligible. None of the previous theories predicts this interactive finding. Thus we believe the evidence to date supports the hypothesis that events occurring in infancy may result in conflicts which are either resolved or expressed in culturally prescribed rituals.

TABLE 18-3 Mother–Infant Contact, Patrilocal Residence, and Male Sex-Role Resolutions

Mother–Infant Contact	Marital Residence	Male Sex-Role Resolutions			
		Circumcision		Couvade	
		Absent	Present	Absent	Present
Close	Patrilocal	22 (17)	32 (16)	31 (20)	5 (4)
	Other	81 (44)	8 (5)	22 (15)	20 (16)
	$\bar{\phi}^2$	0.46	(0.36†)	0.32	(0.26*)
Distant	Patrilocal	13 (13)	2 (2)	3 (3)	2 (2)
	Other	57 (44)	0 (0)	19 (17)	2 (2)
	$\bar{\phi}^2$		(NS)		(NS)

The numbers in parentheses indicate the number of independent cases in each cell, i.e., the number of different language families represented.
*$p < 0.02$.
$^\dagger p < 0.001$.

RESEARCH DIRECTIONS

At the cross-cultural level, possible differences among male solidarity groups, fraternal interest groups, and various patterns of residence, descent, and inheritance should be explored and their differential effect on initiation and the couvade estimated.

The effects of historical factors on the incidence of male initiation and the couvade have long been noted but not adequately discounted. Male initiation rites are limited largely to Africa and Oceania, the couvade to South America. The assumption that these two institutions were invented but once or twice and spread to neighboring societies from the point of origin must be considered more carefully than it has been.

The effect of environmental factors such as climate must also be considered. Both male initiation rites and the couvade are limited almost exclusively to societies situated in the tropics. It has been argued (J. Whiting, 1964, and Chapter 7 in this volume) that this is a consequence of the effect of climate on both sleeping arrangements and infant-carrying practices, but further investigation of environmental factors should be fruitful.

More intensive field studies of initiation and the couvade should be especially valuable. A careful investigation of the nature and duration of the liminal period and its psychological effect on the novice is badly needed. Only two studies—those of Herzog (1973) and Granzberg (1972)—have considered this problem.

A field study of the impact of industrialization and Western schooling on both the independent and dependent variables should be carried out. The shift from the polygynous extended family to the independent nuclear monogamous family has a profound effect on father salience. Pax Britannica and the advent of Western schooling have rendered obsolete the status of junior warrior and perhaps also of fraternal interest groups.

Further field studies of societies that deviate from cross-cultural prediction should be enlightening. What happens in societies that should have initiation rites or the couvade and do not, or in societies that have one or another of these institutions but lack the specified antecedent conditions?

There is much to be done.

ACKNOWLEDGMENTS

The authors are indebted to Charlene Bolton, Ralph Bolton, Karen Paige, Dee Posner, Susan Seymour, and Stella Vlastos for their aid in the preparation of this chapter. The work was also facilitated by a grant from the Research and Development Committee of Pitzer College.

NOTES

1. This account is taken from discussions and visits with Melissa Lewellyn-Davies during the time she was doing a field study of the Masai (1969–1973) and from a documentary film of which she was codirector, "The Masai Warrior" (Grenada Films, 1975).

2. This brings up the interesting question of whether the couvade-practicing Black Carib males, in apparently effecting a disguised and unconscious imitation of the female role through their couvade observances, are thus able to avoid investing

psychic energy in the issue of their essential maleness. Since the Black Carib and the Nilote males are so similar in their sex-identity profiles, a first reading of the question leads to a negative conclusion, but the problem should be investigated further.

3. $\overline{Phi}^2$ is an estimate of the variance accounted for, with adjustment for the skewness of the marginals in the original table. It is obtained by calculating the value of $\overline{phi}^2$ ($\overline{X}^2$) from the observed data and then calculating the maximum value of $\overline{phi}^2$ with the given marginals. This is done by setting the value of the smallest cell in the table at zero and adjusting the values in the remaining cells so that the marginals remain the same.

REFERENCES

Anthony, A. S. *A cross-cultural study of factors relating to male initiation rites and genital operations.* Unpublished doctoral dissertation, Harvard University, 1955.

Bachofen, J. J. *Das Mutterrecht.* Basel: Benno Schwabe, 1861.

Bettelheim, B. *Symbolic wounds.* Glencoe, Ill.: Free Press, 1954.

Biller, H. B. The father and personality development: Paternal deprivation and sex-role development. In M. E. Lamb (Ed.), *The role of the father in child development.* New York: John Wiley & Sons, 1976.

Burton, R. V., & Whiting, J. W. M. The absent father and cross-sex identity. *Merrill-Palmer Quarterly,* 1961, *7,* 85–95.

Carlsmith, L. Some personality characteristics of boys separated from their fathers during World War II. *Ethos,* 1973, *1,* 466–477.

Cohen, Y. A. *The transition from childhood to adolescence.* Chicago: Aldine, 1964.

Crawley, A. E. *The mystic rose.* London: Macmillan, 1902.

D'Andrade, R. G. Father absence, identification, and identity. *Ethos,* 1973, *1,* 440–455.

Daniels, R. E. *By rites a man: A study of the societal and individual foundations of tribal identity among the Kipsigis of Kenya.* Unpublished doctoral dissertation, University of Chicago, 1970.

Douglas, M. *Purity and danger.* London: Routledge & Kegan Paul, 1966.

Eliade, M. *Rites and symbols of initiation* (W. R. Trask, trans.). New York: Harper & Row, 1965. [Originally published in 1958]

Frazer, J. G. *Totemism and exogamy.* London: Macmillan, 1910.

Freud, S. *Moses and monotheism.* New York: Vintage Books, 1939.

Garibay Patron, M. La psicologia del Mexicano. *Revista Mexicana de Psicologia,* 1969, *3,* 350–354.

Goldschmidt, W. *Comparative functionalism: An essay in anthropological theory.* Berkeley: University of California Press, 1966.

Granzberg, G. Hopi initiation rites—A case study of the validity of the Freudian theory of culture. *Journal of Social Psychology,* 1972, *87,* 189–195.

Granzberg, G. The psychological integration of culture: A cross-cultural study of Hopi type initiation rites. *Journal of Social Psychology,* 1973, *90,* 3–7.

Greenstein, J. M. Father characteristics and sex typing. *Journal of Personality and Social Psychology,* 1966, *3,* 271–277.

Harrington, C. *Errors in sex-role behavior in teenage boys.* New York: Teachers College Press, 1970.

Hendrick, S. J. *Gender identity and belief in invariance of gender among boys with gender identity alienated fathers.* Unpublished doctoral dissertation, Harvard University, 1970.

Herzog, J. D. Initiation and high school in the development of Kikuyu youths' self-concept. *Ethos,* 1973, *1,* 478–489.

Hetherington, E. M., & Deur, J. L. The effects of father absence on child development. In W. W. Hartup (Ed.), *The young child* (Vol. 2). Washington, D.C.: National Association for the Education of Young Children, 1972.

Hogbin, H. I. A New Guinea infancy: From conception to weaning in Wogeo. *Oceania,* 1943, *13,* 285–309.

Holmberg, A. R. *Nomads of the long bow.* Washington, D.C.: Smithsonian Institution, Institute of Social Anthropology, Publ. No. 10, 1950.

Howe, J. *Caymanian drinking behavior.* Unpublished honors thesis, Harvard College, 1966.

Karsten, R. Contributions to the sociology of the Indian tribes of Ecuador. *Acta Academiae Aboensis,* 1920, *1,* 1–75.

Kitahara, M. Living quarter arrangements in polygyny and circumcision and segregation of males at puberty. *Ethnology,* 1974, *13,* 401–413.

Mead, M. *Male and female.* New York: New American Library, 1949.

Munroe, R. L. *Some studies of cross-sex identity.* Paper presented at the Annual Meeting of the American Anthropological Association, Philadelphia, November 1961.

Munroe, R. L. *Couvade practices of the Black Carib: A psychological study.* Unpublished doctoral dissertation, Harvard University, 1964.

Munroe, R. L., & Faust, W. L. Psychological determinants of institutions in a laboratory microculture. *Ethos,* 1976, *4,* 449–462.

Munroe, R. L., & Munroe, R. H. Male pregnancy symptoms and cross-sex identity in three societies. *Journal of Social Psychology,* 1971, *84,* 11–25.

Munroe, R. L., & Munroe, R. H. Psychological interpretation of male initiation rites: The case of male pregnancy symptoms. *Ethos,* 1973, *1,* 490–498.

Munroe, R. L., & Munroe, R. H. *Cross-cultural human development.* Monterey: Brooks/-Cole, 1975.

Munroe, R. L., Munroe, R. H., & Nerlove, S. B. Male pregnancy symptoms and cross-sex identity: Two replications. *Journal of Social Psychology,* 1973, *89,* 147–148.

Munroe, R. L., Munroe, R. H., & Whiting, J. W. M. The couvade: A psychological analysis. *Ethos,* 1973, *1,* 30–74.

Murdock, G. P. Ethnographic atlas: A summary. *Ethnology,* 1967, *6,* 109–236.

Murdock, G. P., & White, D. R. Standard cross-cultural sample. *Ethnology,* 1969, *8,* 329–369.

Muriuki, G. *History of the Kikuyu 1500–1900.* Nairobi: Oxford, 1974.

Osgood, C. E., Suci, G. J., & Tannenbaum, P. H. *The measurement of meaning.* Urbana, Ill.: University of Illinois Press, 1957.

Paige, K. E., & Paige, J. M. The politics of birth practices: A strategic analysis. *American Sociological Review,* 1973, *38,* 663–676.

Paige, K. E., & Paige, J. M. *Politics and reproductive rituals.* Berkeley: University of California Press, in press.

Parsons, T., & Bales, R. F. (Eds.). *Family, socialization and interaction process.* Glencoe, Ill.: Free Press, 1955.

Reik, T. Ritual. In M. Mead & N. Calas (Eds.), *Primitive heritage.* New York: Random House, 1953.

Rohrer, J. H., & Edmonson, M. S. (Eds.). *The eighth generation.* New York: Harper & Row, 1960.

Rubel, A., & Spielberg, J. Aspects of the couvade in Texas and northeast Mexico. *Summa anthropologica en homenaje a Roberto J. Weitlaner.* Mexico: Instituto Nacional de Antropologia e Historia, 1966.

Santrock, J. W., & Wohlford, P. Effects of father absence: Influences of, reasons for, and onset of absence. *Proceedings of the 78th Annual Convention of the American Psychological Association,* 1970, *5,* 265–266.

Schlegel, A., & Barry, H., III. *Cultural correlates of adolescent initiation ceremonies.* Paper presented at the Annual Meeting of the Society for Cross-Cultural Research, Chicago, February 1975.

Spiro, M. E. An overview and a suggested reorientation. In F. L. K. Hsu (Ed.), *Psychological anthropology.* Homewood, Ill.: Dorsey Press, 1961.

Turner, V. W. *The forest of symbols: Aspects of Ndembu ritual.* Ithaca, N.Y.: Cornell University Press, 1967.

Tylor, E. B. On a method of investigating the development of institutions: Applied to laws of marriage and descent. *Journal of the Royal Anthropological Institute of Great Britain and Ireland, 1889, 18,* 245–272.

van Gennep, A. *Les rites de passage.* Paris: E. Nourry, 1909.

Whiting, B. B. Sex identity conflict and physical violence: A comparative study. *American Anthropologist,* 1965, *67* (6, part 2), 123 –140.

Whiting, J. W. M. Resource mediation and learning by identification. In I. Iscoe & M. Stevenson (Eds.), *Personality development in children.* Austin: University of Texas Press, 1960.

Whiting, J. W. M. Socialization process and personality. In F. L. K. Hsu (Ed.), *Psychological anthropology.* Homewood, Ill.: Dorsey, 1961.

Whiting, J. W. M. Effects of climate on certain cultural practices. In W. H. Goodenough (Ed.), *Explorations in cultural anthropology.* New York: McGraw-Hill, 1964.

Whiting, J. W. M., & Child, I. L. *Child training and personality.* New Haven: Yale University Press, 1953.

Whiting, J. W. M., Kluckhohn, R., & Anthony, A. The function of male initiation ceremonies at puberty. In E. E. Maccoby, T. M. Newcomb, & E. L. Hartley (Eds.), *Readings in social psychology* (3rd ed.). New York: Holt, Rinehart & Winston, 1958.

Young, F. W. *Initiation ceremonies.* Indianapolis: Bobbs-Merrill, 1965.

Zelditch, M., Jr. Role differentiation in the nuclear family: A comparative study. In T. Parsons and R. F. Bales (Eds.), *Family, socialization and interaction process.* Glencoe, Ill.: Free Press, 1955.

19

The Cultural Management of Sexuality

Gwen J. Broude

Studies of human sexuality range over a number of disciplines, addressing a variety of questions and employing diverse theoretical frameworks and methodologies. Nevertheless, researchers concerned with the study of human sexual behavior agree upon two things. The first has to do with the enormous power of sexuality as a motivating influence upon human behavior; the second concerns the enormous potential of sexuality as both an integrative and a disruptive force in human society. Thus as regards the management of sexuality, society is charged with the performance of a most delicate balancing act. On the one hand, sexual behavior needs to be constrained and channeled in such a way as to minimize its capacity to undermine social cohesiveness; on the other hand, sexual impulses must be allowed sufficient rein so as to insure both the survival of society and the mental well-being of its members.

This view of the role of society in the management of sexuality is borne out by the ethnographic evidence. Thus the regulation of sexual behavior is a cultural universal; no known human culture allows sexuality to be expressed in an entirely unrestrained way. Nevertheless, there is also tremendous variation in how specific societies direct and elaborate the biologic given of human sexuality. This circumstance raises a minimum of three questions. Each has its representation in the cross-cultural literature.

The initial question suggested by the ethnographic data concerns the patterning of sexuality per se; that is, given the fact that cultures differ as to their treatment of sexuality, is there method to their madness? Does a society that prohibits sex play for children also show equal constraint as regards adolescent and adult sexuality? Does a permissive attitude toward extramarital sex predict indulgence of homosexuality or immodesty of dress and speech? In brief, granted that there is diversity in the patterning of sexuality from one society to the next, to what extent do sex norms and practices aspire to consistency within a particular cultural context? This question has special significance inasmuch as academic anthropologists and popular opinion tend to describe societies as essentially permissive or restrictive in their overall sexual orientation.

The second question raised by the ethnographic data concerns the correlates and antecedents of variations in the cultural patterning of sexual behavior. This question goes beyond the issue of consistency in sexual outlook within a particular culture.

Thus, given the latitude in how societies deal with sexuality, it remains for us to account for the specific orientation that an individual society displays. Why are some societies restrictive and others permissive regarding particular aspects of sexuality?

Finally, the question arises as to the implications of specific patterns of sex norms and practices. That is, how does the cultural management of sexuality affect the social and psychological functioning of the individual? Further, in what ways is the structure of society itself affected by its sexual orientation?

Each of these questions has received attention from anthropologists interested in human sexuality, and each will be treated here. The review will begin with a discussion of hypotheses and findings dealing with the antecedents and correlates of cross-cultural variations in a series of sexual attitudes and practices. This will be followed by a consideration of the issue of consistency in the patterning of sex norms and behaviors per se within and across cultures. The specific effects of a culture's sexual orientation upon the psychological and social adjustment of the individual are noted throughout this chapter. Finally, a number of suggestions will be offered regarding future research. It should be noted that the review of the literature is selective; it is confined largely to work that is cross-cultural in nature. Because cross-cultural studies involve a specific methodology and because studies of sexuality present special methodologic problems, a discussion of the cross-cultural method and its implications for the study of human sexuality precedes the review of the literature.

THE CROSS-CULTURAL METHOD

The cross-cultural method is at once a strategy for doing research and a way of formulating questions that research is meant to address. In brief, cross-cultural studies concern the testing of hypotheses by use of statistical procedures. This particular conception of the purpose and strategy of anthropological investigation lends rigor to cross-cultural studies; it also imposes a number of constraints and creates a number of potential problems. The most fundamental constraints upon cross-cultural research are methodologic; they have to do specifically with sampling and measurement. Attempts to conform to these constraints are sometimes hampered by the state of the ethnographic literature; this is especially true for studies on sexuality. The absence of detailed and reliable data not only frustrates the researcher regarding methodology, it also affects the scope and sophistication of the hypotheses that can be tested. Finally, cross-cultural researchers sometimes run into problems of interpretation once a study has been completed.

Methodology

The testing of hypotheses in cross-cultural research involves making inferences about relationships between and among variables in an entire population based upon data taken from a sample. In order for inferences to be legitimate, a number of guidelines must be adopted in the process of sample selection. Thus samples should include cases that are both independent and representative of the population with which the researcher's hypotheses are concerned. Further, there are lower limits in terms of sample size beyond which inferences are no longer justified.

The criteria of independence and representativeness of cases have been a source of some controversy among cross-cultural anthropologists; however, the *Standard Cross-Cultural Sample* (Murdock & White, 1969) has done much to resolve sampling problems and is now being widely used by cross-culturalists. Researchers using the cross-cultural method deal with the problem of reliability in that data are generally rated by a minimum of two independent coders; extent of agreement between coders is then assessed and reported in published studies. On the other hand, demands of sample size and validity of measures remain a potential source of frustration for some cross-cultural researchers, and this is largely attributable to the quality of the ethnographic data. While ethnographic reports are often detailed and accurate as regards their treatment of a variety of aspects of culture and behavior, making it relatively easy to accommodate to criteria of sample size and validity of measures, there are a number of areas of investigation that are of interest to cross-culturalists but for which information is neither extensive nor entirely trustworthy. As a result, samples tend to be small and measurement validity can become problematic. This is particularly true for the domain of sexuality.

Data

The initial problem confronting the study of sexuality is that of sheer availability of data. Many ethnographers neglect any mention of sexual matters, in part because collecting data of this sort is especially ticklish and in part because sexuality is not always considered an appropriate focus of inquiry. When data are reported, accuracy becomes a real problem; this can be a function of suspected distortions on the part of subjects or the ethnographer. Thus verbally elicited data may be overstated or understated, depending upon the inclinations of the informant. As to the observation of sexual behavior, the problems need no elaboration. Ethnographer bias is equally a concern. Much of the available information on sexuality has traditionally come from missionary accounts that tend to take a dim view of indigenous sexual mores and behaviors; the contemporary field worker sometimes tilts in the opposite direction. Even accurate data are seldom detailed, the preponderance of material on sexuality being rather sketchy in nature. These problems of the quality and quantity of data on sexuality make it difficult to conform to the demands of sample size and sampling procedures; they also handicap the researcher in terms of the validity of measures and the degree of detail that codes can reflect.

Coding

Because data on sexuality are often lacking in detail, codes are sometimes quite crude in terms of their ability to distinguish among gradients of attitudes and behaviors. Some scales include only two or three points and therefore make only gross discriminations in terms of the patterning of sex norms and practices across cultures. Codes measuring the frequencies of sexual behaviors are associated with a set of problems as a result of the way that data are reported. Thus it is characteristic of ethnographic accounts to state that a specific sexual activity is "not uncommon"; this can be interpreted to mean that the behavior is almost universal, that it is quite common, or that it is frequent but not pervasive. This kind of reporting makes both code construction and rating extremely cumbersome and reduces the sensitivity of codes on frequencies of sexual behaviors.

It is also the case that while ethnographers will report the presence of a particular sexual attitude or practice, they will fail to report its absence explicitly. A number of cross-cultural studies on sexuality include "present–absent" scales, yet the failure of the ethnographer to make any mention of a particular norm or behavior is not always sufficient reason to infer that it does not exist in a given culture. The result is that "present–absent" codes tend to be skewed; that is, there is a preponderance of cases that are reported as "present" concerning a specific variable and few that are coded as "absent." This makes the analysis of data very difficult, inasmuch as some cells have few cases. Where researchers do take absence of data to mean absence of the phenomenon itself, then ratings become less accurate.

Scope of Hypotheses

The state of the ethnographic data not only imposes methodologic problems upon cross-cultural research, it also affects the formulation of hypotheses. The problem is not idiosyncratic to studies of sexuality; it characterizes much of cross-cultural research. However, problems having to do with the stating of hypotheses are especially salient in investigations of sex norms and practices because of the especially poor quality of these data. The difficulty has to do in particular with formulating hypotheses that take into account the effects of two or more independent variables upon a dependent variable. This problem specifically affects studies that attempt to trace the antecedents and correlates of specific sex norms and practices.

The first limitation having to do with the stating of hypotheses is related to the fact that specific sex norms and practices are characteristically associated with a number of independent variables that are themselves highly correlated. This is recognized by cross-cultural researchers who therefore would prefer to formulate hypotheses in terms of the relative effects of a set of independent measures upon a dependent sex variable. However, the small sample sizes upon which many such studies depend make it impossible to assess the unique variance associated with one independent variable while controlling for others. As a result, hypotheses are generally confined to predicting relationships between one antecedent variable and a consequent variable; further, studies generally fail to jeopardize their research hypotheses by controlling for confounding variables after the fact.

It is also the case with cross-cultural research that, while each of two antecedent variables fails to predict a dependent variable by itself, the conjunction of the two will do so. However, the same problem of small sample sizes makes multivariate analysis difficult. Thus studies attempting to isolate antecedents or correlates of particular sex norms and behaviors sometimes fail to uncover important relationships because these are too complicated for available procedures to handle.

Interpretation of Findings

A final problem associated with cross-cultural research has to do with the interpretation of the underlying significance of a set of findings once a study has been completed. The difficulty can be traced in part to the use, especially in studies testing psychological hypotheses, of what are variously called intervening, mediating, or proxivariables. The terms are more or less synonomous and refer to the particular way in which variables in cross-cultural research are operationalized. Specifically, because it is often impossible to find direct measures of the kinds of variables with which cross-cultural research deals, investigators sometimes resort to indirect measures. This means that the relationship between the proxivariable and its referent is inferred by the researcher. While this can again be attributed in part to the sketchiness of the ethnographic data, it also arises from the fact that psychological anthropologists often deal with aspects of personality for which there are no direct measures. The result is that different studies commonly depend upon identical proxivariables to test entirely different hypotheses; then identical associations between variables are interpreted in various studies according to entirely different explanatory frameworks. While this discrepancy among interpretations of identical findings can be initially confusing, it tends to advance rather than hinder such research, and for a minimum of two reasons. First, varying interpretations of the same correlations do not so much contradict as complement each other; that is, each is likely to deal with a different, but compatible, level of social or psychological reality. Second, it is an axiom of psychological theory that human behavior is overdetermined, which is to say that human thoughts, emotions, and actions are generally motivated by a combination of factors. Thus different interpretations of identical associations often highlight the principle of overdetermination in human motivation.

Summary
Cross-cultural research in general and studies on sexuality in particular are associated with a unique set of goals, demands, and problems. Such studies attempt to conform to a specific set of constraints of sampling, sample size, and measurement. The poor quality of data on sexuality per se makes it difficult to meet these requirements and also frustrates the formulation of hypotheses. The use of proxivariables in a number of studies on sexuality at once complicates and enriches the analysis of variations in sex norms and practices across cultures. As specific studies of sexuality are reviewed, mention will be made of the extent to which each study conforms to the requirements of cross-cultural research and of the ways in which the investigator(s) has tried or failed to resolve problems of hypothesis formulation and interpretation. As cross-cultural studies depend upon statistical procedures in the testing of hypotheses, χ^2 and correlation coefficient values, as well as levels of statistical significance, will be noted when these are reported by the researcher. Readers should be aware that a statistically significant result is not an absolute measure of the power of a hypothesis. Correlation coefficients may reach an accepted level of significance while leaving a major portion of the variance in dependent variables unexplained. Further, as sample size increases, smaller and smaller coefficients are needed in order to reject the null hypothesis. Finally, χ^2 tests, which predominate in cross-cultural research, assess only the degree to which variables are or are not independent; they do not isolate the strength of association between variables. Therefore, in assessing the viability of any hypothesis, the reader should take note of a variety of factors, including sampling procedures, sample size, reliability and validity of measures, and appropriateness of the interpretation of findings proposed by the researcher.

ANTECEDENTS AND CORRELATES OF SEX NORMS AND PRACTICES

Studies attempting to isolate antecedents and correlates of specific sex norms and practices are limited in terms of the kinds of sex variables with which they deal. The major effort has involved hypotheses relating to premarital sex norms for females; this emphasis reflects the relatively thorough coverage of premarital sex in the ethnographic literature. Extramarital sex and homosexuality receive some limited attention, as do a variety of norms and behaviors assumed to measure sex anxiety. Research into the causes and correlates of sex norms and practices will be reviewed topically, beginning with norms of premarital sex for females. To date, no studies have been devoted to a consideration of attitudes towards male premarital sex; this may be a consequence of the generally indulgent way in which societies treat the sexual behavior of unmarried males. Neither has frequency of premarital sex received much attention in the literature.

Premarital Sex Norms for Females

By and large, studies concerned with variations in premarital sex norms across cultures look to social structural explanations to account for differences in how premarital sex is regarded from one society to the next. These studies view attitudes towards premarital sex as essentially pragmatic responses to social structural or economic constraints operating within a culture. A few researchers trace permissiveness and restrictiveness to underlying psychological dispositions, and one researcher looks in particular to child rearing, and specifically to mother–child interaction, as the precursor of premarital sex norms.

The earliest cross-cultural study of variations in premarital sex norms is Murdock's analysis of the social structural correlates of permissiveness and restrictiveness (1964). Murdock's study is based upon data taken from 180 societies representing the major world culture areas; ratings for all variables included in the study were taken from the *Ethnographic Atlas* (Murdock, 1967). Thus his measure of premarital sex norms is a collapsed version of John T. Westbrook's code for rules regarding premarital sex, the first and most extensively used scale codifying attitudes toward premarital sex for females.

Murdock makes three distinctions in terms of cross-cultural variations in rules regarding premarital sex. Restrictive societies are those wherein premarital sex is prohibited and in fact rare. Permissive societies, by contrast, are more or less indulgent as regards the sexual behavior of unmarried girls. Intermediate between these two types are societies where sanctions against premarital sex are not consistently enforced, with the result that sexual activity is relatively frequent, or where restrictive rules are conditional. It should be noted that Westbrook's codes combine a consideration of both norms and frequency of premarital sexual behavior. This is a pronounced strength of the code, since societies that prohibit sexual behavior for unmarried girls nevertheless differ in terms of their responses to contraventions of these rules.

Murdock includes six independent variables in his study, each reflecting an aspect of social structure or economy, and all discriminating between simple and complex cultures. Five of these are reported to predict premarital sex norms with reasonable success, although Murdock does not include formal statistical tests in his study. Thus as societies range from simple to complex in terms of descent rules, residence rules, subsistence economy, community size, and belief in high gods, rules regarding premarital sex become more restrictive. Political organization does not predict norms of premarital sexual behavior.

While Murdock notes the tendency of this set of associations to support the evolutionary hypothesis that premarital sex norms are related to cultural complexity per se, he is himself not entirely persuaded by that argument. Rather, he explains these associations in more pragmatic terms, and in particular as adaptations to the constraints of social structural and economic contingencies. The association between economy and premarital sex norms is thus explained in terms of the relative demands that different types of subsistence activity place upon the individual. Intensive agriculture requires industry and self-discipline, and prohibitions against premarital sex are seen as a mechanism for directing young people toward the acquisition of the skills and traits needed for adult roles. Where, by contrast, subsistence activities require less discipline and rigor, and particularly where success depends upon independence and initiative, then premarital sex becomes less of a problem. Hence the relationship between permissive premarital sex norms and simple tiller and hunter–gatherer societies.

Murdock explains the relationship between demography and premarital sex norms in similarly pragmatic terms. Thus permissiveness is associated with small communities because external regulation is less necessary and less effective in groups of this kind. Further, where small groups are kin based, rules of exogamy decrease the necessity for restrictive premarital sex norms. It should also be noted that knowing your neighbors has another advantage in terms of the consequences of premarital sexual activity, although Murdock does not propose this interpretation. In small communities, where individuals are familiar with one another, premarital pregnancies are more easily managed, inasmuch as it becomes relatively easy to identify the father and to place pressure on him to rectify matters, either by marriage or other compensation. Large communities, on the other hand, tend to be comprised of people who have only superficial acquaintanceship or who are strangers. This makes it more difficult to exert pressure upon the father of an illegitimate child to meet his responsibilities. The problems associated with premarital pregnancies are increased where mobility is introduced; in that case, it becomes less likely that an aggrieved family will find the father at all.

While Murdock proposes no detailed explanation of the association between belief in high gods and premarital sex norms, he does note a number of difficulties related to the interpretation of these data. Presence of a belief in high gods is correlated with restrictive premarital sex norms, while absence of high gods is related to permissive rules regarding premarital sex. However, the correlation is confounded by a minimum of two factors. First, many of the cases coded as including a belief in high gods are Muslims or Christians, so that the association may reflect differences among religious systems rather than the influence of high gods in general. A more damaging indictment of the association has to do with the nature of the scale measuring high gods. Thus one index for determining ratings on this code concerns whether or not a culture has a god who is actively concerned with human morality. High gods falling into this category generally oversee human sexual behavior, including the sexual activity of the unmarried. What this means is that the two variables of high gods and premarital sex norms are not independent.

The final two associations isolated by Murdock are those between descent and residence rules and premarital sex norms. Thus patrilocal, patrilineal societies tend to be restrictive, whereas matrilineal and matrilocal societies are unlikely to be restrictive. Further, permissiveness is associated with neolocal or ambilocal residence. Murdock finds the last correlation puzzling but proposes that where these residence patterns obtain, the absence of a cohesive kind group might tend to undermine the parents' capacity to enforce prohibitions against premarital sex. Murdock notes in passing that the association between patrilineal, patrilocal societies and restrictiveness supports the widely held assumption that consolidation of power and authority by males is likely to result in expectations of virginity in unmarried women. While Murdock suggests no explanation for that assumption, other researchers do elaborate upon the rationale behind the relationship between male authority and restrictive premarital sex norms.

At about the time that Murdock was investigating the relationships between premarital sex norms and measures of social structure and economy, an independent team of researchers, under the direction of John Whiting at Harvard University, was also conducting a study of the causes and correlates of variations in premarital sex norms. The Palfrey House project was responsible for the construction and rating of a number of codes dealing with a variety of sexual beliefs and behaviors as well as with the formulation and testing of a set of hypotheses concerning the antecedents of variations in sexual orientation across cultures. Neither the codes nor the findings originating at Palfrey House have been published in a formal way; however, Goethals (1971) has reported some preliminary hypotheses and trends concerning premarital sex norms as these were isolated by J. Whiting and Goethals.

In his report on the factors affecting premarital sex norms, Goethals notes the congruence of his own findings with those isolated by Murdock; however, the interpretations of these findings differ. He also notes the tentative nature of the trends and interpretations he presents. The report is tentative in a number of ways, and particularly in terms of its lack of methodologic rigor. Data were taken from the Human Relations Area Files; however, there is no mention of sampling procedures or sample size, and no tabulations of data or tests of significance are reported. The Palfrey House code on premarital sex norms does not appear in the article, nor are the sources of other measures used in the study cited. Nevertheless, the associations and interpretations appearing in Goethals' preliminary report are intriguing and provide an extremely provocative starting point for other studies of premarital sex norms.

While the premarital sex code upon which the Goethals article is based has not been published, copies do exist in manuscript. The code measures attitudes towards premarital sex per se and does not take into account the extent to which norms are enforced by a culture. The scale rates societies on a five-point scale in terms of whether premarital sex is strongly approved, accepted without positive or negative sanctions, mildly disapproved, moderately disapproved, or strongly disapproved. Moderate disapproval implies a high valuation of virginity before marriage; where premarital sex is strongly disapproved, virginity is generally required.

The first set of associations reported by Goethals is between premarital sex norms and residence and descent rules. Thus permissive rules regarding premarital sex are found in matrilineal, matrilocal societies, while restrictiveness is characteristic of patrilineal, patrilocal cultures. Regarding the relationship between locality and premarital sex norms, Goethals suggests that in matrilocal societies unmarried mothers still enjoy the economic and social support of their kin groups in raising their children, so that premarital pregnancies are not particularly disruptive in that social structural context. As to lineality, Goethals remarks that where descent is traced through the father the position of an illegitimate child is ambiguous, whereas in matrilineal societies the problem of illegitimacy does not arise. Goethals proposes a further explanation for the association between patricentered societies and restrictiveness which elaborates upon Murdock's interpretation of this relationship. In particular, he suggests that restrictive premarital sex norms may, in fact, be an outcome of universal male anxieties about sexual adequacy which, however, can be practically resolved only in patrifocal cultures where men have sufficient clout to restrict the behavior of women.

A second association reported in this study is that between attitudes toward premarital sex and the presence or absence of bride-price, permissiveness being typical of cultures with no bride-price and restrictiveness being characteristic of societies where bride-price is present. Goethals interprets these findings in terms of the market value of women; thus where bride-price is traditional, virginity becomes an important bargaining chip in the sense that prospective husbands are unlikely to pay premium prices for "damaged goods."

In a set of unpublished papers, Goethals (n.d.) isolates a further association between premarital sex norms and allocation of social status. Specifically, permissiveness is correlated with ascribed status and restrictiveness with achieved status. The relationship is explained in terms of upward mobility; in societies with a fluid class structure, fathers make an effort to prevent their daughters from forming liaisons with males whose credentials might damage the social standing of the girl and her family.

The Goethals and Murdock studies clearly complement each other. Thus both isolate an association between descent and residence rules and premarital sex norms; while Murdock focuses upon the significance of the relationship between neolocal and ambilocal residence and permissiveness, Goethals provides the explanation for the correlation between restrictiveness and patricentered societies that Murdock glosses over. While both researchers propose pragmatic interpretations for the relationship between residence and descent and rules regarding premarital sex, Murdock is concerned with the effects of the absence of cohesive kin groups upon a society's capacity to enforce regulations. Goethals, in contrast, focuses upon the differential significance of premarital pregnancies in cultures with dissimilar social structures. The fact that Goethals replicates Murdock's finding is significant because each study uses different measures of both independent and dependent variables. The Goethals study also supports Murdock's cultural complexity hypothesis; specifically, Goethals' independent measures of bride-price and allocation of status discriminate between simple and complex cultures and predict permissiveness and restrictiveness in accordance with the evolutionary theory suggested by Murdock. The implications of the agreement between these two studies should nevertheless be tempered to some degree with the reminder that neither has entirely conformed to the demands of methodology; since neither has used a sample that is representative of the entire population about which inferences are being made, statements as to the global relationships between premarital sex norms and residence and descent rules, or cultural complexity, are not justified. Murdock explicitly notes this problem in his own study and cites it as his reason for failing to apply statistical procedures to his data.

In his cross-cultural study of premarital permissiveness, Eckhardt (1971) further elaborates a theme explored by Goethals (1971) and also by Coleman (1966) to the effect that premarital sex norms can be best understood in terms of the market place mentality, specifically as it applies to marriage. Eckhardt's hypothesis takes off in particular from exchange theory; within this framework, marriage is seen as a bartering of "goods" wherein potential spouses and their kind attempt to maximize the gains and minimize the costs that each is likely to incur as a result of a match. In this context, Eckhardt distinguishes between two exchange models on the basis of the direction in which resources flow at marriage. Thus there are societies where resources are largely in the hands of males and flow to females; in other societies resources are controlled by women and their kin so that males have little to barter upon marriage. Where females are on the receiving end of exchange arrangements, women and their kin will find it to their advantage to use sex itself as an item of barter in return for the social and economic benefits that will accrue to them from a match

—hence restrictive premarital sex norms to increase the value of sex. Where, by contrast, women and their kin are already in control of major resources, there is little reason to inflate the market value of sex as an additional bartering good; under these circumstances, women are free to indulge their sexual impulses before marriage. Thus variations in premarital sex norms are viewed in terms of the extent to which important goods are controlled by men or by women.

Eckhardt's test of the relationship between premarital sex norms and flow of resources at marriage is based upon a sample of 153 societies drawn from Murdock's *World Ethnographic Sample*. Premarital sex norms are measured using Westbrook's code; the scale is collapsed into the three categories of permissive, semirestrictive, and restrictive as these are defined in Murdock's study. The independent variable of control and flow of resources is measured by three scales as constructed by the author; these are residence and descent rules and the contribution of women to the economy. A fourth variable, degree of autonomy in choice of spouses, is also introduced; this is measured indirectly by the presence or absence of property exchange at marriage. Data for the independent measures were taken from the Human Relations Area Files.

The results of Eckhardt's study are ambiguous. While all findings are in the direction predicted by Eckhardt's overall hypothesis, none of the associations that he reports is especially strong. Matrilineal societies tend to be more permissive than otherwise; 61 percent of these cultures are permissive, 39 percent are semirestrictive, and none are restrictive ($n = 18$). Patrilineal societies, by contrast, tend to be nonpermissive; of 67 societies coded as patrilineal, only 30 percent are permissive, while 28 percent are semirestrictive and 43 percent are restrictive. While there is a clear trend here, the λ value of 0.10 suggests only a weak association between premarital sex norms and descent.

Residence rules similarly tend to be associated with rules regarding premarital sex. Matrilocality is related to permissiveness; of the 32 societies coded as matrilineal, 47 percent are permissive and 30 percent are semirestrictive, while only 16 percent are restrictive. By contrast, patrilocality tends to predict restrictiveness; of the 97 patrilocal societies included in the sample, 29 percent are restrictive and 40 percent are semirestrictive, while only 31 percent are permissive. The λ value is again 0.10, suggesting that this relationship is also weak.

The correlation between premarital sex norms and the relative contribution of women to the economy is even less striking. Thus where women are in the top quartile in terms of their economic importance, 47 percent of societies are permissive, 37 percent are semirestrictive, and 16 percent are restrictive ($n = 43$); while for societies where women are in the bottom quartile, 30 percent are permissive, 40 percent are semirestrictive, and 30 percent are restrictive ($n = 40$). The λ value of 0.04 for this association is the weakest reported by Eckhardt.

The strongest correlation isolated in the study is between premarital sex norms and autonomy of choice of marriage partners as measured by property exchange at marriage. Thus where there is little or no property exchange at marriage, 44 percent of societies are permissive, 37 percent are semirestrictive, and only 19 percent are restrictive ($n = 57$). Where exchange is present, 30 percent are permissive, 38 percent are semirestrictive, and 28 percent are restrictive ($n = 96$). The λ value for this association is 0.19.

As a final test of the hypothesis that restrictive premarital sex norms reflect an inflated valuation of sex as a consequence of male control of resources, Eckhardt also tested the combined effects of his four independent measures upon premarital sex norms. Thus societies were coded in terms of the number of factors present in each that reflect control of resources along the male axis. Thirty-five societies were rated as favoring males over females over all four variables; of these, 31 percent were restrictive, 20 percent were semirestrictive, and 29 percent were permissive. At the other end of the continuum were five societies where all independent variables tilted towards favoring females; none of these societies were restrictive. The γ value for this last test is 0.15, suggesting again a weak correlation. The skew in this sample in the direction of male control of resources to some extent impedes Eckhardt's cumulative test of the exchange theory hypothesis, as Eckhardt himself notes.

While Eckhardt's study makes a significant contribution to the literature on variations in premarital sex norms in terms of its particular explanatory framework, the study is in fact essentially a replication of the Murdock and Goethals examinations of the antecedents and correlates of permissiveness and restrictiveness, at least in terms of the way in which the independent variables in Eckhardt's study are operationalized. In essence, Eckhardt is again testing the associations between premarital sex norms and descent, residence, and the presence or absence of bride-price and other forms of exchange at marriage. The three studies both overlap and diverge to some extent in terms of the particular codes and samples they use; nevertheless, they agree as to the overall significance of their findings to the effect that residence, descent, and property exchange are all modestly associated with permissive and restrictive rules regarding premarital sex.

Eckhardt's proposal that premarital sex norms will be affected by the relative importance of women in the economy complements a set of findings reported by Barry, Josephson, Laurer, and Marshall (1977) concerning permissiveness and restrictiveness. While the Barry et al. study is essentially concerned with introducing a new set of codes on child training, a number of correlations between these new scales and other codes are reported, including the relationship between the relative valuation of males and females in childhood and premarital sex norms. Valuation of the sexes is measured by a new code which distinguishes among societies in terms of whether girls are favored, boys are favored, or boys and girls are valued roughly equally. Premarital sex norms are measured by a new scale (Broude & Greene, 1976); the code is collapsed into three points and distinguished between societies that approve of premarital sex for females, societies that place some restrictions upon sexual behavior, and societies that strongly disapprove of premarital sex and place a high premium upon virginity. The Broude and Greene code is similar to the Goethals scale; however, both Broude and Greene and Barry et al. use the *Standard Cross-Cultural Sample* in making their ratings. While Barry et al. have no particular hypothesis in mind, they do report a relationship between valuation of the sexes in childhood and rules regarding premarital sex; specifically, norms tend to be more permissive where girls are valued at least as highly as boys and restrictive when boys are more highly valued ($n = 124$). Further, valuation of the sexes is itself related to lineality. Using the Murdock and White (1972) code for descent rules, Barry et al. report that only 3 of 72 patrilineal societies value females over males, while only 1 of 24 matrilineal societies favor males over females. This last finding is provocative in terms of its implications for the association between descent and premarital sex norms as this has been isolated by Murdock, Goethals, and Eckhardt. In particular, permissiveness and restrictiveness are predicted by both lineality and valuation of the sexes which variables are, in turn, related to each other. The combined work of

Murdock, Goethals, Eckhardt, and Barry et al. suggests a complicated interrelationship among descent, residence, the valuation of females, and the practical contributions made by women as these affect rules regarding premarital sex. A productive line for future research might involve an examination of the relationships among these independent variables themselves as well as an analysis of the relative importance of each in predicting premarital sex norms per se.

The studies reviewed so far interpret permissive and restrictive rules regarding premarital sex as practical responses to social structural constraints operating within a society. However, a number of researchers take the position that attitudes towards premarital sex reflect, or are at any rate compatible with, certain psychological biases on the part of members of a society. All studies equating premarital sex norms with psychological predispositions incorporate the notion of restrictiveness as a reflection of anxiety, although the nature and source of the anxiety are interpreted differently from one study to the next. Thus Ayres (1967) uses premarital sex norms as a measure of sex anxiety in her study of pregnancy taboos; she finds that permissiveness and restrictiveness, as measured by the Westbrook code, are significantly correlated with sex taboos during pregnancy, so that permissiveness is associated with short pregnancy taboos and restrictiveness with long taboos ($n = 25$, $p < 0.01$). Similarly, in his cross-cultural study of the oedipal complex, Stephens (1962) includes premarital sex norms as an item in his composite sex anxiety scale. Again, Goethals (1971) proposes that restrictive premarital sex norms may be a male defense against anxiety about sexuality.

The proposition that restrictiveness reflects sex anxiety receives some support in a study on premarital sex norms by Broude (1975b); here, a significant relationship is isolated between norms of premarital sexual behavior and sex socialization. Premarital sex norms are measured by the Westbrook scale. Sex socialization is measured by the Whiting and Child composite code, which rates societies in terms of the degree to which they punish immodesty, masturbation, and heterosexual and homosexual play in childhood. This code is assumed by Whiting and Child as well as other researchers to indicate the extent to which cultures promote sex anxiety as an outcome of socialization practices.

Of the 16 societies coded as low on sex socialization in this study, 15 were permissive in their attitudes towards premarital sex and 1 was restrictive. By contrast, of the 14 societies that were high on sex socialization anxiety, 5 were permissive and 9 were restrictive ($\chi^2 = 11.3$, $p < 0.001$). While these findings suggest a clear relationship between sex training and premarital sex norms in this sample, two warnings are in order. The first has to do with interpretation—specifically, the theory that punishment for sexual behavior in childhood creates anxiety about sex is an inference. Thus the findings reported in this study point to a relationship between prohibitions against sexual behavior for children and for the unmarried, but they do not necessarily imply that restrictive premarital sex norms are a reflection or a consequence of sex anxiety per se. The second warning is methodologic. In particular, the size of sample and choice of cases upon which these findings depend mean that inferences about the general relationship between sex socialization and premarital sex norms should be made with caution.

The hypothesis that premarital sex norms are related to sex anxiety is undermined by a second set of findings reported in this study. Specifically, rules regarding premarital sex are found to be unrelated to adult sex anxiety as measured by a composite scale constructed by Minturn, Grosse, and Haider ($n = 63$). Neither are premarital sex norms associated with menstrual or postpartum sex taboos, although the latter are interpreted as reflections of sex anxiety by Stephens. Thus the theory that restrictiveness is a manifestation of anxiety about sexuality receives only inconsistent, and on the whole negative, support.

In the same cross-cultural study of premarital sex norms, Broude tests a second psychological hypothesis to the effect that restrictive rules regarding premarital sex have to do with fear, not about sex per se, but about emotional involvement. Anxiety about emotional involvement is, in turn, traced to inaccessible and unpredictable mothering. Thus where mothering is characterized by inaccessibility, this is predicted to lead to a mistrust in interpersonal relationships in general and to an avoidance of premarital sexual involvement in particular. By contrast, where mothering is accessible and predictable, trust in others and a willingness to risk premarital sexual commitments are predicted. Accessibility of mothering is measured by the Barry and Paxson code which rates societies in terms of the amount of time that babies are held or carried. Where infants are carried for more than half of the day, a society was coded high on accessibility; where infants are carried for half of the day or less, a society was rated as low on accessibility. Premarital sex norms were measured using the Westbrook code; cultures were dichotomized as permissive or restrictive. All societies included in this analysis appear in the *Standard Cross-Cultural Sample.*

Accessibility of mothering was found to be significantly related to premarital sex norms, and in the predicted direction. Thus of the 26 societies coded as high on accessibility, 21 were permissive and 5 were restrictive. By contrast, of the 29 societies rated as low on accessibility, 8 were permissive and 21 were restrictive ($\chi^2 =$ 17.4, $p <$0.001). These findings are congruent with the hypothesis that restrictive premarital sex norms are related to fear of emotional involvements as much as to anxiety about sexuality per se.

In the same study, the relationship of premarital sex norms to a number of other aspects of caretaking is assessed—display of affection by caretakers; age of onset of independence training; ease or difficulty of independence training; number of caretakers; and age of weaning. The first variable is measured by a code constructed by Barry, Bacon, and Child; the last is measured by an unpublished Palfrey House scale. The remaining variables are taken from a set of child-rearing codes constructed by Barry and Paxson. Sample sizes ranged from 37 to 73 cases. None of these child-rearing variables is significantly related to premarital sex norms. Thus of all the child-training measures predicted to influence rules regarding premarital sex, only severity of sex training and accessibility of mothering bear any significant relationship to permissiveness and restrictiveness.

To summarize, premarital sex norms have been found to be associated with varying degrees of significance with descent and residence rules; subsistence economy; level of technology; size of community; belief in high gods; property exchange at marriage; relative valuation of boys and girls; women's contribution to subsistence economy; class stratification; severity of sex training; and accessibility of mothering. Further, these variables all tend to discriminate between simple and complex cultures, and Murdock explains the association between a number of these variables and premarital sex norms in terms of cultural complexity per se. However, the proposition that it is cultural complexity that accounts for variations in rules regarding premarital sex is not entirely satisfying; the question still remains as to why simpler cultures are permissive and more complex societies restrictive. Those studies that focus on a single antecedent variable as it predicts premarital sex norms are more successful in pinpointing a specific underlying rationale for permissiveness and restrictiveness; however, taken as a body, they present a fragmented picture of the factors affecting attitudes toward premarital sex. In fact, studies of premarital sex norms provide an embarrassment of hypotheses with very little synthesis of theoretical positions and propositions from one investigation to the next.

There is a further problem associated with research on variations in premarital sex norms, and particularly with studies focusing on the social structural correlates of permissiveness and restrictiveness. This has to do with the fact that the specific set of antecedent variables upon which these studies depend are themselves highly intercorrelated. As a result, it is impossible to tell whether a particular social structural variable in fact predicts variations in premarital sex norms or whether a significant finding is really an artifact of other, untested, social structural contingencies. The problem is to some extent resolved by a set of findings reported in the study of premarital sex by Broude (1975b). In that study, a regression analysis is run with the specific intention of synthesizing a number of independent investigations of rules regarding premarital sex, and specifically the studies of Murdock, Goethals, Eckhardt, and Broude. The regression analysis assesses the proportion of unique variance in premarital sex norms accounted for by six independent variables— residence rules; descent rules; class stratification; bride-price; belief in high gods; cultural complexity; and accessibility of mothering. Cultural complexity is measured by a composite scale constructed by Murdock subsequent to the publication of his study on premarital sex norms; the other independent variables are measured using the same codes found in the original studies.

The regression analysis suggests that when the predictive power of each independent variable is assessed while holding the others constant, only class stratification, cultural complexity, and accessibility of mothering still account for more than 0.01 of the unique variance in premarital sex norms. Accessibility of mothering accounts for 0.24, class stratification for 0.046, and cultural complexity for 0.027 of the variance. The other social structural variables drop out entirely as predictors of rules regarding premarital sex.

These findings suggest two things about variations in premarital sex norms. As regards the social structural variables, while individual measures reflecting complexity of culture do not in general retain their predictive power in the regression analysis, the composite measure of cultural complexity accounts for some, although not much, of the variance. This suggests that a combination of factors conducive to restrictiveness need to coexist in a given social context for restrictive norms to become operative. The associations that were isolated in the studies reviewed here may in fact be a function of the inclusion in the samples of societies where such a combination of factors existed. Thus Murdock's proposition that it is cultural complexity per se that accounts for restrictiveness is supported, although the particular reason for the association remains unexplained. It is also the case that accessibility of mothering proves to be a better predictor of premarital sex norms than any of the social structural variables; this measure has ten times the predictive power of the next best predictor. The temptation is to infer that a psychological interpretation, and in particular a developmental explanation, of permissiveness and restrictiveness is the most persuasive hypothesis to come out of studies on premarital sex thus far. In any event, even when the combined effects of the social-structural and child-rearing variables are taken into account, two-thirds of the variance in premarital sex norms is still unexplained. Clearly, other factors are operating to influence attitudes toward premarital sex that have been neglected by cross-cultural researchers.

Extramarital Sex Norms

Unlike premarital sex norms, rules regarding extramarital sex tend to be interpreted as much within a psychological as within a social-structural framework. Of the studies reviewed here, two depend upon a social-structural explanation of extramarital sex norms, while three attribute permissiveness and restrictiveness to psychological factors. The research tends to be less elegant for extramarital than for premarital sex in the sense that hypotheses are, in general, not formally tested. Two of the studies are essentially comparative in nature; that is, they depend upon contrasts of two or three cases in the testing of theories. The remaining studies conform in varying degrees to the definition of cross-cultural research.

In his study of mechanisms of political control, Cohen (1969) examines the relationship between extramarital sex norms and levels of political integration. The research is based upon a sample of 60 societies, each case of which represents one of the culture areas in Murdock's *World Ethnographic Sample*. Codes for political integration as well as for attitudes toward extramarital sex and other sex practices are constructed by the author. Cohen bases his conclusions upon trends in his data and performs no statistical tests of his hypotheses.

Cohen begins by making a distinction between forms of state organization. Thus he discriminates between the incorporative and the expropriated state. The incorporative state consists of a number of geographically contiguous and culturally equivalent local groups; in the expropriated state the ruling elite is clearly at a more culturally advanced level than the ruled.

As regards extramarital sex norms per se, Cohen's focus is on the inchoate incorporative state, that is, the transitional state wherein rulers are attempting to consolidate power over culturally equivalent local groups. It is this level of political integration that is associated with severe sanctions against extramarital sex in the form of capital punishment. Cohen explains this association in pragmatic terms. Thus the primary task of leaders of the inchoate state is at once to undermine local allegiances and subordinate local communities to the ruling elite. Severe sanctions against extramarital relations have the effect of isolating and intensifying the marital dyad at the expense of wider kin and community loyalties; therefore punishment for extramarital sex is interpreted as a political weapon serving to fragment the solidarity of existing networks to the benefit of the new rulers.

Cohen also reports a relationship between the inchoate incorporative state and capital punishment for incest and for infringement of vows of celibacy. He explains institutionalized celibacy as a reflection of psychological conflicts about the meaning of marriage and parenthood in states where the cultural definition of marriage is undergoing a profound change. As to punishment for incest, Cohen points out that incestuous relationships, however these are defined by a particular society, tend to create tensions among members of a kin group. Since it is in the interests of the leaders that local groups retain some degree of harmony and integrity while the political system remains in a state of transition, punishment for incest becomes a mechanism for achieving that end. Thus sanctions against extramarital sex serve to undermine local allegiances, which allegiances punishment for incest helps to perpetuate. The reasoning is somewhat strained.

A more straightforward social structural explanation for variations in attitudes towards extramarital sex is found in the Rosenblatt and Hillabrant (1972) study on adultery and divorce for childlessness (see Chapter 17 in this volume). The researchers report a significant relationship between attitudes towards extramarital sex and grounds for divorce. Thus where divorce for childlessness is disallowed, extramarital sex norms tend to be permissive. Indulgence of extramarital relations is in essence an escape hatch for couples who would otherwise be unable to have children.

Abernethy (1974) proposes an alternative interpretation for variations in extramarital sex norms in her study of dominance and sexual behavior. The study is not technically cross-cultural, since she relies upon data from only three societies in the testing of her hypothesis. However, the research she presents draws upon ethologic evidence and psychoanalytic theory and findings as well as cross-cultural comparisons in a way that might be usefully implemented by other social scientists.

It is Abernethy's intention to explore the relationship between relative male–female dominance and male sexual orientations, including attitudes toward extramarital sex. More specifically, Abernethy proposes that where women are dominant over men, there will be a tendency for male sexual behavior to be inhibited. By contrast, male dominance is predicted to result in uninhibited sexuality. Abernethy's cross-cultural evidence is drawn from the Trobriands, Hopi, and Haida. In none of these societies are men dominant over women. Further, there is a trend in these cultures for men to undervalue sex within marriage, for divorce to be frequent, and for expectations of fidelity to be minimal.

Abernethy also notes the power of her dominance hypothesis in explaining the mother–son incest taboo as a cultural universal. Thus by virtue of the fact that mothers are everywhere dominant over their young sons, the incest taboo may be a reflection of the tendency of male subordination to women to extinguish male sexual impulses. Abernethy further extrapolates her hypothesis to the brother–sister incest taboo. Thus in the Trobriands the idea of mother–son incest appears not to create anxiety in males, while brother–sister incest is profoundly threatening. Abernethy suggests that the Trobriand response to brother–sister incest is a function of male–female dominance, inasmuch as sisters are dependent upon their brothers.

Abernethy's dominance hypothesis as it applies to extramarital sex norms is indirectly tested in a study by Broude (1975a). Extramarital sex norms are run against three measures of female dominance, specifically descent and residence rules and the relative contribution of women to the subsistence economy. The first two variables were measured by codes constructed by Murdock and Wilson (1972); the last was taken from the *Ethnographic Atlas*. The study was undertaken with the express intention of testing the Abernethy dominance hypothesis, so that matrilineality, matrilocality, and minimal contribution of males to subsistence were all meant to reflect female dominance. Extramarital sex was measured by a scale constructed by Broude and Greene and distinguishing between permissive and restrictive extramarital sex norms for wives. The 106 societies comprising the sample all appear in the *Standard Cross-Cultural Sample*.

Neither residence rules nor contribution of women to the economy were significantly related to extramarital sex norms. Lineality was found to be significantly related to rules regarding extramarital sex ($\chi^2 = 6.2$, $p = 0.047$). However, this last relationship is accounted for by the strong association between patrilineality and restrictive extramarital sex norms; 11 patrilineal societies in this sample are permissive and 33 are restrictive. Of the 13 matrilineal societies included in the study, 8 are permissive and 5 are restrictive. The trend is not sufficient to indicate a strong relationship between matrilineality and rules regarding extramarital sex. It should be noted that none of these independent measures directly measures relative male–female dominance. They do, on the other hand, reflect the kinds of prerogatives that Abernethy had in mind in the formulation of her original hypothesis. To the extent that descent, residence, and contributions to subsistence do reflect, or are associated with, relative dominance, Abernethy's hypothesis is not supported.

In his long-term study of childhood associations and sexual attraction in Taiwan, Wolf (1966; 1968; 1970) proposes a psychological hypothesis concerning extramarital sex norms and behavior that provides a fascinating parallel to Abernethy's comments on brother–sister incest among the Trobriands and similar societies. Wolf is concerned with exploring a number of conflicting hypotheses relating to the origins of the incest taboo; within that context, he also isolates a number of intriguing relationships between forms of betrothal in Taiwan and extramarital sex. Again, Wolf's study is not cross-cultural; his research is limited to a comparison of couples sharing a single cultural tradition. His hypotheses and findings, however, speak to a central controversy among anthropologists; further, Wolf's work is open to replication on a cross-cultural basis.

It is Wolf's intention to assess the major, and contradictory, theories regarding the meaning of the incest taboo. Briefly, what Wolf calls the sociological and biological interpretation of sanctions against incest states that intimate childhood associations lead to an intensification of sexual attraction; incest taboos are thus seen as social mechanisms serving to counter these impulses. This argument is in contrast to the psychological position, which proposes that for a number of reasons sexual impulses will be inhibited between individuals who have been reared together. According to this line of reasoning, incest taboos are a reflection of the flattening of sexual attraction between childhood intimates. Whereas the argument among anthropologists concerning the effects of childhood association upon sexual attraction has proceeded largely on a theoretical level, Wolf provides concrete evidence in support of the psychological point of view.

Wolf's evidence derives from the differential consequences of two coexisting forms of marriage in Taiwan. In the "grand" or "major" form of marriage, the bride enters her husband's household at the time of the marriage ceremony itself; often the bride and groom are virtually strangers. This is in contrast to the "minor" form of marriage, where future wives are raised by and live with their future husband and in-laws. It is Wolf's contention that the marital histories of couples married by the minor form provide empirical evidence concerning the effects of intimate childhood associations upon sexual attraction. In fact, the relationships of couples married in the minor form differ in a number of important ways from those of couples married in the grand form. Thus for minor marriages males are far more likely to visit prostitutes, to live with mistresses after their wives have had children, to have fewer children of their own, and to divorce. Similarly, wives married in the minor form are more likely to engage in extramarital sexual relations, although adultery for a wife is considered to be a quite serious infringement. Thus where future spouses are reared under the same roof, marriages tend to be brittle, sexual relations strained, and extramarital sex relatively common. What is more, individuals married in the minor mode appear to be indifferent to the infidelities of their spouses.

Wolf interprets the relationship between childhood association and sexual inhibition within marriage in terms of the effects of joint socialization. Thus children who are reared together are taught to inhibit impulses as these are directed towards members of the household. Socialization centers predominantly on the punishment of aggression; however, this becomes generalized to include sexual gratification. Wolf notes here the finding, reported by Beach, to the effect that male mammals tend not to engage in sexual activity in environments where they have formerly been punished. In the human case, socialization environments include and are associated with members of the household. Thus children who are raised together on the one hand are explicitly trained to inhibit instinctual impulses, since these would otherwise be directed to family members, and on the other hand come to equate family members with punishment in general.

Wolf's study is provocative for a number of reasons. First, it is an ingenious test of the origins of the incest taboo. There is also a sense in which Wolf's findings contradict the Abernethy hypothesis concerning the effects of male–female dominance upon brother–sister incest taboos. It is Abernethy's contention that where brothers are dominant over their sisters, sexual attraction, at least for males, ought to increase. In fact, girls who are raised by their in-laws in Taiwan are reported to be treated in the classical stepdaughter mode; their status is less than ideal as compared with that of the other children in the household. If Abernethy's hypothesis were operating here, the prediction would be in favor of increased sexual attraction between couples married in the minor form. In fact, the opposite obtains. Finally, Wolf's study provides a baseline for cross-cultural research into variations in sexual orientation in general and in extramarital sex norms and behavior in particular. In particular, his findings raise the question of the extent to which attitudes toward and frequency of extramarital sex differ cross-culturally as a function of differences in the degree to which married couples have enjoyed a certain familiarity in childhood.

The cross-cultural study of extramarital sex by Broude cited earlier (1975a) complements Wolf's findings in that it focuses specifically upon the relationship between husband–wife intimacy and norms of extramarital sexual behavior. Degree of intimacy between spouses is measured indirectly by men's houses; extramarital sex norms are coded in terms of whether a society holds a single standard or a double standard concerning attitudes toward extramarital sex for males versus females. The men's houses code is taken from the unpublished Palfrey House codes; the extramarital sex code was constructed and rated by Broude and Greene. The sample includes 46 societies, all of which appear in the *Standard Cross-Cultural Sample.*

Presence or absence of men's houses is related significantly to rules regarding extramarital sex as measured by the double standard. Thus of the 16 societies that hold to a single standard (equally permissive or restrictive for husbands and wives), only 4 have men's houses. In contrast, of the 30 societies holding the double standard (wives punished more severely than husbands), 20 have men's houses. In brief, the double standard is typical in societies where husbands spend their time away from their wives and in the company of other men, while the single standard characterizes societies where men have no institutionalized meeting place. The relationship is significant below the 0.01 level ($\chi^2 = 7.2$).

While the independent variable of men's houses is social structural in nature, the association is interpreted by Broude as highlighting a psychological dimension of attitudes toward extramarital sex. Specifically, it is noted that where men's houses are the rule, males are essentially distancing themselves from their spouses, perhaps in part because of an underlying antagonism towards women. Similarly, the double standard can be seen as reflecting some degree of hostility towards women. Double standard societies universally restrict the sexual behavior of females while allowing males relative sexual freedom. Thus the association between men's houses and the double standard is interpreted as a function of the tendency of both to reflect hostility towards females.

In the same study of extramarital sex, Broude also tests the relationship between the double standard and severity of sex socialization as measured by the Whiting and Child composite code. Thus of the 10 societies that had a single standard, 8 were low on sex socialization anxiety and 2 were high. Of the 18 societies that had a double standard, 7 were low on sex socialization anxiety and 11 were high. The results are statistically significant ($p = 0.04$); however, the size of the sample as well as the choice of cases suggests caution in inferring a global relationship between sex training and extramarital sex norms.

Finally, a regression analysis on extramarital sex norms is run by Broude to assess the relative power of a number of independent variables in predicting rules regarding extramarital sex across cultures. The independent measures include residence and descent rules; relative contribution of women to the economy; cultural complexity; sex socialization; and men's houses. Men's houses and sex socialization retain their power to predict extramarital sex norms; however, the remaining variables drop out of the analysis. As a unit, these variables account for 0.26 of the variance in rules regarding extramarital sex.

While anthropologists have proposed a number of hypotheses to account for variations in both extramarital sex norms and behaviors across cultures, the preponderance of these hypotheses have not been tested in a formal sense. It is therefore difficult to assess the viability of these theories. The only variables found to be correlated with permissiveness and restrictiveness by use of the cross-cultural method are lineality, men's houses, and sex socialization. Lineality, however, accounts for less than 0.01 of the unique variance in extramarital sex norms when other factors are held constant. Abernethy's dominance hypothesis receives no support from the indirect test of her proposal by Broude. Further, the dominance hypothesis is to some extent contradicted by Wolf's findings and his interpretation of those findings. Cohen reports interesting trends in terms of the relationship between inchoate incorporative states and restrictive extramarital sex norms; however, his theory applies to a restricted set of circumstances and has no direct bearing upon permissiveness and restrictiveness on a more global level. The association between the double standard and men's houses reported by Broude suggests a connection between extramarital sex norms and intimate versus aloof marital relationships; this theme also appears in the work of Abernethy and Wolf. The association between restrictiveness and permissiveness and sex socialization underscores the power of child training regarding sexuality in its effects upon adult sexual orientation; premarital sex norms were also significantly related to this same measure of sex socialization. In terms of hypotheses and findings appearing in the literature to date, perhaps the most productive line of research for the future might involve a consideration of the interrelationships among sex training, childhood associations, husband–wife relationships, and extramarital sex norms as these affect and are affected by each other.

Homosexuality
While any cross-cultural study of sexuality confronts problems of both methodology and interpretation, the difficulties are especially pronounced for research into homosexuality in particular. On the most basic level, data, regardless of quality or

detail, are less available on homosexuality than they are for many other sex variables. Thus while codes on premarital and extramarital sex have been consistently rated on samples of well over 100 societies at a minimum from one study to the next, attitudes towards homosexuality have been coded on a maximum of 52 societies (Minturn et al., 1969), and frequency of homosexuality has been rated on a maximum of 70 societies (Broude & Greene, 1976). Scales measuring norms of homosexual behavior are capable of making fine discriminations; the Minturn et al. (1969) and Broude and Greene (1976) codes both distinguish among societies where homosexuality is strongly disapproved, mildly disapproved, ridiculed, ignored, accepted, or not understood, although the scales are not identical. On the other hand, data on the incidence of homosexuality are not consistently detailed in the ethnographic literature. Thus while Minturn et al. differentiate among societies in terms of increasing percentages of incidence of homosexuality, Broude and Greene discriminate only between societies where homosexuality is absent or rare and societies where it is present and not uncommon. In fact, actual frequency counts of homosexual activity are uncommon in ethnographic accounts.

As regards attitudes towards homosexuality, researchers also confront a special problem of interpretation. A major issue in anthropology concerns the significance of taboos or prohibitions upon specific behaviors; briefly, these are alternately seen as social mechanisms constraining individuals from engaging in behaviors for which there is strong motivation, or as reflections of profound motivation to avoid certain behaviors because of the anxiety they provoke. This conflict of interpretation underlies the controversy over the meaning of the incest taboo as outlined earlier; it also applies to the study of attitudes towards homosexuality. Thus researchers are faced with the choice between explaining sanctions against homosexuality either as a cultural regulation prohibiting a compelling drive toward homosexuality or as a psychological manifestation of an avoidance response to homosexual behavior.

In fact, there is cross-cultural evidence to support both positions. A study by Broude (1975a) reports the association between norms and incidence of homosexuality, as measured by the Broude and Greene codes, as follows: of 15 societies where homosexuality is rare or absent, 14 also ridicule or condemn the practice and 1 accepts or ignores it; of 19 societies where homosexuality is not uncommon, 8 accept or ignore the behavior and 11 ridicule or condemn it ($\gamma = 0.821$; $p < 0.001$). The finding that a greater number of societies condemn homosexuality when it is present than accept or ignore it suggests that taboos do sometimes serve to counter strong inclinations to engage in homosexuality. On the other hand, the development of a taboo in response to homosexual inclinations is not universal. Thus there are 8 societies in this sample that accept or ignore the relatively frequent practice of homosexuality. One question raised by these findings concerns the divergence in cultural response to strong homosexual tendencies; that is, why do some societies erect taboos prohibiting a prevalent homosexual tendency among its members while other societies allow this same tendency to go unchecked?

The theory that restrictions against homosexuality are a manifestation of anxiety about homosexual behavior also receives some support. In their cross-cultural study of sexual beliefs and behavior, Minturn et al. (1969) assess the relationship between attitudes toward homosexuality—as measured by their own code—and their composite measure of adult sex anxiety. Rules regarding homosexuality are associated significantly with adult sex anxiety in a sample of 45 societies ($r = 0.20$, $p < 0.05$). However, the relationship is quite weak; sex anxiety accounts for only 0.04 of the variance in norms of homosexual behavior. The findings tend to support the results reported by Broude. Specifically, homosexuality is profoundly threatening to some, but not all, societies; when the idea of homosexual behavior does provoke anxiety, severe sanctions against the practice result.

While the relationship between attitudes and incidence of homosexuality is a vital issue for researchers interested in the cultural management of sexuality, most studies have tended to focus upon the antecedents of frequency of homosexuality per se while ignoring the relationship between the regulation and practice of homosexual behavior. Hart (1968) proposes a developmental explanation for the tendency to engage in homosexuality. Specifically, he traces homosexual practive to close and collaborative same-sex friendships; these, in turn, are viewed as a consequence of segregation of the sexes in childhood. In particular, Hart suggests that where male–male chumships predominate, males experience what is in essence an arrested psychosexual development; they become fixated in the same-sex dyad, and this eventually manifests itself in overt homosexuality. Hart derived his theory from his work in the Philippines and did not test it cross-culturally.

In the study cited above, Minturn et al. propose and test a theory of homosexuality that is similar to the hypothesis formulated by Hart. Specifically, they predict that homosexuality will be accepted and frequent in societies where adolescents are segregated into same-sex groups. The hypothesis rests upon essentially the same reasoning proposed by Hart; segregation of the sexes is thus seen as weakening heterosexual impulses and strengthening homosexual relationships. In fact, neither norms ($n = 44$) nor frequency ($n = 59$) of homosexuality are significantly correlated with segregation of the sexes at adolescence. These findings, however, do not refute directly the Hart hypothesis; Hart's argument assumes a separation of the sexes well before adolescence.

Minturn et al. also assess the relationship of norms and incidence of homosexuality and a number of child-training variables, including sex training in childhood, age of independence training, and length of the postpartum sex taboo. None of these variables is significantly related to attitudes toward or frequency of homosexuality.

In her comparative study of dominance and sexuality, Abernethy (1974) explains homosexuality within the same framework used to interpret male sexual orientations in general. Thus homosexuality is seen as an outcome of female dominance over males. Her hypothesis is based upon clinical findings to the effect that homosexuals are characteristically reared in families where mothers are perceived as having maximum power while fathers are seen as distant and ineffectual. Boys thus reject their own masculinity in favor of a feminine identification, which is then acted out in homosexual behavior.

Abernethy does not test the relationship between homosexuality and female dominance; however, the dominance hypothesis is assessed on a cross-cultural sample by Broude (1975a). Female dominance is again measured indirectly by the variables of descent and residence as taken from the Murdock and Wilson codes. Norms and frequency of homosexuality are measured by the Broude and Greene codes. Neither descent nor residence is significantly related to attitudes regarding or frequency of homosexuality. Thus to the extent that these measures reflect female dominance the dominance hypothesis is not supported.

In the same study, the effects of family relationship upon norms and incidence of homosexuality are assessed. Family relationships are measured by the following five independent variables: family structure, father's role as caretaker, mother–child sleeping arrangements, husband–wife rooming, and the postpartum sex taboo. None of the family relationship variables were found to be significantly related to either norms or frequency of homosexuality; however, an interesting trend does emerge. Specifically, homosexuality is largely absent in monogamous nuclear families, in households where husbands and wives room together, and in families where fathers are the regular companions of their children. Homosexuality is also ridiculed or condemned in these circumstances. The findings are interpreted in psychological terms. Where sons are in active competition with their sexually superior fathers for mother's affection, then sexual adequacy becomes a major concern—hence sanctions against behaviors indicating failure in heterosexual relationships. Absence of homosexuality in father-salient, husband–wife intimate families is seen as a consequence of these negative sanctions. While there are clear trends in the data presented in this study, two comments are in order. First, the sample sizes for frequency of homosexuality are too small to allow more than tentative conclusions. More important, these data suggest only trends; no findings were reported to be statistically significant.

To summarize, homosexuality has not been extensively studied by cross-cultural anthropologists. This may be due in part to the absence of data, especially on the frequency of homosexuality, in the ethnographic literature. Societies appear to diverge significantly in terms of their responses to homosexual tendencies in males. Some cultures exhibit a relaxed attitude towards homosexual behavior, while others erect severe sanctions to counter the homosexual inclinations of adult men. The origins of these differences have not been successfully tapped. Thus sex socialization per se appears not to affect either norms or incidence of homosexual behavior in any predictable way; neither does segregation of the sexes at adolescence. There is a tendency for nuclear family households where parents and children interact frequently and intimately to be associated with both condemnation and absence of homosexuality. Perhaps more sensitive measures of family patterns and family relationships will predict variations in homosexuality with more success than has been the case thus far.

Sex Anxiety

A number of cross-cultural studies concerned with human sexuality have attempted to isolate the causes and correlates of what is glossed in the literature as sex anxiety. These studies present a serious problem of interpretation because of the disposition on the part of researchers to assume that any restriction, deviation, preoccupation, or elaboration relating to sexual concerns must reflect an underlying anxiety about sexuality. Ayres (1967), Stephens (1962), and Goethals (1971) all assume that restrictive premarital sex norms are a reflection of sex anxiety. Montgomery (1974) and Bettelheim (1954) both interpret menstrual taboos as a manifestation of castration anxiety which is, in turn, equated with anxiety about sex. Stephens (1962; 1967) proposes a similar interpretation of menstrual taboos and also measures sex anxiety in terms of genital injury, severing, and physical injury as themes in folk tales. In his study of the Oedipus complex, Stephens (1962) also introduces a composite measure of sex anxiety which includes the items of restrictive premarital sex norms; length of pregnancy taboos; punishment for sexual intercourse in folk tales; presence of sexual explanations for illness; and sex avoidance therapy for illness. Minturn et al. (1969) have constructed a composite scale of sex anxiety in adulthood which includes no less than 11 items. These include concern about impotence, genital size, or lack of sexual experience; impotence or sterility as grounds for divorce; impotence or sterility attributed to witchcraft; avoidance of sexual topics in public or around relatives; shame at the sight of someone's genitals; danger associated with having intercourse with pregnant, nursing, or menstruating women; danger associated with excessive indulgence in or thoughts about sex; assumption of a disparity between the sexes in enjoyment of sex; love affairs kept secret; belief that continence is necessary for the success of some important endeavors; and cleansing during or after intercourse. There is some, but not consistent, evidence to the effect that a number of these variables tend to coexist in a given cultural context. This suggests that such variables form a constellation of related customs and preoccupations which may reflect a specific orientation about sexuality. The point is that the relationship of these measures to sex anxiety in particular is only inferred. Therefore studies into the antecedents and consequences of sex anxiety should be viewed with caution. There follows an overview of the cross-cultural research into the consequences of socialization practices assumed to result in anxiety about sexuality. The review will then be expanded to a more general consideration of the causes and correlates of sex anxiety.

The notion of anxiety first appears in the Whiting and Child (1953) study of child rearing and personality. The authors are interested in testing a set of hypotheses concerning the effects of socialization for five behavior systems upon adult patterns of personality. Extrapolating from Freudian theory, Whiting and Child propose that to the degree that a behavior is gratified or frustrated in early life, the result will be a positive or negative fixation concerning that behavior as reflected in a variety of adult projective systems. The childhood behaviors with which the study deals include orality, anality, sexuality, aggression, and dependence. Positive and negative fixations on specific behaviors are measured by the extent to which those behaviors play a role in adult belief systems relating to the origins and treatment of illness.

As regards sexuality per se, Whiting and Child focus upon three aspects of sex training in childhood. Specifically, they are concerned with assessing the degree of sex satisfaction experienced by a child, the degree of sex anxiety fostered by socialization practices, and the age of onset of sex socialization. Societies are assessed in terms of their treatment of four aspects of sexual behavior in childhood; these are modesty, masturbation, and homosexual and heterosexual play. To the extent that these behaviors are punished, it is assumed that anxiety about sexuality will result; to the extent that they are indulged, a society is scored high on sex satisfaction in childhood. Studies assessing the relationship between sex socialization and premarital, extramarital, and homosexual norms and behaviors as reviewed earlier have used the Whiting and Child sex anxiety socialization scale as their independent measure.

The Whiting and Child findings concerning the relationship between sex socialization and the role of sexuality in adult responses to illness are mixed. Punishment for sexual behavior in childhood predicts the avoidance of sexual behavior as a therapeutic treatment for illness ($p = 0.05$), and indulgence of sexuality in childhood is correlated with the belief that sexual activity can be of therapeutic value ($p = 0.01$). Age of onset of two items in the sex socialization scale—specifically, training for modesty and heterosexual play—are related to an individual's predisposition to take the blame for his own illness, so that the later the onset of training, the less likely are patients to attribute their illnesses to their own actions. On the other hand, severe sex training is not related to explanations for illness; adults are no more likely to equate illness with sexual activity in societies with harsh sex socialization than they are in cultures where sex play in childhood is treated with indulgence. Finally, punishment for sexual behavior in childhood is related to paranoia in later life, and specifically to fear of other people. Whiting and Child suggest that fear of others is a defensive maneuver in response to sexual temptation. However, socialization for aggression is a superior predictor of paranoia.

The Whiting and Child study predates the time when sampling procedures became a major preoccupation of cross-cultural anthropologists. Moreover, the samples upon which the conclusions in this study are based are consistently small, and the results are not entirely consistent in supporting the fixation hypothesis proposed by the investigators. Nevertheless, the study provides some evidence in favor of the theory that where sex socialization is severe in childhood, sexuality plays a predictable role in a variety of adult beliefs about the origins and treatment of illness.

Severity of sex training as measured by Whiting and Child subsequently appears as an antecedent variable in a number of other cross-cultural studies. In their study of love magic, Shirley and Romney (1962) extrapolate directly from the Whiting and Child fixation hypothesis in predicting that love magic both reflects and is an outcome of sex anxiety as a function of severity of sex training. Sex socialization is measured by the Whiting and Child code and love magic is rated independently by the authors. Sex anxiety as an outcome of child rearing is significantly related to the presence or absence of love magic; of 20 societies where children are punished for sexual activity, 19 use love magic, while of the 19 societies where sex socialization is mild, only 6 use love magic ($p < 0.001$). Shirley and Romney draw their cases from the Whiting and Child sample, so that interpretation of their results is only tentative. However, these findings clearly coincide with the Whiting and Child fixation hypothesis.

The same negative fixation hypothesis is tested by Barbara Ayres (1967) in her study of pregnancy taboos. In particular, Ayres tests the theory that sex taboos during pregnancy are a reflection of sex anxiety having its origins in child-training techniques. The Whiting and Child severity of sex socialization scale is used as the independent measure; duration of pregnancy taboos is coded by Ayres. Based upon a sample of 33 societies taken from the Whiting and Child sample, Ayres reports a trend in the relationship between childhood sex training and pregnancy taboos; the more severe the punishment for sexual behavior in early life, the longer the sex taboos during pregnancy. However, the results are not statistically significant. It will be remembered that pregnancy taboos are significantly correlated with premarital sex norms as measured by the Westbrook code. Ayres takes this to mean that sex anxiety in adulthood is more directly influenced by punishment for adolescent than for childhood sexuality.

In his cross-cultural study of the Oedipus complex, Stephens (1962) broadens the consideration of the causes and consequences of sex anxiety as this applies to males. Stephens focuses upon the significance of the diluted marriage syndrome, by which he means family constellations where wives are deprived of the sexual attention of their husbands for extended periods of time. Under these circumstances, mothers are predicted to behave in a markedly seductive manner toward their young sons; this is predicted to promote a profound anxiety about and avoidance of sex and women for adult men.

Stephens' central measure of the diluted marriage is the long postpartum sex taboo. His first intention is to determine the relationship between the duration of the postpartum sex taboo and a number of measures of sex anxiety, including extensiveness of menstrual taboos. A subsidiary concern in this study is the compilation of evidence that the menstrual taboo in fact reflects anxiety about sex and women. Thus Stephens simultaneously presents two sets of correlations, the first having to do with the associations between the postpartum sex taboo and sex anxiety measures and the second having to do with the degree of association between menstrual taboos and other variables assumed to reflect sex anxiety.

Stephens' major hypothesis concerning the relationship between the postpartum sex taboo and menstrual taboos is supported. Menstrual taboos are coded in terms of the number of restrictions surrounding menstruation within a society; postpartum sex taboos are dichotomized into long and short. For a sample of 72 societies, the long postpartum sex taboo tends to predict extensiveness of menstrual taboos, while short postpartum sex taboos are associated with few menstrual restrictions ($p = 0.02$). The postpartum sex taboo is also significantly correlated with Stephens' composite measure of sex anxiety as outlined earlier. Thus where the postpartum sex taboo is long, societies also score higher on the sex anxiety code ($n = 36$, $p = 0.03$). Stephens also tests the relationship between duration of the postpartum sex taboo and the Whiting and Child sex socialization scale. While societies with a long postpartum sex taboo tend to be harsh in their sex socialization, the relationship does not reach statistical significance ($n = 41$).

The notion that menstrual taboos in fact reflect an underlying anxiety about sexuality is indirectly supported by a number of associations as these are reported by Stephens. Thus on a sample of 37 societies, extensive menstrual taboos are correlated with high scores on Stephens' composite sex anxiety scale ($p = 0.01$). Similarly, menstrual taboos are less extensive the lower a society scores on both punishment for masturbation ($n = 26$, $p = 0.01$) and on the Whiting and Child sex socialization scale ($n = 41$, $p = 0.05$). Menstrual taboos are also strongly related to a composite measure including a number of items thought to predict castration anxiety in males; the scale reflects a combination of factors relating to father–son relationships and techniques of discipline. The higher a society scored on the composite predictor of castration anxiety, the more extensive the menstrual taboos ($n = 55$, $p < 0.001$). Menstrual taboos were also tested against castration themes in folk tales. Neither genital injury nor severing themes are significantly related to menstrual taboos. Instances of themes of physical injuries of all kinds are significantly related to menstrual taboos, but the relationship is curvilinear, so that societies with a moderate number of menstrual taboos have the highest scores on physical injury in folk tales. Stephens describes these findings as peculiar.

As a whole, the Stephens study presents reasonably consistent evidence in support of the theory that the postpartum sex taboo is associated with menstrual taboos and that menstrual taboos are, in turn, correlated with severity of sex training, themes and childhood experiences evoking castration anxiety, and concern with and restrictions on sexual behavior in general. Whether the first relationship is evidence of Stephens' Oedipus complex hypothesis or whether the other associations support the sex anxiety theory of menstrual taboos is a matter of interpretation. Since the Stephens study depends entirely upon the use of proxivariables, the viability of his interpretations should be weighed against the validity of his measures.

The notion that sex restrictions, deviations, avoidances, and elaborations always reflect an underlying anxiety about sexuality is undermined by a number of cross-cultural findings reported in the literature on sexuality. In their study of the patterning of sexual beliefs and behaviors, Minturn et al. (1969) test the degree of association between nine variables more or less directly reflecting one or another aspect of sexuality. Among these is the Minturn et al. composite adult sex anxiety code outlined earlier. This composite measure of sex anxiety is reported to be significantly associated with two other sex variables—the use of sex charms for a sample of 88 societies ($r = 0.48$, $p = 0.48$) and attitudes toward homosexuality for 45 societies ($r = 0.20$, $p = 0.05$). However, sex anxiety is unrelated to frequency of homosexuality ($n = 61$); frequency of rape ($n = 37$); attitudes toward rape ($n = 26$); segregation of the sexes at adolescence ($n = 84$); or marriage arrangements ($n = 95$). Further, the Minturn sex anxiety scale is unrelated to the Whiting and Child measure of sex socialization (Broude, 1975a). Finally, it was noted in the context of premarital sex norms that while restrictive rules regarding premarital sexual behavior are interpreted by a number of theorists as a reflection of sex anxiety, restrictiveness is not associated with the Minturn sex anxiety scale or with menstrual or postpartum sex taboos.

The research on the causes and correlates of sex anxiety is difficult to evaluate. The Whiting and Child code is a powerful predictor of a number of variables assumed by some researchers to measure sex anxiety in adulthood. However, there is no direct support for the position that sex anxiety per se is functioning as a mediating factor in any of the studies reviewed here. The absence of consistent correlations among variables assumed to reflect sex anxiety complicates the picture. When variables assumed to measure the same underlying psychological orientation are nevertheless not associated with each other, this is often taken to mean that they represent alternate strategies for resolving the particular conflict at issue. However, if it is the case that cultures are selective in their manifestations of sex anxiety, then how does the researcher know beforehand which sex norms and practices will be indicative of anxiety about sexuality in a given cultural context and which will not?

In fact, the notion of a unitary sex anxiety is probably counterproductive; it is not unreasonable to suppose that there exist, not just one kind of sex anxiety, but rather sex anxieties. The proposition that there are a variety of anxieties about sex, each of which can be distinguished by a unique psychological meaning and origin, would explain in part the failure of variables assumed to reflect anxiety about sexuality to correlate with each other. Future studies might therefore change tactics and focus upon the causes and consequences of specific sexual problems and abandon the notion of an overall phobic response to sex as manifested in every observable restrictive or deviant sexual belief or behavior.

THE PATTERNING OF SEX NORMS AND PRACTICES

While most cross-cultural studies on sexuality are concerned with isolating antecedents and correlates of specific norms and behaviors, a number of researchers have also examined the interrelationships among sexual beliefs and behaviors per se. These studies attempt to isolate consistent associations among sex variables as these are patterned within and across cultures. An explicit or implicit hidden agenda of research of this variety is to determine the extent to which societies are consistent in their overall sexual orientation. Moreover, a majority bias can be inferred in favor of the position that there is such consistency in sexual orientation and in particular that societies are either generally permissive or restrictive in their views of and responses to sexuality. In fact, the objective findings do not justify the theory of overall regularity in the patterning of sex norms and practices within a specific cultural context. Rather, it appears that individual cultures tend to place greater restrictions, or to exhibit more concern, or to show greater reserve regarding some aspects of sexuality, than others. On the other hand, societies are not entirely arbitrary in their treatment of sexuality; there are a number of sexual beliefs and behaviors that are consistently interrelated within and across cultures.

Review of the Findings

The best introduction to the cross-cultural patterning of sexuality is the Ford and Beach study *Patterns of Sexual Behavior* (1951). This is an exhaustive and detailed normative description of a wide range of sexual customs and behaviors as they are played out across cultures. The study is not strictly cross-cultural in nature; that is, it is not concerned with testing hypotheses or applying statistical procedures. However, *Patterns of Sexual Behavior* is enormously useful in that it defines the range of possibility in the ways that cultures do and do not elaborate the biologic sex drive. The study has been used extensively as a source of data for other cross-cultural research on sexuality.

Heise's study of sexual socialization (1967) is explicitly concerned with isolating consistencies in sex norms and behaviors across cultures. The issue of consistency is examined from a developmental perspective; specifically, Heise is interested in determining the extent to which societies exhibit regularities in their management of sexuality across the life cycle. The study takes off from a set of hypotheses concerning the specific kinds of regularity that a culture is likely to reflect. Thus Heise predicts that societies will tend toward consistency in their sex norms across developmental stages; that any shifts in attitudes across stages will be minor; that when shifts occur, norms will be more restrictive for later than for earlier stages; and that adolescent sex norms will tend to be relaxed in response to the powerful role of the sex drive at that time of life.

Heise focuses on the four developmental stages of infancy, childhood, adolescence, and adulthood. For each stage, a culture is rated as restrictive, semirestrictive, or permissive in terms of its management of sexuality. Sex norms in infancy are measured by the Whiting and Child sex socialization code. Sex norms for childhood are measured by the extent of segregation of the sexes during latency; the importance attached to virginity before marriage; and attitudes toward sexual activity before puberty. Adolescent sex norms are determined according to the Westbrook code on rules regarding premarital sex. Attitudes toward sexual behavior for adults are measured by extramarital sex norms. The study is based upon a sample of 116 societies, with adequate representation of the major world culture areas.

In terms of the predictions upon which Heise's study rests, the results are mixed. Thus sex norms do tend to become more restrictive from infancy to adulthood, and premarital sex norms for adolescents tend to be less severe than are norms at other points in the life cycle. On the other hand, there is no convincing evidence in support of a theory of overall consistency in sex norms across developmental stages. Rather, there is some, but not overwhelming, regularity in the patterning of sexual beliefs and behaviors within cultures.

Heise's findings are an especially damaging indictment of the cultural consistency theory in light of the specific variables he includes in his study and those that he excludes. His variables focus on unspectacular sexual behaviors and omit such considerations as rape, homosexuality, occasional sex taboos, and the like. Further, his cross-stage indices overlap to some extent; thus childhood and adolescence are both measured in terms of premarital sex norms, while childhood also includes the related measure of valuation of virginity. In view of these methodologic constraints, Heise's failure to isolate regularities among these norms is persuasive evidence against the consistency hypothesis.

In her cross-cultural study of deviations from sex norms, Brown (1952) is primarily concerned with if and why any particular kinds of sexual behavior are punished more severely than others across cultures. Her study is based on a sample of 110 cultures taken from the Human Relations Area Files and representing the major world culture areas. Nineteen sexual behaviors were rated in terms of the severity with which each was punished.

The first question addressed by Brown concerns the issue of which behaviors are most frequently punished across societies. Incest, abduction, and rape were found to be most commonly sanctioned, while homosexuality and premarital sex were punished least frequently. Adultery falls somewhere in between. The correlation between frequency and severity of punishment is 0.87. Brown outlines three contributing factors in explaining this pattern. Thus sexual activities are most likely to be negatively sanctioned if they are aggressive in nature, if the participants are married, and if they affect others besides the partners themselves.

Brown also isolates six significant associations among the 19 sex variables in terms of the severity with which these behaviors are punished. These are (1) premarital and extramarital sex for males ($r = 0.36$); (2) premarital and extramarital sex for females ($r = 0.21$); (3) premarital sex for males and rape of an unmarried girl ($r = 0.59$); (4) premarital sex for males and females ($r = 0.66$); (5) extramarital sex for males and females ($r = 0.83$); (6) extramarital sex for males and rape ($r = 0.77$). Brown takes these correlations as evidence that societies are generally lax, moderate, or severe in their overall sexual orientation; however, her findings are more suggestive of Heise's conclusion to the effect that societies appear not to exhibit any startling regularity in their attitudes towards sexuality.

The cross-cultural study on the patterning of sexual beliefs and behaviors by Minturn et al. (1969) has already received some attention in this review in relation to homosexuality and sex anxiety. The study also examines the question of cultural consistency. Thus in a sample of 135 societies taken from the Human Relations Area Files, nine significant correlations are isolated among a set of nine sex variables: (1) sex charms and sex anxiety ($r = 0.48$, $p = 0.01$); (2) attitude toward homosexuality and marriage arrangements ($r = 0.31$, $p = 0.01$); (3) attitude toward homosexuality and sex anxiety ($r = 0.20$, $p = 0.05$); (4) frequency of homosexuality and marriage arrangements ($r = 0.26$, $p = 0.05$); (5) frequency of homosexuality and sex charms ($r = 0.31$, $p = 0.05$); (6) frequency and norms of homosexuality ($r = 0.39$, $p = 0.01$); (7) frequency of rape and ease of divorce ($r = -0.23$, $p = 0.05$); (8) frequency of rape and frequency of homosexuality ($r = -0.34$, $p = 0.01$); and (9) frequency and punishment for rape ($r = 0.47$, $p = 0.05$). Again, there is some, but not overwhelming, consistency in the patterning of sex norms and practices across cultures.

The application of factors to the study of sexual beliefs and behaviors appears first in Stephens' cross-cultural study of modesty (1972). The research, based upon a sample of 92 societies, is preliminary; no statistical tests are performed and no formal factor analysis is included. Stephens begins with an abbreviated survey of cultural customs concerning modesty, privacy for sexual intercourse, sexual activity in ceremonial contexts, talk about sex, and kin avoidance. Taking off from these data,

Stephens proposes that two factors are operating in terms of the clustering of sex norms and practices. The first is the "modesty-chastity" factor, which includes modesty of dress and speech as well as restrictive premarital and extramarital sex norms for women. The "taboo" factor includes kin avoidances and occasional sex taboos —for instance, those associated with menstruation and birth. The problem with the Stephens study is essentially methodologic. Specifically, the research depends upon a correlational approach to infer interrelationships among sets of beliefs and behaviors. In fact, the extent to which the customs as isolated by Stephens form genuine factors is unknown.

The strategy of searching for clusters of interrelated sex norms and practices is adopted in Broude's study of the patterning of sexual beliefs and behaviors across cultures (1976); further, multidimensional scaling and clustering techniques are used in this study. The research is based upon an analysis of 29 sex variables coded largely by Broude and Greene on the *Standard Cross-Cultural Sample.* A preliminary examination of the pairwise associations among these variables again leads to the conclusion that societies are neither entirely consistent nor entirely quixotic in their overall management of sexuality.

Clustering and multidimensional scaling procedures are applied to a subset of ten sex variables; on the basis of this analysis, three clusters of interrelated norms and practices are isolated. The first cluster includes premarital sex norms for females; frequency of premarital sex for males; frequency of extramarital sex for males; and marriage arrangements. Thus where rules regarding premarital sex for unmarried girls are permissive, males tend to engage in a high incidence of premarital and extramarital sexual activity, and potential spouses have relatively free choice of partners. Frequency of premarital and extramarital sex for females are also highly related to this cluster. Cluster 2 includes the double standard for extramarital sex as well as extramarital sex norms for wives and formal customs of wife sharing. Thus where the single standard obtains, rules regarding extramarital sex for wives tend to be permissive, and wife sharing is also present. Cluster 3 includes incidence of or concern about impotence, frequency of homosexuality, and extramarital sex norms for husbands. Where there is a high frequency of and/or concern about impotence, homosexuality is also frequent and extramarital sex for men is condemned. Attitudes toward homosexuality, boasting, genital injury as a theme in folk tales, and menstrual taboos are also related significantly to variables in this third cluster. Thus where impotence or homosexuality is present, or where extramarital sex is disallowed, homosexuality is likely to be condemned and/or boasting, genital injury, and menstrual taboos are likely to be present.

It is proposed in this study that each of the three clusters represents a different and distinguishable psychological orientation regarding sexuality. Specifically, the first dimension is seen as reflecting an overall disposition toward heterosexual involvement; individuals either approach or avoid opposite-sex attachment. Cluster 2 is viewed as indicating an underlying orientation toward marital exclusivity for wives; males either expect sexual fidelity or they do not. Cluster 3 concerns male orientations about sexual adequacy. Thus males tend to be either secure or insecure about their sexual performance; to the extent that they are insecure, sex anxiety results.

The first and third clusters isolated in this analysis are entirely independent; however, some of the variables in the second cluster are significantly associated with measures in the two remaining clusters. As to the absence of correlation between clusters 1 and 3, it is suggested that anxiety about sexual adequacy is likely to be resolved in either of two diametrically opposed ways; that is, males will either avoid or aggressively pursue heterosexual involvements. The correlation between the second cluster and clusters 1 and 3 is explained as follows: where males form intimate opposite-sex attachments and where men are insecure about their own sexual adequacy, expectations of fidelity are likely to obtain.

To summarize, cross-cultural studies on the patterning of sex norms and practices consistently undermine the theory that societies can be classified as essentially permissive or restrictive in their management of sexuality. Rather, cultures appear to discriminate among various aspects of sexuality in the sense that they treat different dimensions of sexual belief and behavior as though they are, in fact, different. Neither, however, is the patterning of sex norms and practices entirely quixotic. Specific pairs of beliefs and behaviors are treated within and across cultures as in some way equivalent. Further, independent studies essentially agree upon which pairs of beliefs and behaviors are significantly related, in spite of the fact that different scales and samples are used from one investigation to the next.

Research on the cultural management of sexuality nevertheless presents a fragmented picture of the patterning of sex norms and practices. Thus while studies have dealt effectively with the isolation of pairwise associations between sex variables, little work has been done concerning the interrelationships among sets of three or more beliefs and behaviors. The problem is in large part methodologic. Because the quality of data on sexuality is so poor, the use of multidimensional scaling and clustering procedures becomes extremely cumbersome when applied to this domain of human behavior. As a result, investigations can tackle the issue of the degree of regularity in the patterning of sexuality but do not provide comprehensive and coherent data concerning the sophisticated interplay among a wide range of beliefs and behaviors as these reflect views of and responses to human sexuality within and across cultures.

CONCLUSIONS

The cultural management of sexuality has not been explored extensively by cross-cultural anthropologists. Those researchers who have dealt with sex norms and practices within a cross-cultural framework have been hampered by methodologic problems that have tended to limit the scope and significance of their investigations. Nevertheless, a number of important hypotheses and findings have emerged from these studies; further, the recent publication of codes and ratings on a variety of sexual beliefs and behaviors provides the raw material for more ambitious research on human sexuality in the future.

As regards the origins and correlates of specific sex norms and practices, investigators have interpreted variations in sexual orientation across cultures either as practical responses to social structural constraints or as reflections of psychological dispositions. Each of these theoretical perspectives receives some empirical support. Thus premarital sex norms are associated with a variety of social-structural variables which themselves reflect cultural complexity and also with accessibility of mothering and with sex socialization. Similarly, extramarital sex norms are correlated with lineality, men's houses, and sex socialization. While studies on the causes and correlates of homosexual norms and practices have been on the whole unsuccessful, there is some tentative evidence that both absence of and sanctions against homosexuality characterize nuclear family households and particularly families where husbands and wives enjoy a close relationship and where fathers play a significant caretaking role. Regression analyses for premarital and extramarital sex norms suggest that child-rearing variables are at least as powerful as are social-structural variables in predicting variations in sexual attitudes and practices across cultures. For premarital sex norms, accessibility of mothering has ten times the predictive power of the next best predictor in distinguishing between permissive and restrictive societies. Men's houses and sex socialization have roughly equal predictive power concerning extramarital sex norms.

Tables 19–1 through 19–3 summarize the studies reviewed here as they relate to the antecedents of premarital and extramarital sex norms and homosexuality. Because different researchers use different codes to measure identical variables and because independent studies explain the same associations according to different theoretical frameworks, scales and interpretations are summarized for each study. All of the associations outlined in Table 19–1 for premarital sex norms are based upon cross-cultural studies and have been reported or implied to be statistically significant. Since some studies on extramarital sex norms and homosexuality are not strictly cross-cultural, and since some of the findings reported in these studies are not statistically significant, the nature of the sample and the level of significance are summarized for these two sex variables.

A number of researchers have looked into the causes and correlates of sex anxiety; this literature is to some extent ambiguous. Severity of sex socialization as measured by the Whiting and Child composite scale proves to be a powerful predictor of a number of sexual beliefs and behaviors, including premarital and extramarital sex norms, beliefs related to the origins and treatment of illness, love magic, pregnancy sex taboos, and menstrual and postpartum sex taboos. Further, the Whiting and Child negative fixation hypothesis is supported by all of these associations. The notion that sex prohibitions and deviations inevitably reflect anxiety about sexuality is not consistently supported, and it has been suggested here that theories proposing a unitary sex anxiety as reflected in every elaboration of human sexual belief and behavior are probably counterproductive. Table 19–4 summarizes the findings concerning sex anxiety as reported here.

As regards the patterning of sexual attitudes and practices per se, studies have consistently exploded the assumption that cultures are either permissive or restrictive in their overall sexual orientation. Rather, individual societies almost universally distinguish among various dimensions of sexual behavior in the sense that they exhibit greater concern or interest or delight in some aspects of sexuality than in others. On the other hand, researchers have also demonstrated that particular pairs of customs and behaviors are regularly associated with each other from one society to the next. Thus cultures are neither entirely consistent nor entirely arbitrary in their management of sexuality.

FUTURE RESEARCH

In terms of future studies into the cross-cultural management of sexuality, three lines of research are indicated. The first has to do with the systematic collection of data on sex norms and practices, the second involves the elaboration and refinement of existing research, and the third concerns the ways in which single-community studies can contribute to the literature on the patterning and origins of sexual orientation.

TABLE 19–1 Studies on Premarital Sex Norms

Study	Antecedent	Code for Premarital Sex	Code for Antecedent	Interpretation
Murdock (1964)	Descent	Westbrook	Ethnographic Atlas	Patricentered societies tend to be restrictive
	Residence	Westbrook	Ethnographic Atlas	Patricentered societies tend to be restrictive
				Absence of cohesive kin groups in ambilocal and neolocal societies undermine parents' ability to enforce restrictive norms
	Subsistence economy	Westbrook	Ethnographic Atlas	Restrictiveness encourages young people to direct their energies toward subsistence activities in intensive agriculture societies where industry and self-discipline are needed. Simple tilling and hunting–gathering require less discipline; hence permissive norms
	Demography	Westbrook	Ethnographic Atlas	Restrictive norms are less necessary and less effective in small communities
				Small, kin-based communities are generally endogamous, thus minimizing the need for restrictive norms
	High gods	Westbrook	Ethnographic Atlas	The association between presence of high gods and restrictiveness may in part reflect Muslim/Christian morality
Goethals (1971)	Descent	Palfrey House	—	Where descent is traced through the father, the position of an illegitimate child is ambiguous; hence restrictive norms. In matrilineal societies, descent does not depend upon paternity; thus premarital pregnancies need not be avoided
	Residence	Palfrey House	—	In patrilocal societies, unmarried mothers do not enjoy the support of a cohesive kin group; hence restrictive norms to avoid premarital pregnancies. In matrilocal societies, unwed mothers can depend upon their own kin for support; therefore premarital pregnancies need not be avoided
	Bride-price	Palfrey House	—	Where bride-price is present, virginity becomes important because men will not pay premium prices for "damaged goods"

TABLE 19-1 (continued)

Study	Antecedent	Code for Premarital Sex	Code for Antecedent	Interpretation
Goethals (n.d.)	Class structure	Palfrey House	—	In societies with a fluid class structure, fathers attempt to prevent their daughters from marrying men of inferior social standing
Eckhardt (1971)	Descent	Westbrook	Eckhardt	Exchange theory hypothesis. Where males contribute more to marriage than do females, sex becomes an item of exchange for women; hence restrictive norms. Where women contribute more than men, the value of sex is not inflated and premarital sex is allowed
	Residence	Westbrook	Eckhardt	Exchange theory hypothesis
	Property exchange at marriage	Westbrook	Eckhardt	Where bride-price or bride service prevails, then premarital sex is prohibited as sexual intercourse and pregnancy would deflate a woman's value at marriage
	Women's role in subsistence	Westbrook	Eckhardt	Where women make a large contribution to subsistence, then male authority is reduced and men have difficulty enforcing restrictive norms for women
Barry (1977)	Valuation of the sexes	Broude & Greene	Barry	
Broude (1975b)	Accessibility of mothering	Westbrook	Barry & Paxson	High accessibility leads to willingness to risk sexual involvement; hence permissive norms. Low accessibility leads to avoidance of sexual involvements; hence restrictive norms
	Sex socialization	Westbrook	Whiting & Child	Sex anxiety learned in childhood results in anxiety about sex in adulthood as reflected in restrictive norms

TABLE 19-2 Studies on Extramarital Sex Norms

Study	Antecedent	Code for Sex Norms	Code for Antecedent	Kind of Study and Significance	Interpretation
Cohen (1969)	Political integration	Cohen	Cohen	Cross-cultural, no test	Restrictive norms in inchoate incorporative states intensify the marital dyad at the expense of local group solidarity, thus increasing the power of the emerging ruling elite
Abernethy (1974)	Female dominance	None	None	Comparative, no test	Female dominance over males inhibits male sexual impulses which is reflected in minimal expectations of marital fidelity
Wolf (1966; 1968; 1970)	Childhood association	None	None	Comparative, no test	Intimate childhood association between future spouses inhibits sexual attraction and results in high incidence of and little jealousy over infidelity
Broude (1975a)	Descent	Broude & Greene	Murdock & Wilson	Cross-cultural, $p = 0.047$	Test of Abernethy female dominance hypothesis
	Residence	Broude & Greene	Murdock & Wilson	Cross-cultural, NS	Test of Abernethy female dominance hypothesis
	Women's role in subsistence	Broude & Greene	*Ethnographic Atlas*	Cross-cultural, NS	Test of Abernethy female dominance hypothesis
	Men's houses	Broude & Greene	Palfrey House	Cross-cultural, $p = 0.01$	Men's houses and the double standard both reflect an underlying hostility toward women
	Sex socialization	Broude & Greene	Whiting & Child	Cross-cultural, $p = 0.04$	Severe sex training in childhood leads to sex anxiety as reflected in restrictive norms

TABLE 19-3 Studies on Homosexuality

Study	Antecedent	Code for Homosexuality	Code for Antecedent	Kind of Study and Significance	Interpretation
Hart (1968)	Segregation of sexes in latency	None	None	Comparative, no test	Segregation of sexes strengthens same sex friendships. Males thus become fixated in the same-sex dyad, resulting in homosexuality
Minturn (1969)	Segregation of sexes at adolescence	Minturn	Minturn	Cross-cultural, NS	Segregation of the sexes inhibits heterosexual impulses and facilitates homosexual relationships
	Sex socialization	Minturn	Whiting & Child	Cross-cultural, NS	
	Independence training	Minturn	—	Cross-cultural, NS	
	Postpartum sex taboo	Minturn	—	Cross-cultural, NS	
Abernethy (1974)	Female dominance	None	None	Comparative, no test	Where women are dominant over men, men reject their masculinity in favor of feminine identifications as reflected in homosexuality
Broude (1975a)	Descent	Broude & Greene	Murdock & Wilson	Cross-cultural, NS	Test of Abernethy female dominance hypothesis
	Residence	Broude & Greene	Murdock & Wilson	Cross-cultural, NS	Test of Abernethy female dominance hypothesis
	Family structure	Broude & Greene	Murdock & Wilson	Cross-cultural, NS	Homosexuality is condemned and therefore absent where father–son rivalry is present
	Father's role	Broude & Greene	Barry & Paxson	Cross-cultural, NS	Homosexuality is condemned and therefore absent where father–son rivalry is present
	Mother–child sleeping	Broude & Greene	Palfrey House	Cross-cultural, NS	
	Husband–wife rooming	Broude & Greene	Palfrey House	Cross-cultural, NS	Homosexuality is condemned and therefore absent where father–son rivalry is present
	Postpartum sex taboo	Broude & Greene	Palfrey House	Cross-cultural, NS	

667

TABLE 19–4 Studies on Sex Anxiety

Study	Correlate 1	Correlate 2	Code for Correlate 1	Code for Correlate 2	Significance	Interpretation
Whiting & Child (1953)	Sex anxiety potential	Sex avoidance therapy	Whiting & Child	Whiting & Child	$p = 0.05$	Negative fixation hypothesis. Where sexual behavior is punished in childhood, adults will be anxious about sex as reflected in projective systems
	Sex anxiety potential	Paranoia	Whiting & Child	Whiting & Child	$p < 0.05$	Fear of others is a defense against sexual temptation
	Sex anxiety potential	Sexual explanations for illness	Whiting & Child	Whiting & Child	NS	Negative fixation hypothesis
	Early punishment for immodesty	Self-blame for illness	Whiting & Child	Whiting & Child	$p = 0.05$	Early socialization leads to guilt
	Early independence training	Self-blame for illness	Whiting & Child	Whiting & Child	$p = 0.01$	Early socialization leads to guilt
	Sex satisfaction potential	Presence of sex therapy	Whiting & Child	Whiting & Child	$p = 0.01$	Positive fixation hypothesis. Indulgence of sexual behavior in childhood leads to lasting reliance upon sex as a source of security
Shirley & Romney (1962)	Sex anxiety potential	Love magic	Whiting & Child	Shirley & Romney	$p < 0.001$	Negative fixation hypothesis
Ayres (1967)	Sex anxiety potential	Pregnancy sex taboos	Whiting & Child	Ayres	NS	Negative fixation hypothesis

668

TABLE 19-4 (continued)

Study	Correlate 1	Correlate 2	Code for Correlate 1	Code for Correlate 2	Significance	Interpretation
Stephens (1962)	Sex anxiety potential	Postpartum sex taboo	Whiting & Child	Stephens	NS	The postpartum sex taboo is a reflection of sex anxiety
	Sex anxiety potential	Menstrual taboos	Whiting & Child	Stephens	$p = 0.05$	Menstrual taboos are a reflection of sex anxiety
	Postpartum sex taboo	Menstrual taboos	Stephens	Stephens	$p = 0.02$	The postpartum sex taboo is related to intense Oedipus conflicts. Males fear sex and women and this is reflected in extensive menstrual taboos
	Postpartum sex taboo	Composite sex anxiety	Stephens	Stephens	$p = 0.03$	The postpartum sex taboo is an antecedent of sex anxiety
	Menstrual taboos	Composite sex anxiety	Stephens	Stephens	$p = 0.01$	Menstrual taboos reflect sex anxiety
	Menstrual taboos	Punishment for masturbation	Stephens	Whiting & Child	$p = 0.01$	Punishment for masturbation leads to castration anxiety which is reflected in menstrual taboos
	Menstrual taboos	Predictors of castration anxiety	Stephens	Stephens	$p < 0.001$	Castration anxiety is reflected in menstrual taboos
	Menstrual taboos	Castration in folk tales	Stephens	Stephens	NS	Menstrual taboos are a reflection of castration anxiety
Minturn (1969)	Adult sex anxiety	Sex charms	Minturn	Minturn	$p = 0.01$	
	Adult sex anxiety	Norms of homosexuality	Minturn	Minturn	$p = 0.05$	

669

TABLE 19-4 (continued)

Study	Correlate 1	Correlate 2	Code for Correlate 1	Code for Correlate 2	Significance	Interpretation
(Minturn, 1969, *continued*)	Adult sex anxiety	Frequency of homosexuality	Minturn	Minturn	NS	Frequent homosexuality reflects sex anxiety
	Adult sex anxiety	Frequency of rape	Minturn	Minturn	NS	Frequent rape reflects sex anxiety
	Adult sex anxiety	Norms of rape	Minturn	Minturn	NS	
	Adult sex anxiety	Segregation of the sexes	Minturn	Minturn	NS	
	Adult sex anxiety	Marriage arrangements	Minturn	Minturn	NS	
Broude (1975a)	Sex anxiety potential	Adult sex anxiety	Whiting & Child	Minturn	NS	Variables inferred to reflect sex anxiety should be correlated
	Sex anxiety potential	Extramarital sex norms	Whiting & Child	Broude & Greene	$p = 0.04$	Negative fixation hypothesis
Broude (1975b)	Sex anxiety potential	Premarital sex norms	Whiting & Child	Westbrook	$p < 0.001$	Negative fixation hypothesis
	Postpartum sex taboo	Premarital sex norms	Palfrey House	Westbrook	NS	Variables inferred to reflect sex anxiety should be correlated
	Menstrual taboos	Premarital sex norms	Stephens	Westbrook	NS	Variables inferred to reflect sex anxiety should be correlated
	Adult sex anxiety	Premarital sex norms	Minturn	Westbrook	NS	Variables inferred to reflect sex anxiety should be correlated

Data collection

The most pressing problem confronting cross-cultural research on sexuality involves the availability of data and the comparability of ethnographic reports on sex norms and practices. The Marshall and Suggs (1971) collection of studies on human sexual behavior provides a comprehensive guide for field workers, including an outline and definitions of relevant sex variables and strategies for obtaining reliable data. Research on sexuality would be greatly aided if anthropologists were to adopt the Marshall and Suggs outline as a baseline for collecting and reporting data on sexual beliefs and behaviors.

Future Cross-cultural Research

While studies on the antecedents and correlates of sex norms and practices have made an important contribution to the anthropological literature, the scope of this research needs to be expanded and the antecedent and corollary variables refined. A serious problem with this body of research involves the use of intervening variables or proxivariables characterizing most studies on the origins of variations in sexual orientation across cultures. It is the use of mediating variables that accounts for the differing interpretations of identical findings in so many investigations of sexual beliefs and behaviors, and particularly of premarital sex norms. In fact, findings reported in the cross-cultural literature do not usually reflect the hypotheses that they were meant to test in any precise way. Therefore more nearly precise measures of antecedent variables, and particularly of psychological variables, are badly needed.

It has also been noted that, even when the combined effects of all social structural and psychological variables are taken into account as they predict sex variables, the major proportion of the variance in sexual orientation across cultures still remains unexplained. Clearly, new antecedent variables need to be introduced, particularly antecedents having to do with socialization in light of their power to predict a number of sex variables. The Whiting and Child sex socialization codes have had special success in terms of their relationships to other sex variables; however, these scales have been rated on a small and unrepresentative sample of societies. A first step toward the expansion of antecedent variables might therefore involve the construction and rating of new sex socialization codes on the Murdock and White *Standard Cross-Cultural Sample.*

Finally, as regards research on the origins of variations in sexual orientation, the range of sex variables per se needs to be broadened to include beliefs and behaviors other than premarital and extramarital sex norms, homosexuality, and sex anxiety.

Studies on the patterning of sex norms and behavior also need expansion. Thus while this research has been successful in isolating pairwise associations between sex variables, little work has been done concerning the clustering of sets of sexual beliefs and behaviors as these are patterned within and across cultures. Cross-culturalists might make more use of clustering and multidimensional scaling techniques in attempting to map out associations and absences of association in sex variables from one society to the next. Until such techniques are employed, the literature on patterns of sexual attitudes and practices will remain fragmented.

Intracultural Studies

Intracultural studies can advance research on both the origins and the patterning of sexual beliefs and behaviors as they have been addressed in a cross-cultural context. Intraculture studies can be especially useful in testing cross-cultural hypotheses concerning the effects of socialization upon sexual orientation. In particular, field workers have the advantage of being able to collect data that will directly measure child-rearing variables; this obviates the need for proxivariables to test hypotheses. Studies concerning the effects of differences in socialization experiences upon individual sexual orientation can be seen as a way of testing more general cross-cultural hypotheses and as a strategy for assessing the degree to which theories supported by cross-cultural data also gain support within single societies.

Single-culture studies can also contribute to the research on patterns of sex norms and practices per se. Thus field workers might collect individual profiles on a variety of sexual beliefs and behaviors and determine the degree and kinds of associations existing between and among specific beliefs and behaviors across subjects. Thus clusters or dimensions of sex norms and practices can be isolated with reference to a set of variables that is at once more comprehensive and more sensitively measured than has been the case with cross-cultural research.

To date, studies on the patterning and origins of sexual beliefs and behaviors have exploded myths and provided provocative theory and data regarding the cultural management of human sexuality. However, the cross-cultural study of sexuality is still in its infancy. The expansion and refinement of existing research depend in great part upon the acquisition of more and better data on sexuality. In the meantime, researchers can still profitably exploit the cross-cultural codes and ratings that already appear in the literature as these measure sexual, social structural, and socialization parameters.

ACKNOWLEDGMENTS

I would like to thank Ruth and Lee Munroe and Beatrice B. Whiting for their valuable comments on the first draft of this article. Thanks also to George W. Goethals and John W. M. Whiting for their continued and substantial support at every stage of my own work in the field of sexuality.

REFERENCES

Abernethy, V. Dominance and sexual behavior: A hypothesis. *American Journal of Psychiatry*, 1974, *131*, 813–817.

Ayres, B. Pregnancy magic: A study of food taboos and sex avoidances. In C. S. Ford (Ed.), *Cross-cultural approaches.* New Haven: HRAF Press, 1967.

Barry, H., Josephson L., Lauer, E., & Marshall, C. Agents and techniques for child training: Cross-cultural codes 6. *Ethnology*, 1977, *16* (2), 191–230.

Bettelheim, B. *Symbolic wounds.* New York: Collier Books, 1954.

Broude, G. J. *A cross-cultural study of some sexual beliefs and practices.* Unpublished doctoral dissertation, Harvard University, 1975. (a)

Broude, G. J. Norms of premarital sexual behavior: A cross-cultural study. *Ethos*, 1975, *3*, 381–402. (b)

Broude, G. J. Cross-cultural patterning of some sexual attitudes and practices. *Behavior Science Research*, 1976, *11*, 227–262.

Broude, G. J., & Greene, S. J. Cross-cultural codes on twenty sexual attitudes and practices. *Ethnology*, 1976, *15*, 409–429.

Brown, J. S. A comparative study of deviations from sex mores. *American Sociological Review*, 1952, *17* (2), 135–146.

Cohen, Y. Ends and means in political control: State organization and punishment of adultery, incest, and violation of celibacy. *American Anthropologist,* 1969, *71,* 658–687.

Coleman, J. Female status and premarital sex codes. *American Journal of Sociology,* 1966, *1* (4), 440–455.

Eckhardt, K. Exchange theory and sexual permissiveness. *Behavior Science Notes,* 1971, *6* (1), 1–18.

Ford, C. S., & Beach, F. A. *Patterns of sexual behavior.* New York: Harper & Brothers, 1951.

Goethals, G. W. Factors affecting permissive and nonpermissive rules regarding premarital sex. In J. M. Henslin (Ed.), *Sociology of sex: A book of readings.* New York: Appleton-Century-Croft, 1971, pp. 9–26.

Goethals, G. W. Working papers on premarital sex. Harvard University, n.d.

Hart, D. Homosexuality and transvestism in the Philippines: The Cebuan Filipino bayot and lakin-on. *Behavior Science Notes,* 1968, *3* (4), 211–248.

Heise, D. R. Cultural patterning of sexual socialization. *American Sociological Review,* 1967, *32,* 726–739.

Marshall, D. S., & Suggs, R. C. *Human sexual behavior.* New York: Basic Books, 1971.

Minturn, L., Grosse, M., & Haider, S. Cultural patterning of sexual beliefs and behavior. *Ethnology,* 1969, *8,* 301–318

Montgomery, R. A cross-cultural study of menstruation, menstrual taboos, and related social variables. *Ethos,* 1974, *2,* 137–170.

Murdock, G. P. Cultural correlates of the regulation of premarital sex behavior. In R. A. Manners (Ed.), *Process and Pattern in Culture.* Chicago: Aldine, 1964.

Murdock, G. P. Ethnographic atlas. *Ethnology,* 1967, *6,* 109–236.

Murdock, G. P., & White, D. R. Standard cross-cultural sample. *Ethnology,* 1969, *13,* 329–369.

Murdock, G. P., & Wilson, S. F. Settlement patterns and community organization: Cross-cultural codes 3. *Ethnology,* 1972, *11,* 254–295.

Rosenblatt, P., & Hillibrant, W. Divorce for childlessness and the regulation of adultery. *Journal of Sex Research,* 1972, *8,* 117–127.

Shirley, W. R., & Romney, A. K. Love magic and socialization anxiety: A cross-cultural study. *American Anthropologist,* 1962, *64,* 1028–1031.

Stephens, W. N. *The oedipal complex: Cross-cultural evidence.* New York: Glencoe Free Press, 1962.

Stephens, W. N. A cross-cultural study of menstrual taboos. In C. S. Ford (Ed.), *Cross-cultural approaches.* New Haven: HRAF Press, 1967.

Stephens, W. N. A cross-cultural study of modesty. *Behavior Science Notes,* 1972, *7,* 1–28.

Whiting, J. W. M., & Child, I. L. *Child training and personality.* New Haven: Yale University Press, 1953.

Wolf, A. Childhood association, sexual attraction, and the incest taboo: A Chinese case. *American Anthropologist,* 1966, *68,* 883–898.

Wolf, A. Adopt a daughter-in-law, marry a sister: A Chinese solution to the problem of the incest taboo. *American Anthropologist,* 1968, *70,* 864–874.

Wolf, A. Childhood association and sexual attraction: A further test of the westermarck hypothesis. *American Anthropologist,* 1970, *72,* 503–515.

20

Internalization

Roger V. Burton • Janet Reis

Humans since time immemorial have wondered how children come to accept adult society's values and rules. The goal of socialization is to make the members both accept the norms and standards of their society and also feel that such acceptance is right.

Observers of the socialization process have identified an array of techniques used for the inculcation of roles. External contingencies in the form of reward and punishment number highly among the methods of control in the modification and maintenance of children's behavior. Caretakers around the world rely on these time-honored methods to mold their children's behavior in the desired manner.

In the course of normal development, however, initial reliance on external control wanes. The maturing child needs no longer to be coaxed or coerced with reward or punishments. Rather, the child's behavior gradually comes to be governed by internal monitors. These self-control mechanisms appear to function in much the same way as the external controls originally required to manage behavior. The difference is in the locus of control. Somehow the child incorporates the socializing agents' rules concerning proper behavior into him/herself.

This remarkable shift from overt control to cognitive self-control is known as internalization. It is a developmental process of utmost importance for the functioning of a society. Without individual internalization, societies would be forced to rely on external systems of behavioral control for each individual member's lifespan, an inefficient and costly method. Further, it seems likely that the outcome of internalization—individuals regulating their own behavior—is more than just a contributor to societal stability; it is necessary for the persistence of the society. As an important element in the cultural glue of any society, the internalization process has been studied intensively by social scientists.

Often concealed in philosophical treatises dealing with the problem of internalization is the realization that adult moral standards are not inflexible laws imposed by heavenly edict; instead, these codes of both proscibed and prescribed conduct result from a complex interaction of genetic, cultural, and ecologic factors.

Evidence for this role flexibility across cultures is clearly shown in studies of the division of labor by sex. It is commonly accepted that an individual's sex role is one of the most salient among her/his social roles. An important element of these sex roles is the type of work allocated to each sex. Worldwide, there is a tendency for certain tasks to be gender based. When ethnographers describe measurable sex differences in socialization, male children are pressured to be aggressive, self-reliant, and high in achievement, whereas female children are molded to be nurturant,

675

obedient, and responsible (Barry, Bacon, & Child, 1957; Barry, Josephson, Lauer, & Marshall, 1976). Yet there is a tremendous variability among societies as to what constitutes approved feminine and masculine adult behavior (Murdock & Provost, 1973). To illustrate, there was only one occupation delegated exclusively to men in the 324 societies studied, and that was metal working. In some societies even cooking, carrying water, and grinding grain, generally female chores, are assigned to men. (See Chapter 16 in this volume for a more complete discussion of the links between socialization experiences and the development of adult sex roles.)

The socialization task seems to be all the more formidable in the face of these apparently fluid and arbitrary roles. A major question, then, is how do societies convince children to accept constraints and requirements for acceptable adult behavior and also to regulate their own behavior within those standards?

The problem of the development of self-control has been studied from many different theoretical perspectives. Western researchers, in particular, have concentrated on the mechanisms of internalization; that is, the exact means by which children's internalized controls over their behavior are produced and maintained. (For a recent review, see Burton, 1976b.) This approach has produced much useful empirical information on the roles played by specific environmental factors and by observational learning (modeling) in the acquisition and performance of self-control. In their attempts to outline the parameters of internalization, however, Western researchers have sometimes lost sight of the links between this learning process and the culture in which it occurs. Cross-cultural theory and findings offer themselves as a redress to the imbalance of Western research.

In this review we have assumed the theoretical orientation of the socialization process that posits a direct relation between early childhood experiences and adult personality (J. Whiting, 1961; 1964). In brief, this model sees the variations in socialization techniques as having been determined in their gross respects by the maintenance systems constructed according to the mandates of the environment.

Internalization enters the model as one of the means by which individuals learn behavior suited to the environment into which they are born. The content of what is learned will vary widely around the world. The varying social structures adapted to the different ecologies require quite different sets of internalized self-controls. Although the specific details of internalized self-controls differ, these controls share a common function of stabilization in producing adaptive adults.

The model assumes that different patterns of child rearing will lead to differences in children's personalities and eventually to differences in adult personalities. Continuity between child and adult personality allows the impact of the environment to extend to adult behavior and their cultural by-products: folktales, religious beliefs, and theories of disease. The links in the cultural–evolutionary system between ecology and behavior are completed with the final formation of adult personality. Clearly this is a feedback system, since the adult personality determines the way the society will cope with certain major environmental stresses and also the way children will be raised.

The assumption that the dominant causal path in cross-cultural findings leads from childhood experiences to adult personality has been contested by some researchers. Although strong arguments have been made for alternative interpretations (for example, see Chapter 4 in this volume), the assumption that early experiences determine later personality is made in the discussion that follows.

SORCERY

Anthropologists have long recognized that one mechanism for control of socially unacceptable behavior, particularly aggression and crime, is sorcery and witchcraft. B. Whiting (1950) has detailed how the major means for controlling crime among the Paiute is the internalized fear of retaliation from the victim who may have magical powers that would be used for revenge. The cross-cultural test to assess the generality of this function of sorcery revealed a strong relation between the lack of a formal judicial body and the importance of sorcery. The question of why these alternative mechanisms for social control were adopted by various societies remained unanswered.

Subsequently, J. Whiting and Child (1953) explored the relations between early child rearing and sorcery, indexed by a measure of the fear of living human beings who can cause illness. They found that sorcery was associated with severe socialization for aggression and somewhat less so with severity of punishment used in sex training. A later study (J. Whiting, 1959) produced much stronger support for the paranoia hypothesis derived from Freud that the development of sorcery as a mechanism of social control "is a defense against sexual anxiety produced by a combination of seduction in infancy followed by the punishment for sex during childhood" (p. 153). The data indicate that sorcery is important in societies with a long postpartum sex taboo (assumed to result in the mother's unconsciously seducing the infant), especially when severe punishment is used in subsequent sex training during childhood. By contrast, there was no evidence of higher incidence of sorcery for societies which had both a long post partum sex taboo and severe aggression training, despite the fact that each of these variables was independently associated with sorcery.

Although the occurrence of sorcery and witchcraft—is frequently reported in ethnographies of primitive societies, these few cross-cultural surveys are the only ones that have tested the alternative theories offered by anthropologists for the presence of these customs. Clearly the two alternative hypotheses about displaced aggression anxiety and societal paranoia that have been tested by J. Whiting should be explored further. With the development of the individual difference measure for conflict in sex identity that can be used as an index of high female control during infancy (see Chapter 18 in this volume), it should be possible to assess the correspondence between the relations at the social-structural level and at the individual level. Individual assessments of sex-identity conflict, of anxiety about aggression, and of anxiety about sexual performance could be used to relate to the degree to which individuals participate or believe in the practice of sorcery. The contribution of the antecedent measures singly and jointly would provide clarifying evidence for the function that sorcery as a social control mechanism plays both at the institutional level (comparing scores across societies with marked differences in the presence of sorcery) and at the individual level (within each society).

GHOSTS, SPIRITS, AND GODS

Another means that societies have employed for controlling individual behavior is the belief that supernatural beings will punish mortals who engage in prohibited behavior. When we compare the Puritan's belief in a just but righteously punitive god, a spirit to be feared but whose wrath was contingent on a mortal's sinning, with other societies' gods who, although present, have no power over living beings, it is clear that the role played by supernaturals for insuring moral conduct varies dramatically. In the first exploration of the relation of child training to beliefs in supernatural sanctions, J. Whiting and Child (1953) used a scale of the belief that supernatural beings could cause illness. The only association of any magnitude was between punishment for aggression and fear of animal spirits. The authors interpreted this finding as support for a conflict model of displacement: severe physical punishment produced both aggressive motives toward the parent and high anxiety about directly aggressing toward them. The aggression was then displaced to objects dissimilar to the parents. The result, however, was disappointing for understanding the antecedents of the belief that supernaturals punish the living for immoral acts. The authors noted there were problems with the measure: first, it estimated the belief that spirits *could* cause illness instead of the belief that the spirits *do* punish mortals for immoral acts, and, second, it was not scored very reliably.

A more direct test of the role of supernaturals in controlling prohibited behavior was performed by Spiro and D'Andrade (1958). Although their sample was small ($n = 11$), they found that the Whiting and Child measure of high indulgence in child rearing (i.e., during infancy) was associated with powerful gods who could be influenced by ritualized worship or ceremonies to force the gods to help the living. Malevolent gods were not associated with low indulgence but were related to severe weaning and toilet-training practices. Although the authors considered it a pilot study, their findings supported the hypothesis of a relation between child training and the kinds of gods a society believes in.

Lambert, Triandis, and Wolf (1959) also explored the relationship between rearing practices and types of gods with a more adequate sample and found that malevolent gods were present in societies that treated infants harshly (cold baths, rough handling, and physical punishment), that had high pressures for self-reliance and independence in childhood, and where these childhood socialization procedures were inflexible in eliciting punishment for nonperformance. Benevolent gods were associated with a pattern of nurturant practices in infant and child training, specifically absence of pain inflicted by caretakers and a general pattern of high nurturance during infancy.

Extending his study of the function of supernaturals as a means of social control, J. Whiting (1959) explored what early experiences would relate to fear of ghosts at funerals. He hypothesized that children who are often neglected when in a high state of need during early childhood will fantasize their mothers or caretakers taking care of them. This magical thinking is a means of coping with their frustration and is reinforced when the mothers eventually do provide for their needs. This fantasizing behavior becomes part of these children's regular mode of coping with frustrated needs. It is proposed that such fantasies learned in childhood will generalize in adulthood to concerns with spirits and ghosts. In addition to the acquisition of the tendency to produce fantasies of parents, it is also necessary to consider what conditions would lead to these parental spirits being fearful. It was hypothesized that this association of punitiveness with the parental ghosts would occur if the parents punish their children severely for aggression. He found that low indulgence during infancy (a scale from Bacon, Barry, & Child, 1957) combined with punishment for aggression (from J. Whiting & Child, 1953) predicted fear of ghosts at funerals (Friendly, 1956), particularly if just those societies in which both predicted conditions are either present or absent are compared. (15 of 17 scores were in the predicted direction).

J. Whiting acknowledged that there were some loose ends in the theory. First, the rating of ghost fear was not specifically fear of parental ghosts. Second, and more important, this ghost measure did not directly rate the belief that the ghosts were being feared because they would punish for immoral conduct. Although such beliefs about retributive supernaturals are widespread, there is no scale available for directly testing Whiting's hypothesis. In spite of the evidence being indirect, it is strongly in line with the theory that neglected infants who are severely punished for aggression in the childhood years will become adults who fear retributive parental ghosts.

The hypothesis that reliance on harsh physical punishment (reported in interviews) would be related to fear of supernaturals was tested in a field study with a sample of Bahamanian caretakers by Otterbein and Otterbein (1973). They found a consistent association between reported reliance on beatings for disobedience and fear of the supernatural, a finding clearly consonant with the cross-cultural surveys. Neither the Lambert et al. (1959) study at the cultural level nor the Otterbeins (1973) study at the individual level could find any evidence that the pain inflicted on children was based directly on their religious system. The direction of the relationship, then, seems more likely to be that the childhood experiences produced the religious beliefs rather than that the religious system resulted in pain-inflicting rearing practices.

The nature of supernaturals has also been related to the kinds of chores assigned to children. B. Whiting (1961) has shown that where children are responsible for the care of infants and of animals, the consequences of failure are obvious, and the sanctions are harsh and immediate, the society believes that supernaturals punish mortals immediately. By contrast, in societies that require mainly household chores that seem less exigent or where the major chore for children is formal schooling with its long delay in benefits, people are likely to believe the gods punish and reward in a future life.

These studies all demonstrate that generally indulgent, attentively nurturant, and nonpain-producing practices during infancy combined with low childhood socialization pressures produce supernatural projective systems that consist of benevolent, entreatable beings. The emphasis on assigning tasks that from the child's perspective seem to be arbitrary and to involve very delayed consequences produces gods who exert their rewards and punishments in the next life. Malevolent, aggressively punitive supernaturals make up the projective system of societies that treat infants harshly or neglectfully and then employ rigid and punitive socialization pressures during childhood, particularly if the failure to perform required chores has immediately obvious consequences.

These studies suggest research that would shed light on the different roles that beliefs in supernaturals play at both the institutional and individual level. First, additional cross-cultural scales need to be developed that directly rate the extent to which spirits are believed to be punitive for misdeeds rather than just malevolently punitive or present but otiose. Also, the timing of punishment administered to mortals by these supernaturals, whether right now or deferred until after death, would permit a broader test of B. Whiting's (1961) hypothesis to account for data from the *Six Cultures* study. Simultaneously, scales to assess the same dimensions at the individual difference level should be produced. The studies that need to be done would follow the *Six Cultures* model and would test the same hypothesis using the cross-cultural survey analysis, comparisons on observations made on individuals of societies selected for wide variations on the dependent variable of interest, and tests of individual differences within societies.

GUILT

Perhaps the mechanism of social control that is most familiar to members of our society is that of an internalized conscience. The major theoretical guidelines for the antecedents to investigate in assessing the child-rearing influences on conscience development derive mainly from the Freudian formulation of the identification process (Freud, 1933). According to Freud, a major factor in the internalization of parental standards and values, and in the development of feelings of remorse or guilt when these standards are violated, is the affectional bond (warmth) between parent and child. Many studies done within our society, typically based on maternal interview material, have assessed this association. The most common conclusion from these studies is that parental warmth is positively correlated with guilt (Yarrow, Campbell, & Burton, 1968), yet the positive relationships found are based on correlations of antecedent–consequent measures that both come from the same respondent, usually the mother reporting about her own child training and the conscience of her child.

To assess this relation cross-culturally, J. Whiting and Child (1953, p. 227) used as a cultural index of guilt "a measure of the extent to which a person who gets sick blames himself for having gotten sick." They reasoned that "self-recrimination, as a response to illness," was an "index of the degree to which guilt feelings are strong and widely generalized." They found no relation between parental warmth during early childhood, indexed by indulgence of dependency, and their guilt measure of patient responsibility for illness. In contrast, the relative importance of love withdrawal as a disciplinary technique was related positively to guilt.

Although J. Whiting and Child present reasons why the lack of association between general warmth and guilt should not be considered conclusive, a recent review of the evidence concludes that in fact there is probably no consistent relationship between parental warmth and conscience development (Burton, 1976b). Data based on direct observations of mother–child interactions indicate that warmth should be conceptualized as both a long-term affectional relationship and as a resource that can be manipulated in the immediate situation (Burton & Goldberg, described by Burton, 1976a,b; Gill & Burton, 1978). These studies have found that parental warmth does not invariably or inevitably relate to conscience (or any other socially desired behavior) but instead becomes influential when it is contingent in some way on required behavior. Our initial analyses in both studies assessed the relationship between a global measure of maternal warmth when interacting with the child and a measure of the child's compliance to rules of a game. In the Burton and Goldberg study this global warmth measure was obtained in what appeared to the mother to be a play situation but was actually a temptation test for the child. The relationship between overall warmth and the child's tendency to cheat was positive ($r = 0.37$, $p < 0.01$).

Mothers appeared to perceive the honesty test used in these studies as a situation testing their children's achievement. As a consequence many mothers inadvertently manipulated their warmth to shape dishonest behavior in their child. A division of the global warmth measure into warmth contingent on the child's successful performance and warmth unrelated to the game clarified the picture. It was the warmth contingent on success that led to the child's deviation ($r = 0.38$, $p < 0.01$), whereas the noncontingent warmth was unrelated to the child's honesty ($r = 0.08$).

In the subsequent study (Gill & Burton, 1978) the mother taught her own children the rules for playing a game and then the child was tested for deception from these rules when playing alone. The global maternal warmth measure was unrelated to the child's conscience measure. We were able to divide this global warmth measure into success-related and rule-related warmth. Warmth contingent on successful performance led to low resistance to temptation ($r = 0.29$, $p < 0.05$). Mothers high on this measure seemed to insist that it was an achievement study and focused on how well the child was performing even when teaching the child the rules. The measure of warmth contingent on following rules led to the child's resisting the temptation to cheat when alone ($r = 0.25$, $p < 0.05$). Mothers high on this measure did concentrate on the rules and made their warmth contingent on the child's compliance.

Further, the data show that the effectiveness of the immediate manipulation of warmth depends on the long-term affectionate bond or love relationship that has been established. Withdrawal of warmth was most effective in producing behavior in the child that the mother wanted when the mother–child relationship was generally one of high warmth ($r = 0.35$) but was relatively ineffective if the warmth relationship was generally low ($r = 0.14$). This interaction between a generally high-warmth relationship and subsequent punishment has also been demonstrated in experimental studies with puppies (J. Whiting, 1954; Freedman, 1958) and children (Parke & Walters, 1967). But what should be the effect if the parent uses reward rather than punishment as the mode for manipulating warmth? Our experimental study showed the mother's giving warmth contingent on behavior she wanted in the child was effective in a generally low-warmth relationship ($r = 0.51$) but had little immediate effect on the child's behavior if the relationship was usually one of high warmth ($r = -0.14$).

These findings fit nicely with a general principle of learning: If an individual is in a deprived state of a desired resource, giving that resource is an effective reward for shaping behavior. The corollary is that if the individual is used to a high level of the desired resource, the withdrawal of the resource is effective as a punishment for undesirable behavior. This punishment is especially effective in shaping behavior if the termination of the withdrawal is contingent on the desired behavior. Clearly, the giving of warmth and attention as rewards and the withdrawal of warmth and subsequent termination of withdrawn attention conform to this general model.

We have looked again at the analyses of J. Whiting and Child (1953) and find similarities in their findings on conscience with general warmth (no association) and manipulation of warmth (low positive association). These cross-cultural scales seem to permit a partial test at the cultural level of the joint effects found in the experimental studies. We use the measure of initial indulgence for dependency as an index of the general affectional bond or love relationship. The use of love-oriented techniques is the index of the manipulation of warmth at a later age in childhood when children are being taught to comply with standards. The measure of conscience is patient responsibility for illness. Using all cases on which all three measures are available, we find some cross-cultural support for our hypothesis as far as use of love withdrawal in a high warmth context is concerned (Table 20–1). Societies low on the index of general warmth (initial indulgence of dependency) are equally divided as to high and low guilt regardless of their use of love withdrawal. In line with our interpretation, societies high on initial indulgence of dependency show a positive relation between guilt and use of love withdrawal. Certainly this test is suggestive only and needs to be explored further on a larger, more adequate sample. Still, the consistency of the results across the individual and cultural level of analyses provide strong support for the hypotheses being tested.

J. Whiting & Child also assessed the relations between age of beginning socialization and their index of guilt. In predicting that early socialization would result in high guilt, they considered the following possibilities: (1) withdrawal of love when the child was very young and helpless would be more effective than when the child was older; (2) early socialization would be more severe than later socialization; and (3) guilt learned at a very young age would be more likely to generalize inappropriately because of the inability to discriminate adequately and would therefore manifest itself in the belief that one must have done something wrong if one is now ill. Their hypothesis that age of initiating socialization would affect superego strength was consistently supported by strong negative correlations between guilt and age of beginning socialization for weaning, modesty training, sex training, and independence training (av. $r = -0.50$). The evidence also suggested a curvilinear effect (for weaning and toilet training) if training began before 1 year of age. This evidence led

TABLE 20-1   Joint Effect of Initial Indulgence for Dependency and Use of Love-oriented Techniques of Punishment on Patient Responsibility for Illness

Initial Indulgence for Dependency	Use of Love-oriented Techniques of Punishment	Patient Responsibility for Illness	
		Low (1–9)	High (10–21)
Low (9–15)	Low (−20 to −7)	Tikopia Bena Ainu Rwala Chenchu	Pukapukans Dobuans Lakher Dahomeans Chiricahua
	High (−6 to 14)	Marquesans Samoans Kwakiutl Trobrianders	Alorese Hopi Manus Yakut Lepcha $r = 0.096, t = 0.198$, NS
High (16–19)	Low	Azande Kurtachi Comanche Lesu	Chamorro
	High	Siriono Teton Wogeo Tanala	Maori Navaho Kwoma Arapesh Papago $r = 0.238, t = 2.20, p < .05$

$r = 0.10, t = 1.77, p < 0.05$ for relation between love-oriented techniques and patient responsibility for illness (Whiting & Child, 1953, p. 245); $r = -0.06$ for relation between initial indulgence for dependency and patient responsibility for illness (Whiting & Child, 1953, pp. 238–239).

to a rejection of the interpretation that the result was due to a deficiency to discriminate adequately, resulting in inappropriate generalization. Further, the disparity between the magnitudes of association of guilt with these age measures compared to the association with severity of socialization ($r = 0.29$) decreased the persuasiveness of the severity explanation. They concluded that the reasoning based on use of love withdrawal at an early age, which should increase identification with parental standards, was the most plausible explanation for these results.

This hypothesis and supporting evidence is particularly interesting for its developmental implications. When a hypothesis predicts that an experience that occurs early in development, especially during infancy, will affect adult personality, the predicted effect must be robust. Otherwise, the original effect is likely to be overridden or at least much modified by all the intervening events that might independently or interactively influence the same aspect of adult personality being studied. If the theory proposes a continuous or cumulative influence beginning in infancy and continuing into adulthood, the effect is more likely to be manifested. Further exploration of the reasons for this long-term robust effect is certainly warranted.

The cumulative shaping of theory by data has led J. Whiting to propose a theory of identification labeled the status envy hypothesis (J. Whiting, 1959; 1960; Burton & Whiting, 1961). According to this theory, disbarment from controlling coveted resources results in the child's envying the status of and thus identifying with the person who does exercise such control (see Chapter 18 in this volume for a full presentation of this theory and supporting evidence). Testing this theory for predicting superego development, J. Whiting (1959) found that Murdock's (1957) measures of family and household structures strongly related to patient responsibility for illness. Societies with mother–child household structure were lowest, polygynous households were next, and then monogamous extended households; highest were monogamous nuclear household societies. This finding was interpreted as support for the prediction that the more the father exercised control over resources in the child's early development, the stronger would be an internalized conscience as an adult. Strong confirmation of this hypothesis was provided by Bacon, Child, and Barry (1963), who found that crime of all types was associated with low father salience during infancy. This finding was also supportive of the argument made by Burton and Whiting (1961) that early father absence was a contributing factor to juvenile delinquency. (For a different viewpoint, see Chapter 4 in this volume.)

Additional cross-cultural analyses by J. Whiting (1959) showed that early father presence interacts with age of initiating weaning. This analysis showed that although both antecedent measures (early father presence and early weaning) were separately predictive of high conscience, the analysis of their joint effect indicated that early age for initiating socialization may hold only in monogamous societies.

The results of these studies provide support for a conceptualization of the socialization of conscience as involving a process of identification. In most of the current research on self-control and conscience formation, identification processes are benignly neglected. We see here one of the contributions of the cross-cultural method. This method brings to our attention some factors in the socialization process that might be overlooked if our experiments focus only on immediately effective reward and punishment techniques. The influence of current reinforcement contingencies is likely to be powerful and may mask more subtle yet persistent effects from an early identification process. The strongest approach is obviously to pursue the questions at all levels of analysis.

SUMMARY

This review of cross-cultural evidence bearing on the inculcation of mechanisms that different societies have developed for social control supports a model of early childhood experiences leading to adult personality. The data suggest that the structure of a society reinforces the development of some types of moral orientations and frustrates others. Noticeable in our review is the dearth of cross-cultural work in this area over the last 20 years. Certainly there are loose ends and some promising questions to pursue suggested in these studies.

We have already noted the need for more adequate scales to test more directly the theoretical reasoning used to interpret some of the findings. This is recommended not only to provide more understanding of the findings already presented but also to provide more adequate tests of hypotheses that may be rejected from using inadequate, indirect scales. The recommendation for individual difference scales to be used across cultures is not made lightly. Rather than have investigators sidetracked into trying to develop a fully "equivalent" instrument across cultures (probably impossible by definition), the effort should be in developing instruments with comparable face validity that could provide evidence of parallel functional relations at the three levels of analysis recommended. In a recent review (Burton, 1976b), it was noted that analysis of the generality of various behavioral tests of honesty shows that although there is a traitlike factor present there is only a modest amount of overlap across different kinds of individual tests. With the average correlation in the 0.30s, the tests are clearly not alternative equivalent forms of the underlying common factor. Nevertheless, the review found that functional or antecedent–consequent relations, such as the effect of risk on honesty, demonstrated remarkable consistency despite the low overlap across both risk measures and the honesty indices. It is this kind of consistent functional association that is most interesting in the cross-cultural comparisons.

In this review we had intended to include "shame" as a mechanism of social control, particularly since there is currently so much research within our culture on locus of control that seems so parallel to the theoretical conceptualizations of shame (Ausubel, 1955; Benedict, 1946; Gilligan, 1976; Mead, 1937; Piers & Singer, 1953). However, there appear to be no cross-cultural surveys exploring the antececents of "shame" compared to "guilt" and only one small study that was stimulated by the possible theoretical differences between "shame" and "guilt" cultures (Grinder & McMichael, 1962). Perhaps this reflects an attitude by investigators using the cross-cultural survey method that in the projective systems of societies there are represented many types of external orientations that have distinguishable antecedents in childhood. Certainly, as J. Whiting (1959) noted, shame conceptualized as a single typology of external moral orientation is not supported by the cross-cultural data. Control over behavior through learned fear of sorcerers, of retributive gods and parental ghosts, and of inanimate animal spirits do not fit together as equivalent manifestations of a common orientation toward external locus of control. Still, a conceptualization of shame as an internalized self-control mechanism might lead to productive cross-cultural comparisons. Societies may vary in the extent to which an internal moral orientation is egoistic or group focused. Consider, for example, a society like the Hopi that is rated high on the cross-cultural index of superego. Dennis (1955) found that 40 percent of the Hopi children tested cheated on an academic task. Although this evidence may seem at odds with the usual depiction of this society as emphasizing noncompetitive behavior, it may be that this test did not place these children in moral conflict. Academic achievement tests may have low salience in their Hopi moral system. By contrast, there should be significantly higher resistance by the Hopi—and other societies with a strong group orientation—in temptation tests that involve deception for personal gain at another's expense.

The progression of the evidence from the studies indicates that there should be additional consideration of joint or multivariate effects. We found, for example, that the conclusion that early warmth was unrelated to adult superego was not borne out by the interactional analysis. Other examples are the interactions of household and age for guilt, of postpartum sex taboo and sex training for sorcery, and of early nurturance and aggression training for fear of ghosts. Additional interaction effects should be considered and tested.

Some of our recent experimental studies suggest that the language structure of societies might be a determinant in the strength of internalized controls. These studies show, first, that there is a dimension of inclusiveness from specific to general that children use to order common labels of moral conduct (Burton, 1976a). For the youngest children, "cheating" was the most inclusive term for classifying cartoons of moral transgressions, whereas "honesty" was most inclusive, increasingly so from age 7 years on. These studies show us what children can do under experimental conditions, not what they actually do when faced with categorizing real-life situations. The data did support our hypothesis that the adult language community makes hierarchically inclusive distinctions among moral conduct terms and that these distinctive usages are correlated with the cognitive development of children.

Additional experiments show that the use of the more inclusive terms in specific moral training situations can produce greater strength of honesty than will the use of less inclusive terms. In the initial studies, the results were mixed, with the middle level "cheating" being most effective as a critical term to use in teaching children honesty. It appeared that "cheating" may be a term frequently used in real life for punishing moral misconduct, whereas "honesty"—the most inclusive term we used —is a term learned in a more rational, academic context. To test this interpretation we devised films portraying a child's being punished for a transgression (Casey, 1978). The differences among the films were the critical terms used by the punishing agent. Although the results are complex, the more inclusive term of "honesty" produced most generalized honest behavior. It seems likely that the language structures of societies may vary on the dimension of inclusiveness explored in these experiments. Analyses of the terms used by parents when rearing children might reveal significant differences in the inclusiveness of the concepts used across cultures. In some societies, parents may rely on limited, specific terms, such as "do this" and "don't do that." This language would not provide the semantic mediation to serve as discriminative cues for generalization to other situations. Parents in other societies may use more inclusive terms that should contribute to their children's classifying physically different situations as being similar on the abstract conceptual dimension. If this cognitive cue is tied to inhibitory arousal, there should be greater generalization of learned self-control and therefore stronger conscience. Little has yet been done to explore the relationships of language structure, especially the language used in child training, to the mechanisms of self-control. It seems to us a promising area to investigate.

A full consideration of the internalization of standards would deal with both proscribed and prescribed behaviors. Children must learn what actions are taboo in their society, their culture's reasons for designating those actions as forbidden, and what consequences will result if the taboos are broken. These proscriptive, "thou shalt not ..." standards set limits on the motives for immediate gratification. The task of assimilating these imposed restraints is onerous enough, yet the internalization of standards is only half complete. Children must also learn the culture's prescriptive behaviors, what is deemed should be "done unto others." These standards establish the actions required to be in compliance with the cultural norms.

In this chapter, however, we have dealt only with the evidence on certain proscriptive standards, since the prescriptive behavioral systems are covered by other authors of this volume. Our discussion focused on the mechanisms developed by various cultures for achieving acceptance of these norms by their members. We hope that some of the suggestions for exploring questions that seem to us to be especially promising at this time will act to stimulate more research in this important area of human conduct.

REFERENCES

Ausubel, D. F. Relationships between shame and guilt in the socializing process. *Psychological Review,* 1955, *62,* 378–390

Bacon, Margaret, Barry, H., III, & Child, I. L. Rater's instructions for analysis of socialization practices with respect to dependence and independence. In H. Barry, III, M. K. Bacon, & I. L. Child, A cross-cultural survey of some sex differences in socialization. *Journal of Abnormal and Social Psychology,* 1957, *55,* 327–332.

Bacon, M. K., Child, I. L., & Barry, H., III. A cross-cultural study of the correlates of crime. *Journal of Abnormal and Social Psychology,* 1963, *66* (4), 291–300.

Barry, H., III, Bacon, M. K., & Child, I. L. A cross-cultural survey of some sex differences in socialization. *Journal of Abnormal and Social Psychology,* 1957, *55,* 327–332.

Barry, H., III, Josephson, L., Lauer, E., & Marshall, K. Trait inculcated in childhood: Cross-cultural codes 5. *Ethnology,* 1976, *15,* 83–114

Benedict, R. *The chrysanthemum and the sword: Patterns of Japanese culture.* Boston: Houghton Mifflin, 1946.

Burton, R. V. Moral training programs. Where are we going? Invited address, Annual Convention of the American Psychological Association, Washington, D. C., 1976a.

Burton, R. V. Honesty and dishonesty. In T. Lickona (Ed.), *Moral development and behavior.* New York: Holt, Rinehart & Winston, 1976b.

Burton, R. V., & Goldberg, F. G. Cheating related to maternal pressures for achievement. Reported by R. V. Burton, Honesty and dishonesty. In T. Lickona (Ed.) *Moral development and behavior.* New York: Holt, Rinehart & Winston, 1976.

Burton, R. V. & Whiting, J. W. M. The absent father and cross-sex identity. *Merrill-Palmer Quarterly of Behavior and Development,* 1961, *7,* 85–95.

Casey, W. M. Training children to be consistently honest through verbal self-instructions. Unpublished doctoral dissertation, State University of New York at Buffalo, 1978.

Dennis, W. Are Hopi children non-competitive? *Journal of Abnormal and Social Psychology,* 1955, *50,* 99–100.

Freedman, D. G. The effects of indulgent and disciplinary rearing in four breeds of dogs. *Science,* 1958, *127,* 585–586.

Freud, S. *New introductory lectures on psycho-analysis.* New York: Norton, 1933.

Friendly, J. P. A cross-cultural study of ascetic mourning behavior. Unpublished honors thesis, Radcliffe College, 1956.

Gill, P., & Burton, R. V. Parent-child interaction and child self control assessed through direct observation. Paper read at the Eastern Psychological Association Annual Meeting Meeting, Washington, D. C., 1978.

Gilligan, J. Beyond morality: Psychoanalytic reflections on shame, guilt, and love. In T. Lickona (Ed.), *Moral development and behavior.* New York: Holt, Rinehart & Winston, 1976.

Grinder, R. E., & McMichael, R. E. Cultural influence on conscience development: Resistance to temptation and guilt among Samoans and American Caucasians. *Journal of Abnormal and Social Psychology,* 1962, *66,* 503–507.

Lambert, W. W., Triandis, L. M., & Wolf, M. Some correlates of beliefs in the malevolence and benevolence of supernatural beings: A cross-cultural study. *Journal of Abnormal and Social Psychology,* 1959, *58,* 162–169.

Mead, M. *Cooperation and competition among primitive peoples.* New York: McGraw-Hill, 1937.

Murdock, G. P. World ethnographic sample. *American Anthropologist,* 1957, *59,* 664–687.

Murdock, G. P., & Provost, C. Factors in the division of labor by sex. *Ethnology,* 1973, *12,* 203–225.

Otterbein, K. F., & Otterbein, C. S. Believers and beaters: A case study of supernatural beliefs and child rearing in the Bahama Islands. *American Anthropologist,* 1973, *75,* 1670–1681.

Parke, R. D., & Walters, R. H. Some factors influencing the efficacy of punishment training for inducing response inhibition. *Monographs of the Society for Research in Child Development,* 1967, *32* (1).

Piers, G., & Singer, M. B. *Shame and guilt: A psychoanalytic and a cultural study.* Springfield, Ill.: Charles C. Thomas, 1953.

Spiro, M. E., & D'Andrade, R. A cross-cultural study of some supernatural beliefs. *American Anthropologist,* 1958, *60,* 456–466.

Whiting, B. B. *Paiute sorcery.* New York: Viking Fund Publications in Anthropology, No. 15, 1950.

Whiting, B. B. Task assignment and character development. Unpublished manuscript, 1961.

Whiting, J. W. M. Fourth presentation. In J. M. Tanner & B. Inhelder (Eds.), *Discussions on child development: II.* London: Tavistock Publications, 1954.

Whiting, J. W. M. Sorcery, sin and the superego. In M. R. Jones (Ed.), *Nebraska symposium on motivation.* Lincoln: University of Nebraska Press, 1959.

Whiting, J. W. M. Resource mediation and learning by identification. In I. Iscoe & H. W. Stevenson (Eds.), *Personality development in children.* Austin: University of Texas Press, 1960.

Whiting, J. W. M. Socialization process and personality. In F. L. K. Hsu (Ed.), *Psychological anthropology.* Homewood, Ill.: Dorsey Press, 1961.

Whiting, J. W. M. The effects of climate on certain cultural practices. In W. H. Goodenough (Ed.), *Explorations in cultural anthropology: Essays in honor of George Peter Murdock.* New York: McGraw-Hill, 1964.

Whiting, J. W. M., & Child, I. L. *Child training and personality: A cross-cultural study.* New Haven: Yale University Press, 1953.

Yarrow, M. R., Campbell, J. D., & Burton, R. V. *Child rearing: An inquiry into research and methods.* San Francisco: Jossey-Bass, 1968.

21

Affiliation, Social Context, Industriousness, and Achievement

Ronald Gallimore

Describing and explaining human industriousness and achievement has occupied social and behavioral science for a long time. The better known theories treat industriousness as a quality of the individual. For example, individuals with need for achievement or *n* Ach (McClelland, Atkinson, Clark, & Lowell, 1953) are presumed to work hard for self-produced rewards such as feelings of personal mastery. But there are other reasons a person may work hard:

> We found a pervasive preoccupation with achievement and accomplishment, no matter where or what group of Japanese was tested. But their achievement imagery differs from that of American samples. (Wagatsuma, 1956)
>
> Throughout, the Japanese materials show high need affiliation. (DeVos, 1968, p. 359)
>
> Nowhere is the importance of affiliative values more evident than in the incredible energy which Hawaiians will expend in preparing a luau with friends, or helping a friend repair his home, or car, etc. . . . Nothing is more incorrect than the stereotype of the "lazy" Hawaiian; they are an industrious and willing people, but their commitments are always more firm and productive if the goal is an intensification of human relationships rather than an accumulation of personal wealth or some individual achievement. (Gallimore & Howard, 1968, p. 10)

The Japanese and Hawaiian data show that individuals may be motivated to work hard and achieve for a variety of reasons, social as well as personal. The view that individual need for achievement is only one of many possible antecedents of achievement and industriousness is held, among others, by McClelland (1975)—with whom the concept of *n* Ach is most closely identified. Implication? A person may be low in *need for achievement* and yet still be highly industrious and achieving. He/she may be *motivated to work and achieve* because of social rewards, affiliation opportunities, power, fear of failure, delusions of persecution, and so on. A person may have *low achievement motivation* (low *n* Ach) but be *motivated to achieve;* this sentence is contradictory only if the term *achievement motivation* is given surplus meaning. It can be a mischievous term because it is so easily overgeneralized to include all motivations to achieve.

689

The quotations from the Japanese and Hawaiian studies also indicate that affiliation behavior and motivation are among the potential antecedents of industriousness and achievement.

The opportunity to interact with others and the approval of family/peers can have a significant impact. In cultures which make affiliation and social rewards contingent on hard work and achievement, such factors may be relatively more important than individual need for achievement. As this review will demonstrate, the amount of industriousness and achievement may not be less for being encouraged and sustained by affiliation variables; some studies suggest affiliation opportunities and rewards may be more significant in Western societies than the traditional emphasis on individual need achievement would indicate.

But first, a modest recounting is presented of the personality versus setting controversy and its current resolution. This is a proper introduction for a review that assumes that industriousness and achievement may be a function of social setting as well as personality variables.

PERSONALITY, SOCIAL CONTEXT, AND INDUSTRIOUSNESS: AN INTERACTIONIST CONSENSUS

Hotly debated for the past decade has been the issue of social context versus "internalized" state or trait explanations of personality or complex behavior. After reviewing nearly five decades of personality research, Mischel (1968) concluded that the search for "situation-free" theories of personality ought to be abandoned; he suggested there was little evidence that traits or "underlying dispositions" alone can account for complex behavior. Rather, he argued that social factors exert a strong influence on such behaviors as industriousness, achievement, affiliation, introversion, aggression, etc.

Naturally there were rejoinders to Mischel's argument (e.g., Block, 1977). More recently, the social setting personality argument has given way to an interactionist consensus (Bandura, 1977; Magnusson & Endler, 1977; Mischel, 1977). For example, Bandura conceives behavior to be the product of a continuous, reciprocal interaction between person and environment. The environment influences behavior, and behavior influences an individual's environment.

In such a model, behavior construed as industriousness is assumed to be a joint product of environmental variables and internal processes. In some instances, persons who otherwise show little sign of achievement or industry might be induced to work and strive for a reward, such as peer approval or money (Atkinson & Feather, 1966, pp. 317–318).

Others may work hard in the absence of socially mediated incentives: "After individuals learn to set standards for themselves and to generate self-reactions, they can influence their behavior by self-produced consequences. The development of self-reactive functions thus gives humans a capacity for self-direction" (Bandura, 1977, p. 142).

But to imply that any individual, irrespective of culture group, is industrious solely for internal or external reasons is to oversimplify:

> To begin with, one would be hard put to find any situations that lack external inducements for behavior. The physical and social structures of situations, the materials they contain, the expectations of others, and a host of other stimulus determinants all exert a substantial influence on behavior. . . . The activation and

persistence of behavior is therefore best understood as a continuous interaction between personal and situational sources of influences." (Bandura, 1977, pp. 108–109)

Cultural differences in the relative importance of internal versus external sources of behavior determination are likely to be more a matter of degree than kind.

Some discussions attribute variations in industriousness and achievement to differences in social values. Social values are said to define and implement motivated behavior (Rosen, 1956); variables that impel the individual to achieve do not specify the activities through which excellence may be achieved (Rosen, 1956). Although psychological factors may be similar, in one culture school achievement is valued, in another canoe building; what people will work at follows accordingly.

But these accounts do not explain how values regulate behavior. There are two mechanisms identified at present. First, people differ in the values they place on money, approval, material possessions, social status, exemption from restrictions, etc. These represent prized *incentives* which can motivate activities required to secure them; disvalued incentives do not. The higher the incentive value, the higher the level of performance (Watson, 1971).

A second mechanism was described by Bandura—value can be invested in activities themselves as well as in extrinsic incentives:

As we have seen, the value does not inhere in the behavior itself but rather in the positive and negative self-reactions it generates. Evaluative self-reinforcement thus provides a second mechanism by which values influence conduct. The evaluative standards represent the values; the anticipatory self-pride and self-criticism for actions that correspond to, or fall short of, adopted standards serve as the regulatory influences. (Bandura, 1977, pp. 139–140)

FOCUS

In this chapter I am concerned with those antecedents and covariates of achievement and industriousness that have to do with affiliation behavior, including motives and values, social context, work and task organization, and social rewards. The common thread among the diverse studies reviewed is the connection among human industriousness/achievement, individual interest in and concern with social affiliation, and individual response to affiliation opportunities, context, outcomes, and rewards. The studies include both those that focus on the individual and those that focus on the settings in which individuals function.

Industriousness and achievement can be distinguished as means and ends, respectively. Many achievements are the product of skill, creativity, and good fortune as well as industry and effort. Where making the distinction between achievement and industriousness is useful or made by the research reviewed, it is made here.

As much as possible, findings are discussed in terms of the specific variables under study, such as the effect on industriousness of the opportunity to work as a member of a team or the correlation of TAT affiliation themes and school achievement. In most studies achievement is defined in terms of short-term performance on a task or relatively longer period of work, such as production rates and school achievement scores. These various forms of task and work achievement depend partly or largely on, or are assumed to depend on, individual industriousness; often the operational definition of achievement is directly related to attentiveness and effort expenditure.

In some cases it may appear that hard work is its own reward and presumptuous to describe the endproduct as an achievement. Although there is more to these points, they are beyond the scope of the present survey.

As used here the term *affiliation motivation* is a gloss, a matter of convenience. The term refers in this context to a variety of psychological and social variables, not a single dimension or state/trait. I see little value in proposing a motivational dimension which would be the affiliation equivalent of *n* Ach. To suggest a single construct to explain affiliation behavior and its connection to achievement/industriousness is not plausible. I believe this review will demonstrate that a variety of factors, individual as well as social, must be considered in the analysis of achievement and industriousness. If there is eventually a definitive formulation of the antecedents of industriousness, it will be complex, not simple, and it will include affiliation behavior and motivation.

The chapter is divided roughly into two thematic structures. The first half reviews the affiliation motivation/achievement link in two sharply different cultural groups —Japanese and Hawaiians. Although both have been described as affiliation oriented, the former has exhibited high levels of industriousness and achievement while the latter are economically disadvantaged and often stereotyped as "happy-go-lucky natives." These studies have treated affiliation/achievement in terms of personality or individual differences.

The second half reviews a diverse set of studies of the effects of social context variables. Few of these studies have been concerned with individual differences; almost none have interpreted results in terms of affiliation motivation, however defined. But the context variables studied include such things as the effects on performance of group working conditions, group reward, group contingencies, attitudes and preferences of individuals to be with and work as a team, etc. These are social context variables which may influence industriousness and achievement and are thus properly included in this review. Again, including them as referents of affiliation motivation is a matter of convenience; I do not mean to imply that a single state/trait of affiliation motivation explains the effects of social context variables.

CULTURAL STUDIES OF AFFILIATION MOTIVATION AND ACHIEVEMENT

Studies of Native Japanese and Japanese in North America: Group versus Individual Motivation

Testing of the hypothesis that Japanese are group or affiliatively motivated began more than 20 years ago. These data are particularly relevant to the issue at hand because of the striking economic and social achievements in this century of Japanese nationals and immigrants. The success of the Japanese is strong evidence that a variety of psychological and/or social factors, including affiliation motivation, may antecede industriousness and achievement.

In the Japanese studies, the distinction between *group* and *individual* motivation cuts across many discussions of the affiliation motivation/industriousness and achievement linkage—for example, DeVos' (1968) argument that many psychological theories of motivation were "too much dependent on individualistically motivated conceptions of human nature" to apply to Japanese behavior. Among the Japanese, the pursuit of purely personal, individual satisfaction is likely to be viewed as a "sign of excessive immoral egoism" (DeVos, 1968, p. 359). The rewards bestowed by Japanese families and society are more important sources of motivation. Wagatsuma (1956) examined TAT (Thematic Apperception Test) protocols collected from samples of Issei (first-generation Japanese immigrants to the U.S.), residents of three rural communities in Japan, Nisei (second-generation Japanese-Americans), and Anglo-American middle- and upper-class groups. Qualitative content analyses suggested two prevalent values in the Japanese protocols: an emphasis on striving for success and success for the sake of parents. "When an achievement theme is told by Americans on Picture 2 it is usually concerned with the girl's individualistic achievement. Stories about the achievement of a family as a whole are rare in American samples and possibly characteristic for the Japanese. This point becomes clearer if we combine the stories of family's achievement and of family's happily doing hard-work together and compare their number with that of the girl's achievement stories" (Wagatsuma, 1956, pp. 23–25).

Of the Anglo-Americans who included achievement concerns in their stories, 26 percent (5 of 19 stories) involved a family achievement/hard work theme; for rural Japanese villagers the comparable percentage was 45 (28 of 62 stories).[1] The figures for individual-oriented achievement stories are, of course, 74 and 55 percent for Anglo-Americans and Japanese villagers, respectively.

Using an entirely different method Minoura (1975) reports evidence consistent with Wagatsuma's TAT results. Minoura examined Japanese and Canadian (British Columbia) school textbooks in use in the 1920s and 1970s. Among the dimensions rated was "value orientations which governed the interpersonal behavior of a central character." (Minoura, 1975, p. 95). Satisfactory levels of intercoder reliability were achieved. The results indicated that the Japanese texts of the 1920s had a collectivity orientation (main character doing something for nuclear or extended family, local community, country or society)[2]

... which had been somewhat attenuated over the half century, but those of the 1970's were still not as individualistic as the Canadian counterpart. (Minoura, 1975, p. 98) ... Over the half century, individualistic orientation of British Columbia textbooks was basically unchanged, if we put aside the influence of [World] War I. The relational orientation embodied in behavior of Japanese textbook characters was shifting towards the Canadian pattern, but still retained a group orientation. Individualism was said to be an important element of an industrial society. However, our findings suggest that successful industrialization need not necessarily be accompanied by an increasing individualistic orientation. (p. 101)

In addition, Minoura reports that highly achievement-oriented characters in Japanese texts were motivated to achieve because of an other-directed orientation:

In the British Columbia texts, achievement oriented behaviors were depicted not in the comparative contexts of others, but in relation to the goal. One competed to attain the goal. In this sense, the characters acted individualistically. Thus, other-directed personalities in North American societies tended to be related to less achievement oriented behavior, but other-directed personalities in Japanese society were linked to achievement oriented behavior. (p. 105)

Minoura concluded that these data weigh against attributing Japanese achievement and striving solely to individual motivation. Value orientations must be considered. Japanese values focus on the family, the community, the importance of meeting others' expectations—as DeVos wrote earlier about Japanese achievement motivation, "Success for oneself only was considered a sign of excessive immoral egoism"

(DeVos, 1968, p. 359). While Minoura's textbook analysis suggests that there has been some increase in individualism since 1920 contrasted to that of North Americans, there remains a clear orientation to the family and community.

The group versus individual distinction is also prominent in Dore's (1973) comparison of British and Japanese factories. A central question in this study is accounting for the success of highly different industrial patterns; some of the contrasts drawn are relevant to the present question. Part of the difference in industrial pattern is attributed to cultural variables, one of which Dore terms "groupishness." Groupishness is manifested in Japan by such things as organization of employees into work teams, loyalty toward and identification with the company, frequent attendance at company-organized social events, placing company over family concerns, and other features quite unlike the individualistic orientation of British workers.

Once a Japanese worker, at the factories studied by Dore, accepts employment, it is assumed to be permanent. Although monetary rewards are based on education, seniority, and performance, much of the compensation structure acts to increase loyalty to or affiliation with the company. This is a reflection of the general agreement among Japanese employers and employees of a mutual social as well as economic responsibility. At the English company, "Personal crises are dealt with . . . either by the informal assistance of workmates or through a specialized welfare officer; at Hitachi they are the responsibility of the work supervisor" (Dore, 1973, p. 220). The Japanese company is concerned with worker morals, the British company is not: "An English Electric worker's family has very limited contact with the firm; [a] Hitachi worker's family are peripheral members of the enterprise family—a fact recognized in the system of congratulatory gifts, the work superior's assumption of the wedding go-between role, and so on" (p. 220). Of course, it is not possible to unravel the contributions of these cultural practices to the industriousness and productivity of the Japanese and British workers. Rather, these findings are consistent with the general arguments of DeVos (1968), Wagatsuma (1956), and Minoura (1975).

The Japanese studies are persuasive. These data are consistent with the general argument that family/group orientation or affiliation motivation may foster industriousness and achievement equal to or greater than that of individual achievement-oriented cultures, but they provide no evidence of a correlation between individual level of motivation or value orientation and achievement. In other words, the intergroup comparative analyses provided by the Japanese studies suggest an explanation for the high levels of Japanese and Japanese-American achievement. They do not show how individual variations within culture groups relate to achievement. This question will be examined by reviewing studies of Hawaiian-Americans.

Studies of Hawaiian-American Motivation and Achievement

In economic terms the contrast could not be greater between the status of Hawaiians today and that of Japanese in Japan or Japanese-Americans in Hawaii. The familiar pattern of poverty, poor health, delinquency, and low school achievement plague that 20 percent of the Hawaiian Islands population tracing their heritage to the original Polynesian residents. Yet affiliation is as central a theme of Hawaiian life (Gallimore & Howard, 1968) as has been attributed to Japanese culture. Consequently, this provides an opportunity to determine whether the affiliation motivation/achievement linkage holds in a situation in which historical and economic factors have not been as favorable as was the case in Japan.

Sloggett, Gallimore, & Kubany (1970) compared academically successful and unsuccessful Hawaiian boys on a projective test modeled on the TAT (essentially, pictures were redrawn to feature Island themes and eliminate racial cues). The boys wrote stories which were scored following the standard procedure for obtaining n Ach. More than half of the boys in the two Hawaiian groups wrote no n Ach themes; only 15 percent of the high-achieving and 3 percent of the low-achieving boys wrote n Ach themes for two or more of six pictures. Comparisons with samples of Japanese and Filipino American boys in Hawaii showed that both the high- and low-achieving Hawaiian boys had significantly lower n Ach scores. This was the case despite the fact that the high-achieving Hawaiian boys actually had higher achievement test scores (an average reading achievement test scores above the 70th percentile) than the Japanese and Filipino boys. The high-achieving Hawaiians attended a private school endowed by a Hawaiian princess; selection for the school involves statewide competitive examinations, the purpose of which is to enroll academically elite Hawaiian children. Yet these high-achieving boys wrote no more n Ach themes than the low-achieving boys from one of the poorest areas of the state, where the average reading scores are below the 20th percentile.

> The conclusion that Hawaiian males were poor scholars because they lack n Ach is a "deficiency" explanation. . . . It explains why Hawaiian children do not behave as middle-class Caucasian children do, but it does not explain what motivates those among the Hawaiian children who do achieve. Thus the issue becomes what motive, if not n Ach, is associated with achievement. (Sloggett et al., 1970, pp. 59–60)

Using the same measure as Sloggett et al., Gallimore (1974) correlated n Ach and n Affiliation (n Aff) with actual school achievement of Hawaiian students. n Aff is obtained in a manner identical to the n Ach procedure: stories written in response to pictures are scored according to a prescribed system. The scorer examined the stories for evidence of stated need for affiliation, instrumental activity, anticipatory goal states, obstacles, affective states, and affiliation themata.

Samples of male and female Hawaiian high school students from an economically disadvantaged community were used. There was a significant correlation between n Aff and reading achievement tests; there was no correlation between achievement and n Ach. This is evidence that one kind of affiliation motivation can be directly related to achievement and is consistent with the substantial but indirect evidence provided by the Japanese studies.

There is also evidence from a contrived experimental task (Gallimore, 1972) that Hawaiians scoring high on n Aff chose intermediate risks which are typical of high-achievement motivated persons (Atkinson & Feather, 1966). n Ach was not correlated with the dependent variable (number of intermediate risks chosen). Intermediate risks are apparently preferred by achievement-oriented persons because tasks of such difficulty make individual skill and effort a larger determinant of outcome. Easy or hard risks tend to require only minimal effort and skill (easy tasks) or emphasize luck (hard tasks) as an outcome determinant.

In some respects the n Aff/achievement correlation seems reasonable, but its reasonableness is based more on what we know of the culture than on the sort of common sense assumptions that underlie the *n* Ach/achievement linkage. Needing achievement seems a sensible antecedent to achieving; needing affiliation seems a more likely motivation for good times than hard work.

n Aff and Achievement: What Are the Mediating Links?

n Aff scores are correlated with reading achievement among Hawaiian high school students. What does it mean? How does affiliation motivation reflected in *n* Aff scores help a student?

n Aff stories by Hawaiian high school students are highly likely to involve elements which are judged as instrumental activity (successful outcome) according to the standard affiliation motive manual (Heyns, Veroff, & Atkinson, 1958) used by Gallimore, Boggs, and Jordan (1974):

> The picture which stimulated the greatest number of *n* Aff stories portrayed a single boy standing on the curb by a street light with his hands in his pockets. The high *n* Aff boys and girls described his problem as isolation, and projected that he had no friends, no family. . . . The instrumental actions they predicted the boy would take were of two sorts: he would solve the problem by being friendly, making new friends, getting help from parents. . . .
>
> The second class of instrumental activities involved solving the problem by confrontation, discussion, or apology. . . . There is a striking similarity between the tactics proposed by the high *n* Aff group (and the behaviors which our school observations suggested) to be a critical factor in school adjustment and performance. These data suggest that high *n* Aff [Hawaiians] . . . are more likely to conceive solutions to interpersonal problems in terms that would be of great advantage in relationships with teachers. (Gallimore et al., 1974, pp. 258–259)

In addition, more Hawaiian girls produce *n* Aff fantasy material than boys, and girls have significantly higher reading achievement scores (Gallimore, 1974). Girls are also generally better able to relate directly to teachers (Gallimore et al., 1974).

The instrumental uses of affiliation in the pursuit of achievement have also been noted in studies of the academic success of Anglo-American firstborns and only children. Firstborns are more achieving, affiliative, and conforming (Sutton-Smith & Rosenberg, 1970). When the firstborn is still young, achievements are a means to approval and affiliation. As the child matures, Sutton-Smith and Rosenberg hypothesized, the relationship between affiliation and achievement may be reversed:

> It stands to reason that when one's own career is paramount (as in adolescence) rather than one's relationship to parents, the need for achievement would take on a more autonomous role in human behavior. At the same time the particular success of the first born and only born in becoming eminent might well imply that they may ultimately use their affiliative skills in service of their achievement. (Sutton-Smith & Rosenberg, 1970, pp. 106–107)

Hawaiian students who are especially affiliation motivated are more likely to orient to teachers and to be able to relate effectively (Gallimore et. al., 1974). Thus in addition to the social rewards of incentives component of affiliation motivation, another element appears to operate—among people motivated to secure affiliation rewards, some develop more skillful interpersonal behavior which can be bent to a variety of situations, including achievement. This is consistent with evidence from small group research on U.S. college students; Sorrentino (1973) found that high *n* Aff scores are under some conditions related to performance effectiveness in task-oriented situations.

Overall, the mediating lines between affiliation motivation, whether defined as n Aff or in some other way, have not been widely explored; for example, no study of Japanese achievement motivation has to date used the TAT n Aff method, although the system devised by Wagatsuma (1956) was similar in conception. The opportunities for future research are clear, but whether or not work should continue with the n Aff scoring scheme used in the Hawaiian studies is problematical. The advantage is the already available research, although it involves almost exclusively U.S. undergraduates. Perhaps further development of the need for family achievement scoring procedure of Ramirez and Price-Williams (1976) would be a more satisfactory starting point.

Ramirez and Price-Williams used the standard n achievement scoring procedure to obtain need for individual achievement scores, and devised a scheme for coding need for family achievement; in a typical story, coded for family achievement, a child's difficulties in school were quickly overcome after parents visited school and began to encourage the child to work hard. The family achievement code includes the following:

(1) Imagery—reference made to achievement or attainment of an achievement goal (competition with a standard of excellence) from which the family would benefit or that would gain recognition from family members; (2) instrumental activity—any activity independent of the original statement that helps the character achieve for his [or her] family; (3) positive outcome of instrumental activity—activity leads to attainment of the achievement goal; and (4) thema—achievement is the central plot or theme of the story. (Ramirez & Price-Williams, 1976, p. 54)

Ramirez and Price-Williams asked fourth graders in Houston, Texas to write stories about each of seven line drawings of persons depicted in educational settings. Using the family achievement and n Ach scoring procedures, they found that Mexican-American and black-American children scored higher on family achievement; Anglo children scored higher on n Ach. However, the n Ach scores of the Mexican-American and black children were also slightly higher than those of the Anglo children in stories written about pictures that depicted parental figures. They concluded that the ethnic minority children were just as likely to exhibit achievement concerns but that the form in which they are expressed will be determined by cultural factors.

n Affiliation and need for family achievement may be members of a larger class of social approval incentives to achieve. At this point it is not clear if these two variables are related, but it is a plausible assumption.

It is possible also that need for family achievement themes written by Mexican-American youngsters may reflect instrumental skills useful in achievement settings, such as interacting with teachers. Whatever the case, future research should consider the role of affiliation and family approval concerns in terms of instrumental behaviors as well as incentive value.

Finally, despite the contrast in economic situation between Hawaiians and Japanese, it appears that in both areas affiliation-related factors may antecede industriousness and achievement. Of course, available evidence does not allow the conclusion that these apparently similar patterns are in fact composed of identical processes and specific variable linkages. Given the enormous differences between the two cultures, a common factor seems unlikely. But these data do confirm the argument that there may be multiple antecedents of achievement, including social context factors such as social or family approval.

SOCIAL CONTEXT, INDUSTRIOUSNESS, AND ACHIEVEMENT

At this point the focus becomes social context and the setting factors which affect industriousness and achievement. Two major themes are covered—the structure and organization of work and the effects of social rewards and group contingencies.

Structure and Organization of Effort and Work

Unlike what she or he does in Western society, traditional man typically does not separate "tasks from personal relationships. In such societies it is common for working parties, sewing bees, and other task-oriented groups to work willingly because of the inherent social rewards in being together" (Graves & Graves, 1974).

This quotation from Graves and Graves' study of Polynesians in New Zealand summarizes a view held by many social scientists who have contrasted traditional with industrial societies. The emphasis is not on individual motives or needs, which have been featured in the preceding section. Rather, it is the structure, organization, and dynamic of work situations to which are attributed major variations in individual industriousness and achievement.

The quotation underscores an important point—"groups work willingly because of the inherent social rewards in being together." In other words, work is motivated by the *opportunity* for social affiliation and the rewards that affiliation implies. There is no need to belabor this as a rationalization for the present effort to link affiliation, industriousness, and achievement.

But is it only in traditional societies that people are affected in their work by social affiliation opportunities? Terkel's (1972) imaginative study of American workers suggests that affiliation may be as important to some as wages and working conditions, although employers may not always have organized tasks to capitalize upon it:

> The time study men of the General Motors Assembly Division made this discomforting discovery in Lordstown. Gary Bryner, the young union leader, explains it. Occasionally one of the guys will let a car go by. At that point he's made a decision: "Aw, fuck it. It's only a car." It's more important to just stand there and rap. (Terkel, 1972, p. xviii)

Apparently, organization of the work did not capitalize on the desire to interact, and productivity suffered.

Among the dozens of people Terkel interviewed, there are some who like their work, such as a mason who takes pride in his skill and what he creates. But a surprising number of well-paid workers express feelings of alienation, loneliness, boredom, and social isolation, of being not connected with the final product, fellow workers, or the organization. One exception was a firefighter who said that in addition to the social value of his work he enjoyed his job because, "I like everybody working together" (p. 757). This echoes Hawaiian men interviewed by Boggs and Gallimore (1968), who also valued "working together."

Management science research reflects a growing awareness in industrial nations that social features of jobs greatly affect worker productivity and satisfaction (Davis & Taylor, 1972). One of the more interesting approaches to the issue has been explored systematically in Norway. Engelstad (1972) reports the results of an experiment with the autonomous work group (AWG) concept in the chemical pulp department of an integrated paper mill. This situation provided a rigorous test because of the technologic complexity of the industry. Before the experiment began, operations were seriously hampered because the technology required more worker flexibility than permitted by the traditional "segregation of jobs and lack of overlapping skills in the permanent shift teams" (p. 340). These strict limits on individual job specification are traditional in this and many industries and do have many advantages. Training time is shortened; supervision is strengthened by clarity of worker responsibility. But these conventional arrangements segment jobs.

The AWG plan in this instance was designed to achieve two objectives. First, the workers as a group were to take "greater responsibility for the operation of the department as a whole" (p. 345). Second, they must be "enabled and initially encouraged to increase their understanding and control of the processes" (pp. 345–346). Evaluation of several dependent variables, including production indices, indicated important gains were realized by the new approach.

Engelstad provides a number of theoretical principles to account for the benefits of the AWG. There are two classes of principles: task characteristics and psychological job requirements. Among the psychological requirements, which influence worker motivation and attitudes, is "the need for some minimum degree of social support and recognition in the work place" (p. 353).

Does this industrial case support the idea that working as part of a group contributes to worker industriousness and achievement (in the form of productivity)? This particular study provides no direct assessment of the contribution of affiliation satisfaction (access to "inherent social rewards") to productivity. However, an example of the benefits of the AWG suggests that other variables may be more direct mediators of the productivity changes. Engelstad reports his team found post hoc that one machine was particularly good for pulping a certain wood. While this was not public knowledge, one machine operator had discovered the same advantage long before and never communicated the information. It was expected that once the AWG was set up such exchanges of information would be more commonplace; indeed, they found the number of suggestions made by operators increased from an average of 1 per year for 6 years to 53 in approximately 6 months of the experiment. This suggests that better communication may be a more important and direct mediator of change than worker motivation engendered by working in a group.

More recently, Northrup (1977) described the use of AWG in a Swedish automobile assembly plant. The plan was instituted to counteract worker feelings of alienation, high absenteeism, and turnover. The results are mixed. The plant functions, but many suggested it is so much more costly that the gains in productivity are outweighed by increased costs. Also, worker interviews suggest there is a novelty effect that dissipates after time, which one worker described as, "It isn't an experiment any more; it's just a plant for building cars" (Northrup, 1977, p. 29).

Ouchi and Jaeger (1978) report that American workers express liking for a work atmosphere in which "social life is often connected to other employees, that corporate values are adjusted to reflect employee need as well as profit needs, and that high job security is protected above all else" (p. 3). They describe this type of organization, which they call type Z, as a mix of the Japanese and Western European/American models; one that is currently well suited for the U.S. Although the Z models include a "basic cultural commitment to individualistic values," there are also elements of a "highly collective, non-individual pattern of interaction." The Z model simultaneously satisfies "old norms of independence and present needs of affiliation."

The need for affiliation of modern American workers resulted, Ouchi and Jaeger argue, partially as a result of the negative effects on family, house of worship, neighborhood, and friendship networks of the large organizations from which the Z model is now emerging. These large organizations in North American and Western Europe, called type A, "brought about urbanization and its consequent social ills." Work organizations can be arranged to provide the lost affiliation opportunities.

It is an appealing argument given the data presented here. But as Weisner shows (Chapter 25 in this volume), attributing social problems to urbanization is more a matter of opinion than fact. Although Weisner's focus is stress and urbanization, the studies he reviews offer little solid evidence that urban life is as evil as contemporary opinion holds it to be.

Weisner's conclusions, of course, do not contradict Ouchi and Jaeger's argument that U.S. workers prefer work settings in which affiliation opportunities are present or that U.S. workers have "need for affiliation." Rather, at issue is the origin of such needs and whether or not they are the result of urbanization promoted by large organizations. Urban life does provide opportunities for affiliation, although surely in mobile urban life styles it is in the work place that they may be most quickly found and reliably sustained. Weisner's review cautions that urbanization is a complex variable which is better unpacked so that more specific relationships may be examined.

For example, in many urban settings there are ethnically homogeneous neighborhoods in which family, religious, and peer groups are intact, supportive, and functional. Alternative forms of child care are available because of kin proximity; multigeneration households may constitute a large percentage of residences; and the economic base of families may be diverse, with some working in small shops, industry, or in civic services such as refuse collection, police, etc. Each of these qualities can represent a variable, which in turn becomes part of the collection of variables which make up the concept of urbanization. But not all urban households are necessarily part of an immediate affiliation network. It is possible to retain the same job but move to another part of the same urban complex to set up a separate nuclear family residence. Although the subject is still part of the urban setting, the new arrangement effectively untangles family and childhood friendship networks and eliminates many affiliation opportunities. Using the packed variable *urbanization* can conceal the variability found in urban living arrangements.

Whatever else can be concluded from these studies, it is clear that affiliation opportunities and rewards must be taken into account in Western industrial societies as well as in nonindustrial cultures. These industrial studies of the effects of group working conditions add two important elements to a discussion of cross-cultural human development in general and of the affiliation motivation/achievement link in particular. First, they provide a better data base than cross-cultural researchers have tended to use when contrasting traditional and industrial societies; I confess to having contrasted my personal experience of middle-class American industrial culture with my more systematic studies of Hawaiian culture. My undergraduate students like those kinds of contrastive generalizations, but I think better use of industrial psychology and management science research sources can be made in some cultural comparisons and analyses involving Western societies.

Second, the industrial studies (Davis & Taylor, 1972) suggest that the effects on industriousness and achievement of group working conditions vary greatly as a function of many variables. Caution is the watchword for generalizations about the benefits of group working conditions.

This conclusion is an echo of Kelley and Thibaut's (1968) definitive review of group problem-solving research in experimental social psychology. They concluded that the "presence of others increases the individual's level of motivation" (p. 3). However, groups do not have a uniform effect on achievement. In many cases, groups are disruptive of problem solving in terms of both quality and quantity. It appears that a person may become more industrious in the company of others, but what is produced is less than would be achieved on an individual basis.

Structure and Organization of Classrooms: Effects on Student Effort and Achievement

The effects on effort and achievement of group or team working conditions has also been studied in classrooms. DeVries and Slavin (1976) summarized the results of ten experiments on the teams–games–tournament (TGT) instructional process. In general the TGT approach increases student learning, fosters positive nonacademic outcomes (e.g., reducing racial frictions), changes the role of teacher from manager to curriculum expert and resource, and readily complements other kinds of instruction.

Teams consist of four or five students assigned by the teacher to ensure heterogeneity of achievement levels among the members. Teams compete in course content-relevant academic games. Teams practice or study together, during which peer tutoring is encouraged but not required.

The superiority of the team approach over the traditional individual approach is attributable largely to group process variables. Specifically, the team approach increases peer tutoring and alters the normative climate so that students reinforce each other for classroom industry and achievement. The effects of social and peer rewards on classroom performance are reviewed in the next section.

In addition to the DeVries and Slavin studies, there have been a number of investigations which suggest that in some cultures group working conditions do positively influence student industry and achievement.

Graves and Graves (1974) report that Polynesian children display in school settings interaction styles that differ markedly from European (Pakeha) children. Polynesian children tend to be inclusive:

> As we have come to define it, *"Inclusion"* is a principle for interaction which aims at perpetrating a sense of belonging, membership, or solidarity among persons, incorporating them in a *group*. ... Acts of inclusion encompass such behaviors as greetings, welcomes, invitations to join an activity, and organized or spontaneous group activities with a single goal entered into by the participants. (Graves & Graves, 1974)

A preference for working in groups and with peers has also been reported for Hawaiian students. MacDonald and Gallimore (1971) observed six classes twice over a 6-week period. The results indicated that Hawaiian students spontaneously engaged in work with another student about 35 percent of the time. Lenz and Gallimore (1973) used the same observation technique and found a substantially lower rate of spontaneous group work in a nearby Anglo school.

Ramirez and Castaneda (1974) recommended that classroom instruction for Mexican-Americans would be culturally more appropriate if conducted in small groups in an environment that lends itself to group projects (p. 143). Although they do not relate these recommendations to specific cultural observations, their description of traditional Mexican-American communities suggests a connection. They note that Mexican-American children are socialized to *achieve cooperatively* (p. 91).

These studies suggest clearly a preference of some culture groups for working in groups, but they leave an important question unanswered: Does working in groups increase industriousness and/or achievement? Some studies have addressed the question.

MacDonald and Gallimore (1971) reported that very low-achieving Hawaiian boys worked longer and achieved more when working in teams as opposed to individually. However, Chun, Speidel, and Tharp (1974) compared individual and group working conditions and found no difference in number of arithmetic problems finished accurately for a predominantly Hawaiian primary grade group.

Lucker, Rosenfield, Sikes and Aronson (1976) compared the performance of Anglo and minority fifth- and sixth-grade children working in traditional classrooms or in small, interdependent groups. In the interdependent group each student learns a unique portion of the material (in this case a unit on Colonial America) and then teaches fellow group members, each of whom reciprocates. The arrangement places a premium on cooperation and communication, although it retains an individual final reward system because examinations are taken individually. "A covariance analysis indicated that Anglos perform equally in both interdependent and traditional classes. Minorities performed significantly better in interdependent classes than in traditional classes" (Lucker et al., 1976 p. 115). The minorities in this case were Mexican-Americans and Afro-Americans living in Austin, Texas. The authors do not entertain a cultural explanation, but it is plausible, given Ramirez and Castadeda's findings and given the fact that more than half the minority children were Mexican-American. Ramirez and Castaneda (1974) concluded that Mexican-American children were motivated to achieve cooperatively, which suggests they might respond well to an "interdependent group" structure.

On the whole, the classroom studies confirm the argument that for some culture groups the opportunity to work with peers has a salutary effect. What is needed is individual level assessment of the relationship between preference for group organization and industriousness and achievement. The studies reviewed here are based on group classification: Hawaiians have been observed to be affiliation oriented, these children are Hawaiians, therefore their positive response to "classroom teams" must be a result of their "affiliation orientation." In such studies no assessment of an individual's "affiliation orientation" is provided. But there are likely to be intraculture variations in strength of such dimensions as group orientation, as the studies of individual differences in Hawaiian *n* Aff suggested (Gallimore, 1974); individual level measurement would provide a powerful test of the question.

More generally, cultural studies of the effects of working conditions are of largely recent vintage. Most of the citations are in the 1970s. Much remains to be done.

The Effects of Social Rewards on Industriousness and Achievement

Among the reasons teamwork in school is effective is the opportunity such arrangements provide for peer reward. The possibility that social rewards might influence industriousness and achievement has been long recognized:

Atkinson and O'Connor (1966) found that low achievement motivated [U.S.] college students were induced to behave in an achievement-oriented fashion when social approval was available. This hypothesis means that a person in whom the achievement motive is very weak (i.e., a person who produces very little imagery having to do with excellence of performance in thematic apperceptive stories under neutral conditions) might display all of the behavioral symptoms of "an entrepreneurial risk-taker" if some extrinsic reward like love or money, for which he [or she] does have a strong motive, were offered as a general inducement for performance. (Atkinson & Feather, 1966 pp. 317–318)

Kubany, Gallimore, and Buell (1970) found that Filipino high school boys exhibited more achievement-oriented behavior in the presence of an adult experimenter than when the same game was played by isolated individuals. This result was attributed to the motivating effects of implied evaluation by the experimenter and, by implication, the possibility of social approval. Other interpretations are possible— increased attention to the task because of evaluation apprehension, for example. However, the results were consistent with ethnographic descriptions of the importance attached by Filipinos in Hawaii to social approval, interpersonal harmony, and fulfillment of the perceived expectation and needs of others.

Howard (1970) reports that teachers on Rotuma (a Polynesian society) rely on praise to motivate students because Rotumans are socially sensitive. Gallimore et al. (1974) hypothesized that the demonstrated effectiveness of praise for Hawaiian students (and perhaps other Polynesians such as Rotumans) was a partial function of strong habits of attending and orienting to other persons (attending and orienting to others is an operational definition of affiliation); this hypothesis was based partly on a study of ten classrooms and involved over 11,000 observations. MacDonald and Gallimore (1971) found that positive, supportive teacher behavior (e.g., praise) was associated with greater amounts of classroom work. A series of classroom experiments and consultation/interventions with teachers having problems confirmed the positive impact of praise on student effort and achievement.

Gallimore and Tharp (1976) operated a research school for a population of primary grade children mostly of Hawaiian and Polynesian ancestry. A major feature of the program was high rates of teacher praise. Comparisons to control groups demonstrated that project teachers praised more and project children were more industrious as indexed by direct observation of work behavior. Although praise significantly increased student industriousness, reading achievement was still below grade level (Tharp & Gallimore, 1976).

However, Gallimore et al. (1968) found that among some very low-achieving Hawaiian high school students, praise was counterproductive. Students were either embarrassed or angered, in part because of peer norms which devalued school success; it was also possible that the infrequent use of praise by Hawaiian parents may be related to negative reactions to teacher praise. The effects of praise are most dramatic for younger students, while noncontingent, nonevaluative, positive interaction seems more appropriate for older students.

Gallimore et al. (1974) suggested that the affiliation orientation of Hawaiian culture might account partly for the response of younger children to praise. Such children come to school accustomed to being cared for by siblings and other adults as well as parents. Praise helps them to attend to the teacher as is typically required in public classrooms. Gallimore et al. also noted that positive teacher behaviors such as praise are advocated widely in many school programs as a remedy for poor student performance and motivation, but it is possible that positive teacher behavior is more critical for children from cultures which are affiliation oriented or motivated.

One reason for the effectiveness of praise for children from some cultural backgrounds may be the information value of positive teacher—pupil interactions. Teachers who praise often must do so consistently to be effective. To be consistent teachers must have clearly specified rules and expectations themselves as well as for the students. The result may be greatly enhanced information feedback to the students as well as access to the supposed incentive value of praise. For the child who is inclined to approach and interact with others, teachers or peers, well-defined rules and reward contingencies for interpersonal behavior would surely have a significant influence.

Social rewards can have a profound effect on industriousness and achievement. The results are clear, and the implications significant. Motivated students—those who display industriousness and achieve in school—may do so because of environmental conditions. But what of their personal, felt need for achievement? Their levels of n Ach? How do individual motives interact with availability of social rewards for effort and achievement? There are precious few studies of this apparently significant interaction (e.g., Atkinson & O'Connor, 1966). This is primarily because of research traditions; those interested in n Ach and individual motive states do not generally do natural setting classroom research. Those who study the effects of teacher rewards do not attend to the question of individual motive states. There is no cross-cultural research literature on this question.

As for the cultural questions, there is a theme running through the studies reviewed. It appears that children from affiliation- or group-oriented societies may be more responsive to certain forms of interpersonal behavior in achievement settings. For these children frequent, positive feedback (in the form of praise, etc.) appears to have a positive effect on their attention to academic tasks, their diligence, and their achievement. Whether it is the incentive or informative components of social feedback is unclear, since these two functions are nearly always confounded in natural settings. That is, a teacher saying "good job" communicates information about work accuracy and indicates progress toward whatever consequence (incentive) good work produces.

In any event, the diverse reports of the positive effects of social rewards for some culture groups suggest it is an area worthy of further inquiry.

Group Rewards and Contingencies

In the preceding section the arrangements for granting of rewards were considered because this represents an important variable in its own right. Not only is behavior affected by a reward, it is affected by the structure and organization of reward distribution.

In the Soviet Union, teachers reward the achievement of student groups rather than individuals (Bronfenbrenner, 1970). Use of group reward contingencies enhances peer influence, which in turn appears to increase conformity to adult expectations.

Hayes (1976) reviewed the education research on group contingencies in U.S. classrooms. In one approach, group reward is made contingent on an individual's behavior. For example, a second-grade classroom enjoys an ice cream party if the target subject goes 2 days without a tantrum (Carlson, Arnold, Becker, & Madsen,

1968). A second approach employs group reward for group consequences. Hayes' review suggests both approaches to be about equally effective for studies of academic achievement and control of disruptive behavior.

There have been industrial applications of group contingencies. The Engelstad (1972) report of the autonomous work group program at a company in Norway described a group bonus plan. Workers earned extra money when certain total work group production goals were achieved or exceeded. Brown (1965) described the Scanlon Plan: "The general idea is to provide a formula whereby the work force shares in any savings that are produced by reducing the cost of labor" (Brown, 1965 p. 471). There is evidence in many companies that it works.

Groups contingency effects were studied in classrooms organized with some success for low-achieving Hawaiian high school boys (MacDonald & Gallimore, 1971). One of the classrooms was operated for a full semester on a daily basis; during the course of the semester a controlled comparison of group versus individual contingency conditions was conducted (Sloggett, 1968). The boys performed slightly better under group reward conditions as opposed to individual reward; also, under group reward the boys took less time to complete work. An appraisal of the entire semester suggested that the group reward arrangement, which of course included group working conditions, was the most satisfactory form of classroom organization for this population.

Kubany (1971) compared the time spent working on a math test by Hawaiian and Anglo sixth-grade children under group and individual reward conditions. A pretest was administered to all students under no reward conditions. The Hawaiian children showed an average increase from pre- to posttest of 20 min. in the group reward condition, compared to an increase from pre- to posttest of 5 minutes for the Anglo children. Both Hawaiians and Anglos showed increases of 5 minutes in the individual reward condition. Kubany proposes that the data be interpreted cautiously, since the changes in time spent working are relative not absolute culture group differences. The Hawaiian children did not work longer under group conditions than Anglo children, but they showed a far greater increase in time from pretest (no reward all groups) to posttest (group reward condition only).

Although no exhaustive survey is available, group contingencies are sometimes described in ethnographies of nontraditional societies. For example, Wilbert (1976) suggested that an important motive for South American canoe builders was sharing of profits. Sharing of the profits of trade widely among the band was a powerful incentive for the effort necessary to get ready for a difficult voyage.

When my colleagues and I worked in a rural community on Oahu we were told that many Hawaiian workers preferred a group contingency arrangement termed hukipau. "You guys, dig a trench here to here and when you pau (finished), get paid, go home." One informant, a Japanese-American construction foreman, told me that he had great success with such arrangements; although he was slightly derisive in his appraisal of Hawaiian motivation and values in general, he described in extravagant language the amount of work that a Hawaiian work party could do in short time under the hukipau plan. A number of Hawaiian men also told me they liked working on City and County refuse crews because of the hakipau arrangement then in use; curiously, many of these men worked fast in order to finish early enough to take a second job. This was at odds with one version of hakipau we heard which attributed the success of the arrangement to a Hawaiian preference for short working hours and long leisure periods. Many reported enjoying being a member of a team, working together, and relaxing as a group after work. This preference seems consistent with other observations of Hawaiian affiliation orientation.

One of the most remarkable examples of the effects of group contingencies was reported by Spicer (1952). In a relocation camp during World War II, the Japanese and Japanese-Americans interned there were offered jobs as cotton pickers for nearby growers whose usual labor force was absorbed by the wartime economy. Initially it was arranged that money earned by individuals would be placed in a community or campwide trust fund. Although all members of the camp would presumably benefit from the trust fund, the initial response to recruitment was minimal. Some attributed the problem to hostility of the residents toward the U.S. Government for obvious reasons; others argued it was absence of individual incentive or payment. Discussion within organized subareas of the camp (called blocks) led to the reorganization of the payment plan. Instead of payments to a greater community fund, money earned was placed in trust funds set up for camp blocks, social clubs, and churches. The response was immediate. Over a period of days the number of people picking cotton increased by a factor of 4. "Totals in the various block funds began to be known throughout the Center. Some competitive spirit in working for one's block developed" (p. 51). Spicer attributes the effect of the altered plan to strength of local groups or neighborhoods as a "social unit focusing the interests and activities of its members" (p. 52). The relatively greater influence of the local neighborhoods as opposed to the larger group is enhanced in newly forming communities; in such circumstances the solidarity of the larger community may come much later than solidarity of the local, face-to-face group.

In summary, working in groups, social rewards, and group contingencies seem to have an impact in some cases for many sociocultural groups. It remains to be seen how the effects of the structure, organization, and dynamic of work/achievement situations covary with cultural and individual differences in affiliation orientation.

Graves and Graves (1974) suggest that Polynesian children would profit from more group-oriented learning situations because of the opportunity to use culturally shaped social talents—which I have glossed here as affiliation motivation and related instrumental skills.

Gallimore and Tharp (1976) concluded that Hawaiian children, as well as most other students, may but do not necessarily work harder and achieve more in group settings; they argue that behavior in school rooms, as in other work settings, is a function of complex, higher-order interactions of multiple person and setting variables. Simple educational reforms may be attractive and easy to communicate, but they will be inevitably confounded and affected by other factors. The most prudent recommendation is careful assessment of each setting and population before commencing program design. Premature commitment to group work settings, social rewards, and group contingencies can be as limiting as unquestioned acceptance of more traditional-centered schemes.

The Effects of Social Models

There is ample experimental evidence that social models may greatly influence the acquisition and performance of behavior. For example, there are a variety of data to indicate that standards children impose on their own performances may be significantly affected by adult models (Bandura, 1977); thus how long a child might persist at a task may be determined by observation of the standards a model sets. If the model imposes a stern performance contingency which must be met before taking a reward, the child will also set relatively high standards. Modeling and observational learning can thus be added to the list of factors that influence motivation to achieve.

Because this volume is devoted to cross-cultural human development and there are no cross-cultural studies (as far as I know) of modeling cues and achievement motivation, the topic will not be pursued. But it is important to note the substantial advances that have been made in recent years in the study of observational learning; these findings indicate that the phenomenon is far more complex than simple mimicry or imitation. It involves complex cognitive and symbolic processes which can be presumed to have cross-cultural validity. Because of the relative recency of these findings, they have not been absorbed into the cross-cultural literature. That will be soon remedied, I believe, as the study of observational learning processes offers a powerful tool for analysis of behavior antecedents of interest to cross-cultural researchers.

Socialization Antecedents of the Affiliation/Achievement Link

As for general studies of the socialization antecedents of the affiliation motivation/ achievement link, Sutton-Smith and Rosenberg (1970) characterized the field this way: "There are not actually any developmental studies of affiliation, conformity, and achievement. What we have are a few scattered studies on parallel topics at different chronological age levels" (1970 p. 92). Much of current work was stimulated by a classic study by Schachter (1959). He began with experiments designed to show a relationship between anxiety and the desire to be with others. He found that under fearful conditions firstborns showed a stronger preference to be with others even when compared to anxious laterborns. Schachter attributed these results to the differential treatment by parents of firstborn children; e.g., the relatively inexperienced parents who inadvertently trains the growing child to expect immediate, comforting attention and companionship for even minor accidents and wounds. Laterborns, of course are treated differently because the parents have learned, in Sutton-Smith and Rosenberg's (1970) words, to distinguish between a burp and a death rattle.

A review of the developmental literature confirms the generalization that firstborns are more achieving, affiliative, and conforming (Sutton-Smith & Rosenberg, 1970). That these consequences can be attributed to the special relationships between firstborn and parents is also apparently supported, although there is continuing controversy about birth order as a possible artifact: "The firstborns' continuing need for reassurance and guidance appears to evoke contradictory behavior from the parents. The child seeks help but performs well. The parent gives help but is critically expectant of an even higher level of performance" (Sutton-Smith & Rosenberg, 1970, p. 107). As noted earlier, an affiliation/achievement connection is suggested by Sutton-Smith and Rosenberg; affiliative skills are used in service of achievement.

Of course, most of the studies cited by Sutton-Smith and Rosenberg (1970) involve U.S. Anglo-American samples. Whether their conclusions are generalizable to the cultures in which affiliation plays a role in achievement motivation is doubtful. For example, in most traditional societies families are generally larger than in the U.S. Traditional families are also more likely to feature affiliation-motivated achievement (Graves & Graves, 1974). In cultures which would presumably have greater amounts of affiliation motivated persons, the proportion of firstborns to laterborns would be smaller; it seems unlikely that in such cultures the socialization of affiliation motivation is dependent on birth order effects.

Researchers in Polynesia have tended to focus on antecedents of affiliation motivation other than birth order. As noted earlier, in Polynesia and in many traditional societies work and achievement contexts are not separated from the larger context of social relationships, family organization, and the like. The problem of training a child in the family for performance later in life in a wholly different situation is not as sharply defined an issue as in labor-differentiated industrial societies. Indeed, Hawaiian-Americans generally do not conceive childhood and adolescence as a training period for a wholly different life; children do not mature into less dependence but more dependence on the family—the term interdependence is actually more descriptive (Gallimore et al., 1974). A result of the interdependence ethic is sharing of critical family functions by all family members; shared functions include domestic chores, child care, and wage contributions by offspring as well as other-directedness. Such group-directed, collective activity could also be discussed in terms of affiliation motivation.

One of the features of shared functioning is the multiple-caretaker/sibling-caretaker systems which have often been described in Polynesian societies.

Tahitians, Maoris, Samoans, and Hawaiians rely heavily on siblings and others as caretakers (Weisner & Gallimore, 1977), and the effects include a lasting sensitization toward the group (Levy, 1968 p. 595). Graves and Graves (1974, pp. 22–23) suggest multiple caretaking systems place "a great deal of emphasis on sharing and cooperation, behaviors which are highly adaptive in small, closely-knit societies with subsistence economies. By contrast, European children raised within small nuclear families have less opportunity to acquire a level of skill in interpersonal relations and group functioning which is commonly exhibited by Polynesian children."

Gallimore et al. (1974) suggest that affiliative behavior is fostered in multiple caretaking socialization by the reinforcement of attending and orienting to many caretakers. Attending and orienting in this context is equivalent to social dependency behavior; in turn, affiliation motivation can be defined as the frequency of attending and orienting to others (or amount of social dependency). Because the multiple-caretaker system encourages children to attend to many others—for example, the sibling and peer group—as well as parents, the basis for adult affiliation behavior is set. As Levy (1968) noted, Polynesian adult group orientation and affiliation behavior has an analogue in child involvements with siblings and peers. Developmental studies of affiliation motivation and achievement are almost nonexistent (Sutton-Smith & Rosenberg, 1970). Many possibilities exist. For example, the HRAF could be used to check the relationship between sibling caretaking and frequency of cooperative workgroups, nonsolitary work patterns, etc. The hypothesized connection between sibling caretaking or multiple caretaking socialization and affiliation motivation needs study. Fine-grained naturalistic observations of the strategic behaviors associated with birth order might contribute to the interpretation of the studies reviewed by Sutton-Smith and Rosenberg.

In affiliation-motivated achieving societies which do not feature multiple caretaking systems, such as Japan, socialization antecedents need to be identified and examined. Important in all cases is careful attention to social values as well as psychological and socialization factors (Wagatsuma, 1977).

FINAL THOUGHTS

What has been presented here confirms McClelland's (1975) argument that there are many reasons why people will work hard. This review suggests that among these reasons are affiliation opportunities and rewards. It is apparent that the affiliation–achievement link will not soon be reduced to a simple formulation. One reason is the variety of definitions used in previous research. DeVos (1968) used need for affiliation but in a more general sense than Gallimore et al. (1974), who used n Affiliation as defined by Heyns et al. (1958). Minoura (1975) described Japanese motivation as "other-directed" in terms that could be considered affiliation motivation. Graves and Graves (1974) coined the term "inclusive behavior" to describe a pattern of Polynesian child behavior that features elements of affiliation motivation. Ramirez and Price-Williams (1976) described Mexican-American and Afro-American children as family achievement motivated.

To these global personality dimensions could be added a host of more narrowly defined social setting variables. Working in groups or group facilitation, social rewards, and group rewards and contingencies are variables which would surely influence the behavior of other-directed Japanese school children. Indeed, it is likely that in affiliation-oriented cultures/social groups, social rewards and group contingencies would be inherent structural and organizational features. For example, the Hawaiians' preference for working conditions that permit workers to go home as soon as the work team is finished has parallels in family organization (Gallimore et al., 1974).

Study of industriousness in affiliation-oriented cultures has a recent history and a promising future. But if the affiliation–achievement link in cross-cultural reviews is to be more than a one-paragraph qualification of the n Ach/achievement connection, there is work to be done. The first task is to introduce into cross-cultural research the more complex conception of industriousness and achievement behavior that is afforded by behavior X environment interactionism.

Useful would be further studies in Japan because of the high levels of achievement and the group affiliation pattern. In Western industrial societies the impact of affiliation opportunities and rewards might be more appreciated if industrial psychology and management science research were more widely exploited. Another promising line is the analysis of the impact on school behavior of children reared in affiliation-oriented cultures; for example, the attempt by Thomas, Graves, and Graves (1977) to develop cooperative, group-oriented teaching techniques for improving the achievement of Maori and other Polynesian children. Another effort is also in progress to develop school programs appropriate to Hawaiian children (Gallimore & Tharp, 1976), which includes, among other things, efforts to adapt to affiliation orientation. All of these efforts can contribute to understanding the effects of social setting variables on industriousness.

On the person's side of the interaction, more studies of n Aff in Japan and Polynesia would be helpful. Would the correlation between n Aff and school achievement hold in Japan as well as among Hawaiians? What of the suggestive finding that it is the Hawaiian student who writes instrumental affiliation stories that does better in school? Does the affiliation motivation/achievement depend, as Sutton-Smith and Rosenberg (1970) have suggested, on interpersonal skills in achievement situations?

What is the correlation between n Aff and n Ach? Curiously, this question has not been well researched in any group. In general the few studies report correlation coefficients around 0.30 (Groesbeck, 1958; Gallimore, 1974). One interesting possibility is suggested by the relatively greater correlation of n Aff and n Ach among Hawaiian girls as opposed to boys (Gallimore, 1974). Since the girls are more successful in school and write more n Aff themes, it is possible that the joint occurrence of the two motives reflects an interpersonal style in achievement situations. In any event, studies of affiliation motivation which rely on *n* Aff scores should also examine *n* Ach, much as McClelland has measured both *n* Power and *n* Aff in his studies of power motivation (McClelland, 1975). A serious problem, of course, is differential cue value of stimuli used to elicit stories for *n* Aff and *n* Ach scoring; much of fluctuation in reported correlation between the two scores is probably due to the nature of stimuli used. Some pictures "draw" *n* Ach stories, other elicit *n* Aff themes.

There is nothing sacred about the Heyns et al. (1958) definition of *n* Aff. Perhaps future studies ought to score imaginative stories for both the Heyns et al. definition of *n* Aff and for a newly devised system more suitable for cross-cultural work. Wagatsuma (1977), for example, argues that some changes would be necessary for work in Japan and that to his knowledge there are no quantitative studies of Japanese affiliation motivation and achievement. The Graves and Graves (1974) concept of inclusive behavior represents a fresh approach that could be used in a new scoring scheme.

Methodological Issues

It is regrettable but true that many of the concepts in social science are lay terms elevated to pseudoscientific status by repeated association with widely accepted operational definitions. An imaginative researcher devises a measure or test which yields successful and interesting results. The test is described as an operational definition of a putatively important concept or variable. Other investigators report successful use of the test, adding to knowledge about the concept it supposedly measures. Of course, negative results are less likely to be published. Eventually the body of literature that grows up around the test is described in terms of the concept that the test supposedly measures, not in terms of the test. The test has become the concept. Because the concept was intuitively or culturally appealing in the first place, the degree of confidence in the meaning of the test-generated research may become substantial. An effective antidote in many cases is the low or zero correlations between the favored measure and other measures that are also operational definitions of the concept under study (Mischel, 1968). The successful test may measure something important and worth researching but of far less generality and significance than the now-exalted lay term it is used to define operationally

McClelland and his associates provided a crisp, operational definition of *n* Achievement and developed a flexible measurement procedure; in terms of both quality and quantity of research their contributions are awesome. But at times the *n* Ach concept has been overgeneralized and treated as a synonym for all forms of *motivation to achieve.*

I once attended a colloquium presented by McClelland. Several in the audience argued as if *n* Ach was defined by McClelland as the only form of motivation for achievement; to such a notion they objected vigorously and offered multiple instances of culture groups in which social and not personal factors were regnant. Professor McClelland tried in vain to convince his audience that he also conceived of industriousness as a multiply determined behavior—that *n* Ach was only one of many potential antecedents, albeit one of possibly great international significance and one for which there were replicated findings. The discussion never resolved because the critics had so overgeneralized the terms achievement motivation and *n* Ach; they imbued them with more meaning than the authors had originally intended. Of course, one can argue that McClelland's admirers have contributed to the surplus of meanings *n* Ach had acquired.

But the larger lesson is the tendency of appealing terms which are rooted in lay culture to expand in meaning and reference as they get connected to objective measurements (Walters & Parke, 1964). *n* Ach is much like intelligence and IQ tests in this regard. What started as a solution to a practical problem—identifying children who would not profit from ordinary instruction—ended as a great social and political issue. The outcome in both cases can be reified concepts, misapplied instruments, oversimplified accounts of complex behavior, and bad science. These things are true at the same time that we recognize the historical and scientific significance of *n* Ach and IQ research. If there is mischief, it is in the overgeneralizations, not the concepts.

All of this suggests the need to approach the study of achievement and industriousness more broadly than is permitted by measures such as the TAT that have dominated the field. As the review here has shown, there are a variety of approaches to be taken and a diversity of operations to use. An important element lacking especially in psychological studies has been direct, naturalistic observation. Studies using HRAF files and *n* Aff-type scored fantasy materials should be complemented by naturalistic observation and fine-grained ethnographic research. Such approaches are more sensitive to social context and help moderate the almost exclusive focus in achievement motivation studies on internal psychological variables and Western achievement goals.

The traditional qualitative methods of anthropology may begin to be borrowed and adopted by psychologists if recent trends are any indication. In a paper on the future of personality assessment, Mischel (1977) concluded that "one of the most impressive—and obvious—lessons from the history of personality measurement is the recognition that complex human behavior tends to be influenced by many determinants, and reflects the almost inseparable and continuous interaction of a host of variables both in the person and in the situation" (Mischel, 1977, p. 246).

To cope with the complexity and the multiple determinants of behavior, Mischel (1977, p. 247) recommends that psychologists and other social and behavioral scientists accept as respectable multiple methods and multiple perspectives, including idiographic naturalistic research. He suggests that "one may construe the study of persons alternatively from many complementary perspectives" and lists three: environmental conditions, personal variables (competencies, constructs, expectancies, etc., used by the researcher to construe the person), and the subjective viewpoint of the research participants (feelings, thoughts, wishes, etc.).

In cross-cultural research it is useful also to employ multiple methods as well as multiple perspectives. Participant and direct observation, interviews, surveys, psychometric devices, and experiments can be combined to provide a triangulated description and analysis of behavior. A major advantage of the multimethod approach is sensitivity to the complexities of environment X person X phenomenologic interactions. It is a strategy which more closely matches the complexity of multiply determined behavior because it provides complex rather than simple descriptions and explanations.

Maehr (1974) argues as well for the value of naturalistic observation in a multimethod strategy in the study of achievement motivation. He sees this approach as a means of avoiding deficiency explantions, which attribute low motivation to certain culture groups because they score low on tests and tasks validated among majority groups in Western, industrial societies. "Much of the research which attempts to understand the motivational patterns of ethnic and cultural groups involves placing children in a 'middle class biased' performance setting" (Maehr, 1974, p. 847). Instead, Maehr argues that more attention should be devoted to identifying settings in which achievement motivation "occurs or does not occur in various cultures and then proceed to characterize the nature of these settings." By direct observation both settings and patterns of achievement motivation and behavior, as they vary culturally, can be described.

The studies reviewed here indicate that the importance of the affiliation/achievement relationship is not restricted to traditional societies. It would seem to hold in many populations—for example, U.S. college students and industrial workers. There may be more continuities between these variables in industrial and traditional societies than we are accustomed to putting in our contrastive generalizations. To what extent affiliation variables are the same in traditional and industrial groups is difficult to assess because of the differences in theoretical models that have been used. With rare exceptions, the kinds of variables that have been used by social psychologists (e.g., Kelley & Thibaut, 1968) and affiliation motivation researchers (DeVos, 1968; Gallimore, 1974; Minoura, 1975) have not been examined by ethnographers.

In our original work in Hawaii we were inclined to the view that Hawaiians were affiliation oriented and motivated and that appropriate adjustments in the incentives in public schools would be necessary to insure satisfactory academic progress. Our more recent work in a small research school in urban Honolulu suggests that the young Hawaiian children are more flexible. They respond with industry to many kinds of situations (Chun et al., 1974; Gallimore & Tharp, 1976; Tharp & Gallimore, 1976). Using a wide variety of curricula and classroom organizations and with heavy use of teacher praise, we have gotten very high work rates. There is an important message in these data for investigators of cross-cultural motivational differences. At least in young humans there is more plasticity than rigidity, and the variability in cultural differences in motivation to achieve is probably more impressive than the uniformity. Children are adaptive, quick-witted creatures who will work hard, learn, and achieve in any number of reasonable social environments. They may be from groups that feature one or another form of motivation to achieve, but they are not limited to one form.

Finally, I conceived a major purpose of this review to be consciousness raising. As much as anything the affiliation/achievement question needs recognition as a research area. I hope the recognition afforded by this effort has a positive function. I also hope to have reinforced the view that the explanation of achievement and industriousness will require a complicated, multidimensional person X environment formulation.

ACKNOWLEDGMENTS

Yasuko Minoura greatly contributed to this chapter by sharing her bibliographic sources and by our spirited discussions. Hiroshi Wagatsuma, Sara Beth Nerlove, Harold Levine, Douglass Price-Williams, and Jim Turner have talked with me about these issues in many useful ways. Paul Rosenblatt and Manuel Ramirez offered useful comments and references. Tom Weisner provided extensive criticism of the first draft. Many of the original ideas were a product of collaboration with Alan Howard. Finally, I thank the editors for their many comments.

NOTES

1. These percentages calculated from Table 4 of the work by Wagatsuma (1956, p. 26).

2. Only one case of service to country or society was coded for the Japanese 1920s and 1970s texts; there were 16 cases coded for nuclear or extended family and 11 for local community (Minoura, 1975, Appendix A, Table 3, p. 133).

REFERENCES

Atkinson, J. W., & Feather, N. T. (Eds.). *A theory of achievement motivation.* New York: John Wiley & Sons, 1966.
Atkinson, J. W., & O'Connor, P. Effects of ability grouping in schools related to individual differences in achievement-related motivation. In J. W. Atkinson & N. T. Feather (Eds.), *A theory of achievement motivation.* New York: John Wiley & Sons, 1966.
Bandura, A. *Social learning theory.* Englewood Cliffs, N.J: Prentice-Hall, 1977.
Block, J. Advancing the psychology of personality: Paradigmatic shift or improving the quality of research. In D. Magnusson & N. S. Endler (Eds.), *Personality at the crossroads: Current issues in interactional psychology.* Hillsdale, N.J.: Lawrence Erlbaum, 1977 pp. 37–63.
Boggs, S. T., & Gallimore, R. Employment. In R. Gallimore & A. Howard (Eds.), *Studies in a Hawaiian community: Na makamaka o nanakuli.* (Pacific Anthropological Records No. 1.) Honolulu: B. P. Bishop Museum, 1968, pp. 17–27.
Bronfenbrenner, U. *Two worlds of childhood: U.S. and U.S.S.R.* New York: Russell Sage Foundation, 1970.
Brown, R. *Social psychology.* New York: The Free Press, 1965.
Carlson, C. S., Arnold, C. R., Becker, W. C., & Madsen, C. H. The elimination of tantrum behavior of a child in an elementary classroom. *Behavior Research and Therapy,* 1968, *6,* 117–119.
Chun, S., Speidel, G. E., & Tharp, R. G. *Learning centers and study carrels: A comparative study (Technical Report No. 18). Honolulu: The Kamehameha Early Education Program, 1974.*
Davis, L. E., & Taylor, J. C. (Eds.). *Design of jobs.* Baltimore: Penguin Books, 1972.
DeVos, G. A. Achievement and innovation in culture and personality. In E. Norbeck, D. Price-Williams, & W. M. McCord (Eds.), *The study of personality: An interdisciplinary approach.* New York: Holt, Rinehart & Winston, 1968, pp. 348–370.
DeVos, G. A. *Socialization for achievement.* Berkeley: University of California Press, 1973.
DeVries, D. L., & Slavin, R. *Teams-games-tournament: A final report on the research* (Report No. 217 Baltimore: Center for Social Organization of Schools, The Johns Hopkins University, 1976).
Dore, R. *British factory-Japanese factory: The origins of national diversity in industrial relations.* Berkeley: University of California Press, 1973.
Engelstad, P. H. Socio-technical approach to problems of process control. In L. E. Davis & J. C. Taylor (Eds.), *Design of Jobs.* Baltimore: Penguin Books, 1972, pp. 328–356.
Gallimore, R. Variations in the motivational antecedents of achievement among Hawaii's ethnic groups. In W. Lebra (Ed.), *Mental health in Asia and the Pacific* (Vol. 2). Honolulu: East-West Center Press, 1972, pp. 227–248.
Gallimore, R. Affiliation motivation and Hawaiian-American achievement. *Journal of Cross-Cultural Psychology,* 1974, *5,* 481–491.
Gallimore, R., Boggs, J. W., & Jordan, C. *Culture, behavior, and education: A study of Hawaiian-Americans.* Beverly Hills: Sage Publications, 1974.

Gallimore, R., & Howard, A. The Hawaiian life style: Some qualitative considerations. In R. Gallimore & A. Howard (Eds.), *Studies in a Hawaiian community: Na makamaka o nanakuli* (Pacific Anthropological Records No. 1). Honolulu: B. P. Bishop Museum, 1968, pp. 10–16.

Gallimore, R., & Tharp, R. G. *An overview of research strategies and findings of the Kamehameha Early Education Program: 1971–1975* (Technical Report No. 66). Honolulu: The Kamehameha Early Education Program, 1976.

Graves, N. B., & Graves, T. D. *Inclusive versus exclusive behavior in New Zealand school settings: Polynesian-Pakeha contrasts in learning styles.* Auckland: University of Auckland, Deptarment of Anthropology, 1974.

Groesbeck, B. L. Toward description of personality in terms of configuration of motives. In J. W. Atkinson (Ed.), *Motives in fantasy, action, and society.* New York: Van Nostrand, 1958, pp. 383–399.

Hayes, L. A. The use of group contingencies for behavioral control: A review. *Psychological Bulletin,* 1976, *83,* 628–648.

Heyns, R. W., Veroff, J., & Atkinson, J. W. A scoring manual for the affiliation motive. In J. W. Atkinson (Ed.), *Motives in fantasy, action, and society.* Princeton: Van Nostrand, 1958, pp. 205–218.

Howard, A. *Learning to be Rotuman.* New York: Columbia Teachers College Press, 1970.

Kelley, H. H., & Thibaut, J. Group problem solving. In G. Lindzey & E. Aronson (Eds.), *The handbook of social psychology (Vol.2).* Reading, Mass.: Addison-Wesley, 1968, pp. 1–101.

Kubany, E. S. *The effects of incentives on the test performances of Hawaiians and Caucasians. Unpublished doctoral dissertation, University of Hawaii, 1971.*

Kubany, E. S., Gallimore, R., & Buell, J. The effects of extrinsic factors on achievement-oriented behavior: A non-Western case. *Journal of Cross-Cultural Psychology,* 1970, *1,* 77–84.

Lenz, J., & Gallimore, R. A behavioral comparison of two "good" teachers. In S. MacDonald & G. Tanabe (Eds.), *Focus on classroom behavior.* Springfield, Ill.: Charles C. Thomas, 1973, pp. 36–44.

Levy, R. I. Child management structure and its implications in a Tahitian family. In E. Vogel & N. Bell (Eds.), *A modern introduction to the family.* New York: The Free Press, 1968, pp. 590–598.

Lucker, G. W., Rosenfield, D., Sikes, J., & Aronson, E. Performance in the interdependent classroom: A field study. *American Journal of Educational Research.* 1976, *13,* 115–123.

MacDonald, S., & Gallimore, R. *Battle in the classroom.* Scranton, Pa.: Intext, 1971.

McClelland, D. C. Review. *Contemporary Psychology,* 1975, *20,* pp. 876–878.

McClelland, D. C., Atkinson, J. W., Clark, R. A., & Lowell, E. L. *The achievement motive.* New York: Appleton-Century, 1953.

Maehr, M. L. Culture and achievement motivation. *American Psychologist,* 1974, *29,* 887–896.

Magnusson, D. & Endler, N. S. (Eds.). *Personality at the crossroads: Current issues in interactional psychology.* Hillsdale, N.J.: Lawrence Erlbaum, 1977.

Minoura, Y. *Value orientations found in British Columbian and Japanese schoolbooks: The 1920's-the 1970's.* Unpublished master's thesis, University of Victoria, 1975.

Mischel, W. *Personality and assessment.* New York: John Wiley & Sons, 1968.

Mischel, W. On the future of personality measurement. *American Psychologist,* 1977, *32,* 246–254.

Northrup, B. Battling boredom: Auto plant in Sweden scores some success with worker "teams." *Wall Street Journal,* March 1, 1977, pp. 1–29.

Ouchi, W. G., & Jaeger, A. M. Trend for future: The Z organization. *Los Angeles Times,* January 1, 1978, V, p. 3.

Ramirez, M., & Castaneda, A. *Cultural democracy, bicognitive development, and education.* New York: Academic Press, 1974.

Ramirez, M., & Price-Williams, D. R. Achievement motivation in children of three ethnic groups in the United States. *Journal of Cross Cultural Psychology,* 1976, *7,* 49–60.

Rosen, B. C. The achievement syndrome: A psychocultural dimension of social stratification. *American Sociological Review,* 1956, *21,* 203–211.

Schachter, S. *The psychology of affiliation.* Stanford: Stanford University Press, 1959.

Sloggett, B. B. Classroom behavior modification of the rural Hawaiian adolescent as a function of group activities and reinforcement techniques. Unpublished master's thesis, University of Hawaii, 1968.

Sloggett, B. B., Gallimore, R., & Kubany, E. A comparative analysis of fantasy need achievement among high and low achieving male Hawaiian-Americans. *Journal of Cross Cultural Psychology,* 1970, *1,* 53–61.

Sorrentino, R. M. An extension of theory of achievement motivation to the study of emergent leadership. *Journal of Personality and Social Psychology,* 1973, *26* (3), 356–368.

Spicer, E. H. Reluctant cotton-pickers. In E. H. Spicer (Ed.), *Human problems in technological change.* New York: Russell Sage Foundation, 1952.

Sutton-Smith, B., & Rosenberg, B. G. *The sibling.* New York: Holt, Rinehart & Winston, 1970.

Terkel, S. *Working.* New York: Avon Books, 1972.

Tharp, R. G., & Gallimore, R. The uses and limits of social reinforcement and industriousness for learning to read (Technical Report No. 60). Honolulu: The Kamehameha Early Education Program, 1976.

Thomas, D. R., Graves, N. B., & Graves, T. D. *Research on group-oriented teaching methods.* Hamilton & Auckland, New Zealand: Department of Psychology, University of Waikato, and South Pacific Research Institute, 1977.

Wagatsuma, H. *Japanese values of achievement: The study of Japanese inhabitants of three Japanese villages by means of T.A.T.* Unpublished master's thesis, University of Michigan, 1956.

Wagatsuma, H. Personal communication, February 1977.

Walters, R. H., & Parke, R. D. Social motivation, dependency, and susceptibility to social influence. In L. Berkowitz (Ed.), *Advances in experimental social psychology* (Vol. 1). New York: John Wiley & Sons, 1964, pp. 232–276.

Watson, D. Reinforcement theory of personality and social system: Dominance and position in a group power structure. *Journal of Personality and Social Psychology,* 1971, *20,* 180–185.

Weisner, T. S., & Gallimore, R. My brother's keeper: Child and sibling caretaking. *Current Anthropology,* 1977, *18,* 169–190.

Wilbert, J. To become a maker of canoes: An essay in Warao enculturation. In J. Wilbert (Ed.), *Enculturations in Latin America: An anthology.* Los Angeles: UCLA Latin American Center Publications, 1976, pp. 303–358.

❧22 ❧

Cooperation and Competition: Some Issues and Problems in Cross-cultural Analysis

Susan Seymour

The last major effort to investigate cooperative and competitive behavior was an extensive interdisciplinary study prepared for the Social Science Research Council (SSRC) by Mark May, Gordon Allport, and Gardner Murphy in 1937 (May & Doob, 1937). Most relevant to the current review is the cross-cultural component of the study, resulting in a separate publication by Margaret Mead (1937), *Cooperation and Competition Among Primitive Peoples.*

In the SSRC report, cooperation and competition were defined as goal-oriented behaviors—cooperation being the act of working together to one end or sharing goals and competition being the act of working against another or simultaneously trying to gain what another is trying to gain. These definitions have been followed generally in the present paper in our attempt to select relevant literature for review.

The SSRC report also recognized that cooperation and competition were not polar concepts; that the opposite of cooperation is not necessarily competition, and vice versa. In fact, Mead found it necessary to add a third category, individualistic behavior. This was defined as "behavior in which the individual strives toward his [or her] goal without reference to others" (Mead, 1937, p. 16). We shall find these distinctions of use as well.

Few cross-cultural generalizations were arrived at in the SSRC study, perhaps owing to the limited number of cultural cases used (13) and to the emphasis on the uniqueness of each culture. No association was found between the scarcity or abundance of goods and cooperative or competitive behavior. Similarly, there was no correspondence between level of technological development or primary subsistence patterns such as hunting-gathering, agriculture, or pastoralism and patterns of cooperation and competition. Considerations of population density were also deemed irrelevant. Mead, however, did find that more highly integrated societies, characterized by clearly defined status differences among individuals, an emphasis upon group-oriented and highly structured activities, and a deemphasis upon individual

717

activities, were more cooperative than less well integrated societies. The finding has not been followed up with further research.

Since this groundbreaking work, the various social science disciplines have gone their own ways. Psychology has developed an extensive literature, particularly since the late 1960s, most of which is experimental and only some of which is cross-cultural in design. We will restrict this review to those psychological studies that are cross-cultural.[1] Anthropology has concerned itself less directly with cooperation and competition, especially in the area of human development. However, there are a number of ethnographic and cross-cultural studies from which we can extrapolate information, raise questions, and suggest directions for further research.

Cooperation is necessary for the survival of any society, and some competition inevitably occurs, even under the best circumstances, because resources are always limited. Thus settings, situation, and circumstances dictate, in some measure, the likelihood of occurrence of these types of behavior, and motives are difficult to ascertain. Questions therefore arise not only as to the amount and degree of cooperation and competition exhibited by the members of a society but also concerning whether the behaviors are institutionally prescribed, informally pressured, or spontaneous and whether they appear generally or are restricted to particular sociocultural domains. The research literature does not allow us to sort out these issues clearly, but they are implicit in much of the discussion to follow.

In this chapter, we will briefly review some relevant insights and theories from the field of sociobiology in order to suggest an evolutionary perspective from which to view cooperative and competitive behavior. Then we will examine these behaviors at the societal level, selecting from the ethnographic literature societies that may suggest how extensive and varied the cross-cultural range is for these traits. We will also use the ethnographic examples to illuminate some of the problems raised above, such as the assumption of bipolarity and the determination of relevant domains and structures. In the next section, we will examine studies that focus on or measure cooperation and competition at the individual level and relate them to institutional levels of analysis. Finally, we will try to draw some conclusions from the current state of research on cooperation and competition and suggest some directions for future research.

THE SOCIOBIOLOGICAL PERSPECTIVE

One of the underlying assumptions of the 1937 SSRC report was that "human beings by original nature strive for goals, but striving with others (cooperation) or against others (competition) are *learned* forms of behavior" (May & Doob, 1937, p. 23—italics added). Throughout that study learning was emphasized over the possibility of any built-in capacities for cooperative and competitive behavior. Not surprisingly, the study reflected the view of the period that "human nature is almost infinitely plastic," and hence patterns of cooperation and competition were viewed as the result of particular socialization processes.

Recent efforts to examine human behavior from an evolutionary perspective in an attempt to synthesize social and biological processes question that assumption and offer a new perspective from which to view cooperation and competition at the species level. Since the Darwinian period of the 19th century the concept of natural selection through competition has dominated much thought and research, resulting in a widespread view of "man the aggressor" and "man the competitor" rather than "man the cooperator." If built-in characteristics of human behavior were assumed, they tended to be the former rather than the latter. According to Montagu's review of the period, "It was not that the natural selectionists denied the existence of cooperation, but that they passed it by and neglected it in favor of a crass competition" (1970, p. 25).

Montagu (1970) proposes that human behavior is characterized by both competitive drives and social/cooperative ones, the latter being the most dominant and biologically the most important. In support of this thesis Montagu suggests that cooperation makes for more harmonious group activity, which leads to more successful adaptation to the environment, resulting in an increased probability of survival for the individual:

> Cooperation, not conflict, was evidently the selectively most valuable form of behavior for man taken at any stage of his evolutionary history, and surely, quite as evidently never more so than today. . . . It is essentially the experience, the means, that fits human beings not to their external environment so much as to one another. It must never be forgotten that society is fundamentally, essentially, and in all ways a cooperative enterprise, an enterprise designed to keep [people] in touch with one another. Without the cooperation of its members society cannot survive, and the society of man has survived because the cooperativeness of its members made survival possible—it was not an advantageous individual here and there who did so, but the group. In human societies the individuals who are most likely to survive are those who are best enabled to do so by their group. (Montagu, 1965, p. 162)

Montagu has raised several issues above that have become prominent in the recent work of sociobiologists and ethologists and which are relevant to the topic of cooperation and competition. The first issue is to what extent, from an evolutionary perspective, human behavior can be characterized as cooperative and how this relates to survival. The second issue is individual versus group selection. The third issue is the nature of human society and the cooperative activity which it requires.

Wilson (1975), in his stimulating publication *Sociobiology: The New Synthesis,* has spoken to these several issues and has provoked a number of debates. In his cross-species comparison of behavior, Wilson concludes that cooperation is usually rudimentary among vertebrate societies but that human societies alone approach the insect societies in cooperativeness:

> The typical vertebrate society, in short, favors individual and in-group survival at the expense of social integrity. Man has intensified these vertebrate traits while adding unique qualities of his own. In so doing he has achieved an extraordinary degree of cooperation with little or no sacrifice of personal survival and reproduction. (Wilson, 1975, p. 382)

Wilson is suggesting that despite the emphasis upon individual competition and survival in *Homo sapiens'* evolution, humans have been unique in combining these characteristics with cooperation, thus enabling them to build complex societies. In fact, Wilson (1975; 1976) suggests, reviewing the theory of group selection and Trivers' (1971) idea of "reciprocal altruism," that there may be a genetic basis to reciprocally altruistic acts which would result in a population of individuals with increased genetic fitness. The idea here is that if an individual helps another with some reasonable expectation that his or her altruistic act will be reciprocated when he or she is in need, then both individuals will have benefited. This principle can be extended to the group level, increasing the personal fitness of a set of individuals and hence of the entire group. Although such reciprocal altruism has a calculating and self-interested side to it, it may be what has enabled humans to operate in groups successfully enough to have built more complex societies than any other organism to date. Wilson concludes that we have available reasonable genetic mechanisms to explain how such reciprocal altruism is sustained but that "we are still left with the theoretical problem of how the evolution of the behavior gets started." (1975, p. 120)

According to this theory, "reciprocal altruism," or mutual helping behavior, may have been the basis for cooperative behavior among humans. By recognizing that helping one another had a selective advantage, individuals may have developed patterns of working together toward some common goals, such as acquiring and distributing food and protecting one another. Various principles of reciprocity, or exchange, operate in all societies today and are the basis for much anthropological theory concerning kinship and social organization (e.g., Mauss, 1954; Sahlins, 1960; 1965; 1968):

> As a specific institution, exchange penetrates through the social fabric and may be thought of as a network holding society together. This applies whether we think of an isolated family group, the members of which give each other support and the benefit of differentiated services; or of an Oceanic culture in which reciprocal services and obligations link together in reflection of social structure and values; or of modern capitalism or communism in which exchange is rationalized by reference to a price system. (Belshaw, 1965, p. 6)

Wilson's effort to synthesize aspects of biological and social evolution, and particularly his suggestion that altruism may have a genetic base, has stimulated much debate. A prominent example was Campbell's (1975) presidential address to the American Psychological Association and the responses which it, in turn, generated. In his two "controversial conclusions," Campbell essentially called for a separation of social and biological evolutionary perspectives, asserting that we must look to social evolution to understand what has made complex human societies possible. Altruistic and cooperative behavior, he suggests, are the result of social evolution which has had to counter the innate selfish tendencies of man that biological evolution has continued to select for.

Campbell's remarks bring us full circle in the old "nature-nurture" debate regarding this topic, and we tend to agree with Whitney's (1976, p. 370) response to Campbell's address: "Man can have achieved [our] degree of complex social interdependence only through the complementary interplay of genetic *and* social evolution." In fact, no such strict division between biological and social evolution seems theoretically tenable today. For example, the human ethologists have been suggesting that humans have a variety of built-in capacities for social behavior which emerge at birth and during the first few years of life, such as the mechanisms for attachment which make social interdependence and group behavior the rule rather than the exception (e.g., Ainsworth, 1964; 1967; Bowlby, 1958; 1969). A reasonable perspective to take regarding cooperation and competition might be, then, that there has been some genetic selection for both of these behaviors in humans but that as with the expression of other genetically determined capacities the environment can have a profound effect upon them. This approach is compatible with Wilson's (1976, p. 370) comment that "to say that human altruism is genetically based at the species level is not to say that the variation *within* our species has any genetic foundation."

In conclusion, since the SSRC study of 1937 which emphasized learning as the sole mechanism by which cooperative and competitive behaviors were acquired, there has been published much literature suggesting that these behaviors may have their roots in our evolutionary past. An examination of the role of biology is one of the areas, then, where future research may be particularly illuminating to a discussion of cooperation and competition.

THE SOCIETAL LEVEL OF ANALYSIS

Regardless of whether or not one wants to assert innate drives or tendencies for cooperation in *Homo sapiens*, one cannot deny the fact that at the societal level a certain amount of interpersonal cooperation is required. Social institutions, whether at the family level or the level of complex governmental bureaucracies, necessitate certain amounts of cooperation in order to function:

> Without high levels of cooperation there would be no coordination of behavior on highways or sidewalks, in stores, within organizations, or anywhere else. . . . No two individuals could communicate with each other or interact without cooperating to form a common language and agreed-upon norms for behavior. Societies would not exist, exchange of goods and services would not take place, entertainment would not be possible, occupations would not be available, education would be unheard of—complete anarchy would exist without cooperation. Even in fighting wars and conducting competitive activities, there are vast underpinnings of cooperative aggreements concerning how the competition or conflict will be conducted and the ways in which antagonists can express their hostility toward each other. (Johnson & Johnson, 1975, pp. 45–46)

In the most general sense, then, societies require interpersonal cooperation in order to function, but just what the range of variation is and how it relates to competition is open to question. In order to explore these and other questions, we will select from the cross-cultural ethnographic literature some cases to suggest the range of behavior that occurs and to illustrate our points.

One of the dimensions along which societies vary is the degree to which cooperation is institutionalized. At one end of the continuum are societies in which cooperation is intentionally inculcated and overtly valued, while at the other end are societies where people are barely able to cooperate enough to maintain their sociocultural institutions. Intentional communes are perhaps the best examples of societies where cooperation is highly institutionalized in most social domains. For example, the Hutterites, an intensive agricultural society in North America, believe that to live communally and to submit oneself to the will of the community is the divine order of God. As a consequence, all work is shared and tasks are assigned, not chosen by individuals; food is served and eaten in groups according to age and sex; clothing and other items are assigned on the basis of age and need; and families are given sleeping rooms according to their size. There is very little individual ownership of goods, and all activity is oriented to the well-being of the group. The socialization of children is also believed to be the responsibility of the group, and at 3 years of age children are placed in kindergartens in order to wean them from their families and to introduce them to their peer groups:

At the age when children in North American society are exerting their growing individuality and developing a concept of self, the Hutterite child is placed in a setting that minimizes treatment of him [or her] as an individual and maximizes his identity as a member of a group. . . . The Kindergarten teaches the child to respect the authority of the colony in addition to that of his parents and babysitters. . . . In the Kindergarten the child learns to tolerate a limited, restricted environment. . . . He is rewarded for a cooperative, docile, passive response to correction and frustration. (Hostetler & Huntington, 1967, p. 62)

Socialization among the Hutterites is a well-ordered process whereby children are carefully moved through a series of stages into an adulthood that stresses cooperation and interdependence among individuals.

Similarly, in modern Soviet society, where there is also a collective ideology, the socialization of children is planned, and children are frequently reared in communal facilities from a very early age where cooperation is intentionally inculcated:

Nor is such cooperation left to chance. From the very beginning stress is placed on teaching children to share and to engage in joint activity. Frequent reference is made to common ownership. . . . Collective play is emphasized. Not only group games, but special complex toys are designed which require the cooperation of two or three children to make them work. (Bronfenbrenner, 1972, p. 23)

From an early age children are encouraged to evaluate and criticize each other in order to produce a "self-reliant collective" in which they cooperate, discipline themselves, and take on numerous communal responsibilities.

The Hopi, a small-scale agricultural society in Arizona, are an example of a society that is not intentionally communal but where cooperation among kin and villagers is stressed. At an early age children are taught by the members of their extended families and clans that to be a good Hopi is to be nonaggressive, responsible, cooperative, noncompetitive, and self-reliant (Eggan, 1956; Schlegel, 1973). To strive to be better than or to outperform others is to be noncooperative and to risk acquiring the title of kahopi ("*not* Hopi") and being viewed as a threat to the community and possibly a witch. In order to emphasize a group identity, a group of children may share the punishment for the wrongdoing of one (Dennis, 1965). In addition, Hopi communities regularly call on supernatural figures, or bogey kachinas, to chastise uncooperative children. Among the Hopi, cooperation among the members of a community is considered critical to their survival and overt competition a threat to that survival.

By contrast, the !Kung Bushmen, hunters and gatherers of the Kalahari Desert in southern Africa, have few institutionalized forms of cooperation but a number of informal techniques to ensure group harmony. Among the !Kung, who reside in migratory bands whose membership is fluid, cooperation is oriented primarily to the hunting and distribution of large game, a scarce and highly prized resource. Hunting parties are formed voluntarily and not restricted in membership, but once a kill is made the meat is always distributed among the members of the hunting party and from each of them to all other kin and visitors who are residing together at the time (Marshall, 1976). In this way, everyone is assured of a share. However, a kill is believed to be owned by the hunter whose arrow first effectively penetrates the animal, and he has the prerogative of making the first distribution of meat. Once an individual receives a portion of meat, he is believed to own it: "He may give and share it further as he wishes, but it never becomes family or group property"

(Marshall, 1976, p. 363). Similarly, all other material goods, although not plentiful, are privately owned. However, an informal system of reciprocal gift giving ensures that most goods continually circulate among members of a band.

Among the !Kung, then, there are few institutionalized forms of cooperation, but a number of informal techniques are used to ensure a certain level of group harmony and to mitigate discord. According to Marshall (1976, p. 350), "The arduous hunting-gathering life would be insupportable for a single person or a single nuclear family without cooperation and companionship of the larger group." Similarly, there are no institutionalized forms of competition, although it is recognized that some men are better hunters than others and that some individuals are more suited to serve as leaders. However, "no Bushman wants prominence" and, as in the case of one leader, may avoid it by divesting himself of all possessions, winning respect in return (Thomas, 1959, p. 183).

Furthermore, the !Kung do not consciously socialize their children for cooperation and against interpersonal competition. In fact, child care by adults is generally informal and nondirective (Draper, 1976). However, children are rarely without adult supervision and are usually in close proximity to others, where they gradually learn the rules which govern the sharing of food and other goods and the avoidance of serious conflict (Draper, 1971). They can observe that behavior is characterized by reciprocity and interdependence. Similarly, they learn that competitiveness and boasting are not acceptable behavior. They play no competitive games and are not encouraged to evaluate their performance against that of other children. Children play games for fun and to practice their own skills, but not in a spirit of competition.

Even societies that appear to be highly individualistic or atomistic may have subtle devices for counteracting divisive tendencies and promoting cooperation. For example, the pastoral Navajo of Arizona, New Mexico, and Utah are an egalitarian society with a social structure that has been characterized as "ego-centered" (Lamphere, 1970; 1971). Individual autonomy is stressed from an early age, with children being given their own possessions over which they have full authority. The Navajo stress individuals' rights to make decisions regarding the use and disposal of their possessions as well as their own actions and allocation of time. This individualistic social system, however, is combined with a cultural system of generalized reciprocity and universally understood concepts of cooperative and uncooperative behavior. Consequently, the individual is aware of a diffuse set of obligations to help others, and this "ethic of cooperation" is backed up by negative prescriptions which define what it is to be noncooperative, or "anti-Navajo." Gilmore (1975), Balikci (1968), and Piker (1968) have recently pointed out for other seemingly atomistic societies the presence of subtle mechanisms, such as patterns of friendship, that help to promote societal cooperation.[2]

There are, however, in the cross-cultural literature a few examples of societies where cooperation is minimal. Contrary to Marshall's observation for the !Kung, among the Siriono, who subsist largely as hunters and gatherers with some rudimentary agriculture in the forests of eastern Bolivia, cooperation rarely extends beyond the nuclear family, although people live in small bands of intermarrying kin. The nuclear family operates as the primary economic and social unit, although some cooperative hunting, gathering, and food sharing may occur among the members of the matrilineal extended family. Food, however, is scarce, and people are reluctant to share, even going to the extreme of eating at night or off in the forest alone so as not to be obliged to share. What minimal norms of cooperation and reciprocity exist are recognized only reluctantly and result frequently in quarrels (Holmberg, 1969). Children past infancy are taught to be as independent of their families as possible and to fend for themselves. By the age of 8 years, for instance, a boy is actively hunting. "The strong dependency relationships formed in infancy and early childhood do not persist. Gradually but prematurely they are displaced by traits of independence, so that when [a Siriono] has reached adulthood [she or] he displays an individualism and apathy toward his fellows that is remarkable.... The Siriono ... is anything but cooperative, generous, submissive, or kind" (Holmberg, 1969, pp. 259–261).

An even more extreme example of a society characterized by minimal interpersonal cooperation is Turnbull's (1972) celebrated account of the Ik of East Africa. It seems that for this group, under conditions of drought and severe food shortage, nearly all social ties of cooperation have broken down, even at the family level. Children go uncared for, food is stolen from friends and relatives at any opportunity, and an extreme form of individualism has arisen where people consider only their own survival. Turnbull suggests that the Ik are characterized by such rampant individualism and competition for survival that "those 'basic' qualities such as family, cooperative sociality, belief, love, hope and so forth" have been discarded (Turnbull, 1972, p. 289).

Examples of societies characterized by limited interpersonal cooperation are not restricted to small tribal groups. Banfield's (1958) account of a village in southern Italy indicates that even in a complex society where extensive organization is necessary at the national level, at the village level peoples' behavior may be characterized by rampant noncooperation. Banfield describes the villagers of Montegrano as lacking any sense of cooperation with others beyond the nuclear family ("amoral familism"), as having no public-spiritedness, and as being incapable of organized action for the common good. Nuclear families look out for their own interests, and help is seldom offered to anyone outside this small unit. One individual, when asked about persons who might act for the welfare of the whole community, answered:

No one in town is animated by a desire to do good for all of the population. Even if sometimes there is someone apparently animated by this desire, in reality he is interested in his own welfare and he does his own business. Even the saints, for all their humility, looked after themselves. And men, after all, are only made of flesh and spirit. (Banfield, 1958, p. 20)

While the cross-cultural ethnographic literature suggests that there is considerable variation in the extent to which cooperation is emphasized or institutionalized at the societal level, it offers few examples of societies that are highly competitive. The Kwakiutl of the Canadian Pacific Northwest coast represent one of the few cases of a highly competitive society in the ethnographic literature, but recent reinterpretation suggests that the "competitive" feasting and gift giving (potlatch) may have been a method of distribution of seasonally scarce products (Donald & Mitchell, 1975; Netting, 1977; Piddocke, 1965; Suttles, 1962). While examples of institutions organized to foster competition are rare in the non-Western, nonindustrialized world (Munroe & Munroe, 1975), Western, complex societies yield abundant examples of competitive institutions in the form of the educational system, private business and industry, and professional athletic organizations.

The cultural examples cited suggest that there is another dimension relevant to societal cooperation: individualism-collectivism (cf. Mead, 1937). Those societies that clearly institutionalize cooperation also tend to stress group-oriented goals and to deemphasize individual ones. The Hutterites, for instance, allow individuals few personal possessions and little time to themselves; almost all goods belong to the colony and almost all activities are group ones. Kanter (1972), in her analysis of 19th century American utopian communities, notes that the most successful communities combined communal sharing of property, communal labor, and regularized group contact with a renunciation of such divisive bonds between individuals as family and heterosexual ties. They used a variety of "commitment mechanisms" to create a group identity that would outweigh a concern with individuality. However, at the other end of the scale, a cultural value on individualism does not mean that a society will be noncooperative in its emphasis. The Siriono and the Ik combine extreme individualism with low levels of cooperation, but the !Kung and the Navajo are examples of societies where individualism is tempered by informal rules of generalized reciprocity. Similarly, complex societies such as the United States combine an ideology of individualism with elaborate corporate groups in which cooperative endeavors are important. Systematic investigation of the relationship between the degree of cooperativeness in a society and levels of collectivism-individualism should be made.

The cultural examples cited above also indicate that cooperation and competition are not bipolar phenomena, as is frequently assumed. High levels of institutionalized cooperation do not necessarily imply an absence of competition, and low levels of institutionalized cooperation do not imply rampant competition (e.g., Cook & Stingle, 1974; Whyte, 1975).[3] Rather, these two areas of behavior can coexist in a variety of ways. Among the Siriono, where group cooperation is minimal, there is no institutionalized form of competition. Competitive games do not occur, warfare between bands does not exist, and hunters or gatherers are not rewarded for trying to outperform one another. Similarly, among the !Kung and the Navajo, where cooperation is based upon informal patterns of reciprocity rather than being institutionalized, competition between individuals and groups is discouraged. Both societies emphasize individual rights and skills but not competition.

On the other hand, among the Hutterites and in the Soviet Union, where cooperation is highly valued, where it is institutionalized in numerous domains, and where it is carefully inculcated in children, competitive activities do occur. For example, among the Hutterites a certain degree of economic competition between department managers is believed to increase productivity:

> The competition between department managers proves to be healthy for the welfare of the colony. It does not involve direct competition between individuals or their assigned status but between income-producing phases of the operation. (Hostetler & Huntington, 1967, p. 42)

Group competition is often allowed because it is believed to encourage group cooperation and loyalty (Bronfenbrenner, 1972; Eifermann, 1970; Howard, 1970). Team sports is a good example of a situation in which an individual simultaneously cooperates with teammates while competing with the opposing team. The observation that intergroup conflict and/or competition may help to produce intragroup unity has been made by a number of researchers and theorists. For example, Simmel long ago pointed out that "conflict is thus designed to resolve divergent dualism; it is a way of achieving some kind of unity" (1964, p. 13). With regard to competitive games, he says, "One *unites* in order to fight, and one fights under the mutually recognized control of norms and rules" (1964, p. 35, italics in original). In a similar fashion, Evans-Pritchard (1940), in his analysis of the Nuer segmentary lineage system, has pointed out that external conflict results in the temporary unification of larger and larger social units. Gluckman (1965) has made similar observations in his analysis of conflict and ritual in tribal societies.

The sociocultural materials presented above represent one source of information relevant to an investigation of cooperation and competition. They enable us to raise questions about the relationship of cooperation and competition to various sociocultural factors. The next section examines the relationship between these sociocultural factors and individual expressions of cooperative and competitive behavior.

INDIVIDUAL AND INSTITUTIONAL LEVELS OF ANALYSIS

The sociocultural and individual levels of analysis do not always yield congruent results for a given population. We will first present some examples of conflicting results and discuss their implications. Then we will review several different sets of studies which use a variety of research strategies to measure cooperation and/or competition either at the individual level or the institutional level.

There are several striking cases of studies which conflict with one another in their evaluations of cooperation and competition for the same society. For example, we cited the Hopi as a society which strenuously emphasizes cooperation among individuals and deemphasizes competition. This has been the general characterization of the Hopi in the ethnographic record (e.g., Eggan, 1956; Schlegel, 1973). Dennis (1955), however, in a study of 180 Hopi primary and secondary school children, found that they made significantly more competitive responses to a set of paired preference items (e.g., "to make the best grades in your class," or "make the same grades as most of the others") than an Anglo control sample of children. Dennis concluded that "although the Hopi traditionally play down overt expressions of competition, it appears that competitive behavior may nevertheless be elicited" (1955, p. 100).

Several different interpretations of these findings are possible. First, the school-attending sample of children may have been atypical. However, there are numerous studies of other native North American groups which indicate that the traditionally noncompetitive children do not suddenly become competitive in the school setting (e.g., Havighurst, 1957; Sindell, 1974; Wax, Wax, & Dumont, 1964). Second, it is possible that the experimental tasks themselves were producing uncharacteristic behavior. There is no way to determine whether or not that was the case. On the other hand, Dennis' interpretation may be accurate, suggesting that we must distinguish between overt, socially valued expressions of cooperation and competition and covert expressions of such behavior. Societal goals, values, and institutions may not always accurately reflect the underlying motivations of individuals.

Several instances of the above situation come to mind. In India, for example, the joint family is held as an ideal to which all individuals should strive. It is supposed to be characterized by total sharing and cooperation among its members. In actuality, however, the joint family is less common than not and is frequently the arena for bickering and competition among its members, which may result in its dissolution (see Mandelbaum, 1970, for a review of relevant studies). Similar observations have been made for extended families in China. For example, Wolf (1968), in describing the house of Lim, points out that from an outside perspective the family appeared to function smoothly and to be highly cooperative. "To see the less fortunate effects, one has to look beneath the surface of the family's daily routines. As Lim Chiu-ieng once told me, 'If you look at the face of our family, it looks good, but if you look at its bones, it's not like that' " (Wolf, 1968, p. 35). Similarly, although the !Kung overtly value sharing and all goods are regularly distributed among band members, there is often much bickering and argumentation over the actual distribution of goods (Lee, 1969; 1972). As a final example, Balinese society, which generally emphasizes harmony, cooperation, and group-oriented activities, has highly competitive cock fights: "Much of Bali surfaces in a cock ring. For it is only apparently cocks that are fighting there. Actually, it is men" (Geertz, 1973, p. 417).

By contrast, the Kwakiutl, as we have mentioned, have been much celebrated in the ethnographic literature as a highly competitive society. "All the social relations among the Kwakiutl are keyed to the principle of rank, and each individual of any status in the community is motivated by an obsessive drive for prestige. . . . Above all, an individual gains prestige by crushing a rival. It is this intense rivalry that is at the heart of Kwakiutl social relations" (Goldman, 1937, pp. 183–184). "The individual among the Kwakiutl is fitted very early into the competitive pattern" (p. 203). When a child was 1 year old the father distributed gifts to the tribe in the child's name, and by age 10 or 12 years a boy was expected to collect and distribute his own property in a competitive fashion.

Given such an orientation, one might expect Kwakiutl children to adapt easily to the competition that characterizes Western schooling. This seems not to be the case, however. In his description of his year of teaching Kwakiutl children in Alert Bay, British Columbia, Wolcott (1967, p. 108) mentions that he had to avoid "using comparisons and teacher-induced competition as a source of motivation among the pupils." Such efforts were not effective, and although the children initiated some informal competition among themselves, "their self-imposed competition was more than offset . . . by the tendency of pupils constantly to help each other, especially for older pupils to help younger ones to the extent of doing all the work designed for the young pupils and ignoring their own" (1967, p. 104). The children tended to view school work as tasks to be completed with their combined resources, not as something on which to try to outperform one another.

Thus we are again presented with an instance of a society which at the institutional level has been characterized in one fashion but for which at the individual level there are contradictory observations. The fact that the Kwakiutl children did not perceive school as an arena in which to compete may be the result of the introduction of a strange institution. On the other hand, it may be that at the individual level the Kwakiutl are more cooperative than their traditional competitive institutions would indicate. Even the potlatch, although characterized as a competitive institution, actually may have stimulated "social cooperation in production under the management of defined leaders" (Netting, 1977, p. 39).

Madsen and his associates have developed some direct experimental techniques for measuring cooperation and competition among individuals and groups. One is the Madsen Cooperation Board (Madsen, 1967), and another is the Marble-Pull Task (Madsen, 1971). The Madsen Cooperation Board is designed for four subjects to play at once, pulling strings and drawing lines. However, in order for one subject to draw a line toward himself or herself, the other children must cooperate. If all pull at once, no one succeeds. The task can be used to measure cooperation for individuals or for groups by assigning either individual rewards or group rewards. The

Marble-Pull Task is similar in design but uses marbles instead of paper and pen and can be played by only two subjects at once. Again, in order for one subject to pull a marble toward herself or himself, the other person must cooperate by relaxing his or her string; if both persons pull at once, neither can succeed in getting a marble in the hole. It is assumed in these games that a cooperative person will relax the string and allow the other player(s) to pull, and a person's cooperation can be measured by the number of times she or he allows the other(s) to pull the string and get the marble or draw a line through their circles. The competitive person, it is assumed, will not let an opponent(s) pull the string and thus win. Under individual reward conditions, the cooperative solution to these games is to have subjects alternate pulling and relaxing the string so that each one can win. On the Madsen Board, group rewards can be established whereby subjects are rewarded only when they all cooperate so as to allow each one to draw a line through his or her circle.

Using variations on these techniques, it has been found that rural children are generally more cooperative than urban ones in Mexico and in the United States (Kagan & Madsen, 1971; 1972a, b; Madsen, 1967; 1971; Madsen & Shapira, 1970), in Israel (Shapira & Madsen, 1969; 1974), in Canada (Miller & Thomas, 1972), in New Zealand (D. Thomas, 1975), and in Columbia (Marin, Mejia, & de Oberle, 1975). In Mexico poor urban children are more cooperative than middle-class ones (Madsen, 1967). More traditional groups such as the Blackfoot of Canada (Miller & Thomas, 1972), the Australian Aborigines (Sommerlad & Bellingham, 1972), and the Cook Islanders and rural Maori (D. Thomas, 1975) are more cooperative than their European counterparts. Mexican-Americans are more cooperative than non-kibbutz Israelis (Shapira & Madsen, 1969) or Americans (Shapira & Madsen, 1974).

The only exceptions to the general pattern that rural and non-Western, or nonmodal Western, children are more cooperative than urban and Western ones seem to be Zambian schoolchildren and Cuban-Americans. Using the Madsen Board, no significant differences were found between Zambian and European school children (Bethlehem, 1973), while Cuban-Americans proved to be even less cooperative than Anglo-Americans (Concha, Garcia, & Perez, 1975). With regard to the Zambian case, schooling may have had an effect, as has been indicated in several other studies of non-Western groups (Graves & Graves, 1978; Miller, 1973; Sommerlad & Bellingham, 1972). On the other hand, several studies using different measures of cooperation and competition, such as the Prisoner's Dilemma game and the Picture-Frustration test, have also indicated that rural, non-Western, and nonmodal Western children are more cooperative than their counterparts (Alcock, 1974; Meeker, 1970; Miyawaki, 1958; Richmond & Weiner, 1973).

The distinction between individual and group rewards appears to be a significant factor in these experimental tasks. For example, in the study of rural kibbutz and urban Israeli children (Shapira & Madsen, 1969) using the Madsen Board, both groups cooperated adaptively under the group reward condition. It was only with the change to an individual reward condition that the urban children began to compete nonadaptively while the kibbutz children continued to cooperate. In another study (Shapira & Madsen, 1974) Israeli kibbutz children were found to be more group oriented than urban Israelis or urban Americans, even when the group-oriented response was not economically adaptive. Similarly, both Blackfoot and urban Canadian children cooperated under the group reward condition, but under the individual reward condition the Blackfoot subjects continued to cooperate even more effectively while the urban ones began to compete (Miller & Thomas, 1972).

It seems that there are real and significant differences in the underlying motivations of these various groups, with the traditional Blackfoot and the communally reared kibbutz children being more group oriented and potentially more cooperative than their more urban and Western counterparts. These findings support our earlier suggestion that the dimension collectivism–individualism is a factor relevant to cooperation and competition.

In a further study Madsen and Kagan (1973) have identified another factor which perhaps affects the levels of cooperation and competition expressed by children on these experimental tasks. Comparing Mexican and American mothers and their children in two experimental situations, they found that although both sets of mothers rewarded their children for success on a task, the Mexican mothers gave significantly more rewards for failure than did the American mothers. In addition, the American mothers chose significantly more difficult achievement goals for their children and did not lower the goals following failure, as did the Mexican mothers. These behaviors on the part of the mothers suggest that American mothers were training their children to be competitive and achievement oriented, while the Mexican mothers were responding more to their children's feelings.[4] That their mothers' training was effective is indicated by the fact that the American children, despite having fewer successes on these experimental tasks, received more rewards than the Mexican children. This is attributable to the fact that American mothers directed their children into more difficult, higher-risk choices which brought greater rewards.

The research of Madsen and his associates has made a major contribution to the study of cooperation and competition in having developed direct measures of these behaviors which have been used to compare a variety of populations. They do succeed in differentiating sets of individuals of different sociocultural backgrounds both between and within cultures. However, they still leave us with several questions. For instance, because the experimental tasks tend to present cooperation and competition as opposed strategies where competition is actually maladaptive, it is not clear what a cooperative choice means. "A 'cooperative choice' in the Madsen games may reflect either enlightened self-interest, a player's altruistic interest in gratifying his [or her] partner, or both" (Maccoby & Jacklin, 1974, p. 251). McClintock (1972) and his associates (McClintock, Messick, Kuhlman, & Campos, 1973) have responded to this problem by devising a set of tasks which help to determine whether a subject is motivated by self-interest, generosity, or the outright desire to defeat another person.

Another issue raised by the Madsen et al. research is the question of to what extent these experimental tasks reflect real-life situations. For example, Maccoby and Jacklin (1974, pp. 249–251) point out that "on the sports field or among junior executives who covet the same higher job . . . competition is the path to real individual gains." The Madsen games, however, are biased in favor of cooperation; in order to succeed, one must use a cooperative strategy. Thus they do not really tell us much about competition per se other than that more urbanized and Westernized individuals are so thoroughly trained to be competitive that they compete even when it is maladaptive. Even here, however, group versus individual rewards are relevant factors and must be examined further.

These experimental studies, then, still leave us with the problem of how cooperation and competition are interrelated and may be expressed simultaneously by the same person, as in team sports. A striking example of this is Eifermann's (1970) observation that Israeli kibbutz children do not play totally cooperative games but rather games which require cooperation toward a common goal but which have an overall competitive framework. Such games, in fact, are more popular among kibbutz than nonkibbutz children. Thus in real-life situations cooperative and competitive drives and behaviors are probably combined in a variety of complex ways which can be discovered only by means of careful observational as well as experimental research. We also need more research into the antecedents of cooperative and competitive behavior that gets expressed in games and tasks of either the experimental or the cultural variety.

Graves and Graves (1978), in their study of the impact of modernization upon traditional forms of cooperation and generosity among a set of Cook Islanders, have combined some experimental techniques with such other research strategies as participant observation, systematic observation of children's behavior, attitude questionnaires, academic achievement scores, and measures of attitudes towards school. Their purpose was to explore personality changes relative to these dimensions under the impact of modernization and Western schooling. Thus they were concerned with more than just measuring cooperation and competition experimentally. They wanted to relate those measures to changes in the environment and traditional social structure and to discuss personality change at the individual level.

Graves and Graves devised a Coin Game, building on the experiments of Kagan and Madsen (1972a, b), which they administered to a sample of adults and school children. "The technique offers subjects an opportunity to distribute valued goods to themselves and to others in a variety of ways that simulate real life situations" (Graves & Graves, 1978, p. 117). The experiment consists of ten pairs of stimulus cards, each of which offers the subject a unique combination of payoff options. One set of options they categorize as "generous," i.e., they either maximize the other subject's payoff or they equalize payoffs between subjects. The other set of options are categorized as "rivalrous" in that one subject takes more than he or she gives to another or maximizes her or his own payoff by taking more without regard to the other players. They found that for adults there was a change from more traditional generous responses, which were associated with older people who lived in more remote parts of the island, resided in extended families, engaged in traditional subsistence activities, and had less than average formal education, to more rivalrous responses, which were associated with younger people who were involved in the wage economy, resided in nuclear families, and had greater than average formal education. Thus they conclude that rivalry is a Western import, a conclusion which is congruent with the findings for competition mentioned above.

The results of the Coin Game for children are more illuminating, however. On this experimental task they found no association with home, background, household size, or father's performance on the same task. Rather, the critical variables were ones associated with schooling—i.e., high scores for rivalry were correlated with high achievement scores and with ratings for neat hair and complete uniforms in good condition, which were used as measures of positive attitude toward school. The critical variables affecting traditional norms for generosity and cooperation seem to be, then, the introduction of Western schooling and the development on the part of some of a positive attitude toward it. In fact, by testing children of different ages, Graves and Graves were able to determine that at 5 or 6 years of age Polynesian children are highly generous but that by grade 4 for boys and grade 6 for girls more rivalry than generosity is being displayed in the Coin Game. The degree of rivalry continues to increase with each grade in school thereafter. Graves and Graves have further examined these relationships by means of a set of experiments using the Madsen Cooperation Board.

On the basis of their experiments with children and their observations in the schools, Graves and Graves have determined that schooling is associated with an increase in rivalry and competition among individuals. They note that the schools emphasize individual achievement and individual rewards to the possible detriment of group activities and cooperation. This view is supported by the *Six Cultures* study (B. Whiting & Whiting, 1975; J. Whiting & Whiting, 1973), which found that in complex societies, "where no child knows what he is going to be when he grows up, individual achievement and success must be positively valued" (J. Whiting & Whiting, 1973, p. 64). It is in such societies, of course, that schooling receives its maximum emphasis.

Graves and Graves go on to point out the import of these outcomes for the future of the Cook Islanders:

> In this study of modernization, we are interested not only in changes in personality predisposition, but also the implications of these changes for community life. What would happen to social cohesiveness on the island if not only the motivation but also the interpersonal skills necessary to achieve coordination of efforts within groups were decreasing? Our discovery of a high degree of rivalry among primary school children, increasing with each grade, suggested that cooperation could be at least problematic in the future. (Graves & Graves, 1978, p. 127)

In conclusion, they raise the question of why educators have assumed that competition is necessary for motivating learning and suggest that in Polynesian society there are numerous examples of successful group functioning that could serve as models for developing cooperative techniques in the classroom. As it is, they argue, "most of the children learning a competitive, rivalistic style in school will not have an opportunity to go very far academically, nor will they fit into a society which still values and needs communal participation and cooperative effort" (Graves & Graves, 1978, p. 133).

The Graves and Graves (1978) study is important to our discussion of cooperation and competition on several accounts. First of all, by combining experimental measures with a variety of other research strategies they have been able to offer explanations for the scores they found on generosity–rivalry and cooperation–competition scales. Second, they have successfully combined an individual level of analysis with a sociocultural or institutional one. Third, they have identified a specific factor, Western schooling, which is producing important changes in individuals' motivations vis-à-vis cooperation and competition and which may, in turn, affect the social organization of these Cook Islanders.

Finally, we should mention that all of these studies which are concerned with measuring cooperation and/or competition, at either the individual or the institutional level, are pertinent to discussions of personality. They are all concerned with identifying behavioral and motivational differences for these dimensions among a variety of populations. In particular, the Graves and Graves study is suggestive of factors affecting the development of these behaviors. However, at this time we have little evidence as to whether or not these behavioral tendencies are enduring personality characteristics.

Perhaps, the best evidence we have that particular cooperative and/or competitive behaviors can be indicative of enduring personality traits comes from studies of communal societies. We have, for instance, described the values associated with and the training for cooperation among the Hutterites. Kaplan and Plant (1956) in their study of Hutterite personality have confirmed the Hutterite emphasis upon cooperation and deemphasis of competition:

> It is quite remarkable how infrequently responses indicating competitive feeling occur in the psychological tests. Rivalry occurs very rarely in any of the tests. . . . Sibling rivalry too is infrequent. One TAT card that often elicits rivalry in our society does not do so with the Hutterites. On the Sentence Completion Tests, competition and rivalry do occur in both men and women but with a relatively low frequency. Certainly as far as these findings indicate, there are very few covert competitive feelings that would conflict with the Hutterite emphasis on cooperative values. (Kaplan & Plant, 1956, p. 91)

Similarly, a longitudinal, observational study (Plattner & Minturn, 1975) which used the *Six Cultures* study categories (B. Whiting & Whiting, 1975) to compare communally and noncommunally raised children in the United States indicates that even as preschoolers the commune children were more group oriented and less competitive and achievement oriented than the children from nuclear families. These differences persisted in observations of the children a year later. Another study (Rappaport, Bernstein, Hogan, Kane, Plunk, & Sholder, 1972) comparing American college undergraduates who lived in communes with those living in fraternities and sororities also found that in a game situation the commune members were more cooperative than the other students.

When these studies are combined with those by Spiro (1965), Eifermann (1970), and Shapira and Madsen (1969; 1974) for Israeli kibbutz children, there is strong evidence that a communal life style has long-term effects upon individuals' cooperative and competitive behavior. It would seem, then, that we not only need to use a greater variety of measures and techniques to study cooperation and competition, but that we need to examine the cooperative-competitive behavior of sets of individuals at different points in time to determine how enduring it is.

SUMMARY AND CONCLUSIONS

The purpose of this chapter has been to review the cross-cultural literature relevant to the behavioral domain, cooperation–competition, and to identify critical issues and questions. We have concentrated on those psychological and anthropological studies that have been published since the groundbreaking work of the Social Science Research Council in 1937 (May & Doob, 1937; Mead, 1937). Since that study there has been no comparable integrative effort, and with the exception of some experimental work in psychology few studies have focused on this particular behavioral domain. Nonetheless, we have found many studies to be suggestive. In conclusion, then, we wish to summarize some of the issues which we think are critical to cross-cultural analyses of these behaviors and to suggest some directions for further research.

One major issue raised throughout this chapter has been the nonbipolarity of cooperative and competitive behavior. It seems clear that the presence of one kind of behavior does not imply the absence of the other; rather, the two forms of behavior appear to covary in a complex set of ways. An area critical to further research is therefore determination of how these two forms of behavior are inter-related. In order to do that, however, we must devise a variety of techniques for measuring them and identify relevant social domains in which to examine them. To date, only small strides have been made in these directions.

A second important issue is the level—individual or societal—at which we examine cooperative and competitive behavior. Several studies indicate that for the same population these behaviors are not always congruent for both levels of analysis. What this suggests is that in order to understand how these behaviors vary it is critical to examine them at *both* the individual and the societal levels. Furthermore, at the individual level both overt and covert behavior need to be examined. The cross-cultural experimental testing of children indicates that people may be moti-vated by different factors to cooperate and/or compete.

Another issue which has been raised is the relationship of individualism to cooper-ation and competition. In the SSRC report, Mead (1937) proposed a threefold scheme for classifying societies, adding the category of "individualistic behavior" to those of cooperation and competition. It was her belief that some societies stressed individualism more than either cooperation or competition. However, we have pointed out that even highly individualistic or atomistic societies may have subtle devices for promoting cooperation and that, again, our focus should be upon deter-mining the interrelationships of these behaviors rather than opposing them to one another. In this regard, we have suggested several directions for further research. First, we need to identify and distinguish formal and informal structures or mecha-nisms that promote either cooperative or competitive behavior. Then we can investi-gate how the dimension individualism–collectivism is associated with these structures. For example, we have suggested that collective societies tend to have formal structures for cooperation. This is an idea which has received some support from the experimental research of Madsen and his associates—i.e., children from formally cooperative societies, such as the Israeli kibbutzim, were more group ori-ented in their responses to testing than nonkibbutz children, even when that re-sponse was not rewarded.

The study by Graves and Graves (1978) is particularly enlightening. First, they have identified one specific factor, Western formal schooling, that critically affects levels of cooperation and competition and that deserves further exploration. Sec-ond, they have examined changing patterns of cooperation and competition through time at both the individual and the societal level. Third, they have related these behaviors to personality changes, which raises another question requiring further research: To what extent are cooperation and competition enduring personality characteristics, and under what circumstances are they subject to change?

To answer these and other questions raised relative to cooperative and competi-tive behavior we need improved research techniques and more data. Currently, for example, there is no cross-cultural material specifically concerned with the socializa-tion of children for cooperation and/or competition. The cross-cultural codes for training for competition (Barry, Josephson, Lauer, & Marshall, 1976) are based upon a variety of ethnographic materials, none of which was specifically concerned with the collection of such data. Furthermore, there is no cross-cultural coding of ethno-graphic data for cooperative behavior. The experimental research of Madsen and his associates is valuable in that it has produced some direct techniques for measuring cooperation and competition among both individuals and groups. However, ques-tions remain about how cooperative and competitive strategies are interrelated, what motivates individuals to select one strategy over another, and to what extent these experimental tasks reflect real-life situations. Such experimental techniques need to be used in association with other research strategies. Thus there is great need for more data collection, using a variety of research methods.

It is also essential that we try to determine how cooperation and competition are related to other kinds of behavior. Throughout this review of the literature the term "cooperation" has been linked with other terms, describing other behavioral traits, such as reciprocal altruism and generosity. Similarly, the discussion of "competition" has frequently involved the mention of such other behavioral traits as conflict and rivalry. It is not clear just what the interrelationships among these various traits are. This, then, is another area requiring further work—one that is critical to our better understanding of a variety of behaviors.

Finally, we have suggested that the recent efforts to examine human behavior from an evolutionary perspective so as to integrate social and biological perspectives may offer new insights into cooperation and competition at the species level. It may be that learning is not the sole mechanism by which these behaviors are acquired but that they have their roots in our evolutionary past. This, then, is another important direction requiring further research.

ACKNOWLEDGMENTS
I want to thank Ralph Bolton, Charlene Bolton, Donald Brenneis, Robert Munroe, Ruth Munroe, and Beverly Scales for their help in the preparation of this chapter.

NOTES
1. There have been several recent reviews of the psychological literature, especially with regard to the socialization for cooperation and competition (see Bryan, 1975; Cook & Stingle, 1974; Phillips & DeVault, 1957).

2. For a discussion of this phenomenon among a variety of societies see the special issue of *Human Organization*, Vol. 27, No. 3, Fall 1968, Perspectives on the Atomistic-Type Society, with an introduction by A. J. Rubel and H. J. Kupferer.

3. Whyte (1975), in a recent analysis of conflict and cooperation among several Andean communities, has proposed a fourfold model for categorizing these communities. He suggests that cooperation and conflict are not bipolar phenomena and must be viewed in relationship to one another. Therefore he offers a two dimensional-two continua model according to which communities can be arranged into four categories: high cooperation-low conflict, low cooperation-high conflict, and high-high and low-low combinations (1975, p. 376). Although Whyte is concerned with cooperation and conflict rather than competition, some such similar model might be a heuristic device for conceptualizing cooperation and competition at the societal level. Whyte has also devised a series of measures according to which his Peruvian communities can be categorized, a necessary task for examining the interrelationship of cooperation and competition at the societal level.

4. Cross-cultural codes for competitive games (Roberts, Arth, & Bush, 1959; Roberts & Sutton-Smith, 1962) and for the socialization of competitiveness (Barry, Josephson, Lauer, & Marshall, 1976) are available. These codes need to be exploited in the continuing exploration of individual competitive and cooperative behavior.

REFERENCES

Ainsworth, M. D. Patterns of attachment behavior shown by the infant in interaction with his mother. *Merrill-Palmer Quarterly*, 1964, *10*, 51–58.

Ainsworth, M. D. *Infancy in Uganda: Infant care and the growth of love.* Baltimore: Johns Hopkins Press, 1967.

Alcock, J. E. Cooperation, competition, and the effects of time pressure in Canada and India. *Journal of Conflict Resolution*, 1974, *18*, 171–197.

Balikci, A. Bad friends. *Human Organization*, 1968, *27*, 191–199.

Banfield, E. C. *The moral basis of a backward society.* New York: The Free Press, 1958.

Barry, H., III, Josephson, L., Lauer, E., & Marshall, C. Traits inculcated in childhood: Cross-cultural codes. *Ethnology*, 1976, *15*, 83–106.

Belshaw, C. S. *Traditional exchange and modern markets.* Englewood Cliffs, N.J.: Prentice-Hall, 1965.

Bethlehem, D. W. Cooperation, competition and altruism among school children in Zambia. *International Journal of Psychology*, 1973, *8*, 125–135.

Bowlby, J. The nature of the child's tie to his mother. *International Journal of Psychoanalysis*, 1958, *39*, 350–373.

Bowlby, J. *Attachment and loss* (Vol. 1). New York: Basic Books, 1969.

Bronfenbrenner, U. *Two worlds of childhood: U.S. and U.S.S.R.* New York: Simon & Schuster, 1972.

Bryan, J. H. Children's cooperation and helping behaviors. *Review of Child Development Research*, 1975, *5*, 127–182.

Campbell, D. T. On the conflicts between biological and social evolution and between psychology and moral tradition. *American Psychologist*, 1975, *30*, 1103–1126.

Concha, P., Garcia, L., & Perez, A. Cooperation versus competition: A comparison of Anglo-American and Cuban-American youngsters in Miami. *Journal of Social Psychology*, 1975, *95*, 273–274.

Cook, H., & Stingle, S. Cooperative behavior in children. *Psychological Bulletin*, 1974, *81*, 918–933.

Dennis, W. Are Hopi children non-cooperative? *Journal of Abnormal Psychology*, 1955, *50*, 99–100.

Dennis, W. The socialization of the Hopi child. In W. Dennis, *The Hopi child.* New York: John Wiley & Sons, 1965.

Donald, L., & Mitchell, D. H. Some correlates of local group rank among the Southern Kwakiutl. *Ethnology*, 1975, *14*, 325–346.

Draper, P. *!Kung childhood.* Paper presented at the Annual Meeting of the American Anthropological Association, New York, 1971.

Draper, P. Social and economic constraints on child life among the !Kung. In R. B. Lee & I. DeVore (Eds.), *Kalahari hunters-gatherers: Studies of the !Kung San and their neighbors.* Cambridge, Mass.: Harvard University Press, 1976.

Eggan, D. Instruction and affect in Hopi cultural continuity. *Southwestern Journal of Anthropology*, 1956, *12*, 347–370.

Eifermann, R. R. Cooperativeness and egalitarianism in Kibbutz children's games. *Human Relations*, 1970, *23*, 579–587.

Evans-Pritchard, E. E. *The Nuer: A description of the modes of livelihood and political institutions of a Nilotic people.* Oxford: Clarendon Press, 1940.

Geertz, C. Deep play: Notes on the Balinese cockfight. In C. Geertz, *The interpretation of cultures: Selected essays.* New York: Basic Books, 1973.

Gilmore, D. Friendship in Fuenmayor: Patterns of integration in an atomistic society. *Ethnology*, 1975, *14*, 311–324.

Gluckman, M. *Politics, law and ritual in tribal society.* Chicago: Aldine, 1965.

Goldman, I. The Kwakiutl of Vancouver Island. In M. Mead (Ed.), *Cooperation and competition among primitive peoples.* New York: McGraw-Hill, 1937.

Graves, N. B., & Graves, T. D. The impact of modernization on Polynesian personality, or how to make an up-tight, rivalrous Westerner out of an easy-going, generous Pacific Islander. *Human Organization,* 1978, *37,* 115–135.

Havighurst, R. J. Education among American Indians: Individual and cultural aspects. *Annals of the American Academy of Political and Social Science,* 1957, *311,* 105–115.

Holmberg, A. *Nomads of the long bow.* New York: Natural History Press, 1969.

Hostetler, J. A., & Huntington, G. E. *The Hutterites in North America.* New York: Holt, Rinehart & Winston, 1967.

Howard, A. *Learning to be Rotuman.* New York: Teachers College Press, 1970.

Johnson, D. W., & Johnson, R. T. *Learning together and alone: Cooperation, competition and individualization.* Englewood Cliffs, N.J.: Prentice-Hall, 1975.

Kagan, S., & Madsen, M. C. Cooperation and competition of Mexican, Mexican-American, and Anglo-American children of two ages under four instructional sets. *Developmental Psychology,* 1971, *5,* 32–39.

Kagan, S., & Madsen, M. C. Experimental analyses of cooperation and competition of Anglo-American and Mexican children. *Developmental Psychology,* 1972, *6,* 49–59. (a)

Kagan, S., & Madsen, M. C. Rivalry in Anglo-American and Mexican children of two ages. *Journal of Personality and Social Psychology,* 1972, *24,* 214–220. (b)

Kanter, R. M. *Commitment and community.* Cambridge, Mass.: Harvard University Press, 1972.

Kaplan, B., & Plant, T. F. A. *Personality in a communal society: An analysis of the mental health of the Hutterites.* Lawrence: University of Kansas Publications, 1956.

Lamphere, L. Ceremonial co-operation and networks: A reanalysis of the Navajo outfit. *Man,* 1970, *5,* 39–59.

Lamphere, L. The Navajo cultural system: An analysis of concepts of cooperation and autonomy and their relation to gossip and witchcraft. In K. Basso & M. Opler (Eds.), *Apachean culture: History and ethnology.* Tucson: University of Arizona Press, 1971.

Lee, R. B. *!Kung Bushman violence.* Paper presented at the Annual Meeting of the American Anthropological Association, New Orleans, 1969.

Lee, R. B. The intensification of social life among the !Kung Bushmen. In B. J. Spooner (Ed.), *Population growth: Anthropological implications.* Cambridge, Mass.: MIT Press, 1972.

McClintock, C. G. Game behavior and social motivation in inter-personal settings. In C. McClintock (Ed.), *Experimental social psychology.* New York: Holt, Rinehart & Winston, 1972.

McClintock, C. G., Messick, D. M., Kuhlman, D., & Campos, F. Motivational bases of choice in three-choice decomposed games. *Journal of Experimental Social Psychology,* 1973, *9,* 572–590.

Maccoby, E. E., & Jacklin, C. N. *The psychology of sex differences.* Stanford, Calif.: Stanford University Press, 1974.

Madsen, M. C. Cooperative and competitive motivation of children in three Mexican subcultures *Psychological Reports,* 1967, *20,* 1307–1320.

Madsen, M. C. Developmental and cross-cultural differencs in the cooperative and competitive behavior of young children. *Journal of Cross-Cultural Psychology,* 1971, *2,* 365–371.

Madsen, M. C., & Kagan, S. Mother-directed achievement in two cultures. *Journal of Cross-Cultural Psychology,* 1973, *4,* 221–228.

Madsen, M. C., & Shapira, A. Cooperative and competitive behavior of urban Afro-American, Anglo-American, Mexican-American, and Mexican village children. *Developmental Psychology,* 1970, *3,* 16–20.

Mandelbaum, D. G. *Society in India* (Vol. 1). Berkeley: University of California Press, 1970.

Marin, G., Mejia, B., & de Oberle, C. Cooperation as a function of place of residence in Colombian children. *Journal of Social Psychology*, 1975, *95*, 127–128.

Marshall, L. Sharing, talking and giving: Relief of social tensions among the !Kung. In R . B. Lee & I. Devore (Eds.), *Kalahari hunters-gatherers: Studies of the !Kung San and their neighbors.* Cambridge, Mass: Harvard University Press, 1976.

Mauss, M. *The gift.* London: Cohen & West, 1954.

May, M. A., & Doob, L. W. *Competition and cooperation.* New York: Social Science Research Council, 1937.

Mead, M. *Cooperation and competition among primitive people.* New York: McGraw-Hill, 1937.

Meeker, B. Experimental study of cooperation and competition in West Africa. *International Journal of Psychology*, 1970, *5*, 11–19.

Miller, A. G. Integration and acculturation of cooperative behavior among Blackfoot Indians and non-Indian Canadian children. *Journal of Cross-Cultural Psychology*, 1973, *4*, 374–380.

Miller, A. G., & Thomas, R. Cooperation and competition among Blackfoot Indian and urban Canadian children. *Child Development*, 1972, *43*, 1104–1110.

Miyawaki, J. The study of personality traits of rural pupils: Primarily based upon the Picture-Frustration study. *Japanese Journal of Educational Psychology*, 1958, *6*, 77–84.

Montagu, A. *The human revolution.* New York: World Publishing, 1965.

Montagu, A. *The direction of human development* (rev. ed.). New York: Hawthorne, 1970.

Munroe, R. L., & Munroe, R. H. *Cross-cultural human development.* Monterey, Calif.: Brooks/Cole, 1975.

Netting, R. M. *Cultural ecology.* Menlo Park, Calif.: Cummings Publishing, 1977.

Phillips, B. N., & DeVault, M. V. Evaluation of research on cooperation and competition. *Psychological Reports*, 1957, *3*, 289–292.

Piddocke, S. The potlatch system of the Southern Kwakiutl: A new perspective. *Southwestern Journal of Anthropology*, 1965, *21*, 244–264.

Piker, S. Friendship to the death in rural Thai society. *Human Organization*, 1968, *27*, 200–204.

Plattner, S., & Minturn, L. A comparative and longitudinal study of the behavior of communally raised children. *Ethos*, 1975, *3*, 469–480.

Rappaport, J., Bernstein, D. A., Hogan, M., Kane, J., Plunk, M., & Sholder, M. Fraternal and communal living: Values and behavior on the campus. *Journal of Counseling Psychology*, 1972, *19*, 296–300.

Richmond, B. O., & Weiner, G. P. Cooperation and competition among children as a function of ethnic grouping, grade, sex, and reward condition. *Journal of Educational Psychology*, 1973, *64*, 329–334.

Roberts, J. M., Arth, M. J., & Bush, R. R. Games in culture. *American Anthropologist*, 1959, *61*, 597–605.

Roberts, J. M., & Sutton-Smith, B. Child-training and game involvement. *Ethnology*, 1962, *1*, 166–185.

Sahlins, M. D. Political power and the economy in primitive society. In G. E. Dole & R. L. Carneiro (Eds.), *Essays in the science of culture: In honor of Leslie A. White.* New York: Thomas Y. Crowell, 1960.

Sahlins, M. D. On the sociology of primitive exchange. In M. Banton (Ed.), *The relevance of models for social anthropology.* New York: Praeger, 1965.

Sahlins, M. D. *Tribesmen.* Englewood Cliffs, N.J.: Prentice-Hall, 1968.

Schlegel, A. The adolescent socialization of the Hopi girl. *Ethnology*, 1973, *12*, 449–462.

Shapira, A., & Madsen, M. C. Cooperative and competitive behavior of Kibbutz and urban children in Israel. *Child Development,* 1969, *40,* 609–617.

Shapira, A., & Madsen, M. C. Between- and within-group cooperation and competition among kibbutz and nonkibbutz children. *Developmental Psychology,* 1974, *10,* 140–145.

Simmel, G. *Conflict and the web of group-affiliations.* New York: Free Press, 1964.

Sindell, P. S. Some discontinuities in the enculturation of Mistassini Cree children. In G. D. Spindler (Ed.), *Education and cultural process.* New York: Holt, Rinehart & Winston, 1974.

Sommerlad, E. A., & Bellingham, W. P. Cooperation-competition: A comparison of Australian European and Aboriginal school children. *Journal of Cross-Cultural Psychology,* 1972, *3,* 149–158.

Spiro, M. E. *Children and the kibbutz.* New York: Schocken Books, 1965.

Suttles, W. Variation in habitat and culture on the Northwest Coast. In *Proceedings of the 34th International Congress of Americanists.* Vienna: Verlag Ferdinand Berger, 1962.

Thomas, D. R. Cooperation and competition among Polynesian and European children. *Child Development,* 1975, *46,* 948–953.

Thomas, E. M. *The harmless people.* New York: Vintage Books, 1959.

Trivers, R. L. The evolution of reciprocal altruism. *Quarterly Review of Biology,* 1971, *46,* 35–57.

Turnbull, C. M. *The mountain people.* New York: Simon & Schuster, 1972.

Wax, M., Wax, R. H., & Dumont, R. V., Jr. Formal education in an American Indian community. *Supplement to Social Problems,* 1964, *11* (4).

Whiting, B. B., & Whiting, J. W. M. *Children of six cultures: A psychocultural analysis.* Cambridge, Mass.: Harvard University Press, 1975.

Whiting, J. W. M., & Whiting, B. B. Altruistic and egoistic behavior in six cultures. *Anthropological Studies,* 1973, *9,* 56–66.

Whitney, G. The war between the words: Biological versus social evolution and some related issues (Responses to D. T. Campbell's 1975 APA presidential address). *American Psychologist,* 1976, *31,* 369–370.

Whyte, W. F. Conflict and cooperation in Andean communities. *American Ethnologist,* 1975, *2,* 373–392.

Wilson, E. O. *Sociobiology: The new synthesis.* Cambridge, Mass.: Harvard University Press, 1975.

Wilson, E. O. The war between the words: Biological versus social evolution and some related issues (Responses to D. T. Campbell's 1975 APA presidential address). *American Psychologist,* 1976, *31,* 370–371.

Wolcott, H. F. *A Kwakiutl village and school.* New York: Holt, Rinehart & Winston, 1967.

Wolf, M. *The house of Lim: A study of a Chinese farm family.* New York: Appleton-Century-Crofts, 1968.

23
Folktales and Childhood Experience

John L. Fischer

This chapter reviews possible relationships between the content and structure of folktales and techniques of socialization and other variables of childhood experience. Since relatively little has been accomplished directly in the way of systematic cross-cultural study in this field, the chapter begins with a consideration of some problems encountered by anthropologists, folklorists, and others in work focusing primarily on the folktales of single cultures. Several cross-cultural studies of folktales in relation to child development are then considered and evaluated. A concluding section summarizes some of the main issues arising out of the work to date and presents some suggestions for further research.

Recent surveys in the same general area in which the reader can find additional references and points of view include Barnouw's chapter on folktales (1973) and the contribution of Colby and Peacock (1974) on narrative. Some of the ideas presented below have been developed at greater length in an earlier survey article (Fischer, 1963). The contributions of Devereaux (1961) and LaBarre (1961) on art and mythology also present useful comprehensive views.

While these authors agree that the cross-cultural study of folktales in relation to human development appears to bear great promise, research along these lines has been less developed than the promise warrants. Recently the Human Relations Area Files (HRAF) have been making a compendium of all known published hologeistic studies. Out of these only ten deal with variables in folktales or myth, and only some deal directly or indirectly with the relation of folktale variables to variables of childhood experience, according to a computer search performed at my request in October 1976. This search appears to be reasonably complete.

There has, however, been other work suggesting the potential of folktales as indices of modal personality and social values. For some time, for instance, psychoanalysts have noted the similarity of folk narrative to dreams and have regarded them as symptomatic of widespread psychological constellations (see Kardiner, 1939; 1945). The Thematic Apperception Test (TAT) of Henry Murray asks subjects to produce stories about a set of pictures. Some subjects are reminded of folktale material by the pictures, and these responses may be used along with more idiosyncratic responses in interpreting the subject's personality.

Ethnographers have transcribed and translated vast amounts of oral narrative from a wide variety of societies. Some anthropologists have occasionally referred to

739

these as expressive of cultural ethos or as a technique of moral education, in which models or socially appropriate behavior are presented to children with praise and models of inappropriate behavior are held up to ridicule. The psychologist David McClelland has used both folktales and published stories in children's readers in cross-cultural research on the achievement motive and regards both as important means of developing achievement behavior in adults (McClelland, 1961). He has also conducted a second cross-cultural study of folktale content in a comparative investigation of the drinking of alcoholic beverages (McClelland, Davis, Kalin, & Wanner, 1972) and has used folktale content as a source of hypotheses about the psychological significance of heavy drinking.

From a methodological point of view the most ambitious study of folktale content and socialization is that by Child, Storm, and Veroff (1958). However, the associations which the authors found between folktale content and socialization are weaker than earlier, less sophisticated studies, and the authors themselves, as well as some later investigators, appear to have been discouraged by the results.

THE COLLECTION AND ANALYSIS OF FOLKTALES

One of the problems of using folktales, myths, and other oral narratives as evidence of social and psychological variables is the tremendous mass of complex and varied data available for many societies. If one looks in an ethnography for some variables of social structure, such as the existence of hereditary political office, the presence of matrilineal descent groups, the extent of the incest taboo, or the practice of male initiation ceremonies, one can usually refer to the index or table of contents, read a few relevant pages, and promptly form a reasonably reliable judgment about the society in these respects. On the other hand, if one is interested in discovering whether a particular society has an Oedipus-type myth or tale, one ideally should look at a collection containing several hundred fully translated texts, some of them several pages long, and perhaps read a number of them quite carefully. The investigator who finds one such tale still needs to look at all the remaining texts, for if there are several Oedipus narratives in a corpus of 300 this presumably means something more than finding just one. Moreover, there may be several distinct tales with Oedipus-type plots in the culture, and the differences among them may be theoretically relevant. Even if there is only one such tale recognized in the society, versions from several narrators may be available, and they all deserve consideration.

Some folklorists (e.g., Dégh, 1969) have produced excellent studies establishing the variation of repertoires among master narrators according to their positions in the community and individual personalities. Investigators reading these studies might be led to the conclusion that folk narratives tell more about the narrator than about the audience which hears them or the community in which they are told. Certainly narrators can be characterized by their repertoires, as can members of the audience by their individual narrative preferences. Nevertheless, popular narratives in a culture can justly be regarded as diagnostic in some way of salient social conflicts and psychological characteristics of the society. Even the less common traditional narratives must still appeal to enough members of the society to be passed on from one generation to the next and must touch on relatively common social and psychological problems and portray characters who are in some sense relevant to the society.

Ideally the investigator should try to ascertain the relative popularity of narratives in the corpus from each society. The best information on this point would be detailed information as to what narratives were actually told in a community over one or more annual cycles, to what audiences, on what occasions, with what response, etc. A questionnaire administered to a stratified sample of the community about knowledge of traditional narratives and preferences among those most commonly mentioned would also be very helpful. This kind of information is hardly ever available in existing published collections, but at times there are other indices of tale popularity which should be taken into account when available. Tales recorded in two or more versions by an ethnographer can plausibly be inferred to be popular, since most ethnographers are more interested in getting a wide variety of tales from a culture than in recording multiple variants of a single tale; they usually record variants of tales already transcribed only when the informant insists or has no new tale to offer. Other things being equal, the popular tales are usually longer and more explicit. Of course, one must also consider the category of tale: children's tales, for instance, are generally shorter than tales for an adult audience. Occasionally narrators will comment on the popularity of a tale: "Everyone likes this," "This is very important," "I am the only one who tells this story." Such remarks deserve great weight. Sometimes one finds several narratives regarded as distinct by informants because they have characters with different names and take place in different-named localities but which are enough alike with respect to plot that a historically oriented folklorist would catalogue them as belonging to the same tale type. Here again the corpus of tales provides useful evidence as to the popularity of the general plot, at least.

Folklorists recognize a large number of categories or genres of traditional narrative according to function and content: myths, legends, fables, tales, märchen, jokes (humorous anecdotes), personal accounts, etc. In some parts of the world many of these categories are further subdivided, although not all of the finer categories are represented in all cultures. These folkloristic categories of narrative are often derived from categories recognized in one or another culture studied, but since folklorists have worked more with European materials than with those from other parts of the world there is a bias toward European traditional categories. Some non-Western societies have different and perhaps simpler classifications of narrative. For a hologeistic study it will probably be necessary to use fairly broad and simple classifications.

The social and psychological significance of the categories of folktales varies. Ideally the comparative investigator should select for comparison the same general category of narrative from each culture in his sample. It could be very misleading, for instance, to compare an origin myth from one culture with a fairy tale from another and a historical legend from a third. In my own field work in the Caroline Islands, to give a concrete example, I found that on both Truk and Ponape origin myths tended statistically to have anticlimactic plots, i.e., ending in some compromise or accommodation, whereas tales told for entertainment tended to have a climactic plot, with a decisive victory for one of the parties. Other statistically significant differences in content can be found between myths and tales in the two cultures, which probably have parallels in other cultures as well. To compare a myth from Truk with a tale from Ponape on the assumption that they were functionally similar could easily lead to imputing the wrong differences between the social structure and values of the two cultures.

A complete collection of the folklore of a culture will usually include examples of a number of narrative categories, ideally grouped accordingly. A more casual collection, as part of a general ethnography, may have fewer categories represented; these are not carefully distinguished. Cultures vary in the availability of narrative material, whether from informants in the field or, even more, in published collections. In my own field work in the Caroline Islands, for instance, I found that when I asked Trukese informants to tell me a story they would most often start out by telling me the most popular children's tale, "Rat and Crab." If I asked them specifically to tell me an origin myth they would usually profess ignorance and tell me instead an amusing tale of some sort. At Ponape, however, the informants, when asked for a story, would generally start by recounting the story of the conquest of Ponape by the legendary hero Isohkelekel, which is regarded as a myth explaining the origin of certain features of the traditional political system. Even when specifically asked for a children's tale, the Ponapean narrators usually ended up telling me an origin myth on the assumption that I, as a serious adult, should not concern myself with anything as stupid as the silly lies told to children. Moreover, the Ponapean narrators who related the myths would at the same time insist—falsely—that they *were* telling me children's tales. This again was culturally appropriate although initially confusing for the ethnographer, since Ponapeans place a strong value on modesty; since knowledge of myths is prestigious, a Ponapean expresses modesty and humility by denying any knowledge of myth. There is a standard formula to append to a myth recital to the following effect: "What I say is crooked; let him who knows listen and straighten it out later." At the same time other Ponapeans in the audience would freely tell me, "That was not a children's tale you just heard; it was an origin myth." Both cultures have children's tales and both have origin myths; both value origin myths more than children's tales. Yet it is much easier for the investigator to get children's tales on Truk and origin myths on Ponape, even though the most precious parts of the myth from the narrator's point of view are likely to be concealed in either culture. (Fortunately the general outline of the plot is considered less valuable than certain specific details such as names of places and characters; this information is of interest but is mostly redundant for the investigator of psychological variables in myth.)

Granting the importance of paying attention to the category of narrative in comparative studies, how does one proceed? Where the narratives have been classified carefully by the narrators and the ethnographer this is very helpful, but often this information is missing. Sometimes one can find information on the usual social context of the narration or on the context in which the narrator learned the narrative. If the narrator and siblings, cousins, and friends learned it in early childhood from some caretaker, one can provisionally assume it is primarily a children's tale. If it may only be told on special occasions by special individuals one can tentatively classify it as a kind of myth.

The narrator's attitude toward the narrative may give important clues: if he or she (or the local audience) finds it hilarious and seems to be making spontaneous modifications to the narrative to adapt it to the particular audience, it is probably a tale told for entertainment. If the narrator stresses the importance of details in the account and the truth of objectively implausible segments, it is probably a myth.

The content of the narrative also may indicate something about the function of it. If a narrative purports to describe the origin of some important social institution or cultural feature, it is probably an origin myth. Again, it can be regarded as probably a myth if it includes as major characters well-known deities that are currently the object of worship. If it does not deal with any of these and at the same time contains many amusing features and incidents, it is probably a tale told for entertainment.

Folklorists interested primarily in tracing historical origins and contacts have made elaborate catalogues of the specific content of narratives: motifs (Thompson, 1955–1958) and tale types (Thompson, 1961). These catalogues of content, however, cannot be used automatically for identifying the functional category of a given narrative because many detailed items of content (motifs) can appear in several distinct narratives with different functions; also, a single organized narrative (representing a tale type) can change its function within a culture over time or as it moves from one culture to another. Thus part of the popular Ponapean myth of Isohkelekel, for instance (mentioned above; see also Fischer, 1966), has a cognate in a Trukese narrative of a boy who does a number of the same things. But at present the Trukese narrative is simply a tale told for entertainment, although, like many tales, it may have been regarded more seriously some generations back before certain political shifts took place. Since precolonial political organization in Truk was very fragmented and unstable, the myths supporting the political structure were probably subject to frequent revision and replacement. Once a narrative has been rejected as myth and preserved as an entertaining tale, the social pressures on its form and content shift, and this shift in itself may be enough to alter it significantly without much alteration in the basic social structure.

Motifs as defined by folklorists are a kind of minimal distinctive feature of tale content, including distinctive characters or actors, events, material objects, etc. Motifs are distinctive in a special sense, however: that is, they are unusual enough so that if the same motif is found in two tales it is at least plausible that the similarity is ultimately due to historical contact or common origin. Motifs are therefore concerned mostly with unique details rather than with basic features of character and plot. In many cultures, for instance, there are love stories in which a young man after some difficulties marries a young woman and they live happily ever after. Only a few of these, all of European origin, have the specific detail of fitting a slipper to the woman's foot to identify her, and this detail can therefore constitute a motif for folklorists. The basic plot of the narrative, however, is not culturally distinctive enough to constitute either a motif or a tale type in the sense of historically oriented folklorists (taking the basic plot in a most general sense of "boy meets girl; love at first sight; boy loses girl; boy gets girl").

Other analytic concepts somewhat related to the folklorists' concept of motifs are the "functions" of the Russian folklorist Propp (1958)—a limited stock of fixed combinations of actors and events sufficient to generate or account for the plots of a sizable corpus of Russian fairy tales, the "motifemes" of Dundes (1962b), and the "edions" of Colby (1973), the latter two being revisions of Propp's concept of "functions" and extending it to other genres and cultures. Dundes and Colby are explicitly interested in the problem of characterizing what might be called the lexicon of images available for use in the oral literature of a single culture, and they make analogies with the "emic" analysis of language. These functions, motifemes, or edions are defined, however, in sufficiently general terms so that most of them, perhaps even all of them, can be found individually and in meaningful sequences in the folktales of other cultures, although with different frequency, elaboration, and structural salience. These tale components are certainly less distinctive culturally than their closest linguistic analogues, which would seem to be the morphemes of a lexicon. On the other hand, their very lack of cultural uniqueness makes them useful for selecting comparable texts in a hologeistic sample.

Colby (1966) has also used computers to analyze translated texts of folktales for what might be called the frequency of certain minimal semantic elements, coding as equivalent the words in the text that share a common simple meaning, and counting their frequency as a group; e.g., "travel," "walk," "proceed," "sail" (as a verb), etc. might all be regarded as sharing a general concept of "locomotion" and the frequency of words expressing locomotion in the total text could then be computed. Colby finds interesting and culturally distinctive differences in frequency of these basic semantic elements between cultures, which are plausible in terms of the associated social values as analyzed by other investigators. McClelland et al. (1972) have used the same computer technique to analyze a hologeistic sample of folktales in their study of the drinking of alcoholic beverages. The Munroes and colleagues (R. L. Munroe, Munroe, Nerlove, & Daniels, 1969; R. H. Munroe & Munroe, 1973) have used a basically similar technique, although with hand rather than computer coding of folktale texts, in a comparative study of three East African societies. The correlations of these measures of tale content with social and environmental variables in all three studies constitute plausible evidence for the validity of this approach. Anthropological critics of Colby's work have complained that he should have used native language texts and coded these into a neutral metalanguage to avoid the bias of English language categories and concepts. It should be said, however, that these criticisms underestimate the possibility of the translation of elemental general concepts into all languages, if necessary by paraphrase or by the coining of new words. If translation of folktales is possible—and the widespread diffusion of many folktales across cultural and linguistic boundaries demonstrates that it is possible for ordinary people, not just semantic specialists—then equation of concepts across these boundaries must be possible, and the simpler and more elemental the concepts, the easier the equation. If Colby had used the native language texts rather than English translations and had used a supposedly neutral metalanguage to label the analytic semantic elements, he would still need to translate the results eventually into English or some other major world language in order to communicate his findings to other social scientists. Of course, Colby does not claim to be accounting for the full exact nuance of each word in the native language texts; if he did, other methods would be needed and ordinary free translations would be insufficient as data.

The cultural prominence of folk narrative differs from one society to the next. In literate civilizations traditional oral narratives are replaced largely, although not completely, by various forms of written literature: novels, short stories, newspaper comics, children's readers, religious scriptures, and ultimately by drama on radio and television, cinema, etc. Even in nonliterate societies, however, the prominence of traditional oral narrative varies. Some cultures are reported to have a rich traditional oral literature, while others have much less. A few are reported by ethnographers of excellent repute to have practically none (e.g., the Siriono, as reported by Holmberg, 1950; the Ifaluk, as reported by Spiro, 1951; the Baktaman, as reported by Barth, 1975).

The significance of these reports is unclear. In the three examples cited the communities studied were rather small. Since the active narrators in most societies with a rich oral literature are a minority of the adults, it is conceivable that in communities small enough a traditional oral literature could be entirely extinguished by the death of two or three individuals within a short period. Moreover, a sudden shift of environment and economy, as may have occurred historically among the Siriono, might also disrupt an oral narrative tradition. This disruption might be especially likely if the narratives were tied to specific localities in a former habitat and to activities and forms of social organization which were abandoned with a move to a new territory. It may also be the case that there are entire practically oriented societies, as there are individuals in some societies, that consciously reject traditional narratives dealing with deceased individuals, the past, or imaginary situations in favor of "real" accounts of events in the lives of current members of the community. If so, narratives or personal events might be the closest one could come to folktales in such societies.

At the same time, explicit reports of societies with few or no folktales are not common. Further investigation of some of these societies might uncover more folktales than were initially apparent to the ethnographer. In the three examples cited above, the investigators conducted field research for relatively short periods and in spite of their best efforts must have been lacking in fluency in the local language during much of their field stay. If someone had been telling a folktale in their presence they might have missed it. Moreover, traditional oral narratives often are the subject of various restrictions on their narration: they may be limited to a particular season of the year, a particular time of day, or a particular social context. The ethnographer who happens not to sample the right context may get a mistaken impression of the rarity or unimportance of folktales. Also, informants in some cultures who for whatever reason do not want to talk about a certain subject, such as folktales, may be prone to tell the ethnographer that the cultural material in question is nonexistent, even though they know very well that they are lying. This type of response is especially likely for items of expressive culture which are practiced and transmitted only by certain individuals on special occasions before the right audiences. Ethnographers who are convinced of the validity of traditional field methods may be prone to place undue trust in informants' statements on such matters.

In sum, at this point in the development of ethnographic technique the most important thing to keep in mind about folktale data is the desirability of full information on the social context of the tale. If one is an ethnographer who is going to do field work, something should be said for each text about the narrators, audiences, reactions, values, local categorization, etc. If one is analyzing published or manuscript collections, attention should be paid to all scraps of information which may throw some light on these topics.

CROSS-CULTURAL STUDIES OF FOLKTALES

There have been very few cross-cultural studies of folktales in relation to socialization or childhood experience which utilize a worldwide sample. Perhaps the most successful of these is the one by Wright (1954), who studied the expression of aggression in folktales as related to child training. Among his most significant findings, he noted that the hero was less likely to be victorious in tales from societies where the children are punished severely for aggression. Also, he found that if one assumes that human strangers, supernaturals, and animal characters are increasingly remote projects of the self, then the more remote characters are most common as agents of aggression in folktales from societies with great aggression anxiety for children (i.e., high severity of punishment for aggression).

Another study, by the psychologist Child and colleagues (Child, Storm, & Veroff, 1958), investigated achievement imagery in folktales in relation to child training. The authors attempted, using more elaborate and sophisticated techniques, to test the findings of an earlier study by a student of McClelland's (McClelland & Friedman, 1952) concerning achievement imagery in folktales and socialization. The latter study used a sample of tales limited to North American tribal Coyote tales and used socialization ratings from a study by Whiting and Child (1953; ratings made available before publication). McClelland and Friedman had found a clear relationship in their sample between the amount of achievement imagery in folktales and both the severity and earliness of independence training; direct ratings of achievement training were not available. Child et al., using a worldwide sample of societies and a random sample of tales from each of these, found no significant relationship between these same variables, although they did find a relationship between achievement imagery in folktales and training specifically for achievement, involving an attempt to measure up to a standard of excellence, as distinguished from independence. They also found that representations of punishment for achievement in folktales were associated with low indulgence of children and rigid socialization as reported by ethnographers for actual behavior.

Child et al. (1958) suggest that methodological inadequacies in the McClelland and Friedman (1952) study may have led to false positive results. While this possibility cannot be ruled out, it is also possible that the study by Child et al. suffered from too much random "noise" in the sample of folktales and from disagreements among their three judges, whose ratings of tale content were pooled. The authors admit disappointment in the relatively weak findings of their study. Nevertheless, they have probably made an important contribution in the long run by carefully describing their methodology, which should enable future investigators to try new solutions for the problems which they attempted to meet.

They noted, for instance, that McClellend and Friedman, in counting achievement imagery, had failed to control for length of tale. Thus long-winded cultures, other things being equal, had a greater chance of getting a higher achievement score, although the frequency of achievement imagery per fixed length of text might be less. Child et al. tried to control for this by dividing longer tales into more or less self-contained episodes and picking at random only enough episodes to match in length whole tales from short-winded, laconic cultures. While this solves one problem it may create another: In my own work with folktales from Truk and Ponape in the Caroline Islands I have found a contrast between prefinal and final episodes, regardless of length of tales. As noted earlier, in tales told for entertainment the final episode is more likely to contain events which can serve as climax, including, for example, murder and death. However, Trukese tales are more long-winded and tend to have more episodes than Ponapean tales. Thus if one sampled episodes at random rather than whole narratives, one might underestimate the frequency with which the main characters in Trukese tales ultimately die. Colby has also found content differences in different portions of narratives (see Colby, 1973). Probably it would be more valid psychologically to take a fixed number of tales from each culture without bothering to match the length of texts and measure items of content in terms of percents and ratios rather than in absolute frequency figures. The average length of tales in a culture may itself be an index of theoretical interest: are the narrators typically loquacious or terse?

McClelland and Friedman's (1952) restriction of their folktale texts to a single genre, Coyote tales among native North Americans, seems to me an important advantage because it increases the comparability of the tales across the cultures studied. Many of the tales from different cultures were cognate with each other, and the examples the authors cite of the different ways in which different cultures handled the same basic tale are especially convincing. Admittedly, Coyote tales as such are geographically limited, but the investigator who extended the basis for selection to trickster and culture hero tales more generally could get something close to a world sample. Or perhaps the investigator interested in a particular type of behavior, such as achievement, should scan the entire corpus of tales from each society in the sample for the two or three tales most relevant to this behavior and compare these; it might turn out that among many North American tribes achievement imagery is most prominent in trickster tales, whereas in some other culture areas, where the roles of trickster and culture hero are more sharply differentiated, achievement imagery might be more prominent in more strictly heroic tales.

Another cross-cultural hologeistic study relating folktale content to childhood experience has been conducted by Roberts, Sutton-Smith, and Kendon (1963). Results support the hypothesis that folktales depicting competition by strategy (as contrasted with those emphasizing physical skill or chance) are found in societies in which parents strongly reward obedience and, with somewhat less correlation, inculcate anxiety about "nonperformance of obedience." These societies also tend to be politically complex and to possess games of strategy, an example of consonance between two different modes of expressive culture (folktales and games). While such intermodal agreement seems plausible, it needs to be tested repeatedly, since it is conceivable that different modes may be practiced or favored by different segments of the population, which might also differ in personality or values. For instance, certain games might be played entirely by children and transmitted from children to other children, while certain folktales, even if told mostly to children, might be told to them principally by adults, who would have considerable influence on their content. There is also the possibility that some modes are more subject to rapid diffusion and historical change than others and might therefore be more representative of current personality and values. Spencer's (1957) study of Navajo myths and values suggests that any one expressive mode may depict only a selected set of the major social values.

Stephens' (1962) cross-cultural study of the Oedipus complex used judgments of folktale content as one kind of index of modal personality variables. His principal finding regarding folktales was that the intensity of menstrual taboos was positively associated with the frequency of physical injury in folktales. Stephens regarded mention of physical injury in folktales as a measure of castration anxiety, which he considered to be derived from a strong Oedipus conflict in early childhood. Athough neither of these variables is a direct measure of childhood experience, Stephens postulates that the association between them is due to the fact that both are results of a single kind of childhood experience. Stephens reconfirmed this finding in a later article (1967) using additional data.

Other cross-cultural studies involving judgments of folktale content in relation to cultural variables include those of Kalin, Davis, & McClelland (1966) and Bacon and co-workers (Bacon, Barry, & Child, 1965; Bacon, Child, & Barry, 1963). Kalin et al.

found that heavy drinking as reported by ethnographers tended to be absent in societies where the folktales contained direct references to fear and that heavy drinking tended to be present in societies where the folktales had prominent themes of hunting. The first finding could be interpreted as supporting the theory that drinking alcoholic beverages is one way of handling anxiety, i.e., handling fears that cannot be verbalized directly even in folktales. Bacon, Barry, and Child (1965) were also interested in alcohol consumption and found that it was negatively associated with achievement imagery in folktales. McClelland et al. (1972), reviewing earlier work and conducting further investigations of their own, concluded that alcohol consumption was positively correlated with a need for what they call "personalized power" as expressed in folktales and other individual measures. Bacon, Child, and Barry (1963) found that depictions of an unkind environment in folktales were associated with a high reported frequency of theft in real life. To the extent that folktales are told to children, these studies may be regarded as involving childhood experience influencing later adult personality and behavior. However, these studies did not discover strong statistical associations directly between folktale content and variables of socialization or childhood experience.

RELATED STUDIES

There are a number of comparative studies of folktales by folklorists, anthropologists, and others which make psychological and developmental interpretations but do not use statistical tests of hypotheses. The psychoanalyst Rank (1959) used mythic themes as evidence for the presence of the Oedipus complex in a variety of Near Eastern and European cultures. Two works by Dundes (1962a; 1976) deserve special mention for their combination of erudition, intellectual boldness, and insight. These studies admittedly have a geographic bias, since they take whatever ethnographic material is available. They are concerned primarily with the internal analysis of the meaning of folktales (more specifically, of myths) and related folklore (rituals, beliefs) and with universal tendencies in human experience; they are less concerned with accounting for variations between cultures with respect to folklore in relation to culturally distinctive childhood experience or other variables. Nevertheless, the insights expressed could be reformulated in terms of a hypothetical relation between measurable variables; these hypotheses could then be tested statistically on a worldwide sample.

Comparisons of the folktales of a small number of cultures within a single culture area can show up convincing differences between folktales, especially if the investigator focuses on cognate tales or tales dealing with closely related themes. One recent example is given by Hsu (1975), who compares a Chinese and a Japanese version of a story about a man and his snake wife. In the Chinese version the man is virtuous and his snake wife defends him against the suspicions of others; eventually a son is born to the couple. In the Japanese version the snake wife is initially virtuous but her human husband is unfaithful to her, so she kills him in a well-founded jealous rage. The Chinese snake wife has a female snake helper or servant, while the Japanese snake wife acts entirely alone. Hsu sees this tale as illustrating, among other things, the stronger psition of the woman in the Japanese stem family as compared to the Chinese patrilocal extended family.

I have published comparative studies of pairs of cognate folktales from Truk and Ponape in the Caroline Islands (Fischer, 1956; 1960) and the Polynesian outliers of

Nukuoro and Kapingamarangi (1958). In the first of these, comparing the role of men and women, it was found that the women were portrayed in folktales and myths as relatively more competent or powerful in Truk, whereas the men were portrayed as more competent in Ponape. Certain features of the traditional social structure might lead one to expect these differences as a reflection of social life, notably, stronger matrilineages in Truk and a stronger, male-dominated political system in Ponape. The comparison of Nukuoro and Kapingamarangi showed similar differences in the competence of sex roles in cognate tales, again relatable plausibly to social structure: women were portrayed in Nukuoro tales as relatively more competent, whereas men were portrayed as more competent in Kapingamarangi. This contrast appears to be related to the typical nuclear family household with individual land ownership by both sexes in Nukuoro on the one hand and the patrilocal extended family household with family ownership of land under the control of the men in Kapingamarangi. The Nukuoro tales also displayed greater competence, but less virtuous action, for younger characters as compared to those of Kapingamarangi. These differences may be related to a greater emphasis on individualistic achievement in Nukuoro and an emphasis on harmonious family cooperation under the authority of the elders in Kapingamarangi. A further difference is that positive spouse relationships are stressed in Nukuoro tales, whereas sibling relationships are stressed in Kapingamarangi.

In the second paper, comparing Trukese and Ponapean tales (Fischer, 1960), differences in pairs of cognate tales were investigated with respect to dramatic or episodic structure. The variable measured was the extent to which later episodes or segments tended to be essentially repetitions of preceding segments, regardless of the amount of variation in detail, or tended to be essentially opposed to earlier segments, that is, having an outcome opposite to that of a preceding segment. The analysis used mathematical indices of the amount of repetition and opposition for tale texts, measuring length of segments in terms of numbers of sentences in each. In each of five pairs of cognate tales the Trukese tale consistently showed more repetition and less opposition than its Ponapean cognate, although among the five tales in each culture there was great intracultural variation in these respects. It is possible that the tendency to repetition in folktales is a measure of anxiety and lack of self-confidence, just as repetition in a dream is regarded by psychoanalysts as evidence of a special concern.

A number of authors have concentrated on the study of tale collections or selected tales from single cultures and on the relation of tale content to social and psychological variables. Especially notable examples are the study of Nunivak Island Eskimo personality and folktales by Lantis (1953), Jacobs' monograph on Clackamas Chinook myths and tales (1959), the Herskovitses' study of Dahomean narrative (1958), and Halpern's study of Navajo chantway myths (Spencer, 1957). Intensive studies of single cultures such as these should be the source of many hypotheses that are testable hologeistically concerning the relationship among folktales, social structure, and human development.

CONCLUSION

Cross-cultural studies of the relationship of folktales to variables of human development have suffered both from the poverty of some cultural data and the overabundance of other data. Ethnographers have too often reported very cursorily on socialization techniques and the life of children on the often unconscious assumptions that children are unimportant, since they know less than adults and are not interested in talking to the ethnographer anyway; adult informants usually support such views. At the same time, for many cultures oral literature is abundantly recorded and extremely varied, so that it becomes difficult for the comparativist to assimilate it and make valid summaries of it. Investigators relying on library research can do little to make up for inadequate ethnographic descriptions of children's life, but much more remains to be done in the way of experimenting with different techniques for selecting representative samples of folktale material for the societies chosen for a hologeistic study.

Since the total corpus of folktales for most cultures is quite large and varied, it makes sense to search through the entire corpus for the particular kinds of tales in which one is interested instead of picking a small number at random: if one is interested in aggression, for instance, one should look through the entire tale corpus of each culture in the sample for the two or three most aggressive tales; for parent–child, husband–wife, or sibling relationships, one could look through each corpus for tales exemplifying these as central; an investigator interested in episodic structure should look through each corpus for the longest full texts, avoiding abbreviated summaries by the ethnographer.

At the same time that worldwide comparative studies are continued, there is an urgent need for small-scale "controlled comparisons" of neighboring cultures with respect to folktale and social and psychological variables. These small-scale studies can be more intensive and are thus perhaps more likely to generate plausible hypotheses about the relationship of folktale content and structure to other aspects of culture than are worldwide comparative studies at this point. At the same time, those hypotheses that work in a small-scale comparison need to be tested in a larger sample of societies.

Some critics of the usefulness of psychological and sociological interpretations of folktale content charge that while tale content is always related to real life in some fashion, the nature of the relationship is variable and unpredictable: sometimes the tale is a direct reflection of life, while at other times it represents an unrealistic wish which is the opposite of life. Lévi-Strauss at times seems to take this position. In his *Geste d'Asdiwal* (1958), for instance, he regards the plot as derived in part from an exploration of the implications of patterns of marital residence not actually practiced in the society. Nevertheless, in the few cross-cultural studies of folktales and real life that have been made, the relationship between the portrayal of life in folktales and real life seems to be direct: if there is more of a certain behavior portrayed in the folktales of society A than in those of society B, there appears to be more of this behavior in real life in society A as well. Of course, this in itself does not deny the selection and exaggeration of behavior for dramatic effect when represented in folktales; it suggests simply that there is a standard dramatic distortion from the level of reality for comparable genres in all or most cultures. Moreover, this distortion is in the direction of cognitive clarity and wish fulfillment, but the notion of wish fulfillment always involves a compromise with reality, such that wishes that are more difficult to fulfill in reality are fulfilled less lavishly in the tale representation.

Some of the studies discussed above deal with social and psychological variables of adult experience and attempt to relate these to folktale content. To the extent that adult behavior affects the children around the adults and serves as a model for the children, it is also highly relevant to the understanding of childhood experience. In some of the studies associations between adult behavior and folktale content are interpreted in terms of preparing the children for adulthood by modeling suitable adult behavior in folktales or in terms of both the adult behavior and the folktale content being the consequence of some presumed single childhood variable. Studies which involve variables of kinship, household formation, the sex division of labor, and the like, although dealing with adult behavior, should be generally of interest to those exploring childhood experience. As noted above, ethnographic information on adult behavior is often better than that on childhood; thus such studies have a greater hope of attaining statistically significant findings as a result of an adequate base of data.

At the same time, continued research is needed on the nature of the direct relationship between childhood experience as portrayed in folktales of various functional categories and as childhood experience can be observed in real life. If enough clear relationships can be established between these two sets of variables in a series of cultures where the data on both are good, it may be possible in the future to use folktale portraits of childhood as indirect evidence of actual childhood experience in extinct and greatly changed cultures where direct observations are inadequate and further observations are now unobtainable.

ACKNOWLEDGMENTS
Helpful comments and references have been received from B. N. Colby, M. S. Edmonson, F. L. K. Hsu, D. C. McClelland, R. Naroll, and J. M. Roberts.

REFERENCES
Bacon, M. K., Barry, H., III, & Child, I. L. A cross-cultural study of drinking: II: Relations to other features of culture. *Quarterly Journal of Studies on Alcohol, Supplement 3*, 1965, *26*, 29–48.

Bacon, M. K., Child, I. L., & Barry, H., III. A cross-cultural study of correlates of crime. *Journal of Abnormal and Social Psychology*, 1963, *66*, 291–300.

Barnouw, V. *Culture and personality*. Homewood, Ill.: Dorsey, 1973.

Barth, F. *Ritual and knowledge among the Baktaman of New Guinea*. New Haven: Yale University Press, 1975.

Child, I. L., Storm, T., & Veroff, J. Achievement themes in folk tales related to socialization practice. In J. W. Atkinson (Ed.), *Motives in fantasy, action and society*. Princeton: Van Nostrand, 1958.

Colby, B. N. The analysis of culture content and the patterning of narrative concern in texts. *American Anthropologist*, 1966, *68*, 374–388.

Colby, B. N. Analytical procedures in eidochronic study. *Journal of American Folklore*, 1973, *86*, 14–24.

Colby, B. N., & Peacock, J. L. Narrative. In J. J. Honigmann (Ed.), *Handbook of social and cultural anthropology*. Chicago: Rand McNally, 1974.

Dégh, L. *Folktales and society: Story telling in a Hungarian peasant community*. Bloomington, Ind.: Indiana University Press, 1969.

Devereux, G. Art and mythology. In B. Kaplan (Ed.), *Studying personality cross-culturally*. Evanston, Ill.: Row, Peterson, 1961.

Dundes, A. Earth-Diver: Creation of the mythopoeic male. *American Anthropologist*, 1962, *64*, 1032–1051 (a)

Dundes, A. From etic to emic units in the structural study of folktales. *Journal of American Folklore*, 1962, *75*, 95–105 (b)

Dundes, A. A psychoanalytic study of the bullroarer. *Man,* 1976, *11,* 220–238.

Fischer, J. L. The position of men and women in Truk and Ponape. *Journal of American Folklore,* 1956, *62,* 55–62.

Fischer, J. L. Folktales, social structure, and environment in two Polynesian outliers. Journal of the Polynesian Society, 1958, *67,* 11–36.

Fischer, J. L. Sequence and structure in folktales. In A. F. C. Wallace (Ed.), *Selected papers of the Fifth International Congress of Anthropological and Ethnological Sciences, 1956.* Philadelphia: University of Pennsylvania Press, 1960.

Fischer, J. L. The sociopsychological analysis of folktales. *Current Anthropology,* 1963, *4,* 235–295.

Fischer, J. L. A Ponapean Oedipus tale: Structural and sociopsychological analysis. *Journal of American Folklore,* 1966, *79,* 109–129.

Herskovits, M. J., & Herskovits, F. S. *Dahomean narrative.* Evanston, Ill.: Northwestern University Press, 1958.

Holmberg, A. *Nomads of the long bow.* Washington, D.C.: Smithsonian Institution, Institute of Social Anthropology, 1950.

Hsu, F. L. K. *Iemoto: The heart of Japan.* Princeton: Van Nostrand, 1975.

Jacobs, M. The content and style of an oral literature. *Viking Fund Publications in Anthropology,* 1959, *26.*

Kalin, R., Davis, W. N., & McClelland, D. C. The relation between use of alcohol and thematic content of folktales in primitive societies. In P. J. Stone, D. C. Dunphy, M. S. Smith, & D. M. Ogilvie (Eds.), *The general inquirer.* Cambridge, Mass.: MIT Press, 1966.

Kardiner, A. *The individual and his society.* New York: Columbia University Press, 1939.

Kardiner, A. *The psychological frontiers of society.* New York: Columbia University Press, 1945.

LaBarre, W. Art and mythology. In B. Kaplan (Ed.), *Studying personality cross-culturally.* Evanston, Ill.: Row, Peterson, 1961.

Lantis, M. Nunivak Eskimo personality as revealed in mythology. *University of Alaska anthropological papers,* 1953, *2,* 109–174.

Lévi-Strauss, C. *La geste d'Asdiwal.* In *Ecole pratique des hautes etudes, section des sciences religieuses,* Extr. Annuaire 1958–1959, pp. 3–43.

McClelland, D. C. *The achieving society.* Princeton: Van Nostrand, 1961.

McClelland, D. C., & Friedman, G. A. A cross-cultural study of the relationship between child training practices and achievement motivation appearing in folk-tales. In G. E. Swanson, T. M. Newcomb, & E. L. Hartley (Eds.), *Readings in social psychology* (rev. ed.). New York: Holt, 1952.

McClelland, D. C., Davis, W. N., Kalin, R., & Wanner, E. *The drinking man.* New York: Free Press, 1972.

Munroe, R. H., & Munroe, R. L. Population density and movement in folktales. *Journal of Social Psychology,* 1973, *91,* 339–340.

Munroe, R. L., Munroe, R. H., Nerlove, S. B., & Daniels, R. E. Effects of population density on food concerns in three East African societies. *Journal of Health and Social Behavior,* 1969, *10,* 161–171.

Propp, V. *Morphology of the folktale.* Bloomington: Indiana University Research Center in Anthropology, Folklore and Linguistics, 1968.

Rank, O. *The myth of the birth of the hero.* New York: Vintage, 1959.

Roberts, J. M., Sutton-Smith, B., & Kendon, A. Strategy in games and folk tales. *Journal of Social Psychology,* 1963, *61,* 185–199.

Spencer, K. *Mythology and values: An analysis of Navaho chantway myths.* Philadelphia: American Folklore Society, 1957.

Spiro, M. E. Some Ifaluk myths and tales. *Journal of American Folklore,* 1951, *64,* 289–302.

Stephens, W. N. *The Oedipus complex: Cross-cultural evidence.* New York: Free Press, 1962.

Stephens, W. N. A cross-cultural study of menstrual taboos. In C. S. Ford (Ed.), *Cross-cultural approaches to the study of sex.* New Haven: HRAF Press, 1967.

Thompson, S. (Ed.). *Motif-index of folk literature* (rev. ed.). Bloomington, Ind: Indiana University Press, 1955–1958.

Thompson, S. The types of the folktale (2nd rev. ed.). *FF communications No. 184.* Helsinki, 1961.

Whiting, J. W. M., & Child, I. L. *Child training and personality.* New Haven: Yale University Press, 1953.

Wright, G. O. Projection and displacement: A cross-cultural study of folktale aggression. *Journal of Abnormal and Social Psychology,* 1954, *49,* 523–528.

24

Cross-cultural Perspectives on Motivations for Drinking

Margaret K. Bacon

Any discussion of the use of alcoholic beverages must make note of the extensiveness of this human activity. Since fermentation occurs freely in nature, it seems probable that alcoholic beverages were independently discovered or invented many times by early humans. Braidwood, Sayer, Helback, Mangelsdorf, Coon, Linton, Steward, and Oppenheim (1953) summarize archeological evidence regarding this early use of fermented drinks. Certainly written records of human behavior contain references to the use of alcoholic beverages far back into antiquity. The oldest known code of laws, that of Hammurabi of Babylonia (ca. 1700 B.C.), regulated the sale of wine and also forbade riotous assembly in the house of the wine seller. The medicinal use of alcohol was recorded on a clay tablet found at Nippur, dated about 2100 B.C., where directions were given in Sumerian cuneiform for making various remedies; beer was the usual solvent (Keller, 1958). The use of alcohol among the peoples of antiquity has been documented in detail (McKinlay, 1948a, b; 1949a, b; 1951; Heath, 1976, provides an extensive bibliography).

The use of alcoholic drinks is also widely distributed throughout the peoples of the world. In fact, the available evidence suggests that the majority of known cultural groups use some kind of alcoholic beverage in one context or another. Tribal peoples in all major parts of the world (with the exception of Oceania and parts of North America) made use of alcoholic drinks from their aboriginal times onward (Mandelbaum, 1965). Those societies that did not develop a drinking custom in their early history did so readily when introduced to it through contact with Western civilization. There seems, for example, to be no record of any group which did not accept alcoholic drinks, once experienced, as a part of the way of life for significant numbers of the population. The use of alcohol is thus widely prevalent and easily diffused. It is also amazingly persistent. Once accepted by a society the custom of drinking has rarely been relinquished except temporarily.[1] It has persisted in spite of the social problems that often accompany the use of alcohol and in spite of the organized opposition of many reform groups who have sought to eliminate drinking. Control of drinking and intoxication through prohibitory legislation has been tried in different societies since ancient times. Moore (1948) reports that within a period of about 2000 years—between the middle of the Chou dynasty (1134–256 B.C.) and the reign of the fourth emperor of the Yuan Dynasty (about A.D. 1312)—laws against the manufacture, sale, and consumption of wine were passed and repealed 41 times. The Athenians sought to regulate drinking through selling diluted wine and the appointment of wine inspectors to supervise drinking at magistrates' dinners. Plato proposed general restrictions on drinking—for example, complete prohibition of drinking for those under the age of 18 years, slaves, judges, and councilors on duty (McKinlay, 1951).

Many societies in more recent history have experimented with prohibition. Sweden (Marcus, 1946; Skutin, 1959) and Finland (Sariola, 1954) are often noted as examples. In no case has the drinking custom been successfully abolished. A century of effort and the expenditure of millions of dollars by the "Dry" forces in the United States have failed to turn the American public away from the use of alcoholic beverages (McCarthy & Douglass, 1959).

Alcohol is not necessary in any way for human life, and the manufacture of alcoholic drinks requires a considerable expenditure of time and effort. Therefore the accumulated evidence of the antiquity of the use of alcohol, its nearly universal occurrence, and its persistence in the face of organized and powerful opposition clearly raise a question as to the nature of the human satisfactions derived from drinking alcohol. Drinking customs may and do vary enormously in detail. Still there must be a common core of human experience related to the consumption of alcohol that leads people to drink again, to develop customs of drinking as a part of their way of life, and to resist efforts to deprive them of these customs. What are these common factors of motivation or experience that underlie the great variations in other aspects of drinking customs?

Questions as to why people drink have been asked many times and addressed in different ways. Many anthropologists tend to feel that the drinking customs of a given society can be understood only as a part of the totality of the customs of the society. According to this view, attempts to abstract and quantify variables across a sample of societies for the purpose of making general statements about drinking behavior represent a distortion of meaning. Other writers also avoid motivational constructs and see drinking behavior as acquired as a part of the learning of appropriate social behavior, relying only on the concept of norm acquisition to explain drinking (see Davis, 1972). Such an approach, however, does not account for variations on either side of the norm, apparently necessitating different explanations for these different "kinds" of drinking. Thus the tri-ethnic study of Jessor, Graves, Hanson, and Jessor (1968) attempts to explain "heavy drinking" which they conceive as a type of deviance. Aside from the difficulties inherent in the definition of deviance this approach seems to involve separate conceptualizations of differing degrees of participation in the custom—for example, drinking which deviates in the direction of abstinence, as well as "heavy drinking."

Research on the determinants of drinking which has appeared in the sociological literature has emphasized the importance of the contexts in which drinking occurs and the social controls developed in various cultural groups. This approach appears to have developed out of an early interest in the trouble-free characteristics of drinking among Jews (Myerson, 1940; Snyder, 1958) and has led to many comparative studies of drinking in ethnic and religious groups. Examples include, among others, Bales' (1946; 1962) comparisons of Irish and Jewish drinking, Glad's (1947) comparison of drinking in Irish and Jewish male youth, Barnett's (1955) study of drinking among the Cantonese of New York, the description of drinking patterns among Italians in New Haven (Williams & Straus, 1950), Sterne's (1966) investigation of drinking customs in the black ghetto, the report of drinking in Italian culture by Lolli, Serianni, Golder, and Luzzatto-Fegis (1958), *Drinking in French Culture* by Sadoun, Lolli, and Silverman (1965), and "Religious-Ethnic Differences in Alcohol Consumption" by Wechsler, Demone, Thum, and Kasey (1970). From this work has come a conceptualization of "safe" and "unsafe" drinking as a dimension of alcohol consumption significantly related to the contexts of drinking and the degree of social problem. The primary emphasis in this work appears to be on factors which limit or control drinking as opposed to factors which motivate or reinforce drinking.

Other researchers have sought for psychological explanations for drinking. Examples may be found among anthropological studies explicitly directed to the description of drinking customs. Whittaker (1962; 1963), in his study of drinking among the Standing Rock Sioux, attributed drinking problems in this group to increased intrapsychic tension, attitudes toward alcohol that encourage its use to relieve tension, and absence of social sanctions against the heavy drinker. Savard (1968) found excessive use of alcohol among Navaho men related to the suppression of anger (a prominent proscription in Navaho culture). Dailey (1968) related drinking among certain native North American tribes to the cultural value placed on dreaming and other psychic experiences resembling intoxication. Kearney (1970) studied drunkenness and religious conversion in a peasant farming community in Mexico.

Much of this research has focused on possible causal factors associated with "heavy drinking" or "problem drinking," with the implication that this is somehow related to alcoholism, which is in turn perceived as a disease. It is important to emphasize that alcoholism is not synonymous with heavy drinking and is not a necessary consequence of heavy drinking. The concern in this chapter will be to examine evidence related to the question as to why people drink, not why they drink in a manner that labels them as suffering from an illness.

HOLOGEISTIC STUDIES OF THE DETERMINANTS OF DRINKING

A number of large-scale cross-cultural studies have addressed the question of motivation for drinking through the investigation of correlations between variables of drinking behavior and other variables related to societal customs and structure. These studies represent the collection and interpretation of very considerable amounts of data which have been related to various hypotheses concerning the antecedents of different aspects of drinking behavior. The studies are, for the most part, well known to workers in the alcohol field. However, the literature which has included reviews of hologeistic studies on the use of alcohol has placed more emphasis on the hypotheses than on the data reported as supporting these hypotheses. This chapter will present a brief review of the studies and accompanying hypotheses and will attempt to summarize the data (independent of the hypotheses) with a view toward alternate interpretations.

Hypotheses Relating Drinking Behavior to the Availability of Alcohol

One of the recurring ideas in the alcohol literature is that drinking, together with any problems that may be associated with it, is directly related to the availability of alcohol (cf. DeLint & Schmidt, 1976; see also Parker & Herman, 1978, for a critical review). In the extreme case, of course, this must be true. If alcohol is completely absent from the environment, no one will drink and there will be no problems associated with the use of alcoholic beverages. However, since this condition presumably exists only where the climate does not permit vegetation and fermentation to exist and/or legal controls are entirely successful, it seems safe to conclude that complete lack of availability of alcohol rarely occurs. The hypothesis generally implies that the consumption of alcohol, and the problems which often accompany it, varies as a function of the availability of alcoholic beverages.

This hypothesis has not been tested directly by any of the existing cross-cultural studies of drinking. However, a study by Bacon and co-workers (Bacon, Barry, & Child, 1965a; Bacon, Barry, Child & Snyder, 1965b; Bacon, Child & Barry, 1965c) does have data related to this question. This study, which coded ethnographic accounts of drinking customs in 139 societies, included, wherever possible, ratings on the availability of alcohol. Since variations in availability were largely seasonal, the seven-point rating scale was developed in terms of the proportion of the year that alcohol was available. Of the total sample of 139 societies, information was sufficient to make a rating on availability of alcohol for 86 societies. Of this group 81 (96 percent) received ratings by two judges totaling 12, 13 or 14, indicating that alcohol was generally available throughout the year or for all but a month or two. For only five societies was alcohol judged to be available for only half of the year or less: the Chenchu, Choroti, Colorado, Naskapi, and Siriono. This is, of course, a very skewed distribution with respect to availability, and a sample of five societies is too small to permit statistical comparison with a sample of 81. Nevertheless, inspection of the distribution of ratings for the two groups on measures related to the consumption of alcohol when it was available yields information relevant to this hypothesis.

Ratings were obtained on the following aspects of drinking behavior which are related to the hypothesis: (1) Extent of Drinking: an "across-the-board" estimate of the proportion of adults in the society who drink at all, ranging from very few to all adults. (2) General Consumption of alcohol: an estimate of the per capita consumption of beverage alcohol for each society compared with other societies in the sample. (3) Frequency of Drinking: estimated frequency ranging from "daily" at the high end of the scale to "once or twice a year" at the low end. (4) Frequency of Drunkenness: estimated frequency compared with other societies in the sample, ranging from extreme to rare. (5) Procurement Effort: judgment of the proportion of all cultural effort (as indicated by such indices as money, time, and labor) which is typically expended in preparing or procuring alcohol beverages. (6) Extent of Problem: the rater's opinion of the extent to which drinking constitutes a problem —economic, medical, social, moral (as defined by the society), or otherwise—to the society, whether or not the members of the society view it so.

Ratings on all aspects of drinking behavior were made in terms of the behavior which occurred when alcohol was available. The hypothesis relating drinking and problems associated with drinking to availability of alcohol would suggest that when alcohol was available those societies where it was available throughout the year would tend generally to rank high on those variables representing a fixed scale (e.g., Extent of Drinking, Frequency of Drinking, Procurement Effort, and Degree of Problem). The hypothesis would also suggest that societies high in the availability of alcohol would rank higher on all six scales than societies low in availability of alcohol. Inspection of the distribution of ratings on all six scales for both groups of societies indicates that these predictions are not upheld. Societies with alcohol freely available show a wide range of ratings from low to high on all six variables. The small group of societies with low availability shows the same general trend. When there is evidence suggestive of some difference between the two groups, the difference is in the direction opposite to that predicted. For example, with respect to Extent of Drinking, each of the five societies with low availability was given a maximum rating on this scale by both judges, indicating that when alcohol was available all of the adult men of the society drank. For the sample of 81 with high availability of alcohol, only about half of the societies were given a maximum rating.

A similar pattern was observed with respect to the ratings on frequency of drunkenness. For the high-availability group the ratings here ranged widely, with a median rating between 8 and 9. All of the societies where alcohol was rated as limited in availability were rated as above the median in frequency of drunkenness, rather than below as would be expected by this hypothesis. For the remaining measures (Frequency of Drinking, Consumption, Procurement Effort, and Degree of Problem) ratings for the five societies tended to be evenly distributed about the median rating for the larger high-availability group.

In summary, the available cross-cultural data would tend to support the null hypothesis, indicating that there is no relationship between the degree of availability of alcohol and measures of the extent and frequency of drinking, the amount consumed, the effort toward procurement of alcohol, the frequency of drunkenness, and judgments of the degree to which drinking constitutes a problem for the society. These findings must be accepted with reservation because of the small size of the sample of societies with limited availability. However, it should be noted that the findings for all six scales are in complete agreement in *not* supporting the hypothesis.

The Anxiety Reduction Hypothesis

One of the most persistent ideas concerning motivations for drinking is that relating alcohol consumption to anxiety reduction. This idea has long been a part of folk knowledge and is supported in part by clinical evidence. The question has also been addressed in the experimental literature. In much of this research, little distinction is made between anxiety and tension. The so-called measures or indicators of anxiety are also extremely various, ranging in experiments with animals from approach–avoidance conflict (e.g., Masserman, Jacques, & Nicholson, 1945; Masserman & Yum, 1946; Conger, 1951; Barry & Miller, 1962) to avoidance or escape behavior (e.g., Hogans, Moreno, & Brodie, 1961), conditioned suppression of operant responding for food or water (e.g., Estes & Skinner, 1941) and audiogenic seizures (e.g., Greenberg & Lester, 1953). In experiments with human subjects anxiety has been measured by disruption of verbal behavior as a result of delayed auditory feedback (Hughes & Forney, 1963), the galvanic skin response (GSR) (Greenberg & Carpenter, 1957), risk-taking behavior (Teger, Katkin, & Pruitt, 1969), the Thematic Apperception Test (TAT) (Kalin, Davis, & McClelland, 1966), self-ratings of anxiety and depression (A. Williams, 1966), and others.

The results of studies such as these are not in agreement. In some cases they provide support for the anxiety reduction hypothesis, in others they do not. (For a review of the literature dealing with anxiety reduction and alcohol, see Wallgren & Barry [1970]; see also a recent review chapter on the tension reduction hypothesis by Capell [1975].)

A number of ethnographic studies have emphasized the importance of anxiety or tension from various sources as motivating factors in excessive drinking and drunkenness (e.g., Whittaker, 1963; Savard, 1968; Gallagher, 1965; Hamer, 1965; Durgin, 1974). The first large-scale cross-cultural study to test the anxiety reduction function of alcohol was that of Horton (1943). This study represents a pioneering effort not only in the field of alcohol studies but also in the field of holocultural research. It has been reviewed many times and is usually summarized as providing evidence that level of insobriety in a sample of societies varies with the level of anxiety. This in turn is interpreted as favoring the hypothesis that anxiety reduction is an important function of alcohol consumption and that cross-culturally people drink to reduce anxiety. In his test of this hypothesis, Horton made judgements on a three-point scale of the degree of insobriety among men in a sample of 56 societies of wide geographic distribution. Since no direct measure of the anxiety level of a society existed, he sought among environmental variables common to all societies those which might be reasonably expected to be associated with variations in the level of anxiety experienced by the people of the society. By this approach he developed the following "measures" or indices of anxiety: type of subsistence, subsistence insecurity, effects of acculturation, frequency of warfare, belief in sorcery, and degree of premarital sexual freedom. Thus the first two measures were presumed to be related to greater or less anxiety about the food supply. It was assumed that societies whose subsistence depended primarily on fairly well developed agricultural techniques might have a food supply that was more reliable and less anxiety provoking than societies whose subsistence depended on hunting and gathering.

It was also assumed that such anxiety about the food supply would be relatively greater where there were frequent threats of food shortage (as a consequence of drought, floods, crop failure, insect plagues) than where such dangers were rare or did not exist. In addition to these two measures of "subsistence insecurity," the degree of acculturation of the society was also used as an indirect measure of generalized anxiety, as were the frequency of warfare and the prevalence of the belief in sorcery. Sexual anxiety was assumed to be inversely related to the degree of premarital sexual freedom permitted by the society.

Horton's data showed significant positive correlations between his measures of insobriety and his two indices of subsistence insecurity. This association became even stronger when the degree of acculturation was included. No significant association was found between degree of insobriety and either frequency of warfare or prevalence of belief in sorcery. Also, sexual anxiety (as measured by absence of premarital sexual freedom) was not found to be significantly related to degree of insobriety in the total sample. When societies with strong anxiety related to subsistence hazards, which was interpreted as competing with sexual anxiety, were removed from the sample, a positive association between insobriety and sexual anxiety in the remaining 36 societies was found.

With respect to the anxiety reduction hypothesis, Horton's findings can perhaps be best described as indicating that in societies where various threats to the food supply were present the men of the society tended to drink to more prolonged and higher levels of intoxication than where such threats were absent. A positive association was also found with degree of acculturation. The relationships between insobriety and other possible sources of anxiety tested, such as frequency of warfare, belief in sorcery, and suppression of premarital sex, were generally not statistically significant.[2]

Field (1962) questioned Horton's interpretation of his data. He correlated Horton's measures of insobriety with a number of measures (which he interpreted as measures of fear) that were derived from the Whiting and Child (1953) study on child training and personality. On the basis of a lack of association between these two sets of measures (for the 27 overlapping societies from the Horton and Whiting & Child sample), Field concluded that extent of drunkenness in primitive societies is not related to level of fear. This finding does not seem to represent a crucial test of Horton's hypothesis, since the sample is quite small and the so-called measures of fear were actually ratings of explanations for illness which were assumed to be indirect measures of anxiety associated with child-rearing practices in different systems of behavior. In his reanalysis, Field confirmed Horton's findings relating frequency of drunkenness and type of subsistence economy but offered an alternate interpretation (see later discussion.) Field also tested the relationship between insobriety and other psychological variables representing possible indices of anxiety. These included socialization anxiety measures from the Whiting and Child (1953) study for the sexual and aggressive systems of behavior. These measures represented judgments of the severity of socialization in early childhood in these systems. Field found a significant inverse relationship between insobriety and aggression socialization anxiety, which would seem to support Horton's theory. However, a later test of this relationship (Barry, Buchwald, Child, & Bacon, 1965) with a more sensitive test of association did not confirm this finding. Field also found no relationship with various measures of sex socialization anxiety, which he interpreted as refuting Horton's findings. However, the association found by Horton was limited to those societies of his sample that did not show strong anxiety in response to subsistence hazards.

Horton's study was also criticized on methodologic grounds, chiefly because he made all of his ratings on ethnographic data himself and thus did not control for experimenter bias. However, a later cross-cultural study of drinking included the 56 societies of Horton's sample in a larger sample of 139. This procedure provided independent ratings of drinking behavior for the Horton sample and thus a check on similar measures from both sets of data and on the correlates found by both Horton and Field (Barry, et al., 1965). Product moment correlations between Horton's three alcohol-related variables and three similar measures from the later study were statistically significant and confirmed the reliability and validity of the respective alcohol measures in both studies. Horton's findings relating degree of insobriety to measures of anxiety based on subsistence insecurity were supported in part by the new sample. The relationship with type of economy (scaled according to estimated degree of economic insecurity) was confirmed, but other measures of insecure food supply and measures of degree of acculturation did not show statistically significant correlations with frequency of drunkenness. The findings here also agreed with Horton in uncovering no relationship between measures of insobriety and frequency of warfare or belief in sorcery.

On the other hand, the 1965 study did find a significant positive association between frequency of drunkenness and other variables that might be interpreted as indices of anxiety—e.g., unrealistic storing of food and pressures in childhood which would be expected to make children anxious about achievement behavior. Other variables which might be considered possible measures of anxiety did not support the hypothesis—e.g., the Whiting and Child measures of aggression socialization anxiety and anal socialization anxiety, and ratings of childhood anxiety over training in responsibility or nurturance (Bacon et al., 1965a). Possible refinements of the anxiety reduction hypothesis, relating measures of drinking to particular kinds of anxiety rather than a general overall measure, were suggested by these authors.

In this connection Schaefer's (1973) findings are related to an anxiety reduction explanation of the rewarding effects of alcohol consumption. With a carefully selected sample of 57 societies he sought to test the hypothesis that the primary function of alcohol is to help people feel less anxious and powerless. His formulation appears thus to relate drinking cross-culturally to a specific kind of anxiety and at the same time to extend some of the ideas of McClelland, Davis, Kalin, and Wanner (1972) about the function of alcohol.

Schaefer developed two new measures of drinking. The first involved coding drunkenness or insobriety on a three-point scale ranging from Strong Insobriety (defined as excessive drinking for up to several days with drinking to unconsciousness a commonplace occurrence) to Rare Insobriety (where intoxication was "restrained"). A second measure of Drunken Brawling also was used (defined as the regular occurrence of physical assault); this behavior was rated as present or absent. Schaefer's results included the finding that Drunken Brawling was significantly related to Extreme Male Insobriety, which is not surprising, since the presence of brawling must have in part predisposed the report by the ethnographer of extreme insobriety. However, Schaefer also found that Extreme Insobriety was significantly related to the belief that the spirits of dead ancestors were malicious, harmful, and capricious beings. Although the predicted association between drunken brawling and belief in malicious spirits was of doubtful significance, the above association could certainly be interpreted as supporting an anxiety reduction hypothesis. In a more recent publication Schaefer (1976) also reports statistically significant associations between extreme and aggressive drunkenness and the following variables: a hunting and gathering economy, simple division of labor, simple political system, absence of social-class distinction, and low societal complexity. He feels that this correlation pattern fits well Horton's original theory regarding the function of alcohol in reducing anxiety.

In summary, evidence is found both for and against the anxiety reduction hypothesis. It certainly cannot be considered "proven" in any sense. One difficulty, as noted below, lies in the breadth and all-inclusiveness of the construct. This criticism, of course, does not detract from the heuristic value of Horton's pioneering work.

Hypotheses Relating Degree of Insobriety to Variables of Social Control

Cross-cultural findings on the relation of features of social organization to drinking behavior can be interpreted in terms of underlying psychological mechanisms operating to motivate drinking (e.g., Horton, 1943; Schaefer, 1976). They can also be interpreted as factors which limit or control drinking once it has been established as a custom.

In his analysis of Horton's data, Field (1962) suggested that the association which Horton found (and which Field confirmed) between type of subsistence economy and degree of drunkenness could be interpreted in terms other than level of anxiety. He pointed out that the economy measure used by Horton could represent a continuum of variables of social organization as well as one of subsistence insecurity. By this argument, societies depending on hunting and gathering for subsistence were conceptualized as lower on a scale of social organization than societies where subsistence activities depended largely on herding and agriculture. Thus Field chose to intrepret Horton's findings as indicating an association between variation in social organization and sobriety rather than between variation in anxiety and drunkenness.

Field presented other evidence of significant associations between degree of insobriety and aspects of social structure obtained from Murdock (1957). Using Horton's ratings of drunkenness (dichotomized into extreme drunkenness versus moderate or slight drunkenness), he found significant negative correlations with presence of unilineal kin groups, approach to an exogamous clan community, patrilocal exogamy, and presence of bride-price and a positive correlation with nonpatrilocal residence in marriage. These associations led Field to conclude that more highly organized societies tend to have interpersonal relationships organized along hierarchic lines, which leads to greater control of informal drinking bouts. Thus he generalized that increased social organization would be associated with increased control of drinking behavior, leading therefore to decreased drunkenness. Field also reported significant correlations between degree of drunkenness and certain child-training variables that he felt supported this interpretation (e.g., positive correlations with degree of childhood indulgence and pressures toward achievement and self-reliance; Barry, Child, & Bacon, 1959) and a negative correlation with aggression socialization anxiety (Whiting & Child, 1953).

In a reanalysis of the Field data, Barry, Buchwald, Child, and Bacon (1965) made use of product moment correlations which utilize the entire range of scale values and are generally more sensitive and accurate measures of association than those used by Field. He tested Field's findings with the Frequency of Drunkenness measure for both the Horton sample of 57 societies and the remaining sample of 82 societies. The results of the reanalysis failed to confirm many of Field's findings. For the Horton sample, significant negative correlations were found for presence of unilineal kin groups, nonpatrilocal residence in marriage, and a subsistence economy emphasizing agriculture and the accumulation of food. For the alternate sample of societies not in Horton's sample, none of these relationships were confirmed; the only significant association was that between pressures toward self-reliance and achievement in childhood and Frequency of Drunkenness.

Further evidence of the relationship of variables of social organization to measures of drinking was presented by Child, Bacon and Barry (1965). Factor analysis of the correlational matrix of cross-cultural measures of drinking behavior suggested the existence of a type of alcohol consumption which was highly related to drinking in ceremonial and ritual contexts, labeled the Integrated Drinking Factor. Evidence was found that this integrated (or ceremonial) drinking refers to a general pattern of drinking which is quite different from that involved in the other measures used in this study (General Consumption and Frequency of Drunkenness) and which provides a measure of the cultural integration of drinking customs. Sociologists concerned with the study of alcohol have long conceptualized the cultural integration of drinking as a major factor in the social control of alcohol consumption. For example, Snyder's (1958) study of drinking among Jews related the almost complete absence of alcoholism in this group to the religious contexts of their drinking and the integration of their drinking customs into the total cultural pattern. The Bacon et al. study (1965a, b, c) provided data relevant to this conceptualization. If cultural integration of drinking customs operates to inhibit frequency of problems with drinking, then measures of integrated drinking would be expected to be correlated negatively with measures of drunkenness. This relationship, however, was not confirmed. The correlation of all measures of integrated drinking with Frequency of Drunkenness was near zero, indicating that there is no relationship. The presence of integrated drinking does not necessarily eliminate drunkenness, according to these findings.

Results of this study also found a strikingly close relationship between integrated drinking and the presence or absence of aboriginal drinking. It was assumed that the integration of drinking customs into cultural traditions would be to some degree a function of time. It therefore would be expected that the frequency of integrated drinking would be greater in the group accustomed to drinking in the aboriginal period than in the group which drank only after contact with a dominant cultural group. The results strongly confirmed this expectation. Of the 49 societies with aboriginal drinking, 37 were rated as having ceremonial or integrated drinking and only 3 as definitely lacking it. Of the 35 societies listed as drinking only after contact, integrated drinking was found to be present in only 3.

As might be expected, frequency of integrated drinking was found to be positively related to measures reflecting the general level of social organization. Significant positive correlations were found with the following measures, based on ratings by Murdock (1957): level of political integration, degree of social stratification, densely populated settlement patterns, and presence of slavery. General consumption of alcohol was also significantly related to level of political integration and social stratification. However, no relationship, either positive or negative, was found between these measures of social organization and Frequency of Drunkenness. Although Field did not test these relationships, his general hypothesis would seem to predict an inverse relationship between Frequency of Drunkenness and these measures of social complexity.

Klausner (1964) also sought to test in a cross-cultural sample the Bales-Snyder hypothesis that ritual drinking and heavy drinking in secular situations were inversely related. He chose as his sample the first 48 societies in the alphabetic listing of societies in the Human Relations Area Files (HRAF) which had some record of the use of alcoholic beverages in any situation. These societies were analyzed in terms of their use of alcohol in religious and secular situations. Each society was scored as to whether there was light, heavy, or no drinking in each situation. Secular situations were classified as primarily occupational, familial, social, or political. Religious ceremonials were classified according to their orientation (e.g., control of the external world, uncertain outcome of human action, and moral integration) and according to the means employed (e.g., scapegoating, prayer, exorcism, and sacrifice). Klausner's findings did not support the hypothesis. Out of 63 ϕ coefficients, 58 were positive, rather than negative as would have been predicted. This failure to find a negative association between ritual or religious drinking and heavy drinking in secular context seems consistent with the Bacon et al. (1965a, b, c) finding of no relationship between frequency of integrated drinking and Frequency of Drunkenness. In other words, the data from these samples indicate that the presence of ceremonial or religious drinking in a society does not appear to inhibit heavy drinking or Frequency of Drunkenness.

In a further analysis, Klausner cited anthropological evidence indicating the symbolic equivalence of wine and blood. Using the severity of the menstrual taboo as an indicator of a cultural attitude toward and use of blood (and alcohol), he reported a negative relationship between severe menstrual taboos and heavy drinking in secular situations. This he interpreted as evidence that societies that consider blood as sacred will develop avoidance toward it in secular situations and will moderate secular drinking. This he considered support within limits for the Snyder-Bales hypothesis. However, the statistical data on which Klausner based his conclusions are not very convincing. The samples are small (varying from 15 to 27), and the ϕ coefficients are not very high (-0.21 to -0.37). Tests of significance were not reported. In this connection it is of interest that Field (1962) made use of Stephens' (1961) scale of menstrual taboos as a measure of sex anxiety and found no correlation with extent of drunkenness as measured in his sample.

With regard to the social control hypothesis, again there are conflicting findings as well as differing interpretations of the same evidence. Some factors of social organization seem clearly related to measures of degree of insobriety.

The Power Hypothesis

McClelland and his associates (Kalin et al. 1966; McClelland et al., 1972; Boyatzis, 1976) have proposed the hypothesis that drinking in males is related to motivations for power. According to this hypothesis men drink primarily to feel stronger. Feelings of powerlessness are mitigated by alcohol which "cues off thoughts of strength and power . . . apparently for physiological reasons" (McClelland et al., 1972, p. 334). McClelland's findings led him to postulate two kinds of power motivation: "socialized power," revealed by thoughts of having impact on others for their own good, and "personalized power," associated with thoughts of winning personal victories. In younger men these thoughts of personal power are often expressed in terms of "sexual and aggressive conquests." McClelland et al. claim that individuals whose power drives are worked out in other activities tend to drink in moderation and act passively while drunk.

The evidence which McClelland et al. produce in support of this hypothesis is based largely on the assumption that power needs are expressed and can be reliably identified in fantasy material (see recent criticism by Entwhistle, 1972). Their data therefore consist, for the most part, of TAT responses from American males under the influence of alcohol and thematic analysis of the content of folktales obtained from a sample of societies. Their coding system was apparently developed from the analysis of fantasy material produced under conditions assumed by the investigator to arouse motives for power (cf. Winter, 1972). McClelland et al. report that themes of impulsiveness and power, as coded in the TAT's produced by males, increased with alcohol consumption. In their cross-cultural test they indicated that "impulsive power" themes in folk tales correlated significantly with measures of drunkenness (Kalin et al., 1966; McClelland et al.,1972).

The analysis by McClelland et al. of folktales made use of the "general inquirer" computer technique, which is a system of content analysis. Basic to this system is the development of a dictionary of concepts or "tags" which consists of groups of "entry words" that the investigator decides are conceptually related. This dictionary is entered into the computer, which stores the tags and their entry words. When test material is subsequently read into the computer, the program searches the text and records the frequency of occurrence of the entry words. This provides a measure of the relative frequency of the use of the concepts. Obviously the development of the dictionary of conceptually related words is crucial to this type of analysis. McClelland et al. (1972, pp. 53–59) provides some description of the development of these lists of associated words or themes. For example, in searching folktale material for themes relevant to the anxiety reduction hypothesis, McClelland et al., (1972, p. 54) made use of the following tags or concepts designated by these entry words:

Tag (Concept)	Sample Words Classified Under Tag
Fear	Afraid, dread, fright, flinch, scare(d)-ing, fear
Unable	Cannot, incompetent, inept, muddle, ineffective
Fail	Fail, flunk, miss, loss or lost
Not	Not, no, won't, wouldn't

By the use of this method, McClelland et al. claim to have not only found evidence for their hypothesis relating drunkenness to motivations for power but also to have retested competing hypotheses and found no evidence to support them.

The concepts or tags, together with the words most frequently found related to these concepts for Field's (1962) social organization hypothesis and the dependency-conflict hypothesis (Bacon et al., 1965a, b, c), are as follows (McClelland et al., 1972, p. 58):

Formal Organization (Field)

Title (king, priest, queen, prince)
Vertical space (under, above, below)
Old and dead (old, dead, death)
Scheduling (time, after, before, next)
Activity inhibition (not, catch, stop)

Dependency (Bacon et al.)

Give (give, let, help)
Taking (take, seize, collect)
Dependency (ask, carry, help)
Want (want, wish, need)
Capability (make, could, can)
Anal socialization anxiety[3] (dung, excrement = fear or negation)

On the basis of a lack of correlation between the frequency of occurrence of such words and his measure of frequency of drunkenness, McClelland et al. find no support for the dependency-conflict hypothesis.

The cross-cultural measure of drinking used by McClelland et al. as the dependent variable consisted of the summed ratings for the following variables taken from the Bacon et al. study (1965b, pp. 88–89): General Consumption (an estimate of the actual per capita consumption of beverage alcohol) and Frequency of Drunkenness (an estimate of the frequency of drunkenness in this group compared with other groups in the sample). In addition to the findings from their folk tale analysis, McClelland et al. cite in support of their hypothesis a number of variables of social organization which are correlated significantly with this combined measure of drinking: For example, they report as evidence of "low male solidarity" significant correlations with the following variables from Murdock (1960, p. 64): nonlineal descent, small community size, and egalitarian kin terms (collateral terms, few "child" references indicating low hierarchic differentiation). These cultural characteristics are interpreted as representing a situation where there are few organized or structured means for the male to attain a sense of masculinity or to achieve status. This ambiguity over the males' importance or power is assumed to be the significant factor associated with drinking. Similarly, the following measures associated with socioeconomic simplicity are reported as significantly correlated with drinking: degree of dependence on hunting, impermanence of settlement pattern, small size of local community, and degree of dependence on agriculture. Although the possible support for Horton's hypothesis was noted here, the interpretation preferred was that such arrangements described a temporary and uncertain life style in which there are no stable mechanisms present which allow the male to maintain a position of importance. Such a situation presumably leads to feeling of powerlessness and the need to drink.

Another cluster of cultural characteristics described as the "male institutions scale" (cf. Boyatzis, 1976) was found to be negatively correlated with drinking: presence of male initiation, clear initiation impact, strong male solidarity, exclusive mother–infant sleeping arrangements, large sleeping distance of mother and father, warm winter temperature, and wet climate. Aside from the last two, these variables are interpreted to indicate the existence of stable mechanisms for attaining or keeping a position in the male group, which, in turn, is assumed to reduce the pressure on men to assert themselves continually and to seek power through drinking.

The cross-cultural folktale evidence of McClelland et al. has been criticized as unconvincing. It depends in essence on a conceptual analysis (based on the frequency of what are judged to be relevant words) of a sample of folktales translated from the original. The problems of translation alone must be very large. One might wonder to what extent two independent translators might agree with regard to the word content of the same folktale. The question of sampling is also important. As noted by Schaefer (1976), McClelland et al. give us little information about sampling procedures, especially with regard to folktale selection. McClelland et al. report reliability coefficients based on a split-half comparison of frequencies of word combinations, a procedure which is questioned by Masamura (1972). The larger question would appear to be one of validity. Does the type of analysis employed measure what it purports to measure? It seems unlikely, and here again there is criticism, recently reviewed by Schaefer (1976).

As further support for the masculine power hypothesis, Wanner (1972) makes use of findings from the Bacon et al. study (1965a, b, c) with regard to behavior occurring during drinking. In this study, ratings were made of the following kinds of behavior often associated with drinking: sociability (friendly interaction), exhibitionistic behavior (all behavior by which individuals call attention to themselves), hostility and resentment (directly expressed in interpersonal relationships), rule breaking (transgressions from the standard of "good" behavior), and boisterousness (tendencies to be loud and boisterous rather than quiet and inactive). Three aspects of each type of behavior were rated separately in the original study: (1) intensity or degree of the behavior, (2) extent of change of the behavior during drinking as compared with that during the sober state, and (3) occurrence of extreme behavior. (Detailed definitions and directions for coding are described in the original study.) Wanner reported a significant positive correlation between the drinking measure employed in his study (General Consumption of Alcohol plus Frequency of Drunkenness) and each of the following measures of behavior associated with drinking: exhibitionism, boisterousness, and occurrence of extreme hostility. Wanner interprets these findings as indicative of a loud, assertive, often aggressive display, which suggests that drinking provides an immediate means of gratifying the need to feel powerful. On the surface this seems to be a possible interpretation. However, it should be noted that when these measures of drinking behavior are correlated separately with ratings on General Consumption of alcohol and Frequency of Drunkenness, the difference between the two sets of correlations indicates that it is Frequency of Drunkenness that is significantly correlated with these kinds of behavior. Further examination reveals that Frequency of Drunkenness also shows a statistically significant correlation with sociability and sociability change, which is more difficult to rationalize as an expression of a need for power. Also, some note should be made of the fact that all of the types of behavior listed above as associated with drinking showed significant positive correlations with Frequency of Drunkenness. This is not surprising, since the directions to the coders suggested that they use the presence of extreme behavior reactions accompanying the consumption of alcohol in making their judgments as to the frequency of drunkenness. Thus the presence of these kinds of behavior was part of the operational definition of drunkenness.

The hypothesis relating drinking in males to a search for power is provocative and is certainly more acceptable to males than competing hypotheses. It suffers, however, from a number of limitations aside from those already mentioned. It apparently does not apply to drinking among females. Also, the data cited to support it are not convincing in many cases. Further, the power construct is so broadly defined that it is capable of encompassing almost contradictory kinds of behavior (e.g., nurturance and aggression).

The Dependency-Conflict Hypothesis

Another recurring theme in the alcohol literature which has been subjected to cross-cultural study concerns the relationship between drinking behavior and other kinds of behavior often classified as dependent. Lolli (1956) described the alcoholic personality as one who longs for the dependent state of infancy, Bailey (1961) noted a tendency for alcoholics to assume a dependent role in marriage, and Lemert (1962) made similar observations. McCord and McCord (1960) offered a dependency-conflict interpretation of the data they obtained from a longitudinal study of a group of alcoholics. Witkin, Karp, and Goodenough (1959) found evidence of perceptual field dependence in alcoholics. They related this mode of perceiving to basic personality characteristics of passivity, lack of self-esteem, and undifferentiated body image. Blane (1968) described dependence–independence conflict as characteristic of alcoholics. Barry (1974) has reviewed some of the literature related to this question. It should be emphasized that these studies and others relate dependent behavior (variously defined) to the type of drinking behavior known as alcoholism.

It should also be noted that the term dependence has been used to refer to many different kinds of behavior which sometimes seem to have little in common. As with the concept of anxiety, attempts to quantify the construct have led to a wide variety of operational definitions. Most of the research on dependence has focused on the dependent behavior of children where the following kinds of behavior are often classed as dependent: seeking physical contact, seeking praise and approval, resisting separation, seeking help, asking questions (see Gewirtz, 1972, for a discussion of dependence indices). Dependent behavior in adults has been "measured" by affiliative response to threat of shock (Schachter, 1959), self-ratings and interviewer ratings (Kagan & Moss, 1962), and projective tests (for reviews of this literature see Maccoby & Masters, 1970, and Sears, 1972).

There are apparently several versions of the dependency-conflict hypothesis. In recent statements by Bacon (1974; 1976) the rationale underlying this hypothesis has been summarized as follows: Insobriety is conceived to be associated with a type of dependence–independence conflict. In this context, dependence refers to a behavioral complex related to seeking for help which is universally acquired in the course of normal development. Every individual who survives experiences a long period of helplessness at the beginning of life during which nurturant care is provided by older people in the infant's social environment. As a consequence of this universal experience, every child develops an elaborate repertoire of help-seeking sequences of behavior together with a set of expectations regarding the help-giving or nurturant responses of certain individuals or groups. As the child grows older, the help-giving behavior of adults is modified in response to the developing capabilities of the child and the expectations of the society with regard to autonomy. It therefore is assumed that adults in any society may show variations in habits, attitudes, beliefs, expectations, and feelings about asking for help as a function of the nature of this socialization process. Or, stated in the drinking context, individuals in any society who are considered old enough to learn to drink, however this may be defined by their cultural group, will have in their behavioral repertoire a well developed set of help-seeking techniques and feelings about asking for help that have been "shaped" by experiences as members of their social group. Since the human animal lives in groups and no individual is entirely self-sufficient, the need to seek help from others persists in varying degrees throughout life. Thus while the necessity of asking for help is less obvious in adulthood than in infancy, it is nevertheless present universally. This point should be emphasized because in many groups in our own society behavior which is labeled "independent" is highly valued and help-seeking behavior is considered childish and unbecoming in an adult, especially an adult male. Dependent behavior is associated further with "maternal overprotection," which is popularly conceived to be the source of many difficulties in adult adjustment.

Earlier cross-cultural studies of child rearing (Whiting & Child, 1953; Barry, Child, & Bacon, 1959) have demonstrated that societies vary in the degree to which they respond to the dependence needs of infants and in the degree to which the care of infants and children is dispersed among many people or confined to a few. Societies also vary in their expectations for self-reliant and achieving behavior during childhood and the manner in which they enforce these expectations. In the original conceptualization of the dependence–independence conflict, it was assumed that the severity of such conflict would be related in some degree to the strength of opposing motivations generated by the socialization process. Thus the learned motivation for self-reliant and achieving behavior was conceived to be in opposition to previously learned help-seeking behavior. On the other hand, a lower level of satisfaction of physical needs in infancy was viewed as a frustration of dependence needs. Measures of "infant indulgence" (the degree to which physical and emotional needs are judged to be satisfactorily met) were therefore assumed to be *inversely* related to the frustration of dependence and the development of dependence–independence conflict. Evidence in the child development literature that frustration of dependence needs in infancy and early childhood is followed by increased demands for attention in later childhood tends to support such an assumption (cf. Zigler & Child, 1969).

A third set of variables related to the dependency conflict hypothesis concerned the extent to which typical adults in a sample of societies customarily asked for and expected help from each other (without criticism or any other indication of disapproval). An attitude of general expectation and acceptance of help-seeking behavior in adulthood, by this hypothesis, would be associated with a low degree of dependence–independence conflict. As a measure of this adult attitude, ratings were made of the following variables related to help-seeking in adulthood: emotional dependence (defined generally as seeking support from other people in times of crisis, avoiding isolation, seeking security in group contact, etc.), and instrumental dependence (seeking help of others in satisfying needs for food, clothing, shelter, transportation, etc.).

It was hypothesized in the 1965 study (Bacon et al. 1965a, b, c) that measures of dependence–independence conflict might be found in these three areas. Thus when the customs of the society provided adequate response to the dependence needs of infants, mild and nonpunitive socialization pressures toward self-reliance and achievement, and the acceptance of help-seeking behavior in adulthood, then a low level of dependence–independence conflict would be expected to result. When opposite conditions prevailed, a psychological state of conflict associated with help-seeking behavior might be found. It was hypothesized further that the drinking situation might provide the temporary resolution of such conflict by simultaneously permitting the satisfaction of dependent or help-seeking behavior, the enjoyment of fantasies of achievement and success, and the reduction of anxiety associated with the conflict experienced in the sober state. The resolution of such conflict might then operate as a reinforcement of drinking behavior.

Stated in terms of the cross-cultural measures available, the hypothesis would predict that Frequency of Drinking and Drunkenness would be (1) negatively corre-lated with measures of indulgence in infancy, (2) positively correlated with pressures toward self-reliance and achievement in childhood, and (3) negatively correlated with emotional and instrumental dependence in adulthood.

Support for this hypothesis was found in all three of these areas: consumption of alcohol (a general measure referring to the overall amount of alcohol typically drunk by the members of a given society) showed statistically significant negative correla-tions with overall indulgence in infancy, childhood indulgence, instrumental depen-dence in adulthood, and environmental kindness in folktales (a measure representing the relative number of themes in folktales of a given society in which the environment is kind or nurturant to the principal character). Frequency of drunkenness showed statistically significant negative correlations with the following measures related to the indulgence of dependence: diffusion of nurturance (a mea-sure of the number of people in the environment who customarily give nurturant care to the infant and young child), emotional dependence in adulthood, instrumen-tal dependence in adulthood, and communal eating. These findings were inter-preted as suggesting a strong tendency toward a negative relationship between the indulgence of dependence and measures of drinking. In other words, societies rated low in frequency of drinking and drunkenness tended to be those rated as indulgent of dependent help-seeking behavior.

The relationship of these measures of drinking behavior to socialization pressures toward independence also was investigated. Of the 14 resulting correlations, 11 were in the expected positive direction. Frequency of drunkenness yielded a statistically significant relationship with the following: Pressure toward achievment in child-hood, anxiety over achieving in childhood, and assertion versus compliance (a mea-sure of the relative amount of pressure in childhood toward self-reliance and achievement [assertion] at the upper end of a continuum as against responsibility and obedience [compliance] at the lower end of the continuum). These findings tended to agree with the prediction that pressures toward self-reliance and achieve-ment in childhood would be positively correlated with extent of drinking and drunk-enness.

These findings from the 1965 study (Bacon et al., 1965a, b, c) were therefore interpreted as providing support for the dependency-conflict hypothesis. The asso-ciations found upheld the predictions in all three areas of degree of indulgence in infancy, pressures toward achievement and self-reliance in childhood, and custom-ary acceptance of help-seeking behavior in adulthood. The association was strongest for the correlates of Frequency of Drunkenness.

A reexamination of the data from the 1965 study by Bacon (1974) produced further confirmation of the significance of the variables conceptualized as related to a dependence–independence continuum. In the original study the correlations reported between measures of drinking and variables related to dependence and achievement were computed for all societies in the larger sample of 139 for which measures were available for each successive pair of variables. The findings indicated that these variables were, as predicted, individually related to measures of drinking and drunkenness. However, the method of analysis used provided no information with regard to how these variables might interact. The original hypothesis predicted that measures of indulgence of dependence would be correlated negatively with Frequency of Drinking and Drunkenness, while pressures toward achievement in childhood would be positively correlated. Therefore as a step in further analysis a combination rating was made by subtracting the rating for diffusion of nurturance in infancy from the rating for pressure toward achievement in childhood for each of the 53 societies where both measures were available. Diffusion of nurturance was chosen for use in this combination rating because of all the measures of indulgence of dependence available it was most highly correlated (negatively) with Frequency of Drunkenness. According to the hypothesis, the combination of these two measures should be more highly correlated with measures of drinking than would either measure alone. As predicted, the combined measure showed an appreciably higher correlation ($r = 0.45$, $n = 53$, $p < 0.001$) with Frequency of Drunkenness than was found for the separate measures. (diffusion of nurturance: $r = -0.32$, $n = 61$, $p < 0.05$; pressure toward achievement: $r = 0.28$, $n = 56$, $p < 0.05$.) It was also of note that the combined rating showed an essentially zero correlation with the other two measures of drinking (overall consumption and integrated drinking). This finding provides additional support for the earlier findings indicating that these are independent measures of drinking (Child et al., 1965). It also suggested that for purposes of testing the hypothesis it would be better to use the Frequency of Drunkenness measure as a dependent variable rather than a measure combining consumption of alcohol and frequency of drunkenness in spite of the positive correlation between the two. Two other factors supported the choice. In the earlier analysis (Barry, Buchwald, Child, & Bacon, 1965) frequency of drunkenness was highly correlated with Horton's (1943) measure of drunkenness, thus attesting to the validity and reliability of the measure. Also, other cross-cultural studies of drinking used some measure of frequency of drunkenness as the dependent variable.

A more crucial test of the dependency-conflict hypothesis, making use of cross-cultural data, is provided by a multiple-regression analysis. Ordinary least-squares regression is a technique for examining the linear relationship between a dependent variable and a series of possible independent variables which takes into consideration the interrelationship between these predictor variables. By this technique it is possible to determine how much of the total variation in drunkenness can be accounted for by the three sets of variables acting together.

With Frequency of Drunkenness as a dependent variable, the following independent variables were chosen on the basis of the earlier findings as having some predictive relationship: Diffusion of Nurturance in infancy and early childhood, Pressures toward Achievement in childhood, Instrumental Dependence, and Emotional Dependence in adulthood. A total of 38 societies from the original sample had ratings available on all five of these variables. The multiple-regression findings (discussed in detail by Bacon, 1974; 1976) are summarized in Table 24–1, which indicates that the combined interaction of the independent variables entered into the

TABLE 24-1 Results of the Multiple–Regression Analysis

	B	B SE	t	R^*	R^2
Diffusion of nurturance	-0.45	0.21	-2.17	0.41	0.17
Pressures toward achievement	0.46	0.14	3.24	0.52	0.27
Instrumental dependence	-0.05	0.16	-0.33	0.61	0.37
Emotional dependence	-0.34	0.15	-2.30	0.67	0.46
Constant = 13.83		2.48	5.57		

*After variable is entered in the equation.
The dependent variable is frequency of drunkenness (n = 38). Reprinted from Bacon (1974) by courtesy of the editors of *The Quarterly Journal of Studies on Alcohol*.

analysis produced a multiple correlation (R) of 0.67 with the dependent variable, Frequency of Drunkenness. In other words, 46 percent of the variance of the dependent variable is explained by the interaction of the four independent variables. The numerical values recorded in the B value column indicate the direction and degree to which each independent variable contributes to the association with drunkenness when the influence of the other variables is held constant. In all cases the direction of the relationship is as predicted in the hypothesis, i.e., the variables theoretically related to indulgence of dependence are negatively associated with Frequency of Drunkenness, while the achievement variable is positively associated. The t values, which represent a measure of the statistical significance of the contribution of each variable, are all statistically significant except for the Instrumental Dependence. Because this variable is highly correlated with Emotional Dependence ($r = 0.67$), the interpretation of the two in the regression is more complicated.[4]

The results of the multiple-regression analysis thus provided strong confirmation of the significance of these variables in predicting drunkenness in a cross-cultural sample of societies. Since nearly half the variance in Frequency of Drunkenness was accounted for by the interaction of four variables (which can be collapsed to two; Bacon, 1974), the significance of these variables could hardly be questioned. They were interpreted as providing powerful support for a dependency-conflict hypothesis relating Frequency of Drunkenness to societal customs which (1) limit the indulgence of dependence in infancy, especially the diffusion of nurturance among many caretakers, (2) emphasize demands for achievement in childhood, and (3) in some way limit help-seeking behavior in adulthood. Stated conversely, the evidence could be interpreted to indicate that societies whose members drink but tend in general toward sobriety are those in which the dependence needs of infants are indulged by many people, demands for achievement in childhood are not stressed, and adults behave freely in an interdependent manner. Certainly the findings were in essential agreement with the predictions of the original dependency-conflict hypothesis, stated in 1965, with regard to the nature of the significant variables, the direction of their influence, and the effect of their interaction.

Barry (1976) presented additional cross-cultural findings in support of the dependency-conflict hypothesis. He correlated measures of drunkenness from the 1965 study with relevant socialization variables from the Barry and Paxson (1971) sample. High Frequency of Drunkenness was found to be correlated with low general indulgence during infancy, low duration of bodily contact with the caretaker during the later stages of infancy, a high amount of crying during infancy, low ceremonialism centered around the child, and low magical protectiveness of the child. These associations are statistically significant and in the direction predicted by the hypothesis. However, note should be taken of the fact that Barry's (1976) conceptualization of the dependency-conflict hypothesis makes use of a reward–punishment model which is quite different from the original position (Bacon et al., 1965) and the revision outlined here. Barry's formulation has led him to assign an interpretation quite different from that held by the writer to variables and their association with drunkenness. For example, Barry interprets low anal socialization anxiety as reflecting low attentiveness on the part of the nurturant agent and therefore a measure of a low degree of "reward for dependency." Low diffusion of nurturance is interpreted as indicating a low degree of "reward for self-reliance" (Barry, 1976, pp. 255–256).

Criticisms of the dependency-conflict hypothesis have varied according to the interpretation placed on it. Some writers have interpreted the hypothesis as stating that people drink because they wish to be dependent (e.g., Williams, 1976; Boyatzis, 1976). This is not an accurate interpretation of the original Bacon et al. statement and is related even less to recent revisions by Bacon (1974; 1976). Most of the criticisms of this hypothesis have been presented by researchers who support an alternate hypothesis that men are motivated to drink out of needs for power. They report no support for the dependency hypothesis by the measures they have employed to test it.

SUMMARIZING CONSIDERATIONS

A review of the various hypotheses concerning motivations for drinking and the data presented to support them underlines a number of basic problems involved in all of this research. One such problem concerns the nature of the constructs invoked to rationalize the findings. Generally speaking, they are large and inclusive constructs which can be reasonably applied to a wide range of variables related to social organization, maintenance systems, child rearing, and other cultural arrangements. The anxiety construct and its use in the anxiety reduction hypothesis provides a good example. This is a very broad concept that can "explain" many things. Indeed, it seems likely that most environmental variables could be reliably ranged on a continuum of more to less with regard to the degree to which they were conceived to be anxiety provoking.

The power construct provides another example. McClelland et al. include within this construct two classes of behavior: "impulsive power" and "socialized power." Impulsive power comprises all kinds of assertive, competitive, dominating behavior, including sexual conquest. Socialized power includes acts for the benefit of others, often classed in other contexts as nurturant, prosocial, or responsible. Dependency conflict is also a broad concept, especially in Barry's conceptualization (1976). And Field's concept of social control can include many variables of social organization. The breadth and inclusiveness of these various concepts makes it difficult to assess in any objective fashion the degree of support or lack of it provided by cross-cultural findings for any of these hypotheses.

The other side of the problem of the generality of the constructs is the question of the indicators and what they indicate. Examples of this problem are numerous throughout this chapter. Is the presence of a hunting and gathering economy an indicator of high subsistence anxiety (Horton), an indicator of low mechanisms of social control (Field), or an indicator of a temporary and uncertain life style which places males under persistent pressure to assert themselves in situations of low probability of success (Boyatzis, 1976)? Is diffusion of nurturance in early childhood an indicator of the degree of reward for self-reliance (Barry, 1976) or of the degree to which children are taught to expect nurturance and help from a wide circle of people (Bacon, 1974)? Are postpartum sex taboos and exclusive mother–infant sleeping arrangements customs which emphasize the male's membership in the male group and thus indicators of status (Boyatzis, 1976) or conditions which might lead to cross-sex identification and insecurity about male status (Whiting, Kluckhohn, & Anthony, 1958)? This problem of "indicators" or "measures" is, of course, a problem for much of the science of human behavior but is especially marked in cross-cultural studies where the variables are exceedingly complex; there often exists no way of determining what aspect of the variable may have entered into the correlation.

Alternate interpretations of the various findings have been offered. Schaefer (1976) has recently reexamined his own data and the cross-cultural findings of McClelland et al. and Field. He argues that McClelland et al. have not produced convincing evidence to refute competing hypotheses and suggests that the various findings can best be rationalized as supporting a hypothesis relating drinking to anxiety reduction or holocultural stress.

Bacon (1976) has also considered the data base for the dependency-conflict hypothesis from other points of view. She pointed out that the significance of the variable Diffusion of Nurturance in the regression equation suggests that it is not only the degree to which children's dependence needs are adequately met which is an important predictor of degree of sobriety or drunkenness but also the extent to which this nurturance is dispersed among many adults. Thus in societies with high diffusion of nurturance children are not only indulged with respect to their dependence needs but probably learn to expect and ask for help from a large number of nurturant people rather than primarily one (the mother or mother surrogate). This kind of childhood experience may lead to adults who ask freely for help when they feel the need and experience no conflict or hesitance about doing so. In considering the essential nature of this variable as it interacts in this context, it is significant that Diffusion of Nurturance in early childhood is found to be correlated with the following: communal eating, adult nurturance, and adult responsibility. It is possible to view this cluster of associations as an expression of motives toward affiliation or seeking to be with others. Affiliation, of course, can be seen as an aspect of dependence, but this shift in conceptualization might be more useful, especially since it implies a greater mutuality of interaction than that suggested by the term "dependence."

The variable Pressures toward Achievement was also found to be a significant predictor of frequency of drunkenness. This measure assessed ethnographic evidence of encouragement of competitiveness and expectations of individual rather than group attainment of high standards of performance. It is possible that pressures toward individual achievement in childhood involve anxieties specific to this kind of socialization. Measures of anxiety over achieving were also found to be significantly associated with frequency of drunkenness. This variable was defined as the amount of anxiety inherent in the achievement situation, such as fear of arousing hostility in others by winning in any competitive endeavor. Possibly the significant factor involved here is anxiety. On the other hand, it is also possible that the aspect of this variable which is crucial in the interaction is individualistic behavior. Perhaps the significant dimension is group orientation versus individualistically oriented behavior. This would be consistent with the positive association found between pressures toward assertion versus pressures toward compliance and frequency of drunkenness.[5]

Bacon's recent conceptualization has placed less emphasis on the model of opposing motivations (as in the 1965 statement) and focuses instead on the learning conditions surrounding the development in individuals of attitudes and feelings toward their own help-seeking behavior, the situations which might evoke it, and the methods of solution. Thus inadequate or inconsistent satisfaction of realistic dependence needs in infancy would produce conflict and anxiety about help seeking. In contrast, child-rearing arrangements whereby many people give nurturant care should lead to feelings of security about asking for help. Pressures toward achievement would tend to prevent help seeking, since achievement demands (as measured here) emphasize competitive, individualistic behavior which is largely nonaffiliative. Again, in contrast, societal customs which foster free interdependence among adults should encourage feelings of trust in situations which might evoke help-seeking behavior. This conceptualization moves closer to Erikson's (1963) ideas regarding the development of trust and is certainly akin to Bowlby's (1973) formulation of the necessary conditions for the development of adult self-reliance. According to Bowlby, people of all ages are happiest and most able to make use of their abilities when they are confident that standing behind them are one or more trusted persons who will provide them with a secure base, i.e., come to their aid if needed. By this view the healthy adult is not as independent as cultural stereotypes would suppose. Essential ingredients for healthy functioning include a capacity to rely trustingly on others when the occasion demands and to exchange roles in order to provide a secure base for others when the situation changes.

This formulation provides an alternate interpretation for some of the findings of other researchers related to the correlates of moderate drinking. Thus what McClelland et al. view as cultural arrangements which ensure masculine status and provide outlets for men's needs for power can also be seen as conditions fostering affiliation, group orientation, mutual interdependence, and what Bowlby calls a secure base. Strong male solidarity, presence of male initiation, and unilineal descent patterns provide good examples. Also, Field's concept of hierarchic organization of interpersonal relationships, which he feels leads to greater control of drinking, can be reinterpreted in this same way.

On the other hand, variables associated with drinking to drunkenness appear to involve conditions where individuals lack support (e.g., Schaefer's fear of the supernatural, Horton's insecure food supply and acculturation stress) and where individualistic, assertive, nonaffiliative behavior is encouraged (e.g., pressures toward achievement [Bacon et al, 1965a.] and search for personal power [McClelland et al.]). The persistent and strong inverse correlation between degree of societal complexity and frequency of drunkenness is, of course, associated with socialization pressures toward assertive and individualistic behavior in simpler societies. It may also be related to the greater vulnerability of more complex social organizations to the disruptive behavior associated with drunkenness and the consequent development of methods of control. The fact that societal complexity is also positively related to integrated drinking is also significant.

But what is the relationship of these various bodies of data to the original question addressed? All of the studies reviewed here have stated that they seek evidence as to why people drink, and they have agreed further in either implying or stating explicitly the basic assumption, based on learning theory, that the ingestion of alcohol has some kind of reinforcing effect. The research therefore has been directed to the discovery of the nature of this reinforcement. In this connection it is of interest that all of the studies have used as their dependent variable, some variant of a frequency of drunkenness measure. Field used Horton's measure of Frequency of Drunkenness. Schaefer used two measures, one of Frequency of Drunkenness, one of Drunken Brawling. The Bacon et al. study made use of both measures of General Consumption and Frequency of Drunkenness, and McClelland and his associates combined these two measures into one.

The choice of this measure as the dependent variable seems to imply that it is a measure of strength of motivation to drink, but this can certainly be questioned. In many societies daily drinking is the custom and drunkenness is rare, and in such societies the drinking custom has often persisted since aboriginal times and has thus demonstrated the capacity to resist extinction. Are we to assume that these people have little motivation to drink? It seems doubtful. The Frequency of Drunkenness measure also seems to imply that drinking to the point of drunkenness varies in terms of motivation only along a continuum of intensity. Again this seems doubtful. We cannot assume that the reinforcing effect of the seventh drink is the same as that of the second or that the reduction in anxiety or satisfaction of needs for power or resolution of conflict over dependency is more effectively met by seven drinks than by two. Evidence that the emotional response to drinking changes with continued drinking is pertinent here (e.g., Williams, 1966). It would appear, then, that all of the cross-cultural studies reviewed here have investigated motives for drinking to drunkenness rather than motives for drinking. This is an important distinction which seems to have been obscured. Our reasons for emphasizing frequency of drunkenness as a dependent variable are not certain but may be related to an ethnocentric tendency to equate drunkenness with alcoholism and a desire to contribute to the understanding of this social problem. Again, the distinctions should be kept clear. However alcoholism is defined, it is not the same as drunkenness. Furthermore, there is little if any evidence in the ethnographic literature on which these studies were based that yields us any information whatsoever on the cross-cultural incidence of alcoholism.

The nature of the reinforcing effect of alcohol remains in doubt. It seems unlikely that it can be reduced to the removal of some adverse effect such as anxiety, conflict, or feelings of powerlessness. Perhaps the answer can be found in some theoretical model such as that developed by Tomkins (1962) to explain smoking behavior. Tomkins distinguishes positive and negative affects. He proposes that these affects are the primary motives of the human being who is innately motivated to maximize positive affects and minimize negative affect. Tomkins classifies smokers into different types on the basis of their management of affect. Perhaps those who drink in moderation are motivated by positive affects which are linked in some way to the ingestion of alcohol, while those who drink to drunkenness are motivated primarily to remove negative affect.

Hologeistic studies have taught us a great deal about the range of cultural variation in all aspects of the drinking custom. They have also suggested a good deal about the cultural determinants of drinking to drunkenness, however these findings may best be rationalized. We must conclude, however, that cross-cultural studies have so far not taught us very much about the reinforcing effects of alcohol and the learning process whereby people accept, maintain, and perpetuate the drinking custom. Future studies directed to this question must clearly distinguish between drinking and drunkenness. They must also recognize that while frequency of drunkenness may be a measure of motivation to drink to drunkenness it is not a measure of motivation to drink.

NOTES

1. The Moslems are usually cited as an exception to this rule. Most of them do not drink, in keeping with the religious proscription laid down by Mohammed in response to widespread excess (Bales, 1946). However, not all Moslems adhere to this rule, and the number of nonadherents appears to be increasing.

2. In this review the statement of statistical significance will refer to $p < 0.05$.

3. This child-rearing variable from the Whiting and Child study (1953) was found in the 1965 study to show a significant negative correlation with frequency of drunkenness. This finding is contrary to the predictions of the dependency-conflict hypothesis.

4. The t ratio is the ratio between the B value and its standard error. In order to be significant at about the 0.05 level, B should be about twice the size of its standard error at the minimum. The t ratio should therefore have a value of at least 2. The correlation between independent variables (multicollinearity) results in large standard errors and hence in low t values for the coefficients of these particular variables. The consequence of multicollinearity in this case is the joint effect of Instrumental and Emotional Dependence on Frequency of Drunkenness. For this reason it has not been dropped from the regression, even though it has a very low t value.

5. A combination rating of child-rearing variables consisting of pressures toward self-reliance and achievement versus pressures toward responsibility and obedience.

REFERENCES

Bacon, M. K. The dependency-conflict hypothesis and the frequency of drunkenness: Further evidence from a cross-cultural study. *Quarterly Journal of Studies on Alcohol,* 1974, *35,* 863.

Bacon, M. K. Alcohol use in tribal societies. In B. Kissin & H. Begleiter (Eds.), *The biology of alcoholism* (Vol. 4). *Social aspects of alcoholism.* New York: Plenum Press, 1976.

Bacon, M. K., Barry, H., III., & Child, I. L. A cross-cultural study of drinking. II. Relations to other features of culture. *Quarterly Journal of Studies on Alcohol, Supplement 3,* 1965, *26,* 29–48. (a)

Bacon, M. K., Barry, H., III., Child, I. L., & Snyder, C. R. A cross-cultural study of drinking. V. Detailed definitions and data. *Quarterly Journal of Studies on Alcohol, Supplement 3,* 1965, *26,* 78–111. (b)

Bacon, M. K., Child, I. L., Barry, H., III., & Snyder, C. R. A cross-cultural study of drinking. *Quarterly Journal of Studies on Alcohol, Supplement 3,* 1965, *26.* (c)

Bailey, M. Alcoholism and marriage: A review of research and professional literature. *Quarterly Journal of Studies on Alcohol,* 1961, *22,* 81.

Bales, R. F. Cultural differences in rates of alcoholism. *Quarterly Journal of Studies on Alcohol,* 1946, *6,* 480–499.

Bales, R. F. Attitudes toward drinking in Irish culture. In D. J. Pittman & C. R. Snyder (Eds.), *Society, culture and drinking patterns.* New York: John Wiley & Sons, 1962.

Barnett, M. L. Alcoholism in the Cantonese of New York City: An anthropological survey. In O. Diethelm (Ed.), *Etiology of chronic alcoholism.* Springfield, Ill.: Charles C. Thomas, 1955.

Barry, H., III. Psychological factors in alcoholism. In B. Kissin & H. Begleiter (Eds.), *The biology of alcoholism* (Vol. 3). *Clinical pathology.* New York: Plenum Press, 1974.

Barry, H., III. Cross-cultural evidence that dependency conflict motivates drunkenness. In M. W. Everett, J. O. Waddell, & D. B. Heath (Eds.), *Cross-cultural approaches to the study of alcohol: An interdisciplinary perspective.* The Hague: Mouton, 1976.

Barry, H., III, Buchwald, C., Child, I. L., & Bacon, M. K. A cross-cultural study of drinking. IV. Comparisons with Horton's ratings. *Quarterly Journal of Studies on Alcohol, Supplement 3,* 1965, *26,* 62–77.

Barry, H., III, Child, I. L., & Bacon, M. K. Relation of child training to subsistence economy. *American Anthropologist,* 1959, *61,* 51–63.

Barry, H., III, & Miller, N. E. Effects of drugs on approach-avoidance conflict tested repeatedly by means of a "telescope alley." *Journal of Comparative Physiological Psychology,* 1962, *55,* 201.

Barry, H., III, & Paxson, L. M. Infancy and early childhood: Cross-cultural codes 2. *Ethnology,* 1971, *10,* 466–508.

Blane, H. T. *The personality of the alcoholic.* New York: Harper & Row, 1968.

Bowlby, J. Self-reliance and some conditions that promote it. In R. Gosling (Ed.), *Support, innovation and autonomy.* London: Tavestock Publications, 1973.

Boyatzis, R. E. Drinking as a manifestation of power concerns. In M. W. Everett, J. O. Waddell & D. W. Heath (Eds.), *Cross-cultural approaches to the study of alcohol.* The Hague: Mouton, 1976.

Braidwood, R. J., Sayer, J. D., Helback, H., Mangelsdorf, P. C., Coon, C. S., Linton, R., Steward, J., & Oppenheim, A. L. Symposium: Did man once live by beer alone? *American Anthropologist,* 1953, *55,* 515–526.

Capell, H., An evaluation of tension models of alcohol consumption. In *Research advances in alcohol and drug problems* (Vol. 2). New York: John Wiley & Sons, 1975.

Child, I. L., Bacon, M. K., & Barry, H., III. A cross-cultural study of drinking. I. Descriptive measurements of drinking customs. *Quarterly Journal of Studies on Alcohol, Supplement 3,* 1965, *26,* 1–28.

Conger, J. J. The effects of alcohol on conflict behavior in the albino rat. *Quarterly Journal of Studies on Alcohol,* 1951, *12,* 1.

Dailey, R. C. The role of alcohol among North American Indian tribes as reported in the Jesuit Relations. *Anthropologica,* 1968, *10,* 45–59.

Davis, K. E. Drug effects and drug use. In L. S. Wrightsman (Ed.), *Social psychology in the seventies.* Belmont, Calif.: Wadsworth, 1972.

DeLint, J., & Schmidt, W. The distribution of alcohol consumption in Ontario. *Quarterly Journal of Studies on Alcohol,* 1968, *29,* 968–973.

Durgin, E. C. *Brewing and boozing: A study of drinking patterns among the Hare Indians.* Unpublished doctoral dissertation, University of Oregon, 1974.

Entwhistle, D. R. To dispel fantasies about fantasy-based measures of achievement motivation. *Psychological Bulletin,* 1972, *77,* 377–392.

Erikson, E. H. *Childhood and society* (2nd ed.). New York: Norton, 1963.

Estes, W., & Skinner, B. F. Some quantitative properties of anxiety. *Journal of Experimental Psychology,* 1941, *29,* 390.

Field, P. B. A new cross-cultural study of drunkenness. In D. J. Pittman & C. R. Snyder (Eds.), *Society, culture, and drinking.* New York: John Wiley & Sons, 1962.

Gallagher, O. R. Drinking problems among tribal Bihar. *Quarterly Journal of Studies on Alcohol,* 1965, *26,* 617.

Gewirtz, J. L. (Ed.). *Attachment and dependency.* New York: John Wiley & Sons 1972.

Glad, D. D. Attitudes and experiences of American-Jewish and American-Irish male youth as related to differences in adult rates of inebriety. *Quarterly Journal of Studies on Alcohol,* 1947, *8,* 406–472.

Greenberg, L. A., & Carpenter, J. A. The effect of alcoholic beverages on skin conductance and emotional tension. I. Wine, whiskey and alcohol. *Quarterly Journal of Studies on Alcohol,* 1957, *18,* 190.

Greenberg, L. A., & Lester, D. The effect of alcohol on audiogenic seizures of rats. *Quarterly Journal of Studies on Alcohol,* 1953, *14,* 385–389.

Hamer, J. H. Acculturation stress and the function of alcohol among the Forest Patawatomi. *Quarterly Journal of Studies on Alcohol,* 1965, *26,* 285.

Heath, D. B. Anthropological perspectives on the social biology of alcohol. In B. Kissin & H. Begleiter (Eds.), *The biology of alcoholism* (Vol. 4). *Social aspects of alcoholism.* New York: Plenum Press, 1976.

Heath, D. B. A critical review of ethnographic studies of alcohol use. In R. J. Gibbons, Y. Israel, H. Kalant, R. E. Popham, W. Schmidt, & R. Smart (Eds.), *Recent advances in alcohol and drug studies* (Vol. 2). New York: John Wiley & Sons, 1974.

Hogans, A. F., Moreno, O. M., & Brodie, D. A. Effects of ethyl alcohol on EEG and avoidance behavior of chronic electrode monkeys. *American Journal of Physiology,* 1961, *211,* 434.

Horton, D. The functions of alcohol in primitive societies: A cross-cultural study. *Quarterly Journal of Studies on Alcohol,* 1943, *4,* 199.

Hughes, F. W., & Forney, R. B. Delayed audio feedback (DAF) for induction of anxiety. JAMA *(Journal of the American Medical Association),* 1963, *185,* 556.

Jessor, R., Graves, T. D., Hanson, R. C., & Jessor, S. L. *Society, personality, and deviant behavior.* New York: Holt, Rinehart & Winston, 1968.

Kagan, J., & Moss, H. A. *Birth to maturity: A study in psychological development.* New York: John Wiley & Sons, 1962.

Kalin, R., Davis, W. N., & McClelland, D. C. The relationship between use of alcohol and thematic content of folktales in primitive societies. In P. J. Stone, D. C. Dunphy, M. S. Smith, & D. M. Ogilvie (Eds.), *The general inquirer: A computer approach to content analysis.* Cambridge, Mass.: MIT Press, 1966.

Kearney, M. Drunkenness and religious conversion in a Mexican village. *Quarterly Journal of Studies on Alcohol,* 1970, *31,* 132–152.

Keller, M. Beer and wine in ancient medicine. *Quarterly Journal of Studies on Alcohol,* 1958, *19,* 153.

Klausner, S. Z. Sacred and profane meanings of blood and alcohol. *Journal of Social Psychology,* 1964, *64,* 27.

Lemert, E. M. Dependency in married alcoholics. *Quarterly Journal of Studies on Alcohol,* 1962, *23,* 590.

Lolli, G. Alcoholism as a disorder of the love disposition. *Quarterly Journal of Studies on Alcohol,* 1956, *17,* 96.

Lolli, G., Serianni, E., Golder, G., & Luzzatto-Fegis, P. *Alcohol in Italian culture.* Glencoe, Ill.: Free Press, 1958.

McCarthy, R. G., & Douglass, E. M. Prohibition and repeal. In R. G. McCarthy (Ed.), *Drinking and intoxication.* Glencoe, Ill.: Free Press, 1959.

McClelland, D. C., Davis, W. N., Kalin, R., & Wanner, E. *The drinking man.* New York: Free Press, 1972

McCord, W., & McCord, J. *Origins of alcoholism.* Stanford, Calif.: Stanford University Press, 1960

McKinlay, A. P. Early Roman sobriety. *Classic Bulletin,* 1948, *24,* 52. (a)

McKinlay, A. P. Ancient experience with intoxicating drinks: Nonclasscal peoples. *Quarterly Journal of Studies on Alcohol,* 1948, *24,* 388–414. (b)

McKinlay, A. P. Roman sobriety in the later Republic. *Classic Bulletin,* 1949, *25,* 27. (a)

McKinlay, A. P. Ancient experience with intoxicating drinks: Non-Attic Greek states. *Quarterly Journal of Studies on Alcohol,* 1949, *10,* 289–315. (b)

McKinlay, A. P. Attic temperance. *Quarterly Journal of Studies on Alcohol,* 1951, *6,* 61–102.

Maccoby, E. E., & Masters, J. C. Attachment and dependency. In P. H. Mussen (Ed.), *Carmichael's manual of child psychology* (Vol. 2). New York: John Wiley & Sons, 1970.

Mandelbaum, D. G. Alcohol and culture. *Current Anthropology,* 1965, *6,* 281–294.

Marcus, M. *The liquor control system in Sweden.* Stockholm: Norstadt & Suner, 1946.

Masamura, W. T. *Folktales and drunkenness: A critique of McClelland's The Drinking Man.* Missoula: University of Montana, 1972.

Masserman, J. H., Jacques, M. G., & Nicholson, M. R. Alcohol as a preventative of experimental neuroses. *Quarterly Journal of Studies on Alcohol,* 1945, *6,* 281.

Massermann, J. H., & Yum, K. S. An analysis of the influence of alcohol on experimental neurosis in cats. *Psychosomatic Medicine,* 1946, *8,* 36.

Moore, M. Chinese wine. Some notes on its social use. *Quarterly Journal of Studies on Alcohol,* 1948, *9,* 270–279.

Murdock, G. P. World ethnographic sample. *American Anthropologist,* 1957, *59,* 664.

Murdock, G. P. Ethnographic atlas. *Ethnology,* 1960–1964, *1–5.*

Myerson, A. Alcohol: A study of social ambivalence. *Quarterly Journal of Studies on Alcohol,* 1940, *1,* 13–20.

Parker, D. A., & Herman, M. S. The distribution of consumption model of prevention of alcohol problems. *Quarterly Journal of Studies on Alcohol,* 1978, *39,* 377–399.

Sadoun, R., Lolli, G., & Silverman, M. *Drinking in French culture.* New Brunswick, N.J.: Rutgers University Center of Alcohol Studies, 1965.

Sariola, S. Prohibition in Finland, 1919–1932: Its background and consequences. *Quarterly Journal of Studies on Alcohol,* 1954, *15,* 477–490.

Savard, R. J. *Cultural stress and alcoholism: A study of their relationship between Navaho alcoholic men.* Unpublished doctoral dissertation, University of Minnesota, 1968.

Schachter, S. *The psychology of affiliation: Experimental studies of the sources of gregariousness.* Stanford, Calif.: Stanford University Press, 1959.

Schaefer, J. M. Drunkenness and culture stress: A holocultural test. In M. W. Everett, J. O. Waddell, & D. W. Heath (Eds.), *Cross-cultural approaches to the study of alcohol.* The Hague: Mouton, 1976.

Schaefer, J. M. *A hologeistic study of family structure, sentiment, supernatural beliefs and drunkenness.* Unpublished doctoral dissertation, State University of New York, 1973.

Sears, R. R., Attachment, dependency, and frustration. In L. L. Gewirtz (Ed.), *Attachment and dependency.* Washington, D.C.: Winston & Sons, 1972.

Skutin, A. Sweden: Sequel. In R. G. McCarthy (Ed.), *Drinking and intoxication.* Glencoe, Ill.: Free Press, 1959.

Snyder, C. R. *Alcohol and the Jews: A cultural study of drinking and sobriety.* Glencoe, Ill.: Free Press, 1958.

Stephens, W. N. A cross-cultural study of menstrual taboos. *Genetic Psychology Monographs,* 1961, *64,* 385–416.

Sterne, M. E. *Drinking patterns and alcoholism among American Negroes.* St. Louis, Mo.: Washington University, Social Science Institute, 1966.

Teger, A. I., Katkin, E. S., & Pruitt, D. G. Effects of alcoholic beverages and their congener content on level and style of risk taking. *Journal of Personality and Social Psychology,* 1969, *11,* 170–176.

Tomkins, S. *Affect, imagery and consciousness* (Vol. 1). *The positive affects.* New York: Springer-Verlag, 1962.

Wallgren, H., & Barry, H., III. *Actions of alcohol* (Vols. 1 and 2). *Biochemical physiological and psychological aspects; Chronic and clinical aspects.* Amsterdam: Elsevier, 1970.

Wanner, E. Power and inhibition: A revision of the magical potency theory. In D. C. McClelland, W. N. Davis, R. Kalin, & E. Wanner (Eds.), *The drinking man.* New York: Free Press, 1972.

Wechsler, H., Demone, H. W., Jr., Thum, D., & Kasey, E. H. Religious-ethnic differences in alcohol consumption. *Journal of Health and Social Behavior,* 1970, *11,* 21–29.

Whiting, J. W. M., & Child, I. L. Child rearing and personality. New Haven: Yale University Press, 1953.

Whiting, J. W. M., Kluckhohn R., & Anthony, A. The function of male initiation ceremonies at puberty. In E. E. Maccoby, T. Newcomb, & E. L. Hartley (Eds.), *Readings in social psychology* (3rd ed.). New York: Holt, Rinehart & Winston, 1958.

Whittaker, J. O. Alcohol and the Standing Rock Sioux tribe. I. The pattern of drinking. *Quarterly Journal of Studies on Alcohol,* 1962, *23,* 468–479.

Whittaker, J. O. Alcohol and the Standing Rock Sioux tribe. II. Psychodynamic and cultural factors in drinking. *Quarterly Journal of Studies on Alcohol,* 1963, *24,* 80–90.

Williams, A. F. Social drinking, anxiety, and depression. *Journal of Personality and Social Psychology,* 1966, *3,* 689–693.

Williams, A. F. The alcoholic personality. In B. Kissin & H. Begleiter (Eds.), *The biology of alcoholism* (Vol. 4). New York: Plenum Press, 1976.

Williams, P. H., & Straus, R. Drinking patterns of Italians in New Haven. *Quarterly Journal of Studies on Alcohol,* 1950, *11,* 51, 247, 452, 586.

Winter, D. C. The need for power in college men. In D. C. McClelland, W. N. Davis, R. Kalin, & E. Wanner (Eds.), *The drinking man.* New York: Free Press, 1972.

Witkin, H. A., Karp, S. A., & Goodenough, D. R. Dependence in alcoholics. *Quarterly Journal of Studies on Alcohol,* 1959, *20,* 493.

Zigler, E., & Child, I. L. Socialization. In G. Lindzey & E. Aronson (Eds.), *The handbook of social psychology* (2nd ed.) (Vol. 3). Reading, Mass.: Addison-Wesley, 1969.

25

Cities, Stress, and Children: A Review of Some Cross-cultural Questions

Thomas S. Weisner

> Whatever trade, profession or vocation you decide to follow, I hope you will keep an intense interest in land to which you can retire when the pace of life in the modern city becomes intolerable. It will slow the beat of your heart, increase the capacity of your lungs, force patience on the most restless of you, and dependence on the proudest. It is no false romanticism I'm foisting onto you. I'm well aware of the cruelties and treacheries of Nature. But there is also a wisdom to be acquired away from artificialities of city life which I venture to think you may profit by.
>
> Kenneth David Kaunda (1973)

There is a pervasive belief in Western industrial societies that cities are stressful and cause anxiety and that the rural and small town environment (not to mention the "good old days" more generally) offer a bucolic alternative lost to the city dweller. Controlled studies of urban-rural differences in stress do not support this Western folk view. There is little evidence for a systematic, global influence of urban stress on parents. The available evidence suggests that the context in which urbanization occurs, the role of folk beliefs, and acculturation are critical mediating factors in understanding the effects of the city on family and child.

The chapter is not an exhaustive review of current cross-cultural or comparative urban studies, cross-cultural or comparative studies of families or stress, or a review of the concept of stress and acculturation. Indeed, there are few examples of cross-cultural research which combine these three perspectives—urban studies, studies of stress, and studies of children in urban settings. In general, the study of cities by anthropologists includes little on childhood and child rearing. Work in other fields that has examined urban-rural differences in children's behavior, including stress, is similarly uncommon. Thus a chapter for a handbook of cross-cultural human development focusing on cities *and* children *and* stress should redefine, conceptualize, and ask questions.

Lofland (1975) provides one possible interpretation as to why there are relatively few studies of stress, urban life, and families. Lofland reviewed major works in urban sociology on American cities to discover what these studies have told us about the role of women and found relatively little on women in this literature. Lofland suggests that there is so little focus on women because they are "just there"; they (and their children) provide the background, the setting, for the study of men in American urban communities. Just as the study of the lives and careers of women in urban community settings has begun only recently to receive more focused attention, so have studies on children and child rearing.

The paucity of studies specifically in this area encourages a broader look at the general question of city life, stress, and families. The chapter will begin by outlining some definitions and content problems with terms such as stress, urban, rural, and so forth. Some direct rural-urban comparisons of stress are discussed, followed by a review of two general factors implicated in rural-urban differences: life changes due to migration or mobility, and crowding and density. Next, if direct comparisons do not show strong differences between city and country, what cross-cultural mediating variables do appear to affect stress in cities? Consistency between urban and rural settings in child-rearing practices, ecology, and beliefs appears to affect the levels of stress reported. The final section suggests some areas for future research.

CROSS-CULTURAL STUDIES OF CITIES AND STRESS

Cross-cultural Urban Differences

Cities in non-Western settings are not necessarily mirrors of New York or Los Angeles, and the social organization of non-Western cities varies enormously. Students of comparative urbanization and urban anthropologists and sociologists have provided voluminous documentation and typologic analysis of the immense differences in cities around the world (Basham, 1978; Gulick, 1973; Fava, 1968; Fox, 1977; Southall, 1973; Walton & Carns, 1973). There are urban settings where the subsistence mode centers on horticulture and artisan and trading activities (e.g., Bascom, 1955, and Lloyd, 1973, for the Yoruba of West Africa); there are cities with clearly delineated neighborhoods where family relationships center around extended family compounds and ethnic homogeneity much as might characterize rural horticultural communities (e.g., Rowe, 1973, and Seymour, 1976, on India); and there are urban centers which mirror political and economic systems of the colonial and neocapitalist era in often extreme forms yet retain traditional cultural social institutions as well (e.g., Mayer, 1971, for South Africa).

This remarkable variability in city life is a proper starting point for thinking about the effects of cities on new arrivals, and on families, children, and stress. Are there central tendencies—some similarities in most cities most of the time—which might have consistent effects on families and children? If there are some such consistent effects, research must focus on what the specific antecedents were which produced them, since the covering category of "urban" conceals enormous diversity. It is an empirical question whether crowding, density, diverse ethnic contacts, occupational specialization, smaller family size, and other attributes characterizing many urban settings are actually present in any family's environment; clearly this cannot simply be assumed to be the case because families reside within a city's limits. Every city has enclaves, neighborhoods, and life styles of great diversity, including many where the intimate, daily experience of a child or family is not one of crowding and heterogeneity. The conventional term "urban" should not become a convenient gloss for ignoring such variations within or between cities.

Rural–Urban Comparisons Within Cultures

Rural–urban comparisons are also difficult because differences based on ecology or geography or culture area are so often confounded with other critical family variables. Common confounding variables include acculturation levels, education, language use, socioeconomic status, family size and composition, occupational characteristics, and so forth. Which of these vary directly with city and country residence within a culture? It is seldom clear which specific rural–urban difference might influence stress reports, or even what the importance of each is. Just as with city-to-city comparisons, then, it is seldom possible to make tidy rural–urban ecologic distinctions.

Definitions of Stress

Controversy nearly always surrounds a folk concept which has been expropriated for scientific use by many disciplines. The definition of "stress" or a "stressor" is no exception. For convenience in this review, the referents of stress or a stressor will refer both to situations that may tend to be stressful as well as the psychic or physical state within people who are experiencing stress.

Appley and Trumbull (1967, as quoted by Glass & Singer, 1972, pp. 5–6) provide a vivid paragraph describing the presumed urban environmental stressors in the large metropolis and end with a very general definition of psychological stress:

> Life in the city is an endless round of obstacles, conflicts, inconveniences, and bureaucratic routine. The urban dweller is confronted daily with noise, litter, air pollution, and overcrowding. Some of these conditions are pervasive. Others occur only at home, or at work, or in transit. Their incidence is profoundly disturbing, and many commentators on modern urban life allege that such conditions produce behavioral and physiological consequences inimical to the health and well-being of man. The study of these consequences may be subsumed under the category of *stress,* which has been generally defined as the affective, behavioral, and physiological response to aversive stimuli.

The definition of psychological stress includes affective, behavioral, and physiologic reactions; the question of what an "aversive" stimulus is for an individual or group is not defined. If aversive stimuli are defined solely by their outcomes, the outcomes need to be specified before the term can be widely applied; if there are clear physiologic or psychosomatic responses operationally defined as indicating stress, their validation depends on the conventional criteria of content and convergent validity, replicability and so on.

Some stress and resultant anxiety or disturbance are a part of all life and may indeed be essential for effective functioning (Selye, 1956). For example, childhood stresses in some mammals produce stronger, healthier adults; the work on animal handling (but cf. Freedman, 1974, pp. 92–94) and human responses to inoculation (Landauer & Whiting, 1964) illustrate these kinds of stressor effects.

Most urban and cross-cultural research is concerned with excessive amounts of stress for long periods of time resulting in some measurable trouble, concern, or decrement in functioning. "Adjustment" or "adaptation" to stress may be defined simply as habituation to what initially was stressful. These terms may also imply a more active and long-term involvement of individuals in shaping changes in themselves and in their environment, as well as the implication that the adaptation is for the better—it helps persons to function better than before the stress occurred. Cross-cultural research has been concerned particularly with adaptation in the broader functional sense of the term. There have been very few attempts to deal with the folk perceptions of stress, stressors, and adjustment. Using broad and inclusive definitions and operational measures of these concepts is both necessary and probably useful at this early stage of comparative work.

In practice, most cross-cultural studies have measured feelings of stress with some version of a self-report psychophysiologic symptom scale. These scales list a series of items such as biting one's fingernails, having trouble sleeping, or having trembling hands. Among the most widely used have been the Health Opinion Survey (MacMillan, 1957) and a 22-item screening scale (Langner, 1962) derived from the Cornell Medical Index. Inkeles and Smith (1974) review the scope and use of these and similar measures.

Stress and Problem Solving in Specific Environments

Howard and Scott (1965) have reviewed both biologic and sociopsychological approaches to the study of human stress and propose a model which relies on the concept of humans seeking a dynamic equilibrium with their environment. The essential sequence involves humans as presented with problems which lead to disequilibrium and the necessity to expend energy to solve the problems. Problems people must solve can come from (1) the person's own biochemical environment, (2) the external physical environment, (3) the person's own psychological environment, and (4) the person's sociocultural milieu (Howard & Scott, 1965, pp. 145–146). The core idea in Howard and Scott's paper seems intuitively sensible and useful in thinking about stress, adaptation, and adjustment in cities and during sociocultural change: people are faced with a set of *problems,* and personal *energy* is needed to deal with them. Big problems are hard to solve, probably involve physiologic, psychological, and behavioral consequences, and produce some degree of stress and anxiety. Parents and children moving to cities define and are faced with new problems and deal with them with varying degrees of success; the interaction between the urban and other stressors, how these are viewed by families, and the resultant stress experienced by family members are each important foci for research.

DIRECT RURAL–URBAN COMPARISONS OF STRESS REPORTS

What is the direct evidence for rural–urban differences in stress between rural and urban populations in different cultures? Do city residents, or migrants to cities from rural areas, report or experience more stress symptoms than their rural counterparts? The first step is to review studies which have surveyed this question or report cross-cultural work on this topic.

The Dohrenwends (B. P. Dohrenwend & Dohrenwend, 1974a; B. S. Dohrenwend & Dohrenwend, 1974b) have reviewed sociocultural factors related to the occurrence and distribution of all types of psychopathology, extending their own comprehensive study (1969). They report on "ten pairs of rural and urban rates from studies within which uniform procedures were used" (1974a, p. 434). Their rates of pathology are not limited to psychosomatic stress nor are reported by any particular subgroup, such as children, mothers, etc. However, these comparisons do provide the best available summary of general urban-rural differences in psychopathology. On the basis of these studies, the Dohrenwends conclude the following:

> The most reasonable hypothesis appears to be that total rates of psychopathology are somewhat higher in urban than in rural areas, due at least in part to an excess of neurosis and personality disorder in the urban areas. Whether these differences

are a function of harsher stress of residents of urban settings, however, is quite a different matter. (1974a, p. 435)

The absolute differences in prevalence rates are small; the median difference is only 1.1 percent higher in urban centers, with the largest absolute difference of 13.9 percent higher city rates. Psychoses and manic-depressive illnesses were in fact more prevalent in rural samples, while there were no clear urban–rural differences in the prevalence of schizophrenia. The overall implication of "true prevalence" studies for urbanization and stress appears to be that if there is a general, ecologic setting effect of cities, this effect is a small one but does often appear to include psychosomatic stress or anxiety. Further, evidence for urban–rural differences specifically affecting mothers, fathers, children of differing ages and sexes, or differing kinds of family units, is not available for cross-cultural generalization at the present time.

Weisner and Abbott (1977) also reviewed 22 cross-cultural studies of psychophysiologic stress. Stress measures used in these studies ranged from versions of the Cornell Medical Index self-report scale (ten studies), estimates of overall impairment in functioning (four studies), rates of disease implicated in stress (five studies), and blood pressure levels (two studies). The samples ranged widely in geographic distribution and level of sociocultural complexity. Age, educational level, income, sex, and urban–rural residence are all background variables utilized by many of these studies and implicated in acculturative change. The overall pattern of results showed a rather inconsistent relationship between these antecedent variables and stress. One study which directly tested urban–rural differences (controlling for other variables) found that urban subjects reported higher stress; a second found no differences unless the subject had migrated from a rural setting different from the city setting they moved to. Clearly, the variety of stress measures used in these studies influenced the results, and contextual differences in the meaning of stress and stressors play an important role. However, "it is certainly not the case that general background variables taken out of context are conspicuously consistent in their relationships to stress" (Weisner & Abbott, 1977).

Among the most extensive and carefully done cross-cultural studies of the relationships between urban experience and psychosomatic stress symptoms is the work of Inkeles and Smith (1970; 1974). They observed that the notion of the city as a powerful stressor of men, if not a generally evil and noxious place to live, is a common belief among laymen and social scientists alike:

> In our experience, no belief is more widespread among critics of industrialization than that it disrupts basic social ties, breaks down social controls, and therefore produces a train of personal disorientation, confusion, and uncertainty, which ultimately leads to misery and even mental breakdown among those who are uprooted from the farm and herded into great industrial cities. (Inkeles and Smith, 1974, p. 261)

Inkeles and Smith found little support for these popular beliefs about the effects of cities, modernity, or factory work on reported stress. They interviewed large samples (720–1300) of men in six developing countries—Argentina, Chile, India, Israel, Nigeria, and Pakistan. Their complex sampling design included men who were rural farmers, newly arrived urban migrants to various kinds of cities, industrial workers in factory settings, and urban workers employed outside of large productive enterprises. They used items from psychosomatic symptom self-report scales, varied slightly for each country. Inkeles and Smith provide detailed evidence for the internal reliability of scale items and substantial evidence for external validity by comparing psychosomatic report scores to other responses men made during their interview session which indicated some feelings of disturbance or anxiety. In short, given the constraints of self-report symptom techniques for estimated prevalence of stress in cross-cultural work, Inkeles and Smith provide a thorough and careful argument for the usefulness of their measure.

Inkeles and Smith's results for urban–rural differences are presented in detail (1970, pp. 97–101). Their results do not absolve cities of creating stressful effects on young men, but these effects appear to be weak. In addition, reasons for urban–rural differences are not clear from their data. Two of five countries show a significant negative correlation between the years men lived in the city and adjustment scores (Argentina and Pakistan), two others were negative in direction (Chile and Nigeria), and one (India) was slightly positive. A technique of controlling for other background variables (education, factory experience, mass media exposure, and mobility) within each country sample permitted a more direct look at the effect of urban exposure on reported stress; again, four of the five countries on which this analysis could be run showed that men with fewer years of urban exposure did indeed have better adjustment scores, although none of these correlations showed statistically significant differences.

Whatever urban characteristics may make men experience more stress should increase in amount and intensity the larger the urban setting is. Is there, then, a "critical mass," or synergistic effect of living in larger urban centers compared to smaller cities? There is a different atmosphere and feel to the large central capital compared to the small regional center, although what these qualitative differences between big and small cities might be in the aggregate is not well defined. Inkeles and Smith compared the men in their sample living in large cosmopolitan cities to men from smaller regional centers. Four of five countries showed no correlation between larger and smaller cities and stress reports; in India men in the smaller cities reported more stress. Inkeles and Smith's work suggests that there is a weak effect of urban residence on stress but no indication that larger, dense, heterogeneous, and cosmopolitan cities produce more stress.

Men in the Inkeles and Smith study who had migrated to cities from rural settings did not have higher stress scores than men who were low in migration and mobility in their recent pasts. However, what happened to the men after they arrived in the city did produce differences in stress reports. Men who ended up in more secure and higher-status jobs after migrating reported somewhat less stress than men who had been less successful. This finding is to be echoed later in this chapter when discussing correlates of differences in urban–rural stress reports—the degree of fit, or the ecologic and familial match between city and country settings, influences stress experienced by migrants in cities. Large city–country differences and relatively poor urban economic success lead to higher reported stress symptoms.

There are cautions to be kept in mind in evaluating the Inkeles and Smith data: the men surveyed were under 40 years of age; all were employed, thus narrowing the range of variation in class and types of adaptation; and no direct health measures were available. But there is certainly no evidence of a widespread, strong, stressful effect of city life among men in these six countries.

Finally, Fischer (1976, pp. 153–177) has done a recent and comprehensive review of research on the effects of cities on disorder, alienation, and psychological stress. He considered outcome measures as diverse as mental illness, suicide, alcoholism, and personality differences between city and country populations. "The conclusion is important enough to reiterate. Despite widespread notions that city life inflicts psychological damage, we have no evidence that it is so. It probably is not so" (1976, p. 169).

The Dohrenwends contrast a social stress interpretation of urban–rural differences to a social selection model. Are certain situations (lower-class membership; being a man or woman in urban society; living in the city or the country; being a member of an oppressed ethnic minority) productive of stresses and strains which in turn lead to psychopathologies? Or do men and women, migrants and nonmigrants to cities, etc., have different kinds of successful and unsuccessful adjustments to various situations, producing differential class and geographic mobility patterns, leading to selective migration between country and city, or selective upward economic mobility, etc.? Do families who move to a city from a rural, traditional community have a higher level of psychophysiologic stress than those who remain behind? Or do cities raise the level of stress in migrating families which in other respects are no different from those left in the rural community? Even more complex interpretations than these are plausible.

Assume, for example, that cities do produce more stress in mothers but that mothers who migrate to the city are more adaptable and better adjusted than those left behind; the complex interaction of both factors would produce only small differences, or no differences, in rural and urban stress and pathology. And only small differences are found in the results of the Dohrenwends' rural–urban comparison. Rabkin and Struening (1976) raise the same point in their review of life change research; not only might high life changers differ in confounding ways from nonchangers, but changers may seek medical or other help more often than nonchangers. At best, then, there is very weak support for a general rural–urban difference hypothesis.

Weisner and Abbott (1977) explored this problem by comparing women in varying life circumstances in different ethnic groups in Kenya in an attempt to examine the sociocultural contexts which produce psychosomatic stress. They used versions of the Health Opinion Survey and interviewed (1) Kikuyu women living in Nairobi as market traders, (2) Kikuyu women living in a rural horticultural community, and (3) a matched sample of Abaluyia women, some of whom did and some of whom did not commute back and forth between a rural farm and the urban residence of their husbands. These women differed in characteristics other than their urban or rural residence. The Kikuyu urban market women were economically self-supporting, while the full-time Kikuyu rural women were partially dependent on their husband's earning and/or cash crops. The Abaluyia commuting sample had little economic support other than their husbands' wage earnings and their subsistence crops. These commuting women were in contact with city life but were also part of a strong rural-urban kinship network which provided social supports and contacts with other women in similar circumstances. The rural women's husbands were often away, living and working in urban centers. These women bore the burden of maintaining the rural homesteads, plus working in cash crop or other trading activities, and dealing with their husbands' rural-resident kin.

The rural–urban matched sample did not differ on either psychophysiologic stress reports or a questionnaire measure of modernization. Weisner and Abbott comment that "the back and forth movement between city and country and Abaluyia women's economic and familial roles in the rural economy are more important than simple periodic exposure to potentially modernizing urban settings" (1977). The urban market women had stress scores lower than those of their rural counterparts and similar to those of the rural–urban network sample. Thus urban exposure did not in itself produce higher reported stress for these women; rather, the socioeconomic pressures on the women appear to be more influential in producing stress:

> It has long been proposed that urban residence is a high-stress, high-pressure environment for an African woman. It is our finding that urban residence can be much less stressful than rural residence, or equally stressful—depending on the relative autonomy, level of income, and stage in the life cycle of the individual. Urban resident women married to men employed in town who maintain rural homesteads (the urban Abaluyia women) have very different situations than urban women (such as our Kikuyu urban market women) who are independent by and large of rural ties and are essentially entrepreneurs and shopkeepers in their own right. Both differ from women tied to their homesteads through the work demands of their subsistence and cash crops (rural Kikuyu) or subsistence alone (urban Abaluyia). (Weisner & Abbott, 1977, p. 437)

In conclusion, a series of studies comparing urban and rural stress reports have not found strong and consistent differences between city and country samples. There have been some slight differences reported in some of the literature, however. Differential migration and social pressures as causes of what urban–rural differences there are have not been disentangled for stress reports. Variables such as age or sex or family status are related to the experience of stress in city and country settings but do not appear to have a consistent association with stress in city and country locations. Just what the differences are between city and country settings which might produce or reduce stress have not been clearly identified. The next section explores two such differences, which are probably the most striking contrasts between city and country settings—crowding, and life changes and mobility.

URBAN–RURAL SETTING DIFFERENCES AND STRESS

The fact that there are no large-scale measurable differences in stress between most city and country populations ends any hope of a simple ecologic comparison between the two places. This result simply forces the question to a more complex level. Since the concepts of "urban" or "rural" settings hide enormous variability, perhaps there are specific features of some urban settings, under some conditions, which do produce feelings of stress yet which are masked by global cross-cultural comparisons of cities. Further, the relevant comparison may be not strictly between city and country but rather an evaluation of the relative differences between particular urban and rural environments. Perhaps the degree or types of contrast between the two settings is more relevant for producing stress than simply comparing residents in the two places. This section explores the influence of crowding and density and of life change or mobility. Each has been implicated in increasing stress, and each is associated with some, if not all, rural–urban regional environments and urban centers. The next section looks at the question of the fit between city and country settings as an important intervening factor in producing stress in city or country dwellers.

Crowding and Density Effects

A presumed urban characteristic closely studied by psychologists and sociologists is crowding and density. It is worth discussing this variable along with the comparative reviews of urbanism and stress, since the results appear to parallel those for general reviews of global urban effects. J. Freedman (1975) reviewed the literature on direct relationships between crowding, density, and stress responses in man; he concluded that crowding does not have a clear negative or positive effect on stress:

> Controlled experiments in which density is explicitly varied [have] not found negative effects of high density. With one exception, those studies that did find overall effects of density found people responding more positively under high than low density. . . . There is no evidence from this body of work that crowding causes either stress or arousal. It does not affect task performance, it does not make people more anxious or nervous, and it certainly does not make the experiences more unpleasant. If density does have generally negative effects, they should have appeared in these careful experiments. (p. 105)

Freedman does argue that high density makes other people a more important stimulus and therefore *intensifies* typical reactions to them. Intensification, for example, would imply that a high-density situation would elicit more positive responses when the situation was positive, while negative situations would bring out a stronger negative reaction under high—compared to low—density. There is, in short, a strong density-by-affective-valence interaction effect. Freedman also points out that there are complex sex differences in responses to high- and low-density situations. The thrust of his review is that it is the salience of and responsiveness to others, rather than stress, which increases with density.

Bausano (1977, pp. 27–29) reviewed several studies of the effects of density and crowding, both social and spatial, on children, and her review supports the views of Freedman. She suggests that "experiments investigating 'crowding' and its effect on specific classes of behavior have led to contradictory results." Fischer (1976, pp. 154–164) also could find no clear effect of crowding.

Ashcraft and Scheflen (1976) illustrate the complexity of the crowding-density-stress relationship for children and families in naturalistic settings in their work on differences in the use of space among various ethnic groups in the greater New York City area. They comment on a Puerto Rican family, for example, whose members frequently congregate in the same room even if pursuing separate activities. Women and small children are often housebound through much of the day and throughout the evening hours. In fact, "in one home, the housewife did not leave the apartment during eight weeks of continuous observation. She did permit her two young boys to play in the afternoon under close supervision at the church playground" (p. 91). The Puerto Rican family members crowded together in spite of the availability of other space:

> It is not unusual then to witness a Puerto Rican family of six or seven huddled together in one room for the duration of the evening hours. In one household we recall a regular family event of the children and parents packed onto a sectional sofa watching television. After the children went to bed, the husband and wife would remain on the sofa sitting as close together as before with their arms about each other. . . . This habit of sitting close together appeared to us to be a rather consistent part of Puerto Rican home behavior. (Ashcraft & Scheflen, 1976, p. 91)

In contrast, black American families and Anglo-American families tend to spread out in their same apartments and use the whole room. They do not touch each other as much, they use different seats in the same room, and they do activities in different rooms.

Ashcraft and Scheflen are highly critical of studies which measure crowding in terms of square feet per individual, number of rooms, surrounding space of the home, use of the space available for dispersal, and so forth. In general, Ashcraft and Scheflen believe that the results of these kinds of comparisons are largely "uninformative" (p. 94). Ashcraft and Scheflen's comments on New York City building codes, which state that a child requires 60 square feet of living space, are apropos:

> The question is: how much space does a child require for which activities, at what times of the day, and in which portions of the household, and in which portions of the neighborhood that supports the living space within the confines of the household? One of the first steps involved in trying to understand human space requirements is to go where humans can carry out an activity and observe their behavior directly. (p. 192)

Ashcraft and Schflen's message for studies of urban life, families, and stress is that simple urban density measures of square feet can be misleading; that ethnic differences in usage of the same space can be an important variable; and that parent/child behaviors which might be related to some indirect estimates of stress (such as aggression, parental involvement in child disputes, privacy, and so forth) cannot be linked directly to spatial variables. The perception of the external neighborhood setting in New York City as dangerous, however, does appear to be fairly uniform —although the response by families in their use of interior design, or mobility in and out of the home, varies widely. Although this work implies that there is no density factor of powerful pancultural importance, it does not say what *does* produce the urban differences in family interaction which were observed, nor does it compare rural populations to conclusively demonstrate that there is no systematic urban spatial—ecological factor influencing family behaviors. Until this sort of work is carried further, crowding and density remain an undemonstrated urban stressor.

Life Changes, Stress, and Illness

Migrating to a town or city is a major life change. However many important intermediate and supportive institutions there may be, whatever the fit between rural and urban economic and cultural demands, and whatever the known variations in kinds of city environments around the world, the change is profound. Living in a city very likely produces more change and variety in daily life as well. The most important point to be made about life change, urbanization, and stress is how well and how successfully most people make such a change and how little major disruption there is. The great majority of people moving to cities or living in them do not become seriously or even moderately ill, and certainly do not become disabled. There may be a *relatively* greater degree of reported stress, observed medical problems, and the like, but such a finding must be seen against the general background of the overall successful adjustment characteristic of the millions of urbanizing families throughout the world. Exposure to cities as a potential stressor cannot be a sufficient condition for accounting for the onset of illness or increased stress but rather must be viewed as one among many factors and must be seen within the comparative rural–urban context.

The concept of life change, stress, and illness has an extensive literature recently reviewed by Rabkin and Struening (1976) (see also Dohrenwend & Dohrenwend, 1974a, b). Rabkin and Struening talk about the characteristics of external stressors which have been shown to influence the onset of illness. The magnitude of stressors (how far they depart from a baseline condition), the intensity or the rate of change, the length of exposure, preparedness, and absence of prior experience of the particular stressor have all been found to "heighten the impact of stressful events" (Rabkin & Struening, 1976, p. 1018).

The support systems available to individuals undergoing stress have been shown to be of great importance (see Caplan & Killilea, 1976). Rabkin and Struening mention three kinds of social supports or social network mechanisms influencing response to stress: social isolation, social marginality or minority membership, and status inconsistency (p. 1019). Living alone or in an isolated setting can in itself lead to greater vulnerability to chronic disease, for example. "Social marginality" is a more complex variable and in cross-cultural studies is particularly difficult to measure. One piece of evidence for the importance of marginality is an ecologic correlation between the sheer numerical size of a given group, or "ethnic density," and hospitalization rates for psychiatric disorder. If "a given ethnic group constitutes a smaller proportion of the total population in a particular area, diagnosed rates of mental illness increase in comparison both to the rates for other ethnic groups in that area and to the rates of the same ethnic group in neighborhoods where its members constitute a significant proportion or majority" (p. 1019).

Status inconsistency is likely to co-occur with urban migration or urban residence for newcomers to a city. Urban migrants, however, are not necessarily individuals who are always status inconsistent, especially if migration is a common part of the life cycle for members of that rural community (Weisner, 1976a). In addition, whether the status inconsistency of the occupational or employment situation is higher or lower than the family background appears to make a difference (Hinkle & Wolff, 1957). If one's current occupational and employment situation is *lower* than one's own family background, Hinkle found that illness events were greater than where there was a congruence. The same was not true for upwardly mobile individuals.

Individual characteristics are also important as mediating factors in stress—in other words, how the stressors are perceived by individuals. Internal and interpersonal mediating characteristics also influence the perception of stressors. These are summarized by Rabkin and Struening as "biological and psychological threshold sensitivities, intelligence, verbal skills, morale, personality type, psychological defenses, past experience, and a sense of mastery over one's fate" (1976, p. 1018). Glass and Singer (1972), for instance, emphasize the role of perceived control over stressors (noise, in their experiments) as a critical factor in influencing subjects' performances on complex tasks. Berry (1976), Chance (1965), and others also emphasize that the same environmental conditions may be perceived differently by different subcultural groups; these differential perceptions of a situation mediate responses to stressors. The ethnographic literature concentrates on group and cultural differences in perceptions of change and stress, while Rabkin and Struening and the Dohrenwends, reflecting a social-psychological approach, document individual differences in responsiveness. Many demographic characteristics (age, sex, and family size, for instance) have also been shown to be influential in the perception of stressful events.

Migrants to cities in developing countries, or anyone who has recently come to an urban center from a non-Western background, can be assumed to have had a significant number of changes in life experience during the recent preceding years. Rabkin and Struening suggest that there is a "modest but statistically significant relationship" between increasing life changes and physical disease, including psychosomatic symptoms (p. 1015). There is some question as to whether the measures used for studying these relationships are valid; this is thoroughly reviewed by Rabkin and Struening. In addition, it is not clear whether or not life events scores are related to onset of illness or "care-seeking behavior" (Rabkin & Struening, 1976, p. 1016). Life change may simply produce a greater likelihood of seeking medical treatment, rather than producing actual symptoms. Thus, even though

> . . . causal relations have been found between stressful life events and worsening of psychiatric conditions already existing, and between life events and subsequent admission to treatment facilities, [Hudgens] has not found it convincingly demonstrated that ordinary life events cause illness. Instead, it may be that life changes lead people to seek medical treatment, that they are equivalent, perhaps, in their etiological role to the availability of medical facilities or funds with which to pay for treatment. (Rabkin & Struening, 1976, p. 1016)

It should be noted that one of the reasons for short-term visits to cities by many mothers and children in non-Western countries is precisely to seek medical treatment. Therefore differential urban migration of mothers and children seeking treatment may produce a spurious correlation between urban residence and the likelihood of medical records, admissions, and reports of any kind.

Miller, Bentz, Aponte, and Brogan (1974) utilized a version of the life events technique to compare a group of rural and urban adults in North Carolina in their perceptions of life crises. The rank order correlation of the lists of crises was high ($\rho = 0.85$). However, the amount of readjustment these crises required was evaluated differently by urban and rural respondents. Four factors were extracted from the list of life crisis events; for each factor, a core of events was similar for city and country subjects, with others varying between the two samples. In general, differences between the two samples were related to specific features of the meaning of life crises in each context, rather than indicating a general difference in perception of stressful events in the two samples. "The urbanite from a Northwestern city and his [or her] rural counterpart may live in matrices of similar stresses, but with the dimensions of stress slightly involving some events unique to the subculture" (1974, pp. 272–273).

There are some scales of psychiatric impairment, including some stress-related items, becoming available for young children (Langner, Gersten, Eisenberg, McCarthy, Greene, Herson, Jameson, & Temkin, in press), and some work on stressful life events and children's behavior (Gersten, Langner, Eisenberg, and Orzek, 1974). Leighton (1972) measured stress levels in children in public schools in North Carolina and adapted the HOS for use with American children in a large-scale screening program setting. Suepsaman (1973) studied stress in Thai school children, but this study was unavailable for review. On the whole, the work done to date has focused on adults, with very limited attention to children specifically, or to larger family influences.

CONSISTENCY BETWEEN URBAN AND NONURBAN BELIEFS

Each of the sections to this point has given cities a rather good review: cities are not inherently stressful, and factors which often go along with urban residence (such as life changes, migration, and crowding) either have a mixed effect on stress or are as likely to produce stress in nonurban settings. The focus has thus far been on characteristics of city life which are likely to be stressful but which in fact are not or at least seem to be no more stressful in rural areas.

This section looks at the fit between cities and the rural and traditional settings from which migrants come, and particularly at the effects of differing ecologic adaptations of traditional societies and the effects of these adaptations on urban adjustment. The urban–nonurban comparative view asks about the compatibility between city and country settings and the effects of consistency or inconsistency between the two settings on stress. In this area of study, cross-cultural research seems to suggest a general hypothesis concerning the urbanizing experience and its relationship to stress: incompatibility tends to produce more stress.

Consistency and Beliefs

Leis' study of acculturation among the Ijaw provides an illustration of the use of the consistency model. Leis (1964) lists a series of acculturating traits and can see no regularity in the way in which traits have been maintained under conditions of culture contact. Leis suggests that "those traits perceived by a people as being interdependent with others, particularly with other elements unaffected by acculturation, will be less likely to change than those which are recognized by the people as being loosely related to other traits in an indigenous pattern" (p. 41). This raises an interesting question about development and social stress in urban settings.

Some urban settings and/or some traditional cultures from which people have come to cities may encourage this maintenance of an intellectual consistency among preexisting traits—that is, maintenance of a consistent folk interpretation of cultural patterns. If urbanizing cultural groups live in cohesive neighborhoods or retain their indigenous language and are otherwise able to retain these practices, survival is also likely for traditional child-rearing practices and child behaviors which are consistent with the indigenous culture. Settings where these intellectually consistent traditions of explanation are not maintained by the people themselves, or where the urban environment does not promote the use of a native language, neighborhood coresidence, strong urban kinship networks, etc., should be less likely to maintain traditional child-rearing practices.

Loss of stable sets of folk beliefs, in turn, may be related to stress. It is also possible that new urban child-rearing patterns, altered through acculturation, which cannot be subsumed into an existing explanatory system of the indigenous culture will be practiced more inconsistently and produce more stress and anxiety among parents practicing them and among the children on whom they are practiced. Although there is little evidence concerning the direct effects of differences in folk beliefs on children or stress, there are some cross-cultural studies implicating consistency and the degree of fit between traditional and modern/urban settings in reports of stress. This approach suggests that rural–urban comparisons alone find few differences in stress because it is the *relative* degree of change in life circumstances within societies that leads to greater stress.

Howard (1974, p. 183) has compared Hawaiian-American mothers and fathers on several child-rearing dimensions (obedience styles, care and affection, importance of training children, and others) in a periurban community on Oahu. Howard found a relationship between high psychosomatic stress scores on the Cornell Medical Index (CMI) and the use of material rewards and physical punishment. These relationships are not found for men's reported child-rearing styles. Howard also found that women raised in Honolulu are most likely to materially reward their children. "Perhaps," Howard says, "it is in an urban environment that the vulnerability to rejection is greater, owing to the increased ambiguities that characterize loosely knit networks" (p. 184). It is important to note, however, that Howard does not report an association between the CMI and any of the other child-rearing variables for men and women. The influence of stress appears to be limited only to increased use of physical punishment and material rewards for women. The influence of a Honolulu upbringing for women also is reported to influence use of material rewards only. This is a very modest effect, and one that is too specific to offer many general clues to urban effects on families' changing beliefs.

N. Graves (1972; also reviewed by T. Graves and Graves, 1978) compared urban and rural patterns of child rearing and beliefs about children and parenting among Spanish-American, Anglo, and African children. In her first series of studies, N. Graves contrasted rural and urban mothers' beliefs about their efficacy in influencing their children and beliefs mothers had about how malleable or teachable their children were. She found that her urban Spanish-American mothers were not uniformly adopting Anglo child-rearing methods and beliefs about children, even though these Spanish-American mothers were using Anglos as a reference group for acculturation. Denial of social access to Anglo life led to a selective rejection of new child-rearing patterns. Parental feelings and beliefs about efficacy and control of children appear to depend on class, ethnic, and power relationships between subcultures as well as urban residence or acculturation.

Howard (1966) described the adaptation of Rotuman and Fijian Islanders who have been exposed to the urbanized market economy, if not larger urban centers. Part of Howard's argument contrasts child-rearing practices between Fijian and Rotuman societies. Howard's study supports the general model that a closer fit between traditional and modern patterns of child rearing is likely to lead to better adjustment in urban-acculturative situations. Howard suggests that the "parental pressure for and reward of early achievement, an affectionate relationship between parents and children, early encouragement of independence, and low father dominance" (p. 268) are more conducive to acculturation to Western and urban norms.

Following the general model of stress and adaptation as problem solving, Howard suggests that individuals or groups whose models for decision making and whose range of problem-solving settings are broad will be better able to adjust to changing conditions than a group whose decision-making models are highly specific (p. 270):

> This brings us to a key question: How does culture, including social organization, affect the capacity of individuals to adjust to a developing economy or to acculturation circumstances in general? The answer appears to lie in the type of socialization, and hence learning, associated with different types of culture. In a culture characterized by highly specific solutions to recurrent problems, one expects rote learning to predominate and behavioral prescriptions to be explicitly and mechanically taught. To the extent that this is true, the product of learning will be an

alloplastic cognitive structure, or mazeway; i.e., one which cannot easily be altered to accommodate unusual experience or observations contrary to those previously made and incorporated. This in turn constitutes a barrier to learning new skills in acculturation circumstances. (Howard, 1966, p. 271)

The contrast to alloplastic structure is *autoplastic* cognitive development, which favors learning through a set of general principles and provides more easy readjustment to new experience.

Howard argues that Fijian children are taught the specifics of behavior and are alloplastic; in contrast, the Rotumans do not usually learn behavioral specifics and are thus more autoplastic and can learn more easily and less stressfully in novel and Western-type environments.

The alloplastic–autoplastic contrast in teaching and child-rearing styles is difficult to identify in holistic cross-cultural accounts of socialization, and their connection with learning skills (e.g., Cole & Scribner, 1974) or with stress (e.g., Weisner & Abbott, 1977) is far from conclusive. The central point is not the specific validation of Howard's types, but the importance of his design—comparing the consistency between specific features of urban and modern settings to specific situational features of traditional, rural settings.

Folk Child-rearing Beliefs and Urbanization

What happens to conventional folk wisdom when the ecologic/environmental situation may no longer be functionally appropriate for such beliefs? This problem is characteristic of any rapid environmental change, but is especially important in rural-to-urban migration. It is also critical in thinking about the consequences of urbanization for parent–child relationships. Emphasis usually has been placed on showing how conventional folk wisdom meets societal needs for training and socializing children to function effectively in traditional adult societies. In addition, these child-rearing practices have been shown to be part of, to "fit with," other aspects of social and community life. A functional, role-training approach to beliefs and child training would predict rapid change in ideals and practices in urban settings.

Several aspects of folk wisdom and child rearing practices are relevant (Whiting, 1974): (1) the *availability* of such ideas and supports for women coming to cities; (2) the *fit* between city pressures and old beliefs; and (3) the opportunities to *practice* and try out child rearing as an older child or new mother.

First, what is the nature of the social support system and availability of folk wisdom for urban and for rural/traditional mothers? Perhaps urban mothers who have no clear folk wisdom or conventional child care experience available to them, regardless of its content or urban functional utility, may act in a less confident way, or experience more anxiety, than mothers who have such folk wisdom and child care support available to them.

Second, what about folk beliefs that no longer fit? Beliefs about the importance of stern and early responsibility training for children remain unsupported when there are few responsibilities for urban tasks. Beliefs about sex differences in task performance may change when such tasks are no longer required in town and when traditional sex role differences are no longer as sharply defined. Adherence to folk beliefs that are no longer functionally appropriate may be more stressful and anxiety producing for mothers and children alike.

However, any set of folk beliefs and practices may be better than none at all. There is a constant interaction between folk beliefs, support networks, and actual experience new mothers have had with babies. There probably are many parts of folk wisdom which are pancultural or universal in their relevance and clarity (Whiting, 1974), since they are based on universal maturational states. To the extent that this is true, mothers without a support system or without any folk wisdom might be more anxious than mothers with some beliefs and training, even though the traditionally derived folk wisdom may no longer be completely relevant and appropriate. In addition, actual experience in caring for babies and young children may be better than *any* folk wisdom. Opportunities for this experience for children and adolescents may be less common in some cities, leading to less confident, more anxious mothers (and perhaps children).

STRESS AND ACCULTURATION: ECOLOGICAL DIFFERENCES

The general model in ecologic comparisons parallels that for beliefs: the greater the differences between the urban and nonurban ecology, subsistence modes, and settings, the more difficulty will be experienced in the process of acculturation or rural-to-urban migration. Again, it is not the urban settings themselves, but rather how these fit with the settings and cultures which surround them, which is the likely correlate of family stresses.

Ecological Differences: Family and Subsistence Economy

There are many ecologic variations between rural, traditional settings and cities. Those which affect the domestic group and the domestic subsistence economy and the daily routines of families appear to be the most likely candidates for affecting parents and children. Comparing the fit or consistency between city and country settings in these domains is likely to be crucial for socialization and parenting, and possibly for stress, for several reasons.

First, cross-cultural evidence indicates that differences in subsistence economy, as these in turn impinge on the domestic group and the domestic economy, are powerful predictors of general caretaking styles, caretaking practices, pressures for compliance, discipline and responsibility training, sociability, and other factors (Whiting & Whiting, 1975). If nothing else, cities and urban migration tend to alter subsistence economy patterns. To the extent that we can generalize about differences between rural and urban subsistence economies, domestic economies, and daily routines, some testable questions can be raised about the effect of cities on cross-cultural human development and socialization of children.

Variables closely related to these urban–rural differences include the availability of the father during the day, evening, and weekends; the availability of school-age versus nonschool-age children for child care; the availability of the mother during the day; the kinds of tasks and subsistence pressures on women and children alike in city versus country settings; the specific kinds of tasks that family members are asked to perform, especially the ability to perform them independently; the modes by which they are learned; sex differences in their practice and responsibility; and others. It is likely to be in the economic-subsistence domain where the clearest urban–rural differences occur and where available cross-cultural data already show powerful effects on socialization.

Second, these subsistence and daily routine variations are likely to go along with a whole series of changes in the household and in the organization of the family. Such contrasts include the personnel present in the home and the distinction between smaller nuclear and expanded/extended family organizations. To the extent that cities contain families with a nuclear form, with fewer household members actually resident, and with a differing set of normative responsibilities for mothers and fathers within the family unit, cross-cultural research on the influence of family organization on socialization patterns again predicts effects on families and parenting. There is some indication that nuclear households tend to have lower compliance pressures; more shared and "democratic" decision making; more parent–child, especially mother–child, interaction; more verbal interaction; and increased rates of "egoistic" or seeking and requesting behaviors from children (Whiting & Whiting, 1975).

Reductions in family size, especially in the numbers of nonparental and older siblings present, alter the shared caretaking patterns characteristic of extended family settings in rural communities. Mothers have less help in child care from older siblings, who are either in formal schools part of the day or who may less often be living in the city. Weisner (1976b), for instance, found that urban migrant families with rural homes tended to keep their older children on the farm for several purposes—assisting in agricultural work, attending rural schools taught in the native tribal language, or saving the high costs of maintaining children in the city.

N. Graves (1972) looked at maternal child care beliefs and situational pressures in Uganda, using a single African ethnic group, the Baganda, in urban and rural settings. She also studied Anglos and Spanish speakers in Colorado. Graves studied a series of urban "situational constraints" (such as crowding, external dangers for small children, and others) which might account for mothers' feelings of efficacy and control. The Baganda had little direct acculturation experience with a dominant group and were in fact themselves the dominant tribal group in Uganda. Thus to some extent acculturation variables were controlled, and Graves was able to directly look at urban–rural differences by comparing rural Baganda from Masaka district with those in Kampala:

> When the results were analyzed, I found that as suspected the Baganda lower-income mothers had almost no exposure to Anglos and did not identify with them at all. Rural and Urban Baganda were no different in their norms of child rearing, but they differed strongly in the type of child they valued, in their expectations of success in getting such a child, and in their use of future-oriented techniques. In general, the more urban experience a Baganda mother had, the less control she felt and the fewer future-oriented teaching methods she employed with her children. (T. Graves & Graves, 1978, pp. 545–546)

Both Baganda and Spanish mothers complained of crowded city conditions, indoors and out, of physical dangers and bad social influences, and of urban "pleasures" which lured the fathers away from home. They were left alone to cope with the household and small children more often than in country settings, and this may have led to a "harassment" syndrome among urban mothers, since for both city and country groups the more preschool children the mother had in the home, the stronger the effects on child rearing (p. 546).

Graves' study is unusual in that it deals with the mutual effects of ethnicity, acculturation, and urban situational stressors. Unfortunately, however, there are no direct measures of maternal or child stress. Mothers who felt they had little influence on their children's lives and fates as adults *seem* to have experienced more stress or more difficulties and anxieties as parents, but there is no direct way to tell. Graves' ethnographic and interview materials tend to suggest that the urban mothers did feel concerned and disturbed by their urban situation. Whiting (1976, p. 102) emphasizes that new anxieties and responsibilities for women fall on rural resident mothers whose husbands are away in cities as well as on women who move to the city for periods of time with their husband and young children.

Weisner (1979) found a number of clear differences between children and mothers living in Nairobi, Kenya, and in a rural horticultural area in Western Kenya. These behavioral and child care differences were related to differences in subsistence tasks and daily routines in the two locations; changes in family personnel (such as fewer older siblings); and the absence of a kin-based neighborhood organization. Urban-resident children engage in less sociable behavior than do rural children and are more often acting dominantly and aggressively toward their siblings. However, the mothers of these children were not significantly different in their reported psychophysiologic stress compared to a matched sample of rural mothers, nor were they significantly more modern as measured by the modernization scale developed by Inkeles (Weisner & Abbott, 1977). The rural comparison sample had also had considerable urban experience; thus the absence of rural–urban acculturative or stress differences in this particular sample does not reflect a comparison between widely different groups. Although there are clear behavioral changes in children's and mothers' urban and rural behaviors, these are not necessarily accompanied by significanctly more reported stress.

Watson (1968) compared a group of rural, pastoral Guajiro in Venezuela to a group of Guajiro who had spent most or all of their lives in Maracaibo, the capital city. Watson's study represents one of the most detailed studies of socialization and child training comparing rural and urban populations. The traditional socialization complex of the Guajiro includes severe socialization of (1) obedience-compliance, (2) responsibility, (3) vulnerability-dependence, (4) peer- and parent-directed aggression, and (5) low parental warmth (Watson, 1968, p. 79).

Rural Guajiro raise livestock and have minor horticultural and wage work supplements to their pastoral subsistence economy. Urban Guajiro in Watson's sample live in a crowded, low-income barrio occupied largely by Guajiro migrants. Conjugal families subsist on a man's wage earnings, which are often not regular and which take men away from the barrio for extended periods of time for wage labor. Few women are employed, and the father-absent mother–child domestic unit is common in the urban barrio (Watson, 1968, pp. 118–119). Watson lists factors which distinguish urban from rural Guajiro life and which are critical to differences in socialization practices: (1) competitive wage labor replaces pastoralism; (2) urban parents are powerless to control economic resources; (3) there is "disintegration" (p. 131) of the corporate descent group and of interlineage relationships; (4) the conjugal and mother–child family replaces a traditional matrilocal extended family; (5) the mother's economic contribution to the urban family is unimportant compared to that of other family members; (6) bride-payment in cattle disappears in the city; (7) rigid socioeconomic distinctions characteristic of rural life disappear in more egalitarian urban society; and (8) formal education replaces acquisition of cattle or kinship status as a mode of achievement (pp. 129–136).

Each of these characteristics, Watson suggests, has specific effects on the socialization pressures on boys and girls. For example, Watson argues that a mother who no longer made important economic contributions to the home "would be less effective in socializing obedience-compliance and parent-directed aggression because of her inability to invoke strong economic sanctions" (p. 134). Among rural pastoral Guajiro, maintenance and care of the family herds by children is a very important responsibility. Since the family as a unit no longer controls property, there is less parental pressure to train children to be responsible and diligent in task performance. "Training the girl in domestic skills, however, represents something of an exception to this, since it constitutes a direct preparation in many individual cases for the role in life which will eventually be assumed, as in tribal culture" (p. 135).

Watson did not measure or comment on the stressful or anxiety-producing consequences of these urban–rural differences, although he suggests that the life of the urban mother and child is made more difficult because of the wide gap between urban and rural subsistence and family patterns. As in Weisner's and Graves' work, Watson did identify a number of differences in children's behaviors and personality indicators in comparing his rural and urban samples.

Stress, Acculturation, and Ecological Differences

The rural–urban comparisons which emphasize the relative contrast between city and country usually have not measured stress reports directly. Berry and Annis (1974) and Berry (1976), in a series of studies, have compared ecology, acculturation, and stress measures in a number of societies. Although not focused directly on child rearing and children, this work provides further support for the hypothesis that it is the fit between rural and urban settings, and the degree of contrast between them, that is most directly related to familial stress. Berry suggests that acculturative stress experienced by individuals varies as a function of the traditional cultures which characterize a community and as a function of acculturative influences. The greater the disparity in culture and behavior between the two, traditional and modern, the greater will be the stress.

For example, Berry suggests that low-food-accumulation societies will experience more stress than will high-food-accumulation societies. Berry and Annis emphasize food accumulation because low-food-accumulating societies also have low population density and small settlement units and are often migratory, while high-food-accumulating societies are agriculturalists, have higher densities and larger settlement units, and are sedentary (p. 386). There is usually more social stratification evident in the high-food-accumulating societies as well. Achievement, self-reliance, and independence or assertion training appear more important for low-food-accumulating societies, whereas responsibility and compliance appear more important for high-food-accumulation societies (Barry, Child, & Bacon, 1959). Ecological characteristics of the traditional habitats, with fewer similarities to more modern or town settings, should produce more stress. On the side of the more modern, contact culture, Berry emphasizes the density, employment, education, and "urban factors" which characterize the acculturative setting.

Berry defines acculturative stress to relate specifically to culture contact between groups and to refer specifically to affective states or behaviors relating to mental health. Berry and Annis operationalize acculturative stress by using a 20-item psychosomatic checklist for stress, a scale of cultural marginality, and a scale of deviance.

Berry (1976) reviews all of these relationships for a sample of over 40 individuals in each of a widely differing group of native American cultures. Generally, each of the hypotheses was supported: what Berry calls "loose" societies—those based on low food accumulation, hunting, migratory or mobile settlement patterns, and relatively unstratified, egalitarian forms of social organization—had higher stress scores under conditions of Western acculturation and urbanization than did the contrasting "tight" societies. Individuals with more Western education reported fewer stress symptoms than did those with less education, but this effect was true within culture samples more than across the samples. Berry (1976) suggests that "there may be a curvilinear relationship between education in particular (and acculturation level more generally) and the experience of acculturative stress" (p. 190). The level of acculturation of Berry's samples was negatively related to reported stress—that is, at the individual level, more acculturated respondents reported fewer stress symptoms. At the group or cultural level, however, where acculturative influences and ecocultural variations could be directly pitted against each other, the ecocultural variable (loose versus tight societal type) was more strongly related to stress levels.

Finally, Berry's data indicate that individuals with higher scores on measures of psychological differentiation reported fewer stress symptoms across all the societies where both stress and differentiation were tested. He suggests that one intervening variable influencing the stress experienced during acculturation and urbanization is the degree of "psychological differentiation" and field independence. Differentiation is hypothesized by Berry to be related to increase in cultural complexity and has perceptual, cognitive, social functioning, and affective components. Although there are many problems in measuring and conceptualizing psychological differentiation cross-culturally, there does appear to be some relationships between individuals scoring higher on differentiation tests and lower stress reports.

Berry's hypotheses suggest some testable predictions for urban-rural studies of stress and acculturation. Children in urban settings, for example, who are relatively high on scores of field independence and psychological differentiation should experience *less* stress across different urbanizing and acculturating situations than children who are more field dependent. The traditional cultures of origin as well as the urban setting could be ranked and compared on the relative difference score between the two settings. The more similar the two settings are, the less children's field independence or dependence should matter. In addition, traditional cultures may differ in their pressure toward field independence or dependence, and the relative acculturative stress should be measurable in these environments as well. If urban settings generally promote field independence (for which there is some evidence), children who have lived in cities longer should, on these grounds alone, show less acculturative stress. However, this relationship will be mediated through the *parents'* stress level. Parents migrating to an urban center who are (relatively) field dependent, where there is a large gap between urban and rural settings, may socialize and train their children differentially regardless of the child's own field dependence or independence. Relationships here are complex, and there are really no data available at the present to disentangle all the relevant factors involved.

Berry (1976, p. 192–193) and Chance (1965) both find women generally reporting higher psychophysiologic stress symptoms than men, but the sex differences interact with the ecological level of the culture. Women in Berry's "loose" hunting and migratory societies with little social stratification are only slightly more likely to report higher stress symptoms than men, whereas women in the "tight," more highly stratified horticultural societies show much greater differences than men. These data indicate that social role expectations and the culturally defined status of women play an important role in creating stress in women. Since women in Western societies also generally report more stress symptoms than men, there is evidence here for both cultural-ecologic and pancultural sex differences in stress during periods of social change, including urbanization.

These sex differences in reports of stress might also be due to differences in styles of self-disclosure. Women may be more willing to "admit" that they are feeling anxious, or have trouble sleeping, or sometimes sweat or tremble in difficult situations. Women (or men) able to talk about these stress-related symptoms may be less likely to suffer from them as much as someone with similar symptoms who must continually deny them to others. One paradoxic result of this line of argument is that men or women who are able to state that they do indeed have these symptoms, although scoring higher on an overall measure of stress, may in fact suffer less, since they are able to talk about them with others. Mothers able to talk with others about their children's and their own parenting problems certainly experience relief in the sharing and exchange of folk wisdom which results. This entire area of the meaning of stress report scores as a measure is considered in the next section; these speculative comments on the interpretation of sex differences in reports remain for further research to disentangle.

SUMMARY

The focus in this section has been on comparative work which looked at stress reports in terms of the consistency between traditional and acculturating (including urban) settings. The general pattern of findings indicates that the greater the differences between traditional and acculturative settings, the higher the reported psychophysiologic stress tends to be. Some of the global cross-cultural factors likely to influence stress responses during acculturation in urban settings include the ecologic and subsistence modes of the traditional cultural environment (those more different from urban settings produce more stress); global measures of psychological differentiation (more differentiated individuals possibly are more adaptive to stressful settings); levels of acculturation and education (generally a small, negative relationship between reported stress and these variables); and the *relative* degree of acculturation or stress within a given ecologic level (not the absolute level).

CONCLUSIONS: DIRECTIONS FOR FUTURE RESEARCH

Cross-cultural Measures of Stress

The reliance on the one-time, self-report psychophysiologic stress questionnaire in comparative work, and the few alternative field measures available in a form for relatively easy use, is startling. This may be a credit to the clarity, ease of use, and face validity of such items and such a technique, but serious questions as to its validity and usefulness as a measure of stable characteristics persist. Kennedy (1973, pp. 1121–1134) reviews cross-cultural epidemiologic research methods and instruments, many of which use a version of a stress measure. His review is a litany of the potential sources of bias and error in the field. Kennedy concludes by suggesting that "the best approaches will combine the intensive long-term techniques of anthropological observations of groups with the clinical methods of psychiatry" (p. 1185). He also advocates longitudinal work, studies of folk views of disorder, and the use of "culture-free" biochemical or other physiologic measures for purposes of diagnosis.

The psychophysiologic self-report instruments have an important use, and the evidence is fairly good that the methodologic problems are balanced by some pancultural validity in items, but additional, alternative measures of stress among adults and children in cross-cultural research must be developed. As Berry and Inkeles both point out, it may well be true that methods sufficient for cultural-level comparisons using aggregate data may not be usable for intracultural, individual-level data used for inferring stable characteristics in longitudinal studies of a community. However this may be resolved, comparative work on stress and stressors in families must be based on more and improved measures.

Abbott (1977) has looked at the Health Opinion Survey psychosomatic items for sex differences in responses. Surprisingly little work in item analysis has been done on the HOS. Abbott's preliminary work indicates that 13 of 20 items from her sample of Kikuyu men and women do differ by sex. Women tend to report that they are bothered by items related to feelings of depression or hysteria, such as "Don't feel healthy enough to carry out things I want to do," "Trouble sleeping," "Shaky hands," and "Sometimes wonders if anything is worthwhile." Men's frequent items were more related to anxiety with some hysterical and hypochondriacal items as well, such as "tends to feel tired in the morning," "Feels in poor spirits," and "Has trouble breathing when not exerting self." Abbott attempts to relate these different responses to the social pressures men and women are experiencing in rural Kikuyuland. This type of search for specific social situations likely to produce specific kinds of stress-related responses is an important step in both validating and "contextualizing" self-report measures like the HOS.

Howard and Scott's (1965) framework for conceptualizing stress as the product of microadaptation to specific life problems in defined sociocultural settings is a valuable definition for naturalistic studies of stress, but one which has not as yet led to effective measures of different types of adaptation or the resultant problem-solving stress experienced. The study of the personal experiences of specific settings within which parents and children live in cities, and the adaptive problems faced, is a vital next task for the cross-cultural study of stress and urbanization.

Direct Rural–Urban Comparisons of Socialization

Inkeles could not find features of cities which were associated with differences in stress reports. It is no less difficult to find urban–rural situational differences in child-rearing patterns, since there are so few studies which directly compare child rearing and stress in rural and urban settings. The need for a better understanding of just how children and parents differ in matched city and country settings is as great as the need for better measures of stress.

The linkage between urban settings, acculturation and ethnicity, on the one hand, and the specifics of child rearing and mothers' and children's attitudes and feelings, on the other, is very complex. Ethnic homogeneity and rural–urban attachments neutralized stress reports in the Kenya rural–urban study of Weisner, although there were clear changes in children's and mother's social behaviors. Howard (1974) showed specific effects of intraurban variations in Hawaiian-American families in stress reports, but these differ for men and women and are influenced by socioeconomic status. Graves' work is the most detailed and careful in showing the interaction of ethnicity (Spanish-American versus Anglo versus Baganda), levels of acculturation, and urban experience, but the outcomes for measures such as mothers' feelings of efficacy in urban settings and mothers' beliefs about their abilities to control their environment and their children's development are not consistently affected by city life. Hence urban "situational factors" clearly play a role in affecting mothers' and children's feelings and behaviors, but the direction of the effect and its strength cannot be predicted using city residence alone.

Folk and Child Experience of Urban Settings

A central issue in cross-cultural research (certainly such research in anthropology) is the relevance of the individual's own perception of a situation. In the case of a child in a city, urban social-ecologic experiences are filtered through the family; through a larger network within which the family is embedded in the neighborhood and community; and through formal institutions, most preeminently public schools. This methodologic and theoretical orientation in cross-cultural work in anthropology raises at the most fundamental level our perceptions of what cities, as an ecologic, cross-cultural unit, are like in the sense of how they are perceived and lived in by children.

Sociology tells us that cities are dense, complex, heterogeneous, and very large in both size and numbers. Secondary consequences of these physical and population traits of cities may include feelings of isolation and individuation, loss of a multiplex relationship network and such a network's replacement with a series of autonomous, individualized dyadic interactions with strangers, an increased feeling of cosmopolitanism, etc. Looking at the city from the point of view of a maturing child casts serious doubt on the conventional wisdom of what cities are supposed to be like and what influences they are supposed to have. Much research on cities has been designed to study the consequences of size, density, complexity, heterogeneity, and so forth, with their presumed effects on family life, or stress, or acculturation, or whatever. This *ecologic* definition of cities' effects may itself be a variable and may be seriously called into question when we look at the effects of cities on children, taking the *child's* point of view. From a child's point of view, cities may be homogenous socially, may be quiet, may be relatively less complex and elaborate in demands than the rural setting (or at least have qualitatively different sets of demands), and may be no "larger" in appearance or size than many rural or traditional areas. Cities, suburbs, and rural areas are not uniform and may well not provide the ecologic stimulation cities are supposed to encourage. Thus one question raised in this review is, How are the details of city life actually perceived and experienced by children? The very limited available evidence suggests that when education, income differences, and other confounding influences are removed, cities can have familial and ecologic consequences on children running the range from "rural" to the "urban" ends of the ideal ecologic continuum. Thus it is an empirical question whether or not "size, complexity, and heterogeneity" even exist in the child's world. This empirical and descriptive issue must be considered before considering the question of the influence of "urban" environmental features or stress in children.

Future work on city life, children, and stress should focus on the relative contribution of urban situational factors in the context of these other, highly related variables. In addition, urban studies in cross-cultural settings should return to some of the central issues which have been important in cross-cultural work in human development in traditional societies: close naturalistic description of the actual urban situation children and their parents find themselves in; the role of folk beliefs and folk wisdom in integrating attitudes and practices of child rearing; and the role of cities in altering the subsistence mode of the family and the personnel available to care for and shape children. The importance of these issues in other cross-cultural studies of socialization, the clear evidence for the influence of acculturation and folk beliefs interacting with urban situational effects, and the absence of uniform, pancultural urban influences on stress suggest a reduction in large-scale survey work on stress and cities and an increase in intensive, naturalistic, contextual studies of the family and stress in urban settings.

REFERENCES

Abbott, S. *Studies in Kikuyu personality: Sex differences in response to the health opinion survey.* Paper presented at the Annual Meeting, American Anthropological Association, Houston, November 1977.

Appley, M., & Trumbull, R. (Eds.). *Psychological stress; Issues in research.* New York: Appleton-Century-Crofts, 1967.

Ashcraft, N., & Scheflen, A. E. *People space: The making and breaking of human boundaries.* Garden City, N.Y.: Anchor Press, 1976.

Barry, H., Child, I., & Bacon, M. Relation of child training to subsistence economy. *American Anthropologist,* 1959, *61,* 51–63.

Bascom, W. R. Urbanization among the Yoruba. *American Journal of Sociology,* 1955, *60,* 446–454.

Basham, R. *Urban anthropology: The cross-cultural study of complex societies.* Palo Alto, Calif.: Mayfield Publishing, 1978.

Bausano, M. O. *Contributions of environmental psychology in child behavior research.* Unpublished manuscript, 1977.

Berry, J. W. *Human ecology and cognitive style: Comparative studies in cultural and psychological adaptation.* New York: John Wiley & Sons, 1976.

Berry, J. W., & Annis, R. C. Acculturative stress: The role of ecology, culture and differentiation. *Journal of Cross-Cultural Psychology,* 1974, *5,* 382–406.

Caplan, G., & Killilea, M. (Eds.). *Support systems and mutual help: Multidisciplinary explorations.* New York: Grune & Stratton, 1976.

Chance, N. A. Acculturation, self-identification, and personality adjustment. *American Anthropologist,* 1965, *67,* 372–393.

Cole, M., & Scribner, S. *Culture and thought—A psychological introduction.* New York: John Wiley & Sons, 1974.

Dohrenwend, B. P., & Dohrenwend, B. S. Social status and psychological disorder: A causal inquiry. New York: John Wiley & Sons, 1969.

Dohrenwend, B. P., & Dohrenwend, B. S. Social and cultural influences on psychopathology. *Annual Review of Psychology,* 1974, *25,* 417–452 (a).

Dohrenwend, B. S., & Dohrenwend, B. P. (Eds.). *Stressful life events: Their nature and effects.* New York: John Wiley & Sons, 1974 (b).

Fava, S. F. (Ed.). *Urbanism in world perspective: A reader.* New York: Crowell, 1968.

Fischer, C. S. *The urban experience.* New York: Harcourt Brace Jovanovich, 1976.

Fox, R. G. *Urban anthropology: Cities in their cultural settings.* Englewood Cliffs, N.J.: Prentice-Hall, 1977.

Freedman, D. G. *Human infancy: An evolutionary perspective.* Hillsdale, N.J.: Lawrence Erlbaum, 1974.

Freedman, J. L. *Crowding and behavior.* San Francisco: Freeman, 1975.

Gersten, J. C., Langner, T. S., Eisenberg, J. G., & Orzek, L. Child behavior and life events: Undesirable change or change per se? In B. S. Dohrenwend & B. P. Dohrenwend (Eds.), *Stressful life events: Their nature and effects.* New York: John Wiley & Sons, 1974.

Glass, D., & Singer, J. *Urban stress.* New York: Academic Press, 1972.

Graves, N. B. *City, country, and child rearing: A tri-cultural study of mother-child relationships in varying environments.* Unpublished manuscript, 1972.

Graves, T. D., & Graves, N. B. Evolving strategies in the study of culture change. In G. D. Spindler (Ed.), *The making of psychological anthropology.* Berkeley: University of California Press, 1978.

Gulick, J. Urban anthropology. In J. J. Honigmann (Ed.), *Handbook of social and cultural anthropology.* Chicago: Rand McNally, 1973.

Hinkle, L. E., & Wolff, H. G. Health and the social environment: Experimental investigations. In A. Leighton, J. Clausen, & R. Wilson (Eds.), *Explorations in social psychiatry.* New York: Basic Books, 1957.

Howard, A. Plasticity, achievement and adaptations in developing economics. *Human Organization,* 1966, *25,* 265–272.

Howard, A. *Ain't no big thing: Coping strategies in a Hawaiian-American community.* Honolulu: University Press of Hawaii, 1974.

Howard, A., & Scott, R. A. A proposed framework for the analysis of stress in the human organism. *Behavioral Science,* 1965, *10,* 141–160.

Inkeles, A., & Smith, D. H. The fate of personal adjustment in the process of modernization. *International Journal of Comparative Sociology,* 1970, *11,* 81–114.

Inkeles, A., & Smith, D. H. *Becoming modern: Individual change in six developing countries.* Cambridge, Mass.: Harvard University Press, 1974.

Kaunda, K. *Letter to my children.* London: Longman Publishers, 1973.

Kennedy, J. G. Cultural psychiatry. In J. J. Honigman (Ed.), *Handbook of social and cultural anthropology.* Chicago: Rand-McNally, 1973.

Landauer, T. K., & Whiting, J. W. M. Infantile stimulation and adult stature of human males. *American Anthropologist,* 1964, *66,* 1007–1028.

Langner, T. S., Gersten, J., Eisenberg, J. G., McCarthy, E. D., Greene, E. L., Herson, J. H., Jameson, J. D., & Temkin, S. M. A screening score for assessing psychiatric impairment in children six to eighteen. In R. Prince & H. G. M. Murphy (Eds.), *Brief psychosocial stress measures for community studies.* Baltimore: National Education Consultants, in press.

Langner, T. S. A twenty-two item screening score of psychiatric symptoms indicating impairment. *Journal of Health and Human Behavior,* 1962, *3,* 269.

Leighton, D. C. Measuring stress levels in school children as a program-monitoring device. *American Journal of Public Health,* 1972, *62,* 799–806.

Leis, P. E. Ijaw enculturation: A reexamination of the early learning hypothesis. *Southwestern Journal of Anthropology,* 1964, *20,* 32–41.

Lloyd, P. C. The Yoruba: An urban people? In A. Southall (Ed.), *Urban anthropology: Cross-cultural studies of urbanization.* New York: Oxford University Press, 1973.

Lofland, L. H. The "thereness" of women: A selective review of urban sociology. In M. Millman & R. M. Kanter (Eds.), *Another voice: Feminist perspectives on social life and social science.* Garden City, N.Y.: Anchor Press, 1975.

MacMillan, A. M. The health opinion survey: Techniques for estimating prevalence of psychoneurotic and related types of disorder in communities. *Psychological Reports: Monograph Supplement,* 1957, *7,* 325–339.

Mayer, P. *Townsmen or tribesmen* (2nd ed.). Capetown: Oxford University Press, 1971.

Miller, F. T., Bentz, W. K., Aponte, J. F., & Brogan, D. R. Perception of life crisis events: A comparative study of rural and urban samples. In B. S. Dohrenwend & B. P. Dohrenwend (Eds.), *Stressful life events: Their nature and effects.* New York: John Wiley & Sons, 1974.

Rabkin, J. G., & Struening, E. L. Life events, stress, and illness. *Science,* 1976, *194,* 1013–1020.

Rowe, W. L. Caste, kinship, and association in urban India. In A. Southall (Ed.), *Urban anthropology: Cross-cultural studies of urbanization.* New York: Oxford University Press, 1973.

Selye, H. *The stress of life.* New York: McGraw-Hill, 1956.

Seymour, S. Caste/class and child-rearing in a changing Indian town. *American Ethnologist,* 1976, *3,* 783–796.

Southall, A. (Ed.). *Urban anthropology: Cross-cultural studies of urbanization.* New York: Oxford University Press, 1973.

Suepsaman, B. *The study of stress in Thai children: An epidemiological study of school children in Bangkok, Thailand.* Unpublished doctoral dissertation, University of North Carolina at Chapel Hill, 1973.

Walton, J., & Carns, D. E. *Cities in change: Studies on the urban condition.* Boston: Allyn & Bacon, 1973.

Watson, L. C. *Guajiro personality & urbanization.* Los Angeles: University of California at Los Angeles, Latin American Center, 1968.

Weisner, T. S. The structure of sociability: Urban migration and rural-urban ties in Kenya. *Urban Anthropology,* 1976, *5,* 199–223 (a).

Weisner, T. S. Consequences of rural-urban migration for families and children in Kenya: Some results and suggested research orientations. *Kenya Education Review,* 1976, *3,* 108–114 (b).

Weisner, T. S. Urban-rural differences in sociable, aggressive and dominant behaviors of Kenya children. *Ethnology,* 1979, *18,* 153–172.

Weisner, T. S., & Abbott, S. Women, modernity and stress: Three contrasting contexts for change in East Africa. *Journal of Anthropological Research,* 1977, *33,* 421–451.

Whiting, B. Folk wisdom and child rearing. *Merrill-Palmer Quarterly of Behavior and Development,* 1974, *20,* 9–19.

Whiting, B. Rapid social change: Threat or promise? *Kenya Education Review,* 1976, *3,* 99–104.

Whiting, B. B., & Whiting, J. W. M. *Children of six cultures: A psycho-cultural analysis.* Cambridge, Mass.: Harvard University Press, 1975.

26

Abnormal Behavior in Traditional Societies: Labels, Explanations, and Social Reactions

Jane M. Murphy

For nearly 50 years anthropologists have been concerned with questions about abnormal behavior which largely grew out of the work of Ruth Benedict. Benedict (1934) indicated that "most people are shaped to the form of their culture by the enormous malleability of their original endowment" (p. 254). It was her view that all aspects of behavior reflected such plasticity to the "moulding force of culture" and, further, that the shaped behavior which was appropriate and normal to one group could be the abnormal behavior of another group.

Some of the questions of concern are these: How much malleability is enormous malleability? What portion of a population constitutes "most people?" Are there *any* commonalities of abnormal behavior across cultures?

It is not surprising that the answers which have been formulated are partial and complex. Considerably more empirical work now exists regarding normal behavior in different cultural settings than abnormal. I interpret such work as showing that some forms of behavior *are* more plastic than others and that the *mixture* of original endowment and cultural patterning is a great deal more prominent in the findings to date than the weight of one source versus the other.

Caudill's (1972) research, for example, comparing Japanese and American infants by carefully controlled observational methods suggests that some behaviors are similar in the two cultures while others are sufficiently different to say that the "infants have learned some of the rudiments of their respective culture by three to four months of age" and that such learning "takes place well before the development of the ability to use language in the ordinary sense" (p. 43). In the two countries, babies spend about the same amount of time feeding, and in both they spend about the same amount asleep. When unattended by their mothers, the infants have similar rhythms of sleep; that is, they change from being asleep to awake and from being awake to asleep with approximately the same frequency. The behaviors which vary

809

by culture involve mainly vocalization patterns. These appear to be conditioned as a response to the different styles of caregiving typical of Japanese as compared to American mothers.

If human malleability is enormous, why are not the amount and rhythm of sleep also shaped to match the cultural form? The interpretation given by Caudill is that the patterns which show a basic similarity across cultures are those rooted in biologic functioning, while those which vary are by definition cultural. The point of relevance here, however, is that research such as this leads the way for thinking concretely about behavior as a complex phenomenon and provides some information about the potentially malleable and the potentially nonmalleable components of behavior, the potentially highly malleable and the potentially less malleable.

Where abnormal behavior is concerned, there are fewer cross-cultural investigations available to give evidence about how Benedict's ideas *have* or *have not* borne the test of time. Added to this circumstance is the fact that there has recently occurred in psychiatry, psychology, and sociology a recrudescence of interest in cultural relativity, especially as it can be related to mental illness. This interest has come to be called the labeling orientation. A fundamental tenet of labeling is that what is abnormal in one group is normal in another; that mental illness is a myth (Szasz, 1961). Such proponents of this approach as the psychologist Rosenhan (1973) and the sociologists Scheff (1966) and Lemert (1967) explicitly affiliate their work with the anthropological tradition of Benedict.

Scheff's theoretical statements are illustrative. He suggests that "the culture of the group provides a vocabulary of terms for categorizing many norm violations" (p. 33). These designate deviations such as crime and drunkenness. There remains a residual category of diverse kinds of deviations which constitute an affront to the unconscious definition of decency and reality uniquely characteristic of each culture. He posits that the "culture provides no explicit label" for these deviations. Nevertheless, these residual violations form in the minds of societal agents as "stereotypes of insanity." When other people around a deviant respond to him or her in terms of these stereotypes, her or "his amorphous and unstructured rule-breaking tends to crystallize in conformity to these expectations" (p. 82). Scheff further suggests that these cultural stereotypes tend to produce uniformity of symptoms within a cultural group and "enormous differences in the manifest symptoms of stable mental disorder between societies" (p. 82).

The purpose of this chapter is to report studies I have carried out on this topic and to put my work in context with other anthropological investigations on this issue. The point I will make is that my work and my interpretation of the now-expanding literature on this theme suggests that cultural relativity has been greatly overemphasized in regard to mental illness, especially psychotic illness. In cross-cultural investigations of abnormal behavior, there is a parallel to the studies on normal behavior in that the results seem consistently to point to very complex blendings of genetic, biologic, psychological, social, and cultural factors. The challenge now is to bear these factors in mind at one time and in one frame of reference.

In using Benedict as the starting point for this review, it seems appropriate to acknowledge that we are following a scientific trajectory which was well described by Geertz (1973) when he said, "Scientific advancement commonly consists in a progressive complication of what once seemed a beautifully simple set of notions but now seems an unbearably simplistic one" (p. 33).

DESCRIPTION OF A COMPARATIVE STUDY

The data to be presented derive mainly from a year of field work in a village of Yupik-speaking Eskimos on an island in the Bering Sea in 1954-1955 and investigations among Egba Yorubas of Nigeria in 1961 and 1963. I have also had some opportunities for cross-checking observations in other areas: Gambia, Sudan, and South Vietnam. There was, however, no design in the choice of these areas, but merely the happenstance of history, opportunity, and the desire to compare contrasting groups.

The kind of field work on which I draw for this analysis is traditional to anthropology. It is basically the ethnographic method involving participant observation, interviewing key people, and voluminous daily recordings of events, comments, and observations. It does, however, represent a new trend in anthropology which is shown by increased attention to the need for sampling times, places, and persons to strengthen the base for generalization. Among the anthropologists interested in mental illness, this trend is equally exemplified, for example, by Edgerton (1966), Graves (1974), and Levy and Kunitz (1974).

Because *concepts* of abnormality constituted a central point of interest, much of my data derived from a variety of interviewing techniques. In this regard it has some affiliation with the procedures of ethnoscience.

In the Eskimo study, some of the data came from a key person whom I systematically interviewed regarding the life experiences of the 499 Eskimos who constituted a total village census for the 15 years previous to and including the year of investigation. This procedure took 5 months, and during it I made use of a dictionary of Eskimo words for illness and deviance developed by Hughes (1960). The census also provided a structure for accumulating and coordinating comments and observations about these nearly 500 individuals by a wide selection of Eskimos in addition to the one who reviewed the whole census. I originally used these and other materials for an epidemiologic assessment of the 348 individuals living in the village in 1955 (Murphy, 1960; Murphy & Leighton, 1965).

The approach among the Yorubas was different in that I first worked with a group of three native healers and a member of an indigenous cult (A. Leighton & Murphy, 1964). These interviews began at a more abstract level, being concerned initially with an attempt to understand Yoruba concepts of abnormal behavior in a general way. It turned out to be more satisfying, however, to move to the specific mode characteristic of the Eskimo study. Most of what the Yoruba healers described concerned their actual patients and acquaintances. Following this period of interviewing, I participated in a larger study carried out in 1961 with a group of Nigerian and U.S. colleagues in which we gathered data about 416 Yoruba adults, some of them patients in a mental hospital, some patients of native healers, and 245 of whom constitute representative samples of 14 villages (A. Leighton, Lambo, Hughes, D. Leighton, Murphy, & Macklin, 1963).

In the Yoruba study we made use of a structured questionnaire which we had been developing for community studies of mental illness and which we had been adapting for cross-cultural investigations. We had also used such a technique in an exploratory way among the Eskimos (Murphy & Hughes, 1965). Because of the interest here in Eskimo and Yoruba concepts of abnormality and how these groups label mental illness, I draw only from those sources in which an Eskimo or Yoruba described another Eskimo or Yoruba rather than what anyone said about his or her own experiences and feelings in response to a questionnaire item. To supplement this I have in some instances added my own observations about a person who was indigenously labeled as abnormal, or what such a person said to me in circumstances other than a structured interview. A main resource for this approach in the Yoruba study was that we had interviewed the bale—the headman—of each village about each sample member. This provided a systematic outside assessment of each sample member which I have considered to be a counterpart to the systematic census interviews among the Eskimos.

I returned to Nigeria in 1963 to carry out another psychiatric study focused on urban Yoruba women. This allowed for review and refinement of the concepts which emerged in the earlier investigation.

The materials of this study can be described best as a collection of dossiers on specific individuals, observations by Eskimos about specific other Eskimos and by Yorubas about specific other Yorubas. The focus was on indigenous meanings and native interpretations of behavior. Insofar as a general pattern of meaning emerged it was revealed by sifting through a very large number of often small descriptions about particular individuals.

Thus a paramount feature of the methods I employed is that for the most part the data are concerned not with behaviors in the abstract but with behaviors exhibited by actual people known to my native helpers and often to me. When a stable meaning for a certain kind of behavior was revealed, that meaning was then used as a basis for counting similar behavior patterns so that they were defined from within a cultural group rather than by imposed criteria. Often, but not always, these stable meanings were conveyed through labels. Sometimes they were conveyed by means of actions taken in regard to a particular person described as exhibiting various behaviors. In Western societies, official recognition of abnormal behavior is conveyed by commitment of a person to a hospital or prison. It seemed reasonable to consider that official native recognition of abnormality was equally well conveyed in the action of taking a person to an Eskimo shaman or a Yoruba healer or in taking a person to the village fathers for reprimand or punishment among the Eskimos or the native courts among the Yorubas.

The findings are presented in terms of the following categories: (1) labeled behavior patterns, (2) unlabeled behavior patterns, (3) evaluation of behavior patterns, (4) norm violations, and (5) prevalence.

Labeled Behavior Patterns

The first question is, Do Eskimos and Yorubas have labels for psychological and behavioral differences which bear any resemblance to what we mean by mental illness? These groups clearly recognize differences among themselves and describe these in terms of what people do and what they say they feel and believe. Some of the differences arouse sympathy and protection while others elicit disapproval, some of them are called sickness and others health, some are conceived as misconduct and others are good conduct. Some of them are described by a single word or nominative phrase. Other behaviors which seem to have common features are described in varying circumlocutions and sentences. If a word exists for a complex pattern of behavior it seems acceptable to assume that the concept of that pattern has been crystallized out of a welter of specific attributes and that such a word qualifies as an explicit label.

Of first importance is whether or not the Yorubas and Eskimos conceptualize a distinction between body and mind and attribute differences in functioning to one or the other. The first indication of how this was viewed arose in the Eskimo census review when early in the procedure one woman was described in these terms: "Her sickness is getting wild and out of mind . . . but she might have had sickness in her body too." "Getting wild" in this instance meant running out in the winter at night to the lake near the village and struggling with her son when he found her and tried to bring her home. Going "out of mind" meant not knowing where she was and accusing her family of things they did not do. As the pieces began to fit together, it seemed to me that there was indeed a distinction between mind and body. To an Eskimo, a phenomenon which can happen to the mind is *nuthkavihak,* a word which is translated as "crazy."

It became clear from other descriptions that nuthkavihak refers to a complex pattern of multiple possible behavioral processes of which the hallmark is conceived to be that something inside the person—the soul, the spirit, the mind—is out of order. Descriptions of how nuthkavihak is manifest include such phenomena as "talking to oneself," "screaming at somebody who does not exist," "believing that a child or husband was murdered by witchcraft when nobody else believes it," "believing oneself to be an animal," "refusing to eat for fear it will kill the person," "refusing to talk," "running away," "getting lost," "hiding in strange places," "making strange grimaces," "drinking urine," "becoming strong and violent," "killing dogs," and "threatening people." Eskimos say that nuthkavihak means "being crazy."

There is a Yoruba word, *were,* which is also translated as insanity. The phenomena include "hearing voices and trying to get other people to see their source when other people cannot," "laughing when there is nothing to laugh at," "talking all the time or not talking at all," "asking oneself questions and answering them," "picking up sticks and leaves for no purpose except to put them in a pile," "throwing away food because it is thought to contain juju," "tearing off one's clothes," "setting fires," "defecating in public and then mushing around in the feces," "taking up a weapon and suddenly hitting someone," "breaking things in a state of being stronger than normal," "believing that an odor is continuously being emitted from one's body."

The growing anthropological literature on this topic indicates that the concepts of insanity I have presented as reflecting Eskimo and Yoruba beliefs are common throughout many parts of the world. Important among the recent studies is that of Edgerton (1966), who worked with four tribal societies in East Africa. He provides a list of 24 behaviors ascribed to psychosis by these groups, including such patterns as "serious assault," "arson," "abusing people verbally," "shouting, screaming, crying," "running wild," "going naked," "talking nonsense," "wandering aimlessly," "eating and smearing feces," etc. Edgerton noted that "the most obvious aspect of the many behaviors ascribed to 'psychosis' is the agreement between the four tribes" (p. 413). Comparing the African view of psychosis to that of the West, he wrote:

It is remarkable how alike these African conceptions of psychosis are to the Western European psychoses, particularly to the constellation of reactions known as schizophrenia. The Africans of these four tribes do not regard a single behavior as psychotic which could not be so regarded in the West. That is, they do not produce symptoms which are understandable as psychotic only within the context of their own cultures. What is psychotic for them would be psychotic for us. (p. 415)

Another contemporary study which provides similar evidence is that of Selby (1974), who worked among the Zapotecs of Mexico. He found that insanity was indigenously recognized and that the condition was defined as having "something to do with the soul and was symptomized by agitated motor behavior, ataraxia, violent purposeless movement, and the inability to talk in ways that people could readily understand" (p. 41). These investigations, along with other studies (Field, 1960; Kaplan & Johnson, 1964; Prince, 1964; Cawte, 1972; Beiser, Burr, Ravel, & Collomb, 1973; Burton-Bradley, 1975; Carstairs & Kapur, 1976) point to similar behavior patterns being thought of as indicators of psychosis in many and widely scattered areas of the world.

When a person among the Eskimos or Yorubas behaved in the ways or said that he or she believed the kinds of things indicated in nuthkavihak or *were,* the course of action was to take her or him to a healer and have a curing rite performed. In fact, among the Yorubas some native healers specialize in the treatment of *were* (Prince, 1964).

The profile of *were* behaviors is based not only on what the healers described in the abstract but also from data on two members of the sample identified as *were* by the village headman and a group of 28 *were* patients in the custody of native healers and in a Nigerian mental hospital. The profile of nuthkavihak is built from information about four individuals within the 15 year population of 499 persons and six Eskimos from earlier times and from a related Eskimo settlement in Siberia.

Of paramount significance is the fact that *were* and nuthkavihak were never used for a *single* attribute such as hearing voices but rather were applied to a *pattern* in which three or four phenomena existed together even though no one person was described or observed as having the whole set of behaviors given above. I understand this to mean that a pattern or model of behaviors was in mind. No person suffering from nuthkavihak, for example, fit the total pattern perfectly, but neither did any one sufferer have only one component. Since no one feature was considered sufficient reason for using the labels *were* and nuthkavihak, it is possible to examine the situations in which a person exhibited one or another of the components but was not labeled insane.

The ability to see things other people do not see and to look into the future and prophesy is a clearly recognized and highly valued trait in these groups. It is called "thinness" by Eskimos. This ability is used by numerous minor Eskimo diviners and is the outstanding characteristic of the shaman. If "thinness" is the Eskimo way of talking about what we would call "hallucinations," it alone does not constitute their stereotype of insanity, since there were no instances when a "thin" person was also called nuthkavihak.

When a shaman undertakes a curing rite she or he becomes possessed by the spirit of an animal; he "deludes" himself, so to speak, into believing that he or she is an animal. Consider this description which concerns a female shaman among the Eskimos with whom I worked:

"When my brother was sick, my grandmother who was a shamaness tried her best to get him well. She did all her part, acting as though a dog, singing some songs at night, but he died. While she was singing she fell down so hard on the floor, making a big noise. After about fifteen minutes later we heard the tappings of her fingers and her toes on the floor. Slowly she got up, already she had become like a dog. She looks awful. My grandfather told me that he used to hide his face with his drum just because she looks different, changed and awful like a dog, very scary. She used to crawl back and forth on the floor, making big noises. Even though my brother was afraid of her, he tried not to hide his face, he looked at her so that he would become well. Then my grandmother licked his mouth to try to pull up the cough and to blow it away. Then after half hour, she fell down so hard on the floor again." (Murphy, 1964, p. 59)

Compare this to the case of a Baffin Island Eskimo, reported by Teicher (1954), who believed that a fox had entered her body. This was not associated with shaman-izing but was a continuous belief. She barked herself hoarse, tried to claw her husband, thought her feet were turning into fox paws, believed that the fox was moving up in her body, gagged because she thought she could feel its hair in her throat, lost control of her bowels at times, and finally became so excited that she was tied up and put into a coffinlike box with an opening at the head through which she could be fed. This woman was thought to be crazy, but the shaman was not. One Eskimo summarized the distinction this way: "When the shaman is healing he is out of his mind, *but he is not crazy.*"

This suggests that seeing, hearing, and believing things which are not seen, heard, and believed by all members of the group are sometimes linked to insanity and sometimes not. The distinction appears to be the degree to which they are controlled and utilized for a specific social function. The inability to control these processes is what is meant by a mind out of order, and when a mind is out of order it will not only fail to control sensory perception but will also fail to control many other behaviors. Another Eskimo, on being asked to define nuthkavihak, said that it means "the mind does not control the person, *he is crazy.*" I take this to mean that volition is implicated and that hearing voices, for example, can be both voluntarily achieved and involuntarily manifested and that the involuntary aspect is what is associated with *were* and nuthkavihak.

In cultures such as Eskimo and Yoruba, where clairvoyant kinds of mental phe-nomena are encouraged and preternatural experiences are valued, something simi-lar to what we might call hallucinations and delusions can probably be learned or simulated. A favorable social reaction is likely to stabilize the performance of the people who fill the roles of fortune teller and faith healer. For example, the shaman described above was unable to keep her patient alive, but her *performance* was consid-ered to have been well executed; she was said to have done "all her *part, acting* like a dog." The Eskimo believe that a person can *learn* to become a shaman and that the behaviors we might see as indicative of psychosis are highly controlled and limited to the act of shamanizing. Their view of nuthkavihak was of something that befalls the person, a pattern of behavioral processes which can appear and disap-pear, lasting a long time with some people and a short time with others.

A number of researchers in the field of cross-cultural psychiatry take the position that the underlying processes of insanity are the same everywhere but that the specific content varies between cultural groups (deReuck & Porter, 1965; Kiev, 1972; Yap, 1974). Psychotic persons, it is thought, could not make use of the imagery of Christ if they had not been exposed to the Christian tradition; they could not believe themselves to be Napoleon if they did not know about the Napoleonic Wars; and they could not elaborate ideas about the *wittiko* cannibalistic monster if they lacked knowledge of the Cree and Ojibwa cultures. This position makes use of relativism in a modified fashion. It would seem that if a culture-specific stereotype of the content of psychosis exists in a group, it might have the kind of influence suggested by Benedict and elaborated in labeling theory. If the content stereotype were applied to the unstructured delusions of a psychotic, his or her thought products might be shaped and stabilized around the theme of that stereotype.

There have been several attempts to study phenomena such as wittiko, (Parker, 1960; Teicher, 1960) and *pibloktoq* (Gussow, 1960). The former is thought of as the culturally defined content of a psychotic process in which a Cree or Ojibwa believes herself or himself to be a cannibalistic monster and the latter as a culture-specific form of hysteria found in the Arctic. The evidence of their existence comes from early ethnographies, and it has been difficult in the contemporary period to locate people who have these illnesses. There are no recent reports of individuals exhibiting wittiko, and even the existing documentation from early investigations is open to question. After an extensive review of these materials, Honigmann (1967) wrote, "I can't find one [case] that satisfactorily attests to someone being seriously obsessed by the idea of committing cannibalism" (p. 401).

Pibloktoq is a pattern of episodic and transient alteration of consciousness involving running away, jabbering in neologisms, making faces, and, lastly, a seizure. Scattered cases have been reported from Greenland across the Canadian Archipelago to Alaska. Among the Eskimo group with which I worked, I found only one description which was anything like the classical description, and it did not involve seizure. One woman was described as "once in a while having her face go every which way for short moments." People thought she might be on the verge of becoming a shaman. She did not achieve this, but neither was she thought of as having an illness.

Foulks (1972) has carried out a much larger and more comprehensive study of Arctic hysteria. His conclusions are similar to mine in that he found very few cases which could be said to match the prototype. Ten cases were located among 11,000 Unnuit Eskimos. These ten appeared to comprise a heterogeneous group: some had epilepsy, some were diagnosed as schizophrenic, and one was possibly alcoholic.

Thus it appears that these highly particular culturally patterned phenomena are exceedingly rare. If they ever did exist, they represent a kind of cultural patterning which has not been maintained in the way which Benedict suggested. If the availability of a stereotype of the content of a psychosis has the effect one would expect from labeling theory, the stereotype should have sustained the pattern while in fact these content patterns seem to have disappeared.

Prominent in the descriptions of the images and behavior of people labeled *were* and nuthkavihak were cultural beliefs and practices as well as features of the natural environment. Eskimo ideation concerned Arctic animals and Eskimo people, Eskimo objects, and Eskimo spirits. The Yoruba ideation was based on tropical animals and Yoruba figures. The cultural variation was, in other words, general. There was no evidence that if a person were to become *were* or nuthkavihak, he would reveal one specific delusion based on cultural mythology. The lack of cultural specificity was borne home to me when I was introduced to an illiterate psychotic Sudanese. He thought he was Napoleon, an idea which I assume represented his knowledge of national history but which was not tightly linked to his own cultural tradition. In regard to specificity of content, I reach the same conclusion as Brown (1973) did when he set out to see how far labeling ideas would aid his understanding of hospitalized schizophrenics: "Delusions are as idiosyncratic as individual schizophrenics or normals. . . . There seems to be nothing like a standard set of heresies, but only endless variety" (p. 397).

The answer to the first question, whether Eskimos and Yorubas have labels for psychological and behavioral differences resembling what we call mental illness, is to my mind a definite yes. Not only do these Eskimos and Yorubas have an explicit label for insanity; so do most other non-Western groups. From this broad perspective, it appears that (1) phenomenal processes of disturbed thought and behavior similar to schizophrenia are found in most cultures; (2) they are sufficiently distinctive and noticeable that almost everywhere a name has been created for them; and (3) over and above similarity in processes there is variability in content which in a loose and general way is colored by culture.

Unlabeled Behavior Patterns

The next questions are, "Do phenomena labeled mental illness by us go unlabeled elsewhere? If so, what are the consequences? Are there natural experiments of culture which allow us to gain some understanding of the effects of not labeling? From the linguistic relativist's viewpoint, if phenomena are not named they are screened out of the perceptions of the people who speak that language. Not only would mental illness go unrecognized if unlabeled, but also the negative effects of stigmatization could probably not pertain.

Although one cannot speak of mental illness without reference to insanity and psychoses, most people in our culture mean more and include some or all of the phenomena described in a textbook of psychiatry. Although elsewhere I have discussed mental retardation, convulsions, and senility as perceived by the Eskimos and Yorubas (Murphy, 1960), I will focus only on psychoneurosis here.

In working with the Eskimos and Yorubas, I was unable to find a word which could be translated as a general reference to neurosis or words which directly parallel our meaning of anxiety and depression. On the other hand, the number of words for emotional responses which we might classify as manifestations of anxiety or depression constituted a very large vocabulary. The Yoruba concepts include, for example, "unrest of mind which prevents sleep," "fear of being among people," "tenseness and overeagerness," etc. The Eskimo ideas are "worrying too much until it makes a person sick," "too easy to get afraid," "crying with sadness, head down and rocking back and forth," "shaking and trembling all over," "afraid to stay indoors," etc.

The point is that neither group had a single word or explicit label which lumps these phenomena together as constituting a general class of illness by virtue of their underlying similarities or as a pattern in which several components are usually found in association. In the terms of this chapter, these neurotic-appearing symptoms are unlabeled. These emotional reactions do, however, exist. People recognize them and try to do something about them. Some of them are conceived as minor ailments, while others are severely disabling and have caused people to give up their work. One Eskimo stopped being the captain of a hunting boat on these grounds. Some of these reactions are transient episodes; others are lifelong characteristics.

Of special significance to the problem at hand is the fact that most of these emotional phenomena are definitely thought of as remediable illnesses for which the shaman and witchdoctor have effective armamentaria of cures. The number of people who exhibit these patterns is considerably in excess of those labeled *were* and nuthkavihak. Among the Yorubas the ratio is approximately 12 to 1 and among the Eskimos 14 to 1. If one were to look at the clientele of an Eskimo shaman or a Yoruba healer, a healer who had *not* specialized in the treatment of *were*, a very large proportion would be those who come with patterns such as "unrest of mind that prevents sleep" or "shaking and trembling all the time."

The answer to the question about whether or not phenomena we label mental illness go unlabeled elsewhere is thus also yes. These Eskimos and Yorubas point out a large number of psychological and behavioral phenomena which we would call neuroses but which they do not put together under such a rubric. The consequence is not, however, a reduction in the number of people who display the phenomena nor great difference in how they are treated. The fact that these peoples cannot categorically define someone as "a neurotic" appears mainly to be a classification difference, and I am led to conclude that these phenomena exist independently of cultural labels.

Evaluation of Behavior Patterns

Do non-Western groups evaluate the labeled behaviors of mental illness negatively or positively? Do they tolerate deviance better than we do? I shall approach these questions in terms of first the positively and negatively valued institutions of a culture, its roles and ceremonies and then the noninstitutionalized actions and attitudes carried out toward the mentally ill.

It has been hypothesized by a number of researchers that individuals who fill the role of holy person, shaman, or witchdoctor are psychotic (Benedict, 1934; Devereux, 1956; Linton, 1956; Silverman, 1967). Such people are rewarded for their mental illness as incumbents of highly regarded social roles. If this is the case, it means that in some cultures psychosis is noted for its social usability in contrast to the social disability so often associated with it in ours. Still other researchers hold that psychosis is affiliated with an opposite role, that of the witch. The witch is the purveyor of magically evil influences against other human beings. A lunatic, it has been thought, is especially vulnerable to being accused of witchcraft practices and punished in various ways (Sarbin, 1969).

The ideas embedded in these hypotheses underscore the lengths to which relativity can be carried, for they suggest that the social definition of one kind of behavior can turn it into such opposing roles as the defamed witch *or* the renowned shaman.

Beginning with the notion that psychopathology is positively valued in the role of healer, it can be recalled that the Eskimos do not believe that the shaman is nuthkavihak. Therefore it cannot be insanity which invests the role with prestige in their eyes. It could be, however, that some other form of mental illness, possibly a neurotic disorder such as hysteria, is considered essential to what a shaman does; therefore it is accorded the same respect which the role as a whole commands.

Among the 499 Eskimos, 18 had shamanized at some time in their lives. Just as none was thought to be nuthkavihak, similarly no other personality characteristic or emotional response was given as typical of all of them. In these regards the shamans seemed to be a random sample of the whole group with no more and no less of the labeled phenomena than was true for those who did not shamanize. The only feature I was able to determine as common to the group was that they shamanized, and that with variable success.

It is important to note that this does not mean that a mad person has never become a shaman. I am sure that this has happened sometimes. What seems interesting is that it did not occur among a group of Eskimo where the shamans outnumbered the psychotics by better than 4 to 1 (if the minor diviners are included, the ratio can be estimated conservatively as 11 to 1) and where the group partakes of a cultural tradition which has been described as making extremely good use of its disordered members. Even in this society where a role exists which seems well suited to the characteristics of an insane person or a schizophrenic and where the role is common enough to be open to a range of personalities, the fit between individual psychopathology and useful social role did not take place.

The Yoruba healer has not been described in the literature as a mentally ill person, although some of the Yoruba healing cults consist of people who have been cured and thereafter participate in curing others. The healers known to me and my conversations with Yorubas about their healers gave no evidence that mental illness was a requisite. Thus as far as the groups reported here are concerned, they do not appear to venerate mental illness in these roles. If the shaman is to be considered either psychotic or hysterical, it seems necessary that a Western definition be given to that portion of behavior specific to shamanizing.

If not institutionalized in a positively valued role, is mental illness institutionalized in a contemptible role? Both the Yorubas and Eskimos have a clearly defined role of witch. Although feared, the man or woman who is believed to use magic in this way is held in low esteem.

Is insanity or other mental illness prima facie evidence that a person is a witch? If one tries to answer this by identifying the people labeled *were* or nuthkavihak and then identify the people labeled as witches and compare the two groups to see how much they overlap in membership, as I did regarding the shamans, a serious problem arises. The difficulty is in identifying the witches. Unlike shamanizing, which is a public act, the use of evil magic is exceedingly secretive, and there is not necessarily good agreement between people regarding whom they accuse of such acts. I did note, however, that there was no correspondence between the group of Eskimos said to be insane at some point in their lives and the six people named as *auvinak* (witch) by at least one other Eskimo.

In the more generalized information from the Yoruba healers, it was evident that insanity is often believed to result from the use of evil magic, but an insane person rarely uses it against others. Thus my interpretation of whether or not mental illness is built into the negatively valued role of witch is similar to the view presented about the positively valued role of healer. Some insane people have probably been accused of being witches, but this is by happenstance and not because witching and insanity are considered to be the same thing and equally stigmatized.

Another way in which a culture might institutionalize a negative view of mental illness is through a degradation ceremony or ritual slaying. Ceremony is a preservative of custom, and there is voluminous information on ceremonies for healing, for fertility of land, animals and humans, and for rites of passage as well as ceremonies in which various forms of human sacrifice are carried out.

In view of the wide elaboration of customs whereby groups of people enact their negative and positive values, it is perhaps surprising that no groups seem to have developed the idea of *ceremonially* killing an insane person in the prime of life just because he or she is insane. Infanticide has sometimes been conducted when a child was born grossly abnormal in a way which might later have emerged as brain damage, and it is possible that senility might have been a contributing factor in the live burials practiced in some parts of the world (Rivers, 1926). Also, there is no doubt but that insane people have sometimes been "done away with," but such is different from ritual sacrifice. There is no evidence as far as I can determine that killing the insane has ever been standardized as a custom. There are, on the other hand, numerous indications from non-Western data that the ceremony appropriate for people labeled as mentally deranged is healing (Edgerton, 1969; Field, 1960; Kaplan

& Johnson, 1964; Kiev, 1968; Lambo, 1964; Prince, 1964). Even the word lunatic associates the phenomenon with healing, since it was usually the healer who was believed to have power over such cosmic forces as the lunar changes which were thought to cause insanity.

Regarding the problem of informal actions and attitudes toward the mentally ill, it is difficult to draw conclusions because there is evidence of a wide range of behaviors which can be conceptualized as social reactions. Insane people have been the objects of certain restrictive measures among both the Eskimos and Yorubas. The Eskimo physically restrain people in violent phases, follow them around, and force them to return home if they run away, and there is one report of an insane man being killed in self-defense when, after killing several dogs, he turned on his family. In describing the Chukchee, a Siberian group known to these Bering Strait Eskimos, Bogoras (1904–1909) reports the case of an insane woman who was tied to a pole during periods of wildness. Teicher (1954) describes, in addition to the coffinlike box mentioned earlier, the use of an igloo with bars across the opening through which food could be passed.

The Yoruba healers of *were* often have 12–15 patients in custody at one time. Not infrequently they shackle those who are inclined to run off, and they may use various herbal concoctions for sedation. In Nigeria, where population is much denser than it is in the Arctic, it was not uncommon to see *were* people wandering about the city streets, sometimes naked, more often dressed in odd assortments of tattered clothing, almost always with long dirt-laden hair, talking to themselves, picking up objects to save. In studying a group of such vagrant psychotics, Asuni (1968) noted that they usually stayed in one locale and that people fed them generously, allowed them to sleep in the market stalls, teased them mildly or laughed at them for minor deviations, and took action only to control them if the psychotics became violent.

A case I encountered in Gambia serves to illustrate the complexities of the situation and indicates that compassion and rejection are sometimes both engaged. The case is a man, identified as insane, who lived some 500 yards outside a village. The villagers lived in thatched mud houses, while the madman lived on an abandoned anthill about 2.5 meters long and 1.5 meters high; the top had been worn away to match the contours of his body. Except for occasional visits to the village, he remained on this platform through day and night and changing weather. His behavior was said to have become odd when he was a young man, and when I saw him he had not spoken for years, although he sometimes made grunting sounds. In one sense he was as secluded and alienated from his society as patients are in our back wards. On the other hand, the villagers always put food out for him and gave him cigarettes. The latter act was accompanied by laughter because the insane man had a characteristic way of bouncing several leaps into the air to get away from anyone who came close to him. This was considered amusing. Once a year, however, someone would forcibly bathe and put new clothes on him.

If one defines intolerance of mental illness as the use of confinement, restraint, or exclusion from the community (or allowing people to confine or exclude themselves), there does not appear to be a great deal of difference between Western and non-Western groups. Furthermore, there seems to be little that is distinctively "cultural" in the attitudes and actions directed toward the mentally ill, except in the obvious way that an abandoned anthill is not found in the Arctic or a barred igloo in the tropics. There is apparently a common range of possible responses to the mentally ill person, and the portion of the range brought to bear regarding a particular person is determined more by the nature of the behavior than by a preexisting cultural set to respond in a uniform way to whatever is labeled mental illness. If the behavior indicates helplessness, help tends to be given, especially in food and clothes. If the behavior appears foolish or incongruous, even though obviously colored by the distinctive Eskimo and Yoruba views of what is humorous, laughter is the response. If the behavior is noisy and agitated, the response may be to quiet, sometimes by herbs and sometimes by other means. If the behavior is violent or threatening, the response is to restrain or subdue.

The answer to the question posed at the beginning of this section seems to be that the patterns that these groups label *were* or nuthkavihak are not evaluated in either a starkly positive or a starkly negative way. The flavor and variability of the social reactions to mental illness suggest the word "ambivalence."

Norm Violations

If these Eskimo and Yorubas are ambivalent about mental illness, do they give strong negative evaluation to any behaviors at all? Both groups have words for theft, cheating, lying, stinginess, drunkenness, and a large number of other behaviors which they consider to be specific acts of bad conduct. These, like the practice of witchcraft, are thought of as transgressions against social standards and are negatively sanctioned.

In addition, the Eskimos have a word—*kunlangeta*—which means "the mind knows what to do but the person does not do it." This is an abstract term for the breaking of many rules when awareness of the rules is not in question. It might be applied to a male who, for example, repeatedly lies to people and thereby cheats them *and* steals things *and* does not go hunting *and,* when the men are out of the village, takes sexual advantage of many women; someone who does not pay attention to reprimands and who is always being brought to the elders for punishment. One Eskimo among the 499 was called kunlangeta. When asked what would have happened to such a person traditionally, an Eskimo said that probably "somebody would have pushed him off the ice when nobody else was looking." This suggests that permissiveness has a limit even in a cultural group which in some respects, such as heterosexual activity, is very lenient. The Yorubas have a similarly abstract word—*arankan*—which means a person who always goes her or his own way regardless of others, who is uncooperative, full of malice, and bullheaded.

It therefore appears that these groups have a concept of behavior which is similar to what we call "deviance" and that these deviations are evaluated negatively. Further, there are parallels between kunlangeta and arankan and our concept of a "psychopath"—someone who consistently carries out multiple acts which violate the norms of society. Some of the specific acts of wrongdoing which they recognize might in our society be called evidence of "personality disorder." In Western psychiatry this term refers to sexual deviations, excessive use of drugs or alcohol, and a variety of behaviors which cause trouble primarily for other people rather than for the subject.

It is of considerable interest that kunlangeta and arankan are not behaviors which the shamans and healers are believed to be able to cure or change. As a matter of fact, when I pressed this point with the Yoruba healers, they denied that these patterns are illness. Both groups, however, believe that specific acts of wrongdoing may make an individual vulnerable to illness or other misfortune. Eskimos, for example, hold to a hunting ethic which prescribes ownership and sharing of animals.

If a person cheats in reference to the hunting code, this is thought of as a potential cause of physical or mental illness. Although the social codes among the Yorubas are somewhat different, they also believe that breaking taboos can cause illness. It has been recognized by anthropologists for nearly half a century that transgression (as well as witchcraft) ranks high in the accepted etiologies of many non-Western groups (Clements, 1932). Believing that transgression causes illness is nevertheless quite different from believing that transgression *is* illness. The latter equation is typical of labeling theory as exemplified in the statements of Scheff discussed in the opening pages of this chapter.

Even though the Eskimos and Yorubas do not consider these norm violations to be illness and do not send people who exhibit them to healers, they do not lack means for dealing with misconduct. Among the Yorubas, bad conduct is dealt with at many levels, through the kinship system and in native courts. The channels of justice among the Eskimo, although somewhat less formal, follow a similar pattern.

Thus the answer to the question of this section appears to be that these groups do have strong negative sanction for a number of behaviors. A difference between their opinions and those embodied in Western psychiatry is that the Eskimo and Yorubas do not consider these transgressions as symptomatic of illness or responsive to the techniques used by shamans and healers.

Prevalence

Is the net effect of a non-Western way of life such that fewer people suffer from something they label as mental illness than is the case in the West? In view of the focus on *were* and nuthkavihak, attention will be directed mainly to this pattern of behavior and to schizophrenia.

The rates of *were* and nuthkavihak can be compared to rates of schizophrenia in two Western surveys, one in Sweden and one in Canada. The Swedish study was carried out by Essen-Möller (1956) and concerns two rural parishes for which a population register exists. Each member of the population was interviewed by a psychiatrist. A prevalence rate of schizophrenia is reported with figures for cases in the community and cases in a hospital during a specific year. This design is similar to that which I used among the Eskimos, where a census register provided the base for determining the population and each person was systematically described by at least one other Eskimo.

The Canadian study, in which I was one of the investigators, refers to a probability sample of adults in a rural county (D. Leighton, Harding, Macklin, Macmillan, & A. Leighton, 1963). We designed the Yoruba study to explore the possibilities of comparing mental illness rates, and similar sampling procedures were used. The rates in these two surveys are based on compilations of interview data with selected respondents as well as systematic interviews about these respondents with local physicians in Canada and, as noted above, local village headmen in Nigeria.

The results of comparing these studies is that the proportion of people who exhibited the pattern of behavior called schizophrenia, *were*, or nuthkavihak appears to be much the same from group to group (Table 26–1). At the time these studies were carried out, mental hospitals existed all over the world. Canada and Sweden are similar to the United States in having a sizeable number of large mental hospitals. The Eskimo population was considered to be in the catchment area served by a mental hospital in the U.S., and the Yoruba villages were in the vicinity of two mental hospitals. For the Canadian and Yoruba studies, we do not know the number of

TABLE 26-1   Rates of Nonhospitalized Schizophrenia in Two Western Populations and Indigenously Defined Insanity in Two Non-Western Populations

			Cases	
Group	Date	Size	Number	Rate*
Swedish	1948	2550	12	5.7
Eskimo	1954	348	1	4.4
Canadian	1952	1071	7	5.6
Yoruba	1961	245	2	6.8

*Based on the Weinberg (1915) method of age adjustment and presented as rate per 1000 population.

people who might otherwise have been in the communities but were hospitalized during the period when prevalence was surveyed. The Swedish and Eskimo studies, by virtue of starting with a census register, provide information on this point. The age-adjusted prevalence rate in the Swedish survey is 8.1 per 1000 when hospitalized schizophrenics are included (Essen-Möller, 1956, pp. 85–86), and the rate of nuthkavihak is increased to 8.8 per 1000 when one hospitalized case is added.

The number of schizophrenics, *were*, and nuthkavihak in a population is small, but this comparison suggests that the rates are similar. Thus the answer to the last question above seems to be that the non-Western way of life does not offer protection against mental illness to the point of making marked difference in frequency. The rates of mental illness patterns are much more striking for similarity from culture to culture than for difference.

SUMMARY AND CONCLUSIONS

I began this chapter by referring to Benedict's view of the malleability of human endowment and the relativity of abnormal behavior. A conclusion she drew from her studies is this:

> There can be no reasonable doubt that one of the most effective ways in which to deal with the staggering burden of psychopathic tragedies in America at the present time is by means of an educational program which fosters tolerance in society and a kind of self-respect and independence that is foreign to . . . our urban traditions. (pp. 273–274)

The materials reported and reviewed here suggest that in the last 50 years the picture has been vastly complicated in the Geertzian sense. The interpretation I make of the evidence about abnormal behavior is that psychosis, especially a process such as schizophrenia, has remarkably similar features and is widely distributed around the world. This suggests that the causes of insanity, whether genetic or experiential, are ubiquitous in human groups. Because psychosis takes a rather similar form in all the diverse societies in which it is found, it seems to show less malleability to cultural molding than some other forms of behavior. Even its manifestations of imagery and ideation, although colored by cultural patterns, are not inextricably bound to them in any standard way. Although found in most cultural groups, psychosis everywhere seems to be a rather rare phenomenon. Perhaps therefore it lies outside the framework Benedict had in mind when she said that "most people are shaped to the form of their culture."

Three aspects of the indigenous concepts of insanity and abnormality among the groups with whom I worked deserve to be emphasized. One is that the cognitive construct of what people call nuthkavihak and *were* can be described as a pattern, a model, or a configuration. It involves several features which *tend* to be found together but practically never in perfect replication of the construct people carry in their minds as a means of recognizing this phenomenon. Second, insanity appears to be conceived in a different frame of reference from transgression. There does not appear to be a grey area between illness and deviance among the Eskimo and Yorubas. They have a cognitive construct for each, and the boundaries are not conspicuously fuzzy. Finally, the social reactions to the phenomenon of insanity appear to be mixed, ambivalent, and complex. Among the groups described here, as among us, psychosis seems far more commonly associated with social disability than social usability.

In view of this information I am led to a conclusion quite different from Benedict's. It seems to me that insanity is an exceedingly complex, serious, and troubling affliction, troubling to those who exhibit it and troubling to those in the families and communities who must respond to it. Further, there appear to be few if any experiments of cultural tolerance which have solved the problems posed by these afflictions. Surely social attitudes and societal reactions have considerable influence on what happens to people so troubled as they progress through life, but that tolerance alone will cure the trouble is exceedingly doubtful.

ACKNOWLEDGMENTS

This report draws on materials presented by J. Murphy, "Psychiatric Labeling in Cross-Cultural Perspective" [*Science*, 1976, *191*, 1019–1028]. It is adapted here with the permission of the publisher. The Eskimo and Yoruba studies which form the core of this paper have been carried on as part of the Cornell and later Harvard Program in Social Psychiatry, directed by Alexander H. Leighton. Funds for the Eskimo study of 1954–1955 came from a grant to Charles C. Hughes from the Social Science Research Center of Cornell University; for the Yoruba study of 1961 grants from the U.S. National Institute of Mental Health to Alexander H. Leighton and from the Ministry of Health of Nigeria to Thomas Adeoye Lambo; and for the Yoruba study of 1963 a grant to Jane M. Murphy from the Social Science Research Council.

REFERENCES

Asuni, T. Vagrant psychotics in Abeokuta. *Deuxième colloque Africain de psychiatrie.* Paris: Association Universitaire pour le Développement de l'Enseignement et de la Culture en Afrique et à Madagascar, 1968.

Beiser, M., Burr, W., Ravel, J. L., & Collomb, H. Illnesses of the spirit among the Serer of Senegal. *American Journal of Psychiatry*, 1973, *130*, 881–886.

Benedict, R. *Patterns of culture* (with a preface by M. Mead). Boston: Houghton Mifflin, 1959 (Originally published in 1934).

Bogoras, W. *The Chukchee.* New York: Memoirs of the American Museum of Natural History, 1904–1909.

Brown, R. Schizophrenia, language, and reality. *American Psychologist*, 1973, *28*, 395–403.

Burton-Bradley, B. G. *Stone age crisis: A psychiatric appraisal.* Nashville: Vanderbilt University Press, 1975.

Carstairs, G. M., & Kapur, R. L. *The great universe of Kota: Stress, change, and mental disorder in an Indian village.* Berkeley: University of California Press, 1976.

Caudill, W. Tiny dramas: Vocal communication between mother and infant in Japanese and American families. In W. P. Lebra (Ed.), *Transcultural research in mental health.* Honolulu: University of Hawaii Press, 1972.

Cawte, J. *Cruel, poor and brutal nations: The assessment of mental health in an Australian Aboriginal community.* Honolulu: University of Hawaii Press, 1972.

Clements, F. *Primitive concepts of disease.* Berkeley: University of California Publications in American Archeology and Ethnology, 1932.

deReuck, A., & Porter, R. (Eds.) *Transcultural psychiatry: A Ciba Foundation symposium.* London: Churchill, 1965.

Devereux, G. Normal and abnormal: The key problem of psychiatric anthropology. In J. B. Casagrande & T. Gladwin (Eds.), *Some uses of anthropology: Theoretical and applied.* Washington, D.C.: Anthropological Society of Washington, 1956.

Edgerton, R. B. Conceptions of psychosis in four East African societies. *American Anthropologist,* 1966, *68,* 408–425.

Edgerton, R. B. On the recognition of mental illness. In S. C. Plog & R. B. Edgerton (Eds.), *Changing perspectives in mental illness.* New York: Holt, Rinehart & Winston, 1969.

Essen-Möller, E. *Individual traits and morbidity in a Swedish rural population.* Copenhagen: Ejnar Munksgaard, 1956.

Field, M. J. *Search for security: An ethnopsychiatric study of rural Ghana.* Chicago: Northwestern University Press, 1960.

Foulks, E. *The Arctic hysterias of the North Alaskan Eskimo.* Washington, D.C.: American Anthropological Association, 1972.

Geertz, C. *The interpretation of cultures.* New York: Basic Books, 1973.

Graves, T. Urban Indian personality and the "culture of poverty." *American Ethnologist,* 1974, *1,* 65–84.

Gussow, Z. "Pibloktoq" (hysteria) among Polar Eskimos. In W. Muensterberger (Ed.), *Psychoanalysis and the social sciences* New York: International Universities Press, 1960.

Honigmann, J. *Personality in culture.* New York: Harper & Row, 1967.

Hughes, C. C. *An Eskimo village in the modern world.* Ithaca, N.Y.: Cornell University Press, 1960.

Kaplan, B., & Johnson, D. The social meaning of Navaho psychopathology and psychotherapy. In A. Kiev (Ed.), *Magic, faith, and healing.* New York: Free Press, 1964.

Kiev, A. *Curanderismo: Mexican-American folk psychiatry.* New York: Free Press, 1968.

Kiev, A. *Transcultural psychiatry.* New York: Free Press, 1972.

Lambo, T. A. Patterns of psychiatric care in developing African countries. In A. Kiev (Ed.), *Magic, faith, and healing.* New York: Free Press, 1964.

Leighton, A. H., Lambo, T. A., Hughes, C. C., Leighton, D. C., Murphy, J. M., & Macklin, D. B. *Psychiatric disorder among the Yoruba.* Ithaca, N.Y.: Cornell University Press, 1963.

Leighton, A. H., & Murphy, J. M. The problem of cultural distortion. In R. M. Acheson (Ed.), *Comparability in international epidemiology.* New York: Milbank Memorial Fund, 1964.

Leighton, D. C., Harding, J. S., Macklin, D. B., Macmillan, A. M., & Leighton, A. H. *The character of danger: The Stirling County study of psychiatric disorder and sociocultural environment* (Vol. 3). New York: Basic Books, 1963.

Lemert, E. M. *Human deviance, social problems, and social control.* Englewood Cliffs, N.J.: Prentice-Hall, 1967.

Levy, J. E., & Kunitz, S. J. *Indian drinking: Navajo practices and Anglo-American theories.* New York: John Wiley & Sons, 1974.

Linton, R. *Culture and mental disorders.* Springfield, Ill.: Charles C. Thomas, 1956.

Murphy, J. M. (formerly Hughes). *An epidemiological study of psychopathology in an Eskimo village.* Unpublished doctoral dissertation, Cornell University, 1960.

Murphy, J. M. Psychotherapeutic aspects of shamanism on St. Lawrence Island, Alaska. In A. Kiev (Ed.), *Magic, faith, and healing.* New York: Free Press, 1964.

Murphy, J. M., & Hughes, C. C. The use of psychophysiological symptoms as indicators of disorder among Eskimos. In J. M. Murphy & A. H. Leighton (Eds.), *Approaches to cross-cultural psychiatry.* Ithaca, N.Y.: Cornell University Press, 1965.

Murphy, J. M., and Leighton, A. H. Native conceptions of psychiatric disorder. In J. M. Murphy & A. H. Leighton (Eds.), *Approaches to cross-cultural psychiatry.* Ithaca, N.Y.: Cornell University Press, 1965.

Parker, S. The wittiko psychosis in the context of Ojibwa personality and culture. *American Anthropologist,* 1960, *62,* 603–623.

Prince, R. Indigenous Yoruba psychiatry. In A. Kiev (Ed.), *Magic, faith, and healing.* New York: Free Press, 1964.

Rivers, W. H. R. *Psychology and ethnology.* New York: Harcourt, Brace, 1926.

Rosenhan, D. L. On being sane in insane places. *Science,* 1973, *179,* 250–258.

Sarbin, T. R. The scientific status of the mental illness metaphor. In S. C. Plog & R. B. Edgerton (Eds.), *Changing perspectives in mental illness.* New York: Holt, Rinehart & Winston, 1969.

Scheff, T. J. *Being mentally ill: A sociological theory.* Chicago: Aldine, 1966.

Selby, H. A. *Zapotec deviance: The convergence of folk and modern sociology.* Austin: University of Texas Press, 1974.

Silverman, J. Shamans and acute schizophrenia. *American Anthropologist,* 1967, *69,* 21–31.

Szasz, T. S. *The myth of mental illness: Foundations of a theory of personal conduct.* New York: Hoeber-Harper, 1961.

Teicher, M. I. Three cases of psychosis among the Eskimos. *Journal of Mental Science,* 1954, *100,* 527–535.

Teicher, M. I. *Windigo psychosis.* Seattle: American Ethnological Society, 1960.

Weinberg, W. Zur Korrektur des Einflusses der Lebensdauer und Todesauslese auf die Ergebnisse bestimmter Kreuzungen. *Archiv Fur Rassen-Und Gesellschaftsbiologic,* 1915, *11,* 434–444.

Yap, P. M. *Comparative psychiatry: A theoretical framework.* Toronto: University of Toronto Press, 1974.

Author Index

Blount, B. G., & Kempton, W.: (1976) 397, 398
Blount, B. G., & Padgug, E.: (1977) 396–397, 398
Blurton Jones, N. G.: (1972) 600, 601; (1972b) 27
Blurton Jones, N. G., & Konner, M. J.: (1973) 7, 8, 21, 548, 549, 552
Blurton Jones, N. G., & Sibley, R. M.: (1978) 37
Boas, F.: (1898) 298
Bobbitt, J. F.: (1909) 309
Bock, P.: (1967) 589, 604
Bock, R., & Kalokowski, D.: (1973) 481
Bock, R. D., Wainer, H., Petersen, A., Thissen, D., Murray, J., & Roches, A. A.: (1973) 537
Boehm, L.: (1962) 504
Boggs, S. T., & Gallimore, R.: (1968) 698
Bogoras, W.: (1904–1909) 820
Boismier, J. D.: (1977) 184
Boldt, E. D.: (1978) 485
Bonné, B.: (1966) 315, 318
Bourliere, F.: (1955) 16
Boutourline, E., Tesi, G., Kerr, G. R., Stare, F. J., Kallal, Z., Turki, M., & Hemaidan, N.: (1972) 282; (1973) 282
Bovet, M. C.: (1974) 408, 411, 412, 445; (1976) 412, 413
Bovet, M. C., Dasen, P. B., Inhelder, B., & Othenin-Girard, C.: (1972) 219, 220
Bowden, B. D., Johnson, J., Ray, L. J., & Towns, J.: (1976) 307
Bowditch, H. P.: (1879) 309
Bower, L. G. R.: (1974) 4, 5
Bowerman, M.: (1973) 383, 385, 386–387
Bowes, W. A., Jr., Brackbill, Y., Conway, E., & Steinschneider, A.: (1970) 183
Bowlby, J., 4, 8
(1958) 720
(1969) 5, 7, 9–10, 17, 29, 66, 68, 170, 233–234, 235, 720
(1973) 7, 17, 775
Boyatzis, R. E.: (1976) 765, 767, 773, 774
Boyd, D., & Kohlberg, L.: (1973) 507
Brackbill, Y., & Thompson, G. G.: (1967) 204
Braidwood, R. J., Sayer, J. D., Helback, H., Mangelsdorf, P. C., Coon, C. S., Linton, R., Steward, J., & Oppenheim, A. L.: (1953) 755
Brain, R., & Wilkinson, M.: (1959) 186, 187

Braine, M. D. S.: (1963) 379, 380, 381, 385–386; (1974) 385, 391; (1976) 385
Brazelton, T. B., 31
(1961) 183
(1972) 198, 214
(1973) 5, 184, 193
(1977) 198
Brazelton, T. B., & Freedman, D. G.: (1971) 197
Brazelton, T. B., Koslowski, B., & Tronick, E.: (1976) 192, 194
Brazelton, T. B., Robey, J. S., & Collier, G. A.: (1969) 198, 214, 232, 243
Brazelton, T. B., Tronick, E., Lechtig, A., Lasky, R., & Klein, R.: (1977) 198, 241
Brazelton, T. B., Tryphonopoulou, Y., & Lester, B. M.: (1977) 199
Brazziel, W.: (1964) 119
Breer, P. E., & Locke, E. A.: (1965) 557
Brenneis, C. B., & Roll, S.: (1975) 570
Breuton, M. J., Palit, A., & Prosser, R.: (1973) 189
Brody, L.: (1977) 57
Broman, S. H., Nichols, P. L., & Kennedy, W. A.: (1975) 209–210
Bronfenbrenner, U.: (1970) 704; (1972) 722, 725; (1976) 144; (1977) 430
Bronson, G. W.: (1972) 4
Broude, G. J., 155, 633–672
(1975) 588
(1975a) 648, 650, 652–653, 658, 666, 667, 670
(1975b) 644, 646, 665, 670
(1976) 591, 661
Broude, G. J., & Greene, S. J., 648, 650, 653, 661, 665–667 passim, 670
(1976) 105, 107, 542, 543, 643, 652
Broughton, J.: (1978) 509
Brown, A.: (1977) 444, 463
Brown, C.: (1977) 440
Brown, J. K., 155, 581–605
(1962) 582, 583, 585, 604
(1963) 42, 539, 583, 585, 588
(1969a) 585
(1969b) 604
(1970) 604
(1970a) 540, 541, 585
(1970b) 545
(1971) 582, 604
(1975) 604
(1978) 585
Brown, J. S.: (1952) 660

Graves, N. B., 801, 804
(1972) 796, 799
(1976) 136
Graves, N., & Graves, T. D.: (1974) 136,
698, 701, 706–710 *passim;* (1978)
728, 730, 731, 733
Graves, T.: (1974) 811
Graves, T. D., & Graves, N. B.: (1978) 796,
798
Gray, C. R., & Gummerman, K.: (1975) 450
Gray, L.: (1911) 604
Greenacre, P., 173
(1944) 172
Greenbaum, C. G., & Landau, P.: (1977)
217, 227, 228
Greenberg, L. A., & Carpenter, J. A.:
(1957) 759
Greenberg, L. A., & Lester, D.: (1953) 759
Greene, L. S.: (1973) 312
Greenfield, P. M.: (1966) 403–404, 416,
445, 446; (1968) 449; (1974) 411;
(1976) 404, 413
Greenfield, P. M., & Bruner, J.: (1969) 412,
413, 446
Greenfield, P. M., & Childs, C.: (1977) 417;
(in process) 411, 441, 442
Greenfield, P. M., & Smith, J. H.: (1976)
389, 391–392
Greenstein, J. M.: (1966) 620
Gregg, C. L., Haffner, M. E., & Korner, A.:
(1976) 241
Gregory, I.: (1965) 561
Grenada Films: (1975) 629
Grey, A., & Kalsched, D.: (1971) 570
Griffiths, J.: (1969) 186
Griffiths, R.: (1954) 203
Grim, E. R.: (1967) 183
Grinder, R. E.: (1964) 504, 505
Grinder, R. E., & McMichael, R. E.: (1962)
684
Groesbeck, B. L.: (1958) 709
Grossack, M. M.: (1957a,b) 119
Grossman, S., Handlesman, Y., & Davies,
A. M.: (1974) 276
Grotevant, H. D., Scarr, S., & Weinberg, R.
•A.: (1977) 436
Guba, E. G., Jackson, P., & Bidwell, C.:
(1959) 119
Gulick, J.: (1973) 784
Gunders, S. M.: (1961) 359
Gunders, S. M., & Whiting, J. W. M.:
(1964) 367; (1968) 207, 359, 360,
361, 363, 537, 604
Gur'ev, V. I.: (1967) 304, 305

Gussow, Z.: (1960) 816
Guthrie, G. M.: (1966) 243
Guttman, R. (1974) 563
Guzmán, M. A., Scrimshaw, N. S., Bruch,
H. A., & Gordon, J. E.: (1968) 271

Hall, C., & Domhoff, B.: (1963) 570
Hallowell, A. I.: (1935/1955) 481; (1955)
67, 69
Hamer, J. H.: (1965) 760
Hamill, P. V. V., Johnston, F. E., &
Lemeshow, S.: (1973a) 298, 302,
313; (1973b) 293
Hamilton, W. D.: (1964) 13
Hamm, C. M.: (1977) 509
Hampden-Turner, C.: (1974) 144
Hampton, M. C., Huenemann, R. L.,
Shapiro, L. R., Mitchell, B. W., &
Behnke, A. R.: (1966) 309, 321
Hannerz, U.: (1970) 132
Hansen, H.: (1961) 158
Harfouche, J. K.: (1966) 276, 282
Harkness, S.: (1973) 440; (1975) 425, 431,
439; (1977) 240, 397, 398
Harkness, S., Edwards, C. P., & Super, C.
M.: (1977) 511–514 *passim,* 521, 522
Harkness, S., & Super, C. M.: (1977) 243,
425
Harley, J. K.: (1963) 34, 42
Harlow, H. F.: (1960) 359; (1963) 10
Harlow, H. F., & Harlow, M. K.: (1965) 237
Harpending, H.: (1976) 25
Harper, L. V.: (1972) 241
Harrington, C.: (1970) 83, 620
Harris, M.: (1968) 181
Harris, S., Mussen, P., & Rutherford, E.:
(1976) 518
Hart, D. (1968) 653, 667
Harvey, R. G.: (1974) 288; (personal
communication) 288
Hasler, A. D.: (1960; 1974) 11
Haü: (1970) 320
Hautvast, J. G. A. J.: (1961) 289; (1967)
295; (1971a) 536; (1971b) 536
Havighurst, R. J.: (1957) 726
Havighurst, R. J., & Neugarten, B. L.:
(1955) 501, 506
Hawley, T. G., & Jansen, A. A. J.: (1971)
290
Hayes, L. A.: (1976) 704–705
Hayes, R. O.: (1975) 599, 604
Heapost, L.: (1973) 296
Heath, D. B.: (1958) 539, 588; (1974) 779;
(1976) 755

Subject Index